1996 Novel & Short Story Writer's Market

1996

Novel & Short Story Writer's Market

Edited by: Robin Gee

Assisted by: Barbara Kuroff

WRITER'S DIGEST BOOKS
Cincinnati, Ohio

Distributed in Canada by McGraw-Hill Ryerson,
300 Water St., Whitby, Ontario L1N 9B6.
Distributed in Australia by Kirby Books, Private
Bag No. 19, P.O. Alexandria NSW 2015.

Managing Editor, Market Books Department:
Constance J. Achabal; Supervisory Editor:
Mark Garvey; Production Editor: Chantelle
Bentley.

1996 Novel & Short Story Writer's Market.

International Standard Serial Number
ISSN 0897-9812
International Standard Book Number
0-89879-713-6

Cover design: Lamson Design

Cover illustration: Chris O'Leary

Attention Booksellers: This is an annual directory of F&W Publications.
Return deadline for this edition is April 30, 1997.

Contents

The Markets

Resources

From the Editor

It's been another year of changes in the publishing industry, and we've kept our eyes and ears open and gathered all the latest information from writers, editors, publishers and booksellers across the U.S., Canada and even some foreign countries. Now, as we do every year, we pass that information on to you in this, our 1996 edition of *Novel & Short Story Writer's Market*.

What's new this year

As you have probably already noticed, we've gone from soft- to hardcover for our 1996 edition. Inside these covers you'll find nearly 2,000 new and updated markets for fiction along with invaluable resources for writers, articles written by experts on the Craft and Technique of fiction writing, nuts and bolts pieces on the business of Writing and Publishing, and Personal Views from bestselling authors. In the Insider Viewpoints scattered throughout the book, editors discuss their views of the publishing industry and offer helpful tips on getting your fiction published.

In working to bring you the most current information for fiction writers, we are, of course, aware of the movement toward "cyberspace." While many book publishers have not yet ventured into electronic publishing, several of the magazines listed here are exclusively electronic and very open to the work of new writers. Many more now have e-mail addresses and are establishing "home pages" on the World Wide Web, offering a sort of home-base for news and information about the magazine and its readers. We now include this electronic-age information as a routine part of listing formats. In addition, our interview with JF Williams, editor of the electronic publication *Al Aaraaf*, offers a wealth of advice to writers looking to explore this area.

Our Literary and Small Circulation Magazines section and our Small Press section continue to offer new writers the most opportunities. This year we've paid special attention to our Small Press area, bringing you interviews with small press editors Jeff Putman of Baskerville Publishers, Curtis White of FC2/Black Ice Books, Fiona McCrae of Graywolf Press, and Lane Stiles of Mid-List Press.

For both new writers and published authors, we include a Publicists' Roundtable by Don Prues. Prues asks publicists from small and independent presses, as well as commercial publishers, what they do to promote writers and what writers can expect once they've published their first book. In our First Bylines section, newly-published authors offer insights into what it's like to be published for the first time and how they're handling life after publication.

Writers on all levels will appreciate our interviews with well-known authors Belva Plain and Lee Smith, who share their writing and publishing experiences. Plain and Smith discuss their methods for writing and offer tips on the craft of writing fiction, including how to keep the creative process going.

Explore new worlds

If you've been writing a specific type of story, such as mystery or romance, but have been toying with the idea of exploring other areas, now is an excellent time to consider trying to combine or switch genres. As our Commercial Trends Report and many of our introductions indicate, the blending of genres is very popular right now. For instance, some publishers seem more willing to look at romance books with science fiction elements and mysteries set in the Wild West.

For writers of short fiction, we've included a look at anthologies by anthologist and popular horror author J. N. Williamson. While a tougher market to break into than small magazines, anthologies offer short fiction opportunities for book publication, for being published alongside some of the top names in the industry and for a longer shelf-life (more readers!) for their work. As Williamson explains, the anthology market is one both new and established writers may find well worth exploring.

If you've been using *Novel & Short Story Writer's Market* for a while, you may be in the habit of turning to the same areas of the book each year, checking your favorite magazines for changes and perhaps skimming through for some new markets. I urge you, however, to take a look at the book as if you're seeing it for the first time. You may be surprised what other opportunities you'll find in sections you hadn't considered. Look at our Resources section for conferences or workshops in your area or at our burgeoning contest section—there's an opportunity for practically every type of writer, some with very nice publication or monetary rewards.

Also take a look at interviews with editors outside your area of interest. Whether or not you write religious fiction or westerns, you will find valuable insights into the publishing world in interviews with editors such as Trudy Bush from *Christian Century* and Elana Lore of *Louis L'Amour Western Magazine*. Editors at large commercial publishers, such as Jessica Lichtenstein at HarperPaperbacks or Jay Schaefer at Chronicle Books, offer a look behind the scenes that can help any writer better understand the industry and the editors and publishers who run it.

As always, we'd like to tell you, the reader, what an important part you play in our annual creation of an all-new *Novel & Short Story Writer's Market*. Feedback is important to us—not just information about specific markets, but also about your experiences as writers. There are many changes on the horizon and, with your help, *Novel & Short Story Writer's Market* will be there offering you current information on the publishing industry and leads on new markets for your work. We hope you'll use this book as a trusted guide to getting your fiction published. We also look forward to having you join us in years to come as we continue to explore this ever-changing world of writing and publishing.

Robin L. Gee

Editor

How to Get the Most Out of This Book

Like most of the people who use *Novel & Short Story Writer's Market*, chances are you've already put a great deal of time and effort into your writing. Many of you write regularly and are well-read, especially in the area in which you write. Some of you are studying writing formally, while some are receiving feedback on your work by sharing it with a writer's group. You've been spending lots of time on writing and rewriting your work, honing it until it sings and now you feel it's time to share your work with others.

If we could open this book with just one piece of advice it would be this: Take as much care searching for potential markets for your work as you have in crafting it. With this in mind, this book is designed as a tool to help you in your search and we hope you will use it as a starting place, a component, if you will, of your overall marketing plan. The temptation when using any book like this is to go straight to the listings and start sending out your work. Perhaps this is the fastest, but it's not the most efficient route to publication.

While we do offer listings of nearly 2,000 markets and other opportunities for fiction writers, the listings contain only a portion of the information available to you in *Novel & Short Story Writer's Market*. In addition to the listings, we offer interviews with published authors and editors and a wide range of articles and introductory material on the craft of writing and all aspects of marketing and publishing your work. Reading the material covered here, as well as other books on writing and publishing, will help you make informed decisions that will further your writing career.

What you'll find here

Novel & Short Story Writer's Market is divided into three parts, each presenting a different type of information. The first part is Writing Techniques. Here we provide informational pieces on the business of publishing, articles on the craft of writing, and in-depth interviews with established authors. This is where you will find the Business of Fiction Writing and the Commercial Fiction Trends Report, in addition to other articles on writing and publishing fiction.

Following Writing Techniques is The Markets, the heart of our book. This part is divided into five sections. The largest is the Literary and Small Circulation Magazines section, which includes literary journals of all sizes and smaller magazines with circulations under 10,000. Next comes the Commercial Periodicals section, featuring magazines with commercial appeal and circulations of more than 10,000. After this is the Small Press section, which includes small presses and some larger independent presses. Commercial Book Publishers, the next section, features listings of major publishers of commercial hardcover, trade paperback and mass market books. Finally, the Contests and Awards section offers listings for contests, awards and grants available to fiction writers.

Within the two magazine and two book publisher sections, you will find a main section of markets from North America [Canadian markets are noted with a maple leaf symbol (❀)] followed by international markets. Many of these markets are open to writers of English from all over the world. The contest section also includes international markets, but these are not listed separately.

Throughout The Markets, you'll find features called Insider Viewpoints. These are short interviews with editors, publishers and writers designed to give you an inside look at specific writing areas and a behind-the-scenes look at particular publications or publishers. In these pieces those "inside" publishing offer valuable tips on breaking into markets in their areas of expertise.

Resources, the last section of the book, is included for the support and information those listed there provide to writers, including places to make contact with other writers. Here you will find Conferences and Workshops, Retreats and Colonies, Organizations and Resources, and Publications of Interest to Fiction Writers sections.

Developing your marketing plan

After reading the articles and interviews that interest you, the next step in developing your marketing plan is to use the book to come up with a preliminary list of potential markets. If you are not sure in what categories your work fits or if you just want to explore the possibilities, start by reading the introductions and browsing through the sections to find markets that interest you. This approach will familiarize you with the many different types of markets for your writing and may lead you to a market you haven't thought of before.

To help you with your market search, we include a Category Index, beginning on page 588. The Category Index is divided into sections corresponding to the two magazine and two book publisher sections in The Markets. Under each section in the index, you'll find fiction types such as romance, mystery, religious, regional, etc. Subject headings are then followed by the names and page numbers of listings expressing an interest in that specific type of fiction.

You may notice that not all the listings in the magazine and book publisher sections appear in the Category Index. Some said they were only interested in very specific topics such as fiction about hiking or hot air ballooning or about the Civil War. Whether your writing subjects are general or specific, we recommend a combination of the browsing method and the Category Index method.

To further help you narrow your list of potential markets, we include ranking codes that identify the level of openness of each listing. These codes, Roman numerals I through IV, appear just after each listing's name. In the magazine and book sections, codes indicate whether editors are open to work from writers on all levels, are only open to work by established writers, or whether they only accept work by writers from a certain region or who write on a specific subject. In the Contest section, ranking codes let you know if entries should be published or unpublished or should be work from certain groups of writers or about certain regions. The ranking codes and explanations for each are outlined after each section introduction.

You will also notice symbols at the start of some listings. Listings new to our book this year are indicated by a double dagger symbol (‡). Many are newly established markets, and often these are most open to the work of new writers. Some are not new, but have decided to list with us because they have increased their fiction needs. In the book publisher sections, we also use other symbols to indicate different types of publishers. Check the introductions to these sections for more information.

Reading the listings

Once you've come up with a list of potential markets, read each listing carefully. You will find you can further streamline your list based on the market's editorial statement, advice, specific needs, terms, payment and reputation.

While different sections contain slightly different listings, there are some things all listings have in common:

After the name and contact information for each listing, you'll find a brief description of the market's publishing philosophy and intended audience. Following this is often a physical description of the magazine or books published. Physical descriptions can tell you a lot about the market's budget and give you hints about its quality and prestige. There is a brief explanation of printing terms to help you get a better picture of the publications as they are described in the listings. This information is included in The Business of Fiction Writing on page 9. Also check the establishment date, circulation or number of books published.

In some listings, following the profile, we've added our own comment, set off by a bullet. This feature allows us to pass on additional information we've learned about the listing. Included here is information about the market's honors or awards, its treatment of writers and related listings in the book.

Next comes the Needs section of the listing. In addition to a list or description of the type of work the market is seeking, you'll also find how much work the market receives from writers in a given time and how much it publishes. This will help you determine your competition. Also included are specifics on length and other requirements.

After Needs comes How to Contact, where you'll find out how to approach a market and what material to include with your submission. We suggest you follow the requirements for submission carefully. You will notice that some markets have told us they accept disk or e-mail submissions. Although some listings have included e-mail and fax numbers, it is always best to *get permission before submitting a manuscript to a publisher by fax or e-mail*. For more information on submission, presentation and cover letters, see The Business of Fiction Writing on page 9.

After How to Contact is the Payment/Terms section. When possible, we've provided a range of payment, but note that many publications in the Literary and Small Circulation section pay only in copies or subscriptions. We also indicate when you will be paid and for what rights. For more on rights and what to look for concerning terms, see the Business of Fiction Writing.

Your marketing research should begin with a careful study of the listings, but it should not end there. Whenever possible obtain a sample copy or catalog. Editors and successful writers agree there is no substitution for reading copies of magazines that interest you. Likewise, you should familiarize yourself with the books of publishers to whom you'd like to submit.

To find out more about a potential market, send a self-addressed, stamped envelope for submission guidelines. Most magazines have sample copies available for a modest price. For book publishers, check *Books in Print* at the library to find the publishers of books you admire or feel are similar to the one you are writing. The library also has publishing industry magazines such as *Publishers Weekly* as well as magazines for writers. Some of these magazines are listed in Publications of Interest to Fiction Writers beginning on page 578. These can help you keep informed of new publishers and changes in the field.

The follow through

After careful study and narrowing your list of potential markets to those who represent the most suitable places for your work, the next step, of course, is to mail out your work. If you have any questions on how to present your work, see the Business of Fiction Writing. When in doubt, remember to make it as easy as possible for editors to read and respond to your work. They're a busy lot and will not waste time with submissions that are messy and difficult to read. It may be good writing, but the editor may never read a poorly presented manuscript to find that out. If you show you care about your work, the editor will too.

Also keep accurate records. We've asked our listings to indicate how long it will take them to report on a submission, but at times throughout the year the market may get behind. Note that with small magazines and literary journals (especially those published by universities) response time tends to be slower in the summer months. Keeping track of when you sent your manuscript will help you decide when it is time to check on the status of your submission.

About our policies

We occasionally receive letters asking why a certain magazine, publisher or contest is not in the book. Sometimes when we contact a listing, the editor does not want to be listed because they: do not use very much fiction; are overwhelmed with submissions; are having financial difficulty or have been recently sold; use only solicited material; accept work from a select group of writers only; do not have the staff or time for the many unsolicited submissions a listing may bring.

Some of the listings do not appear because we have chosen not to list them. We investigate complaints of unprofessional conduct in editors' dealings with writers and misrepresentation of information provided to us by editors and publishers. If we find these reports to be true, after a thorough investigation, we will delete the listing from future editions. See Important Listing Information on page 70 for more about our listing policies.

If a listing appeared in our book last year but is no longer listed, we list it at the end of each section with an explanation, if provided. Sometimes the listing does not appear because the editor did not respond in time for our press deadline or it may not appear for any of the reasons mentioned above.

If you feel you have not been treated fairly by a market listed in our book, we advise you to take the following steps:
- First, try to contact the listing. Sometimes a phone call or letter can quickly clear up the matter.
- Be sure to document all your correspondence with the listing. When you write to us with a complaint, we will ask for the name of your manuscript, the date of your submission and the dates and nature of your subsequent correspondence.
- We will write to the publisher or editor and ask him to resolve the problem. Then, we will enter your letter into our files.
- The number, frequency and severity of unresolved complaints will be considered in our decision to delete a listing from the book.

Listings appearing in *Novel & Short Story Writer's Market* are compiled from detailed questionnaires, phone interviews and information provided by editors, publishers and awards directors. The publishing industry is volatile and changes of address, editor, policies and needs happen frequently. To keep up with the changes between editions of the book, we suggest you check the monthly Markets column in *Writer's Digest* magazine.

Club newsletters and small magazines devoted to helping writers also list market information. For those writers with access to online services, several offer writers' bulletin boards, message centers and chat lines with up-to-the-minute changes and happenings in the writing community.

We rely on our readers as well, for new markets and information about market conditions. Write us if you have any new information or if you have suggestions on how to improve our listings to better suit your writing needs.

Writing
Techniques

The Business of Fiction Writing

by Robin Gee

It's true there's no substitute for talent and hard work. A writer's first concern must always be attention to craft. No matter how well presented, a poorly written story or novel has little chance of being published. Yet, on the other hand, a well-written piece may be equally hard to sell in today's competitive publishing market. Talent alone is just not enough.

To be successful, writers need to study the field and pay careful attention to finding the right market. While the hours spent perfecting your writing are usually hours spent alone, you're not alone when it comes to developing your marketing plan. *Novel & Short Story Writer's Market* provides you with detailed listings containing the essential information you'll need to locate and contact the markets most suitable for your work.

Yet once you've determined where to send your work, you must turn your attention to presentation. We can help here, too. We've included the basics of manuscript preparation here, along with a compilation of information on submission procedures and approaching markets. In addition we provide information on setting up and giving readings. We also include tips on promoting your work. Canadian writers will find a section with information and sources specifically designed to help them. A section of brief explanations for many of the printing terms describing magazines and books in our listings will help you get a better picture of each publication. No matter where you are from or what level of experience you have, you'll find useful information here on everything from presentation to mailing to selling rights to promoting your work—the "business" of fiction.

Approaching magazine markets: While it is essential for nonfiction markets, a query letter by itself is usually not needed by most magazine fiction editors. If you are approaching a magazine to find out if fiction is accepted, a query is fine, but editors looking for short fiction want to see *how* you write. A cover letter, however, can be useful as a letter of introduction, but it must be accompanied by the actual piece. Include basic information in your cover letter—name, address, a brief list of previous publications—if you have any—and two or three sentences about the piece (why you are sending it to *this* magazine or how your experience influenced your story). Keep it to one page and remember to include a self-addressed, stamped envelope (SASE) for reply. See the winning letter from our Short Story Cover Letter Contest on page 18.

Approaching book publishers: Some book publishers do ask for queries first, but most want a query plus sample chapters or an outline or, occasionally, the complete manuscript. Again, make your letter brief. Include the essentials about yourself—name, address, phone number and publishing experience. Include only the personal information related to your story. Show that you have researched the market with a few sentences about why you chose this publisher.

Book proposals: A book proposal is a package sent to a publisher that includes a cover letter and one or more of the following: sample chapters, outline, synopsis, author bio, publications list. When asked to send sample chapters, send up to three *consecutive* chapters. An outline covers the highlights of your book chapter by chapter. Be sure to include details on main characters, the plot and subplots. Outlines can run up to 30 pages, depending on the length of your novel. The object is to tell what happens in a concise, but clear, manner. A synopsis is a very brief description of what happens in the story. Keep it to two or three pages. The terms synopsis and outline are sometimes used interchangeably, so be sure to find out exactly what each publisher wants.

Agents: Agents are not usually needed for short fiction and most do not handle it unless they already have a working relationship with you. For novels, you may want to consider working with an agent, especially if marketing to publishers who do not look at unsolicited submissions. For more on approaching agents see *The Guide to Literary Agents* (Writer's Digest Books).

Approaching markets outside your own country: When sending return postage to another country, do not send stamps. You must purchase International Reply Coupons (IRCs). The publisher can use the IRCs to buy stamps from his/her own country. In the U.S., IRCs cost $1.05 cents each and can be purchased at the main branch of your local post office.

Main branches of local banks will cash foreign checks, but keep in mind payment quoted in our listings by publishers in other countries is usually payment in their currency. Also note reporting time is longer in most overseas markets. To save time and money, you may want to include a return postcard (and IRC) with your submission and forgo asking for a manuscript to be returned.

Some mailing tips: Manuscripts under five pages long can be folded into thirds and sent in a business-size (#10) envelope. For submissions of five pages or more, however, mail it flat in a 9 × 12 or 10 × 13 envelope. Your manuscript will look best if it is mailed in an envelope only slightly larger. For the return envelope, fold it in half, address it to yourself and add a stamp (or clip IRCs to it with a paper clip).

Mark both of your envelopes in all caps, FIRST CLASS MAIL or SPECIAL FOURTH CLASS MANUSCRIPT RATE. The second method is cheaper, but it is handled the same as Parcel Post (Third Class). First Class mailing assures fastest delivery and better handling.

Book manuscripts should be mailed in a sturdy box (a ream-size typing paper box works well). Tape the box shut and tape corners to reinforce them. To ensure your manuscript's safe return, enclose a self-addressed and stamped insulated bag mailer. You may want to check with the United Parcel Service (UPS) or other mailing services for rates.

If you use an office or personal postage meter, do not date the return envelope—it could cause problems if the manuscript is held too long before being returned. First Class mail is forwarded or returned automatically. Mark Third or Fourth Class return envelopes with "Return Postage Guaranteed" to have them returned.

It is not necessary to insure or certify your submission. In fact, many publishers do not appreciate receiving unsolicited manuscripts in this manner. Your best insurance is to always keep a copy of all submissions and letters.

Manuscript mechanics: A professionally presented manuscript will not guarantee publication. Yet a sloppy, hard-to-read manuscript will not be read—publishers simply do not have the time. Here's a list of suggested submission techniques for polished manuscript presentation:

● Use white, 8½ × 11 bond paper, preferably 16 or 20 lb. weight. The paper should be heavy enough so that it will not show pages underneath it and strong enough to take handling by several people. Do not use onion skin or erasable paper.

● Type your manuscript on a typewriter with a dark ribbon. Make sure the letters are clean and crisp. You can also use a computer printer, but avoid hard-to-read dot matrix.

● Proofread carefully. An occasional white-out is okay, but don't send a marked up manuscript with many typos. Keep a dictionary, thesaurus and stylebook handy.

● Always double space and leave a 1¼ inch margin on all sides of the page. For a short

❦Canadian writers take note

While much of the information contained in this section applies to all writers, here are some specifics of interest to Canadian writers:

Postage: *At press time, the cost of one International Reply Coupon in Canada is $3.50 (Canadian). A 7 percent GST tax is required on postage in Canada and for mail with postage under $5 going to destinations outside the country. Since Canadian postage rates are voted on in January of each year (after we go to press), the Canadian Postage by the Page chart provided may change. Contact a Canada Post Corporation Customer Service Division, located in most cities in Canada, for the most current rates.*

Copyright: *For information on copyrighting your work and to obtain forms, write Copyright and Industrial Design, Phase One, Place du Portage, 50 Victoria St., 5th Floor, Hull, Quebec K1A 0C9 or call (819)997-1936.*

The public lending right: *The Public Lending Right Commission has established that eligible Canadian authors are entitled to payments when a book is available through a library. Payments are determined by a sampling of the holdings of a representative number of libraries. To find out more about the program and to learn if you are eligible, write to the Public Lending Right Commission at 350 Albert St., P.O. Box 1047, Ottawa, Ontario K1P 5V8 or call (613)566-4378 for information. The Commission which is part of The Canada Council, produces a helpful pamphlet,* How the PLR System Works, *on the program.*

Grants available to Canadian writers: *Most province art councils or departments of culture provide grants to resident writers. Some of these, as well as contests for Canadian writers, are listed in our Contests and Awards section. For national programs, contact The Canada Council, Writing and Publishing Section, P.O. Box 1047, Ottawa, Ontario K1P 5V8 or call (613)566-4334 for information. For more information on grants available to writers, contact the Arts Awards Section of the Council at the same address.*

For more information: *More details on much of the information listed above and additional information on writing and publishing in Canada are included in the* Writer's Essential Desk Reference: A Companion to Writer's Market, *2nd edition, published by Writer's Digest Books. In addition to information on a wide range of topics useful to all writers, the book features a detailed chapter for Canadians, "Writing and Selling in Canada," by Fred Kerner.*

See the Organizations and Resources section of Novel & Short Story Writer's Market *for listings of writers' organizations in Canada. Also contact The Writer's Union of Canada, 24 Ryerson Ave., Toronto, Ontario M5T 2P3; call them at (416)703-8982 or fax them at (416)703-0826. This organization provides a wealth of information (as well as strong support) for Canadian writers, including specialized publications on publishing contracts; contract negotiations; the author/editor relationship; author awards, competitions and grants; agents; taxes for writers, libel issues and access to archives in Canada.*

story manuscript, your first page should include your name, address and phone number (single-spaced) in the upper left corner. In the upper right, indicate an approximate word count. Center the name of your story about one-third of the way down, skip two or three lines and center your byline (byline is optional). Skip three lines and begin your story.

● On subsequent pages, put last name and page number in the upper right hand corner.

● For book manuscripts, use a separate cover sheet. Put your name, address and phone number in the upper left corner and word count in the upper right. Some writers list their agent's name and address in the upper right (word count is then placed at the bottom of the page). Center your title and byline about halfway down the page. Start your first chapter on the next page. Center the chapter number and title (if there is one) one-third of the way down the page. Include your last name and page number in the upper right of this page and each page to follow. Start each chapter with a new page.

● If you work on a computer, chances are your word processing program can give you a word count. If you are using a typewriter, there are a number of ways to count the number of words in your piece. One way is to count the words in five lines and divide that number by five to find an average. Then count the number of lines and multiply to find the total words. For long pieces, you may want to count the words in the first three pages, divide by three and multiply by the number of pages you have.

● Always keep a copy. Manuscripts do get lost. To avoid expensive mailing costs, send only what is required. If you are including artwork or photos, but you are not positive they will be used, send photocopies. Artwork is hard to replace.

● Most publishers do not expect you to provide artwork and some insist on selecting their own illustrators, but if you have suggestions, please let them know. Magazine publishers work in a very visual field and are usually open to ideas.

● If you want a reply or if you want your manuscript returned, enclose a self-addressed, stamped envelope (SASE). For most letters, a business-size (#10) envelope will do. Avoid using any envelope too small for an 8½×11 sheet of paper. For manuscripts, be sure to include enough postage and an envelope large enough to contain it. If you are requesting a sample copy of a magazine or a book publisher's catalog, send an envelope big enough to fit.

● When sending electronic (disk or modem) submissions, *contact the publisher first for specific information and follow the directions carefully.* Always include a hard copy with any disk submission. *Fax or e-mail your submissions only with prior approval of the publisher.*

● Keep accurate records. This can be done in a number of ways, but be sure to keep track of where your stories are and how long they have been "out." Write down submission dates. If you do not hear about your submission for a long time—about three weeks to one month longer than the reporting time stated in the listing—you may want to contact the publisher. When you do, you will need an accurate record for reference.

Rights: Know what rights you are selling. The Copyright Law states that writers are selling one-time rights (in almost all cases) unless they and the publisher have agreed otherwise. Below is a list of various rights. Be sure you know exactly what rights you are selling before you agree to the sale.

● Copyright is the legal right to exclusive publication, sale or distribution of a literary work. This right is that of the writer or creator of the piece and you need simply to include your name, date and the copyright symbol © on your piece in order to copyright it. You can also register your copyright with the Copyright Office for additional protection. Request information and forms from the Copyright Office, Library of Congress, Washington DC 20559. To get specific answers to questions about copyright (but not legal advice) you can call the Copyright Public Information Office at (202)707-3000 weekdays between 8:30 a.m. and 5 p.m. EST. Publications listed in *Novel & Short Story Writer's Market* are copyrighted *unless* otherwise stated. In the case of magazines that are not copyrighted, be sure to keep a copy of your manuscript with your notice printed on it. For more information on copyrighting your work see *The Copyright Handbook: How to Protect and Use Written Works* by Stephen Fishman (Nolo Press, 1992).

● First Serial Rights—This means the writer offers a newspaper or magazine the right to publish the article, story or poem for the first time in any periodical. All other rights to the material remain with the writer. The qualifier "North American" is often added to this phrase to specify a geographical limit to the license.

When material is excerpted from a book scheduled to be published and it appears in a magazine or newspaper prior to book publication, this is also called first serial rights.

● One-time Rights—A periodical that licenses one-time rights to a work (also known as simultaneous rights) buys the *nonexclusive* right to publish the work once. That is, there is nothing to stop the author from selling the work to other publications at the same time. Simultaneous sales would typically be to periodicals without overlapping audiences.

● Second Serial (Reprint) Rights—This gives a newspaper or magazine the opportunity to print an article, poem or story after it has already appeared in another newspaper or magazine. Second serial rights are nonexclusive—that is, they can be licensed to more than one market.

● All Rights—This is just what it sounds like. All Rights means a publisher may use the manuscript anywhere and in any form, including movie and book club sales, without further payment to the writer (although such a transfer, or *assignment*, of rights will terminate after 35 years). If you think you'll want to use the material later, you must avoid submitting to such markets or refuse payment and withdraw your material. Ask the editor whether he is willing to buy first rights instead of all rights before you agree to an assignment or sale. Some editors will reassign rights to a writer after a given period, such as one year. It's worth an inquiry in writing.

● Subsidiary Rights—These are the rights, other than book publication rights, that should be covered in a book contract. These may include various serial rights; movie, television, audiotape and other electronic rights; translation rights, etc. The book contract should specify who controls these rights (author or publisher) and what percentage of sales from the licensing of these sub rights goes to the author. For more information, see Selling Subsidiary Rights below.

● Dramatic, Television and Motion Picture Rights—This means the writer is selling his material for use on the stage, in television or in the movies. Often a one-year option to buy such rights is offered (generally for 10% of the total price). The interested party then tries to sell the idea to other people—actors, directors, studios or television networks, etc. Some properties are optioned over and over again, but most fail to become dramatic productions. In such cases, the writer can sell his rights again and again—as long as there is interest in the material. Though dramatic, TV and motion picture rights are more important to the fiction writer than the nonfiction writer, producers today are increasingly interested in nonfiction material; many biographies, topical books and true stories are being dramatized.

Selling subsidiary rights

The primary right in the world of book publishing is the right to publish the book itself. All other rights (such as movie rights, audio rights, book club rights, electronic rights and foreign rights) are considered secondary, or subsidiary, to the right to print publication. In contract negotiations, authors and their agents traditionally try to avoid granting the publisher subsidiary rights that they feel capable of marketing themselves. Publishers, on the other hand, typically hope to obtain control over as many of the sub rights as they can. Philosophically speaking, subsidiary rights will be best served by being left in the hands of the person or organization most capable of—and interested

Printing and Production Terms Defined

In most of the magazine listings in this book you will find a brief physical description of each publication. This material usually includes the number of pages, type of paper, type of binding and whether or not the magazine uses photographs or illustrations.

Although it is important to look at a copy of the magazine to which you are submitting, these descriptions can give you a general idea of what the publication looks like. This material can provide you with a feel for the magazine's financial resources and prestige. Do not, however, rule out small, simply produced publications as these may be the most receptive to new writers. Watch for publications that have increased their page count or improved their production from year to year. This is a sign the publication is doing well and may be accepting more fiction.

You will notice a wide variety of printing terms used within these descriptions. We explain here some of the more common terms used in our listing descriptions. We do not include explanations of terms such as Mohawk and Karma which are brand names and refer to the paper manufacturer. Getting it Printed, by Mark Beach (Writer's Digest Books), is an excellent publication for those interested in learning more about printing and production.

PAPER

acid-free: *Paper that has a low or no acid content. This type of paper resists deterioration from exposure to the elements. More expensive than many other types of paper, publications done on acid-free paper can last a long time.*

bond: *Bond paper is often used for stationery and is more transparent than text paper. It can be made of either sulphite (wood) or cotton fiber. Some bonds have a mixture of both wood and cotton (such as "25 percent cotton" paper). This is the type of paper most often used in photocopying or as standard typing paper.*

coated/uncoated stock: *Coated and uncoated are terms usually used when referring to book or text paper. More opaque than bond, it is the paper most used for offset printing. As the name implies, uncoated paper has no coating. Coated paper is coated with a layer of clay, varnish or other chemicals. It comes in various sheens and surfaces depending on the type of coating, but the most common are dull, matte and gloss.*

cover stock: *Cover stock is heavier book or text paper used to cover a publication. They come in a variety of colors and textures and can be coated on one or both sides.*

CS1/CS2: *Most often used when referring to cover stock, CS1 means paper that is coated only on one side; CS2 is paper coated on both sides.*

newsprint: *Inexpensive absorbent pulp wood paper often used in newspapers and tabloids.*

text: *Text paper is similar to book paper (a smooth paper used in offset printing), but it has been given some texture by using rollers or other methods to apply a pattern to the paper.*

vellum: *Vellum is a text paper that is fairly porous and soft.*

Some notes about paper weight and thickness: *Often you will see paper thickness described in terms of pounds such as 80 lb. or 60 lb. paper. The weight is determined by figuring how many pounds in a ream of a particular paper (a ream is 500 sheets). This can be confusing, however, because this figure is based on a standard sheet size and standard sheet sizes vary depending on the type of paper used. This information is most helpful when comparing papers of the same type. For example, 80 lb. book paper versus 60 lb. book paper. Since the size of the paper is the same it would follow that 80 lb. paper is the thicker, heavier paper.*

Some paper, especially cover stock, is described by the actual thickness of the paper. This is expressed in a system of points. Typical paper thicknesses range from 8 points to 14 points thick.

BINDING

case binding: *In case binding, signatures (groups of pages) are stitched together with thread rather than glued together. The stitched pages are then trimmed on three sides and glued into a hardcover or board "case" or cover. Most hardcover books and thicker magazines are done this way.*

comb binding: *A comb is a plastic spine used to hold pages together with bent tabs that are fed through punched holes in the edge of the paper.*

perfect binding: *Used for paperback books and heavier magazines, perfect binding involves gathering signatures (groups of pages) into a stack, trimming off the folds so that the edge is flat and gluing a cover to that edge.*

saddle stitched: *Publications in which the pages are stitched together using metal staples. This fairly inexpensive type of binding is usually used with books or magazines that are under 80 pages.*

Smythe-sewn: *Binding in which the pages are sewn together with thread. Smythe is the name of the most common machine used for this purpose.*

spiral binding: *A wire spiral that is wound through holes punched in pages is a spiral bind. This is the binding used in spiral notebooks.*

PRINTING

letterpress: *Letterpress printing is printing that uses a raised surface such as type. The type is inked and then pressed against the paper. Unlike offset printing, only a limited number of impressions can be made, as the surface of the type can wear down.*

offset: *Offset is a printing method in which ink is transferred from an image-bearing plate to a "blanket" and from the blanket to the paper.*

sheet-fed offset: Offset printing in which the paper is fed one piece at a time.

web offset: *Offset printing in which a roll of paper is printed and then cut apart to make individual sheets.*

There are many other printing methods but these are the ones most commonly referred to in our listings.

in—exploiting them profitably. Sometimes that will be the author and her agent, and sometimes that will be the publisher.

Larger agencies have experience selling foreign rights, movie rights and the like, and many authors represented by such agents prefer to retain those rights and let their agents do the selling. Book publishers, on the other hand, have subsidiary rights departments, which are responsible for exploiting all sub rights the publisher was able to retain during the contract negotiation. That job might begin with a push to sell foreign rights, which normally bring in advance money which is divided among author, agent and publisher.

Further efforts then might be made to sell the right to publish the book as a paperback (although many book contracts now call for hard/soft deals, in which the original hardcover publisher buys the right to also publish the paperback version). Any other rights which the publisher controls will also be pursued. Publishers, however, usually don't control movie rights to a work, as those are most often retained by author and agent.

The marketing of electronic rights to a work, in this era of rapidly expanding capabilities and markets for electronic material, can be tricky. With the proliferation of electronic and multimedia formats, publishers, agents and authors are going to great pains these days to make sure contracts specify exactly *which* electronic rights are being conveyed (or retained).

Readings: Attending public readings of poetry and fiction has become very popular in many cities. The general public seems to be just now catching on to something writers and avid readers have known for years: Readings offer a unique opportunity for those who love literature to experience it together.

If you are comfortable in front of a crowd and you'd like to share your work with others, try giving a reading. Not only does a reading allow you the opportunity to gauge reaction to your unpublished work, it's also an invaluable tool for promoting published short story collections and novels.

While there are some very prestigious reading series such as the "Main Reading Series" sponsored by The Unterberg Poetry Center of the 92nd Street Y in New York City, many readings are local events sponsored by area writers' clubs. You can start small, if you like, with one of the open-mike readings held in most cities in neighborhood coffee houses and taverns or, if you are published, look for bookstores that offer readings by authors whose books they sell.

Other reading outlets include libraries, churches, hospitals, radio stations and public-access cable television stations. Some series are well-established, while in other cases, you may have to approach a location and suggest a reading. It all depends on the amount of time and effort you'd like to invest.

If you decide to create your own reading opportunity, you may have to supply publicity and refreshments as well as a location. Established authors sometimes charge fees to sponsoring organizations, but newer writers usually feel the exposure is enough. If you have published work, however, you may want to bring copies to sell or arrange with your local bookstore to set up a table to sell your books. If you want to join an established series, keep in mind it can be competitive. You may be asked to submit work for consideration and a formal application.

For listings of sponsored readings, see *Author & Audience* and *Literary Bookstores* by Poets & Writers Inc., 72 Spring St., New York NY 10012. Poets & Writers publishes other publications on readings. Write to them for information. *The Writer's Book of Checklists* by Scott Edelstein (Writer's Digest Books) includes information about giving readings as well.

Promotion tips: Everyone agrees writing is hard work whether you are published or not. Yet, once you arrive at the published side of the equation the work changes.

Most published authors will tell you the work is still hard but it is different. Now, not only do you continue working on your next project, you must also concern yourself with getting your book into the hands of readers. It becomes time to switch hats from artist to salesperson.

While even bestselling authors whose publishers have committed big bucks to promotion are asked to help in promoting their books, new authors may have to take it upon themselves to plan and initiate some of their own promotion, sometimes dipping into their own pockets. Yet, this does not mean that every author is expected to go on tour, sometimes at their own expense. It does mean authors should be prepared to offer suggestions for promoting their books.

Depending on the time, money and the personal preferences of the author and publisher, a promotional campaign could mean anything from mailing out press releases to setting up book signings to hitting the talk-show circuit. Most writers can contribute to their own promotion by providing contact names—reviewers, home-town newspapers, civic groups, organizations—that might have a special interest in the book or the writer.

Above all, when it comes to promotion, be creative. What is your book about? Try to capitalize on it. For example, if you've written a mystery whose protagonist is a wine connoisseur, you might give a reading at a local wine-tasting or try to set something up at one of the national wine events. For an inside look at the role publicists play in promotion, see the article, Publicists' Roundtable, by Don Prues, on page 22. For more suggestions on promoting your work see *The Writer's Guide to Promotion & Publicity*, by Elane Feldman (Writer's Digest Books).

The sample cover letter

For the last two editions of *Novel & Short Story Writer's Market*, we have invited readers to enter our Short Story Cover Letter Contest. This year's winning letter (on page 18) was written by Sandra Black and originally accompanied her submission of "The Poster Man" to *Nocturnal Ecstasy Vampire Coven*. For her efforts, Black received a handwritten letter of acceptance from editor Darlene Daniels on *NEVC*'s "vampire lady" letterhead. In her letter, Daniels says, "I enjoyed ["The Poster Man"] very much and do intend on sharing it with *NEVC*'s readers."

Black's letter incorporates all the basic elements of a good cover letter and more. That is, a cover letter should be no more than one page, proofread carefully and neatly typed. Paragraphs should be single spaced with a double space between paragraphs. Ideally, the letter should be addressed to a specific editor and should include a self-addressed, stamped envelope or postcard for reply.

Here are some additional things to notice about Black's winning cover letter:
● In the first sentence, Black gives the name of the story and the word count (*NEVC* specifically asks that word count be included in the cover letter).
● The remainder of the first paragraph is a short but enticing description of "The Poster Man." By the end of the second sentence, the editor knows that the story fits *NEVC*'s requirement for "vampire-related" fiction.
● In the second paragraph, Black effectively conveys to Daniels her enthusiasm for, and knowledge of, the genre of vampire fiction. This tells the editor that she is dealing with a writer who knows about vampires and whose story will most likely reflect that knowledge.
● In the third paragraph, Black lets the editor know that she is familiar with *NEVC* and appreciates the market it provides for vampire fiction. In an often thankless profession, an editor can find such words of sincere appreciation irresistible.
● Black devotes most of her fourth paragraph to listing previous publishing credits, all in the same genre as *NEVC*. Publishing credits, especially those in a pertinent genre, can

The Short Story Cover Letter

Address
Phone

January 23, 1995

Darlene Daniels, Editor
Nocturnal Ecstasy Vampire Coven Journal
NEVC/Nocturnal Productions
P.O. Box 147
Palos Heights, IL 60463-1047

Dear Ms. Daniels:

Enclosed please find my short story of approximately 2,500 words entitled "The Poster Man." This is a contemporary vampire tale based upon a true happening. It features a Bram Stoker Dracula poster, a man who wants to buy the poster, and a man who is willing to sell the poster.

I am a true-blue vampire buff. I read/research all vampiric material from serious accounts to the utterly preposterous. Of particular interest to me is the evolution of the vampire from a Neanderthal-like creature to a more sophisticated and alluring persona, e.g. Lestat de Lioncourt.

I am happy to find your magazine which features the vampire, as it seems so few reach out into this medium anymore. It would be a shame to throw by the wayside such classic monstrous phenomena.

My past credits include local publications and short stories in *Midnight Zoo*, *Aberations*, *'Scapes*, and the anthology, *Shock Treatment*. Adopting a softer image than horror maven, I also volunteer to read stories to children at the library.

I look forward to your reply. Thank you for your consideration.

Sincerely,

Sandra Black

Enclosures: manuscript, "The Poster Man"
            SASE

Sandra Black *is a fiction writer and graduate of Writer's Digest School's Writing and Selling Short Stories class. Her vampire stories have been published in a number of small magazines. Black is currently trying to find a publisher for her still untitled first novel about—what else?—vampires.*

increase the chances of having your story read by an editor who thinks, "If others have published this writer, perhaps I might like what she's submitting to me."

● In her last paragraph, Black thanks the editor for her consideration of "The Poster Man" and expresses her eagerness to receive a reply. She could have mentioned here that she has enclosed a SASE, but chooses to include that as an enclosure notation.

By the time editor Daniels begins reading "The Poster Man," she has learned a lot about the story and its author from Black's one-page, targeted cover letter. It is no wonder that, having read and liked the story, Daniels' letter of acceptance to Black ends with, "I do hope that you will continue to submit work to *NEVC* in the future."

For more on cover letters and formats, see *The Writer's Digest Guide to Manuscript Formats*, by Dian Dincin Buchman and Seli Groves. If you feel you have a successful cover letter, we hope you will consider entering our 1997 Short Story Cover Letter Contest. The winning letter will be published in the next edition. Our criteria is simple: We're looking for a letter that helped lead to the *acceptance* of a short story between May 1995 and May 1996. Keep in mind the letter must include the elements of a good cover letter as outlined. The deadline is May 15, 1996. Send the letter with your address and phone number and proof of acceptance (a copy of the letter of acceptance will do) to Cover Letter, *Novel & Short Story Writer's Market*, 1507 Dana Ave., Cincinnati OH 45207.

In addition to publication in the 1997 edition of *Novel & Short Story Writer's Market*, the writer will receive a small cash payment for publication of the letter, a copy of the book and the opportunity to select two titles from our Writer's Digest Books catalog.

U.S. Postage by the Page

by Carolyn Lieberg

Mailing costs can be an appreciable part of writing expenditures. The chart below can help save money as well as time by allowing you to figure the fees for sending your manuscripts to prospective publishers.

Postage rates are listed by numbers of pages (using 20 lb. paper) according to the most commonly used envelopes and their self-addressed, stamped envelopes (SASEs). While most writers prefer to send their work First Class, Third Class is becoming a choice for some. Third Class moves more slowly, and currently costs the same as First Class under 12 ounces. However, it is permissible in Third Class to include a letter pertaining to the material inside.

First Class mail weighing more than 33 ounces is assessed according to weight plus geographical zone so it needs to be priced at the Post Office.

Postcards can be a bargain for writers. If the postage costs are higher than another computer printout or photocopied version of a manuscript, a postcard can be used for the editor's reply. The cost is 20¢.

For short manuscripts or long queries, use a #10 (business-size) envelope with a 32¢ stamp. Four pages is the limit if you are including a SASE. Another option is the 6×9 envelope. For 1-3 pages, postage is 32¢ in the U.S. For 4-7 pages with SASE, cost is 55¢. Computer disks may be sent in official mailers or mid-size envelopes with stiffening for 78¢.

Since paper and packaging weights do vary, however, it's always best when possible to have mail weighed at your local post office.

Ounces	9×12 9×12 SASE number of pages	9×12 SASE (for return trips) number of pages	First Class Postage	Third Class Postage	Postage from U.S. to Canada
under 2	. . .	1 to 2	$ .43*	$ .43*	$ .64*
2	1 to 4	3 to 8	.55	.55	.72
3	5 to 10	9 to 12	.78	.78	.95
4	11 to 16	13 to 19	1.01	1.01	1.14
5	17 to 21	20 to 25	1.24	1.24	1.33
6	22 to 27	26 to 30	1.47	1.47	1.52
7	28 to 32	31 to 35	1.70	1.70	1.71
8	33 to 38	36 to 41	2.93	2.93	1.91
9	39 to 44	42 to 46	2.16	2.16	2.09
10	45 to 49	47 to 52	2.39	2.39	2.28
11	50 to 55	53 to 57	2.62	2.62	2.47
12-32	56 to 99	58 to 101	3.00	3.00	2.66

*This cost includes a 11¢ assessment for oversized mail that is light in weight.

Carolyn Lieberg *'s short fiction and essays have appeared in* Four Minute Fictions, The North American Review, Cream City, The Montana Review *and others.*

Canadian Postage by the Page

by Barbara Murrin

The following chart is for the convenience of Canadian writers sending mail and American writers sending a SAE with International Reply Coupons (IRCs) or Canadian stamps for return of a manuscript from a Canadian Publisher. These figures are approximate, because the canadian Postal Service meets to determine new fees in January each year, after we go to press. Check your post office for changes.

In a #10 envelope, you can have up to five pages for 45¢ (on manuscripts within Canada) or 52¢ (on manuscripts going to the U.S.). If you enclose a SAE, four pages is the limit. With 10×13 envelopes, send one page less than indicated on the chart. IRCs are worth 50¢ Canadian postage and 60¢ in U.S. postage but cost $1.05 to buy in the U.S. and $3.50 in Canada.

Canada Post designations for types of mail are:

Standard Letter Mail — Minimum size: 9×14cm (3⅝×5½″); Maximum size: 15×24.5cm (5⅞×9⅝″); Maximum thickness: 5mm (³⁄₁₆″)

Oversize Letter Mail — Max. size: 27×38cm (10⅞×15″); Max. thickness: 2cm (¹³⁄₁₆″)

International Letter Mail — Min. size: 9×14cm (3⅝×5½″); Max. size: Length + width + depth 90cm (36″); Greatest dimension must not exceed 60cm (24″)

Small packets is a category designed to provide an alternative to Parcel Post for items weighing up to 2 kg. They may be sealed and security registered but cannot be insured (unless sent at parcel rates). An "Air Mail" sticker is required on all air mail small packets. All small packets must bear a green Customs label C1 (form no. 43-074-076). Parcels over 1 kg. to U.S. require customs label no. 43-074-013.

Insurance: To U.S.—65¢ for each $100 coverage to a maximum coverage of $1,000. Within Canada—$1 for first $100 coverage; 45¢ for each additional $100 coverage to a maximum coverage of $1,000. International—65¢ for each $100 coverage to the maximum coverage allowed by country of destination. (Not accepted by all countries.)

Registered Mail: $3.15 plus postage (air or surface—Canadian destination). Legal proof of mailing provided. No indemnity coverage.

Weight up to	9×12 envelope, 9×12 SAE number of pages*	9×12 SAE (for return trips) number of pages*	Canada Standard	Oversize	First Class to U.S. Standard	Oversize
30 g/1.07 oz.	. . .	1 to 3	$ .45	$ .90	$ .52	$ 1.17
50 g/1.78 oz.	1 to 4	4 to 7	.71	.90	.96	1.17
100 g/3.5 oz.	5 to 14	8 to 18	. . .	.88	.96	1.17
200 g/7.1 oz.	15 to 46	19 to 49	. . .	1.40	1.43	2.23
300 g/10.7 oz.	47 to 57	50 to 61	. . .	2.00	2.00	3.80
400 g/14.2 oz.	58 to 79	62 to 82	. . .	2.00	2.70	3.80
500 g/17.8 oz.	80 to 101	83 to 104	. . .	2.00	3.55	3.80
1.0 kg/2.2 lbs.	102 to 208	105 to 212	**	**	6.20	***

*Based on 20 lb. paper and 2 adhesive labels per envelope.
**For Canadian residents mailing parcels 1 kg. and over within Canada (domestic mail), rates vary according to destination. Ask your Post Master for the chart for your area.
***Over 1kg rates vary by destination (country and state).

Barbara Murrin *is a recently retired music and business instructor who now does network marketing full time.*

Publicists' Roundtable

by Don Prues

Unpublished writers often wonder what happens to their books once they are published. Of course, you want to be assured everyone will have an opportunity to see, buy and read your book. You'd hate to spend two years arduously writing that long-awaited novel only to find that, even though the publisher has agreed to publish it, no steps will be taken to promote it.

This roundtable discussion will shed light on the darkness behind those closed doors of the enigmatic world of promotion and publicity. We've asked an eclectic group of specialists in the publishing industry, from small presses to an evangelical publisher to one of the biggest players in the publishing game, to reveal the ins and outs of what will happen to your book once it's published.

Participating in this discussion are Sandra Kalagian, Publicity and Subsidiary Rights Manager at Coffee House Press; Lisa Bullard, Publicity and Promotions Director at Graywolf Press; Kathy Jacobs, Public Relations Director at Crossway Books; and Therese Zazycki, Senior Publicist at Penguin USA's Mass Market Division.

What specific steps are taken to promote a book or an author?

Most of us know there are various ways to promote a book—author tours, reviews, guest appearances, in-store displays, etc. These things don't "just happen." Each publishing house uses a structured set of steps designed for each book and its author.

Says Lisa Bullard of Graywolf, "As soon as authors sign a contract, the marketing department sends them an author questionnaire to complete. We ask for all sorts of information—a biography, past reviews, a photo, previous contacts with booksellers and reviewers, availability for touring, ideas for catalog copy, special markets, competition for the book and potential endorsements."

"For me, the first step is to read the book after the editors tell me why they selected the manuscript," says Sandra Kalagian of Coffee House. "Meanwhile, I send a questionnaire to the author to find out why he wrote the book and to get his take on its market. With this information, I plan a marketing strategy that may include bookstore readings, point-of-purchase promotional items, radio interviews, advertising, or even a special gimmick such as a book display contest for booksellers. The manuscript is sent to a printer to be made into bound galleys (rough advance copies of the book). A press release announcing the upcoming publication date with a description of the book and the author is sent to a select list of reviewers. Our catalog announcing the upcoming titles is sent out to a larger list of reviewers so that they may call and request titles of interest. Months later, when the finished book comes off the press, it is sent out with an updated press release to everyone who received the galley as well as to a larger list of potential reviewers."

Likewise, Penguin's Therese Zazycki uses a methodical approach: "When deciding to promote a book I look mainly into five areas: book reviews, off-the-book page articles or mentions, appearances on radio and television shows, author tours, and book and author events [signings, bookfairs, library readings, trade shows, newspaper-sponsored

Don Prues *is the editor of* Guide to Literary Agents *and assistant editor of* Writer's Market.

book and author dinners]." Unfortunately, not all authors get such strong and varied support. "The type of publicity depends on the type of book, the personality and availability of the author, how big the book is in terms of printing and budget, and what has worked well in the past for this author or this type of book."

Kathy Jacobs at Crossway Books says, "I help guide authors through the book promotion process. I always ask authors to do a thorough job of filling out the author information sheet because the information will be used by several different departments including publicity. I interact with authors about a myriad of publicity details. I try to keep them informed about our promotional efforts and the results. Our editorial department often solicits endorsements. Early in the editorial process we ask if the author knows any prominent people or experts on his topic who might favorably comment on the book."

How does promotion for new authors, mid-list authors and established authors differ? Does your company have any special programs for new authors or mid-list authors?

Obviously, if you're having your first book published, you're not going to get the same promotional goodies offered to established authors. Established authors have a following and thus it's worth the risk for a publisher to spend lots of time and money promoting them. Promoting a new author, on the other hand, is very risky, which is why there are varying levels of the promotion campaign. Much does depend on the author's reputation—and hearsay.

Crossway Books recently capitalized on Dr. Marvin Olasky's *The Tragedy of American Compassion*, a book few people knew about until Newt Gingrich recommended it. Immediately after hearing of Gingrich's endorsement, Jacobs sent a news release and phoned key media contacts even though the book was published in 1992. "The Speaker's interest boosted sales which resulted in the book's going back to press and its subsequent release in paperback. Olasky now has been interviewed on network newscasts, on C-Span and on Dateline NBC. And dozens of articles about him have appeared in newspapers and magazines nationwide."

The bigger houses, like Penguin, try to capitalize on authors who will bring in big returns—after all, the publisher probably has paid the author a big advance. Nobody wants to lose money. "The promotion campaign we do for Stephen King is very different than one we would do for a first-time paperback author with a conservative print run," says Zazycki. "What type of promotion we give depends on the type of book and the author and how much the company has budgeted the publicity department for promotion. If the book or author is very media friendly (a juicy biography, autobiography by a famous or controversial person, topic of the moment book, or a novel by a celebrity) more will be planned. If it's a work of fiction, concentration will be on review attention.

"Big books get press kits, multi-city tours, radio and television interviews, bookstore autographings and wider review mailings. Mid-list books will get the above but on a lesser scale. Instead of a press kit sent to media and reviewers, they may get a press release or press packet, fewer autographings and only publicity in the city in which the author lives. Books that are considered small in terms of print run and budget will only get a review mailing and perhaps a local bookstore autographing. Penguin does not have any special programs for new or mid-list authors."

But don't be disappointed if you're no Stephen King. Not all publishers are the same. In fact, many small presses uphold an egalitarian philosophy when promoting. Take, for example, Coffee House Press. "At a small nonprofit literary press, a major effort is made on behalf of all of the authors on its list," says Kalagian. "There is not much chance of getting lost in the shuffle. For us, first-time authors carry with them the advantage of being able to be publicized as 'debut authors,' which makes them newsworthy. And book reviewers, bookstores and the media are interested in discovering a great new talent or hearing about how an author finally made it into print."

Lisa Bullard agrees. "As a nonprofit press, Graywolf is mission-driven, and we select our books based on literary merit and originality of language. We work very hard to promote every title we publish; every book has a marketing plan and goes through the same steps. We very much enjoy publishing and marketing books by new authors; helping writers establish themselves is part of our mission, and new authors often bring great energy and enthusiasm to the publishing process."

How soon in the process does publicity start?

Publicity planning varies from publisher to publisher depending on the book's marketability. At Graywolf "planning and discussion for publicity begin as soon as a book is signed," says Bullard. "But 'hands-on' publicity efforts—writing copy, talking to reviewers, choosing an advertising campaign, talking with booksellers—begin nine months to a year before the publication date."

The process takes a bit longer at Coffee House. "The book should be selected and steps to begin publicity should occur at least 18 months before the anticipated publication date. Sometimes, however, the process begins even before the selection of the book."

"In mass markets," says Zazycki, "a year before publication is when the ball starts rolling at Penguin. That is when the editor will present the book to all departments and the publicity director will then research the book's and author's potential for promotion. Ten months before publication, the publicity director will present ideas for this book as well as others for that month. The final marketing/promotion plans are completed six months before publication, detailing the exact publicity for the book."

So what are the final marketing/promotion plans? That, too, emphasizes Zazycki, depends on the book and its author. "If there is a proposed sell-in tour (where an author meets with agency personnel at accounts that distribute mass market books), work will begin six months before the sale date. Four months before that date, galleys are sent to reviewers. This is when the publicist assigned to the book will be in contact with the author about publicity plans. Dates for an author tour will be plotted and bookstore autographings and book and author events will also be sent to book reviewers. If there is a tour, four to six weeks before it begins, a press kit will be made up, a mailing will be sent, and calls to the media will begin."

How important are reviews and what are the major review publications for fiction?

Publicists agree that reviews often determine whether a book sells 2,000 or 2,000,000 copies. Yes, reviews are *that* important. Says Bullard, "Reviews are so very important that booksellers list them as one of the top reasons that customers come to a store asking for a specific title. For fiction, *The New York Times Book Review* still has the biggest impact, although several other nationally recognized newspapers are also important, such as *The Washington Post, The Los Angeles Times Book Review,* and *The Boston Globe.* A review in a popular magazine such as *MS.* or *Time* also has a big impact. Regional papers and alternative newsweeklies can also make a difference in the author's hometown. One of the best places to get coverage remains National Public Radio."

Adds Kalagian, "A very good review in an important journal can launch a book's success by attracting the attention of readers, other reviewers, media people, and even movie studios. Of course, one dreams of great reviews, but any review—favorable or not—is good for the book. The more reviews the better! We strive for reviews in *Publishers Weekly, Kirkus Reviews, The New York Times Book Review, The Washington Post Book World, The Los Angeles Times Book Review,* and *The Village Voice Literary Supplement.*"

At Penguin, Zazycki primarily focuses on obtaining reviews for hardcovers. "I consider review attention for a hardcover very important. It establishes an author's reputation, brings a reader's attention to the book and provides blurb material for the reprint or next book. Good reviews in major publications work in the author's favor when negotiating with a house for the next book or selling the paperback reprints. On the other hand, it's not so easy to get reviews for paperback originals or reprints."

Even relatively small, targeted publishers can benefit greatly from noteworthy reviews in the most specialized publications. Jacobs of the evangelical publisher, Crossway, tells this recent success story. "After fiction author Frank E. Peretti's novel *This Present Darkness* was favorably reviewed in several Christian publications, the book began to set sales records in the Christian market, and we used existing publicity to help obtain additional publicity in *The New York Times, People, USA Today, The Chicago Tribune* and *The L.A. Times.* Consequently, *This Present Darkness* has sold over 2 million copies."

What are some ways you work with authors to promote their books?

Says Kalagian, "At the very beginning, when the author is sent a contract to sign, he or she is asked to write a statement of purpose about the book. This helps us understand and present the book in the way the author intended. It also helps us write good catalog copy and book jackets. We also ask the author to note local or specialized reviewers, confirm his or her availability for bookstore touring, suggest special markets that fall outside of standard publishing channels, and provide lists of friends, relatives, professors and associates who might buy the book if sent a notice and order form."

According to Zazycki, authors play a key role in book promotion. "Authors are instrumental. A personable and interesting author talking about his or her book in front of an audience at a bookstore event, on a television or radio show, or in a newspaper or magazine article will sell many more books than if the book was simply reviewed. Recently, I worked with a fiction author who was a savvy businesswoman who knew the art of selling. A lot was stacked against promotion: she wasn't known, the book had a modest print run, was a paperback and an ethnic romance, appealing to a specific audience. I had a very hard time getting her publicity on the basis of those cold facts. Yet when this author appeared in front of an audience, none of that mattered—the members of the audience fell for her. Bookstore owners and media personalities who originally told me no to events and interviews would change their minds after meeting her. I may have been the hand that started the publicity wheel, but she was definitely the force that made it spin and sell those books."

Graywolf encourages authors to think about the market for their book and to give the publicity department any leads they can. "Some of our authors have been writing for a long time, and have valuable contacts that can help sell books," says Bullard. "These contacts might be other writers who will provide an early endorsement for catalog copy, or reviewers or booksellers who have helped them in the past. Authors are also more likely to know which of their local reviewers really have clout, and which of their local bookstores stage the best events. Many authors are also teachers or professors, and can give us names of past students or other professors who might use the book in class. Sometimes authors also have connections with special markets. Does the book focus on a particular ethnic group? Is there a connection to a health issue—a character with a disability, for instance?"

At Crossway, Jacobs makes it a point to get to know the author well. "I help authors understand their role and mine in publicizing their books," she says. "In my role as publicist I am often a coach, adviser and encourager. I might advise them to pursue one media opportunity over another. I encourage authors to widen their sphere of influence by becoming experts on their topic. If I learn that an author is not gifted at interviewing I may tactfully suggest he or she hire a professional to teach the necessary skills. I've helped authors become contributing writers for publications. I encourage authors, especially first-time authors, to network with other authors. I interact with a lot of different people and am often a link between people who share the same vision and can aid one another in dispensing and publicizing that vision. I communicate with authors, especially first-time authors, so they have realistic expectations about their book's publicity and sales."

What are some extra things an author can do to help?

While larger publishing houses often front a large advance for promotion and publicity, there are many things authors can do to promote their books without the financial backing of the publisher. "An author can visit local bookstores and libraries to encourage them to carry a book," says Jacobs. "One of my authors is currently visiting a couple of dozen bookstores while vacationing in the East. Known as a western fiction writer, this author has just written his first contemporary fiction, the first book in a new series. He wants to get acquainted with booksellers and wants them to get acquainted with his new work. So that's what he's doing."

Bullard acknowledges that while self-promotion helps increase a book's popularity, Graywolf doesn't expect its authors to invest large amounts of time or money in promoting their books. "Our authors are not required to commit any money or time to book promotion. However, we strongly encourage authors to make themselves available for a few interviews and local events. Some authors choose to spend a great deal of time working on audience development—to the degree that they tell us they no longer have time to write! We also have had authors who've volunteered to travel less expensively (by train or car, and staying with friends along the way), or who have covered their own travel expenses so that they could tour more bookstores, or reach an area where they have friends and family. We're happy to try to arrange for extra events in these cases.

"I've also heard of cases where authors have paid for ads, hired their own freelance publicist, paid for a special bookmark, hired someone to do Internet marketing, etc. I would encourage any of our authors to talk with us before spending their own money. In some cases, they might have an excellent idea that goes beyond our budget capacity. Other times, however, their idea might be one we have already considered and rejected for good reasons."

Kalagian concentrates on what an author can do at each stage in publicity. "An author must meet deadlines throughout the publishing process. Delays in even the earliest stages have a negative impact on the publicity department's ability to properly promote a book," she says.

Regarding promotion once the book is published, Kalagian has two words for authors. "Be available," she advises. "If the publicity department lands a bookstore event or an interview, do your best to be there. Make it easy for the publicity department to get in touch with you. Return messages promptly. Provide a fax number if available. Become comfortable talking about your book. Tell everyone you meet about it. Be prepared to give effective interviews and readings. Explore local angles, professional groups, community organizations and other such places in which you have more experience than your publisher. You are the book's best salesperson."

Zazycki does as much as possible to get to know the author's background and concept of the book, looking for anything that can aid promotion. "Help from an author is extremely important for a publicist. I need to know why this author and/or book is interesting or unique enough so I can effectively approach the media. Does the author have a special talent or unusual life? How did this book originate? My company publishes approximately 28 books a month and we may not catch something that would make this book stand out from the hundreds that are vying for the same attention from reviewers and radio and television producers. To create an effective publicity campaign, I need an author's input about what is important about the book. Sometimes I ask the author to create a synopsis of the book with bullets pointing out interesting facts, a question and answer sheet, and/or bio on herself. And any media contacts the author has are very important. This is the time when authors need to backtrack over their lives and call anyone they ever knew who might help them get a review, an interview or any type of publicity."

What particularly bothers you about working with new authors? What publicity knowledge should an author possess by the time a publisher acquires the book? What are some of the mistakes new authors make?

Publicists agree that first-time authors often make the mistake of thinking publishers have an unlimited budget for promotion, that once their book is published it will automatically become a success. The prominent problems new authors have are unrealistic, grandiose ideas about their book's reception.

"The hardest part about working with new authors is that many of them have unrealistic expectations about publicity and they're easily disappointed," says Bullard. "Instead of being delighted with the good things that happen for their book, they focus on what didn't happen (no interview in *People* magazine, no Pulitzer Prize, no invitation from David Letterman)."

"Having realistic expectations is one of the most important traits a new author should have," echoes Zazycki. "Except for a remarkable few, a first book will not make the bestseller lists, command an audience of 500 at a bookstore event, or make Barbara Walters want to talk to the author. I enjoy working with new authors who have a sense of how publishing works—where their books stand among all the others and exactly what I can and cannot do for their books. They have researched the publishing business, talked to published authors. These are the best authors to work with—those willing to help me in any way to promote their books, even doing it themselves."

But an author must use discretion in how much time and energy he or she invests in promoting the book. Use common sense says Zazycki: "I had a first-time author tell me, very seriously, that he wanted me to work '24 hours a day for the next year' to make his book a bestseller. He would not listen to me either—another big mistake. When I would tell him a certain show producer said no to an interview, he would call the person himself, damaging my relationship with the producer and ruining future possible interviews for him. He insisted the key to the success of his book lay in his traveling around the country doing bookstore autographings. From my experience, I knew it would not work for his type of book, and the few events he did confirmed this. Unfortunately, he created a reputation as a difficult author, and in the publishing business, word travels."

Referring to this story, Zazycki emphasises that authors must understand the demands placed on a publicist. "New authors need to know that book publicists work for the publishing company and are not an author's personal publicist. I work on anywhere from five to ten books a month and may not have that extra time to call an author back immediately." So be patient if your call isn't expediently returned.

It is essential to be professional, cordial and grateful. Says Kalagian, "Don't be annoying just because you're nervous. We know this is your first book. We don't expect you to know everything so don't feel obliged to pretend you do. Share your concerns with us but don't harp on them. Don't intrude too much on the staff's daily work. Do express your willingness to help—tell the publicity department to feel free to call on you. But don't be too demanding. We are working as hard as we can for you. Be a pleasure to work with. Say thank you. Authors so infrequently say thank you that I can't help but feel grateful and want to work extra hard for the ones that do. Radio interviewers, reporters and bookstore personnel are also rarely thanked and will respond warmly to your kindness. I am not just pointing this out as a lesson in good manners. One of our authors stood out for her enthusiasm and genuine appreciation of any efforts made on her behalf. After being impressed and charmed by her, bookstore employees went out of their way to sell her book. Good word-of-mouth on this author and her book spread in large part due to her natural tendency to be nice and to say thank you."

One final word of caution to new authors: Don't get too discouraged by negative reviews. "One of the biggest mistakes new authors make is taking bad reviews too personally," says Bullard. "Every book gets a bad review from somewhere—and I mean it when I tell new authors that even bad reviews can sell books. Some authors let a few negative reviews, or unrealistic expectations, ruin their whole publishing experience. Just because one, two or even ten reviewers don't praise your book does not mean you've failed as a writer and that you should give up promoting that book."

For information on entering the Novel & Short Story Writer's Market *Cover Letter Contest*, see page 19.

Anthologies—Another Place for Your Fiction

by J.N. Williamson

Many writers automatically shy away from the idea of anthologies as another opportunity to place their fiction. They do so either because they fear they cannot adapt their skills to the varied demands of anthology editors; they believe the competition is too stiff; or they just don't know how to locate anthologists. Some writers add, "I have my own magazine markets," ignoring the fact that many anthologies continue to pay royalties on copies sold for years, and most magazine sales pay exactly once.

Yet there are a few likely challenges for the newer writer trying to break in to the anthology market:

1. Some editors have virtual "stables" of writers whose versatility, quickness to complete professional-level work, and overall reliability may leave only a few "slots" open for other authors.

2. Most anthologies are "closed" to begin with, which is to say, "not open to submissions without an invitation."

3. Unlike magazines, which are published with some regularity and include mastheads bearing editors' names and addresses, it can seem impossible to unpublished authors to hear of an anthology in time to make a submission—or to know *where* to send it!

These, obviously, are the drawbacks that give credence to the nay-sayers' point of view. Yet it is true that many anthology editors want to present new writers to the reading public. From the conception of my first anthology, I planned to introduce work by at least one or two new writers, and I have done so in all the books I originally edited. Three contributors to that first anthology were in hardcover for the first time, one earning his first payment. Five more were in hardback for the first time in my second anthology; two were new writers in any form; and so forth. And I know other editors like to allow for the inclusion of relative "unknowns."

What is an anthology?

The word anthology usually refers to a book of short stories, but that is not unfailingly accurate. Annually, many *nonfiction* anthologies are published on a wide variety of topics ranging from nature or politics to sociological concerns, the paranormal, and this very book. My own 1987-released how-to book has no fiction; it comprises, for the most part, 27 chapters of advice about successful writing. Yet it is an anthology and continues to reward its contributors with royalty moneys paid on copies of the book sold since the prior royalty period.

Here, the emphasis is placed on anthologies of short fiction. It is useful to point out that, though professional authors and editors may themselves slip and occasionally refer

J.N. Williamson has edited nine anthologies. His short fiction has appeared in several magazines and anthologies such as Dark Seductions, Vampire Detectives *and* Hot Blood V. *He is also the author of* How to Write Tales of Horror, Fantasy & Science Fiction *(Writer's Digest Books).*

to them as "collections," that term specifically means a gathering of the shorter works of a *single* writer.

Anthologies of fiction feature an editor's (or editors') carefully-assembled choice of short stories—sometimes with a smattering of poems—created by a number of writers. That number varies from as few as three or four writers, when it may be called a "limited anthology," to a more common range of 14 to 20-some contributors. There are, too, weighty anthologies presenting dozens of writers' work. In most instances these very long books exist as "Best of" volumes, customarily tales reprinted from many different magazines or books, or samplings from publications issued for decades, possibly those that are hard-to-find collectors' items.

Anthologists are told by publishers the acceptable maximum length of the book they are contracted to edit, usually in terms of the number of words the planned anthology may contain. It becomes the anthologists' task to decide how they want to use the allotted space (which, to me, will mean keeping a running count as stories are accepted). Contemporary fiction anthologies tend to run between 70,000 and 110,000 words; therefore, an editor whose contract calls for 85,000 words of short fiction may be inclined to seek approximately 14 contributors whose submissions should not exceed 6,000 words in length per story. (Complications develop when work is outstanding and comes from a famous writer whose name may well sell copies, but it runs thousands of words longer.)

Original anthology indicates that the contents were not previously published and therefore is the kind of "antho" for which new writers should look if they want to make submissions. A *reprint* anthology, obviously enough, has short works that have already been published somewhere. Finally, a *theme* anthology presents material connected to and springing from a single, specific subject. Both new and reprinted fiction may comprise these anthologies, occasionally in the same book.

Some further remarks here may be worth noting: I know of original anthologies in which editors concluded that privately-printed stories and poetry, and a story that had been in a publication with fewer than 500 subscribers, could be viewed as making "original" publication. After all, the primary concerns of anthologist and publisher alike are to sell copies and please the readers.

Theme anthologies are often linked to a perceived "hot" trend or topic; a "tie-in" to a currently-popular film or TV program or they "salute" certain occasions. Here, from a list of anthology titles to which I sold my own short fiction, are examples of theme books: *14 Vicious Valentines*, *Phantoms*, *The Bradbury Chronicles*, *Stalkers*, *Murder Most Delicious* (mysteries about food, with recipes), *After the Darkness*, *Vampire Detectives*, *Dark Seductions*, *Voices from the Night*, and—my most recent story sale at this writing—*Holmes for Christmas*, Sherlock Holmes pastiches.

Although there are anthologies published for virtually every genre as well as mainstream interests, there are three common threads that link them: Each editor craves submissions that are *fresh*, or acceptably different, that ideally *fit* his or her needs for that particular anthology, and that are *finished* and need little or no correction or revision.

Make it fresh

Anthologists yearn for submissions that are freshly, acceptably different. By this I do not mean a story conceived in an entirely experimental format such as a yarn without nouns or commas, nor a rhymed tale or autobiographical memoir. I certainly don't mean that the manuscript itself—or the mailer in which it arrives—should have some stylistic strangeness. What I mean to imply is that the writer has read enough fiction in the specified genre that what is crafted seems "new" to the editor in some way. If that just is not possible, the submission needs to have a fresh twist on the more familiar plots and characters within the category and be plausibly written. Without something that sets the newer writer apart, the anthologist is apt to prefer a story that is no fresher by a published writer but who may, at least, have an interested readership.

Make it fit

The second thing anthologists look for in submissions may be the key to breaking into the anthology market. Remember, I described it as creating a story that "ideally fits" the guidelines for "that particular anthology," something even professional writers don't always do. When the editor is disappointed by the invited pro's yarn but pleased by the close "fit" of the newcomer's work, he or she may well accept the latter's story—especially if a deadline is near! (Twice, in fact, I have made such a choice.) That's why fully comprehending the anthology guidelines, then precisely tailoring your talents and ideas to that book should not be considered an irksome task but a bona fide opportunity.

Make it finished

In regard to the tale being finished and "ready to go," I mean that most editors of anthologies generally wear additional hats, unlike editors of commercial magazines, and they simply do not have time to discuss changes. This fact is frequently the reason most anthologists pursue either the work of established professionals and, when they can, already-written, published yarns to be reprinted. A newcomer may very well have completed a draft of a story with a better premise than a few of the professionals who wind up being accepted for an anthology, but unless it is surprisingly polished and free of gaffes, the editor may reluctantly reject it if it seems a few changes are required.

Unfortunately, newcomers often forget that creating a story that is involving, suspenseful and satisfying to read also requires attention to correct spelling and grammar, consistent internal logic and professional sentence and paragraph structure.

Another drawback for beginners is that the deadline for an "antho" is apt to be daunting, particularly if research appears to be needed. Bear in mind that all devoted effort expended to write a good story is worthwhile. Even if you complete it too late or it is rejected, you have had the practice. You will also have a submission either already finished for another publication or one that will be after some unpressured revision.

Having fiction in anthologies can be a significant step for newer writers because it proves helpful in selling to other anthologies and to magazines, perhaps even in getting a book contract. In the first two cases, editors tend to keep up with what their peers are doing, and it seems less chance-taking when somebody else has already bought from a writer. Until 1988, my short fiction had been in nine anthologies not counting my own; since I appeared in Ed Gorman's and Martin H. Greenberg's highly successful *Stalkers* in 1989, my short stories have sold to 47 more anthologies, most of them written to editors' guidelines. It may be additionally interesting to learn that ten people who were first in hardcover in my four fiction anthologies now have published one or more books of their own.

The money

As for the matter of royalties, anthologies can boast where magazines cannot. Quite often, the word rates paid by anthologies are often higher than those offered by regular newsstand publications. Not all anthologies are published first as hardcovers, but any kind of book may well be left on bookstore shelves longer than magazines just because monthly and quarterly publications are replaced when newer issues are distributed. It is also always conceivable that an "antho" first published as a hardcover will enjoy a paperback or foreign sale and most anthology contracts then call for additional payment to contributors.

Finding anthology markets

How do you know where to make a submission to an anthology when you don't know who is editing them? Visit a bookstore or library, identify the editors and publishers of several anthologies in your fields of writing interest, and direct a polite query letter in care of the publishing house. (If a given antho has a Roman numeral in the title or is in its third or fourth printing, the editor may be at work on the *next* "number" or on a completely new anthology.) Various computer networks furnish up-to-date information including contact names. Magazines such as *Writer's Digest* often carry news of upcoming anthologies, as do the short bios many publications run with their stories. If Author A sold a story to Anthologist B, that book may not yet have closed.

Organizations for writers often mention, in newsletters, anthologies under way, and you may be eligible for one kind of membership or another. Joining writers' groups and generally becoming acquainted with other writers may also provide "tips" about anthologies. I have lost count of how many I first heard of from a fellow writer or editor. In writing, too, business acquaintanceships are useful. I often telephone people with similar track records and ask if they are involved with new anthologies. Although you may not be able to do that, you probably can do what two people did, to me, at writer's conventions: introduced themselves and nicely inquired if they could send me samples of their work. I agreed, and each eventually sold fiction to me for anthologies I edited.

Selling your short stories to anthologies is challenging and may take awhile, but what aspect of writing does not? I know the effort can be rewarding.

I know a few other facts, too: Nearly *all* anthologies contain some fiction written by authors whose names are not remotely familiar to most of the world's readers. Indeed, apart from the books I have edited, I can't think of even one anthology in which I was able to identify every contributor, including those with stories I wrote!

Doesn't that suggest that one or two writers of extremely limited fame make it into almost every new fiction anthology? Maybe you should give that some thought.

Commercial Fiction Trends Report

by Robin Gee

Clearly, while the 1980s have been looked upon as a decade of tremendous growth and change for the book publishing industry, the '90s so far are becoming known as a slow-growth period. Since 1990, sales figures for the industry have continued to increase each year, but only by six or seven percent. Last year sales were up again, by an estimated 6.2 percent, but with the cost of paper and other materials on the rise, publishers claim their profits are lower than in previous years.

What does this mean for the writer—especially the new writer? Predictably, all this points to a tightening of the market. Many publishers are cutting back on the number of books they publish each season, consolidating lines, cutting staff and generally taking an even closer look at the bottom line. There's a heavy reliance on the big-name authors both with new books and with reissues of their backlist books. In turn, this leaves less room on publishers' lists for new authors or for those whose work has a stable but less-than-blockbuster following, those known in the industry as "the midlist."

Despite all the talk in the industry press about the decline of support for midlist authors and a general tightening of the market, all is not doom and gloom. Publishers, well aware that tomorrow's bestselling authors must come from a pool of fresh, new voices, are dedicated more than ever to finding new, talented authors. They are also even more committed to building some of their talented midlist authors into big names and promoting newer authors in creative ways.

Some specific areas of growth

Despite a slowing down of the market, some areas of fiction publishing are experiencing solid growth. Religious fiction continues to do well. Sales of religious books, both fiction and nonfiction, are up by nearly 20 percent. One reason religious fiction is doing so well is its growing acceptance within the religious community as a viable way to reach people and "get the word out" without being preachy or dogmatic. Another reason is many new religious fiction titles do well in crossover markets. As one religious fiction author put it, "Good fiction is still good fiction. I think our society is looking for stories with moral dimensions." Christian mysteries, adventure stories and romances are all doing very well, and Christian romances are popular not only with adult romance readers, but also with young adult readers.

With discounting and other marketing strategies, adult hardcover fiction overall is also doing well. Many well-known category authors—those who write mystery, science fiction, romance, horror, western and other genres—are now being published in hardcover and paperback. Many publishers are also reissuing entire backlists of popular authors.

Children's and young adult fiction

The children's book industry is still reeling from the merger of Macmillan and Simon and Schuster and a late 1994 decision by Random House to cut staff and consolidate departments. This merger has resulted in fewer individual book imprints with some being absorbed and others being cut altogether. The changes at Random House included a combining of the company's two hardcover children's imprints, Crown and Knopf, and the letting go of around 20 employees. Another change at Random House was the elimination of a separate library sales force, a move which has librarians and sales people throughout the industry concerned. Many feel libraries and other institutions require a different, more focused type of marketing than retail outlets. Library sales are an important part of children's book sales and the move could affect this area if other publishers decide to follow suit.

Other changes, too, indicate a tightening of the children's book industry. Some publishers are cutting back on the number of titles they publish by up to 25 percent. Others are relying more heavily on backlist books (always a strong area in children's publishing) by repackaging classic books in new formats as games, CD-ROMs, toys and other merchandise.

On the other hand, there is still room for well-written children's and young adult fiction. According to Alice P. Buening, editor of *Children's Writer's & Illustrator's Market*, middle grade fiction, especially chapter books and series, is still doing well as is young adult horror and science fiction. Romance for young adults, she says, is also a growth area. With the emphasis on horror in recent years, young adult romance publishing has suffered some. But now, while the horror market continues to thrive, publishers are looking to expand romance and other areas of interest to those young adults with different tastes.

General fiction books for young adults today do not differ much from their adult counterparts, and writers are finding more freedom to tackle tough issues and themes. Sensitive issues such as suicide, AIDS, unwed pregnancy, rape and guns in schools are no longer taboo.

Fantasy

All types of fantasy continue to do well. Traditional fantasy—sorcerers, dragons, fairies and elves in medieval-type settings—remains the mainstay of the genre, but the market for fantasies which take place in contemporary urban or even futuristic settings has become a major growth area for the field.

Last year we mentioned that fantasy has managed to break apart from its grouping with science fiction to be recognized as a separate genre. Even the Science Fiction Writers of America acknowledged this by changing their name to Science Fiction and Fantasy Writers of America. Science fiction has done well in combination with other genres—mystery and romance in particular—and now fantasy is following suit.

Perhaps the most interesting development has been the melding of science fiction and fantasy. Some fantasy writers also consider themselves science fiction writers. Fantasy writer Ann McCaffrey, for instance, points out that her famous dragons are a product of genetic engineering. Many fantasy authors create their fantasy worlds in space on other planets and mix elements of science into their magic.

One recent development has been the combining of fantasy and the science fiction subgenre cyberpunk to create what is being called "elf punk." These stories involve magical creatures such as elves who behave like urban punks, outsiders and drifters living on the fringe of society in a bleak, industrial urban atmosphere. The market is good right now for writers interested in this darker version of fantasy.

Many fantasy role-playing games recently have been turned into books and series. As mentioned last year, game companies such as Wizards of the Coast (the publishers behind *Magic: The Gathering* collectible card game and book series) are doing very well publishing books based on their games. Magic continues to be such a popular draw that many science fiction and fantasy bookstores are developing "Magic Nights" and other promotions. Books based on these games are strong sellers and popular with publishers.

Horror

Dark fantasy continues to dominate the horror field. After last year's *Interview with the Vampire* movie based on the bestseller by Anne Rice, vampire fiction is a strong area. Vampire erotica, vampire anthologies and vampire series are currently popular. The game publisher, White Wolf, is doing well with its series of books based on a vampire role-playing game and has ventured into publishing books in more areas of dark fantasy and horror. Last year the young company launched its book line and an anthology series, The World of Darkness.

Young adult horror, despite a cluttering of the field, is still very popular with teens and continues to sell well. Publishers remain interested in new properties to compete with big-name authors such as R.L. Stine and Christopher Pike.

Gothic horror is making a comeback. The popularity of this subgenre has never waned much, but, with all the attention to vampires and books like Caleb Carr's *The Alienist*, interest in Gothic horror appears to be on the rise.

Mystery

The mystery field continues to be a strong area for both new and established writers. It's been true in recent years that series books are doing particularly well. Publishers still want to see one book at a time, but they are hungry for books with series potential. With the expansion of superstores and the continued strength of independent mystery bookstores, there's often room to display an author's entire series, resulting in more money for publishers and authors alike.

Big name authors continue to take the lion's share of promotion dollars in the field, and with the emphasis on supporting their backlist, midlist authors are feeling the crunch. This means competition is keen for new authors. Still, publishers want to find the next big name. While unusual, it's no longer impossible for a relatively new mystery author to make it "into the big time" with a first or second book, garnering a big advance and a movie deal. Midlist and newer authors with strong potential now have a slightly better chance of being published in both hardcover and softcover as publishers try to promote those with strong potential.

On the other hand, the demand for extra quality that began in the 1980s continues to dominate the mystery field. Publishers have become highly selective and a new mystery these days must offer something a little different. The writing, of course, has to be top-notch, but mysteries with a unique new twist seem to have the edge. That twist might be an unusual setting such as ancient Egypt or modern-day New Orleans, or it might involve glimpses of a different culture such as rural Appalachians or Native Americans. Protagonists in today's mysteries are flawed and much more interesting than the 1950s gumshoe. They come from all walks of life—bookstore owners, cat sitters, teachers, jazz musicians, park rangers, as well as lawyers and cops.

While mystery readers (and publishers) always look for a strong plot, the emphasis in recent years is on the detective—whether he or she is an amateur or a professional. In an article on the state of mystery in the *Mystery Writers of America Annual* for 1995, author Les Roberts sums it up: "I see all kinds of crime writers veering off in more or less the same direction; i.e., the character-driven mystery."

Also writing in that annual, author Barbara Paul predicted the return of the white male detective. Women detectives and sleuths from a variety of ethnic backgrounds continue to be popular with readers, but Paul says she expects the male private investigator, long a mainstay of the genre, to return. Yet, she says, this time he'll be "more upscale, better educated. He'll be more respectful of women (or will have learned to hide his chauvinism) and he'll be more likely to turn to his computer for information instead of 'the street.' "

Last year also marked the 50th anniversary of the Mystery Writers of America. Since its early days, the organization has fought for respect and better conditions for mystery writers and remains one of the best sources of support and information for the mystery writer. Sisters in Crime, the Crime Writers Association, Private Eye Writers of America and other groups also help keep today's mystery well connected. A recent article in the trade journal *Publishers Weekly* discusses the strong mystery network involving publishers, booksellers, authors and readers. There are also numerous conventions and newsletters for mystery writers. In particular, 1995 marked the first year of Eyecon, a convention sponsored by the Private Eye Writers of America. Online computer services and bulletin boards, such as the popular Dorothy L. service named for author Dorothy L. Sayers (listserve@kentvm.kent.edu) keep everyone in the field in touch. Several book publishers produce their own newsletters, such as Scribner's *Inner Sanctum* and St. Martin's *Murder in the Flatiron Building*. Writers can obtain copies of these newsletters at local bookstores or through the publishers.

Romance

As in the song, R-E-S-P-E-C-T is the buzz word in the romance field these days. After years of being snubbed by critics and ignored by mainstream reviewers, romance authors are finally getting some well-deserved attention. For example, *Library Journal* inaugurated a special column devoted to romance reviews to appear three times a year. *Publishers Weekly* as well as *USA Today* and the *Atlanta Journal-Constitution* have also added more romance reviews.

Nearly half of all mass market paperback sales are in the romance genre, and authors and readers alike agree they are worthy of recognition. More romances than ever have made it onto bestseller lists, and the more popular authors are being published in hardcover as well as paperback. It's been a hard road to this new-found acceptance. Just last year, Jayne Ann Krentz (aka Amanda Quick) wrote, "There hasn't been a bodice ripped in ten years, but we can't shake the stigma."

Along with the ripped bodices, also gone are weak, formulaic plots. Today's romances have much stronger plots and characters than in the past. In fact, in keeping with similar trends in mystery and science fiction, romances are more character-driven than ever.

Word of mouth has always been an important factor to sales in the romance genre. Despite the lack of reviews in established media, romance rose to the top of the mass market mountain. Now, with new attention, the outlook is even better for writers interested in getting a start in this field.

Historical romances, especially western and frontier series are in great demand. Regencies, on the other hand, have changed a bit. While short Regencies are holding their own, there appears to be a demand for more involved books set in the Regency period.

An estimated one-third of all romance buyers are African-American, and, with the development of special lines such as Kensington's Arabasque line and growth in established lines, ethnic romances are doing well. Some market experts feel Terri McMillan's *Waiting to Exhale*, a book about four African-American women looking for love, while not at all a traditional romance, showed the industry how popular a book for and about African-American women can be. This year Arabasque plans to add Hispanic heros and heroines as well as historical fiction to the line.

Time travel remains very popular as a way to transport a heroine with modern-day sensibilities back in time. The trend in this area is to send characters to whom readers can relate into a very different situation. Robin Burcell's *When Midnight Comes*, for example, sends a female police officer back in time.

Modest expansion seems to be the key this year, and there have been a few specific changes to various romance lines. Harlequin has added the Love and Laughter line devoted to humorous romance. Silhouette launched Truly Yours, an interesting line built on the premise of love found through unexpected correspondence such as love letters, a misdirected Dear Jane missive, an invitation, a want ad or a personal ad. Signet/Topaz has absorbed its Dreamspun line into the Topaz line.

The only bad news for the genre came in the May/April 1995 issue of the *Romance Writers Report*, the magazine of the Romance Writers of America. In that report, Kensington publisher Walter Zacharius expressed great concern that the midlist (including newer romance authors) would be squeezed out by too much competition, by emphasis on publishing big-name authors' backlist titles, and by deep discounts on hardcover books. His article, however, was answered by a flood of mail from readers and writers supporting the need for a good midlist, many saying it has been an important proving ground for talented writers. Writers and publishers will do well to listen to Zacharius's warnings, and, as he says, take steps to support newer authors more than ever.

Science fiction

Science fiction remains a strong market, and character-driven stories are taking the lead. Genre-crossing or blending is also popular, especially combining science fiction with mystery, fantasy and, of course, romance. Literary science fiction is also popular, characterized by the work of writers like Gene Wolf and Elizabeth Hand. Despite predictions, cyberpunk and near-future settings continue to attract readers and publishers alike.

More and more science fiction authors are being published in hardcover and have garnered serious attention and reviews. As with other genres, big-name authors are not only published in hardcover with regularity but are also seeing reissues of their books. Series science fiction remains strong and, thanks to the extra space in superstores, you'll find entire series on bookstore shelves.

Perhaps the genre most strongly influenced by outside media, science fiction publishing continues to benefit from the interest built by television, CD-ROM games and movies. Recently *TV Guide* added a special science fiction column, bowing to the popularity of such shows as the "X-Files" and "Babylon 5." The Star Trek saga continues with "Voyager" and "Deep Space Nine" attesting to the resilience of the genre. Along with the publication of books based on these specific series, the interest from television viewers has added to the general popularity of science fiction publications.

Always at the forefront of technology, science fiction writers and readers stay in touch with each other over various online services as well as through conventions. Del Rey has started an online newsletter to communicate with readers and is developing a World Wide Web page. Watch for more of this as other publishers begin to explore the Internet.

Westerns

When Elana Lore became editor of *Louis L'Amour Western Magazine*, she surveyed readers to find out what kind of westerns interested them. She discussed those results in the February issue of *Roundup*, the magazine of the Western Writers of America. In that article, Lore says she found readers were interested in traditional western tales but were also interested in tales involving the Native American point-of-view, westerns laced with historical facts, Civil War stories and frontier stories. (See the interview with Lore on page 340 of this book.)

The trend in western writing today seems to be toward more believable and historically accurate westerns with nontraditional heros and heroines. There still seems to be a market for old-style westerns, but they must be more authentic than earlier books. With this effort to reflect the West as it really was, we are also finding stories involving African-American cowboys, Native Americans and more women.

Complex novels of the West about mining towns, family feuds and sagas of the frontier also remain popular. Often these are set one generation after pioneers settled the West. Western writers are also finding more diversity in subjects as today's westerns deal with corruption, politics, science and business.

Keeping an eye on the market

There are numerous ways to keep an eye on the fiction market. Get to know your local booksellers. These are the people on the front lines of the publishing industry. Not only are they painfully aware of what is not selling well or what seems to be flooding the market, they are also keen observers of what is becoming popular with readers. It's their business to know.

Networking is an excellent way to keep tabs on what's happening in the publishing industry. In addition to your local writer's group, organizations such as the Romance Writers of America, Horror Writers Association, Science Fiction and Fantasy Writers of America, Western Writers of America, Mystery Writers of America and the Society of Children's Book Writers and Illustrators offer writers in these areas support, encouragement and a wealth of "insider" information through newsletters, meetings and conferences. (You'll find information on most of these groups in our Organizations and Resources section.)

Writers' conferences offer other opportunities to learn about what's happening in the industry. These are great places to meet editors and agents as well as other writers. Most include trend topics in their programs. Conferences are held across North America and around the world. See the Conferences and Workshops section of this book for listings organized by regions, or pick up a copy of Writer's Digest magazine's conference issue published each May.

Writers' magazines and trade journals can also help you keep up with the market. In addition to Writer's Digest, which includes a monthly markets column, you'll find a wealth of market information in such publications as Scavenger's Newsletter and The Writers' Nook News. Industry journals such as Publishers Weekly, Small Press and Quill & Quire provide up-to-date news on publishing and bookselling.

If you have a computer and a modem, you also have access to the most current information available on the various online services and bulletin boards. America Online, GEnie, Compuserve and eWorld all include writers' areas, and there are several internet e-mail groups catering to specific genres.

It pays to know your market and your competition, but this trend-watching can only go so far. Every year, as we gather information for this report, we are reminded by writers, editors and agents that quality goes a long way no matter what you are writing. If you believe in what you've written and have taken the time to carefully craft your prose, by all means send it out. Regardless of any trend, there's always room for well-done fiction.

Experience and Imagination: The Sources of Fiction

by Josip Novakovich

Stories come primarily from either experience or imagination, and in most cases from both. The degree to which each is used varies from writer to writer and from tale to tale.

The standard advice to writers seeking sources for their stories is to write about what you know. That is, write about your experience. Still, others advise that you write about what you *don't* know, an approach that requires the use of imagination. It is to a writer's advantage to learn how to draw upon both of these sources—experience and imagination—separately and together.

Experience

Some stories come almost directly from the writer's experience—you experience something, then you write about it. This is the most direct, autobiographical method. The advantage in writing from experience is that you can write vividly, directly and with the authority of your knowledge. There's also a personal advantage to writing from your experience. Following the Socratic dictum, "Know thyself," you may reap the therapeutic and philosophic benefits of introspection. In fact, one of the greatest pleasures of writing for many people is the sensation of grasping for, and reaching, an understanding of the world and self.

Childhood experiences have inspired the literature of many famous authors. Tolstoy was only 22 when he wrote his autobiographical trilogy *Childhood, Boyhood, Youth.* Willa Cather said, "Most of the basic material a writer works with is acquired before the age of fifteen." Dickens wrote *David Copperfield* from memories of his poverty-stricken youth, and Philip Roth's *Goodbye Columbus* is mostly autobiographical.

Adult experiences, of course, are also the source of many stories and novels. Norman Mailer drew heavily from his war experiences to write *The Naked and the Dead.* Paul Theroux recounts his marriage and travels in *My Secret History.*

As a writer, you must be open to your experiences at all times. To be convincing, vivid, believable, your writing must have the texture of life: the details, the sensations, the thoughts and the emotions you experience. To instill life into your imagined story, you will need to provide accurate details of your experiences and perceptions. Many writers keep journals and jot down whatever strikes them as something they might use in their fiction: a character portrait, a description of a group of people, a smell, a thought, a conversation snippet, a joke, the atmosphere of a bus terminal. By doing this, when you need to describe a bus terminal in one of your stories, you can pull it out of your journal as well as out of your memory.

Josip Novakovich is the author of Apricots from Chernobyl, *a collection of narratives, and* Yolk, *a volume of short stories, both published by Graywolf Press in 1995; and* Fiction Writer's Workshop, *a textbook published by Story Press in 1995. Novakovich teaches fiction writing at the University of Cincinnati.*

There are some serious disadvantages to writing exclusively from experience, however. You may soon run out of things to say if you are not an adventurer and if your memory is not amazingly keen. Even if you are an adventurer, you may not have the time to write down all that happens to you.

You can spare your body the pain of wild adventures *and* write, however, if you learn to observe other people. You can write from experience, but not necessarily your own. Look around and when you are intrigued by a particular person's experience, transform it into fiction. If you've observed a struggle someone has gone through, and that struggle has the elements of a good story, then you need not imagine much, except to disguise the fictional characters and places enough to protect the real person's privacy.

At the end of the readings that I give from my fiction, frequently someone asks, "Is this an autobiographical story?" It always seems that the questioner hopes it is—either as a confirmation of that person's own desire to write directly from personal experience, or as a reassurance of having learned something about the real world rather than an imagined one. I usually answer, "No, the story is not autobiographical, but is biographical and topographical." What I mean is I've written about people and places.

In Russia, I once saw a woman send her son to beg. When he came back with a ruble, she would slap him, so he'd be teary, and send him off to beg from another tourist. I think this would make a good starting point for a story. You could transport the mother and her son to another country, a country you know pretty well. And you could write it either from the child's perspective or the mother's. I'd say the one who has more choice about what happens is the better focal point for the story. In this instance, the woman's story intrigues me more than the child's. Suppose she faces the prospect of eviction from her apartment and she can't get a job. She might have to resort either to prostitution or to forcing her child to beg. Later she could come up with some other options, but that would be for you to imagine as you write the story.

Imagination

Working primarily from your imagination does not mean that you must, or can, imagine everything. An imaginative painter does not have to invent colors, lines and geometric shapes—these are the basic things an artist works with. An architect need not reinvent the brick and the window for they are the components of any structure. Imagination takes place in the way an architect and a painter combine and recombine the familiar elements of their work to come up with new images. Imagination, literally, should mean a capability to make images. As a writer, you need not totally reinvent train stations, airplanes, hair styles, human behavior—you work with the elements of the world that you know to construct images of something you have not necessarily experienced.

The crucial thing in working from the imagination is to have an empty canvas. You have all the paints and shapes you need to work with, but you need the freedom to maneuver those elements. That freedom comes from *not* knowing the whole story but wanting to know it. Author David Michael Kaplan says he often works from a moment of experience which he calls a story seed. He keeps a journal of these seed ideas and uses them, not to recall what actually happened, but to imagine what could have happened. For example, he wrote his story "Comfort" after visiting his girlfriend's daughter, a young woman who was living with a female friend. During the visit, nothing out of the ordinary happened. But, as he drove away from them, he wondered what would have happened if he had slept with one of the women—what complications would have come out of that. To ensure he was writing fiction, Kaplan wrote the story from a woman's point of view and created a male protagonist much different from himself. He was not living out his fantasy, but writing a fine story imaginatively.

Many writers who work from the imagination do not want to know where the story is going. The uncertainty itself may work as a stimulant. The process can be as simple as one sentence leading to another or one image to another. All they need is a good start. Short story writer Peggy Shinner says that she works by association. Once she gets a sentence going, that sentence asks for another, and so on. For this string of sentences to work, all she needs is a rhythm, usually clipped and fast paced, with lots of commas and periods.

Mark Richard, author of *Fishboy*, says that he got a whole story from the sentence, "At night, stray dogs come up underneath our house to lick our leaking pipes." It took him a while to come up with the image and the sentence, but once he had it down, he says, the rest of the story came quickly as though he was "just the radio."

To make sure their imaginations are not limited by knowing too much about what actually happened, many writers beg to know just a piece of an intriguing life situation. For example, Patricia Stevens, a short story writer and essayist, says that an acquaintance began telling about a friend who had visited a married couple and been invited by the husband to sleep with his wife. "Stop right there," Stevens said. "I don't want to know the rest. Let me imagine it!" From this situation, Stevens created a story about the people she did not know. She had been sufficiently intrigued to imagine, and she was not limited by what she knew. She refused to hear the life script so she could follow her imagination.

Steve Yarbrough, author of *Mississippi History*, found the idea for his story "Stay-gone Days" in a newspaper account of a woman's confession that she and a male accomplice had robbed a store. After the first sentence, Yarbrough quit reading. He did not want to know how the robbery actually happened. Instead, he imagined it, using as the protagonist one of his childhood friends in disguise.

Emotion: fuel for the imagination

Writers, however, can run into problems when writing mostly from imagination. After many fantastic plots, your characters and places may begin to sound hollow, unreal and lifeless. What happens is that your ideas may be out of touch with what you perceive, observe and, most importantly, what you feel. That's why it is imperative that you fuel your imagination with emotion. Move your stories along with desire, fear, love, grief and other strong motives for your characters' actions. And don't be afraid to make those emotions yours as you write your story—experience them through your characters.

It is, in fact, possible to construct a story largely from an emotion. For example, Stephen Crane wrote "The Blue Hotel" from personifying fear in a character. As a stage for the emotion, Crane uses a vivid setting, a Nebraska inn in the middle of winter. In that setting, the protagonist imagines that he is in the Wild West where people cheat on cards and kill.

Talking about the source for his short story "Firefly," Tobias Wolff says: "What impelled me to write it in the first place is its emotional core—that sense, hardly unique to me, of being outside the circle of light, a feeling so pernicious that, even when you are where you want to be, you shy away from the joy of it and begin to fear banishment and loss."

Tolstoy, both intrigued and terrified by death, wrote "The Death of Ivan Illych" to imagine, step-by-step, what dying might be like. He created one of the most stirring stories ever written because, in the imagined death of a man very much unlike himself, Tolstoy managed to express his own emotion—fear of death—by allowing his fictional character to experience it for him. This catharsis is the basic Aristotelian notion of drama: you purge yourself of your own fears and vices by watching them enacted on the stage.

Filling in the gaps

Other good sources of fiction ideas are gaps in your experience, gaps in what is known about the experiences of others, and even gaps in history. For example, as author Joanna Scott set out to write a story dealing with the history of medicine, she read about Leeuwenhoek's work with the microscope. She was intrigued by his secrecy, but even more by the scant mention of his family life. As a result of her curiosity about this gap in what was known about Leeuwenhoek's family, Scott wrote a story about his daughter, "Concerning Mold Upon the Skin, Etc." This is what she says about the source of that story: "As a fiction writer, I'm interested in the vast silences of history, and like many women, Marie floats silently in the background of her father's biography. So she became the center of the narrative, the presence that enabled me to reshape history into fiction."

Fission, fusion and deportation

No matter where else you get your story ideas or where imagination takes you with those ideas, people are still the greatest source of fiction. If you construct a character and dramatize what makes that character intriguing, you'll have a story, because you'll have to concentrate on several examples of what makes that person what he is. Novelist Norman Mailer says, "Generally, I don't even have a plot. What happens is that my characters engage in an action, and out of the action little bits of plot sometimes adhere to the narrative."

One way of creating interesting characters is the fission method in which you use imagination to view yourself as a split personality. From what you know about the different facets of your own personality, you can create new fictional characters. Dostoyevski used this method to create many characters who, although different, all have Dostoyevski's own overriding temperamental nature of making extreme decisions in moments of passion. In a discussion of the contemporary medium of movies, comedy writer and director Mel Brooks says, "Every human being has hundreds of separate people living under his skin. The talent of a writer is his ability to give them their separate names, identities, personalities, and have them relate to other characters living within him."

Another imaginative way of creating characters, the fusion method, draws from a number of different real people to create one fictional character. You might fuse one person's looks with another's personality and yet with another's predicament. Lillian Hellman, author of *Pentimento*, says "I don't think you start with a person. I think you start with parts of many people."

If your characters come largely out of real life, you must make some major shifts to ensure that you fictionalize them. Author Steve Yarbrough uses what I describe as "the deportation method." When he finds an interesting real character in California, for instance, he might place her in a rural Mississippi setting. The new fictional environment serves as the starting point for a story about a character who probably won't go out for cappuccino and doesn't get stuck in freeway traffic. And, out of the clash between the character and her new environment, tensions and conflicts arise and plots naturally suggest themselves.

Variations on themes

When you feel you have run out of experience and ideas to write about, try writing variations on existing themes. You can borrow from other writers' stories the way composers write variations of musical scores. Taking a theme from literature and playing with it does not mean that your story will not be original, just as musicians never doubt the potential for originality in using variations. Brahms's "A Variation on a Theme of Handel" is, for instance, a highly original work.

Many great writers' imaginations have been sparked by the works of other writers. Shakespeare took many of the basic plots for his plays from Plutarch's *Lives*. However, while he may have taken the core events from Plutarch, the situations and dialogue are Shakespeare's. Most likely Homer composed *The Odyssey* and *The Iliad* from the oral tradition surrounding the battle for Troy. Virgil, then, patterned *The Aeneid* on Homer's work by imagining a character who returns home to Rome rather than to Greece. Dante wrote *Inferno* as a variation on the theme of Odysseus's journey into the underworld. More recently, James Joyce also borrowed from Homer's *Odyssey* in *Ulysses*, his novel about a one-day journey of the mind around the streets of early 20th century Dublin.

In *Notes from the Underground*, Dostoyevski writes, "Only if I could become an insect!" Franz Kafka borrowed from this line for his story, "Metamorphosis": "As Gregor Samsa awoke that morning from uneasy dreams, he found himself transformed in his bed into a gigantic insect." Gabriel Garcia Marquez says, "When I read the line (by Kafka), I thought to myself that I didn't know anyone was allowed to write things like that." Marquez then wrote his story "A Very Old Man with Enormous Wings," strewing the angel's wings with parasites and insects.

Like these famous writers, it's important that you look into literature with an eye to borrow from it. Discover what writers stir you as a reader and, particularly, look for themes that can trigger your imagination. Using your imagination, then, you can add major changes to make those themes your own.

Watch, listen and write

William Faulkner summed up the writer's quest for fiction sources best when he said, "An artist is completely amoral in that he will rob, borrow, beg, or steal from anybody and everybody to get the work done." Observe your family, your friends and your enemies and see whose story intrigues you. Look for themes that excite your imagination. Be patient, like a fisherman—listen, contemplate, and see what arouses your interest and curiosity the most. And then begin writing, for as author Robin Henley says, "Stories generate stories. You write one story and get the idea for another."

Killer-Diller Details Bring Fiction to Life

by Donna Levin

There's an expression, "God is in the details," and it applies to nothing more than it does to the writing of fiction. To that and to the art of telling good lies. And what is fiction but the telling of lies?

Well, not exactly, but fiction writing and lying do have something in common. (Picasso said, "Art is a lie that lets us see the truth.") In both cases you are making something up and trying to make someone believe it. Even when you write about something that "really happened" in your personal life, in fiction you will find that making the reader believe it is one of your chief tasks.

Now, I mean "believe" in a specialized sense. A reader picks up a book in a store knowing it's fiction, or fictionalized. But when the reader actually buys the book, he's in effect saying to the author, "I'm going to give you a chance to tell me a story that I can at least pretend is real for the duration of the book."

Providing the details is how you make your reader into a believer. Why? Because it's how you put your reader into the action.

As a writer, you should know that if you really want the reader to believe he's reading about an African safari, you'd better describe the long purple tongues of the giraffes. You must learn that giraffes have purple tongues, or imagine they do, or remember that detail from your real-life safari or trip to the zoo. The purple tongue of the giraffe lets us see the giraffe. The wind in the face of our heroine lets us stand out on the savannah with her.

A detail doesn't need to be real in the conventional sense in order to have power. Science fiction and horror writers know very well the power of invented, but authentic, details.

One of the most compelling aspects of Anne Rice's *Interview With the Vampire* is that Rice really makes you believe that vampires exist—and she does so by the exquisite detailing of the way they live (or, we might say, *un*live) and function. She casually dismisses any familiar Hollywood notions or even any traditional ones that don't suit her. "Forget that," she says, "this is the way it is." And then she follows her own rules with a steely consistency.

In the same way, the science fiction writer has to let us know that the South Forkorian qebor eats yodels and that yodels eat mordons in order to establish the food chain on the planet Zen.

When writing historical fiction, you must weave in as many of the factual details as you can. But sometimes you will be called upon to fill gaps that history has left. Your inventions—whether they are to surmise the way that the Huns celebrated wedding ceremonies or to recreate dialogue spoken by Charlemagne—will also make history seem real.

Donna Levin *is the author of* Get That Novel Started! *and the forthcoming* Get That Novel Written, *from which this article was adapted, both published by* Writer's Digest Books.

Quality, not quantity

When it comes to details, more is not necessarily better. The number of details you need to describe a person or to dramatize an event is a result of several factors. The first is your writing style. Some writers like to give the reader just enough of the bare facts to keep from getting lost. Others like to write lavish descriptions of every crinoline.

Both the amount and type of details you include will also be a function of the genre you're writing in. The readers of a Judith Krantz-style "sex and shopping" novel will be looking for lots of brand names, especially of designer clothes. A sword-and-sorcery novel will require you to authenticate the magic by inventing the details of how it works. A police procedural requires the details of how evidence is collected, suspects interviewed and bodies autopsied.

Another factor in gauging the amount of details you need is the question of how familiar or unfamiliar the situation you're writing about is. The more unfamiliar, the more details you'll need to give. For example, I had a student who was writing about a mythical colony of semi-humans who lived underground. She needed to describe their underground life in fairly thorough detail. By contrast, a book about modern life may require fewer details because we already know what a McDonald's looks like and how fast the average car can drive.

That doesn't mean you should eliminate all the details about contemporary life. It's the job of literary writers in particular to let us see commonplace occurrences as if for the first time—and they can often do that by their careful choice of details. The novelist Sue Miller has a gift for it. In *The Good Mother*, she describes a laundromat: "The long row of gleaming yellow washers sat silent, lids up, open-mouthed." Elsewhere: "I liked the laundromat—the way it smelled, the rhythmic slosh of the machines, the ticking of buttons, zippers, in the dryers ..." There's more, but not much, because we've all seen laundromats. But by honing in on a few details, Miller brings this ordinary setting to life.

Whether your style and genre dictate that you shovel or sprinkle on the details, it's still important to choose well, to make your details earn their living by revealing much in a few words. One well-chosen detail can do the work of 20 banal ones. And when they do, I call them "killer-diller details."

Specific details

Sometimes you can turn a banal detail into a killer-diller one by being specific. Don't tell us there were flowers in the yard—name them. Don't say the man was wearing a suit—tell us it was double-breasted chalkstripe.

Challenge yourself to see just how specific you can get. "A red scarf" might be adequate, but how about a vermilion, crimson or raspberry one? You might get away with "a brand new car," but a 1996 Mercedes 450SL in aubergine is bound to tell us more about the person behind the wheel.

Metaphors and similes can help make your details more specific, too. To be precise, "He ate like a pig," is a simile, and "He was a pig" is a metaphor. In both cases, the writer is taking a person and comparing him to something else that isn't there (presumably there's no pig in the restaurant).

If you write, "her face was as expressionless as a hard-boiled egg," the image of the woman's face lodges much more solidly in our minds than if you write, "Her face was blank." The latter, being a familiar idiom, passes through the reader's consciousness without even leaving a footprint.

Anne Tyler, in *Dinner at the Homesick Restaurant*, writes of "a spindly, starved cat with a tail as matted as a worn-out bottle-brush." Forever and ever I can perfectly see that cat's tail.

Beyond blue-eyed blondes

Killer-diller details are not the obvious ones. Say your character is walking into a kitchen. Most kitchens have stoves and refrigerators and to tell us that this kitchen does, too, isn't telling us much. In the name of being specific, you might tell us that the kitchen has a restaurant-style oven with a six-burner range top, or an avocado side-opening General Electric refrigerator, and you'd be telling us more. But you might also try to zero in on what's in this kitchen that is not in the usual kitchen. A bowl of strawberries from the owner's own garden. A child's artwork on the refrigerator (and what does the artwork depict?). A manual Smith-Corona typewriter on the Formica table.

When describing people, beginning writers usually check off hair and eye color. "She was a redhead with green eyes." Then, if they have any energy left, they may get onto general physique and cite the character's age.

I had a student once whose character descriptions were so formulaic that I suspected her of having created a format in her computer for them. "The 36-year-old brunette mother of two was five-five." "The 25-year-old blonde beauty was five-foot-eight."

I had a devil of a time breaking her of this habit, which to her seemed efficient, since it covered a character's vital statistics in a few words. When I first encouraged her to vary the description she came up with, "At six-four, the hulky 40-year old had gray hair and blue eyes."

It's true that in real life we often appraise the people we meet casually. If you tried to remember what the waitress at the coffee shop this morning looked like, you might come up with hair color and approximate height, if that. If you're not "into" houses you might not remember much about your neighbor's living room beyond the color of the couch and wing chair.

But paradoxically, in order to make your reader believe in your fiction, it has to be more intense than real life. Documenting only the obvious facts about a character or an environment isn't enough. Sure, we often want to know what a character's hair and eye color are, her age and height. But we also need to know what it is about this character, or this couch, or this bowling ball, that is unlike any other person, couch or bowling ball in the universe. We want to see the one loose button on a man's shirt. The graffiti scratched in the wood (and perhaps what it says). The Band-Aids on the finger-tips of a nail-biter.

Details as information

The facts of how things work are important details, and sometimes they can be killer-diller ones. When Tom Wolfe wrote *The Bonfire of the Vanities* he made us believe that Sherman McCoy was a bond trader by carefully detailing just how bonds are traded, giving us information that only a bond trader (or someone who had done thorough research) would know.

If you ever saw Billy Crystal and Danny DeVito in the movie *Throw Mama From the Train*, you know what I'm talking about from its opposite. Billy Crystal is a teacher of fiction writing (there should be more movies about teachers of fiction), and in an early scene in the film one of his students has written a story about men on a submarine. She reads with great energy, " 'Dive! Dive!' yelled the captain through the thing. So the man who makes it dive pressed a button or something and it dove. And the enemy was foiled again."

Billy Crystal tactfully points out, "When you write a novel that takes place on a submarine, it's a good idea to know the name of the instrument that the captain speaks through."

In this case, knowing the names of the various equipment on a submarine is a necessary starting point. If the writer here can also provide the slang expression that Navy personnel use under stress, that would be a killer-diller detail.

How the part becomes the whole

In a novel by Ken Kulhkin, *The Angel Gang*, an old man, Leo, receives a beating at the hands of some thugs. At one point the author describes how the thugs cut a slit in Leo's eyelid. When Leo closes his eyes, he can see through his eyelid. The image is horrific, but also very specific and concise. The one detail stands in for the whole beating.

That doesn't necessarily mean that you then eliminate all the rest of the description of that beating. As we've discussed, the exact number of details and the amount of description you include is a function of your style, the genre, and the content. But always be on the lookout for the killer-diller detail that can encapsulate a person, environment or incident.

In Barbara Kingsolver's novel, *Animal Dreams*, the narrator describes how her sister Hallie was so honest that, "I'd seen her tape dimes to broken parking meters." This killer-diller detail becomes the whole person for a moment, allowing us to imagine how she'd act in a hundred different situations. That doesn't mean that we don't want or need to know more about Hallie—of course we do, and the more important she is to the book as a whole, the more we'll want to know. Kingsolver in fact gives us many more killer-diller details to describe her.

An exercise for detail-spotting

There's a technique for training yourself to produce these killer-diller details. Around dinnertime or later (if you're a night person), take ten minutes to note the five most interesting things you observed that day. Make this a rigid habit for at least a month.

Now, when I say write down what you observed, I don't mean the weighty insights you had while watching the clerk bag your groceries. I mean the most specific, and sometimes off-beat, details that you see (or hear, or taste, or smell or touch). It doesn't have to be the color of the hold of an alien ship. I'm talking about details you might miss if you weren't paying attention. How *does* the clerk bag the groceries—did he put the bread on the bottom? Did he have any unusual physical features? Did he ask you a too-personal question that made you uncomfortable?

Maybe while walking up and down the aisles at the store you noticed that someone had stuck a package of linguine on top of the canned pineapple. Maybe you overheard a pair of twins fighting over who would get to ride in the cart. Those kind of details are hardly earth-shattering. But they're real, and not immediately obvious, the way that writing, "It was a big, crowded grocery store with Muzak playing," *would* be obvious—and banal. As you learn to add these types of details judiciously to your scenes, your scenes, too, will become more real.

Here are some things I observed in the past couple of days:

- Two women were talking in Vietnamese, peppering their speech with "Wow!" and "Okay."
- The bus driver wore a royal purple cable knit sweater that washed out her pale skin and white-blond eyebrows.
- My wedding ring tapping on the banister as I went down the stairs.
- An old man wearing a cardigan that used to be a woman's; the giveaway was that the buttons were backwards.

● A red Ford pickup covered with bumper stickers: FARMS NOT ARMS, ABOLISH APARTHEID, ARMS ARE FOR HUGGING, ONE NUCLEAR BLAST CAN RUIN YOUR WHOLE DAY, I ♥ MY PSYCHOANALYST.

● A man with a belt-length black beard and a parrot on a leash.

● Walking down the street I heard someone shuffling behind me. The whispery sound made me realize that the person was wearing bedroom slippers.

● At the deli, there was a woman wearing the jumpsuit of an American Airlines mechanic. Her name patch said, "Cupcake."

Remember as you practice observing that it's not a contest to see what offbeat or dramatic occurrences you can witness. (No extra points for going to a hospital emergency room.) Nor is the goal to come up with details that you can actually use in your novel or story, although you may do that in the process. Rather, the point is to become more aware of what's going on around you. The point is to learn to mine even familiar surroundings for what's specific and unique about them. Then use those details in your writing to go beyond blue-eyed blondes, a description that probably fits 15% of the population.

Observing and recording your observations are also helpful exercises to get you back into a writing routine when you've been away for awhile, or when you're feeling stuck. But the greatest value lies in how your observations will translate, over time, to an improved ability to invent precise, informative, unpredictable details—in other words, killer-diller details that make the reader take notice.

And that's no lie.

For information on entering the Novel & Short Story Writer's Market *Cover Letter Contest, see page 19.*

Belva Plain: The "Charmed Life" of a Bestselling Writer

by Anne Bowling

Among fiction writers, Belva Plain has led a charmed life. In the rough-and-tumble world of publishing, where even the most talented writers have had to struggle for attention, Plain has never received a rejection letter. Never. Her ability to spin a good tale has kept this Ivy League-educated, 76-year-old grandmother above the fray. From the first short story she submitted to a woman's magazine in the 1940s, to the first novel she shipped off to Delacorte Press in 1976, each and every piece of fiction she has attempted to have published has been accepted.

"It is highly unusual, and I'm very, very grateful for it," Plain says. "I don't pin any medals on myself—I've just been very fortunate."

Plain began penning fiction at Barnard College in New York City, where she wrote for the college magazine and edited the school paper. Despite a creative writing professor who told her she had "no feeling" for the English language, Plain continued to write, achieving publication in women's magazines such as *McCall's*, *Redbook* and *Cosmopolitan*. Some 25 short stories later, Plain took a 12-year break from her writing to run a household and raise a family.

Plain's winning streak resumed in the 1970s with Delacorte Press publishing *Evergreen*, the story of Jewish immigrant Anna Friedman who comes to New York from Poland to pursue the American dream. A broad family saga which led to two sequels, *Evergreen* became a bestseller and later a television mini-series. Its popularity took Plain by surprise: "I would have been delighted just to have someone publish it, period, let alone have it reach the bestseller list." Since then, eight more of Plain's 12 novels have reached the bestseller list, and there are more than 23 million copies of her books in print in a dozen languages.

Despite her success, Plain says with characteristic modesty that writing hasn't gotten any easier since she first began some 50 years ago. "You have to watch out to see that it doesn't become too easy," she says. "It is true that if you have had some successes, you can feel encouraged . . . but on the other hand, if you get too pleased with yourself, you can end up in disaster, too. But you do have some encouragement in thinking, 'well, I've done it before, so I'm pretty sure I can do it again.' But I'm never 100 percent certain."

Although Plain had no fiction published during her working hiatus, she continued to write while attending to diaper changing, car pooling, and housekeeping. "I think if you like to write, you always walk around with a notebook in your pocket and jot things down," Plain says. "Sometimes I wrote things down—just sketches—and subsequently I've looked them up and utilized many impressions, character sketches and descriptions in just the right places.

"To have published 12 novels in 18 years (all with Delacorte Press) has required a

Anne Bowling *is a Cincinnati-based freelance writer, and frequent contributor to Writer's Digest Books.*

steady, disciplined writing schedule. A self-described "morning person," Plain says she writes every day, from shortly after breakfast until mid-afternoon, at the typewriter she refuses to relinquish for a personal computer.

Getting ideas

When she's not actually writing, the ideas continue to flow, often providing the seed for the next novel, says Plain. "For instance, the subject of my current novel, *Carousel*, is child abuse. You read about it all the time. So of course, having an imagination—I wouldn't be a writer if I didn't—it came to me that it would be very interesting to try to fathom how a parent would feel going to a doctor and being told that their child had been molested. And from that point on," she says enigmatically, "I really can't tell you what the process is any more than I imagine you could get a musician to give you a clear explanation of how he wrote a song."

The idea for *Evergreen*—although planted many years before Plain actually started writing—grew ripe once her children had grown and her family underwent a generational shift. "When the last member of my parent's generation died, I suddenly became the older generation," Plain says. "Although *Evergreen* is not about my family, I think it's true of any generation, that they want to record what life was like, particularly in America, which was an immigrant's country. I thought it would be interesting to use a woman protagonist to trace a family through a whole century. So that's what I did. I wanted to take this woman who grew up in a relatively primitive village in Eastern Europe, where she never even saw a railroad train, and carry her through all the events of the 20th century—the wars and depression, and right up to the jet age."

A second reason Plain decided to write *Evergreen* was that she was tired of reading "the same old story told by Jewish writers about the same old stereotypes: the possessive mothers, the worn-out fathers, and all the rest of the neurotic, rebellious, unhappy, self-hating tribe," she says in an interview with *The New York Times* published shortly after *Evergreen* came out. "I admit that I wanted to write a different novel about Jews, and a truer one."

Creating believable characters

From *Evergreen*'s Anna Friedman to Lynn Ferguson, the central female character in the 1993 novel *Whispers*, Plain develops both male and female characters that have a ring of truth. Her female lead characters are typically competent, dependable, warm and compassionate, yet marked with a flaw—such as Lynn Ferguson's need to please, or Anna Friedman's attraction to a married man—that can bring their ruin.

A *Publishers Weekly* reviewer wrote of *Whispers*, "By getting under the skin of each of her diverse characters, Plain delivers a story of considerable impact." Decades of studying people have trained her to note their mannerisms and actions, and play the writer's game of "I wonder . . . ," which leads to her character composition, Plain says.

"Sometimes you see a person, and you think 'fascinating person. I wonder where he or she comes from, or what he's doing,' " Plain says. "I know a pair of brothers who gave me an idea that I used in *Carousel*, because I was so struck by the differences between them. One is a picture of a handsome man—tall, beautiful hair, personality, everything. His brother is a little fellow, five-foot-four, and not as attractive. The contrast between them is so striking that, every time I see them, I wonder what the less attractive brother truly feels in his heart toward the other one. And I wonder, can he think, 'Why was nature so mean to me? Why me?' There are endless possibilities there."

Creating believable characters is one part imagination and one part craft, Plain says: "You have to see the character, and you don't put words into the character's mouth

©Deborah Feingold

just to fill space. Everything has to express the person in a way that the careful reader won't even notice the art that has been put into it. Everything the person does and says must in a way reflect the person, not just fill up the page with meaningless sentences."

Authenticity plays an important role in the settings for Plain's novels, as well. The Werner family saga, which begins in *Evergreen* and continues through the bestsellers *The Golden Cup* and *Tapestry*, includes a detailed backdrop of history from 19th century Eastern Europe to the United States in the 20th century. *Eden Burning*, set on the fictional island of St. Felice, required research into the geographic, social and political history of the Caribbean. The social lives and political involvement of Jews in the South during the Civil War was the basis for *Crescent City*. Even *Whispers*, set in the contemporary U.S., includes detailed descriptions of antagonist Robert Ferguson's business trips to Hungary.

Details add dimension

Plain, who has called research the fun part of her writing, says that crisp detail—such as the fine points of extracting meat from conch shells, and street scenes in Budapest—requires both research and travel. "I never write about anyplace I haven't seen," she says. "I think it just won't ring true. You have to feel what it's like, feel the air and see the people. Of course, if I'm writing a New York scene, it's easier. I live here, I know where the museums are, and so on, and I don't have to research it. But if I'm writing about a place I have only visited, I want to make sure I know what I'm writing."

Plain definitely writes for readers who love detail. Her scenes are sprinkled with descriptions of costuming, menus, home furnishings—all the details that add dimension to her characters, she says. "When I have a character, I want to know what kind of house that person lives in—whether it's fussy, or very spare. It tells you a lot about the person. If I tell you I met a woman, and to describe her, I say she has a nose, a mouth and two eyes, you don't know much about her. But if I say she laughs a lot, but it's kind of a nervous laugh, so I think she's kind of shy, and she dresses well, but she's kind of roughly built, then you've got something. You're getting to know her. That's what it's all about."

While Plain's attention to detail and character development strengthen her novels, she can get carried away, she admits: "I'm most interested in characters and people, but what I have to be careful about in writing popular fiction is keeping the plot moving. Anthony Trollope was a wonderful character analyst, but the Victorians sometimes got bogged down in a lot of description. Modern readers like a story to move along. They complain about Victorian novels, saying they are turgid, and they take too long. People who read popular fiction don't want to be delayed before finding out what happens next."

To follow her complex plot lines, which in some books move across hemispheres, Plain spends a great deal of time—sometimes as much as five months—preparing for the actual writing. Her preparation includes research, character sketches, and a detailed outline. *Contemporary Authors* quotes Plain as saying she could write the final chapter before the first sentence.

"I like to know exactly where I'm going," Plain says. "I call my outline a road map. It directs me. Let's say you're in New York, and you want to get to Taos, New Mexico. There are many different routes you could take. You might go by way of Colorado, through the mountains, or you might head as far south as Texas, but you have to know where you're going."

On agents

From the time she sold her first short story to her most recent novel, Plain has worked with an agent. While using an agent in the 1940s may have given her work an edge, as publishing becomes increasingly competitive it is more and more important for writers to get representation, she says. "I don't know what would have happened to *Evergreen* if I had just mailed it in," says Plain, who conferred with her long-time agent Dorothy Olding before beginning the novel. "Unless you're very fortunate, and you've written something absolutely stupendous, and you get the right person to read it and recognize how stupendous it is, your manuscript may simply get discarded from the slush pile. I would say definitely get an agent. An agent sifts things through, and since he wants to make money, he won't send anything that he doesn't think stands a chance. In other words, the manuscript has passed one test. And it will get a reading, from the magazine or publisher, simply because an agent has sent it."

Plain concedes that, for inexperienced authors, just finding an agent can be half the work. She likens the process to the old job-ad joke: "Young man wanted—experience only." That Plain connected with her first agent was "a fluke," she says. "It was through a friend of a friend—that's how tenuous it was. But I'm not saying this to be discouraging. Somehow, the young person without a job does find work."

Plain plans to keep working until health prevents her. Her next novel, *Promises*, will be published by Delacorte in April, 1996. Unlike her earlier historical novels, *Promises* will be "very current," Plain says. "Just as *Whispers* was about wife abuse and *Carousel* was about child abuse, *Promises* deals with a serious current problem.

"So many people say 'aren't you going to write more about the Werner family?' And others say they like my newer books because they deal with social problems we face every day," Plain says. "I suppose you can't please all of the people all of the time. For now, I'm not returning to the more historical novels. But I won't ever say never."

What can a self-taught, best-selling author offer by way of instruction to beginning fiction writers? She qualifies her advice by cautioning that it is not very original, but nevertheless true: "Be a reader. If you do a lot of reading among the best writers of the past and present, and you have any inborn talent or feel for words, you are bound to absorb a good deal of information about rhythm, pacing, the building of characters, and showing how they change during their lives. The characters who begin the books are not the same people you finish with, because life has changed them. All of these things you will see if you do serious, careful and extensive reading."

Lee Smith: Writing Down the Voices

by Perri Weinberg-Schenker

Chapel Hill, North Carolina, is in many ways worlds apart from the small towns and hollows of the Appalachian mountain region, but veteran author Lee Smith manages to keep one foot planted firmly in each place. It is in Chapel Hill where she makes her home, maintains her marriage, and teaches creative writing at North Carolina State University. But her roots are plunged deep into the mountains of southwestern Virginia, where she spent her childhood and from where the sounds and voices continue to whisper in her ear, compelling her to write nine novels and countless short stories, each in its own way a tribute to the rich heritage of the region. From her earliest novel, *The Last Day the Dogbushes Bloomed*, to the more well-known *Oral History* and *Fair and Tender Ladies*, Smith's works have been characterized by an authenticity of dialect, place and voice that have been largely unmatched in Southern literature. Two of her short stories—"Mrs. Darcy Meets the Blue-Eyed Stranger at the Beach" and "Between the Lines"—have received O. Henry awards, and her latest novel, *Saving Grace*, which confronts the question of belief against the backdrop of serpent-handling fundamentalism, has been called "lyric, poetic and subtly cosmic" and "a daring, ambitious effort from one of our finest writers."

At the time of this interview, Smith was enjoying a three-year fellowship that allows her to concentrate on new works and, in addition, to conduct adult literacy workshops in the mountains of Eastern Kentucky. She describes the workshops not as a diversion but as an extension of her writing and teaching, and she welcomes the opportunity to revisit the mountains—an area populated with the sort of models who inevitably find their way into her fiction. In fact, Smith herself could serve as a model for her characters: She shares with them a lilting, native dialect, an eagerness to weave fact into story, and an almost disarming openness about herself and her work. She speaks with the quickness of someone whose tongue can barely keep up with her ideas, yet her observations are deliberate and thoughtful. The interview is interrupted only once, by the barking of her dog, Gracie, for whom the protagonist of *Saving Grace* is named.

Perri Weinberg-Schenker: You've been defined as a Southern writer, as an Appalachian writer, as a feminine or feminist or woman's writer. How do you define yourself?

Lee Smith: I personally would just define myself as a writer, period. However, it's true that I'm a writer to whom place matters. Therefore, what something looks like, what the air smells like right before a thunderstorm, how cold the water is—all these things really matter to me. My interest in place is inescapable. And I'm lucky enough to come from one of the most interesting places in the world, which is the Appalachian mountain region. Therefore, I really am an Appalachian writer—much more than a Southern

Perri Weinberg-Schenker *is a Cincinnati freelance writer/editor and frequent contributor to* Novel & Short Story Writer's Market.

© Susan Woodley Raines

writer. Because, frankly, when I first read the stories of Faulkner, I thought they were great, but it was like reading about another country. The part of the South where I grew up had no houses with columns or black people or sense of loss in the Civil War. I couldn't identify with many things we associate with literature of the Deep South.

I do love oral storytelling, though. I consider myself more of a storyteller than a writer, and that's Southern, whether you refer to the mountains or the Deep South.

As far as being a woman's writer, a lot of times when I'm writing, it's like I'm hearing a story being told to me, and that story very often is in a woman's voice. And of course because I am a woman, I think I understand women's lives better. That may be a failure of the imagination, but it also seems completely natural to me.

PW-S: Tell me more about why you consider yourself a storyteller more than a writer.

LS: I always think of a writer as someone who is writing in a more formal style than I can usually muster. I think my style is more oral. It's more as if someone's telling me a story and I'm taping it.

PW-S: I read somewhere that you felt a little guilty of plagiarism when you wrote *Oral History*, because so much of it derived from research and other people's stories.

LS: That's true. Yet, on the other hand, my intent was really to document that culture, with all its stories and lore and songs. Because like every other very isolated regional culture in this country, it's passing. Television has been the great leveler.

Oral History was the first thing I wrote which involved a great deal of research and taking notes and taping. And I kept thinking, "This can't be fair. These are great stories, but I didn't make them up."

PW-S: I know you started writing as a child. Did you always envision yourself to be a professional writer?

LS: I always envisioned myself to be a writer. I don't think I had a sense of what a professional writer was. I didn't know any professional writers growing up. I knew very few real readers.

PW-S: Were you an anomaly among your family and the people you grew up with?

LS: I guess so. But I didn't have a sense of myself as being different at the time. I was an only child born to older parents who encouraged me in anything I was interested in. And I always had teachers who were very interested in the fact that I liked to read and write so much. So I had support in school and at home.

I grew up in a family of people who were world-class talkers. All information was imparted in the form of anecdotes. So I grew up kind of drunk on language. And when you grow up like that, language holds no terrors for you.

PW-S: What can you tell me about your early writing days? You wrote *The Last Day the Dogbushes Bloomed*, which earned you a Book of the Month Club Writing Fellowship, while you were in undergraduate school, didn't you?

LS: I wrote it in its first version as a senior thesis in college. And then after I graduated from college, I was supposed to go to Columbia to study creative writing, but instead I got married.

PW-S: I read that you passed up a second fellowship to get married. Do you have any regrets about that?

LS: Not a one. I'm not very scholarly, and I think I have maybe derived more from life. That's where my stories come from. I'm still a great reader, but I'm not a student in a certain sense. I'm more of an observer.

PW-S: What about some of your other life choices? How do you think they've helped shape your career?

LS: There were many years when I didn't write as much as I wanted because I had little children and I was the one at home with them. There were other years when I had to work and teach and couldn't write things that I was dying to at the time. But in retrospect, I don't regret one minute spent with my children or teaching or working because, as I say, my writing in particular derives from real life. Having children opened up my world more than anything else.

And teaching is the same way. It keeps me in touch with what it's really all about, instead of being around people talking about their agents and how much money they got for that last book. That's not what writing's about. Writing is about examining your soul and looking real hard at the world, and I think to teach is to examine things in that way.

PW-S: You mentioned that you don't surround yourself with people who are preoccupied about agents and book deals. Even though you don't embrace that lifestyle, how has the industry worked for you? Do you have an agent?

LS: I do. But I didn't with my first book. After it was accepted, the publisher—it was Harper & Row—found me an agent whom I kept for a long time. Then I didn't have an agent for a while and in about 1979 I found Liz Darhansoff, who I'm still with.

PW-S: It sounds like the pathway to getting published was fairly easy for you. Am I wrong about that?

LS: It isn't that it was easy for me, it's just that it was easier then than it is today. They were publishing a lot more serious novels by young writers then. If I were starting today, I don't know that my first novel would ever get published. One reason is they're paying so much to writers that they think will get on bestseller lists that there's very little money left over to make an investment in a first novel. Traditionally, a first novel has represented an investment in a young writer, and there are increasingly fewer companies willing to make that investment.

PW-S: Did you get your fair share of rejections when you began?

LS: It's almost like I've had two careers. Early on, I was very lucky—I don't think I realized how lucky I was—and I got my first novel published, then two more. And then, I wrote a very depressing fourth novel. And, in the meantime, the first three books hadn't sold at all. And publishing had changed. Suddenly people had to make some money. They had to justify what they were publishing. And so when I sent in my fourth novel, they just said "Sorry, honey," and that was that. And my agent said pretty much the same thing. So there I was, down in Alabama with two little babies, an unpublishable manuscript and no agent. And I had seven or eight years of being unable to get that book published.

PW-S: That was *Black Mountain Breakdown*?

LS: Yes. I sent it myself to about 20 publishers, and, in the meantime, I was always trying to find an agent. Then I decided to go back to school and get a degree in special education. I was due to start when I found out that Liz Darhansoff had found a publisher that actually liked *Black Mountain Breakdown*.

So I went through with my fourth book what most people go through with their first. And during that time, what kept me writing were the literary magazines. I had a couple of stories accepted, and two of them went on to get into an O. Henry anthology.

PW-S: Many writers are very driven to be published and widely read. But I was struck by a line from *Fair and Tender Ladies*, after Ivy has destroyed the letters, when she says "It was the writing of them, that signified." Is that symbolic of your attitude about your own writing?

LS: It is. I, of course, am a published author and I love to write things that get published, but I've also written a whole lot of material that is not for publication. I have written several novels that I don't intend to publish. People write for all kinds of reasons, and publication to my mind is only one of them. I also write because that's the way I examine my life and my beliefs and what I think about the world. Sometimes I think I write fiction for some of the same reasons that other people write in journals.

PW-S: I've heard other writers express similar sentiments.

LS: Yes. Ann Tyler once said she writes because she wants to have more than one life. Isn't that great? I think what so many people don't understand is that the process itself is valuable, not only the product. I try to tell my students, a writer is a person who is *writing*, not a person who is being published. The very act of writing is empowering. It's important. It's *valid*.

PW-S: I read where you pointed to your first novels and said there were weaknesses that were "typical first-writer kinds of things." What are those things, and is there a way to avoid them? Or are they something every beginner has to wade through?

LS: A lot are things every writer does have to wade through. I think the tone of the first novel is a child's point of view, and the theme is a little simplistic, perhaps. About 90 percent of first novels are about the end of innocence, an initiation story. But maybe that's the first story we all have to write. I guess the only way to avoid it—because a lot of times you have to write your way through some material to get to other material—is to not publish it.

PW-S: What would you say are your strengths as a writer?

LS: My strength is the ability to reproduce the way people speak and think. It's kind of a natural first-person voice. And my weakness is that it's really hard for me to write passages of narration in the third person, where information is being imparted. Yet, there are some stories I want to tell that have to be done inescapably from that point of view. My weakness is a failure to think abstractly enough to take a more temperate, logical, philosophical overview. I'm good at writing close to people, but sometimes I think people get tired of that and would like a breather.

PW-S: It's interesting that you say that, because I think you've had some real success with varying points of view. *Fair and Tender Ladies* is that very close, singular perspective, and it does work beautifully. But you also had those shifting and multiple perspectives in *Oral History* and *Family Linen* that I think were very effective.

LS: Well, thank you. But I know that's real hard for me to do. It's like pulling teeth for me when I get in a more omniscient mode. But I do like to try it.

PW-S: What are you working on these days?

LS: I'm working on short stories, but I'm also doing something else that's a lot of fun. I'm going back up into Eastern Kentucky twice a year, doing some writing workshops with adult literacy students. And that is really exciting, to work with people who have not known all their whole lives how to read and write.

PW-S: It's interesting that you go back and forth between the novel and the short story. A lot of writers sort of progress from the short story to the novel and never return to the more structured short story. What is it that keeps you interested in both?

LS: I've always been in love with short stories. Again, I think it's because I am sort of a storyteller, and that was the way I first heard language. And I really don't think of the short story as being necessarily more structured. I think of a tale as being open-ended. Some of my favorite short stories have as much in them as novels.

I think with a novel, the challenge is simply to finish it. It's like being a long-distance runner. It takes a tremendous amount of stamina and intellectual energy to write a whole novel. You get to that point in the middle where you think that it's just terrible. There may be a part of a novel that works brilliantly and then another 200 pages that just don't work at all. It's very hard.

Stories, on the other hand, are easier. You just have a little window into a life rather than producing the whole life. Yet, a lot of times a voice will start in a short story, then not shut up. Then I have to write the novel.

One thing about the short story: When you're working in a more limited form, you can concentrate more on the level of the language. I think many novels are sloppily written. The language is much more interesting as a rule in the short story.

PW-S: I'd like to know how you generate ideas. It impressed me that *Fair and Tender Ladies* was inspired by a packet of old letters you bought at a flea market.

LS: You never know where it's going to come from. A lot of times, for me—and this is, of course, different for every writer—a strong image will get me going. I have several friends who will start off with a visual image. An example of that would be William Faulkner's remark that he had a visual image of a little girl with muddy drawers climbing up and trying to see in a window, and he wrote a whole novel to find out what it was she was trying so hard to see. And that of course was *The Sound and the Fury*.

With me, though, it's more something that somebody says. The packet of letters was kind of unusual. Usually it's a remark that will kind of grow into a character, and then that character will have more to say.

PW-S: I saw at one point, that your address was on Burlage Circle. Is that where Richard Burlage in *Oral History* came from?

LS: Oh, yeah. You have the life of the fiction and then you have your real life, and inescapably those two things will coincide. When I was writing *The Devil's Dream*, which is about country music, I heard on the radio that Reba McIntyre's whole band had been killed in a wreck, and I found myself immediately having someone killed in a wreck in my novel. It just happened. You plan as much as you can, but then whatever's happening in your own life or in the world finds its way into the novel.

PW-S: So there are elements of you and your life, but you've said that your writing absolutely is not autobiographical.

LS: Not in the sense that I am in any way a main character or a main character is in any way based on me. But bits and pieces of your life will get in there, and I think every character is perhaps autobiographical in some sense. And oftentimes it would surprise your friends to see that, because it would be the part of yourself that is maybe not expressed in what they see of your personality.

PW-S: You've said that you can't choose your material as much as it chooses you. Do you still believe that?

LS: I do. I think we're always straining against that. I believe that the imagination, of course, is unlimited. But our sense of language and our sense of story is in some way given to us by the circumstances we're born into and how we first learn language. And if we want to go beyond that or transcend it completely, it's going to take a lot of effort.

PW-S: You once indicated you were afraid of getting stuck in that voice of the woman in Buchanan County from 50 years ago and that you would like to do more contemporary, even more commercial, writing. Have you accomplished that?

LS: Actually, the stories I'm writing now are very contemporary. But every now and then, I will just be compelled by a voice telling me a story and it's like someone holding a gun to my head. That's what happened to me with *Saving Grace*, which is a story of a girl who is the daughter of a charismatic minister. That's a book I didn't intend to write. I was doing an introduction to a book of photographs for a friend, and some of the photographs were taken way up in the mountains, of people who were serpent-handling believers. I wrote the introduction for my friend, and then it all turned into a novel.

PW-S: Has the Appalachian writer been affected by the growing popularity of minority voices in literature?

LS: I think it's true that the term *regional* is no longer pejorative, whether you're talking about someone who is a Native American, someone who's from the Appalachian region or whatever. It's no longer a reason *not* to publish their book.

PW-S: I read once that you did all your writing in longhand. Is that still true?

LS: Yes, although at a certain point I'll type it on a typewriter. I was struck dead with fear because my husband read in the paper where Smith Corona just made their last typewriter. And I type on a Smith Corona. So I guess I'm obsolete. I mean, I'm *happily* obsolete. To me, writing is a physical act, particularly with a book like *Saving Grace*. It was a completely spoken narration. I felt like I was simply taking down the story, and it was flowing out from my arm onto the page. And I didn't want some machine in there between Gracie and her words, between the page and the voice.

PW-S: What can you tell me about your day-to-day writing process? What's your office like, what's your workday like, do you keep regular hours?

LS: I don't really have an office, and I don't really have structured working hours. I don't write anything until it totally obsesses me, and then I write all the time. I prefer to write in the morning. If that's not possible, I'll do it whenever I can. And I also go long periods of time when I don't write. I don't write until I have something to say.

PW-S: Most writers would consider that writer's block, but you seem very easy with it. What's the longest you've gone without writing?

LS: Oh, maybe four months. Writing is my life—I mean, it's what I do. But I do try to take real breaks. I think it reinvigorates you. I try to be interested in other things.

PW-S: You do quite a bit of nonfiction writing too, don't you?

LS: Yes. I'm always writing a book review, or a little article for someone. I don't think I want to write a nonfiction book, but I like to do the shorter pieces.

PW-S: When you're writing both fiction and nonfiction, is there any conflict?

LS: To me, they're completely different. Writing nonfiction seems a lot more like a game, like an intellectual pursuit. But the fiction is completely different. It's a very emotional pursuit. To write fiction to me is to go into a trance, to go out of yourself entirely. It's like prayer.

PW-S: Are you as commercially successful as you would like to be?

LS: No, I guess not. But on the other hand, to be truly commercially successful is just fraught with dangers for the writing self. The way I write is more a form of self-expression than to create a product. I think if I were going at this strictly to be commercially successful, I wouldn't be able to write the way I write. I haven't tried to write to any perceived market.

PW-S: I guess as a teacher you're bound to be biased about this, but as a writer, how crucial do you think formal writing instruction is?

LS: I think instruction is very helpful. A writer trying to write in isolation can get a lot done, but I'm not sure how good the work would be. I always urge my students to go to a summer writing program. I think we all need to become part of a community of writers. I always show my work to friends who are writers and get feedback. I don't think you ever get to the point where you are any kind of judge of your own work.

PW-S: What's the most important advice you give beginning writers?

LS: Read! As a teacher of creative writing, the most important thing I do is point students to what they should be reading. Find writers who write what you'd like to, take their work apart and see what makes it work. I think any writer would do well to read as much as possible.

First Bylines

by Chantelle Bentley

With the odds stacked against them, thousands of beginning and unpublished writers seek their first sale. Of those thousands, it seems only a lucky few make it into print. However, many writers *are* finding success.

Coming from a variety of experiences, ages and backgrounds, the following four writers, through hard work, persistence and courage, have seen their dreams become reality. Each one took the leap and threw their manuscripts into the publishing ring. And, despite the possibility of rejection, believed in themselves and their work. Their stories are an inspiration for those still awaiting that first acceptance.

Jewel Mogan
Beyond Telling, Ontario Review Press

Heralded as a "late bloomer," Jewel Mogan returned to her love of writing after not writing a word of fiction for over 25 years. Born in Plaquemine, Louisiana, Mogan got her first taste for writing while majoring in English at Louisiana State University. "I graduated from LSU in 1955 after working summers on my hometown weekly and as a staff writer for a Baton Rouge society magazine, where, while writing what purported to be the facts, I first learned how to turn 'the facts' into pure Southern fiction."

During her time at LSU, Mogan also received second place for a story she submitted to *Mademoiselle*'s 1955 College Fiction Contest. However, the time was not right for Mogan to pursue fiction writing. "I got a few rejections after that first story was published (in *Mademoiselle*) and, in those days, I was easily discouraged," she says. "I just quit writing and didn't even want to think about it." After taking a job as book editor for LSU Press, Mogan met her husband-to-be and settled into married life and raising a family.

Finally, with her children raised and more leisure time, Mogan, who now lives in Lubbock, Texas, returned to writing by keeping a journal. Then she read John Toole's *Confederacy of Dunces* and she was smitten. "I loved it and wanted to write like that. The urge began to snowball then, with images crowding out my sleep at night and impelling me to get up and write them down. The next morning, however, they didn't seem all that great."

To improve her writing, Mogan joined a writer's group and enrolled in a creative writing course taught by poet Walter McDonald. And because the majority of her writing group was writing and submitting poetry, Mogan gave that a try. "I began submitting poetry first. After about six hits and 100 strike-outs, I went back to my first love, prose

Chantelle Bentley *is the production editor for* Poet's Market *and* Novel & Short Story Writer's Market.

fiction. Also, I found poetry difficult; every word must be perfect and the expression so concise. In a short story you can expand and people will forgive you for getting off the subject a little bit."

Mogan's first published short story after returning to writing was accepted by *The North American Review* in 1987. The story previously had been rejected by *The New Yorker*, *Antaeus* and *Esquire*. "I sent to those four magazines because those were the ones a member of our group suggested I submit to," Mogan says. "Sounds like picking lottery numbers, but it worked." *The North American Review* held the story six months before accepting it, then published it five months later.

Still submitting her stories to quality literary journals, Mogan's efforts to be published soon tested her determination. Over the next six years, she had one story accepted annually. "I agonized, as everyone does, over piles, mountains, of rejections. It was not unusual to get 13 rejections on a story that I had reworked three times."

One of those stories, however, was read (and rejected) by *Ontario Review*'s associate editor Joyce Carol Oates, who saw something in Mogan's writing and asked to see more. "The first time Joyce Carol Oates wrote me she wondered what happened. Why this big gap in my writing? All I could tell her was that I was really busy getting married and raising a family and so on. There was no deep dark reason. I just quit writing, and when the desire came back, I was compelled to sit down and write. I think the consciousness of time passing does catch up with you, and you say 'I better get into it if I'm ever going to do it.' " So Mogan sent Oates and editor Raymond Smith (also Oates's husband) practically everything she had ever written. The result was the short story collection, *Beyond Telling*, published by Ontario Review Press in 1995.

Ontario Review Press worked with Mogan through every step of production and played a very active role in promoting *Beyond Telling*. The press released 50 review copies and informed Mogan of all incoming reviews. Smith read one of the stories to a meeting of book representatives as a way to promote her book. Ontario Review Press also submitted the book to several annual awards for first collections. "They [Ontario Review Press] have been really supportive and given me good vibes about the stories," says Mogan. "They answer every question no matter how stupid, and working with them has been a very pleasant experience." In fact, the publication of *Beyond Telling* sparked an inquiry from *Story* magazine and from two agents. In early 1996, one of the stories included in the collection is being performed as a dramatic monologue by a New Orleans theater group for their series called "Native Tongues."

Mogan continues to submit stories, but now relies on a database in her computer when she selects markets for her submissions. "I did use market directories and whatever other sources I could find that listed magazines and a little bit about them. Now, I have a whole section on markets in my computer so I don't need to draw on other sources except to update what I already have. I include comments about the magazines—what I think they want and what might work there. Some of them are difficult to pinpoint because they are so eclectic, but with others you at least know what they don't like. For me, submitting has been a whole lot of working in the dark."

Despite her success, Mogan does not base her desire to write on the need to publish. "I try to do it for the enjoyment. I say 'this is interesting to me and I'm going to plummet to the depths and see what I come up with and maybe it will be interesting to someone else.' I try to just write the story and not think of publication." To Mogan, the audience is very important. "Out there is the reader with a capital R, that special reader you're writing to. Otherwise, there is no reason for writing. It pleases me to no end if somebody likes the story I've written, because it means I've connected with that reader. That really helps to keep me going."

To "keep going" is the best advice Mogan has for others working toward their first publication. "Of course, I am called a late bloomer. But I have a word to all you fellow late bloomers: Hang on and don't let them shake you off the bush."

Colleen Curran
Something Drastic, Goose Lane Editions

A professional playwright whose works have been produced across Canada and the U.S., Colleen Curran began writing her first novel on January 6, 1991, after typing on the computer screen a headline from her "strange but true" newspaper clippings collection. "There was one clipping, MAN KILLED BY TURNIP THROWN FROM CAR, that was by my desk for a long time. Why? I really do not know. But I typed the headline out and then this fictional person (Lenore Rutland) began to write a letter to someone who had left her eleven days before. It became a monologue, a very, very long monologue actually." By April of 1993, Curran's monologue was a completed novel.

"Writing the book was quite different from playwriting but I enjoyed it very much," Curran says. "I enjoy books that are letters and clippings and lots of different ingredients, and that's what my book became." Not showing the manuscript to anyone, Curran kept to her May 1, 1993, send-off deadline by mailing her manuscript to a "super" Toronto literary agent who was a friend of a friend.

The agent, Lucinda Vardey, wrote Curran a very encouraging letter, but said she was selling her agency and leaving the business. "She gave me the names of two agents who might be interested in a first novel author." Curran wrote to both the agents Vardey recommended. "The first agent wrote a very nice and sincere letter saying she couldn't take on anyone else but she wished me lots of luck and said my novel sounded like it was lots of fun. The other agent phoned and was very patronizing, but told me to send her the novel."

Curran sent the manuscript right away. The agent called her almost immediately upon receiving the manuscript saying: "I don't like it. With all those letters, it's very epistolary and they're death. They did it with *Griffin and Sabine* and your book, *HA-HA*, is not *Griffin and Sabine*. It's also too Canadian. No one wants to read anything set in Canada by a Canadian." Of the agent's remarks, Curran says, "It was quite cruel and I was devastated, shattered, upset for about half an hour. Then I thought she's ONE person."

With her novel back and no agent, Curran used the encouragement she received from Vardey to gain the confidence to submit the manuscript on her own. "Even though Lucinda [Vardey] wasn't able to get my book to a publisher, she did something great for me: she encouraged me. Lucinda would say if a novel wasn't good." So, Curran sent out about 20 letters, complete with outline and background, to a number of small as well as large publishers. She received rejections from most of them. By the time December ended, she had sent out an additional ten letters with no success.

Determined to find a publisher for her manuscript, Curran contacted the Canadian Publishers Association. "I wrote a 'To Whom It May Concern' letter asking for advice. And this wonderful person, Julia Rhodes, sent me a booklet listing all the small presses with their criteria," Curran says. And, given the description of Curran's book, Rhodes suggested she try Goose Lane Editions.

Curran wrote Goose Lane Editions who said they would be interested in reading the complete manuscript. "Yes, not just sample chapters. I sent it off and received a postcard on August 11, 1994, stating the evaluation process could take as long as six months." By October, Curran received another postcard saying the first reader's report on the manuscript was very positive and it was being sent out for a second read.

Two weeks after Christmas, Curran received a letter from Senior Editor Laurel Boone. "Goose Lane had decided to publish my novel! Yes, the miracle had happened." After a revision to the novel's ending and a title change, *Something Drastic* was published by Goose Lane Editions in October of 1995, 14 months after Curran's first correspondence with Goose Lane.

Curran feels quite positive about her first novel's submission process and about being published. She may even consider turning the book into a play. As a result of her experience, Curran encourages writers to submit their work. "You must never think about the odds or you'll never do it. We all know about those offices with seas of manuscripts cramming the bookshelves, but don't think about it. Somehow your book or play will eventually be accepted. In my case, Goose Lane wanted a novel that was funny to balance their fall list. Mine came along and they bought it."

RaeAnne Thayne
"Special of a Lifetime," *Woman's World Magazine*

Being a mom and newspaper editor hasn't kept RaeAnne Thayne from pursuing her dream of writing romance fiction. Addicted to romance novels since junior high, Thayne first attempted writing romance while on maternity leave. "After the birth of my daughter in 1990, we purchased a cheap computer at a bid sale. I didn't have an excuse not to start anymore, so I wrote an idea that had floated around in my head for a while."

© Mitch Mascaro 1995

After a few chapters, however, Thayne became disenchanted with the story. "I realized the plot had fallen apart and the characters were flatter than paper dolls. So, I put the story away and returned to work." But Thayne wasn't going to give up that easy. She enrolled in a seminar for beginning romance writers. "The major lesson I learned was I had absolutely no clue how to write fiction. So, I borrowed a few books from the library on novel writing and attended a few meetings of the Salt Lake City Chapter of Romance Writers of America." Thayne also contacted a few writers in the area and formed a critique group that meets monthly.

When she tried again, Thayne felt more assured of her idea and the development of her characters. She proceeded with her writing until she had completed six chapters. "My critique group convinced me I was ready to send a query. So, I did." In less than a week, she received a response from the publisher asking to see the entire manuscript. "It took me four months to finish it," Thayne says. "I waited another ten months for the eventual rejection. Apparently, both the outside reader and the junior editor liked the manuscript, but a senior editor found several major problems with it."

While attending the National Writer's Workshop, Thayne was turned to the idea of writing romance short stories by a fellow journalist who worked on a sister newspaper. Thayne says, "She'd sold something like 35 short stories to *Woman's World Weekly* over the past five years. At the time, she had just sold her first novel and she talked about how valuable writing short stories had been to her." After learning about the short story market, Thayne read nearly every issue of *Woman's World Weekly.*

Thayne's first attempt at submitting to the weekly publication came up short, but that didn't extinguish her interest. "After I developed the general idea, my first short story took about two weeks to write. *Woman's World* rejected it, but the editors were kind enough to give me some ideas of why, saying it was 'too low-keyed' for their needs. Despite the rejection, I enjoyed writing the story so much, I had to try again." For her next attempt, Thayne emphasized dialogue, humor and fast-paced action. "Several weeks after I mailed the manuscript, *Woman's World*'s editor Brooke Comer called me and said she liked the story but it was about 800 words too long. Apparently, I'd been using outdated guidelines. Also, she asked me to delete some references to alcohol, since *Woman's World* sells to a somewhat conservative audience."

After rewriting and resubmitting the story, Thayne was contacted by Comer and they went through a line-by-line edit of problems. "I rewrote the story for a second time. A few weeks later Comer called to tell me she would buy it. I was at work and had to try to remain calm until I was off deadline, but I wanted to run out into the parking lot, lock the doors to my car, and scream like crazy."

Since the acceptance of her first short story, Thayne has submitted another story to *Woman's World.* Comer likes it but, again, has suggested a few changes. "I think I am extremely fortunate to have Brooke work with me so extensively—very few editors would be willing to put so much effort into the process," says Thayne. "I don't know what about the story or my writing eventually sold the piece, but I'm thrilled she saw something she apparently wanted to cultivate."

While working on her short stories, Thayne awaited news on two novel manuscripts she'd submitted to the romance publisher, Bantam Loveswept. "My second book, *Endangered Hearts*, had been under consideration with them for several months. Earlier in the summer an editor there called me and said she'd read my manuscript, liked it, and wanted me to send anything else I'd written." Thayne sent her the revamped version of her first novel. Then, she was contacted and asked to make a few revisions to *Endangered Hearts.*

After nearly a three-month wait, Thayne received a call from the editor at Bantam Loveswept and was offered a contract to publish both manuscripts. And, while the specifics have not been worked out, the first manuscript is tentatively scheduled to be published in August of 1996.

Citing her journalism background as an asset to her fiction writing, Thayne advises other writers to branch out and not limit themselves to only one kind of writing. "I believe a beginning fiction writer shouldn't just concentrate on fiction. Nonfiction is a much easier market to break into—anyone with a modicum of talent and a good article idea can find at least one place to publish it, gaining clips and experience in the process.

"I would also say, as if other beginning writers don't already know this, swallow your ego. You may think what you've written is absolutely perfect great literature, but if you are unwilling to change a word or a comma, no one will ever read it but you. Editors know what they want. If you seriously want to be published, you need to be willing to revise and rework—even rewrite the whole thing—if that's what it takes to make the sale."

Caitlin Hamilton
"Tags," *Beloit Fiction Journal*

Growing up in a multigenerational family and traveling widely from an early age have given Caitlin Hamilton a great variety of topics, locations, periods and viewpoints from which to write. However, she does not limit her fiction only to what she knows; she writes what she envisions.

"Travel opened my imagination. I saw a whole new world and it helped me envision my own," says Hamilton. "I am convinced that my family, my travels, and my exposure to history gave me a kind of fearlessness and courage in my early work that allowed my imagination free rein."

Hamilton's imagination and interest in writing have been active since before she could read or write. "Early on, according to my mother, I would bring scribbles of things to her and call them stories. Often, she would ask me to read them to her." By the time Hamilton was 13, she had written her first short story. By age 21, she had completed a novella and three more short stories. "They were lousy, but they have their high points, and I certainly learned a great deal from writing them."

Encouraged by family and teachers, Hamilton continued to write while receiving a BA from Smith College and going on to pursue an MFA from Colorado State. "The early encouragement was essential to me. I was working awfully hard on my writing; without support (readers and others teaching me the fundamentals) I think I would have felt frustrated and thwarted."

Finding inspiration an elusive commodity, Hamilton takes the opportunity to grab it whenever it presents itself. "I write at all hours, especially if I hear a line. If I'm in bed, and a voice or line comes to me, I get up and write. When I do, I usually end up with the kernel of a story, or at least an important realization about a character. When I don't rouse myself, I always wonder if I've let go of an important piece of the puzzle."

Perceiving writing as an "act of will," Hamilton forces herself to sit down and write, even if it's only for short periods of time. "I firmly believe that there is time each week for me to write, but I can't clean the house instead, or write a letter, or read. Writing time is my gift to myself."

In 1992, at the encouragement of a faculty member, Hamilton submitted her first story for publication. It was not until three years later, however, that she received her first acceptance. "Receiving rejection after rejection is not easy. It's tiring and demoralizing. In retrospect, I think the real trial is not rejection but struggling to write well enough to be accepted. The more rejections I received, the more determined I became. After a while, though, the string of rejections took a shift; they came back with remarks scribbled on the bottom, notes that aided me or encouraged me."

That first acceptance came from *Beloit Fiction Journal*, recommended by one of her professors and a publication with which she was familiar. "I met *Beloit*'s editor, Clint McCown, and he said I was welcome to submit. It took me almost a full year to do so," Hamilton says. "I sent a piece I liked, but as time went on I became less confident in the story." Meeting McCown, however, gave Hamilton confidence that he would offer feedback even if her piece was ultimately rejected.

As she hoped, he returned the story with suggested revisions. "I was excited about revising, since I had had, over the intervening months, more ideas about the story. I did, however, rewrite more of the story than was requested, leaving open the possibility that he might not like the revision." McCown approved all of Hamilton's changes and the story was published four to five months after acceptance. Since that first acceptance, Hamilton has had two more stories accepted for publication.

Hamilton credits her MFA degree and attending writers' conferences for the improvement in her writing that led to her first publication. "I attended two writers' conferences that were incredibly helpful—The Bread Loaf Writers' Conference in Middlebury, Vermont, and The Iowa Summer Writing Festival in Iowa City, Iowa. At both, in addition to receiving helpful criticism, I was able to broaden my writing community, go to readings, and talk about books." Hamilton encourages writers to connect with the larger writing community, but she also suggests that writers explore opportunities to meet writers in their own area—through writing groups, local readings, and university classes.

By working in the wee hours of the morning or late at night, Hamilton plans to finish her novel and, perhaps, rewrite five or six stories. In fact, revision is a vital part of Hamilton's writing process, and a step she encourages other writers to take before submitting. "I believe rewriting is crucial, that it is in rewriting that my stories become stories. Knowing about grammar is crucial, of course, but I'm talking about editing more than misplaced modifiers. One has to be able to see what really drives a story, what is essential.

"I may sound like I can't let go of a story, but what I really can't let go of is my vision for the piece. If I feel I can take another leap, risk something more, I do—and the stories are often better for the continued effort. Often, the small changes—the rephrasing that gets to the heart of the story, the telling detail that locks characterization into place—are the greatest triumphs."

The Markets

Important Listing Information

● Listings are not *advertisements. Although the information here is as accurate as possible, the listings are not endorsed or guaranteed by the editor of* Novel & Short Story Writer's Market.

● Novel & Short Story Writer's Market *reserves the right to exclude any listing that does not meet its requirements.*

Key to Symbols and Abbreviations

‡ *New listing in all sections*

* *Subsidy publisher in Small Press and Commercial Book Publishers sections*

■ *Book packager or producer*

● *Comment by editor of* Novel & Short Story Writer's Market

❦ *Canadian listing*

ms—*manuscript;* mss-*manuscripts*

b&w—*black and white*

SASE—*self-addressed, stamped envelope*

SAE—*self-addressed envelope*

IRC—*International Reply Coupon, for use on reply mail from other countries*

(See Glossary for definitions of words and expressions used in writing and publishing.)

The Markets

Literary and Small Circulation Magazines

This, the largest section of *Novel & Short Story Writer's Market*, contains over 700 markets for your short fiction. Over 200 of those markets are new to this edition, and all listings which appeared in last year's edition have been updated to reflect editors' current needs. Listed here are literary journals of all sizes and small magazines with circulations of under 10,000. Although these journals and magazines vary greatly in size, theme, format and management, the editors at each have told us they are actively seeking fiction for their respective publications. Their specific fiction needs present writers of all degrees of expertise and interests with an abundance of publishing opportunities.

While publishing your fiction in one of the magazines listed in this section can yield the important benefits of experience, exposure and prestige, many offer little if any cash payment. Some of the well-established literary journals may pay several hundred dollars for a short story, but most of the small magazines pay only with contributor's copies or a subscription to their publication. However, as Salima Keegan, manager of *Hayden's Ferry Review*, points out in the interview with her on page 152, being published in a literary journal or small magazine can be a stepping stone for new writers "so that they are able to find a voice and an audience."

Diversity in opportunity

Among the diverse publications in this section are magazines devoted to almost every topic, every level of writing and every type of writer—prestigious literary journals, specific genre magazines, regional magazines, highly specialized theme magazines and personal fanzines.

You'll find most of the well-known prestigious literary journals listed here. Many, including *Carolina Quarterly* and *Ploughshares*, are associated with universities, while others such as *The Quarterly* and *The Paris Review* are independently published. Fiction in these journals, although occasionally experimental, tends toward the literary and traditional, and contributors include both prominent as well as previously unpublished writers. Editors of these journals pride themselves on having stories they publish routinely selected for inclusion in prestigious annual prize anthologies such as *The Best American Short Stories*, *Prize Stories: The O. Henry Awards*, *Pushcart Prize: Best of the Small Presses*, and *New Stories from the South: The Year's Best*. *Ploughshares*, in fact, has the distinction of having the most stories from a single issue published in *The Best American Short Stories*.

The staffs of university journals are usually made up of student editors and a managing editor who is also a faculty member. These staffs often change every year. Whenever possible, we indicate this in listings and give the name of the current editor and the length of that editor's term. Also remember that the schedule of university journals usually coincides with the university's academic year, meaning that most offices are difficult or impossible to reach during the summer.

Many of the magazines listed here publish a wide range of fiction with their only criteria being that it is well written, well presented and suitable for their particular readership, while others only publish stories of a specific genre. A few of the specific genre magazines in this section include *Worlds of Fantasy and Horror* (fantasy), *Terror Time Again* (horror), *Nonsense* (humor), *Mystery Time* (mystery), *Peoplenet* (romance), and *Other Worlds* (science fiction).

A number of the listings in this section publish fiction about a particular geographic area or by authors who live in that locale. Some of the regional magazines you'll find here are *Bamboo Ridge*, looking for "writing that reflects the multicultural diversity of Hawaii"; *Big Sky Stories*, publishing "fiction set in Big Sky country prior to 1950"; and *Cayo*, seeking fiction about "Florida Keys-related topics or by Keys authors." Still other magazines only publish stories by or about members of a particular ethnic group: *African American Review* and *Obsidian II* (African-American), *A Gathering of the Tribes* and *Moccasin Telegraph* (Native American), and *Americas Review* and *Bilingual Review* (Hispanic).

Among this year's new listings are a number of publications with highly specialized needs. *Inner Voices* only wants fiction by prisoners while *Legal Fiction*, a new publication of the Temple University School of Law, needs stories by attorneys and for attorneys. In addition, *Liberty* is looking for fiction with "anti-authoritarian themes," *Mail Call* wants pieces that in some way involve the Civil War, and *Mentor* only publishes stories about mentoring. Also new to this section are *Dream Forge* a new "electronic magazine for a thinking and literate readership," and *The Supernatural Magazine on Audiobook* which, as its name suggests, is a "magazine on cassette."

Many of the highly specialized publications listed here are fanzines or micro-press magazines that are often one- or two-person operations whose needs run the gamut from traditional fiction to personal rants to highly experimental work. While these represent the most volatile group of publications in this section, they have offered many writers their first bylines. The editors of these small magazines are often writers themselves who welcome the opportunity to give others a chance at publication.

Selecting the right markets for your work

Your chance for publication begins as you zero in on those markets most likely to be interested in your work. If you write a particular type of fiction, such as fantasy or mystery, check the Category Index (starting on page 588) for the appropriate subject heading. If your work is more general, or, in fact, very specialized, you may wish to browse through the listings, perhaps looking up those magazines published in your state or region.

In addition to browsing through the listings and using the Category Index, check the ranking codes at the beginning of listings to find those most likely to be receptive to your work. This is especially true for beginning writers, who should look for magazines that say they are especially open to new writers (I) and for those giving equal weight to both new and established writers (II). For more explanation about these codes, see the end of this introduction.

Once you have a list of magazines you might like to try, read their listings carefully. Much of the material within each listing carries clues that tell you more about the magazine. How to Get the Most Out of This Book starting on page 3 describes in detail the listing information common to all the markets in our book, but there is some information in this section that pertains only to magazines and especially to literary and small publications.

The physical description appearing near the beginning of the listings can give you clues about the size and financial commitment to the publication. This is not always an indication of quality, but chances are a publication with expensive paper and four-color artwork on the cover has more prestige than a photocopied publication featuring a clip art self-cover. If you're a new writer or your work is considered avant garde, however, you may be more interested in the photocopied publication. For more information on some of the paper, binding and printing terms used in these descriptions, see the sidebar in the Business of Fiction Writing on page 9.

This is the only section in which you will find magazines that do not read submissions all year long. Whether limited reading periods are tied to a university schedule or meant to accommodate the capabilities of a very small staff, those periods are noted within listings.

Furthering your search

It cannot be stressed enough that reading the listing is only the first part of developing your marketing plan. The second part, equally important, is to obtain fiction guidelines and read the actual magazine. Reading copies of a magazine helps you determine the fine points of the magazine's publishing style and philosophy. There is no substitute for this type of hands-on research.

Unlike commercial periodicals available at most newsstands and bookstores, it requires a little more effort to obtain some of the magazines listed here. The new super chain bookstores are doing a better job these days of stocking literaries and you can find some in independent and college bookstores, especially those published in your area. You may, however, need to send for a sample copy. We include sample copy prices in the listings whenever possible.

Another way to find out more about literary magazines is to check out the various prize anthologies and take note of journals whose fiction is being selected for publication there. Studying prize anthologies not only lets you know which magazines are publishing award-winning work, but it also provides a valuable overview of what is considered to be the best fiction published today.

Award-winning publications, as well as other information we feel will help you determine if a listing is the right market for you, are noted in editorial comments identified with a bullet (●). The comments section also allows us to explain more about the special interests or requirements of a publication and any information we've learned from our readers that we feel will help you choose potential markets wisely.

Among the awards and honors we note are inclusion of work in:
● *Best American Short Stories*, published by Houghton Mifflin, 222 Berkeley St., Boston MA 02116.
● *New Stories from the South: The Year's Best*, published by Algonquin Books of Chapel Hill, P.O. Box 2225, Chapel Hill NC 27515.
● *Prize Stories: The O. Henry Awards*, published by Doubleday/Anchor, 1540 Broadway, New York NY 10036.
● *Pushcart Prize: Best of the Small Presses*, published by Pushcart Press, Box 380, Wainscott NY 11975.

The well-respected *Poet* magazine (published by Cooper House Publishing Inc., P.O. Box 54947, Oklahoma City OK 73154) created a new awards program in 1993 to honor the best literary magazines (those publishing both fiction and poetry). The program is titled The American Literary Magazine Awards and most recipients of editorial content awards have listings in this section. To find out more about the awards, see the *Poet*'s fall issue.

For more information

See The Business of Fiction Writing for the specific mechanics of manuscript submission. Above all, editors appreciate a professional presentation. Include a brief cover letter and send a self-addressed envelope for a reply or a self-addressed envelope in a size large enough to accommodate your manuscript, if you would like it returned. Be sure to include enough stamps or International Reply Coupons (for replies from countries other than your own) to cover your manuscript's return.

North American publications are listed in the following main section of listings; it is followed by listings for other English-speaking markets around the world. To make it easier to find Canadian markets, we include a maple leaf symbol (✹) at the start of those listings.

If you're interested in learning more about literary and small magazines, you may want to look at *The International Directory of Little Magazines and Small Presses* (Dustbooks, Box 100, Paradise CA 95967) or contact the Council of Literary Magazines and Presses (3-C, 154 Christopher St., New York NY 10014-2839), a group that supports the small press and publishes a directory of its magazine members, the *Directory of Literary Magazines*.

If your tastes run toward fanzines and the micro-press, you may want to check out *Factsheet Five* (P.O. Box 170099, San Francisco CA 94117-0099) or *Scavenger's Newsletter* (519 Ellinwood, Osage City KS 66523).

The following is the ranking system we have used to categorize the listings in this section.

I **Publication encourages beginning or unpublished writers to submit work for consideration and publishes new writers regularly.**

II **Publication accepts work by established writers and by writers of exceptional talent.**

III **Publication does not encourage beginning writers; prints mostly writers with previous publication credits; very few new writers.**

IV **Special-interest or regional publication, open only to writers in certain genres or on certain subjects or from certain geographical areas.**

‡**A.R.T., Arbitrary Random Thought, (I),** NewHouse Publications, P.O. Box 8128, Janesville WI 53547-8128. Editor: John J. Liptow. Magazine: 8½×11; 25-40 pages; bond paper; C1S cover; illustrations. The philosophy of *A.R.T.* is "to integrate cross-cultural themes for a general literate audience of a 20+ crowd." Quarterly. Estab. 1994. Circ. 100.
Needs: Adventure, condensed/excerpted novel, erotica, ethnic/multicultural, experimental, fantasy (science fantasy, sword and sorcery), feminist, gay, historical (general), horror, humor/satire, lesbian, literary, mainstream/contemporary, mystery/suspense (amateur sleuth, cozy, police procedural, private eye/hardboiled, romantic, suspense), psychic/supernatural/occult, regional, religious/inspirational, romance (contemporary, futuristic/time travel, gothic, historical), science fiction (hard science, soft/sociological), senior citizen/retirement, serialized novel, sports, translations, westerns. Receives 50 unsolicited mss/month. Buys 5-6 mss/issue. Publishes ms 1 year after acceptance. Length: 10,000 words maximum. Publishes short shorts. Also publishes literary essays, literary criticism, poetry.
How to Contact: Submit ms, no cover letter necessary. Place all pertinent information on ms. Reports in 2 weeks on queries; 2 months on mss. Send a disposable copy of the ms. No SASE necessary. No simultaneous submissions. Occasionally considers reprints. Electronic submissions OK. Sample copy for $3.95. Fiction guidelines free.
Payment/Terms: Pays $10 maximum on acceptance and free subscription to the magazine. Buys first North American serial rights.
Advice: "I will look past almost anything—weak structure, negligible word choice, poor characterizations—but the ending will express to me the extent of the writer's commitment to this particular work. Submit with

an understanding of manuscript mechanics—they are both writer's and editor's best friend."

ABOVE THE BRIDGE, (IV), Third Stone Publishing, P.O. Box 416, Marquette MI 49855. (906)228-2964. Editor: Mikel B. Classen. Magazine: 8½×11; 48 pages; 80 lb. text paper; 80 lb. LOE cover stock; illustrations and photos. "For and about the Upper Peninsula of Michigan." Quarterly. Estab. 1985. Circ. 2,500.
Needs: Regional. "Any stories pertaining to the Upper Peninsula of Michigan." Receives 15-20 unsolicited mss/month. Accepts 12-13 mss/year. Publishes ms up to 2 years after acceptance. Length: 800-1,000 words average; 300 words minimum; 2,000 words maximum. Publishes short shorts. Length: 300-400 words. Also publishes literary essays and literary criticism.
How to Contact: Send complete ms with a cover letter. Should include estimated word count, bio, name, address, phone number. Reports in 6-8 months. Send SASE for reply, return of ms or send a disposable copy of ms. Simultaneous and reprint submissions OK. Sample copy for $3.50. Fiction guidelines free.
Payment/Terms: Pays 2¢/word on publication. Buys one-time rights.
Advice: "Make certain that the manuscript pertains to the Upper Peninsula of Michigan. If you've never been there, don't fake it."

ABRUPT EDGE: A Magazine of Horror & Suspense, (I, II), P.O. Box 1227, Eugene OR 97440. Editor: Dean Wesley Smith. Magazine: 8½×11; 64 pages; saddle-stitched; web-printed. Estab. 1994.
Needs: Fantasy, horror, science fiction, speculative fiction. Length: 7,500 words maximum.
• This is a magazine by the publisher of *Pulphouse* and the new magazine, *Full Clip*, listed in this section. The editor is particularly interested in horror and dark fantasy "with an edge."
How to Contact: Send complete ms with a cover letter "that gives publication history, work history, or any other information relevant to the magazine. Don't tell us about the story. The story will tell us about the story." SASE. Reports in 2 months. Sample copy for $4.95. Fiction guidelines for #10 SASE .
Payment/Terms: Pays 4-7¢/word on acceptance for first serial rights.

ABSOLUTE MAGNITUDE, The Magazine of Science Fiction Adventures, (I, II, IV), DNA Publications, P.O. Box 13, Greenfield MA 01302. (413)772-0725. Editor: Warren Lapine. Magazine: 8½×11; 96 pages; illustrations. "We publish technical science fiction that is adventurous and character driven." Quarterly. Estab. 1993. Circ. 9,000.
Needs: Science fiction: adventure, hard science. No fantasy, horror, funny science fiction. Receives 300-500 unsolicited mss/month. Buys 7-10 mss/issue; 28-40 mss/year. Publishes ms 3-6 months after acceptance. Agented fiction 5%. Recently published work by Hal Clement, Allen Steele, C.J. Cherryh, Barry B. Longyear, Janet Kagan. Length: 5,000-12,000 words average; 1,000 words minimum; 25,000 words maximum. Publishes very little poetry. Often critiques or comments on rejected ms.
How to Contact: Do NOT query. Send complete ms with a cover letter. Should include estimated word count and list of publications. Send SASE for reply, return of ms or send a disposable copy of ms. Simultaneous and reprint submissions OK. Sample copy for $4. Reviews novels and short story collections.
Payment/Terms: Pays 3-5¢/word on publication for first North American serial rights; 1¢/word for reprints. Sometimes sends galleys to author.
Advice: "We want good writing with solid characterization, also character growth, story development, and plot resolution. We would like to see more character-driven stories."

ABYSS MAGAZINE, "Games and the Imagination," (II, IV), Ragnarok Enterprises, P.O. Box 140333, Austin TX 78714-0333. (512)472-6535. Fax: (512)472-6220. Editor: David F. Nalle. Fiction Editor: Patricia Fitch. Magazine: 8×10; 48 pages; bond paper; glossy cover; illustrations; photos. "Heroic fantasy fiction: some fantasy, horror, SF and adventure fiction, for college-age game players." Quarterly. Plans special fiction issue. Estab. 1979. Circ. 1,500.
• *Abyss Magazine* can be contacted through Internet online service as well as their own electronic bulletin board.
Needs: Adventure, fantasy, horror, psychic/supernatural/occult, cyberpunk, science fiction, heroic fantasy, sword and sorcery. "Game-based stories are not specifically desired." Upcoming themes: "Horror Issue" (spring); "Review Issue" (summer). Receives 20-30 unsolicited mss/month. Buys 1 ms/issue; 7 mss/year. Publishes ms 1-12 months after acceptance. Published work by Antoine Sadel, Kevin Anderson, Alan Blount; published new writers within the last year. Length: 2,000 words average; 1,000 words minimum; 4,000

Market categories: (I) Open to new writers; (II) Open to both new and established writers; (III) Interested mostly in established writers; (IV) Open to writers whose work is specialized.

words maximum. Publishes short shorts occasionally. Also publishes literary essays and literary criticism. Sometimes critiques rejected mss or recommends other markets.

How to Contact: Send for sample copy first. Reports in 6 weeks on queries; 3 months on mss. "Do send a cover letter, preferably entertaining. Include some biographical info and a precis of lengthy stories." SASE. Simultaneous submissions OK. Prefers electronic submissions by modem or network. "Call our BBS at (512)472-6905 for ASCII info." Internet address: DFN@Infinity.ccsi.com. Sample copy and fiction guidelines $5. Reviews novels and short story collections (especially fantasy novels).

Payment/Terms: Pays 1-3¢/word or by arrangement, plus contributor's copies. Pays on publication for first North American serial rights.

Advice: "We are particularly interested in new writers with mature and original style. Don't send us fiction which everyone else has sent back to you unless you think it has qualities which make it too strange for everyone else but which don't ruin the significance of the story. Make sure what you submit is appropriate to the magazine you send it to. More than half of what we get is completely inappropriate. We plan to include more and longer stories."

ACM, (ANOTHER CHICAGO MAGAZINE), (II), Left Field Press, 3709 N. Kenmore, Chicago IL 60613. Editor: Barry Silesky. Fiction Editor: Sharon Solwitz. Magazine: 5½×8½; 200-220 pages; "art folio each issue." Estab. 1977.

 • *ACM* is best known for experimental work or work with political slants, clear narrative voices. The editor looks for "engaged and unusual writing."

Needs: Contemporary, literary, experimental, feminist, gay/lesbian, ethnic, prose poem, translations and political/socio-historical. Receives 200 unsolicited fiction mss each month. Published work by David Michael Kaplan, Brett Lott, Jean Thompson and Wanda Coleman; published new writers in the last year. Also publishes literary essays.

How to Contact: Unsolicited mss acceptable with SASE. Publishes ms 6-12 months to 1 year after acceptance. Sample copies are available for $8 ppd. Reports in 2-5 months. Receives small press collections.

Payment/Terms: Pays small honorarium plus contributor's copy. Acquires first North American serial rights.

Advice: "Get used to rejection slips, and don't get discouraged. Keep introductory letters short. Make sure ms has name and address on every page, and that it is clean, neat and proofread. We are looking for stories with freshness and originality in subject angle and style, and work that encounters the world and is not stuck in its own navel."

ACORN WHISTLE, (II), 907 Brewster Ave., Beloit WI 53511. Editor: Fred Burwell. Magazine: 8½×11; 75-100 pages; uncoated paper; coated cover; illustrations; photos. "*Acorn Whistle* seeks accessible writing, art and photography that appeals to readers on both emotional and intellectual levels. Our intended audience is the educated non-academic. Semiannually. Estab. 1995. Circ. 500.

 • Editor Fred Burwell is also editor of *Beloit Fiction Journal* listed in this section.

Needs: Ethnic/multicultural, feminist, historical (general), humor/satire, literary, mainstream/contemporary, regional. No erotica, experimental, fantasy, horror, religious or science fiction. Buys 5-7 mss/issue; 10-15 mss/year. Publishes ms within a year after acceptance. Length: open. Publishes short shorts. Also publishes memoir and poetry. Often critiques or comments on rejected ms.

How to Contact: Send complete ms with a cover letter. Should include bio. Reports in 2 weeks on queries; 1-8 weeks on mss. Send SASE for reply, return of ms or send a disposable copy of ms. Simultaneous submissions OK. Sample copy for $5. Fiction guidelines for #10 SASE.

Payment/Terms: Pays 2 contributor's copies. Acquires first North American serial rights. Features expanded contributor's notes with personal comments from each author.

Advice: "We prefer realistic story telling, strong characterization, a vivid presentation. Writing that moves both heart and mind has an excellent chance here. We encourage a friendly working relationship between editors and writers. We seek fiction that communicates and illuminates shared human experience."

‡ACTA VICTORIANA, (I, II), 150 Charles St. West, Toronto, Ontario M5S 1K9 Canada. Editor: Abbie Levin. Editors change each year. Send future submissions to "Editor." Magazine: 9½×13; 40 pages; glossy paper; cornwall cover; illustrations and photos. "We publish the poetry, prose, drawings and photographs of university students as well as of other writers. The magazine reaches the University of Toronto community as well as students of other universities. Semiannually. Estab. 1875. Circ. 1,500+.

 • The editors at *Acta Victoriana* are particularly interested in "Gen-X" stories.

Needs: Contemporary, ethnic, experimental, humor/satire, literary, mainstream, prose poem. Accepts 4-5 mss/issue; 8-10 mss/year. Publishes ms 2 months after acceptance. Published work by Craig Stephenson, Peter McCallum and Douglas Brown; published new writers within the last year. Length: 1,500 words maximum.

How to Contact: Send complete ms with cover letter, which should include information about the writer's previous publishing credits and biography. Reports in 2 months on mss. Simultaneous submissions OK. E-mail address: yumyum2@aol.com. Sample copy and fiction guidelines for $3 and 9×12 SAE.

Payment/Terms: Pays in contributor's copies.
Advice: "University publications such as ours offer beginning fiction writers good opportunities to get published. If your piece is innovative and exciting, yet at the same time well-crafted, you will have a good chance of getting published. Editors change yearly in this student journal, yet our editorial policy remains roughly the same."

ADRIFT, Writing: Irish, Irish American and . . . , (II), 46 E. First St. #4D, New York NY 10003. Editor: Thomas McGonigle. Magazine: 8 × 11; 32 pages; 60 lb. paper stock; 65 lb. cover stock; illustrations; photos. "Irish-Irish American as a basis—though we are interested in advanced writing from anywhere." Semiannually. Estab. 1983. Circ. 1,000.
 • Note *Adrift* has a new address.
Needs: Contemporary, erotica, ethnic, experimental, feminist, gay, lesbian, literary, translations. Receives 40 unsolicited mss/month. Buys 3 mss/issue. Published work by Francis Stuart; published new writers within the last year. Length: open. Also publishes literary criticism. Sometimes critiques rejected mss.
How to Contact: Send complete ms. Reports as soon as possible. SASE for ms. Sample copy for $5. Reviews novels or short story collections.
Payment/Terms: Pays $7.50-300 on publication for first rights.
Advice: "The writing should argue with, among others, James Joyce, Flann O'Brien, Juan Goytisolo, Ingeborg Bachmann, E.M. Cioran, Max Stirner, Patrick Kavanagh."

AETHLON, (I,II,IV), Dept. of English, St. Norbert College, De Pere WI 54115-2099. Editor: E.L. Risden. (414)337-3938. Magazine: 6 × 9; 180-240 pages; illustrations and photographs. "Theme: Literary treatment of sport. We publish articles on that theme, critical studies of author's treatment of sport and original fiction and poetry with sport themes. Most of our audience are academics." Semiannually. Estab. 1983. Circ. 800.
 • In the past due to editorial changes, reporting time has been slow. The current editor is working to reduce this time.
Needs: Sport. "Stories must have a sport-related theme and subject; otherwise, we're wide open." Receives 15-20 fiction mss/month. Accepts 6-10 fiction mss/issue; 12-20 fiction mss/year. Publishes ms "about 1 year" after acceptance. Length: 2,500-5,000 words average; 500 words minimum; 7,500 words maximum. Also publishes literary essays, literary criticism, poetry. Sometimes critiques rejected mss.
How to Contact: Send complete ms and brief cover letter with 1-2 lines for a contributor's note. Reports in 6-12 months. SASE in size to fit ms. No simultaneous submissions. Electronic disk submissions OK. Final copy must be submitted on disk (WordPerfect). Sample copy for $12.50. Reviews novels and short story collections. Send books to Professor Brooke Horvath, Dept. of English, Kent State University, 6000 Frank Ave., Canton OH 44720.
Payment/Terms: Pays 1 contributor's copy and 5 offprints.
Advice: "We are looking for well-written, insightful stories. Don't be afraid to be experimental. Take more care with your manuscript. Please send a legible manuscript free of grammatical errors. Be willing to revise."

‡AFRICAN AMERICAN REVIEW, (II), Indiana State University, Department of English, Root Hall A218, Terre Haute IN 47809. (812)237-2968. Fax: (812)237-3156. Editor: Joe Weixlmann. Fiction Editor: Reginald McKnight. Magazine: 7 × 10; 176 pages; 60#, acid-free paper; 100# skid stock cover; illustrations and photos. "*African American Review* publishes stories and poetry by African American writers, and essays about African American literature and culture." Quarterly. Estab. 1967. Circ. 3,764.
 • *African American Review* is the official publication of the Division of Black American Literature and Culture of the Modern Language Association. The magazine received American Literary Magazine Awards in 1994 and 1995.
Needs: Ethnic/Multicultural: experimental, feminist, gay, lesbian, literary, mainstream/contemporary. "No children's/juvenile/young adult/teen." Receives 10 unsolicited mss/month. Buys 6-8 mss/year. Publishes ms 1 year after acceptance. Agented fiction 10%. Recently published work by Clarence Major, Ann Allen Shockley, Alden Reimoneng. Length: 3,000 words average. Also publishes literary essays, literary criticism, poetry. Sometimes critiques or comments on rejected ms.
How to Contact: Send complete ms with a cover letter. Reports in 2 weeks on queries; 3 months on mss. Send SASE for reply, return of ms or send a disposable copy of ms. E-mail address: aschoal@amber.indstate.edu. Sample copy for $6. Fiction guidelines for #10 SASE. Reviews novels and short story collections. Send books to Keneth Kinnamon, Dept. of English, Univ. of Arkansas, Fayetteville, AR 72701.
Payment/Terms: Pays $50-100 and 10 contributor's copies on publication for first North American serial rights. Sends galleys to author.

AGNI, (II), Creative Writing Program, Boston University, 236 Bay State Rd., Boston MA 02215. (617)353-5389. Editor-in-Chief: Askold Melnyczuk. Magazine: 5½ × 8½; 320 pages; 55 lb. booktext paper; recycled cover stock; occasional art portfolios. "Eclectic literary magazine publishing first-rate poems and stories." Semiannually. Estab. 1972.
 • Work from *Agni* has been selected regularly for inclusion in both *Pushcart Prize* and *Best American Short Stories* anthologies.

Get Connected with Electronic Magazines

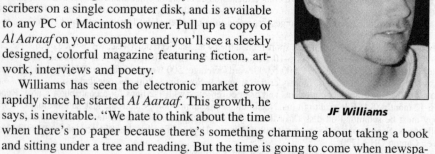

JF Williams, editor and publisher of the electronic literary magazine *Al Aaraaf*, sees the electronic market as a viable way for fiction writers to get their work published. Williams started the magazine three years ago, going the electronic route as an alternative to the high paper costs of printing a conventional magazine. *Al Aaraaf* is sent to subscribers on a single computer disk, and is available to any PC or Macintosh owner. Pull up a copy of *Al Aaraaf* on your computer and you'll see a sleekly designed, colorful magazine featuring fiction, artwork, interviews and poetry.

Williams has seen the electronic market grow rapidly since he started *Al Aaraaf*. This growth, he says, is inevitable. "We hate to think about the time

JF Williams

when there's no paper because there's something charming about taking a book and sitting under a tree and reading. But the time is going to come when newspapers will be delivered over phone lines, and kids are going to be carrying electronic slates that have their science books, math books, everything in them. The price of electronic equipment will drop to where everyone can afford it. I think publishing is going in that direction whether we like it or not."

Whether you're for or against the idea of a computer screen replacing the printed page, one thing you can be sure of is that electronic magazines offer new opportunities for writers. In an electronic medium, Williams says, "you get the chance of getting your work seen by a lot of people who normally wouldn't see it. Only so many people subscribe to literary magazines—basically those interested in fine literature. Whereas on an online service, anyone can see your work. You have a chance of capturing an audience you normally wouldn't capture."

The literary field seems to be warming up to the idea of magazines on disks and online services. "Most people really like *Al Aaraaf* on disk," he says. "I think at first it might be the novelty of it, but I hope after that wears off they actually sit down and read the stories. Acceptance is there but it's slow. We're fighting that age old pen/ink/paper thing . . . some people think if you're not published on paper you're not a real magazine." Williams points out that many large literary magazines are moving toward electronic versions. "*Atlantic Monthly* is on America Online," he says. "A lot of the big magazines have electronic versions now. And with the advent of the World Wide Web, people are putting together their own home pages and sites. They're publishing their own work on the Internet."

Even though it's available to America Online subscribers in a text-only form, Williams prefers to keep *Al Aaraaf* on disk. Online, Williams says, "you can't see everything I want to include because graphics take up so much disk space. It takes a long time to download the information. That's why I keep *Al Aaraaf* on disk, so I can include the graphics. I also don't want to be exclusively online because then subscribers wouldn't be receiving something in the mail."

The fact that *Al Aaraaf* is an electronic magazine shouldn't overshadow the real reason it exists—to present the work of new writers. "We're different because we're electronic," Williams says, "but from a literary standpoint we're different in that we try to present young writers who have not been published before and probably would not be published anywhere else."

The title of the magazine, *Al Aaraaf*, is taken from a work by Edgar Allan Poe and refers to an Arabic term for a netherworld, a place between Heaven and Hell where people are neither rewarded nor punished. Because the reference is taken from Poe, many writers think *Al Aaraaf* publishes mystery or horror, but Williams says this could not be farther from the truth.

He is interested in more literary work in which the language is almost as important as what happens in the story. "Writers need to take more risks and do something different with words. I like words that sound melodic on the page— not plot heavy, genre fiction but true honest fiction. The work has to feel like it's coming from somewhere other than just a pen and a brain. There should be a feeling that kind of bubbles through the words, to the surface . . . it's hard to explain but I know it when I see it.

"Being published in *Al Aaraaf* is an opportunity to be involved in something a little bit different than a regular magazine," Williams continues. "We exist on computer networks and on disk, so it's a different experience for the writers we publish. They can now say they're connected!"

—*Cindy Laufenberg*

❝We're different because we're electronic, but . . . we try to present young writers who have not been published before. . . . ❞

—JF Williams

Needs: Stories, excerpted novels, prose poems and translations. Receives 200 unsolicited fiction mss/month. Buys 4-7 mss/issue, 8-12 mss/year. Reading period October 1 to April 30 only. Published work by Joyce Carol Oates, Stephen Dixon, Andra Neiburga, Ha Jin. Rarely critiques rejected mss.
How to Contact: Send complete ms with SASE and cover letter listing previous publications. Simultaneous submissions OK. Reports in 1-4 months. Sample copy for $6.
Payment/Terms: Pays $10/page up to $150; 2 contributor's copies; one-year subscription. Pays on publication for first North American serial rights. Sends galleys to author. Copyright reverts to author upon publication.
Advice: "Read *Agni* carefully to understand the kinds of stories we publish. Read—everything, classics, literary journals, bestsellers."

THE AGUILAR EXPRESSION, (II), P.O. Box 304, Webster PA 15087. Editor: Xavier F. Aguilar. Magazine: $8\frac{1}{2} \times 11$; 10-16 pages; 20 lb. bond paper; illustrations. "We are open to all writers of a general theme—something that may appeal to everyone." Semiannually. Estab. 1989. Circ. 150.
• The editor is particularly interested in stories about the homeless in the U.S. but publishes fiction on other topics as well.
Needs: Adventure, ethnic/multicultural, experimental, horror, mainstream/contemporary, mystery/suspense (romantic suspense), romance (contemporary). No religious or first-person stories. Will publish annual special fiction issue or anthology in the future. Receives 10 unsolicited mss/month. Acquires 1-2 mss/issue; 2-4 mss/year. Publishes ms 1 month to 1 year after acceptance. Published work by Aphrodite Mitsos, Linda Keegan, Loueva Smith. Length: 1,000 words average; 750 words minimum; 1,500 words maximum. Also publishes poetry.
How to Contact: Send complete ms with cover letter. Reports on queries in 1 week; mss in 1 month. SASE for a reply to a query or send a disposable copy of the ms. No simultaneous submissions. Sample copy for $6. Fiction guidelines for #10 SASE.
Payment/Terms: Pays 1 contributor's copy; additional copies at a reduced rate of $3. Acquires one-time rights. Not copyrighted. Write to publication for details on contests, awards or grants.

AL AARAAF, (II), JFW Publishing, 10 Entrada West, Irvine CA 92720. Phone/fax: (714)544-8274. Editor: JF Williams. Electronic magazine: Hardcopy version is $8\frac{1}{2} \times 6\frac{1}{2}$; 150-200 pages; high quality bond paper; glossy color cover; illustrations and photos. "*Al Aaraaf* doesn't have a particular theme. We're looking for serious fiction, and by that we do not mean boring and without humor. We publish material geared toward an audience which can recognize and enjoy the words themselves." Quarterly. Estab. 1992. Circ. 100 (but thousands can access us online).
• The graphics and presentation of this electronic magazine are high quality.
Needs: Experimental, literary, serialized novel and translations. No genre fiction e.g. romance, westerns, horror, science fiction, mystery, fantasy, etc. Nothing that can be categorized. Receives 25-50 unsolicited mss/month. Buys 2-4 mss/issue; 8-12 mss/year. Publishes ms 3-6 months after acceptance. Recently published work by William Logan, Kevin Coll, Jessica Roder and Jeff Peters. Length: 3,000 words average; 500 words minimum; 5,000 words maximum. Publishes short shorts. Also publishes literary essays, literary criticism and poetry. Often critiques or comments on rejected ms.
How to Contact: Send complete ms with a cover letter or send through America Online at "Al Aaraaf" (alaaraaf@aol.com). Use text only or Word format. Should include estimated word count, Social Security number, and list of publications. Reports on mss in 1-2 months. Send a disposable copy of ms (or electronic submission). Simultaneous and electronic submissions OK. E-mail address: "Al Aaraaf"; (America Online); alaaraff@aol.com (Internet). Sample copy free (sample copy issued only on disk, must state IBM or Mac version) for #10 SAE and 2 first-class stamps. Fiction guidelines for #10 SAE and 1 first-class stamp. Reviews novels and short story collections.
Payment/Terms: Pays $10/page and 1 contributor's copy on publication for first North American serial rights.
Advice: "The main thing we look for in a manuscript is honesty. It is easy to differentiate between a story written for an audience and one written for the author himself. We're looking for the latter. And, above all, the writing must be extremely good. Most writers don't seem to take enough risks. We'd like to see more risky attempts at style and narration; not deliberately wacky, but honestly wacky. Do not send us plot heavy, 'Hollywood' stories or anything that we can lump into a category."

ALABAMA LITERARY REVIEW, (II), Smith 253, Troy State University, Troy AL 36082. (334)670-3286, ext. 3307. Fax: (334)670-3519. Editor: Theron Montgomery. Magazine: $6 \times 11\frac{1}{2}$; 100 pages; top paper quality; some illustrations; photos. "National magazine for a broad range of the best contemporary fiction, poetry, essays, photography and drama that we can find." Semiannually. Estab. 1987.
Needs: Contemporary, experimental, humor/satire, literary, prose poem, science fiction, serialized/excerpted novel, translations. "Serious writing." Receives 50 unsolicited fiction mss/month. Acquires 5 fiction mss/issue. Publishes ms 5-6 months after acceptance. Recently published work by Reina McKeithew, Manette Ansay, Ed Peaco, Pete Fromm, John Holman and Mary Sue Weston; published new writers within the last

year. Length: 2,000-3,500 words average. Publishes short shorts of 1,000 words. Also publishes literary essays, literary criticism, poetry. Sometimes comments on rejected mss.

How to Contact: Send complete ms with cover letter or submit through agent. Reports on queries in 2 weeks; on mss in 2 months (except in summer). SASE. Simultaneous submissions OK. Sample copy for $4 plus 50¢ postage. Reviews novels or short story collections. Send to Steve Cooper.

Payment/Terms: Pays in contributor's copies and honorarium when available. First rights returned to author upon publication. Work published in *ALR* may be read on state-wide (nonprofit) public radio program.

Advice: "Read our publication first. Avoid negative qualities pertaining to gimmickry and a self-centered point of view. We are interested in any kind of writing if it is *serious* and *honest* in the sense of 'the human heart in conflict with itself.' "

ALASKA QUARTERLY REVIEW, (II), University of Alaska, Anchorage, 3211 Providence Dr., Anchorage AK 99508. (907)786-1327. Fiction Editor: Ronald Spatz. Magazine: 6×9; 200 pages; 60 lb. Glatfelter paper; 10 pt. C15 black ink varnish cover stock; photos on cover only. Magazine of "contemporary literary art and criticism for a general literary audience." Semiannually. Estab. 1982.

- Work appearing in the *Alaska Quarterly Review* has been selected for the *Pushcart Prize*, *Best American Essays*, and *Best American Short Stories* anthologies. For more, see "On Target," by Ronald Spatz in the Writing Techniques section of the 1994 *Novel & Short Story Writer's Market*.

Needs: Contemporary, experimental, literary, prose poem and translations. Receives 180 unsolicited fiction mss/month. Accepts 7-13 mss/issue, 15-24 mss/year. Does not read mss May 15-August 15. Published new writers within the last year. Publishes short shorts. Occasionally critiques rejected mss.

How to Contact: Send complete mss with SASE. Simultaneous submissions "undesirable, but will accept if indicated." Reports in 2-3 months "but during peak periods a reply may take up to 5 months." Publishes ms 6 months to 1 year after acceptance. Sample copy for $5.

Payment/Terms: Pays 1 contributor's copy and a year's subscription. Pays honorarium when grant funding permits. Acquires first rights.

Advice: "We have made a significant investment in fiction. The reason is quality; serious fiction *needs* a market. Try to have everything build to a singleness of effect."

‡ALDEBARAN, (I), Roger Williams University, One Old Ferry Rd., Bristol RI 02809. (401)254-3503. Editor: Kym Jones. Magazine: 4¼×5½; 50-75 pages; illustrations; photos. Semiannually. Estab. 1971. Circ. 275.

Needs: "Open to any subject any style. We will consider just about anything." List of upcoming themes available for SASE. Receives 25-30 unsolicited mss/month. Accepts 2-3 mss/issue; 4-6 mss/year. Does not read mss October 1-January 31, April 1-August 31. Publishes ms 1-3 months after acceptance. Length: 2,000 words average; 100 words minimum; 2,500 words maximum. Publishes short shorts. Also publishes poetry.

How to Contact: Send complete ms with a cover letter. Should include estimated word count. Reports in 1-3 weeks on queries; 1-2 months on mss. SASE. Simultaneous submissions OK. Sample copy for $5. Fiction guidelines for legal SASE.

Payment/Terms: Pays 2 contributor's copies for one-time rights.

Advice: "Don't ever be afraid to experiment and let your imagination run wild. Avoid sending personal journal-type essays; would love to see more student work."

‡ALLEGHENY REVIEW, (IV), Commercial Printing, Box 32, Allegheny College, Meadville PA 16335. (814)332-6553. Senior Editor: Christina Read. Editors: Brooke Balta, Tony Bonds. Magazine: 8×5; 82 pages; white paper; illustrations and photos. "The *Allegheny Review* publishes short fiction, poetry and short nonfiction; our intended audience is other college students, professors and interested readers. Annually. Estab. 1980. Circ. 500.

Needs: Adventure, ethnic/multicultural, experimental, fantasy, feminist, gay, historical (general), horror, humor/satire, lesbian, literary, mainstream/contemporary, mystery/suspense, psychic/supernatural/occult, regional, religious/inspirational, science fiction (soft/sociological), westerns. Receives 40 unsolicited mss/month. Buys 7 mss/issue; 7 mss/year. Does not read mss May-August. Publishes ms 2 months after deadline. Length: 2,000 words average; 3,000 words maximum. Publishes short shorts. Also publishes literary essays, poetry.

How to Contact: *Open to work by undergraduate writers only.* Sometimes critiques or comments on rejected ms. Send complete ms with a cover letter. Should include 1 page bio. SASE for reply. Sample copy for $5.

The double dagger before a listing indicates that the listing is new in this edition. New markets are often the most receptive to submissions by new writers.

Payment/Terms: Pays free subscription and 1 contributor's copy; additional copies for $2.
Advice: Looking for "interesting plot, mature style and good technique. Proofread! Avoid clichés."

ALPHA BEAT PRESS, (II, IV), 31 A Waterloo St., New Hope PA 18938. Editor: Dave Christy. Magazine: 7½×9; 95-125 pages; illustrations. "Beat and modern literature—prose, reviews and poetry." Semiannually. Estab. 1987. Circ. 600.
  ● Work from *Alpha Beat Press* appeared in the *Pushcart Prize* anthologies, most recently in 1993. Alpha Beat Press also publishes poetry chapbooks and supplements. The magazine is known for writings associated with modern and beat culture.
Needs: Erotica, experimental, literary and prose poem. Recently published work by Charles Bukowski, Jan Kerouac and Charles Plymell; published new writers within the last year. Length: 600 words minimum; 1,000 words maximum. Also publishes literary essays, literary criticism, poetry.
How to Contact: Query first. Reports on queries within 2 weeks. SASE. Simultaneous and reprint submissions OK. Sample copy for $10. Reviews novels and short story collections.
Payment/Terms: Pays in contributor's copies. Rights remain with author.
Advice: "*ABP* is the finest journal of its kind available today, having, with 15 issues, published the widest range of published and unpublished writers you'll find in the small press scene."

AMATEUR WRITERS JOURNAL, Four Seasons Poetry Club Magazine, (II), R.V. Gill Publishing Co., 3653 Harrison St., Bellaire OH 43906. (614)676-0881. Editor: Rosalind Gill. Magazine: 8½×11; 38 pages; 20 lb. paper; illustrations. "Stories, articles, essays and poetry on all subjects. No avant-garde or porno-type manuscripts of any kind accepted. Poetry, when seasonal, published only in the season for which it is appropriate. Same rule applies to stories. For a family audience." Quarterly. Estab. 1967. Circ. 700.
Needs: Adventure, contemporary, fantasy, humor/satire, mainstream, mystery/suspense, religious/inspirational, romance (contemporary), science fiction, young adult/teen. Receives around 300 fiction mss/month. Accepts 8 fiction mss/issue; 48 mss/year. Publishes ms "within 3 months" after acceptance. Length: 1,200 words average; 1,500 words maximum. Also publishes literary essays, poetry. Sometimes critiques rejected mss.
How to Contact: Send complete ms with cover letter. State whether you are offering first rights, or, if material has been published elsewhere, the name of the publication in which your work appeared. Reports on queries in 1 month; on mss in 1 week. SASE. No simultaneous submissions. Sample copy available for $2.25 and 3 first-class stamps. Fiction guidelines for #10 SAE and 2 first-class stamps.
Payment/Terms: No payment. Acquires one-time rights.
Advice: "I believe that all fiction writers should have a showplace for their work, and my magazine readers prefer fiction to nonfiction, although I accept both."

AMELIA, (II), 329 E St., Bakersfield CA 93304. (805)323-4064. Editor-in-Chief: Frederick A. Raborg, Jr. Magazine: 5½×8½; 124-136 pages; perfect-bound; 60 lb. high-quality moistrite matte paper; kromekote cover; four-color covers; original illustrations; b&w photos. "A general review using fine fiction, poetry, criticism, belles lettres, one-act plays, fine pen-and-ink sketches and line drawings, sophisticated cartoons, book reviews and translations of both fiction and poetry for general readers with eclectic tastes for quality writing." Quarterly. Plans special fiction issue each July. Estab. 1984. Circ. 1,250.
  ● The editor of this well-respected magazine also edits *Cicada* (devoted to Oriental-style writing) and *SPSM&H* (devoted to sonnets and sonnet-inspired work). The magazine also sponsors a long list of fiction awards. Listings for the other publications and for the *Amelia* Awards appear in this book.
Needs: Adventure, contemporary, erotica, ethnic, experimental, fantasy, feminist, gay, historical (general), humor/satire, lesbian, literary, mainstream, mystery/suspense, prose poem, regional, science fiction, senior citizen/retirement, sports, translations, western. Nothing "obviously pornographic or patently religious." Receives 160-180 unsolicited mss/month. Buys up to 9 mss/issue; 25-36 mss/year. Published work by Michael Bugeja, Jack Curtis, Maxine Kumin, Eugene Dubnov and Merrill Joan Gerber; published new writers within the last year. Length: 3,000 words average; 1,000 words minimum; 5,000 words maximum. Usually critiques rejected ms.
How to Contact: Send complete manuscript with cover letter with previous credits if applicable to *Amelia* and perhaps a brief personal comment to show personality and experience. Reports in 1 week on queries; 2 weeks-3 months on mss. SASE. Sample copy for $8.95. Fiction guidelines for #10 SASE. Sends galleys to author "when deadline permits."
Payment/Terms: Pays $35-50 on acceptance for first North American serial rights plus 2 contributor's copies; extras with 20% discount.
Advice: "Write carefully and well, but have a strong story to relate. I look for depth of plot and uniqueness, and strong characterization. Study manuscript mechanics and submission procedures. Neatness does count. There is a sameness—a cloning process—among most magazines today that tends to dull the senses. Magazines like *Amelia* will awaken those senses while offering stories and poems of lasting value."

AMERICAN LITERARY REVIEW, A National Journal of Poems and Stories, (II), University of North Texas, P.O. Box 13827, Denton TX 76203-6827. (817)565-2127. Editor: Barb Rodman. Magazine: 7×10;

128 pages; 70 lb. Mohawk paper; 67 lb. Wausau Vellum cover. "Publishes quality, contemporary poems and stories." Semiannually. Estab. 1990. Circ. 800.

Needs: Mainstream and literary only. No genre works. Receives 50-75 unsolicited fiction mss/month. Accepts 7-10 mss/issue; 14-20 mss/year. Publishes ms within 2 years after acceptance. Published work by Gordon Weaver, Gerald Haslam and William Miller. Length: less than 10,000 words. Critiques or comments on rejected mss when possible. Also accepts poetry and essays.

How to Contact: Send complete ms with cover letter. Reports in 2-3 months. SASE. Simultaneous submissions OK. Sample copy for $8. Fiction guidelines free.

Payment/Terms: Pays in contributor's copies. Acquires one-time rights.

Advice: "Give us distinctive styles, original approaches, stories that are willing to take a chance. We respond to character first, those that have a past and future beyond the page." Looks for "literary quality and careful preparation. There is a sameness to most of the stories that we receive—somebody dies or a relationship ends. We would love to see stories beyond those topics that grab us immediately and keep us interested throughout."

AMERICAN SHORT FICTION, (II), English Dept., Parlin 108, University of Texas at Austin, Austin TX 78712-1164. (512)471-1772. Editor: Joseph Kruppa. Magazine: 5¾×9 1/4; 128 pages; 60 lb. natural paper; 8015 karma white cover. "*American Short Fiction* publishes fiction *only*, of all lengths, from short short to novella." Quarterly. Estab. 1990. Circ. 1,200.

• See the interview with Joseph Kruppa in the 1995 edition of this book. Also, see the short story contest sponsored by *ASF* listed in the Contests and Awards section.

Needs: Literary. "No romance, science fiction, erotica, mystery/suspense and religious." Receives 500 unsolicited mss/month. Acquires 6 mss/issue; 25-30 mss/year. Accepts mss September 1-May 31. Publishes ms up to 1 year after acceptance. Agented fiction 20%. Published work by Reynolds Price, Ursula K. Le Guin and Rick Bass. Length: open.

How to Contact: Send complete ms with cover letter. Reports in 3-4 months on mss. Send SASE for reply, return of ms; or send disposable copy of the ms. Simultaneous submissions OK if informed. Sample copy for $9.95. Fiction guidelines for #10 SASE.

Payment/Terms: Pays $400/story for first rights. Sends galleys to author.

Advice: "We pick work for *American Short Fiction* along simple lines: Do we love it? Is this a story we will be happy reading four or five times? We comment only *rarely* on submissions because of the volume of work we receive."

THE AMERICAS REVIEW, A Review of Hispanic Literature and Art of the USA, (II, IV), Arte Publico Press, 4800 Calhoun, University of Houston, Houston TX 77204-2090. (713)743-2841. Editors: Lauro Flores and Evanglina Vigil-Pinon. Magazine: 5½×8½; 128 pages; illustrations and photographs. "*The Americas Review* publishes contemporary fiction written by U.S. Hispanics—Mexican Americans, Puerto Ricans, Cuban Americans, etc." Triannually. Estab. 1972.

Needs: Contemporary, ethnic, literary, women's, hispanic literature. No novels. Receives 12-15 fiction mss/month. Buys 2-3 mss/issue; 8-12 mss/year. Publishes mss "6 months to 1 year" after acceptance. Length: 3,000-4,500 average number of words; 1,500 words minimum; 6,000 words maximum (30 pages maximum, double-spaced). Publishes short shorts. Sometimes critiques rejected mss.

How to Contact: Send complete manuscript. Reports in 3-4 months. SASE. Accepts electronic submissions via IBM compatible disk. Sample copy for $5; $10 double issue.

Payment/Terms: Pays $50-200; 5 contributor's copies on acceptance for first rights, and rights to 40% of fees if story is reprinted. Sponsors award for fiction writers.

Advice: "There has been a noticeable increase in quality in U.S. Hispanic literature."

THE AMHERST REVIEW, (II, IV), Box 1811, Amherst College, Amherst MA 01002. (413)542-2000. Editor: Molly Lyons. Magazine: 7½×8½; 60-70 pages; illustrations and photographs. "We are a college literary magazine publishing work by students, faculty and professionals. We seek submissions of poetry, fiction, and essay for the college community." Annually.

Needs: Adventure, confession, contemporary, ethnic, experimental, feminist, gay, historical (general), horror, humor/satire, lesbian, mainstream, prose poem, regional, romance, mystery/suspense, translations, western. Receives 10-20 unsolicited mss/month. Does not read mss March-August. Length: 4,500 words; 7,200 words maximum.

How to Contact: Send complete ms with cover letter and SASE. Reports in 4 months on mss. Sample copy for $6.

Payment/Terms: Pays 1 contributor's copy; $6 charge for extras. Acquires first rights.

‡ANARCHY, A Journal of Desire Armed, (II, IV), BAL Press, P.O. Box 2647, New York NY 10009. Editors: Tad Kepley, Alex Trotter. Magazine: 8¼×10¾; 88 pages; Mando Brite paper; 50 lb. offset cover; illustrations and photos. "Libertarian/anarchist fiction—i.e. fiction which does not glorify or reinforce authority, but which demystifies or subverts it, though we also publish fiction which may explore any aspect of life." Quarterly. Estab. 1980. Circ. 5,000.

• *Utne Reader* nominated this magazine to receive an Alternative Press Award. *Anarchy* is a member of COSMEP (an organization of independent publishers) and, of course, the Anarchist Media Network.

Needs: Erotica, ethnic/multicultural, experimental, feminist, gay, lesbian, literary, science fiction (soft/socio-logical). "No religious, inspirational, conventional, romances, uncritical material." Receives 2-4 mss/month. Acquires 1 mss/issue; 4 mss/year. Publishes ms 3-6 months after acceptance. Recently published works by Richard Kostelanetz, Paul Goodman, Nancy Bogen. Length: 2,000 words preferred; 500 minimum; 4,000 words maximum.

How to Contact: Send complete ms with cover letter. Reports in 2-3 months. Send SASE for reply, return of mss or send a disposable copy of the manuscript. Simultaneous, reprint and electronic submissions OK. Sample copy for $3.50.

Payment/Terms: Pays free subscription to the magazine, 5-6 contributor's copies; additional copies for $1.50. Acquires one-time rights. Sends galleys to author. Not copyrighted.

ANTERIOR FICTION QUARTERLY, (II), Anterior Bitewing Ltd.®, 993 Allspice, Fenton MO 63026. (314)343-1761. Editor: Tom Bergeron. Newsletter: 8½×11; 20 pages; 20 lb. bond paper; 20 lb. bond cover; illustrations. "Good, easy-reading stories with a point or punch-line, general interest; audience tends to be over 50." Quarterly. Estab. 1993. Circ. 50.

Needs: Adventure, historical (general), humor/satire, literary, mainstream/contemporary, mystery/suspense, psychic/supernatural/occult, regional, romance, sports. No "protests, causes, bigotry, sickness, fanatacism, soap." Receives 10 unsolicited mss/month. Accepts 10 mss/issue; 40 mss/year. Publishes ms 3-15 months after acceptance. Recently published work by Thomas Lynn, Denise Martinson, J. Alvin Speers. Length: 1,000 words preferred; 500 words minimum; 2,500 words maximum. Publishes short shorts. Length: 100-500 words. Always critiques or comments on rejected mss.

How to Contact: *Charges $2 reading fee per story.* Reports in 1 week on queries; 2 weeks on mss. Send SASE for reply, return of ms or send a disposable copy of ms. Simultaneous, reprint and electronic submissions OK. E-mail address: 72247.1405@compuserve.com. Sample copy for $2. Fiction guidelines for SASE.

Payment/Terms: Pays $0-25 on publication for one-time rights; "$25 prize for best story in each issue. No other payments."

Advice: Looks for "good gimmicks; twists; imagination; departures from the everyday. Read Bernard Mala-mud; James Thurber; Henry James."

ANTIETAM REVIEW, (II, IV), Washington County Arts Council, 7 W. Franklin St., Hagerstown MD 21740. (301)791-3132. Editor: Susanne Kass. Magazine: 8½×11; 60 pages; photos. A literary journal of short fiction, poetry and black-and-white photographs. Annually. Estab. 1982. Circ. 1,500.

• *Antietam Review* has received several awards including First-runner up (1993-94) for Editorial Content from the American Literary Magazine Awards. Work published in the magazine has been included in the *Pushcart Prize* anthology and *Best American Short Stories*.

Needs: Contemporary, ethnic, experimental, feminist, literary and prose poem. "We read manuscripts from our region—Delaware, Maryland, Pennsylvania, Virginia, West Virginia and Washington D.C. only. We read from Sept. 1 to Feb. 1." Receives about 100 unsolicited mss/month. Buys 7-9 stories/year. Published work by Wayne Karlin, Elisavietta Ritchie and Maxine Clair; published new writers within the last year. Length: 3,000 words average.

How to Contact: "Send ms and SASE with a cover letter. Let us know if you have published before and where." Reports in 1-2 months. "If we hold a story, we let the writer know. Occasionally we critique returned ms or ask for rewrites." Sample copy for $5.25. Back issue $3.15.

Payment/Terms: "We believe it is a matter of dignity that writers and poets be paid. We have been able to give $100 a story and $25 a poem, but this depends on funding. Also 2 copies." Buys first North American serial rights. Sends galleys to author if requested.

Advice: "We look for well-crafted work that shows attention to clarity and precision of language. We like relevant detail but want to see significant emotional movement within the course of the story—something happening to the central character. This journal was started in response to the absence of fiction markets for emerging writers. Its purpose is to give exposure to fiction writers, poets and photographers of high artistic quality who might otherwise have difficulty placing their work."

✿THE ANTIGONISH REVIEW, (II), St. Francis Xavier University, P.O. Box 5000, Antigonish, Nova Scotia B2G 2W5 Canada. (902)867-3962. Editor: George Sanderson. Literary magazine for educated and creative readers. Quarterly. Estab. 1970. Circ. 800.

Needs: Literary, contemporary, prose poem and translations. No erotic or political material. Accepts 6 mss/ issue. Receives 50 unsolicited fiction mss each month. Published work by Arnold Bloch, Richard Butts and Helen Barolini; published new writers within the last year. Length: 3,000-5,000 words. Sometimes comments briefly on rejected mss.

How to Contact: Send complete ms with cover letter. SASE ("U.S. postage not acceptable"). No simultane-ous submissions. Accepts disk submissions compatible with WordPerfect (IBM) and Windows. Prefers hard copy with disk submission. Reports in 6 months. Publishes ms 3 months to 1 year after acceptance.

Payment/Terms: Pays 2 contributor's copies. Authors retain copyright.
Advice: "Learn the fundamentals and do not deluge an editor."

ANTIOCH REVIEW, (II), Box 148, Yellow Springs OH 45387. (513)767-6389. Editor: Robert S. Fogarty. Associate Editor: Nolan Miller. Magazine: 6×9; 128 pages; 50 lb. book offset paper; coated cover stock; illustrations "seldom." "Literary and cultural review of contemporary issues in politics, American and international studies, and literature for general readership." Quarterly. Published special fiction issue last year; plans another. Estab. 1941. Circ. 4,500.
Needs: Literary, contemporary, translations and experimental. No children's, science fiction or popular market. Buys 5-6 mss/issue, 20-24 mss/year. Receives approximately 275 unsolicited fiction mss each month. Approximately 1-2% of fiction agented. Length: any length the story justifies.
How to Contact: Send complete ms with SASE, preferably mailed flat. Reports in 2 months. Publishes ms 6-9 months after acceptance. Sample copy for $6. Guidelines for SASE.
Payment/Terms: Pays $10/page; 2 contributor's copies. $3.30 for extras. Pays on publication for first and one-time rights (rights returned to author on request).
Advice: "Our best advice, always, is to *read* the *Antioch Review* to see what type of material we publish. Quality fiction requires an engagement of the reader's intellectual interest supported by mature emotional relevance, written in a style that is rich and rewarding without being freaky. The great number of stories submitted to us indicates that fiction still has great appeal. We assume that if so many are writing fiction, many must be reading it."

‡APHRODITE GONE BERSERK, (IV), A journal of erotic art, Red Wine Press, 233 Guyon Ave., Staten Island NY 10306. Editors: C. Esposito, E Eccleston. Magazine: 8½×11; 50 pages; illustrations and photos. "*AGB* publishes fiction, poetry, memoirs, photography, etc. that deal with the erotic or sexuality in all styles and from any perspective or orientation." Semiannually. Estab. 1996.
Needs: Erotica: condensed/excerpted novel, experimental, feminist, gay, lesbian, literary, translations. Upcoming themes: "Public Exposure" (summer/fall 1996). List of upcoming themes available for SASE. Receives 10 unsolicited mss/month. Buys 3 mss/issue; 6 mss/year. Publishes ms 6-12 months after acceptance. Publishes short shorts. Also publishes literary essays, literary criticism, poetry.
How to Contact: Send complete ms with a cover letter. Reports in 2 weeks on queries; 1 month on mss. Send SASE for reply, return of ms or send a disposable copy of ms. Simultaneous, reprint submissions OK. Reviews novels or short story collections.
Payment/Terms: Pays 1 contributor's copy. Acquires one-time rights.
Advice: "Stay away from the cliché, and always enclose SASE for the return of your work."

APPALACHIAN HERITAGE, (I, II), Hutchins Library, Berea College, Berea KY 40404. (606)986-9341. Editor: Sidney Farr. Magazine: 6×9; 80 pages; 60 lb. stock; 10 pt. Warrenflo cover; drawings and b&w photos. "*Appalachian Heritage* is a southern Appalachian literary magazine. We try to keep a balance of fiction, poetry, essays, scholarly works, etc., for a general audience and/or those interested in the Appalachian mountains." Quarterly. Estab. 1973. Circ. 1,100.
Needs: Regional, literary, historical. Receives 20-25 unsolicited mss/month. Accepts 2-3 mss/issue; 10 or more mss/year. Published work by Robert Morgan, David Whisnant, Denise Giardina, Gurney Norman; published new writers within the last year. Length: 2,000-2,500 word average; 3,000 words maximum. Publishes short shorts. Length: 500 words. Occasionally critiques rejected mss.
How to Contact: Send complete ms with cover letter. Reports in 3-4 weeks on queries; 4-6 weeks on mss. SASE for ms. Simultaneous submissions OK. Sample copy for $6.
Payment/Terms: Pays 3 contributor's copies; $6 charge for extras. Acquires one-time rights. No reading fee, but "would prefer a subscription first."
Advice: "Trends in fiction change frequently. Right now the trend is toward slick, modern pieces with very little regional or ethnic material appearing in print. The pendulum will swing the other way again, and there will be a space for that kind of fiction. It seems to me there is always a chance to have really good writing published somewhere. Keep writing and keep trying the markets. Diligent writing and rewriting can perfect your art. Be sure to study the market. Do not send me a slick piece of writing set in New York City, for example, with no idea on your part of the kinds of things I am interested in seeing. It is a waste of your time and money. Get a sample copy, or subscribe to the publication, study it carefully, then send your material."

ARARAT QUARTERLY, (IV), Ararat Press, AGBU., 585 Saddle River Rd., Saddle Brook NJ 07662. (212)765-8260. Editor: Dr. Leo Hamalian. Magazine: 8½×11; 72 pages; illustrations and b&w photographs. "*Ararat* is a forum for the literary and historical works of Armenian intellectuals or non-Armenian writers writing about Armenian subjects."
Needs: Condensed/excerpted novel, contemporary, historical, humor/satire, literary, religious/inspirational, translations. Publishes special fiction issue. Receives 25 unsolicited mss/month. Buys 5 mss/issue; 20 mss/year. Length: 1,000 words average. Publishes short shorts. Length: 500 words. Also publishes literary essays, literary criticism, poetry. Sometimes critiques rejected mss and recommends other markets.

How to Contact: Send complete ms with cover letter. Reports in 1 month on queries; 3 weeks on mss. SASE. Simultaneous and reprint submissions OK. Sample copy for $7 and $1 postage. Free fiction guidelines. Reviews novels and short story collections.
Payment/Terms: Pays $40-75 plus 2 contributor's copies on publication for one-time rights. Sends galleys to author.

ARBA SICULA, (II, IV), St John's University, Jamaica NY 11439. Editor: Gaetano Cipolla. Magazine: 5½×8½; 85 pages; top-grade paper; good quality cover stock; illustrations; photos. Bilingual ethnic literary review (Sicilian-English) dedicated to the dissemination of Sicilian culture. Published twice a year. Plans special fiction issue. Estab. 1979. Circ. 1,800.
Needs: Accepts ethnic literary material consisting of various forms of folklore, stories both contemporary and classical, regional, romance (contemporary, historical, young adult) and senior citizen. Material submitted must be in the Sicilian language, with English translation desirable. Published new writers within the last year. Critiques rejected mss when there is time. Sometimes recommends other markets.
How to Contact: Send complete ms with SASE and bio. Reports in 2 months. Publishes ms 1-3 years after acceptance. Simultaneous submissions and reprints OK. Sample copy for $8 with 8½×11 SASE and 90¢ postage.
Payment/Terms: 5 free author's copies. $4 for extra copies. Acquires all rights.
Advice: "This review is a must for those who nurture a love of the Sicilian language."

‡ARK/ANGEL REVIEW, (II), NYU Creative Writing Program, 19 University Place, 2nd Floor, New York NY 10003. (212)998-8816. Fax: (212)995-4019. Editor: Jay Papasan. Fiction Editors: Diane Gurman, Kathryn Tarlow. Editors change each year. Magazine: 5½× 8½; 120 pages. Semiannually. Estab. 1987. Circ. 1,000.
Needs: Literary. Accepts 6-8 mss/issue; 12-14 mss/year. Does not read mss April 1-August 15. Publishes ms 6 months after acceptance. Agented fiction 50%. Recently published work by Wesley Brown, Pagan Kennedy, Jonathan Dee. Length: 5,000 words maximum. Publishes short shorts. Also publishes poetry. Sometimes critiques or comments on rejected ms.
How to Contact: Send complete ms with a short cover letter. Reports in 4 months on mss. SASE for return of ms. Simultaneous submissions OK. Sample copy for $5.
Payment/Terms: Pays 3 contributor's copies. Acquires first North American serial rights.
Advice: "Please send polished, proofread manuscripts only."

ARNAZELLA, (II), English Department, Bellevue Community College, Bellevue WA 98007. (206)641-2373. Advisor: Jeffrey White. Editors change each year; contact advisor. Magazine: 5×6; 104 pages, 70 lb. paper; heavy coated cover; illustrations and photos. "For those interested in quality fiction." Annually. Estab. 1976. Circ. 500.
  • The advisor says *Arnazella* needs more fiction manuscripts! (They receive a great deal of poetry and not enough fiction.) The magazine received First Place for Outstanding Literary Arts Publication from the Washington Technical and Community College Humanities Association in 1994.
Needs: Adventure, contemporary, ethnic, experimental, fantasy, feminist, gay, historical, humor/satire, lesbian, literary, mainstream, mystery/suspense, prose poem, regional, translations. Submit in fall and winter for issue to be published in spring. Published new writers within the last year. Publishes short shorts. Also publishes literary essays and poetry. *Preference will be given to Northwest contributors.*
How to Contact: Send complete ms with cover letter. Reports on mss in spring. "The months of June through October are very hard for us to read mss because we have no staff at that time. The best times to submit are October through December." SASE. No simultaneous submissions. Sample copy for $5. Guidelines for SASE.
Payment/Terms: Pays in contributor's copies. Acquires first rights.
Advice: "Read this and similar magazines, reading critically and analytically."

ARTEMIS, An Art/Literary Publication from the Blue Ridge and Virginia, (IV), Box 21281, Roanoke VA 24018-0130. (703)365-4326. Managing Editor: Carol Murphy. Fiction Editor: Rita Ciresi. Magazine: 8×8; 85 pages; heavy/slick paper; colored cover stock; illustrations; photos. "We publish poetry, art and fiction of the highest quality and will consider any artist/writer who lives or has lived in the Blue Ridge or Virginia. General adult audience with literary interest." Annually. Estab. 1976. Circ. 2,000.
Needs: Literary. Wants to see "the best contemporary style." Receives 50 unsolicited fiction mss/year. Accepts 3-4 mss/issue. Does not read mss November-August. Publishes ms 4-5 months after acceptance. Published works by Rosanne Coggeshall, Jeanne Larsen, Kurt Rheinheimer; published work by new writers within the last year. Length: 1,500 words average; 2,500 words maximum. Also publishes poetry.
How to Contact: Submit 2 copies of unpublished ms between September 15-October 16, name, address and phone on title page only. Reports in 2 months. SASE for ms. No simultaneous submissions. Sample copy for $6.50.
Payment/Terms: Pays 2 complimentary copies. Acquires first rights.
Advice: "We look for polished quality work that holds interest, has imagination, energy, voice."

ARTFUL DODGE, (II), Department of English, College of Wooster, Wooster OH 44691. (216)263-2000. Editor-in-Chief: Daniel Bourne. Magazine: 150-200 pages; illustrations; photos. "There is no theme in this magazine, except literary power. We also have an ongoing interest in translations from Eastern Europe and elsewhere." Annually. Estab. 1979. Circ. 1,000.

● A story which first appeared in *Artful Dodge*, "Sister Barbara" by John Azrak, was reprinted in an anthology about growing up in Catholic schools, published by Penguin Books.

Needs: Experimental, literary, prose poem, translations. "We judge by literary quality, not by genre. We are especially interested in fine English translations of significant contemporary prose writers." Receives 40 unsolicited fiction mss/month. Accepts 5 mss/year. Published fiction by Edward Kleinschmidt, Sesshu Foster, David Surface, Greg Boyd and Zbigniew Herbert; and interviews with Tim O'Brien, Lee Smith and Stuart Dybek; published 1 new writer within the last year. Length: 10,000 words maximum; 2,500 words average. Also publishes literary essays, literary criticism, poetry. Occasionally critiques rejected mss.

How to Contact: Send complete ms with SASE. Do not send more than 30 pages at a time. Reports in 5-6 months. Sample copies of older, single issues are $2.75 or five issues for $5; recent issues are double issues, available for $5.75. Fiction guidelines for #10 SASE.

Payment/Terms: Pays 2 contributor's copies and small honorarium. Acquires first North American serial rights.

Advice: "If we take time to offer criticism, do not subsequently flood us with other stories no better than the first. If starting out, get as many *good* readers as possible. Above all, read contemporary fiction and the magazine you are trying to publish in."

‡ARTISAN, a journal of craft, (I, II), P.O. Box 157, Wilmette IL 60091. (708)676-3240. Editor: Joan Daugherty. Tabloid: 8½ × 11; 12-16 pages; colored bond paper; illustrations. "The philosophy behind *artisan* is that anyone who strives to express themselves through their craft is an artist and artists of all genres can learn from each other. For artists and the general public. Estab. 1995. Circ. 100.

Needs: Adventure, condensed/excerpted novel, erotica (mild), ethnic/multicultural, experimental, fantasy (science fantasy, sword and sorcery), feminist, gay, horror, humor/satire, lesbian, literary, mainstream/contemporary, mystery/suspense, psychic/supernatural/occult, science fiction, sports, westerns. "No pornography, or anything too sweet or saccharine." Receives 4 unsolicited mss/month. Accepts 2-3 mss/issue; 12-15 mss/year. Publishes ms 2-6 months after acceptance. Recently published work by Byron Dean, J. James and John Forwald. Length: 1,000 words average; 4,000 words maximum. Publishes short shorts. Also publishes literary essays, literary criticism, poetry. Sometimes critiques or comments on rejected mss.

How to Contact: Send complete ms with cover letter. Should include estimated word count. Reports in 1 month on queries; 3 months on mss. SASE for reply or send a disposable copy of ms. Simultaneous and electronic submissions OK. E-mail address: artisanjnl@aol.com. Sample copy for $2.50. Fiction guidelines for #10 SASE.

Payment/Terms: Pays 3 contributor's copies; additional copies $2. Acquires first rights.

Advice: "Innovative phrasing and subject matter stand out. Strive to use fresh language and situations. I would like to see more definite stories, ones with real themes where something actually happens."

ART:MAG, (II), P.O. Box 70896, Las Vegas NV 89170. Editor: Peter Magliocco. Magazine: 5½ × 8½, some 8½ × 11; 70-90 pages; 20 lb. bond paper; b&w pen and ink illustrations and photographs. Publishes "irreverent, literary-minded work by committed writers," for "small press, 'quasi-art-oriented' " audience. Annually. Estab. 1984. Circ. under 500.

● *Art:Mag* is interested in art-related themes. Recent issues have included a wide range of work from a novel excerpt to freeform experimental work.

Needs: Condensed/excerpted novel, confession, contemporary, erotica, ethnic, experimental, fantasy, feminist, gay, historical (general), horror, humor/satire, lesbian, literary, mainstream, mystery/suspense, prose poem, psychic/supernatural/occult, regional, science fiction, translations and arts. No "slick-oriented stuff published by major magazines." Receives 1 plus ms/month. Accepts 1-2 mss/year. Does not read mss July-October. Publishes ms within 3-6 months of acceptance. Recently published work by R. Sebastian Bennett (Flannery O'Connor Fiction Award Finalist), Kat Ricker, J.B. McKeon, Laurie Stapleton, Gregory Sanders and Alan Catlin. Length: 2,000 words preferred; 250 words minimum; 3,000 words maximum. Also publishes literary essays "if relevant to aesthetic preferences," literary criticism "occasionally," poetry. Sometimes critiques rejected mss.

Market conditions are constantly changing! If you're still using this book and it is 1997 or later, buy the newest edition of Novel & Short Story Writer's Market at your favorite bookstore or order from Writer's Digest Books.

How to Contact: Send complete ms with cover letter. Reports in 3 months. SASE for ms. Simultaneous submissions OK. Sample copy for $4.50, 6×9 SAE and 79¢ postage. Fiction guidelines for #10 SASE.
Payment/Terms: Pays contributor's copies. Acquires one-time rights.
Advice: "Seeking more novel and quality-oriented work, usually from solicited authors. Magazine fiction today needs to be concerned with the issues of fiction writing itself—not just with a desire to publish or please the largest audience. Think about things in the fine art world as well as the literary one and keep the hard core of life in between."

‡ASCENDING SHADOWS, (I, II), Shadow Press, P.O. Box 123, Tankio MO 64491. (816)736-5676. Editor: Lynn McConkie. Magazine: 8×5; 10-40 pages; 20 lb. bond paper; b&w illustrations and photos. "*Ascending Shadows* publishes a wide variety of material. My audience is those who love writing." Semiannually. Estab. 1993. Circ. 20-30.
Needs: Adventure, erotica, experimental, fantasy (science fiction, sword and sorcery), horror, humor/satire, literary, mainstream/contemporary, mystery/suspense, psychic/supernatural/occult, romance, science fiction. "Experimental and psychic/supernatural/occult are my favorites." Publishes annual special fiction issue or anthology. Receives 2-3 unsolicited mss/month. Accepts 4-6 mss/issue; 12-15 mss/year. Publishes ms in next issue after acceptance. Recently published work by John Hudson, J.R. Reeves, Joel Climenhaga. Length: 1,500 words average; 500 words minimum; 2,000 words maximum. Publishes short shorts. Length: 300 words. Also publishes literary essays, literary criticism, poetry. Always critiques or comments on rejected ms.
How to Contact: Send complete ms with a cover letter. Should include estimated word count and bio (around 200 words) with submission. "Include the reason you write." Reports in 2-4 weeks on queries; 6-8 weeks on mss. Send SASE for reply, return of ms or send a disposable copy of ms. Simultaneous, reprint and electronic (disk only) submissions OK. Samples copy for $2, 5×8 SAE and 75¢ postage. Reviews novels and short story collections; mark "For review."
Payment/Terms: Pays 1 contributor's copy; additional copies $1.50. Acquires one-time rights. "Send SASE for information on awards and contests for writers."
Advice: "No spelling errors; neat, numbered pages; personalized cover letter—let me know you through the letter. Always send SASE for reply. Go for it! I love beginning writers!"

‡ASIAN PACIFIC AMERICAN JOURNAL, (I, II, IV), The Asian American Writers' Workshop, 37 St. Marks Place, New York NY 10003-7801. (212)228-6718. Fax: (212)228-7718. Editors: Soo Mee Kwon, Juliana Koo. Magazine: 5½×8½; 150 pages; illustrations. "We are interested in publishing works by writers from all segments of the Asian Pacific American community. The journal appeals to all interested in Asian-American literature and culture." Semiannually. Estab. 1992. Circ. 1,500.
   ● *Asian Pacific American Journal* received a NEA grant in 1995.
Needs: Adventure, condensed/excerpted novel, erotica, ethnic/multicultural, experimental, feminist, gay, historical (general), humor/satire, lesbian, literary, mainstream/contemporary, regional, serialized novel, translations, Asian-American themes. Upcoming themes: "Issues of Difference" (fall 1995), "The Body" (spring 1996). List of upcoming themes available for SASE. Publishes annual special fiction issue or anthology. Receives 75 unsolicited mss/month. Accepts 15 mss/issue; 30 mss/year. Does not read September-October, March-April. Publishes ms 3-4 months after acceptance. Agented fiction 5%. Recently published work by Chang-rae Lee, Katherine Min and Sue Lin Chong. Length: 3,000 words average; 1,500 words minimum; 5,000 words maximum. Publishes short shorts. Also publishes literary essays, poetry. Sometimes critiques or comments on rejected ms.
How to Contact: Query first. Send SASE for guidelines. Should include estimated word count, 3-5 sentence bio, list of publications. Reports in 1 month on queries; 4 months on mss. SASE for reply or send a disposable copy of ms. Simultaneous, reprint, electronic submissions OK. Sample copy for $12. Fiction guidelines for SASE. Reviews novels and short story collections.
Payment/Terms: Pays 2 contributor's copies; additional copies at 40% discount. Acquires one-time rights. Sends galleys to author. Sponsors contests, awards or grants for fiction writers. "Send query with SASE."

ATHENA INCOGNITO MAGAZINE, (II), 1442 Judah St., San Francisco CA 94122. (415)665-0219. Editor: Ronn Rosen. Magazine: 8½×11; approximately 30-40 pages; illustrations; photocopied photos. "Open-format magazine with emphasis on experimental and/or any type of quality writing. Emphasis on poetry and experimental artwork especially." Quarterly. Estab. 1980. Circ. 100.
   ● Work included in *Athena Incognito* tends to be Dada, surrealist, stream-of-consciousness material.
Needs: Any subjects OK. Receives 15 unsolicited mss/month. Publishes ms usually 3-6 months after acceptance. Requires magazine subscription "to cover postage and expense of publication" of $5 (for 1 issue) before reading ms. Published new writers within the last year. Publishes short shorts. No long pieces over 2 pages. Sometimes critiques rejected mss.
How to Contact: *Magazine requires copy purchase before consideration.* Send complete ms with cover letter. Reports in 2 weeks to 1 month. SASE. Simultaneous and reprint submissions OK. Sample copy for $5; fiction guidelines for SASE.

Payment/Terms: Pays in contributor's copies. Acquires all rights. Publication not copyrighted.
Advice: "Experiment and practice eclecticism of all kinds! Discover! Pioneer! Dada lives!"

ATOM MIND, (II), Mother Road Publications, P.O. Box 22068, Albuquerque NM 87154. Editor: Gregory Smith. Magazine: 8½×11; 100 pages; 60 lb. paper; 80 lb. cover; illustrations and photos. "*Atom Mind* reflects the spirit of the 1960s; it is dedicated to the memory of Steinbeck, Hemingway, Kerouac, Bukowski et al." Quarterly. Estab. 1992. Circ. 700.
Needs: Condensed/excerpted novel, erotica, ethnic/multicultural, experimental, historical (general), horror, humor/satire, literary, mainstream/contemporary, serialized novel and translations. No juvenile, romance, science fiction or young adult/teen. Receives 200-300 unsolicited mss/month. Accepts 5-6 mss/issue; 20 mss/year. Publishes ms 6-12 months after acceptance. Recently published work by Sesshu Foster, Wayne Hogan, Tom Dombrock and Michael Phillips. Length: 1,000 words minimum; 6,000 words maximum. Also publishes literary essays, literary criticism and poetry. Sometimes critiques or comments on rejected ms.
How to Contact: Send complete ms with a cover letter. Should include estimated word count. Reports in 2 weeks on queries; 1-2 months on mss. Send SASE for reply, return of ms or send a disposable copy of ms. Simultaneous and reprint submissions OK. Sample copy $5. Fiction guidelines free.
Payment/Terms: Pays in contributor's copies. Some cash payments in certain cases. Acquires first North American serial rights.
Advice: "*Atom Mind* is very much a one-man operation and therefore subject to the whims and personal biases of the editor. I would like to see more satirical short fiction. Read at least one issue of any magazine you intend to submit to. Writers can save an immense amount of time and money by sending their work ONLY to those journals for which it is suitable—study the markets!"

‡ATROCITY, Publication of the Absurd Sig of Mensa, (I), 2419 Greensburg Pike, Pittsburgh PA 15221. Editor: Hank Roll. Newsletter: 8½×11; 8 pages; offset 20 lb. paper and cover; illustrations; photographs occasionally. Humor and satire for "high IQ-Mensa" members. Monthly. Estab. 1976. Circ. 250.
Needs: Humor/satire: Liar's Club, parody, jokes, funny stories, comments on the absurdity of today's world. Receives 20 unsolicited mss/month. Accepts 2 mss/issue. Publishes ms 3-6 months after acceptance. Published new writers within the last year. Length: 50-150 words preferred; 650 words maximum.
How to Contact: Send complete ms. "No cover letter necessary if ms states what rights (e.g. first North American serial/reprint, etc.) are offered." Reports in 1 month. SASE. Simultaneous and reprint submissions OK. Sample copy for 50¢, #10 SAE and 2 first-class stamps.
Payment/Terms: Pays contributor's copies. Acquires one-time rights.
Advice: Manuscript should be single-spaced and copy ready in a horizontal format to fit on one 8½×11 sheet. "Be funny!"

AURA Literary/Arts Review, (II), University of Alabama at Birmingham, Box 76, University Center, Birmingham AL 35294. (205)934-3216. Editor: Steve Mullen. Editors change each year. Magazine: 6×9; 150 pages; b&w illustrations and photos. "We publish various types of fiction with an emphasis on short stories. Our audience is college students, the university community and literary-minded adults, the arts community." Semiannually. Estab. 1974. Circ. 1,000.
Needs: Contemporary, ethnic, feminist, horror, literary, regional, romance and science fiction. Acquires 5-6 mss/issue. Receives 30-50 unsolicited fiction mss each month. Published works by Nickell Romjue, Josephine Marshall and Rodolfo Tomes; published new writers within the last year. Length: up to 5,000 words. Also publishes literary essays, literary criticism, poetry. Critiques rejected mss when there is time.
How to Contact: Send complete ms with SASE. No simultaneous submissions; please include biographical information. Reports in 6 months. Sample copy for $2.50. "Occasionally" reviews novels and short story collections.
Payment/Terms: Pays 2 contributor's copies. Acquires first North American serial rights.
Advice: "We welcome experimental or traditional literature on any subject."

THE AZOREAN EXPRESS, (I, IV), Seven Buffaloes Press, Box 249, Big Timber MT 59011. Editor: Art Cuelho. Magazine: 6¾×8¼; 32 pages; 60 lb. book paper; 3-6 illustrations/issue; photos rarely. "My overall theme is rural; I also focus on working people (the sweating professions); the American Indian and Hobo; the Dustbowl era; and I am also trying to expand with non-rural material. For rural and library and professor/student, blue collar workers, etc." Semiannually. Estab. 1985. Circ. 600.
● *Azorean Express* is published by Art Cuelho of Seven Buffaloes. He also publishes *Black Jack*, *Hill and Holler* and *Valley Grapevine* listed in this book. See also his listing for the press.
Needs: Contemporary, ethnic, experimental, humor/satire, literary, regional, western, rural, working people. Receives 10-20 unsolicited mss/month. Accepts 2-3 mss/issue; 4-6 mss/year. Publishes ms 1-6 months after acceptance. Length: 1,000-3,000 words. Also publishes short shorts, 500-1,000 words. "I take what I like; length sometimes does not matter, even when longer than usual. I'm flexible."
How to Contact: "Send cover letter with ms; general information, but it can be personal, more in line with the submitted story. Not long rambling letters." Reports in 1-4 weeks. SASE. Sample copy for $6.75. Fiction guidelines for SASE.

Payment/Terms: Pays in contributor's copies. "Depends on the amount of support author gives my press." Acquires first North American serial rights. "If I decide to use material in anthology form later, I have that right." Sends galleys to the author upon request.

Advice: "There would not be magazines like mine if I was not optimistic. But literary optimism is a two-way street. Without young fiction writers supporting fiction magazines the future is bleak, because the commercial magazines allow only formula or name writers within their pages. My own publications receive no grants. Sole support is from writers, libraries and individuals."

BABY SUE, (I), Box 8989, Atlanta GA 30306-8989. (404)875-8951. Editor: Don W. Seven. Magazine: 8½×11; 32 pages; illustrations and photos. "*Baby Sue* is a collection of music reviews, poetry, short fiction and cartoons" for "anyone who can think and is not easily offended." Biannually. Plans special fiction issue. Estab. 1983. Circ. 2,500.

● Sometimes funny, very often perverse, this 'zine featuring mostly cartoons and "comix" definitely is not for the easily offended. Note *Baby Sue* has a new post office box.

Needs: Erotica, experimental and humor/satire. Receives 5-10 mss/month. Accepts 3-4 mss/year. Publishes ms within 3 months of acceptance. Publishes short shorts. Length: 1-2 single-spaced pages.

How to Contact: Query with clips of published work. SASE. Simultaneous submissions OK.

Payment/Terms: Pays 1 contributor's copy.

Advice: "If no one will print your work, start your own publication—it's easy and cheap. It's also a great way to make contact with other people all over the world who are doing the same."

‡BACKSPACE, (I, II), A Collection of Queer Poetry & Fiction, Lock the Target Publishing, 33 Maplewood Ave., Suite 201, Gloucester MA 01930-6201. Phone/fax: (508)283-3813. Editor: Kimberley Smith. Fiction Editor: Charlotte Stratton. Magazine: 5½×8½; 48 pages; copy paper; glossy cover; illustrations and photos. "*Backspace* is a literary zine for the gay, lesbian, bisexual and transgender community." Semiannually. Estab. 1991. Circ. 400-600.

Needs: Experimental, gay, humor/satire, lesbian, literary. "No sexually explicit or violent material." Plans to publish special fiction issues or anthologies. Receives 8-10 unsolicited mss/month. Buys 4-8 mss/issue; 16-20 mss/year. Publishes ms 6 months after acceptance. Agented fiction 85%. Recently published work by Jameson Currier, Robert Cataldo, Chriss-Spike Quatrone. Length: 3,000 words average; 1,500-2,000 words minimum; 3,000 words maximum. Also publishes literary essays, poetry.

How to Contact: Send complete ms with a cover letter. Should include estimated word count, 30 word bio, list of publications. Reports in 2 weeks on queries; 3-6 weeks on mss. Send SASE for reply, return of ms or send a disposable copy of ms. Simultaneous, reprint, electronic submissions (3.5 diskette; Word, QuarkXPress, Pagemaker, ASCII) OK. E-mail address: charkim@tiac.com. Sample copy for $1, 6×9 SAE, 2 first-class stamps. Fiction guidelines for #10 SASE. Reviews novels and short story collections. Send books to Charlotte Stratton.

Payment/Terms: Pays 1 contributor's copy; additional copies $2. Acquires one-time rights. Not copyrighted.

Advice: "Fully formed characters are important; topical allusions are distracting."

BAHLASTI PAPERS, The Newsletter of the Kali Lodge, O.T.O., (I), P.O. Box 3096, New Orleans LA 70177-3096. (504)949-2037. Editor: Soror Chén. Newsletter: 8½×11; 12 pages; 20 lb. paper; 20 lb. cover; 2 illustrations; occasional photographs. "Occult, mythological, artistic, alternative and political material for the lunatic fringe." Monthly. Estab. 1986. Circ. 200.

Needs: Condensed/excerpted novel, erotica, ethnic, experimental, fantasy, feminist, gay, horror, humor/satire, lesbian, literary, psychic/supernatural/occult, science fiction, serialized novel, "however our emphasis is on the occult. We do not publish poetry." Plans special compilation issues. Receives 10 unsolicited mss/month. Accepts 2 mss/issue; 24 mss/year. Publishes mss approximately 12-18 months after acceptance. Published work by Nancy Collins, Steve Canon and Darius James. Publishes short shorts. Also publishes literary essays, literary criticism.

How to Contact: Send complete ms with cover letter telling "why author is interested in being published in *Bahlasti Papers*." Reports in 1 month on queries and mss. SASE. Simultaneous and reprint submissions OK. Sample copy for $2.25 with 6×9 SAE and 2 first-class stamps. Occasionally reviews novels and short story collections.

Payment/Terms: Pays subscription to magazine. Publication not copyrighted.

Advice: "We look for the odd point-of-view, the individual, independence of thought, work which breaks down established archetypes and so liberates us from social programming. We are noted for our occult and mystical slant, and our concern for fresh, insightful, and odd points-of-view, with an emphasis on healing."

BAMBOO RIDGE, The Hawaii Writers' Quarterly, (II, IV), P.O. Box 61781, Honolulu HI 96839-1781. (808)599-4823. Editors: Darrell Lum and Eric Chock. "Writing that reflects the multicultural diversity of Hawaii." Published 2-4 times/year. Estab. 1978.

Needs: Ethnic, literary, Hawaii interest. "Writers need not be from Hawaii, but must reflect Hawaii's multicultural ethnic mix." Publishes annual special fiction and poetry issues (special collections by single authors). Publishes ms 6 months-1 year after acceptance. Length: up to 25 typed pages, double-spaced. Publishes short shorts.

How to Contact: Query first. Reports in 1 month on queries; 3-6 months on mss. SASE. Photocopied submissions OK. Fiction guidelines for #10 SASE.

Payment/Terms: Pays 2 contributor's copies, small honorarium and 1 year subscription depending on grant money. Pays on publication for first North American serial rights. Charges for extra copies (40% discount).

✦BARDIC RUNES, (IV), 424 Cambridge St, Ottawa, Ontario K1S 4H5 Canada. (613)231-4311. E-mail address: bn872@freenet.carleton.ca. Editor: Michael McKenny. Magazine. Estab. 1990.

Needs: Fantasy. "Traditional or high fantasy. Story should be set in pre-industrial society either historical or of author's invention." Length: 3,500 words or less.

Payment/Terms: Pays ½¢/word on acceptance. Reports in 2 weeks.

Advice: "Writers, pay keen attention to our stated needs or your story will probably be rejected, however good it may be."

THE BELLETRIST REVIEW, (I, II), Marmarc Publications, Suite 290, 17 Farmington Ave., Plainville CT 06062. Editor: Marlene Dube. Fiction Editor: Marc Saegaert. Magazine: 8½×11; 80 pages. "We are interested in compelling, well-crafted short fiction in a variety of genres. Our title *Belletrist*, means 'lover of literature.' This magazine will appeal to an educated, adult audience that appreciates quality fiction." Semiannually.

• *The Belletrist Review* offers a special fiction contest in September (Deadline, July 1). The award is $200—check with them for details. The editors would like to see more "light" and humorous fiction.

Needs: Adventure, contemporary, erotica, horror (psychological), humor/satire, literary, mainstream, mystery/suspense, regional. No poetry, fantasy, juvenile, westerns, or overblown horror or confessional pieces. Accepts 10-12 mss/issue; approximately 25 mss/year. Publishes ms within 1 year after acceptance. Length: 2,500-5,000 words preferred; 1,000 words minimum; 5,000 words maximum. Comments on or critiques rejected mss when time permits.

How to Contact: Send complete ms with cover which should include brief biographical note and any previous publications. Reports in 1 month on queries; 2 months on mss. SASE. Simultaneous submissions OK. 1996 Fiction Contest Guidelines for SASE.

Payment/Terms: Pays contributor's copies. Acquires one-time rights.

Advice: "Please submit only one story at a time, double-spaced and unstapled. Don't tell us in your cover letter how great the story is or what it's about. In our roles as editors, we commonly find ourselves saying the following when preparing a rejection: 'It was well-written and professionally presented, but we didn't care at all about the characters or what happened to them.' Another frequent cause for rejection: stories that resolve everything on the first page, or don't really get started until the middle."

THE BELLINGHAM REVIEW, (II), Western Washington University, MS9053, Bellingham WA 98225. Editor: Robin Henley. Magazine: 5½×8; 120 pages; 60 lb. white paper; varied cover stock. "A literary magazine featuring original short stories, novel excerpts, essays, short plays and poetry of palpable quality." Semiannually. Estab. 1977. Circ. 700.

• *The Bellingham Review* recently increased its page count from 64 pages to 120 pages and, also, is accepting submissions of up to 10,000 words.

Needs: All genres/subjects considered. Acquires 1-2 mss/issue. Publishes short shorts. Published new writers within the last year. Length: 10,000 words or less. Also publishes poetry.

How to Contact: Send complete ms. Reports in 2 weeks to 3 months. Publishes ms an average of 1 year after acceptance. Sample copy for $5. Reviews novels and short story collections.

Payment/Terms: Pays 1 contributor's copy plus 2-issue subscription. Charges $2.50 for extras. Acquires first North American serial and one-time rights.

Advice: "We look for work that is ambitious, vital, and challenging both to the spirit and the intellect. We hope to publish important works from around the world, works by older, neglected writers, and works by unheralded but talented new writers."

BELLOWING ARK, A Literary Tabloid, (II), Box 45637, Seattle WA 98145. (206)545-8302. Editor: R.R. Ward. Tabloid: 11½×16; 32 pages; electro-brite paper and cover stock; illustrations; photos. "We publish material which we feel addresses the human situation in an affirmative way. We do not publish academic fiction." Bimonthly. Estab. 1984. Circ. 500.

• Work from *Bellowing Ark* appeared in the *Pushcart Prize* anthology. The editor says he's using much more short fiction and prefers positive, life-affirming work. Remember he likes a traditional, narrative approach and "abhors" minimalist and post-modern work.

Needs: Contemporary, literary, mainstream, serialized/excerpted novel. "Anything we publish will be true." Receives 600-800 unsolicited fiction mss/year. Accepts 2-3 mss/issue; 12-18 mss/year. Time varies, but publishes ms not longer than 6 months after acceptance. Published work by Diane Trzcinski, Shelly Uva, Dorothy Worfolk, Jim Bernhard and Robin Sterns; published new writers within the last year. Length: 3,000-

5,000 words average ("but no length restriction"). Publishes short shorts. Also publishes literary essays, literary criticism, poetry. Sometimes critiques rejected mss.

How to Contact: No queries. Send complete ms with cover letter and short bio. "Prefer cover letters that tell something about the writer. Listing credits doesn't help." No simultaneous submissions. Reports in 6 weeks on mss. SASE. Sample copy for $3, 9×12 SAE and $1.21 postage.

Payment/Terms: Pays in contributor's copies. Acquires all rights, reverts on request.

Advice: "*Bellowing Ark* began as (and remains) an alternative to the despair and negativity of the Workshop/ Academic literary scene; we believe that life has meaning and is worth living—the work we publish reflects that belief. Learn how to tell a story before submitting. Avoid 'trick' endings—they have all been done before and better. *Bellowing Ark* is interested in publishing writers who will develop with the magazine, as in an extended community. We find *good* writers and stick with them. This is why the magazine has grown from 12 to 32 pages."

BELOIT FICTION JOURNAL, (II), Box 11, Beloit College WI 53511. (608)363-2028. Editor: Fred Burwell. Magazine: 6×9; 150 pages; 60 lb. paper; 10 pt. C1S cover stock; illustrations and photos on cover. "We are interested in publishing the best contemporary fiction and are open to all themes except those involving pornographic, religiously dogmatic or politically propagandistic representations. Our magazine is for general readership, though most of our readers will probably have a specific interest in literary magazines." Semiannually. Estab. 1985.

 • Work first appearing in *Beloit Fiction Journal* has been reprinted in award-winning collections, including the *Flannery O'Connor* and the *Milkweed Fiction Prize* collections.

Needs: Contemporary, literary, mainstream, prose poem, spiritual and sports. No pornography, religious dogma, political propaganda. Receives 400 unsolicited fiction mss/month. Accepts 8-10 mss/issue; 16-20 mss/year. Replies take longer in summer. Publishes ms within 9 months after acceptance. Length: 5,000 words average; 250 words minimum; 10,000 words maximum. Sometimes critiques rejected mss and recommends other markets.

How to Contact: Send complete ms with cover letter. Reports in 1 week on queries; 2-8 weeks on mss. SASE for ms. Simultaneous submissions OK if identified as such. Sample copy for $6. Fiction guidelines for #10 SASE.

Advice: "Many of our contributors are writers whose work we have previously rejected. Don't let one rejection slip turn you away from our—or any—magazine."

♣**BENEATH THE SURFACE, (I, II)**, McMaster University Society of English, Dept. of English, Chester New Hall, McMaster University, Hamilton, Ontario L8S 4S8 Canada. Editor: Christopher J. Currie. Editors change every four months. Magazine: 21cm × 13.5cm; 25-55 pages; illustrations and photos. "Primarily, university audience intended. Also targets general reading public." Semiannually. Estab. 1984. Circ. varies.

Needs: Ethnic/multicultural, experimental, fantasy (non-formula), feminist, gay, historical (general), horror, humor/satire, lesbian, literary, mystery/suspense (non-formula), psychic/supernatural/occult, science fiction (non-formula), translations. Accepts 5 mss/issue; 10 mss/year. Does not read mss during summer months. Publishes ms 1-4 months after acceptance. Published work by Jill Batson, Jeff Pritchard and Stephen Schryer. Length: 3,000 words maximum. Publishes short shorts. Also publishes literary essays and poetry.

How to Contact: Send complete ms with a cover letter. Should include short bio and list of publications. Reports in 6 months on mss. Send a disposable copy of ms. Electronic submissions OK. E-mail address: u9209263 uss.cis.mcmaster.ca. Sample copy for $4.

Payment/Terms: Pays contributor's copies. Not copyrighted; copyrights belong to authors.

BERKELEY FICTION REVIEW, (II), 703 Eshelman Hall, University of California, Berkeley CA 94720. (510)642-4005. Editors: Rachael Courtier and Jacqueline Carpenter. Magazine: journal size; 200 pages; some visual art and photographs. "We publish fresh, inventive fiction and poetry, as well as non-academic essays." Annually. Estab. 1981. Circ. 500.

Needs: No "self-consciously trendy fiction." Receives up to 50 unsolicited mss/month. Accepts 8-20 mss/ issue. Published work by new writers in the last year. Also publishes literary essays, literary criticism, poetry. Occasionally critiques rejected mss.

How to Contact: Send complete ms with short author's note. SASE. Submission deadlines: March 1, May 1, September 15, December 1. Sample copy for $5.

Payment/Terms: Pays 1 contributor's copy.

Advice: "We are not necessarily looking for polished, professional pieces. This is a forum for new writers to debut their fiction—fiction that shows promise and a sense of the craft. However, we welcome, and we have published, writers of all levels of experience."

‡**BIG SKY STORIES, (II)**, P.O. Box 477, Choteau MT 59422. (406)466-5300. Editor: Happy Feder. "Story-letter": 8½×11; 16 pages; heavy bond paper; illustrations and photos. "We publish fiction set in Big Sky Country (Montana, Wyoming, North and South Dakota) prior to 1950. Don't fake the history or geography. Our readers want to be entertained and educated!" Monthly. Estab. 1996. Circ. 4,000.

Needs: Adventure, historical, westerns. Publishes special fiction issues or anthologies. Accepts 2-4 mss/ issue. Also publishes literary essays and "cowboy poetry only—no contemporary or ranch-life poetry." Always critiques or comments on rejected ms.

How to Contact: Send complete ms with a cover letter. Should include estimated word count and list of publications with submission. Reports in 1-2 months. Send SASE for reply, return of ms or send a disposable copy of ms. Simultaneous and reprint submissions OK. Sample copy for $3, 8½ × 11 SAE and 2 first-class stamps. Fiction guidelines for SASE. Reviews novels and short story collections.

Payment/Terms: Pays minimum 1¢/word on publication for "negotiable" rights.

Advice: "Your first paragraph should introduce where, when, who and what, and the story must be set in Big Sky Country. Don't bluff or offer 'soft' history, i.e., a story that, with a few name/place changes, could take place in Ohio or Maryland or Okinawa. Know your Big Sky history."

BILINGUAL REVIEW, (II, IV), Hispanic Research Center, Arizona State University, Box 872702, Tempe AZ 85287-2702. (602)965-3867. Editor-in-Chief: Gary D. Keller. Scholarly/literary journal of US Hispanic life: poetry, short stories, other prose and short theater. Magazine: 7 × 10; 96 pages; 55 lb. acid-free paper; coated cover stock. Published 3 times/year. Estab. 1974. Circ. 2,000.

Needs: US Hispanic creative literature. "We accept material in English or Spanish. We publish original work only—no translations." US Hispanic themes only. Receives 50 unsolicited fiction mss/month. Accepts 3 mss/issue; 9 mss/year. Publishes ms an average of 1 year after acceptance. Published work by Ernestina N. Eger, Leo Romero, Connie Porter and Nash Candelaria; published work of new writers within the last year. Also publishes literary criticism on US Hispanic themes and poetry. Often critiques rejected mss.

How to Contact: Send 2 copies of complete ms with SAE and loose stamps. Reports in 1-2 months. Simultaneous and high-quality photocopied submissions OK. Sample copy for $6. Reviews novels and short story collections.

Payment/Terms: Pays 2 contributor's copies. 30% discount for extras. Acquires all rights (50% of reprint permission fee given to author as matter of policy).

Advice: "We do not publish literature about tourists in Latin America and their perceptions of the 'native culture.' We do not publish fiction about Latin America unless there is a clear tie to the United States (characters, theme, etc.)."

BIZÁRA, Filling The Void That Wants To Get In Between Your Ears, (II), The Slow X Press, P.O. Box 3118, Albany NY 12203-0118. Editor: Ted Kusio. Magazine: 7 × 8½; 44 pages; illustrations and photos. "Sometimes merely tugging at the reality carpet, while usually pulling it from beneath our feet, *Bizára* shows that some of the best stuff around is that which doesn't exist." Semiannually. Estab. 1993. Circ. 1,500.

Needs: Erotica (non-explicit), experimental, fantasy (surreal), humor/satire (especially absurd, wild, odd material), uncategorizable "weird" material. "No typical, standard, cliché, mainstream, political, 'issue-based,' vulgar." Special issues such as Dark Bizára, She-Bizára and electronic computer-based. Receives 15 unsolicited mss/month. Accepts 15-25 mss/issue/; 30-50 mss/year. Publishes ms 6 months maximum after acceptance. Recently published work by C.F. Roberts, Corrine DeWinter and Janet Kuypers. Length: 800 words average; 100 words minimum; 1,500 words maximum. Publishes short shorts. "Will also consider "one-liners" of about 10-25 words. Also publishes literary essays, literary criticism and poetry (*very* selective). "Style must match the rest of the publication. Content must be non-mainstream." Often critiques or comments on rejected ms.

How to Contact: Send complete ms with a cover letter. Should include estimated word count and bio (50 words maximum) with submission. Reports in 4-8 weeks. Send a disposable copy of ms. Simultaneous, reprint and electronic submissions (MAC or PC text) OK. E-mail address: SlowX@eworld.com. Sample copy for $3 (check made out to "Ted Kusio" or "The Slow X Press," not *Bizára*). Fiction guidelines for #10 SASE. Reviews novels and short story collections. Query editor first.

Payment/Terms: Pays 2 contributor's copies; additional copies available at cost. Acquires one-time rights.

Advice: "Send material that wipes readers with dream-like waves of radiation ranging from kiwi to liver. But understand that if an English teacher likes it, I probably won't. If you're still not sure what *Bizára* seeks, then buy a copy."

‡BLACK BOOKS BULLETIN: WORDSWORK, (IV), Third World Press, P.O. Box 19730, Chicago IL 60422. (312)651-0700. Fax: (312)651-7286. Editor: Haki R. Madhubuti. Magazine: 80 pages. "*Black Books Bulletin: WordsWork* publishes progressive material related to an enlightened African-American audience." Annually.
  ● In addition to publishing fiction, *Black Books Bulletin: WordsWork* is primarily a review publication covering nonfiction, fiction and poetry books by African-American authors.

Needs: Condensed/excerpted novel, ethnic/multicultural, feminist, historical (general). Receives 40 unsolicited mss/month. Accepts 2 mss/issue. Does not read mss January-June. Publishes ms 1 year after acceptance. Agented fiction 20%. Recently published work by Amiri Baraka, Keorapetse Kgositsile. Also publishes literary essays, literary criticism, poetry. Sometimes critiques or comments on rejected ms.

How to Contact: Query first. Should include estimated word count, bio. Reports in 3 weeks on queries; 3 months on mss. Simultaneous, reprint submissions OK. Reviews novels and short story collections. Send books to David Kelley.

Payment/Terms: Pays on publication. Acquires all rights.

BLACK FIRE, (I, IV), BLK Publishing Co., Box 83912, Los Angeles CA 90083. (310)410-0808. Fax: (310)410-9250. Editor: Alan Bell. Magazine: 8½×11; 48 pages; book 60 lb. paper; color glossy cover; illustrations and photographs. Bimonthly. Estab. 1992.
- BLK also publishes *Black Lace*, a magazine featuring lesbian-oriented fiction, listed in this book. BLK is a member of COSMEP.

Needs: Ethnic/multicultural, gay. Accepts 4 mss/issue. Publishes short shorts. Also publishes poetry.
How to Contact: Query first, query with clips of published work or send complete ms with a cover letter. Should include bio (3 sentences). Send a disposable copy of ms. No simultaneous submissions; electronic submissions OK. Sample copy for $7. Fiction guidelines free.
Payment/Terms: Pays free subscription, 5 contributor's copies. Acquires first North American serial rights and right to anthologize.

THE BLACK HAMMOCK REVIEW, A Literary Quarterly, (I, II, IV), 909 Woodgate Trail, Longwood FL 32750. (407)260-2035. Editor: Edward A. Nagel. Magazine: 8½×11; 40 pages; 20 lb. paper; illustrations and photos. "*The Black Hammock Review* is published by Quantum Press, a Florida non-profit cooperative. It was established to publish works which reflect rural motifs, for example, such settings as Oviedo, Geneva, Chuluota and the Black Hammock area in east-central Florida." Quarterly. Estab. 1992.
- Note that *The Black Hammock Review* is published co-operatively with memberships required and members share publishing costs. Editor Edward Nagel recently published a book, *No Entry*, with Four Walls Eight Windows. The magazine has a new address this year.

Needs: Ethnic/multicultural, experimental, fantasy (artistic), humor/satire, literary, mainstream/contemporary, psychic/supernatural, regional, "bucolic themes." Receives 10 unsolicited mss/month. Buys 4 mss/issue; 16 mss/year. Publishes ms 3 months after acceptance. Length: 2,500 words preferred; 1,500 words minimum; 3,500 words maximum. Also publishes literary essays, literary criticism and poetry. Always critiques or comments on returned mss.
How to Contact: Send complete ms with a cover letter. Should include bio (short), list of publications and brief statement of writer's artistic "goals." Reports in 2 weeks. Send SASE for reply, return of mss or a disposable copy of the ms. No simultaneous submissions. Sample copy for $4 and 8½×11 SAE.
Payment/Terms: *Charges membership fee: $25 for individual; $50 for 3 writers.* Fee waivers available for first rate, first time writers. Each member of the cooperative is assured publication of at least one carefully edited piece each year, subject to approval by our editors. Expenses not covered by the fees and subscriptions will be shared by the members, pro rata, not to exceed an amount fixed by the members, prior to the publication each quarter. Pays $50-75 *for selected works of established authors* on publication for one-time rights. Pays 6 contributor's copies; additional copies for $2.
Advice: Looks for "work that evokes in the reader's mind a vivid and continuous dream, vivid in that it has density, enough detail and the right detail, fresh with the author, and shows concern for the characters and the eternal verities. And continuous in that there are no distractions such as poor grammar, purple prose, diction shifts, or change in point of view. Short fiction that has a beginning, middle and end, organically speaking. Immerse yourself in the requested genre, format i.e., bucolic themes; work the piece over and over until it is 'right' for you, does what you want it to do; read the masters in your genre on a stylistic and technical level; begin to 'steal instead of borrow.' Transmute your emotions into the work and 'write short.' "

‡THE BLACK HOLE LITERARY REVIEW, (I), 333 Shoshone Ct., Cincinnati OH 45215. (513)821-6670 or (513)821-6671. Editor: Wm. E. Allendorf. Electronic Bulletin Board. "This is an attempt to revolutionize publishing—no paper, no rejection slips, no deadlines. For any person with access to a home computer and a modem." Estab. 1989. Circ. 8,000.
Needs: "Any or all fiction and nonfiction categories are acceptable. Any size, topic, or inherent bias is acceptable. The only limitation is that the writer will not mind having his piece read, and an honest critique given directly by his readership." Plans future hardcopy anthology. Publishes ms 1-2 days after acceptance. Length: 2,000-10,000 words. Publishes short shorts, poetry, essays and novels. "Critique given if not by editor, then by readers through e-mail."
How to Contact: Upload as EMAIL to the editor. Cover letter should include "titles, description (abstract), copyright notice." Reports in 1-2 days. Simultaneous submissions OK.
Payment/Terms: Pays in royalties, but charges fee for initial inputting. Charges $5 minimum subscription. Royalties are accrued each time the piece is read. Contact editor for details. Buys one-time rights.

A bullet introduces comments by the editor of Novel & Short Story Writer's Market *indicating special information about the listing.*

Advice: "If the concept of the electronic magazine goes over with the public, then the market for fiction is limitless. Any piece that an author has taken the trouble to set to print is worth publishing. However, *The Hole* is looking for writers that want to be read—not ones that just want to write. The electronic magazine is an interactive medium, and pieces are judged on their ability to inspire a person to read them." Writers interested in submitting should: "Do it. You would be the first to be rejected by *The Hole*, if we did not use your piece; to make matters easier for all concerned, submit your piece as a ASCII text file via the modem. If you do not have access to a home computer with a modem, buy one, borrow one, steal one. This is the wave of the future for writers."

BLACK JACK, (I), Seven Buffaloes Press, Box 249, Big Timber MT 59011. Editor: Art Cuelho. "Main theme: Rural. Publishes material on the American Indian, farm and ranch, American hobo, the common working man, folklore, the Southwest, Okies, Montana, humor, Central California, etc. for people who make their living off the land. The writers write about their roots, experiences and values they receive from the American soil." Annually. Estab. 1973. Circ. 750.

● *Black Jack* is published by Art Cuelho of Seven Buffaloes Press. He also publishes *Valley Grapevine* and *Azorean Express* also listed in this book. See also his listing for the press.

Needs: Literary, contemporary, western, adventure, humor, American Indian, American hobo, and parts of novels and long short stories. "Anything that strikes me as being amateurish, without depth, without craft, I refuse. Actually, I'm not opposed to any kind of writing if the author is genuine and has spent his lifetime dedicated to the written word." Receives approximately 10-15 unsolicited fiction mss/month. Acquires 5-10 mss/year. Length: 3,500-5,000 words (there can be exceptions).

How to Contact: Query for current theme with SASE. Reports in 1 week on queries; 2 weeks on mss. Sample copy for $6.75.

Payment/Terms: Pays 1-2 contributor's copies. Acquires first North American serial rights and reserves the right to reprint material in an anthology or future *Black Jack* publications. Rights revert to author after publication.

Advice: "Enthusiasm should be matched with skill as a craftsman. That's not saying that we don't continue to learn, but every writer must have enough command of the language to compete with other proven writers. Save postage by writing first to find out the editor's needs. A small press magazine always has specific needs at any given time. I sometimes accept material from writers that aren't that good at punctuation and grammar but make up for it with life's experience. This is not a highbrow publication; it belongs to the salt-of-the-earth people."

BLACK LACE, (I, IV), BLK Publishing Co., Box 83912, Los Angeles CA 90083. (310)410-0808. Editor: Alycee Lane. Magazine: 8½×11; 48 pages; electrabrite paper; color glossy cover; illustrations and photographs. Quarterly. Estab. 1991.

● BLK also publishes a magazine of gay-oriented fiction, *Black Fire*, listed in this book. BLK is a member of COSMEP.

Needs: Ethnic/multicultural, lesbian. Accepts 4 mss/year. Publishes short shorts. Also publishes literary essays, literary criticism and poetry.

How to Contact: Query first with clips of published work or send complete ms with a cover letter. Should include bio (3 sentences). Send a disposable copy of ms. No simultaneous submissions; electronic submissions OK. Sample copy for $7. Fiction guidelines free.

Payment/Terms: Pays free subscription, 5 contributor's copies. Acquires first North American serial rights and right to anthologize.

BLACK RIVER REVIEW, (II), 855 Mildred Ave., Lorain OH 44052. (216)244-9654. Editors: Deborah Glaefke Gilbert and Kaye Coller. Fiction Editor: Jack Smith. Magazine: 8½×11; 60 pages; mat card cover stock; b&w drawings. "Contemporary writing and contemporary American culture; poetry, book reviews, essays on contemporary literature, short stories." Annually. Estab. 1985. Circ. 400.

Needs: Contemporary, experimental, humor/satire and literary. No "erotica for its own sake, stories directed toward a juvenile audience." Accepts up to 5 mss/year. Does not read mss May 1-December 31. Publishes ms no later than July of current year. Published work by David Shields, Jeanne M. Leiby and Louis Gallo. Length: up to 3,500 words but will consider up to 4,000 maximum. Publishes short shorts. Also publishes literary essays, literary criticism, poetry. Sometimes critiques rejected mss.

How to Contact: Reports on mss no later than July. SASE. No simultaneous submissions. E-mail address: aa1250@freenet.lorain.oberlin.edu. Sample copy for $3.50 plus $1.50 shipping and handling for back issue; $4 plus $1.50 for current issue. Fiction guidelines for #10 SASE. Reviews novels and short story collections.

Payment/Terms: Pays in contributor's copies. Acquires one-time rights.

Advice: "Since it is so difficult to break in, much of the new writer's creative effort is spent trying to match trends in popular fiction, in the case of the slicks, or adapting to narrow themes ('Gay and Lesbian,' 'Vietnam War,' 'Women's Issues,' etc.) of little and literary journals. An unfortunate result, from the reader's standpoint, is that each story within a given category comes out sounding like all the rest. Among positive developments of the proliferation of small presses is the opportunity for writers to decide what to write and how to write it. My advice is to support a little magazine that is both open to new writers and prints fiction you like.

'Support' doesn't necessarily mean 'buy all the back issues,' but, rather, direct involvement between contributor, magazine and reader needed to rebuild the sort of audience that was there for writers like Fitzgerald and Hemingway."

BLACK SHEETS, (II), % Black Books, P.O. Box 31155-NS, San Francisco CA 94131-0155. (415)431-0171. Fax: (415)431-0172. Editor: Bill Brent. Magazine: 8½×11; 52 pages; illustrations and photos. "We are a magazine of sexuality and popular culture intended for a polysexual, sex-positive audience. Our motto is 'kinky/queer/intelligent/irreverent.' We are bisexual owned and operated." Quarterly. Estab. 1993.
   ● Fiction published in *Black Sheets* was included in *Best American Erotica 1995* (Simon & Schuster).
Needs: Bi/polysexual, popular culture-based: erotica, ethnic/multicultural, experimental, feminist, gay, humor/satire, lesbian, psychic/supernatural/occult. "No sex-negative fiction." Upcoming themes: #10 "Bestiality & Glamour" (February); #11 "Sex Pioneers" (May); #12 "Sleaze Revisited!" (August); #13 "Unsafe!" (November). List of upcoming themes available for SASE. Receives 5-10 mss/month. Buys 2-4 mss/issue; 10-20 mss/year. Publishes ms 3-6 months after acceptance. Recently published work by Paul Reed, Cecilia Tan and Thomas Roche. Length: 1,000 words average; 3,000 words maximum (longer can be serialized). Publishes short shorts. Also publishes essays, literary criticism and poetry. Often critiques or comments on rejected ms.
How to Contact: Send complete ms with a cover letter. Should include estimated word count and a brief bio. Reports in 1 month on queries; 2-3 months on mss. Send a disposable copy of ms. Simultaneous, reprint and electronic (IBM-compatible diskette preferred, MAC OK) submissions OK. Sample copy for $6. Fiction guidelines free. Requests for guidelines may be made via e-mail (blackb@105.com), but submissions are *not* accepted through e-mail. Reviews novels and short story collections.
Payment/Terms: Pays $10-50 and 1 contributor's copy on publication for one-time rights; additional copies for $3.
Advice: "We like to see good writing, a unique or different perspective, a sex-positive attitude, humor, irreverence, honesty, intelligence, boldness. We'd like to have more submissions from women of *all* sexual orientations."

BLACK WARRIOR REVIEW, (II), Box 2936, Tuscaloosa AL 35486-2936. (205)348-4518. Editor-in-Chief: Mindy Wilson. Fiction Editor: Mitch Wieland. Magazine: 6×9; 170 pages; illustrations and photos occasionally. "We publish contemporary fiction, poetry, reviews, essays and interviews for a literary audience." Semiannually. Estab. 1974. Circ. 1,300-2,000.
   ● Work that appeared in the *Black Warrior Review* has been included in the *Pushcart Prize* anthology, *Best American Short Stories*, *Best American Poetry* and in *New Short Stories from the South*.
Needs: Contemporary, literary, mainstream and prose poem. No types that are clearly "types." Receives 200 unsolicited fiction mss/month. Buys 5 mss/issue, 10 mss/year. Approximately 25% of fiction is agented. Published work by David Wojahn, Alison Baker and Rita Dove; published new writers within the last year. Length: 7,500 words maximum; 3,000-5,000 words average. Also publishes literary criticism, poetry. Occasionally critiques rejected mss.
How to Contact: Send complete ms with SASE (1 story per submission). Simultaneous submissions OK. Reports in 2-3 months. Publishes ms 2-5 months after acceptance. Sample copy for $6. Fiction guidelines for SASE. Reviews novels and short story collections.
Payment/Terms: Pays $5-10/page and 2 contributor's copies. Pays on publication.
Advice: "Become familiar with the magazine prior to submission. We're not a good bet for genre fiction. Regular submission deadlines are June 1 for the fall issue and November 31 for the spring issue."

‡THE BLACKSTONE CIRCULAR, (II), 26 James St., Suite B-8, Toms River NJ 08753. Editor: Linda Rogers. Magazine: 8½×11; 12-20 pages; copy paper. "Fiction and nonfiction with gay and lesbian themes for all interested readers." Monthly. Estab. 1995.
Needs: Gay, lesbian. No juvenile, young adult, psychic/supernatural/occult, erotica. Plans anthology. Buys up to 10 mss/issue. Publishes ms 1-2 months after acceptance. Recently published work by Steven J. Baeli, David Altier, C.E. Lindstrom and Del Pearl. Length: 10 words minimum; 3,000 words maximum. Publishes short shorts. Also publishes literary essays, literary criticism, poetry. Often comments on rejected ms.
How to Contact: Send complete ms with a cover letter. Reports on mss in 2 months. Simultaneous, reprint submissions OK. Sample copy for $2.
Payment/Terms: Pays 1 contributor's copy. Acquires one-time rights.
Advice: "Think of gay and lesbian themes in the broad sense of the phrase, too."

‡BLACKWATER REVIEW, (II), Tidewater Community College, 1700 College Crescent, Virginia Beach VA 23464. (804)427-7272. Editor: Robert P. Arthur. Fiction Editor: Juliet Crichton. Magazine: 6×9; 150 pages; illustrations and photos. Annually. Estab. 1995. Circ. 1,000.
Needs: Adventure, experimental, feminist, historical (general), horror, humor/satire, literary, regional, science fiction (soft/sociological). Accepts 6-8 mss/issue. Publishes ms September after acceptance. Length: 8,000 words maximum. Publishes short shorts. Also publishes literary essays, literary criticism, poetry. Often critiques or comments on rejected ms.

How to Contact Send complete ms with a cover letter. Should include 3-5 line bio. Reports in 3 weeks on ms. Simultaneous, reprint, electronic submissions OK. Sample copy for $3, 8×11 SAE and $3 postage. Fiction guidelines for $3 and 8×11 SAE. Reviews novels and short story collections.
Payment/Terms: Pays 2 contributor's copies; additional copies $3. Acquires one-time rights. Sponsors contests, awards or grants for fiction writers.
Advice: "We prefer experimental fiction but will print any high-quality work. Writers should avoid sending work that is commonplace or experimental work lacking clarity."

‡**BLINK**, P.O. Box 823, Miami FL 33243-0823. Editor: Fia Dimauro. Magazine. Quarterly. Estab. 1992.
Needs: "Any subject matter presented in an interesting, experimental, avant-garde way." No romance, gay, erotica, mystery. Publishes annual special fiction issue or anthology. Publishes ms 3-5 weeks after acceptance. Recently published work by Mario Cubas and John Sevigny. Often critiques or comments on rejected ms.
How to Contact: Send complete ms with a cover letter. Reports in 1 month on queries; 1 month on mss. SASE. Simultaneous and electronic (disk) submissions OK. Fiction guidelines for SASE.
Payment/Terms: Pays 3 contributor's copies.
Advice: "We would like to see more experimental writing, more loose, crazy material. We'd like to see less slice-of-life vignettes; more hard-hitting, from-the-gut fiction."

✦**BLOOD & APHORISMS, A Journal of Literary Fiction, (II)**, P.O. Box 702, Station P, Toronto, Ontario M5S 2Y4 Canada. Publisher: Tim Paleczny. Fiction Editor: Ken Sparling. Managing Editor: Mark Hickmott. Magazine: 8½×11; 44 pages; bond paper; illustrations. "We publish new and emerging writers whose work is fresh and revealing, and impacts on a literary readership." Quarterly. Estab. 1990. Circ. 1,900.
Needs: Experimental, humor/satire, literary. No gratuitous violence or exploitive fiction. Publishes anthology every 2 years. Receives 50 unsolicited mss/month. Acquires 12-15 mss/issue; 45-55 mss/year. Publishes ms 3-6 months after acceptance. Recently published work by Elise Levine, Natasha Waxman, Christine Slater and Derek McCormack. Length: 2,500-4,000 words average; 150 words minimum; 4,500 words maximum. Publishes short shorts. Often critiques rejected mss.
How to Contact: Send complete ms with a cover letter. Should include estimated word count, short bio, list of publications with submission. Reports in 2 weeks on queries; 2 months on mss. SASE for reply to a query or return of ms. Simultaneous (please advise) and electronic (disk with hard copy) submissions OK. E-mail address: blood@io.org. Home Page: www.io.org:80\~blood. Sample copy for $6. Fiction guidelines for SASE. Reviews novels and short story collections.
Payment/Terms: Pays subscription to the magazine. Additional copies $6. Acquires first North American serial rights, electronic distribution for current issue sampling on Home Page, and the right to use work in anthology.
Advice: "Be honest, take chances, find the strength in your own voice, show us your best and keep an open mind—we're ready for anything. Know the magazine you're sending to."

‡**THE BLOWFISH CATALOG, (I)**, 2261 Market St., #284, San Francisco CA 94114. (415)864-0880. Fax: (415)864-1858. Contact: Editorial Staff. Catalog: 8½×11; 48 pages; newsprint; 50 lb. cover; illustrations and photos. "We buy short fiction for use in our catalog. Our catalog contains erotic books, videos, safer sex products, and so forth, and we add fiction which complements it." Triannually. Estab. 1994. Circ. 5,000.
Needs: Erotica. Plans special fiction issues in the future. Receives 4-7 unsolicited mss/month. Buys 2 mss/ issue; 6 mss/year. Publishes ms 1-4 months after acceptance. Recently published work by Trish Thomas. Length: 200 words average; 500 words maximum. Publishes short shorts. Also publishes poetry. Sometimes critiques or comments on rejected ms.
How to Contact: Send complete ms with a cover letter. Should include estimated word count and Social Security number. Reports in 1 month on queries; 2 months on mss. Send a disposable copy of ms. Simultaneous, reprints and electronic submissions OK. E-mail address: blowfish@blowfish.com. Sample copy for $3. Fiction guidelines for #10 SASE. Reviews novels and short story collections.
Payment/Terms: Pays $10-100 and 5 contributor's copies on acceptance; for one-time rights; additional copies for $1.
Advice: "We look for 'high density' fiction: not just arousing, but thought-provoking or poetic as well, in a very short form. Being erotic is important, but not sufficient: the piece must have merits beyond an ability to arouse."

‡**BLUE MESA REVIEW, (I, IV)**, Creative Writing Program, University of New Mexico, Dept. of English, Albuquerque NM 87131. (505)277-6347. Fax: (505)277-5573. Managing Editor: Patricia Lynn Sprott. Magazine: 6×9; 200 pages; 55 lb. paper; 10 pt C1S; photos. "*Blue Mesa Review* publishes the best/most current creative writing on the market. Annually. Estab. 1989. Circ. 1,200.
Needs: Adventure, ethnic/multicultural, feminist, gay, historical, humor/satire, lesbian, literary, mainstream/ contemporary, regional, westerns. Upcoming theme: "The Approaching Millenium" (effects on culture, technology, education, etc.). Receives 60-120 unsolicited mss/year. Accepts 10 mss/year. Accepts mss May-October; reads mss November-December; responds in January. Publishes ms 5-6 months after acceptance.

Recently published work by Kathleen Spivack, Roberta Swann and Tony Mares. Publishes short shorts. Also publishes literary essays, poetry.

How to Contact: Send complete ms with a cover letter. Should include 1 paragraph bio. Send SASE for reply, return of ms or send a disposable copy of ms. Electronic submissions OK. E-mail address: psprott@pegasus.unm.edu. Sample copy for $12. Reviews novels and short story collections.

Payment/Terms: Pays 2 contributor's copies for one-time rights.

Advice: "Get to the point—fast. A short story does not allow for lengthy intros and descriptions. Take a class and get the teacher to edit you! Now that we are using themes, we would like to see theme-related stories. Avoid thought pieces on 'vacations to our enchanting state.' "

THE BLUE PENNY QUARTERLY, (I, II), Apt 6, 1212 Wertland St., Charlottesville VA 22903-2861. Editor: Doug Lawson. Electronic magazine: Illustrations and photos. Quarterly. Estab. 1994. Circ. 3,000-7,000.
* The editors advise writers to contact them through e-mail because the magazine's address may change.

Needs: Experimental, feminist, gay, lesbian, literary, mainstream/contemporary, regional, translations. No genre fiction. Receives 25-30 unsolicited mss/month. Accepts 7-10 mss/issue; 28-40 mss/year. Publishes ms up to 9 months after acceptance. Recently published work by Edward Falco, Deborah Eisenberg, Robert Sward and Eva Shaderowfsky. Length: open. Publishes short shorts. Also publishes literary essays, literary criticism and poetry. Sometimes critiques or comments on rejected ms.

How to Contact: Send complete ms with a cover letter. Should include a brief bio, list of publications and e-mail address if available. Reports in 1-3 months on mss. Send SASE for reply, return of ms or send a disposable copy of ms. Send e-mail address for reply if available. Simultaneous and electronic submissions OK. E-mail address: dlawson@ebbs.english.vt.edu. Sample copy free on World Wide Web at http://ebbs.english.vt.edu/olp/bpq/front-page.html. Fiction guidelines for 4×9 SASE or free via e-mail. Reviews novels and short story collections.

Payment/Terms: Pays in contributor's copies. Acquires electronic rights.

Advice: "We look for strong use of language or strong characterization. Manuscripts stand out by their ability to engage a reader on an intellectual or emotional level. Present characters with depth regardless of age and introduce intelligent concepts that have resonance and relevance. We recommend our writers be electronically connected to the Internet."

THE BLUE WATER REVIEW, (II), P.O. Box 900428, Homestead FL 33090-0428. (305)248-8222. Editor/Publisher: Dennis M. Ross. Magazine: 5½×7; 45 pages; 60 lb. paper; standard cover stock; illustrations and photos. "No theme. We want quality writing: fiction, interviews with well known writers and critics, poetry, and photos." Semiannually. Estab. 1989. Circ. 5,000.

Needs: Adventure, contemporary, ethnic, experimental, flash fiction, humor/satire, literary, mainstream, mystery/suspense (amateur sleuth, police procedurals, private eye), regional, science fiction (soft/sociological), sports. "No pornography, no handwritten or single-spaced submissions, no manuscripts without SASE." Receives 15 unsolicited mss/month. Accepts 3-4 mss/issue; 10 mss/year. Publishes ms 1-3 months after acceptance. Agented fiction 10%. Length: 3,000 words maximum. Publishes short shorts. Sometimes critiques rejected mss.

How to Contact: Send complete manuscript with cover letter. Reports in 4-5 months. SASE. Simultaneous submissions OK. Fiction guidelines for #10 SASE.

Payment/Terms: Pays 1 contributor's copy; charge for extras. Acquires one-time rights.

Advice: "Manuscripts should have classic elements of short story, such as meaningful character change. Submit your best work no matter the publication. We want quality. Use standard form as illustrated in *Writer's Digest* (short stories)."

BLUELINE, (II, IV), English Dept., SUNY, Potsdam NY 13676. (315)267-2000. Editor: Tony Tyler. Magazine: 6×9; 112 pages; 70 lb. white stock paper; 65 lb. smooth cover stock; illustrations; photos. "*Blueline* is interested in quality writing about the Adirondacks or other places similar in geography and spirit. We publish fiction, poetry, personal essays, book reviews and oral history for those interested in the Adirondacks, nature in general, and well-crafted writing." Annually. Estab. 1979. Circ. 400.

Needs: Adventure, contemporary, humor/satire, literary, prose poem, regional, reminiscences, oral history and nature/outdoors. Receives 8-10 unsolicited fiction mss/month. Accepts 6-8 mss/issue. Does not read January-August. Publishes ms 3-6 months after acceptance. Published fiction by Jeffrey Clapp. Published new writers within the last year. Length: 500 words minimum; 3,000 words maximum; 2,500 words average. Also publishes literary essays, poetry. Occasionally critiques rejected mss.

How to Contact: Send complete ms with SASE and brief bio. Submit mss August 1-November 30. Reports in 2-10 weeks. E-mail address: tylerau@potsdam.edu. Sample copy for $3.50. Fiction guidelines for 5×10 SASE.

Payment/Terms: Pays 1 contributor's copy for first rights. Charges $3 each for 3 or more extra copies.

Advice: "We look for concise, clear, concrete prose that tells a story and touches upon a universal theme or situation. We prefer realism to romanticism but will consider nostalgia if well done. Pay attention to grammar and syntax. Avoid murky language, sentimentality, cuteness or folksiness. We would like to see more good fiction related to the Adirondacks. Please include short biography and word count. If manuscript has potential, we work with author to improve and reconsider for publication. Our readers prefer fiction to poetry (in general) or reviews. Write from your own experience, be specific and factual (within the bounds of your story) and if you write about universal features such as love, death, change, etc., write about them in a fresh way. Triteness and mediocracy are the hallmarks of the majority of stories seen today."

BOGG, A Magazine of British & North American Writing, (II), Bogg Publications, 422 N. Cleveland St., Arlington VA 22201. (703)243-6019. U.S. Editor: John Elsberg. Magazine: 6×9; 64-68 pages; 70 lb. white paper; 70 lb. cover stock; line illustrations. "American and British poetry, prose poems and other experimental short 'fictions,' reviews, and essays on small press." Published triannually. Estab. 1968. Circ. 800.
 • The editors at *Bogg* are most interested in short, wry fiction.
Needs: Very short experimental and prose poem. "We are always looking for work with British/Commonwealth themes and/or references." Receives 25 unsolicited fiction mss/month. Accepts 1-2 mss/issue; 3-6 mss/year. Publishes ms 3-18 months after acceptance. Published 50% new writers within the last year. Length: 300 words maximum. Also publishes literary essays, literary criticism, poetry. Occasionally critiques rejected mss.
How to Contact: Query first or send ms (2-6 pieces) with SASE. Reports in 1 week on queries; 2 weeks on mss. Sample copy for $3.50 or $4.50 (current issue). Reviews novels and short story collections.
Payment/Terms: Pays 2 contributor's copies; reduced charge for extras. Acquires one-time rights.
Advice: "Read magazine first. We are most interested in prose work of experimental or wry nature to supplement poetry, and are always looking for innovative/imaginative uses of British themes and references."

BOHEMIAN CHRONICLE, It's Not for Everyone, (I, II), P.O. Box 387, Largo FL 34649-0387. Editor: Emily Skinner. Assistant Editor: Ellen Williams. Magazine: 8×11 (folded); 12 pages; standard paper; illustrations and photographs. "Experimental, quality works, anything that *isn't* mainstream!" Monthly. Estab. 1991. Circ. 500.
 • The editor is particularly interested in work that is considered experimental. *B.C.* has new, very clear guidelines available.
Needs: Adventure, childrens/juvenile (written by children only), ethnic/multicultural, experimental, gay, humor/satire, literary, mystery/suspense (experimental), psychic/supernatural/occult, romance (conversational), science fiction (light), serialized novel. Receives 100 mss/month. Accepts 5 mss/issue; 60 mss/year. Does not read mss from October-November. Publishes ms 1-10 months after acceptance. Length: 500-1,000 words only! Publishes short shorts. Also publishes literary essays, literary criticism and poetry. Always critiques or comments on rejected mss.
How to Contact: Send complete ms with a cover letter. Should include estimated word count. Reports in 1-3 months months. Send SASE for reply, return of ms or send a disposable copy of ms. No simultaneous or reprint submissions. Sample copy for $1 and 6×9 SASE. Fiction guidelines for #10 SASE.
Payment/Terms: Pays $5 and 5 contributor's copies on publication for all rights, first rights or first North American serial rights.
Advice: "Don't write long introduction letters and don't send clips. Stick to the required length. We would like to see more humor and satire (non-political)!"

‡BOOKLOVERS, (I, II), Jammer Publications, P.O. Box 93485, Milwaukee WI 53203-0485. (414)541-7510. Editor: Jill Lindberg. Magazine: 8½×11; 32 pages; high-grade newsprint paper; photos. "*BookLovers* is a literary magazine aimed at avid readers and writers. Includes book reviews, author interviews, book lists, original short stories, poetry, features on unique book stores and profiles of book discussion groups." Quarterly. Estab. 1992. Circ. 800.
Needs: Adventure, ethnic/multicultural, fantasy (children's), historical, humor/satire, literary, mainstream/contemporary, mystery/suspense (amateursleuth, cozy, police procedural), regional, romance (gothic, historical), serialized novel, sports, young adult/teen (adventure, mystery, science fiction). List of upcoming themes available for SASE. Receives 10 unsolicited mss/month. Buys 3-4 mss/issue; 10-12 mss/year. Publishes ms 6 months after acceptance. Recently published work by Shirley Mudrick, Lois Schmidt and Jane Farrell. Length: 800-1,000 words average; 500 words minimum; 1,500 words maximum. Publishes short shorts. Length: 300 words. Also publishes literary essays, literary criticism, poetry.
How to Contact: Send complete ms with a cover letter. Should include estimated word count and bio (200 words maximum). Reports in 2-3 months. Send SASE for reply, return of ms or send a disposable copy of ms. Simultaneous, reprint, electronic (Macintosh only) submissions OK. E-mail address: rjammer@omnifest. uwm.edu. Sample copy for 9×12 SAE and 5 first-class stamps. Fiction guidelines for #10 SASE.
Payment/Terms: Pays 2-5 contributor's copies. Acquires one-time rights.
Advice: Looking for "unique story line, good grammar, syntax—very important! Story told in succinct manner. Would like to see more fiction *about* men and *by* men."

‡BOSTON LITERARY REVIEW (BLUR), (I, II), P.O. Box 357, West Somerville MA 02144. (617)666-3080. Editor: Gloria Mindock. Magazine: 24-30 pages. Semiannually. Estab. 1985. Circ. 500.

Needs: Condensed/excerpted novel, experimental, humor/satire, literary, mainstream/contemporary, translations. Receives 80 unsolicited mss/month. Accepts 2 mss/issue; 4 mss/year. Publishes ms 6-12 months after acceptance. Length: 2,000 words average; 2,000 words maximum. Also publishes poetry. Often critiques or comments on rejected ms.

How to Contact: Send complete ms with a cover letter. Should include estimated word count, short paragraph bio, list of publications. Reports in 2-4 weeks on queries; 1 month on mss. Send SASE for reply, return of ms or send a disposable copy of ms. Sample copy for $2.

Payment/Terms: Pays free subscription to magazine and 2 contributor's copies. Sends galleys to author.

Advice: Looking for "neatness and fiction that takes risks. If you're not sure what type of fiction we are open to, please query."

BOTTOMFISH MAGAZINE, (II), De Anza College, 21250 Stevens Creek Blvd., Cupertino CA 95014. (408)864-8623. Editor-in-Chief: David Denny. Magazine: 7×8½; 80-100 pages; White Bristol vellum cover; b&w high contrast illustrations and photos. "Contemporary poetry, fiction, b&w graphics and photos." Annually. Estab. 1976. Circ. 500.
  • Note that *Bottomfish* has a new editor. He's interested in publishing more short shorts.

Needs: "Literary excellence is our only criteria. We will consider all subjects." Receives 50-100 unsolicited fiction mss/month. Accepts 5-6 mss/issue. Length: 500 words minimum; 5,000 words maximum; 2,500 words average.

How to Contact: Reads mss September to February. Submission deadline: February 1; publication date: end of March. Send complete mss with cover letter, brief bio and SASE. No simultaneous submissions or reprints. Reports in 3-4 months. Publishes mss an average of 6 months-1 year after acceptance. Sample copy for $5.

Payment/Terms: Pays 2 contributor's copies. Acquires one-time rights.

Advice: "Strive for orginality and high level of craft; avoid clichéd or stereotyped characters and plots."

BOUILLABAISSE, (I, II, IV), Alpha Beat Press, 31 A. Waterloo St., New Hope PA 18938. (215)862-0299. Editor: Dave Christy. Magazine: 11×17; 120 pages; bond paper; illustrations and photos. Semiannually. Estab. 1986. Circ. 600.
  • Work included in *Bouillabaisse* has been selected for inclusion in the Pushcart Prize anthology. *Alpha Beat Press* magazine is listed in this section.

Needs: Beat generation and modern sub-cultures: adventure, condensed/excerpted novel, erotica, literary. Receives 15 unsolicited mss/month. Accepts 2 mss/issue; 4 mss/year. Publishes ms 6 months after acceptance. Published work by Jan Kerouac, Ken Babbs and Stephen Gutirrez. Length: no limit. Publishes short shorts. Also publishes literary essays, literary criticism and poetry. Sometimes critiques or comments on rejected ms.

How to Contact: Query first. Should include bio with submission. Reports in 1 week. Send SASE for reply or return of ms. Simultaneous submissions OK. Sample copy $10. Reviews novels and short story collections.

Payment/Terms: Pays 1 contributor's copy.

‡BOULEVARD, (II), Opojaz Inc., P.O. Box 30386, Philadelphia PA 19103-8386. (215)568-7062. Editor: Richard Burgin. Magazine: 5½×8½; 150-225 pages; excellent paper; high-quality cover stock; illustrations; photos. "*Boulevard* aspires to publish the best contemporary fiction, poetry and essays we can print." Published 3 times/year. Estab. 1986. Circ. about 3,000.
  • *Small Magazine Review*, a new publication by Dustbooks, Inc. selected *Boulevard* for its "Small Magazine Club." Also, a story originally printed in *Boulevard* was included in *Prize Stories 1995: The O. Henry Awards.*

Needs: Contemporary, experimental, literary. Does not want to see "anything whose first purpose is not literary." Receives over 400 mss/month. Buys about 8 mss/issue. Does not accept manuscripts between May 1 and October 1. Publishes ms less than 1 year after acceptance. Agented fiction ⅓-¼. Length: 5,000 words average; 10,000 words maximum. Publishes short shorts. Published work by Lee K. Abbott, Francine Prose, Alice Adams. Also publishes literary essays, literary criticism, poetry. Sometimes critiques rejected mss and recommends other markets.

How to Contact: Send complete ms with cover letter. Reports in 2 weeks on queries; 3 months on mss. SASE. Simultaneous submissions OK. Sample copy for $7 and SAE with 5 first-class stamps.

Payment/Terms: Pays $50-250; contributor's copies; charges for extras. Buys first North American serial rights. Does not send galleys to author unless requested.

Advice: "We are open to different styles of imaginative and critical work and are mindful of Nabokov's dictum 'There is only one school, the school of talent.' Above all, when we consider the very diverse manuscripts submitted to us for publication, we value original sensibility, writing that causes the reader to experience a part of life in a new way. Originality, to us, has little to do with a writer intently trying to make each line or sentence odd, bizarre, or eccentric, merely for the sake of being 'different.' Rather, originality is the result of the character or vision of the writer; the writer's singular outlook and voice as it shines through in the totality of his or her work."

‡BOY'S QUEST, (II), The Bluffton News Publishing & Printing Co., P.O. Box 227, Bluffton OH 45817. (419)358-4610. Fax: (419)358-5027. Editor: Marilyn Edwards. Magazine: 7×9; 50 pages; enamel paper; illustrations and photos. Bimonthly. Estab. 1994.

• This publisher also publishes *Hopscotch* magazine for girls listed in this section.

Needs: Adventure, children's/juvenile (5-9 years, 10-12 years), ethnic/multicultural, historical, sports. List of upcoming themes available for SASE. Receives 300-400 unsolicited mss/month. Accepts 20-40 mss/year. Agented fiction 2%. Recently published work by Jean Patrick, Eve Marar and Linda Herman. Length: 300-500 words average; 500 words maximum. Publishes short shorts. Length: 250-400 words. Also publishes poetry. Always critiques or comments on rejected ms.

How to Contact: Send complete ms with a cover letter. Should include estimated word count, 1 page bio, Social Security number, list of publications. Reports in 2-4 weeks on queries; 6-10 weeks on mss. Simultaneous and reprint submissions OK. Sample copy for $3. Fiction guidelines for #10 SASE. Reviews novels and short story collections.

Payment/Terms: Pays 5¢/word and 1 contributor's copy on publication for first North American serial rights; additional copies $3, $2 for 10 or more.

Advice: Looks for "typewritten, proofread stories under 600 words about boys 6-13 years old."

MARION ZIMMER BRADLEY'S FANTASY MAGAZINE, (II, IV), Box 249, Berkeley CA 94701. (510)644-9222. Editor and Publisher: Marion Zimmer Bradley. Magazine: 8½×11; 64 pages; 60 lb. text paper; 10 lb. cover stock; b&w interior and 4 color cover illustrations. "Fantasy only; strictly family oriented." Quarterly.

• This magazine is named for and edited by one of the pioneers of fantasy fiction. Bradley is perhaps best known for the multi-volume Darkover series.

Needs: Fantasy. May include adventure, contemporary, humor/satire, mystery/suspense and young adult/teen (10-18) (all with fantasy elements). "No avant-garde or romantic fantasy. No computer games!" Receives 50-200 unsolicited mss/week. Buys 8-10 mss/issue; 36-40 mss/year. Publishes 3-12 months after acceptance. Agented fiction 5%. Length: 3,000-4,000 words average; 7,000 words maximum. Publishes short shorts.

How to Contact: Send complete ms. SASE. Reports in 90 days. No simultaneous submissions. Sample copy for $4. Fiction guidelines for #10 SASE.

Payment/Terms: Pays 3-10¢/word on acceptance and contributor's copies for first North American serial rights.

Advice: "If I want to finish reading it—I figure other people will too. A manuscript stands out if I care whether the characters do well, if it has a rhythm. Make sure it has characters I will know *you* care about. If you don't care about them, how do you expect me to? Read guidelines *before* sending ms."

(the) BRAVE NEW TICK, (I, IV), Graftographic Press, P.O. Box 24, S. Grafton MA 01560. (508)799-3769. Editor: Paul Normal Dion-Deitch. Newsletter: 8½×11; 10 pages; standard paper; b&w illustrations. "Civil rights for all, focus on gay rights, activisim. Would very much like to publish gay fiction—no porn." Monthly. Estab. 1993. Circ. 75-100.

• The editor says he's publishing more longer pieces.

Needs: Mild erotica (gay), gay, lesbian short stories; general poetry, art, political commentary. Receives 1-2 unsolicited mss/month. Length: 1 or 2 typed pages maximum. Publishes short shorts. Also publishes literary essays, literary criticism and poetry.

How to Contact: Open to any method of submission. Should include bio. Send SASE for return of ms. Simultaneous, reprint and electronic submissions OK (IBM compatible, ASCII files accepted and preferred). E-mail address: tick@ultranet.com. Sample copy for #10 SAE and 52¢ postage, 2-3 loose first-class stamps.

Payment/Terms: Pays contributor's copies. "Rights remain with contributor."

Advice: Looks for fiction "related to gay rights, growing up gay, living in a straight world, gay culture, gay pride that is well written, thought provoking, visually interesting. Hard core porn is not what I'm looking for."

THE BRIAR CLIFF REVIEW, (II), Briar Cliff College, 3303 Rebecca St., Sioux City IA 51104-2100. (712)279-1651 or 279-5321. Fax: (712) 279-5410. Editors: Tricia Currans-Sheehan and Jeanne Emmons. Fiction Editor: Dennis Sjolie. Magazine: 8½×11; 64 pages; 70 lb matte paper; 10 Pt CIS cover stock; illustrations and photos. "*The Briar Cliff Review* is an eclectic literary and cultural magazine focusing on (but not limited to) Siouxland writers and subjects. We are happy to proclaim ourselves a regional publication. It doesn't diminish us; it enhances us." Annually. Estab. 1989. Circ. 500.

• *The Briar Cliff Review* has received The Gold Crown and Silver Crown awards from the Columbia Scholastic Prize Association and the All-American Award from the Associated Collegiate Press.

Needs: Ethnic/multicultural, feminist, historical, horror, humor/satire, literary, mainstream/contemporary, regional. Accepts 5 mss/year. Reads mss only between August 1 and November 1. Publishes ms 3-4 months after acceptance. Published work by Robley Wilson, Mary Helen Stefaniak, Bill Franzen, and Brian Bedard. Length: 3,000 words average; 2,500 words minimum; 3,500 words maximum. Also publishes literary essays, literary criticism and poetry. Sometimes critiques or comments on rejected ms.

How to Contact: Send complete ms with a cover letter. Should include estimated word count, bio and list of publications. Reports in 3-4 months on mss. Send a SASE for return of ms. No simultaneous submissions.

Sample copy for $4 and 9×12 SAE. Fiction guidelines free for #10 SASE. Reviews novels and short story collections.

Payment/Terms: Pays 2 contributor's copies for first rights; additional copies available for $2.

Advice: "Strong fiction transcends all genres. Send us your best."

THE BRIDGE, A Journal of Fiction & Poetry, (II), The Bridge, 14050 Vernon St., Oak Park MI 48237. Editor: Jack Zucker. Fiction Editor: Helen Zucker. Magazine: $5\frac{1}{2} \times 8\frac{1}{2}$; 192 pages; 60 lb. paper; heavy cover. "Fiction and poetry for a literary audience." Semiannually. Estab. 1990.

• *The Bridge* received a 1995 grant from the Oakland City Office of Cultural Affairs.

Needs: Ethnic, literary, mainstream, regional. Receives 80 unsolicited mss/month. Acquires 9-10 mss/issue; 18-20 mss/year. Publishes ms within one year of acceptance. Length: 3,000 words average; 7,500 words maximum. Publishes short shorts. Length: 1,000 words. Also publishes some short essays, some criticism, poetry.

How to Contact: Send complete manuscript with cover letter. Reports in 1 week on queries; 2-4 months on mss. SASE. Simultaneous submissions OK. Sample copy for $5. Reviews novels and short story collections.

Payment/Terms: Pays in contributor's copies. Acquires first North American serial rights.

Advice: "Don't give us fiction intended for a popular/commercial market—we accept very little comedy and experimental."

BRILLIANT STAR, (II), National Spiritual Assembly of the Baha'is of the U.S., Baha'i, National Center, Wilmette IL 60091. Managing Editor: Pepper Peterson Oldziey. Fiction Editor: Cindy Savage. Magazine: $8\frac{1}{2} \times 11$; 33 pages; matte paper; glossy cover; illustrations; photos. "A magazine for Baha'i children about the history, teachings and beliefs of the Baha'i faith. Manuscripts should reflect spiritual principles of the baha'i" For children approximately 5-12 years old. Bimonthly. Estab. 1969. Circ. 2,300.

Needs: Adventure, children's/juvenile, ethnic, historical, humor/satire, mystery/suspense, spiritual, young adult/teen (10-12 years). "Accepts inspirational fiction if not overtly preachy or moralistic and if not directly Christian and related directly to Christian holidays." Upcoming themes: "World Embracing Vision" (September-October); "Confidence in Action" (January-February 1996); "This Is The Balance" (March-April 1996); "Life of Service" (May-June 1996); "light of Unity" (July-August 1996). Receives 30 unsolicited mss/month. Accepts 1-2 mss/issue; 6-12 mss/year. Publishes ms no sooner than 6 months after acceptance. Published work by Susan Pethick and John Paulits; published new writers within the last year. Length: 100 words minimum; 600 words maximum. "Length should correlate with intended audience—very short mss for young readers, longer mss must be for older readers (ages 10-12), and intended for their interests." Publishes short shorts. Also publishes poetry.

How to Contact: No queries. Send complete ms. Cover letter not essential. Reports in 6-10 weeks on mss. SASE. Simultaneous submissions OK "but please make a notation that it is a simultaneous sub." Sample copy for $2, 9×12 SAE and 5 oz. postage. Fiction guidelines for #10 SASE.

Payment/Terms: Pays in contributor's copies (two); charges for extras.

Terms: "Writer can retain own copyright or grant to the National Spiritual Assembly of the Baha'is of the U.S."

Advice: "We enjoy working with beginning writers and try to develop a constructive collaborative relationship with those who show promise and sensitivity to our aims and focus. We feel that the children's market is open to a wide variety of writers: fiction, nonfiction, science, photo-essays. Our needs for appealing fiction especially for pre-schoolers and young readers make us a good market for new writers. *Please*, have a story to tell! The single main reason for rejection of manuscripts we review is lack of plot to infuse the story with energy and make the reader want to come along, as well as length to age/interest level mismatch. Longer stories must be intended for older children. Only very short stories are useable for young audiences. We love stories about different cultures and ethnic groups. We also welcome submissions that offer solutions to the problems kids face today. We're looking for active, child-oriented writing, not passive, preachy prose."

BROWNBAG PRESS, (II), Hyacinth House Publications, P.O. Box 120, Fayetteville AR 72702-0120. Editors: Shannon Frach and Randal Seyler. Magazine: 30-55 pages; 20 lb. paper; cardstock cover; b&w illustrations. "*Brownbag Press* is a digest of poetry, fiction, and experimental writing that is seeking avant-garde, forceful, and often bizarre literature for a literate, adult audience that is bored to death with the standard offerings of modern mainstream fiction." Semiannually. Estab. 1989. Circ. 375.

• Hyacinth House Publications also publishes *Psychotrain* listed in this book. No need to send to both publications, says the editor, as submissions will be considered for both. Notice the editors have reduced the length to no more than 1,500 words. They are also currently overstocked with fiction.

Needs: Condensed/excerpted novels, contemporary, erotica, ethnic, experimental, feminist, gay, humor/satire, lesbian, literary, prose poem, psychic/supernatural/occult, translations, "Punk, psychedelia, fringe culture, Dada, surrealism. A sense of dark humor is definitely a plus. No religious, romance, or criminally boring mainstream. No tedious formula fiction. No yuppie angst. Nothing saccharine." Receives 300 unsolicited ms/month. Accepts 4-6 ms/issue. Publishes ms 1 year after acceptance. Length: 100-1,500 words maximum. Publishes short shorts. Length: 100 words or longer. Sometimes critiques rejected mss and recommends other markets.

How to Contact: Send complete ms with or without cover letter. "Don't use a cover letter to brag about how great you are; if you're that good, I guarantee we'll have heard of you." Reports in 2-10 months on ms. SASE. Simultaneous and reprint submissions OK. Sample copy for $3 and 4 first-class stamps. Make checks out to "Hyacinth House Publications." Cash is also OK. Fiction guidelines for #10 SASE.
Payment/Terms: No payment. Acquires one-time rights.
Advice: "We're getting a lot of fiction that reads as if it were penned by the living dead. What we need, instead, is writing that is vigorous, unrepentant, and dynamically *alive*. We'd like to see *Brownbag* become more forceful and intense with every issue. Send us the strongest, most compelling material you've got. Keep the weak stuff at home. Short, tight stories always beat long, rambling ones. In fact, as we are nearly overstocked with longer fiction and are primarily interested in short shorts at present. International writers should try their best to obtain U.S. stamps for SASEs. Using IRCs will seriously delay response time. Also, we're receiving too many submissions with postage due. Despite the stacks of them we receive, we do not, under any circumstances, answer queries which arrive without SASE. A great deal of time and postage could be saved by writers if they would actually take the time to read market listings carefully. We receive material every day from people who claim to have seen our entries in this book, but who could not possibly have read them past the initial address."

THE BROWNSTONE REVIEW, (II), 331 16th St., #2, Brooklyn NY 11215. Fiction Editor: Laura Dawson. Magazine: 5½×8½; 60 pages; illustrations. Semiannually. Estab. 1995. Circ. 250.
Needs: Adventure, erotica, ethnic/multicultural, experimental, feminist, gay, historical, horror, humor/satire, lesbian, literary, mainstream/contemporary, mystery/suspense, regional, science fiction, senior citizen/retirement, sports, westerns. No romance, religious, children's stories or occult/gothic horror. Planning future special fiction issue or anthology. Receives 15 unsolicited mss/month. Accepts 3-6 mss/issue; 6-12 mss/year. Publishes ms 6-9 months after acceptance. Length: 1,000-2,000 words average; 250 words minimum; 10,000 words maximum. Publishes short shorts. Also publishes poetry. Sometimes critiques or comments on rejected ms.
How to Contact: Send complete ms with a cover letter. Should include list of publications. Reports in 3 months. Send SASE for reply, return of ms or send a disposable copy of ms. Simultaneous submissions OK.
Payment/Terms: Pays 2 contributor's copies. Acquires first North American serial rights.
Advice: "Revise, revise, revise . . . "

‡BRÚJULA/COMPASS, (I, II, IV), Latin American Writers Institute, % Hostos Community College, 500 Grand Concourse, Bronx NY 10451. (718)518-4195. Fax: (718)518-4294. Editor: Isaac Goldemberg. Tabloid: 10×14; 40 pages; 50 lb. bond paper; illustrations and photos. "*Brújula/Compass* is devoted exclusively to Latino writers living in the U.S. and writing in English and/or Spanish." Quarterly. Estab. 1988. Circ. 10,000.
Needs: Ethnic/multicultural, feminist, gay, humor/satire, lesbian, mainstream/contemporary, translations. Publishes annual special fiction issue or anthology. Receives 25 unsolicited mss/month. Accepts 3 mss/issue; 10-12 mss/year. Publishes ms 3 months after acceptance. Agented fiction 20%. Recently published work by Oscar Hijuelos, Julia Alvarez, Ariel Dorfman. Length: 3,000 words average. Publishes short shorts. Also publishes literary essays, literary criticism, poetry.
How to Contact: Send complete ms with a cover letter. Send SASE for reply, return of ms or send a disposable copy of ms. Simultaneous, reprint, electronic submissions OK. Sample copy free. Reviews novels and short story collections.
Payment/Terms: Pays 10 contributor's copies, free subscription of magazine. Acquires one-time rights.

BRUTARIAN, The Magazine That Dares to be Lame, (I, II), Odium Ent., P.O. Box 25222, Arlington VA 22202-9222. (703)308-9108. Editor: D.J. Salemi. Magazine: 8½×11; 84 pages; illustrations and photos. "Our theme is 'The World of Trash & Weirdness.' Quarterly. Estab. 1991. Circ. 3,000.
Needs: Erotica, experimental, fantasy, feminist, gay, horror, humor/satire, lesbian, literary, mainstream/contemporary, mystery/suspense (police procedural, private eye/hardboiled), psychic/supernatural/occult. Receives 15 unsolicited mss/month. Buys 1-2 mss/issue; 4-8 mss/year. Publishes ms 3 months after acceptance. Agented fiction 20%. Length: 2,000-3,000 words average; 500 words minimum; 5,000 words maximum. Publishes short shorts. Also publishes literary essays.
How to Contact: Send complete ms with a cover letter. Should include estimated word count and list of publications. Reports in 2 weeks on queries, 2 months on mss. Send SASE (or IRC) for reply, return of ms or send a disposable copy of ms. Simultaneous and reprint submissions OK. Sample copy for $5. Fiction guidelines for SAE and 1 first-class stamp. Reviews novels and short story collections.
Payment/Terms: Pays $20-$300 and 3 contributor's copies; additional copies for $2.
Terms: Pays on publication for first rights. Sends galleys to author.
Advice: "The beauty of the language, the depth of ideas make a manuscript stand out. Rewrite it several times."

‡BURNING LIGHT, (II), A Journal of Christian Literature, Burning Light Press, 98 Constitution Way, Franklin NJ 07416-2151. (201)209-0365. Editor: Carl Simmons. Magazine: 5½×8½; 32-48 pages; 50 lb. Nekoosa paper; 80 lb. classic laid cover; illustrations. "*Burning Light* publishes fiction, essays and poetry from a Christian perspective. It's worth noting, though, that we want Christians who write and not 'Christian writing'. No one's going to mistake us for *Christianity Today* or *Guideposts*, although hopefully *Kenyon Review*, et al. will come to mind before they catch on to our drift." Quarterly. Estab. 1993.

Needs: Condensed/excerpted novel, experimental, fantasy (children's, science), humor/satire, literary, religious/inspirational, science fiction (soft/sociological), serialized novel. Receives 10-12 unsolicited mss/month. Accepts 2-3 mss/issue; 8-10 mss/year. Publishes ms 1-9 months (4-6 months typical) after acceptance. Recently published work by Sandra Tucker-Maxwell, Diane Glancy, Jamie Parsley and Judith Dupree. Length: 1,500-2,000 words average; 10,000 words maximum. Publishes short shorts. Also publishes literary essays, poetry. Sometimes critiques or comments on rejected ms.

How to Contact: Send complete ms with a cover letter. Should include estimated word count, 3-4 sentence bio, list of publications. Reports in 3-4 weeks. Send SASE for reply, return of ms or send a disposable copy of ms. Simultaneous and electronic (WordPerfect, PageMaker preferably) submissions OK. Sample copy for $4. Fiction guidelines free. Reviews novels and short story collections.

Payment/Terms: Pays free subscription to magazine, 5-6 contributor's copies; additional copies for $2.50. Acquires all rights (negotiable).

Advice: "Make sure the writing's coming from you; don't write something because you think it's what a publisher wants."

‡BURNT ALUMINUM, (II), P.O. Box 3561, Mankato MN 56001. Editors: Jim Redmond and Brian Batt. Magazine: 8½×7; 60 pages. "*Burnt Aluminum* is a mainstream fiction magazine. We prefer realistic themes." Semiannually. Estab. 1995. Circ. 150.

Needs: Condensed/excerpted novel, literary, mainstream/contemporary. No horror, mystery or science fiction. Receives 10 unsolicited mss/month. Accepts 6-8 mss/issue; 12-16/year. Publishes ms 6 months after acceptance. Recently published work by Terry Davis and Roger Sheffer. No preferred length.

How to Contact: Send complete ms with a cover letter. Should include one-paragraph bio and list of publications with submission. Send SASE for reply, return of ms or send a disposable copy of ms. Simultaneous submissions OK. Sample copy for $4 and $1.50 postage.

Payment/Terms: Pays 2 contributor's copies. Acquires first North American serial rights.

Advice: "We prefer stories with strong characters and strong character development. Plot is secondary. We also prefer realistic fiction—like Ray Carver's or Richard Ford's—stories representative of life in today's world. We do not like anything related to fantasy or horror, or trivial writing."

‡BY THE WAYSIDE, (I), 5 West St., Wilmington MA 01887. Editor: Stephen Brown. Tabloid: 6 pages; plain bond. "*By the Wayside* is intended for those who enjoy P.G. Wodehouse, Robert Benchley and the Marx Brothers." Triannually. Estab. 1995. Circ. 100.

Needs: Humor/satire. Receives 15 unsolicited mss/month. Accepts 3 mss/issue; 10 mss/year. Publishes ms 3 months after acceptance. Recently published work by Boko Fittleworth and Louis Saccocea. Length: 800 words average; 100 words minimum; 1,100 words maximum. Publishes short shorts. Length: 800 words. Sometimes critiques or comments on rejected ms.

How to Contact: Send complete ms with a cover letter. Reports in 1-2 months. Send SASE for reply, return of ms or send a disposable copy of ms. Simultaneous submissions OK. Sample copy for $3, 7×10 or 8×11 SAE and 2 first-class stamps.

Payment/Terms: Pays 5 contributor's copies. Acquires one-time rights. Not copyrighted.

Advice: "I want to provide humor writers, particularly new ones, with an outlet for their work. Attitude is more important than ideas."

BYLINE, (I, II), Box 130596, Edmond OK 73013. (405)348-5591. Editor-in-Chief: Marcia Preston. Managing Editor: Kathryn Fanning. Monthly magazine "aimed at encouraging and motivating all writers toward success, with special information to help new writers." Estab. 1981.

  ● *Byline* is known as an excellent starting place for new writers and the payment for fiction has doubled. The magazine also sponsors the *Byline* Literary Awards listed in this book.

Needs: Literary, genre and general fiction. Receives 100-200 unsolicited fiction mss/month. Buys 1 ms/issue, 11 mss/year. Published work by Susan McKeague Karnes and Michael Bugeja; published many new writers within the last year. Length: 4,000 words maximum; 2,000 words minimum. Also publishes poetry.

How to Contact: Send complete ms with SASE. Simultaneous submissions OK, "if notified. For us, no cover letter is needed." Reports in 6-12 weeks. Publishes ms an average of 3 months after acceptance. Sample copy, guidelines and contest list for $4.

Payment/Terms: Pays $100 on acceptance and 2 contributor's copies for first North American rights.

Advice: "We're very open to new writers. Submit a well-written, professionally prepared ms with SASE. No erotica or senseless violence; otherwise, we'll consider most any theme. We also sponsor short story and poetry contests."

‡CAFE MAGAZINE, (II), 1223 Bomar St., Houston TX 77006. (713)523-3237. Editor: Jeff Troiano. Magazine: 8½×11; 40 pages; 20 lb. paper; 70 lb. cover; illustrations and photos. "*Cafe Magazine* publishes fiction, poetry and essays of contemporary style for an urban audience." Quarterly. Estab. 1995. Circ. 10,000.

Needs: Erotica, ethnic/multicultural, experimental, literary, mainstream/contemporary, translations. No science fiction, romance, mystery, fantasy, inspirational. Receives 50 unsolicited mss/month. Buys 4 mss/issue; 11 issues/year. Publishes ms 3 months after acceptance. Length: 1,000 words average; 1,500 words maximum. Publishes short shorts. Also publishes literary essays and poetry.

How to Contact: Send Complete ms with a cover letter. Should include short bio with submission. Reports in 3 months. Send SASE for reply, return of ms or send a disposable copy of ms. Simultaneous and electronic submissions OK. E-mail address: magazeen@aol.com. Sample copy for $2. Fiction guidelines for SASE.

Payment/Terms: Pays $25 on publication and 5 contributor's copies for one-time rights.

Advice: Sponsors contests for fiction writers and poets. Contests are advertised in the magazine.

CALLALOO, A Journal of African-American and African Arts and Letters, (I, II, IV), Dept. of English, 322 Bryan Hall, University of Virginia, Charlottesville VA 22903. (804)924-6637 Editor: Charles H. Rowell. Magazine: 7×10; 250 pages. Scholarly magazine. Quarterly. Plans special fiction issue in future. Estab. 1976. Circ. 1,500.

- One of the leading voices in African-American literature, *Callaloo* has received NEA literature grants. Work published in *Callaloo* received a 1994 Pushcart Prize anthology nomination and inclusion in *Best American Short Stories*.

Needs: Contemporary, ethnic (black culture), feminist, historical, humor/satire, literary, prose poem, regional, science fiction, serialized/excerpted novel, translations. Also publishes poetry and drama. Themes for 1996: Australian Aboriginal Literature; Dominican Arts and Letters. Acquires 3-5 mss/issue; 10-20 mss/year. Length: no restrictions. Recently published work by Chinua Achebe, Rita Dove, Reginald McKnight, Caryl Philips and John Edgar Wideman.

How to Contact: Submit complete ms in triplicate and cover letter with name, mailing address, e-mail address if possible and SASE. Reports on queries in 2 weeks; 3-4 months on mss. Previously published work accepted "occasionally." E-mail address: callaloo@virginia.edu. Sample copy for $8.

Payment/Terms: Pays in contributor's copies. Acquires all rights. Sends galleys to author.

Advice: "We strongly recommend looking at the journal before submitting."

CALLIOPE, (II, IV), Creative Writing Program, Roger Williams University, Bristol RI 02809. (401)254-3217. Coordinating Editor: Martha Christina. Magazine: 5½×8½; 40-56 pages; 50 lb. offset paper; vellum or 60 lb. cover stock; occasional illustrations and photos. "We are an eclectic little magazine publishing contemporary poetry, fiction, and occasionally interviews." Semiannually. Estab. 1977. Circ. 400.

Needs: Literary, contemporary, experimental/innovative. "We try to include at least 2 pieces of fiction in each issue." Receives approximately 10-20 unsolicited fiction mss each month. Does not read mss mid-March to mid-August. Published new writers within the last year. Length: open. Publishes short shorts under 20 pages. Critiques rejected mss when there is time.

How to Contact: Send complete ms with SASE. Reports immediately or up to 3 months on mss. Sample copy for $2.

Payment/Terms: Pays 2 contributor's copies and one year's subscription beginning with following issue. Rights revert to author on publication.

Advice: "We are not interested in reading anyone's very first story. If the piece is good, it will be given careful consideration. Reading a sample copy of *Calliope* is recommended. Let the characters of the story tell their own story; we're very often (painfully) aware of the writer's presence. Episodic is fine; story need not (for our publication) have traditional beginning, middle and end."

CALYX, A Journal of Art & Literature by Women, (II), Calyx, Inc., P.O. Box B, Corvallis OR 97339. (503)753-9384. Managing Editor: Margarita Donnelly. Editorial Coordinator: Beverly McFarland. Editors: Linda Varsell Smith, Micki Reaman, Lois Cranston, Dorothy Mack and Yolanda Calvillo. Magazine: 7×8; 128 pages per single issue, 250 per double; 60 lb. coated matte stock paper; 10 pt. chrome coat cover; original art. Publishes prose, poetry, art, essays, interviews and critical and review articles. "*Calyx* editors are seeking innovative and literary works of exceptional quality." Biannually. Estab. 1976. Circ. 3,000.

- *Calyx* received an Honorable Mention for editorial content and First Place for cover design in 1993-94 from the American Literary Magazine Awards. An interview with Managing Editor Margarita Donnelly appears in the Small Press section of the 1995 edition of this book.

Needs: Accepts 4-8 prose mss/issue, 9-15 mss/year. Receives approximately 300 unsolicited fiction mss each month. Reads mss October 1-November 15; submit only during these periods. Published works by Beth Bosworth, Eleonora Chiavetta and Ellen Frye; published new writers within the last year. Length: 5,000 words maximum. Also publishes literary essays, literary criticism, poetry.

How to Contact: Send ms with SASE and bio. Simultaneous submissions OK. Reports in up to 6 months on mss. Publishes ms an average of 6 months after acceptance. Sample copy for $8 plus $1.50 postage. Guidelines available for SASE. Reviews novels, short story collections, poetry and essays.

Payment/Terms: "Combination of payment, free issues and 1 volume subscription."

Advice: Most mss are rejected because "the writers are not familiar with *Calyx*—writers should read *Calyx* and be familiar with the publication."

✤**CANADIAN AUTHOR, (IV)**, Canadian Author Association, 27 Doxsee Ave. N., Campbellford, Ontario K0L 1L0 Canada. (705)653-0323. Fax: (705)653-0593. Editor: Welwyn Wilton Katz. Fiction Editor: Bill Valgardson. Magazine: 8¼×10¾; 32 pages; glossy paper; illustrations and photos. "Features in-depth profiles and interviews with the people who influence Canadian literature, as well as articles on the craft and business of writing." Quarterly. Estab. 1919. Circ. 4,000.

Needs: Ethnic/multicultural, experimental, feminist, historical, humor/satire, literary, mainstream/contemporary, regional, senior citizen/retirement. *Must be by a Canadian author only.* Receives 50 unsolicited mss/month. Buys 1 mss/issue; 4 mss/year. Publishes ms 6-9 months after acceptance. Length: 3,000 words average; 2,000 words minimum; 3,000 words maximum. Also publishes literary essays and poetry.

How to Contact: Send complete ms with a cover letter. Should include estimated word count, short bio and list of publication. Reports in 3-5 months. Send SASE for reply, return of ms or send a disposable copy of ms. Simultaneous and reprint submissions OK. Sample copy for $6.50 (Canadian) and 9×12 SAE with 88¢ postage.

Payment/Terms: Pays $125 on publication for first rights. Usually sends galleys to author.

Advice: "We look for quality fiction. Read our magazine. Better yet, subscribe."

‡✤**CAPERS AWEIGH MAGAZINE, (I, II, IV), Cape Breton Poetry & Fiction**, Capers Aweigh Small Press, P.O. Box 96, Sydney, Nova Scotia B1P 6G9 Canada. (902)567-1449. Editor: John MacNeil. Magazine: 5×8; 80 pages; bond paper; Cornwall-coated cover. "*Capers Aweigh* publishes poetry and fiction of, by and for Cape Bretoners." Publication frequency varies. Estab. 1992. Circ. 500.

Needs: Adventure, ethnic/multicultural, fantasy, feminist, historical, humor/satire, literary, mainstream, contemporary, mystery/suspense, psychic/supernatural/occult, regional, science fiction. List of upcoming themes available for SASE. Receives 2 unsolicited mss/month. Buys 30 mss/issue. Publishes ms 9 months after acceptance. Recently published work by C. Fairn Kennedy and Shirley Kiju Kawi. Length: 2,500 words. Publishes short shorts. Also publishes literary criticism and poetry.

How to Contact: Query first. SASE for reply or send a disposable copy of ms. Electronic submissions OK (IBM). Sample copy for $3 and 6×10 SAE.

Payment/Terms: Pays free subscription to the magazine and 1 contributor's copy; additional copies for $3. Acquires first North American serial rights. Sends galleys to author. Sponsors contests only to Cape Bretoners fiction writers.

CAROLINA QUARTERLY, (II), Greenlaw Hall CB #3520, University of North Carolina, Chapel Hill NC 27599-3520. Editor-in-Chief: Amber Vogel. Fiction Editor: Brenda Thissen. Literary journal: 70-90 pages; illustrations. Triannually. Estab. 1948. Circ. 1,400.

● Work published in *Carolina Quarterly* has been selected for inclusion in *Best American Short Stories* and in *Short Stories from the South: The Year's Best.*

Needs: Literary. Receives 150-200 unsolicited fiction mss/month. Acquires 5-7 mss/issue; 15-20 mss/year. Publishes ms an average of 4 months after acceptance. Published work by Barry Hannah, Nanci Kincaid and Doris Betts. Published new writers within the last year. Length: 7,000 words maximum; no minimum. Also publishes short shorts, literary essays, poetry. Occasionally critiques rejected mss.

How to Contact: Send complete ms with cover letter and SASE to fiction editor. No simultaneous submissions. Reports in 2-4 months. Sample copy for $5; writer's guidelines for SASE.

Payment/Terms: Pays in contributor's copies for first rights.

✤**CAROUSEL LITERARY ARTS MAGAZINE, (I, II)**, % CSA, University Centre, University of Guelph, Guelph, Ontario N1G 2W1 Canada. Editor: Michael Carbert. Magazine: 5½×8½; 80 pages; illustrations and photographs. Annually. Estab. 1985. Circ. 500.

Needs: Contemporary, literary. Receives 5 unsolicited mss each month. Accepts 3-4 mss per issue. Publishes ms 1-2 months after acceptance. Published work by Leon Rooke, Clark Blaise, John Metcalf, Hugh Hood, Constance Rooke, Diane Schoemperlen. Length: 3,000 words maximum. Also publishes literary essays, interviews, poetry.

How to Contact: Send complete ms. Include bio with manuscript. No simultaneous submissions. Reports in 2 months on queries; 4 months on mss. SASE. Sample copy for $7 (Canadian).

Payment/Terms: Pays in contributor's copies. Acquires one-time rights.

Advice: "We want work which takes chances in style, point of view, characterization. We are open to new writers."

The maple leaf symbol before a listing indicates a Canadian publisher, magazine, conference or contest.

CAT'S EAR, Poetry and Fiction, (II), Galliard Group Publishers, P.O. Box 946, Kirksville MO 63501. (816)665-6009. Editor: Tim Rolands. Fiction Editors: Tim Rolands and Jack Holcomb. Magazine: 5½×8½; 64-96 pages; 50 lb. recycled paper; one cover photo. "Poety and fiction for intelligent readers, though not exclusively academic." Annually. Estab. 1992. Circ. 100.
Needs: Experimental, horror, humor/satire, literary, mainstream/contemporary, psychic/supernatural/occult, science fiction (soft/sociological). Plans special fiction issue or anthology in the future. Receives 3-5 unsolicited mss/month. Accepts 1 ms/issue. Published work by Alfred Schwaid. Length: 3,000 words average. Publishes short shorts. Length: 500 words.
How to Contact: Send complete ms with a cover letter. Should include estimated word count and list of publications (optional). Reports in 1 month on queries; 3 months on mss. Send SASE for reply, return of ms or send a disposable copy of ms. No simultaneous submissions. Electronic submissions OK. Sample copy for $5. Fiction guidelines for #10 SASE.
Payment/Terms: Pays 2 contributor's copies; additional copies for $4. Acquires first North American serial rights.

‡CAYO, A Chronicle of Life in the Keys, (II, IV), 7 Bay Dr., Key West FL 33040. (305)745-3304. Editor: Alyson Simmons. Magazine: 8½×11; 40-48 pages; gloss paper; 70 lb. cover stock; illustrations and photos. Magazine on Keys-related topics or by Keys authors. Quarterly. Estab. 1993. Circ. 500.
Needs: Condensed/excerpted novel, experimental, literary, regional. Receives 4-5 unsolicited mss/month. Accepts 2-3 mss/issue; 8-12 mss/year. Recently published work by Alma Bond and Robin Shanley. Length: 3,000 words average; 800 words minimum; 3,000 words maximum. Publishes short shorts. Also publishes literary essays and poetry. Often critiques or comments on rejected ms.
How to Contact: Send complete ms with a cover letter. Should include bio and list of publications with submission. Reports in 6 weeks on queries; 3 months on mss. Send SASE for reply, return of ms or send a disposable copy of ms. Simultaneous, reprint and electronic submissions OK. Sample copy for $4. Fiction guidelines for #10 SASE. Reviews novels.
Payment/Terms: Pays in contributor's copies. Acquires one-time rights.
Advice: "The story has to stand on its own and move the reader."

‡CENTURY (I), Century Publishing, Inc., P.O. Box 150510, Brooklyn NY 11215. Editor: Robert K.J. Killheffer. Magazine: 6×9; 144 pages. "*Century* is a magazine devoted to sophisticated, ambitious, speculative fiction, for readers of science fiction, fantasy and horror with a literary bent." Bimonthly. Estab. 1995. Circ. 5,000.
Needs: Experimental, fantasy (science), feminist, historical, horror, literary, mainstream/contemporary, psychic/supernatural/occult, science fiction. "Not interested in unsophisticated formulaic work—we want original, inventive material." Receives 300 unsolicited mss/month. Buys 10-12 mss/issue; 65 mss/year. Publishes mss 6 months after acceptance. Agented fiction 10%. Recently published work by Michael Bishop, Michael Randel, Jonathan Lethem. Length: 1,000 words minimum; 20,000 words maximum. Often critiques or comments on rejected ms.
How to Contact: Send complete ms with a cover letter. Should include estimated word count with list of publications. Reports in 2-3 months on mss. Send SASE for reply, return of ms or send a disposable copy of ms. Sample copy for $5.95, 7×10 SAE and 6 first-class stamps or 4 IRCs. Fiction guidelines free for #10 SAE and 1 first-class stamp or 1 IRC.
Payment/Terms: Pays $40 minimum; $1,200 maximum (4-6¢/word). Pays on acceptance for First World English and nonexclusive reprint rights. Sends galleys to author.
Advice: "Submit your best work. Write from the heart and gut and don't be concerned about genre boundaries—that is, don't aim your story at any particular category. Stories that have a really wonderful science fictional idea and are also written with a high degree of literary skill are very rare and I'd like more. Don't send me formulaic genre stuff."

CHAMINADE LITERARY REVIEW, (II, IV), Chaminade Press, 3140 Waialae Ave., Honolulu HI 96816. (808)735-4723. Editor: Loretta Petrie. Magazine: 6×9; 200 pages; 50 lb. white paper; 10 pt. C1S cover; photographs. "Multicultural, particularly Hawaii—poetry, fiction, artwork, criticism, photos, translations for all English-speaking internationals, but primarily Hawaii." Annually. Estab. 1987. Circ. 350.
Needs: Excerpted novel, ethnic, experimental, humor/satire, literary, religious/inspirational, translations. "We have published a variety including translations of Japanese writers, a fishing story set in Hawaii, fantasy set along the Amazon, but the major point is they are all 'literary.'" Receives 8 unsolicited mss/month. Acquires 5-8 mss/issue. Publishes ms 3-6 months after acceptance. "We haven't published short shorts yet, but would depending on quality." Sometimes critiques rejected ms.
How to Contact: Send complete ms with cover letter. Include short contributor's note. Reporting time depends on how long before deadlines of May 15 and December 15. SASE. Reprint submissions OK. Sample copy for $5.

Payment/Terms: Pays subscription to magazine. Acquires one-time rights.

Advice: "We look for good writing; appeal for Hawaii audience and writers everywhere. *CLR* was founded to give added exposure to Hawaii's writers, both here and on the mainland, and to juxtapose Hawaii writing with mainland and international work."

CHANGING MEN, Issues in Gender, Sex, & Politics, (II), Feminist Men's Publications, Inc., P.O. Box 3121, Kansas City KS 66103. (816)374-5969. Editor: Michael Biernbaum. Fiction Editor: Paul Matalucci. Magazine: 8½×11; 72 pages; bond paper; glossy card stock cover; illustrations and photographs. "Issues in gender, sex and politics for pro-feminist men (largely)." Biannual. Estab. 1979. Circ. 6,000.

● Focusing on the changing roles of men in our society, this publication has been nominated for the *Utne Reader* Alternative Press Award. Note they have a new address.

Needs: Contemporary, erotica, experimental, feminist, gay, humor/satire, lesbian, literary, sports. "Fiction should be pro-feminist or pro-gay/lesbian or deal with issues in leftist/radical politics." Upcoming themes: "Undoing Gender." Receives 5-10 unsolicited mss/month. Acquires 1-2 mss/issue. Publishes ms 6-12 months after acceptance. Published work by Bob Shelby, S. Kolankiewicz, Keith Kelly. Length: 1,500-2,000 words average; 1,000 words minimum; 4,000 words maximum. Sometimes critiques rejected mss.

How to Contact: Send complete ms with cover letter. Include brief description of work. Reports in 6 months on mss. SASE. "May consider" simultaneous submissions. Sample copy for $6. Fiction guidelines for SASE.

Payment/Terms: Pays contributor's copies and one-year subscription. Acquires first North American serial rights. Sends galleys to author.

Advice: "Fresh perspectives on feminist, gay/lesbian and political issues. Writer should ideally be familiar with our magazine, know our topics of interest and know what we have recently published to avoid excessive similarity/duplication."

THE CHARITON REVIEW, (II), Northeast Missouri State University, Kirksville MO 63501. (816)785-4499. Editor: Jim Barnes. Magazine: 6×9; 100+ pages; 60 lb. paper; 65 lb. cover stock; photographs on cover. "We demand only excellence in fiction and fiction translation for a general and college readership." Semiannually. Estab. 1975. Circ. 700.

Needs: Literary, contemporary and translations. Buys 3-5 mss/issue; 6-10 mss/year. Recently published work by Steve Heller, John Deming, Jean Anderson; published new writers within the last year. Length: 3,000-6,000 words. Also publishes literary essays, poetry. Critiques rejected mss when there is time.

How to Contact: Send complete ms with SASE. No book-length mss. No simultaneous submissions. Reports in less than 1 month on mss. Publishes ms an average of 6 months after acceptance. Sample copy for $5 with SASE. Reviews novels and short story collections.

Payment/Terms: Pays $5/page up to $50 maximum and contributor's copy on publication; additional copies for $5.50. Buys first North American serial rights; rights returned on request.

Advice: "Do not ask us for guidelines: the only guidelines are excellence in all matters. Write well and study the publication you are submitting to. We are interested only in the very best fiction and fiction translation. We are not interested in slick material. We do not read photocopies, dot-matrix, or carbon copies. Know the simple mechanics of submission—SASE, no paper clips, no odd-sized SASE, etc. Know the genre (short story, novella, etc.). Know the unwritten laws."

THE CHATTAHOOCHEE REVIEW, (II), DeKalb College, 2101 Womack Rd., Dunwoody GA 30338. (404)551-3166. Editor: Lamar York. Magazine: 6×9; 150 pages; 70 lb. paper; 80 lb. cover stock; illustrations; photographs. Quarterly. Estab. 1980. Circ. 1,250.

Needs: Literary, mainstream. No juvenile, romance, science fiction. Receives 500 unsolicited mss/month. Accepts 5 mss/issue. Published work by Leon Rooke, R.T. Smith; published new writers within the last year. Length: 2,500 words average. Also publishes literary essays, literary criticism, poetry. Sometimes critiques rejected mss.

How to Contact: Send complete ms with cover letter, which should include sufficient bio for notes on contributors' page. Reports in 2 months. SASE. May consider simultaneous submission "reluctantly." Sample copy for $5. Fiction and poetry guidelines available on request. Reviews novels and short story collections.

Payment/Terms: "Pays in contributor's copies. Acquires first rights.

Advice: "Arrange to read magazine before you submit to it." Known for publishing southern regional fiction.

CHELSEA, (II), Chelsea Associates, Inc., Box 773, Cooper Station, New York NY 10276. Editor: Richard Foerster. Magazine: 6×9; 185-235 pages; 60 lb. white paper; glossy cover stock; artwork; occasional photos. "We have no consistent theme except for single special issues. Otherwise, we use general material of an eclectic nature: poetry, prose, artwork, etc., for a sophisticated, literate audience interested in avant-garde literature and current writing, both national and international." Annually. Estab. 1958. Circ. 1,300.

● *Chelsea* sponsors the Chelsea Awards also listed in this book. Entries to that contest will also be considered for the magazine, but writers may submit directly to the magazine as well. The magazine was the recipient of a New York State Council for the Arts grant in 1993-94.

Needs: Literary, contemporary, poetry and translations. "No romance, divorce, racist, sexist material or I-hate-my-mother stories." Receives approximately 100 unsolicited fiction mss each month. Approximately 1% of fiction is agented. Recently published work by Paul West, Rosa Shand, Ha Jin and Peter LaSalle. Length: not over 25 printed pages. Publishes short shorts of 4-6 pages. Critiques rejected mss when there is time.

How to Contact: Send complete ms with with SASE and succinct cover letter with previous credits. No simultaneous submissions. Reports in 3 months on mss. Publishes ms within a year after acceptance. Sample copy for $5 plus postage.

Payment/Terms: Pays contributor's copies and $10 per printed page for first North American serial rights plus one-time non-exclusive reprint rights. Sponsors annual Chelsea Award, $500 (send SASE for guidelines).

Advice: "Familiarize yourself with issues of the magazine for character of contributions. Manuscripts should be legible, clearly typed, with minimal number of typographical errors and cross-outs, sufficient return postage. Most mss are rejected because they are conventional in theme and/or style, uninspired, contrived, etc. We see far too much of the amateurish love story or romance. Writers should say something that has never been said before or at least say something in a unique way. There is too much focus on instant fame and not enough attention to craft. Our audience is sophisticated, international, and eclectic and expects freshness and originality."

CHICAGO REVIEW, 5801 S. Kenwood Ave., Chicago IL 60637. Fiction Editors: Leigh Ann Duck, Lisa McNair and John Roberts. Magazine for a highly literate general audience: 6×9; 128 pages; offset white 60 lb. paper; illustrations; photos. Quarterly. Estab. 1946. Circ. 2,600.

Needs: Literary, contemporary and experimental. Accepts up to 5 mss/issue; 20 mss/year. Receives 80-100 unsolicited fiction mss each week. No preferred length, except will not accept book-length mss. Also publishes literary essays, literary criticism, poetry. Sometimes recommends other markets.

How to Contact: Send complete ms with cover letter. SASE. No simultaneous submissions. Reports in 4-5 months on mss. Sample copy for $5. Guidelines with SASE. Reviews novels and short story collections. Send books to Book Review Editor.

Payment/Terms: Pays 3 contributor's copies and subscription.

Advice: "We look with interest at fiction that addresses subjects inventively, work that steers clear of clichéd treatments of themes. We're always eager to read writing that experiments with language, whether it be with characters' viewpoints, tone or style."

‡THE CHILDREN'S JOURNAL, (I, II), The Morris Publishing Co., 1415 Hemlock St., Cayce SC 29033. (803)603-0430. Fiction Editor: Roy Morris. Magazine: 8½×11; 100 pages; 20 lb. bond paper; illustrations and photos. Publishes "stories for children of all ages." Monthly (may become quarterly). Estab. 1995. Circ. 5,200.

Needs: Children's/juvenile (5-12 years) and young adult/teen: adventure, experimental, fantasy (children's, science, sword and sorcery), literary, mainstream/contemporary, mystery/suspense, religious/inspirational, romance, science fiction, westerns (frontier, traditional). Upcoming themes: Halloween, Thanksgiving, back-to-school, Christmas, New Year. List of upcoming themes available for SASE. Publishes special fiction issues or anthologies. Receives "many" unsolicited mss. Publishes ms 1-12 months after acceptance. Recently published work by Cynthia L. Hansen, Anthony Hill, Kris Erickson, Edward Knowlton and Kathleen Neff. Length: 500-2,000 words average; 500 words minimum; 10,000 words maximum. Publishes short shorts. Also publishes literary essays and poetry. Sometimes critiques or comments on rejected mss.

How to Contact: Send complete ms with a cover letter. "Send a copy of your manuscript because, if accepted, your work will not be returned." Should include estimated word count with submission. Reports in 1-4 weeks. Send SASE for reply, return of ms or send a disposable copy of ms. Simultaneous submissions OK. Sample copy for $2.50, mss-sized envelope. Reviews novels and short story collections.

Payment/Terms: Pays in contributor's copies; additional copies for $2.50. Acquires first North American serial rights.

Advice: Sponsors Annual Children's Author/Poet Awards.

CHIRICÚ, (II, IV), Ballantine Hall 849, Indiana University, Bloomington IN 47405. Editorial Assistant: B. Santos. "We publish essays, translations, poetry, fiction, reviews, interviews and artwork (illustrations and photos) that are either by or about Latinos. We have no barriers on style, content or ideology, but would like to see well-written material. We accept manuscripts written in English, Spanish or Portuguese." Annually. Estab. 1976. Circ. 500.

Needs: Contemporary, ethnic, experimental, fantasy, feminist, humor/satire, literary, mainstream, prose poem, science fiction, serialized/excerpted novel, translations. Published new writers within the last year. Length: 7,000 words maximum; 3,000 words average. Occasionally critiques rejected mss.

How to Contact: Send complete ms with cover letter. "Include some personal information along with information about your story." SASE. No simultaneous submissions. Reports in 5 weeks. Publishes ms 6-12 months after acceptance. Sample copy for $5. Guidelines for #10 SASE.

Advice: "Realize that we are a Latino literary journal so, if you are not Latino, your work must reflect an interest in Latino issues or have a Latino focus." Mss rejected "because beginning writers force their language instead of writing from genuine sentiment, because of multiple grammatical errors and because writers think that naming a character José gives their story a Latino slant."

CHIRON REVIEW, (I, II), 522 E. South Ave., St. John KS 67576-2212. (316)549-3933. Editor: Michael Hathaway. Tabloid: 10×13; minimum 24 pages; newsprint; illustrations; photos. Publishes "all types of material, no particular theme; traditional and off-beat, no taboos." Estab. 1982. Circ. 1,200.
 • *Chiron Review* is known for publishing experimental and "sudden" fiction.
Needs: Contemporary, experimental, humor/satire, literary. Receives 20 mss/month. Accepts 1-3 ms/issue; 4-12 mss/year. Publishes ms within 6-18 months of acceptance. Length: 3,500 words preferred. Publishes short shorts. Sometimes recommends other markets to writers of rejected mss.
How to Contact: Query. Reports in 6-8 weeks. SASE. No simultaneous submissions. Sample copy for $4 ($8 overseas). Fiction guidelines for #10 SASE.
Payment/Terms: Pays 1 contributor's copy; extra copies at 50% discount. Acquires first rights.

❦**CHRISTIAN COURIER, (II, IV)**, Calvinist Contact Publishing Limited, Unit 4, 261 Martindale Rd., St. Catharines, Ontario L2W 1A1 Canada. (905)682-8311. Fax: (905)682-8313. Editor: Bert Witvoet. Tabloid: 11½×14; 20 pages; newsprint; illustrations and photos. Weekly. Estab. 1945. Circ. 5,000.
Needs: Adventure, children's/juvenile (10-12 years), historical, religious/inspirational, senior citizen/retirement, sports and translations. No "sentimental 'religious' stuff; superficial moralizing." Receives 5-10 unsolicited mss/month. Buys 12 mss/year. Does not read mss from the end of July to early August. Publishes ms within a month after acceptance. Length: 1,200 words average; no minimum; 1,400 words maximum. Publishes short shorts. Length 500 words. Also publishes literary essays (if not too technical), literary criticism and poetry. Always critiques or comments on rejected ms.
How to Contact: Send complete ms with a cover letter. Should include word count and bio (100 words maximum). Reports in 3 weeks on queries; 4-6 weeks on mss. Send a disposable copy of ms. Simultaneous, reprint and electronic submissions OK. Sample copy free. Fiction guidelines for SASE. Reviews novels and short story collections.
Payment/Terms: Pays $25-100 on publication and 1 contributor's copy (on request). Buys one-time rights.
Advice: Looks for work "geared to a Christian audience but reflecting the real world, real dilemmas, without pat resolutions—written in an engaging, clear manner."

CHRYSALIS READER, Journal of the Swedenborg Foundation, (II), (formerly *Chrysalis*), The Swedenborg Foundation, P.O. Box 549, West Chester PA 19381-0549. (610)430-3222. Send mss to: Rt. 1, Box 184, Dillwyn VA 23936. (804)983-3021. Editor: Carol S. Lawson. Fiction Editor: Phoebe Loughrey. Book series: 7½×10; 192 pages; archival paper; coated cover stock; illustrations; photos. "A literary magazine centered around one theme per issue. Publishes fiction, essays and poetry for intellectually curious readers interested in spiritual topics." Biannually. Estab. 1985. Circ. 3,000.
 • *Chrysalis Reader* has more than doubled its pages, allowing more room for fiction.
Needs: Adventure (leading to insight), contemporary, experimental, historical, literary, mainstream, mystery/suspense, science fiction, spiritual, sports. No religious, juvenile, preschool. Upcoming themes: "The Good Life" (Summer 1996) and "Symbols" (Winter 1996). Receives 60 mss/month. Buys 6-7 mss/issue; 18 mss/year. Publishes ms within 1 year of acceptance. Published work by Robert Bly, Larry Dossey, John Hitchcock, Betty Bone Schiess and Barbara Marx Hubbard. Length: 2,000 words minimum; 3,500 words maximum. Also publishes literary essays, literary criticism, chapters of novels, poetry. Sometimes critiques rejected mss and recommends other markets.
How to Contact: Query first and send SASE for guidelines. Reports in 2 months. SASE. No simultaneous, reprinted or in-press material. Sample copy for $5. Fiction guidelines for #10 SASE.
Payment/Terms: Pays $75-250 and 5 contributor's copies on publication for one-time rights. Sends galleys to author.
Advice: Looking for "1. *Quality*; 2. appeal for our audience; 3. relevance to/illumination of an issue's theme."

CICADA, (II, IV), 329 "E" St., Bakersfield CA 93304. (805)323-4064. Editor: Frederick A. Raborg, Jr. Magazine: 5½×8¼; 24 pages; matte cover stock; illustrations and photos. "Oriental poetry and fiction related to the Orient for general readership and haiku enthusiasts." Quarterly. Estab. 1985. Circ. 600.
 • *Cicada* is edited by Frederick A. Raborg, Jr., who is also editor of *Amelia* and *SPSM&H* listed in this book. See also the listing for the *Amelia* Magazine Awards.
Needs: *All with Oriental slant:* Adventure, contemporary, erotica, ethnic, experimental, fantasy, feminist, historical (general), horror, humor/satire, lesbian, literary, mainstream, mystery/suspense, psychic/supernatural/occult, regional, contemporary romance, historical romance, young adult romance, science fiction, senior citizen/retirement and translations. "We look for strong fiction with Oriental (especially Japanese) content or flavor. Stories need not have 'happy' endings, and we are open to the experimental and/or avant-garde. Erotica is fine (the Japanese love their erotica); pornography, no." Receives 30 unsolicited mss/month. Buys 1 ms/issue; 4 mss/year. Publishes ms 6 months to 1 year after acceptance. Agented fiction 5%. Published work by Gilbert Garand, Frank Holland and Jim Mastro. Length: 2,000 words average; 500 words minimum;

3,000 words maximum. Critiques rejected ms when appropriate. Also publishes poetry.

How to Contact: Send complete ms with cover letter. Include Social Security number and appropriate information about the writer in relationship to the Orient. Reports in 2 weeks on queries; 3 months on mss (if seriously considered). SASE. Sample copy for $4.95. Fiction guidelines for #10 SASE.

Payment/Terms: Pays $10-25 and contributor's copies on publication for first North American serial rights; charges for additional copies. $5 kill fee.

Advice: Looks for "excellence and appropriate storyline. Strong characterization and knowledge of the Orient are musts. Neatness counts high on my list for first impressions. A writer should demonstrate a high degree of professionalism."

CIMARRON REVIEW, (II), Oklahoma State University, 205 Morrill, Stillwater OK 74078-0135. (405)744-9476. Editor: Edward P. Walkiewicz. Magazine: 6×9; 100 pages. "Poetry and fiction on contemporary themes; personal essay on contemporary issues that cope with life in the 20th century, for educated literary readers. We work hard to reflect quality." Quarterly. Estab. 1967. Circ. 500.

Needs: Literary and contemporary. No collegiate reminiscences or juvenilia. Buys 6-7 mss/issue, 24-28 mss/year. Published works by Peter Makuck, Mary Lee Settle, W. D. Wetherell, John Timmerman; published new writers within the last year. Also publishes literary essays, literary criticism, poetry.

How to Contact: Send complete ms with SASE. "Short cover letters are appropriate but not essential, except for providing *CR* with the most recent mailing address available." No simultaneous submissions. Reports in 3 months on mss. Publishes ms within 1 year after acceptance. Sample copy with SASE and $3. Reviews novels, short story collections, and poetry collections.

Payment/Terms: Pays one-year subscription to author, plus $50 for each prose piece and $15 for each poem. Buys all rights on publication. "Permission to reprint granted freely."

Advice: "Short fiction is a genre uniquely suited to the modern world. *CR* seeks an individual, innovative style that focuses on contemporary themes."

‡THE CIMMERIAN-JOURNAL, (I, II), Tales of the Weird and Unusual, 622 Reeds Bridge Rd., Conway MA 01341. (413)369-4341. Editor: Robert B. Heath. Magazine: 7×8½; 60 pages; 24 lb. paper; 24 lb. color cover; illustrations; b&w photos. "The purpose of *The Cimmerian Journal* is to explore the weird and unusual, the darkness of the human condition via several genres, but we don't want to just horrify or shock. The reader should be led to thought and/or self-examination, even angered; amused while being entertained." Bimonthly. Estab. 1990. Circ. 125.

Needs: Condensed/excerpted novel, ethnic/multicultural, fantasy (science), horror, literary, mystery/suspense, psychic/supernatural, science fiction, serialized novel, translations. "No explicit sex, graphic violence, nothing advocating anti-religion, racism, violence, especially against women and children, although these themes may be explored or depicted in a responsible manner." Receives 20 unsolicited mss/month. Buys 10-15 mss/issue. Publishes ms 4-6 months after acceptance. Recently published Ken Jaworowski, Louise Dragon, Deborah Hunt and Eugene C. Flynn. Length: 2,600 words average; 250 words minimum; 6-7,000 words maximum. Publishes short shorts. Also publishes literary essays, literary criticism, poetry. Often critiques or comments on rejected ms.

How to Contact: Send complete ms with a cover letter. Should include estimated word count, short paragraph bio and list of publications (brief). "Prefer a familiar, friendly, non-technical bio that reveals writer." Reports in 2 weeks on queries; 4-6 weeks on mss. SASE for reply. Simultaneous, reprint and electronic submissions (MAC preferred, query about others) OK. E-mail address: robert.heath@the-spa.com. Sample copy for $3, 9×12 SAE and 4 first-class stamps. Fiction guidelines free for #10 SASE.

Payment/Terms: Pays 5 contributor's copies; additional copies for $2. Acquires one-time rights.

Advice: "I want to be fascinated, puzzled, challenged. A story that makes me think, makes me question, that affects me for a while after I've read it will be accepted. Explore the weirdness, the darkness of the human condition and make the reader sit up and take notice—and think. Let the writing be transparent to the story. Be simple, honest, clear, precise, neat and watch spelling and punctuation. But, even with bad grammar, if your story can reach out from the page with freedom and clarity, that's what's important. Avoid sex, violence, vulgarity and explicitness of language. Shock without being obvious and horrify without graphic descriptions of gore. Make the reader sympathize with your characters so that what happens to them is important. Make the reader feel what your characters feel. Above all, make us think!"

♣THE CLAREMONT REVIEW, The Contemporary Magazine of Young Adult Writers, (I, IV), The Claremont Review Publishers, 4980 Wesley Rd., Victoria, British Columbia V8Y 1Y9 Canada. (604)658-5221. Fax: (604)658-5387. Editors: Terence Young and Bill Stenson. Magazine: 6×9; 110-120 pages; book paper; soft gloss cover; b&w illustrations. "We are dedicated to publishing emerging young writers aged 13-19 from anywhere in the English-speaking world, but primarily Canada and the U.S." Biannually. Estab. 1992. Circ. 350.

Needs: Young adult/teen ("their writing, not writing for them"). Plans special fiction issue or anthology. Receives 10-12 unsolicited mss/month. Accepts 10-12 mss/issue; 20-24 mss/year. Publishes ms 3 months after acceptance. Length: 1,500-3,000 words preferred; 5,000 words maximum. Publishes short shorts. Also publishes prose poetry. Always comments on rejected mss.

How to Contact: Send complete ms with cover letter. Include 2-line bio, list of publications and SASE. Reports in 6 weeks-3 months. Simultaneous submissions OK. E-mail address: aurora@islandnet.com. Sample copy for $5 with 6x9 SAE and $2 Canadian postage. Guidelines free with SAE.

Payment/Terms: Pays 1 contributor's copy on publication for first North American and one-time rights. Additional copies for $6.

Advice: Looking for "good concrete narratives with credible dialogue and solid use of original detail. It must be unique, honest and a glimpse of some truth. Send an error-free final draft with a short covering letter and bio; please, read us first to see what we publish."

‡THE CLIMBING ART, (II, IV), Fairfield Communications, P.O. Box 1378, Laporte CO 80535. (303)221-9210. (800)243-2671. Editor: Scott Titterington. Fiction Editor: Christiana Langenberg. Magazine: 5×7; 150 pages; illustrations and photos. "*The Climbing Art* publishes literature, poetry and art for and about the spirit of climbing." Semiannually. Estab. 1986. Circ. 800.

Needs: Adventure, condensed/excerpted novel, ethnic/multicultural, experimental, fantasy, historical, literary, mainstream/contemporary, mystery/suspense, regional, science fiction, sports. "No religious, rhyming, or non-climbing related." Receives 40 unsolicited mss/month. Buys 2-5 mss/issue; 4-10 mss/year. Publishes ms up to 1 year after acceptance. Agented fiction 10%. Length: 500 words minimum; 10,000 words maximum. Publishes short shorts. Also publishes literary essays. Often critiqes or comments on rejected ms.

How to Contact: Send compelete ms with a cover letter. Should include estimated word count, short paragraph bio and list of publications. Reports in 2 weeks on queries; 2 weeks-2 months on mss. SASE. Simultaneous submissions OK. E-mail address: clang@iastate.edu. Sample copy $10. Reviews novels and short story collections.

Payment/Terms: Pays free subscription and 2 contributor's copies; additional copies for $4. Acquires one-time rights.

Advice: Sometimes sponsors contests. "Read several issues first and make certain the material is related to climbing and the spirit of climbing. We have not seen enough literary excellence. Avoid sending crap—especially handwritten with no SASE."

CLOCKWATCH REVIEW, A Journal of the Arts, (II), Dept. of English, Illinois Wesleyan University, Bloomington IL 61702. (309)556-3352. Editor: James Plath. Magazine: 5½×8½; 64-80 pages; coated stock paper; glossy cover stock; illustrations; photos. "We publish stories which are *literary* as well as alive, colorful, enjoyable—stories which linger like shadows," for a general audience. Semiannually. Estab. 1983. Circ. 1,500.

• *Clockwatch Review* is planning a western issue and would like to see more high-quality genre fiction.

Needs: Contemporary, experimental, humor/satire, literary, mainstream, prose poem and regional. Receives 50-60 unsolicited mss/month. Accepts 2 mss/issue; 4 mss/year. Published work by Ellen Hunnicutt, Beth Brandt, Charlotte Mandel; published new writers within the last year. Length: 2,500 words average; 1,200 words minimum; 4,000 words maximum. Occasionally critiques rejected mss if requested.

How to Contact: Send complete ms. Reports in 6-12 months. SASE. Publishes ms 3-12 months after acceptance. Sample copy for $4.

Payment/Terms: Pays 3 contributor's copies and small cash stipend (currently $50, but may vary) for first serial rights.

Advice: "*Clockwatch* has always tried to expand the audience for quality contemporary poetry and fiction by publishing a highly visual magazine that is thin enough to invite reading. We've included interviews with popular musicians and artists in order to further interest a general, as well as academic, public and show the interrelationship of the arts. We're looking for high-quality literary fiction that brings something fresh to the page—whether in imagery, language, voice or character. Give us characters with meat on their bones, colorful but not clichéd; give us natural plots, not contrived or melodramatic. Above all, give us your *best* work."

COCHRAN'S CORNER, (I), 1003 Tyler Court, Waldorf MD 20602. (210)659-5062. Editor: Jeanie Saunders. Magazine: 5½×8; 52 pages. "We publish fiction, nonfiction and poetry. Our only requirement is no strong language." For a "family" audience. Quarterly. Estab. 1986. Circ. 500.

Needs: Adventure, children's/juvenile, historical, horror, humor/satire, mystery/suspense, religious/inspirational, romance, science fiction and young adult/teen (10-18 years). "Mss must be free from language you wouldn't want your/our children to read." Plans a special fiction issue. Receives 50 mss/month. Accepts 4 mss/issue; 8 mss/year. Publishes ms by the next issue after acceptance. Published work by Juni Dunkin, Ruth Cox Anderson and Becky Knight. Length: 500 words preferred; 300 words minimum; 1,000 words maximum. Also publishes literary essays, literary criticism, poetry.

How to Contact: "Right now we are forced to limit acceptance to *subscribers only*." Send complete ms with cover letter. Reports in 3 weeks on queries; 6-8 weeks on mss. SASE for manuscript. Simultaneous and reprint submissions OK. Sample copy for $5, 9×12 SAE and 90¢ postage. Fiction guidelines for #10 SASE.

Payment/Terms: Pays in contributor's copies. Acquires one-time rights.

Advice: "I feel the quality of fiction is getting better. The public is demanding a good read, instead of having sex or violence carry the story. I predict that fiction has a good future. We like to print the story as the writer submits it if possible. This way writers can compare their work with their peers and take the necessary steps to improve and go on to sell to bigger magazines. Stories from the heart desire a place to be published. We try to fill that need.''

‡COFFEEHOUSE, "A Little Literary Magazine", (II), P.O. Box 77, Berthoud CO 80513. (970)532-3118. Editor: Ray Foreman. Magazine: 5½ × 8½; 20 pages; 20lb. paper and cover. "Our audience consists primarily of writers and their friends. We publish only short-shorts of 1,000 words or less with tight writing free of obscurity dealing with the 'human condition.' " Bimonthly. Estab. 1990. Circ. 600.
Needs: Stories that "deal with people's lives and situations with strong images." Receives 20 unsolicited mss/month. Accepts 3-5 mss/issue; 30 mss/year. Publishes ms 2-4 months after acceptance. Length: 700 words average; 1,000 words maximum. Publishes short shorts. Length: 800-1,000 words. Also publishes literary essays, literary criticism, poetry. Sometimes critiques or comments on rejected ms.
How to Contact: Send complete ms with a cover letter. Reports in 2-3 weeks on mss. SASE or send a disposable copy of the ms. Simultaneous submissions OK. Sample copy for $1 and #10 SAE. Fiction guidelines free for SASE.
Payment/Terms: No payment. Charges $5 for 14 copies of magazine. Acquires one-time rights.
Advice: Looks for "a strong opening and writing quality geared to readers who are writers rather than those who have no interest or recognition of quality. Know the difference between fine writing and cutesy high school composition class work. Learn that difference by reading good collections of short stories. If something rubs off, you'll write good work. If not, keep at it until it does. Short stories are the hardest fiction to write.''

COLD-DRILL MAGAZINE, (IV), English Dept., Boise State University, 1910 University Dr., Boise ID 83725. (208)385-1999. Editor: Tom Trusky. Magazine: box format; various perfect and non-perfect bound inserts; illustrations and photos. Material submitted *must be by Idaho authors or deal with Idaho*. For adult audiences. Annually. Estab. 1970. Circ. 500.
  • *Cold-Drill* has submissions dictate theme. *Factsheet Five* called *Cold-Drill* "by far the most creatively produced literary magazine."
Needs: "For our 1995-96 issue we are looking for poems, short stories, nonfiction, essays, camera-ready artwork. We want material about the sweat and frustration, anger and satisfaction of a day's work." Length: determined by submissions.
How to Contact: Query first. SASE.
Payment/Terms: Pays in contributor's copies. Acquires first rights.

COLLAGES AND BRICOLAGES, The Journal of International Writing, (II), P.O. Box 86, Clarion PA 16214. (814)226-5799. Editor: Marie-José Fortis. Magazine: 8½ × 11; 100-150 pages; illustrations. "The theme, if there is any, is international cultures, with socio-political undertones. The magazine may include essays, short stories, short plays, poems that show innovative promise." Annually. Estab. 1987.
  • This year the editor is focusing on "Beckett, Ionesco and absurdism."
Needs: Contemporary, ethnic, experimental, feminist, humor/satire, literary, philosophical works. "Also symbolist, surrealist b&w designs/illustrations are welcome." Upcoming themes: "George Sand" (1995) (tentative). Receives about 30 unsolicited fiction mss/month. Publishes ms 6-9 months after acceptance. Recently published work by Marilou Awiakta, Rosette Lamont, Eric Basso, Greg Boyd; published new writers within the last year. Publishes short shorts. Also publishes literary essays, literary criticism, poetry. Sometimes critiques rejected ms.
How to Contact: Send complete ms with cover letter that includes a short bio. Reports in 1-3 months. SASE. Simultaneous submissions OK. Sample copy for $6. Reviews novels and short story collections. "How often and how many per issue depends on reviewers available."
Payment/Terms: Pays 2 contributor's copies. Acquires first rights. Rights revert to author after publication.
Advice: "This is a fin-de-siécle—also the end of a millenium—with chaos, conflicts, cruelty, and confusion. The writer should be aware of these elements, and let them enter her every pore. Yet, paradoxically, she should write as if nothing else mattered. On a more pedestrian level: *always include* a SASE that is no smaller than a business envelope."

COLUMBIA: A MAGAZINE OF POETRY & PROSE, (II), 404 Dodge Hall, Columbia University, New York NY 10027. (212)854-4391. Editor-in-Chief: Mike McGreger. Fiction Editors: Ken Foster and Justin Peacock. Editors change each year. Magazine: 5¼ × 8¼; approximately 200 pages; coated cover stock; illustrations, photos. "We accept short stories, novel excerpts, translations, interviews, nonfiction and poetry." Biannually.
Needs: Literary and translations. Accepts 3-10 mss/issue. Receives approximately 125 unsolicited fiction mss each month. Does not read mss May 1 to August 31. Recently published work by Julian Barnes, Rick Moody, Antonya Nelson, Jennifer Egan and Russell Banks; published 5-8 unpublished writers within the year. Length: 20 pages maximum. Publishes short shorts.
How to Contact: Send complete ms with SASE. Accepts computer printout submissions. Reports in 1-2 months. Sample copy for $5.

Payment/Terms: Offers yearly contest with guest editors.

Advice: "Finding publishable work is surprisingly challenging. Often good writers submit work that is below standard, not polished or in some cases too long. We'd rather publish just a few good pieces than compromise the issue with work that doesn't excite us."

COMMON LIVES/LESBIAN LIVES, A Lesbian Quarterly, (IV), Box 1553, Iowa City IA 52244. "*CL/LL* seeks to document the experiences and thoughts of lesbians for lesbian audience." Magazine: 5×8½; 112-128 pages; illustrations; photos. Quarterly.

Needs: *All pertaining to lesbian culture*: Adventure, comics, contemporary, erotica, ethnic, experimental, fantasy, feminist, historical (general), humor/satire, juvenile, lesbian, prose poem, psychic/supernatural/occult, regional, romance, science fiction, senior citizen/retirement, suspense/mystery, western and young adult/teen. Length: 4-10 pages. Also publishes literary essays, literary criticism, poetry. Occasionally critiques rejected mss.

How to Contact: Send complete ms with cover letter; a short bio sketch is required. Reports in 4 months. SASE. Publishes ms up to 4 months after acceptance. Published "many" new writers within the last year. Sample copy for $5. Reviews novels and short story collections.

Payment/Terms: Pays 2 contributor's copies.

Advice: "Readers relate stories to their lives; fiction is an interesting and accessible way for lesbians to document their experience and express their opinions."

COMMUNITIES: JOURNAL OF COOPERATION, (I), 1118 Round Butte Dr., Ft. Collins CO 80524. (303)224-9080. Business Manager: Laird Schaub. Editors change each issue. "Features articles on intentional communities, urban collectives, rural communes," politics, health, alternative culture and workplace democracy for people involved in cooperative ventures." Quarterly. Estab. 1973. Circ. 4,000.

Needs: "Utopian" stories, science fiction (soft/sociological). "Stories set in intentional communities or cooperatively-run organizations." Accepts "maybe 4 manuscripts per year (would do more if we got them)." Length: 1,000 words minimum; 5,000 words maximum. Generally critiques rejected mss.

How to Contact: Query first or send complete ms. Reports in 1 month on queries; 6 weeks on mss. Simultaneous and previously published submissions OK. Sample copy for $5.50.

Payment/Terms: Pays 1 year subscription and 3 contributor's copies. Acquires one-time rights.

Advice: "We receive too many articles and stories which are completely off topic, by people who have no idea what we do and have never seen the magazine."

A COMPANION IN ZEOR, (I, II, IV), 307 Ashland Ave., Egg Harbor Township NJ 08234. Editor: Karen Litman. Fanzine: 8½×11; 60 pages; "letter" paper; heavy blue cover; b&w line illustrations; occasional b&w photographs. Publishes science fiction based on the various Universe creations of Jacqueline Lichtenberg. Occasional features on Star Trek, and other interests, convention reports, reviews of movies and books, recordings, etc. Published irregularly. Estab. 1978. Circ. 300.

- *Companion in Zeor* is one of two fanzines devoted to the work and characters of Jacqueline Lichtenberg. Lichtenberg's work includes several future world, alien and group culture novels and series including the Sime/Gen Series and The Dushau trilogy. She's also penned two books on her own vampire character and she co-authored *Star Trek Lives*. Note the magazine's new address.

Needs: Fantasy, humor/satire, prose poem, science fiction. "No vicious satire. Nothing X-rated. Homosexuality prohibited unless *essential* in story. We run a clean publication that anyone should be able to read without fear." Occasionally receives one manuscript a month. Accepts "as much as can afford to print." Publication of an accepted ms "can take years, due to limit of finances available for publication." Occasionally critiques rejected mss and recommends other markets.

How to Contact: Query first or send complete ms with cover letter. "Prefer cover letters about any writing experience prior, or related interests toward writing aims." Reports in 1 month. SASE. Simultaneous submissions OK. Sample copy price depends on individual circumstances. Fiction guidelines for #10 SASE. "I write individual letters to all queries. No form letter at present." SASE for guidelines required. Reviews science fiction/fantasy collections or titles.

Payment/Terms: Pays in contributor's copies. Acquires first rights.

Advice: "We take fiction based on any and all of Jacqueline Lichtenberg's published novels. The contributor should be familiar with these works before contributing material to my fanzine. Also accepts manuscripts on cassette from visually handicapped if submitted. 'Zines also on tape for those individuals."

✦COMPENIONS, The Quarterly Publication of the Stratford Writer's Workshop, (I), P.O. Box 2511, St. Marys, Ontario N4X1A3 Canada. (519)284-1675. Contact: Marco Balestrin. Magazine: 8½×11; 12-20 pages; bond paper; card stock cover; computer graphics illustrations. "We have expanded the mandate of our magazine to include the work of outside writers. We would like to see serious beginning writers who give original twists to the old forms." Quarterly. Estab. 1983. Circ. 25 issues to members and contributors.

- See listings for other writers clubs and organizations across the U.S. and Canada in the Organizations and Resources section.

Needs: Adventure, ethnic/multicultural, experimental, fantasy (science), feminist, historical, horror, humor/satire, literary, mainstream/contemporary, mystery/suspense (amateur sleuth, private eye/hard-boiled, romantic suspense), psychic/supernatural/occult, regional, romance (contemporary, gothic), science fiction (hard science, soft/sociological), translations, westerns (frontier, traditional). "No pornography, ultra-religious or 'cutesy' stuff." Upcoming themes: "East" (deadline February 1, 1996); "West" (deadline May 1, 1996); "North" (deadline August 1, 1996); "South" (deadline November 1, 1996). Receives 3 unsolicited mss/month. Accepts 5 mss/issue; 15-20 mss/year. Publishes ms 3 months after acceptance. Recently published work by Ray Margulies and Jerry Penner. Length: 800-1,000 words preferred; 100 words minimum; 3,000 words maximum. Publishes short shorts. Length: 300-400 words preferred. Also publishes literary essays and poetry. Often critiques or comments on rejected mss.
How to Contact: *Charges $3.50 reading fee per manuscript* (up to 3,000 words). Send complete ms with a cover letter. Should include estimated word count, 1-page bio and "anything unusual that may be of interest." Reports in 2 months on queries; 3 months on mss. Send SASE for reply, return of ms or send a disposable copy of ms. Simultaneous, reprint and electronic submissions OK. Sample copy for $4, 9×12 SAE and 2 IRCs (if outside Canada). (Make cheques out to "Stratford Writer's Workshop.")
Payment/Terms: Pays 2 contributor's copies; additional copies for $4 and 2 IRCs. Acquires one-time rights.
Advice: "A manuscript must be compelling. We will forgive rawness if it exposes us to a new slant on an old theme."

CONCHO RIVER REVIEW, (I, II, IV), Fort Concho Museum Press, 630 S. Oakes, San Angelo TX 76903. Magazine: 6½×9; 100-125 pages; 60 lb. Ardor offset paper; Classic Laid Color cover stock; b&w drawings. "We publish any fiction of high quality—no thematic specialties—contributors must be residents of Texas or the Southwest generally." Semiannually. Estab. 1987. Circ. 300.
• The magazine is considering featuring "guest editors" with each issue, but manuscripts should still be sent to the editor, Mary Ellen Hartje.
Needs: Contemporary, ethnic, historical, humor/satire, literary, regional and western. No erotica; no science fiction. Receives 10-15 unsolicited mss/month. Accepts 3-6 mss/issue; 8-10 mss/year. Publishes ms 4 months after acceptance. Published work by Robert Flynn, Clay Reynolds, Roland Sodowsky. Length: 3,500 words average; 1,500 words minimum; 5,000 words maximum. Also publishes literary essays, poetry. Sometimes critiques rejected mss and recommends other markets.
How to Contact: *Send submissions to Mary Ellen Hartje, English Dept., Angelo State University, San Angelo, TX 76909.* Send complete ms with SASE; cover letter optional. Reports in 3 weeks on queries; 3-8 weeks on mss. SASE for ms. Simultaneous submissions OK (if noted). Sample copy for $4. Fiction guidelines for #10 SASE. Reviews novels and short story collections. Books to be reviewed should also be sent to Mary Ellen Hartje.
Payment/Terms: Pays in contributor's copies; $4 charge for extras. Acquires first rights.
Advice: "We prefer a clear sense of conflict, strong characterization and effective dialogue."

‡CONDUIT, (II), Conduit, Inc., 3142 Lyndale Ave. S., #6, Minneapolis MN 55408. (612)822-8434. Editor: William Waltz. Fiction Editor: Brett Astor. Magazine: 4¼×11; 40 pages; card stock cover; illustrations and photos. "*Conduit* is primarily a poetry magazine, but we're eager to include lively fiction verbally speaking and otherwise. *Conduit* publishes work that is intelligent, serious, irreverent and daring." Quarterly. Estab. 1993. Circ. 500.
Needs: Experimental, literary, translations. Upcoming themes: "Remembering Generation X"; "Life: The Big Cliché". Receives 25 unsolicited mss/month. Buys 1-2 mss/issue; 4-8 mss/year. Publishes ms 3-6 months after acceptance. Length: 1,500-2,000 words maximum. Publishes short shorts. Also publishes poetry. Sometimes critiques or comments on rejected ms.
How to Contact: Send complete ms with a cover letter. Reports in 2 months. Send SASE for reply, return of ms or send a disposable copy of ms. Electronic submissions OK. E-mail address: conduit47@aol.com. Sample copy for $3, 4¼×11 SAE and 78¢ postage. Fiction guidelines free for SASE. Reviews novels or short story collections.
Payment/Terms: Pays 3 contributor's copies. Acquires first North American serial rights.
Advice: "Write and send work that feels like it is absolutely essential, but avoid the leg-hold traps of self-importance and affectation."

CONFLUENCE, (II), Sponsored by Ohio Valley Literary Group & Marietta College, Box 336, Belpre OH 45714. (614)373-2999. Fiction Editor: Daniel Born. Editors change each year. Magazine: 6½×8; 112-120 pages; acid-free paper; illustrations. Annually. Estab. 1989. Circ. 500.
• *Confluence* sponsors an annual short story contest. Guidelines are available January 1 to March 1 each year.
Needs: Condensed/excerpted novel, ethnic/multicultural, feminist, humor/satire, literary, mainstream/contemporary, mystery/suspense, regional, science fiction, translations. "No romance, homophobia." Receives 75-150 mss/reading period. Accepts 7-15 mss/issue. Does not read ms March 2-December 30. Publishes ms 3-5 months after acceptance. Published work by Mitch Levenberg, Thea Caplan, Frank Tota. Length: 4,500

words maximum. Publishes short shorts. Also publishes literary essays and poetry. Always critiques or comments on rejected ms.

How to Contact: Send complete ms with a cover letter. Should include estimated word count and 2-4 sentence bio. Reports in 1-2 weeks on queries; 1-2 months on mss. Send SASE for reply, return of ms or send a disposable copy of ms. Simultaneous submissions OK if indicated by author; occasionally considers reprints. Sample copy for $3 and 6×9 SAE.

Payment/Terms: Pays 1 contributor's copy. Acquires one-time rights.

Advice: "We like stories grounded in lived detail, regardless of whether they're traditional or experimental narratives."

CONFRONTATION, (II), English Dept., C.W. Post of Long Island University, Brookville NY 11548. (516)299-2391. Editor: Martin Tucker. Magazine: 6×9; 190-250 pages; 70 lb. paper; 80 lb. cover; illustrations; photos. "We like to have a 'range' of subjects, form and style in each issue and are open to all forms. Quality is our major concern. Our audience is made up of literate, thinking people; formally or self-educated." Semiannually. Estab. 1968. Circ. 2,000.

- *Confrontation* has garnered a long list of awards and honors, including the Editor's Award for Distinguished Achievement from CCLM (now the Council of Literary Magazines and Presses) and NEA grants. Work from the magazine has appeared in numerous anthologies including the *Pushcart Prize, Best Short Stories* and *O. Henry Prize Stories*.

Needs: Literary, contemporary, prose poem, regional and translations. No "proseletyzing" literature. Upcoming themes: "New Southern Writing"; "Emerging South Africa." Buys 30 mss/issue; 60 mss/year. Receives 400 unsolicited fiction mss each month. Does not read June-September. Approximately 10-15% of fiction is agented. Published work by Nadine Gordimer, William Styron, Mario Vargas Llosa, Jayne Cortez; published many new writers within the last year. Length: 500-4,000 words. Publishes short shorts. Also publishes literary essays and poetry. Critiques rejected mss when there is time. Sometimes recommends other markets.

How to Contact: Send complete ms with SASE. "Cover letters acceptable, not necessary. We accept simultaneous submissions but do not prefer it." Accepts diskettes if accompanied by computer printout submissions. Reports in 6-8 weeks on mss. Publishes ms 6-12 months after acceptance. Sample copy for $3. Reviews novels and short story collections.

Payment/Terms: Pays $20-250 on publication for all rights "with transfer on request to author"; 1 contributor's copy; half price for extras.

Advice: "Keep trying."

‡CONMOCIÓN, Revista de lesbianas Latinas, (IV), 1521 Alton Rd., #336, Miami Beach FL 33139. (305)751-8385. Editor: Tatiana de la Tierra. Magazine. "*Conmoción* publishes writings by Latina lesbians. We do not censor ideas—we welcome diverse points of view in Spanish, English or Spanglish." Quarterly. Estab. 1994. Circ. 5,000.

Needs: Lesbian: Erotica, ethnic/multicultural, experimental, fantasy. "Must be Latina-lesbian focused—no heterosexual point of view." Buys 10 mss/year. Publishes ms 2 months after acceptance. Length: 3,000 words maximum.

How to Contact: Query with clips of published work. Simultaneous, reprint submissions OK. Sample copy $6. Fiction guidelines free.

Payment/Terms: Pays in contributor's copies. Acquires one-time rights.

‡CONTEXT SOUTH, (II), Box 4504, Kerrville TX 78028. Editor: David Breeden. Fiction Editor: Craig Taylor. Magazine: digest sized; 65 pages; illustrations and photos. Annually. Estab. 1988. Circ. 500.

Needs: Experimental, feminist, literary. List of upcoming themes available for SASE. Receives 10-15 unsolicited mss/month. Does not read in summer. Publishes ms up to 1 year after acceptance. Agented fiction 10%. Length: 500 words minimum; 3,000 words maximum. Publishes short shorts. Also publishes literary essays, literary criticism, poetry. Sometimes critiques or comments on rejected ms.

How to Contact: Send complete ms with a cover letter. Should include short bio. Reports in 2 weeks on queries; 3 months on mss. SASE for return of ms. Simultaneous submissions OK. Sample copy for $5. Reviews novels and short story collections.

Payment/Terms: Pays 2 contributor's copies. Acquires one-time rights. Sends galleys to author.

Advice: "Read a good deal of fiction, current and past. Avoid sending the trite and that which depends merely on shock."

CORONA, Marking the Edges of Many Circles, (II), Dept. of History and Philosophy, Montana State University, Bozeman MT 59717. (406)994-5200. Co-Editors: Lynda Sexson, Michael Sexson. Managing Editor: Sarah Merrill. Magazine: 7×10; 130 pages; 60 lb. "mountre matte" paper; 65 lb. Hammermill cover stock; illustrations; photos. "Interdisciplinary magazine—essays, poetry, fiction, imagery, science, history, recipes, humor, etc., for those educated, curious, with a profound interest in the arts and contemporary thought." Published occasionally. Estab. 1980. Circ. 2,000.

Needs: Comics, contemporary, experimental, fantasy, feminist, humor/satire, literary, prose poem. "Our fiction ranges from the traditional Talmudic tale to fiction engendered by speculative science, from the extended joke to regional reflection—if it isn't accessible and original, please don't send it." Receives varying number of unsolicited fiction mss/month. Accepts 6 mss/issue. Published work by Rhoda Lerman and Stephen Dixon; published new writers within the last year. Publishes short shorts. Also publishes literary essays and poetry. Occasionally critiques rejected mss.

How to Contact: Query. Reports in 6 months on mss. Sample copy for $7.

Payment/Terms: Pays minimal honorarium; 2 free contributor's copies; discounted charge for extras. Acquires first rights. Sends galleys to author upon request.

Advice: "Be knowledgeable of contents other than fiction in *Corona*; one must know the journal."

COSMIC LANDSCAPES, An Alternative Science Fiction Magazine, (I, IV), % Dan Petitpas, D & S Associates, 19 Carroll Ave., Westwood MA 02090. (617)329-1344. Editor: Dan Petitpas. Magazine: 7×8½; 32-56 pages; white bond paper and cover stock; illustrations; photos occasionally. "A magazine which publishes science fiction for science-fiction readers; also articles and news of interest to writers and science fiction fans. Occasionally prints works of horror and fantasy." Annually. Estab. 1983. Circ. 150.

- Submissions will automatically be considered for their promotional newsletter, *CL: Limited Edition*, and their electronic publishing program, *Cosmic Landscapes Online, Electronic SF, Fantasy and Horror*, which accepts "science fiction (all kinds), fantasy and horror stories, as well as articles and discussion about science fiction, fantasy and horror stories, writers, etc."

Needs: Science fiction (hard science, soft/sociological). Receives 15-20 unsolicited mss/month. Accepts 8 mss/issue. Published new writers in the last year. Length: 2,500 words average; 25 words minimum. Will consider all lengths. "Every manuscript receives a personal evaluation by the editor." Sometimes recommends other markets.

How to Contact: Send complete ms with bio. Reports usually in 1 week-3 months. SASE. Simultaneous submissions OK. E-mail address: dslitser@aol.com or danpetitpas@geonetol.com. Sample copy for $3.50. Fiction guidelines for SASE.

Payment/Terms: Pays 2 contributor's copies; $2 for extras. Acquires one-time rights.

Advice: "We're interested in all kinds of science fiction stories. We particularly like stories with ideas we've not seen before. Unfortunately we receive a lot of warmed-over Star Trek plots. Be imaginative. Be wild. Ask yourself 'what if?' and then follow through with the idea. Tell the story through the actions of a character or characters to give the readers someone to identify with. Be careful of creating scientific theories if you don't know much science. Let your imagination go!"

THE COSMIC UNICORN, (I, II, IV), Silver Creation Press, 451 Hibiscus Tree Dr., Lantana FL 33462. (407)588-0907. Editor: Tricia Packard. Fiction Editor: Liz Dennis. Magazine: 5¼×8½; 160 pages; 20 lb. white paper; white index cover stock; cover illustrations only. "*TCU* looks to open doors for both new and well-seasoned writers. We want to make available a forum that has the space for really good science fiction/fantasy works of varying lengths and styles—a forum that offers writers the opportunity to say what they want to say but haven't been able to. Our readers range from 10-70." Semiannually. Estab. 1993. Circ. 100.

Needs: Fantasy, science fiction, young adult/teen (science fiction). No horror. Receives 40-50 unsolicited mss/month. Accepts 12-15 mss/issue; 24-30 mss/year. Does not read mss September 1-April 30. Publishes ms within 1 year after acceptance. Recently published work by Devon Tavern, Edward L. McFadden, Gordon Graves. Length: 4,500 words average; 100 words minimum, 10,000 words maximum. Publishes short shorts. Length: 100-400 words. Also publishes poetry. Sometimes critiques or comments on rejected ms.

How to Contact: Send complete ms with a cover letter; query first for nonfiction or long poetry. Should include estimated word count, bio (100-words maximum), Social Security number and a brief list of related publications. Reports in 1 month on queries; 2 months on mss. Send SASE for reply, return of ms or send a disposable copy of ms. No simultaneous submissions. Reprint and electronic submissions OK. E-mail address: T. Packard (Genie), T. Packard@Genie.geis.com (Internet). Sample copy for $6.75 and 6×9 SAE with 4 first-class stamps or 2 IRCs. (Make checks payable to Tricia Packard.) Fiction guidelines for #10 SASE. Reviews novels and short story collections.

Payment/Terms: Pays ¼-½¢ a word for one-time rights; copies available to contributors at special rate.

Advice: "We look for a strong plot, well-defined characters, unusual story or plot; a manuscript stands out if it can make me interested in what happens to the character(s). We haven't seen enough science fiction/fantasy with romantic characters, or romance. Avoid graphic sex or gore. Our readers range from adolescents to senior citizens."

CRAZYHORSE, (II), Dept. of English, Univ. of Arkansas, Little Rock, AR 72204. (501)569-3161. Managing Editor: Zabelle Stodola. Fiction Editor: Judy Troy. Magazine: 6×9; 140 pages; cover illustration only. "Publishes original, quality literary fiction." Biannually. Estab. 1960. Circ. 1,000.

- Stories appearing in *Crazyhorse* regularly appear in the *Pushcart Prize* and *Best American Short Stories* anthologies.

Needs: Literary. No formula (science fiction, gothic, detective, etc.) fiction. Receives 100-150 unsolicited mss/month. Buys 3-5 mss/issue; 8-10 mss/year. Does not read mss in summer. Published work by Lee K.

Abbott, Frederick Busch, Andre Dubus, Pam Durban, H.E. Francis, James Hannah, Gordon Lish, Bobbie Ann Mason and Maura Stanton; published new writers within the last year. Length: Open. Publishes short shorts. Also publishes literary essays, literary criticism, poetry. "Rarely" critiques rejected mss.

How to Contact: Send complete ms with cover letter. Reports in 1-4 months. SASE. No simultaneous submissions. Sample copy for $5. Reviews novels and short story collections. Send books to fiction editor.

Payment/Terms: Pays $10/page and contributor's copies for first North American serial rights. *Crazyhorse* awards $500 to the author of the best work of fiction published in the magazine in a given year.

Advice: "Read a sample issue and submit work that you believe is as good as or better than the fiction we've published."

CRAZYQUILT, (II), P.O. Box 632729, San Diego CA 92163-2729. (619)688-1023. Editor-in-Chief: Jim Kitchen. Fiction and Drama Editor: Marsh Cassady. Magazine: 5½×8½; 92 pages; illustrations and photos. "We publish short fiction, poems, nonfiction about writing and writers, one-act plays and b&w illustrations and photos." Quarterly. Estab. 1986. Circ. 175.

Needs: Contemporary, ethnic, excerpted novel, fantasy, gay, historical, humor/satire, literary, mainstream, mystery/suspense, science fiction. "Shorter pieces are preferred." Receives 85-100 unsolicited mss/quarter. Accepts 6-8 mss/issue; 25-35 mss/year. Publishes 1 year after acceptance. Published work by Louis Phillips, Geraldine Little and Judson Jerome; published new writers within the last year. Length: 500 words minimum; 4,000 words maximum. Also publishes literary essays, literary criticism, poetry. Occasionally critiques rejected mss.

How to Contact: Send complete ms with cover letter and SASE. Reports in 2 weeks on mss. Simultaneous submissions OK. Sample copy for $6 ($4.50 for back issue). Fiction guidelines for SASE.

Payment/Terms: Pays 2 contributor's copies. Acquires first North American serial rights or one-time rights.

Advice: "Write a story that is well constructed, develops characters and maintains interest."

THE CREAM CITY REVIEW, (II), University of Wisconsin-Milwaukee, Box 413, Milwaukee WI 53201. (414)229-4708. Editors-In-Chief: Andrew Rivera, Matthew Roberson and Cynthia Belmont. Contact: Fiction Editor. Editors rotate. Magazine: 5½×8½; 200-300 pages; 70 lb. offset/perfect-bound paper; 80 lb. cover stock; illustrations; photos. "General literary publication—an eclectic and electric selection of the best we receive." Semiannually. Estab. 1975. Circ. 2,000.

Needs: Ethnic, experimental, humor/satire, literary, prose poem, regional and translations. Receives approximately 300 unsolicited fiction mss each month. Accepts 6-10 mss/issue. Does not read June, July and August. Recently published work by Stephen Dixon, Joyceann Masters, Ron Silliman and Gordon Lish; published new writers within the last year. Length: 1,000-10,000 words. Publishes short shorts. Also publishes literary essays, literary criticism, poetry. Critiques rejected mss when there is time.

How to Contact: Send complete ms with SASE. Simultaneous submissions OK. Reports in 2-6 months. World Wide Web address: http://www.uwm.edu/Dept/English. Sample copy for $4.50. Reviews novels and short story collections.

Payment/Terms: Pays 1 year subscription and $5/page (when funding allows).

Terms: Acquires first rights. Sends galleys to author. Rights revert to author after publication.

Advice: "Read as much as you write so that you can examine your own work in relation to where fiction has been and where fiction is going."

THE CRESCENT REVIEW, (II), The Crescent Review, Inc., P.O. Box 15069, Chevy Chase MD 20825. (301)986-8788. Editor: J.T. Holland. Magazine: 6×9; 160 pages. Triannually. Estab. 1982.

● Work appearing in *The Crescent Review* has been included in recent editions of the *Best American Short Stories*, *Pushcart Prize* and *Black Southern Writers* anthologies and in the *New Stories from the South*.

Needs: "Wellcrafted stories" Does not read submissions May-June and November-December.

How to Contact: Reports in 2 weeks-4 months. SASE. Sample issue for $9.40.

Payment/Terms: Pays 2 contributor's copies; discount for contributors. Acquires first North American serial rights.

CROSSROADS . . . Where Evil Dwells, (I, II), 478 Waters Rd., Jacksonville NC 28546-9756. (910)455-7047. Editor: Pat Nielsen. Magazine: Digest-sized; approximately 68 pages; 20 lb. paper; 64 lb. index cover. "All stories must be about people at a *Crossroad* in their lives, or set at the crossroads themselves—or both. I strongly encourage writers to do research about the crossroad legends. This is an *adult* horror magazine." Triannually. (Published February, June and October.) Estab. 1992. Circ. 100.

● Work appearing in *Crossroads* received three Honorable Mentions in the *The Year's Best Horror and Fantasy*.

Needs: Horror, psychic/supernatural/occult. "No futuristic or fiction set in the past. Every October issue is the Halloween issue—all material must have a Halloween theme." Receives 20 unsolicited mss/month. Accepts 10-15 mss/issue; 30 mss/year. Publishes ms 1-6 months after acceptance. Published work by J.N. Williamson, John Maclay, David Shtogryn and D. Sandy Nielsen. Length: 1,500 words average; 500 words minimum; 2,500 words maximum. Also publishes literary criticism and poetry. Often critiques or comments on rejected ms.

How to Contact: Send complete ms with a cover letter. Should include estimated word count. Reports in 2 weeks on queries; 2-4 weeks on mss. Send SASE for reply, return of ms or send a disposable copy of ms. "I don't like IRCs—please use US stamps whenever possible." No simultaneous submissions. Reprints OK. Sample copy for $4.50. Fiction guidelines for #10 SASE.

Payment/Terms: Pays 1 contributor's copy; additional copies for $3.50 plus postage for multiple copies. Acquires first North American serial rights. Sends galleys to author (time permitting).

Advice: "I publish many kinds of horror, from the mild to the hard core horror. My theme is that of people at a crossroads in their lives or of the crossroads themselves, which is not that unique because most horror stories are about someone at a crossroads of some kind. However, I do find the legends about the crossroads fascinating and would love to see more fiction like that. Do not send science fiction or fantasy in any form."

CRUCIBLE, (I, II), English Dept., Barton College, College Station, Wilson NC 27893. (919)399-6456. Editor: Terrence L. Grimes. Magazine of fiction and poetry for a general, literary audience. Annually. Estab. 1964. Circ. 500.

Needs: Contemporary, ethnic, experimental, feminist, gay, lesbian, literary, regional. Receives 20 unsolicited mss/month. Accepts 5-6 mss/year. Publishes ms 4-5 months after acceptance. Does not normally read mss from April 30 to December 1. Published work by William Hutchins and Guy Nancekeville. Length: 8,000 words maximum. Publishes short shorts.

How to Contact: Send 3 complete copies of ms unsigned with cover letter which should include a brief biography, "in case we publish." Reports in 2 weeks on queries; 2-3 months on mss (by June 15). SASE. Sample copy for $6. Fiction guidelines free.

Payment/Terms: Pays contributor's copies. Acquires first rights.

Advice: "Write about what you know. Experimentation is fine as long as the experiences portrayed come across as authentic, that is to say, plausible."

CUTBANK, (II), English Dept., University of Montana, Missoula MT 59812. (406)243-0211. Editors-in-Chief: Lary Kleeman and Allyson Goldin. Fiction Editor: Eric Simmons. Editors change each year. Terms run from June-June. After June, address to "Fiction Editor." Magazine: 5½×8½; 115-130 pages. "Publishes highest quality fiction, poetry, artwork, for a general, literary audience." Semiannually. Estab. 1973. Circ. 600.

Needs: Receives 200 unsolicited mss/month. Accepts 6-12 mss/year. Does not read mss from February 28-August 15. Publishes ms up to 6 months after acceptance. Published new writers within the last year. Length: 40 pages maximum. Also publishes literary essays, literary criticism, poetry. Occasionally critiques rejected mss.

How to Contact: Send complete ms with cover letter, which should include "name, address, publications." Reports in 1-4 months on mss. SASE. Simultaneous submissions OK. Sample copy for $4 (current issue $6.95). Fiction guidelines for SASE. Reviews novels and short story collections. Send books to fiction editor.

Payment/Terms: Pays 2 contributor's copies. Rights revert to author upon publication, with provision that *Cutbank* receives publication credit.

Advice: "Strongly suggest contributors read an issue. We have published stories by David Long, William Kittredge, Rick DeMarinis, Patricia Henley, Melanie Rae Thon and Michael Dorris in recent issues, and like to feature new writers alongside more well-known names. Send only your best work."

CWM, (II, III, IV), 1300 Kicker Rd., Tuscaloosa AL 35404. (205)553-2284. Editor: David C. Kopaska-Merkel. Co-editor: Geof Huth, 875 Central Pkwy., Schenectady NY 12309. (518)374-7143. Magazine: Variable size; pages, paper quality, cover variable; ink drawings or others possible. "Each issue has a theme. We publish fiction, art and poetry for anyone interested in something a little bit different." Estab. 1990.

Needs: "Any submission fitting the theme." Receives 15-30 mss/issue; 2-10 mss/year. Publishes ms within 2 years of acceptance. Length: 10,000 words maximum. Publishes short shorts; any length is acceptable. Also publishes poetry. Sometimes comments on rejected mss.

How to Contact: Query first or send complete manuscript with cover letter. Reports in 2-4 weeks on queries; 6-20 weeks on mss. SASE. No simultaneous submissions. Accepts electronic submissions via disk. Fiction guidelines for #10 SASE.

Payment/Terms: Pays contributor's copies. Acquires one-time rights.

Advice: "A manuscript must meet our theme for the issue in question. It stands out if it begins well and is neatly and clearly prepared. Given a good beginning, the story must hold the reader's interest all the way to the end and not let go. It helps if a story haunts the reader even after it is put aside."

DAGGER OF THE MIND, Beyond The Realms Of Imagination, (II), K'yi-Lih Productions (a division of Breach Enterprises), 1317 Hookridge Dr., El Paso TX 79925. (915)591-0541. Executive Editor: Arthur William Lloyd Breach. Magazine. 8½×11; 62-86 pages; hibright paper; high glossy cover; from 5-12 illustrations. Quarterly. Estab. 1990. Circ. 5,000.

● Do not send this publication "slasher" horror. The editor's preferences lean toward "Twilight

Original Ideas Replace Horror's Old Blood and Guts

Today's horror stories can't be just blood and guts, according to Wayne A. Harold, editor of *Dark Kiss* magazine. "One thing I am trying to do is publish intelligent horror. Everybody says they want intelligent horror fiction, but I don't think a lot of people publish it. Blood and gore is not what I find to be scary. It's the idea behind the story and the situation that have to be scary."

Harold began *Dark Kiss* in 1994, motivated by what he was reading in the horror field. "When I was putting the magazine together, I was inspired by an editor named Michelle Slung who put out an anthology called *I Shudder at Your Touch*. Basically, it's stories of sex and horror, and I was intrigued by that. The stories aren't pornographic; I wouldn't even go so far as to say they're erotica. They explore the fine line between sex and horror, and after reading the book, I decided I wanted to do a magazine of stories like that."

And, Harold adds, that doesn't mean misogyny. "I'm surprised at the stories I get in from some writers which are just descriptions of women being decapitated and all these horrible things being done to them. I'm in no way looking for wimpy stories or even G-rated stuff, but I'm also not looking to go in that direction, because it just isn't interesting."

Not every story in the magazine is sex and horror, however. Once in a while, Harold throws in something different. "There's a story in Issue One called 'The Cemetery,' by Gary Lovisi, and it's basically the story of a guy who is visiting his childhood home and meets the ghost of his great-grandmother." The character sees ghosts, but they are peaceful spirits, not vengeful demons. There are no situations involving, or references to, sex. So, while not every story has to deal with sex, they do have to be stories that fit the framework of an adult horror magazine.

Harold can usually tell within the first page or so if a story is something he's going to be interested in. "Occasionally, I'll be losing interest midway, then the author will pull something off that will make it seem worthwhile," he says. Usually, however, the seemingly clichéd rule applies; you must grab Harold with the first line or two. "If I see the standard line, like a blonde walking into a P.I.'s office, I know I'm in trouble. I want to give the person a chance, I want to like the story and want to buy it, but if it's the same thing I've seen a thousand times over, I end up getting bored halfway through."

What Harold definitely doesn't want to see is the tired plot of the vampire stalking the victim who turns out to be another vampire, or an alien, or a werewolf. "I've heard people laugh about that," he says, "but I get stories like that on a weekly basis. That's the one thing that leaves me completely cold, and I think that the writer who comes up with something like that obviously hasn't read that much. Those sorts of stories I won't run whatsoever, unless somebody would be totally outrageous with it. But that's rare."

Harold's advice to writers wishing to publish in *Dark Kiss* or other horror magazines is to read as much as you possibly can. "It's another cliché that they tell everybody, but it's true. Otherwise, you fall into the trap of thinking you've written something great and fresh and new, only to find out it's been done to death years before." In addition to reading, Harold says you must write as much as possible, but keep in mind that less is more. "I get too much stuff that is too verbose. The way fiction is going, you don't want to have pages and pages of describing someone's clothes and the threading that goes into their pants and everything else. Paint with broad strokes and let the reader fill in the blanks. I'm basically looking for an original idea and interesting characters that aren't stereotypes. The best story evolves from seeing what happens when that idea is let go."

—*David Borcherding*

Zone" and similar material. He says he added mystery to his needs last year but has received very little quality material in this genre.
Needs: Lovecraftian. Adventure, experimental, fantasy, horror, mystery/suspense (private eye, police procedural), science fiction (hard science, soft/sociological). Nothing sick and blasphemous, vulgar, obscene, racist, sexist, profane, humorous, weak, exploited women stories and those with idiotic puns. Plans special paperback anthologies. Receives 400 unsolicited mss/month. 8-15 mss/issue; 90-100 mss/year depending upon length. Publishes ms 2 years after acceptance. Agented fiction 30%. Published work by Sidney Williams, Jessica Amanda Salmonson, Donald R. Burleson. All lengths are acceptable; from short shorts to novelette lengths. Also publishes literary essays, literary criticism, poetry. Sometimes comments on rejected mss.
How to Contact: Send complete manuscript with cover letter. "Include a bio and list of previously published credits with tearsheets. I also expect a brief synopsis of the story." Reports in 5-5½ months on mss. SASE. Simultaneous submissions OK "as long as I am informed that they are such." Accepts electronic submissions. Sample copy for $3.50, 9×12 SAE and 5 first-class stamps. Fiction guidelines for #10 SASE.
Payment/Terms: Pays ½-1¢/word plus 1 contributor's copy on publication for first rights (possibly anthology rights as well).
Advice: "I'm a big fan of the late H.P. Lovecraft. I love reading through Dunsanian and Cthulhu Mythos tales. I'm constantly on the lookout for this special brand of fiction. If you want to grab my attention immediately, write on the outside of the envelope 'Lovecratian submission enclosed.' There are a number of things which make submissions stand out for me. Is there any sensitivity to the tale? I like sensitive material, so long as it doesn't become mushy. Another thing that grabs my attention are characters which leap out of the pages at you. Move me, bring a tear to my eye; make me stop and think about the world and people around me. Frighten me with little spoken of truths about the human condition. In short, show me that you can move me in such a way as I have never been moved before."

✤**THE DALHOUSIE REVIEW, (II),** Room 314, Dunn Building, Dalhousie University, Halifax, Nova Scotia B3H 3J5 Canada. Editor: Dr. Alan Andrews. Magazine: 15cm×23cm; approximately 140 pages; photographs sometimes. Publishes articles, book reviews, short stories and poetry. Published 3 times a year. Circ. 600.
Needs: Literary. Length: 5,000 words maximum. Also publishes essays on history, philosophy, etc., and poetry.
How to Contact: Send complete ms with cover letter. SASE (Canadian stamps). Prefers submissions on computer disk (WordPerfect). Sample copy for $8.50 (Canadian) plus postage. Occasionally review novels and short story collections.

DAN RIVER ANTHOLOGY, (I), Box 298, S. Thomaston ME 04861. (207)354-0998. Editor: R. S. Danbury III. Book: 5½×8½; 156 pages; 60 lb. paper; gloss 65 lb. full-color cover; b&w illustrations. For general/adult audience. Annually. Estab. 1984. Circ. 1,200.
• See the listing for the Dan River Press in the Small Press section of this book.
Needs: Adventure, contemporary, ethnic, experimental, fantasy, historical, horror, humor/satire, literary, mainstream, prose poem, psychic/supernatural/occult, regional, romance (contemporary and historical), science fiction, senior citizen/retirement, suspense/mystery and western. No "evangelical Christian, pornography or sentimentality." Receives 150 unsolicited fiction mss each submission period (January 1-March 31).

"We generally publish 12-15 fiction writers." Reads "mostly in April." Length: 2,000-2,400 words average; 800 words minimum; 2,500 words maximum. Also publishes poetry.

How to Contact: *Charges reading fee: $1 for poetry; $3 for prose* (cash only, no checks). Send complete ms with SASE. Reports by May 15 each year. Sample copy for $12.95 paperback, $19.95 cloth, plus $2.50 shipping. Fiction guidelines for #10 SASE.

Payment/Terms: Pays $5/page, minimum *cash advance on acceptance* against royalties of 10% of all sales attributable to writer's influence: readings, mailings, autograph parties, etc., plus up to 50% discount on copies, plus other discounts to make total as high as 73%. Buys first rights.

DARK KISS, (II), Scarlett Fever Press, 3160 Brady Lake Rd., Ravenna OH 44266. Editor: Wayne A. Harold. Magazine: 8½×11; 40 pages; 20 lb. paper; cardstock cover; illustrations and photos. "The best in adult and erotic horror." Semiannually. Estab. 1994. Circ. 200.

   • Scarlett Fever Press also publishes *Naked Kiss* which is listed in this section and features hard boiled crime, mystery and suspense fiction. Avoid sending vampire/serial killer stories to *Dark Kiss*. They prefer more original treatments. See the interview with Wayne Harold in this section.

Needs: Fantasy (science), horror, psychic/supernatural/occult, science fiction (soft/sociological). No "porno, slasher stories, or misogynistic fiction." List of upcoming themes available for SASE. Plans special fiction issues or anthologies in the future. Receives 15-20 unsolicited mss/month. Buys 5-7 mss/issue; 10-20 mss/year. Publishes ms 6-36 months after acceptance. Recently published work by Gary Lovisi, J.D. Hunt, Charlee Jacob, Scott Urban. Length: 2,000 words minimum; 6,000 words maximum. Often critiques or comments on rejected ms.

How to Contact: Send complete ms with a cover letter. Should include estimated word count, bio (1 paragraph), Social Security number and list of publications. Reports in 1 month on queries; 2-4 months on mss. Send SASE for reply, return of ms or send a disposable copy of ms. Simultaneous and electronic submissions OK. Sample copy for $5 (payable to Scarlett Fever Press). Fiction guidelines for #10 SASE. E-mail address: MrWHarold@aol.com. Reviews novels and short story collections.

Payment/Terms: Pays $5-15 and 1-2 contributor's copies on publication for first North American serial rights.

Advice: Looks for "original, interesting horror fiction for adults. Erotic horror with strong emotional content."

‡DARK REGIONS, (II), P.O. Box 6301, Concord CA 94524. Editor: Joe Morey. Fiction Editors: Mike Olson and John Rosenman. Magazine: 8½×11; 100 pages; newsprint; full color cover ; illustrations and photographs. "Science fiction, fantasy, horror and all subgenres. Our philosophy is to publish the most professional, fresh, original work we can find." Triannually. Estab. 1985. Circ. 3,000.

   • *Dark Regions* is a member of the Small Press Writers and Artists Organization and recently received SPWAO's Best Fiction Award for the story "Darby's Bone," by Albert J. Manachino.

Needs: Fantasy, horror, science fiction, young adult/teen (horror, science fiction). Upcoming themes: "Virtual Reality" (March 1996). List of upcoming themes available for SASE. Receives 200 unsolicited mss/month. Accepts 10-15 mss/issue; 30-45 mss/year. Publishes ms 6-12 months after acceptance. Recently published work by Mike Resnick, Kevin J. Anderson and Joe R. Lansdale. Length: 3,500 words average; 500 words minimum; 5,000 words maximum. Also publishes poetry. Sometimes critiques rejected mss.

How to Contact: Send complete ms with a cover letter. Should include estimated word count, brief bio, Social Security number and list of publications. Reports in 3-8 weeks on queries; 3-12 weeks on mss. Send SASE for reply, return of ms or send a disposable copy of ms. No simultaneous submissions. Considers reprints for "The Year's Best Fantastic Fiction." Sample copy for $4.95, 9×12 SAE and 2 first-class stamps. Fiction guidelines free for SASE.

Payment/Terms: Pays ½-6¢/word and 1 contributor's copy; additional copies $2.50 (plus $1.28 shipping). Pays on publication. Buys first North American serial rights.

Advice: "We want fiction with good short story elements and good short story structure—stories that move through action/description and employ elements of suspense, inventive tales which push the boundaries of weirdness. The more original, the better." Avoid "overused themes such as Friday the 13th, Conan, Invaders from Mars, werewolves and vampires (unless highly original). No racism, no hard pornography and definitely no children in sexual situations."

‡DAUGHTERS OF NYX, A Magazine of Goddess Stories, Mythmaking, and Fairy Tales, (I, IV), Ruby Rose's Fairy Tale Emporium, P.O. Box 1100, Stevenson WA 98648. Fiction Editor: Kim Antieau. Magazine: 8½×11; 32 pages; illustrations. "We are a woman-centered publication, interested in stories that retell legends, myths and fairy tales from a matristic viewpoint. Feminist, women's spirituality, pagan." Semiannually. Estab. 1993. Circ. 2,000.

Needs: Ethnic/multicultural, fantasy, feminist, lesbian, literary, mainstream/contemporary, psychic/supernatural/occult, science fiction, goddess stories, fairy tales, myths. No "anti-woman, slasher, violent" material. Receives 15 unsolicited mss/month. Accepts 7-10 mss/issue; 20 mss/year. Publishes ms within 24 months after acceptance. Length: 1,000 words minimum; 7,000 words maximum. Sometimes critiques or comments on rejected mss.

How to Contact: Send complete ms with a cover letter. Should include estimated word count, short bio and list of publications. Reports in 3-12 weeks. Send SASE for reply, return of ms or send a disposable copy of ms. Simultaneous and reprint submissions OK, "but please tell us." Sample copy for $4.50. Fiction guidelines for #10 SASE. Reviews novels and short story collections.
Payment/Terms: Pays ½¢/word ($10 minimum) and 2 contributor's copies on publication for first North American serial rights, or one-time rights.
Advice: A manuscript stands out "if the author understands goddess stories and their power for women. Read the field—Starhawk, Merlin Stone, Barbara Walker, Z. Budapest. Avoid sending sword and sorcery fantasy masquerading as retellings of fairy tales. Our fiction is women-centered, imaginative. We seek to challenge and/or transcend patriarchal ideas, institutions, traditions and myths."

‡DAVIDS' PLACE JOURNAL, An AIDS Experience Journal, (IV), P.O. Box 632759, San Diego CA 92103. (619)294-5775. Fax: (619)683-9230. Editor: R. Osborne. Magazine: 8½×7; 125 pages; illustrations and photos. The philosophy of *David's Place Journal* is "to communicate the HIV/AIDS experience, to reach the whole community. Submissions may be popular or scholarly." Quarterly. Estab. 1994. Circ. 500.
   ● *David's Place Journal* was named for a not-for-profit cafe in San Diego supportive of people with HIV/AIDS and their friends.
Needs: HIV/AIDS experience. "No erotica." Receives 15 unsolicited mss/month. Buys 10-15 mss/issue; 40-60 mss/year. Publishes ms 3-6 months after acceptance. Recently published work by Jameison Currior, Crystal Bacon, Gary Eldon Peter. Length: 5,000 words maximum. Publishes short shorts. Also publishes literary essays, poetry. Sometimes critiques or comments on rejected ms.
How to Contact: Send complete ms with a cover letter. Send complete ms with a cover letter. Should include 1-paragraph bio with submission. Send SASE for reply. Simultaneous submissions, reprints OK. Sample copy $4.
Payment/Terms: Pays 2 contributor's copies. Acquires one-time rights.
Advice: Looking for "authentic experience or artistic relevance to the AIDS experience."

DEAD OF NIGHT™ MAGAZINE, (II), 916 Shaker Rd., Suite 228, Longmeadow MA 01106-2416. (413)567-9524. Editor: Lin Stein. Magazine: 8½×11; 64-96 pages; newsprint paper; slick 2-color cover stock; illustrations, and occasionally photographs. "*Dead of Night Magazine* publishes horror, fantasy, mystery, science fiction and vampire-related fiction. If we had a 'motto' it might be 'horror/fantasy/mystery/science fiction in a different vein'." Quarterly. Estab. 1989. Circ. 3,000.
   ● The editor of *Dead of Night Magazine* is a member of the Small Press Genre Association and Horror Writers Association. If $4 for a sample copy is beyond the writer's budget, back issues for $2.50 may be available. The magazine is known for "atmospheric, dark, character-oriented fiction." Note acceptable word-count has increased.
Needs: Condensed novel, fantasy (science fantasy, sword and sorcery), horror, mystery/suspense (mysteries need supernatural element), psychic/supernatural/occult, science fiction (soft/sociological). "We don't care for fantasy with an overabundance of elves, wizards, etc." Receives 90 unsolicited mss/month. Accepts 8-12 mss/issue. Does not read mss during June, July, August. Publishes ms 6-18 months after acceptance. Published work by Janet Fox, J.N. Williamson, Mort Castle, Gary Braunbeck. Length: 2,500-2,800 words preferred; 500 words minimum; 4,000 words maximum. Publishes literary essays, literary criticism and poetry. Often critiques or comments on rejected mss.
How to Contact: Send complete ms with a cover letter. Should include estimated word count, bio (1-2 paragraphs), Social Security number and list of publications (if available). Reports in 3 weeks on queries; 4-8 weeks on mss. Send SASE for reply, return of ms or send a disposable copy of ms. No simultaneous submissions. "No reprints except novel/book excerpts." Sample copy for $4. Fiction guidelines for #10 SASE. Reviews novels or short story collections.
Payment/Terms: Pays 3-7¢/word and 1 contributor's copy (2 to cover artists) on publication for first North American serial rights; additional copies for 10% discount off cover price.
Advice: "We think our magazine takes a somewhat 'literary' approach to the dark genres; that is, we avoid unnecessary gore and splatter. Instead, we aim for moody, atmospheric tales that are genuinely frightening and that will give the reader a lasting jolt rather than a momentary gross-out type of reaction. We look for truly frightening horror, believable fantasy, mysteries with some 'mysteriousness,' and character-oriented science fiction. Vampire tales should add some fresh or unique slant to the legend. We'd like to see stories that are not so 'media-influenced'; that is, tales that don't re-hash the latest horror movie/thriller the writer has seen at the box office or on television. Horror, fantasy, mystery and science fiction in our magazine are not the same as that in films. Also, we see too many vampire stories in which the writer tries to take the gothic atmosphere too far; for example, making vampire characters speak in 'Olde English'—annoying, and often poorly done."

DEATHREALM, (II), 2210 Wilcox Dr., Greensboro NC 27405-2845. (910)621-8160. Editor: Mark Rainey. Magazine: 8½×11; 50-60 pages; 20 lb. bond paper; 8 pt. glossy coated cover stock; pen & ink, screened illustrations; b&w photos. Publishes "fantasy/horror," for a "mature" audience. Quarterly. Estab. 1987. Circ. 3,000.

● This horror and dark fantasy magazine has won the Small Press Writers and Artists Organization's "Best Magazine" award (1990, 1994) and the editor won the "Best Editor" award (1990). Right now the editor is looking for fiction with supernatural-based plots.

Needs: Experimental, fantasy, horror, psychic/supernatural/occult and science fiction. "Sci-fi tales should have a horror slant. *Strongly* recommend contributor buy a sample copy of *Deathrealm* before submitting." Receives 200-300 mss/month. Buys 6-8 mss/issue; 30 mss/year. Does not read mss January 1 to May 1. Publishes ms within 1 year of acceptance. Published work by Joe R. Lansdale, Fred Chappell, Kevin J. Anderson, Jessica Amanda Salmonson. Length: 5,000 words average; 10,000 words maximum. Publishes short shorts. Also publishes literary criticism, poetry. Sometimes critiques rejected mss.

How to Contact: Send complete ms with cover letter, which should include "publishing credits, some bio info, where they heard about *Deathrealm*. Never reveal plot in cover letter." May accept simultaneous submissions, but "not recommended." Reports in 2 weeks on queries; 9-12 weeks on ms. SASE. E-mail address: s.rainey@genie.com. Sample copy for $4.95. Fiction guidelines for #10 SASE. Reviews novels and short story collections.

Payment/Terms: Pays 1¢/word; higher rates for established professionals; contributor's copies.

Advice: "Concentrate on characterization; development of ideas; strong atmosphere, with an important setting. I frown on gratuitous sex and violence unless it is a mere side effect of a more sophisticated story line. Stay away from overdone themes—foreboding dreams come true; being a frustrated writer; using lots of profanity and having a main character so detestable you don't care what happens to him."

DENVER QUARTERLY, (II, III), University of Denver, Denver CO 80208. (303)871-2892. Editor: Bin Ramke. Magazine: 6×9; 144-160 pages; occasional illustrations. "We publish fiction, articles and poetry for a generally well-educated audience, primarily interested in literature and the literary experience. They read *DQ* to find something a little different from a strictly academic quarterly or a creative writing outlet." Quarterly. Estab. 1966. Circ. 1,000.

● *Denver Quarterly* received an Honorable Mention for Content from the American Literary Magazine Awards.

Needs: "We are now interested in experimental fiction (minimalism, magic realism, etc.) as well as in realistic fiction and in writing about fiction." Also publishes poetry.

How to Contact: Send complete ms with SASE. Does not read mss May-September 15. Do not query. Reports in 3 months on mss. Publishes ms within a year after acceptance. Published work by Joyce Carol Oates, T.M. McNally, Charles Baxter; published new writers within the last year. No simultaneous submissions. Sample copy for $5 with SASE.

Payment/Terms: Pays $5/page for fiction and poetry and 2 contributor's copies for first North American serial rights.

Advice: "We look for serious, realistic and experimental fiction; stories which appeal to intelligent, demanding readers who are not themselves fiction writers. Nothing so quickly disqualifies a manuscript as sloppy proofreading and mechanics. Read the magazine before submitting to it. Send clean copy and a *brief* cover letter. We try to remain eclectic, but the odds for beginners are bound to be long considering the fact that we receive nearly 8,000 mss per year and publish only about 10 short stories."

❦DESCANT, (II), Box 314, Station P, Toronto, Ontario M5S 2S8 Canada. (416)603-0223. Editor: Karen Mulhallen. Magazine: 5¾×8¾; 100-300 pages; heavy paper; good cover stock; illustrations and photos. "High quality poetry and prose for an intelligent audience who wants to see a broad range of literature." Quarterly. Estab. 1970. Circ. 1,200.

● In past years *Descant* has won Canada's National Magazine Award for both poetry and fiction. Work published in *Descant* was selected for the *Journey Prize* anthology.

Needs: Literary, contemporary, translations. "Although most themes are acceptable, all works must have literary merit." Upcoming themes: "Women in Film," "Reading Pictures," "Caribbean Writers." Receives 100-200 unsolicited mss/month. Recently published work by Michael Ondaatje, Douglas Glover, Margaret Atwood. Publishes short shorts. Also publishes literary essays, poetry. Critiques rejected mss when there is time.

How to Contact: Send complete ms with cover letter. SASE. Simultaneous submissions OK ("but we only print unpublished material"). Reports in 3 months on mss. Sample copy for $7.50 plus $2 for postage to U.S.

Payment/Terms: Pays a modest honorarium and 1 year subscription. Extra contributor's copies at discount.

Advice: "*Descant* has plans for several special issues in the next two years. Unsolicited work is less likely to be accepted in the coming months, and will be kept on file for longer before it appears."

DESCANT, (II), Department of English, Texas Christian University, P.O. Box 32872, Fort Worth TX 76129. (817)921-7240. Editors: Neil Easterbrook, Stanley Trachtenberg, Harry Opperman, Steve Sherwood. "*Descant* publishes fiction and poetry. No restriction on style, content or theme. *Descant* is a 'little' literary magazine, and its readers are those who have interest in such publications." Semiannually. Estab. 1955. Circ. 500.

● *Descant* offers a $500 annual prize for fiction—the Frank O'Connor Prize listed in the Contests and Awards section of this book. The award is made to the story considered (by a judge not connected to the magazine) to be the best published in a given volume of the journal.

Needs: Literary, contemporary and regional. No genre or category fiction. Receives approximately 50 unsolicited fiction mss each month. Length: 1,500-5,000 words.

How to Contact: Send complete ms with SASE. Sample copy for $8 (old copy).

Payment/Terms: Pays 2 contributor's copies; charges $8 for extra copies.

Advice: "Submit good material. Even though a small publication, *Descant* receives many submissions, and acceptances are few compared to the total number of mss received." Mss are rejected because they "are badly written, careless in style and development, shallow in characterization, trite in handling and in conception."

THE DISABILITY RAG & RESOURCE, (IV), The Advocado Press, P.O. Box 145, Louisville KY 40201. Phone/fax: (502)459-5343. Editor: Eric Francis. Fiction Editor: Anne Finger. Magazine: 8 × 10½; 40 pages; newsprint paper; illustrations and occasionally photos. "To discern the causes of the discrimination, devaluation and disenfrachisement of disabled people by the nondisabled majority and communicate the true nature of the relationship between American society and its disabled members to both." Bimonthly. Estab. 1980. Circ. 4,000.

● *The Disability Rag & Resource* received an Utne Reader Alternative Press Award for Best Special Interest Publication.

Needs: All need to bear some relation to disability/disability rights: erotica, ethnic/multicultural, experimental, feminist, gay, lesbian, literary, science fiction (soft/sociological). "We want stories that reflect the concerns of the disability movement without resorting to the stereo-typical attitudes of pity, shame, miracle cures, etc. We are not interested in sentimental or 'inspirational' material." Receives 5 unsolicited mss/month. Buys 2 mss/year. Publishes ms 6-12 months after acceptance. Published work by Helen Cline and Robert Perretz-Rosales. Length: Open. Publishes short shorts. Also publishes poetry. Sometimes critiques or comments on rejected ms.

How to Contact: Send complete ms with a cover letter. Should include Social Security number. Reports in 1 months on queries. Send SASE for reply, return of ms or send a disposable copy of ms. If the ms is disposable, please do include a SASE for our response. No simultaneous submissions. Reprint submissions OK (reprint material that hasn't previously appeared in the disability press). Sample free. Fiction guidelines for SAE. Occasionally reviews novels or short story collections.

Payment/Terms: Pays $25/page and 2 contributor's copies; additional copies sliding discount according to quantity. Pays on publication. Buys all rights (unless otherwise negotiated).

Advice: "We seek work of high literary quality which explores the social and political aspects of disability, as well as the personal ones. We give a thorough and prompt reading to all work submitted. Please do familiarize yourself with our outlook before submitting fiction. I would love to see work from writers exploring the intersections of ethnicity and disability, sexual identity and disability; work which is experimental in nature. I'd like to see work in which its clear that the writers have thought about disability culture and aesthetic practice."

‡DISTURBED GUILLOTINE, (I, II), P.O. Box 14871, University Station, Minneapolis MN 55414-0871. Editor: Fredrik Hausmann. Magazine: 6 × 9; 120-140 pages; 60 lb. paper; 10 pt. C1S cover; illustrations and photos. "*Disturbed Guillotine* is a magazine/journal of exploratory writing and art—mindful transgression with an emphasis on creating rather than destroying." Semiannually. Estab. 1994. Circ. 500.

Needs: Erotica, Experimental, feminist, gay, lesbian, literary, translations. Receives 10-15 unsolicited mss/month. Accepts 7 mss/issue; 15 mss/year. Publishes ms 4-5 months after acceptance. Recently published work by Harold Jaffe, Ronald Sukenick, Patricia Eakins and Mark Amerika. Length: open. Publishes short shorts. Also publishes literary essays, literary criticism, poetry. Often critiques or comments on rejected ms.

How to Contact: Send complete ms with a cover letter. Should include short paragraph bio and list of publications. Reports in 7 weeks. No simultaneous submissions. Reprint submissions OK. Sample copy for $4.

Payment/Terms: Pays 3 contributor's copies. Sends galleys to author.

Advice: Looks for "well-written exploration of themes, style, etc.—exploratory, not necessarily avant-garde. We are interested in literary exploration, not immature rants."

‡DIVERSIONS, Erotic Fiction for the Mainstream, (I, II), A'n'D Enterprises, P.O. Box 70581, Richmond VA 23255. (804)740-7437. Fax: (804)740-7437. Editor: Don Mason. Magazine: 8½ × 5½; 64 pages; white laser paper; illustrations and photos. "We publish erotic stories, illustrations and photos intended to arouse/interest straight men and women 18 to 68 years old." Quarterly. Estab. 1995. Circ. 250.

Needs: Erotica. "No ultra violence or children." Plans to publish special fiction issues or anthologies. Receives 10-15 unsolicited mss/month. Accepts 8-12 mss/issue; 30-50 mss/year. Publishes ms 3 months after acceptance. Length: 1,500 words average; no minimum or maximum. Also publishes literary essays and poetry. Sometimes critiques or comments on rejected mss (with SASE).

How to Contact: Send complete ms with a cover letter. Should include estimated word count, 35-word bio and Social Security number with submission. Reports in 4-6 weeks. Send SASE for reply, return of ms or send a disposable copy of ms. Simultaneous, reprint and electronic submissions OK. E-mail address:

dmason@freente.vcu.edu. Sample copy for $3, 6×9 SAE and 2 first-class stamps. Fiction guidelines for #10 SASE.

Payment/Terms: Pays ¼-5¢/word on publication and 2 contributor's copies; additional copies half price. Pays on publication for one-time rights.

Advice: "Looks for real characters in new situations. Must be *mainstream* erotica. Revise and edit at least three times. Spell check. Grammar check. Show, don't tell. We would like to see more interesting locations and circumstances. We've seen too many 'boy cutting grass gets seduced' stories."

DJINNI, (II), 29 Front St., #2, Marblehead MA 01945. Fax: (617)639-1889. Editors: Kim A. Pederson and Kalo Clarke. Magazine: digest-sized; 60-100 pages; perfect bound; matte card cover. "An international magazine, *Djinni* publishes contemporary poetry, short fiction (including novel excerpts), short drama, essays, and drawings by well-knowns and new talent. The annual issue is published when sufficient quality material has been selected—usually late fall or early winter." Annually. Estab. 1990.

Needs: "The editors are especially interested in short work (1,200-3,000 words) that explores new directions."

How to Contact: Send ms including brief bio (and/or comment on the work). Open submissions are read May-November. Reports in 1-3 months on mss. SASE. Simultaneous submissions OK. Accepts hard copy, disk, e-mail or fax. E-mail address: kaloclarke@aol.com. Sample copy for $5.

Payment/Terms: Pays 1 contributor's copy.

Terms: Acquires first North American serial rights.

Advice: Looks for "intensity, originality, striking use of language in dealing with contemporary issues."

DODOBOBO, A New Fiction Magazine of Washington D.C., (I), Dodobobo Publications, P.O. Box 57214, Washington DC 20037. Editor: Brian Greene. Magazine: 5½×8½; 20-35 pages; illustrations and photos. "We're a literary fiction magazine which intends to give voice to writers the more well-known literary magazines would not be open to." Quarterly. Estab. 1994. Circ. 500.

• *Dodobobo*'s accepted word-length for stories has been changed from 7,500 words to 3,000 words maximum.

Needs: Experimental, feminist, gay, historical, humor/satire, lesbian, literary, mystery/suspense, psychic/supernatural/occult, regional, science fiction and serialized novel. Receives 20 unsolicited mss/month. Accepts 2-4 mss/issue; 8-16 mss/year. Publishes ms 1-12 months after acceptance. Published work by Michael K. White, Abigail Hoffman, Matthew Langley and Paul Boland. Length: 3,000 words maximum. Sometimes critiques or comments on rejected ms.

How to Contact: "Send complete ms, with or without cover letter." Reports in 2 months on mss. Send SASE for reply, return of ms or send a disposable copy of ms. Simultaneous and reprint submissions OK. Sample copy for $2 (including postage). Fiction guidelines for SASE.

Payment/Terms: Pays 2 contributor's copies. Acquires one-time rights. Sends galleys to author if requested.

Advice: "We like stories which illustrate the reality of the humor experience—people's existential crises, their experiences with other people, with their own psyches. Get a copy or two of the magazine and read the stories we've printed."

DOGWOOD TALES MAGAZINE, For the Fiction Lover in All of Us, (I), Two Sisters Publications, P.O. Box 172068, Memphis TN 38187. Editor: Linda Ditty. Fiction Editor: Peggy Carman. Magazine: 5½×8½; 50-75 pages; 20 lb. paper; 60 lb. cover stock; illustrations. "Interesting fiction that would appeal to all groups of people. Each issue will have a Special Feature Story about a Southern person, place or theme." Bimonthly. Estab. 1993.

• *Dogwood Tales* sponsors a short story contest at least twice a year with cash awards and publication.

Needs: Adventure, mainstream/contemporary, mystery/suspense, romance. No erotica, children and westerns. Accepts 7-9 mss/issue; 42-54 mss/year. Publishes ms within 1 year after acceptance. Length: 1,350 words preferred; 200 words minimum; 6,000 words maximum. Publishes short shorts. Length: 200-500 words. Sometimes critiques or comments on rejected mss.

How to Contact: Send complete ms with a cover letter. Should include estimated word count and list of publications. Reports within 10 weeks on mss. Send SASE for reply, return of ms or send a disposable copy of ms. Simultaneous submissions OK. E-mail address: write2me@aol.com. Sample copy for $3.25. Fiction guidelines for #10 SASE.

Payment/Terms: Pays 1 contributor's copy; 2 copies for special feature story; additional copies at reduced rate. Acquires first North American serial rights and reprint rights.

Advice: "We like fresh and action moving stories with a strong ending. Must be tightly written and reach out and grab the reader. Revise and send your best. Don't be afraid to submit. Don't be discouraged by rejections."

DOWNSTATE STORY, (II, IV), 1825 Maple Ridge, Peoria IL 61614. (309)688-1409. Editor: Elaine Hopkins. Magazine: illustrations. "Short fiction—some connection with Illinois or the Midwest." Annually. Estab. 1992. Circ. 500.

Needs: Adventure, ethnic/multicultural, experimental, historical, horror, humor/satire, literary, mainstream/contemporary, mystery/suspense, psychic/supernatural/occult, regional, romance, science fiction, westerns. Accepts 10 mss/issue. Publishes ms up to 1 year after acceptance. Length: 300 words minimum; 2,000 words maximum. Publishes short shorts. Also publishes literary essays.
How to Contact: Send complete ms with a cover letter. Reports "ASAP." SASE for return of ms. Simultaneous submissions OK. E-mail address: ehopkins@prairienet.org. World Wide Web address: http://www.wiu. bqu.edu/users/mfgeh/dss. Sample copy for $8. Fiction guidelines for SASE.
Payment/Terms: Pays $50 maximum.
Terms: Pays on acceptance for first rights.

‡DREAM FORGE, The Electronic Magazine for Your Mind!, (I), Dream Forge, Inc., 6400 Baltimore National Pike, #201, Baltimore MD 21228. (410)437-3463. Editor: Rick Arnold. Humor Editor: Dave Bealer. Magazine: 80 pages; electronic. "*Dream Forge* is a general interest electronic magazine for a thinking and literate readership." Monthly. Estab. 1995. Circ. 1,600.
Needs: Fantasy, humor/satire, mainstream/contemporary, science fiction (hard science, soft/sociological), computer/technical, humor, satire. Plans special fiction issues or anthologies. Receives 10 unsolicited mss/month. Accepts 6 mss/issue; 72 mss/year. Publishes ms 1-2 months after acceptance. Recently published work by Greg Borek, Gay Bost, Mary Soan Lee and Larry Tritten. Length: 3,500 words average; 1,000 words minimum; 6,000 words maximum. Publishes short shorts (humorous only). Also publishes poetry. Sometimes critiques or comments on rejected ms.
How to Contact: Query or send complete ms (electronic submissions only). Should include bio (40-60 words) with submission. E-mail addresses: dbealer@dreamforge.com (humor); 77537.1415@compuserve.c om. (other submissions). Sample copy for $2, SAE disk mailer and 2 first-class stamps. Fiction guidelines for SASE; e-mail address: writers@dreamforge.com.
Payment/Terms: Pays $10-100 on publication for first electronic rights.
Advice: "We look for stories with a positive message, even if the message is hidden deep within the fabric of the work."

DREAM INTERNATIONAL/QUARTERLY, (I, II, IV), U.S. Address: Charles I. Jones, #H-1, 411 14th St., Ramona CA 92065-2777. Australia address: 256 Berserker St., No. Rockhampton, Queensland 4701, Australia. Editor: Charles I. Jones. Magazine: 5×7; 80-135 pages; Xerox paper; parchment cover stock; some illustrations and photos. "Publishes fiction and nonfiction that is dream-related or clearly inspired by a dream. Also dream-related fantasy." Quarterly. Estab. 1981. Circ. 80-100.
Needs: Adventure, confession, contemporary, erotica, ethnic, experimental, fantasy, historical, horror, humor/satire, literary, mainstream, mystery/suspense, prose poem, psychic/supernatural/occult, romance, science fiction, translations, young adult/teen (10-18). Upcoming themes: dream control; lucid dreaming; dream journal experiences; recurring dreams. Receives 20-30 unsolicited mss/month. Publishes ms 6-8 months after acceptance. Length: 1,000 words minimum; 1,500 words maximum. Publishes short shorts. Length: 500-800 words. Recently published work by Ursela K. Leguin, Lyn Lifshin, Hillary Rodham Clinton and Norman Stephens. Also publishes literary essays, poetry (poetry submissions to Tim Scott, 4147 N. Kedvale Ave., #2B, Chicago IL 60641; send SASE for poetry guidelines).
How to Contact: Submit ms *and* computer disk; ms hardcopies accepted. Write editor for details. Reports in 6 weeks on queries; 3 months on mss. SASE. Simultaneous and reprint submissions OK. E-mail address: dreamintlq@aol.com. Sample copy for $8. Guidelines free with SAE and 2 first-class stamps. "Accepted mss will not be returned unless requested at time of submission."
Payment/Terms: Pays in contributor's copies (contributors must pay $2.95 for postage and handling). Offers magazine subscription. Acquires one-time rights.
Advice: "Use your nightly dreams to inspire you to literary flights. Avoid stereotypes and clichés. When contacting U.S. editor, make all checks, money orders, and overseas drafts payable to *Charles Jones*. When contacting senior poetry editor, make checks and money orders payable to Tim Scott."

DREAMS & NIGHTMARES, The Magazine of Fantastic Poetry, (IV), 1300 Kicker Rd., Tuscaloosa AL 35404. (205)553-2284. Editor: David C. Kopaska-Merkel. Magazine: 5½×8½; 20 pages; ink drawing illustrations. "*DN* is mainly a poetry magazine, but I *am* looking for short-short stories. They should be either fantasy, science fiction, or horror." Estab. 1986. Circ. 250.
Needs: Experimental, fantasy, horror, humor/satire, science fiction. "Try me with anything *except*: senseless violence, misogyny or hatred (unreasoning) of any kind of people, sappiness." Receives 4-8 unsolicited fiction mss/month. Buys 1-2 mss/issue; 1-5 mss/year. Publishes ms 1-9 months after acceptance. Published work by Ron McDowell, D.F. Lewis. Length: 500 words average; 1,000 words maximum. Publishes short

---

Check the Category Indexes, located at the back of the book, for publishers interested in specific fiction subjects.

shorts. Length: 500 or fewer words. Sometimes critiques rejected mss. Also publishes poetry.
How to Contact: Send complete manuscript. Reports in 1-3 weeks on queries; 1-6 weeks on mss. SASE. No simultaneous submissions. Accepts electronic submissions. E-mail address: d.kopasks-me@genie.com. Sample copy for $2. Fiction guidelines for #10 SASE.
Payment/Terms: Pays $3 on acceptance and 2 contributor's copies for one-time rights.
Advice: "A story must grab the reader and hold on to the end. I want to be *involved*. Start with a good first line, lead the reader where you want him/her to go and end with something that causes a reaction or provokes thought." Looking for "very short science fiction and fantasy, subtle but with a kick."

❦**DREAMS & VISIONS, New Frontiers in Christian Fiction, (II)**, Skysong Press, RR1, Washago, Ontario L0K 2B0 Canada. Editorial Address: 35 Pete St. S., Orillia, Ontario L3V 5AB Canada. Editor: Steve Stanton. Magazine: 5½×8½; 56 pages; 20 lb. bond paper; glossy cover. "Contemporary Christian fiction in a variety of styles for adult Christians." Triannually. Estab. 1989. Circ. 200.
Needs: Contemporary, experimental, fantasy, humor/satire, literary, religious/inspirational, science fiction (soft/sociological). "All stories should portray a Christian world view or expand upon Biblical themes or ethics in an entertaining or enlightening manner." Receives 20 unsolicited mss/month. Accepts 7 mss/issue; 21 mss/year. Publishes ms 2-6 months after acceptance. Length: 2,500 words; 2,000 words minimum; 6,000 words maximum.
How to Contact: Send complete ms with cover letter. "Bio is optional: degrees held and in what specialties, publishing credits, service in the church, etc." Reports in 1 month on queries; 2-4 months on mss. SASE. Simultaneous submissions OK. Sample copy for $4.95. Fiction guidelines for SASE.
Payment/Terms: Pays ½¢/word and contributor's copy. Acquires first North American serial rights and one-time, non-exclusive reprint rights.
Advice: "In general we look for work that has some literary value, that is in some way unique and relevant to Christian readers today. Our first priority is technical adequacy, though we will occasionally work with a beginning writer to polish a manuscript. Ultimately, we look for stories that glorify the Lord Jesus Christ, stories that build up rather than tear down, that exalt the sanctity of life, the holiness of God, and the value of the family."

‡**THE DRINKIN' BUDDY MAGAZINE, A Magazine for Art and Words, (I)**, Pimperial Productions, P.O. Box 7615, Laguna Niguel CA 92677. (714)452-8720. Editor: K.C. Bradshaw. Magazine: 5½×8½; 40 pages; 20 lb. paper and cover; illustrations and photos. Quarterly. Estab. 1994. Circ. 1,000.
Needs: Adventure, condensed/excerpted novel, erotica, ethnic/multicultural, fantasy, feminist, gay, historical, horror, humor, lesbian, literary, mainstream, mystery/suspense, psychic/supernatural, regional, romance, science fiction, senior citizen/retirement, serialized novel, sports, translations, westerns, young adult/teen. Receives 2 unsolicited mss/month. Recently published work by Groundhog and C. Darner. Publishes short shorts. Also publishes literary essays, literary criticism, poetry.
How to Contact: Sometimes critiques or comments on rejected ms. Send complete ms with a cover letter. Send SASE for reply or a disposable copy of the ms. Simultaneous, electronic submissions OK. E-mail address: kc@kaiwan.com. Sample copy for 5½×8½ SAE and 3 first-class stamps. Reviews novels and short story collections.
Payment/Terms: Pays free subscription to the magazine. Acquires one-time rights.
Advice: "A manuscript stands out when its subject and writing style are unique."

EAGLE'S FLIGHT, A Literary Magazine, (I, II), P.O. Box 832, Granite OK 73547. Editor: Shyamkant Kulkarni. Fiction Editor: Rekha Kulkarni. Tabloid: 8½×11; 4-8 pages; bond paper; broad sheet cover. Publication includes "fiction and poetry for a general audience." Quarterly.
Needs: Literary, mainstream, mystery/suspense, romance. Plans to publish special fiction issue in future. Buys 2-4 mss/year. Does not read mss June-December. Published work by Bal Swami, Anee H. Baker, Nancy Sweetland and O'Bannan M. Cook. Length: 1,500 words preferred; 1,000 words minimum; 2,000 words maximum. Publishes short shorts. Also publishes literary criticism, poetry.
How to Contact: Query first. Reports in 6 weeks on queries; 3-4 months on mss. SASE. Sample copy or fiction guidelines for $1 and #10 SASE. Reviews novels and short story collections.
Payment/Terms: Pays $5-20 on publication for first North American serial rights or one-time rights or subscription to magazine, contributor's copies; charge for additional copies.
Advice: "We look for form, substance and quality. Read and study what you want to write and work at. Our Annual Best Story Award is given in March/April for the best short story published during the previous year."

‡**EARTHSONGS, By People Who Love the Earth, (I, IV)**, Sweetlight Books, 16625 Heitman Rd., Cottonwood CA 96022. (916)529-5392. Editor: Guy Mount. Booklet: 5½×8½; 48-80 pages; 20 lb. bond; parchment cover; illustrations and occasional photos. "We publish poems, stories and illustrations that perpetuate the Earth, not an empire." Annually. Estab. 1993. Circ. 120.
Needs: Adventure, condensed/excerpted novel, erotica, ethnic/multicultural, experimental, feminist, gay, historical, lesbian, literary, mainstream/contemporary, psychic/supernatural/occult, religious/inspirational

(non-Christian), Native American, "Earthpeople." Upcoming theme: "Erotic Earth Stories." Publishes special fiction issues or anthologies. Publishes ms in November after acceptance. Recently published work by Conger Beasley. Length: 500 words minimum; 5,000 words maximum. Publishes short shorts. Also publishes literary essays and poetry. Sometimes critiques or comments on rejected ms.

How to Contact: Send complete ms with a cover letter. Should include 1-paragraph bio and list of publications with submission. Reports in 1 month. SASE for reply. Simultaneous and reprint submissions OK. Sample copy for $5, 6×9 SAE.

Payment/Terms: Pays 1 contributor's copy. Acquires non-exclusive rights. Sends galleys to author.

Advice: Looking for fiction that "reveals a love of the Earth and her people. Challenge and question the Empire."

‡ECHOES, (I, II), Echoes Magazine, P.O. Box 3622, Allentown PA 18106. Fax: (610)776-1634. Editor: Peter Crownfield. Magazine: 6×9; 64 pages.; 60 lb. offset paper; 65-80 lb. cover; illustrations and photos. "*Echoes* publishes stories, poetry, and drawings from people in all walks of life—beginners and professionals, students and teachers. We look for writing that is creative and thought-provoking—writing that speaks to the ideas and feelings that connect us all." Bimonthly. Estab. 1994.

Needs: "*Echoes* will consider any genre as long as the work is thought-provoking and interesting to readers." The following categories are of special interest: ethnic/multicultural, fantasy, humor/satire, literary, mainstream/contemporary, regional, senior citizen/retirement, young adult/teen. "We will not print any work containing gratuitous profanity, sex, or violence." Annual Memorial Day issue "features work about veterans and people in the military. Should have personal appeal—no strident pro- or anti-war themes." Publishes annual special fiction issue or anthology. Receives 25-30 unsolicited mss/month. Buys 5 mss/issue; 30 mss/year. Publishes ms 6 weeks-4 months after acceptance. Length: 3,000 average; 200 words minimum; 7,500 words maximum. Publishes short shorts. Also publishes poetry and drawings. Usually critiques or comments on rejected ms.

How to Contact: Send complete ms with a cover letter. Should include estimated word count and 50-word bio. Reports in 6-8 weeks. Send SASE for return of ms and/or comments. Reprints and electronic submissions OK. E-mail address: echoesmag@aol.com or 73200.1446@compuserve.com. Sample copy $5. Fiction guidelines for SASE.

Payment/Terms: Pays 6 contributor's copies; additional copies for $3.50 plus postage. Sponsors contests. Send SASE for guidelines.

Advice: "We appreciate stories with a personal viewpoint, well-developed characters and a clear story line—writing that makes us care what happens to the characters. Make your story clear and complete, and make sure it has a point that others will understand. Avoid rambling personal reminiscences."

EIDOS: Sexual Freedom and Erotic Entertainment for Women, Men & Couples, (IV), Box 96, Boston MA 02137-0096. (617)262-0096. Fax: (617)364-0096. Toll Free: 1-800-4U-EIDOS. Editor: Brenda Loew Tatelbaum. Tabloid: 10×14; 96 pages; web offset printing; illustrations; photos. Magazine of erotica for women, men and couples of all sexual orientations, preferences and lifestyles. "Explicit material regarding language and behavior formed in relationships, intimacy, moment of satisfaction—sensual, sexy, honest. For an energetic, well informed, international erotica readership." Quarterly. Estab. 1984. Circ. 7,000.

• *Eidos* was named "Publication of the Year" by *Caress*, a British newsletter.

Needs: Erotica. Humorous or tongue-in-cheek erotic fiction is especially wanted. Publishes at least 10-12 pieces of fiction/year. Published new writers within the last year. Length: 1,000 words average; 500 words minimum; 2,000 words maximum. Also publishes literary criticism, poetry. Occasionally critiques rejected mss.

How to Contact: Send complete ms with SASE. "Cover letter with history of publication or short bio is welcome." Reports in 1 month on queries; 1 month on mss. Simultaneous submissions OK. E-mail address: eidos@netcom.com. Sample copy for $15. Fiction guidelines for #10 SASE. Reviews novels and short story collections, "if related to subject of erotica (sex, politics, religion, etc.)."

Payment/Terms: Pays in contributor's copies. Acquires first North American serial rights.

Advice: "We receive more erotic fiction manuscripts now than in the past. Most likely because both men and women are more comfortable with the notion of submitting these manuscripts for publication as well as the desire to see alternative sexually explicit fiction in print. Therefore we can publish more erotic fiction because we have more material to choose from. There is still a lot of debate as to what erotic fiction consists of. This is a tough market to break into. Manuscripts must fit our editorial needs and it is best to order a sample issue prior to writing or submitting material. Honest, explicitly pro-sex, mutually consensual erotica lacks unwanted power, control and degradation—no unwanted coercion of any kind."

‡8, Dancing With Mr. D, (II), Screaming Toad Press/ Dancing With Mr. D Publications, P.O. Box 830, Westminster ND 21158. Editor: Llori Steinberg. Fiction Editor: Greg Bryant. Magazine: 5×7; illustrations and photos. Monthly. Estab. 1994. Circ. 200.

Needs: Adventure, erotica, experimental, fantasy (children's, science), horror, humor/satire, literary, mystery/suspense (amateur sleuth, police procedural, private eye/hardboiled. romantic), psychic/supernatural/occult. List of upcoming themes available for SASE. Receives 100 unsolicited mss/month. Buys 2-5 mss/issue; 6-

9 mss/year. Recently published work by Steven Conan, Regent Kyler and Tom Head. Length: 5,000 words minimum; 8,000 words maximum. Publishes short shorts. Also publishes literary essays, literary criticism, poetry. Sometimes critiques or comments on rejected ms.

How to Contact: Query with clips of published work and SASE with proper postage. Should include bio with list of publications. Reports in 5 weeks on queries; 6-8 weeks on mss. Send SASE for reply. Simultaneous submissions and electronic submissions OK (Windows only). Sample copy for $6 and 6×9 SAE with 5 first-class stamps. Fiction guidelines free for #10 SAE with 2 first-class stamps.

Payment/Terms: None. Sponsors contests; guidelines for SASE.

Advice: "Be original—don't try to prove a thing other than your honest self. Just send 'talk' to me—tell me your goals and 'loves.' " Does not want to see "Gothic vampire horror. There's already too much of it."

1812, A Literary Arts Magazine, (I, II), P.O. Box 1812, Amherst NY 14226-7812. Fiction Editor: Richard Lynch. Magazine: 5½×8½; 150 pages; coated cover stock; illustrations and photographs. "We want to publish work that has some *bang*." Annually. Estab. 1994.

• Work published in *1812* has been described as "experimental, surreal, bizarre."

Needs: Experimental, humor/satire, literary, mainstream/contemporary, translations. Does not want to see "stories about writers, stories about cancer, stories containing hospitals or stories that sound like they've been told before." Also publishes literary essays, literary criticism and poetry. Often critiques or comments on rejected mss.

How to Contact: Send complete ms with a cover letter. Should include brief list of publications. Reports in 2 months. SASE for return of ms. Simultaneous and reprint submissions OK. Reviews novels and short story collections.

Payment/Terms: Payment is "arranged." Buys one-time rights.

Advice: "Our philosophy can be summed up in the following quote from Beckett: 'I speak of an art turning from it in disgust, weary of its puny exploits, weary of pretending to be able, of being able, of doing a little better the same old thing, of going a little further along a dreary road.' Too many writers copy. We want to see writing by those who aren't on the 'dreary road.' "

ELDRITCH TALES, (II, IV), Yith Press, 1051 Wellington Rd., Lawrence KS 66049. (913)843-4341. Editor-in-Chief: Crispin Burnham. Magazine: 6×9; 120 pages (average); glossy cover; illustrations; "very few" photos. "The magazine concerns horror fiction in the tradition of the old *Weird Tales* magazine. We publish fiction in the tradition of H.P. Lovecraft, Robert Bloch and Stephen King, among others, for fans of this particular genre." Semiannually. Estab. 1975. Circ. 1,000.

Needs: Horror and psychic/supernatural/occult. "No mad slasher stories or similar nonsupernatural horror stories." Receives about 8 unsolicited fiction mss/month. Buys 12 mss/issue, 24 mss/year. Published work by J.N. Williamson, William F. Wu, Ron Dee and Charles Grant. Published new writers within the last year. Length: 50-100 words minimum; 20,000 words maximum; 10,000 words average. Occasionally critiques rejected mss.

How to Contact: Send complete ms with SASE and cover letter stating past sales. Previously published submissions OK. Prefers letter-quality submissions. Reports in 4 months. Publication could take up to 5 years after acceptance. Sample copy for $7.25.

Payment/Terms: ¼¢/word; 1 contributor's copy. $1 minimum payment. Pays in royalties on publication for first rights.

Advice: "Buy a sample copy and read it thoroughly. Most rejects with my magazine are because people have not checked out what an issue is like or what type of stories I accept. Most rejected stories fall into one of two categories: non-horror fantasy (sword & sorcery, high fantasy) or non-supernatural horror (mad slasher stories, 'Halloween' clones, I call them). When I say that they should read my publication, I'm not whistling Dixie. We hope to up the magazine's frequency to a quarterly. We also plan to be putting out one or two books a year, mostly novels, but short story collections will be considered as well."

THE ELEPHANT-EAR, (II, IV), Irvine Valley College, 550 Irvine Center Dr., Irvine CA 92720. (714)559-3327 ext. 299. Editor: Lisa Alvarez. Magazine: 6×9; 150 pages; matte paper and cover stock; illustrations and photos. "The journal prints the work of Orange County writers only." Annually. Estab. 1983. Circ. 2,000.

Needs: Contemporary, ethnic, experimental, feminist, humor/satire, literary, regional. Receives 100 mss/year. Accepts 5 mss/issue. Publishes ms within 5 months of acceptance. Length: 25 pages maximum. Publishes short shorts and novel excerpts. Sometimes critiques rejected mss.

How to Contact: Send completed ms with cover letter, which should include the name, address and phone number of author and the title(s) of work submitted. "Author's name must not appear on manuscript." SASE. Deadline January 23 each year. Reports by May. Sample copy for 6×9 SAE. Free fiction guidelines.

Payment/Terms: Pays in contributor's copies. Acquires one-time rights.

ELF: ECLECTIC LITERARY FORUM, (II), P.O. Box 392, Tonawanda NY 14150. (716)693-7006. Editor: C.K. Erbes. Magazine: 8½×11; 56 pages; 60 lb. offset paper; coated cover; 2-3 illustrations; 2-3 photographs.

"Well-crafted short stories, poetry, literary essays for a sophisticated audience." Quarterly. Estab. 1991. Circ. 5,000.

Needs: Adventure, contemporary, ethnic, fantasy, feminism, historical, humor/satire, literary, mainstream, mystery/suspense (private eye), prose poem, regional, science fiction (hard science, soft/sociological), sports, western. No violence and obscenity (horror/erotica). Accepts 4-6 mss/issue; 16-24 mss/year. Publishes ms up to 1 year after acceptance. Recently published work by W. Edwin Verbecke, Sandra Gould Ford, John Dickson, Gary Earl Ross, Bridget Quinn. Length: 3,500 words average. Publishes short shorts. Length: 500 words. Sometimes critiques rejected mss.

How to Contact: Send complete ms with optional cover letter. Reports in 4-6 weeks on mss. SASE. Simultaneous submissions OK (if so indicated). Sample copy for $5.50 ($8 foreign). Fiction guidelines for #10 SASE.

Payment/Terms: Pays contributor's copies. Acquires first North American serial rights.

Advice: "Short stories stand out when dialogue, plot, character, point of view and language usage work together to create a unified whole on a significant theme, one relevant to most of our readers. We also look for writers whose works demonstrate a knowledge of grammar and how to manipulate it effectively in a story. Each story is read by an Editorial Board comprised of English professors who teach creative writing and are published authors."

EMRYS JOURNAL, (I, II), The Emrys Foundation, Box 8813, Greenville SC 29604. Editor: Jeanine Halva-Neubauer. Magazine: 6×9; 120 pages; 70 lb. paper and cover stock. "We publish short fiction, poetry, and essays. We are particularly interested in hearing from women and other minorities. We are mindful of the southeast but not limited to it." Annually. Estab. 1984. Circ. 400.

Needs: Contemporary, feminist, literary, mainstream and regional. "We read from August 15 to December 1. During reading periods we receive around 1,400 manuscripts." Accepts 15-25 mss/issue. Publishes mss each spring. Length: 3,500 words average; 2,500 words minimum; 6,000 words maximum. Publishes short shorts. Length: 1,600 words. Also publishes poetry.

How To Contact: Send complete ms with cover letter. Reports in 6 weeks. SASE. Sample copy for $10 and 7×10 SAE with 4 first-class stamps. Fiction guidelines for #10 SASE.

Payment/Terms: Pays in contributor's copies. Acquires first rights. "Send to managing editor for guidelines."

Advice: Looks for "fiction by women and minorities, especially but not exclusively southeastern."

‡ENTELECHY, The Chronicle of the New Renaissance, (I, II), Flat Earth Media, Inc., 602 South Gay St., Suite 501, Knoxville TN 37902. Editor: Steven Horn. Fiction Editor: Karin Beuerlein. Magazine: 6×9; 224 pages; 60 lb. paper; 100 lb. cover; illustrations and photos. "*Entelechy* publishes poetry, fiction and literary nonfiction which is able to evoke an emotive response whether it is happiness, revulsion or sadness. Our audience is a diverse group of individuals who appreciate and applaude experimentation." Semiannually. Estab. 1993. Circ. 200.

Needs: Condensed/excerpted novel, erotica, experimental, feminist, gay, literary, regional, serialized novel, translations. "No gushy romance or mystery." Upcoming themes: "Vancouver (the writers of)" (Fall 1995). List of upcoming themes available for SASE. Receives 100 unsolicited mss/month. Buys 8 mss/issue; 20 mss/year. "We read only in January-March and June-August." Publishes ms 3 months after acceptance. Recently published work by Lynn Suderman, Susan Wickstrom and Marilyn Kallet. Length: 3,000 words average; 250 words minimum; 5,000 words maximum. Publishes short shorts. Also publishes poetry. Sometimes critiques or comments on rejected ms.

How to Contact: Send complete ms with a cover letter. Should include (75 words maximum) bio and list of publications. Send SASE for reply. Simultaneous and electronic submissions OK. E-mail address: entelechy@aol.com. Sample copy for $8 and 5 first-class stamps. Fiction guidelines for #10 SASE.

Payment/Terms: Pays 3 contributor's copies; additional copies 25% off cover price. Acquires first North American serial rights.

Advice: "We seek purely emotive responses from our readers. If through your writing you are able to evoke an emotion, please send it in. So many people who submit are unfamiliar with our editorial content, so please read the publication before submitting. We are a vibrant, young, and surprisingly esoteric publication. We would much prefer work that makes the reader have to work a little. We want more color, touch, taste and less 'storytelling.' "

EPOCH MAGAZINE, (II), 251 Goldwin Smith Hall, Cornell University, Ithaca NY 14853. (607)255-3385. Editor: Michael Koch. Submissions should be sent to Michael Koch. Magazine: 6×9; 80-100 pages; good quality paper; good cover stock. "Top level fiction and poetry for people who are interested in good literature." Published 3 times a year. Estab. 1947. Circ. 1,000.

● Work originally appearing in this quality literary journal has appeared in numerous anthologies including *Best American Short Stories*, *Best American Poetry*, *Pushcart Prize*, *The O. Henry Prize Stories*, *Best of the West* and *New Stories from the South*.

Needs: Literary, contemporary and ethnic. Buys 4-5 mss/issue. Receives approximately 100 unsolicited fiction mss each month. Does not read in summer. Published work by Denis Johnson, Harriet Doerr, Lee K.

Abbott; published new writers in the last year. Length: 10-30 typed, double-spaced pages. Also publishes literary essays (usually solicited), poetry. Critiques rejected mss when there is time. Sometimes recommends other markets.

How to Contact: Send complete ms with SASE. May accept simultaneous submissions if indicated in cover letter ("but prefer not to"). Reports in 2-8 weeks on mss. Publishes ms an average of 3 months after acceptance. Sample copy for $5.

Payment/Terms: Pays $5-10/printed page on publication for first North American serial rights.

Advice: "Read the journals you're sending work to."

EUREKA LITERARY MAGAZINE, (I, II), Eureka Printing Company, P.O. Box 280, Eureka College, Eureka IL 61530. (309)467-6336. Editor: Loren Logsdon. Fiction Editor: Nancy Perkins. Magazine: 6×9; 72 pages; 70 lb. white offset paper; 80 lb. gloss cover; photographs (occasionally). "No particular theme or philosophy—general audience." Semiannually. Estab. 1992. Circ. 310.

Needs: Adventure, ethnic/multicultural, experimental, fantasy (science), feminist, historical, humor/satire, literary, mainstream/contemporary, mystery/suspense (private eye/hardboiled, romantic), psychic/supernatural/occult, regional, romance (historical), science fiction (soft/sociological), translations. "We try to achieve a balance between the traditional and the experimental. We do favor the traditional, though." Receives 15 unsolicited mss/month. Accepts 4 mss/issue; 8-9 mss/year. Does not read mss mainly in late summer (August). Publishes ms usually within the year after acceptance. Recently published work by Ray Bradbury, Jack Matthews, Nancy Perkins, Gary Pacernick and Ralph Mills, Jr. Length: 4,500 words average; 7,000-8,000 words maximum. Publishes short shorts. Also publishes poetry.

How to Contact: Send complete ms with a cover letter. Should include estimated word count and bio (short paragraph). Reports in 1 week on queries; 4 months on mss. Send SASE for reply, return of ms or send a disposable copy of ms. Simultaneous submissions OK. Sample copy for $5.

Payment/Terms: Pays free subscription to the magazine and 2 contributor's copies. Acquires first rights or one-time rights.

Advice: "Does the writer tell a good story—one that would interest a general reader? Is the story provocative? Is its subject important? Does the story contain good insight into life or the human condition? We don't want anything so abstract that it seems unrelated to anything human. We appreciate humor and effective use of language, stories that have powerful, effective endings."

✦EVENT, (II), Douglas College, Box 2503, New Westminster, British Columbia V3L 5B2 Canada. Editor: David Zieroth. Fiction Editor: Christine Dewar. Assistant Editor: Bonnie Bauder. Magazine: 6×9; 144 pages; quality paper and cover stock; illustrations; photos. "Primarily a literary magazine, publishing poetry, fiction, reviews; for creative writers, artists, anyone interested in contemporary literature." Triannually. Estab. 1970. Circ. 1,000.

Needs: Literary, contemporary, feminist, humor, regional. "No technically poor or unoriginal pieces." Receives approximately 100 unsolicited fiction mss/month. Buys 6-8 mss/issue. Published work by Tom Wayman, George Woodcock and Heather Spears; published new writers within the last year. Length: 5,000 words maximum. Also publishes poetry. Critiques rejected mss "when there is time."

How to Contact: Send complete ms, bio and SAE with Canadian postage or IRC. Reports in 1-4 months on mss. Publishes ms 6-12 months after acceptance. Sample copy for $5.

Payment/Terms: Pays $22/page and 2 contributor's copies on publication for first North American serial rights.

Advice: "A good narrative arc is hard to find."

THE EVERGREEN CHRONICLES, A Journal of Gay, Lesbian, Bisexual & Transgendered Arts & Cultures, (II), Box 8939, Minneapolis MN 55408. Managing Editor: Susan Raffo. Magazine: 7×8½; 90-100 pages; linen bond paper; b&w line drawings and photos. "We look for work that addresses the complexities and diversities of gay, lesbian, bisexual and transgendered experiences." Triannually. Estab. 1985. Circ. 1,000.

● The magazine held a contest on the theme of "Collaborations" and will spotlight various other themes this year.

Needs: Gay or lesbian: adventure, confession, contemporary, ethnic, experimental, fantasy, feminist, humor/satire, literary, romance (contemporary), science fiction, serialized/excerpted novel, suspense/mystery. "We are interested in works by artists in a wide variety of genres. The subject matter need not be specifically lesbian, gay, bisexual or transgender-themed, but we do look for a deep sensitivity to that experience." Accepts 10-12 mss/issue; 30-36 mss/year. Publishes ms approx. 2 months after acceptance. Published work by Terri Jewel, Lev Raphael and Ruthann Robson; published new writers in the last year. Length: 3,500-4,500 words average; no minimum; 5,200 words maximum. 25 pages double-spaced maximum on prose. Publishes short shorts. Sometimes comments on rejected mss.

How to Contact: Send 4 copies of complete ms with cover letter. "It helps to have some biographical information included." Reports on queries in 3 weeks; on mss in 3-4 months. SASE. E-mail address: bzsura@aol.com. Sample copy for $8 and $1 postage. Fiction guidelines for #10 SASE.

Payment/Terms: Pays $50 for one-time rights.

‡EVERY SO OFTEN . . . , (I), Brand New Publications, 13 Cuttermill Rd., #154, Great Neck NY 11021. (516)829-5704. Editor: Adam F. Comen. Magazine: 8½×11; 20-50 pages, 20 lb. paper; 20 lb. cover; illustrations and photos. "*Every So Often* strives for work that is thought provoking. No genre is taboo, save for overly 'lovey-dovey' poetry. Audience is composed of authors, teachers and literate, intelligent people." Bimonthly. Estab. 1993. Circ. 200.

Needs: Adventure, children's/juvenile (1-4 years, 5-9 years), condensed/excerpted novel, erotica, ethnic/multicultural, experimental, fantasy, feminist, gay, historical, horror, humor/satire, lesbian, literary, mainstream/contemporary, mystery/suspense, psychic/supernatural/occult, regional, religious/inspirational, romance (contemporary), science fiction (soft/sociological), young adult/teen. Upcoming themes: "Winter Blue(s)" (December/January—erotica); "Poetry in Motion" (June/July—poetry). Plans special fiction issue or anthology. Receives 20 unsolicited mss/month. Buys 2 mss/issue; 26 mss/year. Publishes ms 1-2 months after acceptance. Recently published Mark Louis Feinson and Kathleen McDonald. Length: 8,500 words average; 8,500 words maximum. Publishes short shorts. Also publishes literary essays, literary criticism, poetry. Often critiques or comments on rejected ms.

How to Contact: Send complete ms with a cover letter. Should include 100-word bio and list of publications. Reports in 1 month on queries; 6 weeks on mss. Send SASE for reply to query or return of ms. Simultaneous, reprint and electronic submissions OK. E-mail address: adamfcohen@aol.com. Sample copy for $2 and 8½×11 SAE. Fiction guidelines free for #10 SASE.

Payment/Terms: Pays free subscription to the magazine and 2 contributor's copies. Acquires one-time rights. Not copyrighted.

Advice: "Pieces should have a pulse, mood or ideas within them. Nothing banal or overly wordy. Our writers have evolved with the publication. We like to see material and writers develop in their own time. Send material because you want to and believe in it, not because you want it printed. Be gutsy. Avoid 'I love my wife and girlfriend' slush at all costs. I want to see at least two pieces at once to get an idea of what interests and provokes a writer."

EXCURSUS, Literary Arts Journal, (II), P.O. Box 1056 Knickerbocker Station, New York NY 10002. Publisher: Giancarlo Malchiodi. Magazine: 8½×11; 100 pages; 28 lb. paper; glossy card cover; illustrations and photographs. "Eclectic, takes creative risks without lapsing into absurdity. The reader should 'travel' through the narrative with interest." Annually. Estab. 1995. Circ. 1,000.

● Publisher Giancarlo Malchiodi has been involved in small press publishing through his work with *The New Press* where he served as associate publisher, essay editor and co-poetry editor. Fiction is selected for *Excursus* by an editorial collective.

Needs: Condensed/excerpted novel, ethnic/multicultural, experimental, feminist, humor/satire, literary, mainstream/contemporary, mystery/suspense (private eye/hardboiled), regional. No romance, religious ("unless atypical in thought and non-soapbox"). Upcoming themes: "Between-The-Hyphens: Work of, about, and for Immigrant America" (fall 1996). Receives 60-70 unsolicited mss/month. Accepts 4-7 mss/year. Does not read mss July 1-August 31 (returned unread during this time). Publishes ms up to a year after acceptance. Length: 2,500 words average; 1,700 words minimum; 3,500 words maximum. Also publishes literary essays, literary criticism and poetry. Sometimes critiques or comments on rejected ms.

How to Contact: Send complete manuscript with a cover letter. Should include estimated word count and an informational and friendly cover letter. Reports in 4-6 weeks on queries; 3-4 months on mss. SASE for return of ms. Simultaneous and electronic disk (WordPerfect 6.0) submissions OK. Sample copy for $7.50. Fiction guidelines for #10 SASE.

Payment/Terms: Pays 1 contributor's copy. Additional copies for $5. Acquires one-time rights. Sends galleys to author for proofing.

Advice: Looks for "insight, positive or negative, into the human condition. New twists on 'old' themes. No pablum! Nothing overly trite or sentimental. No gratuitous violence. Want to see work that tackles, in any way subtle or obvious, issues affecting society. Take risks in content and form, but try to 'work the balance' between convention and avant-garde. Seek power through your characters, their interplay, and their setting. No first drafts."

EXPLORATIONS '96, (I, II), University of Alaska Southeast, 11120 Glacier Highway, Juneau AK 99801. (907)465-6418. Editor: Art Petersen. Magazine: 5½×8¼; 44 pages; heavy cover stock; illustrations and photographs. "Poetry, prose and art—we strive for artistic excellence." Annually. Estab. 1980. Circ. 750.

Needs: Experimental, humor/satire, traditional quality fiction, poetry, and art. Receives 1,000 mss/year.

How to Contact: Send name, address and short bio on *back* of first page of each submission. All submissions entered in contest. Reading/entry fee $4/story required. Submission deadline is March 21, postmarked by. Reports in 2-3 months. Mss cannot be returned. Simultaneous and reprint submissions OK. Sample copy for $5 ($4 for back issues).

Payment/Terms: Pays 2 contributor's copies. Acquires one-time rights (rights remain with the author). *Charges $4 reading/entry fee.* Also awards 4 annual prizes of $500 for prose, $500 for poetry and $125 for art ($100, $50 and $25).

Advice: "Concerning poetry and prose, standard form as well as innovation are encouraged; appropriate and fresh *imagery* (allusions, metaphors, similes, symbols . . .) as well as standard or experimental form draw editorial attention. 'Language really spoken by men' and women and authentically rendered experience are encouraged. Unfortunately, requests for criticism usually cannot be met. The prizes for 1996 will be awarded by a writer of reputation (*to be announced*)."

EXPLORER MAGAZINE, (I), Flory Publishing Co., Box 210, Notre Dame IN 46556. (219)277-3465. Editor: Ray Flory. Magazine: 5½×8½; 20-32 pages; 20 lb. paper; 60 lb. or stock cover; illustrations. Magazine with "basically an inspirational theme including love stories in good taste." Christian writing audience. Semiannually. Estab. 1960. Circ. 200.

● In 1993 the editor added The Joseph Flory Memorial Award in honor of his late father, a writer and editor and recipient of several Freedom Foundation Awards. He also awards the Angel Light Award to the author whose prose or poetry most emphasizes the spiritual. Awards are $10 and a plaque.

Needs: Literary, mainstream, prose poem, religious/inspirational, romance (contemporary, historical, young adult) and science fiction. No pornography. Buys 2-3 mss/issue; 5 mss/year. Length: 600 words average; 300 words minimum; 900 words maximum. Also publishes literary essays. Occasionally critiques rejected mss.

How to Contact: Send complete ms with SASE. Reports in 1 week. Publishes ms up to 3 years after acceptance. Simultaneous submissions OK. Sample copy for $3. Fiction guidelines for SASE.

Payment/Terms: Cash prizes of $25, $20, $15 and $10 and a plaque based on subscribers' votes.

Advice: "I need short material, preferably no longer than 700 words—the shorter the better. I always like 'slice of life' with a message, without being preachy. I look for fiction with a 'message' in all styles that are written with feeling and flair. Just keep it short, 'camera-ready' and always in good taste."

EXPRESSIONS, Literature and Art by People with Disabilities and Ongoing Health Problems, (IV), Serendipity Press, P.O. Box 16294, St. Paul MN 55116-0294. (612)552-1209. Fax: (612)552-1209. Editor: Sefra Kobrin Pitzele. Magazine: 5½×8½; 72-96 pages; 60 lb. biodegradable paper; 80 lb. glossy cover; illustrations and photographs. "*Expressions* provides a quality journal in which to be published when health, mobility, access or illness make multiple submissions both unreachable and unaffordable." Semiannually. Estab. 1993. Circ. 750.

Needs: Material from writers with disabilities or ongoing health problems only. Adventure, ethnic/multicultural, experimental, fantasy, feminist, gay, historical, horror, humor/satire, lesbian, literary, mainstream/contemporary, mystery/suspense, psychic/supernatural/occult, regional, religious/inspirational, romance, science fiction, senior citizen/retirement, sports and westerns. "We have no young readers, so all fiction should be intended for adult readers." Does not read mss from December 15 to February 1. Publishes ms 3-5 months after acceptance. Length: 1,250-1,500 words average. Publishes short shorts. Also publishes literary essays, literary criticism and poetry. Sometimes critiques or comments on rejected ms.

How to Contact: Write for fiction guidelines; include SASE. Reports in 2-6 weeks on queries; 2-4 months on mss. SASE for reply to query or return of ms. Simultaneous, reprint and electronic submissions OK. Sample copy for $6, 6×9 SAE and 5 first-class stamps.

Payment/Terms: Pays 2 contributor's copies. Acquires one-time rights.

Advice: Every 3rd issue is a fiction contest. Send #10 SASE for more information. "Eight to ten reader/scorers from across the nation help me rank each submission on its own merit." Awards are $50 (first place), $25 (second place) and a year's subscription (third place).

‡THE EXTREME, a magazine for three finkers, (I), 49 Summit Ave., Garfield NJ 07026. (201)478-6810. Editor: Andersen Silva. Magazine: 5½×8½; 32 pages; 20 lb. white paper and cover; photos. "*The Extreme* is written by and for people whose minds remain open. If you enjoy thinking, if you can admit that your most deeply held beliefs may be wrong, then welcome!" Monthly. Estab. 1995.

Needs: Adventure, experimental, gay, horror, humor/satire, literary, mystery/suspense (private eye/hard-boiled), science fiction. Plans special fiction issue or anthology. Receives 4-6 unsolicited mss/month. Buys 2-3 mss/issue; 36-40 mss/year. Publishes ms 1-2 months after acceptance. Recently published work by Justin Fallin, Peter Quinones and Jerry Finch. Length: 1,400 words average; 600 words minimum; 2,200 words maximum. Publishes short shorts. Length: 300 words. Also publishes literary essays, poetry. Always critiques or comments on rejected ms.

How to Contact: Send complete ms with a cover letter. Should include estimated word count. Reports in 2 weeks on queries; 1 month on mss. Send a disposable copy of ms. Simultaneous, reprint and electronic submissions OK. E-mail address: extrememag@aol.com. Sample copy for $1. Fiction guidelines for SASE.

Payment/Terms: Pays 5 contributor's copies. Acquires one-time rights.

Advice: "Submit away! If I don't use it right away, I'll tell you what I did like about it, as well as explaining what I didn't like. So far, I haven't hated anything I've seen! I look for the unusual; the surprise ending or an ending with no resolution, the story that can't be pigeonholed, stuff that makes you think! I'm surprised by the dearth of science fiction being submitted. Don't bother sending strong, opinionated pieces about politics or religion unless you can take criticism and possibly lampooning."

EYES, (I), Apt. 301, 2715 S. Jefferson Ave., Saginaw MI 48601. (517)752-5202. Editor: Frank J. Mueller, III. Magazine: 8½×11; 36 pages; 20 lb. paper; Antiqua parchment, blue 65 lb. cover. "No specific theme.

Speculative fiction and surrealism most welcome. For a general, educated, not necessarily literary audience."
Estab. 1991. Circ. 30-40.

• This editor is especially looking for speculative fiction and surrealism, but is no longer interested in fantasy.

Needs: Contemporary, experimental, horror, mainstream, prose poem, romance (gothic). Nothing pornographic; no preachiness; children's fiction discouraged. Accepts 4-7 mss/issue. Publishes ms up to 1 year or longer after acceptance. Length: up to 6,000 words, occasionally longer. Sometimes critiques rejected mss.

How to Contact: Query first or send complete ms. Reports in 1 month (or less) on queries; 3 months on mss. SASE. No simultaneous submissions. Sample copy for $4; extras $4. (Checks to Frank J. Mueller III.) Fiction guidelines for #10 SASE.

Payment/Terms: Pays one contributor's copy. Acquires one-time rights.

Advice: "Write and write again. If rejected, try again. If you have a manuscript you like and would like to see it in *Eyes*, send it to me. If rejected, please try again. Above all, don't let rejections discourage you. Try to have your manuscript say something. I would encourage the purchase of a sample to get an idea of what I'm looking for."

‡FAR GONE, Stalking the giants of tomorrow, (III), P.O. Box 43745, Lafayette LA 70504-3745. Editor: Todd Brendan Fahey. Magazine: 11×8½; 48 pages; 24 lb. laser paper; 64 lb. laid-grain cover. *Far Gone*'s philosophy is "great fiction announces itself and needs no announcement." Annually. Estab. 1995. Circ. 100.

Needs: Black humor, will consider the novella. Plans special fiction issue or anthology. Receives 40 unsolicited mss/year. Buys 3-4 mss/issue. Publishes ms up to 1 year after acceptance. Agented fiction 15%. Recently published work by Sean-Brendan Brown and Alex Kolker. Publishes short shorts. Also publishes poetry.

How to Contact: Often critiques or comments on rejected ms. Send complete ms with a cover letter or submit through an agent. Should include estimated word count and 1-paragraph bio. Reports in 1 month on mss. Send SASE for return of ms or send a disposable copy of ms. Simultaneous and electronic submissions OK (ASCII or WordPerfect). Sample copy for $7.

Payment/Terms: Pays 1 contributor's copy. Acquires first North American serial rights.

Advice: "Good satire does not wink at the reader."

THE FARMER'S MARKET, (II), Midwestern Farmer's Market, Inc., Elgin Community College, 1700 Spartan Dr., Elgin IL 60123-7193. Magazine: 5½×8½; 100-200 pages; 60 lb. offset paper; 65 lb. cover; b&w illustrations and photos. Magazine publishing "quality fiction, poetry, nonfiction, author interviews, etc., in the Midwestern tradition for an adult, literate audience." Semiannually. Estab. 1982. Circ. 500.

• *The Farmer's Market* has received numerous honors including Illinois Arts Council Literary Awards and grants. Work published in the magazine has been selected for the *O. Henry Prize* anthology.

Needs: Contemporary, feminist, humor/satire, literary, regional and excerpted novel. "We prefer material of clarity, depth and strength with strong plots and good character development." No "romance, juvenile, teen." Reading periods: March-May, September-November. Accepts 10-20 mss/year. Published work by Mary Maddox, David Williams; published new writers within the last year. Also publishes literary essays, poetry. Occasionally critiques rejected mss or recommends other markets.

How to Contact: Send complete ms with SASE. Reports in 1-3 months. No simultaneous submissions. Publishes ms 4-8 months after acceptance. Sample copy for $5.50 and $1 postage and handling.

Payment/Terms: Pays 2 contributor's copies plus one-year subscription. (Other payment dependent upon grants). Authors retain rights.

Advice: "We're always interested in regional fiction but that doesn't mean cows and chickens and home-baked apple pie, please. We are publishing more fiction and we are looking for exceptional manuscripts. Read the magazine before submitting. If you don't want to buy it, ask your library. We receive numerous mss that are clearly unsuitable. We're not sweet; we're not cute and we're not 'precious!' "

FAT TUESDAY, (I), 560 Manada Gap Rd., Grantville PA 17028. Editor-in-Chief: F.M. Cotolo. Editors: B. Lyle Tabor and Thom Savion. Associate Editors: Lionel Stevroid and Kristen vonOehrke. Journal: 8½×11 or 5×8; 27-36 pages; good to excellent paper; heavy cover stock; b&w illustrations; photos. "Generally, we are an eclectic journal of fiction, poetry and visual treats. Our issues to date have featured artists like Patrick Kelly, Charles Bukowski, Joi Cook, Chuck Taylor and many more who have focused on an individualistic nature with fiery elements. We are a literary mardi gras—as the title indicates—and irreverancy is as acceptable to us as profundity as long as there is fire! Our audience is anyone who can praise literature and condemn it at the same time. Anyone too serious about it on either level will not like *Fat Tuesday*." Annually. Estab. 1981. Circ. 700.

• *Fat Tuesday* is best known for first-person "auto fiction."

Needs: Comics, erotica, experimental, humor/satire, literary, prose poem, psychic/supernatural/occult, serialized/excerpted novel and dada. "Although we list categories, we are open to feeling out various fields if they are delivered with the mark of an individual and not just in the format of the particular field." Receives 20 unsolicited fiction mss/month. Accepts 4-5 mss/issue. Published new writers within the last year. Length:

1,000 words maximum. Publishes short shorts. Occasionally critiques rejected mss and usually responds with a personal note or letter.

How to Contact: Send complete ms with SASE. "No previously published material considered." No simultaneous submissions. Reports in 1 month. Publishes ms 3-10 months after acceptance. Sample copy for $5.

Payment/Terms: Pays 1 contributor's copy. Acquires one-time rights.

Advice: "As *Fat Tuesday* crawls through its second decade, we find publishing small press editions more difficult than ever. Money remains a problem, mostly because small press seems to play to the very people who wish to be published in it. In other words, the cast is the audience, and more people want to be in *Fat Tuesday* than want to buy it. It is through sales that our magazine supports itself. This is why we emphasize buying a sample issue ($5) before submitting. As far as what we want to publish—send us shorter works that are 'crystals of thought and emotion which reflect your individual experiences—dig into your guts and pull out pieces of yourself. Your work is your signature; like time itself, it should emerge from the penetralia of your being and recede into the infinite region of the cosmos,' to coin a phrase, and remember *Fat Tuesday* is mardi gras—so fill up before you fast. Bon soir."

‡FATHOMS, A Journal of Poetry and Prose, (II, III), Doors West, 2020 W. Pensacola, Unit 46, #549, Tallahassee FL 32304. Editor: Rex West. Fiction Editors: Todd Pierce, Kerry Davies. Magazine: quarto; 48 pages; library bond paper; 80 lb. color cover. Triannually. Estab. 1992. Circ. 800.

Needs: Literary, short short fiction. "We are planning a trade paperback anthology of short short fiction." Receives 200 unsolicited mss/month. Accepts 3-6 mss/issue; 12 mss/year. Publishes ms 6 months after acceptance. Agented fiction 30%. Recently published work by David Shields, Ronald Wallace, Sesshu Foster. Length: 1,000 words average; 2,000 words maximum. Also publishes poetry.

How to Contact: Send complete ms with a cover letter. "Send for a sample issue ($3.50) or look at a library copy—it's best to see the specific type of work we publish." Should include 4-sentence bio and list of publications. Reports in 2-8 months on mss. Send SASE for reply, return of ms or send a disposable copy of ms.

Payment/Terms: Pays 2 contributor's copies on publication. Acquires first North American serial rights.

Advice: "Read good writers every day. Attend workshops. Revise your work over months, even years. Submit only your best work. Work on your fiction continually. Be kind to all editors—it's a hard and thankless job."

‡FAULT LINES, Dedicated to the Image and the Idea, (I, II), Club Mad Publishing, Box 152, 1211 Greenland Dr., Murfreesboro TN 37130. (615)356-6591. Editors: Rex McCulloch, Mark Roberts. Fiction Editor: Rex McCulloch. Magazine: 5½×8½; 32 pages; 20 lb. white bond paper; 60 lb. cover; illustrations. Semiannually. Estab. 1994. Circ. 300.

Needs: Ethnic/multicultural, experimental, humor/satire, literary, translations. "We feel that film is one of the most powerful artistic mediums available today and are always interested in fiction and nonfiction with a film theme." Receives 10-20 unsolicited mss/month. Accepts 4-5 mss/issue; 10 mss/year. Publishes ms 1 month after acceptance. Length: 2,500 words maximum. Publishes short shorts. Also publishes literary essays, poetry. Sometimes critiques or comments on rejected ms.

How to Contact: Send complete ms with a cover letter. Should include estimated word count and brief bio with list or partial list of previous publications. Reports in 2-3 months on mss. Simultaneous, reprint, electronic (Macintosh compatible) submissions OK. E-mail address: rextasy@aol.com. Sample copy for $2. Fiction guidelines for #10 SASE. Reviews novels and short story collections. Send books to Rex McCulloch, 915 Ewing Blvd., B11, Murfreesboro TN 37130.

Payment/Terms: Pays 1 contributor's copy. Acquires one-time rights.

Advice: "It's better to write interesting fiction about an unassuming subject than to try to fake an exciting story. Neatness and careful editing always make a good impression. In any genre, the elements of good fiction are always the same: idea, character development, and above all, the ability to make the reader care."

FEDERATION STANDARD, A *StarTrek: The Next Generation* fanzine, (I, II, IV), Millennium Publications, 610 Church St., Thibodaux LA 70301. Editor: Michelle Benoit. Magazine: 8½×11; 150-200 pages; 20 lb. paper; 50 lb. cover (occasional color); illustrations. "All material deals with characters from the series *Star Trek: The Next Generation*. Short stories should be original. Some DS9 and Voyager material." Quarterly. Estab. 1991.

Needs: *Star Trek: The Next Generation*, also some DS9 and Voyager. No farce or satire in stories; only *Star Trek*. Upcoming theme: Special project devoted to Data character. Accepts 8-12 mss/year. Publishes ms within 1 year after acceptance. Published work by Barbara Caldwell, Cyndi Bayless Overstreet, Jennifer Adams and Julia Fraser. Length: open. Always critiques or comments on rejected mss.

How to Contact: Query first or send complete ms with a cover letter. Should include bio (3-5 paragraphs). Reports in 3 weeks on queries; 6 weeks on mss. Send SASE for reply, return of ms or send a disposable copy of ms. No simultaneous submissions. E-mail address: michelle_walker@lagn.com. Sample copy for $10-15. Fiction guidelines for legal SASE.

Payment/Terms: Pays 1 contributor's copy. Acquires all rights. Sends galleys to author.

Advice: "Stories must present realistic portrayals of characters seen on the television series. Character insight and development are paramount. Watch the *Star Trek: The Next Generation* episodes and know the characters inside and out. Have a point to your story and have something accomplished by the end of the story. We need more character material, such as stories that revolve around some inner turmoil that is hinted at in the series. Don't try to write an episode in a short story." *Federation Standard* is looking for reliable writers who have the time to contribute consistently. "I cultivate writers, but some drop out of fandom."

FELICITY, (I), Weems Concepts, HCR-13, Box 21AA, Artemas PA 17211. (814)458-3102. Editor: Kay Weems-Winter. Newsletter: 8½×11; 20 lb. bond paper; illustrations. "Publishes articles, poetry and short stories. Poetry has different theme each issue. No theme for stories." Quarterly. Estab. 1988. Circ. 200.

Needs: Open. Short stories, any genre in good taste. No erotica, translations. All submissions treated as contest entries. Entry fee is $5 and the deadline is the 30th of each month. Length: 800-2,500 words. Publishes short shorts. Length up to 800 words; entry fee $2. Editor will consider stories that do not win for *My Legacy* or recommends other markets. Publishes ms 3-4 months after acceptance.

How to Contact: Send complete ms with cover letter or enter bimonthly contests. "Send SASE for return of ms or tell me to destroy it if not accepted." Reports in 4-5 months. SASE. Simultaneous and reprint submissions OK as long as author still retains rights. Sample copy for $2, #10 SAE and 65¢ postage. Fiction guidelines for #10 SASE or check *The Bottom Line*, market listing for contests.

Payment/Terms: Pays in contributor's copies and ½ of entry fee collected for Short Story Contest. All entries receive copy of the issue. Acquires one-time rights. "We sponsor bimonthly contests. Winner receives half of entry fees collected for the short story contest. Submit ms along with entry fee and you will be entered in the contest. Deadline is the 30th of each month. Read both of our publications—*Felicity* and *The Bottom Line Publications*. Our contests are listed there."

Advice: Looks for "good opening sentence, realistic characters, nice descriptions, strong plot with believable ending. Use natural conversations. Let me *feel* your story. Keep me interested until the end. Keep trying. A lot of mss I read are from new writers. Personally I enjoy stories and articles which will create a particular emotion, build suspense, or offer excitement or entertainment. Don't spell out everything in detail—keep me guessing."

FEMINIST STUDIES, (II), Women's Studies Program, University of Maryland, College Park MD 20742. (301)405-7415. Editor: Claire G. Moses. Fiction Editor: Alicia Ostriker. Magazine: journal-sized; about 200 pages; photographs. "Scholarly manuscripts, fiction, book review essays for professors, graduate/doctoral students; scholarly interdisciplinary feminist journal." Triannually. Estab. 1974. Circ. 7,500.

Needs: Contemporary, ethnic, feminist, gay, lesbian. Receives about 15 poetry and short stories/month. Acquires 2-3 mss/issue. "We review fiction twice a year. Deadline dates are May 1 and December 1. Authors will receive notice of the board's decision by June 30 and January 30, respectively." Sometimes comments on rejected ms.

How to Contact: Send complete ms with cover letter. No simultaneous submissions. Sample copy for $12. Fiction guidelines free.

Payment/Terms: Pays 2 contributor's copies and 10 tearsheets. Sends galleys to authors.

‡FIBEROPTIC ETCHINGS, A compilation of teenagers' writing from the information super highway, (IV), Platapus Press, 6645 Windsor Court, Columbia MD 21044. (410)730-2319. Editor: Stacy Cowley. Fiction Editor: Marcello Teson. Magazine: 8½×11; 100 pages. "*FiberOptic Etchings* publishes writing by teenagers, intended for a general audience." Annually. Estab. 1995.

Needs: Adventure, condensed/excerpted novel, ethnic/multicultural, experimental, fantasy (science fiction, sword and sorcery), feminist, historical, horror, humor/satire, literary, mainstream/contemporary, mystery/suspense, psychic/supernatural/occult, regional, romance, science fiction, sports, westerns, young adult/teen. "Nothing extraordinarily violent, vulgar, or explicit; no erotica." Receives 5 unsolicited mss/month. Accepts 10-15 mss/issue. Publishes ms 1-10 months after acceptance. Length: 700 words average. Publishes short shorts. Also publishes literary essays, poetry. Always critiques or comments on rejected ms.

How to Contact: Send complete ms with a cover letter (must send via e-mail). Should include 1-2 paragraph bio, list of publications. Reports in 2 weeks. Simultaneous, reprint, electronic submissions (required). E-mail address: foetchings@aol.com. Sample copy for $6. Fiction guidelines free.

Payment/Terms: Pays 1 contributor's copy; additional copies 50% discount. Acquires one-time rights. Not copyrighted.

Advice: "We look for manuscripts with a unique viewpoint and clear, fluid writing. Don't be afraid to submit unusual or experimental pieces, and don't be afraid to submit again and again. We're always delighted to look at anything that comes our way—we never know where a treasure will be found."

FICTION, (II), % Dept. of English, City College, 138th St. & Convent Ave., New York NY 10031. (212)650-6319/650-6317. Editor: Mark J. Mirsky. Managing Editor: Caryn Stabinsky. Magazine: 6×9; 150-250 pages; illustrations and occasionally photos. "As the name implies, we publish *only* fiction; we are looking for the best new writing available, leaning toward the unconventional. *Fiction* has traditionally attempted to make accessible the unaccessible, to bring the experimental to a broader audience." Biannually. Estab. 1972. Circ. 4,500.

- Stories first published in *Fiction* have been selected for inclusion in the *Pushcart Prize* and *Best of the Small Presses* anthologies.

Needs: Contemporary, experimental, humor/satire, literary and translations. No romance, science-fiction, etc. Receives 200 unsolicited mss/month. Acquires 12-20 mss/issue; 24-40 mss/year. Does not read mss May-October. Publishes ms 1-12 months after acceptance. Agented fiction 10-20%. Published work by Harold Brodkey, Joyce Carol Oates, Peter Handke, Max Frisch, Susan Minot and Adolfo Bioy-Casares. Length: 6,000 words maximum. Publishes short shorts. Sometimes critiques rejected mss and recommends other markets.

How to Contact: Send complete ms with cover letter. Reports in approximately 3 months on mss. SASE. Simultaneous submissions OK, but please advise. Sample copy for $5. Fiction guidelines for SASE.

Payment/Terms: Pays in contributor's copies. Acquires first rights.

Advice: "The guiding principle of *Fiction* has always been to go to terra incognita in the writing of the imagination and to ask that modern fiction set itself serious questions, if often in absurd and comic voices, interrogating the nature of the real and the fantastic. It represents no particular school of fiction, except the innovative. Its pages have often been a harbor for writers at odds with each other. As a result of its willingness to publish the difficult, experimental, unusual, while not excluding the well known, *Fiction* has a unique reputation in the U.S. and abroad as a journal of future directions."

FICTION INTERNATIONAL, (II), English Dept., San Diego State University, San Diego CA 92182. (619)594-6220. Editor: Harold Jaffe. "Serious literary magazine of fiction, extended reviews, essays." Magazine: 200 pages; illustrations; photos. "Our twin biases are progressive politics and post-modernism." Semiannually. Estab. 1973. Circ. 1,000.

Needs: Literary, political and innovative forms. Receives approximately 300 unsolicited fiction mss each month. Unsolicited mss will be considered only from September 1 through December 15 of each year. Published new writers within the last year. No length limitations but rarely use manuscripts over 25 pages. Portions of novels acceptable if self-contained enough for independent publication.

How to Contact: Send complete ms with SASE. Reports in 1-3 months on mss. Sample copy for $9: query Harry Polkinhorn, managing editor.

Payment/Terms: Pays in contributor's copies.

Advice: "Study the magazine. We're highly selective. A difficult market for unsophisticated writers."

♣THE FIDDLEHEAD, (I, II), University of New Brunswick, Campus House, Box 4400, Fredericton, New Brunswick E3B 5A3 Canada. (506)453-3501. Editor: Don McKay. Fiction Editors: Diana Austin, Banny Belyea and Ted Colson. Magazine: 6×9; 104-128 pages; ink illustrations; photos. "No criteria for publication except quality. For a general audience, including many poets and writers." Quarterly. Estab. 1945. Circ. 1,000.

- *The Fiddlehead* celebrated its 50th Anniversary in 1995.

Needs: Literary. No non-literary fiction. Receives 100-150 unsolicited mss/month. Buys 4-5 mss/issue; 20-40 mss/year. Publishes ms up to 1 year after acceptance. Small percent agented fiction. Recently published work by C.R. Crackel; published new writers within the last year. Length: 50-3,000 words average. Publishes short shorts. Occasionally critiques rejected mss.

How to Contact: Send complete ms with cover letter. Send SASE and *Canadian* stamps or IRCs for return of mss. Reprint submissions OK. No simultaneous submissions. Reports in 2-6 months. Sample copy for $6.50 (US). Reviews novels and short story collections—*Canadian only.*

Payment/Terms: Pays $10-12 (Canadian)/published page and 1 contributor's copy on publication for first or one-time rights.

Advice: "Less than 5% of the material received is published."

♣FILLING STATION, (I, II), Filling Station Publications Society, Box 22135, Bankers Hall, Calgary, Alberta T2P 4J5 Canada. Contact: Editorial Collective. Magazine: 8½×11; 48 pages; 70 lb. offset paper; 80 lb. glossy cover; illustrations and photos. "We are interested in all types of challenging fiction." Triannually. Estab. 1993. Circ. 500.

- *Filling Station* received a Western Magazine Award (Vancouver) in 1995.

Needs: Ethnic/multicultural, experimental, feminist, gay, lesbian, literary, mainstream/contemporary, regional and translations. Receives 10-15 unsolicited submissions/month. Accepts 3-4 mss/issue; 10 mss/year. Publishes ms within 1 year after acceptance. Recently published work by Roberta Rees, M.A. Laberge, Julia Gaunce, Suzette Mayr and Rick Wenman. Length: 2,000 words average; 5,000 words maximum. Publishes short shorts. Also publishes literary essays, literary criticism and poetry.

How to Contact: Send complete ms with cover letter. Should include bio (20-30 words). Reports in 1 month on queries; 3 months on mss. Send SASE for reply, return of ms or send a disposable copy of ms. Simultaneous and electronic submissions OK. Sample copy for $6, 9×12 SAE, 4 first-class stamps and 2 IRCs. Fiction guidelines for #10 SASE. Reviews novels and short story collections.

Payment/Terms: Pays 2 contributor's copies. Acquires first North American serial rights.

FISH DRUM MAGAZINE, (II), % 626 Kathryn Ave., Santa Fe NM 87501. Editor: Robert Winson. Magazine: 5½×8½; 40-odd pages; glossy cover; illustrations and photographs. "Lively, emotional vernacular modern fiction, art and poetry." Published 2-4 times/year. Estab. 1988. Circ. 500.
Needs: Contemporary, erotica, ethnic, experimental, fantasy, gay, lesbian, literary, prose poem, regional, science fiction. "We're interested in material by New Mexican writers; also on the practice of Zen. Most of the fiction we've published is in the form of short, heightened prose-pieces." Receives 6-10 unsolicited mss/ month. Accepts 1-2 mss/issue; 2-8 mss/year. Publishes ms 6-12 months after acceptance. Also publishes literary essays, literary criticism, poetry.
How to Contact: Send complete manuscript. No simultaneous submissions. Reports on mss in 1-3 months. SASE. Sample copy for $5. Reviews novels and short story collections.
Payment/Terms: Pays in contributor's copies. Charges for extras. Acquires first North American serial rights. Sends galleys to author.

‡FISH STORIES, Collective II, (II), WorkShirts Writing Center, 5412 N. Clark St., South Suite, Chicago IL 60640. Editor: Amy G. Davis. Magazine: 5⅜×8½; 224 pages; 60 lb. white paper; 4-color C1S cover. "We are seeking vivid stories that stand up to a second reading, but don't require it. While our fiction is literary, we have readers outside that audience. *Fish Stories* strives for a diverse collection of work." Annually. Estab. 1995. Circ. 1,200.
Needs: Ethnic/multicutural, experimental, feminist, gay, lesbian, literary, regional. No mainstream, science fiction or any other genre fiction. "We seek experimental or traditional literary work." Receives 65 unsolicited mss/month. Buys 15-20 mss/issue. Does not read April-September. Publishes ms 2-8 months after acceptance. Recently published work by Robert Olen Butler, Charles Baxter, Susan Power and Lan Samantha Chang. Length: 3,000-5,000 words average; 10,000 words maximum. Publishes short shorts. Also publishes poetry. Sometimes critiques or comments on rejected ms.
How to Contact: Send for guidelines. "Read a sample copy first, then send mss." Should include estimated word count, brief bio, Social Security number, list of publications. Reports in 6 months on mss. Send SASE for reply, return of ms or send a disposable copy of ms. Simultaneous and reprint submissions, OK. Sample copy for $10.95. Fiction guidelines free for #10 SASE.
Payment/Terms: Pays 2 contributor's copies; additional copies half-price. Acquires one-time rights. Sponsors a contest; send SASE for guidelines.
Advice: Looks for "a strong introduction that is followed through by the rest of the story. The manuscripts that stand out are polished with careful attention to the holistic use of language, point of view, etc."

FLIPSIDE, (II), Professional Writing Program, Dixon 109, California University, California PA 15419. (412)938-4082. Editor: David R. Eltz. Tabloid: 11½×17; 45-60 pages; illustrations; photos. "Emphasis on 'new journalism,' fiction, nonfiction, poetry and humor." Semiannually. Estab. 1987. Circ. 5,000.
• Stories published in *Flipside* tend to be plot-driven and heavily descriptive.
Needs: Contemporary, experimental, literary. No genre fiction. Receives 5-6 unsolicited mss/month. Accepts 2-3 mss/issue; 6-8 mss/year. Publishes ms 1-6 months after acceptance. Length: 1,000-5,000 words average; 8,000 words maximum. Also publishes literary essays, literary criticism, some poetry.
How to Contact: Send complete ms with cover letter. Reports in 2-4 weeks on queries; 1-2 months on mss. SASE. Simultaneous submissions OK. Sample copy and fiction guidelines for 9×12 SAE and $2 postage.
Payment/Terms: Pays 3 contributor's copies. Acquires first North American serial rights.
Advice: "Experimental and alternative fiction are always welcome here. Traditional fiction, darkly executed, is also encouraged."

THE FLORIDA REVIEW, (II), Dept. of English, University of Central Florida, Orlando FL 32816. (407)823-2038. Contact: Russell Kesler. Magazine: 5½×8½; 128 pages. Semiannually. Estab. 1972. Circ. 1,000.
• Work from this quality literary journal was selected for the *Editor's Choice III: Fiction, Poetry & Art From the US Small Presses* (1984-1990), published by the Spirit That Moves Us Press.
Needs: Contemporary, experimental and literary. "We welcome experimental fiction, so long as it doesn't make us feel lost or stupid. We aren't especially interested in genre fiction (science fiction, romance, adventure, etc.), though a good story can transcend any genre." Receives 200 mss/month. Acquires 8-10 mss/ issue; 16-20 mss/year. Publishes ms within 3-6 months of acceptance. Published work by Stephen Dixon, Richard Grayson and Liz Rosenberg. Publishes short shorts. Also publishes literary criticism, poetry and essays.
How to Contact: Send complete ms with cover letter. Reports in 2-4 months. SASE. Simultaneous submissions OK. Sample copy for $4.50; fiction guidelines for SASE. Reviews novels and short story collections.
Payment/Terms: Pays in contributor's copies. Small honorarium occasionally available. "Copyright held by U.C.F.; reverts to author after publication. (In cases of reprints, we ask that a credit line indicate that the work first appeared in the *F.R.*)"

Advice: "We publish fiction of high 'literary' quality—stories that delight, instruct, and aren't afraid to take risks."

THE FLUMMERY PRESS, (I), P.O. Box 244, Glen Ellyn IL 60138-0244. (708)627-4272. Fax: (708)386-9069. Editors: Keith McClow, Chris Baugher and Brian Dunk. Magazine: 5½×8½; 40-60 pages; 20 lb. paper; 80 lb. cover; illustrations. "*The Flummery Press* will print quality stories from new writers and will return to the writers any comment we receive. We would like to help writers begin a career and provide readers with a good magazine." Quarterly. Estab. 1993. Circ. 125.
Needs: Fantasy, horror, science fiction. Receives 30-40 unsolicited mss/month. Accepts 3-8 mss/issue. Length: 5,000 words maximum. Publishes short shorts. Also publishes poetry.
How to Contact: Submissions by mail should include complete disposable ms with a cover letter, including a half-page bio, and SASE. Prefers electronic submission via e-mail at FlumPress@aol.com or send disposable 3.5″ disk, IBM-formatted, with ms in ASCII, Word, or WordPerfect format.
Payment/Terms: Pays 1 contributor's copy. Acquires one-time rights. Not copyrighted.

THE FLYING ISLAND, (II, IV), Writers' Center of Indianapolis, P.O. Box 88386, Indianapolis IN 46208. (317)929-0625. Editor: Jerome Donahue. Tabloid: 24 pages; illustrations and photos. "A magazine of fiction, essays, reviews and poetry by Indiana-connected writers." Semiannually. Estab. 1979. Circ. 700.
Needs: Ethnic/multicultural, experimental, fantasy, feminist, gay, lesbian, literary, mainstream/contemporary, mystery/suspense, psychic/supernatural/occult, science fiction. Receives 1,000 unsolicited mss/year. Accepts 4-5 mss/issue; 8-10 mss/year. Does not read mss March-May and September-November. Publishes ms 2 months after acceptance. Length: 4,000 words average. Publishes short shorts. Also publishes literary essays, literary criticism and poetry.
How to Contact: Send two copies of complete ms with a cover letter. Should include short bio explaining Indiana connection. Write for guidelines. Reports in 3-5 months on mss. SASE for return of ms. Simultaneous submissions OK. Fiction guidelines for #10 SASE. Reviews novels and short story collections "if story or author has some connection to Indiana."
Payment/Terms: Pays 2 contributor's copies plus honorarium. Pays on publication.
Advice: "We have published work by high school and college students as well as work by 1994 Pulitzer Prize winner Yusef Komunyakaa and Edgar nominee Terence Faherty. Our readers enjoy a wide variety of settings and situations. We're looking for quality and we tend to overlook gimmicky and sentimental writing."

FOLIO: A LITERARY JOURNAL, (II), Department of Literature, American University, Washington DC 20016. (202)885-2990. Editor changes yearly. Send mss to attention: Editor. Magazine: 6×9; 64 pages. "Fiction is published if it is well written. We look for language control, skilled plot and character development." For a scholarly audience. Semiannually. Estab. 1984.
Needs: Contemporary, literary, mainstream, prose poem, translations, essay, b&w art or photography. No pornography. Occasional theme-based issues. See guidelines for info. Receives 150 unsolicited mss/month. Accepts 3-5 mss/issue; 6-40 mss/year. Does not read mss during May-August. Published work by Henry Taylor, Kermit Moyer, Linda Pastan; publishes new writers. Length: 2,500 words average; 4,500 words maximum. Publishes short shorts. Occasionally critiques rejected mss.
How to Contact: Send complete ms with cover letter, which should include a brief bio. Reports in 1-2 weeks on queries; 1-2 months on mss. SASE. Simultaneous and reprint submissions OK (if noted). Sample copy for $5. Guidelines for #10 SASE.
Payment/Terms: Pays in contributor's copies. Acquires first North American rights. "$75 award for best fiction and poetry. Query for guidelines."

FOOTWORK, The Paterson Literary Review, (I, II), Passaic County Community College, One College Blvd., Paterson NJ 07505. (201)684-6555. Editor: Maria Mazziotti Gillan. Magazine: 8½×11; 300 pages; 60 lb. paper; 70 lb. cover; illustrations; photos. Plans fiction issue in future.
• *Footwork* was chosen by *Library Journal* as one of the 10 best literary magazines in the US.
Needs: Contemporary, ethnic, literary. "We are interested in quality short stories, with no taboos on subject matter." Receives about 60 unsolicited mss/month. Publishes ms about 6 months-1 year after acceptance. Published new writers within the last year. Length: 2,000-3,000 words. Also publishes literary essays, literary criticism, poetry.
How to Contact: SASE. Simultaneous submissions OK. Sample copy for $12. Reviews novels and short story collections.
Payment/Terms: Pays in contributor's copies. Acquires first North American rights.

THE FOUR DIRECTIONS, American Indian Literary Quarterly, (II, IV), Snowbird Publishing Company, P. O. Box 729, Tellico Plains TN 37385. (423)253-3680. Senior Editor: Joanna Meyer. Assistant Editor: William Meyer. Magazine: 8×11½; 68 pages; 70 lb. paper; 100 lb. cover; 10-20 illustrations; 2-6 photographs. "All writing must be by American Indian authors. We prefer writing that furthers the positive aspects of the American Indian spirit. We publish poetry, fiction, essays and reviews." Estab. 1992. Circ 1,600.

• *Four Directions* was a runner-up for editorial content from the 1993-94 American Literary Magazine Awards.

Needs: American Indian only: adventure, children's/juvenile; erotica; ethnic/multicultural; experimental; fantasy; feminist; historical; horror; humor/satire; literary; mystery/suspense; psychic/supernatural/occult; regional; science fiction; sports; transalations; westerns; young adult/teen (10-18 years). "Writing should reflect Indian issues and views in all categories." Will publish special fiction issue or anthology. Receives 10 mss/month. Buys 8-12 mss/issue; 32-48 mss/year. Publishes ms 2-9 months after acceptance. Published Lise McCloud, Mary Lockwood, Joe Bruchac. Length: 2,000 words; 300 words minimum; 6,000 words maximum. Publishes short shorts. Length: 350 words. Also publishes literary essays, criticism, poetry. Often critiques rejected mss.

How to Contact: Query with clips of published work or send complete ms with a cover letter. Should include estimated word count, 1-page or less bio, list of publications, tribal affiliation. Reports in 2-6 weeks on queries; 2-10 weeks on mss. Send SASE for reply, return of ms, or send a disposable copy of the ms. Simultaneous, reprint or electronic submissions OK. Sample copy for 8½ × 11 SAE and 4 first-class stamps. Fiction guidelines for #10 SASE.

Payment/Terms: Pays 2¢/word plus 4 contributor's copies on publication for one-time rights. Sends galleys to author, when schedule allows.

Advice: "Writing we'll consider must be relevant, creative, original and of interest to a wide readership, both Indian and non-Indian. We seek professional quality writing, and work, if *about* Indians, that is accurate and authentic. We want work that shows positive spiritual strengths. We've not seen enough theater scripts/drama. We'd like to see more. And we *know* there's more humorous writing than has been submitted."

‡FRAYED, (II), X-it press, P.O. Box 3756, Erie PA 16508. Editor: Bobby Star. Magazine: 8 × 5; Xerox paper; offset opaque cover; illustrations and photos. "This is an 'adult' beat zine for radical-thinking people." Semiannually. Estab. 1994. Circ. 180.

Needs: Adventure, erotica, experimental, fantasy (science), gay, humor/satire, lesbian, literary, psychic/supernatural/occult, romance, science fiction (soft/sociological). Publishes special fiction issues or anthologies. Receives 3-4 unsolicited mss/month. Does not read from mid-September to mid-February. Publishes ms 1 week-1 year after acceptance. Recently published work by Terence Bishop, Robert Howington and Ben Ohmart. Length: 750 words average; 300 words minimum; 1,500 words maximum. Publishes short shorts. Length 200 words. Also publishes literary criticism and poetry.

How to Contact: Send complete ms with a cover letter. Should include estimated word count with submission. Reports in 1-4 weeks on queries; 1 week-5 months on mss. Send SASE for reply, return of ms or send a disposable copy of ms. Simultaneous and reprint submissions OK. Sample copy for $4, 6 × 9 SAE and 4 first-class stamps.

Payment/Terms: Pays 2 contributor's copies; additional copies for $2. Aquires one-time rights.

Advice: Looks for "a knowledge of language without bombast. Write about what you know."

FREE FOCUS/OSTENTATIOUS MIND, Wagner Press, (I, II), Bowbridge Press, P.O. Box 7415, JAF Station, New York NY 10116-7415. Editor: Patricia Denise Coscia. Editors change each year. Magazine: 8 × 14; 10 pages; recycled paper; illustrations and photos. "*Free Focus* is a small-press magazine which focuses on the educated women of today, and *Ostentatious Mind* is designed to encourage the intense writer, the cutting reality." Bimonthly. Estab. 1985 and 1987. Circ. 100 each.

• *Free Focus* sponsors a contest for work submitted to the magazine.

Needs: Experimental, feminist, humor/satire, literary, mainstream/contemporary, mystery/suspense (romantic), psychic/supernatural/occult, westerns (traditional), young adult/teen (adventure). "X-rated fiction is not accepted." List of upcoming themes available for SASE. Plans future special fiction issue or anthology. Receives 1,000 unsolicited mss/month. Does not read mss February to August. Publishes ms 3-6 months after acceptance. Recently published work by Edward Janz, A. Anne-Marie Ljung, Christine Warren. Length: 500 words average; 1,000 words maximum. Publishes short shorts. Also publishes literary essays, literary criticism and poetry. Always critiques or comments on rejected ms.

How to Contact: Query with clips of published work or send complete ms with a cover letter. Should include 100-word bio and list of publications. Reports in 3 months. Send SASE for reply. Simultaneous submissions OK. Sample copy for $3, #10 SAE and $1 postage. Fiction guidelines for #10 SAE and $1 postage. Reviews novels and short story collections.

Payment/Terms: Pays $2.50-5 and 2 contributor's copies on publication for all rights; additional copies for $2. Sends galleys to author.

Advice: "This publication is for beginning writers. Do not get discouraged; submit your writing. We look for imagination and creativity; no x-rated writing."

THE FUDGE CAKE, A Children's Newsletter, (IV), Francora DTP, P.O. Box 197, Citrus Heights CA 95611-0197. Fiction Editor: Jancarl Campi. Newsletter: 5 × 8½; 20 pages; 20 lb. bond paper; illustrations. "Our purpose is to provide a showcase for young writers age 6-17. We value the work of today's children and feel they need an outlet to express themselves." Bimonthly. Estab. 1994. Circ. 125.

Needs: Young adult/teen. No erotica. Receives 2-3 unsolicited mss/month. Accepts 3 mss/issue; 18 mss/year. Publishes ms 2 months after acceptance. Length: 400 words average; 250 words minimum; 500 words maximum. Publishes short shorts. Also publishes poetry. Often critiques or comments on rejected ms.
How to Contact: Send complete ms with a cover letter. Should include estimated word count and age. Reports in 1 month. Send SASE for reply, return of ms or send a disposable copy of ms. Simultaneous and reprint submissions OK. Sample copy for $3 and 1 first-class stamp. Fiction guidelines for #10 SASE.
Payment/Terms: Pays 1 contributor's copy; additional copies for $3. Acquires one-time rights.

‡FUEL MAGAZINE, (II), Anaconda Press, P.O. Box 146640, Chicago IL 60614. Editor: Andy Lowry. Magazine: 5½ × 8½; 70 pages; 60 lb. offset paper; 10 pt. cast coat cover stock; illustrations. "*Fuel* is a very eccentric, eclectic magazine. We do not consider ourselves an academic publication; rather, we prefer to publish underground lesser-known writers." Quarterly. Estab. 1992. Circ. 3,000.
• *Fuel*'s fiction needs have gone from 50% of the magazine to 75-80%. The magazine is best known for dark, realistic fiction.
Needs: Ethnic/multicultural, experimental, feminist, literary. No science fiction, romance, horror, humor/satire. List of upcoming themes available for SASE. Publishes special fiction issue or anthology. Receives 50 unsolicited mss/month. Accepts 5 mss/issue; 20-25 mss/year. Publishes ms 3-5 months after acceptance. Recently published work by Nicole Panter, Larry Oberc, CC Chapman, Sesshu Foster. Length: 1,500 words preferred; 500 words minimum; 3,000 words maximum. Publishes short shorts. Length: 250 words. Also publishes poetry.
How to Contact: Query first. Should include estimated word count and list of publications. Reports in 4 weeks on queries; 6 weeks on mss. SASE. No simultaneous submissions. Reprint and electronic submissions OK. E-mail address: aolwry@mcs.com. Sample copy for $3. Fiction guidelines for #10 SASE. Reviews novels and short story collections.
Payment/Terms: Pays contributor's copies; additional copies at cost. Rights revert to authors.
Advice: "We are not your normal publication—we want intelligent, cutting edge, strongly written works."

FUGUE, Literary Digest of the University of Idaho, (I), English Dept., Rm. 200, Brink Hall, University of Idaho, Moscow ID 83843. (208)885-6156. Executive Editor: Eric Isaacson. Editors change each year. Send to Executive Editor. Magazine: 5½ × 8½; 40-60 pages; 20 lb. stock paper. "We are interested in all classifications of fiction—we are not interested in pretentious 'literary' stylizations. We expect stories to be written in a manner engaging for anyone, not just academics and the pro-literatae crowd." Semiannually. Estab. 1990. Circ. 200.
Needs: Adventure, ethnic/multicultural, experimental, fantasy, historical, horror, humor/satire, literary, mainstream/contemporary, mystery/suspense, regional, romance, science fiction, sports, westerns. Receives 50 unsolicited mss/month. Buys 4-8 mss/issue; 8-16 mss/year. Does not read May-September. Publishes ms 3-8 months after acceptance. Length: 3,000 words average; 50 words minimum; 7,000 words maximum. Publishes short shorts. Also publishes literary essays and poetry. Sometimes critiques or comments on rejected mss.
How to Contact: Send complete ms with cover letter. "Obtain guidelines first." Should include estimated word count, Social Security number and list of publications. Report in 2 weeks on queries; 2 months on mss. SASE for a reply to a query or return of ms. No simultaneous submissions. Sample copy for $3. Fiction guidelines for #10 SASE.
Payment/Terms: Pays $5-20¢. All contributors receive a copy; extra copies $3.
Terms: Pays on publication for first North American serial rights.
Advice: Looks for "competent writing, clarity and consideration for the reader above stylism. Do not send us the traditional themes considered to be 'literary'."

‡FULL CLIP: A MAGAZINE OF MYSTERY & SUSPENSE, (II, IV), (formerly *Mystery Street* and *Mean Streets*), P.O. Box 1227, Eugene OR 97440. Editor: Dean Wesley Smith. Magazine: 8½ × 11; 64 pages; electrabright paper; slick cover; illustrations on cover. "For a general mystery audience. We publish short stories: mystery, police procedural, private-eye, espionage, suspense and thrillers in all forms—hardboiled, softboiled and traditional British cozy." Quarterly. Estab. 1995. Circ. 6,000.
• This is a new magazine from the publishers of *Pulphouse* and *Absolute Edge* also listed in this book.
Needs: Mystery/suspense (private eye/hard-boiled, amateur sleuth, cozy, police procedural, espionage). Receives 100 unsolicited mss/month. Buys 10 mss/issue; 40 mss/year. Publishes ms 2-6 months after acceptance. Agented fiction 20%. Length: 5,000 words preferred; 250 words minimum; 10,000 words maximum. Often critiques or comments on rejected mss.
How to Contact: Send complete ms with cover letter. Should include estimated word count, 50-word bio, list of publications, list of organizations (M.W.A.) Reports in 2 months on mss. Send SASE for reply, return of ms. No simultaneous submissions. Sample copy for $3.95, 9 × 12 SAE and 4 first-class stamps. Fiction guidelines for #10 SASE. Reviews novel and short story collections.
Payment/Terms: Pays 4-7¢/word, subscription and 3 contributor's copies on acceptance for first rights. Sends galleys to author.

‡FULL-TIME DADS, The Magazine For Caring Fathers, (I, II), Big Daddy Publications, P.O. Box 577, Cumberland ME 04021. (207)829-5260. Editor: Stephen Harris. Magazine: 8½×11; 24 pages; bond paper; illustrations and photos. "*Full-Time Dads* publishes anything relating to fathers/fatherhood with a positive point of view." Bimonthly. Estab. 1991. Circ. 400.

Needs: Children's/juvenile, fantasy (children's), humor/satire, literary, mainstream/contemporary, religious/ inspirational, young adult/teen. "No violence, sex, abuse, etc." Plans themed issues next year; list available for SASE. Plans special fiction issue or anthology. Accepts 6 mss/year. Publishes ms 2-6 months after acceptance. Length: 600-1,200 words average. Publishes short shorts. Also publishes literary essays, literary criticism, poetry. Often critiques or comments on rejected ms.

How to Contact: Query first. Send complete ms with a cover letter. Should include estimated word count and 3-4 sentence bio. Reports in 4-6 weeks on queries. Send SASE for reply, return of ms or send a disposable copy of ms. Simultaneous, reprint and electronic submissions OK. E-mail address: fulltdad@aol.com. Sample copy for $5. Fiction guidelines for #10 SASE. Reviews novels and short story collections.

Payment/Terms: Pays 1 contributor's copy. Acquires one-time rights, possibly anthology rights.

Advice: "Take your time. Reread, reread, reread. Make sure what you send is exactly what you want me to read."

THE G.W. REVIEW, (II), The George Washington University, Box 20B, The Marvin Center, 800 21st St., N.W., Washington, DC 20052. (202)994-7288. Editor: Merrell Maschino. Magazine: 6×9; 64 pages; 60 lb. white offset paper; 65 lb. Patina cover; cover illustration. "*The G.W. Review* publishes poetry, short fiction and essays for the Washington DC metropolitan area and national subscribers." Semiannually. Estab. 1980. Circ. 4,000 (annually).

Needs: Condensed/excerpted novel, contemporary, experimental, humor/satire, literary, mainstream, prose poem, translations. "*The G.W. Review* does not accept previously published material. No pornography or proselytizing religious manuscripts." Does not read mss May 15-August 15. Publishes ms up to 6 months after acceptance. Published work by Linda McCarriston and John Haines. Length: 2,500 words average; 6,000 words maximum. Sometimes critiques rejected mss.

How to Contact: Send complete ms with cover letter. Include biographical information, places previously published, previous books, etc. Reports in 3-6 weeks on queries; 4-10 weeks on mss. SASE. Simultaneous submissions OK. Sample copy for $3. Fiction guidelines for SASE.

Payment/Terms: Pays in contributor's copies. Acquires one-time rights.

Advice: "*The G.W. Review* seeks to publish the best contemporary writing from outside the Washington, DC literary community as well as the best from within. Initially intended for distribution to the surrounding Washington, DC metropolitan area, *The G.W. Review* has since attained a more widespread national distribution and readership."

‡GALAXY MAGAZINE, (II), I.D.H.H.B., Inc., P.O. Box 370, Nevada City CA 95959. Editor: E.J. Gold. Magazine: 8½×11; 96 pages; 35 lb. Mando paper; 50 lb. vellum cover; illustrations and photos. "*Galaxy Magazine*'s intended audience is science fiction readers." Bimonthly. Estab. 1994. Circ. 6,000.

Needs: Fantasy (science fiction, sword and sorcery), psychic/supernatural/occult, science fiction, translations, young adult/teen (science fiction). Plans special fiction issue or anthology. Receives 200 unsolicited mss/month. Accepts 15 mss/issue; 90 mss/year. Agented fiction 5%. Recently published work by Linea-weaver, Lictenburg, Zelaeny. Length: 3,000 words average; 300 words minimum; 10,000 words maximum. Publishes short shorts. Sometimes critiques or comments on rejected ms.

How to Contact: Send complete ms with a cover letter. Should include estimated word count, short bio, Social Security number, list of publications, address and phone number. Reports in 2 months on mss. Send SASE for return of ms or send a disposable copy of ms. Sample copy for $2.50. Reviews novels and short story collections. Send books to publisher, David G. Franco.

Payment/Terms: Pays 6-8¢/word on acceptance and 6 contributor's copies; additional copies $1.25. Buys first North American serial rights. Sends galleys to author.

Advice: "Have other writers read your manuscript first, then self-review and submit, submit, submit. Don't send cyberpunk or dark dark fiction."

‡A GATHERING OF THE TRIBES, (II), A Gathering of the Tribes, Inc., P.O. Box 20693, Tompkins Square Station, New York NY 10009. (212)674-3778. Editor: Steve Cannon. Fiction Editor: Angelina Lukacin. Magazine: 8×10; 100-200 pages; glossy paper and cover; illustrations and photos. A "multicultural and multigenerational publication." Estab. 1992. Circ. 2,000-3,000.

   • *A Gathering of the Tribes* received a 1995 American Literary Award for editorial content.

Needs: Erotica, ethnic/multicultural, experimental, fantasy (science), feminist, gay, historical, horror, humor/ satire, lesbian, literary, mainstream/contemporary, romance (futuristic/time travel, gothic), science fiction (soft/sociological), senior citizen/retirement, translations. "We are open to all; just no poor writing/grammar/ syntax." List of upcoming themes available for SASE. Receives 100 unsolicited mss/month. Publishes ms 3-6 months after acceptance. Recently published work of Ishmael Reed, Edwin Torres and David Henderson. Length: 500 words average; 200 words minimum; no maximum. Publishes short shorts. Also publishes literary essays, literary criticism and poetry.

How to Contact: Send complete ms with a cover letter. Should include estimated word count, half-page bio, list of publications, phone and fax numbers and address with submission. Send SASE for reply, return of ms or send a disposable copy of ms. Simultaneous, reprint and electronic submissions OK. E-mail address: tribesnterport.net. Sample copy for $10. Reviews novels and short story collections. Send books to Angelina Lukacin.

Payment/Terms: Pays 1 contributor's copy; additional copies $5. Sponsors contests, awards or grants for fiction writers. "Watch for ads in *Poets & Writers* and *American Poetry Review*."

Advice: Looks for "unique tone and style, offbeat plots and characters, and ethnic and regional work. Type manuscript well: readable font (serif) and no typos. Make characters and their dialogue interesting. Experiment with style, and don't be conventional. Do not send dragged-out, self-indulgent philosophizing of life and the universe. Get specific. Make your characters soar!"

GAY CHICAGO MAGAZINE, (II), Gernhardt Publications, Inc., 3121 N. Broadway, Chicago IL 60657-4522. (312)327-7271. Publisher: Ralph Paul Gernhardt. Associate Publisher: Jerry Williams. Magazine: 8½×11; 80-144 pages; newsprint paper and cover stock; illustrations; photos. Entertainment guide, information for the gay community.

Needs: Erotica (but no explicit hard core), lesbian, gay and romance. Receives "a few" unsolicited mss/month. Acquires 10-15 mss/year. Published new writers within the last year. Length: 1,000-3,000 words.

How to Contact: Send complete ms with SASE. Accepts 3.5 disk submissions and Macintosh or ASCII Format. Reports in 4-6 weeks on mss. Free sample copy for 9×12 SAE and $1.45 postage.

Payment/Terms: Minimal. 5-10 free contributor's copies; no charge for extras "if within reason." Acquires one-time rights.

GEORGETOWN REVIEW, (II), G & R Publications, Box 227, 400 East College St., Georgetown KY 40324. (502)863-8308. Editor: Steven Carter. Magazine: 5¼×8¼; 112 pages; 60 lb. offset paper; 80lb. cover. "We want to publish quality fiction and poetry." Published twice a year. Estab. 1993. Circ. 1,000.

Needs: Literary. No romance, juvenile, fantasy. Receives 1,000 mss/year. Does not read mss May-August. Publishes 3-6 months after acceptance. Length: open. Publishes short shorts. Length: 400-500 words. Also publishes poetry.

How to Contact: Send complete ms with a cover letter. Reports in 1-4 months on mss. SASE. Simultaneous submissions OK. Sample copy for $5, 9×12 SAE and 5 first-class stamps.

Payment/Terms: Pays 2 contributor's copies. All rights revert to author. Sends galleys to author.

Advice: "We simply look for quality work, no matter what the subject or style."

THE GEORGIA REVIEW, (I, II), The University of Georgia, Athens GA 30602-9009. (706)542-3481. Editor-in-Chief: Stanley W. Lindberg. Associate Editor: Stephen Corey. Assistant Editor: Jani Wondra. Journal: 7×10; 208 pages (average); 50 lb. woven old-style paper; 80 lb. cover stock; illustrations; photos. "*The Georgia Review*, winner of the 1986 National Magazine Award in Fiction, is a journal of arts and letters, featuring a blend of the best in contemporary thought and literature—essays, fiction, poetry, visual art and book reviews—for the intelligent nonspecialist as well as the specialist reader. We seek material that appeals across disciplinary lines by drawing from a wide range of interests." Quarterly. Estab. 1947. Circ. 6,000.

● This magazine has an excellent reputation for publishing high-quality fiction.

Needs: Experimental and literary. "We're looking for the highest quality fiction—work that is capable of sustaining subsequent readings, not throw-away pulp magazine entertainment. Nothing that fits too easily into a 'category.'" Receives about 400 unsolicited fiction mss/month. Buys 3-4 mss/issue; 12-15 mss/year. Does not read unsolicited mss in June, July or August. Would prefer *not* to see novel excerpts. Recently published work by Louise Erdrich, Frederick Busch, Kelly Cherry; published new writers within the last year. Length: Open. Also publishes literary essays, literary criticism, poetry. Occasionally critiques rejected mss.

How to Contact: Send complete ms (one story) with SASE. No multiple submissions. Usually reports in 2-3 months. Sample copy for $6; guidelines for #10 SASE. Reviews short story collections.

Payment/Terms: Pays minimum $35/printed page on publication for first North American serial rights, 1 year complimentary subscription and 1 contributor's copy; reduced charge for additional copies. Sends galleys to author.

THE GETTYSBURG REVIEW, (II), Gettysburg College, Gettysburg PA 17325. (717)337-6770. Editor: Peter Stitt. Assistant Editor: Jeff Mock. Magazine: 6¾×10; 170 pages; acid free paper; full color illustrations. "Quality of writing is our only criterion; we publish fiction, poetry, and essays." Quarterly. Estab. 1988. Circ. 4,500.

● Work appearing in *The Gettysburg Review* has also been included in *Prize Stories: The O. Henry Awards*, the *Pushcart Prize* anthology, and *New Stories from the South.*

Needs: Contemporary, experimental, historical, humor/satire, literary, mainstream, regional and serialized novel. "We require that fiction be intelligent, and aesthetically written." Receives 160 mss/month. Buys 4-6 mss/issue; 16-24 mss/year. Publishes ms within 1 year of acceptance. Recently published work by Alison Baker, Frederick Busch. Length: 3,000 words average; 1,000 words minimum; 20,000 words maximum.

Occasionally publishes short shorts. Also publishes literary essays, some literary criticism, poetry. Sometimes critiques rejected mss.

How to Contact: Send complete ms with cover letter, which should include "education, credits." Reports in 3-6 months. SASE. No simultaneous submissions. Sample copy for $7 (postage paid). Does not review books per se. "We do essay-reviews, treating several books around a central theme." Send review copies to editor.

Payment/Terms: Pays $25/printed page, subscription to magazine and contributor's copy on publication for first North American serial rights. Charge for extra copies.

Advice: "Reporting time can take more than three months. It is helpful to look at a sample copy of *The Gettysburg Review* to see what kinds of fiction we publish before submitting."

‡**THE GLASS CHERRY, A poetry magazine, (II)**, The Glass Cherry Press, 901 Europe Bay Rd., Ellison Bay WI 54210-9643. (414)854-9042. Editor: Judith Hirschmiller. Magazine: 5×7; 60 pages; high-tech laser paper; cover stock varies; illustrations and photos. "Our goal is to combine diversity with quality and promote good literature by a variety of writers. New writers are encouraged to submit. We have diversity combined with quality." Quarterly. Estab. 1994. Circ. 500.

Needs: Condensed/excerpted novel, gay, historical, horror, lesbian, literary, mainstream/contemporary, science fiction, serialized novel, translations. "No pornography." Publishes special fiction issues or anthologies. Receives 6-12 unsolicited mss/month. Accepts 1-2 mss/issue; 4-8 mss/year. Does not read books May-December; reads fiction for magazine all year. Publishes ms 1 year after acceptance. Recently published work by Christopher Woods, John Taylor and Alan Elyshevitz. Length: 1,000 words maximum. Publishes short shorts. Also publishes literary essays, literary criticism and poetry. Critiques or comments on rejected ms "only if requested to do so by author."

How to Contact: Query first. Should include short bio and list of publications with submission. Reports in 3 weeks on queries; 3 months on mss. SASE for reply. Sample copy for $5; back issue, $6. Fiction guidelines for #10 SASE. Reviews novels and short story collections.

Payment/Terms: Pays 1 contributor's copy. Acquires one-time rights.

Advice: "We are interested in tasteful writing of superior quality. Request guidelines and buy a sample issue to see what we publish. Send your best work—something you would be proud to have outlive you. We would like more translations, book reviews, plays and short fiction of personal glimpses (individual, unusual events of a personal nature)."

GLIMMER TRAIN STORIES, (II), Glimmer Train Press, #1205, 812 SW Washington St., Portland OR 97205. Editors: Susan Burmeister and Linda Davies. Magazine: 6¾×9¼; 168 pages; recycled, acid-free paper; 20 illustrations; 12 photographs. Quarterly. Estab. 1991. Circ. 21,000.

● The magazine also sponsors an annual short story contest for new writers. See listing in the Contests and Awards section.

Needs: Literary. Plans to publish special fiction issue or anthology. Receives 3,000 unsolicited mss/month. Accepts 10 mss/issue; 40 mss/year. Reads in January, April, July, October. Publishes ms 4-9 months after acceptance. Agented fiction 20%. Published work by Joyce Thompson, Richard Bausch, Stephen Dixon, Joyce Carol Oates, Mary McGarry Morris, Charles Baxter, Ann Beattie, Louise Erdrich. Length: 1,200 words minimum; 8,000 words maximum.

How to Contact: Send complete ms with a cover letter. Should include estimated word count and list of publications. Reports in 3 months. Send SASE for return or send a disposable copy of ms (with stamped postcard or envelope for notification). Simultaneous submissions OK. Sample copy for $9. Fiction guidelines for #10 SASE.

Payment/Terms: Pays $500 and 10 contributor's copies on acceptance for first rights.

GOTTA WRITE NETWORK LITMAG, (I, II), Maren Publications, 612 Cobblestone Circle, Glenview IL 60025. Editor: Denise Fleischer. Fax: (708)296-7631 after 6 pm or call to set up Fax appointment. Magazine: 8½×11; 48-76 pages; saddle-stapled ordinary paper; matte card or lighter weight cover stock; illustrations. Magazine "serves as an open forum to discuss new markets, successes and difficulties. Gives beginning writers their first break into print and promotionally supports established professional novelists." Distributed through the US, Canada and England. Semiannually. Estab. 1988. Circ. 200.

● In addition to publishing fiction, *Gotta Write Network Litmag* includes articles on writing techniques, small press market news, writers' seminar reviews, science fiction convention updates, and features a "Behind the Scenes" section in which qualified writers can conduct mail interviews with small press editors and professional writers. Writers interviewed in this manner in the past have included Frederik Pohl, Jody Lynn Nye, Lawrence Watt-Evans and artist Michael Whelan. Articles may be selected to be reprinted by Warner Books/Aspect for Time Warner's online forum for writers.

Needs: Adventure, contemporary, fantasy, historical, humor/satire, literary, mainstream, prose poem, romance (gothic), science fiction (hard science, soft/sociological). "Currently seeking work with a clear-cut message or a twist at the very end, preferably Twilight Zone and ghost stories. All genres accepted with the exception of excessive violence, sexual overtones or obscenity." Receives 75-150 unsolicited mss per month.

Accepts 1-6 mss per issue; up to 20 mss a year. Publishes mss 6-12 months after acceptance. Length: 10 pages maximum for short stories. Also publishes poetry.

How to Contact: Send complete ms with cover letter. Include "who you are, type of work submitted, previous publications and focused area of writing." Reports in 2-4 months (later during publication months). SASE ("no SASE, no repsonse"). Reports on fax submissions within days. Responds by fax. No simultaneous submissions or reprints. Sample copy for $5. Fiction guidelines for SASE.

Payment/Terms: Pays $10 or 2 contributor's copies for first North American serial rights.

Advice: "If I still think about the direction of the story after I've read it, I know it's good. Organize your thoughts on the plot and character development (qualities, emotions) before enduring ten drafts. Make your characters come alive by giving them a personality and a background, and then give them a little freedom. Let them take you through the story."

‡GRAFFITI OFF THE ASYLUM WALLS, An Illiterary Journal, (II, IV), P.O. Box 1653, Hot Springs AR 71902-1653. Curator: Bryan Westbrook. Magazine: Digest-sized; 20 pages; colored paper cover; illustrations. "The stuff you would be afraid to show your mother, priest and/or psychiatrist. Humor preferred." Publishes "whenever enough material and funds are available." Estab. 1992. Circ. 200.

Needs: Erotica, experimental, feminist, humor/satire, fetishism, perversion, political (anti-Republican). "Nothing pro-religious, pro-animal rights, anything high fallutin'." Recently published work by Robert W. Howington, Allen Renfro, Marc Swan. Length: 1,000 words maximum. Submit no more than 2 mss at a time. Also publishes literary essays and poetry. Often critiques or comments on rejected mss.

How to Contact: Send complete ms with cover letter. Should include bio (personal bio, not publication list). Reports within 2 months. Send SASE for reply, return of ms or send a disposable copy of ms. Simultaneous and reprint submissions OK. Sample copy for $3. Reviews novels and short story collections.

Payment/Terms: No payment; contributor's copies available for discounted price of $2. Acquires one-time rights.

Advice: "If it can make me laugh (not an easy task) or shock me (also a challenge) it will make it. Non-narrative stories have a harder time here. Forget everything you've ever read in school or been told in writing classes. I want to hear from the real you."

♣GRAIN, (I, II), Saskatchewan Writers' Guild, Box 1154, Regina, Saskatchewan S4P 3B4 Canada. Editor: J. Jill Robinson. Literary magazine: 6×9; 144 pages; Chinook offset printing; chrome-coated stock; illustrations; some photos. "Fiction and poetry for people who enjoy high quality writing." Quarterly. Estab. 1973. Circ. 1,800-2,000.

Needs: Contemporary, experimental, literary, mainstream and prose poem. "No propaganda—only artistic/literary writing." No mss "that stay *within* the limits of conventions such as women's magazine type stories, science fiction; none that push a message." Receives 80 unsolicited fiction mss/month. Buys 8-12 mss/issue; 32-48 mss/year. Agented fiction approximately 1%. Published 2 short stories by emerging writers selected for the third *Journey Prize Anthology*. Length: "No more than 50 pages." Also publishes poetry. Occasionally critiques rejected mss.

How to Contact: Send complete ms with SASE (or IRC) and brief letter. "Let us know if you're just beginning to send out." No simultaneous submissions. Reports within 6 months on ms. Publishes ms an average of 4 months after acceptance. E-mail address: grain@bailey2.unibase.com. Sample copy for $6.95 plus postage.

Payment/Terms: Pays $30-100; 2 contributor's copies.

Terms: Pays on publication for first Canadian serial rights. "We expect acknowledgment if the piece is republished elsewhere."

Advice: "Submit a story to us that will deepen the imaginative experience of our readers. *Grain* has established itself as a first-class magazine of serious fiction. We receive submissions from around the world. If Canada is a foreign country to you, we ask that you *do not* use US postage stamps on your return envelope. If you live outside Canada and neglect the International Reply Coupons, we *will not* read or reply to your submission."

GRAND STREET, (II), 131 Varick St., #906, New York NY 10013. (212)807-6548. Fax (212)807-6544. Editor: Jean Stein. Managing Editor: Deborah Treisman. Magazine: 7×9; 240-270 pages; illustrations; art portfolios. "We seek new fiction and nonfiction of all types. We welcome experimental work. The only real criterion for acceptance is quality." Quarterly. Estab. 1981. Circ. 7,000.

● Work published in *Grand Street* has been included in the *Best American Short Stories*.

Sending to a country other than your own? Be sure to send International Reply Coupons instead of stamps for replies or return of your manuscript.

Needs: Fiction, poetry, essays, translations. Receives 400 unsolicited mss/month. Buys 12 mss/issue; 48 mss/year. Time between acceptance of the ms and publication varies. Agented fiction 90%. Published work by David Foster Wallace, Stephen Millhauser, Dennis Hopper, Paul Auster, John Ashbery, Duong Thu Huong, William T. Vollman. Length: 4,000 words average; 9,000 words maximum. Sometimes critiques or comments on rejected mss.

How to Contact: Send complete ms with a cover letter. Reports in 2 months on mss. Send SASE for return of the ms or a disposable copy of the ms. Simultaneous and electronic submissions OK. Sample copy for $15; $18 overseas and Canada.

Payment/Terms: Pays $250-1,000 and 2 contributor's copies on publication for first North American serial rights. Sends galleys to author.

Advice: What magazine looks for is "hard to say, other than first-rate writing. We are fairly eclectic in our publishing policies. Look at a copy of the magazine first. That will give you a good idea of what we're looking for."

GRASSLANDS REVIEW, (I, II), Mini-Course—University of North Texas, P.O. Box 13706, Denton TX 76203-3827. Editor: Laura B. Kennelly. Magazine: 6×9; 80 pages. *Grasslands Review* prints creative writing of all types; poetry, fiction, essays for a general audience. Semiannually. Estab. 1989. Circ. 300.

Needs: Adventure, contemporary, ethnic, experimental, fantasy, horror, humor/satire, literary, mystery/suspense, prose poem, regional, science fiction and western. Nothing pornographic or overtly political or religious. Accepts 5-8 mss/issue. Reads only in October and March. Publishes ms 6 months after acceptance. Recently published work by Catherine deCuir, K.V. Wright, Mark Nigara, A. Roach, Valerie Jeremijenko and Lily Gill. Length: 1,500 words average; 100-3,500 words. Publishes short shorts (100-150 words). Also publishes poetry. Sometimes critiques rejected mss and recommends other markets.

How to Contact: Send complete ms in October or March *only* with cover letter. No simultaneous submissions. Reports on mss in 3 months. SASE. E-mail address: fa40@jove.acs.unt.edu. Sample copy for $2. May review novels or short story collections.

Payment/Terms: Pays in contributor's copies. Acquires one-time rights. Publication not copyrighted.

Advice: "We are looking for fiction which leaves the reader with a strong feeling or impression—or a new perspective on life. The *Review* began as an in-class exercise to allow experienced creative writing students to learn how a little magazine is produced. We now wish to open it up to outside submissions so that our students can gain an understanding of how large the writing community is in the United States and so that they may have experience in working with other writers."

GREEN EGG/HOW ABOUT MAGIC?, (IV), Church of All Worlds, Box 1542, Ukiah CA 95482. (707)485-7787. Editor: Maerian "Sun" Morris. Magazine: 8½×11; 72 pages; H.A.M. 12-16 pages; recycled paper; 4-color glossy cover; b&w illustrations; and photographs. "Magical fantasy, ecological, historical having to do with pagan civilizations." Quarterly. Estab. 1988. Circ. 8,000.

• *Green Egg* has won both Gold and Bronze awards from the Wiccan Pagan Press Alliance including a Gold Award in 1994 for Best Publication.

Needs: Magical, pagan and ecological themes: adventure, children's/juvenile (5-9 and 10-12 years), erotica, ethnic/multicultural, experimental, fantasy (science fantasy, sword and sorcery, children's fantasy), historical, humor/satire, psychic/supernatural/occult, religious/inspirational (pagan). "No porn, sports, western, evil and painful." Upcoming themes: "Love Goddesses" (Spring 1996); "African Diaspora" (Summer 1996); "Buddheo-Pagans"; and "Healing the Earth." Receives 5-6 unsolicited mss/month. Acquires 10 mss/year. Recently published work by Ivo Dominguez, Tim Waggoner, Robert Anton Wilson, Starhawk, Daniel Blair Stewart and Bill Beattie. Length: 600 words minimum; 3,000 words maximum. Publishes short shorts. Length: 500 words. Also publishes poetry. Sometimes critiques or comments on rejected mss.

How to Contact: Send complete ms with cover letter. Should include estimated word count and bio (1 paragraph—50 words). Reports in 2 months. Send SASE for reply, return of ms or send disposable copy of the ms. Include photo of author, if possible, and graphics, if available. Simultaneous, reprint and electronic submissions OK. E-mail address: gemagazine@aol.com (general business); maerian@aol.com (to the editor). Sample copy of *Green Egg* $6.75; sample copy of H.A.M. $2.25. Fiction guidelines for SASE. Reviews novels and short story collections.

Payment/Terms: Pays subscription to the magazine or contributor's copies. Acquires one-time rights.

Advice: "Looks for economy of prose, artistic use of language, but most important is that the subject matter be germaine to our pagan readership. Magical stories teaching ethics for survival as healthy biosphere heroines, human/animal/otherworld interface; transformative experiences; tidy plots; good grammar, spelling, punctuation; humor; classical deities and ethnic stuff. We're especially fond of science fiction and fantasy."

THE GREEN HILLS LITERARY LANTERN, (I, II), The North Central Missouri Writer's Guild, P.O. Box 375, Trenton MO 64683. (816)359-3948, ext. 324. Editors: Jack Smith and Ken Reger. Fiction Editor: Sara King. Magazine: 5½×8½; 120 pages; 60 lb. white opaque offset paper; 80 lb. matte cover. "We are interested in writers whose voices make the reader listen, who offer no definite solutions—but who state the problem well. We want fiction that makes readers look more closely at their own lives." Annually. Estab. 1990.

Needs: Ethnic/multicultural, experimental, feminist, humor/satire, literary, mainstream/contemporary and regional. "Our main requirement is literary merit." Receives 15 unsolicited mss/month. Accepts 6-7 mss/issue. Publishes ms 6-12 months after acceptance. Recently published work by Doug Rennie, Walter Cummins, Robert C.S. Downs and D.L. Olson. Length: 3,000 words average; 5,000 words maximum. Publishes short shorts. Also publishes poetry. Sometimes critiques or comments on rejected ms.
How to Contact: Send complete ms with a cover letter. Should include bio (50-100 words) and list of publications. Reports in 3 months on mss. SASE for return of ms. No simultaneous submissions. Sample copy for $5.95 (includes envelope and postage).
Payment/Terms: Pays two contributor's copies. Acquires one-time rights. Sends galleys to author.
Advice: "Send stories with all the subtleties of ordinary life. Make sure the language is striking. Don't tell the story. Let the story tell itself. We look for fiction which speaks to the heart, the mind, the soul—fiction which is as complex, as dense, as layered as the most simple of human existences and as subtle and as provocative as the best of literary art."

GREEN MOUNTAINS REVIEW, (II), Johnson State College, Box A-58, Johnson VT 05656. (802)635-2356, ext. 350. Editor: Neil Shepard. Fiction Editor: Tony Whedon. Magazine: digest-sized; 125-150 pages. Semiannually. Estab. 1975 (new series, 1987). Circ. 1,500.
• *Green Mountains Review* has received grants from the NEA and the Vermont Council of the Arts.
Needs: Adventure, contemporary, experimental, humor/satire, literary, mainstream, serialized/excerpted novel, translations. Receives 80 unsolicited mss/month. Accepts 6 mss/issue; 12 mss/year. Publishes ms 6-12 months after acceptance. Recently published work by Lynn Sharm Schwartz, Alix Kates Shulman, Francois Comoin, David Huddle and Nzotake Sharge. Length: 25 pages maximum. Publishes short shorts. Also publishes literary criticism, poetry. Sometimes critiques rejected mss.
How to Contact: Send complete ms with cover letter. Reports in 1 month on queries; 3-4 months on mss. SASE. Simultaneous submissions OK (if advised). Sample copy for $5.
Payment/Terms: Pays contributor's copies and small honorarium, depending on grants. Acquires first North American serial rights. Sends galleys to author upon request.
Advice: "The editors are open to a wide spectrum of styles and subject matter as is apparent from a look at the list of fiction writers who have published in its pages. One issue was devoted to Vermont fiction, and another issue filled with new writing from the People's Republic of China. The Spring/Summer 1994 issue was composed entirely of women's fiction."

❧GREEN'S MAGAZINE, Fiction for the Family, (II), Green's Educational Publications, Box 3236, Regina, Saskatchewan S4P 3H1 Canada. Editor: David Green. Magazine: 5¼×8; 100 pages; 20 lb. bond paper; matte cover stock; line illustrations. Publishes "solid short fiction suitable for family reading." Quarterly. Estab. 1972.
Needs: Adventure, fantasy, humor/satire, literary, mainstream, mystery/suspense and science fiction. No erotic or sexually explicit fiction. Receives 20-30 mss/month. Accepts 10-12 mss/issue; 40-50 mss/year. Publishes ms within 3-6 months of acceptance. Agented fiction 2%. Recently published work by Gerald Standley, Arthur Winfield Knight and Vivian Scheffler Locklin. Length: 2,500 words preferred; 1,500 words minimum; 4,000 words maximum. Also publishes poetry. Sometimes critiques rejected mss.
How to Contact: Send complete ms. "Cover letters welcome but not necessary." Reports in 2 months. SASE. "Must include international reply coupons." No simultaneous submissions. Sample copy for $4. Fiction guidelines for #10 SASE. Reviews novels and short story collections.
Payment/Terms: Pays in contributor's copies. Acquires first North American serial rights.

GREENSBORO REVIEW, (II), University of North Carolina at Greensboro, Dept. of English, Greensboro NC 27412. (910)334-5311. Editor: Jim Clark. Fiction Editor: Keith Morris. Fiction editor changes each year. Send future mss to the editor. Magazine: 6×9; approximately 136 pages; 60 lb. paper; 65 lb. cover. Literary magazine featuring fiction and poetry for readers interested in contemporary literature. Semiannually. Circ. 600.
Needs: Contemporary and experimental. Accepts 6-8 mss/issue, 12-16 mss/year. Published work by Jill McCorkle, Robert Morgan and Peter Taylor. Published new writers within the last year. Length: 7,500 words maximum.
How to Contact: Send complete ms with SASE. No simultaneous submissions. Unsolicited manuscripts must arrive by September 15 to be considered for the winter issue and by February 15 to be considered for the summer issue. Manuscripts arriving after those dates may be held for the next consideration. Reports in 2 months. Sample copy for $4.
Payment/Terms: Pays in contributor's copies. Acquires first North American serial rights.
Advice: "We want to see the best being written regardless of theme, subject or style. Recent stories from *The Greensboro Review* have been included in *The Best American Short Stories*, *Prize Stories: The O. Henry Awards*, *New Stories from the South* and *Best of the West*, anthologies recognizing the finest short stories being published."

GREG'S GOOD GAZETTE, (I), 3735 Brownstone Lane, Winston-Salem NC 27106. (910)924-5863. Editor: Greg Knollenberg. Newsletter: 8½×11; 7-10 double-sided pages. "Our theme is really only to laugh, but we are serious when we see potential newbie humorists and are eager to help them get started. For all ages except babies." 4-6 times/year. Estab. 1993. Circ. 150.

Needs: All fiction categories, "but has to be funny or bizarre. No extreme violence, pornography or excessive swearing. No shock-value-only fiction. No specific themes, but we are always interested in seasonal fiction." Receives 15-20 unsolicited mss/month. Accepts 2-3 mss/issue; 25 mss/year. Publishes ms 3-4 months after acceptance. Published work by Dee Tomczyk, Troy Hughes, Lincoln Grant. Length: 500-600 words average; 10 words minimum; 1,200 words maximum. Publishes short shorts. Also publishes literary essays and poetry. Often critiques or comments on rejected ms.

How to Contact: Send complete ms with a cover letter. Should include estimated word count, brief bio and list of publications. "Just a story and SASE is fine, but it is nice to know more." Reports in 3 weeks on queries; 2-3 months on mss. Send SASE for reply, return of ms or send a disposable copy of ms. Simultaneous submissions OK. E-mail address (for queries and questions only): ngjr45@prodigy.com. Sample copy for $1.50. Fiction guidelines for #10 SASE.

Payment/Terms: Pays 1 contributor's copy; additional copies for 75¢. Acquires one-time rights.

Advice: "Material stands out if it is easy to laugh with, flows and is enjoyable. Good dialogue can really help fiction, especially humor fiction. Exaggerate. You do not need to write about what you know, and I encourage you not to. I would like to see more fantasy and science fiction humor."

GRUE MAGAZINE, (II, IV), Hell's Kitchen Productions, Box 370, New York NY 10108. Editor: Peggy Nadramia. Magazine: 5½×8½; 96 pages; 60 lb. paper; 10 pt. C1S film laminate cover; illustrations; photos. "We look for quality short fiction centered on horror and dark fantasy—new traditions in the realms of the gothic and the macabre for horror fans well read in the genre, looking for something new and different, as well as horror novices looking for a good scare." Triannually. Estab. 1985.

● Two stories from *Grue* were chosen for *The Year's Best Fantasy and Horror Anthology*. The editor says she expects to be buying "more aggressively" this year. This is "cutting-edge" horror.

Needs: Horror, psychic/supernatural/occult. Receives 250 unsolicited fiction mss/month. Accepts 10 mss/issue; 25-30 mss/year. Publishes mss 1-2 years after acceptance. Published work by Thomas Ligotti, Joe R. Lansdale, Don Webb; published new writers within the last year. Length: 4,000 words average; 6,500 words maximum. Sometimes critiques rejected ms.

How to Contact: Send complete ms with cover letter. "I like to hear where the writer heard about *Grue*, his most recent or prestigious sales, and maybe a word or two about himself." Reports in 3 weeks on queries; 6 months on mss. Send SASE for return of ms. E-mail address: nadramia@panix.com. Sample copy for $4.50. Fiction guidelines for #10 SASE.

Payment/Terms: Pays ½¢/word on publication and 2 contributor's copies for first North American serial rights.

Advice: "Remember that readers of *Grue* are mainly seasoned horror fans, and *not* interested or excited by a straight vampire, werewolf or ghost story—they'll see all the signs, and guess where you're going long before you get there. Throw a new angle on what you're doing; put it in a new light. How? Well, what scares *you*? What's *your* personal phobia or anxiety? When the writer is genuinely, emotionally involved with his subject matter, and is totally honest with himself and his reader, then we can't help being involved, too, and that's where good writing begins and ends."

GULF COAST, A Journal of Literature & Fine Arts, (II), Dept. of English, University of Houston, Houston TX 77204-3012. (713)743-3013. Contact: Fiction Editors. Editors change each year. Magazine: 6×9; 144 pages; stock paper, gloss cover; illustrations and photographs. "Innovative fiction for the literary-minded." Estab. 1984. Circ. 1,500.

● Work published in *Gulf Coast* has been selected for inclusion in the Pushcart Prize anthology.

Needs: Excerpted novel, contemporary, ethnic, experimental, literary, regional, unconventional. "We are attuned to work representing the Caribbean, Latin America and the Deep South." No children's, religious/inspirational. Receives 150 unsolicited mss/month. Accepts 8-10 mss/issue; 16-20 mss/year. Publishes ms 6 months-1 year after acceptance. Agented fiction 5%. Recently published work by Barry Hannah, Daniel Stern, Lydia Davis and Stuart Dybeck. Length: no limit. Publishes short shorts. Sometimes critiques rejected mss.

How to Contact: Send complete manuscript with cover letter. "List previous publications; please notify us if the submission is being considered elsewhere." Reports in 3-6 months. Simultaneous submissions OK. Back issue for $5, 7×10 SAE and 4 first-class stamps. Fiction guidelines for #10 SASE.

Payment/Terms: Pays contributor's copies and *small* honorarium for one-time rights.

Advice: "We are most intrigued by those who take risks, and experiment with forms."

GULF STREAM MAGAZINE, (II), Florida International University, English Dept., North Miami Campus, N. Miami FL 33181. (305)940-5599. Editor: Lynne Barrett. Editors change every 1-2 years. Magazine: 5½×8½; 96 pages; recycled paper; 80 lb. cream cover; cover illustrations. "We publish *good quality*—fiction, nonfiction and poetry for a predominately literary market." Semiannually. Estab. 1989. Circ. 500.

Needs: Contemporary, literary, mainstream. Nothing "radically experimental." Plans special issues. Receives 100 unsolicited mss/month. Acquires 5 mss/issue; 10 mss/year. Does not read mss during the summer. Publishes ms 6 weeks-3 months after acceptance. Recently published work by Alan Cheuse, Ann Hood and David Kranes. Length: 5,000 words average; 7,500 words maximum. Publishes short shorts. Also publishes poetry. Sometimes critiques rejected mss.

How to Contact: Send complete manuscript with cover letter including list of previous publications and a short bio. Reports in 3 months. SASE. Simultaneous submissions OK "if noted." Sample copy for $4. Free fiction guidelines.

Payment/Terms: Pays in gift subscriptions and contributor's copies. Acquires first North American serial rights.

Advice: "Looks for good concise writing—well plotted with interesting characters."

HABERSHAM REVIEW, (I, II), Piedmont College, P.O. Box 10, Demorest GA 30535. (706)778-3000. Editors: David L. Greene and Lisa Hodgens Lumpkin. Magazine. "General literary magazine with a regional (Southeastern U.S.) focus for a literate audience." Semiannually. Estab. 1991.

Needs: Contemporary, experimental, literary, mainstream, regional. Receives 100 unsolicited mss/month. Acquires 6-10 mss/issue. Publishes short shorts. Sometimes critiques rejected mss.

How to Contact: Send complete ms with cover letter. Reports in 6 months on mss. SASE. No simultaneous submissions. Sample copy for $6.

Payment/Terms: Pays in contributor's copies. Acquires first rights.

HALF TONES TO JUBILEE, (II), English Dept., Pensacola Junior College, 1000 College Blvd., Pensacola FL 32504. (904)484-1416. Editor: Walter Spara. Magazine: 6×9; approx. 100 pages; 70 lb. laid stock; 80 lb. cover. "No theme, all types published." Annually. Estab. 1985. Circ. 500.

Needs: Open. Accepts approx. 6 mss/issue. "We publish in September." Recently published work by Rachel Cann, Dusty Sklar, Jorie Green, Mark Spencer. Length: 1,500 words average. Publishes short shorts. Also publishes poetry. Sometimes critiques rejected mss and recommends other markets.

How to Contact: Send complete ms with cover letter. SASE. Sample copy for $4. Free fiction guidelines.

Payment/Terms: Pays 2 contributor's copies. Acquires one-time rights.

‡HAPPY, (I, II), The Happy Organization, 240 E. 35th St., 11A, New York NY 10016. (212)689-3142. Editor: Bayard. Magazine: 68 pages; 60 lb. text paper; 100 lb. cover; illustrations and photos. Quarterly. Estab. 1995. Circ. 500.

Needs: Erotica, ethnic/multicultural, experimental, fantasy, feminist, gay, horror, humor/satire, lesbian, literary, psychic/supernatural/occult, science fiction. Receives 150-300 unsolicited mss/month. Accepts 20 mss/issue; 80-100 mss/year. Publishes ms 6-12 months after acceptance. Length: 1,000-3,500 words average; 5,000 words maximum. Publishes short shorts. Often critiques or comments on rejected ms.

How to Contact: Send complete ms with a cover letter. Should include estimated word count. Reports in 1 months on mss. Send SASE for reply, return of ms or send a disposable copy of ms. Simultaneous submissions OK. Sample copy for $7.

Payment/Terms: Pays $5 on publication and 1 contributor's copy for one-time rights.

Advice: "Ignore all the rules—defy conventional boredom. Avoid nuns, nurses, librarians, hunters, fishers and Monday Night Football."

HARD ROW TO HOE DIVISION, (II), Misty Hill Press, P.O. Box 541-I, Healdsburg CA 95448. (707)433-9786. Editor: Joe Armstrong. Newspaper: 8½×11; 12 pages; 60 lb. white paper; illustrations and photos. "Book reviews, short story and poetry of rural USA including environmental and nature subjects." Triannually. Estab. 1982. Circ. 150.

● *Hard Row to Hoe* was called "one of ten best literary newsletters in the U.S." by *Small Press* magazine.

Needs: Rural America. Receives 8-10 unsolicited mss/month. Acquires 1 ms/issue; 3-4 mss/year. Publishes ms 6-9 months after acceptance. Length: 1,500 words average; 2,000-2,200 words maximum. Publishes short shorts. Sometimes critiques rejected mss.

How to Contact: Send complete ms with cover letter. Reports in 3-4 weeks on mss. SASE. No simultaneous submissions. Sample copy for $2. Fiction guidelines for legal-size SASE.

Payment/Terms: Pays 3 contributor's copies. Acquires one-time rights.

Advice: "Be certain the subject fits the special need."

‡HARDBOILED, (I, II), Gryphon Publications, Box 209, Brooklyn NY 11228-0209. Editor: Gary Lovisi. Magazine: Digest-sized; 100 pages; offset paper; color cover; illustrations. Publishes "cutting edge, hard, noir fiction with impact! Query on nonfiction and reviews." Quarterly. Estab. 1988.

● By "hardboiled" the editor does not mean rehashing of pulp detective fiction from the 1940s and 1950s but, rather, realistic, gritty material. Lovisi could be called a pulp fiction "afficionado," however. He also publishes *Paperback Parade* and holds an annual vintage paperback fiction convention each year.

Needs: Mystery/suspense (private eye, police procedural, noir). Receives 40-60 mss/month. Buys 20-25 mss/year. Publishes ms within 6 months-2 years of acceptance. Recently published work by Andrew Vachss, Joe Lansdale, Bill Nolan, Richard Lupoff, Bill Pronzini and Eugene Izzi; published many new writers within the last year. Length: 2,000 words minimum; 4,000 words maximum. Sometimes critiques rejected mss and recommends other markets.

How to Contact: Query first or send complete ms with cover letter. Query with SASE only on anything over 3,000-4,000 words. No full-length novels. Reports in 2 weeks on queries; 2-6 weeks on mss. SASE. Simultaneous submissions OK, but query first. Sample copy for $6.

Payment/Terms: Pays $5-50 on publication and 2 contributor's copies for first North American serial rights. Copyright reverts to author.

HAUNTS, Tales of Unexpected Horror and the Supernatural, (II, IV), Nightshade Publications, Box 8068, Cranston RI 02926-0068. (401)781-9438. Editor: Joseph K. Cherkes. Magazine: 6×9 digest; 80-100 pages; 50 lb. offset paper; perfect-bound; pen and ink illustrations. "We are committed to publishing only the finest fiction in the genres of horror, fantasy and the supernatural from both semi-pro and established writers. We are targeted towards the 18-35 age bracket interested in tales of horror and the unknown." Triannually. Plans special fiction issue. 1984. Circ. 1,200.

Needs: Fantasy, horror, psychic/supernatural/occult. No pure adventure, explicit sex, or blow-by-blow dismemberment. Receives 700-750 unsolicited fiction mss/month. Buys 10-12 mss/issue; 50-75 mss/year. Published work by Mike Hurley, Kevin J. Anderson, Frank Ward; published new writers within the last year. Length: 3,500 words average; 1,000 words minimum; 8,500 words maximum. Critiques rejected mss and recommends other markets when possible.

How to Contact: Query first. "Cover letters are a nice way to introduce oneself to a new editor." Open to submissions January 1 to June 1, inclusive. Reports in 2-3 weeks on queries; 3-4 months on mss. SASE for query. Accepts magnetic media (IBM PC-MS/DOS 2.0 or higher), and most major word processing formats. E-mail address: josephkcherkes76520.56@compuserve.com. Sample copy for $4.95 plus $1 postage and handling. Fiction guidelines for #10 SASE.

Payment/Terms: Pays $5-50 (subject to change) on publication and contributor's copies; charge for additional copies. Buys first North American serial rights.

Advice: "Follow writers' guidelines closely. They are a good outline of what your publisher looks for in fiction. If you think you've got the 'perfect' manuscript, go over it again—carefully. Check to make sure you've left no loose ends before sending it out. Keep your writing *concise*. If your story is rejected, don't give up. Try to see where the story failed. This way you can learn from your mistakes. Remember, success comes to those who persist."

HAWAII PACIFIC REVIEW, (II), Hawaii Pacific University, 1060 Bishop St., Honolulu HI 96813. (808)544-0214. Editor: Elizabeth Fischel. Magazine: 6×9; 100-150 pages; quality paper; glossy cover; illustrations and original artwork. "The *Review* seeks to reflect the cultural diversity that is the hallmark of Hawaii Pacific University. Consequently, we welcome material on a wide variety of themes and we encourage experimental styles and narrative techniques. Categories: fiction, poetry, personal essays." Annually. Estab. "nationwide in 1988."

Needs: Adventure, contemporary, ethnic, experimental, fantasy, humor/satire, literary, mainstream, regional, science fiction, translations. No romance, confessions, religious or juvenile. Receives approx. 50 unsolicited fiction mss/month. Accepts 4-8 mss/issue. Deadline for the Spring annual issue is January 1. Does not read in summer. Publishes ms 3-12 months after acceptance. Published new writers within the last year. Length: 5,000 words maximum. Publishes short shorts. Also publishes literary essays, poetry. Sometimes critiques rejected mss or recommends other markets.

How to Contact: Send complete manuscript with cover letter, which should include a brief bio. Reports in 4 months. SASE. Simultaneous submissions OK. Fiction guidelines for #10 SASE.

Payment/Terms: Pays in contributor's copies. Acquires first North American serial rights. Rights revert to author upon publication.

Advice: Known for "ethnic fiction and work that delves into unique characters, themes and ethical choices. In all, the unique rather than the universal."

HAWAII REVIEW, (II), University of Hawaii English Dept., 1733 Donaghho Rd., Honolulu HI 96822. (808)956-3030. Fax: (808)956-9962. Editor: Michelle Viray. Magazine: 6½×9½; 150-170 pages; illustrations; photos. "We publish short stories as well as poetry and reviews by new and experienced writers. As an international literary journal, we hope to reflect the idea that cultural diversity is of universal interest." For residents of Hawaii and non-residents from the continental US and abroad. Triannually. Estab. 1972. Circ. 5,000.

Needs: Contemporary, ethnic, experimental, humor/satire, literary, prose poem, regional and translations. Receives 50-75 mss/month. Buys no more than 40 mss/issue; 130 mss/year. Published work by William Pitt Root, Ursule Molinaro and Ian Macmillan; published new writers within the last year. Length: 4,000 words average; no minimum; 8,000 words maximum. Occasionally critiques mss. Also publishes poetry.

New Writers Find Success Beside the Well-known

Although Rick Bass, Raymond Carver, Rita Dove, and Ken Kesey are among the writers who have been published in *Hayden's Ferry Review*, that shouldn't discourage beginning writers. "Our goal is to publish unpublished writers as well as well-known writers," says Managing Editor Salima Keegan, who has been with *HFR* since its inception in 1986. "We try to give new writers a chance because we feel there are not enough publishing opportunities out there for their work. We want to be that stepping stone for them, a place where they are able to find a voice and an audience."

The circulation of *HFR* is only 600, but that number should increase soon. Plans are being made to have the review represented by a distribution company, a move which could possibly double its circulation. And, though the print run isn't large, the publication is high quality and the editors make sure it is read by people who can help open doors for new writers. Keegan says, "The well-known writers we publish get the magazine noticed and read by people in publishing who might see a piece by one of our new writers and say 'that sounds like someone we'd like to talk to.' "

Keegan sends the magazine to a long list of indexes, reviews and anthologies such as the *Best of the West* series. She also nominates work to the Pushcart Prize every year. "We get it (*HFR*) out to the reviewers and the people who create these anthologies." Keegan also trades subscriptions with 50 literary magazines around the country, not only to have *HFR* and its writers read, but also to read other magazines and writers "to see what's out there."

HFR was chosen last year as one of the six magazines in the country to publish the winners of the Associated Writing Program writing competition. "We were their (AWP's) number one choice and the youngest publication they've ever selected. We were very excited about that," says Keegan. Now, once a year *HFR* expands its standard 128 pages to accommodate 30 additional pages of AWP winners.

Each year a new group of editors, selected from among Arizona State University graduate students, work on two editions of *HFR*. Keegan is the constant year-to-year managing editor who provides direction to the student editors. She prepares the budgets and determines how many pages the editors should aim for, then gives them free rein. "We tell them at the beginning of the year 'whatever you want to do with it, it's really up to you.' "

HFR publishes fiction, essays, art and nonfiction. Everything submitted is read first by one of the associate editors. Those editors then rate submissions and pass them on to the fiction editors who must also agree on a piece before it is chosen for publication. Editors will usually write comments or encouragement on pieces that made it through a few cuts but didn't make it to publication. They would like to write something to each author, says Keegan, but due to the volume of submissions—5,000 per issue—that is physically impossible.

> Although Keegan has no experience with other literary magazines, she reads many of them. She feels that it's of primary importance for writers to know the magazine they're submitting to. She advises writers to ask for or buy a sample copy, but to be sure to have a feel for the publication before submitting. "A lot of writers who submit to us have seen our magazine, or they'll send for a sample so that they know that it's a quality publication," says Keegan.
>
> Keegan understands how hard it is for new writers trying to get published and how discouraging rejection can be. Her advice? "Keep trying, keep sending work out, try not to get discouraged. If one magazine rejects you, try another." Keegan says that, although there are new editors each year at *HFR*, and so no specific "type" of work that appeals most to the staff, that also means that each year brings a new chance that someone will like your story. She also advises, "Even though rejection is discouraging, the odds are that eventually your work is going to be seen and someone's going to like it."
>
> —*Donna Collingwood*

How to Contact: Send complete ms with SASE. Reports in 3-4 months on mss. Sample copy for $5. Fiction guidelines for SASE.
Payment/Terms: Payment "varies depending upon funds budgeted. Last year, we paid $35-70 per story;" 2 contributor's copies. Pays on publication for all rights. Sends galleys to author upon request. After publication, copyright reverts to author upon request.

HAYDEN'S FERRY REVIEW, (II), Box 871502, Arizona State University, Tempe AZ 85287-1502. (602)965-1243. Managing Editor: Salima Keegan. Editors change every 1-2 years. Magazine: 6×9; 128 pages; fine paper; illustrations and photographs. "Contemporary material by new and established writers for a varied audience." Semiannually. Estab. 1986. Circ. 600.
• Work from *Hayden's Ferry Review* was selected for inclusion in the *Pushcart Prize* anthology.
Needs: Contemporary, ethnic, experimental, fantasy, feminist, gay, historical, humor/satire, literary, mainstream, prose poem, psychic/supernatural/occult, regional, romance (contemporary), science fiction, senior citizen/retirement. Possible special fiction issue. Receives 150 unsolicited mss/month. Accepts 5 mss/issue; 10 mss/year. Publishes mss 3-4 months after acceptance. Published work by Raymond Carver, Ken Kesey, Rita Dove, Chuck Rosenthal and Rick Bass. Length: No preference. Publishes short shorts. Also publishes literary essays.
How to Contact: Send complete ms with cover letter. No simultaneous submissions. Reports in 3-5 months from deadline on mss. SASE. E-mail Address: HFR@asuvm.inre.asu.edu. World Wide Web address: http:llas pin.asu.edu/provider/HFR/. Sample copy for $6. Fiction guidelines for SAE.
Payment/Terms: Pays 2 contributor's copies. Acquires first North American serial rights. Sends page proofs to author.

THE HEARTLANDS TODAY, (II), The Firelands Writing Center, Firelands College of BGSU, Huron OH 44839. (419)433-5560. Editors: Larry Smith and Nancy Dunham. Magazine: 6×9; 160 pages; b&w illustrations; 25-30 photographs. Material must be set in the Midwest. "We prefer material that reveals life in the Midwest today for a general, literate audience." Annually. Estab. 1991.
Needs: Ethnic, humor, literary, mainstream, regional (Midwest). Upcoming theme: "Power and Passion." Receives 15 unsolicited mss/month. Buys 6 mss/issue. Does not read mss August-December. Publishes ms 6 months after acceptance. Published work of Wendell Mayo, Tony Tomassi, Gloria Bowman. Length: 4,500 words maximum. Also publishes literary essays, poetry. Sometimes critiques rejected mss.
How to Contact: Send complete ms with cover letter. Reports in 2 months on mss. SASE for ms, not needed for query. Simultaneous submissions OK, if noted. Sample copy for $5.
Payment/Terms: Pays $20-25 on publication and 2 contributor's copies for first rights.
Advice: "We look for writing that connects on a human level, that moves us with its truth and opens our vision of the world. If writing is a great escape for you, don't bother with us. We're in it for the joy, beauty or truth of the art. We look for a straight, honest voice dealing with human experiences. We do not define the Midwest, we hope to be a document of the Midwest. If you feel you are writing from the Midwest, send your work to us. We look first at the quality of the writing."

HEAVEN BONE, (IV), Heaven Bone Press, Box 486, Chester NY 10918. (914)469-9018. Editors: Steven Hirsch and Kirpal Gordon. Magazine: 8½×11; 49-78 pages; 60 lb. recycled offset paper; full color cover;

computer clip art, graphics, line art, cartoons, halftones and photos scanned in tiff format. "New consciousness, expansive, fine literary, earth and nature, spiritual path. We use current reviews, essays on spiritual and esoteric topics, creative stories and fantasy. Also: reviews of current poetry releases and expansive literature." Readers are "spiritual seekers, healers, poets, artists, musicians, students." Semiannually. Estab. 1987. Circ. 2,500.

Needs: Esoteric/scholarly, experimental, fantasy, psychic/supernatural/occult, regional, religious/inspirational, spiritual. "No violent, thoughtless or exploitive fiction." Receives 45-110 unsolicited mss/month. Accepts 5-15 mss/issue; 12-30 mss/year. Publishes ms 2 weeks-10 months after acceptance. Published work by Fielding Dawson, Janine Pommy Vega, Charles Bukowski and Marge Piercy; published new writers within the last year. Length: 3,500 words average; 1,200 words minimum; 6,000 words maximum. Publishes short shorts. Also publishes literary essays, literary criticism, poetry. Sometimes critiques rejected mss.

How to Contact: Send complete ms with cover letter, which should include short bio of recent activities. Reports in 2 weeks on queries; 2 weeks-6 months on mss. SASE. Reprint submissions OK. Accepts electronic submissions via "Apple Mac versions of Macwrite, Microsoft Word 5.1 or Writenow 3.0." Sample copy for $6. Fiction guidelines free. Reviews novels and short story collections.

Payment/Terms: Pays in contributor's copies; charges for extras. Acquires first North American serial rights. Sends galleys to author, if requested.

Advice: "Our fiction needs are temperamental, so please query first before submitting. We prefer shorter fiction. Do not send first drafts to test them on us. Please refine and polish your work before sending. Always include SASE. We are looking for the unique, unusual and excellent."

‡❋**HECATE'S LOOM, Canada's International Pagan Magazine, (II, IV)**, Box 5206, Station B, Victoria, British Columbia V8R 6N4 Canada. (604)383-0410. Editor: Yvonne Owens. Fiction Editors: John Threlfall and Michela Scheuerman. Magazine: 8½×11; 46-52 pages; 60 lb. paper, 50% recycled; 70 lb. coated cover stock; illustrations and photos. Publishes stories about "wiccans, pagans, women's spirituality, men's spirituality, goddess consciousness, alternative politics/spirituality/healing and shamanism." Quarterly. Estab. 1986.Circ. 2,000.

• *Hecate's Loom* is a member of the Canadian Magazine Publishers Association and the Wiccan/Pagan Press Alliance.

Needs: Condensed/excerpted novel, erotica, ethnic/multicultural, fantasy (science, sword and sorcery, historic), feminist, gay, historical, humor/satire, lesbian, literary, mainstream/contemporary, psychic/supernatural/occult, religious/inspirational, romance (contemporary, futuristic/time travel, gothic, historical), science fiction (soft/sociological), serialized novel, "green politics," eco-feminism, shamanic. Upcoming themes: "Pagan Poetry" (February); "Erotic/Spirituality" (May); "Ritual Theatre" (August); "Mystical Death/Rebirth (Initiation)" (October). List of upcoming themes available for SASE. Receives 10-20 unsolicited mss/month. Accepts 1-2 mss/issue; 4-6 mss/year. Publishes ms 3-12 months after acceptance. Recently published work by Diana Michaelis, Yvonne Owens, Robin Skelton, John Threlfall and Michela Scheuerman. Length: 1,500 words average; 1,000 words minimum; 2,000 words maximum. Publishes short shorts. Also publishes literary essays, literary criticism and poetry.

How to Contact: Send complete ms with a cover letter. Should include estimated word count, bio (75-250 words), Social Security number and list of publications with submission. Reports in 3 months. Send SASE for reply, return of ms or send a disposable copy of ms. Simultaneous and electronic submissions OK. Sample copy for $3, SAE. Fiction guidelines for SAE.

Payment/Terms: Pays 1 contributor's copy; additional copies for $3. Acquires one-time rights.

Advice: Pieces "must be well written, with strong character development and memorable imagery to reflect Wiccan/pagan values and goddess/earth spirituality. Please write clearly to *communicate*, rather than to experiment with literary technique. Lyricism is fine where it serves the imagery or plot, but writing should not be too flowery. We would like to see more of the inside of the pagan 'mind.' True pagan sensibilities offer a radically alternative perspective and subtle differences in perception. Nothing trite, shallow or sleazy."

HELIOCENTRIC NET ANTHOLOGY, (II), (formerly *Heliocentric Net*), Three-Stones Publications Ltd., P.O. Box 68817, Seattle WA 98168-0817. Editor: Lisa Jean Bothell. Magazine: 8½×11; 80 pages; 20 lb. offset white paper; glossy 2-color cover; illustrations. Anthology of "horror/dark fantasy fiction; poetry and artwork for an adult audience. We look for horrific/dark fantasy themes based on boundary-pushing experiences and ideas—paranormal, supernatural, mystical, mythical. Eclectic." Annually. Estab. 1996.

• Note *Heliocentric Net* is now *Heliocentric Net Anthology* and has gone from quarterly to annual publication. The editor plans to begin paying small cash payments in 1997. In addition to the magazine, Three Stones Publications also publishes a bimonthly newsletter, *The Network*. Work included in *Heliocentric Net* tends to be more character-driven than idea-based.

Needs: Experimental (dark fantasy and horror), feminist (constructive only), horror, psychic/supernatural/occult, romance (dark fantasy related), science fiction (horrific). "No nihilistic horror; no erotica, pornography or anything intentionally discriminatory." Plans to publish chapbooks. Receives 200 unsolicited mss/month. Publishes mss 14 months maximum after acceptance. Recently published work by Edward Lee, Jessica Amanda Salmonson, Charlee Jacob and Jeff Vander Meer. Length: 2,000 words preferred; 3,000 words maximum. Publishes short shorts. Also publishes poetry. Always comments on rejected mss.

How to Contact: Send complete ms with a cover letter. Should include estimated word count, bio (around 50 words), and list of publications; "mention where you heard of *Heliocentric Net*." Reports in 4-6 weeks on queries; 4-6 weeks on mss. Send SASE for reply, return of ms or send a disposable copy of ms. Simultaneous, reprint and electronic submissions OK (with query). Sample copy for $9.95 plus book rate postage for your country. Fiction guidelines for SASE.

Payment/Terms: Pays 2 contributor's copies. Acquires first North American anthology rights. Sends galleys to author (if author sends SASE).

Advice: "We look for fiction with a constructive outlook and with ideas of real depth and insight, strong plotlines, realistic and believable characters, and complete story boundaries and resolutions. Don't be afraid to send thoughtful and intelligent horror/dark fantasy as opposed to the common action, shock value, and nihilistic horror that is flooding the market. A ms stands out when readers *care about and empathize* with characters, and when the concept is unique."

‡HEROIC TIMES, (I), Millenium, 3681 Offutt Rd., #203, Randallstown MD 21133. Editor: Gary Abraham. Magazine: 8½×11; 24 pages; HQ laser paper. Illustrations. *Heroic Times* covers "comics, entertainment and pop culture." Bimonthly. Estab. 1994. Circ. 200.

Needs: Adventure, erotica, ethnic/multicultural, experimental, fantasy, horror, mystery/suspense, science fiction. Receives 4 mss/month. Buys 8 mss/year. Publishes ms 2-3 months after acceptance. Publishes short shorts. Also publishes literary essays, literary criticism, poetry. Critiques or comments on rejected ms.

How to Contact: Send complete ms with a cover letter. Should include estimated word count. Reports in 2-3 weeks on queries; 1-2 months on mss. Send SASE for reply, return of ms or send a disposable copy of ms. Simultaneous submissions OK. Sample copy for $3.50. Fiction guidelines available with sample copy. Reviews novels and short story collections.

Payment/Terms: Pays 2-3 contributor's copies on publication. Acquires first rights.

HIGH PLAINS LITERARY REVIEW, (II), 180 Adams Street, Suite 250, Denver CO 80206. (303)320-6828. Editor-in-Chief: Robert O. Greer, Jr. Magazine: 6×9; 135 pages; 70 lb. paper; heavy cover stock. "The *High Plains Literary Review* publishes poetry, fiction, essays, book reviews and interviews. The publication is designed to bridge the gap between high-caliber academic quarterlies and successful commercial reviews." Triannually. Estab. 1986. Circ. 1,100.

Needs: Most pressing need: outstanding essays, serious fiction, contemporary, humor/satire, literary, mainstream, regional. No true confessions, romance, pornographic, excessive violence. Receives approximately 300 unsolicited mss/month. Buys 4-6 mss/issue; 12-18 mss/year. Publishes ms usually 6 months after acceptance. Published work by Richard Currey, Joyce Carol Oates, Nancy Lord and Rita Dove; published new writers within the last year. Length: 4,200 words average; 1,500 words minimum; 8,000 words maximum; prefers 3,000-6,000 words. Also publishes literary essays, literary criticism, poetry. Occasionally critiques rejected mss.

How to Contact: Send complete ms with cover letter, which should include brief publishing history. Reports in 10 weeks. SASE. Simultaneous submissions OK. Sample copy for $4.

Payment/Terms: Pays $5/page for prose and 2 contributor's copies on publication for first North American serial rights. "Copyright reverts to author upon publication." Sends copy-edited proofs to the author.

Advice: "*HPLR* publishes *quality* writing. Send us your very best material. We will read it carefully and either accept it promptly, recommend changes or return it promptly. Do not start submitting your work until you learn the basic tenets of the game including some general knowledge about how to develop characters and plot and how to submit a manuscript. I think the most important thing for any new writer interested in the short story form is to have a voracious appetite for short fiction, to see who and what is being published, and to develop a personal style."

HILL AND HOLLER: Southern Appalachian Mountains, (II), Seven Buffaloes Press, Box 249, Big Timber MT 59011. Editor: Art Cuelho. Magazine: 5½×8½; 80 pages; 70 lb. offset paper; 80 lb. cover stock; illustrations; photos rarely. "I use mostly rural Appalachian material: poems and stories, and some folklore and humor. I am interested in heritage, especially in connection with the farm." Annually. Published special fiction issue. Estab. 1983. Circ. 750.

● Art Cuelho of Seven Buffaloes Press also edits *Azorean Express*, *Black Jack* and *Valley Grapevine* listed in this book.

Needs: Contemporary, ethnic, humor/satire, literary, regional, rural America farm. "I don't have any prejudices in style, but I don't like sentimental slant. Deep feelings in literature are fine, but they should be portrayed with tact and skill." Receives 10 unsolicited mss/month. Accepts 4-6 mss/issue. Publishes ms 6 months-1 year after acceptance. Length: 2,000-3,000 words average. Also publishes short shorts of 500-1,000 words.

How to Contact: Query first. Reports in 2 weeks on queries. SASE. Sample copy for $6.75.

Payment/Terms: Pays in contributor's copies. Acquires first North American serial rights "and permission to reprint if my press publishes a special anthology." Sometimes sends galleys to author.

Advice: "In this Southern Appalachian rural series I can be optimistic about fiction. Appalachians are very responsive to their region's literature. I have taken work by beginners that had not been previously published.

Be sure to send a double-spaced clean manuscript and SASE. I have the only rural press in North America; maybe even in the world. So perhaps we have a bond in common if your roots are rural."

‡hip MAMA, The parenting zine, (I, II, IV), P.O. Box 9097, Oakland CA 94613. Phone/fax: (510)658-4508. Editor: Ariel Gore. Magazine: 8½×11, 36 pages; uncoated paper; glossy cover; illustrations and photos. " 'Zine for progressive/liberal/feminist parents." Quarterly. Estab. 1993. Circ. 5,000.
• *hip Mama* was a finalist in the 1995 Annual Alternative Press Awards
Needs: Condensed/excerpted novel, erotica, ethnic/multicultural, experimental, feminist, humor/satire, lesbian, literary, mainstream/contemporary. Nothing "anti-mother." Receives 5 unsolicited fiction mss/month. Accepts 1-2 mss/issue; 6 mss/year. Publishes ms 1 week-1 year after acceptance. Recently published work by Lara Candland and Constance Garcia-Barrio. Length: 1,000 words average; 400 words minimum; 2,000 words maximum. Publishes short shorts. Length: 300-400 words. Also publishes literary essays and poetry. Sometimes critiques or comments on rejected ms.
How to Contact: Send complete ms with a cover letter. Should include estimated word count and short bio with submission. Reports in 1 month on queries; 6 months on mss. Send SASE for reply, return of ms or send a disposable copy of ms. Simultaneous and reprint submissions OK. Sample copy for $4. Reviews novels and short story collections.
Payment/Terms: Pays $50 maximum, free subscription to magazine and 3 contributor's copies on publication for one-time rights. Sends galleys to author if requested.
Advice: Wants "concise, evocative stories about some aspect of mothering in these times. We don't see enough stories about unusual but positive mothering experiences. We're tired of stories about bad mothers."

HOBSON'S CHOICE, (I), Starwind Press, Box 98, Ripley OH 45167. (513)392-4549. Editor: Susannah West. Magazine: 8½×11; 16 pages; 60 lb. offset paper and cover; b&w illustrations; line shot photos. "We publish science fiction and fantasy for young adults and adults with interest in science, technology, science fiction and fantasy." Bimonthly. Estab. 1974. Circ. 2,000.
Needs: Fantasy, science fiction (hard science, soft/sociological). "We like science fiction that shows hope for the future and protagonists who interact with their environment rather than let themselves be manipulated by it." No horror, pastiches of other authors, stories featuring characters created by others (i.e. Captain Kirk and crew, Dr. Who, etc.). Receives 50 unsolicited mss/month. Buys 2-4 mss/issue; 16-24 mss/year. Publishes ms between 4 months-2 years after acceptance. Published work by Robert Gray, Stuart Napier, Doug Beason; published new writers within the last year. Length: 2,000-8,000 words. Also publishes literary criticism and some literary essays. Occasionally critiques rejected mss.
How to Contact: Send complete ms. Reports in 2-3 months. "If an author hasn't heard from us by 4 months, he/she should feel free to withdraw." Send SASE for return of ms. No simultaneous submissions. Accepts electronic submissions via disk for the IBM PC or PC compatible in ASCII format and Macintosh. Sample copy for $2.25. Fiction guidelines for #10 SASE. Tipsheet packet (all guidelines plus tips on writing science fiction) for $1.25 and SASE. Checks should be payable in U.S. funds only.
Payment/Terms: Pays 1-4¢/word (25% on acceptance, 75% on publication) and contributor's copies. "We pay 25% kill fee if we decide not to publish story." Rights negotiable. Sends galleys to the author.
Advice: "I certainly think a beginning writer can be successful if he/she studies the publication *before* submitting, and matches the submission with the magazine's needs. Get our guidelines and study them before submitting. Don't submit something *way over* or *way under* our word length requirements. Be understanding of editors; they can get swamped very easily, *especially* if there's only one editor handling all submissions. You don't need to write a synopsis of your story in your cover letter—the story should be able to stand on its own."

‡HOME GIRL PRESS, Pink Ink, (I, II), ZEB Publications, P.O. Box 651, New York NY 10035. Editor: Ms. Zulma E. Brooks. Magazine: 8½×11; 12-25 pages; recycled 20 lb. bond, colored paper; illustrations and photos. "The theme of *Home Girl Press* is urban American women. Material focuses on the lifestyle of 'big city' women. Our audience is women 18-30, career-oriented and housewives." Quarterly. Estab. 1996.
• This is a very new publication debuting Spring 1996.
Needs: Adventure, ethnic/multicultural, fantasy (science, sword and sorcery, urban), humor/satire, literary, mainstream/contemporary, regional, romance (contemporary), science fiction (hard science, urban). "No lesbian, feminist, male bashing or excessive profanity." Upcoming themes: "The little people's view of High Society," "Sista vs. Sista: Class Clash." Accepts 6-8 mss/issue; 24-32 mss/year. Publishes ms 3-6 months after acceptance. Length: 2,500 words average; 500 words minimum; 3,000 words maximum. Also publishes literary criticism, poetry. Sometimes critiques or comments on rejected ms.
How to Contact: Query first. Send complete ms with a cover letter. Should include estimated word count, 200-word bio and 2×3 photo. Reports in 6-20 weeks on queries; 2-10 months on mss. SASE. Samples copy for $2.50, 9×12 SAE and 5 first-class stamps. Fiction guidelines for #10 SAE and 2 first-class stamps.
Payment/Terms: Pays 3 contributor's copies on acceptance for one-time rights; additional copies $3. Sends galleys to author.

Advice: "Go over it with a fine tooth comb and work out the bugs because I definitely will! Avoid clichés, formulative writing, predictable plots and ends. I would like to see more dramatic writing and more imaginative fiction from the urban woman writer."

HOME OFFICE OPPORTUNITIES, (I, IV), Deneb Publishing, P.O. Box 780, Lyman WY 82937. (307)786-4513. Editor: Diane Wolverton. Magazine: 6½×10; 24 pages; newsprint paper; illustrations and photographs. "Bimonthly digest of help, information and nurturing for people who operate a home office." Bimonthly. Estab. 1989. Circ. 500.
- Deneb also publishes the popular *Housewife Writer's Forum*, also listed in this book. The *Housewife Writer's Forum* Short Fiction Contest is listed in the Contest and Awards section. Editor Diane Wolverton received first place from the National Federation of Press Women for her "personal from the editor" column.

Needs: "Business-oriented fiction. Strong business savvy, central character." Accepts 1 ms/issue; 6 mss/year. Publishes ms 3-6 months after acceptance. Length: 1,500-2,000. Publishes short shorts.
How to Contact: Send complete ms with cover letter. Should include estimated word count, bio (35-50 words), and list of publications. Reports in 4-8 weeks. Send SASE for reply, return of ms or send a disposable copy of ms. Simultaneous, reprint and electronic submissions OK. Sample copy for $2. Fiction guidelines for business size SASE.
Payment/Terms: Pays 1¢/word minimum; 5 contributor's copies; additional copies for $1.50 each. Pays on acceptance for first rights or one-time rights.
Advice: "We are a very open market to new writers—we don't care as much about publication credits as we do about finding writers who can send us fiction that makes our readers feel good about being in business." Looking for more "writers who have a real sense of what it means to be in business—who understand what it's like to make payroll, file tax forms and deal with competitors. Communicate some of that in a short story and you'll have a winner with us."

HOME PLANET NEWS, (II), Home Planet Publications, P. O. Box 415, New York NY 10009. (718)769-2854. Tabloid: 11½×16; 24 pages; newsprint; illustrations; photos. "*Home Planet News* publishes mainly poetry along with some fiction, as well as reviews (books, theater and art), and articles of literary interest. We see *HPN* as a quality literary journal in an eminently readable format and with content that is urban, urbane and politically aware." Triannually. Estab. 1979. Circ. 1,000.
- *HPN* has received a small grant from the Puffin Foundation for its focus on AIDS issues.

Needs: Ethnic/multicultural, experimental, feminist, gay, historical, lesbian, literary, mainstream/contemporary, science fiction (soft/sociological). No "children's or genre stories (except rarely some science fiction)." Upcoming themes: "AIDS." Publishes special fiction issue or anthology. Receives 12 mss/month. Buys 1 ms/issue; 3 mss/year. Reads fiction mss only from February to May. Publishes 1 year after acceptance. Recently published work by Maureen McNeil, Eugene Stein, B.Z. Niditch and Layle Silbert. Length: 2,500 words average; 500 words minimum; 3,000 words maximum. Publishes short shorts. Also publishes literary criticism, poetry.
How to Contact: Send complete ms with a cover letter. Reports in 3-6 months on mss. Send SASE for reply, return of ms or send a disposable copy of the ms. Sample copy for $3. Fiction guidelines for SASE.
Payment/Terms: Pays 3 contributor's copies; additional copies $1. Acquires one-time rights.
Advice: "We use very little fiction, and a story we accept just has to grab us. We need short pieces of some complexity, stories about complex people facing situations which resist simple resolutions."

THE HOPEWELL REVIEW 1995: New Work by Indiana's Best Writers, (III, IV), Arts Indiana, Inc., #701, 47 S. Pennsylvania St., Indianapolis IN 46204. (317)632-7894. Editor: Joseph F. Trimmer. Magazine: 5½×8½; 128 pages; perfect bound. "*The Hopewell Review* is an annual anthology of fiction, poetry and essays. The primary criterion for selection is high literary quality." Annually. Estab. 1989.
Needs: Condensed/excerpted novel, contemporary, experimental, humor/satire, literary, prose poem, regional, translations. "Writers must currently live in Indiana or have an extraordinary tie." Receives 1,200 unsolicited mss/year. Buys 4-6 mss/issue. Publishes annually (September). Published work by Scott Russell Sanders, Yusef Komunyaka and Roger Mitchell. Length: 4,000 words maximum. Sometimes critiques rejected mss.
How to Contact: Send complete ms with cover letter which should include brief biography. Annual deadline: March 1. Notification: June. SASE. Simultaneous submissions OK with notification. Sample copy for $6.95 and $2 postage. Fiction guidelines for SASE.
Payment/Terms: Pays $125-625 ($500 award of excellence) and 2 contributor's copies on publication; charges for additional copies. Buys first rights and one-time rights.
Advice: "Fresh perspectives and use of the English language make a manuscript stand out."

HOPSCOTCH: THE MAGAZINE FOR GIRLS, (II), The Bluffton News Publishing & Printing Co., P.O. Box 164, Bluffton OH 45817. (419)358-4610. Fax: (419)358-5027. Editor: Marilyn Edwards. Magazine: 7×9; 50 pages; enamel paper; pen & ink illustrations; photographs. Publishes stories for and about girls ages 5-12. Bimonthly. Estab. 1989. Circ. 9,000.

• *Hopscotch* is indexed in the *Children's Magazine Guide* and *Ed Press* and has received a Parents' Choice Gold Medal Award and Ed Press Awards.

Needs: Children's/juvenile (5-9, 10-12 years): adventure, ethnic/multicultural, fantasy, historical (general), sports. Upcoming themes: "Bears" (Feb. '96); "Pets" (Apr. '96); "Brothers" (June '96); "Inventions" (Aug. '96); "Dogs" (Oct. '96); "The Post Office" (Dec. '96). Receives 300-400 unsolicited mss/month. Buys 20-40 mss/year. Agented fiction 2%. Recently published work by Lois Grambling, Betty Killion, Jean Patrick, VaDonna Jean Leaf. Length: 500-750 words preferred; 300 words minimum; 750 words maximum. Publishes short shorts. Length: 250-400 words. Also publishes poetry, puzzles, hidden pictures and crafts. Always comments on rejected mss.

How to Contact: Send complete ms with cover letter. Should include estimated word count, 1-page bio, Social Security number and list of publications. Reports in 2-4 weeks on queries; 6-10 weeks on mss. Send SASE for reply, return of ms or send disposable copy of the ms. Simultaneous and reprint submissions OK. Sample copy for $3. Fiction guidelines for #10 SASE. Reviews novels and short story collections.

Payment/Terms: Pays 5¢/word (extra for usable photos or illustrations) before publication and 1 contributor's copy; additional copies $3; $2 for 10 or more. Buys first North American serial rights.

HOUSEWIFE-WRITER'S FORUM, (I), P.O. Box 780, Lyman WY 82937. (307)782-7003. Editor: Emma Bluemel. Fiction Editor: Edward Wahl. Magazine: 6½×10; 32-48 pages; glossy cover; illustrations. Offers "support for women and house husbands of all ages who juggle writing with family life. We publish short fiction, poetry, essays, nonfiction, line drawings, humor and hints." Bimonthly. Estab. 1988. Circ. over 2,000.

• This magazine also includes fiction marketing tips and information. See also our listing for the contest sponsored by the magazine, *Housewife Writer's Forum* Short Story Contest.

Needs: Contemporary, experimental, historical, humor/satire, literary, mainstream, mystery/suspense, romance (contemporary, historical). No pornographic material. Receives 100-200 mss/month. Buys 1-2 mss/issue; 6-12 mss/year. Publishes ms within 6 months-1 year after acceptance. Published work by Elaine McCormick, Carol Shenold and Carole Bellacera. Length: 1,500 words preferred; 500 words minimum; 2,000 words maximum. Publishes short shorts. Publishes critiques of accepted mss.

How to Contact: Send complete ms with cover letter. Reports in 3-4 months on mss. SASE "with *adequate* postage." Simultaneous and reprint submissions OK. Sample copy for $4. Fiction guidelines for #10 SASE.

Payment/Terms: Pays 1¢/word on acceptance and 1 contributor's copy; additional copies half price. Buys first North American rights. Sponsors annual contest "geared to the interests of housewife-writers. First place winners are published in the magazine." Entry fee: $4. Prize: $30. Send #10 SASE for guidelines and further information."

Advice: "All mss are read and sometimes suggestions are offered on the rejections. All published materials are printed with Fiction Editor Edward Wahl's critiques. Here are a few samples of our critiques to show you what we're looking for: 'Life is made up of small details. Writing often consists of finding the right ones out of the thousands that make up even the briefest moment and using them to convey information to the reader. There's more to this than just a bunch of required items and small details, though. There is also believable dialogue, controlled pacing, and a fine ending that fits the tone and the action and the narrator just right. I look for the overall effect of the story—the product of its theme, its narrative skill, its handling of detail and pace and dialogue, its felicity of beginning, transition and ending. The degree to which all these things mesh and contribute to a whole meaning that surpasses the mere sum of the constituents is the degree to which a story succeeds.' "

THE HUNTED NEWS, (I, II), The Subourban Press, P.O. Box 9101, Warwick RI 02889. (401)739-2279. Editor: Mike Wood. Magazine: 8½×11; 25-30 pages; photocopied paper. "I am looking for good writers in the hope that I can help their voices be heard. Like most in the small press scene, I just wanted to create another option for writers who otherwise might not be heard." Biannually. Estab. 1991. Circ. 200.

Needs: Erotica, experimental, literary, mainstream/contemporary, serialized novel, translations. No science fiction, romance or politically-biased work. Publishes annual special fiction issue or anthologies. Receives 15-20 unsolicited mss/month. Acquires 1-2 mss/issue; 6 mss/year. Publishes ms within 3 months after acceptance. Published work by Darryl Smyers and Charles Bukowski. Length: 500 words minimum; 900 words maximum. Publishes short shorts. Length: 300 words. Also publishes literary essays, literary criticism and poetry. Always critiques or comments on rejected mss.

How to Contact: Send complete ms with cover letter. Should include bio. Reports in 1 month. Send SASE for reply, return of ms or send disposable copy of the ms. Simultaneous and reprint submissions OK. Sample copy for 8½×11 SAE and 3 first-class stamps. Fiction guidelines free. Reviews novels or short story collections.

Payment/Terms: Pays up to 3 contributor's copies. Acquires one-time rights.

Advice: "I look for an obvious love of language and a sense that there is something at stake in the story, a story that somehow needs to be told. Write what you need to write, say what you think you need to say, no matter the subject, and take a chance and send it to me. A writer will always find an audience if the work is true."

HURRICANE ALICE, A Feminist Quarterly, (II), Hurricane Alice Fn., Inc., 207 Church St. SE, Minneapolis MN 55455. Executive Editors: Martha Roth and Patricia Cumbie. Fiction is collectively edited. Tabloid: 11×17; 12-16 pages; newsprint stock; illustrations and photos. "We look for feminist fictions with a certain analytic snap, for serious readers, seriously interested in emerging forms of feminist art/artists." Quarterly. Estab. 1983. Circ. 600-700.
Needs: Erotica, experimental, feminist, gay, humor/satire, lesbian, science fiction, translations. No coming-out stories, defloration stories, abortion stories. Upcoming themes: "Legend(s) of Bad Women" (Winter 1996); "Women & Film" (Summer 1996); "Faith & Feminism" (Fall 1996). Receives 80 unsolicited mss/month. Publishes 8-10 stories annually. Publishes mss up to 1 year after acceptance. Published work by Beth Brant, Nona Caspers, Gretchen Legler, Joanna Kadi, Toni McNaron; published new writers within the last year. Length: up to 3,000 words maximum. Publishes short shorts. Occasionally critiques rejected mss.
How to Contact: Send complete ms with cover letter. "A brief biographical statement is never amiss. Writers should be sure to tell us if a piece was commissioned by one of the editors." Reports in 3-4 months. SASE for ms. Simultaneous submissions OK. Sample copy for $2.50, 11×14 SAE and 2 first-class stamps.
Payment/Terms: Pays 5 contributor's copies. Acquires one-time rights.
Advice: "Fiction is a craft. Just because something happened, it isn't a story; it becomes a story when you transform it through your art, your craft."

‡I.E. MAGAZINE, (II), P.O. Box 73403, Houston TX 77273-3403. Managing Editor: Yolande Gottlieb. Fiction Editor: Belle Griffith. Nonfiction Editor: John Gorman. Magazine: digest-sized; 48-50 pages; 70 lb. glossy paper; 80 lb. glossy cover; illustrations and photos. "*i.e. Magazine* is open to different themes. We want quality, innovative, imaginative stories for a literary audience." Quarterly. Estab. 1990. Circ. 200.
Needs: Adventure, experimental, fantasy, historical, humor/satire, literary, mainstream/contemporary, mystery/suspense, romance, science fiction, translations, westerns, play reviews (with photos; "large metropolitan area theaters only"), visual arts. "No pornography." Receives 30-40 unsolicited mss/month. Accepts 4-5 mss/issue; 46-48 mss/year. Publishes ms 3-6 months after acceptance. Recently published work by John Gorman and Eric Muirhead. Publishes short shorts. Also publishes poetry, literary essays, literary criticism, poetry. Sometimes critiques or comments on rejected ms.
How to Contact: Send complete ms with a cover letter. Should include estimated word count, bio (maximum ½ page), Social Security number, list of publications and 2×2 photo to include with bio if story is printed. Reports in 3-4 weeks on queries; 2-4 months on mss. Send SASE for reply, return of ms or send a disposable copy of ms. Simultaneous and reprint submissions OK. Sample copy for $4 and $2.10 postage. Guidelines for #10 SAE and 2 first-class stamps.
Payment/Terms: Pays 1-2 contributor's copies on publication; additional copies $4 and $2.10 postage. Acquires one-time rights. Sponsors contests: fiction, nonfiction, poetry, poetry chapbooks and visual arts.

THE ICONOCLAST, (II), 1675 Amazon Rd., Mohegan Lake NY 10547. Editor: Phil Wagner. Journal. 8½×5½; 24-28 pages; 20 lb. white paper; 20 lb. cover stock; illustrations. "*The Iconoclast* is a self-supporting, independent, unaffiliated general interest magazine with an appreciation of the profound, absurd and joyful in life. Material is limited only by *its* quality and *our* space. We want readers and writers who are open-minded, unafraid to think, and actively engaged with the world." Published 8 times/year. Estab. 1992. Circ. 500.
● *The Iconoclast* has grown from a 16-page newsletter to a 24-28-page journal and is, subsequently, buying more fiction.
Needs: Adventure, ethnic/multicultural, humor/satire, literary, mainstream/contemporary, science fiction. "Nothing militant, solipsistic, or silly." Receives 50 unsolicited mss/month. Accepts 2-3 mss/issue; 15-20 mss/year. Publishes ms 1-6 months after acceptance. Length: 1,500-2,000 words preferred; 100 words minimum; 2,500 words maximum. Publishes short shorts. Also publishes literary essays, literary criticism and poetry. Often critiques or comments on rejected mss.
How to Contact: Send complete ms. Reports in 1 month. Send SASE for reply, return of mss or send a disposable copy of the ms. Simultaneous and reprint submissions OK. Sample copy for $1.75. Reviews novels and short story collections.
Payment/Terms: Pays 1-2 contributor's copies; additional copies $1.05 (40% discount). Acquires one-time rights.
Advice: "We like fiction that has something to say (and not about its author). We hope for work that is observant, intense and multi-leveled. Follow Pound's advice—'make it new.' Write what you want in whatever style you want without being gross, sensational, or needlessly explicit—then pray there's someone who can appreciate your sensibility."

THE ILLINOIS REVIEW, (II), Illinois Writers, Inc., 4240/English Dept., Illinois State University, Normal IL 61790-4240. Editor: Jim Elledge. Magazine: 5½×8½; 72 pages; matte cover stock; cover illustrations only. "We're open to any work of literary merit by unknown or established authors. Mainstream and alternative works are equally desired. Marginalized individuals welcome. Our only bias is for excellence." Semiannually. Estab. 1993. Circ. 500.
● The *Illinois Review* received a 1995 Illinois Arts Council Award for fiction.

Needs: Ethnic/multicultural, experimental, feminist, gay, lesbian, literary and mainstream/contemporary. Length: rarely longer than 15 double-spaced pages. Very interested in short shorts and prose poems. Fall 1995 issue was a double issue devoted to prose poems and short short fiction. Also publishes literary essays, literary criticism and poetry.

How to Contact: Send complete ms with a cover letter. "Cover letters are not required but are read. An author may mention anything in his/her cover letter, but the piece will be accepted only if it's good." Reports in 1-2 weeks on queries; 2-4 months on mss. Send SASE for reply, return of ms or send a disposable copy of ms. Sample copy for $6. No guidelines available. Submissions are returned unread from May 1 through August 1.

Payment/Terms: Pays free subscription to the magazine and 2 contributor's copies. Acquires first North American serial rights. Rights revert to author upon publication.

Advice: "Buy a copy and see the varied styles of the work we publish. Avoid sending religious, romance, nostalgia and sentimental work."

‡**THE INDIA PAPERS, Short Stories by Middle and High School Authors, (I, IV)**, Bradford, Cook and Michaels Publishing, 790 W. 40 Hwy., Blue Springs MO 64015. (816)374-5901. Editor: Randy M. Combs. Tabloid: 7¼×10⅝; 48 pages; newsprint paper; newsprint cover; illustrations. The philosophy of *The India Papers* is "to give young writers (teens, middle and high school) a publishing forum for their imagination." Quarterly. Estab. 1994. Circ. 1,000.

Needs: Young adult/teen. Plans special fiction issue or anthology. Receives 30-50 unsolicited mss/month. Accepts 10-15 mss/issue; 40-60 mss/year. Publishes ms 3-6 months after acceptance. Recently published work by Jennifer Simon, Jacqueline Leigh Ross and Sam Ramsey. Publishes short shorts. Often critiques or comments on rejected ms (if SASE included, always).

How to Contact: Send complete ms with a cover letter. Reports in 4-6 weeks on mss. Send SASE for reply, return of ms or send a disposable copy of ms. Simultaneous and electronic submissions OK. E-mail address: indiapap@aol.com. Sample copy for $3. Fiction guidelines for #10 SASE.

Payment/Terms: Pays 2 contributor's copies; additional copies for $3. Acquires one-time rights.

Advice: "We look for imaginative stories which are daring. Push your imagination, type your manuscript. Don't send 'this summer I did' stories."

INDIANA REVIEW, (II), 316 N. Jordan Ave., Indiana University, Bloomington IN 47405. (812)855-3439. Editor: Shirley Stephenson. Associate Editor: Geoffrey Pollock. Editors change every 2 years. Magazine: 6×9; 200 pages; 50 lb. paper; Glatfelter cover stock. *Indiana Review* is a "magazine of contemporary fiction and poetry in which there is a zest for language, a relationship between form and content, and awareness of the world. For fiction writers/readers, followers of lively contemporary prose." Semiannually. Estab. 1976. Circ. 2,000.

● Work published in *Indiana Review* was selected for inclusion in the *O. Henry Prize Stories* anthology.

Needs: Literary, contemporary. Also considers novel excerpts. Buys 8-12 prose mss/issue. Recently published work by Alberto Ríos, Neal Karlen, Ursula LeGuin and Pamela Painter. Length: 1-35 magazine pages. Also publishes literary essays, poetry.

How to Contact: Send complete ms with cover letter. "Cover letters need to be concise and to the point. Encapsulating a piece's theme or content is unacceptable." SASE. Simultaneous submissions OK (if notified *immediately* of other publication). Reports in 3 months. Publishes ms an average of 4-10 months after acceptance. Sample copy for $7.

Payment/Terms: Pays $5/page for North American serial rights.

Advice: "We look for prose that is well-crafted, socially relevant. We are interested in innovation, unity and social context. All genres that meet some of these criteria are welcome."

‡**INNER VOICES, A New Journal of Prison Literature, (IV)**, Inner Voices, P.O. Box 4500, #219, Bloomington IN 47402. Editor: C. Nolan Williams. 8½×5½; 40 pages; matte paper; card stock cover; illustrations. Publishes literature written by prisoners. Semianually. Estab. 1995. Circ. 200.

Needs: Open to all fiction except heavy erotica and novels. Receives 2 unsolicited mss/month. Accepts 2-3 mss/issue; 4-6 mss/year. Time between acceptance and publication varies. Length: 3,000 words average; 10,000 words maximum. Publishes short shorts. Also publishes poetry. Sometimes critiques or comments on rejected ms.

How to Contact: Send complete ms with a cover letter. Should include a personal statement (100 words or less) with submission. Reports in 1 month on queries; 3 months on mss. Send a disposable copy of ms. Simultaneous, reprint and electronic (Mac) submissions OK. E-mail address: cnwillia@indiana.edu. Fiction guidelines free. Reviews novels and short story collections.

Payment/Terms: Pays with free subscription to magazine or 1-2 contributor's copies. Acquires "shared" rights.

Advice: "Find someone who isn't afraid to critique your work and treat that person like gold. Then, give us a try. Please, no explicit descriptions of crimes. These may be banned from prison libraries. Avoid using past issues as a guideline—we want to show the range of talent in prisons." Sometimes enters writers' work in other organizations' contests.

INTERNATIONAL QUARTERLY, Essays, Fiction, Drama, Poetry, Art, Reviews, (II), P.O. Box 10521, Tallahassee FL 32302-0521. (904)224-5078. Fax: (904)224-5127. Editor: Van K. Brock. Magazine: 7½×10; 176 pages; 50 lb. text paper; 60 lb. gloss cover; fine art illustrations. *"International Quarterly* seeks to bridge boundaries between national, ethnic and cultural identities, and among creative disciplines, by providing a venue for dialogue between exceptional writers and artists and discriminating readers. We look for work that reveals character and place from within." Quarterly. Estab. 1993.

Needs: Ethnic/multicultural, experimental, humor/satire, literary, mainstream/contemporary, regional, translations. "We would consider work in any of the genres that transcends the genre through quality of language, characterization and development. Our sympathies are strongly feminist. Many of the genre categories imply simplistic and limited literary purposes. Any genre can transcend its limits." No issue is limited to work on its regional or thematic focus." Accepts 5 mss/issue; 20 mss/year. "We read all year, but fewer readers are active in July and August." Publishes ms 3-9 months after acceptance. Published work by Edmund Keeley, Iván Mándy, Gary Corgeri, S.P. Elledge. Publishes short shorts. Also publishes literary essays, literary criticism (for general readers), poetry. Sometimes critiques or comments on rejected mss.

How to Contact: Query first or send complete ms with a cover letter. Should include estimated word count, bio, list of publications. Include rights available. "We prefer first rights for all original English texts." Reports in 1-2 weeks on queries; 2-4 months on mss. Send SASE for reply, return of ms or send a disposable copy of ms. Simultaneous, reprint (please specify) and electronic submissions OK. Sample copy for $6 (a reduced rate) and 4 first-class stamps. Fiction guidelines for #10 SASE. Reviews novels and short story collections. Send books to Book Review Editor.

Payment/Terms: Pays free subscription to magazine and 1 contributor's copy. Acquires first North American serial rights. Sends galleys to author.

Advice: "Read the four varied stories in our first issue. Also the two nonfiction 'stories' in the Essay section by Anneliese Wagner and Wayne Brown, which would have been accepted if they had been offered as stories. We like their quality of language, skill and discipline, sensitivity, wit or seriousness, and their careful, effortless-seeming development. And read a wide range of other good fiction. If you are really a beginning writer, persistently seek out and listen to the suggestions of other intelligent, practiced readers and writers. We would like to see more fiction break out of conventional thinking and set fictional modes without straining or trying to shock and fiction that presents the world of its characters from inside the skin of the culture, rather than those outside of the culture, tourists or short-termers, as it were, commenting on the world of a story's subjects from outside, lamenting that it has fallen into our consumerist ways, etc., lamentable as that may be. Works we publish do not have to be foreign, they may arise out of a profound understanding of any culture or locale, as long as they provide the reader with an authentic experience of that locale, whatever the origin of the author. We have no taboos, but we want writing that understands and creates understanding, writers who want to go beyond cultural givens."

INTO THE DARKNESS, The Magazine of Extreme Horror, (I, II, IV), Necro Publications, P.O. Box 677205, Orlando FL 32867-7205. (407)671-4822. Fiction Editor: David G. Barnett. Asistant Editors: Aaron Vest and Debbie Tomasetti. Magazine: 8½×11; 72 pages; 20 lb. paper; 100 lb. full-color cover; illustrations and photos. *"ITD* is dedicated to extreme horror that is dark, disturbing, graphic, sexy, violent and leaves a scar on the reader. Fiction from the darkest minds in horror. A magazine for writers who were always afraid to let their darkside show through. A magazine for new writers with new ideas. Nothing tame or weak, only pure evil thrust in the face of the reader. Fiction that invades the mind and harms the soul. *ITD* is not for the faint of heart." Quarterly. Estab. 1994. Circ. 2,000.

● *Into the Darkness* has doubled its circulation and is looking for longer, more complex horror.

Needs: Horror only. List of upcoming themes available for SASE. Receives 50 unsolicited mss/month. Accepts 12-15 mss/issue; 48-60 mss/year. Publishes ms 6-12 months after acceptance. Published work by D.F. Lewis, Charlee Jacob, Edward Lee, Scott Urban, Gerard Houarner, Deidre Cox and S. Darnbrook Colson. Length: 4,000 words average; 2,000 words minimum; 10,000 words maximum. Often critiques or comments on rejected ms.

How to Contact: Send complete ms with a cover letter. "Should query about guidelines and special issues, but always open to submissions." Should include estimated word count, brief bio, Social Security number, list of publications and phone number. "I sometimes call people about rewrites." Reports in 2 weeks on queries; 2 months on mss. Simultaneous submissions OK. E-mail address: necrodave@aol.com or D.Barnett2 @genie.geis.com. Sample copy for $4.95. Reviews novels, short story collections and magazines (horror only).

Payment/Terms: Pays ¼¢/word and 1 contributor's copy for first North American serial rights with "the right to publish in an anthology if one is produced."

Advice: "Concentrate on making believable characters and dialogue. Make sure the plot is well thought out. I like closure. I want longer pieces with complex plots and well-developed characters. I'm more interested in stories with supernatural elements, especially monsters, witches, demons, etc. If you create a new world, creature, or object, explain it. Don't just drop it in and expect the reader to just accept your creation without explanation."

‡INTUITIVE EXPLORATIONS, A Journal of Intuitive Processes, (I, II, IV), Intuitive Explorations, P.O. Box 561, Quincy IL 62306-0561. (217)222-9082. Editor: Gloria Reiser. Magazine: 8½×11; 28 pages. "*Intuitive Explorations* publishes mind explorations for an audience very interested in exploring the unknown and inner worlds." Bimonthly. Estab. 1987. Circ. 1,000.
Needs: Ethnic/multicultural, psychic/supernatural/occult, religious/inspirational (futuristic/time travel), ancient worlds, future worlds, other realms. Accepts 1 mss/issue; 6 mss/year. Publishes ms 1-2 issues after acceptance. Recently published work by Father John Groff. Length 700-1,000 words average; 300 words minimum; 2,000 words maximum. Publishes short shorts. Also publishes literary essays, poetry. Sometimes critiques or comments on rejected ms.
How to Contact: Send complete ms with a cover letter. Should include estimated word count and short bio. Reports in 2 months on queries; 2-3 months on mss. Send SASE for reply, return of ms or send a disposable copy of ms. Simultaneous and reprint submissions OK. Sample copy for $1, 9×12 SAE and 4 first-class stamps. Reviews novels and short story collections.
Payment/Terms: Pays up to 6 contributor's copies; additional copies 75¢ each. Acquires one-time rights.
Advice: "I'd like to see more fiction in which tarot is woven into the story line as well as stories honoring intuition and/or the earth."

THE IOWA REVIEW, (II), University of Iowa, 308 EPB, Iowa City IA 52242. (319)335-0462. Editor: David Hamilton. Magazine: 6×9; 200 pages; first-grade offset paper; Carolina C1S 10-pt. cover stock. "Stories, essays, poems for a general readership interested in contemporary literature." Triannually. Estab. 1970. Circ. 1,200.
• Work published in *Iowa Review* regularly has been selected for inclusion in the *Pushcart Prize* and *Best American Short Stories* anthologies. The editors are expecially interested in work from minority writers or those whose "voices have been marginalized."
Needs: Literary, ethnic. Receives 150-200 unsolicited fiction mss/month. Agented fiction less than 10%. Buys 4-5 mss/issue, 12-16 mss/year. Does not read mss April-August. Recently published work by Curtis White, Kathy Acker, and Sherley Anne Williams; published new writers within the last year. Also publishes literary essays, literary criticism, poetry.
How to Contact: Send complete ms with SASE. "Don't bother with queries." Simultaneous submissions OK. Reports in 2-4 months on mss. Publishes ms an average of 4-12 months after acceptance. Sample copy for $5. Reviews novels and short story collections (3-6 books/year).
Payment/Terms: Pays $10/page on publication and 2 contributor's copies; additional copies 30% off cover price. Buys first North American serial rights.

IOWA WOMAN, P.O. Box 680, Iowa City IA 52244. Contact: Editorial Collective. Nonprofit magazine "dedicated to encouraging and publishing women writers and artists internationally." Quarterly. Estab. 1979. Circ. 2,500.
• *Iowa Woman* has received numerous awards and honors including Iowa Community Cultural Grant Awards. The magazine has also had essays and fiction included in the *Best American Essays* and *Best American Short Stories*. See the *Iowa Woman* Writing Contest listed also in this book. In 1995 the magazine celebrated the 75th Anniversary of the suffrage movement with features and memoirs by Midwestern participants.
Needs: Historical, literary, regional, women's. Receives 200 unsolicited mss/month. Buys 3 mss/issue; 12 mss/year. Length: 6,500 words maximum. Also publishes literary essays, book reviews, and sponsors contest.
How to Contact: Send complete ms. Reports in 3 months. SASE. E-mail address: rbailey@blue.weeg.uiowa .edu. Sample copy for $6.95. Fiction or contest guidelines for SASE. Reviews novels and short story collections. Send books to Coleen Maddy, Books Editor.
Payment/Terms: Pays $5/published page and 2 contributor's copies; additional copies $4. Buys first serial rights. Offers advertising discounts to writers and artists published in *Iowa Woman*.
Advice: "Our editorial collective often responds critically with rejections. We want stories with women or women's experience as the center."

IRIS: A Journal About Women, (II, IV), Box 323 HSC, University of Virginia, Charlottesville VA 22908. (804)924-4500. Fiction Editor: Kristen Staby Rembold. Magazine: 8½×11; 72 pages; glossy paper; heavy cover; illustrations and photographs. "Material of particular interest to women. For a feminist audience, college educated and above." Semiannually. Estab. 1980. Circ. 3,500.
• An interview with Kristen Staby Rembold appeared in the 1994 edition of *Novel & Short Story Writer's Market*.
Needs: Experimental, feminist, lesbian, literary, mainstream. "I don't think what we're looking for particularly falls into the 'mainstream' category—we're just looking for well-written stories of interest to women (particularly feminist women)." Receives 300 unsolicited mss/year. Accepts 5 mss/year. Publishes ms within 1 year after acceptance. Length: 4,000 words average. Sometimes critiques rejected mss.

How to Contact: Send complete ms with cover letter. Include "previous publications, vocation, other points that pertain. Make it brief!" Reports in 3 months on mss. SASE. Simultaneous submissions OK. Accepts electronic submissions via disk or modem. Sample copy for $5. Fiction guidelines for #10 SASE.
Payment/Terms: Pays in contributor's copies and 1 year subscription. Acquires one-time rights.
Advice: "I select mss which are lively imagistically as well as in the here-and-now; I select for writing which challenges the reader. My major complaint is with stories that don't elevate the language above the bland sameness we hear on the television and everyday. Read the work of the outstanding women writers, such as Alice Munroe and Louise Erdrich."

ITALIAN AMERICANA, (II, IV), URI/CCE 199 Promenade St., Providence RI 02908-5090. (401)277-3824. Editor: Carol Bonomo Albright. Poetry Editor: Dana Gioia. Magazine: 7×9; 150 pages; varnished cover; photographs. "*Italian Americana* contains historical articles, fiction, poetry and memoirs, all concerning the Italian experience in the Americas." Semiannually. Estab. 1974. Circ. 1,000.
Needs: Italian American: literary. Receives 10 mss/month. Buys 3 mss/issue; 6-7 mss/year. Publishes up to 1 year after acceptance. Agented fiction 5%. Published work by Salvatore LaPuma and Rita Ciresi. Length: 20 double-spaced pages. Publishes short shorties. Also publishes literary essays, literary criticism, poetry. Sometimes critiques rejected mss.
How to Contact: Send complete manuscript (in triplicate) with a cover letter. Should include 3-5 line bio, list of publications. Reports in 1 month on queries; 2-4 months on manuscripts. Send SASE for reply, return of ms or send a disposable copy of ms. No simultaneous submissions. Sample copy for $6. Fiction guidelines for SASE. Reviews novels and short story collections. Send books to Professor John Paul Russo, English Dept., Univ. of Miami, Coral Gables, FL 33124.
Payment/Terms: Pays $25-50 (dependent on funding) on publication plus free subscription to magazine and 1 contributor's copy; additional copies $7. Buys first North American serial rights.
Advice: "Please individualize characters, instead of presenting types (i.e., lovable uncle, aunt, etc.). No nostalgia."

‡IT'S YOUR CHOICE MAGAZINE, International Journal of Ethics and Morality, (I, II), FutureWend Publications, P.O. Box 7135, Richmond VA 23221-0135. Editor: Dr. James Rogers. Newsletter: 8½×11; 8-20 pages; 20 lb. bond paper. "*It's Your Choice*— where science meets religion." Monthly. Estab. 1993.
Needs: Adventure, children's/juvenile (10-12 years), ethnic/multicultural, experimental, fantasy (science), feminist, gay, historical, horror, humor/satire, lesbian, mystery/suspense, psychic/supernatural/occult, religious/inspirational, science fiction (soft/sociological), young adult/teen. Special interests: ethics, morality. Publishes annual special fiction issue or anthology. Recently published work by Bill Lockwood, Kris Kincaid and Kris Neri. Length: 1,000 words maximum. Publishes short shorts.
How to Contact: Send complete ms with a cover letter. Should include estimated word count. Reports in 1 month on mss. (Retention indicates continued interest. Mss returned on request.) Simultaneous and reprint submissions OK. Sample copy for $2 and #10 SASE. Fiction guidelines for #10 SASE.
Payment/Terms: Pays up to $1/word and 10 contributor's copies; additional copies $1. Sponsors annual contest. Send $2 for mss registration form.
Advice: "Do not overwrite. Follow guidelines and precisely. No clips."

‡JACARANDA, (I, II), 110 Press, Department of English, California State University, Fullerton, Fullerton CA 92634. (714)773-3163. Editor: Cornel Bonca. Magazine: 8½×5½; 150-175 pages; Gladfelter 55 lb. paper; 10 pt. cover; illustrations and photos. Semiannually. Estab. 1985. Circ. 1,200.
● *Jacaranda* is a member of the Council of Literary Magazines and Presses (CLMP).
Needs: Erotica, ethnic/multicultural, experimental, gay, humor/satire, lesbian, literary, mainstream/contemporary, mystery/suspense, science fiction (soft/sociological, good cyberpunk), translations. "No traditional science fiction, fantasy or romance." Plans special fiction issue or anthology. Receives 30 unsolicited mss/month. Accepts 2-3 mss/issue; 4-6 mss/year. Publishes ms 3-4 months after acceptance. Recently published work by Miguel Asturias and Ann Scott Knight. Length: 5,000 words average. Publishes short shorts. Also publishes literary essays, literary criticism, poetry. Sometimes critiques or comments on rejected ms.
How to Contact: Send complete ms with a cover letter. Should include short bio. Reports in 3 months on mss. SASE for return of ms. Simultaneous submissions OK. Sample copy for $6, 6×9 SAE and 2 first-class stamps. Fiction guidelines for 4½×10½ SASE. Reviews novels and short story collections.
Payment/Terms: Pays 3 contributor's copies; additional copies 20% discount. Acquires one-time rights. Sends galleys to author. Sponsors contests, awards or grants for fiction writers.
Advice: "Don't be so eager. Hone your craft for a while before entering the market. Reade Rilke's *Letters To A Young Poet*. We'd like to see more attention to character."

‡JACK MACKEREL MAGAZINE, (I, II), Rowhouse Press, P.O. Box 23134, Seattle WA 98102-0434. Editor: Greg Bachar. Magazine: 5½×8½; 40-60 pages; Xerox bond paper; glossy card cover stock; b&w illustrations and photos. "We publish unconventional art, poetry and fiction." Quarterly. Estab. 1993. Circ. 1,000.
Needs: Condensed/excerpted novel, erotica, experimental, literary, surreal, translations. "No realism." List of upcoming themes available for SASE. Publishes special fiction issues or anthologies. Receives 20-100

unsolicited mss/month. Accepts 2-10 mss/issue; 8-40 mss/year. Publishes ms 2-3 months after acceptance. Length: 250 words minimum; 5,000 words maximum. Publishes short shorts. Also publishes literary essays, literary criticism and poetry. Sometimes critiques or comments on rejected ms.

How to Contact: Send complete ms with a cover letter. Should include bio with submission. Send SASE for reply, return of ms or send a disposable copy of ms. Sample copy for $4. Reviews novels and short story collections.

Payment/Terms: Pays 2 contributor's copies.

Advice: "Avoid sending conventional fiction that obeys the rules."

‡JAMBALAYA MAGAZINE, Spotlighting People of African Descent, (IV), Jambalaya, Inc., P.O. Box 1142, Columbia MD 21044. (410)312-7972. Editor: Pamela Woolford. Magazine: 8⅛ × 10¾; 40-56 pages; newsprint; 50 lb. white cover; illustrations and photos. "We showcase and promote the accomplishments of people of African descent from diverse fields of study, backgrounds, and age groups. We publish fiction, poetry, profiles, Q&A interviews, and a variety of other nonfiction articles." Semiannually. Estab. 1993. Circ. 8,000.

Needs: All submissions must be by or about people of African descent: condensed/excerpted novel, ethnic/multicultural, feminist, humor/satire, literary, mainstream/contemporary, regional. "No erotica." Receives less than 1 unsolicited mss/month. Buys 1 or 2 mss/issue; 2 or 3 mss/year. Publishes ms up to 5 months after acceptance. Length: 1,500-3,000 words average; 4,000 words maximum. Publishes short shorts. Also publishes literary essays, literary criticism, poetry.

How to Contact: Send complete ms with a cover letter. Should include estimated word count and bio (5 lines or less), list of publications. "Send 2 copies of ms and all other materials. If your manuscript is published or scheduled for publication elsewhere, include publication name and date." Reports in 4 months. Send SASE for reply. Simultaneous submissions and reprints OK. Sample copy free for 9 × 12 SAE and 3 first-class stamps. Fiction guidelines for SASE. Reviews novels or short story collections. "We publish short summaries (not reviews) of recently released books that may be of special interest to people of African descent."

Payment/Terms: Pays 2 contributor's copies; additional copies free. Acquires one-time rights.

Advice: "We are looking for quality work that may be of special interest to people of African descent."

JANUS, A JOURNAL OF LITERATURE, (II), Janus, P.O. Box 376, Collingswood NJ 08108. Editor: David Livewell. Fiction Editors: Edward Pettit and Edward Cilurso. Magazine: 5½ × 8½; 30 pages. "We are interested in the well-crafted fiction of new and established writers and offer a forum where the two can coexist in an exciting way." Biannually. Estab. 1993. Circ. 500.

Needs: Literary, mainstream/contemporary. "We do not accept pornography, autobiography, or nonsense fiction in the guise of 'stream of consciousness' prose." Receives 20 unsolicited mss/month. Accepts 2-3 mss/issue. Publishes ms in next available issue. Published work by Claude Koch and Joseph Chelius. Length: 10-15 typed pages. Also publishes literary essays, literary criticism and poetry. Always critiques or comments on rejected ms.

How to Contact: Send complete ms with a cover letter. Should include 1-paragraph bio and list of publications. Reports in 2 weeks on queries; 3-5 months on mss. SASE for reply. No simultaneous submissions. Disk submissions OK.

Payment/Terms: Pays in contributor's copies. Acquires first North American serial rights.

Advice: "We like to see that a great deal of time and attention went into a story, that all elements—characterization, plot, imagery, rhetorical devices—are fittingly assembled in order to create a moving story. We especially encourage young and new writers. We would be pleased to serve as the first publisher of talented newcomers."

JAPANOPHILE, (I, II, IV), Box 223, Okemos MI 48864. (517)349-1795. Editor-in-Chief: Earl Snodgrass. Magazine: 5¼ × 8½; 58 pages; illustrations; photos. Magazine of "articles, photos, poetry, humor, short stories about Japanese culture, not necessarily set in Japan, for an adult audience, most with a college background and who like to travel." Quarterly. Estab. 1974. Circ. 800.

  ● Most of the work included in *Japanophile* is set in recent times, but the magazine will accept material set back as far as pre-WWII. See the *Japanophile* Short Story Contest listed in this book.

Needs: Adventure, historical, humor/satire, literary, mainstream, and mystery/suspense. Published special fiction issue last year; plans another. Receives 40-100 unsolicited fiction mss/month. Buys 12 ms/issue, 20-30 mss/year. Recently published work by Barbara Fuller, Mary McCormack and Steve Redford; published new writers within the last year. Length: 4,000 words average, 2,000 words minimum; 6,000 words maximum. Also publishes essays, book reviews, literary criticism and poetry.

How to Contact: Send complete ms with SASE and cover letter with bio and information about story. Simultaneous and reprint submissions OK. Reports in 3 months on mss. E-mail address: xtxp32b@prodigy.com. Sample copy for $4; guidelines for #10 SASE.

Payment/Terms: Pays $20 on publication for all rights, first North American serial rights or one-time rights (depends on situation). Stories submitted to the magazine may be entered in the annual contest. A *$5* *entry fee must accompany each submission* to enter contest. Prizes include $100 plus publication for the best short story. Deadline December 31.

Advice: "Short stories usually involve Japanese and 'foreign' (non-Japanese) characters in a way that contributes to understanding of Japanese culture and the Japanese people. However, a *good* story dealing with Japan or Japanese cultural aspects anywhere in the world will be considered, even if it does not involve this encounter or meeting of Japanese and foreign characters. Some stories may also be published in an anthology."

‡JEOPARDY, Literary Arts Magazine, (II), CH 132, Western Washington University, Bellingham WA 98225. (206)676-3118. Editor: Richard Law. Fiction Editor: Greg Heffron. Editors change every year (next term's editor is Chris Russell). Magazine: 6×9; 192 pages; 70 lb. paper; glossy cover stock; illustrations and photographs. "*Jeopardy Magazine*'s intended audience is an intelligent readership which enjoys risks, surprises and subtlety. Our philosophy is that reputation is nothing and words/images are everything." Annually. Estab. 1965. Circ. 1,500.

Needs: Adventure, contemporary, erotica, ethnic, experimental, feminist, gay, historical, humor/satire, lesbian, literary. No long stories. Receives 50-100 unsolicited mss/month. Accepts 4-8 mss/year. Does not read mss January 15-September 1. Publishes ms 3 months after acceptance. Length: 1,500 words average; 250 words minimum; 5,000 words maximum. Also publishes literary essays, poetry.

How to Contact: Send complete ms with cover letter and 50-word bio. SASE and disposable copy of the ms. Does not return mss. Simultaneous submissions OK. Reports in 1-6 months. Sample copy for $5. Fiction guidelines for #10 SASE.

Payment/Terms: Pays 1 contributor's copy. Acquires one-time rights.

Advice: "A clear, insightful voice and style are major considerations. Things that will get your manuscript recycled: tired representations of sex and/or death and/or angst. We like writers who take risks! Know your characters thoroughly—know why someone else would want to read about what they think or do. Then, submit your work and don't give up at initial failures. Don't send us stories about being a writer/artist and/ or a college student/professor. We would like to see more fiction pieces which involve unique or unexpected situations and characters."

JEWISH CURRENTS MAGAZINE, (IV), 22 E. 17th St., New York NY 10003. (212)924-5740. Editor-in-Chief: Morris U. Schappes. Magazine: 5½×8½; 48 pages. "We are a progressive monthly, broad in our interests, printing feature articles on political and cultural aspects of Jewish life in the US and elsewhere, reviews of books and film, poetry and fiction, Yiddish translations; regular columns on Israel, US Jewish community, current events, Jewish women today, secular Jewish life. National audience, literate and politically left, well educated." Monthly. Estab. 1946. Circ. 2,600.

● This magazine may be slow to respond. They continue to be backlogged.

Needs: Contemporary, ethnic, feminist, historical, humor/satire, literary, senior citizen/retirement, translations. "We are interested in *authentic* experience and readable prose; Jewish themes; humanistic orientation. No religious, political sectarian; no porn or hard sex, no escapist stuff. Go easy on experimentation, but we're interested." Upcoming themes: "Black History Month" (February); "International Women's Day"; "Purim"; "Jewish Music Season" (March); "Holocaust and Resistance Commemoration" (April); "Israeli Independence Day" (May); "Jewish Book Month" (November). Receives 6-10 unsolicited fiction mss/ month. Accepts 0-1 ms/issue; 8-10 mss/year. Recently published work by Arthur J. Sabin, Adrienne Cooper; published new writers within the last year. Length: 1,000 words minimum; 3,000 words maximum; 1,800 words average. Also publishes literary essays, literary criticism, poetry.

How to Contact: Send complete ms with cover letter. "Writers should include brief biographical information, especially their publishing histories." SAE. No simultaneous submissions. Reports in 2 months on mss. Publishes ms 2 months-2 years after acceptance. Sample copy for $3 with SAE and 3 first-class stamps. Reviews novels and short story collections.

Payment/Terms: Pays complimentary one-year subscription and 6 contributor's copies. "We readily give reprint permission at no charge." Sends galleys to author.

Advice: Noted for "stories about Jewish family life, especially intergenerational relations, and personal Jewish experience—e.g., immigrant or Holocaust memories, assimilation dilemmas, etc. Matters of character and moral dilemma, maturing into pain and joy, dealing with Jewish conflicts OK. Space is increasingly a problem. Tell the truth, as sparely as possible."

THE JOURNAL, (I, II), Poetry Forum, 5713 Larchmont Dr., Erie PA 16509. (814)866-2543. Fax: (814)866-2543 (Faxing hours: 8-10 a.m. and 5-8 p.m.) Editor: Gunvor Skogsholm. Newspaper: 7×8½; 18-20 pages;

A bullet introduces comments by the editor of Novel & Short Story Writer's Market *indicating special information about the listing.*

card cover; photographs. Looks for "good writing—for late teens to full adulthood." Quarterly. Estab. 1989. Circ. 200.

- *The Journal* is edited by Gunvor Skogsholm, the editor of *Poetry Forum Short Stories* and, new to this edition, *Short Stories Bimonthly*. Although this magazine is not strictly a pay-for-publication, "subscribers come first." See the listings for *Poetry Forum Short Stories* and *Short Stories Bimonthly*.

Needs: Mainstream. Plans annual special fiction issue. Receives 25-30 unsolicited mss/month. Accepts 1 ms/issue; 7-10 mss/year. Publishes mss 2 weeks-7 months after acceptance. Agented fiction 1%. Length: 500 words preferred; 300 words average; 150 words minimum. Publishes short shorts. Length: 400 words.

How to Contact: Send complete ms. Reports in 2 weeks-7 months on mss. SASE. Simultaneous submissions OK. Accepts electronic disk submissions. E-mail address: 75562.670@compuserve.com. Sample copy for $3. Fiction guidelines for SASE.

Payment/Terms: No payment. Acquires one-time rights. Not copyrighted.

Advice: "Subscribers come first!" Looks for "a good lead stating a theme, support of the theme throughout and an ending that rounds out the story or article. Make it believable, please don't preach, avoid propaganda, and don't say, 'This is a story about a retarded person'; instead, prove it by your writing. Show, don't tell."

JOURNAL OF POLYMORPHOUS PERVERSITY, (I), Wry-Bred Press, Inc., 10 Waterside Plaza, Suite 20-B, New York NY 10010. (212)689-5473. Editor: Glenn Ellenbogen. Magazine: 6¾×10; 24 pages; 60 lb. paper; antique india cover stock; illustrations with some articles. "*JPP* is a humorous and satirical journal of psychology, psychiatry, and the closely allied mental health disciplines." For "psychologists, psychiatrists, social workers, psychiatric nurses, *and* the psychologically sophisticated layman." Semiannually. Estab. 1984.

Needs: Humor/satire. "We only consider materials that are funny or that relate to psychology *or* behavior." Receives 50 unsolicited mss/month. Acquires 8 mss/issue; 16 mss/year. Most writers published last year were previously unpublished writers. Length: 1,500 words average; 4,000 words maximum. Comments on rejected mss.

How to Contact: Send complete ms *in triplicate*. Reports in 1-3 months on mss. SASE. Sample copy for $7. Fiction guidelines for #10 SASE.

Payment/Terms: Pays 2 contributor's copies; additional copies $7.

Advice: "We will *not* look at poetry. We only want to see intelligent spoofs of scholarly psychology and psychiatry articles written in scholarly scientific language. Take a look at *real* journals of psychology and try to lampoon their *style* as much as their content. There are few places to showcase satire of the social sciences, thus we provide one vehicle for injecting a dose of humor into this often too serious area. Occasionally, we will accept a piece of creative writing written in the first person, e.g. 'A Subjective Assessment of the Oral Doctoral Defense Process: I Don't Want to Talk About It, If You Want to Know the Truth' (the latter being a piece in which Holden Caulfield shares his experiences relating to obtaining his Ph.D. in Psychology). Other creative pieces have involved a psychodiagnostic evaluation of The Little Prince (as a psychiatric patient) and God being refused tenure (after having created the world) because of insufficient publications and teaching experience."

JUST WRITE, (I, II), Write Away Literary, P.O. Box 385, Hebron IL 60034. (815)455-6404. Fax: (815)455-6484. Editor: Gloria J. Urch. Fiction Editor: E.J. Shumak. Magazine: 8½×11; 36 pages; 60 lb. paper; classic laid card stock cover; illustrations and photos. "The focus of the magazine is instruction and motivation for writers. We use short fiction and novel excerpts in each issue." Quarterly. Estab. 1993. Circ. 500.

- *Just Write* is affiliated with McHenry County College. The magazine sponsors a contest. Send SASE for guidelines.

Needs: Adventure, condensed/excerpted novel, ethnic/multicultural, experimental, fantasy, feminist, historical, horror, humor/satire, literary, mainstream/contemporary, mystery/suspense "No extreme violence, profanity, bigotry, war, satanic." Publishes special fiction issue or anthology. Receives 5-10 unsolicited mss/month. Buys 2-3 mss/issue; 25-36 mss/year. Publishes ms 3-4 months after acceptance. Recently published work by Carla Fortier, Tom Gardner, Thomas Canfield. Length: 400-1,500 words average; 400 words minimum; 2,000 words maximum. Publishes short shorts. Also publishes literary essays; literary criticism and poetry. Always critiques or comments on rejected ms.

How to Contact: Send complete ms with a cover letter. Should include estimated word count, ¼-page bio, Social Security number, list of publications and b&w glossy photo to run with work. Reports in 8-10 weeks on queries; 4-8 weeks on mss. Send SASE for reply, return of ms or send a disposable copy of ms. Simultaneous, reprint and electronic submissions (call first for modem) OK. Sample copy for $4. Reviews novels and short story collections.

Payment/Terms: Pays $5-35 on publication and 1 contributor's copy for first North American serial rights. Occasionally sends galleys to author.

Advice: "We like dialogue, strong characterization, tight writing. Get to the story quickly. Cut the flowery language and give us the guts of the story. We would like to see more contemporary or mainstream fiction." No horror or science fiction "unless it is strongly character-based."

KALEIDOSCOPE: International Magazine of Literature, Fine Arts, and Disability, (II, IV), 326 Locust St., Akron OH 44302. (216)762-9755. Editor-in-Chief: Darshan Perusek, Ph.D. Senior Editor: Gail

Willmott. Magazine: 8½×11; 56-64 pages; non-coated paper; coated cover stock; illustrations (all media); photos. "*Kaleidoscope* creatively explores the experiences of disability through fiction, essays, poetry, and visual arts. Challenges and transcends stereotypical and patronizing attitudes about disability." Semiannually. Estab. 1979. Circ. 1,500.

- *Kaleidoscope* has received awards from the Great Lakes Awards Competition and Ohio Public Images. The editors are looking for more fiction .

Needs: Personal experience, drama, fiction, essay, artwork. Upcoming themes: "Disability and Violence in the Family" (deadline March 1996); "Disability and Caregivers" (deadline August 1996). Receives 20-25 unsolicited fiction mss/month. Buys 10 mss/year. Approximately 1% of fiction is agented. Recently published work by Martin F. Norden and Stephen Jay Gould. Published new writers within the last year. Length: 5,000 words maximum. Also publishes poetry.

How to Contact: Query first or send complete ms and cover letter. Should include author's educational and writing background and author has a disability, how it has influenced the writing. Simultaneous submissions OK. Reports in 1 month on queries; 6 months on mss. Sample copy for $4. Guidelines for #10 SASE.

Payment/Terms: Pays $10-125 and 2 contributor's copies on publication; additional copies $4. Buys first rights. Reprints permitted with credit given to original publication.

Advice: "Read the magazine and get submission guidelines. We prefer that writers with a disability offer original perspectives about their experiences; writers without disabilities should limit themselves to our focus in order to solidify a connection to our magazine's purpose."

KALLIOPE, A Journal of Women's Art, (II), Florida Community College at Jacksonville, 3939 Roosevelt Blvd., Jacksonville FL 32205. (904)381-3511. Editor: Mary Sue Koeppel. Magazine: 7¼×8¼; 76-88 pages; 70 lb. coated matte paper; Bristol cover; 16-18 halftones per issue. "A literary and visual arts journal for women, *Kalliope* celebrates women in the arts by publishing their work and by providing a forum for their ideas and opinions." Short stories, poems, plays, essays, reviews and visual art. Triannually. Estab. 1978. Circ. 1,250.

- Kalliope has received the Frances Buck Sherman Award from the local branch of the National League of Pen Women. The magazine has also received awards and grants for its poetry, grants from the Florida Department of Cultural Affairs and the Jacksonville Club Gallery of Superb Printing Award.

Needs: "Quality short fiction by women writers." Accepts 2-4 mss/issue. Receives approximately 100 unsolicited fiction mss each month. Published work by Layle Silbert, Robin Merle, Claudia Brinson Smith and Colette; published new writers within the last year. Preferred length: 750-2,500 words, but occasionally publishes longer (and shorter) pieces. Also publishes poetry. Critiques rejected mss "when there is time and if requested."

How to Contact: Send complete ms with SASE and short contributor's note. No simultaneous submissions. Reports in 2-3 months on ms. Publishes ms an average of 1-3 months after acceptance. Sample copy: $7 for current issue; $4 for issues from '78-'88. Reviews short story collections.

Payment/Terms: Pays 3 contributor's copies or year's subscription for first rights. $7 charge for extras, discount for 4 or more. "We accept only unpublished work. Copyright returned to author upon request."

Advice: "Read our magazine. The work we consider for publication will be well written and the characters and dialogue will be convincing. We like a fresh approach and are interested in new or unusual forms. Make us believe your characters; give readers an insight which they might not have had if they had not read you. We would like to publish more work by minority writers." Manuscripts are rejected because "1) nothing *happens*!, 2) it is thinly disguised autobiography (richly disguised autobiography is OK), and 3) ending is either too pat or else just trails off."

‡KARMA LAPEL, The Fifth Man Review, (I), Fifth Man Press, P.O. Box 5467, Evanston IL 60204. Editor: Heath Row. Magazine or newsletter: size and paper varies. "*Karma Lapel* is a little magazine of new writing and critical analysis of do-it-yourself media." Published infrequently. Estab. 1992. Circ. 1,000.

Needs: Translations, semi-autobiographical, new journalism, gonzo journalism. Plans science fiction issue. Buys 2-3 mss/issue. Recently published work by Will Sarvis and Thomas Lee Farnsworth. Publishes short shorts. Also publishes literary essays, literary criticism. Always critiques or comments on rejected ms.

How to Contact: Send complete ms with a cover letter. Should include estimated word count, bio and list of publications. Reports in 3-4 months. SASE. No simultaneous submissions. Reprints and electronic submissions OK. E-mail address: heathr@ais.net. Sample copy for $2. Reviews novels or short story collections.

Payment/Terms: Pays contributor's copies. Not copyrighted.

Advice: A manuscript stands out "if the story is true, close to true or plausibly true, reveals a truth, shows substantial personal growth (positive or negative) or surprises me. Be as honest with yourself and the reader as possible. Don't fear to use your true voice. Don't be stingy with your perceptions and feelings."

KELSEY REVIEW, (I, II, IV), Mercer County College, P.O. Box B, Trenton NJ 08690. (609)586-4800. Editor: Robin Schore. Magazine: 7×14; 70 pages; glossy paper; soft cover. "Must live or work in Mercer County, NJ." Annually. Estab. 1988. Circ. 1,500.

Needs: Open. Regional (Mercer County only). Receives 120 unsolicited mss/year. Acquires 24 mss/issue. Reads mss only in May. Publishes ms 1-2 months after acceptance. Length: 2,000 words maximum. Publishes short shorts. Also publishes literary essays, literary criticism and poetry. Always critiques or comments on rejected mss.

How to Contact: Send complete ms with cover letter. SASE for return of ms. No simultaneous submissions. Reports in 1-2 months. Sample copy free. Reviews "anything."

Payment/Terms: Pays 5 contributor's copies. Rights revert to author on publication.

Advice: Looks for "quality, intellect, grace and guts."

KENNESAW REVIEW, (II), Kennesaw State College, English Dept., P.O. Box 444, Marietta GA 30061. (404)423-6297. Editor: Dr. Robert W. Hill. Magazine. "Just good fiction, all themes, for a general audience." Semiannually. Estab. 1987.

Needs: Excerpted novel, contemporary, ethnic, experimental, feminist, gay, humor/satire, literary, mainstream, regional. No romance. Receives 25-60 mss/month. Accepts 2-4 mss/issue. Publishes ms 12-18 months after acceptance. Published work by Julie Brown, Stephen Dixon, Robert Morgan, Carolyn Thorman. Length: 9-30 pages. Length: 500 words. Rarely comments on or critiques rejected mss.

How to Contact: Send complete ms with cover letter. Include previous publications. Reports 2 months on mss. SASE. Simultaneous submissions OK. Sample copy and fiction guidelines free.

Payment/Terms: Pays in contributor's copies. Acquires first publication rights only. Acknowledgment required for subsequent publication.

Advice: "Use the language well and tell an interesting story. Send it on. Be open to suggestions."

THE KENYON REVIEW, (II), Kenyon College, Gambier OH 43022. (614)427-3339. Editor: David H. Lynn. "Fiction, poetry, essays, book reviews." Triannually. Estab. 1939. Circ.5,000.

● Work published in the *Kenyon Review* has been selected for inclusion in the *Pushcart Prize* anthology.

Needs: Condensed/excerpted novel, contemporary, ethnic, experimental, feminist, gay, historical, humor/satire, lesbian, literary, mainstream, translations. Upcoming theme: "American Memory, American Forgetfulness" (Winter 1997; deadline: March 1996. Guest editor: Lewis Hyde). Receives 400 unsolicited fiction mss/month. Does not read mss April-August. Publishes ms 12-18 months after acceptance. Length: 3-15 typeset pages preferred.

How to Contact: Send complete ms with cover letter. Reports on mss in 2-3 months. SASE. No simultaneous submissions. Sample copy for $8.

Payment/Terms: Pays $10/page on publication for first-time rights. Sends copy-edited version to author for approval.

Advice: "Read several issues of our publication. We remain invested in encouraging/reading/publishing work by writers of color, writers expanding the boundaries of their genre, and writers with unpredictable voices and points of view."

‡KEREM, Creative Explorations in Judaism, (IV), Jewish Study Center Press, Inc., 3035 Porter St. NW, Washington DC 20008. Fax: (202)364-3806. Editors: Sara Horowitz and Gilah Langner. Magazine: 6×9; 128 pages; 60 lb. offset paper; glossy cover; illustrations and photos."*Kerem* publishes Jewish religious, creative, literary material—short stories, poetry, personal reflections, text study, prayers, rituals, etc." Annually. Estab. 1992. Circ. 2,000

Needs: Jewish: ethnic/multicultural, feminist, humor/satire, literary, religious/inspirational. Receives 1-2 unsolicited mss/month. Accepts 1-2 mss/issue. Publishes ms 2-10 months after acceptance. Recently published work by Mark Mirsky. Length: 6,000 words maximum. Publishes short short stories. Also publishes literary essays, poetry.

How to Contact: Send complete ms with a cover letter. Should include 1-2 line bio. Reports in 2 months on queries; 4-5 months on mss. Send SASE for reply, return of ms or send a disposable copy of ms. Simultaneous submissions OK. Sample copy for $8.50.

Payment/Terms: Pays free subscription and 2-10 contributor's copies. Acquires one-time rights.

Advice: "We want to be moved by reading the manuscript!"

KESTREL, A Journal of Literature and Art in the New World, (II), Division of Language and Literature, Fairmont State College, 1201 Locust Ave., Fairmont WV 26554. (304)367-4717. Editors: Martin Lammon, Valerie N. Colander, John King. Magazine: 6×9; photographs. "An eclectic journal publishing the best fiction, poetry, creative nonfiction and artwork for a literate audience. We strive to present contributors' work in depth." Semiannually. Estab. 1993. Circ. 500.

● *Kestrel* has received funding grants from the NEA and the West Virginia Commission of the Arts.

Needs: Ethnic/multicultural, experimental, feminist, literary, mainstream/contemporary, regional, translations. "No pornography, children's literature, romance fiction, pulp science fiction—formula fiction in general." Receives 50 unsolicited mss/month. Acquires 3-5 mss/issue; 6-10 mss/year. Publishes ms 6-12 months after acceptance. Published work by Donald McCaig, Elisabeth Rose, Meredith Sue Willis, Cary Holladay,

Joe Schall and Jim Gorman. Length: 5,000 words maximum. Publishes short shorts. Also publishes literary essays and poetry. Sometimes critiques or comments on rejected mss.

How To Contact: Send complete ms with cover letter. Should include estimated word count, brief bio and list of publications with submission. Reports in 3 weeks on queries; 3 months on mss. SASE for return of ms or disposable copy of ms. No simultaneous submissions. Sample copy for $5. Fiction guidelines for #10 SASE.

Payment/Terms: Pays 2 contributor's copies. Rights revert to contributor on publication.

‡KIDS' WORLD, The Magazine That's All Kids!, (I, II), Stone Lightning Press, 1300 Kicker Rd., Tuscaloosa AL 35404. (205)553-2284. Editor: Morgan Kopaska-Merkel. Magazine: digest size; 16 pages; standard white Xerox paper; illustrations. Publishes stories written by children under 17: "fantasy and 'kid stuff'—themes by kids, about kids and for kids." Quarterly. Estab. 1992.

Needs: Children's/juvenile (4-12 years): adventure, fantasy (children's), mystery/suspense (amateur sleuth), science fiction (hard science, soft/sociological); young adult/teen (adventure, mystery, science fiction). No horror or romance. Receives 5-15 unsolicited mss/month. Accepts 10-15 mss/issue; 40-60 mss/year. Publishes ms in next issue after acceptance. Recently published work by Aubry Hopkins, Amanda Howell and Brie Ann Prestorious. Length: 50 words minimum; 500 words maximum. Publishes short shorts. Also publishes poetry.

How to Contact: Send complete ms with a cover letter including your age. Reports in 3-4 weeks on mss. Send SASE for reply, return of ms or send a disposable copy of ms. Sample copy for $1 and SAE. Fiction quidelines for SASE.

Payment/Terms: Pays 1 contributor's copy. Acquires first North American serial rights.

Advice: "Stories must be appropriate for kids. Have an adult check spelling, grammar and punctuation."

KINESIS, The Literary Magazine For The Rest of Us, (I), P.O. Box 4007, Whitefish MT 59937. (406)756-1195. Editor: Leif Peterson. Magazine: 8½ × 11; 56 pages; Mondo Supreme paper; Mondo cover; illustrations and photographs. "Our magazine is wide open. We publish fiction, poetry, essays and reviews as well as several regular columnists. Our audience is anyone with a heartbeat." Monthly. Estab. 1992. Circ. 5,000.

● *Kinesis* is a member of the Council for Literary Magazines & Presses (CLMP). The magazine also sponsors a contest. Send a SASE for details.

Needs: Experimental, humor/satire, literary, mainstream/contemporary and regional. Receives 50 unsolicited submissions/month. Accepts 4 mss/issue; 48 mss/year. Publishes ms 1 month after acceptance. Length: 5,000 words average; 1,000 words minimum; 7,000 words maximum. Publishes short shorts. Also publishes literary essays, literary criticism and poetry.

How to Contact: Send complete ms with a cover letter. Should include estimated word count, short bio and list of publications. Reports in 1 month. Send SASE for reply, return of ms or send a disposable copy of ms. Simultaneous, reprint and electronic submissions OK. E-mail address: AOL:KINESIS1 and eworld:kinesis. Sample copy for $3, 10 × 13 SAE and $1 postage. Fiction guidelines for #10 SASE. Reviews novels and short story collections. Send books to Books Editor.

Payment/Terms: Pays free subscription and 5 contributor's copies. Acquires one-time rights.

Advice: "Make sure it moves!"

KIOSK, (II), English Department, S.U.N.Y. at Buffalo, 306 Clemens Hall, Buffalo NY 14260. Editor: Lia Vella. Fiction Editor: Jonathan Pitts. Magazine: 5½ × 8½; 150 pages; 80 lb. cover; illustrations. "We seek innovative, non-formula fiction and poetry." Annually (may soon be Biannually). Estab. 1986. Circ. 750.

● *Kiosk* is expecting some staff changes. If in doubt, submit to "Editor-in-Chief." The current editor says *Kiosk* is moving away from hard-core experimental work.

Needs: Literary. "While we subscribe to no particular orthodoxy, our fiction editors are most hospitable to stories with a strong sense of voice, narrative direction and craftsmanship." Receives 50 mss/month. Accepts 10-20 mss/issue. Publishes ms within 6 months of acceptance. Published work by Ray Federman, Richard Russo, Daniel Kanyandekwe, Carol Berge and Dennis Tedlock; published new writers within the last year. Length: 3,000 words preferred; 7,500 words maximum. Publishes short shorts, "the shorter the better." Also publishes poetry. Sometimes critiques rejected mss.

How to Contact: Send complete mss with cover letter. Does not read from June-August. Reports in 3-4 months on mss. SASE. Simultaneous and reprint submissions OK. Sample copy for $5. Guidelines for SASE.

Payment/Terms: Pays in contributor's copies. Acquires one-time rights.

Advice: "First and foremost *Kiosk* is interested in sharp writing. There's no need to be dogmatic in terms of pushing a particular style or form, and we aren't. At the same time, we get tired of reading the same old story, the same old poem. Make it new, but also make it worth the reader's effort. Our last issue, 'RUST BELT,' focused upon a pretty specific theme. Because we are anticipating changes in our editorial staff, it would be a good idea to send a self-addressed stamped envelope for the most recent writer's guidelines."

‡LACTUCA, (I, II), % Mike Selender, 159 Jewett Ave., Jersey City NJ 07304-2003. Editor: Mike Selender. Magazine: Folded 8½ × 14; 72 pages; 24 lb. bond; soft cover; saddle-stapled; illustrations. Publishes "poetry, short fiction and b&w art, for a general literary audience." Published 0-3 times/year. Estab. 1986. Circ. 700.

Needs: Adventure, condensed/excerpted novel, confession, contemporary, erotica, literary, mainstream, prose poem and regional. No "self-indulgent writing or fiction about writing fiction." Receives 30 or more mss/month. Accepts 3-4 mss/issue; 10-12 mss/year. Publishes ms within 3-12 months of acceptance. Published work by Douglas Mendini, Tom Gidwitz and Ruthann Robson; published new writers within the last year. Length: around 12-14 typewritten double-spaced pages. Publishes short shorts. Often critiques rejected mss and recommends other markets.

How to Contact: "Query first to see if we're reading before sending manuscripts. We are backlogged and probably won't resume accepting work until mid-1996 or later." Cover letter should include "just a few brief notes about yourself. Please no long 'literary' résumés or bios. The work will speak for itself." Reports in 6 weeks-3 months. SASE. No simultaneous or previously published work. Accepts electronic submissions via "MS DOS formatted disk. We can convert most word-processing formats." E-mail address: Lactuca@aol.com. Sample copy for $4. Fiction guidelines for #10 SASE.

Payment/Terms: Pays 2-5 contributor's copies, depending on the length of the work published. Acquires first North American serial rights. Sends galleys to author. Copyrights revert to authors.

Advice: "We want fiction coming from a strong sense of place and/or experience. Work with an honest emotional depth. We steer clear of self-indulgent material. We particularly like work that tackles complex issues and the impact of such on people's lives. We are open to work that is dark and/or disturbing."

‡LACUNAE, (II), Lacunae Publications/CFD Productions, 32 Tallow Wood Dr., Clifton Park NY 12065. (518)383-1856 or (516)285-5545. Fax: (518)383-1781. Editor: Pamela Hazelton. Magazine: 6⅝ × 10¼; 40-64 pages; 50 lb. offset paper; slick, glossy cover; illustrations and photos. "*Lacunae* is for mature readers of fiction, poetry, comics, reviews, interviews and news." Bimonthly. Estab. 1994. Circ. 2,500-5,000.

Needs: Adventure, erotica, fantasy, horror, humor/satire, literary, mainstream/contemporary, mystery/suspense (amateur sleuth, cozy, police procedural, private eye/hardboiled), psychic/supernatural/occult, science fiction, comic books. "No romance." List of upcoming themes available for SASE. Receives 50-60 unsolicited mss/month. Accepts 5-15 mss/issue; 30-75 mss/year. Publishes ms 1-6 months after acceptance. Recently published work by H.W. Sierra, Joe Monks and Peter Quinones. Length: 2,000 words average; 400 words minimum; 4,000 words maximum. Publishes short shorts. Also publishes literary essays, literary criticism, poetry. Always critiques or comments on rejected ms.

How to Contact: Send complete ms with a cover letter or upload via modem. Should include estimated word count, short bio, Social Security number, list of publications. Reports in 1 week on queries; 3-6 weeks on mss. Send SASE for reply, return of ms or send a disposable copy of ms. Simultaneous, reprint and electronic submissions OK. E-mail address: lacunaemag@aol.com or 75221.560@compuserve.com. Sample copy for $3.25. Fiction guidelines for SASE. Reviews novels and short story collections. Send books to Attention: Reviews.

Payment/Terms: Pays 5-50 contributor's copies; additional copies $1. Acquires one-time rights. Writer retains all rights. Sponsors contests, awards or grants for fiction writers. Charges $5/story, $2/poem; include SASE.

Advice: "Read *Lacunae* to see if you want your work spotlighted with us. Then, read your work out loud to make sure the reader will understand it. Be clear and concise. Make sure to include name and address on the manuscript and SASE. I like to read horror that makes me squirm, mystery that makes me think, and humor that makes me laugh. I don't want to see lovey-dovey stories—aaachk!"

THE LAMPLIGHT, (II), Beggar's Press, 8110 N. 38 St., Omaha NE 68112. (402)455-2615. Editor: Richard R. Carey. Fiction Editor: Sandy Johnsen. Magazine: 8½ × 11; 40 pages; 20 lb. bond paper; 65 lb. stock cover; some illustrations; a few photographs. "Our purpose is to establish a new literature drawn from the past. We relish foreign settings in the 19th century when human passions transcended computers and fax machines. We are literary but appeal to the common intellect and the mass soul of humanity." Semiannually.

● Beggar's Press publishes *Raskolnikov's Cellar*, which alternates with *The Lamplight*, and also publishes *Beggar's Folios* and *The Beggar's Review*. Write them for information on these other publications.

Needs: Historical (general), humor/satire, literary, mystery/suspense (literary), romance (gothic, historical). "Settings in the past. Psychological stories." Plans special fiction issue or anthology in the future. Receives 60-70 unsolicited mss/month. Acquires 2 mss/issue; 4 mss/year. Publishes ms 4-12 months after acceptance. Published work by Fredrick Zydek, John J. McKernan. Length: 2,000 words preferred; 500 words minimum; 3,500 words maximum. Publishes short shorts. Length: 300 words. Also publishes literary criticism and poetry. Sometimes critiques or comments on rejected mss.

How to Contact: Send complete ms with cover letter. Should include estimated word count, bio (a paragraph or two) and list of publications. Reports in 1 month on queries; 2½ months on mss. SASE. Simultaneous and reprint submission OK. Sample copy for $7, 9 × 12 SAE and 2 first-class stamps. Fiction guidelines for $1, #10 SASE. Reviews novels and short story collections.

Payment/Terms: Pays 2 contributor's copies. Additional copies at a reduced rate of 40% discount up to 5 additional copies. Acquires first North American serial rights.

Advice: "We deal in classical masterpieces. Every piece must be timeless. It must live for five centuries or more. We judge on this basis. These are not easy to come by. But we want to stretch authors to their fullest capacity. They will have to dig deeper for us, and develop a style that is different from what is commonly read in today's market."

THE LAMP-POST, of the Southern California C.S. Lewis Society, (II, IV), 29562 Westmont Ct., San Juan Capistrano CA 92675. Editor: James Prothero. Magazine: 5½×8½; 34 pages; 7 lb. paper; 8 lb. cover; illustrations. "We are a literary review focused on C.S. Lewis and like writers." Quarterly. Estab. 1977. Circ. 200.

● C.S. Lewis was an English novelist and essayist known for his science fiction and fantasy featuring Christian themes. He is especially well-known for his children's fantasy, *The Chronicles of Narnia*. So far, the magazine has found little fiction suitable to its focus, although they remain open.

Needs: "Literary fantasy and science fiction for children to adults." Publishes ms 9 months after acceptance. Length: 2,500 words average; 1,000 words minimum; 5,000 words maximum. Also publishes literary essays, literary criticism and poetry. Sometimes critiques or comments on rejected ms.

How to Contact: Query first or send complete ms with a cover letter. Should include bio (50 words). Reports in 6-8 weeks. Send SASE for reply, return of ms or send a disposable copy of ms. No simultaneous submissions. Reprints and electronic submissions OK. Sample copy for $3. Fiction guidelines for #10 SASE. Reviews fiction or criticism having to do with Lewis or in his vein. Send books to: M.J. Logsdon, Book Review Editor, The Lamp-Post, 119 Washington Dr., Salinas CA 93905.

Payment/Terms: Pays 3 contributor's copies; additional copies $3. Acquires first North American serial rights or one-time rights.

Advice: "We look for fiction with the supernatural, mythic feel of the fiction of C.S. Lewis and Charles Williams. Our slant is Christian but we want work of literary quality. No inspirational. Is it the sort of thing Lewis, Tolkien and Williams would like—subtle, crafted fiction? If so, send it. Don't be too obvious or facile. Our readers aren't stupid."

‡LAUGHING TIMES, (I, II, IV), P.O. Box 723176, Atlanta GA 31139-0176. Fax: (404)428-0073. Editor: Diane Carter. Newsletter: 8½×11; 8 pages; 60 lb. offset paper; illustrations. "*Laughing Times* is devoted to humor and the promotion of comedy. We are geared to helping aspiring comics and writers gain exposure and get that first 'big break.'" Bimonthly. Estab. 1993. Circ. 1,000.

Needs: Humor/satire. List of upcoming themes available for SASE. Receives 30 mss/month. Accepts 6 mss/issue; 35 mss/year. Publishes ms 1-3 months after acceptance. Length: 600 words average; 500 words minimum; 800 words maximum. Sometimes critiques or comments on rejected ms.

How to Contact: Query with clips of published work or unprinted material. Should include estimated word count, brief bio. Reports in 2-3 months. SASE for reply to query or send a disposable copy of ms. Simultaneous, reprint and electronic (MacWrite Pro or ASCII or TEXT file/DOS) submissions OK. Always include a hard copy of material. E-mail address: premier@mindspring.com. Sample copy for $3, 9×12 SAE and $1.01 postage. Guidelines for #10 SASE.

Payment/Terms: Pays 3 contributor's copies; additional copies $1.50. Acquires one-time rights.

Advice: "*Laughing Times* actively solicits articles on humor, satire, and profiles on established and up-and-coming comedians. Although the magazine is upbeat and humorous, Di draws the line on bawdy and blue pieces. We want to keep our comedy clean. Submit material double-spaced, typed and neat! It always helps if you review a copy of the publication. I see a lot of material with potential (for humor) but they lose the joke in all the words. Just get to the punch and move to the next one. Edit. Edit. Edit."

THE LAUREL REVIEW, (III), Northwest Missouri State University, Dept. of English, Maryville MO 64468. (816)562-1265. Co-editors: William Trowbridge, David Slater and Beth Richards. Associate Editors: Nancy Vieira Couto, Randall R. Freisinger, Steve Heller. Magazine: 6×9; 124-128 pages; good quality paper. "We publish poetry and fiction of high quality, from the traditional to the avant-garde. We are eclectic, open and flexible. Good writing is all we seek." Biannually. Estab. 1960. Circ. 900.

● The Laurel Review received a Special Merit Award for Graphic Design from the 1995 American Literary Magazine Awards.

Needs: Literary and contemporary. Accepts 3-5 mss/issue, 6-10 mss/year. Receives approximately 120 unsolicited fiction mss each month. Approximately 1% of fiction is agented. Length: 2,000-10,000 words. Sometimes publishes literary essays; also publishes poetry. Reads September to May.

How to Contact: Send complete ms with SASE. No simultaneous submissions. Reports in 1-4 months on mss. Publishes ms an average of 1-12 months after acceptance. Sample copy for $3.50.

Payment/Terms: Pays 2 contributor's copies and 1 year subscription. Acquires first rights. Copyright reverts to author upon request.

Advice: Send $3.50 for a back copy of the magazine.

THE LEDGE POETRY AND FICTION MAGAZINE, (II), 64-65 Cooper Ave., Glendale NY 11385. Editor/Publisher: Timothy Monaghan. Magazine: 5½×8¾; 144 pages; typeset and perfect-bound; gloss cover. Semiannually. Estab. 1988. Circ. 1,000.

● *The Ledge Poetry and Fiction Magazine* received grants from the Queens Council on the Arts through the New York State Council on the Arts and the Department of Cultural Affairs.

Needs: "We are wide open." Receives approximately 120 unsolicited fiction mss/month. Accepts 5 mss/issue; 10-12 mss/year. Publishes mss 2-12 months after acceptance. Recently published work by Charlie G. Hughes, Wendell Mayo, Susann Wilbur, Tara L. Masin, Jacoba Hood and Alfred Schwaid. Length: maximum 30 pages, double-spaced. Publishes short shorts. Also publishes poetry. Occasionally comments on rejected mss.

How to Contact: Send complete ms with cover letter (optional). Reports in 1-2 weeks on queries; 2 months or less on mss. SASE. Sample copy for $5. Fiction guidelines for #10 SASE.

Payment/Terms: Pays 2 contributor's copies; discount on additional copies.

Terms: Acquires one-time rights.

Advice: "We want stories that refuse to let go, stories of significance or consequence."

LEFT BANK, (II, IV), Blue Heron Publishing, 24450 NW Hansen Rd., Hillsboro OR 97124. (503)621-3911. Editor: Linny Stovall. Book Form: 6×9; 160 pages; book paper; illustrations; photographs. "We take only a few short stories—mostly essay format." Published in the fall. Estab. 1991. Circ. 7,000.

Needs: Ethnic/multicultural, feminist, gay, humor/satire, lesbian, literary, mainstream/contemporary, regional. "Each issue is themed. Guidelines must be sent for since each issue is thematic. We also take excerpts from books in progress or recently in print (latter particularly if well-known author)." List of upcoming themes available for SASE. Buys 2-6 fiction mss/issue. Publishes ms 4-6 months after acceptance. Agented fiction 50%. Published work by Ursula Le Guin, Ken Kesey. Length: 1,500-4,000 words maximum. Also publishes literary essays.

How to Contact: Query first and get guidelines for SASE. Should include bio (1 page maximum), list of publications. Reports in 2-3 weeks on queries; 2 months on mss. SASE for a reply to a query or send a disposable copy of the ms. Simultaneous and electronic submissions OK. Sample copy for $5 plus $2 (postage and handling). Fiction guidelines for SASE.

Payment/Terms: Pays $50-150 and 1 contributor's copy. Buys first North American serial rights or one-time rights.

LEFT CURVE, (II), Box 472, Oakland CA 94604. (510)763-7193. Editor: Csaba Polony. Magazine: 8½×11; 112 pages; 60 lb. paper; 100 pt. C1S Durosheen cover; illustrations; photos. "*Left Curve* is an artist-produced journal addressing the problem(s) of cultural forms emerging from the crises of modernity that strive to be independent from the control of dominant institutions, based on the recognition of the destructiveness of commodity (capitalist) systems to all life." Published irregularly. Estab. 1974. Circ. 2,000.

Needs: Contemporary, ethnic, experimental, historical, literary, prose poem, regional, science fiction, translations, political. Upcoming theme: "Post-Communist Culture." Receives approximately 12 unsolicited fiction mss/month. Accepts approximately 1 ms/issue. Publishes ms a maximum of 12 months after acceptance. Length: 1,200 words average; 500 words minimum; 2,500 words maximum. Publishes short shorts. Sometimes comments on rejected mss.

How to Contact: Send complete ms with cover letter, which should include "statement of writer's intent, brief bio and reason for submitting to *Left Curve*." No simultaneous submissions. Reports in 3-6 months. SASE. Sample copy for $8, 9×12 SAE and 90¢ postage. Fiction guidelines for 1 first-class stamp.

Payment/Terms: Pays in contributor's copies. Rights revert to author.

Advice: "Be honest, realistic and gorge out the truth you wish to say. Understand yourself and the world. Have writing be a means to achieve or realize what is real."

‡LEGAL FICTION, (I, IV), Temple University School of Law, Box L6A5, 1719 N. Broad St., Philadelphia PA 19122. (215)204-3993. Editor: Ann Bartow. Newsletter. "The purpose of *Legal Fiction* is to offer attorneys a creative outlet." Quarterly. Estab. 1995.

Needs: Humor/satire, legal thriller, literary, mainstream/contemporary. Publishes ms 3-6 months after acceptance. Length: 150 words minimum; 3,000 words maximum. Also publishes poetry (humorous/satirical). Sometimes critiques or comments on rejected ms.

How to Contact: Send complete ms with a cover letter. Should include estimated word count; bio, indicating legal credentials, if any; and Social Security number with submission. Reports in 2-4 weeks on mss. Send SASE for reply, return of ms or send a disposable copy of ms. Simultaneous and electronic disk submissions OK. Sample copy for $5. Reviews novels and short story collections with legal themes.

Payment/Terms: Pays 3 contributor's copies; additional copies for $3. Acquires first rights. Sends galleys to author.

Advice: "Make sure legal themes are accurately portrayed, because publication will be read by lawyers. Don't send courtroom scenes if you can't portray them accurately, and don't romanticize the courtroom. If your work makes the editor laugh out loud, she will definitely publish it."

THE LETTER PARADE, (I), Bonnie Jo Enterprises, P.O. Box 52, Comstock MI 49041. Editor: Bonnie Jo. Newsletter: legal/letter-sized; 6 pages. Quarterly. Estab. 1985. Circ. 113.

Needs: "Anything short." Receives 5-6 unsolicited mss/month. Accepts 1-2 mss/issue. Publishes ms up to a year after acceptance. Published work by Mimi Lipson, Ann Keniston and Chuck Jones. Length: 250-750 words preferred; 2,000 words maximum. Publishes short shorts. Also publishes literary essays.

How to Contact: Send complete ms with a cover letter. "Please single space so I can publish pieces in the form I receive them." Send disposable copy of ms. Reports in 2 months. Simultaneous and reprint submissions OK. Sample copy for $1. Reviews novels or short story collections. Send review copies to Christopher Magson.

Payment/Terms: Pays subscription to magazine. Not copyrighted.

Advice: "We receive too many stories dealing with suicide, random violence and abuse. Even tragic stories should contain some life-affirming elements. We like humor that's not too light, not too dark. What ridiculous thing happened on the way to the hardware store? What did you do when your cows got loose? What makes you think your husband is in love with Maggie Thatcher?"

‡LIBERTY, (II), Invisible Hand Foundation, P.O. Box 1181, Port Townsend WA 98368. (360)385-3704. Editor: R.W. Bradford. Fiction Editor: Stephen Cox. Magazine: 8½×11; 72 pages; non-coated paper; self-cover; illustrations; some photos. "We are a libertarian magazine that publishes mostly nonfiction with no more than one short story per issue. We are interested in intelligent, nondidactic fiction with individualistic and anti-authoritarian themes." Bimonthly. Estab. 1987. Circ. 13,000.

• *Liberty* received the Mencken Award for the Best Feature Story ("Journalists and the Drug War," 1992); and has also received several Pushcart Prize nominations.

Needs: Experimental, fantasy (science), feminist, gay, horror, humor/satire, lesbian, literary, mainstream/contemporary, mystery/suspense (private eye/hardboiled), science fiction. Receives 5-10 unsolicited mss/month. Accepts 0-1 mss/issue. Recently published work by Greg Jenkins, J. Orlin Crabbe, Karen Michalson and Richard Kostelanetz. Publishes short shorts. Also publishes literary essays, literary criticism and poetry.

How to Contact: Send complete ms with a cover letter. Should include estimated word count and bio (1-2 sentences) with submission. Send SASE for reply, return of ms or send a disposable copy of ms. Electronic (ASCII disk) submissions OK. E-mail address: virkkala@olympus.net. Sample copy for $4. Fiction guidelines for SASE. Reviews novels and short story collections. Send books to Jesse Walker, Books Editor.

Payment/Terms: Pays 3 contributor's copies; additional copies for $2. Acquires first serial rights, plus right to reprint or anthologize.

Advice: "We prefer stories with themes that don't wear their politics on their sleeve. Good writing is more important than a good message. Read the magazine first to see the kind of *non*fiction we publish. Don't try to imitate the fiction you see, but make yourself aware of the audience you're writing for. We'd like to see more subtlety, less overt moralizing. Messages are fine—but don't insert yourself into the story to announce them."

LIBIDO, The Journal of Sex and Sensibility, (II, IV), Libido, Inc., P.O. Box 146721, Chicago IL 60614. (312)281-5839. Editors: Jack Hafferkamp and Marianna Beck. Magazine: 6½×9¼; 88 pages; 70 lb. non-coated; b&w illustrations and photographs. "Erotica is the focus. Fiction, poetry, essays, reviews for literate adults." Quarterly. Estab. 1988. Circ. 9,000.

• Specializing in "literary" erotica, this journal has attracted a number of top-name writers.

Needs: Condensed/excerpted novel, confession, erotica, gay, lesbian. No "dirty words for their own sake, violence or sexual exploitation." Receives 25-50 unsolicited mss/month. Buys about 5/issue; about 20 per year. Publishes ms up to 1 year after acceptance. Published work by Marco Vassi, Anne Rampling (Ann Rice) and Larry Tritten. Length: 1,000-3,000 words; 300 words minimum; 3,000 words maximum. Also publishes literary essays, literary criticism. Sometimes critiques rejected ms and recommends other markets.

How to Contact: Send complete ms with cover letter including Social Security number and brief bio for contributor's page. Reports in 6 months on mss. SASE. No simultaneous submissions. Reprint submissions OK. Sample copy for $7. Free fiction guidelines. Reviews novels and short story collections.

Payment/Terms: Pays $15-50 and 2 contributor's copies on publication for one-time or anthology rights.

Advice: "Humor is a strong plus. There must be a strong erotic element, and it should celebrate the joy of sex."

LIGHT QUARTERLY, (II), P.O. Box 7500, Chicago IL 60680. Editor: John Mella. Magazine: 8½×11; 32 pages; Finch opaque (60 lb.) paper; 65 lb. color cover; illustrations. "Light and satiric verse and prose, witty but not sentimental. Audience: intelligent, educated, usually 'professional.' " Quarterly. Estab. 1992. Circ. 1,000.

Needs: Humor/satire, literary. Receives 10-20 unsolicited fiction mss/month. Accepts 2-4 mss/issue. Publishes ms 6 months-2 years after acceptance. Published work by X.J. Kennedy, J.F. Nims and John Updike. Length: 1,200 words preferred; 600 words minimum; 2,000 words maximum. Publishes short shorts. Also publishes literary essays, literary criticisms and poetry. Sometimes critiques or comments on rejected mss.

How to Contact: Query first. Should include estimated word count and list of publications. Reports in 1 month on queries; 2-4 months on mss. Send SASE for reply, return of ms or send a disposable copy of ms. No simultaneous submissions. Electronic submissions OK. Sample copy for $4. Fiction guidelines for #10 SASE. Reviews novels and short story collections. Send review copies to review editor.

Payment/Terms: Pays contributor's copies (2 for domestic; 1 for foreign). Acquires first North American serial rights. Sends galleys of longer pieces to author.

Advice: Looks for "high literary quality; wit, allusiveness, a distinct (and distinctive) style. Read guidelines first."

LIGHTHOUSE, (II), Box 1377, Auburn WA 98071-1377. Editor: Tim Clinton. Magazine: 5½×8½; 56 pages. "Timeless stories and poems for family reading—G rated." Quarterly. Estab. 1986. Circ. 300.
Needs: Adventure, contemporary, historical, humor/satire, juvenile (5-9 years), mainstream, mystery/suspense, prose poem, regional, romance (contemporary, historical and young adult), senior citizen/retirement, sports, western, young adult/teen (10-18 years). Receives 300 mss/month. Buys 15 mss/issue; 60 mss/year. Publishes ms within 2 years of acceptance. Recently published work by Julie Jacob, Michael Senuta and Neil C. Fitzgerald; published new writers within the last year. Length: 5,000 words maximum. Publishes short shorts.
How to Contact: Send complete mss; include Social Security number. No queries, please. Reports in 3 months or more on mss. SASE. No simultaneous submissions. Sample copy for $3 (includes guidelines). Fiction guidelines for #10 SASE.
Payment/Terms: Pays up to $50 for stories and up to $5 for poetry on publication for first rights and first North American serial rights. Author's copies discounted at $1.50 each.
Advice: "If there is a message in the story, we prefer it to be subtly hidden in the action. We feel there is a market for quality fiction stories that are entertaining and have standards of decency as well."

‡LIME GREEN BULLDOZERS, (I), Oyster Publications, P.O. Box 4333, Austin TX 78765. Phone/fax: (512)458-8628. Editor: Alaina Duro. Magazine: 8½×11; 50 pages; regular white paper; illustrations and photos. "*LGB* looks for honest works of short fiction. Anything with a degree of integrity is sought." Semiannually. Estab. 1986. Circ. 250.
Needs: Condensed/excerpted novel, feminist, gay, historical, horror, humor/satire, lesbian, literary, mainstream/contemporary, mystery/suspense, psychic/supernatural/occult, serialized novel. "Nothing religious." Publishes annual special fiction issue or anthology. Receives 2-3 unsolicited mss/month. Accepts 2-3 mss/issue; 4-6 mss/year. Publishes ms 6 months after acceptance. Publishes short shorts. Also publishes literary essays, poetry. Sometimes critiques or comments on rejected ms.
How to Contact: Query first. Should include a "nice, personal letter." Reports in 1 month. Send SASE for reply, return of ms or send a disposable copy of ms. Simultaneous, reprint and electronic submissions OK. Sample copy for $5. Reviews novels and short story collections. Send books to Drucilla B. Blood.
Payment/Terms: Pays 1 contributor's copy.
Advice: "I don't like boring, academic crap. I like true stories and interesting twists."

LIMESTONE: A LITERARY JOURNAL, (II), University of Kentucky, Dept. of English, 1215 Patterson Office Tower, Lexington KY 40506-0027. (606)257-7008. Contact: Editorial Committee. Magazine: 6×9; 50-75 pages; standard text paper and cover; illustrations; photos. "We publish a variety of styles and attitudes, and we're looking to expand our offering." Annually. Estab. 1981. Circ. 1,000.
Needs: "Quality poetry and short fiction, literary, mainstream, thoughtful. No fantasy or science fiction. No previously published work." Receives 200 mss/year. Acquires 15 mss/issue. Does not read mss May-September. Publishes ms an average of 6 months after acceptance. Publishes new writers every year. Length: 3,000-5,000 words preferred; 5,000 words maximum. Publishes short shorts. Sometimes critiques rejected mss.
How to Contact: Send complete ms with cover letter, which should include publishing record and brief bio. Reports in 1 month on queries; 7 months or longer on mss. SASE. Simultaneous submissions OK. Sample copy for $4.
Payment/Terms: Pays 2 contributor's copies. Rights revert to author.

LINES IN THE SAND, (I, II), LeSand Publications, 890 Southgate Ave., Daly City CA 94015. (415)992-4770. Editor: Nina Z. Sanders. Fiction Editors: Nina Z. Sanders and Barbara J. Less. Magazine: 5½×8½; 32 pages; 20 lb. bond; King James cost-coated cover; illustrations. "Stories should be well-written, entertaining and suitable for all ages. Our readers range in age from 7 to 90. No particular slant or philosophy." Bimonthly. Estab. 1992. Circ. 100.
● The editor would like to see shorter stories, especially 250-1,200 words. Humorous and slice-of-life fiction has a good chance here.
Needs: Adventure, experimental, fantasy, horror, humor/satire, literary, mainstream/contemporary, mystery/suspense (private eye/hard-boiled, amateur sleuth, cozy, romantic), science fiction (soft/sociological), senior citizen/retirement, westerns (traditional, frontier, young adult), young adult/teen (10-18 years). "No erotica, pornography." Receives 70-80 unsolicited mss/month. Buys 8-10 mss/issue; 50-60 mss/year. Publishes ms 2-4 months after acceptance. Published work by Timothy Martin, Anthony P. McAnulla, Mel Tharp, Roxanna Chalmers. Length: 1,200 words preferred; 250 words minimum; 2,000 words maximum. Publishes short shorts. Length: 250 words. Also publishes poetry. Often critiques or comments on rejected mss.
How to Contact: Send complete ms with cover letter. Should include estimated word count, bio (3-4 sentences). Reports in 2-6 months on mss. Send SASE for reply, return of ms or disposable copy of themes. Simultaneous and reprint submissions OK. Sample copy for $3.50. Fiction guidelines for #10 SASE.

Payment/Terms: Pays one contributor's copy. Acquires first North American serial rights. Sponsors contests. To enter contest submit 2 copies of story, 2,000 words maximum, double-spaced, typed and $5 reading fee for each story submitted.

Advice: "Use fresh, original approach, 'show, don't tell' conform to guidelines, use dialogue when appropriate; and be grammatically correct. Stories should have some type of conflict. Read a sample copy (or two). Study the guidelines. Use plain language; avoid flowery, 'big' words unless appropriate in dialogue."

‡**LIQUID OHIO, Voice of the Unheard, (I)**, Blue Fish Publications, P.O. Box 60265, Bakersfield CA 93386-0265. (805)871-0586. Editor: Amber Goddard. Fiction Editor: Michelle Leôn. Magazine: 8×11; 13-25 pages; copy paper; illustrations and photos. *"Liquid Ohio* is a fairly new publication whose goal is to publish new writers that others might toss in the trash. Our main audience is creatively eccentric people who feel what they do." Monthly. Estab. 1995. Circ. 500.

Needs: Adventure, children's/juvenile, condensed/excerpted novel, ethnic/multicultural, experimental, fantasy (children's, science fiction), horror, humor/satire, literary, mystery/suspense (amateur sleuth, private eye/hardboiled), regional, religious, science fiction (cyberpunk), serialized novel, young adult/teen (horror). "No erotica, gay, lesbian, occult." Receives 15-20 unsolicited mss/month. Accepts 2 mss/issue; 24-30 mss/year. Publishes ms 1-3 months after acceptance. Recently published work by Joe Morrissey, Justin Haynes and Michelle Leôn. Length: 1,500-1,800 words average; 2,500-3,000 words maximum. Publishes short shorts. Also publishes literary essays, literary criticism, poetry.

How to Contact: Send complete ms with a cover letter. Should include estimated word count. Reports in 3-4 weeks on queries; 3 months on mss. Send SASE for reply, return of ms or send a disposable copy of ms. Simultaneous submissions, reprint and electronic submissions OK. E-mail address: lornawritr@aol.com. Sample copy for $1, 11×14 SAE and 3 first-class stamps. Fiction guidelines for #10 SASE.

Payment/Terms: Pays 3 contributor's copies. Acquires one-time rights.

Advice: "We like things that are different, but not too abstract or 'artsy' that one goes away saying, 'huh?' Write what you feel, not necessarily what sounds deep or meaningful—it will probably be that naturally if it's real. Send in anything you've got—live on the edge. Stories that have no ties to romance or psychosis are good. Stories that are relatable, that deal with those of us trying to find a creative train in the world. We also love stories that are extremely unique e.g., talking pickles, etc."

LITE, Baltimore's Literary Newspaper, (I, II), P.O. Box 26162, Baltimore MD 21210. (410)719-7792. Editor: David W. Kriebel. Tabloid: 8½×11; 8 pages; 30 lb. newsprint paper; 2-4 illustrations; some photographs. "Satire, poetry, short fiction, occasional nonfiction pieces. Our audience is intelligent, literate, and imaginative. They have the ability to step back and look at the world from a different perspective." Bimonthly. Estab. 1989. Circ. 10,000.

Needs: Experimental, fantasy, historical (general), horror, humor/satire, literary, mystery/suspense (private eye), psychic/supernatural/occult, science fiction (hard science, soft/sociological). "No erotica, gay, lesbian. Nothing demeaning to any ethnic or religious group. No stories with an obvious or trite 'message.' No violence for its own sake." Receives 20-30 unsolicited mss/month. Accepts 1-2 mss/issue; 12-18 mss/year. Publishes mss 1-3 months after acceptance. Published work by Richard Gardner, Bill Jones. Length: 1,500 words preferred; 3,000 words maximum (however, will consider serializing longer pieces). Publishes short shorts. Also publishes poetry. Sometimes comments on or critiques rejected mss.

How to Contact: Request guidelines, then send ms and cover letter. Include "information on the writer, focusing on what led him to write or create visual art. We want to know the person, both for our contributors guide 'Names in Lite' and to help build a network of creative people." Reports in 6-12 months. SASE. Simultaneous submissions OK, but prefer them not to be sent to other Baltimore publications. Sample copy for 9×12 SAE and 3 first-class stamps. Fiction guidelines for #10 SASE.

Payment/Terms: Pays 5 contributor's copies; 5 extras for 9×12 SAE with 4 first-class stamps. Acquires one-time rights.

Advice: "We first look for quality writing, then we look at content and theme. It's not hard to tell a dedicated writer from someone who only works for money or recognition. Fiction that resonates in the heart makes us take notice. It's a joy to read such a story." Known for "offbeat, creative, but not overtly sexual or violent. We like characterization and the play of ideas. We don't like contrived plots or political propaganda masquerading as literature."

‡**LITERAL LATTÉ, A Journal of Prose, Poetry & Art, (II)**, 61 E. Eighth St., Suite 240, New York NY 10003. (212)260-5532. Editor: Jenine Gordon. Fiction Editor: Jeffrey Bockman. Tabloid: 11×17; 24 pages; 35 lb. Jet paper; 50 lb. cover; illustrations and photos. *"LL* is a high-quality journal of prose, poetry and art distributed free in cafés and bookstores in New York and by subscription ($15/year)." Bimonthly. Estab. 1994. Circ. 20,000.

Needs: Experimental, fantasy (science), humor/satire, literary, science fiction. Receives 2,500 mss/year. Accepts 30-60 mss/year. Publishes ms within 1 year after acceptance. Recently published work by John Updike, Stephen Dixon, Harlan Ellison and Allen Ginsberg. Length: 6,000 words maximum. Publishes short shorts. Also publishes literary essays, poetry. Sometimes critiques or comments on rejected ms.

How to Contact: Send complete ms with a cover letter. Should include estimated word count, bio, list of publications. Reports in 2-3 months on mss. SASE for reply. Simultaneous submissions OK. Sample copy for $5. Fiction guidelines for #10 SASE.

Payment/Terms: Pays free subscription and 5 contributor's copies. Acquires first rights. Sponsors contests, awards or grants for fiction writers; send #10 SASE marked "Fiction Contest" or "Poetry Contest."

Advice: "Reading our paper is the best way to determine our preferences. We judge work on quality alone and accept a broad range of extraordinary stories, personal essays, poems and graphics. Include a SASE large enough to house our comments (if any), and news on contests, readings or revised guidelines. Don't send a postcard. Include a phone number, in case we have questions like 'Is this still available?' "

‡LITERARY FRAGMENTS, (I, II, IV), Cedar Bay Press, L.L.C., P.O. Box 751, Beaverton OR 97075. Editor: Susan Roberts. Monthly electronic magazine and periodic pulp magazine. "*Literary Fragments* accepts unpublished writers and is distributed worldwide through Internet. New, unpublished writers are the mainstay of our magazine." Estab. 1980.

Needs: Open. Periodically publishes pulp fiction issue or anthology. Length: 300-10,000 words. Publishes short shorts. Also publishes novellas, poetry.

How to Contact: Send complete ms with cover letter with ASCII text on diskette or e-mail. E-mail address: cedar.bay@comm-dat.com. Sample issue (pulp) and guidelines for $6. Fiction guidelines for $2 and #10 SASE or free via e-mail request.

Payment/Terms: Payment depends on grant/award money available or copy when pulp issue is available. Buys one-time rights for both electronic and pulp issues.

Advice: "Read a current copy of either our electronic or pulp edition to get the flavor of our eclectic style."

THE LITERARY REVIEW, An International Journal of Contemporary Writing, (II), Fairleigh Dickinson University, 285 Madison Ave., Madison NJ 07940. (201)593-8564. Editor-in-Chief: Walter Cummins. Magazine: 6×9; 128-152 pages; illustrations; photos. "Literary magazine specializing in fiction, poetry, and essays with an international focus." Quarterly. Estab. 1957. Circ. 2,500.

• This magazine has received grants from a wide variety of international sources including the Spanish Consulate General in New York, the Program for Cultural Cooperation between Spain's Ministry of Culture and U.S. Universities, Pro Helvetia, the Swiss Center Foundation, The Luso-American Foundation. Work published in *The Literary Review* has been included in *Editor's Choice*, *Best American Short Stories* and the *Pushcart Prize* anthologies.

Needs: Works of high literary quality only. Upcoming themes: "Writers of Iranian Exile" (Spring 1996); "World Nature Writing" (Summer 1996); and "Benelux Writing" (Winter 1997). Receives 50-60 unsolicited fiction mss/month. Approximately 1-2% of fiction is agented. Published Irvin Faust, Ivan Stavans, Dazai Qsamu, John Bovey; published new writers within the last year. Acquires 10-12 mss/year. Also publishes literary essays, literary criticism, poetry. Occasionally critiques rejected mss.

How to Contact: Send complete ms with SASE. "Cover letter should include publication credits." Reports in 3 months on mss. Publishes ms an average of 1-1½ years after acceptance. E-mail address: tlr@fdu.edu. Sample copy for $5; guidelines for SASE. Reviews novels and short story collections.

Payment/Terms: Pays 2 contributor's copies; 25% discount for extras. Acquires first rights.

Advice: "Too much of what we are seeing today is openly derivative in subject, plot and prose style. We pride ourselves on spotting new writers with fresh insight and approach."

THE LONGNECK, (I), North Bank Writer's Group, P.O. Box 659, Vermillion SD 57069. (605)624-4837. Editor: J.D. Erickson. Tabloid: 11×17; 32-40 pages; 50 lb. news white paper; b&w illustrations and photographs. "We want your best short fiction, poetry, and essays. *The Longneck* speaks to a broad spectrum of college-educated readers. We have a sense of humor, with room for good, serious writing." Annually. Estab. 1993. Circ. 1,000.

• Each issue of *Longneck* features an interview and the work of a nationally-known writer as well as new writers. In 1995 the focus was on Dan O'Brien and in 1996 it is James MacPherson.

Needs: Adventure, erotica, ethnic/multicultural, experimental, fantasy (science, sword and sorcery), feminist, gay, historical, horror, humor/satire, lesbian, literary, mainstream/contemporary, mystery/suspense (amateur sleuth, private eye/hard-boiled, romantic), psychic/supernatural/occult, regional. No religious material. Accepts 10-20 mss/year. Publishes ms 10 weeks after acceptance. Length: "generally" 2,000 words maximum. "We will publish one longer story each issue." Publishes short shorts. Length: 250-500 words. Also publishes literary essays and poetry. Sometimes critiques or comments on rejected mss.

How to Contact: Deadline February 1. Send complete ms with a cover letter. Include word count, bio and publications list. Reports in 3-6 months on mss. SASE "always." Simultaneous, reprint and electronic

---

Read the Business of Fiction Writing section to learn the correct way to prepare and submit a manuscript.

submissions OK. E-mail address: jerickso@usd.edu. Sample copy for $3.50.
Payment/Terms: Pays 2 contributor's copies. Acquires first North American serial rights.
Advice: "If we see a beginning, middle, and end with qualities of passion or conviction, we might work with the author."

LOONFEATHER, (II), P.O. Box 1212, Bemidji MN 56601. (218)751-4869. Editors: Betty Rossi, Marsh Muirhead, Elmo Heggie. Magazine: 6×9; 48 pages; 60 lb. Hammermill Cream woven paper; 65 lb. vellum cover stock; illustrations; occasional photos. A literary journal of short prose, poetry and graphics. Mostly a market for Northern Minnesota, Minnesota and Midwest writers. Semiannually. Estab. 1979. Circ. 300.
Needs: Literary, contemporary, prose and regional. Accepts 2-3 mss/issue, 4-6 mss/year. Published new writers within the last year. Length: 600-1,500 words (prefers 1,500).
How to Contact: Send complete ms with SASE, and short autobiographical sketch. Reports within 4 months of submission deadlines (January 31 and July 31). Sample copy for $2 back issue; $5 current issue.
Payment/Terms: Free author's copies. Acquires one-time rights.
Advice: "Send carefully crafted and literary fiction. The writer should familiarize himself/herself with the type of fiction published in literary magazines as opposed to family magazines, religious magazines, etc."

THE LOOP, A Young Look at Life, Literature & Music, (I, II), Still Ill Enterprises, 8812 Mayberry Court, Potomac MD 20854. (301)983-6741. Editor: John East. Magazine: 8½×11, 15 pages; illustrations and photos. "*The Loop* is designed to be a showcase of youth-culture. We publish anything literary except criticisms, and are open to computer artwork and comics. We target a teenage audience, but sell to adults as well." Bimonthly. Estab. 1994. Circ. 150.
Needs: Adventure, condensed/excerpted novel, experimental, fantasy (science fantasy, sword and sorcery), historical (general), horror, humor/satire, mainstream/contemporary, mystery/suspense, regional, religious/inspirational, romance, science fiction, serialized novel, translations, westerns, young adult/teen (adventure, horror, mystery, science fiction, western, journalism). Upcoming themes include rape, abortion, gun control. Plans future special fiction issue or anthology. Receives 15 unsolicited mss/month. Buys 3-5 mss/issue; 30 mss/year. Publishes ms 1-3 months after acceptance. Published work by Kevin Barrett and Emily Beach Jason. Length: 1,000 words average. Publishes short shorts. Also publishes poetry. Always critiques or comments on rejected ms.
How to Contact: Query with clips of published work or send complete ms with a cover letter. Reports in 1 week on queries; 1 month on mss. Send SASE for reply, return of ms or send a disposable copy of ms. Simultaneous, reprint and electronic submissions (American Online or computer-disk copy—IBM WordPerfect or Apple) OK. E-mail address: Fentry. Sample copy for $1, 8½×11 SAE and 2 first-class stamps. Fiction guidelines for legal SASE. Rarely reviews novels or short story collections.
Payment/Terms: Pays $1 and 1-2 contributor's copies on publication for one-time rights. "We may request other rights."
Advice: "We look for clear, concise work with correct grammar. It should be interesting, innovative and stand out as not just 'some composition I had to write for class.' Send as much work as possible. As long as three or more things are sent in, it is likely one will be good enough to consider publishing. Don't give up, we're here for you."

LOST AND FOUND TIMES, (II), Luna Bisonte Prods, 137 Leland Ave., Columbus OH 43214. (614)846-4126. Editor: John M. Bennett. Magazine: 5½×8½; 56 pages; good quality paper; good cover stock; illustrations; photos. Theme: experimental, avant-garde and folk literature, art. Published irregularly (twice yearly). Estab. 1975. Circ. 375.
Needs: Contemporary, experimental, literary, prose poem. Prefers short pieces. Also publishes poetry. Accepts approximately 2 mss/issue. Published work by Spryszak, Steve McComas, Willie Smith, Rupert Wondolowski, Al Ackerman; published new writers within the last year.
How to Contact: Query with clips of published work. SASE. No simultaneous submissions. Reports in 1 week on queries, 2 weeks on mss. Sample copy for $5.
Payment/Terms: Pays 1 contributor's copy. Rights revert to authors.

LOST WORLDS, The Science Fiction and Fantasy Forum, (I, IV), HBD Publishing, P.O. Box 605, Concord NC 28025. (704)933-7998. Editor: Holley B. Drye. Newsletter: 8½×11; 32 pages; 24 lb. bond paper; b&w illustrations. "General interest science fiction and fantasy, as well as some specialized genre writing. For broad-spectrum age groups, anyone interested in newcomers." Monthly. Estab. 1988. Circ. 150.
Needs: Experimental, fantasy, horror, psychic/supernatural/occult, science fiction (hard science, soft/sociological), serialized novel. Publishes annual special fiction issue. Receives 20-45 unsolicited mss/month. Accepts 7-10 mss/issue; 100 and up mss/year. Publishes ms 1 year after acceptance (unless otherwise notified). Length: 3,000 words preferred; 2,000 words minimum; 5,500 words maximum. Publishes short shorts. Sometimes critiques rejected mss and recommends other markets. "Although we do not publish every type of genre fiction, I will, if asked, critique anyone who wishes to send me their work. There is no fee for reading or critiquing stories."

How to Contact: Query first. "Cover letters should include where and when to contact the author, a pen name, if one is preferred, as well as their real name, and whether or not they wish their real names to be kept confidential. Due to overwhelming response, we are currently unable to predict response time to mss or queries." SASE for return of ms. Simultaneous and reprint submissions OK. Accepts electronic submissions via disk or modem. Sample copy for $2. Fiction guidelines free.

Payment/Terms: Pays contributor's copies. Acquires one-time rights.

Advice: "I look for originality of story, good characterization and dialogue, well-written descriptive passages, and over-all story quality. The presentation of the work also makes a big impression, whether it be good or bad. Neat, typed manuscripts will always have a better chance than hand-written or badly typed ones. All manuscripts are read by either three or four different people, with an eye towards development of plot and comparison to other material within the writer's field of experience. Plagiarism is not tolerated, and we do look for it while reading a manuscript under consideration. If you have any questions, feel free to call—we honestly don't mind. Never be afraid to send us anything, we really are kind people."

LOUISIANA LITERATURE, A Review of Literature and Humanities, (I, IV), Southeastern Louisiana University, SLU 792, Hammond LA 70402. (504)549-5022. Editor: David Hanson. Magazine: 6¾×9¾; 100 pages; 70 lb. paper; card cover; illustrations. "Essays should be about Louisiana material; preference is given to fiction and poetry with Louisiana and Southern themes, but creative work can be set anywhere." Semiannually. Estab. 1984. Circ. 400 paid; 500-700 printed.

Needs: Literary, mainstream, regional. "No sloppy, ungrammatical manuscripts." Upcoming themes: Louisiana nature writing, jazz and literature (planned for Fall 1996 and Spring 1997). Receives 100 unsolicited fiction mss/month. Buys mss related to special topics issues. May not read mss June-July. Publishes ms 6-12 months maximum after acceptance. Published work by Kelly Cherry and Louis Gallo; published new writers within the last year. Length: 3,500 words preferred; 1,000 words minimum; 6,000 words maximum. Also publishes literary essays (Louisiana themes), literary criticism, poetry. Sometimes comments on rejected mss.

How to Contact: Send complete ms. Reports in 1-3 months on mss. SASE. Sample copy for $5. Reviews novels and short story collections (mainly those by Louisiana authors).

Payment/Terms: Pays usually in contributor's copies. Acquires one-time rights.

Advice: "Cut out everything that is not a functioning part of the story. Make sure your manuscript is professionally presented. Use relevant specific detail in every scene."

THE LOUISVILLE REVIEW, (II), Department of English, University of Louisville, Louisville KY 40292. (502)852-6801. Editor: Sena Jeter Naslund. Managing Editor: Karen J. Mann. Magazine: 6×8¾; 100 pages; Warren's Old Style paper; cover photographs. Semiannually. Estab. 1976. Circ. 750.

Needs: Contemporary, experimental, literary, prose poem. Upcoming themes: "Our Spring 1996 issue will be a contest issue; $500 prize for fiction; $10 entry fee; Deadline: December 31, 1995. SASE for guidelines. Our Fall 1996 issue will showcase Kentucky authors." Receives 30-40 unsolicited mss/month. Acquires 6-10 mss/issue; 12-20 mss/year. Publishes ms 2-3 months after acceptance. Published work by Maura Stanton, Patricia Goedicke and Michael Cadnum. Length: 50 pages maximum. Publishes short shorts.

How to Contact: Send complete ms with cover letter. Reports on queries in 2-3 weeks; 2-3 months on mss. SASE. Sample copy for $4. Fiction guidelines for #10 SASE.

Payment/Terms: Pays in contributor's copies. Acquires first North American serial rights.

Advice: Looks for "integrity and vividness in the language."

THE LOWELL PEARL, (II), University of Massachusetts Lowell, English Dept., 1 University Ave., Lowell MA 01854. (508)934-4182. Contact: Fiction Editor. Editors revolve each year. Magazine: 5½×8½; 70 pages; heavy cover; illustrations and photographs. "We offer a forum for new and published writers. In addition to distributing the journal to local businesses and libraries, we mail copies to universities across the country. Our philosophy: good writing is good no matter who the author is." Semiannually. Estab. 1989. Circ. 1,500.

• *The Lowell Pearl* received the University of Massachusetts Organization of the Year Award for 1994. Watch for their upcoming fiction contest to be advertised in the magazine.

Needs: Adventure, condensed/excerpted novel, erotica, ethnic/multicultural, experimental, feminist, gay, historical (general), horror, humor/satire, lesbian, literary, mainstream/contemporary, regional, science fiction (soft/sociological), senior citizen/retirement, sports and translations. Nothing "racist, sexist, discriminatory or violent for no particular reason." Publishes annual special fiction issues or anthologies. Receives 30 unsolicited mss/month. Accepts 2-4 mss/issue; 4-8 mss/year. Publishes ms 1-2 months after acceptance. Agented fiction 2%. Published work by Joseph Zaitchik, Richard Zidonas, Lewis Hamond Stone and Mary Mackic Wiles. Length: 1,000 words average; 5,000 words maximum. Publishes short shorts. Also publishes literary essays, literary criticism and poetry. Sometimes critiques or comments on rejected ms.

How to Contact: Send complete ms with a cover letter. Submission deadlines are September 30 and February 28 each year. Include 2 copies of ms; one with *no* identifying marks on it. Include a separate cover page with name, address, phone and bio (under 50 words). Reports in 2-3 weeks on queries; 1-3 months on mss. SASE for return of ms. Simultaneous and reprint submissions OK. Sample copy free.

Payment/Terms: Pays 2 contributor's copies; additional copies $3. Acquires one-time rights.

Advice: "Has the writer considered every word he/she has written? Is there a reason why an action, thought or description has been included? Revise. Revise. Revise. When I read fiction, I want the story to seem so real and flow so smoothly that I forget it's fiction. I don't want anything like an extraneous detail distracting me from the story. If you haven't thought about every word, every piece of punctuation, don't send it."

LUNA NEGRA, (IV), S.P.P.C., Kent State University, Box 26, Student Activities, Kent OH 44242. (216)672-2676. Editor: James Hrusovsky. Magazine: 8½×11; 50 pages; b&w illustrations and photographs. "The *Luna Negra* is a poetry, short story, photography and art biannual." Biannually. Estab. 1975. Circ. up to 2,000.

Needs: Only accepts mss from Kent State students, faculty and alumni. Receives 3-4 unsolicited mss/month. Does not read mss in summer months. Publishes short shorts. Sometimes comments on rejected mss.

How to Contact: Send complete ms with cover letter. SASE. Simultaneous, photocopied and reprint submissions OK. Accepts computer printout submissions. Free sample copy. Fiction guidelines for #10 SAE.

Payment/Terms: Pays in contributor's copies. Acquires one-time rights. Rights revert to author after 60 days.

‡LYNX EYE, (I, II), ScribbleFest Literary Group, 1880 Hill Dr., Los Angeles CA 90041. Editors: Pam McCully and Kathryn Morrison. Magazine: 5½×8½; 120 pages; 60 lb. book paper; varied cover stock; illustrations. "*Lynx Eye* is dedicated to showcasing visionary writers and artists, particularly new voices." Quarterly. Estab. 1994. Circ. 300.

Needs: Adventure, condensed/excerpted novel, erotica, ethnic/multicultural, experimental, fantasy (science), feminist, gay, historical, horror, humor/satire, lesbian, literary, mainstream/contemporary, mystery/suspense, romance, science fiction, serialized novel, translations, westerns. Receives 200 unsolicited mss/month. Buys 30 mss/issue; 120 mss/year. Publishes ms approximately 3 months after acceptance (contract guarantees publication within 12 months or rights revert and payment is kept by author). Recently published work by K.S. Nymoen, Vince Zandri and Julie McCracken. Length: 2,500 words average; 500 words minimum; 5,000 words maximum. Also publishes literary essays, poetry. Often critiques or comments on rejected ms.

How to Contact: Send complete ms with a cover letter. Should include name and address on page one; name on *all* other pages. Reports in 2 months. Send SASE for reply, return of ms or send a disposable copy of ms. Simultaneous submissions OK. Sample copy for $5. Fiction guidelines for #10 SASE. Reviews novels and short story collections.

Payment/Terms: Pays $10 on acceptance and 5 contributor's copies for first North American serial rights; additional copies $3.75.

Advice: "We consider any well-written manuscript. Characters who speak naturally and who act or are acted upon are greatly appreciated. Your high school English teacher was correct. Basics matter. Imaginative, interesting ideas are sabotaged by lack of good grammar, spelling and punctuation skills. Most submissions are contemporary/mainstream. We could use some variety. Please do not confuse confessional autobiographies with fiction."

THE MACGUFFIN, (II), Schoolcraft College, Department of English, 18600 Haggerty Rd., Livonia MI 48152. (313)462-4400, ext. 5292 or 5327. Editor: Arthur J. Lindenberg. Fiction Editor: Elizabeth Hebron. Magazine: 5½×8½; 144 pages; 60 lb. paper; 110 lb. cover; b&w illustrations and photos. "*The MacGuffin* is a literary magazine which publishes a range of material including poetry, nonfiction and fiction. Material ranges from traditional to experimental. We hope our periodical attracts a variety of people with many different interests." Triannual. Quality fiction a special need. Estab. 1984. Circ. 500.

Needs: Adventure, contemporary, ethnic, experimental, fantasy, historical (general), humor/satire, literary, mainstream, prose poem, psychic/supernatural/occult, science fiction, translations. No religious, inspirational, confession, romance, horror, pornography. Upcoming theme: "Magic Science and the Occult" (June 1996). Receives 25-40 unsolicited mss/month. Accepts 5-10 mss/issue; 10-30 mss/year. Does not read mss between July 1 and August 15. Publishes 6 months to 2 years after acceptance. Agented fiction: 10-15%. Published work by Arlene McKanic, Joe Schall, Joseph Benevento; published new writers within the last year. Length: 2,000-2,500 words average; 400 words minimum; 4,000 words maximum. Publishes short shorts. Length: 400 words. Also publishes literary essays. Occasionally critiques rejected mss and recommends other markets.

How to Contact: Send complete ms with cover letter, which should include: "1. *brief* biographical information; 2. note that this *is not* a simultaneous submission." Reports in 2-3 months. SASE. Reprint submissions OK. Sample copy for $4; current issue for $4.50. Fiction guidelines free.

Payment/Terms: Pays 2 contributor's copies. Acquires one-time rights.

Advice: "Be persistent. If a story is rejected, try to send it somewhere else. When we reject a story, we may accept the next one you send us. When we make suggestions for a rewrite, we may accept the revision. There seems to be a great number of good authors of fiction, but there are far too few places for publication. However, I think this is changing. Make your characters come to life. Even the most ordinary people become fascinating if they live for your readers."

‡MAGIC CHANGES, (II), Celestial Otter Press, P.O. Box 5892, Naperville IL 60567. (708)416-3111. Editor: John Sennett. Magazine: 8½×11; 110 pages; 60 lb. paper; construction paper cover; illustrations; photos. "Theme: transformation by art. Material: poetry, songs, fiction, stories, reviews, art, essays, etc. For the entertainment and enlightenment of all ages." Biannually. Estab. 1979. Circ. 500.
Needs: Literary, prose poem, science fiction (soft/sociological), sports fiction, fantasy and erotica. "Fiction should have a magical slant." Accepts 8-12 mss/year. Receives approximately 15 unsolicited fiction mss each month. Published work by J. Weintraub, David Goodrum and Anne F. Robertson; published new writers within the last year. Length: 3,500 words maximum. Also publishes literary essays, literary criticism, poetry.
How to Contact: Send complete ms with SASE. Simultaneous submissions OK. Accepts disk submissions compatible with IBM or Macintosh; prefers hard copy with disk submissions. Reports in 3 months. Publishes ms an average of 8 months after acceptance. Sample copy for $5. Make check payable to John Sennett. Reviews novels and short story collections.
Payment/Terms: Pays 1-2 contributor's copies; $5 charge for extras. Acquires first North American serial rights.
Advice: "Write about something fantastic in a natural way, or something natural in a fantastic way. We need good stories—like epic Greek poems translated into prose."

‡MAGIC REALISM, (III, IV), Pyx Press, P.O. Box 922648, Sylmar CA 91392-2648. Editor and Publisher: C. Darren Butler. Associate Publisher: Lisa S.Laurencot. Managing Editor: Julie Thomas. Magazine: 5½×8½; 80 pages; 20 lb. paper; card stock or bond cover; b&w illustrations. "Magic realism, exaggerated realism, some genre fantasy/dark fantasy, literary fantasy, occasionally glib fantasy of the sort found in folk, fairy tales and myths; for a general, literate audience." Quarterly. Estab. 1990. Circ. 600.
● See the listing for Pyx Press in the Small Press section and their related magazines *A Theater of Blood* and *Writer's Keeper* in this section. The magazine also sponsors a new contest, *The Magic Realism* Short-Fiction Award. See the Contest and Awards section.
Needs: Condensed novel excerpts, experimental, fantasy, literary, magic realism, serialized novel, translations. "No sorcery/wizardry, witches, sleight-of-hand magicians, or occult." Receives 200 unsolicited mss/month. Accepts 15-25 mss/issue; 40-80 mss/year. Publishes ms 4-24 months after acceptance. Recently published work by Robert Pope, Daniel Quinn and Jessica Amanda Salmonson. Length: 4,000 words preferred; 100 words minimum; 8,000 words maximum. "Fiction is considered at any length, but query for more than 8,000 words. Short shorts and microfictions are also needed." Length: 500-1,500 words. Rarely critiques rejected mss and recommends other markets.
How to Contact: Send complete ms with cover letter. Include bio, list of credits. "Response time is generally within 3 months, but acceptance can take up to 6 months." SASE. Simultaneous submissions OK. Back issue: $4.95; current issue: $5.95. Fiction guidelines for SASE.
Payment/Terms: Pays ¼¢/word and 3 contributor's copies on acceptance for first North American serial rights or one-time rights and nonexclusive reprint rights "in case we want to use the work in an anthology." Sends galleys to author.
Advice: "I like finely-controlled feats of association; works wherein the human imagination defines reality. Magic realism subverts reality by shaping it into a human mold, bringing it closer to the imagination and to the subconscious. For example, people used to believe that swans migrated to the moon in autumn or that high-speed vehicles would be useless because human bodies would break apart at high speeds. We are especially interested in encouraging new writers working in this difficult genre, and try to feature at least one unpublished writer in every issue."

‡MAIL CALL, Delivery Civil War Correspondence, (IV), Distant Frontier Press, P.O. Box 5031, South Hackensack NJ 07606. Phone/fax: (201)296-0419. Editor: Anna Pansini. Newsletter: 8½×11; 8 pages; 20 lb. paper; illustrations. *Mail Call* publishes pieces on the Civil War. Bimonthly. Estab. 1990. Circ. 500.
Needs: Historical (the Civil War). Receives 20 unsolicited mss/month. Accepts 1 mss/issue; 6 mss/year. Publishes ms up to 1½ years after acceptance. Length: 500 words minimum; 1,500 words maximum. Publishes short shorts. Also publishes literary essays, literary criticism and poetry. Sometimes critiques or comments on rejected ms.
How to Contact: Send complete ms with a cover letter mentioning "any relations from the Civil War period." Reports in 6 months. SASE for return of ms. Simultaneous, reprint and electronic submissions OK. Sample copy and fiction guidelines are included in a writer's packet for $5.

Market conditions are constantly changing! If you're still using this book and it is 1997 or later, buy the newest edition of Novel & Short Story Writer's Market *at your favorite bookstore or order from Writer's Digest Books.*

Payment/Terms: Pays in contributor's copies. Acquires one-time rights.
Advice: Wants more "personal accounts" and no "overused themes."

MAJESTIC BOOKS, (I, IV), P.O. Box 19097A, Johnston RI 02919. Fiction Editor: Cindy MacDonald. Bound soft cover short story anthologies; 5½ × 8½; 192 pages; 60 lb. paper; C1S cover stock. "Majestic Books is a small press which was formed to give children an outlet for their work. We publish soft cover bound anthologies of fictional stories by children, for children and adults who enjoy the work of children." Triannually. Estab. 1993. Circ. 250.
  ● Although Majestic Books is a small publisher, they are in the market for short fiction for their anthologies. They do a book of stories by children.
Needs: Stories written on any subject by children (under 18) only. Children's/juvenile (10-12 years), young adult (13-18 years). Receives 50 unsolicited mss/month. Buys 80 mss/year. Publishes ms 1 year maximum after acceptance. Length: 100 words minimum; 2,500 words maximum. Publishes short shorts. Also publishes literary essays. Always critiques or comments on rejected mss.
How to Contact: Send complete ms with a cover letter. Should include estimated word count and author's age. Reports in 3 weeks. Send SASE for reply. Simultaneous submissions OK. Sample copy for $3. Fiction guidelines for #10 SASE.
Payment/Terms: Pays $2 and 1 contributor's copy on publication for first rights.
Advice: "We judge our manuscripts against other manuscripts we have received from the same age group. Since we have received hundreds of entries thus far from kids ranging in age from 6-17, we use anything that is considered good for that age. We love stories that will keep a reader thinking long after they have read the last word. Be original. We have received some manuscripts of shows we have seen on television or books we have read. Write from inside you and you'll be surprised at how much better your writing will be. Use *your* imagination."

‡❧**MALAHAT REVIEW**, University of Victoria, P.O. Box 1700, Victoria British Columbia V8W 2Y2 Canada. Editor: Derk Wynand. Quarterly. Circ. 2,000.
Needs: "General fiction and poetry, book reviews." Publishes 3-4 stories/issue. Length: 10,000 words maximum.
How to Contact: "Enclose proper postage on the SASE." Sample copy: $7 available through the mail; guidelines available upon request.
Payment/Terms: Pays $25/page and contributor's copies.

‡**MANGROVE, Fiction, Interviews and Poetry from Around the World, (I, II)**, Americonsult Inc., University of Miami, English Dept., Box 248145, Miami FL 33124-4632. (305)284-2182. Editors change each year. Magazine: 120 pages. *Mangrove* is "a literary magazine publishing short fiction, poetry, memoirs and interviews." Semiannually. Estab. 1994. Circ. 500.
Needs: Ethnic/multicultural, literary, mainstream/contemporary, regional, translations. Receives 60-100 unsolicited mss/month. Accepts 6-8 mss/issue; 12-15 mss/year. Publishes ms 4-6 months after acceptance. Recently published work by Robert Olen Butler, Maxine Kumin and Catherine Bowman. Length: 5,000 words maximum. Publishes short shorts. Also publishes poetry. Sometimes critiques or comments on rejected ms.
How to Contact: Send complete ms with a cover letter. Should include estimated word count, one-paragraph bio and list of publications with submission. SASE for reply. Simultaneous submissions OK. Sample copy for $5, SAE. Fiction guidelines for SASE.
Payment/Terms: Pays 1 contributor's copy. Acquires one-time rights.
Advice: "We look for stories with a distinct voice that make us look at the world in a different way. Send only one story at a time and send us your best work. Form and content should strengthen each other. Writers often give more importance to how they say things than to what they are saying, especially in poetry. We appreciate a beautiful style, but the writer has to have something to say."

‡**manna, The Literary-Professional Quarterly of manna forty, inc., (I, IV)**, manna forty, inc., Route 1, Box 548, Sharon OK 73857-9761. (405)254-2660 (evenings). Fax: (405)256-5777. Editor: Richard D. Kahoe. Newsletter: 8½ × 11; 8 pages; 72 lb. recycled paper and cover; illustrations. "*manna* is interested only in nature/religion/psychology, and especially in interfaces of two or three of these subjects." Quarterly. Estab. 1987. Circ. 300-350.
Needs: Ethnic/multicultural, feminist, religious/inspirational, senior citizen/retirement. "We have room for only short-short fiction: parables, personal experience, etc." List of upcoming themes available for SASE. Receives 1 unsolicited mss/month. Buys 1 mss/issue; 4-8 mss/year. Publishes ms 1-11 months after acceptance. Recently published work by Jo Anna Peard. Length: 500 words average; 150 words minimum; 750 words maximum. Also publishes literary essays, poetry. Always critiques or comments on rejected ms.
How to Contact: Send complete ms with a cover letter. Should include cover letter "telling who you are." estimated word count and 100-word bio. Reports in 1 month on mss. SASE for return of ms or send a disposable copy of the ms. Simultaneous and reprint submissions OK. Sample copy for SASE.

Payment/Terms: Pays 2 contributor's copies; additional copies for 25¢ plus postage. Acquires one-time rights.

Advice: Looking for "human interest, touching on two or more of our subject areas (nature, religion, psychology) and presuming good literary quality, grammar, word selection, etc. Don't send anything that is not relevant to at least one of our basic subjects."

MANOA, A Pacific Journal of International Writing, (II), English Dept., University of Hawaii, Honolulu HI 96822. (808)956-3070. Editor: Frank Stewart. Fiction Editor: Ian MacMillan. Magazine: 7×10; 240 pages. "An American literary magazine, emphasis on top US fiction and poetry, but each issue has a major guest-edited translated feature of recent writings from an Asian/Pacific country." Semiannually. Estab. 1989.

 • *Manoa* has received numerous awards, and work published in the magazine has been selected for prize anthologies.

Needs: Contemporary, excerpted novel, literary, mainstream and translation (from nations in or bordering on the Pacific). "Part of our purpose is to present top US fiction from throughout the US, not only to US readers, but to readers in Asian and Pacific countries. Thus we are not limited to stories related to or set in the Pacific—in fact, we do not want exotic or adventure stories set in the Pacific, but good U.S. literary fiction of any locale." Accepts 8-10 mss/issue; 16-20/year. Publishes ms 6 months-2 years after acceptance. Agented fiction 10%. Recently published work by Anne Beattie, Ron Carlson, H.E. Francis and Barry Lopez. Publishes short shorts. Also publishes essays, book reviews, poetry.

How to Contact: Send complete ms with cover letter or through agent. Reports in 4-6 months. SASE. Simultaneous submissions OK. Sample copy for $10. Reviews novels and short story collections. Send books or reviews to Reviews Editor.

Payment/Terms: "Highly competitive rates paid so far," Plus contributor's copies. Pays for first North American serial rights and one-time reprint rights. Sends galleys to author.

Advice: "Hawaii has come of age literarily and can contribute to the best of US mainstream literature. Its readership is (and is intended to be) mostly national, not local. It also wants to represent top US writing to a new international market, in Asia and the Pacific. Altogether we hope our view is a fresh one; that is, not facing east toward Europe but west toward 'the other half of the world.' "

‡MANY LEAVES ONE TREE, Stories of the Surviving Spirit, (I), MLOT, Inc., P.O. Box 36302, Towson MD 21286. (410)628-0732. Fax: (410)628-1522. Editor: Bent Lorentzen. Fiction Editor: Judith Stoltenberg. Magazine: 8½×11; 18-28 pages; 70 lb. bond paper; 90 lb. cover; illustrations and photos. "*Many Leaves One Tree* is intended for a general public audience and mental health professionals." Quarterly. Estab. 1993. Circ. 600.

 • *Many Leaves One Tree* received a Ben & Jerry's Foundation Award in 1995.

Needs: Adventure, ethnic/multicultural, experimental, fantasy (science fantasy), feminist, gay, humor/satire, lesbian, literary, mainstream/contemporary, religious/inspirational, romance, science fiction (soft-sociological), serialized novel, translations, "stories of the surviving spirit (both personal and social). No graphic violence or material prejudicial to any social group." Upcoming themes: "Finish the Story Literary Contest" (winter 95/96). List of upcoming themes available for SASE. Receives 24 unsolicited mss/month. Buys 7 mss/ issue; 30 mss/year. Publishes ms 3 months after acceptance. Recently published work by Grace Thunderock, Dr. Nancy J. Cole and Meg Nugent. Length: 5,000 words average; 100 words minimum; 10,000 words maximum. Publishes short shorts. Length: 200 words. Also publishes literary essays, literary criticism, poetry. Often critiques or comments on rejected ms.

How to Contact: Send complete ms with a cover letter. Should include estimated word count. Reports in 3-6 weeks on queries; 2 months on mss. Send SASE for reply, return of ms or send a disposable copy of ms. Simultaneous, reprint and electronic (IBM, ASCII, WordPerfect) submissions OK. Sample copy for $2.50, 9×12 SAE and 4 first-class stamps. Fiction guidelines free for legal SASE. Reviews novels and short story collections. Send books to A.R. Norgaard.

Payment/Terms: Pays $15 maximum on publication, free subscription to the magazine and 2 contributor's copies; additional copies for $1.50. Acquires first North American serial rights. Sponsors contests.

Advice: Looking for "characters who rise above his/her challenges either in a legendary or realistic way—but believable within the setting created by the author. Read your story out loud to yourself a week after writing it. Edit accordingly, let it sit another week, then read it out loud to real friends. Do not send semi-plagiarized material."

‡MANY MOUNTAINS MOVING, (II), a literary journal of diverse contemporary voices, 420 22nd St., Boulder CO 80302. (303)545-9942. Fax: (303)444-6510. Editors: Naomi Horii and Marilyn Krysl. Fiction Editor: Naomi Horii. Magazine: 6×9; 176 pages; acid-free paper; color/heavy cover; illustrations and photos. "We publish fiction, poetry, general-interest essays and art. We try to seek contributors from all cultures to promote appreciation of diverse cultures." Triannually. Estab. 1994. Circ. 1,000.

Needs: Ethnic/multicultural, experimental, feminist, gay, historical, humor/satire, lesbian, literary, mainstream/contemporary, translations. "No science fiction or horror, please." Plans special fiction issue or anthology. Receives 240 unsolicited mss/month. Buys 3-5 mss/issue; 9-15 mss/year. Publishes ms 2-8 months after acceptance. Agented fiction 5%. Recently published work by Sherman Alexie, Tony Ardizzone and

Mark McCloskey. Length: 3,000-5,000 words average. Publishes short shorts. Also publishes literary essays, poetry. Sometimes critiques or comments on rejected ms.

How to Contact: Send complete ms with a cover letter. Should include estimated word count, list of publications. Reports in 2 weeks on queries; 4-8 weeks on mss. Send SASE for reply, return of ms or send a disposable copy of ms. Simultaneous submissions OK. Sample copy for $6.50 and enough IRCs for 1 pound of airmail/printed matter. Fiction guidelines free for #10 SASE.

Payment/Terms: Pays 3 contributor's copies; additional copies for $3. Acquires first North American serial rights. Sends galleys to author "if requested." Sponsors a contest. Send SASE for guidelines. Deadline: December 31.

Advice: "We look for top-quality fiction with fresh voices and verve. Read at least one issue of our journal to get a feel for what kind of fiction we generally publish."

MARK, A Journal of Scholarship, Opinion, and Literature, (II), University of Toledo, 2801 W. Bancroft SU2514, Toledo OH 43606. (419)537-2072. Editor: Danielle Demuth. Magazine: 6×9; 72 pages; acid-free paper; some illustrations; photographs. Annually. Estab. 1967. Circ. 3,500.

Needs: Contemporary, ethnic, humor/satire, literary, regional and science fiction. Also accepts pen and ink drawings and b&w photos. "We do not have the staff to do rewrites or heavy copyediting—send clean, legible mss only." No "typical MFA first-person narrative—we like stories, not reportage." Receives 20-25 unsolicited fiction mss/month. Acquires 7-10 mss/year. Does not read June to September. Publishes ms 6 months after acceptance. Publishes short shorts.

How to Contact: Send complete ms with cover letter, name, address and phone. Reports in January each year. Sample copy for $3 plus 7x10 SAE with 72¢ postage.

Payment/Terms: Pays 2 contributor's copies. Acquires one-time rights.

THE MARYLAND REVIEW, Department of English and Modern Languages, University of Maryland Eastern Shore, Princess Anne MD 21853. (410)651-6552. Editor: Chester M Hedgepeth. Magazine: 6×9; 100-150 pages; quality paper stock; heavy cover; illustrations; "possibly" photos. "We have a special interest in black literature, but we welcome all sorts of submissions. Our audience is literary, educated, well-read." Annually. Estab. 1986. Circ. 500.

Needs: Contemporary, humor/satire, literary, mainstream, black literature. No genre stories; no religious, political or juvenile material. Accepts approximately 12-15 mss/issue. Publishes ms "within 1 year" after acceptance. Published work by John K. Crane, David Jauss; published new writers within the last year. Publishes short shorts. "Length is open, but we do like to include some pieces 1,500 words and under." Also publishes poetry.

How to Contact: Send complete ms with cover letter, which should include a brief autobiography. Reports "as soon as possible." SASE, *but does not return mss*. No simultaneous submissions. "No fax copies, please." E-mail address: chedgeph@ume53.umd.edu. Sample copy for $6.

Payment/Terms: Pays in contributor's copies. Acquires all rights.

Advice: "Think primarily about your *characters* in fiction, about their beliefs and how they may change. Create characters and situations that are utterly new. We will give your material a careful and considerate reading. Any fiction that is flawed by grammatical errors, misspellings, etc. will not have a chance. We're seeing a lot of fine fiction these days, and we approach each story with fresh and eager eyes. Ezra Pound's battle-cry about poetry refers to fiction as well: 'Make it New!' "

THE MASSACHUSETTS REVIEW, (II), Memorial Hall, University of Massachusetts, Amherst MA 01003. (413)545-2689. Editors: Mary Heath, Jules Chametzky, Paul Jenkins. Magazine: 6×9; 172 pages; 52 lb. paper; 65 lb. vellum cover; illustrations and photos. Quarterly.

Needs: Short stories. Does not read mss June 1-October 1. Published new writers within the last year. Approximately 5% of fiction is agented. Critiques rejected mss when time permits.

How to Contact: Send complete ms. No ms returned without SASE. Simultaneous submissions OK, if noted. Reports in 2 months. Publishes ms an average of 9-12 months after acceptance. Sample copy for $5.50. Guidelines available for SASE.

Payment/Terms: Pays $50 maximum on publication for first North American serial rights.

Advice: "Shorter rather than longer stories preferred (up to 28 pages)."

‡MATRIARCH'S WAY; JOURNAL OF FEMALE SUPREMACY, (I, II), Artemis Creations, 3395 Nostrand Ave., 2J, Brooklyn NY 11229-4053. (718)648-8215. Editor: Shirley Oliveira. Magazine: 5½×8½; illustrations and photos. *Matriarch's Way* is a "matriarchal feminist" publication. Quarterly. Estab. 1995.

Needs: Condensed/excerpted novel, erotica (quality), ethnic/multicultural, experimental, fantasy (science, sword and sorcery), feminist (radical), gay, horror, humor/satire, lesbian, literary, psychic/supernatural/occult, religious/inspirational, romance (futuristic/time travel, gothic, historical), science fiction (soft/sociological), serialized novel. Receives 4 unsolicited mss/month. Often critiques or comments on rejected ms.

How to Contact: Query first, query with clips of published work or query with synopsis plus 1-3 chapters of novel. Should include estimated word count, bio and list of publications with submission. Reports in 1 week on queries; 6 weeks on mss. SASE for reply or send a disposable copy of ms. Simultaneous and reprint submissions OK. E-mail address: nohel@aol.com. Sample copy for $4. Reviews novels and short story collections.

Payment/Terms: Pays 1-2 contributor's copies; additional copies for $4. Acquires one-time rights. Sends galleys to author.

Advice: Looks for "a knowledge of subject, originality and good writing style."

‡**THE MAVERICK PRESS, (I, II)**, Box 4915, Rt. 2, Eagle Pass TX 78852. (210)773-1836. Editor: Carol Cullar. Magazine: 8½×5½; 76-80 pages; recycled paper; hand-printed, block print cover; illustrations. Semi-annually. Estab. 1992. Circ. 200.

Needs: Experimental, literary, mainstream/contemporary, sudden fiction (1-5 pages). "No children's/juvenile, gothic, horror, religious diatribe, yound adult/teen." November issue is always thematic; write with SASE for guidelines. Receives 6-10 mss/month. Accepts 6-8 mss/issue; 12-16 mss/year. Reads mss every 2 months. Publishes ms 6 months-1 year after acceptance. Recently published work by J.W. Mgebroff, Bruce McCandless III, Sean Connolly and Matt Friedson. Length: 1,500 words maximum. Publishes short shorts. Also publishes poetry. Sometimes critiques or comments on rejected ms.

How to Contact: Send complete ms with a cover letter. Should include estimated word count, half-page bio and list of publications with submission. Reports immediately on queries; 2 months on mss. Send SASE for reply, return of ms or send a disposable copy of ms. Simultaneous and electronic submissions OK. Sample copy for $7.50. Fiction guidelines for #10 SASE.

Payment/Terms: Pays 1 contributor's copy. Acquires one-time rights. Occasionally sends galleys to author.

Advice: "Figurative language always attracts this editor. Avoid cliches, pedestrian adjectives or hackneyed adverbs. In fact, avoid adverbs that qualify, weaken or cripple your verbs; use a stronger verb or an original metaphor instead. I see too many stories written from a child's point of view or about children or teens."

‡**MEDICINAL PURPOSES, Literary Review, (I, II)**, Poet to Poet Inc., 86-37 120 St., #2D, % Catterson, Richmond Hill NY 11418. (718)776-8853. Editors: Robert Dunn and Thomas M. Catterson. Fiction Editor: Andrew Clark. Magazine: 8½×5½; 60 pages; illustrations. "*Medicinal Purposes* publishes quality work that will benefit the world, though not necessarily through obvious means." Triannually. Estab. 1995. Circ. 1,000.

Needs: Adventure, erotica, ethnic/multicultural, experimental, fantasy, feminist, gay, historical, horror, humor/satire, lesbian, literary, mainstream/contemporary, mystery/suspense, psychic/supernatural/occult, regional, romance, science fiction, senior citizen/retirement, sports, westerns, young adult/teen. "Please no pornography, or hatemongering." Receives 5 unsolicited mss/month. Buys 2-3 mss/issue; 8 mss/year. Publishes ms up to four issues after acceptance. Length: 2,000 words average; 50 words minimum; 3,000 words maximum. "We prefer maximum of 10 double-spaced pages." Publishes short shorts. Also publishes literary essays, literary criticism, poetry. Sometimes critiques or comments on rejected ms.

How to Contact: Send complete ms with a cover letter. Should include estimated word count, brief bio, Social Security number. Reports in 6 weeks on queries; 8 weeks on mss. SASE. Simultaneous and electronic submissions OK. E-mail address: ptpmedpur@aol.com. Sample copy for $6, 6×9 SAE and 4 first-class stamps. Fiction guidelines free for #10 SASE.

Payment/Terms: Pays 2 contributor's copies. Acquires first rights.

Advice: "One aspect of the better stories we've seen is that the writer enjoys (or, at least, believes in) the talestale being told. Also, learn the language—good English can be a beautiful thing. We long for stories that only a specific writer can tell, by virtue of experience or style. Expand our horizons. Clichés equal death around here."

MEDIPHORS, A Literary Journal of the Health Professions, (I, IV), P.O. Box 327, Bloomsburg PA 17815. Editor: Eugene D. Radice, MD. Magazine: 8½×11; 73 pages; 20 lb. white paper; 70 lb. cover; illustrations and photos. "We publish broad work related to medicine and health including essay, short story, commentary, fiction, poetry. Our audience: general readers and health care professionals." Semiannually. Estab. 1993. Circ. 900.

Needs: "Short stories related to health." Adventure, experimental, historical, humor/satire, literary, mainstream/contemporary, science fiction (hard science, soft/sociological) and medicine. "No religious, erotica, fantasy." Receives 50 unsolicited mss/month. Accepts 14 mss/issue; 28 mss/year. Publishes ms 10 months after acceptance. Agented fiction 2%. Length: 2,500 words average; 3,500 words maximum. Publishes short shorts. Also publishes literary essays and poetry. Sometimes critiques or comments on rejected mss.

How to Contact: Send complete ms with a cover letter. Should include estimated word count, bio (paragraph) and any experience/employment in the health professions. Reports in 4 months on mss. Send SASE for reply, return of ms or send a disposable copy of ms. No simultaneous submissions. Sample copy for $5.50. Fiction guidelines for #10 SASE.

Payment/Terms: Pays 2 contributor's copies; additional copies for $5.50 Acquires first North American serial rights.

Advice: Looks for "high quality writing that shows fresh perspective in the medical and health fields. Accurate knowledge of subject material. Situations that explore human understanding in adversity. Order a sample copy for examples of work. Start with basic quality writing in short story and create believable, engaging stories concerning medicine and health. Knowledge of the field is important since the audience includes professionals within the medical field. Don't be discouraged. We enjoy receiving work from beginning writers."

MEN AS WE ARE, A Celebration of Men, (II), P.O. Box 150615, Brooklyn NY 11215-0615. (718)499-2829. Editor: Jonathan Running Wind. Magazine: 8⅜ × 10⅞; 48 pages; 100% post-consumer recycled paper; illustrations and photographs. "Honest, vulnerable portrayal of the male experience in all its forms. Types of material: essay, fiction, poetry, journalism, drama excerpts, photography, illustration, fine art. Intended audience: men and women interested in examining and transforming the male gender roles in North American cultures, and in reading fine literature." Quarterly. Estab. 1991. Circ. 1,000.
Needs: Ethnic/multicultural, literary, mainstream/contemporary, regional, translations. Upcoming themes: "Elders, Ancestors & Fools"; "Why Men Do Ugly Things." Publishes special fiction issue or anthology. Receives 50-100 unsolicited mss/month. Accepts 2-3 mss/issue; 8-12 mss/year. Publishes ms 3-9 months after acceptance. Published work by Anne Fausto-Steeling, Taylor Mali and Paul Milenski. Length: 1,500-3,000 words preferred; 500 words minimum; 9,000 words maximum. Publishes short shorts. Also publishes literary essays and poetry. Sometimes critiques or comments on rejected mss.
How to Contact: Send complete ms with a cover letter. Should include estimated word count, 200-word bio and list of publications. Reports in 1 month on queries; 3-6 months on mss. Send SASE for reply, return of ms or send a disposable copy of ms. Simultaneous, reprint and electronic submissions OK. E-mail address: menasweare@aol.com. Sample copy for $3, 9 × 12 SAE and 98¢ postage. Fiction guidelines for #10 SASE. Reviews novels and short story collections.
Payment/Terms: Pays $0-50 and 3 contributor's copies on publication for first rights, first North American serial rights or one-time rights.
Advice: A manuscript stands out with "original and simple use of language, engrossing stories and characters; relationships that change (epiphanies), moments of self-realization and knowledge; original and descriptive metaphor; simple and convincing evocation of time and place; stories that make me laugh, cry or that leave me bewildered, hopeful and confused." Would like to see more "non-white ('minority') and gay characters and writers; stories about infant, adolescent, and elder (50 +) characters; stories that do more than describe and celebrate traditional self-destructive male behavior. Yes, we can be very self-destructive as men, but why, and is there hope for change?"

‡MENTOR, Recreating Community Through the Art and Practice of Mentoring, (I, IV), P.O. Box 4382, Overland Park KS 66204. (913)362-7889. Editor: Maureen Waters. Newsletter: 8½ × 11; 12 pages. Quarterly. Estab. 1989. Circ. 250.
Needs: "Submissions must be mentoring related." Receives 1 unsolicited ms/month. "I would run more fiction if I received more." Length: 1,200 words. Also publishes literary essays. Sometimes critiques or comments on rejected ms.
How to Contact: Query first or send complete ms with a cover letter. Should include bio with submission. Reports in 1 month on queries; 2 months on mss. Send SASE for reply, return of ms or send a disposable copy of ms. Simultaneous, reprint and electronic submissions OK. Sample copy for $6. Fiction guidelines for #10 SASE.
Payment/Terms: Pays 2 contributor's copies.
Advice: "The writer should understand the mentoring concept and the whole story should revolve around mentoring. If it's a good or fixable story, I'll work with the writer."

MERLANA'S MAGICKAL MESSAGES, (I, II, IV), Navarro Publications/Literary Services, P.O. Box 1107, Blythe CA 92226-1107. Editor: Marjorie E. Navarro. Executive Editor: Richard Navarro. Magazine: digest-sized; 50-75 pages; "desk-top published;" soft cover; black-and-white, pen-and-ink illustrations. "*MMM* is a New-Age style pagan publication featuring short stories, articles and poetry." Published 3 times/year (March, July, October).
Needs: New Age, pagan, goddess/god related works. Short stories up to 3,500 words, "with positive uplifting material." No mystery or science fiction. Plans fiction issue in 1996 (July). Recently published work by Dorothy Marie Rice, Diane M. Navicky, S.P. Elledge and J.C. Marrs.
How to Contact: *Charges reading fee to nonsubscribers: $1/article, $1/6 poems, $3 short story (refundable).* Send complete ms with cover letter. "I like to know a little bit about the author, including publishing credits. (Don't worry if you have none; we enjoy discovering new talent.) Also, what prompted you to write this particular story?" Reports in 6-10 weeks. SASE. Will look at simultaneous and reprint submissions, but rarely use. Sample copy for $6 (payable to Navarro Publications). Fiction guidelines for #10 SASE.
Payment/Terms: Pays 1 contributor's copy. Tearsheets available on request for SASE.
Advice: "Looking for fresh originality! Give me an uplifting/healing message of the spirit and together we shall create real magick in ours and others' lives. (If there is artwork to go along with the story/article/poem, I would like to see it.)"

MERLYN'S PEN: The National Magazines of Student Writing, Grades 6-12, (IV), Box 1058, East Greenwich RI 02818. (401)885-5175. Editor: R. Jim Stahl. Magazines: 8⅛ × 10⅞; 40 pages; 50 lb. paper;

70 lb. gloss cover stock; illustrations; photos. Student writing only (grades 6 through 12) for libraries, homes and English classrooms. Bimonthly (September-April). Estab. 1985. Circ. 35,000 (combined).

• *Merlyn's Pen* now comes in two editions: Intermediate for grades 6-9 and Senior for grades 9-12.

Needs: Adventure, fantasy, historical, horror, humor/satire, literary, mainstream, mystery/suspense, romance, science fiction, western, young adult/teen, editorial reviews, puzzles, word games, poetry. Must be written by students in grades 6-12. Receives 1,200 unsolicited fiction mss/month. Accepts 25 mss/issue; 100 mss/year. Publishes ms 3 months to 1 year after acceptance. Length: 1,500 words average; 25 words minimum; 4,000 words maximum. Publishes short shorts. Responds to rejected mss.

How to Contact: Send for cover-sheet template. Reports in 10-12 weeks. Sample copy for $5.

Payment/Terms: Pays $10 for works of 1 magazine page or more; $5 for works shorter than 1 magazine page and 3 contributor's copies, charge for additional copies. Published works become the property of Merlyn's Pen, Inc.

Advice: "Write what you *know*; write where you are."

MESHUGGAH, Thoughts and Tales for the New Dark Ages, (IV), Feh! Press, 200 E. 10th St., #603, New York NY 10003. Editor: Simeon Stylites. Magazine: 40 pages; offset; illustrations. "We publish what interests us, which tends to be unusual and offbeat in subject matter, though not experimental in style. Eclectic. Our audience: a mixed bunch." Quarterly. Estab. 1991. Circ. 1,000.

• Note *Meshuggah* has changed its address and is publishing humor only.

Needs: Humor/satire. Special interests: surreal fiction, political fiction, very short fiction. Receives 15 unsolicited mss/month. Buys 6-7 mss/issue; 25 mss/year. Publishes ms 6 months after acceptance. Published work by Crad Kilodney and Al Ackerman. Length: 1,000 words average; 50 words minimum; 4,000 words maximum. Publishes short shorts. Sometimes critiques or comments on rejected mss.

How To Contact: Send complete ms with cover letter. Reports in 6-8 weeks. Send SASE for reply, return of ms or send disposable copy of the ms. Will consider simultaneous submissions, reprints and electronic submissions. Sample copy for $2. Fiction guidelines for SASE.

Payment/Terms: Pays contributor's copies. Additional copies for 50%. Acquires one-time rights.

Advice: Looks for "interesting, short, thought-provoking, unconventional subject matter; intelligent, offbeat fiction on unusual subjects."

MICHIGAN QUARTERLY REVIEW, University of Michigan, 3032 Rackham, Ann Arbor MI 48109-1070. (313)764-9265. Editor: Laurence Goldstein. "An interdisciplinary journal which publishes mainly essays and reviews, with some high-quality fiction and poetry, for an intellectual, widely read audience." Quarterly. Estab. 1962. Circ. 1,800.

Needs: Literary. No "genre" fiction written for a "market." Upcoming themes: Special issue celebrating the 100th Anniversary of Movies (Fall 1995-Winter 1996). Receives 200 unsolicited fiction mss/month. Buys 2 mss/issue; 8 mss/year. Published work by Charles Baxter, Joan Silber and Jay Neugeboren; published new writers within the last year. Length: 1,500 words minimum; 7,000 words maximum; 5,000 words average. Also publishes poetry, literary essays.

How to Contact: Send complete ms with cover letter. "I like to know if a writer is at the beginning, or further along, in his or her career. Don't offer plot summaries of the story, though a background comment is welcome." Reports in 6-8 weeks. SASE. No simultaneous submissions. Sample copy for $2.50 and 2 first-class stamps.

Payment/Terms: Pays $8-10/printed page on publication for first rights. Awards the Lawrence Foundation Prize of $1,000 for best story in *MQR* previous year.

Advice: "Read back issues to get a sense of tone; level of writing. *MQR* is very selective; only send the very finest, best-plotted, most-revised fiction."

MID-AMERICAN REVIEW, (II), Department of English, Bowling Green State University, Bowling Green OH 43403. (419)372-2725. Fiction Editor: Rebecca Meacham. Magazine: 5½×8½; 200 pages; 60 lb. bond paper; coated cover stock. "We publish serious fiction and poetry, as well as critical studies in contemporary literature, translations and book reviews." Biannually. Estab. 1981.

• *Mid-American Review* sponsors the Sherwood Anderson Short Fiction Prize listed in this book. Works published in the magazine have been reprinted in *Best American Short Stories* and *O. Henry Award Series*.

Needs: Excerpted novel, experimental, literary, prose poem, traditional and translations. Receives about 120 unsolicited fiction mss/month. Buys 5-6 mss/issue. Does not read June-August. Approximately 5% of fiction is agented. Recently published work by Alberto Ríos, François Camoin, Philip Graham, William Goyen and Melissa Malouf; published new writers within the last year. Also publishes literary essays, literary criticism, poetry. Occasionally critiques rejected mss.

How to Contact: Send complete ms with SASE. No simultaneous submissions. Reports in about 3 months. Publishes ms an average of 6 months after acceptance. Sample copy for $5. Reviews novels and short story collections. Send books to reviews editor.

Payment/Terms: Pays $10-50 on publication and 2 contributor's copies for one-time rights; charges for additional copies.

Advice: "We just want *quality* work of whatever vision and/or style. We are not a regional publication. We are now looking for more translated fiction."

MIDLAND REVIEW, (II), Oklahoma State University, English Dept., Morrill Hall, Room 205, Stillwater OK 74078. (405)744-9474. Editors change every year. Send to "Editor." Magazine: 6½×9½; 128 pages; 80 lb. paper; perfect bond cover stock; illustrations; photos. "A mixed bag of quality work." For "anyone who likes to read and for those that want news that folks in Oklahoma are alive. Publishes 25-30% OSU student material." Annually. Estab. 1983. Circ. 300.
Needs: Ecletic, ethnic, experimental, feminist, historical (general), literary, prose poem, regional, translations. Receives 15 unsolicited fiction mss/month. Accepts 4 mss/issue. Publishes ms 6-10 months after acceptance. Does not read in May, June or July. Published work by Jene Friedemann, Steffie Corcoran, Bruce Michael Gans; published new writers within the last year. Length: 4-10 pages double-spaced, typed. Publishes short shorts of 2-4 pages. Also publishes literary essays, literary criticism, poetry.
How to Contact: Send complete ms with cover letter. Reports in 8-10 weeks on queries. SASE for ms. Simultaneous submissions OK. Sample copy for $5 plus, 90¢ postage and 9×12 SAE. Fiction guidelines for #10 SASE.
Payment/Terms: Pays 1 contributor's copy. Copyright reverts to author.
Advice: "We want to encourage good student stories by giving them an audience with more established writers."

MINAS TIRITH EVENING-STAR, (IV), W.W. Publications, Box 373, Highland MI 48357-0373. (813)585-0985. Editor: Philip Helms. Magazine: 8½×11; 40 pages; typewriter paper; black ink illustrations; photos. Magazine of J.R.R. Tolkien and fantasy—fiction, poetry, reviews, etc. for general audience. Quarterly. Published special fiction issue; plans another. Estab. 1967. Circ. 500.
• *Minas Tirith Evening-Star* is the official publication of the American Tolkein Society. Contact the magazine for information on joining. The publisher, W.W. Publications also appears in this book in the small press section.
Needs: "Fantasy and Tolkien." Receives 5 unsolicited mss/month. Accepts 1 ms/issue; 5 mss/year. Published new writers within the last year. Length: 1,000-1,200 words preferred; 5,000 words maximum. Publishes short shorts. Also publishes literary essays, literary criticism, poetry. Occasionally critiques rejected ms.
How to Contact: Send complete ms and bio. Reports in 1-2 months. SASE. No simultaneous submissions. Reprint submissions OK. Sample copy for $1. Reviews novels and short story collections.
Terms: Acquires first rights.
Advice: Goal is "to expand knowledge and enjoyment of J.R.R. Tolkien's and his son Christopher Tolkien's works and their worlds."

MIND IN MOTION, A Magazine of Poetry and Short Prose, (II), Box 1118, Apple Valley CA 92307. (619)248-6512. Editor: Céleste Goyer. Magazine: 5½×8½; 64 pages; 20 lb. paper; 50 lb. cover. "We prefer to publish works of substantial brilliance that engage and encourage the reader's mind." Quarterly. Estab. 1985. Circ. 350.
• This magazine is known for surrealism and poetic language.
Needs: Experimental, fantasy, humor/satire, literary, prose poem, science fiction. No "mainstream, romance, nostalgia, un-poetic prose; anything with a slow pace or that won't stand up to re-reading." Receives 50 unsolicited mss/month. Acquires 10 mss/issue; 40 mss/year. Publishes ms 2 weeks-3 months after acceptance. Recently published work by Robert E. Brimhall, Mitchell Zucker, A.W. DeAnnuntis and M. Kettner. Length: 2,000 words preferred; 250 words minimum; 3,500 words maximum. Also publishes poetry. Sometimes critiques rejected mss.
How to Contact: Send complete ms. "Cover letter or bio not necessary." SASE. Simultaneous (if notified) submissions OK. Sample copy for $3.50. Fiction guidelines for #10 SASE.
Payment/Terms: Pays 1 contributor's copy when financially possible; charge for additional copies. Acquires first North American serial rights.
Advice: "We're now taking more stories per issue, and they may be a bit longer, due to a format modification. *Mind in Motion* is noted for introspective, philosophical fiction with a great deal of energy and originality."

MIND MATTERS REVIEW, (I,II), Box 234, 2040 Polk St., San Francisco CA 94109. (415)775-4545. Editor: Carrie Drake. Magazine: 8 1/2×11; 30-64 pages; illustrations and photos. "*MMR* is basically a philosophical publication. We have published two short stories that were written in the form of parables." Audience is "conservative intellectually, but liberal fiscally." Quarterly. Estab. 1988. Circ. 1,000.
Needs: Historical (general), literary, prose poem. No "utopian" fiction. Buys 1 ms/issue; 4 mss/year. Publishes ms 6-12 months after acceptance. Published Manuel Dominguez and Charles Corry. Length: 800 words preferred; 400 words minimum; 2,000 words maximum.
How to Contact: Query first. Reports in 3 weeks. SASE. Simultaneous and reprint submissions OK. Sample copy for $3.50. Fiction guidelines for SASE.

Payment/Terms: Pays contributor's copies. Acquires one-time rights. Sends galleys to author.
Advice: "A beginning fiction writer for *MMR* should first be familiar with the overall frame of reference of *MMR* and its range of flexibility and limitations. We seek writers who are able to tap moral principles as a source of imagination and inspiration. The moral principle can be atheistic or Christian or Buddhist—whatever—as long as there is a logical structure. Characters and plots do not have to be complex or have strong emotional appeal as long as they draw attention to life experiences that give the reader something to think about."

MINDSPARKS, The Magazine of Science and Science Fiction, (I, II, IV), Molecudyne Research, P.O. Box 1379, Laurel MD 20725-1379. Editor: Catherine Asaro. Magazine: 8½×11; 44 pages; 20 lb. white paper; 60 lb. cover; illustrations and photos. "We publish science fiction and science articles." Quarterly. Estab. 1993. Circ. 1,000.
Needs: Science fiction (hard science sf, soft/sociological sf), young adult (science fiction). "No pornography." Receives 50 unsolicited submissions/month. Buys 2-4 mss/issue; 12-14 mss/year. Publishes ms 1-24 months after acceptance. Recently published work by Hal Clement, G. David Nordley, Lois Gresh, Jonathan Post and Paul Levinson. Length: 4,000 words average; 8,000 words maximum. Publishes short shorts. Also publishes literary essays, literary criticism and poetry. Often critiques or comments on rejected mss.
How to Contact: Send complete ms with a cover letter. Should include estimated word count, bio (1 paragraph), Social Security number and list of publications. Reports in 1-2 months. Send SASE for reply, return of ms or send a disposable copy of ms. No simultaneous submissions. Sample copy for $4.50, 8½×11 SAE and $1 postage or 2 IRCs. Fiction guidelines for #10 SASE. Reviews novels and short story collections.
Payment/Terms: Pays 2¢/word on publication for first North American serial rights; additional copies for $3.50. Sends galleys to author.
Advice: Looks for "well-written, well-researched, interesting science ideas with good characterization and good plot. Read a copy of the magazine. We receive many submissions that don't fit the intent of *Mindsparks*."

MINISTRY TODAY, (IV), Missionary Church, Inc., P.O. Box 9127, Ft. Wayne IN 46899-9127. (219)747-2027. Fax: (219)747-5331. Editor: Robert L. Ransom. Tabloid: 11×17; 4 pages; offset with matte finish; illustrations."Religious/church constituency, age 25-45 target." Bimonthly. Estab. 1993. Circ. 5,000.
Needs: Religious/inspirational. Receives 10-15 unsolicited mss/month. Buys 2 mss/year. Publishes ms 3-6 months after acceptance. Published work by Debra Wood. Length: 500 words average; 200 words minimum; 1,000 words maximum. Publishes short shorts. Length: 200-250 words.
How to Contact: Send complete ms with a cover letter. Should include estimated word count, bio and Social Security number. Reports in 2-3 months on ms. Send SASE for reply, return of ms or send a disposable copy of ms. Simultaneous, reprint and electronic submissions OK. Sample copy for 9×12 SAE.
Payment/Terms: Pays $10-50 and 5 contributor's copies on publication for one-time rights.

‡MINK HILLS JOURNAL, (II), 700 Elves Press, 36 W. Main St., Warner NH 03278.(603)456-3036. Editor: Frederick Moe. Magazine: 8×11; 38-44 pages. "*Mink Hills Journal* publishes personal essays and short fiction that center on a sense of time and place and a celebration of the earth and rural lifestyle." Semiannually. Estab. 1995. Circ. 250.
Needs: Literary, regional. Does not want "polished, anonymous writer's workshop material." Receives 10 unsolicited mss/month. Accepts 4 mss/issue; 6-8 mss/year. Does not read mss July-August. Publishes ms 6-9 months after acceptance. Recently published work by William J. Vernan. Length: 1,800 words average; 100 words minimum; 2,500 words maximum. Publishes short shorts. Also publishes literary essays and poetry. Sometimes critiques or comments on rejected ms.
How to Contact: Send complete ms with a cover letter. Reports in 3 weeks. Send SASE for return of ms. Reprint submissions OK. Sample copy for $6 (payable to Frederick Moe). Fiction guidelines free.
Payment/Terms: Pays 2 contributor's copies; additional copies for $4.50. Acquires first North American serial rights.
Advice: "I am very interested in seeing work that reflects some of the philosophies of people like Thomas Moore, Joseph Campbell, Annie Dillard, and Helen and Scott Nearing. The more eclectic and 'mysterious,' the better!"

THE MINNESOTA REVIEW, A Journal of Committed Writing, (II), Dept. of English, East Carolina University, Greenville NC 27858. (919)328-6388. Editor: Jeffrey Williams. Magazine: 5¼×7½; approximately 200 pages; some illustrations; occasional photos. "We emphasize socially and politically engaged work." Semiannually. Estab. 1960. Circ. 1,500.
Needs: Experimental, feminist, gay, historical, lesbian, literary. Receives 50-75 mss/month. Accepts 3-4 mss/issue; 6-8 mss/year. Publishes ms within 6 months-1 year after acceptance. Recently published work by Joan Frank, Carolyn Parkhurst, Michelle Fogus and John Berger. Length: 1,500-6,000 words preferred. Publishes short shorts. Also publishes literary essays, literary criticism, poetry. Occasionally critiques rejected mss and recommends other markets.

How to Contact: Send complete ms with optional cover letter. Reports in 2-3 weeks on queries; 2-3 months on mss. SASE. Simultaneous submissions OK. Reviews novels and short story collections. Send books to book review editor.
Payment/Terms: Pays in contributor's copies. Charge for additional copies. Acquires first rights.
Advice: "We look for socially and politically engaged work, particularly work that stretches boundaries."

‡**MINORITY LITERARY EXPO (The Journal), (IV),** Minority Literary Expo, 421 10th Terrace North, Birmingham AL 35204. (205)324-7947. Editor: Kervin Fondren. Editors change each year. Tabloid: 8-16 pages; newsprint. "*Minority Literary Expo* is a professional national journal publishing quality literature, poems, essays, etc. for minority writing novices and professionals." Annually. Estab. 1990. Circ. 1,500-5,000.
Need: Children's/juvenile (10-12 years), ethnic/multicultural, literary. Upcoming themes: "College Literature and Black Studies" (Fall 1996). Plans anthology. Receives 8-16 unsolicited mss/month. Buys 3-4 mss/issue; 2 mss/year. Accepts but does not read mss during summer. Publishes ms in the fall. Length: 2,500 words average; 1,500 words minimum; 2,500 words maximum. Publishes short shorts. Also publishes literary essays, literary criticism, poetry.
How to Contact: Sometimes critiques or comments on rejected ms. Query first. Should include estimated word count, 1-page bio, list of publications. Reports in 6-8 weeks on queries; 8-12 weeks on mss. SASE for return of ms. Simultaneous and reprint submissions OK. Sample copy for $12, 8½×11 SAE. Fiction guidelines free for 8½×11 SAE. Reviews novels and short story collections.
Payment/Terms: Pays $5-150, free subscription to the magazine and 1 contributor's copy on publication. Acquires one-time rights. Sends galleys to author. Sponsors contests.
Advice: "Inquire with SASE first. Membership increases your networking and our interest. I solicit college students to submit literature. I want professional literature."

THE MIRACULOUS MEDAL, (IV), The Central Association of the Miraculous Medal, 475 E. Chelten Ave., Philadelphia PA 19144. (215)848-1010. Editor: Rev. John W. Gouldrick, *C.M. Magazine.* Quarterly.
Needs: Religious/inspirational. Receives 25 unsolicited fiction mss/month. Accepts 2 mss/issue; 8 mss/year. Publishes ms up to two years or more after acceptance.
How to Contact: Query first with SASE. Sample copy and fiction guidelines free.
Payment/Terms: Pays 2¢/word minimum. Pays on acceptance for first rights.

MISSISSIPPI REVIEW, (III), University of Southern Mississippi, Box 5144, Hattiesburg MS 39406-5144. (601)266-4321. Editor: Frederick Barthelme. "Literary publication for those interested in contemporary literature—writers, editors who read to be in touch with current modes." Semiannually. Estab. 1972. Circ. 1,500.
 • *Mississippi Review* has been devoting entire issues to single authors and may not be accepting manuscripts. Check with them before submitting.
Needs: Literary, contemporary, fantasy, humor, translations, experimental, avant-garde and "art" fiction. No juvenile. Buys varied amount of mss/issue. Does not read mss in summer. Length: 100 pages maximum.
How to Contact: *See editor's note above.* Send complete ms with SASE including a short cover letter. Sample copy for $8.
Payment/Terms: Pays in contributor's copies. Acquires first North American serial rights.

THE MISSOURI REVIEW, (II), 1507 Hillcrest Hall, University of Missouri, Columbia MO 65211. (314)882-4474. Editor: Speer Morgan. Managing Editor: Greg Michalson. Magazine: 6×9; 256 pages. Theme: fiction, poetry, essays, reviews, interviews, cartoons, "all with a distinctly contemporary orientation. For writers, and the general reader with broad literary interests. We present nonestablished as well as established writers of excellence. The *Review* frequently runs feature sections or special issues dedicated to particular topics frequently related to fiction." Published 3 times/academic year. Estab. 1977. Circ. 6,500.
Needs: Literary, contemporary; open to all categories except juvenile, young adult. Receives approximately 300 unsolicited fiction mss each month. Buys 6-8 mss/issue; 18-25 mss/year. Published new writers within the last year. No preferred length. Also publishes personal essays, poetry. Critiques rejected mss "when there is time."
How to Contact: Send complete ms with SASE. Reports in 10 weeks. Sample copy for $6.
Payment/Terms: Pays $20/page minimum on signed contract for all rights.
Advice: Awards William Peden Prize in fiction; $1,000 to best story published in *Missouri Review* in a given year. Also sponsors Editors' Prize Contest with a prize of $1,000 and the Tom McAfee Discovery Prize in poetry for poets who have not yet published a book.

MOBIUS, The Journal of Social Change, (II), 1149 E. Mifflin, Madison WI 53703. (608)255-4224. Editor: Fred Schepartz. Magazine: 8½×11; 32-64 pages; 60 lb. paper; 60 lb. cover. "Looking for fiction which uses social change as either a primary or secondary theme. This is broader than most people think. Need social relevance in one way or another. For an artistically and politically aware and curious audience." Quarterly. Estab. 1989. Circ. 1,500.

Needs: Contemporary, ethnic, experimental, fantasy, feminist, gay, historical, horror, humor/satire, lesbian, literary, mainstream, prose poem, science fiction. "No porn, no racist, sexist or any other kind of ist. No Christian or spiritually proselytizing fiction." Receives 15 unsolicited ms/month. Accepts 3-5 mss/issue. Publishes ms 3-9 months after acceptance. Length: 3,500 words preferred; 500 words minimum; 5,000 words maximum. Publishes short shorts. Length: 300 words. Always critiques rejected mss.

How to Contact: Send complete ms with cover letter. Reports in 2-4 months. SASE. Simultaneous and reprint submissions OK. E-mail address: smfred@aol.com. Sample copy for $2, 9 × 12 SAE and 3 first-class stamps. Fiction guidelines for 9 × 12 SAE and 4-5 first-class stamps.

Payment/Terms: Pays contributor's copies. Acquires one-time rights.

Advice: Looks for "first and foremost, good writing. Prose must be crisp and polished; the story must pique my interest and make me care due to a certain intellectual, emotional aspect. Second, *Mobius* is about social change. We want stories that make some statement about the society we live in, either on a macro or micro level. Not that your story needs to preach from a soapbox (actually, we prefer that it doesn't), but your story needs to have *something* to say."

‡MOCCASIN TELEGRAPH, (IV), Wordcraft Circle of Native Writers and Storytellers, 2951 Ellenwood Dr., Fairfax VA 22031-2038. Phone/fax: (703)280-1028. Editor: Lee Francis. Newsletter: 8½ × 11; 20 pages; photographs. *Moccasin Telegraph* publishes work by Native American writers and storytellers who are members of Wordcraft Circle. Bimonthly. Estab. 1992. Circ. 800.

Needs: Native American. Publishes special fiction issues or anthologies. Accepts 1-2 mss/issue; 6-12 mss/year. Publishes ms 2 weeks after acceptance. Length: open. Publishes short shorts. Also publishes literary essays, literary criticism and poetry.

How to Contact: "Send a sample of your writing with your application to Wordcraft Circle." Should include estimated word count and list of publications with submission. Simultaneous and electronic submissions OK. E-mail address: wordcraft@ase.com. Sample copy for $2.50. Reviews novels and short story collections.

Payment/Terms: Pays 2 contributor's copies.

THE MONOCACY VALLEY REVIEW, (II), Mt. St. Mary's College, Emmitsburg MD 21727. (301)447-6122. Editor: William Heath. Magazine: 8½ × 11; 72 pages; high-quality paper; illustrations and photographs. For readers in the "Mid-Atlantic region; all persons interested in literature." Annually. Estab. 1986. Circ. 500.

● *The Monocacy Valley Review* won the American Literary Magazine Award of Special Merit for Editorial Content in 1995.

Needs: Adventure, contemporary, experimental, historical, humor/satire, literary, mainstream, prose poem reviews. "We would not exclude any categories of fiction, save pornographic or obscene. Our preference is for realistic fiction that dramatizes things that matter." Receives 20-25 unsolicited mss/month. Buys 3-5 mss/issue. Published work by Ann Knox, Maxine Combs and Doris Selinsky. Length: 3,000-4,000 words preferred; no minimum; 10,000 words maximum. Also publishes poetry. Sometimes critiques rejected mss.

How to Contact: Send 50-word bio. SASE. Simultaneous submissions OK. Sample copy for $5. Fiction guidelines for #10 SASE. Reviews novels and short story collections.

Payment/Terms: Pays $10-25 and contributor's copies on publication.

Advice: "Send manuscripts in December and January. Responses are sent out by May, at the latest."

‡MONOLITH MAGAZINE, Science Fiction Stories and Computer Games, (II), Izsa Designs, 12221 Quince Valley Dr., North Potomac MD 20878. Editor: D.A. Alindogan. Fiction Editor: Andre Villanueva. Magazine: 5½ × 8½; glossy paper; illustrations and photos. Semiannually.

Needs: Adventure, ethnic/multicultural, experimental, fantasy (science, sword and sorcery), horror, humor/satire, mystery/suspense (amateur sleuth, cozy), psychic/supernatural/occult, science fiction. Receives 50 unsolicited mss/month; 5-10 mss/issue. Publishes ms 6 months after acceptance. Length: 500 words minimum; 10,000 words maximum. Publishes short shorts. Also publishes poetry. Critiques or comments on rejected ms.

How to Contact: Send complete ms with a cover letter. Should include estimated word count and list of publications. Reports in 4-6 weeks on queries; 2-4 months on mss. Send SASE for reply, return of ms or send a disposable copy of ms. Simultaneous, reprint and electronic submissions OK. Sample copy for $5. Fiction guidelines for #10 SASE.

Payment/Terms: Pays 3 contributor's copies; additional copies for $2.75. Acquires first North American serial rights.

Advice: "The manuscript must be submitted professionally with SASE and dark, clean type. I have no criteria for the story—if I like it I like it."

THE MONTHLY INDEPENDENT TRIBUNE TIMES JOURNAL POST GAZETTE NEWS CHRONICLE BULLETIN, The Magazine to Which No Superlatives Apply, (I), 80 Fairlawn Dr., Berkeley CA 94708-2106. Editor: T.S. Child. Fiction Editor: Denver Tucson. Magazine: 5½ × 8; 8 pages; 60 lb. paper; 60 lb. cover; illustrations and photographs. "In the past, we have published short stories, short short stories, the world's shortest story, plays, game show transcriptions, pictures made of words, teeny-weeny novelinis." Published irregularly. Estab. 1983. Circ. 500.

Needs: Adventure, experimental, humor/satire, mystery/suspense (amateur sleuth, private eye), psychic/supernatural/occult. "If it's serious, literary, perfect, well-done or elegant, we don't want it. If it's bizarre, unclassifiable, funny, cryptic or original, we might." Nothing "pretentious; important; meaningful; honest." Receives 20 unsolicited mss/month. Accepts 3-4 mss/issue. Accepted manuscripts published in next issue. Length: 400 words preferred. 1,200 words maximum. Publishes short shorts. Length: 400 words. Sometimes critiques rejected mss.

How to Contact: Send complete ms with cover letter. Reports in 1 month. SASE. "May" accept simultaneous submissions. Sample copy for 50¢, and SASE.

Payment/Terms: Pays subscription (2 issues); 3 contributor's copies. Not copyrighted.

Advice: "First of all, work must be *short*—1,200 words maximum, but the shorter the better. It must make me either laugh or scream or scratch my head, or all three. Things that are slightly humorous, or written with any kind of audience in mind are returned. We want writing that is spontaneous, unconscious, boundary-free. If you can think of another magazine that might publish your story, send it to them, not us. Send us your worst, weirdest stories, the ones you're too embarrassed to send anywhere else."

‡**MORE DEAD TREES,(I)**, Casa De Toad, P.O. Box 45065, Cleveland OH 44145. Phone/fax: (216)892-0208. Editor: Dave Miyares. Fiction Editors: Pete Hall/Jill Allington. Magazine: 3×8; 30-40 pages; 20% post consumer recycled paper; matte finish; illustrations and photos. "Ugh, I hate to say it, but our audience is a gen-x audience with topics all over the board—computers, music, art, etc." Bimonthly. Estab. 1994. Circ. 138.

Needs: Adventure, condensed/excerpted novel, ethnic/multicultural, experimental, fantasy (science), horror, humor/satire, mainstream/contemporary, psychic/supernatural/occult, science fiction (soft sociological). Upcoming themes: "Encounters with famous persons, true or false." Receives 2-3 mss/month. Buys 1 mss/issue; 6 mss/year. Publishes ms 2 months after acceptance. Recently published work by Twyla Bennett, Jonathan Falls and Pete Iello. Length: 2,500 words average. Publishes short shorts. Also publishes literary essays, poetry.

How to Contact: Send complete ms with a cover letter. Send SASE for reply, return of ms or send a disposable copy of ms. Simultaneous submissions, electronic submissions OK. E-mail address: cdtoad@nacs. net. "Preferred way of submission is electronic (ASCII is best)." Sample copy for 9×11 SAE and 3 first-class stamps.

Payment/Terms: Pays 5 contributor's copies; additional copies for postage. Acquires one-time rights. Not copyrighted.

Advice: "Submit on 3.25 disk, IBM or Mac format, in either MSWORD, WordPerfect or Quark. We see way too much neo-romantic stories. We don't see enough action."

MOSTLY MAINE, A Writer's Journal, (I), Susan Jo Publishing, P.O. Box 8805, Portland ME 04104. Editor: Peter McGinn. Magazine: 5½×8; 44 pages; 20 lb. stock paper; card stock cover and illustrations. "Our goal is to support and encourage writers, while maintaining a high standard of quality in what we accept." Bimonthly. Estab. 1992. Circ. 80.

● This publication is especially sensitive to the needs of new writers.

Needs: Feminist, gay, historical, humor/satire, lesbian, literary, mainstream/contemporary, regional. No erotica. Accepts 4-6 mss/issue; 24-36 mss/year. Publishes ms 6-12 months after acceptance. Recently published work by Sherrie Michael Bast and Peter Anastas. Length: 4,000 words maximum. Publishes short shorts. Also publishes literary essays, literary criticism, poetry. Always critiques or comments on rejected mss.

How to Contact: Send complete ms with a cover letter. Should include bio. Reports in 1-3 weeks on queries; 1-3 month on mss. Send a disposable copy of ms and a SASE for reply. Simultaneous and reprint submissions OK. Sample copy for $2.50. Fiction guidelines for #10 SASE.

Payment/Terms: Pays 1 contributor's copy to first-time submitters only; additional copies for $2.

Terms: Acquires one-time rights. Sends galleys to author (upon request only).

Advice: "We're looking for crisp writing—vivid images, realistic dialogue, characters we can believe in. We want old fashion storytelling that achieves some sort of closure. It's that simple. *Mostly Maine* is a magazine without an ego. So don't send us stilted cover letters or a list of publishing credits as a bio. Be creative and natural. Often we talk about potential rather than quality when commenting on submissions. A well-written story may be an imaginative rewrite away from being a great story. A plot twist or focusing on a different character, for example, can invigorate a story that rushes in a straight line from start to finish. Uncover what your story is really about."

‡**MOUNTAIN LUMINARY, (I)**, P.O. Box 1187, Mountain View AR 72560. (501)585-2260. Editor: Anne Thiel. Magazine; photos. "*Mountain Luminary* is dedicated to bringing information to people about the New Age; how to grow with its new and evolutionary energies and how to work with the resultant changes in our spirituality, relationships, environment and the planet. *Mountain Luminary* provides a vehicle for people to share ideas, philosophies and experiences that deepen understanding of this evolutionary process and human-kind's journey on Earth." Quarterly. Estab. 1985.

Needs: Humor/satire, new age. Buys 8-10 mss/year. Publishes ms 6 months after acceptance.
How to Contact: Query with clips of published work. SASE for return of ms. Simultaneous and electronic submissions (Mac IIci, Quark XP) OK. Sample copy, fiction guidelines free.
Payment/Terms: Pays 2 contributor's copies. Acquires first rights.

THE MUSING PLACE, The Literary & Arts Magazine of Chicago's Mental Health Community, (IV), The Thresholds, 4101 N. Ravenswood, Chicago IL 60613. (312)281-3800, ext. 2465. Fax: (312)281-8790. Editor: Linda Krinsky. Magazine: 8½×11; 36 pages; 60 lb. paper; glossy cover; illustrations. "All material is composed by mental health consumers. The only requirement for consideration of publication is having a history of mental illness." Semiannually. Estab. 1986. Circ. 1,000.
Needs: Adventure, condensed/excerpted novel, ethnic/multicultural, experimental, fantasy (science fantasy, sword and sorcery), feminist, gay, historical (general), horror, humor/satire, lesbian, literary, mainstream/contemporary, mystery/suspense, regional, romance, science fiction and serialized novel. Publishes ms up to 6 months after acceptance. Published work by Allen McNair, Donna Willey and Mark Gonciarz. Length: 500 words average; 700 words maximum. Publishes short shorts. Length: 500 words. Also publishes poetry. Sometimes critiques and comments on rejected mss.
How to Contact: Send complete ms with a cover letter. Should include bio (paragraph) and statement of having a history of mental illness. Reports in 6 months. Send a disposable copy of ms. Simultaneous and reprint submissions OK. Sample copy free.
Payment/Terms: Pays contributor's copies. Acquires one-time rights.

‡❤MUSK GLAND SALLY, 21st Century Zine for Grrrls, (II), 150 Barrington Ave., Toronto Ontario M4C 4Z2 Canada. (416)699-4665. Editors: Yuki Hayashi and Sigrun Wister. Magazine: 8½×11; 30 pages; cream 20 lb. bond; 40 lb. bond cover; illustrations and photos. "*Musk Gland Sally* is a non-doctrinaire feminist/riot grrl magazine. We print critical essays, poetry, reviews, stories, everything else." Triannually. Estab. 1995. Circ. 150.
Needs: Adventure, condensed/excerpted novel, erotica, feminist, humor/satire, lesbian, literary, serialized novel, politically motivated. "No science fiction, romance, fantasy." List of upcoming themes available for SASE. Receives 10 unsolicited mss/month. Buys 1 mss/issue; 3 mss/year. Publishes ms 4 months after acceptance. Recently published work by Sassy Whiskers, Portnoy Boccolucci and Pheasant Ellakowski. Length: 1,000 words average; 2,000 words maximum. Publishes short shorts. Also publishes literary essays, literary criticism, poetry.
How to Contact: Sometimes critiques or comments on rejected ms. Send complete ms with a cover letter. Should include estimated word count and 30-word bio. Reports in 3 weeks on queries; 1½ months on mss. SASE for reply or send a disposable copy of ms. Simultaneous submissions OK. Sample copy for 9×12 SAE and 2 IRCs. Fiction guidelines for #10 SAE and IRC. Reviews novels or short story selections.
Payment/Terms: Pays 2 contributor's copies. Acquires one-time rights.
Advice: "Don't write morbid, café zombic crap—it's been done. Enclose International Reply Coupons with your SAE. Try to sell the writing, not your own worldliness, weltsmerz, knowledge of obscure shoes, etc. Don't send in your attempt to be the new Chuck Bukowski. We don't see enough honesty. Just give me some truth, man."

MYSTERIOUS WYSTERIA, (I, II), #2, 1136 Prospect, Ann Arbor MI 48104. Editor: Eric E. Scott. Magazine: digest-sized; 37-42 pages; photocopy paper; illustrations. Publishes poetry, fiction (short) and artwork. Intended audience: anybody (but usually college age). Quarterly. Estab. 1993. Circ. 100.
• Note the magazine has a new address.
Needs: Adventure, condensed/excerpted novel, experimental, fantasy, horror, psychic/supernatural/occult, romance (gothic), young adult (horror, romance). Receives 3-4 unsolicited mss/month. Acquires 2-3 mss/issue; 5-6 mss/year. Publishes ms 3 months after acceptance. Recently published work by Terence Bishop, J.R. Campbell, Clint Gustavson and Greg Nyman. Length: 1,000 words average. Publishes short shorts. Also publishes literary essays and poetry.
How to Contact: Always critiques or comments on rejected ms. Query with clips of published work. Reports in 2 weeks on queries. Send SASE for reply, return of ms or send a disposable copy of ms. Sample copy for $2.
Payment/Terms: Pays 1 contributor's copy; additional copies for $2. Acquires all rights.
Advice: "Writers should avoid sending me boring stories of suburbia, white picket fences and the like. I want hard, gritty, street-style stories of sex, drinking, drugs, strip joints, city, etc. . . . ."

MYSTERY TIME, An Anthology of Short Stories, (I), Box 2907, Decatur IL 62524. Editor: Linda Hutton. Booklet: 5½×8½; 44 pages; bond paper; illustrations. "Biannual collection of short stories with a suspense or mystery theme for mystery buffs." Estab. 1983.
• *Mystery Time* is now coming out twice a year and the editor is buying twice as much fiction. The magazine is known for stories featuring older women as protagonists.
Needs: Mystery/suspense only. Receives 10-15 unsolicited fiction mss/month. Buys 20-24 mss/year. Recently published work by Leigh Fox, Kristin Neri and Sylvia Roberts. Published new writers within the last

year. Length: 1,500 words maximum. Occasionally critiques rejected mss and recommends other markets.
How to Contact: Send complete ms with SASE. "No cover letters." Simultaneous and previously published submissions OK. Reports in 1 month on mss. Publishes ms an average of 6-8 months after acceptance. Reprint submissions OK. Sample copy for $3.50. Fiction guidelines for #10 SASE.
Payment/Terms: Pays ¼-1¢/word and 1 contributor's copy; additional copies $2.50. Buys one-time rights.
Advice: "Study a sample copy and the guidelines. Too many amateurs mark themselves as amateurs by submitting blind."

MYSTIC FICTION, (II), P.O. Box 40625, Bellevue WA 98015-4625. (206)649-0926. Editor: Su Llewellyn. Magazine: 8½×11; 32-56 pages; 60 lb. bond paper; soft-cover. "*MF* publishes short stories of almost any genre that demonstrate transformation, especially psychological and emotional. We reject stories with static characters." Quarterly. Estab. 1993.
Needs: Adventure, erotica, ethnic/multicultural, experimental, (science fantasy, sword and sorcery), feminist, historical, horror, humor/satire, literary, mainstream/contemporary, mystery/suspense, psychic/supernatural/occult, science fiction, westerns (frontier, traditional). No romance. Publishes special fiction issue or anthology. Receives 12-15 unsolicited mss/month. Accepts 7-13 mss/issue; 28-52 mss/year. Publishes ms 6 months to a year after acceptance. Published work by Mike James, Carol Meredith, Sheryll Watt, Joe Murphy and Mark McLaughlin. Length: 3,700 words preferred; 500 words minimum; 5,000 words maximum. Publishes short shorts. Length: 450 words. Also publishes poetry. Always critiques or comments on rejected mss.
How to Contact: Send complete ms with a cover letter. Should include estimated word count and cover letter with "a few words justifying how the main character changes in the story." Reports in 1-2 weeks on queries; 2 months on mss. Send SASE for reply, return of ms or send a disposable copy of ms. No simultaneous submissions. Reprint and electronic submissions OK. E-mail address: Su Llewellyn 76170,2266@compuserve.com. Sample copy for $5.75. Fiction guidelines for SASE. Not accepting mss until January, 1996.
Payment/Terms: Pays $20 on acceptance for first North American serial rights or one-time rights (in the case of a reprint). Sometimes pays in contributor's copies;; additional copies for $2.50.
Advice: Looks for: "character transformation demonstrated; writing craft/thorough line editing; distinctive characters. Read William Sloane's *The Craft of Writing*!" Would like to see more "careful attention to prose. Too often writers talk *at* us, the reader is constantly aware of the author. Writers should ask themselves if the sentence, word, paragraph is coming from the author—would the character think of that? Also remember that scene is not scenery!"

THE MYTHIC CIRCLE, (I), The Mythopoeic Society, Box 6707, Altadena CA 91001. Co-Editors: Tina Cooper and Christine Lowentrout. Magazine: 8½×11; 50 pages; high quality photocopy paper; illustrations. "A triannual fantasy-fiction magazine. We function as a 'writer's forum,' depending heavily on letters of comment from readers. We have a very occasional section called 'Mythopoeic Youth' in which we publish stories written by writers still in high school/junior high school, but we are not primarily oriented to young writers. We give subscribers' submissions preference." Triannually. Estab. 1987. Circ. 150.
Needs: Short fantasy. "No erotica, no graphic horror, no 'hard' science fiction." Receives 25 unsolicited ms/month. Accepts 19-20 mss/issue. Publishes ms 1-2 years after acceptance. Published work by Charles de Lint, Gwyneth Hood and Angelee Sailer Anderson; published new writers within the last year. Length: 3,000 words average. Publishes short shorts. Length: 8,000 words maximum. Always critiques rejected mss.
How to Contact: Send complete ms with cover letter. "We give each ms a personal response. We get many letters that try to impress us with other places they've appeared in print—that doesn't matter much to us." Reports in 6 months. SASE. No simultaneous submissions. Sample copy for $6.50; fiction guidelines for #10 SASE.
Payment/Terms: Pays in contributor's copies; charges for extras. Acquires one-time rights.
Advice: "There are very few places a fantasy writer can send to these days. *Mythic Circle* was started because of this; also, the writers were not getting any kind of feedback when (after nine or ten months) their mss were rejected. We give the writers personalized attention—critiques, suggestions—and we rely on our readers to send us letters of comment on the stories we publish, so that the writers can see a response. Don't be discouraged by rejections, especially if personal comments/suggestions are offered."

NAKED KISS, (II), Scarlett Fever Press, 3160 Brady Lake Rd., Ravenna OH 44266. Editor: Wayne A. Harold. Magazine: 8½×11; 40-48 pages; 20 lb. paper; cardstock cover; illustrations and photos. "Hardboiled crime, mystery and suspense fiction. Some stories are intended for mature readers only. Hard-hitting, mature fiction." Triannually. Estab. 1994. Circ. 500.
  • Scarlett Fever Press publishes *Dark Kiss*, a magazine of adult and erotic horror fiction. See the listing in this section.
Needs: Adventure, mystery/suspense (police procedural, private eye/hardboiled. No cozy mystery. Upcoming theme: for Halloween, "Tricks or Treats," Halloween-oriented crime fiction. List of upcoming themes available for SASE. Receives 25-30 unsolicited mss/month. Buys 5-8 mss/issue; 15-25 mss/year. Publishes ms 6-24 months after acceptance. Published work by Gary Lovisi, Mike Black, J.D. Hunt, M.M. Lopiccolo. Length: 4,000 words average; 2,000 words minimum; 6,000 words maximum. Often critiques or comments on rejected mss.

How to Contact: Send complete ms with a cover letter. Should include estimated word count, bio (1 paragraph) and list of publications. Reports in 1 month on queries; 2-3 months on mss. SASE for return of ms. Simultaneous, reprint and electronic submissions OK. E-mail address: mrwharold@aol.com. Sample copy for $5 (make payable to Scarlett Fever Press). Fiction guidelines for #10 SASE. Reviews novels and short story collections.

Payment/Terms: Pays $5-25 and 1-3 contributor's copies on publication for first North American serial rights.

Advice: "Looking for originality; interested in stories with a strong emotional content. No satires! We want hard-hitting crime and suspense. Be original, be creative, and use standard manuscript format. Enclose a cover letter (we want to know about you!) and a SASE."

NASSAU REVIEW, (I, II), Nassau Community College, State University of New York, Stewart Ave., Garden City NY 11530-6793. (516)572-7792. Editor: Paul A. Doyle. Magazine: 5½×8½; 80-120 pages; heavy stock paper; b&w illustrations and photographs. For "college teachers, libraries, educated college-level readers." Annually. Estab. 1964.

Needs: Contemporary, fantasy, historical (general), literary, mainstream, serialized novel. Receives 500 unsolicited mss/year. Accepts 15 mss/issue. Does not read mss January-August. Publishes ms 6 months after acceptance. Published work by Dick Wimmer, Louis Phillips and Norbert Petsch. Length: 800-1,500 words preferred; 1,000 words minimum; 1,500 words maximum. Publishes short shorts.

How to Contact: Send complete ms with cover letter. Include basic publication data. Reports in 1 month on queries; 8 months on mss. SASE. No simultaneous submissions. Sample copy for 9×12 SAE.

Payment/Terms: No payment. Acquires first rights or one-time rights.

Advice: Looks for "imaginative, concrete writing on interesting characters and scenes." Send story ms before October 15. $150 prize to best story published each year.

NEBO, A Literary Journal, (II), Arkansas Tech University, Dept. of English, Russellville AR 72801. (501)968-0256. Editors change each year. Contact Editor or Advisor: Dr. Michael Karl Ritchie. Literary, fiction and poetry magazine: 5×8; 50-60 pages. For a general, academic audience. Annually. Estab. 1983. Circ. 500.

Needs: Literary, mainstream, reviews. Receives 20-30 unsolicited fiction mss/month. Accepts 2 mss/issue; 6-10 mss/year. Does not read mss May 1-September 1. Published new writers within the last year. Length: 3,000 words maximum. Also publishes literary essays, literary criticism, poetry. Occasionally critiques rejected mss.

How to Contact: Send complete ms with SASE and cover letter with bio. Simultaneous submissions OK. Reports in 3 months on mss. Publishes ms an average of 6 months after acceptance. Sample copy for $5. "Submission deadlines for all work are November 15 and January 15 of each year." Reviews novels and short story collections.

Payment/Terms: Pays 1 contributor's copy. Acquires one-time rights.

Advice: "A writer should carefully edit his short story before submitting it. Write from the heart and put everything on the line. Don't write from a phony or fake perspective. Frankly, many of the manuscripts we receive should be publishable with a little polishing. Manuscripts should *never* be submitted with misspelled words or on 'onion skin' or colored paper."

THE NEBRASKA REVIEW, (I, II), University of Nebraska at Omaha, Omaha NE 68182-0324. (402)554-2771. Fiction Editor: James Reed. Magazine: 5½×8½; 72 pages; 60 lb. text paper; chrome coat cover stock. "*TNR* attempts to publish the finest available contemporary fiction and poetry for college and literary audiences." Publishes 2 issues/year. Estab. 1973. Circ. 700.

- *The Nebraska Review* has published a number of award-winning writers.

Needs: Contemporary, humor/satire, literary and mainstream. Receives 40 unsolicited fiction mss/month. Acquires 4-5 mss/issue, 8-10 mss/year. Reads for the *Nebraska Review* Awards in Fiction and Poetry September 1-November 30; Open to submissions January 1-April 30; does not read May 1-August 31. Published work by Elizabeth Evans, Joseph Geha, Stewart O'Nan, E.S. Goldman, and Stephen Pett; published new writers within the last year. Length: 5,000-6,000 words average. Also publishes poetry.

How to Contact: Send complete ms with SASE. Reports in 1-4 months. Publishes ms an average of 6-12 months after acceptance. Sample copy for $2.50.

Payment/Terms: Pays 2 contributor's copies plus 1 year subscription; $2 charge for extras. Acquires first North American serial rights.

Advice: "Write 'honest' stories in which the lives of your characters are the primary reason for writing and techniques of craft serve to illuminate, not overshadow, the textures of those lives. Sponsors a $500 award/year—write for rules."

NERVE, (I, II), P.O. Box 124578, San Diego CA 92112-4578. Editor: Geoffrey N. Young. Magazine: 5½×8½; 32-40 pages; 60 lb. cover stock; illustrations. "We are eager to work with un- or underpublished writers. We publish pieces that have something to say and that say it well." Triannually. Estab. 1994. Circ. 300.

Needs: Adventure, erotica, ethnic/multicultural, experimental, feminist, gay, historical (general), humor/satire, lesbian, literary, mainstream/contemporary, regional, sports. "No pornography. Nothing that insults the reader's intelligence." Receives 10-15 unsolicited mss/month. Accepts 1-3 mss/issue; 3-9 mss/year. Publishes ms 1-4 months after acceptance. Recently published work by Peggy A. Johnson, Selena Anne Shephard and Chris Sturhann. Length: 1,500 words average; 2,500 words maximum. Publishes short shorts. Also publishes literary essays and poetry. Sometimes critiques or comments on rejected ms.
How to Contact: Send complete ms with a cover letter. Should include estimated word count and 2-5 line bio. Reports in 2-4 months. Send SASE for reply, return of ms or send a disposable copy of ms. No simultaneous submissions. Sample copy for $2 (checks to Geoffrey N. Young). Reviews novels and short story collections.
Payment/Terms: Pays 3 contributor's copies. Sends galleys to author upon request. Not copyrighted.
Advice: "Strong characters, good use of dialogue make a manuscript stand out. We want to see dialogue that advances the story. We see a lot of stories without dialogue, or with dialogue that merely chatters. Show us an exciting new topic, a fresh angle on an old topic. Take risks. Practice your craft. We receive too many submissions from authors with wonderful ideas, but who have not yet found their voice. And, of course, once you have a product, research the markets diligently. We encourage submissions of short shorts."

NEURONET, Stories from the Cyberland, (I, II, IV), Stygian Vortex Publications, 6634 Atlanta St., Hollywood FL 33024-2965. Editor-in-Chief: Glenda Woodrum. Fiction Editor: Coyote Osborne. Magazine: digest-sized; 40-60 pages; 20 lb. bond paper; 67 lb. Bristol cover. "*NeuroNet* is a mature readers publication which specializes in the cyberpunk genre." Annually. Estab. 1995. Circ. 75.
Needs: Science fiction (cyberpunk). No pornographic material. Publishes annual special fiction issue or anthology. Receives 8-15 unsolicited submissions/month. Accepts 6-12 mss/year. Publishes ms 6-18 months after acceptance. Recently published work by Charles Saplak. Length: 4,000 words average; 2,500 words minimum; 10,000 words maximum. Also publishes poetry. Often critiques or comments on rejected mss.
How to Contact: Send complete ms with a cover letter "if over 10,000 words, query before submitting." Should include estimated word count, bio (75-150 words). Reports in 1-2 on queries; 1-3 months on mss. Send SASE for reply, return of ms or send a disposable copy of ms. Simultaneous and electronic submissions OK. Sample copy for $5.25 (payable to G. Woodrum). Fiction guidelines for SAE and 2 first-class stamps or 4 IRCs. Reviews novels and short story collections. Send books attn: John Everson.
Payment/Terms: Pays $8 maximum, 1 contributor's copy on publication for one-time rights; additional copies $2.10 each plus 75¢ postage/copy (payable to G. Woodrum).
Advice: Looks for "neatness. We also prefer that no manuscript by submitted using fancy fonts, or type sizes smaller than 12 point/pitch. Make certain that your story conforms to our needs. If in doubt, read *Neuromancer* by William Gibson. Make you characters live and breathe the harsh reality of the grim cyberpunk future. We don't print anything that isn't cyberpunk."

NEW DELTA REVIEW, (II), English Dept./Louisiana State University, Baton Rouge LA 70803-5001. (504)388-4079. Contact: Fiction Editor. Magazine: 6×9; 75-125 pages; high quality paper; glossy card cover; b&w illustrations and artwork; photographs. "No theme or style biases. Poetry, fiction primarily; also literary interviews and reviews." Semi-annual. Estab. 1984.
● *New Delta Review* also sponsors the Eyster Prizes for fiction and poetry. See the listing in the Contest and Awards Section of this book. Work from the magazine has been included in the *Pushcart Prize* anthology.
Needs: Contemporary, experimental, humor/satire, literary, mainstream, prose poem, translations. No novel excerpts. Receives 120 unsolicited mss/ month. Accepts 4-8 mss/issue. Recently published work by Steve Stern, Cliff Yudell, Wendy Bremer and Rita Ciresi. Published new writers within the last year. Length: 20 ms pages average; 250 words minimum. Publishes short shorts. Also publishes poetry. Sometimes critiques rejected mss.
How to Contact: Send complete ms with cover letter. Cover letter should include "credits, if any; no synopses, please." No simultaneous submissions. Reports on mss in 2-3 months. SASE (or IRC). Mss deadlines September 1 for fall; February 15 for spring. Sample copy for $4. Reviews novels and short story collections.
Payment/Terms: Pays in contributor's copies. Charge for extras.
Terms: Acquires first North American serial rights. Sponsors award for fiction writers in each issue. Eyster Prize-$50 plus notice in magazine. Mss selected for publication are automatically considered.
Advice: "Make sparks fly off your typewriter. Send your best work, even if others have rejected it. Don't let our address mislead you: We like fiction and poetry that explore national and international sensibilities, not just Southern regionalism. And don't forget the SASE if you want a response."

NEW ENGLAND REVIEW, (III), Middlebury College, Middlebury VT 05753. (802)388-3711, ext. 5119. Editor: Stephen Donaldio. Magazine: 6×9; 180 pages; 70 lb paper; coated cover stock; illustrations; photos. A literary quarterly publishing fiction, poetry and essays with special emphasis on contemporary cultural issues, both in the limited states and abroad. For general readers and professional writers. Quarterly. Estab. 1977. Circ. 2,000.

● *New England Review* has long been associated with Breadloaf Writer's Conference, held at Middlebury College.

Needs: Literary. Receives 250 unsolicited fiction mss/month. Accepts 5 mss/issue; 20 mss/year. Does not read ms June-August. Published work by Robert Olen Butler, Grace Paley, Charles Baxter, Joyce Carol Oates and Marge Piercy; published new writers within the last year. Publishes ms 3-9 months after acceptance. Agented fiction: less than 5%. Publishes short shorts. Sometimes critiques rejected mss.

How to Contact: Send complete ms with cover letter. "Cover letters that demonstrate that the writer knows the magazine are the ones we want to read. We don't want hype, or hard-sell, or summaries of the author's intentions. Will consider simultaneous submissions, but must be stated as such." Reports in 8-10 weeks on mss. SASE.

Payment/Terms: Pays $10/page, subscription to magazine and contributor's copies on publication; charge for extras. Acquires first rights and reprint rights. Sends galleys to author.

Advice: "It's best to send one story at a time, and wait until you hear back from us to try again."

NEW FRONTIER, (IV), P.O. Box 17397, Asheville NC 28806. (704)251-0109. Fax: (704)251-0727. Editor: Sw. Virato. Magazine: 8×10; 48-60 pages; pulp paper stock; illustrations and photos. "We seek new age writers who have imagination yet authenticity." Bimonthly. Estab. 1981. Circ. 60,000.

Needs: New age, body/mind consciousness. "A new style of writing is needed with a transformation theme." Receives 10-20 unsolicited mss/month. Accepts 1-2 mss/issue. Publishes ms 3 months after acceptance. Agented fiction "less than 5%." Published work by John White, Laura Anderson; published work by new writers within the last year. Length: 1,000 words average; 750 words minimum; 2,000 words maximum. Publishes short shorts. Length: 150-500 words. Occasionally critiques rejected mss and recommends other markets.

How to Contact: Send complete ms with cover letter, which should include author's bio and credits. Reports in 2 months on mss. SASE for ms. Simultaneous and reprint submissions OK. Sample copy for $2.95. Fiction guidelines for #10 SASE.

Terms: Acquires first North American serial rights and one-time rights.

Advice: "The new age market is ready for a special kind of fiction and we are here to serve it. Don't try to get an A on your term paper. Be sincere, aware and experimental. Old ideas that are senile don't work for us. Be fully alive and aware—tune in to our new age audience/readership."

NEW FRONTIERS OF NEW MEXICO, A Magazine of Exploration, (II), New Frontiers, P.O. Box 1299, Tijeras NM 87059. (505)281-1990. Editor: Wally Gordon. Magazine: 8¼×10¾; 32 pages; 50 lb. paper; illustrations and photos. "Elite audience, primarily in New Mexico, secondarily elsewhere in Southwest. General interests." Quarterly. Estab. 1993. Circ. 3,000.

● See the interview with Wally Gordon in this section.

Needs: Adventure, contemporary western issues and conflicts, excerpted novel, ethnic/multicultural, experimental, feminist, historical (general), humor/satire, literary, mainstream/contemporary, regional, translations, westerns. "Prefer fiction that highlights the kind of cultural, ethnic and environmental conflicts that concern New Mexicans today." Receives 25-50 unsolicited mss/month. Buys 2-3 mss/issue. Publishes ms 1-4 months after acceptance. Recently published work by Kate Horsley, Mary Marquez, Katherine Beebe and Kate Besser. Length: 1,500 words average; 3,000 words maximum. Publishes short shorts. Also publishes literary essays, literary criticism and poetry. Often critiques or comments on rejected mss.

How to Contact: Send complete ms with a cover letter. "Query if not already written. Send ms if already done." Should include brief bio. Reports in 1 month on queries; 2 months on mss. Send SASE for reply, return of ms or send a disposable copy of ms. Simultaneous, reprint and electronic submissions OK. Sample copy for $2.95 and 8×11 SAE. Fiction guidelines for #10 SASE. Reviews novels and short story collections.

Payment/Terms: Pays $25-200 and 1 contributor's copy on publication for one-time rights.

Advice: "Put yourself in the shoes of a college-educated, middle-aged man or woman living in Albuquerque or Santa Fe and looking for role models on how to cope with the stress of a radically changing way of life. I want to see more lively fiction, with vivid characters, a sense of humor and strong social relevance."

NEW LAUREL REVIEW, (II), 828 Lesseps St., New Orleans LA 70117. (504)947-6001. Editor: Lee Meitzen Grue. Magazine: 6×9; 120 pages; 60 lb. book paper; Sun Felt cover; illustrations; photo essays. Journal of poetry, fiction, critical articles and reviews. "We have published such internationally known writers as James Nolan, Tomris Uyar and Yevgeny Yevtushenko." Readership: "Literate, adult audiences as well as anyone interested in writing with significance, human interest, vitality, subtlety, etc." Published irregularly. Estab. 1970. Circ. 500.

Needs: Literary, contemporary, fantasy and translations. No "dogmatic, excessively inspirational or political" material. Acquires 1-2 fiction mss/issue. Receives approximately 50 unsolicited fiction mss each month. Length: about 10 printed pages. Also publishes literary essays, literary criticism, poetry. Critiques rejected mss when there is time.

How to Contact: Send complete ms with SASE. Reports in 3 months. Sample copy for $7. "Authors need to look at sample copy before submitting." Reviews novels and short story collections.

Payment/Terms: Pays 1 contributor's copy. Acquires first rights.

Advice: "We are interested in international issues pointing to libraries around the world. Write fresh, alive 'moving' work. Not interested in egocentric work without any importance to others. Be sure to watch simple details such as putting one's name and address on manuscript and clipping all pages together. Caution: Don't use over-fancy or trite language."

NEW LETTERS MAGAZINE, (I, II), University of Missouri-Kansas City, 5100 Rockhill Rd., Kansas City MO 64110. (816)235-1168. Fax: (816)235-2611. Editor: James McKinley. Magazine: 14 lb. cream paper; illustrations. Quarterly. Estab. 1971 (continuation of *University Review*, founded 1935). Circ. 2,500.
Needs: Contemporary, ethnic, experimental, humor/satire, literary, mainstream, translations. No "bad fiction in any genre." Published work by Tess Gallagher, Jimmy Carter and Amiri Barak; published work by new writers within the last year. Agented fiction: 10%. Also publishes short shorts. Rarely critiques rejected mss.
How to Contact: Send complete ms with cover letter. Does not read mss May 15-October 15. Reports in 3 weeks on queries; 2-3 months on mss. SASE for ms. No simultaneous or multiple submissions. Sample copy: $8.50 for issues older than 5 years; $5.50 for 5 years or less.
Payment/Terms: Pays honorarium—depends on grant/award money; 2 contributor's copies. Sends galleys to author.
Advice: "Seek publication of representative chapters in high-quality magazines as a way to the book contract. Try literary magazines first."

NEW METHODS, The Journal of Animal Health Technology, (IV), Box 22605, San Francisco CA 94122-0605. (415)664-3469. Editor: Ronald S. Lippert, AHT. Newsletter ("could become magazine again"): 8½ × 11; 4-6 pages; 20 lb. paper; illustrations; "rarely" photos. Network service in the animal field educating services for mostly professionals in the animal field; e.g., animal health technicians. Monthly. Estab. 1976. Circ. 5,608.
Needs: Animals: contemporary, experimental, historical, mainstream, regional. No stories unrelated to animals. Receives 12 unsolicited fiction mss/month. Buys one ms/issue; 12 mss/year. Length: Open. "Rarely" publishes short shorts. Occasionally critiques rejected mss. Recommends other markets.
How to Contact: Query first with theme, length, expected time of completion, photos/illustrations, if any, biographical sketch of author, all necessary credits or send complete ms. Report time varies (up to 4 months). SASE for query and ms. Simultaneous submissions OK. Sample copy and fiction guidelines for $2.90.
Payment/Terms: No payment. Acquires one-time rights.
Advice: Sponsors contests: theme changes but generally concerns the biggest topics of the year in the animal field. "Emotion, personal experience—make the person feel it. We are growing."

NEW ORLEANS REVIEW, (II), Box 195, Loyola University, New Orleans LA 70118. (504)865-2295. Editor: Ralph Adama. Magazine: 8½ × 11; 100 pages; 60 lb. Scott offset paper; 12+ King James C1S cover stock; photos. "Publishes poetry, fiction, translations, photographs, nonfiction on literature and film. Readership: those interested in current culture, literature." Quarterly. Estab. 1968. Circ. 1,000.
Needs: Literary, contemporary, translations. Buys 9-12 mss/year. Length: under 40 pages.
How to Contact: Send complete ms with SASE. Does not accept simultaneous submissions. Accepts disk submissions; inquire about system compatibility. Prefers hard copy with disk submission. Reports in 3 months. Sample copy for $9.
Payment/Terms: "Inquire." Pays on publication for first North American serial rights. Sends galleys to author.

THE NEW PRESS LITERARY QUARTERLY, (II), 53-35 Hollis Court Blvd., Flushing NY 11365. (212)592-3196. Editor: Joe Sullivan. Magazine: 8½ × 11; 40 pages; medium bond paper and thick cover stock; illustrations and photographs. "Poems, short stories, commentary, personal journalism. Original, informative and entertaining." Quarterly. Estab. 1984. Circ. 2,000.
Needs: Experimental, humor/satire, mainstream, mystery/suspense. No gratuitous violence. Receives 25 unsolicited mss/month. Accepts 5 mss/issue; 20 mss/year. Publishes ms 12 months after acceptance. Published new writers within the last year. Length: 4,000 words maximum; 100 words minimum. Also publishes literary essays, literary criticism and poetry. Sometimes critiques rejected mss.
How to Contact: Send complete ms with cover letter. Reports in 2 months. SASE. Simultaneous and reprint submissions OK. Sample copy for $4; fiction guidelines for SASE. $15 for one-year (4 issues) subscription.
Payment/Terms: Pays 3 contributor's copies, $15 maximum for each prose piece for first rights.

♣THE NEW QUARTERLY, New Directions in Canadian Writing, (II, IV), ELPP, University of Waterloo, Waterloo, Ontario N2L 3G1 Canada. (519)885-1212, ext. 2837. Managing Editor: Mary Merikle. Fiction Editors: Peter Hinchcliffe Kim Jernigan. Magazine: 6 × 9; 80-120 pages; perfect-bound cover, b&w cover photograph; photos with special issues. "We publish poetry, short fiction, excerpts from novels, interviews.

INSIDER VIEWPOINT

Be Specific When Writing Regional Fiction

The biggest challenge to a writer of regional fiction, according to Wally Gordon, editor and publisher of *New Frontiers of New Mexico*, is "to do two things at the same time: to express universal concerns, and do it in the context and with the metaphors of a specific place."

New Frontiers of New Mexico, a literary magazine started by Gordon more than two years ago, focuses on the interests of people living in the Southwest. "We are trying to use different forms of expression—fiction, nonfiction and poetry—to elucidate problems, lifestyles and concerns here in New Mexico," Gordon says. "I'm looking for writers who are concerned with the kind of conflicts that underlie contemporary life in the Southwest."

Wally Gordon

When writing for a regional publication, Gordon says, one of the first things a writer must do is read the publication to identify its audience. "I believe writing is a process of communication between the writer and the reader. It's important for a writer to keep in mind who his reader is." When speaking specifically about the readers of *New Frontiers*, he says, "There is a myth that the Southwest is largely a rural area. It is, in fact, the most urbanized part of the whole United States. Most people who subscribe to magazines here live either in or on the periphery of one of the four major cities in the Southwest. So you're not writing for a cowboy who spends his evenings reading a magazine or someone living on a mountaintop somewhere. There are such people and some subscribe to the magazine, but the concerns of the Southwest are increasingly those of people who live either in or near major metropolitan areas. You need to understand the region; you need to keep in mind the peculiarities of the audience."

Once you understand exactly who you're writing for, Gordon suggests, incorporate regional aspects into the story to capture the reader's attention. "It's not simply a matter of somebody taking a story that is set in Boston and changing the name Boston to Albuquerque," Gordon says of the distinction between regional and general fiction. Writers need to understand the dilemmas that people living in a particular region face on a day-to-day basis. "In the Southwest you are dealing with a lot of newcomers, people who have come to a new place they don't yet understand. Most of the concerns in the Southwest are the concerns of people everywhere—with a few additions. For example, this is a water-short part of the world; people dream of water out here. You see it in the way people write about the region, in the metaphors they use. A lot of times writers will include a paragraph or two of description in their stories to try to localize a region, but the description is so starry-eyed it's clear they don't really have a sense of the place. If a writer is going to include descriptions of the Southwest in his story, he needs to have a real sense of the place, a sense of not only the beautiful sunsets but of the harshness of the land, of the depth and complexity of it all."

Writing about the specific interests of a particular region offers a distinct challenge and new opportunities for writers. "We are open to far more different things than the commercial magazines," Gordon says. "Things like stream of consciousness pieces, or stories that can be difficult to penetrate and may require a second or third reading to fully understand—work that is more about character than action, that may appeal to a narrower, more specific audience than those who read magazines like *Playboy* or *Esquire*. Our average audience has a master's degree or beyond; it's an audience interested in ideas and willing to spend a little time pursuing them." Knowing this audience and understanding its lifestyles and concerns is key to getting published in regional magazines.

—Cindy Laufenberg

We are particularly interested in writing which stretches the bounds of realism. For those interested in Canadian literature." Quarterly.

Needs: "We look for writing which is fresh, innovative, well crafted. We promote beginning writers alongside more established ones. Ours is a humanist magazine—no gratuitous violence, though we are not afraid of material which is irreverent or unconventional. Our interest is more in the quality than the content of the fiction we see." Published recent special issues on magic, realism in Canadian writing, family fiction and Canadian Mennonite writing. Receives approximately 50 unsolicited mss/month. Buys 5-6 mss/issue; 20-24 mss/year. Publishes ms usually within 6 months after acceptance. Published work by Di Brandt, Patrick Roscoe and Steven Heighton; published new writers within the last year. Length: up to 20 pages. Publishes short shorts. Also publishes poetry.

How to Contact: Send complete ms with cover letter, which should include a short biographical note. Reports in 1-2 weeks on queries; approximately 3 months on mss. SASE for ms. Sample copy for $5.

Payment/Terms: Pays $100 and contributor's copies on publication for first North American serial rights.

Advice: "Send only one well-polished manuscript at a time. Persevere. Find your own voice. The primary purpose of little literary magazines like ours is to introduce new writers to the reading public. However, because we want them to appear at their best, we apply the same standards when judging novice work as when judging that of more established writers."

‡the new renaissance, (II), 9 Heath Rd., Arlington MA 02174. Fiction Editors: Louise T. Reynolds, Michal Anne Kuchauki and Patricia Michaud. Magazine: 6×9; 144-182 pages; 70 lb. paper; laminated cover stock; artwork; photos. "An international magazine of ideas and opinions, emphasizing literature and the arts, *tnr* takes a classicist position in literature and the arts. Publishes a variety of very diverse, quality fiction, always well crafted, sometimes experimental. *tnr* is unique among literary magazines for its marriage of the literary and visual arts with political/sociological articles and essays. We publish the beginning as well as the emerging and established writer." Biannually. Estab. 1968. Circ. 1,500.

• Work recently published in *the new renaissance* has been chosen for inclusion in *Editor's Choice III*, *Editor's Choice IV* and *Sudden Fiction*.

Needs: Serious, quality literary, humorous, off-beat fiction, occasionally prose poems and experimental fiction. Buys 4-5 mss/issue, 6-10 mss/year. Receives approximately 80-140 unsolicited fiction mss each month. Reads only from January 2 through February 28/29 and from September 1 through October 31. Agented fiction approx. 6-10%. Recently published work by Marvin Mandell, Richard Lynch, G.P. Vimal, Bennett Capers and Nicholas Emmett. Length of fiction: 3-36 pages. Also publishes articles, literary essays, literary criticism, poetry. Comments on rejected mss "if we feel we might be helpful or to let the writer know where we're coming from. If writers prefer not to have their mss very briefly commented on, we ask that they let us know at the time they submit."

How to Contact: Send complete ms with SASE of sufficient size for return. "Inform us if multiple submission. If you query, enclose SASE, IRC or stamped post card." Reluctantly accepts simultaneous submissions but "we ask that you notify us if the ms has been accepted elsewhere. If we haven't yet read your story, we will accept a substitution either at the time of notification of acceptance by another magazine or within 2 months." Reports in 7-10 months on mss. Publishes ms an average of 12-18 months after acceptance. Sample copy for $6.75 for 2 back issues, $7.50 or $9 for recent issue. Reviews novels and short story collections, also biography, poetry collections, etc.

Payment/Terms: Pays $42-85 after publication; 1 contributor's copy. Query for additional copies, discount with 5 or more copies. All fiction and poetry submissions are now tied into our awards program for best fiction and poetry published in a three-issue volume of *tnr*. Subscribers: $10 entry fee, non-subscribers, $15/year, for which writers will receive 2 back issues or a recent/current issue. Buys all rights in case of a later *tnr* book collection; otherwise, rights return to the writer.

Advice: "We're still seeing a lot of heavily plotted stories with stock and/or one-dimensional characters, and, all too often, predictable situations. These pieces are as wrong for us as the self-conscious 'poetic' or beautiful writing that simply describes an incident that matters only to the author. We're getting much too much 'So what?' fiction and fiction that is self-indulgent. We also don't want to see the heavily academic fiction that is well done but which has nothing to say. Nor do we want to see erotic or pornographic fiction whether or not it has 'classic' over or undertones. We're open on styles and subjects but we're not an 'anything goes' little/literary magazine. Study one or two issues and see what we're doing in fiction. We want writing that is personal, compelling, with that individual signature that shouts that it's your writing and not the writing of a classmate in a 'creative' writing class. The best fiction has a lasting quality—its appeal goes across generations, across boundaries. Writers who aren't interested in literature—whether it's contemporary, modern, 19th century or earlier—are, all too often, focused inward and on the things that the self feels are important. But the outside world may not agree. At *tnr*, we see writing more as a lens than a mirror. The external verities of our human experience remain very much the same one generation after another despite all our pretentions to being in a 'unique' age. What we look for is a story that has a singular view and a highly individualized way of expressing that view. If you feel compelled to share your vision, you're probably a writer we'd like to see."

NEW VOICES IN POETRY AND PROSE, (I), New Voices Publishing, P.O. Box 52196, Shreveport LA 71135. (318)865-2537. Editor: Cheryl White. Magazine: 8½×11; 16-24 pages; linen paper; illustrations. "Dedicated to publishing new writers; accept many types of fiction." Semiannual. Estab. 1991. Circ. 400.

Needs: Adventure, fantasy, historical (general), horror, humor/satire, literary, mainstream/contemporary, mystery/suspense, psychic/supernatural/occult, regional, religious/inspirational, romance, science fiction (soft/sociological). No "controversial themes; political; racist." Receives 20 unsolicited mss/month. Buys 3 mss/issue; 6-8 mss/year. Publishes ms 6 months after acceptance. Recently published work by William Parsons, Steffan Postaer and Susan Vreeland. Length: 4,000 words maximum. Publishes short shorts. Also publishes poetry. Often critiques or comments on rejected mss.

How to Contact: *Charges $5 reading fee for up to 2 short stories.* Send complete ms with cover letter. Should also send estimated word count, very brief bio and list of publications with submission. Reports in 2 months on mss. Send SASE for return of ms. Will consider simultaneous submissions and reprints. Sample copy for $5. Fiction guidelines free. Reviews novels and short story collections.

Payment/Terms: Pays 1 contributor's copy. Acquires one-time rights.

Advice: "A short story appeals to us when it *really tells a story* about human nature, or offers up a basic lesson about life. Develop characters well, so they are fleshed-out and real to life. Complicated plots can be a hindrance; stick to the simple."

✦**NeWEST REVIEW, (II, IV)**, Box 394, R.P.O. University, Saskatoon, Saskatchewan S7N 4J8 Canada. Editor: Gail Youngberg. Magazine: 40 pages; book stock; illustrations; photos. Magazine devoted to western Canada regional issues; "fiction, reviews, poetry for middle- to high-brow audience." Bimonthly (6 issues per year). Estab. 1975. Circ. 1,000.

Needs: "We want fiction of high literary quality, whatever its form and content. But we do have a heavy regional emphasis." Receives 15-20 unsolicited mss/month. Buys 1 ms/issue; 10 mss/year. Length: 2,500 words average; 1,500 words minimum; 5,000 words maximum. Sometimes recommends other markets.

How to Contact: "We like *brief* cover letters." Reports very promptly in a short letter. SAE, IRCs or Canadian postage. No multiple submissions. Sample copy for $5.

Payment/Terms: Pays $100 maximum on publication for one-time rights.

Advice: "Polish your writing. Develop your story line. Give your characters presence. If we, the readers, are to care about the people you create, you too must take them seriously."

NEXT PHASE, (I, II), 5A Green Meadow Dr., Nantucket MA 02554. (508)325-0411. Editor: Kim Guarnaccia. 8½×11; 48 pages. "Features the best of fiction, poetry and illustration by up-and-coming writers and artists. We publish quality work as long as it is environmentally and humanely oriented." Triannually. Estab. 1989. Circ. 2,200.

● *Next Phase* is known for its environmentally-conscious fiction.

Needs: Experimental, fantasy. Receives 15-25 unsolicited mss/month. Accepts 9 mss/issue; 25 mss/year. Publishes short shorts. Also publishes poetry (but poetry should be sent to Holly Day, University of Tampa, Box 1041, Tampa FL 33606). Critiques rejected mss.

How to Contact: Send complete manuscript with cover letter. SASE. Simultaneous and reprint submissions OK. Reports in 6 weeks. E-mail address: 76603.2224@compuserve.com. Sample copy for $4.95 includes postage.
Payment/Terms: Pays contributor's copies. Acquires one-time rights.
Advice: "We accept a broad range of fiction up to 4,000 words. We only accept environmentally or humanely-oriented fiction of all genres."

‡**NEXUS, (I)**, Wright State University, W016a Student Union, Dayton OH 45435. (513)873-5533. Editor: Tara Miller. Magazine: 7×10; 90-140 pages; good coated paper; heavy perfect-bound cover; b&w illustrations and photography. "International arts and literature for those interested." 3 times per year. Circ. 2,000.
  • *Nexus* has received the Gold Crown Award from the Columbia Scholastic Press Association for the past three years.
Needs: Contemporary, experimental, literary, regional, translations. No sci-fi, western, romance. Receives 25-30 unsolicited mss/month. Accepts 2-3 mss/issue; 6-10 mss/year. Does not read mss June-Sept. Publishes ms 2-6 months after acceptance. Length: 4,000 words average; 500 words minimum; 7,500 words maximum. Publishes short shorts of any length. Also publishes literary essays, literary criticism and poetry. Sometimes critiques rejected mss and recommends other markets.
How to Contact: Send complete manuscript with cover letter including "any previous publishers of your work. *Do not* explain anything about the story." Reports in 2-4 weeks on queries; 1-2 months on mss. SASE. Simultaneous, photocopied and reprint submissions OK. Sample copy for $5. Fiction guidelines for #10 SASE.
Payment/Terms: Pays contributor's copies. Acquires first North American serial rights.
Advice: "Simplicity and a perfection of style (description, simile, dialogue) always make a lasting impression. Good, careful translations receive favored readings."

‡**NIGHT SHADOWS, Tales to be Afraid of, (I, II)**, 13575 58th St. N., Clearwater FL 34620. Editor: Tom Hubbard. Magazine: 8½×11; 40-60 pages; 20 lb. paper, with heavy cover; b&w artwork and photos. "We are a forum for new or under published writers. At least 50% of each issue will feature new writers." Quarterly. Beginning circulation 200.
Needs: Horror, psychic/supernatural/occult only. No pornographic, racist or sexist material. Gore and violence should be kept to a minimum. Accepts 10-12 mss/issue; 40-50 mss/year. Length: 500 words minimum; 2,000 words maximum. Original b&w art accepted on occasion. Sometimes comments on rejected mss.
How to Contact: Send complete ms with cover letter. Should include estimated word count, and short bio. Please list publications, if any. Reports in 1-3 months on mss or art. Send SASE for reply, return of ms or art, or send disposable copies. No simultaneous submissions.
Payment/Terms: Pays 2 contributor's copies. Acquires one-time rights.
Advice: "It has to be frightening! If it's not, don't bother sending it. Good openings and believable characters are essential. No rip-offs of TV or movies, and no predictable endings. We are extremely familiar with the genre, so make sure it's your own creation. Also, a dull story, with only a few twists at the end, is no good to us. Our readers are well read and educated, so writers should keep that in mind. Sample copies and checks should be made payable to Tom Hubbard. Watch the magazine for upcoming contests and special theme issues."

NIGHTMARES, (I, II), New Illiad Publishing, P.O. Box 587, Rocky Hill CT 06067. Editor: Ed Kobialka, Jr. Magazine: 8½×11; 40-60 pages; 20 lb. paper; 80 lb. cover; illustrations. "*Nightmares* publishes horror, from the modern age or gothic. We publish any writer, beginning or established, who submits good material." Quarterly. Estab. 1994. Circ. 1,000.
  • The editor says he'd love to be able to wear a T-shirt that says "so many good stories, so little space."
Needs: Horror, supernatural/occult. Receives 50-70 unsolicited mss/month. Buys 8 mss/issue; 35 mss/year. Does not read during December. Publishes ms 1 year after acceptance. Length: 2,500 words average; 500 words minimum; 6,000 words maximum. Usually critiques or comments on rejected mss.
How to Contact: Send complete ms with a cover letter. Should include estimated word count, bio (1-2 paragraphs), Social Security number and list of publications. Reports in 1 month on queries; 2 months on mss. Send SASE for reply, return of ms or send a disposable copy of ms. Simultaneous and reprint submissions OK. Sample copy for $2.95. Fictions guidelines free.
Payment/Terms: Pays $10 maximum and 2 contributor's copies for first rights.
Advice: "It must be scary! Grab the reader's attention with a good opening; make your characters and places seem real; and don't make your ending predictable. Don't forget about the old, classic monsters—vampires, ghosts and demons still scare people. Graphic brutal violence and descriptive sex are unacceptable. Your goal as a writer should be to terrorize your reader without being disgusting or offensive."

‡**NIGHTSUN**, Department of English, Frostburg State University, Frostburg MD 21532. Editor: Douglas DeMars. Magazine: 6×9; 64 pages; recycled paper. "Although *Nightsun* is primarily a journal of poetry

and interviews, we are looking for excellent short-short fiction (5 pgs. maximum)." Annually. Estab. 1981. Circ. 300-500.

How to Contact: Send inquiry with SASE. No simultaneous submissions. Reports within 2-3 months. Sample copy for $6.50.

Payment/Terms: Pays 2 contributor's copies. Acquires one-time rights (rights revert to author after publication).

NIMROD, International Journal of Prose and Poetry, (II), Arts & Humanities Council of Tulsa, 2210 S. Main, Tulsa OK 74114. Editor-in-Chief: Francine Ringold. Magazine: 6×9; 160 pages; 60 lb. white paper; illustrations; photos. "We publish one thematic issue and one awards issue each year. A recent theme was 'Points North: The Arctic Circle,' a compilation of poetry, prose and fiction by authors from Alaska, Canada, Iceland, Norway and Siberia. We seek vigorous, imaginative, quality writing." Semiannually. Estab. 1956. Circ. 3,000.

● *Nimrod* received an Honorable Mention from the 1995 American Literary Magazine Awards.

Needs: "We accept contemporary poetry and/or prose. May submit adventure, ethnic, experimental, prose poem, science fiction or translations." Upcoming theme: "The City" (1996). Receives 120 unsolicited fiction mss/month. Published work by Janette Turner Hospital, Josephine Jacobson, Alice Walker, Francois Camoin and Gish Jen; published 15 new writers within the last year. Length: 7,500 words maximum. Also publishes poetry.

How to Contact: Reports in 3-5 months. Sample copy: "to see what *Nimrod* is all about, send $6 for a back issue. To receive a recent awards issue, send $8 (includes postage)."

Payment/Terms: Pays 2 contributor's copies, plus $5/page up to $25 total per author per issue for one-time rights.

Advice: "We have not changed our fiction needs: quality, vigor, distinctive voice. We have, however, increased the number of stories we print. See current issues. We look for fiction that is fresh, vigorous, distinctive, serious and humorous, seriously-humorous, unflinchingly serious, ironic—whatever. Just so it is quality. Strongly encourage writers to send #10 SASE for brochure for annual literary contest with prizes of $1,000 and $500."

96 Inc., (II), P.O. Box 15559, Boston MA 02215. (617)267-0543. Fiction Editors: Julie Anderson and Nancy Mehegan. Magazine: 8½×11; 50 pages; 20 lb. paper; matte cover; illustrations and photos. "*96 Inc.* promotes the process; integrates beginning/young with established writers; reaches out to audiences of all ages and backgrounds." Semiannually. Estab. 1992. Circ. 3,000.

● *96 Inc.* is a member of the Council of Literary Magazines and Presses and has received grants from numerous sources. Note they will consider long stories.

Needs: Gay, historical (general), humor/satire, lesbian, literary and translations. Receives 200 unsolicited mss/month. Buys 12-15 mss/issue; 30 mss/year. Agented fiction 10%. Published work by Teri Keough, M.E. McDonald, Martha Lufkin, Peter Keough and David Weiher. Length: 1,000 words minimum; 7,000 words maximum. Publishes short shorts. Also publishes literary essays, literary criticism and poetry. Sometimes critiques or comments on rejected mss.

How to Contact: Query first. Should include estimated word count, bio (100 words) and list of publications. Reports in 3 weeks on queries; 6-12 months on mss. Send SASE for reply, return of ms or send a disposable copy of ms. Simultaneous and electronic submissions OK. Sample copy for $5.50. Fiction guidelines for #10 SASE. Reviews novels and short story collections.

Payment/Terms: Pays $20-100 (depending on funds, not length or merit), free subscription and 4 contributor's copies on publication for one-time rights.

Advice: Looks for "good writing in any style. Pays attention to the process. Read at least one issue."

‡NITE-WRITER'S LITERARY ARTS JOURNAL, (I, II), Nite Owl Press, 3101 Schieck St., Suite 100, Pittsburgh PA 15227-4151. (412)882-2259. Editor: John A. Thompson, Sr. Magazine: 8½×11; 30-50 pages; bond paper; illustrations. "*Nite-Writer's Literary Arts Journal* is dedicated to the emotional intellectual with a creative perception of life." Quarterly. Estab. 1993. Circ. 100.

Needs: Adventure, erotica, historical, humor/satire, literary, mainstream/contemporary, religious/inspirational, romance, senior citizen/retirement, sports, young adult/teen (adventure). Plans special fiction issue or anthology. Receives 3-5 unsolicited mss/month. Buys 1-2 mss/issue; 5-8 mss/year. Publishes ms within 1 year after acceptance. Recently published work by Alan Britt and Robert Boucheron. Length: 150 words average; 150 words minimum; 250 words maximum. Publishes short shorts. Also publishes literary essays, literary criticism, poetry.

How to Contact: Often critiques or comments on rejected ms. Send complete ms with a cover letter. Should include estimated word count, 1-page bio, list of publications. Reports in 4-6 weeks. Send SASE for return of ms. Simultaneous submissions OK. Sample copy for $6, 9×13 SAE and 6 first-class stamps. Fiction guidelines for legal size SASE.

Payment/Terms: Does not pay. Acquires first North American serial rights. Sponsors contests.

NOCTURNAL ECSTASY, Vampire Coven, (I, II, IV), Nocturnal Productions, P.O. Box 147, Palos Heights IL 60463-0147. Editor: Darlene Daniels. Magazine: 8½×11; 75 pages; 20 lb. white paper; glossy cover; illustrations and photos. "We publish material on vampires, music, movies, gothic esoteria, erotica, horror, sado-masochism." Triannually. Estab. 1990. Circ. 10,000.

Needs: Vampire related: adventure, children's/juvenile (10-12 years), erotica, experimental, gay, horror, humor/satire, lesbian, mystery/suspense (romantic suspense), psychic/supernatural/occult; romance (gothic), science fiction (hard science sf), young adult/teen (horror, romance). Plans to publish special fiction issue or anthology. Receives 100 unsolicited mss/month. Accepts 6 mss/issue; 40 mss/year. Published work by PJ Roberts, Jeffrey Stadt and Dale Hochstein. Length: 2,000 words average; 500 words minimum; 4,000 words maximum. Publishes short shorts. Also publishes literary essays, literary criticism and poetry. Sometimes critiques or comments on rejected ms.

How to Contact: Send complete ms with a cover letter. Should include estimated word count and ¼-page bio. Reports in 1 month on queries; 2 months on mss. Send SASE for reply, return of ms or send a disposable copy of ms. Simultaneous, reprint and electronic submissions OK. Sample copy for $6. Fiction guidelines for $1 or 4 first-class stamps. Reviews novels and short story collections. Send books to NEVC Reviews.

Payment/Terms: No payment. Acquires one-time rights. Not copyrighted.

Advice: Looks for "originality, ability to hold reader's interest." Would like to see "more erotica, originality; no previously established characters of other authors."

THE NOCTURNAL LYRIC, (I), Box 115, San Pedro CA 90733. (310)519-9220. Editor: Susan Moon. Digest: 5½×8½; 40 pages; illustrations. "We are a non-profit literary journal, dedicated to printing fiction by new writers for the sole purpose of getting read by people who otherwise might have never seen their work." Bimonthly. Estab. 1987. Circ. 400.

Needs: Experimental, fantasy, horror, humor/satire, psychic/supernatural/occult, science fiction, poetry. "We will give priority to unusual, creative pieces." Receives 50 unsolicited mss/month. Publishes ms 10-12 months after acceptance. Publishes short shorts. Length: 2,000 words maximum. Also publishes poetry.

● The editors are most interested in cutting edge, bizarre horror.

How to Contact: Send complete ms with cover letter. Cover letter should include "something about the author, areas of fiction he/she is interested in." Reports in 2 weeks on queries; 4-6 months on mss. SASE. Simultaneous and reprint submissions OK. Sample copy for $3 (checks to Susan Moon). Fiction guidelines for #10 SASE.

Payment/Terms: Pays in gift certificates for subscription discounts. Publication not copyrighted.

Advice: "Please stop wasting your postage sending us things that are in no way bizarre. We're getting more into strange, surrealistic horror and fantasy, or silly, satirical horror. If you're avant-garde, we want you! We're mainly accepting things that are bizarre all the way through, as opposed to ones that only have a surprise bizarre ending."

‡NONSENSE, "Hofstra University's Only *Intentional* Humor Magazine", (II), Hofstra University Press, Room 203, Student Center, 200 Hofstra University, Hempstead NY 11550-1022. (516)463-2442. Fax: (516)463-6030. Editor: Jeff Belanger. Editors change periodically. Magazine: approximately 7×10; 24 pages; 50 lb. offset paper; illustrations and photos. "*Nonsense*'s intended audience is college-aged, give or take a few years." Appears 6 times per year. Estab. 1983. Circ. 5,000.

● *Nonsense* won second place in the Society of Collegiate Journalists awards for "Special Interest Magazine" in 1993-1994.

Needs: Humor/satire. List of upcoming themes available for SASE. Receives 10-12 unsolicited mss/month. Buys 5-6 mss/issue; 30 mss/year. Does not read between June and August. Recently published work by Sam Toperoff. Length: 800 words average; 300 words minimum; 1,000 words maximum. Publishes short shorts. Length: 300 words. Also publishes poetry. Sometimes comments on rejected ms.

How to Contact: Send complete ms with a cover letter. Send a disposable copy of ms. Simultaneous and electronic submissions OK. E-mail address: nonsense@vaxc.hofstra.edu. Sample copy for $2, 9×12 SASE. Fiction guidelines free for any size SASE.

Payment/Terms: Pays free subscription to the magazine and 5 contributor's copies; additional copies for $1. Acquires one-time rights.

Advice: "We don't want our writers to try and be politically correct or incorrect—just funny. Don't hold back. Read the magazine and get a feel for our style. Avoid sending stories about marriage, erotica and stories that are too politically oriented."

✝ *The double dagger before a listing indicates that the listing is new in this edition. New markets are often the most receptive to submissions by new writers.*

NON-STOP MAGAZINE, The Magazine of Alternative SF, (I, II), Non-Stop Magazine, P.O. Box 981, Peck Slip Station, New York NY 10272-0981. Editor: K.J. Cypret. Magazine: 8½×11; 52 pages; glossy cover, illustrations and photos. Quarterly. Estab. 1993.
Needs: Fantasy (modern), science fiction, translations. Science fiction with strong literary/idea content. Planning special issue on alternative history science fiction. Also planning future special all fiction issue or anthology. Receives 300-450 unsolicited mss/month. Buys 3-5 mss/issue; 18 mss/year. Does not read mss July, August or December. Publishes ms 3-18 months after acceptance. Published work by Don Webb, Barry N. Malzberg and Paul Di Filippo. Length: 4,000 words average; 1,000 words minimum; 9,000 words maximum. Publishes literary essays, science articles and literary criticism. Sometimes critiques or comments on ms.
How to Contact: Send complete ms with a cover letter. Should include estimated word count, 1- or 2-page bio and list of publications. Reports in 2-3 weeks on queries; 3 months on mss. SASE for reply. Send a disposable copy of ms. No simultaneous submissions. Reprint submissions OK from outside North America. Sample copy for $4.95. Reviews novels and short story collections.
Payment/Terms: Pays 3-6¢/word and 2 contributor's copies for first North American serial rights. Sends galleys to author.
Advice: Looks for "strong writing with believable characters and new science extrapolation. Read *Non-Stop* to see what we're publishing. We're seeing too many science fiction ideas coming from watching movies or TV shows. We will reject these instantly. We like to see science and technology used as a springboard for a story."

THE NORTH AMERICAN REVIEW, University of Northern Iowa, Cedar Falls IA 50614. (319)273-6455. Editor: Robley Wilson. Publishes quality fiction. Bimonthly. Estab. 1815. Circ. 4,500.
• This magazine has been backlogged, but editors say they plan to begin reading fiction in January 1997.
Needs: Open (literary).
How to Contact: Send complete ms with SASE. Sample copy for $4.
Payment/Terms: Pays approximately $20/printed page; 2 contributor's copies on publication for first North American serial rights. $3.50 charge for extras.
Advice: "We stress literary excellence and read 3,000 manuscripts a year to find an average of 35 stories that we publish. Please *read* the magazine first."

NORTH ATLANTIC REVIEW, (II), North Eagle Corp. of NY, 15 Arbutus Lane, Stony Brook NY 11790. (516)751-7886. Editor: John Gill. Magazine: 7×9; 320 pages; glossy cover. "General interest." Estab. 1989. Circ. 1,000.
• *North Atlantic Review* tends to accept traditional fiction.
Needs: General fiction. Has published special fiction issue. Accepts 40 mss/year. Publishes ms 6-10 months after acceptance. Length: 3,000-7,000 words average. Publishes short shorts. Sometimes critiques rejected mss.
How to Contact: Send complete ms with cover letter. Reports in 5-6 months on queries. SASE. Simultaneous and photocopied submissions OK. Sample copy for $10.

NORTH DAKOTA QUARTERLY, (II), University of North Dakota, Box 7209, University Station, Grand Forks ND 58202. (701)777-3321. Editor: Robert W. Lewis. Fiction Editor: William Borden. Poetry Editor: Jay Meek. Magazine: 6×9; 200 pages; bond paper; illustrations; photos. Magazine publishing "essays in humanities; some short stories; some poetry." University audience. Quarterly. Estab. 1910. Circ. 800.
• Work published in *North Dakota Quarterly* was selected for inclusion in *The O. Henry Awards* anthology. The editors are especially interested in work by Native American writers.
Needs: Contemporary, ethnic, experimental, feminist, historical, humor/satire and literary. Receives 20-30 unsolicited mss/month. Acquires 4 mss/issue; 16 mss/year. Recently published work by Naguib Mahfouz, Jerry Bumpus, Carol Shields, Rilla Askew and Chris Mazza; published new writers within the last year. Length: 3,000-4,000 words average. Also publishes literary essays, literary criticism, poetry.
How to Contact: Send complete ms with cover letter. "But they need not be much more than hello; please read this story; I've published (if so, best examples) . . ." SASE. Reports in 3 months. Publishes ms an average of 1 year after acceptance. Sample copy for $5. Reviews novels and short story collections.
Payment/Terms: Pays 5 contributor's copies; 20% discount for extras; year's subscription. Acquires one-time rights.

NORTHEAST ARTS MAGAZINE, (II), Boston Arts Organization, Inc., J.F.K. Station, P.O. Box 6061, Boston MA 02114. Editor: Mr. Leigh Donaldson. Magazine: 6½×9½; 32-40 pages; matte finish paper; card stock cover; illustrations and photographs. Bimonthly. Estab. 1990. Circ. 750.
Needs: Ethnic, gay, historical, literary, mystery/suspense (private eye), prose poem (under 2,000 words). No obscenity, racism, sexism, etc. Upcoming themes: "the culinary arts, window-dressing, unique boat building, jazz history . . ." Receives 50 unsolicited mss/month. Accepts 1-2 mss/issue; 5-7 mss/year. Publishes

ms 2-4 months after acceptance. Agented fiction 20%. Length: 750 words preferred. Publishes short shorts. Sometimes critiques rejected mss.

How to Contact: Send complete ms with cover letter. Include short bio. Reports in 1 month on queries; 2-4 months on mss. SASE. Simultaneous submissions OK. Sample copy for $4.50, SAE and 75¢ postage. Fiction guidelines free.

Payment/Terms: Pays 2 contributor's copies. Acquires first North American serial rights. Sometimes sends galleys to author.

Advice: Looks for "creative/innovative use of language and style. Unusual themes and topics."

NORTHEAST CORRIDOR, (II), Beaver College, 450 S. Easton Rd., Glenside PA 19038. (215)572-2963. Editor: Susan Balée. Fiction Editor: Peggy Finn. Magazine: 6¾×10; 120-180 pages; 60 lb. white paper; glossy, perfect-bound cover; illustrations and photos. "Interested in writers and themes treating the Northeast Corridor region of America. Literary fiction, poetry, essays." Semiannually. Estab. 1993. Circ. 1,000.

● *Northeast Corridor* publishes an annual theme issue. Check the magazine and *Poets & Writers* for announcements. The magazine has received grants from the Daphne Foundation and the Ruth and Robert Satter Foundation.

Needs: Literary: excerpted novel, ethnic/multicultural, feminist, humor/satire, literary, regional, translations. No religious, western, young adult, science fiction, juvenile, horror. Planning special issue on "Autobiography" in 1996. List of upcoming themes available for SASE. Planning future special fiction issue or anthology. Receives 100 unsolicited mss/month. Buys 2-6 mss/issue; 4-12 mss/year. Reads mss infrequently during June, July and August. Publishes ms 6 months after acceptance. Recently published work by Glen Weldon, Eleanor Wilner and Stephen Dobyns. Length: 2,500 words average; 1,000 words minimum; 4,500 words maximum. Publishes literary essays, literary criticism and poetry. Often critiques or comments on rejected ms.

How to Contact: Send complete ms with a cover letter. Include word count, 1-2 line bio and publications list. Reports in 2-4 months on mss. SASE for reply, return of ms or send a disposable copy of ms. Simultaneous submissions OK if indicated. Sample copy for $5, 9×12 SAE and $1.21 postage. Fiction guidelines for #10 SASE.

Payment/Terms: Pays $10-100 and 2 contributor's copies on publication for first North American serial rights; additional copies for $3.50/copy.

Advice: "In selecting fiction we look for love of language, developed characters, believable conflict, metaphorical prose, satisfying resolution. Read everything from Chekov to Alice Munro and write at least 10-20 stories before you start trying to send them out. We would like to see more humor. Writers should avoid sending work that is 'therapy' rather than 'art.' "

NORTHERN CONTOURS, (I, II, IV), Plumas County Arts Commission, P.O. Box 618, Quincy CA 95971. (916)283-3402. Fax: (916)283-4626. Editor: Cindy Robinson. Magazine: 5f4×7½; 94 pages; recycled paper; glossy cover; b&w artwork and photos. Semiannually. Estab. 1994.

Needs: Literary, mainstream/contemporary, regional. *Only publishes work from residents of northern California or northwestern Nevada*. List of upcoming deadlines available for SASE. Accepts up to 2,500 words for short fiction. Publishes ms 3-6 months after acceptance. Published work by Victoria Ashley and Greg Gonzales. Publishes short shorts. Also publishes poetry. Sometimes critiques or comments on rejected ms.

How to Contact: Submit complete ms with brief cover letter. Reports in 3 months. Send SASE for return of ms or send a disposable copy of ms. Simultaneous submissions OK, "but please inform." Sample copy for $5. Fiction guidelines for #10 SASE.

Payment/Terms: Pays 2 contributor's copies; additional copies available for a discount. Acquires one-time rights.

Advice: "Obtain a sample copy. Read our guidelines. Please don't submit if you don't reside within northern California or northwestern Nevada."

NORTHWEST REVIEW, (II), 369 PLC, University of Oregon, Eugene OR 97403. (503)346-3957. Editor: John Witte. Fiction Editor: Elizabeth Claman. Magazine: 6×9; 140-160 pages; high quality cover stock; illustrations; photos. "A general literary review featuring poems, stories, essays and reviews, circulated nationally and internationally. For a literate audience in avant-garde as well as traditional literary forms; interested in the important writers who have not yet achieved their readership." Triannually. Estab. 1957. Circ. 1,200.

● *Northwest Review* has received the Governor's Award for the Arts regularly. The work included in *Northwest Review* tends to be literary, heavy on character and theme.

Needs: Contemporary, experimental, feminist, literary and translations. Accepts 4-5 mss/issue, 12-15 mss/year. Receives approximately 100 unsolicited fiction mss each month. Published work by Diana Abu-Jaber, Madison Smartt Bell, Maria Flook and Charles Marvin; published new writers within the last year. Length: "Mss longer than 40 pages are at a disadvantage." Also publishes literary essays, literary criticism, poetry. Critiques rejected mss when there is time. Sometimes recommends other markets.

How to Contact: Send complete ms with SASE. "No simultaneous submissions are considered." Reports in 3-4 months. Sample copy for $3.50. Reviews novels and short story collections. Send books to John Witte.

Payment/Terms: Pays 3 contributor's copies and one-year subscription; 40% discount on extras. Acquires first rights.

NORTHWOODS JOURNAL, A Magazine for Writers, (I), Conservatory of American Letters, P.O. Box 298, Thomaston ME 04861. (207)354-0998. Editor: R.W. Olmsted. Fiction Editor: Ken Sieben. Magazine: 5½×8½; 32-64 pages; white paper; 65 lb. card cover; some illustrations and photographs. "No theme, no philosophy—for people who read for entertainment." Quarterly. Estab. 1993. Circ. 500.
- Conservatory of American Letters is also connected with *Dan River Anthology* listed in this section and the Dan River Press listed in the Small Press section.

Needs: Adventure, erotica, experimental, fantasy (science fantasy, sword and sorcery), literary, mainstream/contemporary, mystery/suspense (amateur sleuth, police procedural, private eye/hard-boiled, romantic suspense), psychic/supernatural/occult, regional, romance (gothic, historical), science fiction (hard science, soft/sociological), sports, westerns (frontier, traditional). Publishes special fiction issue or anthology. Receives 50 unsolicited mss/month. Accepts 12-15 mss/year. Length: 2,500 words maximum. Also publishes literary essays, literary criticism and poetry.

How to Contact: Read guidelines *before* submitting. Send complete ms with a cover letter. Include word count and list of publications. Reports in 1-2 days on queries; by next deadline plus 5 days on mss. Send SASE for reply, return of ms or send a disposable copy of ms. No simultaneous submissions. Electronic submissions OK. Sample copies: $5 next issue, $7.50 current issue, $10 back issue (if available) all postage paid. Fiction guidelines for #10 SASE. Reviews novels and short story collections. Send books to James A. Freeman, review editor.

Payment/Terms: Varies, "minimum $5/published page on acceptance for first North American serial rights."

Advice: "Read guidelines, read the things we've published. Know your market."

‡❦**NORTHWORDS, The Journal of Canadian Content in Speculative Literature, (II)**, The Society for Canadian Content in Speculative Arts and Literature, P.O. Box 5752, Merivale Depot, Nepean Ontario K2C 3M1 Canada. (613)596-4105. Editor: James M. Botte. Magazine: 8½×11; 56-60 pages; white offset (120m) paper; 10 pt. Cornwall cover; illustrations and photos. "*Northwords* publishes great fiction, news, reviews, articles, essays, interviews and poetry by Canadians, with a distinctive Canadian slant, or of general interest to everyone who reads or writes speculative literature." Quarterly. Estab. 1993. Circ. 250.

Needs: Fantasy (science fantasy, sword and sorcery), horror, psychic/supernatural/occult, science fiction. Plans special fiction issue or anthology. Receives 10 unsolicited mss/month. Buys 3-6 mss/issue; 16-20 mss/year. Publishes ms 2-6 months after acceptance. Recently published work by Edovan Belkom, Dr. David Stephenson and Christina Morgan. Length: 10 word minimum; 10,000 words maximum. Publishes short shorts. Also publishes literary essays, literary criticism and poetry. Often critiques or comments on rejected ms.

How to Contact: Query first. Should include estimated word count, 500-word bio, list of publications. "If Canadian, include a full bio and list of published works (for possible bio article)." Reports in 3 months. Send SASE for reply, return of ms or send a disposable copy of ms. Simultaneous, reprint and electronic submissions OK. E-mail address: northwords@diana.ocunix.on.ca. Sample copy for $6. Fiction guidelines for #10 SASE. Reviews novels and short story collections. Send books to Attn: Book Review Coordinator. (Works must be by a Canadian or have some demonstratably Canadian angle to be reviewed.)

Payment/Terms: Pays $3/final printed page in magazine and 1 copy of magazine; additional copies for $3.50 (varies depending on issue). "We reserve the right to reprint the story." Sponsors contests for Canadian writers only. Send SASE for info.

Advice: "Get guidelines (send SASE). They contain current requirements and trends, deadlines, and other advice. Buy a sample copy. We want better characterization; 'stronger' material that ruthlessly tackles today's ethical and moral dilemmas within a speculative fiction framework."

NUTHOUSE, Essays, Stories and Other Amusements, (II), Twin Rivers Press, P.O. Box 119, Ellenton FL 34222. Editor: D.A. White. Magazine: digest-sized; 12-16 pages; bond paper; illustrations and photos. "Humor of all genres for an adult readership that is not easily offended." Published every 6 weeks. Estab. 1993. Circ. 100.

Needs: Humor/satire: erotica, experimental, fantasy, feminist, historical (general), horror, literary, mainstream/contemporary, mystery/suspense, psychic/supernatural/occult, romance, science fiction and westerns. Plans annual "Halloween Party" issue featuring humorous verse and fiction with a horror theme. Receives 12-30 unsolicited mss/month. Accepts 3-5 mss/issue; 30 mss/year. Publishes ms 6 months after acceptance. Published work by Ken Rand, Don Webb and P. Andrew Miller. Length: 500 words average; 100 words minimum; 1,000 words maximum. Publishes short shorts. Length: 100-250 words. Also publishes literary essays, literary criticism and poetry. Often critiques or comments on rejected mss.

How to Contact: Send complete ms with a cover letter. Should include estimated word count, bio (paragraph) and list of publications. Reports in 2-4 weeks on mss. SASE for return of ms or send disposable copy of ms. Simultaneous and reprint submissions OK. E-mail address: Nuthous499@aol.com. Sample copy for $1 (payable to Twin Rivers Press). Fiction guidelines for #10 SASE.

Payment/Terms: Pays 1 contributor's copy. Acquires one-time rights. Not copyrighted.
Advice: Looks for "laugh-out-loud prose. Strive for original ideas; read the great humorists—Saki, Woody Allen, Robert Benchley, Garrison Keillor, John Irving—and learn from them. We are turned off by sophomoric attempts at humor built on a single, tired, overworked gag or pun; give us a story with a beginning, middle and end."

THE OAK, (I), 1530 7th St., Rock Island IL 61201. (309)788-3980. Editor: Betty Mowery. 8½×11; 8-14 pages. "Anything of help to writers." Bimonthly. Estab. 1991. Circ. 385.
Needs: Adventure, contemporary, experimental, humor/satire, mainstream, mystery/suspense, prose poem. No erotica. Receives about 12 mss/month. Accepts up to 6 mss/issue. Publishes ms within 3 months of acceptance. Published new writers within the last year. Length: 500 words maximum. Publishes short shorts. Length: 200 words.
How to Contact: Send complete ms. Reports in 1 week. SASE. Simultaneous and reprint submissions OK. Sample copy for $2. Subscription $10 for 6 issues.
Payment/Terms: None, but not necessary to buy a copy in order to be published. Acquires first rights.
Advice: "Just send a manuscript, but first read a copy of our publication to get an idea of what type of material we take. Please send SASE. If not, manuscripts *will not* be returned. Be sure name and address is on the manuscript."

OASIS, A Literary Magazine, (I, II), P.O. Box 626, Largo FL 34649-0626. (813)449-8126. Editor: Neal Storrs. Magazine: 70 pages. "Literary magazine first, last and always—looking for styles that delight and amaze, that are polished and poised. Next to that, content considerations relatively unimportant—open to all." Quarterly. Estab. 1992. Circ. 500.
Needs: High-quality writing (literary). Receives 150 unsolicited mss/month. Accepts 6 mss/issue; 24 mss/year. Publishes ms 4-6 months after acceptance. Published work by Vijay Dan Detha, Alberto Fuguet, Mark Wisniewski and James Sallis. Length: 5,000 words preferred; no minimum or maximum. Also publishes literary essays and poetry. Often critiques or comments on rejected mss.
How to Contact: Send complete ms with or without a cover letter. Reports "in same day." Send SASE for reply, return of ms or send a disposable copy of ms. Simultaneous and reprint submissions OK. Sample copy for $6.50. Fiction guidelines for #10 SASE.
Payment/Terms: Pays $15-50 and 1 contributor's copy on publication for first rights.

OBSIDIAN II: BLACK LITERATURE IN REVIEW, (II, IV), Dept. of English, North Carolina State University, Raleigh NC 27695-8105. (919)515-4153. Editor: Gerald Barrax. Fiction Editor: Susie R. Powell. Magazine: 6×9; approx. 130 pages. "Creative works in English by black writers, scholarly critical studies by all writers on black literature in English." Published 2 times/year (spring/summer, fall/winter). Estab. 1975. Circ. 500.
Needs: Ethnic (pan-African), feminist. No poetry, fiction or drama mss not written by black writers. Accepts 7-9 mss/year. Published new writers within the last year. Length: 1,500-10,000 words.
How to Contact: Send complete ms in duplicate with SASE. Reports in 3 months. Publishes ms an average of 4-6 months after acceptance. Sample copy for $5.
Payment/Terms: Pays in contributor's copies. Acquires one-time rights. Sponsors contests occasionally; guidelines published in magazine.

‡OFFICE NUMBER ONE, (I, II), 2111 Quarry Rd., Austin TX 78703. Editor: Carlos B. Dingus. Magazine: 8½×11; 12 pages; 60 lb. standard paper; b&w illustrations and photos. "I look for short stories, imaginary news stories or essays (under 400 words) that can put a reader on edge—but *not* because of profanity or obscenity, rather because the story serves to jolt the reader away from a consensus view of the world." Quarterly. Estab. 1989. Circ. 1,000.
Needs: Fictional news articles, experimental, fantasy, horror, humor/satire, literary, psychic/supernatural/occult, also fictional reviews. Upcoming themes: "I have a generic bad news page, and generic good news. Need articles about escaping from somewhere or something, or capturing and defeating through transformation. Limericks about fishing and fish, harvests & dogs." Receives 6 unsolicited mss/month. Buys 1-3 mss/issue; 6 mss/year. Publishes ms 4-6 months after acceptance. Recently published work by Jim Sullivan. Length: 30 word minimum; 400 words maximum. Also publishes literary essays, literary criticism and poetry. Sometimes critiques or comments on rejected mss.
How to Contact: Send complete ms with optional cover letter. Should include estimated word count and summary of article and intent ("How does this reach who?") with submission. Reports in 4-6 weeks on mss. Send SASE (or IRC) for reply, return of ms or send disposable copy of ms. Will consider simultaneous submissions, reprints. E-mail address: onocdingus@aol.com. Sample copy for $2 with SAE and 3 first-class stamps or 3 IRCs. Fiction guidelines for SAE and 1 first-class stamp or 1 IRC.
Payment/Terms: Pays 1 contributor's copy. Additional copies for $1 plus postage. Acquires one-time rights.
Advice: "Clean writing, no unnecessary words, perfect word choice, clear presentation of an idea. Make the piece perfect. Express *one* good idea. Write for an audience that you can identify. Be able to say why you write what you write. I'm planning to publish more *shorter* fiction. I plan to be more up-beat and to

focus on a journalistic style—but I will broaden what can be accomplished within this style."

THE OGALALA REVIEW, P.O. Box 628, Guymon OK 73942. Magazine: all issues are different but an example of a recent issue is digest-sized; 80-120 pages; flat-spined; glossy cover. "Mainstream literature for a general and academic audience." Semiannually. Estab. 1990. Circ. 400.
  • The magazine is now primarily interested in mainstream or experimental literary fiction.
Needs: Mainstream and experimental literary fiction. Receives 30-50 unsolicited mss/month. Buys 3 mss/issue. Publishes ms 1 year after acceptance. Length: Up to 10,000 words. Publishes short shorts. Also publishes poetry and essays.
How to Contact: Send complete ms with SASE. "Cover letter OK but not required." Reports in up to 4 months. "Considers simultaneous submissions, but writer should notify us promptly of acceptance elsewhere. No previously published material." Sample copy for $5.
Payment/Terms: Pays in contributor's copies, plus small honorarium when funds are available. Acquires first rights.
Advice: "Besides mainstream fiction, we use much material that is hard to place in mainstream markets—long stories, prose poems, unusual subjects and approaches. We are also interested in seeing creative nonfiction and work that bridges the gap between fiction and essay. Many of the stories we receive are competent; few are exciting."

THE OHIO REVIEW, (II), 209C Ellis Hall, Ohio University, Athens OH 45701-2979. (614)593-1900. Editor: Wayne Dodd. Assistant Editor: Robert Kinsley. Magazine: 6×9; 144 pages; illustrations on cover. "We attempt to publish the best poetry and fiction written today. For a mainly literary audience." Triannually. Estab. 1971. Circ. 3,000.
Needs: Contemporary, experimental, literary. "We lean toward contemporary on all subjects." Receives 150-200 unsolicited fiction mss/month. Buys 3 mss/issue. Does not read mss June 1-August 31. Publishes ms 6 months after acceptance. Also publishes poetry. Sometimes critiques rejected mss and/or recommends other markets.
How to Contact: Query first or send complete ms with cover letter. Reports in 6 weeks. SASE. Sample copy for $6. Fiction guidelines for #10 SASE.
Payment/Terms: Pays $5/page, free subscription to magazine and 2 contributor's copies on publication for first North American serial rights. Sends galleys to author.
Advice: "We feel the short story is an important part of the contemporary writing field and value it highly. Read a copy of our publication to see if your fiction is of the same quality. So often people send us work that simply doesn't fit our needs."

‡OLD CROW REVIEW, (I, II), FKB Press, P.O.Box 662, Amherst MA 01004-0662. Editor: John Gibney. Magazine: 5½×8½; 100 pages; 20 lb. paper; 90 lb. cover stock; illustrations and photos. Semiannually. Estab. 1991. Circ. 500.
Needs: Erotica, experimental, literary, mainstream/contemporary, psychic/supernatural/occult, regional, translations. Receives 20-40 unsolicited mss/month. Accepts 3-5 mss/issue; 6-10 mss/year. Publishes ms 1-3 months after acceptance. Agented fiction 25%. Recently published work by William Monahan, Bernard Hewitt and Elizabeth Borden-Haltwell. Length: 3,000 words average; 6,000 words maximum. Publishes short shorts. Also publishes literary essays, literary criticism and poetry.
How to Contact: Send complete ms with a cover letter. Should include estimated word count, bio (2-5 sentences) and list of publications. Reports in 1 month on queries; 2 months on mss. Send SASE for reply, return of ms or send a disposable copy of ms. Simultaneous, reprint and electronic submissions OK. E-mail address: tkelley@ais.smith.edu. Sample copy for $5. Fiction guidelines for #10 SASE.
Payment/Terms: Pays 1 contributor's copy; additional copies for $5.
Advice: "A piece must seem true to us. If it strikes us as a truth we never even suspected, we build an issue around it. Visions, or fragments of visions, of a new myth emerging at the millenial end are welcome. We haven't seen enough writers taking risks with their stories. Avoid sending pieces which sound just like somebody else's."

THE OLD RED KIMONO, (II), Box 1864, Rome GA 30162. (706)295-6312. Editors: Valerie Gilreath and Jonathan Hershey. Magazine: 8×11; 65-70 pages; white offset paper; 10 pt. board cover stock. Annually. Estab. 1972. Circ. 1,200.
Needs: Literary. "We will consider good fiction regardless of category." Receives 20-30 mss/month. Accepts 6-8 mss/issue. Does not read mss March 15-September 1. "Issue out in May every year." Recently published work by Ruth Moon Kempher, David Huddle and Peter Huggins. Length: 2,000-3,000 words preferred. Publishes short shorts. Also publishes poetry.
How to Contact: Send complete ms with cover letter. Reports in 2 weeks on queries; 2-3 months on mss. SASE. Simultaneous submissions OK, but "we would like to be told." Fiction guidelines for #10 SASE.
Payment/Terms: Pays in contributor's copies. Acquires first rights.

THE OLYMPIA REVIEW, (II), 3430 Pacific Ave. SE, Suite A-6254, Olympia WA 98501. Editor: Michael McNeilley. Managing Editor: Stephanie Brooks. Fiction Editor: Frank Till. Magazine: 5½×8½; 64 pages;

60 lb. text paper; C1S coated cover; perfect-bound; with stampings, illustrations and photos. "Our motto: 'Barrier-free writing for the 90s.' Educated, intelligent audience, in our community and nationwide: bartenders, attorneys, teachers, librarians, gillnetters, hard rock miners, artists, city council members, cashiers, computer operators and members of congress." Published 2-4 times yearly. Estab. 1993. Circ. 750-1,000.

Needs: Adventure, erotica, ethnic/multicultural, experimental, feminist, historical, humor/satire, literary, mainstream/contemporary, regional, science fiction (speculative fiction), translations. "No religious, genre, formula fiction, MFA minimalist autojournalism, first drafts." Publishes anthology. Accepts 2-3 mss/issue; 4-8 mss/year. Publishes ms up to 6 months after acceptance. Length: 3,500 words maximum. Publishes short shorts. Also publishes literary essays, literary criticism, poetry.

How to Contact: Send complete ms with a cover letter. Should include estimated word count, bio (25-50 words), Social Security number and list of publications. Reports in 2 months on mss. Send SASE for reply or return of ms. Simultaneous and electronic submissions OK. Sample copy for $4.95. Fiction guidelines for #10 SASE. Reviews novels and short story collections.

Payment/Terms: Pays 1 contributor's copy; additional copies for $3.50. Acquires one-time rights. Sends galleys to author.

Advice: "I look for fiction that draws me in. An authentic voice. An interesting character, setting, situation. A story I want to read over again. There are no set criteria. Make your own critera . . . let the excellence of your writing speak for itself. *OR* promises to listen. We recommend patience. Giving everything a thorough reading takes time. Take time yourself—in manuscript preparation, in editing and proofreading, to make sure your story says exactly what you mean it to say. Wait a bit after completing it before sending it out—sometimes new meanings appear in time, that ask for further development. Patience. Additionally, support the small presses you like best. Small press subscriptions make all this possible."

✦ON SPEC, The Canadian Magazine of Speculative Writing, (II), The Copper Pig Writers' Society, Box 4727, Edmonton, Alberta T6E 5G6 Canada. (403)413-0215. Magazine: 5×8; 96 pages; illustrations. "Provides a venue for Canadian speculative writing—science fiction, fantasy, horror, magic realism." Quarterly. Estab. 1989. Circ. 2,000.

Needs: Fantasy and science fiction. Receives 50 mss/month. Buys 8 mss/issue; 32 mss/year. "We read manuscripts during the month after each deadline: February 28/May 31/August 31/November 30. Please note that we want mss in competition format." Publishes ms 6 months after acceptance. Published work by Peter Watts, M.A.C. Farrant, Leslie Gadallah and Dave Duncan. Length: 4,000 words average; 1,000 words minimum; 6,000 words maximum. Also publishes poetry. Sometimes critiques or comments on rejected mss.

How to Contact: Send complete ms with a cover letter. "No queries!" Should include estimated word count 2-sentence bio and phone number. Reports in 5 months on mss. SASE for return of ms or send a disposable copy of ms plus #10 SASE for response. No simultaneous submissions. Sample copy for $6. Fiction guidelines for #10 SASE.

Payment/Terms: Pays $25-150 and 2 contributor's copies; additional copies for $4. Pays on acceptance for first North American serial rights. Sends galleys to author.

Advice: "Please note we only accept work by Canadian writers. Tend to prefer character-driven stories." Looking for "more humour, good hard science; less dinosaurs and VR."

‡ONCE UPON A WORLD, (IV), Route 1, Box 110A, Nineveh IN 46164. Editor: Emily Alward. Magazine: 8½×11; 80-100 pages; white paper; card stock cover; pen & ink illustrations. "A science fiction and fantasy magazine with emphasis on alternate-world cultures and stories of idea, character and interaction. Also publishes book reviews and poems for an adult audience, primarily readers of science fiction and fantasy. We're known for science fiction and fantasy stories with excellent wordbuilding and a humanistic emphasis." Annually. Estab. 1988. Circ. 100.

● The science fiction and fantasy published in *Once Upon a World* tends to be "centered on the human element" and explores the individual in society.

Needs: Fantasy, science fiction. No realistic "stories in contemporary settings"; horror; stories using Star Trek or other media characters; stories with completely negative endings." Upcoming theme: "Love Stories Set in Science Fiction or Fantasy Worlds" (Spring 1996). List of upcoming themes available for SASE. Receives 20 unsolicited mss/month. Accepts 8-12 mss/issue; per year "varies, depending on backlog." Publishes ms from 2 months to 1½ years after acceptance. Published work by Janet Reedman and Mark Andrew Garland. Length: 3,000 words average; 400 words minimum; 10,000 words maximum. Publishes short shorts. Also publishes poetry. Sometimes critiques rejected mss and recommends other markets.

How to Contact: Send complete manuscript. Reports in 2-4 weeks on queries; 2-16 weeks on mss. SASE. "Reluctantly" accepts simultaneous submissions, if noted. Sample copy for $8.50; checks to Emily Alward. Fiction guidelines for #10 SASE. Reviews novels and short story collections.

Payment/Terms: Pays contributor's copies. Acquires first rights. "Stories copyrighted in author's name; copyrights not registered."

Advice: "Besides a grasp of basic fiction technique, you'll need some familiarity with the science fiction and fantasy genres. We suggest reading some of the following authors whose work is similar to what we're looking for: Isaac Asimov, Poul Anderson, Norman Spinrad, David Brin, Anne McCaffrey, Marion Zimmer Bradley, Mercedes Lackey, Katharine Kimbriel."

ONE HUNDRED SUNS, (II), Burlap Swan Press, P.O. Box 30186, Long Beach CA 90853. Editor: Glenn Bach. Magazine: 5½×8½; 72 pages; bond paper; matte card cover; illustrations and photos. "I tend to use strong-willed and emotionally rich poetry, and I expect the same of fiction." Semiannually. Estab. 1993. Circ. 200.
Needs: Condensed/excerpted novel, ethnic/multicultural, experimental, feminist, literary, science fiction (soft/sociological). Does not want to see "most standard genres." Plans special fiction issue or anthology in the future. Receives 5-10 unsolicited mss/month. Accepts 1-2 mss/issue; 2-4 mss/year. Publishes ms 1-6 months after acceptance. Published work by B.Z. Niditch, Frank Merenda, Christien Gholson and David Frank. Length: 750-1,000 words average; 2,500 words maximum. Publishes short shorts. Also publishes literary essays, literary criticism and poetry. Sometimes critiques or comments on rejected mss.
How to Contact: Send complete ms with a cover letter. Should include bio (paragraph). Reports in 1 month on queries; 3 months on mss. Send SASE for reply, return of ms or send a disposable copy of ms. No simultaneous submissions. Reprint submissions OK. Sample copy for $5. Fiction guidelines for #10 SAE.
Payment/Terms: Pays 1 contributor's copy; additional copies for $4. Acquires one-time rights.
Advice: Looks for "a strong and clear voice. Readable experimentation. Believability. Specificity. Self-sufficiency (does not necessarily mean beginning-middle-end). Buy a sample copy. Don't adhere to strict divisions between poetry and fiction. Nail images down firmly. I'd like to see good, sociological cyberpunk, poetic experimentation. Don't bother me with a story written for a beginning fiction class. I'd rather see Harvey Pekar than Bukowski, John Coltrane than Benny Goodman."

ONIONHEAD, (II), Literary Quarterly, Arts on the Park, Inc., 115 N. Kentucky Ave., Lakeland FL 33801. (813)680-2787. Editors: Charles Kersey and Dudley Uphoff. Editorial Assistant: Anna Wiseman. Magazine: Digest-sized; 40 pages; 20 lb. bond; glossy card cover. "Provocative political, social and cultural observations and hypotheses for a literary audience—an open-minded audience." Estab. 1989. Circ. 250.
Needs: Contemporary, ethnic, experimental, feminist, gay, humor/satire, lesbian, literary, prose poem, regional. "Must have a universal point (International)." Publishes short fiction in each issue. Receives 100-150 unsolicited mss/month. Acquires approximately 28 mss/issue; 100 mss (these numbers include: poetry, short prose and essays)/year. Publishes ms within 18 months of acceptance. Published work by Lyn Lifshin, A.D. Winans, Jessica Freeman, Laurel Speer. Length: 3,000 words average; 4,000 words maximum. Publishes short shorts. Also publishes poetry.
How to Contact: Send complete manuscript with cover letter that includes brief bio and SASE. Reports in 2 weeks on queries; 2 months on mss. No simultaneous submissions. Sample copy for $3 postpaid. Fiction guidelines for #10 SASE.
Payment/Terms: Pays in contributor's copy. Charge for extras. Acquires first North American serial rights.
Advice: "Review a sample copy of *Onionhead* and remember *literary quality* is the prime criterion. Avoid heavy-handed approaches to social commentary—be subtle, not didactic."

ORACLE STORY, (I, II), Rising Star Publishers, 2105 Amherst Rd., Hyattsville MD 20783. (301)422-2665. Fax: (301)422-2720. Editor: Obi H. Ekwonna. Magazine: 5½×8½; 38 pages; white bond paper; 60 lb. Ibs cover. "Didactic well-made stories; basically adults and general public (mass market)." Quarterly. Estab. 1993. Circ. 500.
  • *Oracle Story* is a member of the Association of African Writers. The editors are interested in all genres of fiction but with an African-cultural slant.
Needs: Condensed/excerpted novel, ethnic/multicultural, historical, horror, humor/satire, literary, mainstream/contemporary, mystery/suspense (romantic suspense), serialized novel, young adult/teen (horror and mystery), folklore (African). "No gay or lesbian writings." List of upcoming themes available for SASE. Publishes annual special fiction issue or anthology. Receives 60 unsolicited mss/month. Accepts 8 mss/issue; 26 mss/year. Publishes ms 6-12 months after acceptance. Length: "not more than 20 type-written pages." Publishes short shorts. Also publishes literary essays, literary criticism and poetry. Sometimes critiques or comments on rejected mss.
How to Contact: Send complete ms with a cover letter. Should include bio with SASE. Reports in 4-6 weeks. SASE for reply or return of ms. No simultaneous submissions. Electronic submissions OK. Sample copy for $5 plus $1.50 postage. Fiction guidelines for SASE. Reviews novels and short story collections.
Payment/Terms: Pays contributor's copy. Acquires first North American seial rights.
Advice: Looks for work that is "well-made, well-written, and has good language." Especially interested in African folklore.

ORANGE COAST REVIEW, (II), Dept. of English, 2701 Fairview Rd., Orange Coast College, Costa Mesa CA 92628-5005. (714)432-5043. Advisor: Raymond Obstfeld. Fiction Editor: Angela Powell. Editors change every 6 months. Magazine: 5½×8½; 70 pages; 60 lb. paper; medium/heavy cover; illustrations and photos. "We look for quality, of course. The genre, style, and format take second place to intelligence and depth. Our largest audience consists of students and writers." Annually. Estab. 1990. Circ. 750.
Needs: Condensed novel, ethnic/multicultural, experimental, feminist, gay, humor/satire, lesbian, literary, mainstream/contemporary, serialized novel, translations. No mainstream short fiction and poetry. Receives 100 unsolicited mss/month. Accepts 5-10 mss/issue. Mss accepted December to April only. Publishes ms 6

months after acceptance. Published work by Jo-Ann Mapson, Meredith Moore, Mark Seyi. Length: Open. Publishes short shorts. Also publishes literary essays, poetry. Sometimes critiques or comments on rejected mss.

How to Contact: Send complete ms with a cover letter. Should include estimated word count, short paragraph bio, list of publications with submission. Reports in 2-3 weeks on queries; 2-3 month on mss. SASE for return ms. Simultaneous submissions OK. Sample copy for $4. Fiction guidelines for #10 SASE.

Payment/Terms: Pays $1/published page fiction, 2 contributor's copies on publication for one-time rights.

Advice: "A manuscript stands out when it actually has a beginning, middle and end; a coherent theme that isn't vague or preachy; and characters that come to life. Check your grammar, punctuation, and spelling—three times. If you don't care about the easy stuff, why should we expect you to have cared about the story or poem. Never single space." Looks for "writing that involves their own voice or style, not Raymond Carver's or whoever else impresses them."

‡OREGON EAST, (II, IV), Hoke College Center, EOSC, La Grande OR 97850. (503)962-3787. Editor: R.S. Kromwall. Magazine: 6×9; 80 pages; illustrations and photographs. "*Oregon East* prefers fiction about the Northwest. The majority of our issues go to the students of Eastern Oregon State College; staff, faculty and community members receive them also, and numerous high school and college libraries." Annually. Estab. 1950. Circ. 900.

Needs: Humor/satire, literary, prose poem, regional, translations. No juvenile/children's fiction. Receives 20 unsolicited mss/issue. Accepts 3-6 mss/issue. Does not read April to August. Publishes ms an average of 5 months after acceptance. Recently published work by Tracy Terrell, Jessica Mills and George Venn. Published new writers within the last year. Length: 2,000 words average; 3,000 words maximum. Publishes short shorts. Sometimes critiques rejected mss.

How to Contact: Send complete ms with cover letter which should include name, address, brief bio. Reports in 1 week on queries; 3 months on mss. SASE. Sample copy for $5; fiction guidelines for #10 SASE.

Payment/Terms: Pays 2 contributor's copies. Rights revert to author.

Advice: "Follow our guidelines, please! Keep trying: we have limited space because we must publish 50% on-campus material. *Oregon East* has been around for almost 40 years, and it has always strived to represent the Northwest's great writers and artists, as well as several from around the world."

OTHER VOICES, (II), The University of Illinois at Chicago, Dept of English (M/C 162), 601 S. Morgan St., Chicago IL 60607. (312)413-2209. Editors: Sharon Fiffer and Lois Hauselman. Magazine: 5⅞×9; 168-205 pages; 60 lb. paper; coated cover stock; occasional photos. "Original, fresh, diverse stories and novel excerpts" for literate adults. Semiannually. Estab. 1985. Circ. 1,500.

● *Other Voices* received an Illinois Arts Council Award for the 1993/94 year.

Needs: Contemporary, excerpted novel, experimental, humor/satire and literary. No taboos, except ineptitude and murkiness. No fantasy, horror, juvenile, psychic/occult. Receives 300 unsolicited fiction mss/month. Accepts 20-23 mss/issue. Published work by Lynne Sharon Schwartz, Karen Karbo, James McManus and Terry McMillan; published new writers within the last year. Length: 4,000 words average; 5,000 words maximum.

How to Contact: Send mss with SASE or submit through agent October 1 to April 1 only. Mss received during non-reading period are returned unread. Cover letters "should be brief and list previous publications. Also, list title of submission. Most beginners' letters try to 'explain' the story—a big mistake." Simultaneous submissions OK. Reports in 10-12 weeks on mss. Sample copy for $7 (includes postage). Fiction guidelines for #10 SASE.

Payment/Terms: Pays in contributor's copies and modest cash gratuity (when possible). Acquires one-time rights.

Advice: "There are so *few* markets for *quality* fiction! We—by publishing 40-45 stories a year—provide new and established writers a forum for their work. Send us your best voice, your best work, your best best."

‡OTHER WORLDS, The Paperback Magazine of Science Fiction-Science Fantasy, (II), Gryphon Publications, Box 209, Brooklyn NY 11228. Editor: Gary Lovisi. Magazine: 5×8; 100+ pages; offset paper; card cover; perfect-bound; illustrations and photographs. "Adventure—or action-oriented SF—stories that are fun to read." Annually. Estab. 1988. Circ. 300.

Needs: Science fiction (hard science, sociological) "with impact." No fantasy, sword and sorcery. Receives 24 unsolicited mss/month. Accepts 4-6 mss/issue. Publishes ms 1-2 years (usually) after acceptance. Length: 3,000 words maximum. Publishes short shorts. Length: 500 words. Sometimes critiques rejected mss and recommends other markets.

How to Contact: Send complete ms with cover letter. Simultaneous submissions OK. Reports in 2 weeks on queries; 1 month on mss. SASE. Sample copy for $9.95 (100 pages perfect bound).

Payment/Terms: Pays 2 contributor's copies. Acquires first North American serial rights. Copyright reverts to author.

Advice: Looks for "harder science fiction stories, with *impact!*"

‡OTISIAN DIRECTORY, (II), IGHF, P.O. Box 390783, Cambridge MA 02139-0783. (617)441-0904. Editor: Jeff Stevens. Magazine: 8½×11; 40 pages; 20 lb. bond paper; 50 lb. bond cover; illustrations and photos. "*Otisian Directory* is an alternative publication—mostly reviews but with the occasional piece of art/fiction/ articles. Anything outside the mainstream will be considered." Quarterly. Estab. 1988. Circ. 500.

Needs: Condensed/excerpted novel, ethnic/multicultural, experimental, fantasy, feminist, gay, historical, humor/satire, lesbian, literary, psychic/supernatural/occult, regional, religious/inspirational, romance (gothic), science fiction, serialized novel, translations. List of upcoming themes available for SASE. Plans special fiction issue or anthology. Receives 5 unsolicited mss/month. Accepts 1 ms/issue; 6 mss/year. Publishes ms 3 months after acceptance. Publishes short shorts. Also publishes literary essays, literary criticism and poetry. Always critiques or comments on rejected ms.

How to Contact: Send complete ms with a cover letter. Should include 1 paragraph bio and list of publications. Reports in 2 months. Send SASE for reply, return of ms or send a disposable copy of ms. Simultaneous, reprint and electronic submissions OK. E-mail address: ighf@netcom.com. Sample copy for $5. Reviews novels and short story collections.

Payment/Terms: Pays 2 contributor's copies. Acquires one-time rights.

Advice: "Beginning writers should feel unfettered by the wishes of editors. Try me."

‡OUROBOROS, (II), 3912 24th St., Rock Island IL 61201-6223. Editor and Publisher: Erskine Carter. Magazine: 6×9; 76 pages; 60 lb. offset paper; 80 lb. cover; b&w illustrations. "We publish fiction (short stories), poetry and art for thoughtful readers." Published irregularly. Estab. 1985. Circ. 400.

Needs: Adventure, contemporary, experimental, fantasy, historical, horror, humor/satire, literary, mainstream, mystery/suspense, psychic/supernatural/occult, science fiction. "We are mainly interested in stories about people, in situations of conflict or struggle. We want to see *real* characters at odds with others, themselves, their universe. No racist/right-wing/anti-minority material." Receives 40-50 unsolicited mss/month. Accepts 8-10 mss/issue; 32-40 mss/year. Publishes ms 3 months to 1 year after acceptance. Published work by W. Rose, C. Stevenson, D. Starkey; published new writers within the last year. Length: 2,500 words average; 3,500 words maximum. Publishes short shorts. Length: 500 words. Also publishes poetry. Sometimes critiques rejected mss and recommends other markets.

How to Contact: Request guidelines and a sample copy. Reports in 2 weeks. SASE. Reprint submissions OK. Sample copy of current issue $4.50. Back issues available.

Payment/Terms: Pays in contributor's copies. Rights revert to author. Sends galleys to author.

Advice: "The beginning writer *can* break in here and learn valuable lessons about writing and publishing. Obtain a sample copy, write something you think will grab us, then submit. Get to know the markets. Don't waste time, energy and postage without researching."

OUTERBRIDGE, (II), English 25-28, The College of Staten Island (CUNY), 2800 Victory Blvd., Staten Island NY 10314. (718)982-3651. Editor: Charlotte Alexander. Magazine: 5½×8½; approx. 110 pages; 60 lb. white offset paper; 65 lb. cover stock. "We are a national literary magazine publishing mostly fiction and poetry. To date, we have had several special focus issues (the 'urban' and the 'rural' experience, 'Southern,' 'childhood,' 'nature and the environment,' 'animals'). For anyone with enough interest in literature to look for writing of quality and writers on the contemporary scene who deserve attention. There probably is a growing circuit of writers, some academics, reading us by recommendations." Annually. Estab. 1975. Circ. 500-700.

Needs: Literary. "No *Reader's Digest* style; that is, very popularly oriented. We like to do interdisciplinary features, e.g., literature and music, literature and science and literature and the natural world." Upcoming themes: "Love and Friendship"; "Send-ups of PC," (politically correct language). Accepts 8-10 mss/year. Does not read in July or August. Published work by William Davey, Ron Berube, Patricia Ver Ellen; published new writers within the last year. Length: 10-25 pages. Also publishes poetry. Sometimes recommends other markets.

How to Contact: Query. Send complete ms with cover letter. "Don't talk too much, 'explain' the work, or act apologetic or arrogant. If published, tell where, with a brief bio." SASE (or IRC). Reports in 8-10 weeks on queries and mss. No multiple submissions. Sample copy for $5 for annual issue.

Payment/Terms: Pays 2 contributor's copies. Charges ½ price of current issue for extras to its authors. Acquires one-time rights. Requests credits for further publication of material used by *OB*.

Advice: "Read our publication first. Don't send out blindly; get some idea of what the magazine might want. A *short* personal note with biography is appreciated. Competition is keen. Read an eclectic mix of classic and contemporary. Beware of untransformed autobiography, but *everything* in one's experience contributes."

OWEN WISTER REVIEW, (II), ASUW Student Publications Board, P.O. Box 4238, University of Wyoming, Laramie WY 82071. (307)766-3819. Fax: (307)766-4027. Editor: Cari Taplin. Fiction Editors: "Fiction Selection Committee." Editors change each year, contact selection committee. Magazine: 6×9; 92 pages; 60 lb. matte paper; 80 lb. glossy cover; illustrations; photographs. "Though we are a university publication, our audience is wider than just an academic community." Semiannually. Estab. 1978. Circ. 500.

• *Owen Wister Review* has won numerous awards and honors far surpassing many student-run publications. Nine poems from *OWR* were nominated for inclusion in the *Pushcart Prize* anthology (1992-1993). The magazine received Best of Show award from the Associated Collegiate Press/College Media Advisors and six individual Gold Circle Awards from the Columbia Scholastic Press Association.

Needs: Ethnic/multicultural, experimental, humor/satire, literary, translations. No science fiction or fantasy. Plans special fiction issue or anthology. Receives 12-15 unsolicited mss. Acquires 3 mss/issue; 6-8 mss/year. "Summer months are generally down time for *OWR*." Publishes ms 2-3 months after acceptance. Published work by Mark Jenkins, John Bennet, the Kunstwaffen art collaborative, Sue Thornton. Length: 1,300 words average; 3,500 words maximum. Publishes short shorts. Also publishes literary essays, literary criticism and poetry.

How to Contact: Send complete ms with cover letter. Should include estimated word count, bio, list of publications. Reports in 2-3 weeks on queries; 2-3 months on mss. Send SASE for reply, return of ms or send disposable copy of the ms. Simultaneous and electronic submissions OK. E-mail address: owr@uwyo.edu. Sample copy for $5. Free fiction guidelines.

Payment/Terms: Pays 1 contributor's copy. 10% off additional copies. Acquires one-time rights.

Advice: "In the last few issues we have geared the material toward what we think of as 'underpublished' groups—minorities, veterans, the gay community—survivor groups. This has broadened our audience to include just about anyone who wishes to be challenged by his reading material. Our committee likes to hear a fresh voice. Experimental fiction is encouraged. Consistency is very important. We look for and encourage young writers but insist on quality. Metafiction and short humor stand out among the longer works. We want to be hooked and not let go; regardless of subject matter, the approach should be compelling and relentless."

THE OXFORD AMERICAN, A Magazine from the South, (II), P.O. Drawer 1156, Oxford MS 38655. (601)236-1836. Editor: Marc Smirnoff. Magazine: 8½×11; 100 pages; glossy paper; glossy cover; illustrations and photos. Bimonthly. Estab. 1992. Circ. 50,000.

• *The Oxford American* is now published by author John Grisham whose support has enabled the magazine to increase its publication frequency. Its circulation has grown from 2,000 to 50,000 within the last year.

Needs: Regional (Southern); stories set in the South. Published work by Barry Hannah, Willie Morris, Madison Jones and Cynthia Shearer. Also publishes literary essays. Sometimes critiques or comments on rejected mss.

How to Contact: Send complete ms. Send SASE for reply, return of ms or send a disposable copy of ms. No simultaneous submissions. Sample copy for $4.50. "We review Southern novels or short story collections only."

Payment/Terms: Pays $100 minimum on publication for first rights. Sends galleys to author.

Advice: "I know you've heard it before—but we appreciate those writers who try to get into the spirit of the magazine which they can best accomplish by being familiar with it."

OXFORD MAGAZINE, (II), Bachelor Hall, Miami University, Oxford OH 45056. (513)529-1809. Fiction Editors: Tayna Allen, Michael Parker. Editors change every year. Send submissions to "Fiction Editor." Magazine: 6×9; 85-100 pages; illustrations. Biannually. Estab. 1985. Circ. 500-1,000.

Needs: Ethnic, experimental, feminist, gay, humor/satire, lesbian, literary, translations. Receives 50-60 unsolicited mss/month. Does not read mss May through Sepetember. Published work by Tony Earley and Ann Harleman; published new writers within the last year. Length: 2,000-3,000 words average. "We will accept long fiction (over 10,000 words) only in cases of exceptional quality." Publishes short shorts. Also publishes literary essays, literary criticism, poetry.

How to Contact: Send complete ms with cover letter, which should include a short bio or interesting information. No simultaneous submissions. Reports in 3-4 months, depending upon time of submissions; mss received after January 1 will be held over for following year's issue, with author's permission. SASE. Sample copy for $5, 10×12 SAE and 4 first-class stamps.

Payment/Terms: Pays in contributor's copies. Acquires one-time rights.

Advice: "*Oxford Magazine* is looking for humbly vivid fiction; that is to say, fiction that illuminates, which creates and inhabits an honest, carefully rendered reality populated by believable, three-dimensional characters. We see far too many glib, sitcom-ish stories, too many saccharine hospital tales, too many brand-name-laden records of GenX angst, too many stories which are really overeager European travelogues. Send us stories which are unique; we want fiction no one else but you could possibly have written."

OXYGEN, A Spirited Literary Magazine, (II), 535 Geary St., #1010, San Francisco CA 94102. (415)776-9681. Editor/Publisher: Richard Hack. Magazine: 8½×11; 40-50 pages; bond paper; 80 lb. color cover; perfect-bound. "We are an eclectic, community-spirited magazine looking for vivid, meaningful writing. We welcome fiction and poetry in modes realistic, surreal, expressionistic, beat, devotional, erotic, satiric, and invective. We stand for inclusive, democratic values and social equality." Publishes 3-4 issues/year. Estab. 1991. Circ. 300.

Needs: Erotica, ethnic/multicultural, experimental, feminist, literary, mainstream/contemporary, religious/inspirational, translations (especially from Spanish; bilingual contributions preferred). "Nothing overly commercial, insincere, or mocking, though we enjoy satire and 'black humor'." Receives 40 unsolicited mss/month. Accepts 3-4 mss/issue; 12-16 mss/year. Publishes ms up to 3 or 4 months after acceptance. Recently published work by Robert Anbian, Eugene Wildman, David Fisher, Jerry Ratch and Poe Ballantine. Length: 500-7,500 words. Publishes short shorts. Also publishes poetry, occasional essays and reviews.

How to Contact: Send complete ms with a cover letter. Should include bio (1-2 paragraphs), list of publications (not necessary). Reports in 2-8 weeks. Send SASE for reply or return of ms. Simultaneous, reprint and electronic submissions OK. Sample copy for $4 (make check out to Richard Hack, not to *Oxygen*). Fiction guidelines for #10 SASE.

Payment/Terms: Pays 2 contributor's copies. All rights revert to contributors.

Advice: "We want vivid, efficient, honest fiction. It can be a short story, tale, fragment, experimental piece, or an excerpt from a novel. We like meaningful writing with inclusive values, hopefully rich and suggestive writing, or a style with a nice feel to it. Does it believe in something, does it love life? Does it satirize injustice and abuse? What kind of personal quality does it demonstrate?"

PABLO LENNIS, The Magazine of Science Fiction, Fantasy and Fact, (I, IV), Deneb Press, Fandom House, 30 North 19th St., Lafayette IN 47904. Editor: John Thiel. Magazine: 8½×11; 22 pages; standard stock; illustrations and "occasional" photos. "Science fiction, fantasy, science, research and mystic for scientists and science fiction and fantasy appreciators." Monthly.

Needs: Fantasy, science fiction. Receives 25 unsolicited mss/year. Accepts 3 mss/issue; 35 mss/year. Publishes ms 6 months after acceptance. Published work by P.M. Fergusson, Michael Kube-McDowell, Darrin Kidd; published new writers within the last year. Length: 1,500 words average; 3,000 words maximum. Also publishes literary criticism, poetry. Occasionally critiques rejected mss and recommends other markets.

How to Contact: "Method of submission is author's choice but he might prefer to query. No self-statement is necessary." No simultaneous submissions. Reports in 2 weeks. Does not accept computer printouts.

Payment/Terms: Pays 1 contributor's copy. Publication not copyrighted.

Advice: "I have taboos against unpleasant and offensive language and want material which is morally or otherwise elevating to the reader. I prefer an optimistic approach, and favor fine writing. With a good structure dealt with intelligently underlying this, you have the kind of story I like. I prefer stories that have something to say to those which have something to report."

PACIFIC COAST JOURNAL, (I, II), French Bread Publications, P.O. Box 355, Campbell CA 95009-0355. Editor: John S.F. Graham. Fiction Editor: Stephanie Kylkis. Magazine: 5½×8½; 56 pages; 20 lb. paper; 67 lb. cover; illustrations; photos. "We just want quality material. Slight focus towards western US/Pacific Rim." Quarterly (or "whenever we have enough money"). Estab. 1992. Circ. 200.

● The editors are now looking for shorter pieces of fiction.

Needs: Ethnic/multicultural, experimental, feminist, historical, humor/satire, literary, science fiction (soft/sociological, magical realism). Receives 30-40 unsolicited mss/month. Accepts 3-4 mss/issue; 10-12 mss/year. Publishes ms 6-18 months after acceptance. Length: 2,500 words preferred; 5,000 words maximum. Publishes short shorts. Also publishes literary essays and poetry. Sometimes critiques or comments on rejected mss.

How to Contact: Send complete ms with a cover letter. Should include bio (less than 50 words) and list of publications. Reports in 2-4 months. Send SASE for reply, return of ms or send a disposable copy of ms. Simultaneous, reprint and electronic submissions OK (Mac or IBM). E-mail address: paccoastj@aol.com. Sample copy for $2.50, 6×9 SASE. Reviews novels and short story collections.

Payment/Terms: Pays 1 contributor's copy. Acquires one-time rights.

PACIFIC REVIEW, (II), Dept. of English and Comparative Lit., San Diego State University, San Diego CA 92182-0295. (619)594-5443. Contact: Sinclair Gregory, advisor. Magazine: 6×9; 100-150 pages; book stock paper; paper back, extra heavy cover stock; illustrations, photos. "There is no designated theme. We publish high-quality fiction, poetry, and familiar essays: academic work meant for, but not restricted to, an academic audience." Biannual. Estab. 1973. Circ. 1,000.

Needs: "We do not restrict or limit our fiction in any way other than quality. We are interested in all fiction, from the very traditional to the highly experimental. Acceptance is determined by the quality of submissions." Does not read June-August. Published new writers within the last year. Publishes short shorts. Length: 4,000 words max.

How to Contact: Send original ms with SASE. No unsolicited submissions. Reports in 3-5 months on mss. Sample copy for $6.

Payment/Terms: 1 contributor's copy. "First serial rights are *Pacific Review*'s. All other rights revert to author."

THE PAGAN REVIEW A Literary Magazine, (I, II), 1291A South Powerline Rd., Suite 149, Pompano Beach FL 33069-4329. Editor: Susan L. Carr. Magazine: 7×8; 32-64 pages; white bond paper; illustrations. "One person operation publishing a small literary magazine." Quarterly. Estab. 1994. Circ. 500.

Needs: Adventure, ethnic/multicultural, fantasy, feminist, gay, historical, horror, humor/satire, lesbian, literary, mainstream/contemporary, mystery/suspense, psychic/supernatural/occult, religious/inspirational, sci-

ence fiction (soft/sociological), pagan, nature, ecological. No racist, fanatical religious. Publishes annual special fiction issue or anthology. Receives 10 unsolicited mss/month. Buys 5-7 mss/issue. Length: 5,000 words maximum (will serialize longer works). Also publishes literary essays, literary criticism and poetry.
How to Contact: Send complete ms with a cover letter. Should include estimated word count, 1-page bio, Social Security number and list of publications. Reports in 6 weeks on queries; 2 months on mss. Send SASE for reply, return of ms or send a disposable copy of ms. Simultaneous and electronic submissions (IBM or Mac) OK. E-mail address: z004625b@bcfreenet.seflin.fl.us (Internet). Fiction guidelines for #10 SASE.
Payment/Terms: Pays ⅛¢/word on publication for first North American serial rights. Sends galleys to author (if requested).
Advice: "I need stories that present paganism in a positive light. I get many good stories, but without a pagan theme."

PAINTED BRIDE QUARTERLY, (II), Painted Bride Art Center, 230 Vine St., Philadelphia PA 19106. (215)925-9914. Editor: Kathy Volk-Miller. Literary magazine: 6×9; 96-100 pages; illustrations; photos. Quarterly. Estab. 1975. Circ. 1,000.
Needs: Contemporary, ethnic, experimental, feminist, gay, lesbian, literary, prose poem and translations. Published new writers within the last year. Length: 3,000 words average; 5,000 words maximum. Publishes short shorts. Also publishes literary essays, literary criticism, poetry. Occasionally critiques rejected mss.
How to Contact: Send complete ms. Reports in 3 weeks-3 months. SASE. Sample copy for $6. Reviews novels and short story collections. Send books to editor.
Payment/Terms: Pays 1 contributor's copy, 1 year free subscription, 50% off additional copies. Acquires first North American serial rights.
Advice: Looks for "freshness of idea incorporated with high-quality writing. We receive an awful lot of nicely written work with worn-out plots. We want quality in whatever—we hold experimental work to as strict standards as anything else. Many of our readers write fiction; most of them enjoy a good reading. We hope to be an outlet for quality. A good story gives, first, enjoyment to the reader. We've seen a good many of them lately, and we've published the best of them."

PALO ALTO REVIEW, A Journal of Ideas, (I, II), Palo Alto College, 1400 West Villaret, San Antonio TX 78224. (210)921-5255 (or 921-5017). Fax: (210)921-5277. Editor: Bob Richmond and Ellen Shull. Magazine: 8½×11; 60 pages; 60 lb. natural white paper (50% recycled); illustrations and photographs. "Not too experimental nor excessively avant-garde, just good stories (for fiction). Ideas are what we are after. We are interested in connecting the college and the community. We would hope that those who attempt these connections will choose startling topics and interesting angles with which to investigate the length and breadth of the teaching/learning spectrum." Semiannually (spring and fall). Estab. 1992. Circ. 500-600.
Needs: Adventure, ethnic/multicultural, experimental, fantasy, feminist, historical, humor/satire, literary, mainstream/contemporary, mystery/suspense, regional, romance, science fiction, translations, westerns. Also "education—in its broadest sense." Upcoming themes: "Reunions" (spring 1996). Upcoming themes available for SASE. Receives 1,005 unsolicited mss/month. Accepts 2-4 mss/issue; 4-8 mss/year. Does not read mss March-April and October-November when putting out each issue. Publishes ms 2-15 months after acceptance. Published work by Sonia Gernes, Jo LeCoeur, Craig Loomis. Length: 3,500 words preferred; 4,500 words maximum. Publishes short shorts. Also publishes literary essays, literary criticism and poetry. Always critiques or comments on rejected mss.
How to Contact: Send complete ms with a cover letter. "Request sample copy and guidelines." Should include brief bio and brief list of publications. Reports in 3-4 months. Send SASE for reply, return of ms or send a disposable copy of ms. Simultaneous and electronic (Macintosh disk) submissions OK. Sample copy for $5. Fiction guidelines for #10 SASE.
Payment/Terms: Pays 2 contributor's copies; additional copies for $5. Acquires first North American serial rights.
Advice: "Good short stories have interesting characters confronted by a dilemma working toward a solution. Generally, the characters are interesting because the readers can identify with them and know much about them. Edit judiciously. Cut out extraneous verbage. Set up a choice that has to be made. Then create tension—who wants what and why they can't have it."

PANGOLIN PAPERS, (II), Turtle Press, P.O. Box 241, Nordland WA 98358. (360)385-3626. Editor: Pat Britt. Magazine: 5½×8½; 80 pages; 24 lb. paper; 80 lb. cover. "Best quality literary fiction for an informed audience." Triannually. Estab. 1994. Circ. 500.
Needs: Condensed/excerpted novel, experimental, humor/satire, literary, translations. No "genre such as romance or science fiction." Plans to publish special fiction issues or anthologies in the future. Receives 20 unsolicited mss/month. Accepts 7-10 mss/issue; 20-30 mss/year. Does not read mss in July and August. Publishes ms 4-12 months after acceptance. Agented fiction 10%. Recently published work by Summer Brenner and Christopher Woods. Length: 3,500 words average; 100 words minimum; 7,000 words maximum. Publishes short shorts. Length: 400 words. Also publishes literary essays. Sometimes critiques or comments on rejected mss.

How to Contact: Send complete ms with a cover letter. Should include estimated word count and short bio. Reports in 2 weeks on queries; 2 months on mss. Send SASE for reply, return of ms or send a disposable copy of ms. No simultaneous submissions. Electronic and reprint submissions OK. Sample copy for $4.95 and $1 postage. Fiction guidelines for #10 SAE.

Payment/Terms: Pays 2 contributor's copies. Offers annual $200 prize for best story. Acquires first North American serial rights. Sometimes sends galleys to author.

Advice: "We are looking for original voices. Follow the rules and be honest in your work."

PARADOX MAGAZINE, (II), Paradox Communications, 36 E. Loraine St., Oberlin OH 44074-1128. Editor: Dan Bodah. Magazine: 8½×11 or 4¼×5¼; 30 pages; 20 lb. paper; illustrations and photos. "*Paradox* exists to publish adventurous, bizarre, experimental and difficult work, as long as it has an accessible power. I prefer to support work that has a hard time getting published." Publication varies from semiannually to annually. Estab. 1991. Circ. 150.

Needs: Condensed/excerpted novel, erotica, experimental, horror, humor/satire, literary, psychic/supernatural/occult, religious/inspirational, science fiction (hard science sf, soft/sociological sf), serialized novel. Receives 30-60 unsolicited mss/month. Publishes ms 1-11 months after acceptance. Published work by Terry Chuba. Publishes short shorts. Also publishes literary essays, literary criticism and poetry. Sometimes critiques or comments on rejected mss.

How to Contact: "Send any work you feel is appropriately representative." Should include SASE. Reports in 2 months. Send SASE for reply, return of ms or send a disposable copy of ms. Simultaneous, reprint and electronic submissions OK. E-mail address: ZBODAH@ocvaxa.cc.oberlin.edu. Sample copy for $5.

Payment/Terms: Pays 1-2 contributor's copies. Acquires first rights.

Advice: "I prefer work that gets right into it, without a lot of superfluous or patience-demanding setup."

THE PARADOXIST LITERARY MOVEMENT, Anti-literary Journal, (IV), Xiquan Publishing House, 2456 S. Rose Peak Dr., Tucson AZ 85710. Editor: Florentin Smarandache. Magazine: 8½×11; 100 pages; illustrations. "The paradoxist literary movement is an avant-garde movement set up by the editor in the 1980s in Romania. It tries to generalize the art, to make the unliterary become literary." Annually. Estab. 1993. Circ. 500.

● Note the magazine's new address.

Needs: "Crazy, uncommon, experimental, avant-garde"; also ethnic/multicultural. Plans specific themes in the next year. Publishes annual special fiction issue or anthology. Receives 3-4 unsolicited mss/month. Accepts 10 mss/issue. Published work by Arnold Skemer, Marian Barbu and Constantin Urucu. Length: 500 words minimum; 1,000 words maximum. Publishes short shorts. Also publishes literary essays, literary criticism and poetry.

How to Contact: Query with clips of unpublished work. Reports in 2 months on mss. Send a disposable copy of ms. Sample copy for $19.95 and 8½×11 SASE.

Payment/Terms: Pays 1 contributor's copy. Not copyrighted.

PARAGRAPH, A Magazine of Paragraphs, (II), 18 Beach Point Dr., East Providence RI 02915. (401)437-9573. Co-Editors: Walker Rumble and Karen Donovan. Magazine: 4¼×5½; 38 pages. "No particular theme—we publish collections of paragraphs for a general audience." Published 3 times/year. Estab. 1985. Circ. 700.

Needs: "Any topic is welcome, including experimental writing. Our only requirement is that paragraphs must be 200 words or less." Receives 30-40 unsolicited mss/month. Accepts 30-33 mss/issue; 90 mss/year. Publishes ms 2-3 months after acceptance. Published work by Lisa Shea, Laurel Speer, Conger Beasley Jr., Deborah Bayer and Gary Fincke. Length: 200 words. Also publishes literary essays, but 200 words maximum, of course. Sometimes critiques rejected mss.

How to Contact: Send complete ms with cover letter. Reports in 2 weeks on queries; 2 months on mss. SASE. Simultaneous submissions OK. Sample copy for $3. Fiction guidelines for SASE.

Payment/Terms: Pays contributor's copies and charges for extras. Acquires first rights. Sends galleys to author.

PARAMOUR MAGAZINE, Literary and Artistic Erotica, (IV), P.O. Box 949, Cambridge MA 02140-0008. (617)499-0069. Publisher/Editor: Amelia Copeland. Senior Editor: Marti Hohmann. Magazine: 9×12; 36 pages; matte coated stock; illustrations and photos. "*Paramour* is a quarterly journal of literary and artistic erotica that showcases work by emerging writers and artists. Our goal is to provoke thought, laughter, curiosity and especially, arousal." Quarterly. Estab. 1993. Circ. 12,000.

● Work published in *Paramour* has been selected for inclusion in *Best American Erotica*.

Needs: Erotica. Receives 40 unsolicited mss/month. Accepts 3-5 mss/issue; 12-20 mss/year. Recently published work by Annie Regrets, Thomas Roche, Steve Bonvissuto and Bart Plantenga. Length: 2,000 words average; 1 word minimum; 4,000 words maximum. Publishes short shorts. Also publishes literary essays, literary criticism and poetry.

How to Contact: Send complete ms with a cover letter. Should include estimated word count, name, address and phone number. Reports in 3 weeks on queries; 2-4 months on mss. SASE (or IRC) for return of ms and send disposable copy of ms. No simultaneous submissions. E-mail address: paramour@xensei.com. Web site address: http://www2.xensei.com/paramour/. Sample copy for $4.95. Fiction guidelines for #10 SAE and 1 first-class stamp. Reviews novels and short story collections.

Payment/Terms: Pays free subscription to the magazine plus contributor's copies. Acquires first rights.

Advice: "We look for erotic stories which are well-constructed, original, exciting and dynamic. Clarity, attention to form and image, and heat make a ms stand out. Seek striking and authentic images and make the genre work for you. We see too many derivative rehashes of generic sexual fantasies. We love to see fresh representations that we know will excite readers."

THE PARIS REVIEW, (II), 45-39 171 Place, Flushing NY 11358 (*business office only, send mss to address below*). Editor: George A. Plimpton. Managing Editor: Daniel Kunitz. Magazine: 5¼×8½; about 260 pages; illustrations and photographs (unsolicited artwork not accepted). "Fiction and poetry of superlative quality, whatever the genre, style or mode. Our contributors include prominent, as well as less well-known and previously unpublished writers. 'The Art of Fiction' interview series includes important contemporary writers discussing their own work and the craft of writing." Quarterly.

● George Plimpton, editor of the well-respected *Paris Review*, also edits a popular series of interviews with well-known writers whose work has appeared in the magazine.

Needs: Literary. Receives about 1,000 unsolicited fiction mss each month. Published work by Raymond Carver, Elizabeth Tallent, Rick Bass, John Koethe, Sharon Olds, Derek Walcott, Carolyn Kizer, Tess Gallagher, Peter Handke, Denis Johnson, Bobbie Ann Mason, Harold Brodkey, Joseph Brodsky, John Updike, Andre Dubus, Galway Kinnell, E.L. Doctorow and Philip Levine. Published new writers within the last year. No preferred length. Also publishes literary essays, poetry.

How to Contact: *Send complete ms with SASE to Fiction Editor, 541 E. 72nd St., New York NY 10021.* Reports in 2 months. Simultaneous submissions OK. Sample copy for $11.50.

Payment/Terms: Pays for material. Pays on publication for first North American serial rights. Sends galleys to author.

PARTING GIFTS, (II), 3413 Wilshire, Greensboro NC 27408. Editor: Robert Bixby. Magazine: 5×8; 40 pages. "High-quality insightful fiction, very brief and on any theme." Semiannually. Estab. 1988.

Needs: "Brevity is the second most important criterion behind literary quality." Publishes ms within one year of acceptance. Length: 250 words minimum; 1,000 words maximum. Also publishes poetry. Sometimes critiques rejected mss.

How to Contact: Send complete ms with cover letter. Simultaneous submissions OK. Reports in 1 day on queries; 1-7 days on mss. SASE.

Payment/Terms: Pays in contributor's copies. Acquires one-time rights.

Advice: "Read the works of Amy Hempel, Jim Harrison, Kelly Cherry, C.K. Williams and Janet Kauffman, all excellent writers who epitomize the writing *Parting Gifts* strives to promote. I need more than ever for my authors to be better read. I sense that many unaccepted writers have not put in the hours reading."

PARTISAN REVIEW, (II), 236 Bay State Rd., Boston MA 02215. (617)353-4260. Editor-in-Chief: William Phillips. Executive Editor: Edith Kurzweil. Magazine: 6×9; 160 pages; 40 lb. paper; 60 lb. cover stock. "Theme is of world literature and contemporary culture: fiction, essays and poetry with emphasis on the arts and political and social commentary, for the general intellectual public; scholars." Quarterly. Estab. 1934. Circ. 8,000.

Needs: Contemporary, experimental, literary, prose poem, regional and translations. Receives 100 unsolicited fiction mss/month. Buys 2 mss/issue; 8 mss/year. Published work by José Donoso, Isaac Bashevis Singer, Doris Lessing; published new writers within the last year. Length: open. Publishes short shorts.

How to Contact: Send complete ms with SASE and cover letter listing past credits. No simultaneous submissions. Reports in 4 months on mss. Sample copy for $6 and $1.50 postage.

Payment/Terms: Pays $25-200 and 1 contributor's copy. Pays on publication for first rights.

Advice: "Please, research the type of fiction we publish. Often we receive manuscripts which are entirely inappropriate for our journal. Sample copies are available for sale and this is a good way to determine audience."

PASSAGER, A Journal of Remembrance and Discovery, (II, IV), University of Baltimore, 1420 N. Charles, Baltimore MD 21201-5779. Editors: Kendra Kopelke, Mary Azrael and Ebby Malmgren. Magazine: 8¼ square; 32 pages; 70 lb. paper; 80 lb. cover; photographs. "We publish stories and novel excerpts to 4,000 words, poems to 50 lines, interviews with featured authors." Quarterly. Estab. 1990. Circ. 750.

Needs: "Special interest in discovering new older writers, but publishes all ages." Receives 200 unsolicited mss/month. Accepts 3-4 prose mss/issue; 12-15/year. Publishes ms up to 1 year after acceptance. Published work by Thomas Fitzsimmons, Will Inman, Wayne Karlin, Hilda Morley, Ruth Daigon. Length: 250 words minimum; 4,000 words maximum. Publishes short shorts. Also publishes personal essays, poetry.

How to Contact: Send complete ms with cover letter. Reports in 3 months on mss. SASE. Simultaneous submissions OK, if noted. Sample copy for $3.50. Fiction guidelines for #10 SASE.

Payment/Terms: Pays subscription to magazine and contributor's copies. Acquires first North American serial rights. Sometimes sends galleys to author.

Advice: "*Get a copy* so you can see the quality of the work we use. We often reject beautifully written work that is bland in favor of rougher work that has the spark we're looking for."

PBW, (I), 130 W. Limestone, Yellow Springs OH 45387. (513)767-7416. Editor: Richard Freeman. Electronic disk magazine: 700 pages; illustrations. "*PBW* is an experimental floppy disk and B.B. publication that 'prints' strange and 'unpublishable' in an above-ground-sense writing." Quarterly. Estab. 1988.

● *PBW* is an electronic magazine which can be read using MacWrite (Mac disk) or it is available over modem on BBS. Write for details.

Needs: Erotica, experimental, gay, lesbian, literary. No "conventional fiction of any kind." Receives 3 unsolicited mss/month. Accepts 40 mss/issue; 160 mss/year. Publishes ms within 3 months after acceptance. Published work by Lisa Baumgardner, Susan Wolf, Marie Markoe, Susannah Manley and Jeff Jarvie. Length: open. Publishes short shorts and novels in chapters. Publishes literary essays, literary criticisms and poetry. Always critiques or comments on rejected mss.

How to Contact: Send complete ms with a cover letter. Reports in 2 weeks. Send SASE for reply, return of ms or send a disposable copy of ms. Simultaneous, reprint and electronic (Mac) submissions OK. Sample copy for $2. Reviews novels and short story collections.

Payment/Terms: Pays 1 contributor's copy. All rights revert back to author. Not copyrighted.

PEACE MAGAZINE, (I, II, IV), P.O. Box 902404, Palmdale CA 93590-2404. (805)267-7364. Editor: Linda James. Magazine: 8½×11; 30 pages; recycled paper; illustrations and photos. Publishes material of "the 1960s—written by and for the people who were there and those who wish they were." Quarterly. Estab. 1994.

● The work published in *Peace Magazine* tends to be written in first-person. The editor would like to see more stories about the women's movement, civil rights and music.

Needs: 1960s oriented: condensed/excerpted novel, feminist; all issues dealing with the 1960s. Planning special theme issues on Motown, civil rights; dates to be determined. List of upcoming themes available for SASE. Receives 3-10 unsolicited mss/month. Buys 5-10 mss/issue; 40-50 mss/year. Publishes ms 3-6 months after acceptance. Length: 2,000 words average; 500 words minimum; 6,000 words maximum. Occasionally publishes short shorts. Also publishes poetry on occasion. Sometimes critiques or comments on rejected ms.

How to Contact: Send complete ms with a cover letter. Should include estimated word count and 50-word bio. Reports in 2 months on queries, 3-6 months on mss. Send SASE for reply, return of ms or send a disposable copy of ms. No simultaneous submissions. Reprint and electronic submissions (Macintosh format) OK. Sample copy for $4 and 9×12 SASE. Fiction guidelines for SASE.

Payment/Terms: Pays 5¢/word-$100 maximum and 1 contributor's copy on publication for one-time rights. Sends galleys to author time permitting.

Advice: "We look for style and voice that says, 'I was there, I saw and I did.' We want to feel your passion, anger, commitment or indignation. You probably should be over 40 and lived through the '60s—or be a history buff. We are wide open to all styles, voices and opinions of the 1960s and what they meant to you."

PEARL, A Literary Magazine, (II, IV), Pearl, 3030 E. Second St., Long Beach CA 90803. (310)434-4523. Editors: Joan Jobe Smith, Marilyn Johnson and Barbara Hauk. Magazine: 5½×8½; 96 pages; 60 lb. recycled, acid-free paper; perfect-bound; coated cover; b&w drawings and graphics. "We are primarily a poetry magazine, but we do publish some *very short* fiction and nonfiction. We are interested in lively, readable prose that speaks to *real* people in direct, living language; for a general literary audience." Triannually. Estab. 1974 ("folded" after 3 issues but began publishing again in 1987). Circ. 600.

● *Pearl* sponsors a short story contest listed in the Contests and Awards section of this book.

Needs: Contemporary, humor/satire, literary, mainstream, prose poem. "We will only consider short-short stories up to 1,200 words. Longer stories (up to 4,000 words) may only be submitted to our short story contest. All contest entries are considered for publication. Although we have no taboos stylistically or subject-wise, obscure, predictable, sentimental, or cliché-ridden stories are a turn-off." Publishes an all fiction issue each year. Receives 10-20 unsolicited mss/month. Accepts 1-10 mss/issue; 12-15 mss/year. Publishes ms 6 months to 1 year after acceptance. Recently published work by MacDonald Harris, Josephine Marshall, Gerald Locklin, Lisa Glatt and Richard Farrell. Length: 1,000 words average; 500 words minimum; 1,200 words maximum. Also publishes poetry.

How to Contact: Send complete ms with cover letter including publishing credits and brief bio. Simultaneous submissions OK. Reports in 6-8 weeks on mss. SASE. Sample copy for $6 (postpaid). Fiction guidelines for #10 SASE.

Payment/Terms: Pays 2 contributor's copies. Acquires first North American serial rights. Sends galleys to author. Sponsors an annual short story contest. Submission period: December 1-March 15. Award: $50, publication in *Pearl*, 10 copies. $7 entry fee. Maximum length: 4,000 words. Send SASE for complete guidelines.

Advice: "We look for vivid, *dramatized* situations and characters, stories written in an original 'voice,' that make sense and follow a clear narrative line. What makes a manuscript stand out is more elusive, though—more to do with feeling and imagination than anything else ..."

THE PEGASUS REVIEW, (I, IV), P.O. Box 88, Henderson MD 21640-0088. (201)927-0749. Editor: Art Bounds. Magazine: 5½×8½; 6-8 pages; illustrations. "Our magazine is a bimonthly, entirely in calligraphy, illustrated. Each issue is based on specific themes." Estab. 1980. Circ. 250.
 • Because *The Pegasus Review* is done in calligraphy, submissions must be very short. Two pages, says the editor, is the ideal length.
Needs: Humor/satire, literary, prose poem and religious/inspirational. Upcoming themes: "Language" (January/February); "Animals" (March/April); "Childhood" (May/June); "America" (July/August); "Old Age" (September/October); "Ideas" (November/December). "Themes may be approached by humor, satire, inspirational, autobiographical, prose. Nothing like a new slant on an old theme." Receives 50 unsolicited mss/month. Accepts "about" 70 mss/year. Published work by new writers within the last year. Publishes short shorts of 2-3 pages; 500 words. Themes are subject to change, so query if in doubt. "Occasional critiques."
How to Contact: Send complete ms. SASE "a must." Brief cover letter with author's background, name and prior credits, if any. Simultaneous submissions acceptable, if so advised. Reports in 1-2 months. Sample copy for $2.50. Fiction guidelines for SAE.
Payment/Terms: Pays 2 contributor's copies. Occasional book awards. Acquires one-time rights.
Advice: "Read what is being offered today, adhere to any publication's guidelines—they are indicated for a specific reason, otherwise you are wasting everyone's time. Keep active by joining (or organizing) a writers group, attend workshops. Above all, keep reviewing the markets and continue to circulate your work. Do not be afraid of rewriting. Often it can be necessary."

PEMBROKE MAGAZINE, (I, II), Box 60, Pembroke State University, Pembroke NC 28372. (910)521-6000. Editor: Shelby Stephenson. Fiction Editor: Stephen Smith. Magazine: 9×10; 225 pages; illustrations; photos. Magazine of poems and stories plus literary essays. Annually. Estab. 1969. Circ. 500.
Needs: Open. Receives 120 unsolicited mss/month. Publishes short shorts. Published work by Fred Chappell, Robert Morgan; published new writers within the last year. Length: open. Occasionally critiques rejected mss and recommends other markets.
How to Contact: Send complete ms. No simultaneous submissions. Reports in up to 3 months. SASE. Sample copy for $5 and 9×10 SAE.
Payment/Terms: Pays 1 contributor's copy.
Advice: "Write with an end for *writing*, not publication."

PENNSYLVANIA ENGLISH, (II), English Department, Penn State University—Erie, Humanities Division, Erie PA 16563. (814)898-6231. Editor: Dean Baldwin. Fiction Editor: Chris Dubbs. Magazine: 7×8½; 100 pages; 20 lb. bond paper; 65 lb. matte cover. For "teachers of English in Pennsylvania at the high school and college level." Semiannually. Estab. 1985. Circ. 300.
Needs: Literary, contemporary mainstream. Does not read mss from May to August. Publishes ms an average of 6 months after acceptance. Length: 5,000 words maximum. Publishes short shorts. Also publishes literary essays, literary criticism, poetry. Sometimes critiques rejected mss.
How to Contact: Send complete ms with cover letter. Reports in 2 months. SASE. Simultaneous submissions OK.
Payment/Terms: Pays in contributor's copies. Acquires first North American serial rights.

PEOPLENET, "Where People Meet People," (IV), Box 897, Levittown NY 11756. (516)579-4043. Editor: Robert Mauro. Newsletter: 8½×11; 8 pages; 20 lb. paper; 20 lb. cover stock. "Romance stories featuring disabled characters." Triannual. Estab. 1987. Circ. 200.
Needs: Romance, contemporary and disabled. Main character must be disabled. Upcoming theme: "Marriage between disabled and non-disabled." Accepts 1 ms/issue; 3 mss/year. Publishes ms up to 2 years after acceptance. Length: 500 words. Publishes short shorts. Length: 750 words. Also publishes literary criticism, poetry. Especially looking for book reviews on books dealing with disabled persons.
How to Contact: Send complete ms and SASE. Reports in 1 month "*only* if SASE there." No simultaneous submissions. Sample copy for $3.55. Fiction guidelines for #10 SASE
Payment/Terms: Pays 1¢/word on acceptance. Acquires first rights.
Advice: "We are looking for stories of under 1,000 words on romance with a disabled man or woman as the main character. No sob stories or 'super crip' stories. Just realistic romance. No porn. Love, respect, trust, understanding and acceptance are what I want."

‡PEQUOD, A Journal of Contemporary Literature and Literary Criticism, (II), 19 University Place, Room 200, New York University, New York NY 10003. Editor: Mark Rudman. Magazine 8½×5½; 150 pages; glossy cover. Semiannually. Estab. 1974. Circ. 2,500-4,000.
Needs: Condensed/excerpted novel, ethnic/multicultural, literary, mainstream/contemporary, translations. List of upcoming themes available for SASE. Publishes annual special fiction issue or anthology. Receives

150 unsolicited mss/month. Accepts 2 mss/issue; 4 mss/year. Does not read mss May-August. Publishes ms 3-6 months after acceptance. Recently published work by Stephen Dixon, John Harvey and Joyce Carol Oates. Publishes short shorts. Also publishes literary essays, literary criticism and poetry. Sometimes critiques or comments on rejected ms.

How to Contact: Send complete ms with a cover letter. Should include estimated word count and list of publications. Reports in 6-8 weeks on queries; 3-4 months on mss. Send SASE for reply, return of ms or send a disposable copy of ms. Simultaneous and electronic submissions OK. Sample copy for $5. Reviews novels and short story collections.

Payment/Terms: Pays 2 contributor's copies. Rights revert back to author upon publication.

Advice: "Please subscribe to or get a sample copy of *Pequod* first to see what we're about."

‡PERCEPTION WRITINGS, (I, II), P.O. Box 246, Fairfax CA 94978. (415)258-0562. Editor: Robert Cesaretti. Magazine: 4×6; 30-50 pages; illustrations. Estab. 1996.

Needs: Experimental, literary. Receives 5 unsolicited mss/month. Length: 6,000 words maximum. Publishes short shorts. Also publishes poetry. Always critiques or comments on rejected ms.

How to Contact: Send complete ms with a cover letter. Send SASE for reply, return of ms or send a disposable copy of ms. Simultaneous and reprint submissions OK.

Payment/Terms: Payment policy "undetermined" at this time. Acquires one-time rights.

‡PERCEPTIONS, The Journal of Imaginative Sensuality, (I, II, IV), Sensuous SIG, Inc., 2111 Lido Circle, Stockton CA 95207. Editor: Alexander Lloyd. Editorial Address: P.O. Box 2210, Livermore CA 94550. Magazine: 5½×8½; 52 pages; 20 lb. bond paper; 60 lb. cover; illustrations; photographs. "*Perceptions* is a journal celebrating the nature of sensuality. We celebrate a realization that virtually everything sexual is sensual, but that sensuality's diversity far exceeds only a sexual purview." Quarterly. Estab. 1988. Circ. 250.

Needs: Erotica, gay, humor/satire, lesbian, psychic/supernatural/occult. "Any fiction with a sensual slant. We do not accept pornography or graphically obscene fiction." Receives 10 unsolicited mss/month. Acquires 4-5 mss/issue; 20 mss/year. Publishes ms 2-6 months after acceptance. Published work by Vlasa Glen, Bud Martin, Bart Geraci, Alan Schwartz. Length: 1,000 words preferred; 400 words minimum; 2,000 words maximum. Publishes short shorts. Length: 400-800 words. Usually publishes literary essays, literary criticism and poetry. Usually critiques or comments on rejected mss.

How to Contact: Submit to editorial address. US writers send $3 for sample issue and submission guidelines (cost is $4 to Canada and Mexico, and $6 overseas). Should include 3-4 sentence bio. Reports in 2 weeks on queries; 2 months on mss. SASE required for reply. Simultaneous and reprint submissions OK.

Payment/Terms: Pays 1 contributor's copy; additional copies $2. Acquires one-time rights.

Advice: "We prefer fiction that has an original or unusual story or angle. We attempt to publish fiction from a variety of viewpoints. Steer away from the temptation to depict sexuality or erotic issues in a graphic or obscene way. We prefer more sensual or 'intellectual' stories. Spelling counts."

PEREGRINE, The Journal of Amherst Writers and Artists, (I, II), Amherst Writers and Artists Press, Box 1076, Amherst MA 01004. (413)253-3307. Editor: Pat Schneider. Fiction Editor: Anna Kirwan. Translation Editor: Enid Santiago Welch. Magazine: 5×7; 90 pages; sturdy matte white paper; heavier cover stock. "Poetry and prose—short stories, short short stories, and occasionally short prose fantasies, essays or reflections. Publishes two pages in each issue of work in translation." Annually.

● *Peregrine* was awarded a Graphic Design Honorable Mention from the 1995 American Literary Magazine Awards. Note the magazine now has a permanent fiction editor.

Needs: "No specific 'category' requirements; we publish what we love." Accepts 2-4 mss/issue. Publishes ms an average of 6 months after acceptance. Published work by Anna Kirwan Vogel, Jane Yolen and Barbara VanNoord; published new writers within the last year. Length: 1,000-2,500 words preferred. Publishes short shorts. "Short pieces have a better chance of publication. Prefer 10 pages or less."

How to Contact: Send complete ms with cover letter, which should include brief biographical note. "May take one year to report." SASE. Simultaneous submissions are encouraged. Sample copy for $4.

Payment/Terms: Pays contributor's copies. All rights return to writer upon publication.

Advice: "Every manuscript is read by 3 or more readers. We publish what we love most—and it has varied widely."

PHANTASM, (I, II), Iniquities Publishing, 235 E. Colorado Blvd., Suite 1346, Pasadena CA 91101. Editor: J.F. Gonzalez. Magazine: 8½×11; 4-8 pages; b&w gloss cover; illustrations and photographs. "Horror fiction (see guidelines) for anybody who has an interest in horror (books, film, etc.)." Quarterly. Estab. 1990. Circ. 1,000.

● Work published in *Phantasm* has been included in the *Year's Best Fantasy and Horror.*

Needs: Horror, mystery/suspense and science fiction (soft sociological). No sword and sorcery, romance, confessional, pornography. Receives 250 unsolicited mss/month. Buys 6-8 mss/issue; 30-35 mss/year. Publishes ms 6 months-1½ years after acceptance. Recently published work by A.R. Murlan, Mick Garris, S.K. Epperson and Ramsey Campbell. Length: 4,000-6,000 words preferred; 10,000 words maximum. Publishes short shorts. Sometimes critiques rejected mss and recommends other markets.

How to Contact: Send complete ms with cover letter. Include "credits, if any, name, address and phone number. I don't want the writer to tell me about the story in the cover letter." Reports in 1-3 weeks on queries; 3 months on mss. SASE. Simultaneous and reprint submissions OK. E-mail address: jgrive@aol.com. Sample copy for $4 plus $1 p&h (payable to *Iniquities Publishing*). Fiction guidelines for #10 SASE.

Payment/Terms: Pays 1¢/word on publication for first North American serial rights. Sends galleys to author.

Advice: Looks for "believable characters and original ideas. Good writing. Fantastic writing. Make the words flow and count for the story. If the story keeps us turning the pages with bated breath, it has a great chance. If we get through the first two pages and it's sloppy, displays weak, or uninteresting characters or a contrived plot, we won't even finish it. Chances are the reader won't either. Know the genre and what's been done. *Invest in a sample copy.* While we are open to different styles of horror, we have high expectations for the fiction we publish. The only way a beginner will know what we expect is to buy the magazine and read what we've published."

PHANTASM, (I, II), 1530 Seventh St., Rock Island IL 61201. (309)788-3980. Editor: Betty Mowery. 5½ × 8½; 16 pages; illustrations. "To provide, especially the beginner a market. Soft horror, fantasy and mystery. No gore or violence." Quarterly. Estab. 1993. Circ. 50.

Needs: Fantasy, horror, mystery/suspense. Receives 20 unsolicited mss/month. Accepts 4 mss/issue; 16 mss/year. Publishes ms next issue after acceptance. Length: 500 words average; 200 words minimum; 500 words maximum. Publishes short shorts. Also publishes poetry. Sometimes critiques or comments on rejected mss.

How to Contact: Send complete ms. Reports in 1 week on queries. SASE for return of ms or send a disposable copy of ms. Simultaneous and reprint submissions OK. Sample copy for $2. Fiction guidelines for #10 SASE.

Payment/Terms: No payment ("but purchase isn't necessary to be published"). Acquires first rights.

Advice: "Either send for a sample and see what has been published—or just go ahead and submit. Always enclose SASE, for there is no response without one."

PHOEBE, An Interdisciplinary Journal of Feminist Scholarship, (II, IV), Theory and Aesthetics, Women's Studies Program, State University of New York, College at Oneonta, Oneonta NY 13820. (607)436-3500, ext. 2014. Editor: Kathleen O'Mara. Journal: 7 × 9; 140 pages; 80 lb. paper; illustrations and photos. "Feminist material for feminist scholars and readers." Semiannually. Estab. 1989. Circ. 400.

Needs: Feminist: ethnic, experimental, gay, humor/satire, lesbian, literary, translations. Receives 25 unsolicited mss/month. "One-third to one-half of each issue is short fiction and poetry." Does not read mss in summer. Publishes ms 3-4 months after acceptance. Length: 1,500-2,500 words preferred. Publishes short shorts. Sometimes critiques rejected mss and recommends other markets.

How to Contact: Send complete ms with cover letter. Reports in 1 month on queries; 15 weeks on mss. Sample copy for $7.50. Fiction guidelines free.

Payment/Terms: Pays in contributor's copies. Acquires one-time rights.

Advice: "We look for writing with a feminist perspective. *Phoebe* was founded to provide a forum for cross-cultural feminist analysis, debate and exchange. The editors are committed to providing space for all disciplines and new areas of research, criticism and theory in feminist scholarship and aesthetics. *Phoebe* is not committed to any one conception of feminism. All work that is not sexist, racist, homophobic, or otherwise discriminatory, will be welcome. *Phoebe* is particularly committed to publishing work informed by a theoretical perspective which will enrich critical thinking."

PHOEBE, A Journal of Literary Arts, (II), George Mason University, 4400 University Dr., Fairfax VA 22030. (703)993-2915. Editor: Graham Foust. Fiction Editors: Scott Berg, Patricia Fuentes. Editors change each year. Magazine: 6 × 9; 116 pages; 80 lb. paper; 0-5 illustrations; 0-10 photographs. "We publish fiction, poetry, photographs, illustrations and some reviews." Published 2 times/year. Estab. 1972. Circ. 3,000.

Needs: "Looking for a broad range of poetry, fiction and essays. Encourage writers and poets to experiment, to stretch the boundaries of genre." No romance, western, juvenile, erotica. Receives 20 mss/month. Accepts 3-5 mss/issue. Does not read mss in summer. Publishes ms 3-6 months after acceptance. Length: no more than 35 pages. Also publishes literary essays, literary criticism, poetry.

How to Contact: Send complete ms with cover letter. Include "name, address, phone. Brief bio." SASE. Simultaneous submissions OK. Sample copy for $6.

Payment/Terms: Pays 2 contributor's copies. Acquires one-time rights. All rights revert to author.

Advice: "We are interested in a variety of fiction, poetry and nonfiction. We suggest potential contributors study previous issues. Each year *Phoebe* sponsors poetry and fiction contests, with $500 awarded to the winning poem and short story. The deadline for the Greg Grummer Award in Poetry is December 15; the deadline for the Phoebe Fiction Prize is December 15. Those interested in entering should write for full contest guidelines."

‡PICA, (I, II), 165 N. Ashbury Ave., Bolingbrook IL 60440. Editor: Lisa Green. Magazine: 5½ × 8½; 50-75 pages; 24 lb. paper; 30-38 lb. cover stock; b&w illustrations and photos. "*Pica* attempts to publish the best of avant-garde fiction, essays and poetry. Our audience is generally academic: passionate about the language." Triannually. Estab. 1995. Circ. 100.

Needs: Condensed/excerpted novel, experimental, feminist, gay, humor/satire, lesbian, literary. "No pornography, nothing 'fluffy,' and nothing you would see published in any magazine you'd find in the checkout aisle at the grocery store." Receives 30 unsolicited mss/month. Accepts 10 mss/issue; 30 mss/year. Publishes ms 6-8 months after acceptance. Recently published work by Michael David Martin, David Moses Fruchter and Steve Moore. Length: 10,000 words maximum. Publishes short shorts. Also publishes literary essays, literary criticism and poetry. Often critiques or comments on rejected ms.

How to Contact: Send complete ms. "Only include a cover letter if there is something you *really* need to tell us." Reports in 2 months on mss. Send SASE for return of ms. Simultaneous, reprint and electronic (WordPerfect compatible disk) submissions OK. Sample copy for $3. Fiction guidelines for SASE.

Payment/Terms: Pays 3 contributor's copies; additional copies for $1. Acquires one-time rights. Sends galleys to author.

Advice: "We are looking for writers with a broad base of knowledge. We love variety and wit, passion and opinion. We adore works that seek out ambiguity and exploit detail. Suck up as much life as you can. Gorge yourself on it. Then let us see what you've got to say. And always read a sample copy of any magazine you submit to." Needs "more good fiction by women!"

PIG IRON, (II), Box 237, Youngstown OH 44501. (216)747-6932. Fax: (216)747-0599. Editor: Jim Villani. Magazine: 8½×11; 128 pages; 60 lb. offset paper; 85 pt. coated cover stock; b&w illustrations; b&w 120 line photographs. "Contemporary literature by new and experimental writers." Annually. Estab. 1975. Circ. 1,000.

• *Pig Iron* sponsors the Kenneth Patchen Competition listed in the Contests and Awards section.

Needs: Literary and thematic. No mainstream. Upcoming themes: "Frontier: Custom and Archtype" (October 1996); "Years of Rage: 1960s" (October 1997). Buys 10-20 mss/issue. Receives approximately 75-100 unsolicited mss/month. Recently published work by John Druska, Joel Climenhaga, Larry Smith, Wayne Hogan and Andrena Zawinski. Length: 8,000 words maximum. Also publishes literary nonfiction, poetry.

How to Contact: Send complete ms with SASE. No simultaneous submissions. Reports in 4 months. Sample copy for $4.

Payment/Terms: Pays $5/printed page and 2 contributor's copies on publication for first North American serial rights; $5 charge for extras.

Advice: "Looking for works psychological, new critical, aggressive, poised for a new century unfolding, unveiling." Rejects manuscripts "lacking modern style, experimental style. Editors look for stylistic innovation."

‡PIKEVILLE REVIEW, (I), Pikeville College, Sycamore St., Pikeville KY 41501. (606)432-9200. Editor: James Alan Riley. Magazine: 8½×6; 120 pages; illustrations and photos. "Literate audience interested in well-crafted poetry, fiction, essays and reviews." Annually. Estab. 1987. Circ. 500.

Needs: Ethnic/multicultural, experimental, feminist, humor/satire, literary, mainstream/contemporary, regional, translations. Receives 25 unsolicited mss/month. Accepts 3-4 mss/issue. Does not read mss in the summer. Publishes ms 6-8 months after acceptance. Length: 5,000 words average; 15,000 words maximum. Publishes short shorts. Also publishes literary essays and poetry. Often critiques rejected mss.

How to Contact: Send complete ms with cover letter. Should include estimated word count. Send SASE for reply, return of ms or send a disposable copy of ms. Simultaneous submissions OK. Sample copy for $3. Reviews novels and short story collections.

Payment/Terms: Pays 5 contributor's copies; additional copies for $3. Acquires first rights. Sponsors occasional fiction award: $50.

Advice: "Send a clean manuscript with well-developed characters."

‡THE PINK CHAMELEON, (I, II), 170 Park Ave., Hicksville NY 11801. (516)939-0457. Editor: Dorothy (Paula) Freda. Magazine: 5½×8½; 100 pages; 20 lb. bond paper; laminated card stock cover; illustrations and photographs. *The Pink Chameleon* is an "upbeat, family-oriented magazine that publishes any genre as long as the material submitted is in good taste and gives hope for the future, even in sadness." Annually. Estab. 1985.

Needs: Adventure, children's/juvenile (1-12 years), condensed/excerpted novel, ethnic/multicultural, experimental, fantasy (children's, science), historical, humor/satire, literary, mainstream/contemporary, mystery/ suspense (amateur sleuth, cozy, romantic), religious/inspirational, romance (contemporary, futuristic/time travel, gothic, historical), science fiction (soft/sociological), senior citizen/retirement, sports, westerns (frontier, traditional), young adult/teen (adventure, mystery, romance, science fiction, western). "No pornography or graphic language." Accepts 12 mss/year. Publishes ms 6-12 months after acceptance. Recently published work by Sr. Mary Ann Henn, Sigmund Weiss, J. Richard Reed, Dorothy R. Brown, Denise Noe and Paula Freda. Length: 3,500 words maximum. Publishes short shorts. Also publishes literary essays and poetry. Often critiques or comments on rejected ms.

How to Contact: *Subscribers only* should send complete ms with a cover letter. Send SASE for reply, return of ms or send a disposable copy of ms. Reprint submissions OK. Sample copy for $5. Fiction guidelines free.
Payment/Terms: Pays 1 contributor's copy. Acquires one-time rights.
Advice: "Avoid wordiness; use simple, evocative language; and remember that *The Pink Chameleon* is a family-oriented magazine."

THE PIPE SMOKER'S EPHEMERIS, (I, II, IV), The Universal Coterie of Pipe Smokers, 20-37 120 St., College Point NY 11356. Editor: Tom Dunn. Magazine: 8½×11; 54-66 pages; offset paper and cover; illustrations; photos. Pipe smoking and tobacco theme for general and professional audience. Irregular quarterly. Estab. 1964.
Needs: Pipe smoking related: historical, humor/satire, literary. Publishes ms up to 1 year after acceptance. Length: 2,500 words average; 5,000 words maximum. Also publishes short shorts. Occasionally critiques rejected mss.
• The Universal Coterie of Pipe Smokers has published two large, hardbound books, collections of work from the magazine.
How to Contact: Send complete ms with cover letter. Reports in 2 weeks on mss. Simultaneous and reprints OK. Sample copy for 8½×11 SAE and 6 first-class stamps.
Payment/Terms: Acquires one-time rights.

PIRATE WRITINGS, Tales of Fantasy, Mystery & Science Fiction, (II), Pirate Writings Publishing, 53 Whitman Ave., Islip NY 11751. Editor: Edward J. McFadden. Assistant Editor: Tom Piccirilli. Magazine: full size, saddle stapled. "We are looking for poetry and short stories that entertain." Quarterly. Estab. 1992. Circ. 8,000.
• The magazine has increased its circulation by more than half and the editor is now accepting longer materials.
Needs: Fantasy (dark fantasy, science fantasy, sword and sorcery), mystery/suspense, science fiction (all types). Receives 300-400 unsolicited mss/month. Buys 8 mss/issue; 30-40 mss/year. Publishes ms 6 months-1 year after acceptance. Length: 2,500 words average; 250 words minimum; 8,000 words maximum. Also publishes poetry. Sometimes critiques or comments on rejected mss.
How to Contact: Send complete ms with cover letter. Should include estimated word count, 1 paragraph bio, Social Security number, list of publications with submission. Reports in 1 week on queries; 2 months on mss. Send SASE for reply or return of ms or disposable copy of ms. Will consider simultaneous submissions. Sample copy for $5 (make check payable to Pirate Writings Publishing). Fiction guidelines for #10 SAE.
Payment/Terms: Pays 1-5¢/word for first North American serial rights.
Advice: "My goal is to provide a diverse, entertaining and thought provoking magazine featuring all the above stated genres in every issue. Hints: I love a good ending. Move me, make me laugh, surprise me, and you're in. Read *PW* and you'll see what I mean."

PKA'S ADVOCATE, (I, II), (formerly *The Advocate*), PKA Publications, 301A Rolling Hills Park, Prattsville NY 12468. (518)299-3103. Editor: Remington Wright. Tabloid: 9⅜×12¼; 32 pages; newsprint paper; line drawings; b&w photographs. "Eclectic for a general audience." Bimonthly. Estab. 1987.
• *PKA's Advocate* editors tend to like positive, upbeat, entertaining material.
Needs: Adventure, contemporary, ethnic, experimental, fantasy, feminist, historical, humor/satire, juvenile (5-9 years), literary, mainstream, mystery/suspense, prose poem, regional, romance, science fiction, senior citizen/retirement, sports, western, young adult/teen (10-18 years). Nothing religious, pornographic, violent, erotic, pro-drug or anti-environment. Receives 24 unsolicited mss/month. Accepts 6-8 mss/issue; 36-48 mss/year. Publishes ms 4 months to 1 year after acceptance. Length: 1,000 words preferred; 2,500 words maximum. Sometimes critiques rejected mss.
How to Contact: Send complete ms with cover letter. Reports in 2 weeks on queries; 2 months on mss. SASE. No simultaneous submissions. Sample copy for $4 (US currency for inside US; $5.25 US currency for Canada). Writers guidelines for SASE.
Payment/Terms: Pays contributor's copies. Acquires first rights.
Advice: "The highest criterion in selecting a work is its entertainment value. It must first be enjoyable reading. It must, of course, be original. To stand out, it must be thought provoking or strongly emotive, or very cleverly plotted. Will consider only previously unpublished works by writers who do not earn their living principally through writing."

‡A PLACE TO ENTER, Contemporary Fiction by Emerging Writers of African Descent, (I, II, IV), Drayton-Iton Communications, Inc. (DICOM), 1328 Broadway, Suite 1054, New York NY 10001. (212)714-7032. Editor: Brian Iton. Fiction Editor: Odessa Drayton. Magazine: 8½×11; 44 pages; 55 lb. Glatfelter paper; Kiyar 9 chrom cover. "*A Place to Enter* publishes contemporary short fiction with the aim of entertaining and validating the experiences of persons of African descent." Quarterly. Estab. 1995. Circ. 1,000.

Needs: Adventure, condensed/excerpted novel, ethnic/multicultural, humor/satire, literary, mainstream/contemporary, mystery/suspense, religious/inspirational, romance. Receives 25-30 unsolicited mss/month. Buys 4-5 mss/issue; 16-20 mss/year. Publishes ms 4 months after acceptance. Agented fiction 0-10%. Recently published work by Jackie Joice, Peter Harris and Gary Earl Ross. Length: 5,000 words average; 1,000 words minimum; 10,000 words maximum. Sometimes critiques or comments on rejected ms.

How to Contact: Send complete ms with a cover letter. Should include estimated word count, 1-page bio. Reports in 10-12 weeks on mss. Send SASE for return of ms or send disposable copy of ms. Sample copy for $8.50, 8½ × 11 SAE and 5 first-class stamps. Fiction guidelines for #9 SASE.

Payment/Terms: Pays $100 and 1 contributor's copy on publication for first North American serial rights.

Advice: "Take the time to make it look as clean as possible. We want stories that entertain and remove the reader from their 'day-to-day.' Edit it. Workshop it. Please proofread it. Tell the story, don't describe your way out of the teller's seat. I don't want to see in-depth explorations of unresolved low-living."

PLÉIADES MAGAZINE/PHILAE, (I, II), Box 357, 6677 W. Suite D, Colfax, Lakewood CO 80215. John Moravec, Pléiades Productions. Magazine: 8½ × 11; 30-50 pages; 30 lb. paper; illustrations. "We want well thought out material; no sex stories, and good rhymed poetry and carefully written prose. We want articles about national issues." Both magazines will, in the future, be published twice a year; *Philae* more often depending on material. *Philae* estab. 1947, *Pléiades*, estab. 1984. Circ. 10,000.

Needs: Literary, fantasy, horror, mystery/suspense, senior citizen/retirement, serialized/excerpted novel, western. Receives 50-100 unsolicited mss/month. Publishes ms 3 months or less after acceptance. Length: 1,200-1,800 words average; 500-800 words minimum.

How to Contact: Send complete ms with short cover letter. SASE. Reports in 1 month. Simultaneous submissions OK. Sample copy for $3.75. (Checks made out to John L. Moravec). Fiction guidelines for #10 SASE.

Payment/Terms: Pays in contributor's copies, awards, trophies.

Advice: "Learn to write, and take lessons on punctuation. Shorter fiction and articles considered first."

PLOUGHSHARES, (II), Emerson College, 100 Beacon St., Boston MA 02116. (617)578-8753. Editor: Don Lee. "Our mission is to present dynamic, contrasting views on what is valid and important in contemporary literature, and to discover and advance significant literary talent. Each issue is guest-edited by a different writer. We no longer structure issues around preconceived themes." Triquarterly. Estab. 1971. Circ. 6,000.

• *Ploughshares* also sponsors a writing seminar in Holland. Work published in *Ploughshares* has been selected continuously for inclusion in the *Best American Short Stories* and *O. Henry Prize* anthologies. In fact the magazine has the honor as having the most stories selected from a single issue (three) to be included in *B.A.S.S.* Guest editors for 1996 include Marilyn Hacker (spring), Richard Ford (fall) and Ellen Bryant Voight (winter).

Needs: Literary, prose poem. "No genre (science fiction, detective, gothic, adventure, etc.), popular formula or commercial fiction whose purpose is to entertain rather than to illuminate." Buys 25 mss/year. Receives 400-600 unsolicited fiction mss each month. Published work by Rick Bass, Joy Williams and Andre Dubus; published new writers within the last year. Length: 300-6,000 words.

How to Contact: Query with #10 SASE for guidelines and examine a sample issue (sample issue order form included in guidelines). Reading period: postmarked August 1 to March 31. Cover letter should include "previous pubs." SASE. Reports in 3-5 months on mss. Sample copy for $6. (Please specify fiction issue sample.) Current issue for $8.95.

Payment/Terms: Pays $10/page, $40 minimum per title; $200 maximum, plus copies and a subscription on publication for first North American serial rights. Offers 50% kill fee for assigned ms not published.

Advice: "Be familiar with our fiction issues, fiction by our writers and by our various editors (e.g., Sue Miller, Tobias Wolff, Rosellen Brown, Tim O'Brien, Jay Neugeboren, Jayne Anne Phillips, James Alan McPherson) and more generally acquaint yourself with the best short fiction currently appearing in the literary quarterlies, and the annual prize anthologies (*Pushcart Prize, O. Henry Awards, Best American Short Stories*). Also realistically consider whether the work you are submitting is as good as or better than—in your own opinion—the work appearing in the magazine you're sending to. What is the level of competition? And what is its volume? (In our case, we accept about 1 ms in 200.) Never send 'blindly' to a magazine, or without carefully weighing your prospect there against those elsewhere. Always keep a copy of work you submit."

‡THE PLOWMAN, (II), Box 414, Whitby Ontario L1N 5S4 Canada. Editor: Tony Scavetta. Tabloid: 56 pages; illustrations and photos. Monthly. Estab. 1988. Circ. 15,000.

• The publisher of *The Plowman* also produces several hundred chapbooks each year.

Needs: "An international journal publishing all holocaust, relition, didactic, ethnic, eclectic, love and other stories."

How to Contact: Send complete ms with cover letter. Reports in 1 week. Simultaneous and reprint submissions OK. Sample copy and fiction guidelines for SAE.

Payment/Terms: Pays in contributor's copies; charges for extras. Acquires one-time rights. Sends galleys to author.

POETRY FORUM SHORT STORIES, (I, II), Poetry Forum, 5713 Larchmont Dr., Erie PA 16509. (814)866-2543. Fax: (814)866-2543 (fax hours 8-10 a.m., 5-8 p.m.). Editor: Gunver Skogsholm. Newspaper: 7×8½; 34 pages; card cover; illustrations. "Human interest themes (no sexually explicit or racially biased or blasphemous material) for the general public—from the grassroot to the intellectual." Quarterly. Estab. 1989. Circ. 400.

• Note the publication policy charging for membership to the magazine for publication and, says the editor, "subscribers come first!" Editor Skogsholm also publishes *The Journal* and *Short Stories Bimonthly* listed in this book.

Needs: Confession, contemporary, ethnic, experimental, fantasy, feminist, historical, literary, mainstream, mystery/suspense, prose poem, religious/inspirational, romance, science fiction, senior citizen/retirement, young adult/teen. "No blasphemous, sexually explicit material." Publishes annual special fiction issue. Receives 50 unsolicited mss/month. Accepts 12 mss/issue; 40 mss/year. Publishes ms 6 months after acceptance. Agented fiction less than 1%. Length: 2,000 words average; 500 words minimum; 5,000 words maximum. Also publishes literary essays, literary criticism, poetry.

How to Contact: *This magazine charges a "professional members" fee of $36.* The fee entitles you to publication of a maximum of 3,000 words. Send complete ms with cover letter. Reports in 3 weeks to 2 months on mss. SASE. Simultaneous and reprint submissions OK. "Accepts electronic submissions via disk gladly." E-mail address: 75562.670@compuserve.com. Sample copy for $3. Fiction guidelines for SASE. Reviews novels and short story collections.

Payment/Terms: Preference given to submissions by subscribers. Acquires one-time rights.

Advice: "Tell your story and tell it to a person standing in the door about to run out."

‡✦POETRY WLU, (I), Wilfrid Laurier University, Wilfrid Laurier University, Waterloo, Ontario N2L 3C5 Canada. (519)884-1970. Managing Editor: Ed Jewinski. Editors change each year. Magazine: 8½×7; 50-60 pages; standard bond paper; illustrations. "*Poetry WLU* is a place for the new, young, unknown and talented." Annually. Estab. 1981. Circ. 250.

Needs: Literary. Receives 5-10 unsolicited mss/month. Accepts 2-3 mss/issue. "All reading and assessing is done between January and March." Publishes ms 2 months after acceptance. Length: 100 words minimum; 1,500 words maximum. Publishes short shorts. Also publishes poetry.

How to Contact: Send complete ms with a cover letter and SASE. Reports in 2 months. SASE for reply or return of ms. Sample copy for $2.

Payment/Terms: Pays 1 contributor's copy; additional copies for $2. Sponsors contests, awards or grants for fiction writers. "The applicant must be a registered Wilfrid Laurier University student."

‡POET'S FANTASY, (I, II), 227 Hatten Ave., Rice Lake WI 54868. (715)234-7472. Editor: Gloria Stoeckel. Magazine: 8½×4½; 40 pages; 20 lb. paper; colored stock cover; illustrations. *Poet's Fantasy* is a magazine of "fantasy, but not conclusive." Bimonthly. Estab. 1992. Circ. 180.

Needs: Fantasy (science). List of upcoming themes available for SASE. Receives 2-3 unsolicited mss/month. Accepts 6 mss/year. Recently published work by Bernard Hewitt and Bobbe Quinlan. Length: 1,000 words average; 500 words minimum; 1,500 words maximum. Publishes short shorts. Also publishes literary essays and poetry. Sometimes critiques or comments on rejected ms.

How to Contact: Send complete ms with a cover letter. Should include estimated word count and list of publications. Reports in 3 weeks. Send SASE for reply, return of ms or send a disposable copy of ms. Simultaneous and electronic submissions OK. Sample copy for $3. Fiction guidelines free.

Payment/Terms: Pays $3 coupon toward purchase of magazine on publication for first North American serial rights.

Advice: Wants fiction with "tight writing, action and ending twist. Edit and re-edit before sending."

THE POINTED CIRCLE, (II), Portland Community College-Cascade, 705 N. Killingsworth St., Portland OR 97217. (503)244-6111 ext. 5230. Editors: Student Editorial Staff. Magazine: 80 pages; b&w illustrations and photographs. "Anything of interest to educationally/culturally mixed audience." Annually. Estab. 1980.

Needs: Contemporary, ethnic, literary, prose poem, regional. "We will read whatever is sent, but encourage writers to remember we are a quality literary/arts magazine intended to promote the arts in the community." Acquires 3-7 mss/year. Accepts submissions only December 1-February 15, for October 1 issue. Length: 3,000 words maximum.

How to Contact: Send complete ms with cover letter and brief bio. SASE. E-mail address: rstevens@pcc.edu. Sample copy for $4.50. Fiction guidelines for #10 SASE.

The maple leaf symbol before a listing indicates a Canadian publisher, magazine, conference or contest.

Payment/Terms: Pays in contributor's copies. Acquires one-time rights.

Advice: "Looks for quality—topicality—nothing trite. The author cares about language and acts responsibly toward the reader, honors the reader's investment of time and piques the reader's interest."

‡POOR KATY'S ALMANAC, Home of Pulp Fiction . . . and More!, (I, II), Katy's Kab Publications, P.O. Box 913, Hayfork CA 96041. Phone/fax: (916)628-4714. Editor: Katy Lawson. Magazine: 8½×5½; 40-50 pages; 20 lb. paper; card stock cover; occasionally illustrations and photos. "*Poor Katy's Almanac* applauds individuals who serve others, especially as their vocation." Monthly. Estab. 1994. Circ. 500.

● Katy's Kab Publications also publishes *Tribute to Officer Dallies* listed in this section.

Needs: Adventure, humor/satire, literary, mystery/suspense (amateur sleuth, police procedural, private eye/hardboiled), science fiction, westerns, patriotic, slice-of-life. "No hateful, negative, depressing, bashing." Upcoming themes: "Dispatcher Appreciation" (April); "Peace Officer Appreciation" (May). "We publish an annual anthology for stories that were too adult, or otherwise didn't fit, the *Almanac*." Receives 100 unsolicited mss/month. Accepts 12 mss/issue; 144 mss/year. Publishes ms 1-12 months after acceptance. Recently published work by Carole Hall, J. Lee Bragg, Glenn Sparks and Catherine Robinson. Length: 500 words average; 200 words minimum; 1,000 words maximum. Publishes short shorts. Length: 200-500 words. Also publishes literary essays and poetry. Often critiques or comments on rejected ms.

How to Contact: Send complete ms with a cover letter. Should include estimated word count, 100-word bio, list of publications and adequate return postage. Reports in 2-6 months. Send SASE for reply, return of ms or send a disposable copy of ms. Simultaneous, reprint and electronic submissions OK. E-mail address: katy.lawson@trnet.org. Sample copy for $2. Fiction guidelines for #10 SASE.

Payment/Terms: Pays 2 contributor's copies; additional copies 50% off. Acquires one-time rights (unless otherwise negotiated). "This year we will sponsor our first contest. We're still in the planning stage. Writers should query with SASE."

Advice: "We love humor. Wit. 'O. Henry' plot twists. Conciseness will win me over. I don't have time to rewrite stories. Don't 'dumb-down' your writing. Our audience can assume most of the plot exposition from your well-crafted dialogue. This is *not* an English composition class. Don't write about something that bores you. If you had fun writing about a subject you feel passionately about, chances are we'll enjoy reading it. Maybe we'll agree with you, maybe not. But you are the writer."

THE PORTABLE WALL, (II), Basement Press, 215 Burlington, Billings MT 59101. (406)256-3588. Editor: Daniel Struckman. Magazine: 6×9¼; 64 pages; cotton rag paper; best quality cover; line engravings; illustrations. "We consider all kinds of material. Bias toward humor." Semiannually. Estab. 1977. Circ. 400.

Needs: Adventure, contemporary, ethnic, experimental, feminist, historical, humor/satire, literary, mainstream, prose poem, regional, science fiction, senior citizen, sports, translations. Upcoming themes: "Human Rights" (1996); "Household Pets" (1997). "We favor short pieces and poetry." Receives 5-10 unsolicited mss/month. Accepts 3-4 mss/issue; 6-8 mss/year. Publishes ms 6-12 months after acceptance. Published works by Gray Harris and Wilbur Wood. Length: 2,000 words preferred. Publishes short shorts. Also publishes literary essays, literary criticism, poetry. Sometimes critiques rejected mss.

How to Contact: Send complete ms with cover letter. No simultaneous submissions. Reports within 3 months on mss. SASE. Sample copy for $6.50.

Payment/Terms: Pays subscription to magazine. Acquires one-time rights.

Advice: "We like language that evokes believable pictures in our minds and that tells news. We are definitely leaning toward idiomatic voices."

‡BERN PORTER INTERNATIONAL, Bern Porter Books, 22 Salmond St., Belfast ME 04915. (207)338-6798. Editor: Bern Porter. Magazine: 8½×11; 98-132 pages; illustrations and photographs. "High literary quality with international flavor." Bimonthly. Estab. 1991.

Needs: Experimental, literary, prose poem, translations, international. Publishes special fiction issue. Receives 30-50 unsolicited mss/month. Buys 10-15 mss/issue. Publishes ms immediately after acceptance. Length: open. Publishes short shorts. Comments on or critiques rejected mss and recommends other markets.

How to Contact: Query first. Reports in 1 week. SASE. Simultaneous and reprint submissions OK. Sample copy and fiction guidelines free.

Payment/Terms: Pays 6¢/word on publication. Buys world rights. Sends galleys to author.

PORTLAND REVIEW, (I, II), Portland State University, Box 751, Portland OR 97207. (503)725-4533. Editors: Lois Breedlove and Barry Rich. Magazine: 9×12; 80 pages; 40 lb. paper; 60 lb. cover stock; b&w drawings and photos. "We seek to publish fiction in which content takes precedence over style." Published 2 times/year. Estab. 1955. Circ. 1,500.

● The editors say they are looking for experimental work "with darker, harsher, more introspective tones."

Needs: Contemporary, literary, regional, humor/satire, experimental. "No porno, sci fi, mood pieces/vignettes, or material which advocates political or religious ideologies." Publishes within 1 year of acceptance. Length: 3,500 words average; 5,000 words maximum. Critiques ms when time allows. Also publishes critical essays, poetry, drama, interviews and reviews.

How to Contact: Submit complete ms with short bio and publishing credits. SASE. Simultaneous submissions OK (if noted). Reports in 6-8 weeks. Sample copy for $5 plus $1 postage.
Payment/Terms: Pays 1 contributor's copy. Acquires one-time rights.
Advice: "Our editors, and thus our tastes/biases change annually, so keep trying us."

POSKISNOLT PRESS, Yesterday's Press, (I, II, IV), Yesterday's Press, JAF Station, Box 7415, New York NY 10116-4630. Editor: Patricia D. Coscia. Magazine: $7 \times 8\frac{1}{2}$; 20 pages; regular typing paper. Estab. 1989. Circ. 100.
Needs: Contemporary, erotica, ethnic, experimental, fantasy, feminist, gay, humor/satire, lesbian, literary, mainstream, prose poem, psychic/supernatural/occult, romance, senior citizen/retirement, western, young adult/teen (10-18 years). "X-rated material is not accepted!" Plans to publish a special fiction issue or anthology in the future. Receives 50 unsolicited mss/month. Accepts 30 mss/issue; 100 mss/year. Publishes ms 6 months after acceptance. Length: 200 words average; 100 words minimum; 500 words maximum. Publishes short shorts. Length: 100-500 words. Sometimes critiques rejected mss and recommends other markets.
How to Contact: Query first with clips of published work or send complete manuscript with cover letter. Reports in 1 week on queries; 6 months on mss. SASE. Accepts simultaneous submissions. Sample copy for $5 with #10 SAE and $2 postage. Fiction guidelines for #10 SAE and $2 postage.
Payment/Terms: Pays with subscription to magazine or contributor's copies; charges for extras. Acquires all rights, first rights or one-time rights.

‡✽**POSSIBILITIIS LITERARY ARTS MAGAZINE, (I, II, IV)**, 109-2100 Scott St., Ottawa, Ontario K1Z 1A3 Canada. (613)761-1177. Editor: Maureen Henry. Magazine: $8\frac{1}{2} \times 11$; 48 pages; illustrations and photos. Semiannually. Estab. 1993. Circ. 600.
Needs: Condensed/excerpted novel, ethnic/multicultural, humor/satire, literary, mainstream/contemporary, romance (contemporary), translations, young adult/teen (mystery, science fiction). Upcoming themes: "Book Review"; "Latin American"; "Young authors, age 18-24." Publishes special fiction issues or anthologies. Receives 20 unsolicited mss/month. Accepts 3 mss/issue; 12 mss/year. Publishes ms 6 months after acceptance. Recently published work by Cecil Foster, Austin Clarke and Makeda Silvera. Publishes short shorts. Also publishes literary essays, literary criticism and poetry. Often critiques or comments on rejected ms.
How to Contact: Send complete ms with a cover letter. Should include 4-line bio with submission. Reports in 6 months. Send SASE for return of ms. Simultaneous and reprint submissions OK. Sample copy for $5. Fiction guidelines free.
Payment/Terms: Pays contributor's copies. Acquires one-time rights. Sponsors contests, awards or grants for fiction writers.

THE POST, (II), Publishers Syndication International, 1413 K St. NW, First Floor, Washington DC 20005. Editor: A.P. Samuels. Magazine: $8\frac{1}{2} \times 11$; 32 pages. Monthly. Estab. 1988.
Needs: Adventure, mystery/suspense (private eye), romance (romantic suspense), western (traditional). "No explicit sex, gore, extreme violence or bad language." Receives 75 unsolicited mss/month. Buys 1 ms/issue; 12 mss/year. Time between acceptance and publication varies. Agented fiction 10%. Length: 10,000 words average.
How to Contact: Send complete ms with cover letter. Reports on mss in 5 weeks. No simultaneous submissions. Fiction guidelines for #10 SASE.
Payment/Terms: Pays $\frac{1}{2}$¢ to 4¢/word. Pays on acceptance for all rights.

POSTMODERN CULTURE, (I, IV), Box 8105, North Carolina State University, Raleigh NC 27695. (919)515-4127. Co-Editors: Eyal Amiran and John Unsworth. Magazine. "Works that are postmodern." Triannually. Estab. 1990. Circ. 3,300.
Needs: Postmodern, any genre. Receives 30 unsolicited mss/month. Accepts 3 mss/year. Publishes ms 3 months after acceptance. Agented fiction 25%. Published work by Robert Coover, Kathy Acker and Alice Fulton. Length: 10,000 words maximum. Publishes short shorts. Also publishes literary essays, literary criticism, poetry.
How to Contact: Send complete ms with a cover letter. E-mail address: pmc@unity.NCSU.edu. Reports in 6 weeks on mss. Send a disposable copy of ms. Simultaneous and electronic submissions OK. Sample copy free.
Payment/Terms: Free subscription to the magazine. Author holds copyright. Sends galleys to author.

POTATO EYES, (II), Nightshade, P.O. Box 76, Troy ME 04987-0076. (207)948-3427. Editors: Carolyn Page and Roy Zarucchi. Magazine: $5\frac{1}{2} \times 8\frac{1}{2}$; 108 pages; 60 lb. text paper; 80 lb. Curtis flannel cover. "We tend to showcase Appalachian talent from Alabama to Quebec, and in doing so, we hope to dispel hackneyed stereotypes and political borders. However, we don't limit ourselves to this area, publishing always the best that we receive." Estab. 1988. Circ. 800.
● The publishers of *Potato Eyes* also operate Nightshade Press listed in the Small Press section of this book.

Needs: Contemporary, humor/satire, literary, mainstream, regional, feminist and ecological themes. A *Nightshade Nightstand Short Story Reader* with forward by Fred Chappell was scheduled for Fall 1995. Receives 500 unsolicited mss/month. Accepts 5 mss/issue; 10 mss/year. Publishes ms 2 months-2 years after acceptance. Recently published work by Shirley G. Cochrane, Richard Abron, Rachel Piccione, Edward M. Holmes, Robert Chute and George Singleton. Length: 3,000 words maximum; 2,000 average. Publishes short shorts. Length: 450 words. Also publishes poetry (looking for English/French translations of Franco poems) plus one or two novels. Sometimes critiques rejected mss.

How to Contact: Send complete ms with cover letter. Reports in 4 weeks-4 months on mss. SASE. Sample copy for $5, including postage. Fiction guidelines for #10 SAE.

Payment/Terms: Pays in contributor's copies. Acquires first North American serial rights.

Advice: "We care about the larger issues, including pollution, ecology, bio-regionalism, uncontrolled progress and 'condominia,' and women's issues, as well as the rights of the individual. We care about television, the great sewer pipe of America, and what it is doing to America's youth. We are exploring these issues with writers who have originality, a reordered perspective, and who submit to us generous sprinklings of humor and satire. Although we do occasionally comment on valid fiction, we have walked away unscathed from the world of academia and refuse to correct manuscripts. We respect our contributors and treat them as professionals, however, and write personal responses to every submission if given a SASE. We expect the same treatment—clean copy without multi folds or corrections. We like brief non-Narcissistic cover letters containing the straight scoop. We suggest that beginning fiction writers spend the money they have set aside for creative writing courses or conferences and spend it instead on subscriptions to good little literary magazines."

‡POTOMAC REVIEW, A Journal of Fiction and Poetry, (I, II), Potomac Review, Inc., P.O. Box 134, McLean VA 22101. (703)556-0578. Editor: Jack Harrison. Magazine: 5½×8½; 80-100 pages; 20 lb. paper; 60 lb. cover; illustrations. "*Potomac Review* is a mainstream literary quarterly." Estab. 1994. Circ. 750.

Needs: Condensed/excerpted novel, ethnic/multicultural, experimental, feminist, literary, mainstream/contemporary, translations. Plans special fiction issue or anthology. Receives 100 unsolicited mss/month. Accepts 20-30 mss/issue; 80-120 mss/year. Publishes ms 2-4 months after acceptance. Agented fiction 10%. Recently published work by Joyce Renwick, Karen Loeb, Paul Estaver and Charlotte Manning. Length: 2,000 words average; 100 words minimum; 3,000 words maximum. Publishes short shorts. Length: 250 words. Also publishes literary essays, literary criticism and poetry.

How to Contact: Send complete ms with a cover letter. Should include estimated word count, 2-4 sentence bio, list of publications and SASE. Reports in 2 weeks on queries; 2 months on mss. Send SASE for reply, return of ms or send a disposable copy of ms. Simultaneous, reprint and electronic submissions (IBM) OK. E-mail address: jgh6265@aol.com. Sample copy for $3. Fiction guidelines for #10 SASE. Reviews novels and short story collections.

Payment/Terms: Pays 1 contributor's copy; additional copies for $3.

Advice: "Send your best work—we have no bias against beginners."

POTPOURRI, (II), P.O. Box 8278, Prairie Village KS 66208. (913)642-1503. Fax: (913)642-3128. Senior Editor: Polly W. Swafford. Magazine: 8×11; 64 pages; glossy cover. "Literary magazine: short stories, verse, essays, travel, prose poetry for a general adult audience." Quarterly. Estab. 1989. Circ. 4,000.

● *Potpourri* offers annual awards (of $100 each) in fiction and poetry; more depending on grants received. Potpourri Publications Co. also publishes *Potpourri Petites*, "little books," and *Red Herring Mystery* magazine. Sponsors the Annual Council on National Literatures Award of $100 each for poetry and fiction on alternating years. "Manuscripts must celebrate our multicultural and/or historic background." 1996 fiction entry deadline: June 30, 1996. Reading fee: $3. Send SASE for guidelines.

Needs: Adventure, contemporary, ethnic, experimental, fantasy, historical (general), humor/satire, literary, mainstream, mystery/suspense (private eye), prose poem, romance (contemporary, historical, romantic suspense), science fiction (soft/sociological), western (frontier stories). "*Potpourri* accepts a broad genre; hence its name. Guidelines specify no religious, confessional, racial, political, erotic, abusive or sexual preference materials unless fictional and necessary to plot." Publishes annual special all-fiction issue. Receives 75 unsolicited mss/month. Accepts 6-8 mss/issue; 60-80 mss/year. Publishes ms 3-10 months after acceptance. Agented fiction 1%. Recently published work by Thomas E. Kennedy, David Ray, Lloyd van Brunt, Dorie La Rue, Marilynne Robinson, Lance Olsen and Arthur Winfield Knight. Length: 3,500 words maximum. Also publishes poetry and essays. Sometimes critiques on rejected mss.

How to Contact: Send complete ms with cover letter. Include "complete name, address, phone number, brief summary statement about submission, short bio on author." Reports in 2-4 months. SASE. Simultaneous submissions OK. Sample copy for $3.50 with 9×12 envelope plus $1 postage and hangling. Fiction guidelines for #10 SASE.

Payment/Terms: Pays contributor's copies. Acquires first rights.

Advice: "We look for well-crafted stories of literary value and stories with reader appeal. First, does the manuscript spark immediate interest and the introduction create the effect that will dominate? Second, does the action in dialogue or narration tell the story? Third: does the conclusion leave something with the reader to be long remembered? We look for the story with an original idea and an unusual twist."

‡✽**THE POTTERSFIELD PORTFOLIO, (I, II)**, The Gatsby Press, 5280 Green St., P.O. Box 27094, Halifax, Nova Scotia B3H 4M8 Canada. (902)443-9178. Editor: Ian Colford. Fiction Editor: Karen Smythe. Magazine: 6×9; 100 pages; recycled acid-free paper and cover; illustrations. "Literary magazine interested in well-written fiction and poetry. No specific thematic interests or biases." Triannually. Estab. 1979. Circ. 300.
Needs: Receives 30-40 fiction mss/month. Buys 4-8 fiction mss/issue. Recently published work by Elin Elgaard, Christian Petersen and Marilyn Gear Pilling. Length: 3,500 words average; 500 words minimum; 5,000 words maximum. Publishes short shorts. Sometimes comments on rejected mss.
How to Contact: Send complete ms with cover letter. Should include estimated word count and 50-word bio. No simultaneous submissions. Reports in 3 months. SASE. Sample copy for $7 (US), 10½×7½ SAE and 4 first-class stamps.
Payment/Terms: Pays contributor's copy on publication for first Canadian serial rights.
Advice: "Neatness counts. Don't let the way your work looks on the page be a barrier to the reader. If you want to challenge the reader, do it with language, style and characterization."

‡**POWER TOOL, (I, II, IV)**, 1317 S. 19th, #1, Lincoln NE 68502. (402)475-8749. Contact: Collective Editorship. Magazine: 40-50 pages; illustrations and photos. "*Power Tool* is the brainchild of women in need of a really loud bullhorn. We publish poetry, short stories, essays/editorials, photographs, graphic art, opinions, questions, educational information and just about anything else regarding life as a woman. We hope our audience is unlimited, though it may appeal only to a certain group of women and men." Quarterly. Estab. 1995. Circ. 300.
Needs: "We're open to most anything of quality. However, we accept submissions from women only; no other specific policies. We'd like to help publish authors who may not get published elsewhere." List of upcoming themes available for SASE. Receives 10-15 unsolicited mss/month. Buys 7-10 mss/issue; 30-40 mss/year. Publishes ms 1 week-3 months after acceptance. Recently published work by Lynda Clause, Tina Koeppe, Trixie, Tara Bremer, Maura McLoughlin, Andrea Wehre and Cinnamon Dokken. Length: 750 words maximum. Publishes short shorts. Length: 250 words. Also publishes literary essays, literary criticism and poetry.
How to Contact: Send complete ms with a cover letter. Should include bio (50 words maximum) and graphic art, "if they want it included." Send SASE for reply or send a disposable copy of ms. Simultaneous, reprint and electronic submissions OK. E-mail address: neckersl@herbie.unl.edu. Sample copy for $5. Fiction guidelines for #10 SASE. Reviews novels or short story collections. Send books to Trixie Truex.
Payment/Terms: "Not possible at this time." Acquires one-time rights.
Advice: "Proofread, well-edited, solid work, that's structurally sound, but creative, has the best chance with us. Because this is all work for women, work showing a unique perspective is especially appealing."

PRAIRIE DOG, A Quarterly for the Somewhat Eccentric, (II), P.O. Box 470757, Aurora CO 80047-0757. (303)696-0490. Editor-in-Chief: John Hart. Magazine: 8½×11; 40 pages; bond paper; parchment cover; illustrations and photos. Quarterly. Estab. 1988 as *Infinity Limited*. Circ. 1,000.
Needs: Adventure, contemporary, erotica, ethnic, experimental, fantasy, historical, humor/satire, literary, prose poem, regional, science fiction, translations. "No space opera, gratuitous violence, or pornography." Receives approximately 50 unsolicited mss/month. Acquires 5-7 mss/issue; 20-28 mss/year. Publishes ms 2-12 months after acceptance. Published work by Daniel Green, Thomas Kretz, I.B. Nelson, Andrew Kong Knight and Ken Johnson. Length: 10,000 words maximum. Publishes short shorts, poetry, essays and occasional book reviews. Sometimes critiques rejected mss.
How to Contact: Send complete ms with cover letter. Include brief bio and $2 reading fee per story, essay or ten poems. Reports in 3-5 months on mss. SASE. Simultaneous submissions OK, "if noted in cover letter." Sample copy for $4.95 plus $1 p&h and 9×12 SAE. Fiction guidelines for #10 SASE.
Payment/Terms: Pays 2 contributor's copies. Acquires one-time and reprint rights.
Advice: "Because we just acquired *Prairie Dog* in March, please be patient. We read everything and will respond if you provide an SASE. We accept double-sided and photocopied manuscripts (save the trees) but will not read faint dot matrix and single-spaced manuscripts. Don't summarize your plot in your cover letter. We would like to feature one 'youthful new voice' (under 25, just beginning to be published) per issue, but our standards are high. Mass submissions based on class assignments are sure to be rejected."

✽**PRAIRIE FIRE, (II)**, Prairie Fire Press Inc., 100 Arthur St., Room 423, Winnipeg, Manitoba R3B 1H3 Canada. (204)943-9066. Managing Editor: Andris Taskans. Magazine: 6×9; 128 pages; offset bond paper; sturdy cover stock; illustrations; photos. "Essays, critical reviews, short fiction and poetry. For writers and readers interested in Canadian literature." Published 4 times/year. Estab. 1978. Circ. 1,500.
● *Prairie Fire* recently received the Gold Award-Manitoba at the 1995 Western Magazine Awards for "Surrational Dreams: A.E. van Vogt and Mennonite Science Fiction."
Needs: Literary, contemporary, experimental, prose poem, reviews. "We will consider work on any topic of artistic merit, including short chapters from novels-in-progress. We wish to avoid gothic, confession, religious, romance and pornography." Upcoming themes: Jewish Writing Issue (Fall 1996). Buys 3-6 mss/issue, 12-24 mss/year. Does not read mss in summer. Published work by Sandra Birdsell, Christopher Dewdney, Heather Spears and Elisabeth Vonarburg; published new writers within the last year. Receives 70-80

unsolicited fiction mss each month. Publishes short shorts. Length: 5,000 words maximum; 2,500 words average. Also publishes literary essays, literary criticism, poetry. Critiques rejected mss "if requested and when there is time."

How to Contact: Send complete ms with IRC w/envelope and short bio. No simultaneous submissions. Reports in 4-5 months. Sample copy for $10 (Canadian). Reviews novels and short story collections. Send books to Andris Taskans.

Payment/Terms: Pays $40 for the first page, $35 for each additional page; 1 contributor copy; 60% of cover price for extras. Pays on publication for first North American serial rights. Rights revert to author on publication.

Advice: "We are publishing more fiction, and we are commissioning illustrations. Read our publication before submitting. We prefer Canadian material. Most mss are not ready for publication. Be neat, double space, and put your name and address on everything! Be the best writer you can be."

✸THE PRAIRIE JOURNAL OF CANADIAN LITERATURE, (I, II, IV), Prairie Journal Press, Box 61203, Brentwood Postal Services, Calgary, Alberta T2L 2K6 Canada. Editor: A.E. Burke. Journal: 7 × 8½; 50-60 pages; white bond paper; Cadillac cover stock; cover illustrations. Journal of creative writing and scholarly essays, reviews for literary audience. Semiannually. Published special fiction issue last year. Estab. 1983.

Needs: Contemporary, literary, prose poem, regional, excerpted novel, novella, typed single space. Canadian authors given preference. No romance, erotica, pulp. Publishes genre series open to submissions: *Prairie Journal Poetry II* and *Prairie Journal Fiction III*. Receives 20-40 unsolicited mss each month. Accepts 10-15 mss/issue; 20-30 mss/year. Suggests sample issue before submitting ms. Published work by Nancy Ellen Russell, Carla Mobley, Patrick Quinn; published new writers within the last year. Length: 2,500 words average; 100 words minimum; 3,000 words maximum. Also publishes literary essays, literary criticism, poetry. Sometimes critiques rejected mss and recommends other markets.

How to Contact: Send complete ms. Reports in 1 month. SASE. Sample copy for $6 (Canadian) and SAE with $1.10 for postage or IRC. Include cover letter of past credits, if any. Reply to queries for SAE with 48¢ for postage or IRC. No American stamps. Reviews novels and short story collections.

Payment/Terms: Pays contributor's copies and modest honoraria. Acquires first North American serial rights. In Canada author retains copyright.

Advice: Interested in "innovational work of quality. Beginning writers welcome. There is no point in simply republishing known authors or conventional, predictable plots. Of the genres we receive fiction is most often of the highest calibre. It is a very competitive field. Be proud of what you send. You're worth it."

PRAIRIE SCHOONER, (II), University of Nebraska, English Department, 201 Andrews Hall, Lincoln NE 68588-0334. (402)472-0911. Editor: Hilda Raz. Magazine: 6 × 9; 176 pages; good stock paper; heavy cover stock. "A fine literary quarterly of stories, poems, essays and reviews for a general audience that reads for pleasure." Quarterly. Estab. 1927. Circ. 3,200.

● *Prairie Schooner*, one of the oldest publications in this book, has garnered several awards and honors over the years. Work appearing in the magazine has been selected for various anthologies.

Needs: Good fiction (literary). Accepts 4-5 mss/issue. Receives approximately 200 unsolicited fiction mss each month. Mss are read September through May only. Recently published work by Julia Alverez, Reynolds Price, Maxine Kumin and Robley Wilson; published new writers within the last year. Length: varies. Also publishes poetry.

How to Contact: Send complete ms with SASE and cover letter listing previous publications—where, when. Reports in 3 months. Sample copy for $5. Reviews novels and short story collections.

Payment/Terms: Pays in contributor's copies and prize money awarded. Acquires all rights. Will reassign rights upon request after publication.

Advice: "*Prairie Schooner* is eager to see fiction from beginning and established writers. Be tenacious. Accept rejection as a temporary setback and send out rejected stories to other magazines. *Prairie Schooner* is not a magazine with a program. We look for good fiction in traditional narrative modes as well as experimental, meta-fiction or any other form or fashion a writer might try." Annual prize of $1,000 for best fiction, $1,000 for best new writer (poetry or fiction), two $500 awards for best poetry; additional prize $300.

PRIMAVERA, (II, IV), Box 37-7547, Chicago IL 60637. (312)324-5920. Editorial Board. Magazine: 5½ × 8½; 128 pages; 60 lb. paper; glossy cover; illustrations; photos. Literature and graphics reflecting the experiences of women: poetry, short stories, photos, drawings. Readership: "an audience interested in women's ideas and experiences." Annually. Estab. 1975. Circ. 1,000.

● *Primavera* has won grants from the Illinois Arts Council and from Chicago Women in Publishing.

Needs: Literary, contemporary, fantasy, feminist, gay/lesbian, humor and science fiction. "We dislike slick stories packaged for more traditional women's magazines. We publish only work reflecting the experiences of women, but also publish mss by men." Accepts 6-10 mss/issue. Receives approximately 40 unsolicited fiction mss each month. Recently published work by Dorothy S. Clark, Megan Olden, Candyce Barnes, Paddy Reid; published new writers within the last year. Length: 25 pages maximum. Also publishes poetry. Critiques rejected mss when there is time. Often gives suggestions for revisions and invites re-submission of revised ms. Occasionally recommends other markets.

How to Contact: Send complete ms with SASE. No post cards. Cover letter not necessary. No simultaneous submissions. Reports in 1-6 months on mss. Publishes ms up to 1 year after acceptance. Sample copy for $5; $10 for recent issues. Guidelines for SASE.
Payment/Terms: Pays 2 contributor's copies. Acquires first rights.
Advice: Looks for "an original slant on a well-known theme, an original use of language, and the highest literary quality we can find."

❖**PRISM INTERNATIONAL, (I, II)**, E462-1866 Main Mall, University of British Columbia, Vancouver, British Columbia V6T 1Z1 Canada. (604)822-2514. Executive Editor: Andrew Gray. Editor: Leah Postman. Magazine: 6×9; 72-80 pages; Zephyr book paper; Cornwall, coated one side cover; photos on cover. "A journal of contemporary writing—fiction, poetry, drama, creative non-fiction and translation. *Prism's* audience is world-wide, as are our contributors." Readership: "Public and university libraries, individual subscriptions, bookstores—an audience concerned with the contemporary in literature." Quarterly. Estab. 1959. Circ. 1,200.
 • *Prism International* received a Journey Prize Award and work published in the magazine has been selected for inclusion in the 1995 *Journey Prize Anthology*.
Needs: Literary, contemporary, prose poem or translations. "Most any category as long as it is *fresh*. No overtly religious, overtly theme-heavy material or anything more message- or category-oriented than self-contained." Buys approximately 70 mss/year. Receives 50-100 unsolicited fiction mss each month. Published new writers within the last year. Length: 5,000 words maximum "though flexible for outstanding work." Publishes short shorts. Also publishes poetry. Critiques rejected mss when there is time.
How to Contact: Send complete ms with SASE or SAE, IRC and cover letter with bio, information and publications list. "Keep it simple. US contributors take note: US stamps are not valid in Canada and your ms will not likely be returned if it contains US stamps. Send International Reply Coupons instead." E-mail address: prism@unixg.ubc.ca Reports in 4 months. Sample copy for $5 (U.S./Canadian).
Payment/Terms: Pays $20 (Canadian)/printed page, 1 year's subscription on publication for first North American serial rights.
Advice: "Too many derivative, self-indulgent pieces; sloppy construction and imprecise word usage. There's not enough attention to voice and not enough invention. We are committed to publishing outstanding literary work in all genres. We are on the lookout for strong, believable characters; real 'voices'; interesting ideas/plots. We *do not* want 'genre' fiction (i.e., romance, horror) . . . which does not mean genres should be avoided . . . rather, they should be integrated." Sponsors annual short fiction contest. Contest issue comes out in April. Grand prize is $2,000 (Canadian). Send SASE for details.

PRISONERS OF THE NIGHT, An Adult Anthology of Erotica, Fright, Allure and . . . Vampirism, (II, IV), MKASHEF Enterprises, P.O. Box 688, Yucca Valley CA 92286-0688. Editor: Alayne Gelfand. Magazine: 8½×11; 50-80 pages; 20 lb. paper; slick cover; perfect-bound; illustrations. "An adult, erotic vampire anthology of original character stories and poetry. Heterosexual and homosexual situations." Annually. Estab. 1987. Circ. 5,000.
Needs: "All stories must be vampire stories, with unique characters, unusual situations." Adventure, contemporary, erotica, fantasy, feminist, gay, lesbian, literary, mystery/suspense, prose poem, psychic/supernatural/occult, science fiction (soft/sociological). No fiction that deals with anyone else's creations, i.e., no "Dracula" stories. Receives 80-100 unsolicited fiction mss/month. Buys 5-12 mss/issue. Publishes ms 1-11 months after acceptance. Recently published work by A.R. Morlan, Jacqueline Carey, Della Van Hise and Wendy Rathbone; published new writers within the last year. Length: under 10,000 words. Publishes short shorts. Sometimes critiques rejected mss.
How to Contact: Send complete ms with short cover letter. "A brief introduction of author to the editor; name, address, *some* past credits if available." Reports in 1-3 weeks on queries; 2-4 months on mss. Reads *only* September-March. SASE. No simultaneous submissions. Accepts electronic submissions via IBM Word Perfect (4.2 or 5.1) disk. Sample copy #1-4, $15; #5, $12; #6-#9, $9.95. Fiction guidelines for #10 SASE.
Payment/Terms: Pays 1¢/word for fiction on acceptance for first North American serial rights.
Advice: "They say there's nothing new under the sun. Well, maybe . . . but *POTN* is looking for what's new under the *moon*! Although *POTN* is limited in its topic to vampires, there is no limitation within its pages on imagination. *POTN* is looking for new twists on the old theme; new perspectives, unique angles, alien visions and newborn music. *POTN* is *not* looking for re-hashes of old plots and characterizations; no 'counts' or 'countesses,' please. The pick-up in a singles bar has been beaten into the ground. The hitchhiker-turned-vampire/victim gives new meaning to the word 'boring.' *POTN* wants material that breaks all molds, that severs ties to old concepts of the vampire and creates utterly new images. *POTN* wants to read your story and be delighted, intrigued, startled in fresh, imaginatively new ways. *POTN* does *not* want to be put off by pornography or obscenity. Please do not add sex to an existing story just to fit POTN's definition of itself as 'an erotic vampire anthology'; sex must be an integral part of the tale. Explicitness is not necessary, but it is acceptable. *POTN* stresses the romantic (but not 'gothic') aspects of the vampire as opposed to the bloody, gory, horrific aspects; no 'slasher' stories, please. And, although it is an important, contemporary subject, *POTN* prefers not to address the issue of AIDS as it relates to vampires at this time. Please be sure to SASE for guidelines before submitting; *POTN's* needs are extremely specific."

PROCESSED WORLD, (II), 41 Sutter St., #1829, San Francisco CA 94104. (415)626-2979. Editor: collective. Magazine: 8½×11; 64 pages; 20 lb. bond paper; glossy cover stock; illustrations; photos. "Magazine about work, office work, computers and hi-tech (satire)." Biannually. May publish special fiction issue. Estab. 1981. Circ. 5,000.

Needs: Comics, confession, "tales of toil," contemporary, fantasy, humor/satire, literary, science fiction. Acquires 1-2 mss/issue; 3-6 mss/year. Published work by James Pollack. Published new writers within the last year. Length: 1,250 words average; 100 words minimum; 1,500 words maximum. Occasionally critiques rejected ms.

How to Contact: Send complete ms. Reports in 4 months. SASE. Simultaneous submissions OK. E-mail address: pwmag@well.com. Sample copy for $5.

Payment/Terms: Pays subscription to magazine. Acquires one-time rights.

Advice: "Make it real. Make it critical of the status quo. Read the magazine before you send us a story."

PROVINCETOWN ARTS, (II), Provincetown Arts, Inc., 650 Commercial St., P.O. Box 35, Provincetown MA 02657. (508)487-3167. Editor: Christopher Busa. Magazine: 9×12; 184 pages; 60 lb. uncoated paper; 12 pcs. cover; illustrations and photographs. "*PA* focuses broadly on the artists, writers and theater of America's oldest continuous art colony." Annually. Estab. 1985. Circ. 8,000.

• *Provincetown Arts* won First Place for Editorial Content and Cover Design from the American Literary Magazine Awards in 1992, 1993 and 1994, and is a recipient of a CLMP seed grant. Provincetown Arts Press has an award-winning poetry series.

Needs: Plans special fiction issue. Upcoming theme: "Writing Well About Sex." Receives 300 unsolicited mss/year. Buys 5 mss/issue. Publishes ms 3 months after acceptance. Published work by Carole Maso and Hilary Masters. Length: 3,000 words average; 1,500 words minimum; 8,000 words maximum. Publishes short shorts. Length: 1,500-8,000 words. Also publishes literary essays, literary criticism, poetry. Sometimes critiques rejected mss and recommends other markets.

How to Contact: Send complete ms with cover letter including previous publications. No simultaneous submissions. Reports in 2 weeks on queries; 3 months on mss. SASE. Sample copy for $7.50. Reviews novels and short story collections.

Payment/Terms: Pays $75-300 on publication for first rights. Sends galleys to author.

PSI, (I, II), 1413 K Street NW, First Floor, Washington DC 20005. Editor: A.P. Samuels. Magazine: 8½×11; 32 pages; bond paper; self cover. "Mystery and romance." Bimonthly. Estab. 1987.

Needs: Romance (contemporary, historical, young adult), mystery/suspense (private eye), western (traditional). Receives 35 unsolicited mss/month. Buys 1-2 mss/issue. Length: 10,000 words average. Critiques rejected mss "only on a rare occasion."

How to Contact: Send complete ms with cover letter. Reports in 2 weeks on queries; 4-6 weeks on mss. SASE. No simultaneous submissions. Accepts electronic submissions via disk.

Payment/Terms: Pays 1-4¢/word plus royalty on acceptance for first North American serial rights.

Advice: "Manuscripts must be for a general audience. Just good plain story telling (make it compelling). No explicit sex or ghoulish violence."

PSYCHOTRAIN, (II), Hyacinth House Publications, P.O. Box 120, Fayetteville AR 72702-0120. Editor: Shannon Frach. Magazine: 8½×11; 25-35 pages; 20 lb. paper; cardstock; illustrations. "*PsychoTrain* is a journal of poetry, fiction, and art that welcomes intense, earthy, decadent, and often risqué work from a wide array of authors, including both beginners and more established. I publish for a generally left-of-center audience that appreciates humor noir, radical writing, and tough, edgy fiction." Estab. 1991. Circ. 250.

• Hyacinth House Publications also publishes *Brownbag Press*. There is no need to submit to both, says the editor, because manuscripts will be considered for all.

Needs: Condensed/excerpted novel, erotica, ethnic, experimental, feminist, gay, humor/satire, lesbian, literary, prose poem, psychic/supernatural/occult, translations, "Pagan, Dada/surrealism, counterculture, subcultural writing of any and all persuasions." No candy-coated, dandyfied fiction here. Just pure, old-fashioned decadence. Nothing didactic. No hand-wringing sentimentalism. No whining unless it's really damned funny." Plans special fiction issue. Receives 350 unsolicited mss/month. Accepts 3-5 mss/issue. Publishes ms 1 year after acceptance. Published work by Gomez Robespierre, C.F. Roberts, Barbara Peck. Length: 50 words minimum; 1,500 words maximum; short shorts preferred. Sometimes critiques rejected mss and recommends other markets.

How to Contact: Send complete ms. "A cover letter is not necessary. If you send one, don't give me a mere list of credits or whine about how nobody understands you because you're a sensitive artist. A friendly note always beats a cold, pedantic, computerized form letter. And no plot synopses, please." Reports in 2-8 months on mss. SASE. Simultaneous and reprint submissions OK. Sample copy for $3 and 4 first-class stamps. Fiction guidelines for #10 SASE.

Payment/Terms: No payment. Acquires one-time rights.

Advice: "*Psychotrain* is a publication that we're attempting to make more outrageous with each issue. Given this, it makes little sense to keep sending us tame, boring, sterile manuscripts. We need weirder, shorter fiction. We are noted for printing the unprintable. We specialize in the bizarre. Also, do not even think about sending us mss or queries without an accompanying SASE. Just like everybody else on the planet, we refuse to answer any mail arriving without a SASE. Don't send us submissions with postage due. You'd think even the lowest, drooling, knuckle-scraping sub-moron would realize these things, but we've got mountains of inappropriate submissions, SASE-less queries, and postage-due submissions which seem to suggest otherwise. Be sure your name and address is on the manuscript itself, as well as an approximate word count. Please tell us whether your ms is disposable. And finally, if you send us anything over 1,500 words, it will end up back in your mailbox unread."

PUCK, The Unofficial Journal of the Irrepressible, (II), Permeable Press, 47 Noe St., #4, San Francisco CA 94114-1017. (415)648-2175. Editor: Brian Clark. Magazine: 8½×11; 96 pages; recycled uncoated paper; coated cover; illustrations and photos. "Our audience does not accept mainstream media as presenting anything even vaguely resembling reality. We publish poetry, prose and dozens of reviews in our humble attempt to counteract the hogwash of *Time, Paris Review,* et al." Triannually. Estab. 1984. Circ. 8,000.
- See the listing for Permeable Press in the Small Press section. *Puck*'s circulation has grown and so has its page count enabling the editor to buy more fiction.
Needs: Condensed novel, erotica, ethnic/multicultural, experimental, fantasy (science fantasy), feminist, gay, historical, horror, humor/satire, lesbian, literary, psychic/supernatural/occult, regional, religious/inspirational, science fiction (cyberpunk, hard science, soft/sociological), translations. Upcoming theme: Science Fiction (summer 1996). List of upcoming themes available for SASE. Receives 300 unsolicited mss/month. Buys 20 mss/issue; 100 mss/year. Publishes ms within 6 months after acceptance. Agented fiction 10%. Published work by Stan Henry, Hugh Fox and Paul di Fillipo. Publishes short shorts. Also publishes literary essays, literary criticism, poetry. Sometimes critiques or comments on rejected mss.
How to Contact: Send complete ms with cover letter. Should include bio (under 50 words), list of publications. Reports in 2 months. Send SASE for reply or return of ms. No simultaneous submissions. Accepts reprints and electronic (disk or modem) submissions. E-mail address: bcclark@igc.apc.org. Sample copy for $6.50. Fiction guidelines for #10 SAE and 2 first-class stamps. Reviews novels and short story collections. Send review copies to Attn: Reviews Editor at above address.
Payment/Terms: Pays 2 or more contributor's copies plus honorarium (40%) on publication. Buys first North American serial rights.
Advice: Looks for "a certain 'je ne sais quois'—as if the work has been channeled or written in a fit of brilliant rage. Keep trying to pull your head out of this ocean of bogus media we're being drowned in. Subscribe."

PUCKERBRUSH REVIEW, (I, II), Puckerbrush Press, 76 Main St., Orono ME 04473. (207)866-4868/581-3832. Editor: Constance Hunting. Magazine: 9×12; 80-100 pages; illustrations. "We publish mostly new Maine writers; interviews, fiction, reviews, poetry for a literary audience." Semiannually. Estab. 1979. Circ. approx. 500.
Needs: Belles-lettres, experimental, gay (occasionally), literary. "Nothing cliché." Receives 30 unsolicited mss/month. Accepts 6 mss/issue; 12 mss/year. Publishes ms 1 year after acceptance. Published work by Deborah Pease and James Kelman. Sometimes publishes short shorts. Also publishes literary essays, literary criticism, poetry. Sometimes critiques rejected mss.
How to Contact: Send complete ms with cover letter. Reports in 2 months. SASE. Simultaneous submissions OK. Sample copy for $2. Fiction guidelines for SASE. Sometimes reviews novels and short story collections.
Payment/Terms: Pays in contributor's copies.
Advice: "Just write the story as it would like you to do."

PUERTO DEL SOL, (I), New Mexico State University, Box 3E, Las Cruces NM 88003. (505)646-3931. Editors: Antonya Nelson and Kevin McIlvoy. Magazine: 6×9; 200 pages; 60 lb. paper; 70 lb. cover stock; photos sometimes. "We publish quality material from anyone. Poetry, fiction, art, photos, interviews, reviews, parts-of-novels, long poems." Semiannually. Estab. 1961. Circ. 1,500.
Needs: Contemporary, ethnic, experimental, literary, mainstream, prose poem, excerpted novel and translations. Receives varied number of unsolicited fiction mss/month. Acquires 8-10 mss/issue; 12-15 mss/year. Does not read mss March-August. Published work by Ricardo Augilar Melantzon, Steven Schwartz and Judith Ortiz Cofer; published new writers within the last year. Also publishes poetry. Occasionally critiques rejected mss.
How to Contact: Send complete ms with SASE. Simultaneous submissions OK. Reports in 3 months. Sample copy for $7.
Payment/Terms: Pays 2 contributor's copies. Acquires one-time rights (rights revert to author).
Advice: "We are open to all forms of fiction, from the conventional to the wildly experimental, as long as they have integrity and are well written. Too often we receive very impressively 'polished' mss that will dazzle readers with their sheen but offer no character/reader experience of lasting value."

PULPHOUSE, A Fiction Magazine, (I, II), Box 1227, Eugene OR 97440. Publisher/Editor: Dean Wesley Smith. Magazine: 8½×11; 64 pages; saddle-stitched; web-printed. Estab. 1988. Has 10,000 copies in print.

● Pulphouse Publishing has several lines of books, mostly featuring short stories or novellas by single authors. Submissions are by invitation *only*. Smith also publishes *Full Clip* listed in this book.

Needs: Fantasy, horror, mainstream, mystery, romance, science fiction, speculative fiction, western. Published work by Harlan Ellison, Kate Wilhelm, Michael Bishop, Charles de Line, George Alec Effinger; published new writers within the last year. Length: 7,500 words maximum.

How to Contact: Send complete ms with cover letter "that gives publication history, work history, or any other information relevant to the magazine. Don't tell us about the story. The story will tell us about the story." SASE. Reports in 2 months. Sample copy for $4.95. Fiction guidelines for #10 SASE.

Payment/Terms: Pays 4-7¢/word on acceptance for first serial rights.

Advice: "*Pulphouse* needs fiction that takes risks, that presents viewpoints not commonly held in the field. Although such fiction can include experimental writing, it is usually best served by clean, clear prose. We are looking for strong characterization, fast-moving plot, and intriguing settings."

‡Q MAGAZINE, (II, IV), 1350-E4 Mahan Dr., #201, Tallahassee FL 32308-5101. (904)681-8917. Publisher: Melanie Anni. Editor: A.E. Ardley. Magazine. "Covers arts, leisure and entertainment in and around Tallahassee, North Florida and South Georgia." Monthly. Estab. 1992. Circ. 12,000-15,000.

Needs: Adventure, historical, slice-of-life vignettes. "Submit seasonal/holiday material six months in advance." Publishes ms 2 months after acceptance. Reports in 1 month. Simultaneous and reprint submissions OK. E-mail address: annis@freenet.scri.fsu.edu. Sample copy for 9×12 SASE.

Payment/Terms: Acquires one-time rights.

Advice: "*Q Magazine* seeks to provoke, arouse and encourage readers to take part in local activities and personal expression. Our emphasis is on the written word and bringing arts, leisure and entertainment to a more mainstream audience. If it's tasty or interesting reading we'll like it."

‡QUANTA, (I), 1509 R St. NW, #3, Washington DC 20009. Editor: Daniel K. Appelquist. Electronic magazine: 8½×11; 35-40 pages; illustrations; photos. "*Quanta* is primarily an electronic publication, distributed across computer networks to an international audience. It is dedicated to bringing the works of new and amateur authors to a wide readership." Bimonthly. Estab. 1989. Circ. 3,500.

● *Quanta* was runner-up for "Best Regular Literary Publication" in the Disktop Publishing Associations' Digital Quill Awards.

Needs: Fantasy (science fantasy), psychic/supernatural/occult, science fiction (hard science, soft/sociological). Plans special fiction issue or anthology. Receives 20 mss/month. Accepts 5 mss/issue; 20 mss/year. Publishes 1-2 months after acceptance. Published work by J. Palmer Hall, Michael C. Berch, Jason Suell and Phillip Nolte. Publishes short shorts. Also publishes literary essays, literary criticism, poetry. Always critiques rejected manuscripts.

How to Contact: Send complete ms with a cover letter; send ms in electronic form (disk or e-mail). Should include estimated word count, short bio and list of publications. Reports in 3 weeks on queries; 2 months on manuscripts. Send SASE for reply, return of ms or send disposable copy of ms. Simultaneous, reprint and electronic submissions OK. Sample copy for SAE and 5 first-class stamps. Fiction guidelines for 8½×11 SAE. E-mail address: quanta@quanta.org.

Payment/Terms: Pays 1 contributor's copy. Acquires one-time rights.

Advice: "Interesting or novel narratorial style or good content. I shy away from 'formula' pieces (e.g., hack 'n' slash fantasy). Send electronic manuscript if possible."

✦QUARRY, (II), Quarry Press, Box 1061, Kingston, Ontario K7L 4Y5 Canada. (613)548-8429. Editor: Mary Cameron. Magazine: 7¼×9¼; 120 pages; #1 book 120 paper; 160 lb. Curtis Tweed cover stock; illustrations; photos. "Quarterly anthology of new Canadian poetry, prose. Also includes graphics, photo essays, travelogues, photographs and book reviews. We seek readers interested in vigorous, disciplined, new Canadian writing." Published special fiction issue; plans another. Estab. 1952. Circ. 1,100.

Needs: Experimental, fantasy, literary, serialized/excerpted novel and translations. "We do not want highly derivative or clichéd style." Receives 80-100 unsolicited fiction mss/month. Buys 4-5 mss/issue; 20 mss/year. Does not read in July. Less than 5% of fiction is agented. Published work by Diane Schoemperlen, David Helwig, Joan Fern Shaw; published new writers within the last year. Length: 3,000 words average. Publishes short shorts. Usually critiques rejected mss and recommends other markets.

How to Contact: Send complete ms with SAE, IRC and brief bio. Publishes ms an average of 3-6 months after acceptance. Sample copy for $6.95 Canadian with 4×7 SAE and 46¢ Canadian postage or IRC.

Payment/Terms: Pays $10/page; 1 year subscription to magazine and 1 contributor's copy on publication for first North American serial rights.

Advice: "Read previous *Quarry* to see standard we seek. Read Canadian fiction to see Canadian trends. We seek aggressive experimentation which is coupled with competence (form, style) and stimulating subject matter. We also like traditional forms. Our annual prose issue (spring) is always a sellout. Many of our selections have been anthologized. Don't send US stamps or SASE (if outside Canada). Use IRC. Submit with brief bio."

THE QUARTERLY, The Magazine of New Writing, (I, II), 650 Madison Ave., Suite 2600, New York NY 10022. Editor: Gordon Lish. Managing Editors: Dana Spiotta and Jodi Davis. Magazine: 6×9; 246 pages; matte cover; illustrations. Quarterly. Estab. 1987. Circ. 8,000.

● *The Quarterly* recently received the George Andrew Memorial Award.

Needs: Literary. Receives 1,200 mss/month. Accepts 40-80 mss/issue; 160-340 mss/year. Publishes ms usually within 6 months. Recently published work by Thomas Glynn, Ben Marcus and Barry Hannah. Publishes short fiction and poetry. Sometimes critiques and comments on rejected mss.

How to Contact: Send complete ms. Reports in 5 days on receipt of ms. SASE for return of ms. Simultaneous and electronic submissions OK. Sample copy for $10. E-mail address: shiyate@alias.com.

Payment/Terms: Pays in contributor's copies. Acquires one-time and anthology rights.

QUARTERLY WEST, (II), University of Utah, 317 Olpin Union, Salt Lake City UT 84112. (801)581-3938. Editors: Marty Williams and Lawrence Coates. Fiction Editor: Wendy Mai Rawlings. Editors change every 2 years. Magazine: 6×9; 200 pages; 60 lb. paper; 5-color cover stock; illustrations and photographs rarely. "We try to publish a variety of fiction and poetry from all over the country based not so much on the submitting author's reputation but on the merit of each piece. Our publication is aimed primarily at an educated audience interested in contemporary literature and criticism." Semiannually. "We sponsor a biennial novella competition." Estab. 1976. Circ. 1,400.

● *Quarterly West* recently received a grant from the NEA. In 1995 work published in the magazine was selected for inclusion in the *Pushcart Prize* anthology and *Quarterly West* received Third Place for Editorial Content from the American Literary Magazine Awards. See the listing for their novella competition in the Contests and Awards section.

Needs: Literary, contemporary, experimental translations. Buys 6-10 mss/issue, 12-20 mss/year. Receives 100 unsolicited fiction mss each month. Published work by Andre Dubus, John Gardner and Chuck Rosenthal; published new writers within the last year. No preferred length; interested in longer, "fuller" short stories, as well as short shorts. Critiques rejected mss when there is time.

How to Contact: Send complete ms. Brief cover letters welcome. SASE. Simultaneous submissions OK with acknowledgement. Reports in 2-3 months; "sooner, if possible." Sample copy for $6.50.

Payment/Terms: Pays $15-500 on publication for all rights (negotiable).

Advice: "We publish a special section or short shorts every issue, and we also sponsor a biennial novella contest. We are open to experimental work—potential contributors should read the magazine! We solicit quite frequently, but tend more toward the surprises—unsolicited. Don't send more than one story per submission, but submit as often as you like."

QUEEN OF ALL HEARTS, (II), Queen Magazine, Montfort Missionaries, 26 S. Saxon Ave., Bay Shore NY 11706. (516)665-0726. Managing Editor: Roger M. Charest, S.M.M. Magazine: 7¾×10¼; 48 pages; self cover stock; illustrations; photos. Magazine of "stories, articles and features on the Mother of God by explaining the Scriptural basis and traditional teaching of the Catholic Church concerning the Mother of Jesus, her influence in fields of history, literature, art, music, poetry, etc." Bimonthly. Estab. 1950. Circ. 4,000.

● *Queen of All Hearts* received a second-place award for "Best Catholic Magazine on Prayer and Spirituality" from the Catholic Press Association in 1994.

Needs: Religious/inspirational. "No mss not about Our Lady, the Mother of God, the Mother of Jesus." Length: 1,500-2,000 words. Sometimes recommends other markets.

How to Contact: Send complete ms with SASE. No simultaneous submissions. Reports in 1 month on mss. Publishes ms 6-12 months after acceptance. Sample copy for $2.50 with 9×12 SAE.

Payment/Terms: Varies. Pays 6 contributor's copies.

Advice: "We are publishing stories with a Marian theme."

✦QUEEN'S QUARTERLY, A Canadian Review, (I, IV), Queen's University, Kingston, Ontario K7L 3N6 Canada. (613)545-2667. Editor: Boris Castel. Magazine: 6×9; 800 pages/year; illustrations. "A general interest intellectual review, featuring articles on science, politics, humanities, arts and letters. Book reviews, poetry and fiction." Published quarterly. Estab. 1893. Circ. 3,000.

Needs: Adventure, contemporary, experimental, fantasy, historical, humor/satire, literary, mainstream, science fiction and women's. "*Special emphasis on work by Canadian writers.*" Buys 2 mss/issue; 8 mss/year. Published work by Janette Turner Hospital; published new writers within the last year. Length: 5,000 words maximum. Also publishes literary essays, literary criticism, poetry.

How to Contact: "Send complete ms with SASE." No simultaneous or multiple submissions. Reports within 3 months. Sample copy for $6.50. Reviews novels and short story collections. E-mail address: qquartly-@qucon.bitnet.

Payment/Terms: Pays $100-300 for fiction, 2 contributor's copies and 1-year subscription; $5 charge for extras. Pays on publication for first North American serial rights. Sends galleys to author.

RACONTEUR, (I, II), Susan Carroll Publishing, P.O. Box 3529, Williamsburg VA 23187-3529. Phone/fax: (804)220-1639. Editor: Susan Carroll. Magazine: 8½×11; 32-45 pages; 24 lb. glossy paper; glossy cover-weight cover; illustrations; photos (on occasion). "There is a lost joy of fresh literature simply because there is no forum to publish the hundreds of manuscripts I have critiqued over the years. My publication was born to provide an open forum for budding writers who actually improve considerably after they have been published. My audience is as open as my publication—from 15 yrs. old to 90 yrs. old—from students to scientists—most of them 'would-be' writers." Monthly. Estab. 1993. Circ. 250.

Needs: Adventure, children's/juvenile (10-12 years), fantasy, historical (general), horror, humor/satire, literary, mainstream/contemporary, mystery/suspense, psychic/supernatural/occult, romance, science fiction, westerns, young adult. Plans to publish an annual special fiction issue or anthology in the future. Receives 75-100 unsolicited mss/month. Accepts 10-12 mss/issue; 135 mss/year. Publishes ms 3-12 months after acceptance. Published work by Phil Stent, Harold Huber and S.L. Rodman. Length: 3,000 words average; 5,000 words maximum. Publishes short shorts. Also publishes poetry. Always critiques rejected mss (charges fee if detailed critique is requested).

How to Contact: Send complete ms with a cover letter. "Recommend sending for guidelines first." Reports in 1-2 weeks on queries; 1 month or less on mss. SASE for reply or return of ms. Simultaneous and electronic submissions OK. Sample copy for $5. Fiction guidelines for #10 SASE.

Payment/Terms: Pays 3 contributor's copies or 3-month subscription. Acquires first North American serial rights; sometimes accepts one-time rights.

Advice: "If I like the story, I publish it. Unique, well-thought out, well-written stories with the traditional beginning, middle, and plot resolution catch my eye. Count the number of times you use 'was' and 'it.' More than two on a page is boring! Substitute more colorful verbs for 'was,' and tell what 'it' is. Also, use passive voice as little as possible. Use lots of creative dialogue and less narrative to spoon-feed info. I would like to see writers make better use of language with solid imagery. Show me how the air smells, don't tell me. Please do not send character sketches and vignettes. Absolutely no pornography!." Sponsors contest; send for current rules.

‡RACS/Rent-A-Chicken Speaks, A little little magazine, (I, II), Rent-A-Chicken, P.O. Box 1501, Wappingers Falls NY 12590-8501. (914)297-9307. Editor: Garth Coogan. Magazine: 5½×8½; 50 pages; laser bond paper; card stock cover; illustrations. *RACS/Rent-A-Chicken Speaks* is for readers of serious contemporary literature (students, educators, and adult public). "A copy of *RACS* is mailed to each of 100 small press and literary magazine publishers." Quarterly. Estab. 1994.

Needs: Experimental, humor/satire, literary. Receives 2 unsolicited mss/month. Accepts 1 ms/issue; 4-5 mss/year. Publishes ms 2-3 months after acceptance. Recently published work by Joe Malone and Diana K. Munson. Length: 1,500 words maximum. Publishes short shorts. Also publishes literary essays, literary criticism and poetry. Always critiques or comments on rejected ms.

How to Contact: Send complete ms with a cover letter. Should include bio (50-100 words) and list of publications. Reports in 10 weeks. Send SASE for return of ms. Simultaneous submissions OK. Sample copy for $5. Fiction guidelines free.

Payment/Terms: Pays 3 contributor's copies; additional copies $2.75 (plus $1 postage/handling for first copy and 80c postage/handling for each additional copy).

Advice: Looks for "insight, freshness and current social/cultural relevance. It is harder to find something important enough to say than something importantly said."

RAFALE, Supplement Littéraire, (II, IV), Franco-American Research Organization Group, University of Maine, Franco American Center, 164 College Ave., Orono ME 04473-1578. (207)581-3789. Editor: Rhea Cote Robbins. Tabloid size, magazine format: 4 pages; illustrations and photos. Publication was founded to stimulate and recognize creative expression among Franco-Americans, all types of readers, including literary and working class. This publication is used in university classrooms. Circulated internationally. Quarterly. Estab. 1986. Circ. 5,000.

Needs: "We will consider any type of short fiction, poetry and critical essays having to do with Franco-American experience. They must be of good quality in French as well as English. We are also looking for Canadian writers with French-North American experiences." Receives about 10 unsolicited mss/month. Accepts 2-4 mss/issue. Published work by Robert Cormier; published new writers within the last year. Length: 1,000 words average; 750 words minimum; 2,500 words maximum. Occasionally critiques rejected mss.

How to Contact: Send complete ms with cover letter, which should include a short bio and list of previous publications. Reports in 3 weeks on queries; 1 month on mss. SASE. Simultaneous and reprint submissions OK.

Payment/Terms: Pays $10 and 3 copies for one-time rights.

Advice: "Write honestly. Start with a strongly felt personal Franco-American experience. If you make us feel what you have felt, we will publish it. We stress that this publication deals specifically with the Franco-American experience."

‡RAG MAG, (II), Box 12, Goodhue MN 55027. (612)923-4590. Publisher/Editor: Beverly Voldseth. Magazine: 6×9; 60-112 pages; varied paper quality; illustrations; photos. "We are eager to print poetry, prose and art work. We are open to all styles." Semiannually. Estab. 1982. Circ. 300.

Needs: Adventure, comics, contemporary, erotica, ethnic, experimental, fantasy, feminist, literary, mainstream, prose poem, regional. "Anything well written is a possibility. No extremely violent or pornographic writing." Receives 100 unsolicited mss/month. Accepts 4 mss/issue. Recently published work by Carol Susco, Myra Longstreet Sullivan and Brian Raszka; published new writers within the last year. Length: 1,000 words average; 2,200 words maximum. Occasionally critiques rejected mss. Sometimes recommends other markets.

How to Contact: Send 3-6 pages and brief bio. SASE. Reports in 3-4 weeks. Simultaneous and previously published submissions OK. Single copy for $6.

Payment/Terms: Pays 1 contributor's copy; $4.50 charge for extras. Acquires one-time rights.

Advice: "Submit clean copy on regular typing paper (no tissue-thin stuff). We want fresh images, sparse language, words that will lift us out of our chairs. I like the short story form. I think it's powerful and has a definite place in the literary magazine."

‡RALPH'S REVIEW, (I), RC Publications, 280 State St., #9, Albany NY 12210-2138. Editor: Ralph Cornell. Newsletter: 8½×11; 20-35 pages; 20 lb. bond paper and cover. "To let as many writers as possible get a chance to publish their works, fantasy, sci-fi, horror, poetry." Monthly. Estab. 1988. Circ. 100.

Needs: Adventure, fantasy (children's fantasy, science fantasy), horror, humor/satire, literary, psychic/supernatural/occult, romance (futuristic/time travel), science fiction, young adult/teen (adventure, horror, science fiction), stamp collecting, dinosaurs, environmental, fishing. No extreme violence, racial, gay/lesbian/x-rated. Upcoming themes: "Spring" issue (April 1996). "Christmas" issue (Dec./Jan. 1996). Publishes annual special fiction issue or anthology. Receives 10-15 unsolicited mss/month. Buys 1-2 mss/issue; 12-15 mss/year. Publishes ms 1-2 months after acceptance. Recently published work by Andy Prunty, Ralph Cornell Kim Laico, John Binns (England) and Rory Morse. Length: 500-1,000 words average; 50 words minimum; 2,000 words maximum. Publishes short shorts. Also publishes poetry. Sometimes critiques or comments on rejected ms.

How to Contact: Send complete ms with a cover letter. Should include bio (1 paragraph) and list of publications. Reports in 1-2 weeks on queries; 1-2 months on mss. Send SASE for reply, return of ms or send a disposable copy of ms. Simultaneous and reprint submissions OK. Sample copy for $2, 9×12 SAE and 5 first-class stamps. Fiction guidelines for #10 SASE. Reviews novels or short story collections.

Payment/Terms: Pays 2 contributor's copies; additional copies for $1. Acquires first North American serial rights.

Advice: Looks for manuscripts "that start out active and continue to grow until you go 'Ahh!' at the end. Something I've never read before. Make sure spelling is correct. Content is crisp and active. Characters are believable."

‡RAMBUNCTIOUS REVIEW, (I, II), Rambunctious Press, Inc., 1221 W. Pratt Blvd., Chicago IL 60626. Editor: Mary Alberts. Fiction Editor: Nancy Lennon. Magazine: 10×7; 48 pages; illustrations and photos. Annually. Estab. 1983. Circ. 300.

● *Rambunctious Review* sponsors a contest; see the listing in the Contests and Awards section.

Needs: Experimental, feminist, humor/satire, literary, mainstream/contemporary. List of upcoming themes available for SASE. Receives 30 unsolicited mss/month. Accepts 4-5 mss/issue. Does not read mss May-August. Publishes ms 5-6 months after acceptance. Recently published work by Jacqueline Disler, Richard Calisch and Sean Lawrence. Length: 1,200 words maximum. Publishes short shorts. Also publishes poetry. Sometimes critiques or comments on rejected ms.

How to Contact: Send complete ms with a cover letter. Should include estimated word count. Reports in 9 months. Send SASE for reply, return of ms or send a disposable copy of ms. Simultaneous submissions OK. Sample copy for $4.

Payment/Terms: Pays 2 contributor's copies. Acquires one-time rights. Sponsors contests, awards or grants for fiction writers. Query.

RANT, A Journal of Fiction, Poetry, and Nonfiction Rants, (I, II), Yorkville Press, P.O. Box 6872, Yorkville Station, New York NY 10128. Editor: Alfred Vitale. Magazine: 5½×8½; 82 pages; 20 lb. white paper; illustrations. "Raw and bombastic ranting. Short bursts of literary vocalizations! The audience is a wide group of people who are looking for new and different writing." Triannually. Estab. 1993. Circ. 1,000.

Needs: Erotica, experimental, fantasy (science fantasy), feminist, historical, horror, humor/satire, psychic/supernatural/occult, avant-garde, post-modern satire. No "long, mainstream fiction. Fiction that whines quietly. Boring or academic literature." Receives 60-80 unsolicited mss/month. Accepts 5-8 mss/issue; 15-25 mss/year. Publishes ms 3 months after acceptance. Published work by C.F. Roberts, Joe Maynard, Dave Breithaupt and Rob Hardin. Length: 1,000 words average; 1,200 words maximum. Publishes short shorts. Also publishes literary essays, literary criticism and poetry. Often critiques or comments on rejected mss.

How to Contact: Send complete ms with a cover letter. Should include estimated word count. Reports in 1-3 months on mss. Send SASE for reply, return of ms or send a disposable copy of ms. Simultaneous, reprint and electronic submissions OK. E-mail address: rant@pipeline.com. Sample copy for $5, 6½×9½ SAE and 6 first-class stamps. Fiction guidelines for #10 SASE.

Payment/Terms: Pays 1 contributor's copy; additional copies for $2. Rights remain with author.
Advice: Looks for "strong voice and intentions. Fearless work. Stands out. Challenge! Be unconventional. Be autonomous. Experiment and be daring—don't worry about 'standards of literature.' Fiction is a strong reflection of the writer and if you feel that you're work is powerful and vocal and daring, send it here! Take risks with subject matter and risks with style. Devalue the traditions! I'd like to see a lot more humor and satire . . . I'd also like to see more experimentation in satirical prose. Writers should avoid mainstream 'New Yorker' type stuff—save that for the boring journals."

THE RAVEN CHRONICLES, A Magazine of Multicultural Art, Literature and the Spoken Word, (I, II), The Raven Chronicles, P. O. Box 95918, Seattle WA 98145. (206)543-0249. Managing Editor: Phoebe Bosché. Fiction Editors: Annie Hansen, Lourdes Orive and Stephan Magcosta. Poetry Editor: John Olson, Tiffany Midge and Jody Aliesan. Magazine: 8½×11; 48-64 pages; 50 lb. book paper; glossy cover; b&w illustrations; photos. *"The Raven Chronicles* is designed to promote multicultural art, literature and the spoken word." Triannually. Estab. 1991. Circ. 2,500-5,000.
  ● This magazine is a frequent winner of Bumbershoot Bookfair awards. The magazine also received grants from the Washington State Arts Commission, the Seattle Arts Commission, the King County Arts Commission and ATR, a foundation for social justice projects.
Needs: Ethnic/multicultural, literary, regional. Upcoming theme: "Masks of the Gods" (The writer in contemporary society). Receives 300-400 mss/month. Buys 2-3 mss/issue; 8 mss/year. Publishes 3-6 months after acceptance. Published work by David Romtvedt, Sherman Alexie, D.L. Birchfield and Bill Ransom. Length: 2,000 words average; 2,500 words maximum. Publishes short shorts. Length: 300-500 words. Also publishes literary essays, literary criticism, poetry. Sometimes critiques rejected mss.
How to Contact: Send complete ms with a cover letter. Should include estimated word count. Reports in 4-8 months on manuscripts. Send SASE for return of ms. Simultaneous submissions OK. Sample copy for $2 plus $1.21 postage. Fiction guidelines for #10 SASE.
Payment/Terms: Pays $10-40 plus 2 contributor's copies; additional copies at half cover cost. Pays on publication for first North American serial rights. Sends galleys to author.
Advice: Looks for "clean, direct language, written from the heart. Read sample copy, or look at *Before Columbus* anthologies, *Greywolf Annual* anthologies."

‡❧RAW FICTION, (II), Oppidan Publications, Box 4065, Edmonton, Alberta T6E 4S8 Canada. (403)431-0771. Editor: Timothy Campbell. Magazine: 8½×11; 30 pages; 60 lb. paper; 100 lb. cover stock. *Raw Fiction* publishes "stories with an edge, about life without artifice and pretension." Bimonthly. Estab. 1995. Circ. 500.
Needs: Erotica, experimental, literary, mainstream/contemporary. No stories "with a mandate." Plans special fiction issues or anthologies. Accepts 6-8 mss/issue. Publishes ms 4 months after acceptance. Length: 500 words minimum; 5,000 words maximum. Publishes short shorts. Sometimes critiques or comments on rejected ms.
How to Contact: Send complete ms with a cover letter. Should include quarter-page bio and list of publications with submission. Reports in 3 months. Send SASE for reply, return of ms or send a disposable copy of ms. Reprint submissions OK. Sample copy for $5. Fiction guidelines for #10 SASE.
Payment/Terms: Pays $5/page minimum and free subscription to the magazine on publication. Acquires anthology rights. Sponsors contests; guidelines advertised in *Raw Fiction* and elsewhere.
Advice: Wants "fiction that is forthright and honest, with a style that rattles the viscera. Write from your gut, not your head."

RE ARTS & LETTERS [REAL], (II), "A Liberal Arts Forum," Stephen F. Austin State University, P.O. Box 13007, Nacogdoches TX 75962. (409)468-2101. Fax: (409)468-2190. Editor: Lee Schultz. Academic journal: 6×10; perfect-bound; 120-150 pages; "top" stock. "65-75% of pages composed of fiction (2-4 stories per issue), poetry (20-60 per issue), an occasional play, book reviews (assigned after query) and interviews. Other 25-35% comprised of articles in scholarly format. Work is reviewed based on the intrinsic merit of the scholarship and creative work and its appeal to a sophisticated international readership (U.S., Canada, Great Britain, Ireland, Brazil, Puerto Rico, Italy)." Semiannually. Estab. 1968. Circ. 400.
Needs: Adventure, contemporary, genre, feminist, science fiction, historical, experimental, regional. No beginners. Receives 1,400-1,600 unsolicited mss/2 issues. Accepts 2-5 fiction mss/issue. Publishes 1-6 months after acceptance; one year for special issues. Published work by Joe R. Lansdale, Lewis Shiner, Walter McDonald, Peter Mattheisson. Length 1,000-7,000 words. Occasionally critiques rejected mss and conditionally accepts on basis of critiques and changes. Recommends other markets.
How to Contact: Send complete ms with cover letter. No simultaneous submissions. Reports in 2 weeks on queries; 3-4 weeks on mss. SASE. Sample copy and writer's guidelines for $5. Guidelines for SASE.
Payment/Terms: Pays 1 contributor's copy; charges for extras. Rights revert to author.
Advice: "Please study an issue. Have your work checked by a well-published writer—who is not a good friend."

RED CEDAR REVIEW, (II), Dept. of English, 17C Morrill Hall, Michigan State University, East Lansing MI 48824. (517)355-9656. Editors change. Fiction Editor: Tom Bissell. Magazine: 5½×8½; 100 pages. Theme: "literary—poetry and short fiction." Biannual. Estab. 1963. Circ. 400.
Needs: Literary. "Good stories with character, plot and style, any genre, but with a real tilt toward literary fiction." Accepts 3-4 mss/issue, 6-10 mss/year. Recently published work by Diane Wakoski, Tom Paine and Mark Jacobs. Length: Open. Also publishes poetry, 4 poems per submission.
How to Contact: Query with unpublished ms with SASE. No simultaneous submissions. Reports in 2-3 months on mss. Publishes ms up to 4 months after acceptance. Sample copy for $5.
Payment/Terms: Pays 2 contributor's copies. $5 charge for extras. Acquires first rights.
Advice: "Literary fiction often gets pegged as staid and boring. Not true. Rewrite as much as you can, read, and submit. If it's good, you'll know soon enough. I like stories that are exciting and insightful. I would recommend to anyone writing short fiction to study the work of Thom Jones, Tim O'Brien, Bobbie Ann Mason and Ursula Hegi, to name a few, for a sense of tone, character, and style. We are not a good market for capital-E 'experimental' fiction."

RED HERRING MYSTERY MAGAZINE, (II), Potpourri Publications Co., P.O. Box 8278, Prairie Village KS 66208. (913)642-1503. Fax: (913)642-3128. Editors: Juliet Kinkaid, Kitty Mendenhall and Donna Trombla. Magazine: 7½×10; 92 pages; newsprint; 70 lb. gloss cover. "Our goal is to expand the genre to include more diverse suspense and mystery." Quarterly. Estab. 1994. Circ. 1,200.
 • Potpourri Publications also publishes *Potpourri* magazine listed in this section.
Needs: Mystery/suspense. "No true crime. No gratuitous sex or violence." Receives 90 unsolicited mss/month. Accepts 15 mss/issue. Publishes mss 6-12 months after acceptance. Published work by Jan Burke, J. Madison Davis, Susan Dunlap and Michael W. Sherer. Length: 6,000 words maximum. Publishes short shorts. Always critiques or comments on rejected mss.
How to Contact: Send complete ms with a cover letter. Should include estimated word count, brief bio and list of publications. "When accepted, we require a copy on Macintosh or IBM 3.5 disk in Word, WordPerfect, QuarkExpress or PageMaker." Reports in 1 month on queries; 2-3 months on mss. Send SASE for reply, return of ms or send a disposable copy of ms. Simultaneous and electronic submissions OK. Sample copy for $5 including shipping and handling. Fiction guidelines for #10 SASE.
Payment/Terms: Pays $5 plus 1 contributor's copy on publication for first rights.
Advice: Looks for "intricate, unique plots in which clues are well-placed and which have well-developed characters and suspense. Read the magazine. Send for guidelines. Work on tone and structure while developing your own particular ability to tell a story."

THE REDNECK REVIEW OF LITERATURE, (I, II), 1556 S. Second Ave., Pocatello ID 83201. (208)232-4263. Editor: Penelope Reedy. Magazine: 8½×11; 80 pages; offset paper; cover varies from semi-glossy to felt illustrations; photos. "I consider *Redneck* to be one of the few—perhaps the only—magazines in the West seeking to bridge the gap between literate divisions. My aim is to provide literature from and to the diverse people in the western region. Readership is extremely eclectic including ranchers, farmers, university professors, writers, poets, activists, civil engineers, BLM officers, farm wives, attorneys, judges, truck drivers." Semiannually. Estab. 1975. Circ. 500.
 • Much of the fiction included in *The Redneck Review of Literature* deals with contemporary western themes but *not* traditional genre westerns.
Needs: "Publishes poetry, fiction, plays, essays, book reviews and folk pieces." Receives 30 "or so" unsolicited mss/month. Accepts 4-5 mss/issue. Published work by Rafael Zepeda, Clay Reynolds and Gerald Haslam; published new writers within the last year. Length: 1,500 words minimum; 2,500 words maximum. Also publishes literary essays, literary criticism, poetry.
How to Contact: Send complete ms. SASE. May accept simultaneous submissions. Reprint submissions from established writers OK. Reports in 6 months. Sample copy for $8.
Payment/Terms: Pays in contributor's copies. Rights returned to author on publication.
Advice: "Give characters action, voices. Tell the truth rather than sentimentalize. *Redneck* deals strictly with a contemporary viewpoint/perspective, though the past can be evoked to show the reader how we got here. Nothing too academic or sentimental reminiscences. I am not interested in old-time wild west gunfighter stories."

REFLECT, (II, IV), 3306 Argonne Ave., Norfolk VA 23509. (804)857-1097). Editor: W.S. Kennedy. Magazine: 5½×8½; 48 pages; pen & ink illustrations. "Spiral Mode fiction and poetry for writers and poets—professional and amateur." Quarterly. Estab. 1979.
Needs: Spiral fiction. "The four rules to the Spiral Mode fiction form are: (1) The story a situation or condition. (2) The outlining of the situation in the opening paragraphs. The story being told at once, the author is not overly-involved with dialogue and plot development, may concentrate on *sound, style, color*—the superior elements in art. (3) The use of a concise style with euphonic wording. Good poets may have the advantage here. (4) The involvement of Spiral Fiction themes—as opposed to Spiral Poetry themes—with love, and presented with the mystical overtones of the Mode." No "smut, bad taste, socialist . . ." Accepts 2-6 mss/issue; 8-24 mss/year. Publishes ms 3 months after acceptance. Published work by Ruth

Wildes Schuler, Joyce Carbone and Susan Tanaka. Length: 1,500 words average; 2,500 words maximum. Publishes short shorts. Sometimes critiques rejected mss.
How to Contact: Send complete mss with cover letter. Reports in 2 months on mss. SASE. No simultaneous submissions. Sample copy for $2. Fiction guidelines in each issue of *Reflect*.
Payment/Terms: Pays contributor's copies. Acquires one-time rights. Publication not copyrighted.
Advice: "Subject matter usually is not relevant to the successful writing of Spiral Fiction, as long as there is some element or type of *love* in the story, and provided that there are mystical references. (Though a dream-like style may qualify as 'mystical.')"

RENEGADE, (II), Box 314, Bloomfield MI 48303. (313)972-5580. Editor: Michael E. Nowicki. Co-editors: Larry Snell and Miriam Jones. Magazine: 5½×8½; 50 pages; 4-5 illustrations. "We are open to all forms except erotica and we publish whatever we find good." Estab. 1988. Circ. 100.
Needs: Adventure, condensed/excerpted novel, contemporary, experimental, fantasy, feminist, historical, horror, humor/satire, literary, mainstream, mystery/suspense, prose poem, psychic/supernatural/occult, religious/inspirational, romance, science fiction, translations and western. Receives 40-50 unsolicited mss/month. Accepts 3 mss/issue; 6 mss/year. Publishes ms 6 months after acceptance. Published work by Sam Astrachan. Length: 400-4,000 words; 3,000 average. Publishes short shorts. Length: 400 words. Also publishes literary essays, literary criticism, poetry. Sometimes critiques rejected mss and recommends other markets.
How to Contact: Send complete ms with a cover letter. Simultaneous submissions OK. Reports in 2 weeks-1 month on queries; 3 weeks-6 months on mss. SASE. Sample copy for $5. Fiction guidelines for #10 SASE. Reviews novels and short story collections.
Payment/Terms: Pays in contributor's copies. All rights revert to author. Publication not copyrighted.
Advice: "We look for characters which appear to be real and deal with life in a real way, as well as the use of plot to forefront the clash of personalities and the theme of the work. Take advice cautiously and apply what works. Then submit it. We are always happy to critique work we read."

RENOVATED LIGHTHOUSE, (II), P.O. Box 340251, Columbus OH 43234-0251. Editor: R. Allen Dodson. 5½×8½; 72 pages; card cover; illustrations. "Trying to define the cutting edge of literary—what modern society wants to read in quality work. Not the stuffy image of a coffee table publication, but engaging articles and stories, poetry and reviews, that are liberal and in good taste." Estab. 1986. Circ. 200.
• The editor is using more stories "thick with plot and suspense."
Needs: Adventure, experimental, fantasy, historical, literary, mainstream, New Age, science fiction (soft/sociological). Receives 60 unsolicited mss/month. Buys 36 mss/year. Publishes ms 1 year average after acceptance. Also publishes literary essays, literary criticism, poetry. Sometimes critiques rejected mss and recommends other markets.
How to Contact: Query with cover letter and credits, when applicable. "Personal information and comments about the story—I like to get to know my writers." Reports in 1-2 months. SASE. Rarely use previously published work and no simultaneous submissions. Sample copy for $4.25. Guidelines available.
Payment/Terms: Pays $1.25 and 1 contributor's copy for first rights.

‡REPORT TO HELL, (II), Maxrat Press, P.O. Box 44089, Calabash NC 28467. (910)579-0567. Editor: Paul Saur. Fiction Editor: Mike O'Shaughnessy. Magazine: digest size; 40-48 pages; standard paper; illustrations and photos. *Report to Hell* publishes stories, poems, essays and art for "twenty-somethings—anyone." Its tone is that of those who are "angry, disillusioned, sarcastic, humorous, cynical." Bimonthly. Estab. 1993. Circ. 100.
Needs: Erotica, experimental, humor/satire, literary, psychic/supernatural/occult. "We'll consider anything." Plans all prose issues and all poetry issues. Receives 10 unsolicited mss/month. Accepts 6-7 mss/issue; 30 mss/year. Publishes ms 2-4 months after acceptance. Length: 1,500 words average; 3,000 words maximum. Publishes short shorts. Also publishes literary essays, literary criticism and poetry. Often critiques or comments on rejected ms.
How to Contact: Send complete ms with a cover letter. Should include bio (25-50 words) with submission. Reports in 1-2 weeks on queries; 1 month on mss. Send SASE for reply, return of ms or send a disposable copy of ms. Simultaneous and reprint submissions OK. Sample copy for $2, 6×9 SAE and 2 first-class stamps. Reviews novels and short story collections.
Payment/Terms: Pays 1 contributor's copy. Acquires one-time rights.
Advice: Looking for material that is "very simple, original and well written. Avoid sending stuff with typos—some of what I get appears to come straight out of the typewriter without proofreading."

‡RESPONSE, A Contemporary Jewish Review, (II, IV), 27 W. 20th St., 9th Floor, New York NY 10011. (212)675-1168. Editors: David R. Atler, Yigal Schleifer. Magazine: 6×9; 120 pages; 70 lb. paper; 10 pt. C1S cover; illustrations; photos. "Fiction, poetry and essays with a Jewish theme, for Jewish students and young adults." Quarterly. Estab. 1967. Circ. 2,000.
• *Response* received an award from *Jewish Currents Magazine* (also listed in this section) for outstanding Jewish journalism in 1995.

Needs: Contemporary, ethnic, experimental, feminist, historical (general), humor/satire, literary, prose poem, regional, religious, spirituals, translations. "Stories in which the Holocaust plays a major role must be exceptional in quality. The shrill and the morbid will not be accepted." Receives 10-20 unsolicited mss/ month. Accepts 5-10 mss/issue; 10-15 mss/year. Publishes ms 2-4 months after acceptance. Length: 15-20 pages (double spaced). Publishes short shorts. Sometimes recommends other markets.
How to Contact: Send complete ms with cover letter; include brief biography of author. "Do not summarize story in cover letter." Reports in 2-3 months on mss. SASE. No simultaneous submissions. E-mail address: response@panix.com. Sample copy for $6; free guidelines.
Payment/Terms: Pays in contributor's copies. Acquires all rights.
Advice: "In the best pieces, every word will show the author's conscious attention to the craft. Subtle ambiguities, quiet ironies and other such carefully handled tropes are not lost on *Response*'s readers. Pieces that also show passion that is not marred by either shrillness or pathos are respected and often welcomed. Writers who write from the gut or the muse are few in number. *Response* personally prefers the writer who thinks about what he or she is doing, rather than the writer who intuits his or her stories."

REVIEW: LATIN AMERICAN LITERATURE AND ARTS, 680 Park Ave., New York NY 10021. (212)249-8950, ext. 366. Editor: Alfred MacAdam. Managing Editor: Daniel Shapiro. "Magazine of Latin American fiction, poetry and essays in translation for academic, corporate and general audience." Biannual.
● See the interview with Alfred MacAdam in the 1995 edition of this book.
Needs: Literary. No political or sociological mss. Receives 5 unsolicited mss/month. Buys 20 mss/year. Length: 1,500-2,000 words average. Occasionally critiques rejected mss.
How to Contact: Query first. Reports in 3 months. Previously published submissions OK if original was published in Spanish. Simultaneous submissions OK, if notified of acceptance elsewhere. Sample copy free. Reviews novels and short story collections. Send books to Daniel Shapiro, Managing Editor.
Payment/Terms: Pays $50-200, and 2-3 contributor's copies on publication.
Advice: "We are always looking for good translators."

RFD, A Country Journal for Gay Men Everywhere, (I, II, IV), Short Mountain Collective, P.O. Box 68, Liberty TN 37095. (615)536-5176. Contact: The Collective. Magazine: 8½×11; 64-80 pages. "Focus on radical faeries, gay men's spirituality—country living." Quarterly. Estab. 1974. Circ. 3,600.
Needs: Gay: Erotica, ethnic/multicultural, experimental, fantasy, feminist, humor/satire, literary, mainstream/ contemporary, mystery/suspense, psychic/supernatural/occult, regional, romance. Receives 10 unsolicited mss/month. Acquires 3 mss/issue; 12 mss/year. Length: open. Publishes short shorts. Also publishes literary essays, literary criticism and poetry.
How to Contact: Send complete ms with cover letter. Should include estimated word count. Usually reports in 6-9 months. Send SASE for reply, return of ms or send disposable copy of ms. Sample copy for $6. Free fiction guidelines.
Payment/Terms: Pays 1 or 2 contributor's copies. Not copyrighted.

‡RHINO, (II), 1808 N. Larrabee, Chicago IL 60614. Fiction Editor: Kay Meier. Magazine: 5½×8; 80 pages; "best" quality paper; 65 lb. Tuscani cover stock; cover illustrations only. "Exists for writers of short prose and poetry—for new writers whose eyes and ears for language are becoming practiced, and whose approaches to it are individualistic. Aimed toward the poetically inclined." Annually. Estab. 1976. Circ. 500.
● Note *Rhino* has a new address.
Needs: "Short prose (up to 10 pages). We aim for artistic writing; we also accept the well-written piece of wide or general appeal." Receives approximately 100 unsolicited fiction mss each month. Published work by Gary Fincke and Lois Hauselmann; published new writers within the last year. Also publishes poetry. Critiques rejected mss "when there is time." Sometimes recommends other markets.
How to Contact: *Charges $3 reading fee.* Send complete ms with cover letter with credits and SASE. No simultaneous submissions. Sample copy for $6 plus $1.30 postage.
Payment/Terms: Pays 1 contributor's copy. Acquires one-time rights.
Advice: "We recommend you know how to construct a variety of idiomatic English sentences; take as fresh an approach as possible toward the chosen subject; and take time to polish the ms for its keenest effect. Don't be afraid to experiment with form. We like strong writing—human warmth, humor, originality, beauty!"

RIVER CITY, (II), Dept. of English, The University of Memphis, Memphis TN 38152. (901)678-4509. Editor: Paul Naylor. Magazine: 6×9; 150 pages. Semiannually. Estab. 1980. Circ. 1,200.
Needs: Novel excerpts, short stories. Upcoming themes: "The Southern/Caribbean Connection." Recently published work by Fred Busch and Lucille Clifton; published new writers within the last year.
How to Contact: Send complete ms with SASE. Reports in 2 months on ms. Sample copy for $7.
Payment/Terms: Awards an annual $100 prize for best poem or best short story and 2 contributor's copies. "We pay if grant monies are available." Acquires first North American serial rights.
Advice: "We're soliciting work from writers with a national reputation, and are occasionally able to pay, depending on grants received. I would prefer no cover letter. *River City* Writing Awards in Fiction: $2,000 1st prize, $500 2nd prize, $300 3rd prize. See magazine for details."

‡**RIVER STYX, (II)**, Big River Association, 3207 Washington Ave., St. Louis MO 63103-1218. Contact: Richard Newman. Magazine: 6×8; 90 pages; b&w visual art. "No theme restrictions, high quality, intelligent work." Triannual. Estab. 1975.
Needs: Excerpted novel chapter, contemporary, ethnic, experimental, feminist, gay, satire, lesbian, literary, mainstream, prose poem, translations. "Avoid 'and then I woke up' stories." Receives 15 unsolicited mss/ month. Buys 1-3 mss/issue; 3-8 mss/year. Reads only in September and October. Published work by John High, Fanny Howe and Constance Urdang. Length: no more than 20-30 manuscript pages. Publishes short shorts. Also publishes poetry. Sometimes critiques rejected mss and recommends other markets.
How to Contact: Send complete manuscript with name and address on every page. Reports in 4 months on mss. Simultaneous submissions OK. Sample copy for $7. Fiction guidelines for #10 SASE.
Payment/Terms: Pays $8/page maximum and contributor's copies on publication for first North American serial rights.
Advice: Looks for "writer's attention to the language and the sentence; responsible, controlled narrative."

RIVERSEDGE, A Journal of Art & Literature, (II), UT-PA, 1201, W. University Dr., CAS 266, Edinburg TX 78539-2999. (210)381-3638. Fax: (210)381-2177. Editor: Dorey Schmidt. Magazine: 100 pages; b&w illustrations and photos. "As a 'Third Coast' publication, *RiverSedge* prints regional and national creative voices whose origin or content speaks specifically to the unique multicultural reality of the southwest, while retaining a commitment to the universality of quality art and literature." Semiannually. Estab. 1972. Circ. 300.
Needs: Ethnic/multicultural, experimental, feminist, historical, literary, mainstream/contemporary, regional, translations. Upcoming theme: "Homeland" (April 96). List of upcoming themes available for SASE. Plans annual special fiction issue or anthology in the future. Receives 10-12 unsolicited mss/month. Accepts 6-8 mss/issue; 12-16 mss/year. Does not read mss in summer. Publishes ms 4-6 weeks after acceptance. Length: 1,600 words preferred; 100 words minimum; 2,600 words maximum. Also publishes literary essays and poetry. Sometimes critiques or comments on rejected mss.
How to Contact: Send complete ms with a cover letter. Should include bio (not over 200 words). Reports in 4 months on mss. Send SASE for reply, return of ms or send a disposable copy of ms. No simultaneous submissions. Sample copy for SASE.
Payment/Terms: Pays 2 contributor's copies; additional copies for $4. Acquires one-time rights.
Advice: Looks for "general literariness—a sense of language as link, not lectern. Characters who look and act and speak in believable ways. Stories which are not simply outpourings of human angst, but which acknowledge life. Read several issues of the publication first!" Would like to see more "stories which do not depend on excessive profanity, violence, pain and sexist attitudes. If everyone is screaming at a high pitch, no one hears anything. How about just a few quiet helpful whispers?"

RIVERSIDE QUARTERLY, (I, II, IV), Box 958, Big Sandy TX 75755. (903)636-5505. Editor: Leland Sapiro. Magazine: 5½×8½; 64 pages; illustrations. Quarterly. Estab. 1964. Circ. 1,100.
Needs: Fantasy and science fiction. Accepts 1 ms/issue; 4 mss/year. Publishes ms 9 months after acceptance. Length: 3,500 words maximum; 3,000 words average. Publishes short shorts. Also publishes essays, literary criticism, poetry. Critiques rejected mss.
How to Contact: Send complete ms with a cover letter. Reports in 2 weeks. SASE. Simultaneous submissions OK. Sample copy for $2.50. Reviews novels and short story collections.
Payment/Terms: Pays in contributor's copies. Acquires one-time rights. Sends galleys to author.
Advice: "We print only science fiction and fantasy, with the first requiring no specific 'approach.' However, a fantasy story is deemed relevant only if it expresses some aspect of human behavior that can't be expressed otherwise. See, for example, Kris Neville's 'The Outcasts' in our 2nd issue or Algis Budrys': 'Balloon, Oh, Balloon' in the 3rd."

RIVERWIND, (I, II), General Studies/Hocking College, 3301 Hocking Pkwy., Nelsonville OH 45764. (614)753-3591 (ext. 2375). Editors: Denni Naffziger and Jane Ann Devol-Fuller. Fiction Editor: Robert Clark Young. Magazine: 7×7; 60 lb. paper; cover illustrations. "College press, small literary magazine." Annually. Estab. 1975.
 ● In addition to receiving funding from the Ohio Arts Council since 1985, *Riverwind* has won the Septa Award and a Sepan Award.
Needs: Contemporary, ethnic, feminist, historical, horror, humor/satire, literary, mainstream, prose poem, spiritual, sports, regional, translations, western. No juvenile/teen fiction. Receives 30 mss/month. Does not read during the summer. Published work by Roy Bentley and Greg Anderson; published new writers within the last year. Sometimes critiques rejected mss.
How to Contact: Send complete ms with a cover letter. No simultaneous submissions. Reports on mss in 1-4 months. SASE. Sample back issue: $1.
Payment/Terms: Pays in contributor's copies.
Advice: "Your work must be strong, entertaining. It helps if you are an Ohio/West Virginia writer. We hope to print more fiction. We now publish mainly regional writers (Ohio, West Virginia, Kentucky)."

ROANOKE REVIEW, (II), English Department, Roanoke College, Salem VA 24153. (703)375-2500. Editor: Robert R. Walter. Magazine: 6×9; 40-60 pages. Semiannually. Estab. 1967. Circ. 300.
Needs: Receives 50-60 unsolicited mss/month. Accepts 2-3 mss/issue; 4-6 mss/year. Publishes ms 6 months after acceptance. Length: 2,500 words minimum; 7,500 words maximum. Publishes short shorts. Occasionally critiques rejected mss.
How to Contact: Send complete ms with a cover letter. Reports in 1-2 weeks on queries; 10-12 weeks on mss. SASE for query. Sample copy for $2.
Payment/Terms: Pays in contributor's copies.

‡ROBIN'S NEST, (I, II), Pometaphysics Publishing, 215 Treherne Rd., Lutherville MD 21093-1244. Editor: Robin Bayne. Magazine: 8½×11; 25-50 pages; bond paper; plastic over paper cover; illustrations. *Robin's Nest* prints "stories, essays and poems of quality that speak to all ages. We want to give new writers an opportunity to be published." Quarterly. Estab. 1995.
Needs: Adventure, ethnic/multicultural, experimental, fantasy (science, sword and sorcery), historical, horror, humor/satire, literary, mainstream/contemporary, mystery/suspense (romantic), psychic/supernatural/occult, regional, religious/inspirational, romance (contemporary, futuristic/time travel, gothic, historical), science fiction (hard science, soft/sociological), senior citizen/retirement. No "explicit sex, drug abuse or violence." Plans special fiction issues or anthologies. Receives 20 unsolicited mss/month. Accepts 5-10 mss/issue. Publishes ms 2-3 months after acceptance. Recently published work by William Orem, Lynn Stearns and T.R. Healy. Length: 2,000 words average; 3,000 words maximum. Publishes short shorts. Also publishes literary essays and poetry.
How to Contact: Send complete ms with a cover letter. Should include estimated word count, 2-line bio and list of publications with submission. Reports in 3-4 weeks. Send SASE for reply, return of ms or send a disposable copy of ms. Simultaneous and electronic submissions OK. Sample copy for $5.
Payment/Terms: Pays 1 contributor's copy. Acquires first North American serial rights. Sponsors contests for writers. Send SASE for current contest guidelines.
Advice: "Neatly done manuscripts with word counts stated are read first. Please proofread all work. Make certain that stories make sense with a logical flow from beginning to end. Please don't submit stories loaded with foul language or violence."

ROCK FALLS REVIEW, (I), Unicorn Tree Press, P.O. Box 104, Stamford NE 68977. (308)868-3545. Editor: Diana L. Lambson. Magazine: 8½×11; 20-24 pages; 20-24 lb. bond paper; 60-80 lb. bond cover; b&w illustrations. "We are a general interest publication. We accept poetry (short is better for us), short fiction, nonfiction articles, essays, science fiction, fantasy, reviews, how-tos, puzzles (occasionally). We are roughly seasonal but not hidebound about it. Most of our readers are middle of the road, average folks. We are expanding our readership." Quarterly. Estab. 1989. Circ. 100.
 • *Rock Falls Review* is affiliated with Authors' Ink and the Great Plains Writers Club.
Needs: Adventure, ethnic/multicultural, fantasy (science fantasy, sword and sorcery), historical, humor/satire, mainstream/contemporary, mystery/suspense (amateur sleuth, cozy, police procedural, private eye/hard-boiled, romantic suspense), regional, religious/inspirational, romance (contemporary, gothic, historical), science fiction (hard science, soft/sociological), senior citizen/retirement, sports, westerns (frontier, traditional). No gay, lesbian, occult, erotica, experimental, vulgarity or obscenity. Publishes special fiction issue or anthology. Receives 15-20 unsolicited mss/month. Accepts 5-7 mss/issue; 20-28 mss/year. Publishes ms "sometimes up to one year" after acceptance. Recently published work by Tom Brown, Karen Kavanagh, Jeff Lacey and Don Stockard. Length: 1,500-2,500 words preferred; 500 words minimum; 2,500 words maximum. Also publishes literary essays and poetry. Often critiques or comments on rejected mss.
How to Contact: Send complete ms with a cover letter. Should include estimated word count and bio ("brief but newsy. We want to know the real person."). Reports in 1-2 weeks on queries; 3-5 weeks or 1-3 months on ms (depends on the editor's work load). Send SASE for reply, return of ms or send a disposable copy of ms. Simultaneous and reprint submissions OK (with proper credits). Sample copy for $3.50 and 9½×11 SASE. Fiction guidelines for #10 SASE. Reviews novels and short story collections.
Payment/Terms: Pays 1 contributor's copy. Acquires one-time rights. Not copyrighted.
Advice: "Even though our guidelines are quite clear about profanity and vulgarity, we continue to receive inappropriate submissions. We don't care for experimental, overly erotic, gory or occult/horror. We'd like to think parents wouldn't ban our publication from their homes although we don't aim it at children."

ROCKET PRESS, (I, II), P.O. Box 672, Water Mill NY 11976. (516)287-4233. Editor: Darren Johnson. Magazine: 4¼×11; 24-40 pages; white 24 lb. paper; color 67 lb. cover. "A Rocket is a transcendental, celestial traveler—innovative and intelligent fiction and poetry aimed at opening minds—even into the next century." Quarterly (plus one special issue). Estab. 1993. Circ. 300-500.
 • This editor prefers to be contacted via e-mail rather than phone. You can also submit to his e-mail address. Although the circulation has been around 500, Johnson recently published a 2,000 circulation issue.
Needs: Erotica, experimental, humor/satire, literary, special interests (prose poetry). "No genre, autobiographical fiction, writing without a story, anything derivative in the least." Publishes annual special fiction

issue or anthology. Receives 20 unsolicited mss/month. Accepts 2-4 mss/issue; 8-16 mss/year. Recently published work by Chris Woods, Paddy Reid and Brian Skinner. Length: 1,000 words average; 500 words minimum; 1,500 words maximum. Publishes short shorts. Length: 400 words. Also publishes poetry. Always critiques or comments on rejected mss.

How to Contact: Send complete ms with a cover letter. Should include estimated word count and bio (100 words) with submission. Reports in 2 weeks on queries; 1 month on mss. Send SASE for reply, return of ms or send a disposable copy of ms. Simultaneous, submissions OK. E-mail address: rocketusa@delphi.com. Sample copy for $1.50. Reviews novels and short story collections. Send books to editor. Checks to D. Johnson, please.

Payment/Terms: Pays 1 copy or free subscription to the magazine; additional copies for $1. Acquires one-time rights.

Advice: "Very few people who submit to me seem to understand the small, basement press. Slick form cover letters and even slicker prose have driven me to chop off one of my ears (the left, if you must know). I urge all writers to subscribe to a few idiosyncratic, low-budget litmags, like *Rocket*. They're cheap—and what they lack in gloss, they make up for in integrity and sincerity."

THE ROCKFORD REVIEW, (II), The Rockford Writers Guild, Box 858, Rockford IL 61105. Editor-in-Chief: David Ross. Magazine: 5⅜×8½; 50 pages; b&w illustrations; b&w photos. "We look for prose and poetry with a fresh approach to old themes or new insights into the human condition." Triquarterly. Estab. 1971. Circ. 750.

Needs: Ethnic, experimental, fantasy, humor/satire, literary, regional, science fiction (hard science, soft/sociological). Upcoming theme: "The Next Decade"—How the human condition is apt to change in the future. Published work by David Olsen, Judith Beth Cohen, Thomas E. Kennedy and Michael Driver. Length: Up to 2,500 words. Also publishes one-acts and essays.

How to Contact: Send complete ms. "Include a short biographical note—no more than four sentences." Simultaneous submissions OK. Reports in 6-8 weeks on mss. SASE. Sample copy for $5. Fiction guidelines for SASE.

Payment/Terms: Pays contributor's copies. "Two $25 editor's choice cash prizes per issue." Acquires first North American serial rights.

Advice: "Any subject or theme goes as long as it enhances our understanding of our humanity."

ROSEBUD™, For People Who Enjoy Writing, (I), P.O. Box 459, Cambridge WI 53523. Phone/fax: (608)423-9609. Editor: Roderick Clark. Magazine: 7×10; 136 pages; 60 lb. matte; 100 lb. cover; illustrations. Quarterly. Estab. 1993. Circ. 7,000.

● The editor says he occasionally uses longer pieces and novel excerpts (prepublished).

Needs: Adventure, condensed/excerpted novel, ethnic/multicultural, experimental, historical (general), humor/satire, literary, mainstream/contemporary, psychic/supernatural/occult, regional, romance (contemporary), science fiction (soft/sociological sf), serialized novel, translations. Each submission must fit loosely into one of the categories below to qualify: City and Shadow (urban settings), Songs of Suburbia (suburban themes), These Green Hills (nature and nostalgia), En Route (any type of travel), Mothers, Daughters, Wives (relationships), Ulysses' Bow (manhood), Paper, Scissors, Rock (childhood, middle age, old age), The Jeweled Prize (concerning love), Lost and Found (loss and discovery), Voices in Other Rooms (historic or of other culture), Overtime (involving work), Anything Goes (humor), I Hear Music (music), Season to Taste (food), Word Jazz (wordplay), Apples to Oranges (miscellaneous, excerpts, profiles). Publishes annual special fiction issue or anthology. Receives 400 unsolicited mss/month. Buys 16 mss/issue; 64 mss/year. Publishes ms 1-3 months after acceptance. Recently published work by Florence Parry Heide, Christi Killien, Judith Beth Cohen and Russell King. Length: 1,200-1,800 words average. Publishes short shorts. Also publishes literary essays. Often critiques or comments on rejected mss.

How to Contact: Send complete ms with a cover letter. Should include estimated word count and list of publications. Reports in 3 months on mss. SASE for return of ms. Simultaneous and reprints submissions OK. Sample copy for $5.50 plus $1.05 postage. Fiction guidelines for legal SASE.

Payment/Terms: Pays $45 and 2 contributor's copies on publication for one-time rights; additional copies for $4.40.

Advice: "Each issue will have six or seven flexible departments (selected from a total of sixteen departments that will rotate). We are seeking stories, articles, profiles, and poems of: love, alienation, travel, humor, nostalgia, and unexpected revelation. Something has to 'happen' in the pieces we choose, but what happens inside characters is much more interesting to us than plot manipulation. We like good storytelling, real emotion and authentic voice."

THE ROUND TABLE, (II), A Journal of Poetry and Fiction, P.O. Box 18673, Rochester NY 14618. Editors: Alan and Barbara Lupack. Magazine: 6×9; 64 pages. "We publish serious poetry and fiction based on or alluding to the Arthurian legends." Annually. Estab. 1984. Circ. 150.

Needs: "Any approach with a link to Arthurian legends. The quality of the fiction is the most important criterion." Accepts 3-7 mss/year. Published new writers within the last year. Publishes ms 9 months after acceptance. Publishes short shorts. Occasionally publishes chapbooks.

How to Contact: Send complete ms with cover letter. Reports usually in 2-3 months, but stories under consideration may be held longer. SASE for ms. Simultaneous submissions OK—if notified immediately upon acceptance elsewhere. Sample copy for $4 (specify fiction issue). Fiction guidelines for SASE.
Payment/Terms: Contributor's copy, reduced charge for extras.

RUBY'S PEARLS, (I, II), 9832-1 Sandler Rd., Jacksonville FL 32222. Editor: Del Freeman. Assistant Editor: Michael Hahn. Electronic magazine; page number varies. "All fiction, no porn, no poetry, general interest." Monthly. Estab. 1991. "Uploaded electronically to BBSs nationwide and internationally, via satellite. Soon to be on the World Wide Web of Internet."
- *Ruby's Pearls* has received the Digital Quill Award (sponsored by the Disktop Publishing Association). The editor publishes an annual year-end hard copy anthology called *Ruby's Pearl's: A Single, A Double and 94-A Triple Perfect Strand.* By using other bulletin boards and "echoing" across the country the magazine is accessible to the 50 states, on Genie and Compuserve and on boards in London, France, Hong Kong, Japan and Singapore, Paraguay, Ireland and Finland.
Needs: Contemporary, experimental, humor/satire, mainstream, mystery/suspense. "Stories can be submitted on either size disk, ASCII, IBM format only. Will return if mailer (pre-paid) is enclosed." No porn, erotica. Buys 1-2 mss/issue; 24-30 mss/year. Publishes ms 1-2 months after acceptance. Publishes short shorts. Length: 250 up (unless it's really killer). Sometimes comments on rejected ms.
How to Contact: Submissions are by 5.25 or 3.5 disk; stories in IBM-ASCII format only or they can be made by modem by calling "Ruby's Joint BBS," 1-904-777-6799 and uploading. Contact by mail, by disk, complete story. Reports in 1-2 months. "Prepaid disk mailer is required." Simultaneous submissions OK. Accepts electronic submissions via disk or modem. E-mail address: ruby@gate.net or del.freeman@rubysbbs. gate.net (for Freeman) and mrhahn@net.com (for Hahn). For sample copy: "Write me and I'll respond with name and number of nearest BBS where it can be found."
Payment/Terms: No payment. Only the privilege to reproduce electronically once. All rights remain with author.
Advice: "We're looking for something different. March to a different drummer."

S.L.U.G.FEST, LTD., A Magazine of Free Expression, (I, II), P.O. Box 1238, Simponville SC 29681-1238. Editor: M.T. Nowak. Magazine: 8½ × 11; 60-80 pages; b&w illustrations. "We are dedicated to publishing the best poetry and fiction we can find from writers who have yet to be discovered." Quarterly. Estab. 1990. Circ. 300.
Needs: Adventure, ethnic/multicultural, experimental, historical, horror, humor/satire, literary, mainstream/contemporary, psychic/supernatural/occult, regional, religious/inspirational, "philosophies, ramblings." Receives 20-25 unsolicited mss/month. Accepts 5-6 mss/issue; 20-25 mss/year. Publishes mss 4 months maximum after acceptance. Length: 2,500-4,000 words preferred. Publishes short shorts. Also publishes literary essays, literary criticism and poetry. Often critiques and comments on rejected mss.
How to Contact: Send complete ms with a cover letter. Should include estimated word count. Reports in 2 weeks on queries; 4 months on mss. Send SASE for reply, return of ms or send a disposable copy of ms. Simultaneous and reprint submissions OK. Sample copy for $5. Fiction guidelines free. Reviews novels and short story collections.
Payment/Terms: Pays 1 contributor's copy. Rights revert to author upon publication.
Advice: "Style and content must grab our editors. Strive for a humorous or unusual slant on life."

SALT LICK PRESS, (II), Salt Lick Foundation, Salt Lick Press/Lucky Heart Books, 3530 SE Madison St., Portland OR 97214-4255. (503)238-8580. Editor: James Haining. Magazine: 8½ × 11; 100 pages; 70 lb. offset stock; 65 lb. cover; illustrations and photos. Irregularly. Estab. 1969.
Needs: Contemporary, erotica, ethnic, experimental, feminist, gay, lesbian, literary. Receives 25 unsolicited mss each month. Accepts 4 mss/issue. Length: open. Occasionally critiques rejected mss.
How to Contact: Send complete ms with cover letter. Reports in 2 weeks on queries; 1 month on mss. SASE. Simultaneous and reprint submissions OK. Sample copy for $6, 9 × 12 SAE and 3 first-class stamps.
Payment/Terms: Pays in contributor's copies. Acquires first North American serial rights. Sends galleys to author.

SAMSARA, The Magazine of Suffering, (IV), P.O. Box 367, College Park MD 20741-0367. Editor: R. David Fulcher. Magazine: 8½ × 11; 50-80 pages; Xerox paper; poster stock cover; illustrations. "*Samsara* publishes only stories or poems relating to suffering." Semiannually. Estab. 1994. Circ. 250.
- *Samsara* is a member of the Small Press Genre Association.
Needs: Condensed/excerpted novel, erotica, experimental, fantasy (science fantasy, sword and sorcery), horror, literary, mainstream/contemporary, science fiction (hard science, soft/sociological). Receives 40 unsolicited mss/month. Accepts 17-20 mss/issue; 40 mss/year. "*Samsara* closes to submission after the publication of each issue. However, this schedule is not fixed." Publishes ms 4 months after acceptance. Recently published work by D.F. Lewis and John Grey. Length: 2,000 words average; no minimum or maximum. Publishes short shorts. Also publishes poetry. Sometimes critiques or comments on rejected ms.

How to Contact: Send complete ms with a cover letter. Should include estimated word count, 1-page bio and list of publications. Reports in 3 months on queries. Send SASE for reply, return of ms or send a disposable copy of ms. Simultaneous, reprint and electronic submissions OK. Sample copy for $2.50. Fiction guidelines for #10 SASE.
Payment/Terms: Pays 1 contributor's copy. Acquires first North American serial rights and reprint rights.
Advice: "Symbolism and myth really make a manuscript stand out. Read a sample copy. Too many writers send work which does not pertain to the guidelines. Writers should avoid sending us splatter-punk or gore stories."

SANSKRIT, Literary Arts Publication of UNC Charlotte, (II), University of North Carolina at Charlotte, Highway 49, Charlotte NC 28223. (704)547-2326. Editors: Scott Hubbard. Magazine: 9×12, 60-90 pages. "We are a general lit/art mag open to all genres, if well written, for college students, alumni, writers and artists across the country." Annually. Estab. 1968.
   • *Sanskrit* has received the Pacemaker Award, Associated College Press, Gold Crown Award and Columbia Scholastic Press Award.
Needs: Contemporary, erotica, ethnic, experimental, feminist, gay, humor/satire, lesbian, mainstream, prose poem, regional, translations. No formula, western, romance. Receives 2-4 unsolicited mss/month. Acquires 3-6 mss/issue. Does not read mss in summer. Publishes in late March. Deadline: January 15. Published work by Nann Budd, P.L. Thomas, Jerry Saviano. Length: 250 words minimum; 5,000 words maximum. Publishes short shorts. Also publishes poetry. Sometimes critiques rejected mss.
How to Contact: Send complete manuscript with cover letter. SASE. Simultaneous submissions OK. Sample copy for $6. Fiction guidelines for #10 SAE.
Payment/Terms: Pays contributor's copies. Acquires one-time rights. Publication not copyrighted.

‡SANTA BARBARA REVIEW, Literary Arts Journal, (II), 104 La Vereda Lane, Santa Barbara CA 93108. (805)969-0861. Fax: (805)965-3049. Editor: Patricia Stockton Leddy. Fiction Editor: Diane de Avalle-Arce. Magazine: 6×9; 184 pages, 60 lb. opaque paper; 10 pt. CS1; illustrations and photos. "The goal of *The Santa Barbara Review* is to find stories that entertain, surprise, and shed light on the vast human condition." Triannually. Estab. 1993.
   • *Santa Barbara Review* is a member of the Council of Literary Magazines and Presses.
Needs: Literary. "No children's fiction. We try to avoid topics for their news value or political correctness." Publishes annual special fiction issue or anthology. Receives 15-20 unsolicited fiction mss/month. Accepts 3-5 mss/issue; 9-15 mss/year. Publishes ms 3-6 months after acceptance. Recently published work by John Sanford and Jerry Freeman. Length: 6,500 words average. Occasionally publishes short shorts. Length: 500 words. Also publishes literary essays and poetry. Often critiques or comments on rejected ms.
How to Contact: Send complete ms with a cover letter. Should include 2-3 line bio and list of publications. "Always send a disk upon acceptance, Macintosh or IBM." Reports in 2 weeks on queries; 3 months on mss. Send SASE for reply, return of ms or send a disposable copy of ms. Electronic submissions OK. Sample copy for $3.60 and $2.40 postage. Reviews novels and short story collections.
Payment/Terms: Pays 2 contributor's copies; additional copies for $3.60. Acquires one-time rights.
Advice: "First thing we look for is voice. Make every word count. We want to see immediate involvement, convincing dialogue, memorable characters. Show us connection between things we had previously thought disparate. The self-indulgent, feel sorry for yourself polemic we really don't like. We are very fond of humor that is not mean spirited and wish to see more."

‡SCORPIO MOON, A Literary Magazine for the New Age, (I, II, IV), 73 Prospect St., #4, Northampton MA 01060. (413)582-0303. Editor: Cathryn McIntyre. Magazine: illustrations and photos. *Scorpio Moon* "publishes fiction, poetry, articles, essays and interviews involving such topics as astrology, tarot, meditation, past lives, extra-sensory perception, supernatural phenomena, UFOs, dreams and new age spirituality." Triannually. Estab. 1996.
Needs: Condensed/excerpted novel, experimental, fantasy (science, sword and sorcery), literary, mainstream/contemporary, psychic/supernatural/occult, romance (contemporary, futuristic/time travel), science fiction (soft/sociological), new age, UFO. No religious. List of upcoming themes available for SASE. Plans special fiction issues or anthologies. Accepts 4-6 mss/issue; 15-20 mss/year. Publishes ms 1-6 months after acceptance. Length: 600 words minimum; 2,500 words maximum. Publishes short shorts. Also publishes literary essays and poetry. Often critiques or comments on rejected mss.
How to Contact: Send complete ms with a cover letter. Reports in 1 month. SASE for reply. Simultaneous and reprint submissions OK. Sample copy for $4. Fiction guidelines for SASE.
Payment/Terms: Pays 2 contributor's copies; "other payment will be made as funds are available." Acquires one-time rights.

SCREAMING TOAD PRESS, Dancing with Mr. D. Publications, (II), P.O. Box 830, Westminster MD 21158-0830. Editor: Llori Steinberg. Magazine: 6×9; 20-30 pages; 60 lb. cover; illustrations and photos. "Fiction/nonfiction—usually warped, mind ripping gore or truelife experience." Quarterly. Estab. 1993. Circ. 500.

Needs: Erotica (horror), experimental, fantasy (children's fantasy, science fantasy), horror, humor/satire, mystery/suspense (amateur sleuth). No religion/Christian. List of upcoming themes available for SASE. Receives 100-350 unsolicited mss/month. Accepts 2 mss/issue; 2-8 mss/year. Published work by Gregory Bryant and Keith Cummings. Length: 1,000 words average; 300-500 words minimum; 1,000 words maximum. Publishes short shorts. Also publishes literary essays and literary criticism. Sometimes critiques or comments on rejected mss.
How to Contact: Should include bio (any length). Reports in 2-6 weeks on queries; 6-12 weeks on mss. Send SASE for reply, return of ms or send a disposable copy of ms. Simultaneous and reprints submissions OK. Sample copy for $5 (payable to Llori Steinberg), #10 SAE and 2 first-class stamps. Fiction guidelines for #10 SAE and 2 first-class stamps.
Payment/Terms: No payment. Copies $5. All rights revert to author.
Advice: "I got to enjoy it—it's gotta be you!"

THE SEATTLE REVIEW, (II), Padelford Hall Box 354330, University of Washington, Seattle WA 98195. (206)543-9865. Editor: Colleen J. McElroy. Fiction Editor: Charles Johnson. Magazine: 6×9. "Includes general fiction, poetry, craft essays on writing, and one interview per issue with a Northwest writer." Semiannual. Published special fiction issue. Estab. 1978. Circ. 1,000.
Needs: Contemporary, ethnic, experimental, fantasy, feminist, gay, historical, horror, humor/satire, lesbian, literary, mainstream, prose poem, psychic/supernatural/occult, regional, science fiction, excerpted novel, mystery/suspense, translations, western. "We also publish a series called Writers and their Craft, which deals with aspects of writing fiction (also poetry)—point of view, characterization, etc., rather than literary criticism, each issue." Does not want to see "anything in bad taste (porn, racist, etc.)." Receives about 100 unsolicited mss/month. Buys about 3-6 mss/issue; about 4-10 mss/year. Does not read mss June-August. Agented fiction 25%. Published work by David Milofsky, Lawson Fusao Inada and Liz Rosenberg; published new writers within the last year. Length: 3,500 words average; 500 words minimum; 10,000 words maximum. Publishes short shorts. Sometimes critiques rejected mss. Occasionally recommends other markets.
How to Contact: Send complete ms. Reports in 6-8 months. SASE. Sample copy "half-price if older than one year." Current issue for $5; some special issues $5.50-6.50.
Payment/Terms: Pays 0-$100, free subscription to magazine, 2 contributor's copies; charge for extras. Pays on publication for first North American serial rights. Copyright reverts to writer on publication; "please request release of rights and cite *SR* in reprint publications." Sends galleys to author.
Advice: "Beginners do well in our magazine if they send clean, well-written manuscripts. We've published a lot of 'first stories' from all over the country and take pleasure in discovery.

THE SECRET ALAMEDA, (II), P.O. Box 527, Alameda CA 94501. (510)521-5597. Editor: Richard Whittaker. Fiction Editor: Wm. Dudley. Magazine: 8½×11; 64-72 pages; 70 lb. coated paper; illustrations and photographs. "We're a magazine put together by artists. We publish art portfolios, interviews, articles, and fiction." Audience is "hard to define. We think we have an educated audience, probably over 30 years old for the most part. People who appreciate the visual arts as well as the literary arts." Triquarterly. Estab. 1991. Circ. 1,500-2,500.
Needs: "Literary work—sometimes serious, sometimes humorous—but always work of substance and depth. We prefer honest, personal work based on lived experience. Will consider nonfiction along these lines also. Not interested in most 'genres' of writing." Length: 500-2,500 words. Sometime critiques rejected mss.
How to Contact: Send complete ms with cover letter. Reports in 4-6 weeks. SASE. Simultaneous and reprint submissions OK. Sample copy for $5.
Payment/Terms: Pays 4 contributor's copies. Acquires one-time rights.
Advice: "Read a copy of the magazine."

SEEMS, (II), Lakeland College, Sheboygan WI 53082-0359. (414)565-3871. Editor: Karl Elder. Magazine: 7×8½; 40 pages. "We publish fiction and poetry for an audience which tends to be highly literate. People read the publication, I suspect, for the sake of reading it." Published irregularly. Estab. 1971. Circ. 300.
Needs: Literary. Accepts 4 mss/issue. Receives 12 unsolicited fiction mss each month. Published work by John Birchler; published new writers within the last year. Length: 5,000 words maximum. Publishes short shorts. Also publishes poetry. Critiques rejected mss when there is time.
How to Contact: Send complete ms with SASE. Reports in 2 months on mss. Publishes ms an average of 1-2 years after acceptance. Sample copy for $4.
Payment/Terms: Pays 1 contributor's copy; $4 charge for extras. Rights revert to author.
Advice: "Send clear, clean copies. Read the magazine in order to help determine the taste of the editor." Mss are rejected because of "lack of economical expression, or saying with many words what could be said in only a few. Good fiction contains all of the essential elements of poetry; study poetry and apply those elements to fiction. Our interest is shifting to story poems, the grey area between genres."

SEMIOTEXT(E), (II), P.O. Box 568, Brooklyn NY 11211. (718)963-2603. Editor: Jim Fleming. Magazine: 7×10; 160 pages; 50 lb. paper; 10 pt. cover; illustrations and photos. "Radical/marginal for an arts/academic audience." Annually. Estab. 1974. Circ. 8,000.

Needs: Erotica, ethnic, experimental, fantasy, feminist, gay, literary, psychic/supernatural/occult, science fiction, translations. Published work by Kathy Acker and William Burroughs. Publishes short shorts. Sometimes recommends other markets.

How to Contact: Query first. Reporting time varies. SASE for ms. Simultaneous submissions OK. Accepts electronic submissions. E-mail address: semiotexte@aol.com. Sample copy for $10.

Payment/Terms: Pays in contributor's copies. Acquires first North American serial rights. Sends galleys to author.

‡SENSATIONS MAGAZINE, (I,II), 2 Radio Ave., A5, Secaucus NJ 07094. Founder: David Messineo. Magazine: $8\frac{1}{2} \times 11$; 100 pages; 20 lb. paper; full color cover; color photography. "We publish short stories and poetry, no specific theme." Magazine also includes the Rediscovering America in Poetry research series. Semiannually. Estab. 1987.

● *Sensations* received an Honorable Mention for Editorial Comment from the American Literary Magazine Awards. This is one of the few markets accepting longer work.

Needs: Fantasy, gay, historical, horror, humor/satire, lesbian, literary, mystery/suspense (private eye), science fiction, western (traditional). "We're not into gratuitous profanity, pornography, or violence. Sometimes these are needed to properly tell the tale. We'll read anything unusual, providing it is submitted in accordance with our submission policies. No abstract works only the writer can understand." Accepts 2-4 mss/issue. Publishes ms 2 months after acceptance.

How to Contact: Send SASE for guidelines. Simultaneous submissions OK. Accepts electronic submissions (Macintosh only). *Must first purchase* sample copy $12. Check payable to David Messineo. *"Do not submit material before reading submission guidelines."* Next deadline: December 30.

Payment/Terms: Pays $25-75 per story on acceptance for one-time rights.

Advice: "Each story must have a strong beginning that grabs the reader's attention in the first two sentences. Characters have to be realistic and well-described. Readers must like, hate, or have some emotional response to your characters. Setting, plot, construction, attention to detail—all are important. We work with writers to help them improve in these areas, but the better the stories are written before they come to us, the greater the chance for publication. Purchase sample copy first and read the stories."

SEQUOIA, Stanford Literary Magazine, Storke Publications Bldg., Stanford CA 94305. Poetry and Managing Editor: Carlos Rodriguez. Fiction Editor: Mark Clevenger. "Literary journal ranges from traditional to avant-garde for newly published to established writers." Semiannually. Estab. 1887. Circ. 500.

Needs: "Literary excellence is the primary criterion. We prefer literary, ethnic, experimental, and 'short' short fiction." Receives 50 mss/month. Accepts 2-3 mss/issue. Publishes ms 2-8 months after acceptance. Length: 8,000 words or 20 pages maximum.

How to Contact: Send complete ms with SASE. Tries to report in 3 months "during academic year." Sample copy for $6.

Payment/Terms: Pays 1-2 contributor's copies. Contributor's rates on request. Author retains rights.

‡THE SEWANEE REVIEW, (III), University of the South, Sewanee TN 37383. (615)598-1245. Editor: George Core. Magazine: 6×9; 192 pages. "A literary quarterly, publishing original fiction, poetry, essays on literary and related subjects, book reviews and book notices for well-educated readers who appreciate good American and English literature." Quarterly. Estab. 1892. Circ. 3,200.

Needs: Literary, contemporary. Buys 10-15 mss/year. Receives 100 unsolicited fiction mss each month. Does not read mss June 1-August 31. Published new writers within the last year. Length: 6,000-7,500 words. Critiques rejected mss "when there is time." Sometimes recommends other markets.

How to Contact: Send complete ms with SASE and cover letter stating previous publications, if any. Reports in 1 month on mss. Sample copy for $6 plus 50¢ postage.

Payment/Terms: Pays $10-12/printed page; 2 contributor's copies; $3.50 charge for extras. Pays on publication for first North American serial rights and second serial rights by agreement. Writer's guidelines for SASE.

Advice: "Send only one story at a time, with a serious and sensible cover letter. We think fiction is of greater general interest than any other literary mode."

‡SHADOW, Between Parallels, (I, II), Shadow Publications, P.O. Box 5464, Santa Rosa CA 95402. Phone/fax: (707)542-7114. Editor: Brian Murphy. Magazine: $8\frac{1}{2} \times 5\frac{1}{2}$; 32 pages; standard white paper; card stock cover. "*Shadow* is aimed at teen readers. Our goal is to provide well-written fiction for young adults. We also support teen writers and make a special point to respond to their work." Quarterly. Estab. 1995.

Needs: Young adult/teen. Receives 20-45 unsolicited mss/month. Accepts 3-5 mss/issue; 15-20 mss/year. Publishes ms 3 months after acceptance. Agented fiction 6%. Length: 3,000 words average; 750 words minimum; 10,000 words maximum. Also publishes literary essays and literary criticism. Often critiques or comments on rejected ms.

How to Contact: Send complete ms. Should include estimated word count, bio (1 page or less), Social Security number and list of publications. Reports in 2 weeks on queries; 1 month on mss. Send SASE for reply. Simultaneous, reprint and electronic submissions OK. E-mail address: brianwts@aol.com. Sample copy for $2 and 2 first-class stamps. Fiction guidelines for #10 SASE.

Payment/Terms: Pays 3 contributor's copies; additional copies for a reduced price. Acquires one-time rights. Sponsors contest. Send SASE for details.

Advice: "We want fiction that has depth to it and that will make our readers stop and think. Work that leaves a lasting impression. Don't be shy. We're very open and comment often. You'll never know if you could have been published if you never try. We'd also like more science fiction and fantasy that deal with teens."

SHADOW SWORD, The Magazine of Fantasy Fiction and Role Playing, (I, II, IV), Stygian Vortex Publications, 6634 Atlanta St., Hollywood FL 33024-2965. (305)653-9458. Editor: Glenda Woodrum. Magazine: 8½×11; 50-60 pages; 20 lb. bond paper; 67 lb. Bristol or 80 lb. glossy cover stock; b&w illustrations. "*Shadow Sword* is geared to a mature audience which is primarily male." Quarterly. Estab. 1993. Circ. 200.

Needs: Fantasy (heroic fantasy, sword and sorcery). "No modern world fantasy, romance oriented fantasy, 'cute' stories, stories with evil wizards. Every year I release a heroines of fantasy issue which features all female lead characters." List of upcoming themes available for SASE. Publishes special fiction issue or anthology. Receives 30-110 unsolicited mss/month. Accepts 6-10 mss/issue; 32-40 mss/year. Publishes ms 6-12 months after acceptance. Recently published work by Lyn McConchie, L.S. Silverthorne and Mitchell Diamond. Length: 5,000 words preferred; 800 words minimum; 10,000 words maximum. Also publishes literary essays and literary criticism. Always critiques or comments on rejected mss.

How to Contact: Send complete ms with a cover letter. Query first if the work is a reprint. Should include estimated word count, 200 word bio and list of publications. Reports in 1-2 weeks on queries; 1-4 months on mss. Send SASE for reply, return of ms or send a disposable copy of ms. Simultaneous and reprint submissions OK. Sample copy for $5.25. Fiction guidelines for SASE. Reviews novels and short story collections. Send review copies to ATTN: Review Staff (address same).

Payment/Terms: Pays $10 maximum plus 1 contributor's copy; additional copies for $2.50 and $1.50 p&h. Checks must be payable to G. Woodrum. Acquires one-time rights and reprint rights.

Advice: "Read the guidelines carefully. A large portion of my rejections are due to the writer submitting an inappropriate work to my publication." Looks for "stories with larger than life heroes/heroines. Avoid evil sorcerers/sorceresses out to conquer the world and sociological plots that contain no real conflict."

‡SHADOW SWORD PRESENTS: LAUGHTER, THE BEST MAGIC OF ALL, Humorous Fantasy for Adults, (I, II, IV), Stygian Vortex Publications. 6634 Atlanta St., Hollywood FL 33024-2965. (305)964-5952. Editor: Glenda Woodrum. Magazine: 8½×11; 60 pages; 20 lb. bond paper; 90 lb. card stock cover; illustrations. "This specific theme issue of our fantasy title *Shadow Sword* features humorous fantasy stories for a mature audience." Annually. Estab. 1993. Circ. 200.

Needs: Fantasy (science, sword and sorcery), humor/satire. "All stories must be of a humorous nature." List of upcoming themes available for SASE. Publishes special fiction issues or anthologies. Receives 50-100 unsolicited mss/month. Accepts 10-15 mss/issue. Publishes ms 10-18 months after acceptance. Recently published work by Lyn McConchie, Frank O. Dodge, Mitchell Diamond, Kathryne Kennedy and Janet Fox. Length: 5,000 words average; 2,500 words minimum; 8,500 words maximum. "Query for works over this length." Also publishes poetry. Always critiques or comments on rejected ms.

How to Contact: Send complete ms with a cover letter. Should include estimated word count and bio (150-200 words) with submission. Sample copy (of *Shadow Sword*, not the humor zine) for $5.25 (payable to Glenda Woodrum). Fiction guidelines for SASE. Reviews novels and short story collections. Send books to Review Department.

Payment/Terms: Pays $1-10 on publication for one-time rights and 1 contributor's copy; additional copies for $2.50 plus $1.25 postage per every 3 zines ordered. Sends galleys to author.

Advice: "Stories should be set in a world of your own creation, contain magic and be peopled with beings and creatures who are not all *human*! I want to see unicorns, elves, dragons and other creatures. Remember, this is fantasy fiction so use the genre to your advantage. Do not copy from the works of others; create your own settings. All stories must contain a strong element of humor and should preferably send our editor-in-chief into a fit of hysterical laughter. Erotic content and clever innuendos are okay, pornography is not."

‡SHADOW SWORD PRESENTS: THE HEROINES OF FANTASY, (I, II, IV), Stygian Vortex Publications. 6634 Atlanta St., Hollywood FL 33024-2965. (305)964-5952. Editor: Glenda Woodrum. Magazine: 8½×11; 60 pages; 20 lb. bond paper; 90 lb. card stock cover; illustrations. This is "an adult publication specializing in stories, articles and artwork by and for fantasy enthusiasts." Annually. Estab. 1994. Circ. 100.

Needs: Fantasy (heroic fantasy, high fantasy). "All submissions must have a female protagonist. No romance-oriented or modern fantasy." List of upcoming themes available for SASE. Publishes special fiction issues or anthologies. Receives 20-30 unsolicited mss/month. Accepts 8-15 mss/issue. Publishes ms 6-18 months after acceptance. Recently published work by Lyn McConchie, Frank O. Dodge, William Marden and Buzz Louko. Length: 5,000 words average; 3,800 words minimum; 8,500 words maximum. "Query for longer works." Also publishes literary essays, literary criticism and poetry. Always critiques or comments on rejected ms.

How to Contact: Send complete ms with a cover letter. Should include estimated word count and bio (100-200 words) with submission. Reports in 1-2 weeks on queries; 1-3 months on mss. Send SASE for reply, return of ms or send a disposable copy of ms. Simultaneous, reprint and electronic submissions OK. Sample copy for $5.25 (payable to Glenda Woodrum). Fiction guidelines for SASE. Reviews novels and short story collections. Send books to Review Department.

Payment/Terms: Pays $1-10 and 1 contributor's copy on publication; additional copies for $2.50 plus $1.25 postage per every 3 copies ordered. Buys one-time rights. Sends galleys to author.

Advice: "Create your own world; do not copy from the realms of fantasy created by others. Passive fantasy without strong conflict (emotional, physical or both), or fiction with poorly done characterization is unacceptable. Don't be afraid to fully develop your world setting and the people who live there. If you overdo the culture descriptions, I can help you fix that, but I can't correct a total lack thereof. I do not accept fantasies set in a version of the real technological world."

‡SHADOWDANCE, (II, IV), Shadowfox Publications, P.O.Box 474, Hinckley OH 44233. (216)225-8298. Editor: Michelle Belanger. Magazine: digest size; 50 pages; 20 lb. bond paper; burgundy card stock; illustrations. "*Shadowdance* is a magazine dedicated to the dark side of creativity. Vampires, decadence and horrerotica can be found in lavish abundance within our pages." Quarterly. Estab. 1992. Circ. 1,000.

Needs: Erotica (soft), experimental, fantasy (dark), gay, horror, lesbian, psychic/supernatural/occult. No "western, sword and sorcery, Christian." Publishes special fiction issues or anthologies. Receives 50 unsolicited mss/month. Accepts 3-5 mss/issue; 20 mss/year. Publishes ms 3-5 months after acceptance. Recently published work by D.F. Lewis, Charles Saplak, Wilum Pugmire and Deidre Cox. Length: 1,500 words average; 500 words minimum; 2,000 words maximum. Publishes short shorts (250-500 words). Also publishes poetry. Often critiques or comments on rejected ms.

How to Contact: Send complete ms with a cover letter. Should include estimated word count and list of publications with submission. Reports in 6-8 weeks on queries; 2-3 months on mss. Send SASE for reply, return of ms or send a disposable copy of ms. Reprint submissions OK. Sample copy for $5. Fiction guidelines for #10 SASE. Reviews novels and short story collections.

Payment/Terms: Pays 1 contributor's copy; additional copies for $5. Acquires one-time rights.

Advice: Looks for "unique styles of writing, strong sense of atmosphere, well-developed characters and, if not fresh plots and themes, at least innovative takes on old ones. Send for our guidelines prior to submitting work. *Shadowdance* is an unusual publication and it may be wise to purchase a sample copy to really get a feel for our style and theme. I like stories that take risks, that break the boundaries of the genre and challenge our concept of prose. I'd like to see a successful synthesis of poetry and prose. Avoid writing a story anyone could have written."

SHATTERED WIG REVIEW, (I, II), Shattered Wig Productions, 2407 Maryland Ave., #1, Baltimore MD 21218-1930. (410)243-6888. Editor: Collective. Magazine: 70 pages; "average" paper; cardstock cover; illustrations and photos. "Open forum for the discussion of the absurdo-miserablist aspects of everyday life. Fiction, poetry, graphics, essays, photos." Semiannually. Estab. 1988. Circ. 500.

Needs: Confession, contemporary, erotica, ethnic, experimental, feminist, gay, humor/satire, juvenile (5-9 years), lesbian, literary, preschool (1-4 years), prose poem, psychic/supernatural/occult, regional, young adult/teen (10-18), meat, music, film, art, pickles, revolutionary practice. Does not want "anything by Ann Beattie or John Irving." Receives 15-20 unsolicited mss/month. Publishes ms 2-4 months after acceptance. Published work by Al Ackerman, Jake Berry and Bella Donna; published new writers within the last year. Publishes short shorts. Also publishes literary criticism, poetry. Sometimes critiques rejected mss and recommends other markets.

How to Contact: Send complete ms with cover letter. Reports in 2 months. SASE for ms. Simultaneous and reprint submissions OK. Sample copy for $5.

Payment/Terms: Pays in contributor's copies. Acquires one-time rights.

Advice: "The arts have been reduced to imploding pus with the only material rewards reserved for vapid stylists and collegiate pod suckers. The only writing that counts has no barriers between imagination and reality, thought and action. Send us at least 3 pieces so we have a choice."

❧SHIFT MAGAZINE, (II), Solomon-Heintzman, 174 Spadina Ave., Suite 407, Toronto, Ontario M5T 2C2 Canada. (416)504-1887. Fax: (416)504-1889. Publisher: Andrew Heintzman. Editor: Evan Solomon. Magazine: 8½×11; 48-60 pages; 20 lb. glossy paper; 80 lb. glossy cover; illustrations; photographs. "Writers are encouraged to send submissions with an insider's feel to media culture: emphasis on independent media." Bimonthly. Estab. 1992. Circ. 30,000.

Needs: Adventure, condensed novel, erotica, ethnic/multicultural, experimental, feminist, gay, historical, humor/satire, lesbian, literary, mainstream/contemporary, regional, serialized novel, translations. Nonfiction also needed. No pornography. Plans special fiction issue or anthology in the future. Receives 50-80 unsolicited fiction mss/month. Acquires 1 ms/issue; 20-35 mss/year. Publishes ms 1-5 months after acceptance. Published work by Michael Coren, Eliza Clark, Evan Solomon, John Sullivan. Length: 4,000 words maximum. Publishes short shorts. Also publishes essays and literary commentary. Often critiques or comments on rejected mss.

How to Contact: Send complete ms with cover letter. Should include estimated word count, bio (2 lines), list of publications. Reports in 2 weeks on queries; 2 months on mss. SASE. Simultaneous submissions, reprint (if noted) and electronic submissions (3.5 disks with hard copy) OK. Sample copy for $4 (Canadian) and 8½×11 SAE. Fiction guidelines for 8½×11 SAE. Reviews novel and short story collections.
Payment/Terms: Pays 1 contributor's copy. Acquires one-time rights.
Advice: Looks for "new, exciting stories on media-related subjects which speak to generation X culture. It should be clearly written. No jargon. Loose but informative feel is encouraged. *But* all styles are examined. Story must be good on its own terms."

‡SHORT STORIES BIMONTHLY, (I, II), Poetry Forum, 5713 Larchmont Dr., Erie PA 16509. Phone/fax: (814)866-2543. Editor: Gunvor Skogsholm. Newsletter: 11×17; 14 pages; 20 lb. paper; illustrations. Estab. 1992. Circ. 400.
   • Gunvor Skogsholm also publishes *The Journal* and *Poetry Forum Short Series* listed in this section. She tends to favor submissions from subscribers.
Needs: Literary, mainstream. Receives 30 unsolicited mss/month. Accepts 8-10 mss/issue; 48-60 mss/year. Publishes ms 1-9 months after acceptance. Recently published work by Terry Dean, John McClusky, Frank Scozzari and Joseph Sivak. Length: 1,800 words average; 600 words minimum; 4,000 words maximum. Publishes short shorts. Length: 600 words. Also publishes literary essays and literary criticism.
How to Contact: Send complete ms with a cover letter. Should include estimated word count. Reports in 3 weeks to 6 months on mss. Send SASE for reply, return of ms or send a disposable copy of ms. Simultaneous and electronic submissions OK. E-mail address: 75562.670@compuserve.com. Sample copy for $3. Fiction guidelines free. Reviews novels and short story collections.
Payment/Terms: Acquires one-time rights. Sponsors contests, awards or grants for fiction writers. Send SASE.

SHORT STUFF MAGAZINE FOR GROWN-UPS, (II), Bowman Publications, P.O. Box 7057, Loveland CO 80537. (970)669-9139. Editor: Donna Bowman. Magazine: 8½×11; 40 pages; bond paper; enamel cover; b&w illustrations and photographs. "Nonfiction is regional—Colorado and adjacent states. Fiction and humor must be tasteful, but can be any genre, any subject. We are designed to be a 'Reader's Digest' of fiction. We are found in professional waiting rooms, etc." Monthly.
   • The editor says she'd like to see more young (25 and over) humor and finds "clean" humor "hard to come by."
Needs: Adventure, contemporary, historical, humor/satire, mainstream, mystery/suspense (amateur sleuth, English cozy, police procedural, private eye, romantic suspense), regional, romance (contemporary, gothic, historical), western (frontier). No erotica. "We use holiday themes." Receives 150 unsolicited mss/month. Buys 9-12 mss/issue; 76 mss/year. Publishes accepted work immediately. Published work by Dean Ballenger. Length: 1,000 words average; 1,800 words maximum.
How to Contact: Send complete ms with cover letter. SASE. Reports in 3-6 months. Sample copies with SAE and $1.50 postage. Fiction guidelines for SASE.
Payment/Terms: Pays $10-50 and subscription to magazine on publication for first North American serial rights. "We do not pay for single jokes or poetry, but do give free subscription if published."
Advice: "We seek a potpourri of subjects each issue. A new slant, a different approach, fresh viewpoints— all of these excite us. We don't like gore, salacious humor or perverted tales. Prefer third person. Be sure it is a story with a beginning, middle and end. It must have dialogue. Many beginners do not know an essay from a short story. Essays occasionally used if *humorous*."

SIDE SHOW, Short Story Annual, (II), Somersault Press, P.O. Box 1428, El Cerrito CA 94530-1428. (510)215-2207. Editor: Shelley Anderson, Kathe Stolz and Marjorie K. Jacobs. Book (paperback): 5½×8½; 300 pages; 50 lb. paper. "Quality short stories for a general, literary audience." Annually. Estab. 1991. Circ. 1,000.
   • Work published in *Side Show* has been selected for inclusion in the Pushcart Prize anthology and reprinted in *Harper's*.
Needs: Contemporary, ethnic, feminist, gay, humor/satire, lesbian, literary, mainstream. Nothing genre, religious, pornographic. Receives 50-60 unsolicited mss/month. Buys 25-30 mss/issue. Does not read mss in August. Publishes ms up to 9 months after acceptance. Recently published work by Dorothy Bryant, Susan Welch and Ann Hood. Length: Open. Critiques rejected mss.
How to Contact: All submissions entered in contest. *$10 entry fee* (includes subscription to next *Side Show*). Deadline: June 30, 1996. No guidelines. Send complete ms with cover letter and entry fee. Reports

Sending to a country other than your own? Be sure to send International Reply Coupons instead of stamps for replies or return of your manuscript.

in 3-4 weeks on mss. SASE. Simultaneous submissions OK. Multiple submissions encouraged. Sample copy for $10 and $2 postage and handling ($.83 sales tax CA residents).

Payment/Terms: Pays $5/printed page on publication for first North American serial rights. Sends galleys to author. All submissions entered in our contest for cash prizes $30 (1st); $25 (2nd); $20 (3rd).

Advice: Looks for "readability, vividness of characterization, coherence, inspiration, interesting subject matter, point of view, originality, plausibility."

✦SIDETREKKED, (I, IV), Science Fiction London, Unit 78, 320 Westminster, London, Ontario Canada. (519)434-9588. Editor: James Jarvis. Editors change by election. Newspaper: 7×8½; 36-40 pages; bond paper; b&w drawings, halftone photographs. "Science fiction for science fiction readers, mostly adults." Quarterly. Estab. 1980. Circ. 200.

Needs: Fantasy, science fiction (hard science, soft/sociological). "We will consider any story with a science fictional slant. Because science fiction tends to be all-embracing, that could include horror, humor/satire, romance, suspense, feminist, gay, ethnic, etc.—yes, even western—but the science fiction classification must be met, usually by setting the story in a plausible, futuristic universe." Receives 3-5 unsolicited fiction mss/month. Accepts 3-8 mss/issue. Time between acceptance and publication varies. Published work by Joe Beliveau and Dave Seburn. Length: 1,000-5,000 words preferred. "No hard-and-fast rules, but we can't accommodate novelettes or novellas." Publishes short shorts. Critiques or comments on rejected mss, if requested by the author. Recommends other markets on occasion.

How to Contact: Send complete ms with cover letter. No simultaneous submissions. Reports in 3 weeks on queries; in 1 month on mss. SASE. Sample copy for $2 (Canadian) and 9×10 SAE.

Payment/Terms: Pays in contributor's copies. Acquires first North American serial rights.

Advice: "We are more forgiving than most fiction markets and we try to work with new writers. What makes us want to work with a writer is some suggestion that he or she understands what makes a good story. What makes a manuscript stand out? Tell a good story. The secondary things are fixable if the story is there, but if it is not, no amount of tinkering can fix it."

SIDEWALKS, (II), P.O. Box 321, Champlin MN 55316. (612)421-3512. Editor: Tom Heie. Magazine: 5½×8½; 60-75 pages; 60 lb. paper; textured recycled cover. "*Sidewalks* . . . place of discovery, of myth, power, incantation . . . places we continue to meet people, preoccupied, on our way somewhere . . . tense, dark, empty places . . . place we meet friends and strangers, neighborhood sidewalks, place full of memory, paths that bring us home." Semiannually. Estab. 1991. Circ. 500.

Needs: Experimental, humor/satire, literary, mainstream/contemporary, regional. No violent, pornographic kinky material. Acquires 6-8 mss/issue; 12-16 mss/year. Work is accepted for 2 annual deadlines: May 31 and December 31. Publishes ms 10 weeks after deadline. Published work by Jonathan Gillman and Jean Ervin. Length: 2,500 words preferred; 3,000 words maximum. Publishes short shorts. Also publishes poetry.

How to Contact: Send complete ms with cover letter. Should include estimated word count, very brief bio, list of publications. Reports in 1 week on queries; 1 month after deadline on mss. Send SASE for reply, return of ms or send a disposable copy of the ms. No simultaneous submissions. Accepts electronic submissions. Sample copy for $5.

Payment/Terms: Pays 1 contributor's copy. Additional copies $5. Acquires one-time rights.

Advice: "We look for a story with broad appeal, one that is well-crafted and has strong narrative voice, a story that leaves the reader thinking after the reading is over."

SIERRA NEVADA COLLEGE REVIEW, (II), Sierra Nevada College, P.O. Box 4269, Incline Village NV 89450. (702)831-1314. Editor: June Sylvester. Magazine: 5×8; 75-100 pages. "We are open to many kinds of work but avoid what we consider trite, sentimental, contrived . . . ." Annually. Estab. 1990. Circ. 200-250 (mostly college libraries).

Needs: Experimental, literary, mainstream/contemporary, regional. Receives 5 unsolicited mss/month. Accepts 2-3 mss/year. Does not read mss April 1-September 1. Work is published by next issue (published in May, annually). Recently published work by R. Nikolas Macioci and Leslie Whitten. Length: 500 words average; 1,000 words maximum. Publishes short shorts. Also publishes literary essays, literary criticism and poetry. Sometimes critiques or comments on rejected mss.

How to Contact: Send complete ms with a cover letter. Should include estimated word count and bio. Send SASE for reply, return of ms or send a disposable copy of ms. Simultaneous submissions OK. Sample copy for $2.50.

Payment/Terms: Pays 2 contributor's copies. Acquires one-time rights. .

Advice: Looks for "memorable characters, close attention to detail which makes the story vivid. We are interested in flash fiction. Also regional work that catches the flavor of place and time—like strong characters. No moralizing, inspirational work. No science fiction. No children's stories. Tired of trite love stories—cynicism bores us."

SIGN OF THE TIMES, A Chronicle of Decadence in the Atomic Age, (II), 3355 Spring Mountain Rd., Suite #267, Las Vegas NE 89102. (702)871-4461. Publisher/Editor: Daniel Jacobs. Tabloid: 8×10; 32 pages; book paper; 120 lb. cover stock; illustrations; photos. "Decadence in all forms for those seeking literary

amusement." Semiannual. Published special fiction issue last year; plans another. Estab. 1980. Circ. 750.
Needs: Comics, erotica, experimental, gay, lesbian. No religious or western manuscripts. Receives 6 unsolicited mss/month. Buys 10 mss/issue; 20 mss/year. Published work by Gary Smith, Willie Smith, Ben Satterfield. Length: 3,000 words average; 500 words minimum, 5,000 words maximum. Publishes short shorts. Sometimes comments on rejected mss and recommends other markets.
How to Contact: Send complete ms with cover letter and bio. Reports in 6 weeks on mss. SASE. Sample copy for $3.50. Fiction guidelines for #10 SASE.
Payment/Terms: Pays up to $20, subscription to magazine, 2 contributor's copies; 1 time cover price charge for extras. Pays on publication for first rights plus anthology in the future.

‡THE SILENCE, A Literary Journal for Emerging Writers, (II), 12 W. Willow Grove, Box 175, Philadelphia PA 19118-3952. Editor: Gregory Martino. Fiction Editor: Jeffrey Boyer. Electronic magazine: illustrations and photos. "The silence confounds and conquers us all in time, but occasionally a work speaks out of passionate necessity and so creates its own life. We seek young writers who have found their voice but have yet to receive the recognition due them. We look for material that can stand on its own as an artifact of the truth-telling imagination that created it." Quarterly. Estab. 1995. Circ. available to all Internet users.
Needs: Condensed/excerpted novel, ethnic/multicultural, experimental, feminist, literary, mainstream/contemporary, translations. "No formula fiction, juvenile or coming-of-age stories, no genre fiction, no propaganda, no stories full of grammatical errors, no beginners' essays." Plans special fiction issue or anthology. Receives less than 20 mss/month. Buys 1-3 mss/issue; 4-12 mss/year. Publishes ms 1-2 months after acceptance. Length: 2,500 words average; no minimum. Publishes short shorts. Also publishes literary essays, literary criticism and poetry. Often critiques or comments on rejected ms.
How to Contact: Send mss with cover letter and disk formatted to windows 6.0 or WordPerfect. Should include estimated word count, short bio and list of publications. Send SASE for return of ms or send a disposable copy of the ms. Simultaneous and electronic submissions OK. E-mail address: silence@cs.widener.edu. Sample copy free on Internet at http://shirley.cs.widener.edu. Reviews novels or short story collections.
Payment/Terms: Acquires one-time rights.
Advice: "Many young writers are too convinced of their own importance and sincerity, and so neglect the requirements of plot and characterization. Or else they employ a reflexive irony that gives their work a superficial polish but no depth. The writer is nothing; the work is everything. Juveniles of all ages should hold onto their stories until the stories no longer belong to them."

THE SILVER WEB, A Magazine of the Surreal, (II), Buzzcity Press, Box 38190, Tallahassee FL 32315. Editor: Ann Kennedy. Magazine: 8½×11; 64 pages; 20 lb. paper; glossy cover; b&w illustrations and photographs. "Looking for unique character-based stories that are off-beat, off-center and strange. But not inaccessible." Semiannually. Estab. 1989. Circ. 1,000.
● Work published in *The Silver Web* has appeared in *The Year's Best Fantasy and Horror* (DAW Books) and *The Year's Best Fantastic Fiction*.
Needs: Experimental, horror, science fiction (soft/sociological sf). No "traditional storylines, monsters, vampires, werewolves, etc." Receives 500 unsolicited mss/month. Accepts 8-10 mss/issue; 16-20 mss/year. Publishes ms within 6-12 months after acceptance. Published work by Sean Brendan-Brown, Juleen Brantingham and Mark Rreh. Length: 6,000 words average; 100 words minimum; 8,000 words maximum. Publishes short shorts. Also publishes poetry. Sometimes critiques rejected ms.
How to Contact: Send complete ms with a cover letter. Should include estimated word count. Reports in 1 week on queries; 6-8 weeks on mss. Send SASE for reply, return of ms or send a disposable copy of ms plus SASE for reply. Simultaneous and reprint submissions OK. Sample copy for $5.95. Fiction guidelines for #10 SASE. Reviews novels and short story collections.
Payment/Terms: Pays 2-3¢/word and 2 contributor's copies; additional copies for $3.50. Acquires first North American serial rights, reprint rights or one-time rights.
Advice: "The kind of work I look for is a piece that will stay with me long after I've finished reading it. It must paint pictures in my mind that are not easily erased. Read a copy of the magazine, at least—get the writer's guidelines. *The Silver Web* publishes surrealistic fiction and poetry. Work too bizarre for mainstream, but perhaps too literary for genre. NOTE: This is not a straight horror/sci-fi magazine. No typical storylines."

SILVERFISH REVIEW, (II), Box 3541, Eugene OR 97403. (503)344-5060. Editor: Rodger Moody. High quality literary material for a general audience. Published in June and December. Estab. 1979. Circ. 750.
Needs: Literary. Accepts 1-2 mss/issue. Also publishes literary essays, poetry, interview, translations.
How to Contact: Send complete ms with SASE. No simultaneous submissions. Reports in 2-3 months on mss. Sample copy for $4 and $1.50 postage.
Payment/Terms: Pays 3 contributor's copies and one year subscription; $5/page when funding permits. Rights revert to author.
Advice: "We publish primarily poetry; we will, however, publish good quality fiction. *SR* is mainly interested in the short short story (one-minute and three-minute)."

Small Magazines Can Be Stepping Stones

Within the tight-knit science fiction, fantasy and horror community, Ann Kennedy, editor of *The Silver Web*, has, perversely, made her mark by blurring the demarcations between literary and category fiction while providing a home for stories that might otherwise go unpublished. For writers in this field especially, publication in small journals can lead to bigger things—not only publication in larger, more commercial magazines, but also inclusion in prestigious anthologies and attention from book publishers.

Ann Kennedy

For Kennedy, working with writers is more satisfying than any other aspect of her role as editor of the magazine. "It is actually very exciting. Each day when I open my mailbox, it's like my birthday. I never know what I'll get next. Also, it is very gratifying to get thank you notes from submitters and letters from those who enjoy the magazine. And, when I can assist in bringing the work of a new talent to an appreciative audience, it's terrific!"

The Silver Web, she points out, has been a stepping stone for several new writers. The magazine's iconoclasm and its striking visual sense (including artwork by such notables as J.K. Potter) have brought it an avid readership and the reprinting of stories in *The Year's Best Horror Stories* and *The Year's Best Fantastic Fiction*. Such honors have not come at the expense of up-and-coming writers. In fact, most writers published by Kennedy have sold fewer than three stories.

"I don't set out to publish new writers, but it works out that way. Perhaps it is because when I read the submissions only the story matters—not the writer's name and not the writer's previous credits and experience."

Kennedy points to two examples she is most proud of: a first sale by Martin Simpson that was cited in the introduction to *The Year's Best Fantasy & Horror* as one of the very best stories published in 1994; and horror writer Yvonne Navarro's decision, at Kennedy's urging, to turn a story published in *The Silver Web* into a novel, which eventually resulted in a three-book deal with Bantam.

Like most small press editors, Kennedy has a "regular job" in addition to the magazine. By day, she works as a software manager for a national computer company. By night, as editor of *The Silver Web*, she sits down at her kitchen table and spends at least three hours responding to the day's mail.

"Tenacity has helped me succeed . . . I have built the magazine slowly but surely, planning improvements each step of the way. I believe that my magazine is top quality and I don't cut corners. I also pay very well for a small press magazine and I treat each submitter with respect, regardless of age or experience."

Kennedy stresses that she expects such respect and extra effort from her potential contributors as well. "If my guidelines say no vampire stories, don't send me a vampire story and tell me it's different, because that shows a lack of respect for me and the guidelines. Any standard plot devices turn me off immediately. Show the same respect for the editors as you would wish to receive as a writer."

The Silver Web's subtitle, "A Magazine of the Surreal," was carefully chosen by Kennedy midway through the magazine's run of six years. "The academic definition of 'surrealism' is the liberation of the subconscious mind. Surreal art, whether visual or written, is the result of such a liberation. My interpretation for *The Silver Web* is fiction that is slightly off-center, weird, unusual and unique. To steal a phrase from Monty Python, 'Something Completely Different.' " Kennedy looks for fiction with a "strong emotional base yet a touch of the bizarre."

The best way to get into *The Silver Web* according to Kennedy is through a finely-honed style and by surprising her. "Beautiful writing always catches my eye. The use of language and how words are put together are so important to me. But the story must interest me enough to compel me to turn the page. I must want to know what's going to happen next."

More generally, Kennedy believes that breaking into any small press magazine takes the same commitment as breaking into the larger markets: Writers must put in the necessary time to improve their work. There are no shortcuts in Kennedy's book.

"At the top of the list is *write*. No matter how much talent a writer has, it doesn't take the place of practice. Reading is second on my list, and don't only read fiction. Make your reading as broad as possible—history, biography, science, politics—and when you do read fiction, read all genres, all types. Read fiction from all over the world. Don't limit yourself. Next, rewrite. You must learn to edit what you have written. Polish, refine, and perfect what you write by rewriting. Study writing books or take classes for technique, but not for inspiration or you will get trapped into paint-by-numbers writing."

—*Jeff VanderMeer*

66. . . when I read the submissions only the story matters—not the writer's name and not the writer's previous credits and experience. **99**

—**Ann Kennedy**

SING HEAVENLY MUSE!, (I, IV), Box 13320, Minneapolis MN 55414. Editor: Sue Ann Martinson. Magazine: 6×9; 125 pages; 55 lb. acid-free paper; 10 pt. glossy cover stock; illustrations; photos. Women's poetry, prose and artwork. Annually. Estab. 1977.

Needs: Literary, feminist, prose poem and ethnic/minority. Receives approximately 30 unsolicited fiction mss each month. Published work by Patricia Hampl, Kate Green and June Jordan. Publishes short shorts. Also publishes literary essays, poetry. Sometimes recommends other markets.

How to Contact: Query for information on theme issues, reading periods or variations in schedule. Include cover letter with "brief writing background and publications." No simultaneous submissions. Reports in 1-6 months. Publishes ms an average of 1 year after acceptance. Sample copy for $4.

Payment/Terms: Pays 2 contributor's copies and honorarium, depending on funding, for first rights.

SINISTER WISDOM, (IV), Box 3252, Berkeley CA 94703. Editor: Akiba Onada-Sikwoia. Magazine: 5½×8½; 128-144 pages; 55 lb. stock; 10 pt C1S cover; illustrations; photos. Lesbian-feminist journal, providing fiction, poetry, drama, essays, journals and artwork. Quarterly. Past issues included "Lesbians of Color," "Old Lesbians/Dykes" and "Lesbians and Religion." Estab. 1976. Circ. 3,000.

Needs: Lesbian: adventure, contemporary, erotica, ethnic, experimental, fantasy, feminist, historical, humor/satire, literary, prose poem, psychic, regional, science fiction, sports, translations. No heterosexual or male-oriented fiction; nothing that stereotypes or degrades women. Receives 50 unsolicited mss/month. Accepts 25 mss/issue; 75-100 mss/year. Publishes ms 1 month to 1 year after acceptance. Published work by Sapphire, Melanie Kaye/Kantrowitz, Adrienne Rich, Terri L. Jewell and Gloria Anzaldúa; published new writers within the last year. Length: 2,000 words average; 500 words minimum; 4,000 words maximum. Publishes short shorts. Also publishes literary essays, literary criticism, poetry. Occasionally critiques rejected mss. Sometimes recommends other markets.

How to Contact: Send 1 copy of complete ms with cover letter, which should include a brief author's bio to be published when the work is published. Simultaneous submissions OK, if noted. Reports in 2 months on queries; 9 months on mss. SASE. Sample copy for $7.50. Reviews novels and short story collections. Send books to "Attn: Book Review."

Payment/Terms: Pays in contributor's copies. Rights retained by author.

Advice: The philosophy behind *Sinister Wisdom* is "to reflect and encourage the lesbian movements for social change, especially change in the ways we use language."

THE SIREN, Literary Magazine of Eckerd College, (II), Eckerd College, 4200 54th Ave. S., St. Petersburg FL 33711. (813)864-8238. Editor changes each year. Magazine: 9×6; 108 pages; photos. Annually. Estab. 1994. Circ. 1,400.

Needs: Literary, mainstream/contemporary, regional, translations. No science fiction, fantasy, horror, romance. Accepts 2-3 mss/issue. Does not read mss February-August. Publishes ms 2-3 months after acceptance. Published work by Mike Picone, Carlos Pecheco, Karen Friswell. Length: 5-10 pages. Also publishes literary essays and poetry.

How to Contact: Send complete ms with a cover letter. Should include bio and list of publications. Reports in 1-6 months on mss. Send SASE for return of ms. Simultaneous submissions OK. Sample copy for $6. Reviews novels and short story collections.

Payment/Terms: Pays 2 contributor's copies. Acquires one-time rights.

Advice: "We look for the highest quality, intelligent writing with plot."

‡sixpack: poems & stories, (I), Lemon Dog Press, c/o Don Lee, 93 S. Duncan, #1, Fayetteville AR 72701. (501)521-2833. Editor: Donald Lee. Magazine: 5½×8½; 40 pages; white paper; illustrations and photos. Triannually. Estab. 1995. Circ. 40.

Needs: Experimental, literary, translations, "Bukowski-type" pieces. No science fiction, mystery, horror. "I am presently soliciting manuscripts for our first few issues from writers I'm familiar with." Accepts 2 mss/issue; 6 mss/year. Publishes ms 6 months after acceptance. Length: 1,500 words average; 2,000 words maximum. Publishes short shorts. Also publishes literary essays, literary criticism and poetry. Often critiques or comments on rejected ms.

How to Contact: Send complete ms with a cover letter. Should include estimated word count, bio, Social Security number and list of publications with submission. Reports in 6 weeks. Send SASE for reply, return of ms or send a disposable copy of ms. Simultaneous and reprint submissions OK. E-mail address: donlee@co mp.uark.edu. Sample copy for $2, SAE and 3 first-class stamps; make checks payable to Don Lee. Fiction guidelines for SASE. Reviews novels and short story collections.

Payment/Terms: Pays 2 contributor's copies. Acquires one-time rights. Not copyrighted.

Advice: "Keep it short. Be funny. Be professional. Read Bukowski first. If not funny, go for that element of the strange that makes a story irresistible. If you send a cover letter, keep it short and friendly."

‡SKIPPING STONES: A Multicultural Children's Magazine, (I), P.O. Box 3939, Eugene OR 97403. (541)342-4956. Editor: Arun N. Toké. Magazine: 8½×11; 36 pages; recycled 50 lb. halopaque paper; 80 lb. text cover; illustrations and photos. "*Skipping Stones* is a multicultural, international, nature awareness magazine for children 8-16, and their parents and teachers." Published 5 times a year. Estab. 1988. Circ. 3,000.

Needs: Children's/juvenile (8-16 years): ethnic/multicultural, feminist, religious/inspirational, young adult/teen, international, nature. List of upcoming themes available for SASE. Receives 20 mss/month. Accepts 3-5 mss/issue; 15-25 mss/year. Publishes ms 3-6 months after acceptance. Recently published work by Norma G. Fisher, Amy Wu, Brandon A. Jones and Jeffrey Lewis. Length: 750 words average; 250 words minimum; 1,000 words maximum. Publishes short shorts. Also publishes literary essays and poetry. Often critiques or comments on rejected ms.

How to Contact: Send complete ms with a cover letter. Should include 50-100 word bio with background, international or intercultural experiences. Reports in 1 month on queries; 3 months on mss. Send SASE for reply, return of ms or send a disposable copy of ms. Simultaneous submissions OK. Sample copy for $5, 9×12 SAE and 4 first-class stamps. Fiction guidelines for #10 SASE.

Payment/Terms: Pays 1-3 contributor's copies; additional copies for $3. Acquires first North American serial rights and nonexclusive reprint rights. Sponsors contests, awards or grants for fiction writers under 16 years of age.

Advice: Looking for stories with "multicultural/multi-ethnic theme, use of other languages when appropriate. Realistic and suitable for 10 to 15 year olds. Promoting social and nature awareness."

SKYLARK, (I), Purdue University, 2200 169th St., Hammond IN 46323. (219)989-2262. Editor-in-Chief: Pamela Hunter. Prose Editor: Nancy Conner. Magazine: 8½×11; 100 pages; illustrations; photos. Fine arts magazine—short stories, poems and graphics for adults. Annually. Estab. 1971. Circ. 600-1,000.

Needs: Contemporary, ethnic, experimental, fantasy, feminist, humor/satire, literary, mainstream, mystery/suspense (English cozy), prose poem, regional, romance (gothic), science fiction, serialized/excerpted novel, spiritual, sports and western (frontier stories). Upcoming theme: "Anniversaries" (submit April 1996). Receives 20 mss/month. Accepts 8 mss/issue. Recently published work by Greta Holt, Joanne Zimmerman, Joan Peternel and Virginia Deweese; published new writers within the last year. Length: 4,000 words maximum. Also publishes essays and poetry.

How to Contact: Send complete ms. SASE for ms. Reports in 4 months. No simultaneous submissions. Sample copy for $7; back issue for $5.

Payment/Terms: Pays 1 contributor's copy. Acquires first rights. Copyright reverts to author.

Advice: "The goal of *Skylark* is to encourage *creativity* and give beginning and published authors showcase for their work. Manuscripts *must* be carefully prepared and proofread."

‡THE SLATE, (II), P.O. Box 581189, Minneapolis MN 55458-1189. (612)823-5279. Editors: Chris Dall, Rachel Fulkerson, Jessica Morris. Magazine: 6×9; 100 pages; 60 lb. Spring Hill paper; illustrations. "*The Slate* is a literary journal that has been created with both the writer and reader in mind. We are dedicated to promoting the written word and to nourishing the bond between the writer and the reader. We are open to all styles of writing." Triannually. Estab. 1995.

Needs: Ethnic/multicultural, experimental, feminist, historical, humor/satire, literary, mainstream/contemporary, regional, translations. Accepts 4-6 mss/issue. Publishes ms 4 months after acceptance. Publishes short shorts. Also publishes literary essays, poetry. Often critiques or comments on rejected ms.

How to Contact: Send complete ms with a cover letter. Should include half-page bio and list of publications. Reports in 2 weeks on queries; 6-8 weeks on mss. Send SASE for reply. Electronic submissions OK. Sample copy for $4.95. Guidelines for SASE.

Payment/Terms: Pays 2 contributor's copies. Acquires one-time rights.

SLATE AND STYLE, Magazine of the National Federation of the Blind Writers Division, (I, IV), NFB Writer's Division, 2704 Beach Dr., Merrick NY 11566. (516)868-8718. Fax: (516)868-9076. Fiction Editor: Loraine Stayer. Newsletter: 8×10; 32 print/40 Braille pages; cassette and large print. "Articles of interest to writers, and resources for blind writers." Quarterly. Estab. 1982. Circ. 200.

● The magazine runs an annual contest for fiction, limit 2,000 words. There is a $10 entry fee and the contest runs from September 1 to May 1. Write for details.

Needs: Adventure, contemporary, fantasy, humor/satire, blindness. No erotica. "Avoid theme of death." Does not read mss in June or July. Length: 1,000-3,000 words. Publishes short shorts. Also publishes literary criticism and poetry. Critiques rejected mss only if requested.

How to Contact: Reports in 3-6 weeks. Sample copy for $2.50. Large print copies also available. "Sent Free Matter For The Blind. If not blind, send 2 stamps."

✝ ***The double dagger before a listing indicates that the listing is new in this edition. New markets are often the most receptive to submissions by new writers.***

Payment/Terms: Pays in contributor's copies. Acquires one-time rights. Publication not copyrighted. Sponsors contests for fiction writers.

Advice: "Keep a copy. Editors can lose your work. Consider each first draft as just that and review your work before you send it. SASE a must."

‡**SLIGHTLY WEST, (II)**, Evergreen State College, Cab 320, Olympia WA 98505. (206)866-6000, ext. 6879. Editor: Ethan Salter. Magazine: 8½×12; 50 pages; 70 lb. paper; 80 lb. cover; illustrations and photos. "*Slightly West* offers exposure for all types of writers, any subject barring offensive material, community at large." Quarterly. Estab. 1985. Circ. 1,500.

Needs: Condensed/excerpted novel, erotica, ethnic/multicultural, experimental, feminist, gay, historical, humor/satire, lesbian, literary, mainstream/contemporary, regional, translations. "No children's fantasy." Receives 120 unsolicited mss/month. Accepts 4 mss/issue; 12 mss/year. Does not read mss in the summer. Publishes ms 1 month after acceptance. Recently published work by Holly Day, Lyn Lifshin, DM Kumfermann. Publishes short shorts. Publishes literary essays, literary criticism and poetry. Sometimes critiques or comments on rejected ms.

How to Contact: Send complete ms with a cover letter. Should include 1-paragraph bio (note if work has been published). Send SASE for reply, return of ms or send a disposable copy of ms. Simultaneous submissions OK. Sample copy for $2.50, 10×13 SAE and 3 first-class stamps. Fiction guidelines for SASE.

Payment/Terms: Pays 2 contributor's copies; additional copies for $1. Acquires one-time rights.

SLIPPERY WHEN WET, A Magazine of Sex & Fun, (IV), More! Productions, P.O. Box 3101, Berkeley CA 94703. Editor: Sunah Cherwin. Electronic magazine: illustrations and photos. "Sex is fun; the scene is fun. Here's how to publish; open to erotica, humor, observations and how-tos." Quarterly. Estab. 1991.

Needs: Erotica. Receives 5-10 unsolicited mss/month. Acquires 3 mss/issue; 12 mss/year. Publishes ms 3 months after acceptance. Published work by Carol Queen, Mark Pritchard and Kris Kovick. Length: 750 words minimum; 5,000 words maximum. Publishes short shorts. Often critiques or comments on rejected mss.

How to Contact: Send complete ms with a cover letter and diskette for Mac. Should include estimated word count and bio (1 paragraph). Reports in 1 month on queries; 2 months on mss. Send SASE (or IRC) for reply, return of ms or send a disposable copy of ms. Simultaneous, reprint and electronic (Mac diskette preferred with/hard copy) submissions OK. World Wide Web address: http://www.best.com./~slippery/18.html. Fiction guidelines free.

Payment/Terms: Payments are arranged. Acquires one-time rights.

Advice: Looks for "hot, funny, new ideas. Ask yourself, 'what does the reader discover?'"

SLIPSTREAM, (II, IV), Box 2071, New Market Station, Niagara Falls NY 14301. (716)282-2616. Editor: Dan Sicoli. Fiction Editors: R. Borgatti, D. Sicoli and Livio Farallo. Magazine: 7×8½; 80-100 pages; high quality paper and cover; illustrations; photos. "We use poetry and short fiction with a contemporary urban feel." Estab. 1981. Circ. 500.

Needs: Contemporary, erotica, ethnic, experimental, humor/satire, literary, mainstream and prose poem. No religious, juvenile, young adult or romance. Occasionally publishes theme issues; query for information. Receives over 75 unsolicited mss/month. Accepts 2-4 mss/issue; 6 mss/year. Length: under 15 pages. Publishes short shorts. Recently published work by Richard Stockton Rand, Katherine Katsens and Robert Perchan. Rarely critiques rejected mss. Sometimes recommends other markets.

How to Contact: "Query before submitting." Reports within 2 months. SASE. Sample copy for $5. Fiction guidelines for #10 SASE.

Payment/Terms: Pays 2 contributor's copies. Acquires one-time rights on publication.

Advice: "Writing should be honest, fresh; develop your own style. Check out a sample issue first. Don't write for the sake of writing, write from the gut as if it were a biological need. Write from experience and mean what you say, but say it in the fewest number of words."

THE SMALL POND MAGAZINE, (II), Box 664, Stratford CT 06497. (203)378-4066. Editor: Napoleon St. Cyr. Magazine: 5½×8½; 42 pages; 60 lb. offset paper; 65 lb. cover stock; illustrations (art). "Features contemporary poetry, the salt of the earth, peppered with short prose pieces of various kinds. The college educated and erudite read it for good poetry, prose and pleasure." Triannually. Estab. 1964. Circ. 300.

Needs: "Rarely use science fiction or formula stories you'd find in *Cosmo*, *Redbook*, *Ladies Home Journal*, etc." Buys 10-12 mss/year. Longer response time in July and August. Receives approximately 40 unsolicited fiction mss each month. Length: 200-2,500 words. Critiques rejected mss when there is time. Sometimes recommends other markets.

How to Contact: Send complete ms with SASE and short vita. Reports in 2 weeks-3 months. Publishes ms an average of 2-12 months after acceptance. Sample copy for $3; $2.50 for back issues.

Payment/Terms: Pays 2 contributor's copies for all rights; $2.50/copy charge for extras.

Advice: "Send for a sample copy first. All mss must be typed. Name and address and story title on front page, name of story on succeeding pages and paginated." Mss are rejected because of "tired plots and poor grammar; also over-long—2,500 words maximum. Don't send any writing conference ms unless it got an A or better."

SNAKE NATION REVIEW, (II), Snake Nation Press, Inc., #2 West Force St., 110, Valdosta GA 31601. (912)249-8334. Editor: Roberta George. Fiction Editor: Nancy Phillips. 6×9; 110 pages; acid free 70 lb. paper; 90 lb. cover; illustrations and photographs. "We are interested in all types of stories for an educated, discerning, sophisticated audience." Quarterly. Estab. 1989. Circ. 1,000.

• *Snake Nation Review* receives funding from the Georgia Council of the Arts, the Georgia Humanities Council and the Porter/Fleming Foundation for Literature.

Needs: "Short stories of 5,000 words or less, poems (any length), art work that will be returned after use." Condensed/excerpted novel, contemporary, erotica, ethnic, experimental, fantasy, feminist, gay, horror, humor/satire, lesbian, literary, mainstream, mystery/suspense, prose poem, psychic/supernatural/occult, regional, science fiction, senior citizen/retirement. "We want our writers to have a voice, a story to tell, not a flat rendition of a slice of life." Plans annual anthology. Receives 50 unsolicited mss/month. Buys 8-10 mss/issue; 20 mss/year. Publishes ms 3-6 months after acceptance. Agented fiction 1%. Published work by Judith Oitiz Cofer and Victor Miller. Length: 3,500 words average; 300 words minimum; 5,500 words maximum. Publishes short shorts. Length: 500 words. Also publishes literary essays, poetry. Sometimes critiques rejected mss and recommends other markets.

How to Contact: Send complete ms with cover letter. Reports on queries in 3 months. SASE. Sample copy for $5, 8×10 SAE and 90¢ postage. Fiction guidelines for SASE.

Payment/Terms: Pays $100 maximum and contributor's copies for first rights. Sends galleys to author.

Advice: "Looks for clean, legible copy and an interesting, unique voice that pulls the reader into the work." Spring contest: short stories (5,000 words); $300 first prize, $200 second prize, $100 third prize; entry fee: $5 for stories, $1 for poems. Contest Issue with every $5 fee.

SNOWY EGRET, (II), The Fair Press, P.O. Box 9, Bowling Green IN 47833. (812)829-1910. Publisher: Karl Barnebey. Editor: Philip Repp. Magazine: 8½×11; 50 pages; text paper; heavier cover; illustrations. "Literary exploration of the abundance and beauty of nature and the ways human beings interact with it." Semiannually. Estab. 1922. Circ. 500.

Needs: Nature writing, including 'true' stories, eye-witness accounts, descriptive sketches and traditional fiction. "We are particularly interested in fiction that celebrates abundance and beauty of nature, encourages a love and respect for the natural world, and affirms the human connection to the environment. No works written for popular genres: horror, science fiction, romance, detective, western, etc." Receives 25 unsolicited mss/month. Buys up to 6 mss/issue; up to 12 mss/year. Publishes ms 6 months-1 year after acceptance. Published works by Jane Candia Coleman, Stephen Lewandowski and Margarita Mondrus Engle. Length: 1,000-3,000 words preferred; 500 words minimum; 10,000 words maximum. Publishes short shorts. Length: 400-500 words. Sometimes critiques rejected mss.

How to Contact: Send complete ms with cover letter. "Cover letter optional: do not query." Reports in 2 months. SASE. Simultaneous submissions OK if noted. Sample back issues for $8, 9×12 SAE. Send #10 SASE for writer's guidelines.

Payment/Terms: Pays $2/page and 2 contributor's copies on publication; charge for extras. Purchases first North American serial rights and reprint rights. Sends galleys to author.

Advice: Looks for "honest, freshly detailed pieces with plenty of description and/or dialogue which will allow the reader to identify with the characters and step into the setting. Characters who relate strongly to nature, either positively or negatively, and who, during the course of the story, grow in their understanding of themselves and the world around them."

SO TO SPEAK, A Feminist Journal of Language and Art, (II, IV), George Mason University, Sub1, Room 254A, 4400 University Dr., Fairfax VA 22030. (703)993-3625. Editor: Anne Marie Yerks. Editors change every 2 years. Magazine: 7×10; approximately 70 pages. "We are a feminist journal of high-quality material geared toward an academic/cultured audience." Semiannually. Estab. 1988. Circ. 1,300.

Needs: Ethnic/multicultural, experimental, feminist, lesbian, literary, mainstream/contemporary, regional, translations. "No science fiction, mystery, genre romance, porn (lesbian or straight)." Receives 100 unsolicited mss/month. Buys 2-3 mss/issue; 6 mss/year. Publishes ms 6 months after acceptance. Length: 4,000 words average; 6,000 words maximum. Publishes short shorts. Also publishes literary essays, literary criticism and poetry. Sometimes critiques or comments on rejected mss.

How to Contact: Send complete ms with a cover letter. Should include bio (50 words maximum), Social Security number and SASE. Reports in 6 months on mss. SASE for return of ms or send a disposable copy of ms. Simultaneous submissions OK. Sample copy for $5. Fiction guidelines for #10 SASE.

Payment/Terms: Pays $25 maximum, plus 5 contributor's copies on publication for first North American serial rights. Sends galleys to author on request.

Advice: "We look for skill with language, feeling behind the words. All our fiction should mean something. Make sure it is polished and pertinent to women's lives. We do not want housewife fantasy or baby-boomer nostalgia."

‡THE SOFT DOOR, (I, II), 202 S. Church St., Bowling Green OH 43402. Editor: T. Williams. Magazine: 8½×11; 30 pages; bond paper; heavy cover; illustrations and photos. "We publish works that explore human relationships and our relationship to the world." Irregularly.
Needs: Literary, mainstream/contemporary. "I will look at anything as long as it has a heart and achieves a complexity that mirrors the human condition." Upcoming theme: "Custer And The Indians." Receives 25 mss/month. Buys 5 mss/year. Does not read mss November-December. Publishes ms up to 1 year after acceptance. Length: 5,000 words average; 10,000 words maximum. Publishes short shorts. Also publishes poetry. Sometimes critiques or comments on rejected ms.
How to Contact: Send complete mss with a cover letter. Should include "short statement about who you are and why you write, along with any successes you have had. Please write to me like I am a human being." Send SASE for reply, return of ms or send a disposable copy of ms. Simultaneous submissions OK.
Payment/Terms: Pays 1 contributor's copy. Acquires one-time rights.
Advice: "Write about what you know or can vividly imagine. I prefer not to see romance or science fiction. Always interested in works by Native American writers."

SONORA REVIEW, (I, II), University of Arizona, Department of English, Tucson AZ 85721. (520)626-8383. Co-Editors: Julie Newman and Alicia Saposnik. Fiction Editor: Becky Hagenston. Editors change each year. Magazine: 6×9; 150 pages; 16 lb. paper; 20 lb. cover stock; photos seldom. *Sonora Review* publishes short fiction and poetry of high literary quality. Semiannually. Estab. 1980. Circ. 900.
  ● Work published in *Sonora Review* has been selected for inclusion in the *Pushcart Prize*, *O. Henry Awards*, *Best of the West* and *Best American Poetry* anthologies. See the listing for their fiction contest in the Contests and Awards section.
Needs: Literary. "We are open to a wide range of stories with accessibility and vitality being important in any case. We're not interested in genre fiction, formula work." Acquires 4-6 mss/issue. Agented fiction 10%. Recently published work by Alison Baker, Alison Hawthorne Deming and Dagdoerto Gilb. Length: open, though prefers work under 25 pages. Also publishes literary essays, literary criticism and poetry.
How to Contact: Send complete ms with SASE and cover letter with previous publications. Simultaneous submissions OK. Reports in 3 months on mss, longer for work received during summer (May-August). Publishes ms an average of 2-6 months after acceptance. Sample copy for $6.
Payment/Terms: Pays 2 contributor's copies; $5 charge for extras. Acquires first North American serial rights. Annual short story contest: 1st prize, $500. Send #10 SASE for submission guidelines.
Advice: "All mss are read carefully, and we try to make brief comments if time permits. Our hope is that an author will keep us interested in his or her treatment of a subject by using fresh details and writing with an authority that is absorbing." Mss are rejected because "we only have space for 6-8 manuscripts out of several hundred submissions annually."

SOUNDINGS EAST, (II), English Dept., Salem State College, Salem MA 01970. (508)741-6270. Advisory Editors: Joseph Salvatore and Sarah Messer. Magazine: 5½×8½; 64 pages; illustrations; photos. "Mainly a college audience, but we also distribute to libraries throughout the country." Biannual. Estab. 1973. Circ. 2,000.
Needs: Literary, contemporary, prose poem. No juvenile. Publishes 4-5 stories/issue. Receives 30 unsolicited fiction mss each month. Submissions limited to 2 fiction pieces, 5 poems, and/or 5 photos/illustrations. Does not read April-August. Deadlines: November 20, Fall/Winter issue; April 20, Spring/Summer issue. Recently published work by Antonya Nelson, Philip Gerard and Joe Salvatore; published new writers within the last year. Length: 250-4,000 words. "We are open to short pieces as well as to long works."
How to Contact: Send complete ms with SASE (or IRC) between September and April. Accepts partial novels and multiple submissions if notified. Reports in 1-3 months on mss. Sample copy for $3.
Payment/Terms: Pays 2 contributor's copies. All publication rights revert to author.
Advice: "We're impressed by an excitement—coupled with craft—in the use of the language. It also helps to reach in and grab the reader by the heart."

SOUTH CAROLINA REVIEW, (II), Clemson University, Clemson SC 29634-1503. (803)656-3151. Editors: Frank Day and Carol Johnston. Magazine: 6×9; 200 pages; 60 lb. cream white vellum paper; 65 lb. cream white vellum cover stock; illustrations and photos rarely. Semiannually. Estab. 1967. Circ. 700.
Needs: Literary and contemporary fiction, poetry, essays, reviews. Receives 50-60 unsolicited fiction mss each month. Does not read mss June-August or December. Published work by Joyce Carol Oates, Rosanne Coggeshall, Stephen Dixon; published new writers within the last year. Rarely critiques rejected mss.
How to Contact: Send complete ms with SASE. Reports in 6-9 months on mss. Sample copy for $5.
Payment/Terms: Pays in contributor's copies.
Advice: Mss are rejected because of "poorly structured stories, or stories without vividness or intensity. The most celebrated function of a little magazine is to take a chance on writers not yet able to get into the larger magazines—the little magazine can encourage promising writers at a time when encouragement is vitally needed. (We also publish 'name' writers, like Joyce Carol Oates, Stephen Dixon, George Garrett.) Read the masters extensively. Write and write more, with a *schedule*. Listen to editorial advice when offered. Don't get discouraged with rejections. Read what writers say about writing (e.g. *The Paris Review* interviews

with George Plimpton; Welty's *One Writer's Beginnings*, etc). Take courses in writing and listen to, even if you do not follow, the advice."

SOUTH DAKOTA REVIEW, (II), University of South Dakota, Box 111, University Exchange, Vermillion SD 57069. (605)677-5966. Editor: Brian Bedard. Editorial Assistant: Geraldine Sanford. Magazine: 6×9; 150 pages; book paper; glossy cover stock; illustrations sometimes; photos on cover. "Literary magazine for university and college audiences and their equivalent. Emphasis is often on the West and its writers, but will accept mss from anywhere. Issues are generally essay, fiction, and poetry with some literary essays." Quarterly. Estab. 1963. Circ. 500.

• A story by Richard Plant, published in *SDR* was selected for inclusion in the *Sudden Fiction* anthology published in Spring 1996.

Needs: Literary, contemporary, ethnic, experimental, excerpted novel, regional. "We like very well-written stories. Contemporary western American setting appeals, but not necessary. No formula stories, sports or adolescent 'I' narrator." Receives 30 unsolicited fiction mss/month. Accepts about 30 mss/year, more or less. Assistant editor accepts mss in June-July, sometimes August. Agented fiction 5%. Publishes short shorts of 5 pages double-spaced typescript. Recently published work by Dan O'Brien, Max Evans and Linda Hasselstrom; published several new writers within the last year. Length: 1,000-1,300 words minimum; 6,000 words maximum. (Has made exceptions, up to novella length.) Sometimes recommends other markets.

How to Contact: Send complete ms with SASE. "We like cover letters that are not boastful and do not attempt to sell the stories but rather provide some personal information about the writer." No multiple submissions. Reports in 5-7 weeks. Publishes ms an average of 1-6 months after acceptance. Sample copy for $5.

Payment/Terms: Pays 1-year subscription, plus 2-4 contributor's copies, depending on length of ms; $3 charge for extras. Acquires first rights and reprint rights.

Advice: Rejects mss because of "careless writing; often careless typing; stories too personal ('I' confessional), adolescent; working manuscript, not polished; subject matter that editor finds sensationalized, pretentious or trivial. We are trying to use more fiction and more variety."

SOUTHERN CALIFORNIA ANTHOLOGY, (II), Master of Professional Writing Program—USC, MPW-WPH 404 USC, Los Angeles CA 90089-4034. (213)740-3252. Contact: Editor. Magazine: 5½×8½; 142 pages; semi-glossy cover stock. "The *Southern California Anthology* is a literary review that is an eclectic collection of previously unpublished quality contemporary fiction, poetry and interviews with established literary people, published for adults of all professions; of particular interest to those interested in serious contemporary literature." Annually. Estab. 1983. Circ. 1,500.

Needs: Contemporary, ethnic, experimental, feminist, historical, humor/satire, literary, mainstream, regional, serialized/excerpted novel. No juvenile, religious, confession, romance, science fiction or pornography. Receives 30 unsolicited fiction mss each month. Accepts 10-12 mss/issue. Does not read February-September. Publishes ms 4 months after acceptance. Length: 10-15 pages average; 2 pages minimum; 25 pages maximum. Publishes short shorts.

How to Contact: Send complete ms with cover letter or submit through agent. Cover letter should include list of previous publications. Reports on queries in 1 month; on mss in 4 months. SASE. Sample copy for $4. Fiction guidelines for #10 SASE.

Payment/Terms: Pays in contributor's copies. Acquires first rights.

Advice: "The *Anthology* pays particular attention to craft and style in its selection of narrative writing."

SOUTHERN EXPOSURE, (II, IV), Institute for Southern Studies, P.O. Box 531, Durham NC 27702. (919)419-8311. Editor: Jo Carson. Magazine: 8½×11; 64 pages. "Southern politics and culture—investigative reporting, oral history, fiction for an audience of Southern changemakers—scholars, journalists, activists." Quarterly. Estab. 1972. Circ. 5,000.

• *Southern Exposure* has won numerous awards for its reporting including the Sidney Hillman Award for reporting on racial justice issues.

Needs: Contemporary, ethnic, feminist, gay, humor/satire, lesbian, literary, regional. Receives 50 unsolicited mss/month. Buys 1 mss/issue; 4 mss/year. Publishes ms 3-6 months after acceptance. Agented fiction 25%. Published work by Clyde Egerton, Jill McCorkle and Larry Brown. Length: 3,500 words preferred.

How to Contact: Send complete ms with cover letter. No simultaneous submissions. Reports in 4-6 weeks on mss. SASE for ms. Sample copy for $4, 8½×11 and $1.85 postage. Fiction guidelines for #10 SASE.

Payment/Terms: Pays $250, subscription to magazine and contributor's copies on publication for first rights.

SOUTHERN HUMANITIES REVIEW, (II, IV), Auburn University, 9088 Haley Center, Auburn University AL 36849. Co-editors: Dan R. Latimer and Virginia M. Kouidis. Magazine: 6×9; 100 pages; 60 lb. neutral pH, natural paper, 65 lb. neutral pH med. coated cover stock; occasional illustrations and photos. "We publish essays, poetry, fiction and reviews. Our fiction has ranged from very traditional in form and content to very experimental. Literate, college-educated audience. We hope they read our journal for both enlightenment and pleasure." Quarterly. Estab. 1967. Circ. 800.

Needs: Serious fiction, fantasy, feminist, humor and regional. Receives approximately 25 unsolicited fiction mss each month. Accepts 1-2 mss/issue, 4-6 mss/year. Slower reading time in summer. Published work by Anne Brashler, Heimito von Doderer and Ivo Andric; published new writers within the last year. Length: 3,500-15,000 words. Also publishes literary essays, literary criticism, poetry. Critiques rejected mss when there is time. Sometimes recommends other markets.

How to Contact: Send complete ms (one at a time) with SASE and cover letter with an explanation of topic chosen—"special, certain book, etc., a little about author if he/she has never submitted." Reports in 90 days. Sample copy for $5. Reviews novel and short story collections.

Payment/Terms: Pays 2 contributor's copies; $5 charge for extras. Rights revert to author upon publication. Sends galleys to author.

Advice: "Send us the ms with SASE. If we like it, we'll take it or we'll recommend changes. If we don't like it, we'll send it back as promptly as possible. Read the journal. Send a typewritten, clean copy carefully proofread. We also award annually the Hoepfner Prize of $100 for the best published essay or short story of the year. Let someone whose opinion you respect read your story and give you an honest appraisal. Rewrite, if necessary, to get the most from your story."

THE SOUTHERN REVIEW, (II), Louisiana State University, 43 Allen Hall, Baton Rouge LA 70803. (504)388-5108. Editors: James Olney and Dave Smith. Magazine: 6¾×10; 240 pages; 50 lb. Glatfelter paper; 65 lb. #1 grade cover stock; occasional photos. "A literary quarterly publishing critical essays, poetry and fiction for a highly intellectual audience." Quarterly. Published special fiction issue. Estab. 1935. Circ. 3,000.

Needs: Literary and contemporary. "We emphasize style and substantial content. No mystery, fantasy or religious mss." Buys 4-5 mss/issue. Receives approximately 400 unsolicited fiction mss each month. Agented fiction 5%. Published work by Gloria Naylor, Wendell Berry and James Dickey; published new writers within the last year. Length: 2,000-10,000 words. Also publishes literary essays, literary criticism, poetry. Sometimes recommends other markets.

How to Contact: Send complete ms with cover letter and SASE. "Prefer brief letters giving information on author concerning where he/she has been published before, biographical info and what he/she is doing now." Reports in 2 months on mss. Publishes ms an average of 6-12 months after acceptance. Sample copy for $6. Reviews novels and short story collections.

Payment/Terms: Pays $12/printed page; 2 contributor's copies on publication for first North American serial rights. "We transfer copyright to author on request." Sends galleys to author.

Advice: "Develop a careful, clear style." Sponsors annual contest for best first collection of short stories published during the calendar year.

SOUTHWEST REVIEW, (II), Box 374, 307 Fondren Library West, Southern Methodist University, Dallas TX 75275. (214)768-1037. Editor: Willard Spiegelman. Magazine: 6×9; 144 pages. "The majority of our readers are college-educated adults who wish to stay abreast of the latest and best in contemporary fiction, poetry, literary criticism and books in all but the most specialized disciplines." Quarterly. Estab. 1915. Circ. 1,600.

Needs: "High literary quality; no specific requirements as to subject matter, but cannot use sentimental, religious, western, poor science fiction, pornographic, true confession, mystery, juvenile or serialized or condensed novels." Receives approximately 200 unsolicited fiction mss each month. Recently published work by Reynolds Price, Elizabeth Graver, Lisa Sandlin, Thomas Beller and Jill Koenigsdorf. Length: prefers 3,000-5,000 words. Also publishes literary essays and poetry. Occasionally critiques rejected mss.

How to Contact: Send complete ms with SASE. Reports in 6 months on mss. Publishes ms 6-12 months after acceptance. Sample copy for $5. Guidelines for SASE.

Payment/Terms: Payment varies; writers receive 3 contributor's copies. Pays on publication for first North American serial rights. Sends galleys to author.

Advice: "We have become less regional. A lot of time would be saved for us and for the writer if he or she looked at a copy of the *Southwest Review* before submitting. We like to receive a cover letter because it is some reassurance that the author has taken the time to check a current directory for the editor's name. When there isn't a cover letter, we wonder whether the same story is on 20 other desks around the country."

SOU'WESTER, (II), Southern Illinois University-Edwardsville, Edwardsville IL 62026-1438. (618)692-3190. Managing Editor: Fred W. Robbins. Magazine: 6×9; 120 pages; Warren's Olde Style paper; 60 lb. cover. General magazine of poetry and fiction. Biannually. Estab. 1960. Circ. 300.

● Work published in *Sou'wester* has received an Illinois Arts Council literary award for "Best Illinois Fiction" and the Daniel Curley Award.

Needs: Receives 40-50 unsolicited fiction mss/month. Accepts 6 mss/issue; 12 mss/year. Published work by Robert Wexelblatt and Robert Solomon; published new writers within the last year. Length: 10,000 words maximum. Also publishes poetry. Occasionally critiques rejected mss.

How to Contact: Send complete ms with SASE. Simultaneous submissions OK. Reports in 6 months. Publishes ms an average of 6 months after acceptance. Sample copy for $5.

Payment/Terms: Pays 2 contributor's copies; $5 charge for extras. Acquires first serial rights.

‡SPECTRUM, (I, II), Box 14800, University of California, Santa Barbara CA 93107. Contact: Editor. Magazine 6×9; 100-150 pages; illustrations and photos. "Interested in quality work. Poetry, fiction and essay." Annually. Estab. 1957. Circ. 750.

Needs: Literary, experimental. Does not read mss January 15-August. Publishes short short stories. Also publishes literary essays, literary criticism, poetry.

How to Contact: Send complete ms. SASE. Simultaneous submissions OK. Sample copy for $6 and 7×10 SAE. Fiction guidelines for #10 SASE. E-mail address: uwatsh@mclousb.edu.

Payment/Terms: Contributor's copies.

SPECTRUM, (II), Box 72-C, Anna Maria College, Sunset Lane, Paxton MA 01612. (508)849-3300. Editor: Robert H. Goepfert. Magazine: 6×9; 64 pages; illustrations and photos. "An interdisciplinary publication publishing fiction as well as poetry, scholarly articles, reviews, art and photography. Submissions are especially encouraged from those affiliated with liberal arts colleges." Semiannually. Estab. 1985. Circ. 1,000.

Needs: Contemporary, experimental, historical, literary, mainstream. No western, mystery, erotica, science fiction. Receives an average of 15 unsolicited fiction ms/month. Accepts 4-6 mss/issue. Publishes ms approximately 6 months after acceptance. Length: 2,000-5,000 words preferred; 3,000 words average; 10,000 words maximum. Publishes short shorts. Also publishes literary essays, literary criticism, poetry. Sometimes critiques rejected mss.

How to Contact: Send complete ms with cover letter. Reports in 6 weeks. SASE for ms. No simultaneous submissions. Sample copy for $3. Fiction guidelines with SASE.

Payment/Terms: Pays $20 and 2 contributor's copies on publication for first North American serial rights. Sends to author. Publication not copyrighted.

Advice: "Our chief aim is diversity."

SPINDRIFT, (I, II), Shoreline Community College, 16101 Greenwood Ave. North, Seattle WA 98133. (206)546-4785. Editor: Carol Orlock, adviser. Magazine: 140 pages; quality paper; photographs; b&w artwork. "We look for fresh, original work that is not forced or 'straining' to be literary." Annually. Estab. around 1967. Circ. 500.

● *Spindrift* has received awards for "Best Literary Magazine" from the Community College Humanities Association both locally and nationally and awards from the Pacific Printing Industries.

Needs: Contemporary, ethnic, experimental, historical (general), prose poem, regional, science fiction, serialized/excerpted novel, translations. No romance, religious/inspirational. Receives up to 150 mss/year. Accepts up to 20 mss/issue. Does not read during spring/summer. Publishes ms 3-4 months after acceptance. Published work by David Halpern and Jana Harris; published new writers within the last year. Length: 250 words minimum; 3,500-4,500 words maximum. Publishes short shorts.

How to Contact: Send complete ms, and "bio, name, address, phone and list of titles submitted." Reports in 2 weeks on queries; juries after February 1 and responds by March 15 with SASE. Sample copy for $6, 8×10 SAE and $1 postage.

Payment/Terms: Pays in contributor's copies; charge for extras. Acquires first rights. Publication not copyrighted.

Advice: "The tighter the story the better. The more lyric values in the narrative the better. Read the magazine, keep working on craft. Submit by February 1."

‡SPIRIT MAGAZINE, Exploring Alternative Ideas, (I), P.O. Box 27244, Minneapolis MN 55427. Editor: C.W. Youssef. Magazine: 8½×11; 40-52 pages; 50 lb. paper; 70 lb. cover; illustrations and photos. "*Spirit* is committed to encouraging awareness of alternative spiritual and healing ways as well as being a part of developing a new consciousness regarding humanitarian and environmental one world issues. We're also about love." Bimonthly. Estab. 1993. Circ. 3,500.

Needs: Children's/juvenile, ethnic/multicultural, experimental, fantasy, feminist, literary, regional, religious/inspirational, New Age, alternative spirituality and healing. List of upcoming themes available for SASE. Plans annual special fiction issue or anthology. Receives 3-6 unsolicited mss/month. Accepts 6 mss/year. Publishes ms 3 months after acceptance. Recently published work by Susan Draughon and Ayal Hurst. Length: 500 words average; 2,000 words maximum. Publishes short shorts. Length: 500 words. Also publishes literary essays and poetry. Sometimes critiques or comments on rejected ms.

How to Contact: Send complete ms with a cover letter. Should include 75-word bio. Reports in 1 month on queries; 2 months on mss. Send SASE for reply, return of ms or send a disposable copy of ms. Reprint and electronic submissions OK. Sample copy for $3 plus legal SAE. Fiction guidelines for legal SAE and 2-3 first-class stamps.

Payment/Terms: Pays 3 contributor's copies.

SPITBALL, (I), 5560 Fox Rd., Cincinnati OH 45239. (513)385-2268. Editor: Mike Shannon. Magazine: 5½×8½; 96 pages; 55 lb. Glatfelter Natural, Neutral, pH paper; 10 pt. C1S cover stock; illustrations; photos. Magazine publishing "fiction and poetry about *baseball* exclusively for an educated, literary segment of the baseball fan population." Quarterly. Estab. 1981. Circ. 1,000.

Needs: Confession, contemporary, experimental, historical, literary, mainstream and suspense. "Our only requirement concerning the type of fiction written is that the story be *primarily* about baseball." Receives 100 unsolicited fiction mss/year. Accepts 16-20 mss/year. Published work by Dallas Wiebe, Michael Gilmartin and W.P. Kinsella. Published new writers within the last year. Length: 20 typed double spaced pages. The longer it is, the better it has to be.

How to Contact: Send complete ms with SASE, and cover letter with brief bio about author. Reporting time varies. Publishes ms an average of 3 months after acceptance. Sample copy for $5.

Payment/Terms: "No monetary payment at present. We may offer nominal payment in the near future." 2 free contributor's copies per issue in which work appears. Acquires first North American serial rights.

Advice: "Our audience is mostly college educated and knowledgeable about baseball. The stories we have published so far have been very well written and displayed a firm grasp of the baseball world and its people. In short, audience response has been great because the stories are simply good as stories. Thus, mere use of baseball as subject is no guarantee of acceptance. We are always seeking submissions. Unlike many literary magazines, we have no backlog of accepted material. Fiction is a natural genre for our exclusive subject, baseball. There are great opportunities for writing in certain areas of fiction, baseball being one of them. Baseball has become the 'in' spectator sport among intellectuals, the general media and the 'yuppie' crowd. Consequently, as subject matter for adult fiction it has gained a much wider acceptance than it once enjoyed."

‡THE SPITTING IMAGE, (II), P.O. Box 931435, Los Angeles CA 90093. (213)668-0080. Editor: Julia Solis. Magazine: 8½×7; 80 pages; 60 lb. paper; heavy cover stock; illustrations. Semiannually. Estab. 1994. Circ. 500.

Needs: Erotica, experimental, literary, occult, translations. Receives 100 unsolicited mss/month. Accepts 10 mss/issue. Recently published work by Henri Michaux, Unica Zurn, Bob Flanagan and Kurt Schwitters. Length: 1,500 words. Also publishes poetry. Sometimes critiques or comments on rejected ms.

How to Contact: Send complete ms with a cover letter. Should include bio. Send SASE for reply, return of ms or send a disposable copy of ms. Simultaneous submissions OK. Sample copy for $5.50.

Payment/Terms: Pays 1 contributor's copy. Not copyrighted.

Advice: "*The Spitting Image* seeks dioramas for schizophrenic peeping toms—fiction that is explosive, absurd or strangely beautiful. Originality counts above all else."

‡SPOUT, (I, II), Spout Press, 28 W. Robie St., St. Paul MN 55107. (612)298-9846. Editors: John Colburn and Michelle Filking. Fiction Editor: Chris Watercott. Magazine: 8½×11; 40 pages; 70 lb. flat white paper; colored cover; illustrations. "We like the surprising, the surreal and the experimental. Our readers are well-read, often writers." Triannually. Estab. 1989. Circ. 300-500.

● *Spout* editors submit work to the Pushcart anthology.

Needs: Condensed/excerpted novel, erotica, ethnic/multicultural, experimental, feminist, gay, humor/satire, lesbian, literary, psychic/supernatural/occult, regional, science fiction (hard science, soft/sociological), translations. Publishes special fiction issues or anthologies. Receives 6-7 unsolicited mss/month. Accepts 4-5 mss/issue; 15 mss/year. Publishes ms 1-3 months after acceptance. Agented fiction 5%. Recently published work by Mario Benedetti (translation), Susanna Shaio, Michael Little and Richard Kostelanetz. Length: open. Publishes short shorts and "sudden" fiction. Also publishes poetry. Often comments on rejected ms.

How to Contact: Send complete ms with a cover letter. Should include short bio and list of publications with submission. Reports in 1 month on queries; 2 months on mss. Send SASE for reply, return of ms or send a disposable copy of ms. Simultaneous and electronic submissions OK. E-mail address: colb0018@gold.t c.umn.edu. Sample copy for $2, 8½×11 SAE and 5 first-class stamps. Fiction guidelines for SASE.

Payment/Terms: Pays 1 contributor's copy; additional copies for $2 plus postage. Acquires one-time rights.

Advice: Looks for "imagination, surprise and attention to language. We often publish writers on their third or fourth submission, so don't get discouraged. We need more weird, surreal fiction that lets the reader make his/her own meaning. Don't send moralistic, formulaic work."

SPSM&H, (II, IV), *Amelia* Magazine, 329 "E" St., Bakersfield CA 93304. (805)323-4064. Editor: Frederick A. Raborg, Jr. Magazine: 5½×8¼; 24 pages; Matte cover stock; illustrations and photos. "*SPSM&H* publishes sonnets, sonnet sequences and fiction, articles and reviews related to the form (fiction may be romantic or Gothic) for a general readership and sonnet enthusiasts." Quarterly. Estab. 1985. Circ. 600.

● This magazine is edited by Frederick A. Raborg, Jr., who is also editor of *Amelia* and *Cicada*. See also the listing for the *Amelia* Magazine Awards.

Needs: Adventure, confession, contemporary, erotica, ethnic, experimental, fantasy, feminist, gay, historical, horror, humor/satire, lesbian, literary, mainstream, mystery/suspense, regional, contemporary and historical romance, science fiction, senior citizen/retirement, translations and western. All should have romantic element. "We look for strong fiction with romantic or Gothic content, or both. Stories need not have 'happy' endings, and we are open to the experimental and/or avant-garde. Erotica is fine; pornography, no." Receives 30 unsolicited mss/month. Buys 1 ms/issue; 4 mss/year. Publishes ms 6 months-1 year after acceptance. Agented fiction 5%. Published work by Brad Hooper, Mary Louise R. O'Hara and Clara Castelar Bjorlie. Length: 2,000 words average; 500 words minimum; 3,000 words maximum. When appropriate critiques rejected ms; recommends other markets.

How to Contact: Send complete ms with cover letter. Should include Social Security number. Reports in 2 weeks. SASE. Sample copy for $4.95. Fiction guidelines for #10 SASE.
Payment/Terms: Pays $10-25 on publication for first North American serial rights; contributor's copies; charge for extras.
Advice: "A good story line (plot) and strong characterization are vital. I want to know the writer has done his homework and is striving to become professional."

SQUARE, (I), P.O. Box 8535, Clearwater FL 34618. Editor: Frank Drouzas. Magazine: 8½×11; 16-20 pages; 70 lb. glossy paper; photos. Monthly. Estab. 1994. Circ. 5,000.
Needs: Experimental, humor/satire, literary, mainstream/contemporary. No romance or science fiction. Planning future special fiction issue or anthology. Receives 10-20 unsolicited mss/month. Accepts 2-5 mss/issue; 25-35 mss/year. Publishes ms 3-6 months after acceptance. Length: 1,500 words average; 300 words minimum; 2,500 words maximum. Publishes short shorts. Also publishes literary essays, literary criticism and poetry. Often critiques or comments on rejected ms.
How to Contact: Send complete ms with a cover letter. Should include estimated word count. Reports in 1-2 months on mss. Send a disposable copy of ms. Simultaneous submissions OK. Sample copy for $3. Reviews novels and short story collections.
Payment/Terms: Pays 1 contributor's copy; additional copies for $3. Acquires one-time rights.
Advice: "Make it interesting and original and I'll publish it."

SQUARE ONE, A Magazine of Dark Fiction, (I, II), Tarkus Press (in conjunction with Ozark Triangle Press), Box 11921, Milwaukee WI 53211-0921. Editor: William D. Gagliani. Magazine: 7×8½; 75-90 pages; 20 lb. white bond paper; 80 lb. colored linen cover; illustrations; pen and ink drawings or any black on white. "There is no specific theme at *Square One*, but we publish only fiction and illustrations. Aimed at a general literate audience—people who *enjoy* reading fiction." Annually. Estab. 1984. Circ. 250.
● See the interview with Editor William Gagliani in the 1994 edition of this book. The editor says he would like to see more work that explores darker themes.
Needs: Open to all categories including mainstream, mystery, science fiction, horror (all subgenres), fantasy, magic realism, suspense, etc. "We like exciting stories in which things happen and characters *exist*." Receives 40-50 unsolicited fiction mss/month. Does not read mss between May and September. Accepts 6-12 mss/issue, depending on lengths; 6-12 mss/year. Publishes ms generally 1-14 months after acceptance. Published new writers within the last year. Length: 3,000 words average; 7,500 words maximum. Occasionally publishes short shorts but not vignettes. "It is editorial policy to comment on at least 75% of submissions rejected, but *please* be patient—we have a very small staff. Due to financial hiatus and editor's move, a backlog has occurred . . . it will take a while to read all manuscripts."
How to Contact: Send complete ms with cover letter. "Too many letters explain or describe the story. Let the fiction stand on its own. If it doesn't, the letter won't help. We like a brief bio and a few credits, but some writers get carried away. Use restraint and plain language—don't try to impress (it usually backfires)." Reports in 1-14 months on mss. SASE for ms. Simultaneous (if so labeled) and reprint submissions OK. Can accept electronic submissions via disk, HD or DS/DD 3.5″ disks (using Microsoft Word 5.0, Works, or WordPerfect 2.0+ for Macintosh). "Hard copy should always accompany any electronic submissions." Sample copies of older issues for $2.50, 9×12 SAE and 7 first-class stamps. Fiction guidelines for #10 SASE. Please make checks payable to William D. Gagliani.
Payment/Terms: Pays 2 contributor's copies. Acquires one-time rights.
Advice: "*Square One* is not a journal for beginners, despite what the name may imply. Rather, the name refers to the back-to-basics approach that we take—fiction must first and foremost be compelling. We want to see stories that elicit a response from the reader. We are currently seeking more horror/dark fantasy (all subgenres welcome), as well as genre blends, but still like to see variety—strong fiction in any genre remains an overall theme. We must stress that, since we are an irregular publication, contributors should expect long response lags. Our staff is small and *Square One* is still a part-time endeavor. Patience is the best advice we can offer. Financial difficulties have delayed our new issue several times, but it is in production and we are reading for future issues. Our new partnership with Ozark Triangle Press may lead to an anthology (rather than magazine) format, as well as future anthology and/or chapbook projects. Also, we oppose the absurdity of asking that writers subscribe to every magazine they would like to write for, especially given most writers' financial state. Check local public and college libraries and bookstores to see what's going on in the small press and literary markets, and—as a matter of dignity—consider carefully before submitting to magazines that routinely charge reading fees."

STARBLADE, (I, IV), P.O. Box 400672, Hesperia CA 92340. Editor: Stephanie O'Rourke. Magazine: 8½×11; 30 pages; 24 lb. paper; illustrations. "Starblade is for fantasy readers, from science fiction to sword and sorcery." Estab. 1994.
Needs: Fantasy (science fantasy, sword and sorcery) and science fiction. "No porn or gore." Length: 3,500 words average. Publishes short shorts. Also publishes literary essays, literary criticism and poetry. Always critiques or comments on rejected mss.

How to Contact: Send complete ms and short bio. Should include estimated word count. Reports in 2 months on queries; 4 months on mss. Send SASE for reply, return of ms or send a disposable copy of ms. Simultaneous submissions OK. Sample copy for 9×12 SAE and 6 first-class stamps. Reviews novels and short story collections.
Payment/Terms: Pays 2 contributor's copies. Acquires one-time rights.
Advice: "I like good dialogue and a good sense of humor in my stories. I prefer them typed with legible, with a beginning, middle, and ending, hopefully in that order. A writer should remember that the worst thing they can do is not try; after all, I can't accept it if I haven't read it. Even if a story isn't accepted I try to give advice on how to fix it, so send it in!"

STONE SOUP, The Magazine By Young Writers and Artists, (I, IV), Children's Art Foundation, Box 83, Santa Cruz CA 95063. (408)426-5557. Editor: Gerry Mandel. Magazine: $6 \times 8\frac{3}{4}$; 48 pages; high quality paper; Sequoia matte cover stock; illustrations; photos. Stories, poems, book reviews and art by children through age 13. Readership: children, librarians, educators. Published 5 times/year. Estab. 1973. Circ. 20,000.
   ● This is known as "the literary journal for children." *Stone Soup* has previously won the Edpress Golden Lamp Honor Award and the Parent's Choice Award.
Needs: Fiction by children on themes based on their own experiences, observations or special interests. Also, some fantasy, mystery, adventure. No clichés, no formulas, no writing exercises; original work only. Receives approximately 1,000 unsolicited fiction mss each month. Accepts approximately 15 mss/issue. Published new writers within the last year. Length: 150-2,500 words. Also publishes literary essays and poetry. Critiques rejected mss upon request.
How to Contact: Send complete ms with cover letter. "We like to learn a little about our young writers, why they like to write, and how they came to write the story they are submitting." SASE. No simultaneous submissions. E-mail address: gmandel@stonesoup.com. Reports in 1 month on mss. Does not respond to mss that are not accompanied by an SASE. Publishes ms an average of 1-6 months after acceptance. Sample copy for $4. Guidelines for SASE. Reviews children's books.
Payment/Terms: Pays $10 plus 2 contributor's copies; $2 charge for extras. Buys all rights.
Advice: Mss are rejected because they are "derivatives of movies, TV, comic books; or classroom assignments or other formulas."

STORY, (II), F&W Publications, 1507 Dana Ave., Cincinnati OH 45207. (513)531-2222. Editor: Lois Rosenthal. Magazine: $6\frac{1}{4} \times 9\frac{1}{2}$; 128 pages; uncoated, recycled paper; uncoated index stock. "We publish the finest quality short stories. Will consider unpublished novel excerpts if they are self-inclusive." Quarterly. Estab. 1931.
   ● *Story* won the National Magazine Award for Fiction in 1992 and 1995. *Story* holds an annual contest for short short fiction. See the listing in the Contests and Awards section.
Needs: Literary, experimental, humor, mainstream, translations. No genre fiction—science fiction, detective, young adult, confession, romance, etc. Buys approximately 12 mss/issue. Agented fiction 50-60%. Recently published work by Joyce Carol Oates, Bobbie Ann Mason, Tobias Wolff, Madison Smartt Bell, Rick DeMarinis, Antonya Nelson, Rick Bass, Charles Baxter, Tess Gallagher, Rick Moody, Ellen Gilchrist and Thom Jones; published new writers within the last year. Length: up to 8,000 words.
How to Contact: Send complete ms with or without cover letter, or submit through agent. SASE necessary for return of ms and response. "Will accept simultaneous submissions as long as it is stated in a cover letter." Sample copy for $6.95, 9×12 SAE and $2.40 postage. Fiction guidelines for #10 SASE.
Payment/Terms: Pays $750 plus 5 contributor's copies on acceptance for first North American serial rights. Sends galleys to author.
Advice: "We accept fiction of the highest quality, whether by established or new writers. Since we receive over 300 submissions each week, the competition for space is fierce. We look for original subject matter told through fresh voices. Read issues of *Story* before trying us."

STORYHEAD MAGAZINE, (I, II), 1340 W. Granville, Chicago IL 60660. (312)702-6674. Editors: Mike Brehm and Joe Peterson. Magazine: $7 \times 8\frac{3}{4}$; 40-60 pages; 70 lb. stock paper; 80 lb. stock cover; illustrations and photos. "What we try to do at StoryHead is bring writers and artists together to create illustrated stories and poems. We are therefore looking for short story writers, and graphic artists who are interested in illustrating stories. No other magazine exploits the energy and tension between the artist and writer quite like ours does." Quarterly. Estab. 1993. Circ. 300-500.
Needs: Short stories, essays and poetry. Receives 20 unsolicited mss/month. Accepts 3-5 mss/issue; 12-20 mss/year. Publishes ms 3-6 months after acceptance. Recently published work by David Greenberger, Joe Maynard, Kevin Riordin and Nina Marks. Length: 3,000 words average.
How to Contact: Send complete ms with a cover letter or send electronic mss on ASCII. Reports in 6 months on mss. Send SASE for reply, return of ms or send a disposable copy of ms. Simultaneous and electronic submissions OK. E-mail address: mb@press.uchicago.edu; Website at: http://www.digimark.net/wraith/zines.html. Sample copy for $4.

Payment/Terms: Pays 2 contributor's copies. All rights revert to author.
Advice: "We're interested in the basics: good writing on compelling subjects. Make sure the manuscript is complete. We try not to do too much editing."

STORYQUARTERLY, (II), Box 1416, Northbrook IL 60065. (708)564-8891. Co-editors: Anne Brashler and Diane Williams. Magazine: approximately 6×9; 130 pages; good quality paper; illustrations; photos. A magazine devoted to the short story and committed to a full range of styles and forms. Semiannually. Estab. 1975. Circ. 3,000.
Needs: Accepts 12-15 mss/issue, 20-30 mss/year. Receives 200 unsolicited fiction mss/month. Published new writers within the last year.
How to Contact: Send complete ms with SASE. Simultaneous submissions OK. Reports in 3 months on mss. Sample copy for $5.
Payment/Terms: Pays 3 contributor's copies for one-time rights. Copyright reverts to author after publication.
Advice: "Send one manuscript at a time, subscribe to the magazine, send SASE."

‡STREET BEAT QUARTERLY, (I, II), Wood Street Commons, 301 Third Ave., Pittsburgh PA 15222. (412)765-3302. Fax: (412)765-2646. Editor: Jay Katz. Magazine: 8½×11; 32 pages; newsprint paper; newsprint cover; illustrations and photos. "*Street Beat Quarterly* publishes (primarily) literary works by those who have experienced homelessness or poverty. We reach those interested in literary magazines and others interested in homelessness issues." Quarterly. Estab. 1990. Circ. 2,000-3,000.
Needs: Adventure, ethnic/multicultural, experimental, fantasy, feminist, historical, humor/satire, literary, mainstream/contemporary, mystery/suspense, stories by children. "No religious." Receives 2 unsolicited mss/month. Buys 2-5 mss/issue. Publishes ms 1-3 months after acceptance. Recently published work by Freddy Posco, James Burroughs and Mel Spivak. Length: 750 words average; 100 words minimum; 10,000 words maximum. Publishes short shorts. Also publishes literary essays and poetry. Sometimes critiques or comments on rejected ms.
How to Contact: Send complete ms with a cover letter. Should include bio. Reports in 1 month on mss. Send a disposable copy of ms. Simultaneous, reprint and electronic submissions OK. E-mail address: ah151@freenet.uchsc.edu. Sample copy for 3 first-class stamps.
Payment/Terms: Pays $3 plus 1 contributor's copy on publication for one-time rights.
Advice: "We are pretty flexible. Our mission is to publish work by those who have experienced homelessness and poverty; we will consider a limited amount of works by others if it is on the topic (homelessness/poverty). Don't be afraid of us! We are very much a grass-roots publication. Be patient with us; as we sometimes take a short while to respond. We publish some very polished work; we also publish some very 'rough' yet energetic work. We are looking for stories that truly capture the experience of homelessness and poverty on a personal level."

STROKER MAGAZINE, (II), 124 N. Main St., #3, Shavertown PA 18708. Editor: Irving Stettner. Magazine: 5½×8½; average 48 pages; medium paper; 80 lb. good cover stock; illustrations; photos. "*An un-literary* literary review interested in sincerity, verve, anger, humor and beauty. For an intelligent audience—non-academic, non-media dazed in the US and throughout the world." Published 3-4 times/year. Estab. 1974. Circ. 600.
Needs: Literary, contemporary. Published new writers within the last year. Also publishes poetry. No academic material. Length: 10 pages (double-spaced) maximum.
How to Contact: Send complete ms with SASE (disposable mss not accepted). Simultaneous submissions OK. Reports in 5 weeks. Sample copy for $5.50.
Payment/Terms: Pays 2 contributor's copies. $1 charge for extras. Acquires one-time rights.

STRUGGLE, A Magazine of Proletarian Revolutionary Literature, (I, II, IV), Box 13261, Detroit MI 48213-0261. Editor: Tim Hall. Magazine: 5½×8½; 24-48 pages; 20 lb. white bond paper; colored cover; illustrations; occasional photographs. Publishes material related to "the struggle of the working class and all progressive people against the rule of the rich—including their war policies, racism, exploitation of the workers, oppression of women, etc." Quarterly. Estab. 1985.
Needs: Contemporary, ethnic, experimental, feminist, historical (general), humor/satire, literary, mystery/suspense, prose poem, regional, science fiction, senior citizen/retirement, translations, young adult/teen (10-18). "The theme can be approached in many ways, including plenty of categories not listed here." No romance, psychic, western, erotica, religious. Receives 10-12 unsolicited fiction mss/month. Publishes ms 6 months or less after acceptance. Recently published work by Billie Louise Jones, Tamar Diana Wilson, Pamela Bond and Edward T. Marquardt; published new writers within the last year. Length: 1,000-3,000 words average; 4,000 words maximum. Publishes short shorts. Normally critiques rejected mss.
How to Contact: Send complete ms; cover letter optional but helpful. "Tries to" report in 3-4 months. SASE. Simultaneous and reprint submissions OK. Sample copy for $2.50. Checks to Tim Hall-Special Account.

Payment/Terms: Pays 2 contributor's copies. No rights acquired. Publication not copyrighted.

Advice: "Write about the oppression of the working people, the poor, the minorities, women, and if possible, their rebellion against it—we are not interested in anything which accepts the status quo. We are not too worried about plot and advanced technique (fine if we get them!)—we would probably accept things others would call sketches, provided they have life and struggle. Just describe for us a situation in which some real people confront some problem of oppression, however seemingly minor. Observe and put down the real facts. We have increased our fiction portion of our content in the last 2 years. We get poetry and songs all the time. We want 1-2 stories per issue. In the past year, the quality of fiction that we have published has improved radically—and mostly from new authors."

♣SUB-TERRAIN, (I,II), Box 1575, Bentall Centre, Vancouver BC V6C 2P7 Canada. (604)876-8710. Fiction Editors: D.E. Bolen and Brian Kaufman. Magazine: 7½×10½; 40 pages; offset printed paper; illustrations; photos. "*Sub-Terrain* provides a forum for work that pushes the boundaries in form or content." Estab. 1988.

Needs: "We are looking for work that expresses the experience of urban existence as we approach the closing of the century. Primarily a literary magazine; also interested in erotica, experimental, humor/satire." Receives 20-30 unsolicited mss/month. Accepts 15-20 mss/issue. Publishes ms 1-4 months after acceptance. Length: 200-3,000 words; 400-500 average. Publishes short shorts. Length: 200 words. Also publishes literary essays, literary criticism, poetry. Sometimes critiques rejected mss and "at times" recommends other markets.

How to Contact: Send complete ms with cover letter. Simultaneous submissions OK, if notify when ms is accepted elsewhere. Reports in 3-4 weeks on queries; 2-3 months on mss. SASE. Sample copy for $4. Also features book review section. Send books marked "Review Copy, Managing Editor."

Payment/Terms: Pays in contributor's copies. Acquires one-time rights.

Advice: "We look for something special in the voice or style. Not simply something that is a well-written story. A new twist, a unique sense or vision of the world. The stuff that every mag is hoping to find. Write about things that are important to you: issues that *must* be talked about; issues that frighten, anger you. The world has all the cute, well-made stories it needs."

‡SUFFUSION MAGAZINE, An Unconventional Literary Experience, (II), (formerly *The Subterranean Quarterly*), Brownhouse Graphic Arts, P.O. Box 57183, Lincoln NE 68505-7183. (402)465-5839. Editor: Cris Trautner. Magazine: 8½×11; 20 pages; 70 lb. white vellum paper; 70 lb. tan vellum cover; illustrations and photos. "Our goal is to be a stepping stone for new and unpublished writers as well as a fresh venue for established writers. Our audience includes anyone who has an open mind to the creative spirit." Quarterly. Estab. 1988. Circ. 500.

Needs: Ethnic/multicultural, experimental, feminist, humor/satire, literary, mainstream/contemporary, mystery/suspense (amateur sleuth, police procedural), regional, science fiction. "No erotica, religious/inspirational, romance." Receives 8-10 mss/month. Buys 3 mss/issue; 12 mss/year. Publishes ms 6-12 months after acceptance. Recently published work by Deborah Christian, Paul Sanders and C. Mulrooney. Length: 3,500 words maximum. Publishes short shorts. Also publishes literary essays, literary criticism and poetry. Sometimes critiques or comments on rejected ms.

How to Contact: Send complete ms with a cover letter. Should include 5-7 sentence bio, estimated word count, list of publications. Reports in 2 months on queries; 4 months on mss. Send SASE for reply, return of ms or send a disposable copy of ms. Simultaneous, reprint and electronic submissions OK. E-mail address: suffusion@aol.com. Sample copy for $2. Fiction guidelines for #10 SASE. Reviews novels or short story collections.

Payment/Terms: Pays 1-3 contributor's copies; additional copies for $1.50. "All rights revert back to author upon publication."

Advice: "Always include a cover letter neatly typed or laser print manuscript. Read a sample copy first. I would like to see more characters that aren't two-dimensional; please refrain from sending violent/pornographic writing that has no justification within the plot for being so."

SULPHUR RIVER LITERARY REVIEW, (II), P.O. Box 402087, Austin TX 78704-5578. (512)447-6809. Editor: James Michael Robbins. Magazine: 5½×8½; 110 pages; illustrations and photos. "*SRLR* publishes literature of quality—poetry and short fiction with appeal that transcends time. Audience includes a broad spectrum of readers, mostly educated, many of whom are writers, artists and educators." Semiannually. Estab. 1978. Circ. 200.

Needs: Ethnic/multicultural, experimental, feminist, humor/satire, literary, mainstream/contemporary and translations. No "religious, juvenile, teen, sports, romance or mystery." Receives 10-12 unsolicited mss/month. Accepts 2-3 mss/issue; 4-6 mss/year. Publishes ms 1-2 years after acceptance. Recently published work by Michael Berberich Marcial Gonzalez and Harry Watnik. Publishes short shorts. Also publishes literary essays, literary criticism and poetry. Often critiques or comments on rejected mss.

How to Contact: Send complete ms with a cover letter. Should include bio (short) and list of publications. Reports in 1 week on queries; 1 months on mss. Send SASE for reply, return of ms or send a disposable copy of ms. No simultaneous submissions. Sample copy for $4.50.

Payment/Terms: Pays 2 contributor's copies; additional copies for $3. Acquires first North American serial rights.

Advice: Looks for "originality, mastery of the language, imagination."

SUN DOG: THE SOUTHEAST REVIEW, (II), English Department, 406 Williams, Florida State University, Tallahassee FL 32306. (904)644-4230. Editor: Ron Wiginton. Magazine: 6×9; 60-100 pages; 70 lb. paper; 10 pt. Krome Kote cover; illustrations; photos. Biannually. Estab. 1979. Circ. 2,000.
Needs: "We want stories which are well written, beautifully written, with striking images, incidents and characters. We are interested more in quality than in style or genre." Accepts 20 mss/year. Receives approximately 60 unsolicited fiction mss each month. Reads less frequently during summer. Critiques rejected mss when there is time. Occasionally recommends other markets (up to 5 poems or 1 story.)
How to Contact: Send complete ms with SASE. "Short bio or cover letter would be appreciated." Publishes ms an average of 2-6 months after acceptance. Sample copy for $4.
Payment/Terms: Pays 2 contributor's copies. $2 charge for extras. Acquires first North American serial rights which then revert to author.
Advice: "Avoid trendy experimentation for its own sake (present-tense narration, observation that isn't also revelation). Fresh stories, moving, interesting characters and a sensitivity to language are still fiction mainstays. Also publishes winner and runners-up of the World's Best Short Short Story Contest sponsored by the Florida State University English Department."

‡THE SUPERNATURAL MAGAZINE ON AUDIOBOOK, (I, II), The Morris Publishing Co., 1415 Hemlock St., Cayce SC 29033. (803)603-0430. Editor: Roy Morris-Bollinger. Magazine on cassette: 90 minutes, 10-12 stories. Monthly. Estab. 1963. Circ. 10,500.
Needs: Erotica, experimental, fantasy (adult), horror, humor/satire, mainstream/contemporary, mystery/suspense (amateur sleuth, cozy, police procedural, private eye/hardboiled, psychic/supernatural/occult, romantic suspense), romance (contemporary, gothic), science fiction (hard science, soft/sociological), serialized novel, westerns (frontier, traditional), young adult/teen. Upcoming themes: Halloween, Christmas, Thanksgiving, New Year. Publishes special fiction issues or anthologies. Also publishes "Audiobook Collection," and "New and Beginner Writers and Poets Book Publishing Program." Receives "many" unsolicited mss/month. Publishes ms 1 month-1 year after acceptance. Recently published work by Frank Allen, Lawrence Belman, Christie Perfetti, Bernadette Monarelli, Heather Holick, Jouna Schloz, Donna Sunday, Tom Jennings, Elijah St. Ives and Hindy Cizffer. Length: 100 words minimum; 2,000 words maximum. Publishes short shorts. Also publishes literary essays, literary criticism and poetry. Critiques or comments on rejected ms.
How to Contact: Send complete ms with a cover letter. "Send a copy of your manuscript because, if it is accepted, it will not be returned." Should include estimated word count and list of publications with submission. Send SASE for reply, return of ms or send a disposable copy of ms. Simultaneous and reprint submissions OK. Sample copy for $3.50. Fiction guidelines free. Catalog free for large, brown SASE.
Payment/Terms: Pays 1 contributor's copy; additional copies for $2.50. Acquires first North American serial rights. Sponsors annual author/poet awards.
Advice: Looks for "new and beginner writers/poets. I can always use horror, science fiction, fantasy and erotic thrillers."

‡SURPRISE ME, (I, II, IV), Surprise Me Publications, P.O. Box 1762, Claremore OK 74018-1762. Editor: Lynda J. Nicolls. Magazine: 8½×11; 16-20 pages; illustrations and photos. "*Surprise Me* is founded on the hope of providing a home for those souls who believe life's purpose is to serve Truth and Beauty. Our main interests are mysticism, the arts and nature. Prisoners, teenagers, the disabled and the elderly are especially welcomed here. Our intended audience is college students, college professors, prisoners, teenagers, the disabled, the elderly and people who do not like most of what is being published now." Biannual. Estab. 1994. Circ. 150.
Needs: Adventure, children's/juvenile, condensed/excerpted novel, erotica, ethnic/multicultural, fantasy, literary, psychic/supernatural/occult, religious/inspirational, romance (futuristic/time travel, gothic), science fiction, senior citizen/retirement, serialized novel, young adult/teen (adventure, romance, science fiction), art, music, mysticism, nature, dance. "I am not interested in profanity, pro-violence, racism, intolerance and pornography. I'm very open to style, form and subject matter." Receives 200 unsolicited mss/month. Accepts 5 mss/issue; 20 mss/year. Publishes ms 1-2 years after acceptance. Recently published work by Jane Stuart, Sara DeLuca, and J. Mallet-Eakin. Also publishes literary essays, literary criticism and poetry. Sometimes critiques or comments on rejected ms.
How to Contact: Send complete ms with a cover letter. Should include 5-line bio, list of publications. "Submissions without cover letters are too impersonal for me, so at least please include a note just to say, 'Hi. This is what I'm sending you.' " Send SASE for reply, return of ms or send a disposable copy of ms. Simultaneous, reprint and electronic submissions OK. "Disks are OK, but I don't have a modem yet." Sample copy for $4. Fiction guidelines for #10 SASE.
Payment/Terms: Pays 2 contributor's copies. Acquires one-time rights.
Advice: "I would suggest a beginning fiction writer examine a sample copy of our magazine before submitting to us. Writers also should not take a rejection too hard, since it is only one person's opinion. One editor may call it trash and another editor may call it a masterpiece. I would also suggest reading James Joyce, Hermann Hesse, Colin Wilson, Thomas Moore and Rollo May. I'm very open to subject matter, style and

form, but I don't like a lot of what is being published now because it often lacks spirituality and has shock value as its motive. I would like to see more writing about the visual arts (i.e. Vincent van Gogh, Georgia O'Keeffe, Ansel Adams and Edward Weston), as well as more writing about philosophy and poetry (i.e. Soren Kierkegaard, William James, William Blake and W.B. Yeats). I would also like to see more children's literature (for or by children)."

SWIFT KICK, (II), 1711 Amherst St., Buffalo NY 14214. (716)837-7778. Editor: Robin Kay Willoughby. Magazine: size, number of pages, paper quality and cover stock vary; illustrations; photos, b&w line art, xerographs. "Specializes in unusual formats, hard-to-classify works, visual poetry, found art, etc. for pataphysical, rarified audience." Published special fiction issue; plans another. Estab. 1981. Circ. 100.
Needs: Open. "If it doesn't seem to fit a regular category, it's probably what we'd like! No boring, slipshod, everyday stuff like in mass-market magazines." Receives 5 unsolicited fiction mss/month. Accepts 1-2 mss/ issue. Does not read just before Christmas. Publishes ms depending on finances (6 months-1 year) after acceptance. Publishes short shorts of 1,000 words (or 1 picture). Sometimes recommends other markets.
How to Contact: Query first for longer works or send complete ms with cover letter for short work. Reports in 2 months to 1 year. SASE ("or include reply card with OK to toss enclosed work"). Simultaneous submissions OK. Will consider reprints of astoundingly good work (out of print). Sample copy for $7; make checks payable to the editor; "sample purchase recommended to best understand magazine's needs."
Payment/Terms: Pays in contributor's copies; half price for extras. Acquires one-time rights. Rights revert to artists/authors. Sends galleys to author if requested.
Advice: "We always get less fiction than poetry—if a story is good, it has a good chance of publication in little mags. Editorially, I'm a snob, so don't write like anyone else; be *so* literate your writing transcends literature and (almost) literacy. Don't submit over 10 pages first time. Submit a 'grabber' that makes an editor ask for more. Don't neglect the stories in your own life for someone else's castles-in-the-air."

SYCAMORE REVIEW, (II), Department of English, Purdue University, West Lafayette IN 47907. (317)494-3783. Editor-in-Chief: Rob Davidson. Editors change every two years. Send fiction to Fiction Editor, poetry to Poetry Editor, all other correspondence to Editor-in-Chief. Magazine: 5½×8½; 150-200 pages; heavy, textured, uncoated paper; heavy laminated cover. "Journal devoted to contemporary literature. We publish both traditional and experimental fiction, personal essay, poetry, interviews, drama and graphic art. Novel excerpts welcome if they stand alone as a story." Semiannually. Estab. 1989. Circ. 1,000.
• Work published in *Sycamore Review* has been selected for inclusion in the *Pushcart Prize* anthology. The magazine was also named "The Best Magazine from Indiana" by the *Clockwatch Review.*
Needs: Contemporary, experimental, humor/satire, literary, mainstream, regional, translations. "We generally avoid genre literature, but maintain no formal restrictions on style or subject matter. No science fiction, romance, children's." Publishes ms 3 months-1 year after acceptance. Length: 3,750 words preferred; 250 words minimum. Also publishes poetry. Sometimes critiques rejected mss and recommends other markets.
How to Contact: Send complete ms with cover letter. Cover letter should include previous publications, address changes. Does not read mss May through August. Reports in 4 months. SASE. Simultaneous submissions OK. E-mail address: sycamore@expert.cc.purdue.edu. Sample copy for $4. Fiction guidelines for #10 SASE.
Payment/Terms: Pays in contributor's copies; charge for extras. Acquires one-time rights.
Advice: "We publish both new and experienced authors but we're always looking for stories with strong emotional appeal, vivid characterization and a distinctive narrative voice; fiction that breaks new ground while still telling an interesting and significant story. Avoid gimmicks and trite, predictable outcomes. Write stories that have a ring of truth, the impact of felt emotion. Don't be afraid to submit, send your best."

‡TALES FROM THE VORTEX, (I, II, IV), Stygian Vortex Publications, 6634 Atlanta St., Hollywood FL 33024-2965. (305)964-5952. Editor: Glenda Woodrum. Magazine: 8½×11; 60 pages; 20 lb. bond paper; 90 lb. card stock cover; illustrations. Annually. Estab. 1996. Circ. 100.
Needs: Fantasy (dark modern), psychic/supernatural/occult. No romance-oriented material "stories pertaining to serial killers, child molesters or rape." Publishes special fiction issues or anthologies. Receives 5-20 unsolicited mss/month. Accepts 8-15 mss/year. Will not be reading until October 1996. Recently published work by Lyn McConchie, Frank O. Dodge and D. Sandy Nielsen. Length: 4,500 words average; 3,500 words minimum; 12,000 words maximum. Publishes short shorts (800 words). Also publishes literary essays, literary criticism and poetry. Always critiques or comments on rejected ms.

Market categories: (I) Open to new writers; (II) Open to both new and established writers; (III) Interested mostly in established writers; (IV) Open to writers whose work is specialized.

How to Contact: Send complete ms with a cover letter. Should include estimated word count and bio with submission. Reports in 1-2 weeks on queries; 1-3 months on mss. Send SASE for reply, return of ms or send a disposable copy of ms. Simultaneous, reprint and electronic submissions OK. Sample copy for $5.25 (payable to Glenda Woodrum). Fiction guidelines for SASE. Reviews novels and short story collections. Send books to Review Department.

Payment/Terms: Pays $1-10 and 1 contributor's copy on publication; additional copies for $2.50 plus $1.25 postage per every 3 copies ordered. Buys one-time rights. Sends galleys to author.

Advice: "Strong characterization and a solid plot are crucial. I am willing to work with new writers on rewrites of stories where both of these elements are present but where narrative, dialogue or flow may be weak." Looking for "ghost stories that would have fit into the old *Twilight Zone* TV series and science fiction with aliens that are more than just cardboard cutouts."

TAMAQUA, (I, II), C120, Humanities Dept., Parkland College, Champaign IL 61821. (217)351-2380. Editor-in-Chief: Bruce Morgan. Magazine: 5½×8½; 160-256 pages; 80 lb. paper; 12 point cover; some illustrations; 12-20 photos every issue. "No theme; top quality fiction, poetry, nonfiction (reviews, thoughtful essays, autobiography, biography, insightful travel, etc.) for a literate audience." Semiannually. Estab. 1989. Circ. 1,500.

Needs: Literary, contemporary, ethnic, experimental, feminist, gay, humor/satire, prose poem, regional. Special interest in Latin American translations. "No stupid writing, no polemics, no demagogues—that is, we want good, solid, intelligent, *professional* writing." Publishes special fiction issues (Native American issue, Pan American issue). Buys 4-10 mss/issue; 8-20 mss/year. Publishes ms 6 months after acceptance. Recently published work by Edith Grossman, William Maxwell and Philip Deaver. Length: 10,000 words maximum. Publishes short shorts. Length: under 1,000 words. Sometimes critiques rejected mss.

How to Contact: Send complete ms with cover letter. Reports in 3-4 weeks on queries; 8-10 weeks on mss. SASE. Simultaneous submissions OK. Accepts electronic submissions. Sample copy for $6, 8½×11 SAE and 72¢ postage. Fiction guidelines for #10 SASE.

Payment/Terms: Pays $10-50, subscription to magazine, contributor's copies on publication for first North American serial rights; charge for extras.

Advice: "The most influential ingredient for the growing market in fiction (as well as all other writing) is the reduced costs of production because of desktop publishing. Purchase a copy and *study* the magazine, or others of similar quality, to distinguish between good, solid professional writing and that which is not."

TAMPA REVIEW, (III), 401 W. Kennedy Blvd., Box 19F, University of Tampa, Tampa FL 33606-1490. (813)253-3333, ext. 6266. Editor: Richard Mathews. Fiction Editor: Andy Solomon. Magazine: 7½×10½; approximately 70 pages; acid-free paper; visual art; photos. "Interested in fiction of distinctive literary quality." Semiannually. Estab. 1988.

Needs: Contemporary, ethnic, experimental, fantasy, historical, humor/satire, literary, mainstream, prose poem, translations. "We are far more interested in quality than in genre. Nothing sentimental as opposed to genuinely moving, nor self-conscious style at the expense of human truth." Buys 4-5 mss/issue. Publishes ms within 7 months-1 year of acceptance. Agented fiction 60%. Recently published work by Elizabeth Spencer, Lee K. Abbott, Lorrie Moore, Tim O'Connor and Naomi Nye. Length: 1,000 words minimum; 6,000 words maximum. Publishes short shorts "if the story is good enough." Also publishes literary essays (must be labeled nonfiction), poetry.

How to Contact: Send complete mss with cover letter. Should include brief bio and publishing record. No simultaneous submissions. SASE. Reads September-December; reports January-March. Sample copy for $5 (includes postage) and 9×12 SAE. Fiction guidelines for #10 SASE.

Payment/Terms: Pays $10/printed page on publication for first North American serial rights. Sends galleys to author upon request.

Advice: "There are more good writers publishing in magazines today than there have been in many decades. Unfortunately, there are even more bad ones. In T. Gertler's *Elbowing the Seducer*, an editor advises a young writer that he wants to hear her voice completely, to tell (he means 'show') him in a story the truest thing she knows. We concur. Rather than a trendy workshop story or a minimalism that actually stems from not having much to say, we would like to see stories that make us believe they mattered to the writer and, more importantly, will matter to a reader. Trim until only the essential is left, and don't give up belief in yourself. And it might help to attend a good writers' conference, e.g. Wesleyan or Bennington."

TAPROOT LITERARY REVIEW, (I, II), Taproot Writer's Workshop, Inc., 302 Park Rd., Ambridge PA 15003. (412)266-8476. Editor: Tikvah Feinstein. Magazine: 5½×10½; 80 pages; #20 paper; glossy cover; illustrations and photographs. "We select on quality, not topic. We have published excellent work other publications have rejected due to subject matter, style or other bias. Variety and quality are our appealing features." Annually. Estab. 1987. Circ. 500.

Needs: Literary. Upcoming themes available for SASE. Publishes special fiction issue or anthology. Receives 20 unsolicited mss/month. Accepts 6 mss/issue. Publishes mss 3 months after acceptance. Recently published work by Marjorie Levenson, Elizabeth Howkins, Sally Levin and Mike Murray. Length: 2,000 words preferred; 250 words minimum; 3,000 words maximum (no longer than 10 pages, double-spaced maximum).

Publishes short shorts. Length: 300 words preferred. Sometimes critiques or comments on rejected mss.

How to Contact: Send for guidelines first. Send complete ms with a cover letter. Should include estimated word count and bio. Reports in 6 months. Send SASE for return of ms or send a disposable copy of ms. No simultaneous submissions. Sample copy for $5, 6×12 SAE and 5 first-class stamps. Fiction guidelines for #10 SASE.

Payment/Terms: Awards prize money for winners each issue; free subscription; 1 contributor copy. Acquires first rights.

Advice: "If the story speaks in its own voice and reveals something about us that's important and memorable, we publish it."

‡❧"TEAK" ROUNDUP, The International Quarterly, (I, II), West Coast Paradise Publishing, #5-9060 Tronson Rd., Vernon, British Columbia V1T 6L7 Canada. (604)545-4186. Fax: (604)545-4192. Editors: Yvonne and Robert Anstey. Magazine: 8½×5½; 60 pages; 20 lb. copy paper; card stock cover; illustrations and photos. " *'Teak' Roundup* is a general interest showcase for prose and poetry. No uncouth material." Quarterly. Estab. 1994. Circ. 100.

Needs: Adventure, children's/juvenile, condensed/excerpted novel, ethnic/multicultural, historical, humor/satire, literary, mainstream/contemporary, mystery/suspense (police procedural), regional, religious/inspirational, romance (contemporary, historical), sports, westerns, young adult/teen (adventure). "No uncouth or porn." List of upcoming themes available for SASE. Receives 25 unsolicited mss/month. Accepts 20 mss/issue. Publishes ms 3-6 months after acceptance. Recently published work by Marian Ford Park, Angie Monnens, Alice Cundiff and B.A. Stuart. Length: 1,000 words average; 2,000 words maximum. Publishes short shorts. Also publishes literary essays, literary criticism and poetry. Often critiques or comments on rejected ms.

How to Contact: Query first or send complete ms with a cover letter. Should include estimated word count and brief bio. Reports in 1 week. Send SASE for reply, return of ms or send a disposable copy of ms. Simultaneous, reprint and electronic submissions OK. Sample copy for $5. Fiction guidelines for #10 SASE. Reviews novels and short story collections.

Payment/Terms: Acquires one-time rights (unreserved reprint if "Best of" edition done later.)

Advice: "Subscribe and see popular work which is enjoyed by our growing audience. Many good writers favor us with participation in subscribers-only showcase for prose and poetry. No criticism of generous contributors."

TERMINAL FRIGHT, The Journal of Traditional Haunts and Horrors, (I), P.O. Box 100, Black River NY 13612. Editor: Kenneth E. Abner Jr. Magazine: 8½×11; 76 pages; 60 lb. white paper; 80 lb. cover stock. "Traditional gothic and modern occult horror." Quarterly. Estab. 1993.

● The editor says he is *not* interested in experimental, splatter punk horror. *Deathrealm* named *Terminal Fright* "Fiction Magazine of the Year" in 1994.

Needs: Horror, supernatural/occult. Publishes ms 1 year after acceptance. Length: 1,500 words minimum; 10,000 words maximum.

How to Contact: Send complete ms with a cover letter. Should include estimated word count and 1-2 page bio; if available, on IBM compatible floppy disk (after acceptance). Reports in 6-8 weeks. Send SASE for return of ms or send a disposable copy of ms. Simultaneous submissions OK. Sample copy for $5. Fiction guidelines for #10 SASE.

Payment/Terms: Pays ½-2¢/word; 1 contributor copy on publication for first North American serial rights.

Advice: "The most important thing is to truly scare me. Stories should be unique, well-thought out and well-written. I highly discourage excessive vulgarity, explicit sex and graphic gore. All have their place in horror but only if used sparingly and with purpose, not as a crutch to an otherwise weak story."

TERROR TIME AGAIN, (I, II), Nocturnal Publications, 11 W. Winona St., St. Paul MN 55107. Editor: Donald L. Miller. Magazine: 5×8; 52-60 pages; 20 lb. paper; 67 lb. cover stock; illustrations. *"Terror Time Again*'s objective is to provoke a sense of fear in our readers." Quarterly. Estab. 1987. Circ. 200.

Needs: Only wants fear-inducing stories. No science fiction or sword and sorcery. Receives up to 35 unsolicited mss/month. Accepts 15-20 mss/issue. Publishes ms in 4-6 months. Published work by Steve Berman, D.A. Sale, Michael Floyd, Bob Madia and Steve Vernon; published new writers within the last year. Length: 1,000 words average; 250 words minimum; 2,000 words maximum. Publishes short shorts. Length: 250-700 words. Also publishes poetry. Sometimes critiques rejected mss; recommends other markets.

How to Contact: Send complete ms with brief bio about yourself. Reports in 2-4 weeks on mss. Remember to enclose a SASE. Simultaneous and reprint submissions OK. Sample copy for $4.50; fiction guidelines free. Reviews novels and short story collections in newsletter.

Payment/Terms: Pays ¼-½¢/word on acceptance for one-time and reprint rights. Sponsors contest for writers through *The Nightmare Express*. *"Terror Time Again* has a cover contest via *The Nightmare Express* in which the cover illustration of the July/August issue of *TNE* is used by the writer to develop a story under 2,000 words. *TNE* is a newsletter for horror writers and is published bimonthly. A sample copy of *Nightmare Express* is $1.50."

THE TEXAS REVIEW, (II), Sam Houston State University Press, Huntsville TX 77341. (409)294-1992. Editor: Paul Ruffin. Magazine: 6×9; 148-190 pages; best quality paper; 70 lb. cover stock; illustrations; photos. "We publish top quality poetry, fiction, articles, interviews and reviews for a general audience." Semiannually. Estab. 1976. Circ. 700.

Needs: Literary and contemporary fiction. "We are eager enough to consider fiction of quality, no matter what its theme or subject matter. No juvenile fiction." Accepts 4 mss/issue. Receives approximately 40-60 unsolicited fiction mss each month. Does not read June-August. Published work by George Garrett, Ellen Gilchrist and Fred Chappell; published new writers within the last year. Length: 500-10,000 words. Critiques rejected mss "when there is time." Recommends other markets.

How to Contact: Send complete ms with cover letter. SASE. Reports in 3 months on mss. Sample copy for $5.

Payment/Terms: Pays contributor's copies plus one year subscription. Acquires all rights. Sends galleys to author.

‡TEXAS YOUNG WRITERS' NEWSLETTER, (I, II, IV), Texas Young Writers' Association, P.O. Box 942, Adkins TX 78101-0942. Editor: Susan Currie. Newsletter: 8½×11; 8 pages; 20 lb. white paper; illustrations. "*TYWN* teaches young writers about the art and business of writing, and also gives them a place to publish their best work. We publish articles by adults with experience in publishing, and poetry and short stories by young writers 12-19." Monthly during summer, bimonthly during school year (August-May). Estab. 1994. Circ. 300.

Needs: Open to authors ages 12-19 only. Adventure, ethnic/multicultural, fantasy (children's fantasy, science fantasy), historical, humor/satire, literary, mainstream/contemporary, mystery/suspense, romance, science fiction, young adult/teen. "Anything by young writers, 12-19. No erotica, horror, gay/lesbian, or occult." List of upcoming themes available for SASE. Receives 6 unsolicited mss/month. Accepts 1 ms/issue; 9 mss/ year. Publishes ms 6 months after acceptance. Recently published work by Sarah Elezian, Lillette Hill, Caroline Beever and Anthony Twistt. Length: 900 words average; 500 words minimum; 1,100 words maximum. Publishes short shorts. Also publishes poetry. Sometimes critiques or comments on rejected ms.

How to Contact: Send complete ms with a cover letter. Should include estimated word count and 50-100 word bio. Reports in 6 weeks. Send SASE for reply, return of ms or send a disposable copy of ms. Electronic submissions OK. E-mail address: tywn1@aol.com. Sample copy for $1. Guidelines for #10 SASE; "please specify adult or young writer's guidelines."

Payment/Terms: Pays 2 contributor's copies for poetry, 5 for articles and short stories. Acquires first North American serial rights. Not copyrighted.

Advice: "Please read back issues and study the sort of fiction we publish, and make sure it fits our newsletter. Since *TYWN* is sent to schools and young people, we prefer upbeat, nonviolent stories. I look for work the is highly original, creative, and appropriate for our audience. Manuscripts that are professional and striking stand out. I haven't seen enough stories with strong characters and involving plots. I don't want to see dull stories with dull characters. We want to show our young writers terrific examples of stories that they can learn from."

‡❦TEXTSHOP, A Collaborative Journal of Writing, (II), Dept. of English, University of Regina, Regina, Sasketchewan S4S 0A2 Canada. (306)585-4316. Editor: Andrew Stubbs. Magazine: 8½×11; 50 pages; illustrations. *Textshop* is "eclectic in form and open to fiction, poetry and mixed genres, including creative nonfiction." Annually. Estab. 1993.

Needs: Ethnic/multicultural, experimental, literary. Plans special fiction issues or anthologies. Receives 3-4 unsolicited mss/month. Accepts 3 mss/issue. Publishes ms in next issue after acceptance. Length: 500 words minimum; 1,000 words maximum. Also publishes literary essays, literary criticism and poetry. Sometimes critiques or comments on rejected ms.

How to Contact: Send complete ms with a cover letter. Should include estimated word count and 25-word bio with submission. Reports in 1 month on queries; 3 months on mss. SASE. Reprint submissions OK. Sample copy for $2. Reviews material published in each issue.

Payment/Terms: Pays 1 contributor's copy; additional copies for $2. Rights remain with the writer.

Advice: Looks for "risk-taking, mixed genre, experimental fiction. Trust your own voice and idiom. Blur the distinction between life and writing."

TEXTURE, (II), Texture Press, P.O. Box 720157, Norman OK 73070. (405)366-7730. Fax: (405)364-3627. Editor: Susan Smith Nash. Magazine: 8½×11; 100 pages; high-quality offset, matte finish paper; perfect-bound matte cover; illustrations and photos. "*Texture* is interested in all writing, art and photography which probes end-of-the-millenium anxieties. Essays, reviews, and critical articles provide theoretical and philosophical underpinnings for new trends in experimental writing." Annually. Estab. 1989. Circ. 750.

● *Texture* was a finalist for the Oklahoma Book Award in 1995.

Needs: Experimental, feminist, "short-short fiction which has a playful, ironic, subversive element." Publishes special fiction issue or anthology. Receives 25-50 unsolicited mss/month. Accepts 25 mss/issue. Publishes ms 6-9 months after acceptance. Agented fiction 10%. Published work of Cydney Chadwick, Laura

Feldman and Rillo. Length: 200 words minimum; 5,000 words maximum. Also publishes literary essays, literary criticism and poetry.

How to Contact: Send complete ms with a cover letter. Should include 1/2-page bio. Reports in 4-6 months. Send SASE for reply, return of ms or send a disposable copy of ms. No simultaneous submissions. E-mail address: smithnash@aol.com. Sample copy with fiction guidelines for $6. Reviews novels and short story collections.

Payment/Terms: Pays 1 contributor's copy; additional copies for half price. Acquires one-time rights.

‡❦THALIA: STUDIES IN LITERARY HUMOR, (II), Thalia: Association for the Study of Literary Humor, English Dept., University of Ottawa, Ottawa, Ontario K1N 6N5 Canada. (613)230-9505. Fax: (613)565-5786. Editor: J. Tavernier-Courbin. Magazine: illustrations and photos. Semiannually. Estab. 1978. Circ. 500.

Needs: Humor/satire. Upcoming theme: "Humor in the Movies." Publishes short shorts. Also publishes literary essays, literary criticism and poetry. Often critiques or comments on rejected ms.

How to Contact: Send complete ms with a cover letter. Should include list of publications. Reports in 4 months on mss. Send SASE for reply. Reviews novels and short story collections.

Payment/Terms: Acquires first rights.

‡A THEATER OF BLOOD, (III, IV), Pyx Press, P.O. Box 922648, Sylmar CA 91392-2648. Editor: C. Darren Butler. Associate Editor: Lisa S. Laurencot. Book: 100-180-page limited edition, annual book serial. "This will appear in a numbered run of about 500-1,000 copies." Estab. 1990.

 • *A Theater of Blood* has recently switched to a new book format. The first of the new format will appear in 1996. See also the Pyx Press listing in the Small Press section and *Magic Realism* and *Writer's Keeper* in this section.

Needs: Horror. "All types of horror fiction: cosmic, dark fantasy, quiet, supernatural (though not using Lovecraft's creations). It is unlikely that I will accept any purely realistic horror; an otherworldly or fantasy element should be included. I have a bias against excessive gore or anything gratuitous." Receives 400 unsolicited mss/month. Accepts 8-15 mss/book. Open to unsolicited mss from September 1 through November 30 only. Publishes ms 4-24 months after acceptance. No reprints. Length: 3,000-20,000 words. Rarely critiques or comments on rejected mss.

How to Contact: Query first for works over 8,000 words. Send complete ms with a cover letter. Should include estimated word count, 1 paragraph bio and list of publications. Reports in 2 months on queries; 3-6 months on mss. Send SASE for reply, return of ms or send a disposable copy of ms. Simultaneous submissions OK. Sample copy for $2.50 (old format). Fiction guidelines for #10 SASE.

Payment/Terms: Pays $2-10, "unless piece is very long, and 1 copy of the trade-paperback." Acquires first rights.

THEMA, (I, II), Box 74109, Metairie LA 70033-4109. Editor: Virginia Howard. Magazine: 5½×8½; 200 pages; Grandee Strathmore cover stock; b&w illustrations. "Different specified theme for each issue—short stories, poems, b&w artwork must relate to that theme." Triannually. Estab. 1988.

 • *Thema* recently received a Certificate for Excellence in the Arts from the Arts Council of New Orleans.

Needs: Adventure, contemporary, experimental, humor/satire, literary, mainstream, mystery/suspense, prose poem, psychic/supernatural/occult, regional, science fiction, sports, western. "Each issue is based on a specified premise—a different unique theme for each issue. Many types of fiction acceptable, but must fit the premise. No pornographic, scatologic, erotic fiction." Upcoming themes: "A visit from the imp" (March 1, '96); "*I Know Who You Are!*" (July 1, '96); "Too proud to ask" (November 1, '96). Publishes ms within 3-4 months of acceptance. Recently published work by Jeffrey Klausman, Eva C. Schegulla, Merilyn Wakefield, Ted L. Huppert and Susan Moore Williams. Length: fewer than 6,000 words preferred. Publishes short shorts "if very clever." Length: 300-900 words. Also publishes poetry. Sometimes critiques rejected mss and recommends other markets.

How to Contact: Send complete ms with cover letter, which should include "name and address, brief introduction, specifying the intended target issue for the mss." Simultaneous submissions OK. Reports on queries in 1 week; on mss in 5 months after deadline for specified issue. SASE. Sample copy for $8. Free fiction guidelines.

Payment/Terms: Pays $25; $10 for short shorts on acceptance for one-time rights.

Advice: "Do not submit a manuscript unless you have written it for a specified premise. If you don't know the upcoming themes, send for guidelines first, before sending a story. We need more stories told in the Mark Twain/O. Henry tradition in magazine fiction."

❦THIS MAGAZINE, (II), Red Maple Foundation, 16 Skey Lane, Toronto, Ontario M6J 3S4 Canada. (416)588-6580. Editor: Clive Thompson. Send mss Attn: Fiction Editor. Magazine: 8½×11; 42 pages; bond paper; coated cover; illustrations and photographs. "Alternative general interest magazine." Estab. 1973. Circ. 12,000.

Needs: Ethnic, contemporary, experimental, fantasy, feminist, gay, lesbian, literary, mainstream, prose poem, regional. No "commercial/pulp fiction." Receives 15-20 unsolicited mss/month. Buys 1 mss/issue; 8 mss/

year. Published work by Margaret Atwood and Peter McGehee. Length: 1,500 words average; 2,500 words maximum. Sometimes critiques rejected mss.

How to Contact: Query with clips of published work. Reports in 6 weeks on queries; 3-6 months on mss. SASE. No simultaneous submissions. Sample copy for $4 (plus GST). Fiction guidelines for #9 SASE with Canadian stamps or IRC.

Payment/Terms: Pays $100 (Canadian) fiction; $25/poem published for one-time rights.

Advice: "It's best if you're familiar with the magazine when submitting work; a large number of mss that come into the office are inappropriate. Style guides are available. Manuscripts and queries that are clean and personalized really make a difference. Let your work speak for itself—don't try to convince us."

THRESHOLDS QUARTERLY, School of Metaphysics Associates Journal, (I, II, IV), SOM Publishing, School of Metaphysics National Headquarters, HCR1, Box 15, Windyville MO 65783. (417)345-8411. Editor: Dr. Barbara Condron. Senior Editor: Dr. Laurel Fuller Clark. Magazine: 7×10; 32 pages; line drawings and b&w photos. "The School of Metaphysics is a nonprofit educational and service organization invested in education and research in the expansion of human consciousness and spiritual evolution of humanity. For all ages and backgrounds. Themes: dreams, healing, science fiction, personal insight, morality tales, fables, humor, spiritual insight, mystic experiences, religious articles, creative writing with universal themes." Quarterly. Estab. 1975. Circ. 5,000.

● *Thresholds Quarterly* has doubled its circulation.

Needs: Adventure, fantasy, humor/satire, psychic/supernatural/occult, religious/inspirational and science fiction. Upcoming themes: "Dreams, Visions, and Creative Imagination" (February 1996); "Health and Wholeness" (May 1996); "Intuitive Arts" (August 1996); "Man's Spiritual Consciousness" (November 1996). Receives 5 unsolicited mss/month. Length: 4-10 double-spaced typed pages. Publishes short shorts. Also publishes literary essays and poetry. Often critiques or comments on rejected mss.

How to Contact: Query with outline; will accept unsolicited ms with cover letter; no guarantee on time length to respond. Should include bio (1-2 paragraphs). Send SASE for reply, return of ms or send a disposable copy of ms. Sample copy for 9×12 SAE and $1.50 postage. Fiction guidelines for #10 SASE.

Payment/Terms: Pays up to 5 contributor's copies. Acquires all rights.

Advice: "Since 1993 our readership has become increasingly international. We want to appeal to people of diverse backgrounds and cultures; therefore fiction (especially humor) needs to have a universal appeal. We publish other articles in addition to fiction. Use of imagery, inspiration, spiritual message or moral is appreciated in well-written fiction pieces."

✤TICKLED BY THUNDER, The magazine that set fiction free, (II), Tickled by Thunder Pub. Co., 7385 129th St., Surrey, British Columbia V3W 7B8 Canada. (604)591-6095 (phone, voice or fax). Editor: Larry Lindner. Magazine: Digest-sized; bond paper; card stock cover; illustrations and photographs. "Totally open. For writers." Published 3 times/year. Estab. 1990. Circ. 5,000.

Needs: Adventure, contemporary, fantasy, humor/satire, literary, mainstream, mystery/suspense, prose poem, psychic/supernatural, religious/inspirational, science fiction, western. "No pornography." Receives 20 unsolicited mss/month. Buys 1-4 mss/issue; 4-16 mss/year. Length: 1,500 words average; 2,000 words maximum. Publishes short shorts. Length: No preference. Also publishes poetry. Sometimes critiques rejected mss.

How to Contact: Query with clips of published work, if any, including "brief resume/history of writing experience, photo, credits, etc." Reports in 2-4 months. SASE. Simultaneous submissions OK. Sample copy for $2.50 (Canadian) or 3 IRCs. Fiction guidelines for legal SASE.

Payment/Terms: Pays 20¢/column inch to maximum of $10. Buys first rights.

Advice: "Send for guidelines, read a sample copy and ask questions. Send SASE for info on contest for fiction and poetry. *Tickled by Thunder* is known for stories that surprise readers, either with unusual themes or twists."

TIGER MOON, (IV), Tigermoon Enterprises, 1249 Palm St. #5, San Luis Obispo CA 93401. (805)544-3456. Editor: Terry Kennedy. Newspaper/newsletter. Publishes material on "spirituality, truth; hard news related to these themes." Semiannually. Estab. 1981.

Needs: Spirituality, truth: literary. Planning future special fiction issue or anthology. Receives 1 unsolicited ms/month. Accepts 1 ms/year. Publishes ms 1 year after acceptance.

How to Contact: Send SASE for reply, return of ms or send a disposable copy of ms. Simultaneous submissions OK. Reviews novels and short story collections.

Payment/Terms: Pays contributor's copies. Acquires one-time rights.

Advice: "If I like it, can't put it down, and feel it is useful as a tool for readers to gain insight into their souls, I might publish it. We are not for beginners or first-timers. Most fiction I receive is workshop learned. I'd like to see purposeful stories."

‡TIMBER CREEK REVIEW, (III), 612 Front St. East, Glendora NJ 08029-1133. (609)863-0610. Editor: J.M. Freiermuth. Newsletter: 5½×8½; 60-80 pages; copy paper; some illustrations and photographs. "Fiction, satire, humerous poetry and travel for a general audience —80% of readers have B.A." Quarterly. Circ. 120.

Needs: Adventure, contemporary, ethnic, feminist, historical, humor/satire, mainstream, mystery/suspense (cozy, private eye), regional, western (adult, frontier, traditional). No religion, children's, gay, romance. Plans third "All Woman Author" issue (July 1996) and "all Harley-Davidson short story" issue (January 1997). Receives 40-50 unsolicited mss/month. Accepts 15-20 mss/issue; 60-70 mss/year. Publishes ms 2-6 months after acceptance. Recently published work by Cliff Morrison, Bruce Bair, Taylor Graham, Debra Purdy Kong, Rene Savage and Wendy Tokunaga; published first time writers last year. Length: 2,000-3,000 words average; 1,200 words minimum; 9,000 words maximum. Publishes short shorts. Length: "Long enough to develop a good bite." Sometimes critiques rejected mss and recommends other markets.

How to Contact: Send complete manuscript copy and/or DOS floppy with cover letter including "name, address, SASE." Reports in 3-6 weeks on mss. SASE. Simultaneous and reprint submissions OK. Accepts electronic submissions. Sample copy for $3 postpaid. Reviews novels and short story collections.

Payment/Terms: Pays subscription to magazine for first publication and contributor's copies for subsequent publications. Acquires one-time rights. Publication not copyrighted.

Advice: "If your story has a spark of life or a degree of humor that brings a smile to my face, you have a chance here. Most stories lack these two ingredients. Don't send something you wrote ten years ago."

TIME PILOT, (I, II, IV), The New Legends Group, P.O. Box 2567, Bellingham WA 98227. (360)738-9759. Editor: Gary Bryant. Newsletter: 8½ × 11; 12-20 pages; illustrations and photos. "Our mission is to create a unique meeting place for a few forward thinking people. We want to take an educated guess on how the people of Earth will actually be living in the 25th century." Monthly. Estab. 1993. Circ. 9,000.

Needs: Fantasy (science fantasy), humor/satire, literary, science fiction (hard science, soft/sociological). Receives 30-50 unsolicited mss/month. Accepts 10 mss/issue; 100-140 mss/year. Publishes ms 2-3 months after acceptance. Length: 500 words average; 200 words minimum; 1,200 words maximum. Publishes short shorts. Also publishes literary essays and literary criticism.

How to Contact: Request guidelines and sample issue. Reports in 1 month on queries; 2 months on mss. Send SASE for reply, return of ms or send a disposable copy of ms. Simultaneous, reprint and electronic submissions OK. E-mail address: newlegends@aol.com. Sample copy for $1.50, 9 × 12 SAE and 4 first-class stamps. Fiction guidelines for #10 SASE.

Payment/Terms: Pays free subscription to the magazine and up to 25¢/word for accepted serials for one-time rights.

Advice: "We want to take an educated guess on how the people of Earth will actually be living in the 25th century. Will we have resolved the issue of abortion, AIDS, racism and aggression? Will we still be living in democracy? *Time Pilot* is an educational tool disguised as a newsletter for people with active minds and something to contribute. It is a chance for students, scientists, philosophers and environmentalists to hypothesize future strategies for dealing with the problems of growth and technological advancement."

TOMORROW Speculative Fiction, (I), Unifont Co., P.O. Box 6038, Evanston IL 60204. (708)864-3668. Editor and Publisher: Algis Budrys. Magazine: 8¼ × 10¾; 80 pages; newsprint; slick cover; illustrations. "Any good science fiction, fantasy and horror, for an audience of fiction readers." Bimonthly. Estab. 1992.

• *Tomorrow* has been nominated for a Hugo two years in a row. For more on this publication and the editor, see *Science Fiction Writer's Marketplace and Sourcebook* (from Writer's Digest Books). Budrys also publishes a series of articles on writing in his magazine.

Needs: Fantasy, horror, science fiction. Receives 100 mss/month. Buys 8-12 mss/issue; 48-82 mss/year. Publishes within 1 year of acceptance. Agented fiction 5%. Recently published works by Ursula K. Le Guin, M. Shayne Bell, Rob Chilson and Norman Spinrad. Length: 4,000 words average. Publishes short shorts. Always critiques rejected mss.

How to Contact: Send complete ms. Should include estimated word count and Social Security number. No covering letters. Reports in 2 weeks. Send SASE for reply, return of ms or send a disposable copy of the ms. No simultaneous submissions. Sample copy for $4.50 plus postage.

Payment/Terms: Pays $75 minimum; 7¢/word maximum plus 3 contributor's copies between acceptance and publication. Acquires first North American serial rights. Sends galleys to author.

Advice: "Read my book, 'Writing to the Point,' $10.50 from Unifont."

TOUCHSTONE LITERARY JOURNAL, (II), P.O. Box 8308, Spring TX 77387-8308. Editor/Publisher: William Laufer. Managing Editor: Guida Jackson. Fiction Editor: Julia Gomez-Rivas. Magazine: 5½ × 8½; 40-104 pages; linen paper; kramkote cover; perfect bound; b&w illustrations; occasional photographs. "Literary and mainstream fiction, but enjoy experimental work and multicultural. Audience middle-class, heavily academic. We are eclectic and given to whims—i.e., two years ago we devoted a 104-page issue to West African women writers." Annually (with occasional special supplements). Estab. 1976. Circ. 1,000.

• Touchstone Press also publishes a chapbook series. Send a SASE for guidelines.

Needs: Humor/satire, literary, mainstream/contemporary, translations. No erotica, religious, juvenile, "stories written in creative writing programs that all sound alike." List of upcoming themes available for SASE. Publishes special fiction issue or anthology. Receives 20-30 mss/month. Accepts 2-10 mss/issue. Does not read mss in December. Publishes ms within the year after acceptance. Published work by Ann Alejandro, Lynn Bradley, Roy Fish and Julia Mercedes Castilla. Length: 2,500 words preferred; 250 words minimum;

5,000 words maximum. Publishes short shorts. Length: 300 words. Also publishes literary essays, literary criticism and poetry. Sometimes critiques or comments on rejected mss.

How to Contact: Send complete ms with a cover letter. Should include estimated word count and 3 sentence bio. Reports in 3 months. Send SASE for return of ms. Simultaneous and electronic submissions OK. Sample copy for $3 or 10 first-class stamps. Fiction guidelines for #10 SASE.

Payment/Terms: Pays 2 contributor's copies; additional copies at 40% discount. Acquires one-time rights. Sends galleys to author (unless submitted on disk).

Advice: "We like to see fiction that doesn't read as if it had been composed in a creative writing class. If you can entertain, edify, or touch the reader, polish your story and send it in. Don't worry if it doesn't read like our other fiction."

TRAFIKA, (I, II), P.O. Box 250413, Columbia Station, New York NY 10025-1536. Contact: Editors. Magazine: 6×9; 224 pages. "An international periodical of current prose and poetry from new and emerging writers." Quarterly. Estab. 1993. Circ. 7,000.

• *Trafika* is a member of the Council of Literary Magazines and Presses.

Needs: Quality short stories, excerpted novels, translations. Receives 50 unsolicited mss/month. Accepts 10-15 mss/issue; 40-60 mss/year. Publishes ms 1-6 months after acceptance. Agented fiction less than 10%. Recently published work by Lars Jakobson, Do Phuoc Tien, Kristien Hemmerechts, Yves Simon and Mia Couto. Length: 10,000 words maximum. Also publishes literary essays and poetry. Sometimes critiques or comments on rejected mss.

How to Contact: Send ms. Should include bio and list of publications. Reports in 2-3 weeks on queries; 2-3 months on mss. SASE for reply only. Simultaneous submissions must be identified. Sample copy for $10. Fiction guidelines for #10 SASE.

Payment/Terms: Pays $15 per printed page plus 2 contributor's copies. Acquires first world serial rights in English.

‡♥TRANSITION, (IV), Canadian Mental Health Association, 2707 12th Ave., Regina, Sasketchewan S4T 1J2 Canada. (306)525-5601. Fax: (306)569-3788. Editor: Lori Wiens. Magazine: 8½×5½; 72 pages; matte 70 lb. paper; glossy cover; illustrations and photos. "The theme of *Transition* is to promote understanding of issues surrounding mental health." Quarterly. Estab. 1989. Circ. 3,000.

Needs: Relating to mental health—all areas. List of upcoming themes available for SASE. Receives 100 unsolicited mss/month. Accepts 15-20 mss/issue; 100 mss/year. Publishes ms up to 6 months after acceptance. Publishes short shorts. Also publishes poetry. Sometimes critiques or comments on rejected ms.

How to Contact: Query first. Should include estimated word count. Reports in 3 months on queries; 6 months on mss. Send SASE for reply, return of ms or send a disposable copy of ms. Simultaneous and electronic submissions OK. Sample copy free.

Payment/Terms: Pays $15-75 plus 2 contributor's copies on publication for one-time rights.

Advice: "Start with short submissions or clips—ask for feedback if interested."

‡TREASURE HOUSE, Stories & Verse, (I, II), Treasure House Publishing, 1106 Oak Hill Ave., #3A, Hagerstown MD 21742. Editor-in-Chief: J.G. Wolfensberger. Fiction Editor: Owen H. Green. Magazine: 8½×11; 28-36 pages; 60 lb. white paper; heavier cover; illustrations. "*Treasure House* publishes fiction, memoirs that read like stories, and poetry, all by real people. We simply believe that we can remain dedicated to literary art forms without growing self-indulgent. We strive to provide readers with a truly diverse range of material in every issue. We publish on time, and we maintain respect for writers." Triannually. Estab. 1994. Circ. 300.

Needs: Literary. "No stories about writers or writing, and no stories about tormented artists or misunderstood new bohemians." Receives more than 60 unsolicited mss/month. Accepts 5 mss/issue; 15 mss/year. Publishes ms within a year after acceptance. Recently published work by Charles Rammelkamp, Margo Perin and Richard Hine. Length: 3,000 words average; 6,000 words maximum. Publishes short shorts. Also publishes poetry. Sometimes critiques or comments on rejected ms.

How to Contact: Send complete ms with a cover letter. Should include estimated word count and brief bio. "Cover letters should serve as personal introductions, not resumés. Reports in 2 weeks on queries; 2-12 weeks on mss. Send SASE for reply, return of ms or send a disposable copy of ms. Simultaneous submissions OK. Sample copy for $4. Fiction guidelines for #10 SASE.

Payment/Terms: Pays 2 or more contributor's copies; additional copies for $3. Acquires first rights. Sends galleys to author. "We sponsor our annual Emerging Writers Fiction Contest. The 1995 prize was $250. Interested writers should query with SASE for current guidelines."

Advice: "We seek stories that surprise us in some way, that make us pace the room or laugh aloud, or that possibly make us uncomfortable with our own opinions. The best work lingers in one's mind long after the reading is finished. A beginner cannot move forward without fully comprehending one essential rule of fiction: show, don't tell. Next, decide, 'Am I a writer or an aspiring artist?' If the former, do reasonable market research, then send your work out like crazy. If you are the latter, exercise greater care. Determine the handful of publications you admire, read them critically, and submit to them consistently. Follow Hemingway's rule: write deliberately. We would love to see more work which crosses and transcends genres, work exhibiting greater imagination when it comes to plotting 'ordinary' characters into extraordinary conflicts. But we're not interested in fantasy! Also, don't send us any New Age spiritual material. No religious material. No agenda-driven material."

‡THE TREKKER NEWS & VIEWS, (I), Cosmic Dolphin, Ltd., 72 Wood Stream Dr., Norristown PA 19403. (610)630-0510. Fax: (610)630-0180. Publisher: Kathy Kimmel. Editor: Colin Stewart. Magazine: 8½×11; 20 pages; glossy paper; glossy cover; b&w illustrations and photos. Bimonthly. Estab. 1988. Circ. 10,000.
Needs: Children's/juvenile, experimental, fantasy (science fantasy), horror, literary, mainstream/contemporary, psychic/supernatural/occult, romance (futuristic/time travel), science fiction, young adult/teen. "Our publication is for all ages." List of upcoming themes available for SASE. Publishes ms 2-3 months after acceptance. Recently published work by Phil Farrand, Jeri Taylor, Don Barrett and Colin Stewart. Also publishes literary essays, literary criticism and poetry. Sometimes critiques or comments on rejected ms.
How to Contact: Send complete ms with a cover letter. Should include estimated word count, 3-4 line bio, list of publications with any experience or published works, knowledge of subject. Reports in 6-8 weeks on queries. Send SASE for reply, return of ms or send a disposable copy of ms. Simultaneous and electronic submissions OK. Send 3.5 disk and hard copy. E-mail address: rrjm78a@prodigy.com. Sample copy for $4. Reviews novels and short story collections.
Payment/Terms: Pays 1 contributor's copy; additional copies for $2.
Advice: "Send pieces that cover science fiction series and films. We cover reviews of film, TV and features, videos, books, interviews with actors, poetry and environmental themed pieces. We love to inspire and discover new and talented writers. We have professional contributors and only print terrific pieces. We're always looking for a new column idea. *The Trekker* is sent to the producers and writers of these series. Send positive views, we don't like to insult the producers/writers/directors of these films and series. Our magazine is a great way for a writer to connect with Hollywood and the entertainment writing field. Our look is like *The Hollywood Reporter*, our content is like *Starlog* magazine."

‡TRIBUTE TO OFFICER DALLIES, "The Man Behind Badge 126," (I, II, IV), Katy's Kab Publications, P.O. Box 913, Hayfork CA 96041. Phone/fax: (916)628-4714. Editor: Katy Lawson. Magazine: 5½×8½; 20 lb. paper; illustrations and photos. "*Tribute to Officer Dallie*s is an ongoing tribute to Garden Grove (CA) Master Officer II Howard E. Dallies. Includes a wanted poster of his killer." Semiannually. Estab. 1993. Circ. 100-500.
Needs: Experimental, historical, mystery/suspense (amateur sleuth, police procedural, private eye/hardboiled, experimental). "Try to solve the still-open murder case via creative fiction. We will supply the necessary data for writers." Publishes annual special fiction issue or anthology. Publishes ms 1-3 months after acceptance. Length: 500 words average; 500 words minimum; 2,000 words maximum. Publishes short shorts. Length: 500 words. Also publishes literary essays and poetry. Often critiques or comments on rejected ms.
How to Contact: Query first. Should include estimated word count, bio and list of publications. Reports in 1-6 months. Send SASE for reply, return of ms or send a disposable copy of ms. Simultaneous, reprint and electronic submissions OK. E-mail address: katy.lawson@trnet.org. Sample copy for 9×12 SAE and 3 first-class stamps. Fiction guidelines free.
Payment/Terms: Pays 1 contributor's copy. Acquires one-time rights. Not copyrighted. Sponsors contest for fiction writers. Query for details.
Advice: "Our goal is to promote awareness of this case and to show the human side of Howard E. Dallies, Jr. Ask for our information kit. We want to help you write a commercially viable story that you can turn around and sell to high-paying markets. A mutual win-win situation. Since this is a new project, we haven't had a chance to gauge the feedback. We want all the stories we can get. God bless us every one."

TRIQUARTERLY, (II), Northwestern University, 2020 Ridge Ave., Evanston IL 60208. (708)491-7614. Fiction Editors: Reginald Gibbons and Susan Hahn. Magazine: 6×9¼; 240-272 pages; 60 lb. paper; heavy cover stock; illustration; photos. "A general literary quarterly especially devoted to fiction. We publish short stories, novellas or excerpts from novels, by American and foreign writers. Genre or style is not a primary consideration. We aim for the general but serious and sophisticated reader. Many of our readers are also writers." Triannual. Estab. 1964. Circ. 5,000.
Needs: Literary, contemporary and translations. "No prejudices or preconceptions against anything *except* genre fiction (romance, sci fi, etc.)." Buys 10 mss/issue, 30 mss/year. Receives approximately 500 unsolicited fiction mss each month. Does not read April 1-September 30. Agented 10%. Published work by Stanley Elkin, Chaim Potok and Alice Fulton; published new writers within the last year. Length: no requirement. Publishes short shorts.

Check the Category Indexes, located at the back of the book, for publishers interested in specific fiction subjects.

How to Contact: Send complete ms with SASE. No simultaneous submissions. Reports in 3-4 months on mss. Publishes ms an average of 6-12 months after acceptance. Sample copy for $5.
Payment/Terms: Pays $30/page (fiction); 2 contributor's copies on publication for first North American serial rights. Cover price less 40% discount for extras. Sends galleys to author.

‡TROIKA MAGAZINE, Wit, Wisdom, and Wherewithal, (I, II), Lone Tout Publications, Inc., P.O. Box 1006, Weston CT 06883. (203)227-5377. Fax: (203)222-9332. Editor: Celia Meadow. Magazine: 8⅛×10⅝; 100 pages; 45 lb. Expression paper; 100 lb. Warren cover; illustrations and photographs. "Our magazine is geared toward an audience aged 30-50 looking to balance a lifestyle of family, community and personal success." Quarterly. Estab. 1994. Circ. 100,000.
  • *Troika* was listed among Samir Husni's *Guide to New Magazines 1995* Top 50 most notable launches and received a 1995 *Print Magazine* Award for Excellence (design).
Needs: Adventure, condensed/excerpted novel, ethnic/multicultural, experimental, feminist, gay, historical, humor/satire, lesbian, literary, mainstream/contemporary, mystery/suspense, psychic/supernatural/occult, regional, religious/inspirational, romance, science fiction. List of upcoming themes available for SASE. Receives 25 unsolicited mss/month. Accepts 2-5 mss/issue; 8-20 mss/year. Publishes ms 3-6 months after acceptance. Agented fiction 10%. Recently published work by Alan Stevens, Gil Jackman and Jamie Shenkman. Length: 2,000-3,000 words. Also publishes literary essays and literary criticism. Sometimes critiques or comments on rejected ms.
How to Contact: Send complete ms with a cover letter giving address, phone/fax number and e-mail address. Should include estimated word count, brief bio and list of publications with submission. Reports in 1 month. Send SASE for reply to query or return of ms or send a disposable copy of ms. Simultaneous and electronic submissions OK. E-mail address: troikamag@aol.com. Sample copy for $5. Fiction guidelines for #10 SASE. Reviews novels and short story collections.
Payment/Terms: Pays $250 maximum on publication and 1 contributor's copy for first North American serial rights.

TUCUMCARI LITERARY REVIEW, (I, II), 3108 W. Bellevue Ave., Los Angeles CA 90026. Editor: Troxey Kemper. Magazine: 5½×8½; 36 pages; 20 lb. bond paper; 67 lb. cover stock; few illustrations; Xerox photographs. "Old-fashioned fiction that can be read and reread for pleasure; no weird, strange pipe dreams and no it-was-all-a-dream endings." Bimonthly. Estab. 1988. Circ. small.
Needs: Adventure, contemporary, ethnic, historical, humor/satire, literary, mainstream, mystery/suspense, regional (southwest USA), senior citizen/retirement, western (frontier stories). No science fiction, drugs/acid rock, pornography, horror, martial arts. Accepts 6 or 8 mss/issue; 35-40 mss/year. Publishes ms 2-6 months after acceptance. Length: 400-1,200 words preferred. Also publishes rhyming poetry.
How to Contact: Send complete ms with or without cover letter. Reports in 2 weeks. SASE. Simultaneous and reprint submissions OK. Sample copy for $2. Fiction guidelines for #10 SASE.
Payment/Terms: Pays in contributor's copies. Acquires one-time rights. Publication not copyrighted.

TWISTED, (II), P.O. Box 1249, Palmetto GA 30268-1249. (404)463-1458. Editor: Christine Hoard. Magazine: 8½×11; approximately 152 pages; 60 lb. paper; 67 lb. cover stock; illustrations; photos. "Emphasis on contemporary horror and fantasy, anything on the dark side of reality." For readers of horror, "weird," fantasy, etc. Published irregularly. Estab. 1985. Circ. 300.
Needs: "We are mostly interested in adult-oriented horror." Fantasy, horror, prose poem, psychic/supernatural/occult. "No hard science fiction, no sword and sorcery. Graphic horror or sex scenes OK if tastefully done. Sexist-racist writing turns me off." Receives approximately 30 unsolicited fiction mss/month. Accepts 10 mss/issue. Publishes ms 2-24 months after acceptance. Published work by David Bruce, Joe Faust, Bentley Little and Kathleen Jurgens; publishes new writers. Length: 2,000 words average; 200 words minimum; 5,000 words preferred. Sometimes critiques rejected mss and recommends other markets.
How to Contact: Reporting time varies, usually 2-3 months. Cover letters not necessary but appreciated. No simultaneous or multiple submissions. Sample copy for $6. Fiction guidelines for #10 SASE.
Payment/Terms: Pays in contributor's copies. Acquires first rights.
Advice: "Sometimes we are overstocked or temporary closed for submissions so probably best to inquire first."

2 AM MAGAZINE, (I, II, IV), Box 6754, Rockford IL 61125-1754. Editor: Gretta M. Anderson. Magazine: 8½×11; 60 or more pages; 60 lb. offset paper; 70 lb. offset cover; illustrations; photos occasionally. "Horror, science fiction, fantasy stories, poetry, articles and art for a sophisticated adult audience." Quarterly. Summer fiction issue planned. Estab. 1986. Circ. 2,000.
  • See the interview with Gretta Anderson in the 1995 edition of this book.
Needs: Experimental, fantasy, horror, humor/satire, mystery/suspense (police procedurals, romantic suspense), prose poem, psychic/supernatural/occult, romance (gothic), science fiction (hard science, soft/sociological). No juvenile. Receives 400 unsolicited mss/month. Buys 12-14 mss/issue; 50 mss/year. Publishes ms an average of 6-9 months after acceptance. Published work by Darrel Schweitzer, Avram Davidson, John Coyne and Larry Tritten; published new writers within the last year. Length: 3,000 words average; 500 words

minimum; 5,000 words maximum. Publishes short shorts. Sometimes critiques rejected mss.

How to Contact: Send complete ms with cover letter (cover letter optional). Simultaneous submissions OK. Reports in 1 month on queries; 10-12 weeks on mss. SASE. Sample copy for $4.95 and $1 postage. Fiction guidelines for #10 SASE.

Payment/Terms: Pays ½¢/word minimum, negotiable maximum on acceptance for one-time rights with nonexclusive anthology option; 1 contributor's copy; 40% discount on additional copies. Sends prepublication galleys to author.

Advice: "Publishing more pages of fiction, more science fiction, and mystery, as well as horror. Put name and address on ms, double-space, use standard ms format. Pseudonym should appear under title on first ms page. True name and address should appear on upper left on first ms page."

THE UNFORGETTABLE FIRE, (IV), 530 Riverside Dr., Suite 5G, New York NY 10027. Editor: Jordan O'Neill. Newsletter: 8½×11; 35 pages; illustrations. "Feminist, humanist publication, by, for and about women. We do accept submissions from men, however." Quarterly. Estab. 1992. Circ. 3,000.

• The editors are now more interested in short short fiction.

Needs: Ethnic/multicultural, feminist, gay, humor/satire, lesbian. "Nothing sexist, racist, homophobic, violent, pornographic." Publishes special fiction issue or anthology. Receives 10-15 unsolicited mss/month. Accepts 8 mss/issue; 10 mss/year. Published work by Lyn Lifshin and Elisavietta Ritchie. Length: 1,200 words maximum. Publishes short shorts. Publishes literary essays, literary criticism and poetry. Sometimes critiques and comments on rejected mss.

How to Contact: Send complete ms with a cover letter. Should include 1 paragraph bio. Reports in 2 weeks on queries; 3-4 weeks on mss. Send SASE for reply, return of ms or send a disposable copy of ms. Simultaneous, reprint and electronic submissions OK. Sample copy and fiction guidelines for SAE and 64¢ postage. Reviews novels and short story collections.

Payment/Terms: Pays 1-2 contributor's copies on acceptance.

Advice: Looks for work "usually with a strong feminist/humanist tone—compassionate stories pertaining to everyday life—stories related to overcoming hardships and, most importantly, empowerment. Write from the heart with a female angle, writing, speaking to and about other women so our readers feel connected to the story."

UNMUZZLED OX, (III), Unmuzzled Ox Foundation Ltd., 105 Hudson St., New York NY 10013. Editor: Michael Andre. Tabloid. "Magazine about life for an intelligent audience." Quarterly. Estab. 1971. Circ. 20,000.

• Recent issues of this magazine have included poetry, essays and art only. You may want to check before sending submissions or expect a long response time.

Needs: Contemporary, literary, prose poem and translations. No commercial material. Receives 20-25 unsolicited mss/month. Also publishes poetry. Occasionally critiques rejected mss.

How to Contact: "Cover letter is significant." Reports in 1 month. SASE. Sample copy for $7.50.

Payment/Terms: Contributor's copies.

‡UNO MAS MAGAZINE, (I, II), P.O. Box 1832, Silver Spring MD 20915. Fax: (301)770-3250. Editor: Jim Saah. Fiction Editor: Ron Saah. Magazine: 8½×11; 50 pages; 60 lb. offset paper; glossy cover; illustrations and photos. "*Uno Mas Magazine* specializes in popular culture. Bringing new and established artists of all dimensions (music, literature, photography, poetry, etc.) together in one magazine." Quarterly. Estab. 1990. Circ. 3,500.

Needs: Condensed/excerpted novel, erotica, ethnic/multicultural, experimental, feminist, gay, historical, humor/satire, lesbian, literary, mystery/suspense (private eye/hardboiled, romantic suspense). Plans special fiction issue or anthology. Receives 4 unsolicited mss/month. Buys 2 mss/issue; 8 mss/year. Publishes ms 1-3 months after acceptance. Agented fiction 20%. Recently published work by George Logothetis and Tom Hamill. Length: 1,500-3,000 words average; 500 words minimum; 3,500 words maximum. Publishes short shorts. Also publishes literary essays, literary criticism and poetry. Sometimes critiques or comments on rejected ms.

How to Contact: Send complete ms with a cover letter. Should include estimated word count, short bio and SASE. Reports in 2 weeks on queries; 1-3 months on mss. Send SASE for reply, return of ms or send a disposable copy of ms. Simultaneous, reprint and electronic submissions OK. Sample copy for $3, 9×11 SAE and 5 first-class stamps. Fiction guidelines free for #10 SASE. Reviews novels or short story collections.

Payment/Terms: Pays 3 contributor's copies; additional copies for $1.50. Acquires one-time rights. Sends galleys to author, "if requested."

Advice: "Short, tight pieces have the best chance of being published. Include word count and address on manuscript."

THE URBANITE, A Journal of City Fiction & Poetry, (II, IV), Urban Legend Press, P.O. Box 4737, Davenport IA 52808. Editor: Mark McLaughlin. Magazine. "We look for quality fiction in an urban setting with a surrealistic tone. Contributors include modern masters of surrealism and talented newcomers. Our audience is urbane, culture-oriented and hard to please!" Published three times a year. Estab. 1991. Circ. 500.

- A story published in *The Urbanite* was selected for inclusion in the *Year's Best Fantasy and Horror* (No.6). More of the magazine's fiction and poetry have received Honorable Mentions in the anthology series.

Needs: Experimental, fantasy (dark fantasy), horror, humor/satire, literary, psychic/supernatural/occult, science fiction (soft/sociological). "We love horror, but please, no tired, gore-ridden horror plots. Horror submissions must be subtle and sly." Upcoming themes: "Strange Fascinations," "Transformations" and "Urban Deities." List of upcoming themes available for SASE. Receives over 60 unsolicited mss/month. Accepts 15 mss/issue; 45 mss/year. Publishes ms 6 months after acceptance. Recently published work by Pamela Briggs, Thomas Ligotti, Jeanne Cavelos, Hugh B. Cave and Nina Kiriki Hoffman. Length: 2,000 words preferred; 500 words minimum; 3,000 words maximum. Publishes short shorts. Length: 350 words preferred. Also publishes poetry. Sometimes critiques or comments on rejected mss.

How to Contact: Query first; each issue has its own theme and guidelines for that theme. Should include estimated word count, 4-5 sentence bio, Social Security number and list of publications. Reports in 1 month on queries; 4-5 months on mss. Send SASE for reply, return of ms or send a disposable copy of ms. Sample copy for $5. Fiction guidelines for #10 SASE.

Payment/Terms: Pays 2-3¢/word and 2 contributor's copies for first North American serial rights and nonexclusive rights for public readings.

Advice: "The tone of our magazine is unique, and we strongly encourage writers to read an issue to ascertain the sort of material we accept. The number one reason we reject many stories is because they are inappropriate for our publication: in these cases, it is obvious that the writer is not familiar with *The Urbanite*. We want to see more slipstream fiction and more bizarre (yet urbane and thought-provoking) humor."

URBANUS/RAIZIRR, (III), Urbanus Press, P.O. Box 192921, San Francisco CA 94119. Editor: Peter Drizhal. Magazine: 5½×8½; 64 pages; 60 lb. offset paper; 10 pt. coated cover; illustrations; a few photographs. "We seek writing for an audience that is generally impatient with mainstream at the same time, not falling into the underground literary mode. Contemporary macabre, we've seen described." Semiannually. Estab. 1988. Circ. 1,000.

Needs: Ethnic/multicultural, experimental, feminist, gay, horror, humor/satire, lesbian, literary, mainstream/contemporary, science fiction (soft/sociological). "Nothing generic slice-of-life—far too much of it out there." Receives 200-300 unsolicited mss/month. Buys 10 mss/year. Publishes ms 6-18 months after acceptance. Published work by Pat Murphy, James Sallis, Sherril Jaffe, Sarah Schulman and Edward Kleinschmidt. Length: 5,000 words maximum. Publishes short shorts. Also publishes poetry. Sometimes comments on or critiques rejected mss.

How to Contact: Send complete ms with a cover letter. Should include estimated word count, list of publications (3-5 sentences). Reports in 2-4 weeks on queries; 1-3 months on mss. Send SASE for reply, return of ms or send a disposable copy of the ms. No multiple or simultaneous submissions. Sample copy for $5. Writer's guidelines available for #10 SASE. "In 1996, unless a reading period has been announced, *please query* before sending a manuscript."

Payment/Terms: Pays 1¢/word and 2 contributor's copies for first North American serial rights.

Advice: "Sample an issue to get a sense for our content; brisk, compelling narrative, and a story not bogged down with prologue, will get our attention; a story incongruous with our focus often loses its footing on page 1. Prefer to see no more than 2 submissions from a writer, per reading period."

US1 WORKSHEETS, (II), % Postings, Box 1, Ringoes NJ 08551. (908)782-6492. Editor: Rotating board. Magazine: 11½×17; 20-25 pages. Publishes poetry and fiction. Annually. Estab. 1973.

Needs: "No restrictions on subject matter or style. Good story telling or character deliniation appreciated. Audience does not include children." Published work by Alicia Ostriker, Richard Kostelanetz, Geraldine C. Little, Robin Clipper Sethi, J.A. Perkins, David Keller and Judith McNally. Publishes short shorts.

How to Contact: Query first "or send a SAE postcard for reading dates. We read only once a year." Reports on queries "as soon as possible." SASE. Sample copy for $4.

Payment/Terms: Pays in contributor's copies. Acquires one-time rights. Copyright "reverts to author."

VALLEY GRAPEVINE, (I, IV), Seven Buffaloes Press, Box 249, Big Timber MT 59011. Editor/Publisher: Art Cuelho. Theme: "poems, stories, history, folklore, photographs, ink drawings or anything native to the Great Central Valley of California, which includes the San Joaquin and Sacramento valleys. Focus is on land and people and the oil fields, farms, orchards, Okies, small town life, hobos." Readership: "Rural and small town audience, the common man with a rural background, salt-of-the-earth. The working man reads *Valley Grapevine* because it's his personal history recorded." Annually. Estab. 1978. Circ. 500.

- *Valley Grapevine* is published by Art Cuelho of Seven Buffaloes Press. He also publishes *Azorean Express*, *Black Jack, Hill and Holler*, listed in this book. See also his listing for the press.

Needs: Literary, contemporary, ethnic (Arkie, Okie), regional and western. No academic, religious (unless natural to theme), or supernatural material. Receives approximately 4-5 unsolicited fiction mss each month. Length: 2,500-10,000 (prefers 5,000) words.

How to Contact: Query. SASE for query, ms. Reports in 1 week. Sample copy available to writers for $6.75.

Payment/Terms: Pays 1-2 contributor's copies. Acquires first North American serial rights. Returns rights to author after publication, but reserves the right to reprint in an anthology or any future special collection of Seven Buffaloes Press.

Advice: "Buy a copy to get a feel of the professional quality of the writing. Know the theme of a particular issue. Some contributors have 30 years experience as writers; most 15 years. Age does not matter; quality does."

‡**VENUS MAGAZINE, (I, II)**, Venus Publishing, Inc., 880 Almaden St., Eugene OR 97402. (503)683-6070 or (503)686-5168. Fax: (503)334-5191, (503)465-1751 or (503)484-0049. Editor: Angela Gass-Gilchrist. Magazine: 8¾×11; 75-150 pages; glossy paper; 100 lb. glossy cover; illustrations and photos. "Mostly Northwest writers and artists—all types of material considered. We do not censor anything we accept. Audience 18-65." Bimonthly. Estab. 1995. Circ. 50,000-75,000.

Needs: Adventure, erotica, ethnic/multicultural, experimental, feminist, gay, historical, horror, humor/satire, lesbian, literary, mainstream/contemporary, mystery/suspense (police procedural, private eye/hardboiled), psychic/supernatural/occult, regional (Northwest). Particularly interested in work from Northwest writers and about Northwest subjects. "No religious, science fiction." List of upcoming themes available for SASE. Plans special fiction issue or anthology. Publishes ms 2-4 months after acceptance. Length: 500 words average; no minimum; 2,000 words maximum. Publishes short shorts. Length: 200-300 words. Also publishes literary essays, literary criticism and poetry. Sometimes critiques or comments on rejected ms.

How to Contact: Send complete ms with a cover letter via fax, US mail or e-mail. Should include estimated word count, 100-word bio, "phone number, address, name on each page, please." Reports in 2 months. Send SASE for reply, return of ms or send a disposable copy of ms. Simultaneous, reprint and electronic submissions OK (IBM Pagemaker 5.0 only at this time). E-mail address: venusmag@aol.com. Fiction guidelines free. Reviews novels or short story collections.

Payment/Terms: Pays 3 contributor's copies; additional copies for $1. Acquires one-time rights. Not copyrighted.

Advice: "We are open minded and will accept most subject matter. We prefer 'on the edge' stories. We do not censor any material we accept. We haven't seen enough 'on the edge' writing. Many submissions seem too controlled and stiff. Avoid sending rhyming poetry."

‡**VERVE, (II)**, P.O. Box 3205, Simi Valley CA 93093. Editor: Ron Reichick. Fiction Editor: Marilyn Hochheiser. Magazine: Digest-sized, 40 pages, 70 lb. paper, 80 lb. cover, cover illustrations or photographs. "Each issue has a theme." Quarterly. Estab. 1989. Circ. 700.

Needs: Contemporary, experimental, fantasy, humor/satire, literary, mainstream, prose poem. No pornographic material. Upcoming themes: "Walking Toward The Roar" (deadline: March 1, 1996); "Out of the Dark" (deadline: August 1, 1996). Receives 100 unsolicited fiction mss/month. Accepts 4-6 mss/issue; 8-12 mss/year. Publishes ms 2 months after acceptance. Length: 1,000 words maximum. Publishes short shorts. Also publishes literary criticism, poetry.

How to Contact: "Request guidelines before submitting manuscript." Reports 4-6 weeks after deadline. SASE. Simultaneous submissions OK. Sample copy for $3.50. Fiction guidelines for #10 SASE. Reviews short story collections.

Payment/Terms: Pays in contributor's copies. Acquires one-time rights.

VIDEOMANIA, The Video Collectors Newspaper, (I, II), LegsOfStone Publishing Co., Box 47, Princeton WI 54968. (414)295-4377. Editor: Bob Katerzynske. Tabloid; 10½×16; 32 pages; newsprint paper; ground wood cover; b&w/color illustrations, photographs. "Slanted towards the home entertainment buff, with a *real* interest in home video and entertainment. Publishes *anything* we feel is of interest to our readers—fiction and non-fiction. Audience is mostly male (90%), but female readership is always increasing." Bimonthly. Estab. 1982. Circ. 5-6,000.

Needs: Movie-related themes. Experimental, fantasy, feminist, horror, humor/satire, lesbian, mainstream, science fiction (soft/sociological), video/film. Receives 3-4 unsolicited mss/month. Buys 1-2 mss/issue; 6-9 mss/year. Publishes ms 2-6 months after acceptance. Publishes short shorts. Length: 300-500 words. Sometimes critiques rejected mss and recommends other markets.

How to Contact: Send complete ms with cover letter. No simultaneous submissions. Reports in 1-2 months. SASE. Sample copy for $2.50, 9×12 SAE and $1 postage. Fiction guidelines for #10 SASE.

Payment/Terms: Pays $2.50 token payment in certain cases on publication for all rights or as writer prefers; contributor's copies.

Advice: "If the editor likes it, it's in. A good manuscript should not be too heavy; a *touch* of humor goes a long way with us. Don't expect to get rich off of us. On the other hand, we're more willing than other publications to look at the first-time, non-published writer. We've published established writers in the past that wanted to use our publication as sort of a sounding board for something experimental."

‡VIGNETTE, (II), Vignette Press, 4150-G Riverside Dr., Toluca Lake CA 91505. (818)955-5368. Fax: (818)848-0585. Editors: Dawn Baillie, Deborah Clark. Magazine: 6×9; 120 pages; 60 lb. smooth opaque, paper; 10 pt. C1S glossy; perfect bound. "*Vignette* provides imaginative short fiction based on a quarterly theme. For example, 'Home' and 'Vegetable' were our first and second themes. Audience is mostly writers and fiction enthusiasts." Estab. 1995. Circ. 500.

Needs: Adventure, erotica, ethnic/multicultural, experimental, feminist, gay, historical, humor/satire, lesbian, literary, mainstream/contemporary, psychic/supernatural/occult, regional. List of upcoming themes available for SASE. Publishes special fiction issue or anthology. Receives 150 unsolicited mss/month. Accepts 10 mss/issue; 40 mss/year. Publishes ms 2 months after acceptance. Agented fiction 10%. Recently published work by Barry Yourgrau, Thomas E. Kennedy, Enid Harlow and Janice Levy. Length: 4,000 words average; 5,000 words maximum. Publishes short shorts. Always critiques or comments on rejected ms.

How to Contact: Send complete ms with a cover letter. Should include estimated word count and bio. Reports in 6 weeks on mss. Send SASE for reply, return of ms or send a disposable copy of ms. Sample copy for $9.95 plus $3.50 postage (CA residents add 8.25% tax). Fiction guidelines for #10 SASE.

Payment/Terms: Pays $100-300 and 1 contributor's copy on publication for first rights plus one-time additional "best of" anthology. Sends galleys to author.

Advice: "Be inventive and use well-rounded characters. Looking for stories that have a unique point of view, unique voice and/or location. More fiction than personal essay."

THE VILLAGER, 135 Midland Ave., Bronxville NY 10708-1800. (914)337-3252. Editor: Amy Murphy. Fiction Editor: Mrs. Ahmed Hazzah. Magazine: 28-40 pages. "Magazine for a family audience." Monthly. Estab. 1928. Circ. 1,000.

Needs: Adventure, historical, humor/satire, literary, mystery/suspense, prose poem, romance (historical). Length: 1,500-1,800 words. Also publishes poetry.

How to Contact: Send complete ms with cover letter. SASE. Sample copy for $1.25.

Payment/Terms: Pays 2 contributor's copies.

Advice: "*The Villager* is known for it's focus on local history and people."

THE VINCENT BROTHERS REVIEW, (II), Vincent Brothers Publishing, 4566 Northern Circle, Riverside OH 45424-5733. Editor: Kimberly Willardson. Magazine: 5½×8½; 64-84 pages; 60 lb. white coated paper; 60 lb. Oxford (matte) cover; b&w illustrations and photographs. "We publish two theme issues per year. Writers must send SASE for information about upcoming theme issues. Each issue of *TVBR* contains poetry, b&w art, at least 3 short stories and usually 1 nonfiction piece. For a mainstream audience looking for an alternative to the slicks." Triannually. Estab. 1988. Circ. 400.

• *The Vincent Brothers Review* has received grants from the Ohio Arts Council for the last five years. The magazine sponsors a fall fiction contest; deadline in October. Contact them for details.

Needs: Adventure, condensed/excerpted novel, contemporary, ethnic, experimental, feminist, historical, humor/satire, literary, mainstream, mystery/suspense (amateur sleuth, cozy, private eye), prose poem, regional, science fiction (soft/sociological), senior citizen/retirement, serialized novel, translations, western (adult, frontier, traditional). Upcoming themes: "Dreams and Nightmares" (April 96); "Humor" (November 96). "We focus on the way the story is presented rather than the genre of the story. No racist, sexist, fascist, etc. work." Send SASE for themes. Receives 200-250 unsolicited mss/month. Buys 3-5 mss/issue; 9-15 mss/year. Publishes ms 2-4 months after acceptance. Published work by Kim Cushman, Tawna Wheeler and Susan Streeter Carpenter. Length: 2,500 words average; 250 words minimum; 3,500 words maximum. Publishes short shorts. Length: 250-1,000 words. Also publishes literary essays, literary criticism, poetry. Often critiques rejected mss and sometimes recommends other markets.

How to Contact: "Send query letter *before* sending novel excerpts or condensations! Send only 1 short story at a time—unless sending short shorts." Send complete ms. Simultaneous submissions OK, but not preferred. Reports in 3-4 weeks on queries; 1-2 months on mss. SASE. Sample copy for $6.50. Fiction guidelines for #10 SASE. Reviews novels and short story collections.

Payment/Terms: Pays $10 minimum and 2 contributor's copies for one-time rights. Charge (discounted) for extras.

Advice: "The best way to discover what *TVBR* editors are seeking in fiction is to read at least a couple issues of the magazine."

VINTAGE NORTHWEST, (I, IV), Northshore Senior Center (Sponsor), Box 193, Bothell WA 98041. (206)823-9189. Editors: Jane Kaake and Sylvia Tacker. Magazine: 7×8½; 68 pages; illustrations. "We are a senior literary magazine, published by and for seniors. All work done by volunteers except printing." For "all ages who are interested in our seniors' experiences." Published winter and summer. Estab. 1980. Circ. 500.

Needs: Adventure, comedy, fantasy, historical, humor/satire, inspirational, mystery/suspense, poetry, senior citizen/retirement, western (frontier). No religious or political mss. Receives 10-12 unsolicited mss/month. Length: 1,000 words maximum. Also publishes literary essays. Occasionally critiques rejected mss.

How to Contact: Send complete ms. SASE. Simultaneous and previously published submissions OK. Reports in 3-6 months. Sample copy for $3.25 (postage included). Guidelines with SASE.

Payment/Terms: Pays 1 contributor's copy.
Advice: "Our only requirement is that the author be over 50 when submission is written."

VIRGIN MEAT, (I), 2325 W.K 15, Lancaster CA 93536. (805)722-1758. Editor: Steve Blum. Gothic interactive computer e-zine. Published irregularly. Estab. 1987. Circ. 5,000.
Needs: Horror. Receives 3-4 mss/day. Length: 2,000 words maximum. Also publishes poetry, art, sound & QTM's.
How to Contact: Request writers guidelines before your first submission. E-mail ms to: virginmeat@aol.com. Sample copy for $5.
Payment/Terms: Pays in contributor's copies. Acquires one-time rights. Publication not copyrighted.
Advice: "Horror fiction should be horrific all the way through, not just at the end. Avoid common settings, senseless violence and humor."

VIRGINIA QUARTERLY REVIEW, (III), One West Range, Charlottesville VA 22903. (804)924-3124. Fax: (804)924-1397. Editor: Fax: (804)924-1397. Staige Blackford. "A national magazine of literature and discussion. A lay, intellectual audience; people who are not out-and-out scholars but who are interested in ideas and literature." Quarterly. Estab. 1925. Circ. 4,500.
Needs: Adventure, contemporary, ethnic, feminist, humor, literary, romance, serialized novels (excerpts) and translations. "No pornography." Buys 3 mss/issue, 20 mss/year. Length: 3,000-7,000 words.
How to Contact: Query or send complete ms. SASE. No simultaneous submissions. E-mail address: jco73@virginia.edu. Reports in 2 weeks on queries, 2 months on mss. Sample copy for $5.
Payment/Terms: Pays $10/printed page on publication for all rights. "Will transfer upon request." Offers Emily Clark Balch Award for best published short story of the year.
Advice: Looks for "stories with a somewhat southern dialect and/or setting."

‡VOICES WEST, A Literary Journal, (I, II), West Los Angeles College, 4800 Freshman Dr., Culver City CA 90230. (310)287-4200. Editors: R. Weinstein and B. Goldberg. Magazine: 6×9, 80-100 pages; 20 lb. bond paper; 70 lb. cover stock; illustrations and photos. *Voices West* is "a forum for most kinds of interesting and provocative writing. Primarily a college audience." Semiannually.
Needs: Adventure, erotica, ethnic/multicultural, experimental, humor/satire, literary, mainstream/contemporary, regional. No science fiction, children's or teen. Accepts 10 mss/issue; 20 mss/year. Does not read in summer. Publishes ms 3-6 months after acceptance. Length: no minimum; 5,000 words maximum. Publishes short shorts. Length: 1,500 words. Also publishes literary essays, literary criticism and poetry. Sometimes critiques or comments on rejected ms.
How to Contact: Send complete ms with a cover letter. Should include 50-word bio with submission. Reports in 1-2 months. Send SASE for reply, return of ms or send a disposable copy of ms. Simultaneous submissions OK.
Payment/Terms: Pays $50 maximum/story, $25 minimum/poem and 2 contributor's copies on publication for first North American serial rights; additional copies for $3.
Advice: "We look for fiction that is carefully worked out and that has a satisfying solution, and for poetry that is both original and accessible. Nothing can beat an involving story told in an original way with fresh language."

‡VOX, Because reaction is a sound, (I, II), Cleave Press, 2118 Central SE, Suite 6, Albuquerque NM 87106. Fax: (505)842-0533. Editor: Robbyn Sanger. Magazine: 8½×11; 40 pages; newsprint paper; newsprint cover; illustrations and photos. "Say it like it is. (Enough said.)" Triannually. Estab. 1994. Circ. 2,000.
Needs: Condensed/excerpted novel, erotica, ethnic/multicultural, experimental, feminist, gay, humor/satire, lesbian, literary, psychic/supernatural/occult, translations. "No formula fiction." Receives 50 mss/month. Buys 35 mss/issue; 105 mss/year. Publishes ms 1-4 months after acceptance. Recently published work by Hal Sirowitz, Ron Kolm, Alfred Vitale and Joe Maynard. Length: 500 words average; 5 words minimum; 1,500 words maximum. Publishes short shorts. Length: 25 plus words. Also publishes literary essays and poetry. Sometimes critiques or comments on rejected ms.
How to Contact: Send complete ms with a cover letter. Send first 20 pages only for longer works. Should include estimated word count and brief bio. Reports in 2-4 weeks on queries; 1-2 months on mss. Send SASE for reply, return of ms or send a disposable copy of ms. Simultaneous, reprint and electronic submissions OK. E-mail address: cleavepres@aol.com. Sample copy for $2. Fiction guidelines free for legal SASE.
Payment/Terms: Pays free subscription to magazine and 5 contributor's copies. Acquires one-time rights. Sends galleys to author (if requested). Not copyrighted. Sponsors contests.
Advice: "Get a sample copy before submitting! I love short shorts, novellas, too. Avoid long dull, overdone stuff."

♣WASCANA REVIEW OF CONTEMPORARY POETRY AND SHORT FICTION, (II), University of Regina, Regina, Saskatchewan S4S 0A2 Canada. Editor: Kathleen Wall. "Literary criticism, fiction and poetry for readers of serious fiction." Semiannually. Estab. 1966. Circ. 500.

Needs: Literary and humor. Upcoming themes: "30th Anniversary" issue (1996). Buys 8-10 mss/year. Receives approximately 20 unsolicited fiction mss/month. Agented fiction 5%. Length: no requirement. Occasionally recommends other markets.

How to Contact: Send complete ms with SASE. All contributors must include 3.5 floppy disk compatible with one of the following programs: ASCII; WordStar 3.0, 4.0 or 5.0; MS Word; MordPerfect 4.0, 5.0, 5.1, 6.1; SY Write; 8-bit ASCII; Writer; Multimate; DCL. Reports in 2 months on mss. Publishes ms an average of 6 months after acceptance. Sample copy for $5. Guidelines with SASE.

Payment/Terms: Pays $3/page for prose; $10/page for poetry; 2 contributor's copies on publication for first North American rights.

Advice: "Stories are often technically incompetent or deal with trite subjects. Usually stories are longer than necessary by about one-third. Be more ruthless in cutting back on unnecessary verbiage. All approaches to fiction are welcomed by the *Review* editors—but we continue to seek the best in terms of style and technical expertise. As our calls for submission state, the *Wascana Review* continues to seek . . . short fiction that combines craft with risk, pressure with grace."

WEBSTER REVIEW, (II), SLCC—Meramec, Meramec, % English Dept. 11333 Big Bend Rd., St. Louis MO 63122. (314)984-7542. Editors: Greg Marshall, Robert Boyd and Nancy Schapiro. Magazine: 5×8; 120 pages; 60 lb. white paper; 10pt. C1S; cover illustrations and photographs. "Literary magazine, international, contemporary. We publish many English translations of foreign fiction writers for academics, writers, discriminating readers." Annually. Estab. 1974.

Needs: Contemporary, literary, translations. No erotica, juvenile. Receives 100 unsolicited mss/month. Accepts 6-10 mss/year. Publishes ms 1 year or more after acceptance. Agented fiction less than 1%. Published work by Marco Lodoli and Barbara Eldridge. Publishes short shorts. Sometimes critiques rejected mss.

How to Contact: Send complete manuscript with cover letter. Reports in 2-4 months on mss. SASE. Simultaneous submissions OK. Sample copy for 6×9 SAE and 2 first-class stamps.

Payment/Terms: Pays contributor's copies. Acquires first rights.

WEIRDBOOK, (II), Box 149, Amherst Branch, Buffalo NY 14226. (716)839-2415. Editor: W. Paul Ganley. Magazine: 8½×11; 64 pages; self cover; illustrations. "Latter day 'pulp magazine' along the lines of the old pulp magazine *Weird Tales*. We tend to use established writers. We look for an audience of fairly literate people who like good writing and good characterization in their fantasy and horror fiction, but are tired of the clichés in the field." Semiannually. Estab. 1968. Circ. 1,000.

Needs: *Presently overstocked. Inquire first.* Fantasy, gothic (not modern) horror and psychic/supernatural. "No psychological horror; mystery fiction; physical horror (blood); traditional ghost stories (unless original theme); science fiction; swords and sorcery without a supernatural element; or reincarnation stories that conclude with 'And the doctor patted him on . . . THE END!' " Buys 8-12 mss/issue. Length: 15,000 words maximum. Also publishes poetry. Sometimes recommends other markets.

How to Contact: Send complete ms with SASE. Reports in 3 months on mss. Sample copy for $6.80. Guidelines for #10 SASE.

Payment/Terms: Pays 1¢/word minimum and 1 contributor's copy on publication ("part on acceptance only for solicited mss") for first North American serial rights plus right to reprint the entire issue.

Advice: "Read a copy and then some of the best anthologies in the field (such as DAW's 'Best Horror of the Year,' Arkham House anthologies, etc.) Occasionally we keep mss longer than planned. When sending a SASE marked 'book rate' (or anything not first class) the writer should add 'Forwarding Postage Guaranteed.' "

WELTER, (I, II), School of Communication Design, University of Baltimore, 1420 N. Charles St., Baltimore MD 21201-5779. (410)837-4200. Editors: Michael J. Cuneo and Stephen Greene. Editors' term ends 1996. Editors change each year. Magazine: 5½×8; 80 pages; 65 lb. paper; 80 lb. cover; illustrations. Annually. Estab. 1975. Circ. 500.

Needs: Ethnic/multicultural, experimental, feminist, gay, humor/satire, lesbian, literary. "No genre fiction." Receives 10 unsolicited mss/month. Accepts 3 mss/issue. Does not read mss between February 1 and August 1. Length: 2,500 words maximum. Publishes short shorts. Also publishes poetry. Sometimes critiques or comments on rejected ms.

How to Contact: Send complete ms with a cover letter. Should include estimated word count and 1-paragraph bio. "We look for bios that are as creative and individual as the author's work." Send SASE (or IRC) for return of ms or, preferably, send a disposable copy of ms. No simultaneous submissions. Sample copy for $2. Fiction guidelines for #10 SAE and 1 first-class stamp.

Payment/Terms: Pays 2 contributor's copies; additional copies for $2. Acquires one-time rights.

Advice: "All submissions are carefully read by the editors and the editorial board. The only thing that will make a piece stand out is high quality writing. Get a sample copy and see what we have just published. Avoid any hint of genre fiction."

WEST BRANCH, (II), Bucknell Hall, Bucknell University, Lewisburg PA 17837. Editors: K. Patten and R. Taylor. Magazine: 5½×8½; 96-120 pages; quality paper; illustrations; photos. Fiction and poetry for readers of contemporary literature. Biannually. Estab. 1977. Circ. 500.
Needs: Literary, contemporary, prose poems and translations. No science fiction. Accepts 3-6 mss/issue. Published work by Chuck Martin, David Milofsky and Sharon Sheehe Stark; published new writers within the last year. No preferred length.
How to Contact: Send complete ms with cover letter, "with information about writer's background, previous publications, etc." SASE. No simultaneous submissions. Reports in 6-8 weeks on mss. Sample copy for $3.
Payment/Terms: Pays 2 contributor's copies and one-year subscription; cover price less 25% discount charge for extras. Acquires first rights.
Advice: "Narrative art fulfills a basic human need—our dreams attest to this—and storytelling is therefore a high calling in any age. Find your own voice and vision. Make a story that speaks to your own mysteries. Cultivate simplicity in form, complexity in theme. Look and listen through your characters."

✦**WEST COAST LINE, A Journal of Contemporary Writing & Criticism, (II)**, 2027 E. Academic Annex, Simon Fraser University, Burnaby, British Columbia V5A 1S6 Canada. (604)291-4287. Fax: (604)291-5737. Managing Editor: Jacqueline Larson. Magazine: 6×9; 128-144 pages. "Poetry, fiction, criticism—modern and contemporary, North American, cross-cultural. Readers include academics, writers, students." Triannual. Estab. 1990. Circ. 600.
Needs: Ethnic/multicultural, experimental, feminist, gay, literary. "We do not publish journalistic writing or strictly representational narrative." Upcoming theme: "Contemporary American/British." Receives 30-40 unsolicited mss/month. Accepts 2-3 mss/issue; 3-6 mss/year. Publishes ms 2-6 months after acceptance. Length: 3,000-4,000 words. Publishes short shorts. Length: 250-400 words. Also publishes literary essays and literary criticism.
How to Contact: Send complete ms with a cover letter. "We supply an information form for contributors." Reports in 3 months. Send SASE for return of ms. No simultaneous submissions. Electronic submissions OK. Sample copy for $10. Fiction guidelines free.
Payment/Terms: Pays $3-8/page (Canadian); subscription; 1 contributor copy; additional copies for $6-8/copy, depending on quantity ordered. Pays on publication for one-time rights.
Advice: "Special concern for contemporary writers who are experimenting with, or expanding the boundaries of conventional forms of poetry, fiction and criticism; also interested in criticism and scholarship on Canadian and American modernist writers who are important sources for current writing. We recommend that potential contributors send a letter of enquiry or read back issues before submitting a manuscript."

WEST WIND REVIEW, (I), English Dept., Southern Oregon State College, Ashland OR 97520. (503)552-6518. Editor: Mitzi Miles-Kubota (1995-1996 school year). Editors change each year. Magazine: 5¾×8½; 150-250 pages; illustrations and photos. "Literary journal publishing prose/poetry/art. Encourages new writers, accepts established writers as well, with an audience of people who like to read anthologies." Annually. Estab. 1980. Circ. 500.
Needs: Adventure, erotica, ethnic/multicultural, experimental, fantasy, feminist, gay, historical (general), horror, humor/satire, lesbian, literary, mainstream/contemporary, mystery/suspense, psychic/supernatural/occult, regional, religious/inspirational, romance, science fiction, senior citizen/retirement, sports, translations, westerns, young adult/teen—"just about anything." Receives 6-60 unsolicited mss/month. Accepts 15-20 mss/issue. Does not read mss during summer months. Publishes ms almost immediately after acceptance. Published work by Lon Schneider, Bette Hosted and Christopher Danowski. Length: 3,000 words maximum. Publishes short shorts. Also publishes literary essays and poetry. Sometimes critiques or comments on rejected ms.
How to Contact: Send complete ms with a cover letter. Should include estimated word count and short bio. Reports in 2 weeks on queries; by May 1 on mss. Send SASE for reply, return of ms or send a disposable copy of ms. No simultaneous submissions. Sample copy for $12.50. Fiction guidelines free. Rarely reviews novels or short story collections.
Payment/Terms: Awards $25 prize for best fiction. Accepted authors receive 1 free copy. Authors retain all rights.
Advice: "Good writing stands out. Content is important but style is essential."

WESTERN HUMANITIES REVIEW, (III), % English Department, University of Utah, Salt Lake City UT 84112. (801)581-6070. Fax: (801)581-3392. Editor: Barry Weller. Fiction Editor: Karen Brennen. Magazine: 95-120 pages. Quarterly. Estab. 1947. Circ. 1,200.
Needs: Experimental, literary. Receives 75 unsolicited mss/month. Accepts 4-8 mss/issue; 15-25 mss/year. Does not read mss July-September. Publishes ms within 1-4 issues after acceptance. Published work by Stephen Dixon, Mark Halliday, Gary Krist, Diane Lefer and Joyce Carol Oates. Length: open. Publishes short shorts. Also publishes literary essays, literary criticism and poetry. Sometimes critiques or comments on rejected mss.

How to Contact: Send complete ms with a cover letter. Should include list of publications. Reports in 3 weeks on queries; 1-6 months on mss. Send SASE for reply, return of ms or send a disposable copy of ms. Simultaneous submissions OK. Sample copy for $6.
Payment/Terms: Pays 2 contributor's copies; additional copies for $3.50. Acquires first North American serial rights. Sends galleys to author.

‡**THE WESTERN POCKET, (I, IV)**, The 21st Communications Corp., 1415 Wewatta, Suite 102, Denver CO 80202. (303)623-6421. Fax: (303)623-7643. Editor: Glenn Meyers. Fiction Editor: Carson Reed. Magazine: 4×7; 64 pages; 60 lb. paper; 90 lb. coated cover; perfect-bound; illustrations and photos. Quarterly. Estab. 1995. Circ. 5,782.
Needs: Ethnic/multicultural, experimental (western based), historical, humor/satire, literary, regional, westerns. "No psychic, romance, science fiction, children's." Publishes special fiction issue or anthology. Receives 20-30 unsolicited mss/month. Accepts 3 mss/issue; 12 mss/year. Publishes ms 3-6 months after acceptance. Recently published work by Jean Huff, Carson Reed and Jess Quinlan. Length: 1,200 words average; 700 words minimum; 2,200 words maximum. Publishes short shorts. Also publishes literary essays and poetry. Sometimes critiques or comments on rejected ms.
How to Contact: Send complete ms with a cover letter. Phone calls or faxes acceptable. Should include estimated word count, short bio, Social Security number and list of publications. Reports in 4-6 weeks on queries; 2-3 months on mss. Send SASE for reply, return of ms or send a disposable copy of ms. Simultaneous, reprint and electronic submissions OK. E-mail address: xx1comm@aol.com. Sample copy for $3.95, 5×7 or 6×9 SAE and 78¢ postage. Fiction guidelines for #10 SASE. Reviews novels and short story collections. Send books to Mark Stevens.
Payment/Terms: Pays $50-300 and 2 contributor's copies on publication for first North American serial rights; additional copies for $2.35.
Advice: "Quality and imagination are good starting points. I want to have something stick with me when I've finished reading a story, some image or sentence that I can remember."

‡**WESTERN TALES MAGAZINE, (II)**, P.O. Box 33842, Granada Hills CA 91394. Editor: Dorman Nelson. Magazine: 8½×11; 100 pages; 60 lb. cover stock; b&w illustrations. Looks for "western stories and poetry for a family audience of all ages." Quarterly. Estab. 1993.
Needs: Westerns (frontier, traditional, young adult western). No porn or hard core violence. Publishes special fiction issue or anthology. Receives 150-200 mss/month. Accepts 26 mss/issue; 100 mss/year. Publishes ms 6 months after acceptance. Agented fiction 10%. Length: 4,000-5,000 words preferred. Publishes short shorts. Length: 1,000 words. Also publishes poetry.
How to Contact: Query first, send complete ms with a cover letter or submit through an agent. Should include short bio and social security number. Reports in 6 weeks. Send SASE for reply, return of ms or send a disposable copy of ms. Simultaneous and reprint submissions OK. Sample copy for $6. Fiction guidelines for #10 SAE.
Payment/Terms: Pays $100 (story); $25 (poetry); 1 contributor's copy on acceptance for first North American serial rights.
Advice: "*Western Tales* is a story, a fib, a trail-riding yarn, a boast or an embellishment of what really happened. We are looking for fiction stories with romance, laughter, shoot-em-ups, mystery and intrigue laced with boot'n'spurs'n'feathers, livestock, the wind-swept reaches, cowboys, Indians, soldiers, pioneering women and others that settled and moved about the land as well. These could be stories set in the past or in present day."

WESTVIEW, A Journal of Western Oklahoma, (II), Southwestern Oklahoma State University, 100 Campus Dr., Weatherford OK 73096-3098. (405)774-3168. Editor: Fred Alsberg. Magazine: 8½×11; up to 44 pages; 24 lb. paper; slick cover; illustrations and photographs. Quarterly. Estab. 1981. Circ. 800.
Needs: Contemporary, ethnic (especially Native American), humor, literary, prose poem. No pornography, violence, or gore. No overly sentimental. "We are particularly interested in writers of the Southwest; however, we accept work of quality from elsewhere." Receives 2-5 unsolicited mss/month. Accepts 10 ms/issue; 40 mss/year. Publishes ms 1 month-2 years after acceptance. Recently published work by Diane Glancy, Wendell Mayo, Jack Matthews and Pamela Rodgers. Length: 2,000 words average; 100 words minimum; 3,000 words maximum. Also publishes literary essays, literary criticism, poetry. Occasionally critiques rejected mss and sometimes recommends other markets.
How to Contact: Simultaneous submissions OK. Send complete ms with SASE. Reports in 1-2 months. "We welcome submissions on a 3.5 disk formatted for WordPerfect 5.0, IBM or Macintosh. Please include a hard copy printout of your submission."
Payment/Terms: Pays contributor's copies for first rights.

♣**WHETSTONE, (II)**, English Dept., University of Lethbridge, Lethbridge, Alberta T1K 3M4 Canada. (403)329-2373. Contact: Professor Martin Oordt. Magazine: 6×9; 90-140 pages; superbond paper; photos. Magazine publishing "poetry, prose, drama, prints, photographs and occasional music compositions for a general audience." Biannually. Estab. 1971. Circ. 500.

Needs: Experimental, literary, mainstream. "Interested in works by native writers/artists. Interested in multi-media works by individuals or collaborators." Write for upcoming themes. Accepts 1-2 ms/issue, 3-4 mss/year. Published new writers within the last year. Also publishes poetry, drama and art.

How to Contact: Send 2 short fictions or 6 poems maximum with SASE. Should include cover letter with author's background and experience. No simultaneous submissions. Reports in 5 months on mss. Publishes ms an average of 3-4 months after acceptance. Sample copy for $7 (Canadian) and 7½ × 10½ or larger SAE and 2 Canadian first-class stamps or IRCs.

Payment/Terms: Pays 1 contributor's copy. Holds copyright but allows work to revert back to writer.

Advice: "We seek most styles of quality writing. Avoid moralizing."

WHISKEY ISLAND MAGAZINE, (II), University Center 7, Cleveland State University, Cleveland OH 44115. (216)687-2056. Editor: Julie Candela. Editors change each year. Magazine of fiction and poetry, including experimental works, with no specific theme. Biannually. Estab. 1978. Circ. 2,500.

Needs: Receives 100 unsolicited fiction mss/month. Acquires 3-4 mss/issue. Length: 6,500 words maximum. Also publishes poetry (poetry submissions should contain no more than 10 pages).

How to Contact: Send complete ms with SASE. No simultaneous or previously published submissions. Reports in 2-4 months on mss. Sample copy for $5.

Payment/Terms: Pays 2 contributor's copies. Acquires one-time rights.

Advice: "Please include brief bio."

WHISPER, (II), Scream Press, P.O. Box 2345, Rohnert Park CA 94927. Editor: Anthony Boyd. Magazine: 8½ × 11; 20 pages; 20 lb. paper; illustrations and photographs. "Horror is *not* a theme. *Whisper* is general interest. Audience: youngest reader 10, oldest reader 75—all ages, all professions." Quarterly. Estab. 1987. Circ. 2,000.

● *Whisper* has become best known for "science fiction adventures."

Needs: Adventure, contemporary, fantasy, humor/satire, mystery/suspense, science fiction. "No gore, no porn." Receives 20 unsolicited mss/month. Accepts 1 ms/issue; 4 mss/year. Publishes ms 3-6 months after acceptance. Length: up to 1,700 words.

How to Contact: Send complete ms with cover letter. Include "anything I may find interesting. Tell me a joke so I'm in a good mood to read your story." Reports in 1 month on mss. SASE. Reprint submissions OK, if stated. No simultaneous submissions. E-mail address: whisper@crl.com. Sample copy for $2, but free on the World Wide Web: http://www.crl.com/~whisper/SPhome.html.

Payment/Terms: Pays in contributor's copies. Acquires one-time rights.

Advice: "I like a lot of what *Pandora* publishes, good plot, and some strong twists. I look for neatness, and appropriateness—I'm not interested in crude, violent drivel and stories that don't follow guidelines (length, etc.) are sent back unread."

WHISPERING PINES QUARTERLY, An Electronic Magazine of Character-Based Fiction, (I, II), Rose Creek Publishing, #201, 41 West Arlington Ave., St. Paul MN 55117. Editor: Craig Hansen. Electronic magazine: (currently in Macintosh and Windows formats; CD-ROM in 2-3 years); illustrations and photos. "Stories are a series of events that happen to people. *WPQ* seeks to promote character-based fiction of high quality, encouraging new and established writers to forget literary trends and return to the basics of good storytelling." Quarterly. Estab. 1994. Circ. 250-500.

Needs: Adventure, fantasy (contemporary, Twilight Zone-style), horror, mainstream/contemporary, mystery/suspense (amateur sleuth, private eye/hardboiled, romantic suspense), science fiction (soft/sociological sf, near future, sports. No erotica, westerns, or pure romances. No sword and sorcery. List of upcoming themes available for SASE. Publishes annual special fiction issue or anthology. Buys 6-12 mss/issue; 24-48 mss/year. Publishes ms 6 weeks-1 year after acceptance. Recently published work by Julia Numally Duncan, Charles Ghinga and Ruth Moose. Length: 5,000 words average; 500 words minimum; 25,000 words maximum. Also publishes poetry (usually by invitation only). Sometimes critiques or comments on rejected mss.

How to Contact: Send complete ms with a cover letter. Download fiction guidelines from fiction library of America Online. Should include estimated word count, bio (one page) and list of publications. Send computer disk with story on it in a Macintosh or Windows text-only file. Reports in 1-4 weeks on queries; 2-4 months on mss. SASE (or IRC) for reply or return of ms. Simultaneous, reprint and electronic submissions OK. E-mail address: wpines@winternet.com. World Wide Web address: http://www.winternet.com/~wpinesq/. Sample copy for $5; specify Mac or Windows format. Fiction guidelines for 9 × 13 SAE and 3 first-class stamps.

Payment/Terms: Pays $5-10 and 1 contributor's copy on publication. Acquires one-time electronic rights.

Advice: Looks for "strong, interesting characters in a well-told tale—it'll hook me every time. I'm not into gimmicks or tends, just tell an entertaining story as best you know how. Read good writers, good storytellers. Read Stephen King, John Irving, Max Allen Collins, William Goldman. Notice how they build character and plot—and emulate those lessons in your own work. I've seen too much trendy, stylistic, multicultural, and gimmicky fiction. I want to see more stories that grab me by the throat and don't let go until the final paragraph. Keep my attention—tell the best story you know how to tell."

THE JAMES WHITE REVIEW, A Gay Men's Literary Quarterly, (II, IV), The James White Review Association, 3356 Butler Quarter Station, Minneapolis MN 55403. (612)339-8317. Editors: Phil Willkie and David Rohlfing. Tabloid: 17×26; 16 pages; illustrations; photos. "We publish work by *male* gay writers—any subject for primarily gay and/or gay sensitive audience." Quarterly. Estab. 1983. Circ. 4,500.
Needs: Adventure, contemporary, experimental, gay, humor/satire, literary, prose poem, translations. No pornography. Receives 50 unsolicited fiction mss/month. Buys 3 mss/issue; 12 mss/year. Publishes ms 3 months or sooner after acceptance. Published work by Felice Picano and George Stambolian; published new writers within the last year. Length: 30 pages, double-spaced. Sometimes critiques rejected mss. Recommends other markets "when we can."
How to Contact: Send complete ms with cover letter and short bio. SASE. No simultaneous submissions. Reports in 2-3 months. Sample copy for $3. Fiction guidelines for $1.
Payment/Terms: Pays 2 contributor's copies and $50. Buys one-time rights; returns rights to author.
Advice: "We are publishing longer stories and serializing."

‡✿WHITE WALL REVIEW, 63 Gould St., Toronto, Ontario M5B 1E9 Canada. (416)977-1045. Editors change annually. Send mss to "Editors." Magazine: 5¾×8¾; 144-160 pages; professionally printed with glossy card cover; b&w photos and illustrations. "An annual using interesting, preferably spare art. No style is unacceptable." Annually. Estab. 1976. Circ. 500.
Needs: Nothing "boring, self-satisfied, gratuitously sexual, violent or indulgent." Accepts 10 mss/book. Accepts mss from September to 1st week in December of a given year. Recently published work by James Fitchette, Joe Peretz and Ruth Olsen Latta. Length: 3,000 words maximum.
How to Contact: Send complete ms with cover letter, SASE and $5 non-refundable reading fee. Include a short bio. Reports on mss "as soon as we can (usually in April or May)." Always comments on ms. No simultaneous submissions. Sample copy for $8.
Payment/Terms: Pays 1 contributor's copy. Acquires first or one-time rights.
Advice: "Keep it *short*. We look for creativity but not to the point of obscurity."

WICKED MYSTIC, (I, II, IV), P.O. Box 3087, Astoria NY 11103. (718)545-6713. Editor: Andre Scheluchin. Magazine: Full-sized; 76 pages; 20 lb. paper; 60 lb. 4-color cover. "Horror, gothic, gore, sex, violence, blood, death." Published 3 times/year. Estab. 1990. Circ. 10,000.
Needs: Explicit, gut-wrenching, brutally twisted, warped, sadistic, deathly, provocative, nasty horror. Receives 120 unsolicited mss/month. Acquires 10-15 mss/issue; 30-45 mss/year. Time between acceptance of the ms and publication varies. Recently published work by Michael Arnzen, Gregory Nyman, Michael Hemmingson and Scott Thomas. Length: 2,500 words preferred; 1,000 words minimum; 3,500 words maximum. Also publishes literary essays, literary criticism, art and poetry.
How to Contact: Send complete ms with cover letter. Should include estimated word count, short and basic bio, list of publications. Reports in 2-12 weeks. Send SASE for reply, return of mss or send a disposable copy of the ms. No simultaneous submissions. Electronic submissions OK. Sample copy for $5.95. Free fiction guidelines.
Payment/Terms: Pays 1 contributor's copy. Acquires first rights.
Advice: "Your story must have a bizarre twist to it and involve both sex and death. No predictability and no slow-moving pieces."

‡WIDENER REVIEW, (II), Widener University, One University Place, Chester PA 19013. (610)499-4342. Managing Editor: Leslie Cronin. Magazine: 5¼×8½; 80 pages. Fiction, poetry, essays, book reviews for general audience. Annually. Estab. 1984. Circ. 250.
Needs: Contemporary, experimental, literary, mainstream, regional, serialized/excerpted novel. Receives 15 unsolicited mss/month. Publishes 3-4 mss/issue. Does not read mss in summer. Publishes ms 3-9 months after acceptance. Length: 1,000 words minimum; 5,000 words maximum. Occasionally critiques rejected mss.
How to Contact: Send complete ms with cover letter. Reports in 3 months on mss. SASE for ms. No simultaneous submissions or reprints. Sample copy for $4.
Payment/Terms: Pays 1 contributor's copy; charge for extras. Acquires first serial rights.

THE W!DOW OF THE ORCH!D, (I, II, IV), Maudit Publications, 2101 Hazel Ave., Virginia MN 55792-3730. (218)749-8645. Editor: Emella Loran. Fiction Editor: Brad Meyers. Magazine: 7½×8; 40 pages; 20 lb. white paper; b&w illustrations, when available. Quarterly. Estab. 1994. Circ. 100.
● The magazine's name is written as the *W!DOW of the ORCH!D.*
Needs: Dark sykotic and experimental tales or poetry of erotica, fantasy, horror and psychic/supernatural/occult with no happy endings .... without a price, that is. "All tales must include one of the following: angels, demons, devils, ghouls, gods, monsters, shapeshifters, sykoz (psychos), vampires, wizardry, and whatever your devious mind in an utter state of severe sykosis can devise! None need to be of the supernatural." Upcoming themes: Oh Baby!; W!DOW of the ROSES?!?; dreamland; Blood; Short, Sweet, and Sour. List of upcoming themes available for SASE. Publishes annual fiction issue or anthology. Publishes ms 1-5 issues after acceptance. Length: 3,000 words average; 100 minimum; 5,000 words maximum. Publishes short

short stories. Also publishes poetry. Often critiques or comments on rejected mss.

How to Contact: Send complete ms with a cover letter or mail disk. (All tales longer than 5 pages send on disk. Can accept: ASCII, WP 6.0, and Microsoft Works 3.1 or less.) Must include estimated word count, bio (more than a list of publications!!) of about 30 words, and words that will blow us off our duffs. Reports in 3 weeks on queries; 1-4 months on mss; 1-2 months on artwork. Send SASE for reply, return of ms or send a disposable copy of ms. No simultaneous submissions. Sample copy $3 (make checks payable to Raquel Bober), 6×9 SAE and 3 first-class stamps. Fiction guidelines for #10 SASE.

Payment/Terms: Pays 1 contributor's copy; additional copies for $2 for 1-5; $1.50 for 6-10; and $1 for 11 or more. Acquires first North American serial rights or one-time rights.

Advice: "Don't worry about offending us. We want tales that are unique, highly imaginative, and well written. Mss are rejected here because they didn't stop our hearts, fry our minds, or claw at our souls. Don't bother sending us tales without structure or tales blatantly stolen from that great TV show you saw that night!"

WILDE OAKS, (II, IV), Billy DeFrank Lesbian/Gay Community Center, 175 Stockton Ave., San Jose CA 95126. (408)293-2429. Editor: Bill Olver. Magazine: 8½×5¼; 100 pages; 20 lb. white paper; glossy cover stock; 5-10 photographs/issue. "Wilde Oaks publishes work with lesbian, gay, bisexual or transgender themes only. With that in mind, we remain wide open to all genre, subjects, and forms. We seek work that speaks to our lives in all our diversity, appeals to our many interests, enlightens and entertains." Semiannually. Estab. 1992. Circ. 300.

Needs: Gay and lesbian: adventure, erotica, ethnic/multicultural, experimental, fantasy (science fantasy, sword and sorcery), feminist, humor/satire, literary, mainstream/contemporary, mystery/suspense, psychic/supernatural/occult, regional, science fiction, westerns. "We are not especially interested in children's/young adult—nothing dogmatically religious." List of upcoming themes available for SASE. Accepts 2-4 mss/issue; 6-8 mss/year. Does not read May, June, July, November, December, January. Publishes ms 1-2 months after acceptance. Published work by Klaus Merrell, Florence Pontius, Marc Lynx and Jason Whitaker. Length: 3,000 words preferred; Publishes short shorts. Also publishes literary essays and poetry; also photography, artwork, comics/cartoons. Sometimes critiques or comments on rejected mss.

How to Contact: Send complete ms with a cover letter. Should include estimated word count, 50-75 word bio and list of publications. Reports in 4 weeks on queries; 3 months on mss. Send a disposable copy of ms. Reprint and electronic submissions OK. Sample copy for $10. Fiction guidelines for #10 SAE and 2 first-class stamps.

Payment/Terms: Pays 1 contributor's copy; additional copies for $8. Acquires one-time rights.

Advice: "We look for excellence. We appreciate work that knows its target, aims squarely for it, and hits it. We do not judge detective fiction on the same scale as erotica or literary prose, etc." Looks for "work that reveals the person inside the writer while avoiding the see me/feel me clichés. Honesty is very attractive, but whining is not. We prefer literary work, but genre work is OK. We'd like more humor. We don't see near enough from people of color."

THE WILLIAM AND MARY REVIEW, (II), P.O. Box 8795, Campus Center, The College of William and Mary, Williamsburg VA 23187-8795. Contact: Editor. Magazine: 110 pages; graphics; photography. "We publish high quality fiction, poetry, essays, interviews with writers, and art. Our audience is primarily academic." Annually. Estab. 1962. Circ. 3,500.

● This magazine has received numerous honors from the Columbia Scholastic Press Association's Golden Circle Awards.

Needs: Literary, contemporary and humor. Receives approximately 90 unsolicited fiction mss/month. Accepts 9 mss/issue. Published work by Paul Wood, W.S. Penn, Amy Clampitt, Robert Hershon and Dana Gioia; published new writers within the last year. Length: 7,000 words maximum. Also publishes poetry. Usually critiques rejected mss.

How to Contact: Send complete ms with SASE and cover letter with name, address and phone number. "Cover letter should be as brief as possible." Simultaneous submissions OK. Reports in 2-4 months. All departments closed in June, July and August. Sample copy for $5.50. May review novels, poetry and short story collections.

Payment/Terms: Pays 5 contributor's copies; discounts thereafter. Acquires first rights.

Advice: "We want original, well-written stories. Staff requests names be attached separately to individual works. Page allotment to fiction will rise in relation to quality fiction received. The most important aspect of submitting ms is to be familiar with the publication and the types of material it accepts. For this reason, back copies are available."

‡WILLOW SPRINGS, (II), Eastern Washington University, 526 Fifth St., MS-1, Cheney WA 99004-2431. (509)458-6429. Editor: Nance Van Winckel. Magazine: 9×6; 128 pages; 80 lb. glossy cover. "*Willow Springs* publishes literary poetry and fiction of high quality, a mix of new and established writers." Semiannually. Estab. 1977. Circ. 1,200.

● *Willow Springs* is a member of the Council of Literary Magazines and Presses and AWP. The magazine has received grants from the NEA and a CLMP excellence award.

Needs: Parts of novels, short stories, literary, prose poems, poems and translations. "No genre fiction please." Receives 150 unsolicited mss/month. Accepts 2-4 mss/issue; 4-8 mss/year. Does not read mss May 15-September 15. Publishes ms 6 months to one year after acceptance. Recently published work by Alberto Rios, Alison Baker and Robin Hemley; published new writers within the last year. Length: 5,000 words minimum; 11,000 words maximum. Also publishes literary essays, literary criticism and poetry. Rarely critiques rejected mss.

How to Contact: Send complete ms with cover letter. Include short bio. No simultaneous submissions. Reports in 2 weeks on queries. Sample copy for $5.

Payment/Terms: Pays $20-50 and 2 contributor's copies for first North American rights.

Advice: "We hope to attract good fiction writers to our magazine, and we've made a commitment to publish three-four stories per issue. We like fiction that exhibits a fresh approach to language. Our most recent issues, we feel, indicate the quality and level of our commitment."

WIND MAGAZINE, (II), P.O. Box 24548, Lexington KY 40524. (606)885-5342. Co-editors: Charlie G. Hughes and Steven R. Cope. Magazine: 5½×8½; 100 pages. "Eclectic literary journal with stories, poems, book reviews from small presses, essays. Readership is students, professors, housewives, literary folk, adults." Semiannually. Estab. 1971. Circ. 450.

Needs: Literary, mainstream/contemporary, translations. Accepts 6 fiction mss/issue; 12 mss/year. Publishes ms less than 1 year after acceptance. Published work by Carolyn Osborn, Jane Stuart, David Shields, Lester Goldberg and Elisabeth Stevens. Length: 5,000 words maximum. Publishes short shorts, length: 300-400 words. Also publishes literary essays, literary criticism and poetry. Sometimes critiques or comments on rejected mss.

How to Contact: Send complete ms with a cover letter. Should include estimated word count and bio (50 words). Reports in 2 weeks on queries; 2 months on mss. Send SASE for reply, return of ms or send a disposable copy of ms. No simultaneous submissions. E-mail address: leafk@aol.com. Sample copy for $3.50. Reviews novels and short story collections from small presses.

Payment/Terms: Pays 1 contributor's copy; additional copies for $3.50. Acquires first North American serial rights and anthology reprint rights.

Advice: "The writing must have an impact on the reader; the reader must come away changed, perhaps haunted, or maybe smiling. There is nothing I like better than to be able to say 'I wish I had written that.' "

✦WINDSOR REVIEW, A Journal of the Arts, (II), Faculty of Arts, Dept. of English, University of Windsor, Windsor, Ontario N9B 3P4 Canada. Fiction Editor: Alistair MacLeod. Magazine/perfect bound book: 6×9; 110 pages; illustrations and photos. Semiannually. Estab. 1965. Circ. 250.

Needs: Literary. Publishes ms 6-9 months after acceptance. Length: 14,450 words average. Also publishes poetry. Length: 14,450 words average.

How to Contact: Send complete ms with a cover letter. Reports in 1 month on queries; 2 months on mss. Send SASE for reply, return of ms or send a disposable copy of ms. No simultaneous submissions. E-mail address: uwrevu@uwindsor.ca. Sample copy for $8. Free fiction guidelines.

Payment/Terms: Pays $50 and 1 contributor's copy on publication for all rights; additional copies available for $5.

WISCONSIN ACADEMY REVIEW, (II, IV), Wisconsin Academy of Sciences, Arts & Letters, 1922 University Ave., Madison WI 53705. (608)263-1692. Editor-in-Chief: Faith B. Miracle. Magazine: 8½×11; 48-52 pages; 75 lb. coated paper; coated cover stock; illustrations; photos. "The *Review* reflects the focus of the sponsoring institution with its editorial emphasis on Wisconsin's intellectual, cultural, social and physical environment. It features short fiction, poetry, essays, nonfiction articles and Wisconsin-related book reviews for people interested in furthering regional arts and literature and disseminating information about sciences." Quarterly. Estab. 1954. Circ. approximately 2,000.

Needs: Experimental, historical, humor/satire, literary, mainstream, prose poem. "Author must have a Wisconsin connection or fiction must be set in Wisconsin." Receives 5-6 unsolicited fiction mss/month. Accepts 1-2 mss/issue; 6-8 mss/year. Published new writers within the last year. Length: 1,000 words minimum; 4,000 words maximum; 3,000 words average. Also publishes poetry; "will consider" literary essays, literary criticism.

How to Contact: Send complete ms with SAE and state author's connection to Wisconsin, the prerequisite. Sample copy for $2. Fiction guidelines for SASE. Reviews books on Wisconsin themes.

Payment/Terms: Pays 3-5 contributor's copies. Acquires first rights on publication.

Advice: "Manuscript publication is at the discretion of the editor based on space, content, and balance. We do not use previously published poetry and fiction. We publish emerging as well as established authors; fiction and poetry, without names attached, are sent to reviewers for evaluation."

WISCONSIN REVIEW, (II), University of Wisconsin, Box 158, Radford Hall, Oshkosh WI 54901. (414)424-2267. Editor: Troy Schultz. Editors change every year. Send submissions to "Fiction Editor." Magazine: 6×9; 60-100 pages; illustrations. Literary prose and poetry. Triannual. Estab. 1966. Circ. 2,000.

Needs: Literary and experimental. Receives 30 unsolicited fiction mss each month. Published new writers within the last year. Length: up to 5,000 words. Publishes short shorts.

How to Contact: Send complete ms with SASE and cover letter with bio notes. Simultaneous submissions OK. Reports in 2-4 months. Publishes ms an average of 1-3 months after acceptance. Sample copy for $2.

Payment/Terms: Pays in contributor's copies. Acquires first rights.

Advice: "We look for well-crafted work with carefully developed characters, plots and meaningful situations. The editors prefer work of original and fresh thought when considering a piece of experimental fiction."

WOMEN'S HARPOON, (I, II), Women's Free Press, 57 S. Triangle Rd., Somerville NJ 08876. (908)359-1185. Editor: Holly Abbott. Magazine: 8½×11; 40 pages; 60 lb. paper; 80 lb. cover; illustrations and photos. "We publish women's humor by women for women." Bimonthly. Estab. 1993. Circ. 6,500.

• *Women's Harpoon* sponsors a "Funniest Woman in the World Contest." Write for information.

Needs: Humor. Planning future special fiction issue or anthology. Receives 50-100 unsolicited mss/month. Accepts 10-15 mss/issue. Publishes short shorts. Also publishes literary essays and literary criticism. Sometimes critiques or comments on rejected ms. Offers humor writer's group online with subscriptions.

How to Contact: Query first. Reports in 4-6 weeks. Send SASE for reply, return of ms or send a disposable copy of ms. No simultaneous submissions. Sample copy for $3.95, 9×12 SAE and $1.05 postage. Guidelines for #10 SASE.

Payment/Terms: Pays 3 contributor's copies. Acquires one-time rights.

Advice: "Make us laugh. Read your story to a friend—if they laugh (not smile, not snicker, but *laugh*), send it. We want originality—no preaching. No poetry, please. No sagas. No 'how to' unless it's wacky."

‡WOMEN'S WORK, The Sound Alternative to Good Housekeeping, (II), 606 Avenue A, Snohomish WA 98290. (206)568-5914. Fax: (206)568-1620. Editor: Andrea Damm. Magazine: 8×10½; 48 pages, bookstock paper; illustrations and photos. "A forum for dialogue among women of diverse cultural, economic, and generational backgrounds, celebrating women's creative expressions." Quarterly. Estab. 1991. Circ. 3,000.

Needs: Feminist, lesbian, women's issues. "No religious proselytizing." List of upcoming themes available for SASE. Receives 10 unsolicited mss/month. Buys 1-2 mss/issue; 6-12 mss/year. Publishes ms 2-6 months after acceptance. Recently published work by Sibyl James. Length: 3,000 words average; 5,000 words maximum. Publishes short shorts. Also publishes literary essays, literary criticism and poetry.

How to Contact: Send complete ms with cover letter. Should include estimated word count and 3-4 sentence bio. Reports in 2-3 months on queries; 3-4 months on mss. Send SASE for return of ms. Simultaneous, reprint and electronic submissions OK. E-mail address: dammit@eskimo.com. Sample copy for $4. Fiction guidelines for #10 SASE. Reviews novels or short story collections. Send books to Attn: Kathleen Waterbury, Book Editor.

Payment/Terms: Pays free subscription to the magazine and 2 contributor's copies; additional copies for $1. Acquires first North American serial rights.

Advice: Looking for "work that obviously 'touches a nerve'; both revealing the risks the writer is taking (revealing herself in her work) and challenging the audience to openly react to the work. Many of our writers are just beginning and many have gone on from being first published with us to publishing their first novel! We wish to nurture the creative process; even if we cannot publish their work, we encourage them to continue trying—other publishers, other manuscripts. Don't despair!"

THE WORCESTER REVIEW, Worcester Country Poetry Association, Inc., 6 Chatham St., Worcester MA 01609. (508)797-4770. Editor: Rodger Martin. Magazine: 6×9; 100 pages; 60 lb. white offset paper; 10 pt. C1S cover stock; illustrations and photos. "We like high quality, creative poetry, artwork and fiction. Critical articles should be connected to New England." Annually. Estab. 1972. Circ. 1,000.

Needs: Literary, prose poem. "We encourage New England writers in the hopes we will publish at least 30% New England but want the other 70% to show the best of writing from across the US." Receives 20-30 unsolicited fiction mss/month. Accepts 2-4 mss/issue. Publishes ms an average of 6 months to 1 year after acceptance. Agented fiction less than 10%. Published work by Debra Friedman and Carol Glickfeld. Length: 2,000 words average; 1,000 words minimum; 4,000 words maximum. Publishes short shorts. Also publishes literary essays, literary criticism, poetry. Sometimes critiques rejected mss and recommends other markets.

How to Contact: Send complete ms with cover letter. Reports in 2 weeks on queries; 5-6 months on mss. SASE. Simultaneous submissions OK if other markets are clearly identified. Sample copy for $4; fiction guidelines free.

✝ *The double dagger before a listing indicates that the listing is new in this edition. New markets are often the most receptive to submissions by new writers.*

Payment/Terms: Pays 2 contributor's copies and honorarium if possible for one-time rights.
Advice: "Send only one short story—reading editors do not like to read two by the same author at the same time. We will use only one. We generally look for creative work with a blend of craftsmanship, insight and empathy. This does not exclude humor. We won't print work that is shoddy in any of these areas."

‡WORDPLAY, (I, II), Wordplay Publishing, P.O. Box 2248, South Portland ME 04116-2248. (207)799-7041. Editor: Helen Peppe. Magazine: 8½×11; 24 pages; 60 lb. paper; medium to heavy cover; illustrations."*Wordplay*'s audience expectations are simply enjoyable stories—I do not accept what is considered 'sophisticated' or 'New Age.' " Quarterly. Estab. 1995. Circ. 500.
Needs: Condensed/excerpted novel, ethnic/multicultural, feminist, historical, humor/satire, literary, mainstream/contemporary, mystery/suspense. "No erotica, horror, gothic romance." Plans special fiction issue or anthology. Receives 150 unsolicited mss/month. Accepts 6-10 mss/issue; 30-50 mss/year. Publishes ms 6-12 months after acceptance. Recently published work by Jean Harmon, Dennis Salem, Thomas Carper and Betsy Sholl. Length: 12-1,500 words average; 7,500 words maximum. Publishes short shorts. Also publishes literary essays and poetry. Always critiques or comments on rejected ms.
How to Contact: Send complete ms with a cover letter. Should include estimated word count and bio. Reports in 2 weeks on queries; 1-2 months on mss. Send SASE for reply, return of ms or send a disposable copy of ms. Simultaneous and reprint submissions OK. Sample copy for $4. Fiction guidelines free.
Payment/Terms: Pays 1 contributor's copy; additional copies for $3.50. Acquires one-time rights. Sends galleys to author.
Advice: "Quality always makes a manuscript stand out. Even if I do not like the actual plot line, if it is well-written, I'll give it serious consideration. Submit again and again and do not get discouraged."

WORDS OF WISDOM, (II), 612 Front St., Glendora NJ 08029-1133. (609)863-0610. Editor: J.M. Freiermuth. Newsletter: 5½×8½; 60-80 pages; copy paper; some illustrations and photographs. "Fiction, satire, humorous poetry and travel for a general audience—80% of readers have B.A." Estab. 1981. Circ. 150.
Needs: Adventure, contemporary, ethnic, feminist, historical, humor/satire, mainstream, mystery/suspense (cozy, private eye), regional, western (adult, frontier, traditional). No religion, children's, gay, romance. Plans third "All Woman Author" issue (October). Receives 50-60 unsolicited mss/month. Accepts 15-20 mss/issue; 60-80 mss/year. Publishes ms 2-6 months after acceptance. Recently published work by Will Sarvis, Jay Liveson, Mary Winters, Lois Greene Stone, June King, Elissa Mathews, Ron Sklar and Irv Rosenthal; published first time writers last year. Length: 2,000-3,000 words average; 1,200 words minimum; 9,000 words maximum. Publishes short shorts. Length: "Long enough to develop a good bite." Sometimes critiques rejected mss and recommends other markets.
How to Contact: Send complete manuscript copy and/or DOS floppy with cover letter including "name, address, SASE." Reports in 2-12 weeks on mss. SASE. Simultaneous submissions OK. Accepts electronic submissions. Sample copy for $3 postpaid. Reviews novels and short story collections.
Payment/Terms: Pays subscription to magazine for first publication of story. Acquires one-time rights. Publication not copyrighted.
Advice: "If your story has a spark of life or a degree of humor that brings a smile to my face, you have a chance here. Most stories lack these two ingredients. Don't send something you wrote ten years ago."

WORLDS OF FANTASY & HORROR, (II), Terminus Publishing Co., Inc., 123 Crooked Lane, King of Prussia PA 19406-2570. Editor: Darrell Schweitzer. Magazine: 8½×11; 164 pages; white, non-glossy paper; glossy 4-color cover; illustrations. "We publish fantastic fiction, supernatural horror for an adult audience." Quarterly. Estab. 1923 (*Weird Tales*); 1994 (*Worlds of Fantasy & Horror*). Circ. 8,000.
Needs: Fantasy (science fantasy, sword and sorcery), horror, psychic/supernatural/occult, translations. "We want to see a wide range of fantasy, from sword and sorcery to supernatural horror. We can use some unclassifiables." Receives 400 unsolicited mss/month. Buys 8 mss/issue; 32 mss/year. Publishes ms 6-18 months after acceptance. Agented fiction 10%. Published work by Joyce Carol Oates, Ian Watson and Ramsey Campbell. Length: 4,000 words average; 15,000 words maximum (very few over 8,000). "No effective minimum. Shortest we ever published was about 100 words." Publishes short shorts. Also publishes poetry. Always critiques or comments on rejected ms.
How to Contact: Send complete ms with a cover letter. Should include estimated word count and list of publications (if relevant). Reports in 2-3 weeks on mss. Send SASE for reply, return of ms or send a disposable copy of ms. No simultaneous submissions. No reprint submissions, "but will buy first North American rights to stories published overseas." Sample copy for $4.95. Fiction guidelines for #10 SASE. Reviews novels and short story collections relevant to the horror/fantasy field. Send books to S.T. Joshi, 10 W. 15th St., #312, New York NY 10011 or Douglas Winter, 506 Crown View Dr., Alexandria VA 22314.
Payment/Terms: Pays 3¢/word minimum and 2 contributor's copies for first North American serial rights plus anthology option. Sends galleys to author.
Advice: "We look for imagination and vivid writing. Read the magazine. Get a good grounding in the contemporary horror and fantasy field through the various 'best of the year' anthologies. Avoid the obvious cliches of technicalities of the hereafter, the mechanics of vampirism, generic Tolkien-clone fantasy. In

general, it is better to be honest and emotionally moving rather than clever. Avoid stories which have nothing of interest save for the allegedly 'surprise' ending."

THE WORMWOOD REVIEW, (II, IV), P.O. Box 4698, Stockton CA 95204. (209)466-8231. Editor: Marvin Malone. Magazine: 5½×8½; 48 pages; 60 lb. matte paper; 80 lb. matte cover; illustrations. "Concentrated on the prose-poem specifically for literate audience." Quarterly. Estab. 1959. Circ. 700.
Needs: Prose poem. No religious or inspirational. Receives 500-600 unsolicited mss/month. Buys 30-40 mss/issue; 120-160 mss/year. Publishes 6-18 months after acceptance. Published work by Charles Bukowski and Dan Lenihan. Length: 300 words preferred; 1,000 words maximum. Critiques or comments on rejected mss.
How to Contact: Send complete ms with cover letter. Reports in 1-2 months. SASE. No simultaneous submissions. Sample copy for $4. Fiction guidelines for #10 SASE.
Payment/Terms: Pays $12-140 or equivalent in contributor's copies for all rights, but reassigns rights to author on written request.
Advice: A manuscript that stands out has "economical verbal style coupled with perception and human values. Have something to say—then say it in the most effective way. Do *not* avoid wit and humor."

WRITERS' FORUM, (II), University of Colorado at Colorado Springs, Colorado Springs CO 80933-7150. Editor: C. Kenneth Pellow. "Ten to fifteen short stories or self-contained novel excerpts published once a year along with 25-35 poems. Highest literary quality only: mainstream, avant-garde, with preference to western themes. For small press enthusiasts, teachers and students of creative writing, commercial agents/publishers, university libraries and departments interested in contemporary American literature." Estab. 1974.
Needs: Contemporary, ethnic (Chicano, Native American, not excluding others), literary and regional (West). Receives approximately 40 unsolicited fiction mss each month and will publish new as well as experienced authors. Published fiction by Robert Olen Butler, Charles Baxter and Gladys Swan; published many new writers within the last year. Length: 1,500-8,500 words. Also publishes literary essays, literary criticism, poetry. Critiques rejected mss "when there is time and perceived merit."
How to Contact: Send complete ms and letter with relevant career information with SASE. Prefers submissions between September and February. Simultaneous submissions OK. Reports in 3-5 weeks on mss. Publishes ms an average of 6 months after acceptance. Sample back copy $7 to *NSSWM* readers. Current copy $10. Check payable to "Writers' Forum."
Payment/Terms: Pays 2 contributor's copies. Cover price less 50% discount for extras. Acquires one-time rights. Rights revert to author.
Advice: "Read our publication. Be prepared for constructive criticism. We especially seek submissions that show immersion in place (trans-Mississippi West) and development of credible characters. Turned off by slick content. Probably the TV-influenced fiction with trivial dialogue and set-up plot is the most quickly rejected. Our format—a 5½×8½ professionally edited and printed paperback book—lends credibility to authors published in our imprint."

WRITER'S GUIDELINES, A Roundtable for Writers and Editors, (I, II), Salaki Publishing, Box 608, Pittsburg MO 65724. Phone/fax: (417)993-5544. Editor: Susan Salaki. Magazine: 8½×11; 16 pages; 60 lb. opaque; illustrations and photos. Bimonthly. Estab. 1988. Circ. 1,000.
Needs: Open. Receives 20 unsolicited mss/month. Buys 1 ms/issue; 6 mss/year. Publishes ms-3 months after acceptance. Length: 1,000 words maximum. Also publishes literary essays and literary criticism. Critiques or comments on rejected mss.
How to Contact: Send complete ms. Should include estimated word count and bio (100 words). Reports in 1 week. SASE for reply or send a disposable copy of ms. Sample copy for $4. Reviews novels or short story collections.
Payment/Terms: Pays $0-25 and 1 contributor's copy on acceptance for first rights.
Advice: "Don't try to write. Just tell a story."

WRITERS' INTERNATIONAL FORUM, (I), (formerly *Writers' Open Forum*), Bristol Publishing, P.O. Box 516, Tracyton WA 98393. Editor: Sandra E. Haven. Magazine: 7½×8½; 40 pages; slick cover; illustrations. "*Writers' International Forum* is the only international magazine specifically designed to help new writers improve their marketability and writing skills through our unique peer critique process. We offer detailed information on writing, market listings plus print several stories and essays per issue. Some critiques on our printed stories are published; all are mailed on to originating author." Bimonthly. Estab. 1990.
● For more, see the article, "The Ethical Dilemma in Fiction" by Sandra Haven in the 1995 edition of this book.
Needs: Adventure, childrens/juvenile (8-12 years), fantasy, historical, humor/satire, mainstream/contemporary, mystery/suspense, psychic/supernatural/occult, regional, romance (contemporary, young adult), science fiction, senior citizen/retirement, sports, westerns, young adult/teen. "No graphic sex, violence, vignettes or wildly experimental formats." Prints special Juniors Edition issue. Buys 7-12 mss/issue; 42-72 mss/year. Publishes ms 4 months after acceptance. Length: 100 words minimum; 2,000 words maximum. Publishes

short shorts. Includes personal response on rejected mss "that have followed our guidelines" and critique on subscribers' mss.

How to Contact: Send complete ms with a cover letter. Should include brief bio. Reports in 2 months on mss. Send SASE for reply. Sample copy for $3.50; $5 for sample of a special Juniors Edition issue. Fiction guidelines for #10 SASE.

Payment/Terms: Pays $5 minimum plus 2 contributor's copies on acceptance; additional copies for authors at discounted rates. Acquires first rights.

Advice: "We emphasize the classic storyline: a protagonist who faces an immediate challenge, confronts obstacles, and finally resolves the situation. It may be a chapter from a book or journal, but must be so stated in the cover letter and still suit our requirements."

WRITER'S KEEPER, (I, II, IV), Pyx Press, P.O. Box 922648, Sylmar CA 91392-2648. Editor: C. Darren Butler. Newsletter: 8½×11; 2-4 pages, 20 lb. paper. "All works must be about writing." Quarterly. Estab. 1993. Circ. 800.

● Pyx Press is a member of the Council of Literary Magazines and Presses. See listings for *A Theater of Blood* and *Magic Realism* also published by Pyx Press.

Needs: Writing-related: fantasy, humor/satire, literary. Receives 50 unsolicited mss/month. Buys 0-3 mss/issue; 2-6 mss/year. Publishes ms within 8 months after acceptance. Publishes short shorts only. Length: 200 words preferred; 300 words maximum. Also publishes literary essays and poetry. Sometimes critiques or comments on rejected ms.

How to Contact: Send complete ms with a cover letter. Should include estimated word count, 1-paragraph bio and list of publications. Reports in 4 weeks on queries; 1-3 months, occasionally longer, on mss. Send SASE for reply, return of ms or send a disposable copy of ms. Simultaneous and reprint submissions OK. Sample copy for #10 SASE. Fiction guidelines for #10 SASE. Reviews novels and short story collections.

Payment/Terms: Pays $1 and 3-issue subscription including 1 contributor's copy on publication for first North American serial rights or one-time rights.

‡WRITES OF PASSAGE, The Literary Journal for Teenagers, (I, II, IV), , Writes of Passage USA, Inc., 817 Broadway, 6th Floor, New York NY 10003. (212)473-7564. Editor: Laura Hoffman. Fiction Editor: Wendy Mass. Magazine: 5½×8½; 100 pages; 60 lb. offset paper; 10 pt. cover; illustrations/photos only on cover; no artwork within magazine. "*Writes of Passage* is designed to publish the creative writing (poems and short stories) of teenagers across the country. We review work from high school and Junior high school students across the country on all topics." Semiannually. Estab. 1994. Circ. 2,000.

Needs: "We accept short stories on all topics written by preteens and teens." Adventure, children's/juvenile (10-12 years), ethnic/multicultural, experimental, fantasy, feminist, gay, historical, horror, humor/satire, lesbian, literary, mainstream/contemporary, mystery/suspense, psychic/supernatural/occult, regional, religious/inspirational, romance, science fiction, sports, westerns, young adult/teen. Receives 50 unsolicited mss/month. Buys 50 mss/issue; 100 mss/year. "Issues are published in the fall and spring so publication of mss depend on when they are received." Length: 2,000 words average; 5,000 words maximum. Publishes short shorts. Also publishes poetry.

How to Contact: Send complete ms with a cover letter. Teachers may submit the work of their students as a group. Should include bio with SASE and contact information. Send SASE for reply or send disposable copy of the ms. Simultaneous and electronic submissions OK. E-mail address: wp usa@aol.com. Sample copy for $6.

Payment/Terms: Pays 2 contributor's copies; additional copies $6 for each copy up to 10; 10 or more copies are $5 each. Rights revert back to the author.

Advice: Looking for "original work, clearly written, poignant subject matter for teen readers. We are interested in more short stories, particularly about teens."

WRITING FOR OUR LIVES, Creative Expressions in Writing by Women, (I, IV), Running Deer Press, 647 N. Santa Cruz Ave., Annex, Los Gatos CA 95032. (408)354-8604. Editor: Janet M. McEwan. Magazine: 5¼×8¼; 80 pages; 70 lb. recycled white paper; 80 lb. recycled cover. "*Writing For Our Lives* is a periodical which serves as a vessel for poems, short fiction, stories, letters, autobiographies, and journal excerpts from the life stories, experiences and spiritual journeys of women. Audience is women and friends of women." Semiannually. Estab. 1992. Circ. 700.

Needs: Ethnic/multicultural, experimental, feminist, humor/satire, lesbian, literary, translations, "autobiographical, breaking personal or historical silence on any concerns of women's lives. Women writers only, please. We have no preannounced themes." Receives 15-20 unsolicited mss/month. Accepts 10 mss/issue; 20 mss/year. Publishes ms 2-24 months after acceptance. Length: 2,100 words maximum. Publishes short shorts. Also publishes poetry. Sometimes critiques or comments on rejected mss.

How to Contact: Send complete ms with a cover letter. Reports in 1-8 months. "Publication dates are May and November. Closing dates for mss are 2/15 and 8/15. I report on mss within 2 months following each closing date." Send 2 SASE's for reply, and also sufficient for return of ms if desired. Simultaneous and reprint submissions OK. Sample copy for $6 (in California add 7.75% sales tax), $8 overseas. Fiction guidelines for #10 SASE.

Payment/Terms: Pays 2 contributor's copies; additional copies for 50% discount and 1 year subscription at 50% discount. Acquires one-time rights in case of reprints and first world-wide English language serial rights.

Advice: "I welcome your writing. I like many more pieces than I can print. If I don't select yours this time, try again!"

THE WRITING ON THE WALL, (I), P.O. Box 8, Orono ME 04473. Editor: Scott D. Peterson. Magazine: 8½×11; 22 pages; 70 lb. paper; 70 lb. cover; illustrations and photographs. "Our goal is to combat the negativity of the mass media, build community, and provide a voice for the 20-something generation." Semiannually. Estab. 1992. Circ. 100.

Needs: Literary, mainstream/contemporary. Will also consider novel excerpts. List of upcoming themes available for SASE. Receives 20-30 unsolicited mss/month. Accepts 3-4 mss/issue; 6-8 mss/year. Publishes ms 2-3 months after acceptance. Published work by Lenore Baeli Wang, Carolee Brockmann and Greg Laughlin. Length: 2,000 words preferred; 500 words minimum; 3,000 words maximum. Publishes short shorts. Publishes literary essays, literary criticism and poetry. Sometimes critiques or comments on rejected mss.

How to Contact: Send complete ms with a cover letter. Should include estimated word count and bio (less than 50 words). Reports in 2 weeks on queries; 3 months on mss. Send SASE for reply, return of ms or send a disposable copy of ms. Reprint and electronic submissions OK. E-mail address: scottp@Maine.Maine.edu. Sample copy for $3. Fiction guidelines for #10 SASE.

Payment/Terms: Pays 2 contributor's copies; additional copies for $2. Acquires one-time rights.

Advice: "We're looking for fiction that edifies as well as entertains—especially stories that send readers away with a sense of positive action. Write honestly and examine your stuff for TV sitcom or movie plot/ characters."

XAVIER REVIEW, (I, II), Xavier University, Box 110C, New Orleans LA 70125. (504)486-7411, ext. 7481. Editor: Thomas Bonner, Jr. Magazine of "poetry/fiction/nonfiction/reviews (contemporary literature) for professional writers/libraries/colleges/universities." Semiannually. Estab. 1980. Circ. 500.

Needs: Contemporary, ethnic, experimental, historical (general), literary, Latin-American, prose poem, Southern, religious, serialized/excerpted novel, translations. Receives 30 unsolicited fiction mss/month. Accepts 2 mss/issue; 4 mss/year. Length: 10-15 pages. Occasionally critiques rejected mss.

How to Contact: Send complete ms. SASE. Sample copy for $5.

Payment/Terms: Pays 2 contributor's copies.

XIB, (II), P.O. Box 262112, San Diego CA 92126. Editor: Tolek. Magazine: 7×8½; 68 pages; offset basis 70 paper; 12 point gloss cover; 25-30 illustrations; 15-20 b&w photos. "Audience mostly of poets, hence prefer fiction concise and compact, more like prose-poem form. Published every 9 months. Estab. 1991. Circ. 300.

Needs: Ethnic/multicultural, experimental, fantasy (science fantasy, sword and sorcery), feminist, gay, historical (general), horror, humor/satire, lesbian, literary, psychic/supernatural/occult, regional, science fiction (hard science, soft/sociological), senior citizen/retirement, translations. No childrens or romance. Receives 5-10 unsolicited mss/month. Accepts 2-4 mss/issue; 4-8 mss/year. Publishes ms 1-6 months after acceptance. Recently pubilshed work by Robert Nagler, D.F. Lewis, Richard Ploetz, Jean E. Bennett and Stephen Fried. Length: 1,000 words average; 2,000 words maximum. Publishes short shorts. Also publishes poetry. Seldom critiques or comments on rejected mss.

How to Contact: Send complete ms with a cover letter. Reports in 2-3 weeks. Send SASE (or IRC) for reply, return of ms or send a disposable copy of ms. Sample copy for $5. Fiction guidelines for #10 SASE. Please make checks payable to *Tolek*.

Payment/Terms: Pays 1 contributor's copy; additional copies for $3 each plus $2 s&h. Acquires one-time rights.

XTREME, The Magazine of Extremely Short Fiction, P.O. Box 678383, Orlando FL 32867-8383. Editor: Rho Wiley. Magazine: 8½×11; 4 pages; heavy bond paper and cover. "Xtreme, the magazine of extremely short fiction, publishes fiction of EXACTLY 250 words. Fiction is considered on the basis of merit only. We feel that the 250 word format affords an opportunity for all writers to push the limits of the language." Semiannually. Estab. 1993. Circ. 500.

Needs: Humor/satire, literary, mainstream/contemporary. Receives 25-30 unsolicited mss/month. Accepts 10 mss/issue; 20 mss/year. Publishes ms 6 months after acceptance. Length: exactly 250 words. Sometimes critiques or comments on rejected mss.

How to Contact: Send complete ms with a cover letter. Reports in 6 weeks on queries; up to 6 months on mss. Send SASE for reply or return of ms. No simultaneous submissions. E-mail address: rhowiley@aol.com. Sample copy for 9×12 SAE and 2 first-class stamps. Fiction guidelines included with sample copy.

Payment/Terms: Pays 3 contributor's copies for first North American serial rights.

Advice: Looks for "the ability to tell a complete story in the boundaries of the 250 word format. A succinct use of the language always stands out. Work with the form. Try to push the limits of what can happen in only 250 words."

‡YARNS AND SUCH, (I, IV), Creative With Words Publications, Box 223226, Carmel CA 93922. Editors: Brigitta Geltrich and Bert Howes. Editors rotate. Booklet: 5½×8½; approximately 60 pages; bond paper; illustrations. Folklore. Annually. Estab. 1975. Circ. varies.

Needs: Ethnic, humor/satire, mystery/suspense (amateur sleuty, private eye), regional, folklore. "Once a year we publish an anthology of the writings of young writers, titled: *We are Writers Too!*" No violence or erotica, religious fiction. Upcoming themes: "Life's Important Things," "Pets," "Nature." List of upcoming themes available for SASE. Receives 100 unsolicited fiction mss/month. Does not read mss July-August. Publishes ms 2-6 months after acceptance. Publishes after set deadlines: after July 31 or December 31 of any given year. Published new writers within the last year. Length: 1,000 words average. Critiques rejected mss "when requested, *then we charge $20/prose, up to 1,000 words.*"

How to Contact: Query first or send complete ms with cover letter and SASE. "Reference has to be made to which project the manuscript is being submitted. Unsolicited mss without SASE will be destroyed after holding them 1 month." Reports in 2 weeks on queries; 2 months on mss; longer on specific seasonal anthologies. No simultaneous submissions. Accepts electronic submissions via Radio Shack Model 4/6 disk and Macintosh. Sample copy price $5 for children's issues, $6 for adult issues. Fiction guidelines for #10 SASE.

Payment/Terms: No payment. Acquires one-time rights. 20% reduction on each copy ordered.

Advice: "We have increased the number of anthologies we are publishing and offer a greater variety of themes. We look for clean family-type fiction."

YELLOW SILK: Journal of Erotic Arts, (II), Verygraphics, Box 6374, Albany CA 94706. (510)644-4188. Editor/Publisher: Lily Pond. Magazine: 8½×11; 60 pages; matte coated stock; glossy cover stock; 4-color illustrations; photos. "We are interested in nonpornographic erotic literature: joyous, mad, musical, elegant, passionate. 'All persuasions; no brutality' is our editorial policy. Literary excellence is a priority; innovative forms are welcomed, as well as traditional ones." Quarterly. Estab. 1981. Circ. 16,000.

Needs: Comics, erotica, ethnic, experimental, fantasy, feminist/lesbian, gay, humor/satire, literary, prose poem, science fiction and translations. No "blow-by-blow" descriptions; no hackneyed writing except when used for satirical purposes. Nothing containing brutality. Buys 4-5 mss/issue; 16-20 mss/year. Recently published work by Angela Carter, Robert Silverberg, Louise Erdrich and Galway Kinnell; published new writers within the last year. Length: no preference. Occasionally critiques rejected ms.

How to Contact: Send complete ms with SASE and include short, *personal* bio notes. No queries. No pre-published material. No simultaneous submissions. Name, address and phone number on each page. Submissions on disk OK *with* hard copy only. Reports in 3 months on mss. Publishes ms up to 3 years after acceptance. Sample copy for $7.50.

Payment/Terms: Pays 3 contributor's copies plus competitive payment on publication for all periodical and anthology rights for one year following publication, at which time rights revert back to author; and nonexclusive reprint and anthology rights for the duration of the copyright.

Advice: "Read, read, read! Including our magazine—plus Nabokov, Ntozake Shange, Rimbaud, Virginia Woolf, William Kotzwinkle, James Joyce. Then send in your story! Trust that the magazine/editor will not rip you off—they don't. As they say, 'find your own voice,' then trust it. Most manuscripts I reject appear to be written by people without great amounts of writing experience. It takes years (frequently) to develop your work to publishable quality; it can take many rewrites on each individual piece. I also see many approaches to sexuality (for my magazine) that are trite and not fresh. The use of language is not original, and the people do not seem real. However, the gems come too, and what a wonderful moment that is. Please don't send me anything with blue eye shadow."

YOUNG JUDAEAN, (IV), Hadassah Zionist Youth Commission, 50 W. 58th St., New York NY 10019. (212)303-4575. National Education Supervisor: Sharon Schoenfeld. Magazine: 8½×11; 16 pages; illustrations. "*Young Judaean* is for members of the Young Judaea Zionist youth movement, ages 8-12." Quarterly. Estab. 1910. Circ. 4,000.

Needs: Children's fiction including adventure, ethnic, fantasy, historical, humor/satire, juvenile, prose poem, religious, science fiction, suspense/mystery and translations. "All stories must have Jewish relevance." Receives 10-15 unsolicited fiction mss/month. Publishes ms up to 2 years after acceptance. Buys 1-2 mss/issue; 10-20 mss/year. Length: 500 words minimum; 800 words maximum.

How to Contact: Send complete ms with SASE. Reports in 3 months on mss. Sample copy for 75¢. Free fiction guidelines.

Payment/Terms: Pays 5 free contributor's copies.

Advice: "Stories must be of Jewish interest—lively and accessible to children without being condescending."

INSIDER VIEWPOINT

Writing Erotica Requires Using Your Senses

Sex was not the first thing on editor Lily Pond's mind in 1981 when she founded *Yellow Silk: Journal of Erotic Arts.* "I wanted to start a literary magazine," she says, "but one that would stand out from the competition. Since most of my favorite stuff is erotica, it seemed a natural fit."

It is important to Pond that a writer working in this area be "comfortable with the subject matter. Some writers feel the only way to write about sex is via the limited format and vocabulary of what is already available. Even they (in addition to American culture in general) do not feel sex is a legitimate topic for serious writing."

Lily Pond

A staunch defender of the genre, Pond makes her point succinctly, "Why should good literature be about death and how deeply you feel about someone dying and not about making out in the back seat of a car and how deeply you feel about that?"

The result is perhaps the most venerated publication in its field, often imitated in its 15-year history, but never matched for its insistence on quality writing, including that of William Kotzwinkle and Gary Soto. The content focuses on erotica but this can, Pond insists, take many forms.

"Each issue has a theme. Examples are old age, science fiction, nature/botanical issues," explains Pond. When writing erotica, she says, writers should think about sex as another sense. They should imbue their stories with yet another form of sensual detail—the sense of sex—as well as that of sight, touch or taste.

Despite the magazine's unique niche in publishing, Pond says her requirements are not unusual. "I look for good writing, a clear and honest voice, original use of language and strength of style—the same criteria any literary editor uses when selecting fiction." She has accepted submissions that vary in length from one page to nearly an entire issue. "The story has to be complete, the characters have to be real. If the writing is good, there are no other requirements."

Yellow Silk receives about 10,000 submissions a year, most of which are unsolicited. Unfortunately, many of these are not appropriate for the magazine. "I read the first page . . . maybe," she confesses. "No cover letter telling me how much my readers will enjoy your work is going to convince me of anything. Either the writing is good or it isn't, and it simply does not take an experienced editor long to determine that."

Though not a fan of experimental writing (she says she feels it's often a coverup for weak writing), Pond insists there is no one way to write about sex, no one way to tell any story. "There are as many different ways to write as there are writers."

Pond offers a word of caution and encouragement to aspiring writers: "Writing is just like any other skill—baking bread or playing the piano. You can't expect your first effort to be your best effort. It is a skill that can be learned only by hard work and diligence, taking the time to find out what works and what doesn't, developing the courage to write honestly. Give your writing as much respect as you give any other work you do."

—*Katie Carroll*

‡**ZEPHYR, A Literary and Arts Magazine, (II)**, P.O. Box 435, Middletown CT 06457. Phone/fax: (203)349-9082. Editor: Desirée Bermani. Magazine: 8½×11; 16-20 pages; 40 lb. paper; 80 lb. patina cover; illustrations and photos. "Our policy is merely to publish the best quality fiction, poetry, artwork and photographs possible. We expect to reach a literary/academic audience but are also trying to broaden our audience beyond the usual pool of writers and gain more interest in the community and among youth. We want to offer a place where readers can turn to for consistently good writing as well as a new outlet in which writers can publish." Estab. 1995. Circ. 500.

Needs: Condensed/excerpted novel, ethnic/multicultural, feminist, gay, lesbian, literary, serialized novel, translations. Plans special fiction issue or anthology. Receives 20-30 unsolicited mss/month. Buys 3-4 mss/issue; 15-20/year. Publishes ms 3-6 months after acceptance. Also publishes poetry. Sometimes critiques or comments on rejected ms ("if author requests").

How to Contact: Query first. Should include bio. Reports in 4-6 weeks on queries; 2-3 months on mss, only if SASE included. Send SASE for reply, return of ms or send disposable copy of ms. Sample copy for $4, SAE and 5 first-class stamps. Fiction guidelines for SASE. Reviews novels or short story collections.

Payment/Terms: Pays 3 contributor's copies; additional copies for $4. Acquires first North American serial rights. Sends galleys to author.

Advice: "Quality is our foremost criterion. Manuscripts that stand out are well-written, well thought out, with new ideas, and a sense of self and purpose. Although we are interested in helping unpublished writers as much as possible, we are mostly geared toward serious writers who know their craft. Please avoid contrite, pretentious works that may be of interest to you and concentrate on refining thoughtful and thought-provoking pieces with a broad human appeal. Avoid sending haphazard works in progress. We are willing to work with writers when we are able to help direct them toward a better manuscript, but this does not mean that we are in a position to rewrite. Please send only your best, polished work."

ZERO HOUR, "Where Culture Meets Crime," (I, II, IV), Box 766, Seattle WA 98111. (206)621-8829. Editor: Jim Jones. Newsprint paper; illustrations and photos. "We are interested in fringe culture. We publish fiction, poetry, essays, confessions, photos, illustrations and interviews, for young, politically left audience interested in current affairs, non-mainstream music, art, culture." Semiannually. Estab. 1988. Circ. 3,000.

Needs: Confessions, erotica, ethnic, experimental, feminist, gay, humor/satire, psychic/supernatural/occult and translations. "Each issue revolves around an issue in contemporary culture: cults and fanaticism, addiction, pornography, etc." No romance, inspirational, juvenile/young, sports. Upcoming themes: "True Life," "Lived-to-Tell," "Exposés," "Pulp Thrillers," "Celebrity Secrets," "Modern Urban Folk Tales," "Rock 'n' Roll." Receives 5 unsolicited mss/month. Accepts 3 mss/issue; 9 mss/year. Publishes ms 2-3 months after acceptance. Published work by Jesse Bernstein, Rebecca Brown, Denise Ohio and Vaginal Davis. Length: 1,200 words average; 400 words minimum; 5,000 words maximum. Publishes short shorts. Length: 400 words. Sometimes critiques rejected mss.

How to Contact: Query first. Reports in 2 weeks on queries; 1 month on mss. SASE. Simultaneous submissions OK. Sample copy for $3, 9×12 SAE and 5 first-class stamps. Fiction guidelines free. Reviews novels and short story collections.

Payment/Terms: Pays $25 per short story, $650 for novels for one-time rights. Sends galleys to author.

Advice: "Does it fit our theme? Is it well written, from an unusual point of view or on an unexplored/underexplored topic?"

ZUZU'S PETALS ANNUAL, A Yearly Anthology of the Written Arts, (II), P.O. Box 4476, Allentown PA 18105. (610)821-1324. Editor: T. Dunn. Magazine: 8½×11; 200 pages; 20 lb. paper; 64 lb. cover stock; black and white illustrations and photographs. "Arouse the senses; stimulate the mind." Estab. 1992. Circ. 350.

● *Zuzu's Petals* has been garnering praise from a variety of sources including *Library Journal* and *Factsheet 5.*

Needs: Ethnic/multicultural, feminist, gay, humor/satire, lesbian, literary, regional. No "romance, sci-fi, the banal, TV style plotting." Receives 110 unsolicited mss/month. Accepts 1-3 mss/issue; 4-12 mss/year. Publishes ms 4-6 months after acceptance. Agented fiction 10%. Recently published work by Norah Labiner, Jean Erhardt and LuAnn Jacobs. Length: 1,000 words minimum; 6,000 words maximum. Publishes short shorts. Length: 350 words. Also publishes literary essays, literary criticism and poetry. Sometimes critiques or comments on rejected mss.

How to Contact: Send complete ms with a cover letter. Should include estimated word count and list of publications. Reports in 2 weeks on queries; 2 weeks-2 months on mss. Send SASE (or IRC) for reply, return of ms or send a disposable copy of ms. Simultaneous and electronic submissions OK. E-mail address: zuzu@epix.net. Back issue for $5. Fiction guidelines free. Reviews novels and short story collections. Send to Doug DuCap, Reviewer.

Payment/Terms: Pays 1 contributor's copy for one-time rights; additional copies for $5.

Advice: Looks for "strong plotting and a sense of vision. Original situations and true to life reactions."

ZYZZYVA, the last word: west coast writers & artists, (II, IV), 41 Sutter St., Suite 1400, San Francisco CA 94104. (415)255-1282. Editor: Howard Junker. Magazine: 6×9; 160 pages; graphics; photos. "Literate" magazine. Quarterly. Estab. 1985. Circ. 4,500.

Needs: Contemporary, experimental, literary, prose poem. West Coast US writers only. Receives 300 unsolicited mss/month. Buys 5 fiction mss/issue; 20 mss/year. Agented fiction: 10%. Recently published work by Kate Braverman, Greg Sarris and William T. Vollmann; published new writers within the last year. Length: varies. Also publishes literary essays.

How to Contact: Send complete ms. "Cover letters are of minimal importance." Reports in 2 weeks on mss. SASE. No simultaneous submissions or reprints. Sample copy for $5. Fiction guidelines on masthead page.

Payment/Terms: Pays $50-250 on acceptance for first North American serial rights.

Advice: "Keep the faith."

International literary and small circulation magazines

The following is a list of literary and small circulation publications from countries outside the U.S. and Canada that accept or buy short fiction in English (or in the universal languages of Esperanto or Ido).

Before sending a manuscript to a publication in another country, it's a good idea to query first for information on the magazine's needs and methods of submission. Send for sample copies, or try visiting the main branch of your local library, a nearby college library or bookstore to find a copy.

All correspondence to markets outside your own country must include International Reply Coupons, if you want a reply or material returned. You may find it less expensive to send copies of your manuscript for the publisher to keep and just enclose a return postcard with one IRC for a reply. Keep in mind response time is slow for many overseas publishers, but don't hesitate to send a reply postcard with IRC to check the status of your submission. You can obtain IRCs from the main branch of your local post office. The charge for one in U.S. funds is $1.05.

THE ABIKO LITERARY PRESS (ALP), 8-1-8 Namiki, Abiko-Shi, Chiba-Ken 270-11 Japan. Phone/fax: (0471)84-7904. Editors: Anna Livia Plaurelbelle and Laurel Sycks. Fiction Editor: Laurel Sycks. Quarterly. Circ. 500. Publishes 8 stories/issue. "We are a semi-bilingual (Japanese/English) magazine for Japanese and foreigners living in Japan." Needs: contemporary, erotica, experimental, historical, humor, literary, mainstream, regional. Length: 3,000 average; 5,000 maximum. Send entire scannable manuscript with SAE and IRCs. Pays 1 contributor's copy. "Stories influenced by James Joyce wanted. A story submitted in both English and Japanese receives special consideration. I look for strong character development as well as a good plot. Most stories I receive are exclusively character development or plot, but both are necessary to stand a good chance of being published." Follow proper format and submission procedures. Sponsors contest ($1,000). Write for details. 500-page sample copy for $15 plus $15 postage.

‡AMBIT, 17 Priory Gardens, Highgate, London N65QY United Kingdom. Fiction Editor: J.G. Ballard. Quarterly. Circ. 7,000. Publishes 3-5 short stories/issue. Publishes contemporary and experimental poetry, fiction and short prose. Length: 1,000 words minimum; 5,000 words maximum. Pays £5/printed page and contributor's copies. "Look at a copy of the magazine first." Sample copy available for £6 or $16. Make cheque payable to *Ambit*.

AMMONITE, 12 Priory Mead, Bruton Somerset BA100DZ (UK). Fiction Editor: John Howard-Greaves. Occasionally. Circ. 200. Publishes 3-7 stories/issue. "Myth, legend, science fiction to do with the current passage of evolution towards the possibilities of the Aquarian Age." Length: no minimum; 2,500 words maximum. Pays 2 contributor's copies.

AQUARIUS, Flat 10, Room-A, 116 Sutherland Ave., Maida-Vale, London W9 England. Fiction Editor: Sean Glackin. Editor: Eddie Linden. Circ. 5,000. Publishes 5 stories/issue. Interested in humor/satire, literary, prose poem and serialized/excerpted novels. "We publish prose and poetry and reviews." Payment is by agreement. "We only suggest changes. Most stories are taken on merit." Price in UK £5 plus postage and packing; in US $18 plus $3 postage. "We like writers who buy the magazine to get an idea of what we publish."

‡AUGURIES, Morton Publishing, P.O. Box 23, Gosport, Hants P012 2XD England. Editor: Nik Morton. Circ. 300. Averages 15 stories/year. "Science fiction and fantasy, maximum length 4,000 words." Pays £2 per 1,000 words plus complimentary copy. "Buy back issues, then try me!" Sample copy for $10. Subscription (2 issues) $30 to 'Morton Publishing.' Member of the New SF Alliance.

AUREALIS, Australian Fantasy and Science Fiction, P.O. Box 2164, Mt. Waverley, Victoria 3149 Australia. Fiction Editors: Dirk Strasser and Stephen Higgins. Semiannually. Circ. 2,500. Publishes 6 stories/issue: science fiction, fantasy and horror short stories. Length: 1,500 words minimum; 6,000 words maximum. "No reprints; no stories accepted elsewhere. Send one story at a time." Pays 2-6¢ (Australian)/word and contributor's copy. "Read the magazine. It is available in the UK and North America." Sample copy for $8 (Australian). Writer's guidelines available for SAE with IRC.

BBR MAGAZINE, P.O. Box 625, Sheffield, S1 3GY, UK. Editor: Chris Reed. Annually. Circ. 3,000. Publishes 20,000-30,000 words/issue. "BBR is a magazine of new speculative fiction. We are particularly interested in material that is too adventurous or thought-provoking for big publishers to handle, but that is no justification for explicit sex and/or violence irrelevant to the story. Plot is of paramount importance. We receive too many stories that contain very good ideas which are weakly and loosely handled, especially with endings that are meaningless or irrelevant to the rest of the story." Length: 2,000 words minimum; 10,000 words maximum. "If word-processed, do not use right justification or proportional spacing, as the variable spacing of words is harder to read. Dot-matrix printout must be clearly legible, especially if photocopied. Never send your only copy! Mark the first sheet clearly with the number of words, plus your name and address. Number each subsequent sheet of the manuscript. Submissions will also be accepted on 3.5 or 5.25 diskettes suitable for IBM compatibles, or 3.5 Apple Mac diskettes. Alternatively, you can e-mail your submission % C.S.Reed@sh effield.ac.uk. In each case, please use a straightforward single column ASCII text file. Pays £5/1,000 words or equivalent in US dollars and contributor's copies. Obtain and read guidelines, and consult recent issues to see what we're publishing. Enclose a SASE for the return of your manuscript if it is not accepted. We are unable to reply to writers who do not send return postage. We recommend IRCs plus disposable copy for overseas submissions. One US dollar is an acceptable (and cheaper!) alternative to IRCs." Sample copy available in US for $10 from Anne Marsden, 31192 Vaseo Amanavolia, San Juan Capistrano CA 92675-2227. (Checks payable to Anne Marsden).

BLACK TEARS, Adam Bradley, 28 Treaty St., Islington, N1 0SY England. Fiction Editor: Adam Bradley. Quarterly. Publishes 8-9 stories/issue. "Small press fiction magazine, all types of horror fiction." Length: 2,500 words maximum. Pays in contributor's copies. Send $5 (US) for sample copy. Send postage and SAE for guidelines.

BLOODSONGS, P.O. Box 7530, St. Kilda Rd., Melbourne Vic, 3004, Australia. Fiction Editors: Chris A. Masters and Steve Proposch. Quarterly. Circ. 6,000 (Australian), 2,000 (US). Publishes 4-6 stories/issue. "Horror magazine." Length: 1,000 words minimum; 10,000 words maximum. "Always attach a cover sheet to the front of the ms stating: the name of the piece; the name of the author (if a pen name is used, make it clear which is which); author's address and phone number (phone number not necessary but preferred); if the piece has been published previously or is due to be published elsewhere (include when and where); if it is a multiple submission; who owns the rights, and what rights are being offered. Include a cover letter stating that you are offering the piece for publication. Also include a paragraph or two about yourself (which will be used to make up an author's bio note which will go at the end of each story). Also let us know if the piece is available on computer disk and in what format. Pays $20 (Australian) for first Australian rights and contributor's copies. "We are only interested in well written, original stories that contain strong elements of horror. It's okay to use a fantasy/science fiction/crime background or setting, but it must be a horror story first to be considered. When dealing with sub-genres (i.e., vampires, Cthulhu Mythos, serial killers, demonic possession, etc.) that have become cliché-ridden, be original. If you can't take an overused genre and offer it something new, turn it inside out, or rework it in such a way to give it your own voice, don't bother." Writer's guidelines available for SASE (IRC). Sample copy for $8 (US)—surface to anywhere in the world. Make payable to "Barmbada Press."

CAMBRENSIS, 41 Heol Fach, Cornelly, Bridgend, Mid-Glamorgan, CF33 4LN Wales. Editor: Arthur Smith. Quarterly. Circ. 500. "Devoted solely to the short story form, featuring short stories by writers born or resident in Wales or with some Welsh connection; receives grants from the Welsh Arts' Council and the Welsh Writers' Trust; uses artwork—cartoons, line-drawings, sketches etc." Length: 2,500 words maximum. Writers receive 3 copies of magazine. Writer has to have some connection with Wales. SAE and IRCs or similar should be enclosed "Air mail" postage to avoid long delay. Send IRCs for a sample copy. Subscriptions via Blackwell's Periodicals, P.O. Box 40, Hythe Bridge Street, Oxford, OX1 2EU, UK or Swets & Zeitlinger B V, P.O. Box 800, 2160 S Z Lisse, Holland.

CHAPMAN, 4 Broughton Place, Edinburgh EH1 3RX Scotland. Fiction Editor: Joy Hendry. Quarterly. Circ. 2,000. Publishes 4-6 stories/issue. "Founded in 1970 *Chapman*, Scotland's quality literary magazine, is a dynamic force in Scotland, publishing poetry, fiction, criticism, reviews; articles on theatre, politics. language and the arts." Length: 1,000 words minimum; 6,000 words maximum. Include SAE and return postage (or IRC) with submissions. Pays £9-50/page.Sample copy available for £3.50 (includes postage).

CHILLS, 46 Oxford Rd., Acocks Green, Birmingham B27 6DT, England. Fiction Editor: Peter Coleborn. Annually. Circ. 300-500. Publishes 5-8 stories/issue. "We are a small press horror fiction magazine. The definition of horror is as wide as the author's imagination. Also uses occasional poetry." Length: 8,000-10,000 words maximum. Pays contributor's copies. Send ms with a brief covering note and IRCs for return of ms or acknowledgement if ms is disposable. Sample copy for large SAE and 5 IRCs.

‡DAM (Disability Arts Magazine), Unit 48, Enterprise Centre, King Edward St., Grimsby DN31 3JH England. Editor: Kit Wells. Quarterly. Circ. 1,500. "Disability-based writing only (personal experiences or work that is informed disability)." Length: 350 words mimimum; 1,000 maximum. Pays in pounds sterling and contributor's copies. "Please submit a short sample of your writing (300 words maximum) for consideration. Avoid 'Americanisms' whenever possible—although we speak English we understand American!" Phone, fax or write and follow the style(s) in the magazine. Phone/fax: (01430)430540 and code for England.

‡DREAMS FROM THE STRANGERS' CAFE, 15 Clifton Grove, Clifton, Rotherham, South-Yorkshire, S65-2AZ England. Fiction Editor: John Gaunt. Published irregularly. Circ. 500. Publishes 10-12 stories/issue. "*DFTSC* is a professionally produced magazine, aiming its fiction at the 'cracks between' most other genre publications. I like strange stories, or as they are sometimes called 'fantastic' or magic realism." Length: 100 words minimum; 8,000 maximum. Include cover letter. "We recommend seeing the magazine before blindly submitting work." Pays in copies. "Be sure to know what I'm looking for by either writing with a SAE (IRC's) for guidelines, or buying a recent issue." Guidelines are available with a SAE (and IRC's). Sample copies: £2.50/$7 for one; £9/$25 for four. English money may be sent. Dollar cheques, payable to Jeff VanderMeer, should be sent to the following address: Dreams From The Strangers' Cafe, % Leviathan, P.O. Box 4248 Tallahassee, FL 32315, USA.

‡FICTION FURNACE, 17 Ankermoor Close, Shard End, Birmingham B34 6TF England. Fiction Editor: John Williams. Quarterly. Publishes 4-6 stories/issue. "*Fiction Furnace* uses all forms of short fiction—any genre except small children's or mills-plus-boon-type romance." Length: 2,000 minimum. Pays approximately £30 and contributor's copy. "Plot, plot and more plot, then do the same for characterization. After I've read it I like to feel it was worth its effort!" Send 2 IRC's minimum. "I get dollar bills all the time—these are useless to me." Send envelope and 1 IRC for guidelines. Send $10 U.S. for single copy; Send $20 U.S. for 4-issue subscription.

FORESIGHT, (IV), 44 Brockhurst Rd., Hodge Hill, Birmingham B36 8JB England. Editor: John Barklam. Fiction Editor: Judy Barklam. Quarterly. Magazine including "new age material, world peace, psychic phenomena, research, occultism, spiritualism, mysticism, UFOs, philosophy, etc. Shorter articles required on a specific theme related to the subject matter of *Foresight* magazine." Length: 300-1,000 words. Pays in contributor's copies. Send SAE with IRC for return of ms. Sample copy for 30p and 35p postage.

‡FRANK, An International Journal of Contemporary Writing and Art, 32 rue Edouard Vaillant, 93100 Montreuil, France. Editor: David Applefield. Semiannual. Circ. 3,000. Publishes 20 stories/issue. "At *Frank*, we publish "fiction, poetry, literary and art interviews, and translations. We like work that falls between existing genres and has social or political consciousness." Send IRC or $3 cash. Must be previously unpublished in English (world). Pays 2 copies and $10 (US)/printed page. "Send your most daring and original work. Be prepared to wait for long periods; some publishers will not answer or return manuscripts. At *Frank*, we like work that is not too parochial or insular, however, don't try to write for a 'French' market." Sample copy $10 (US/air mail included); guidelines available upon request.

‡THE FROGMORE PAPERS, 6 Vernon Rd., London N8 OQD United Kingdom. Fiction Editor: Jeremy Page. Semi-annual. Circ. 200. "A little magazine which publishes poetry, reviews, short stories and novel extracts, both traditional and experimental." Length: 1,000 words minimum; 3,000 words maximum. Pays in contributor's copies. "Study a sample copy before submission." Current issue available for 5 U.S. dollars (bills only) from: The Frogmore Press, 42 Morehall Ave., Folkestone, Kent CT19 4EF UK.

GHOSTS & SCHOLARS, Flat One, 36 Hamilton St., Hoole, Chester CH2 3JQ England. Fiction Editor: Rosemary Pardoe. Semiannually. Circ. 400. Publishes 6-7 stories/year. "Publishes fiction in the M.R. James tradition, and articles/discussion of same." Length: 2,000 words minimum; 8,000 words maximum. Pays in copies. "Submissions should be of ghost stories in the M.R. James tradition only. I will not consider other types of ghost stories." Sample copy for $7 cash (US) or £4 cheque (payable to R. Pardoe). Guidelines for SASE (overseas: 2 IRCs).

‡GOING DOWN SWINGING, P.O. Box 24, Clifton Hill, Victoria 3068 Australia. Fiction Editors: Louise Craig and Lyn Boughton. Circ. 1,000. Annual. Publishes approximately 80 pages of fiction/year. "We publish short stories, prose poetry, poetry, interviews and reviews. We try to encourage young or new writers as well as established writers." Payment: $20 (Australian) per contribution. Writers receive 1 contributor's copy. Send ms, 2 International Reply Coupons and a short biographical note. Include 2-3 stories. Deadline: December 15. "We are interested in innovative, contemporary and experimental writing with the aim of publishing an equal balance of female and male writers of considerable talent." Sample copies $10 (Australian). Writer's guidelines available. Send SAE and IRC.

THE HARDCORE, P.O. Box 1899, London N9 8JT England. Fiction Editor: J. Nuit. Quarterly. Circ. 500. Publishes 3 stories/issue. "The magazine at the edge of contemporary culture. We print high-speed, hard-edged, glitteringly intelligent stories set in the absolute present or near future (cyberpunk). Black and white computer art especially welcome." Length: 1,500 words minimum; 3,000 words maximum. "Complimentary copy always sent to writer/artist." Write to enquire. Send US $4 cash/International Money Order to editorial address.

‡HECATE, Box 99, St. Lucia Q4067 Australia. Fiction Editor: Carole Ferrier. Circ. 2,000. Publishes 5-8 stories annually. "Socialist feminist; we like political stories (broadly defined)." Writers receive $50 (Australian) and 5 copies. "We only rarely publish non-Australian writers of fiction."

HORIZON, Stationsstraat 232A, 1770 Liedekerke Belgium. Fiction Editor: Johnny Haelterman. Quarterly. Circ. 200. Publishes at least a few stories/issue. "*Horizon* is a cultural magazine for a general public, therefore fiction should be suitable for a general public. Preference is given to stories which can happen, although slightly fantastic fiction is sometimes accepted." Length: 300 words minimum; 1,000 words maximum. "A realistic treatment is preferred but a touch of fantasy is sometimes acceptable. The content should be suitable for a general public, therefore no extreme violence or sex." Enclose money or IRCs if you want your work back. Payment in Belgian funds for original fiction in Dutch only. No payment for fiction in other languages but the writers receive two copies in that case. English fiction can be translated into Dutch without payment (two copies). Submitting outside your country is mainly the same as in your own country, except that the postage costs are higher. Puns are usually not translatable, so avoid writing stories with an essential part based on puns if you want your work to be translated." Sample copy available for $8 (US).

HRAFNHOH, 32 Strŷd Ebeneser, Pontypridd, Mid Glamorgan CF37 5PB Wales. Fiction Editor: Joseph Biddulph. Circ. 200. Published irregularly. "Now worldwide and universal in scope. Suitable: fictionalized history, local history, family history. Explicitly Christian approach. Well-written stories or general prose opposed to abortion, human embryo experimentation and euthanasia particularly welcome. No payment made, but free copies provided. Be brief, use a lot of local colour and nature description, in a controlled, resonant prose or in dialect. Suitable work accepted in esperanto, français, español, and other languages, including Creole. "US stamps are of no use to me, but US banknotes acceptable." IRC will cover a brief response, but mss however small are expensive to return, so please send copy." Sample copy free, but 3 IRCs would cover real cost of sending it overseas.

HU (THE HONEST ULSTERMAN), 14 Shaw Street, Belfast BT4 1PT, Northern Ireland. Fiction Editor: Tom Clyde. 3 times/year. Circ. 1,000. Publishes 1-4 stories/issue. "Northern Ireland's premier literary magazine. Prime focus is poetry, but continues to publish prose (story, novel extract). 3,000 words maximum. "Must include sufficient means of return (IRCs, etc.). If we decide to publish, an IBM-type floppy disk version would be very helpful." Writers receive small payment and two contributor's copies. For 4 issues send UK £14 airmail or sample issue US $7. "Contributors are strongly advised to read the magazine before submitting anything."

IMAGO, School of Media & Journalism, QUT, GPO Box 2434, Brisbane 4001 Australia. Contact: Dr. Philip Neilsen or Helen Horton. Published 3 times/year. Circ. 750. 30-50% fiction. *Imago* is a literary magazine publishing short stories, poetry, articles, interviews and book reviews. "While content of articles and interviews should have some relevance either to Queensland or to writing, stories and poems may be on any subject. The main requirement is good writing." Length: 1,000 words minimum; 3,000 words maximum;

2,000 words preferred. Pays on publication in accordance with Australia Council rates: short stories, $A90 minimum; articles, $A90 minimum; poems $A40; reviews, $A60. Also provides contributor's copy. "Contributions should be typed double-spaced on one side of the paper, each page bearing the title, page number and author's name. Name and address of the writer should appear on a cover page of longer mss, or on the back, or bottom, of single page submissions. A SAE and IRCs with sufficient postage to cover the contents should be sent for the return of ms or for notification of acceptance or rejection. No responsibility is assumed for the loss of or damage to unsolicited manuscripts." Sample copy available for $A7. Guidelines, as above, available on request.

INDIAN LITERATURE, Sahitya Akademi, National Academy of Letters, Rabindra Bhavan, 35 Ferozeshah Rd., New Delhi 110 001 India. Editor: Professor K. Sachidanandan. Circ. 4,100. Publishes 6 issues/year; 200 pages. "Presents creative work from 22 Indian languages including Indian English." Sample copy available for $7.

IRON MAGAZINE, (II), Iron Press, 5 Marden Ter., Cullercoats, North Shields, Tyne & Wear NE30 4PD England. Editor: Peter Mortimer. Circ. 1,000. Published 3 times/year. Publishes 14 stories/year. "Literary magazine of contemporary fiction, poetry, articles and graphics." Length: 6,000 words maximum. Pays approximately £10/page. No simultaneous submissions. Five poems, two stories/submission the limit. No submissions during July and August please. Sample copy for $10 (US) (no bills-no checks). "Please see magazine before submitting and don't submit to it before you're ready! Many stories submitted are obviously only of interest to the domestic market of the writer. Always try there first! And do try to find something out about the publication, or better, see a sample copy, before submitting."

JEWISH QUARTERLY, P.O. Box 2078, London W1A1JR England. Editor: Elena Lappin. Quarterly. Publishes 1 contribution of fiction/issue. "It deals in the broadest sense with all issues of Jewish interest." Length: 1,500 words minimum; 7,000 words maximum. Payment for accepted items £50. Work should have either a Jewish theme in the widest interpretation of that phrase or a theme which would interest our readership. The question which contributors should ask is 'Why should it appear in the *Jewish Quarterly* and not in another periodical?' "

KRAX MAGAZINE, 63 Dixon Lane, Leeds LS12 4RR, Yorkshire, Britain, U.K. Fiction Editor: Andy Robson. Appears 9 monthly. Publishes 1 story/issue. "We publish mostly poetry of a lighthearted nature, but use comic or spoof fiction, witty and humorous essays." Length: 2,000 words maximum. Pays contributor's copies. "Don't spend too long on scene-setting or character construction as this inevitably produces an anticlimax in a short piece. Send IRCs or currency notes for return postal costs—stamps are sadly unusable outside their own country and checques for small sums uncashable. If unable to send IRCs or currency notes, then assume non-return of mss." Sample copy for $1 direct from editor. No specific guidelines.

LA KANCERKLINIKO, (IV), 162 rue Paradis, 13006 Marseille France. Phone: 91-3752-15. Fiction Editor: Laurent Septier. Circ. 300. Quarterly. Publishes 40 pages of fiction annually. "An esperanto magazine which appears 4 times annually. Each issue contains 32 pages. *La Kancerkliniko* is a political and cultural magazine. General fiction, science fiction, etc. Short stories or very short novels. The short story (or the very short novel) must be written only in esperanto, either original or translation from any other language." Length: 15,000 words maximum. Pays in contributor's copies. Sample copy on request with 3 IRCs from Universal Postal Union.

‡LANDFALL/OXFORD UNIVERSITY PRESS, University of Opago Press, P.O. Box 56, Dunedin New Zealand. Editor: Chris Price. Publishes fiction, poetry, commentary and criticism. Length: maximum 10,000 words. Pays NZ $11 per page for fiction. "Without wishing to be unduly nationalist, we would normally give first preference to stories which contain some kind of New Zealand connection."

‡LONDON MAGAZINE, 30 Thurloe Place, London SW7 England. Editor: Alan Ross. Bimonthly. Circ. 5,000. Publishes 3-4 stories/issue. "Quality is the only criteria." Length: 1,500-5,000 words. Pays £50-100, depending on length, and contributor's copy. "Send only original and literary, rather than commercial, work."

‡MANUSHI, A Journal About Women and Society, C/202 Lajpat Nagar 1, New Delhi 110024 India. Editor: Madhu Kishwar. Bimonthly. Circ. up to 8,000. Publishes one fiction story/issue. "*Manushi* is a magazine devoted to human rights and women's rights issues with a focus on the Indian subcontinent and the situation of Indian communities settled overseas. It includes poetry, fiction, historical and sociological studies, analysis of contemporary politics, review of mass media and literature, biographies, profiles and histories of various movements for social change." Length: 12,000 words maximum. Duplicate mss preferred.

‡MATTOID, Centre for Research in Cultural Communication, Deakin University, Geelong, Victoria 3217 Australia. Fiction Editor: Prof. Brian Edwards. Published 3 times/year. Circ. 650. Publishes 5-7 stories/issue. "*Mattoid* publishes short fiction, poetry, essays, interviews, reviews and graphics. At present we are running a series of special issues ('The Body,' 'Revisions in Romanticism,' 'Crossing Cultures,' 'Masculinism') but we are interested in innovative fiction." Length: 300 words minimum; 3,000 words maximum. Pays in copies. "Our main criterion is interest value, though we are pleased to see innovative/experimental writing that is well-crafted. Take some care with the choice of destination. Research the writing. Include a brief biographical statement." Single copies available for $18 overseas. Annual subscription (3 issues) $40.

MEANJIN, University of Melbourne, Parkville, Victoria 3052 Australia. Fiction Editor: Christina Thompson. Circ. 3,000. "*Meanjin*'s emphasis is on publishing a wide range of writing by new and established writers. Our primary orientation is toward Australian writers, but material from overseas sources is also published." Writer receives approx. $60 (Australian)/1,000 words and 2 copies. "Please submit typed manuscript and enclose return addressed envelope with IRCs."

‡MIDNIGHT IN HELL, (CULT MEDIA JOURNAL), The Cottage, Smithy Brae, Kilmacolm, Renfrewshire, PA134EN Scotland. Fiction Editor: George N. Houston. Quarterly. Circ. 200. Publishes 2-5 short stories/issue. "We accept fiction, art, poetry and articles within the horror/science fiction/fantasy genres and any crossover thereof. We exist to give the fan writer an outlet with which to stretch their talents and maybe make it to the professional writing scene and not forgetting keeping people abreast of the cult film world." Length: 500 words minimum; 4,000 words maximum. "Fiction described above should be accompanied by a return envelope with the correct postage." Pays 1 contributor's copy. "Don't censor yourself in any way! Keep plugging at it, and send out to as many as possible!" Write for guidelines. No subscriptions.

NEW HOPE INTERNATIONAL, 20 Werneth Ave., Gee Cross, Hyde, SK14 5NL England. Fiction Editor: Gerald England. Circ. 750. Publishes 2-6 stories annually. Publishes "mainly poetry. Fiction used must be essentially literary but not pretentious. Only short fiction used (max 2,000 words). "Most submissions are too long and often too essentially American for an international audience. A brief covering letter should be sent. 1 IRC covers a reply if mss is disposable (please state) otherwise 1 IRC per 2 sheets. Don't send return envelope or US postage stamps." Payment: 1 complimentary copy. Guidelines available for IRC. Sample copy £3. Payment in sterling only payable to "G. England." Send cash equivalent in any currency or International Giro (available from post offices worldwide).

PANURGE, (I), Crooked Holme Farm Cottage, Brampton, Cumbria CA8 2AT UK. Tel. 016977-41087. Fiction Editor: John Murray. Circ. 1,700. Published twice/year. Perfect-bound, 200 pages. "Dedicated to short fiction by new and up-and-coming names. Each issue features several previously unpublished names. Several *Panurge* writers have been included in major anthologies, approached by agents, offered contracts by publishers. All lengths, styles and attitudes given serious consideration. US submissions welcomed. New editor is founder-editor and winner of the Dylan Thomas Award 1988. We are also bringing back hard-hitting features on fiction publishing; third world fiction etc." Pays 1 month after publication, 1 contributor's copy. Pays £10/3 printed pages. Overseas subscription $15; Airmail $20. Sample copy for $7.

PARIS TRANSCONTINENTAL, A Magazine of Short Stories, Institut des Pays Anglophones, Sorbonne Nouvelle, 5, rue de l'Ecole de Médecine, 75006 Paris, France. Editor-in-Chief: Claire Larrière. Assistant Editors: Albert Russo and Devorah Goldberg. Semiannually. Circ. 500. Publishes short stories exclusively; no poetry, nonfiction or artwork. "*Paris Transcontinental*, purports to be a forum for writers of excellent stories whose link is the English language, wherever it is spoken. It purports thus to be global in scope and to introduce the best among today's authors, whether they hail from Europe or the Americas, from Oceania, Africa or Asia, for new literatures are evolving that reflect our post-colonial and computerized societies in ways that do not necessarily converge but certainly enrich our common space, hopefully also spurring our mutual understanding." Average length: 2,000-4,000 words maximum. "Submitters should send us no more than 3 unpublished stories at a time, along with a few lines about themselves and their work (approx. 100 words), one IRC to let them know of our decision, and *extra* IRCs (at least 3) for the return of their manuscripts. (No stamps please!)" Pays 2 contributor's copies. "Have an authentic voice and be professional. Write with your gut and read from all quarters. Author's featured include Stephen Dixon, Herbert Liebman,

---

Sending to a country other than your own? Be sure to send International Reply Coupons instead of stamps for replies or return of your manuscript.

Jayanta Mahapatra, Joyce Carol Oates, Albert Russo, Alan Sillitoe and Michael Wilding." Send IRC for guidelines. For a sample copy, send a check for FF75 payable on a French bank, or $11 drawn on your own local bank.

PLANET-THE WELSH INTERNATIONALIST, P.O. Box 44, Aberystwyth, Dyfed, Cymru/ Wales UK. Fiction Editor: John Barnie. Bimonthly. Circ. 1,300. Publishes 1-2 stories/issue. "A literary/cultural/political journal centered on Welsh affairs but with a strong interest in minority cultures in Europe and elsewhere." Length: 1,500-4,000 words maximum. No submissions returned unless accompanied by an SAE. Writers submitting from abroad should send at least 3 IRCs. Writers receive 1 contributor's copy. Payment is at the rate of £40 per 1,000 words (in the currency of the relevant country if the author lives outside the UK). "We do not look for fiction which necessarily has a 'Welsh' connection, which some writers assume from our title. We try to publish a broad range of fiction and our main criterion is quality. Try to read copies of any magazine you submit to. Don't write out of the blue to a magazine which might be completely inappropriate to your work. Recognize that you are likely to have a high rejection rate, as magazines tend to favor writers from their own countries." Sample copy: cost (to USA & Canada) £2.87. Writers' guidelines for SAE.

THE PLAZA, A Space for Global Human Relations, U-Kan Inc., Yoyogi 2-32-1, Shibuya-Ku, Tokyo, Japan 151. Tel: (81)3-3379-3881. Fax: (81)3-3379-3882. Editor: Joel Baral. Fiction Editor: Hemanshu Lakhani. Quarterly. Circ. 6,000. Publishes about 3 stories/issue. "*The Plaza* is an intercultural and bilingual magazine (English and Japanese). Our focus is the 'essence of being human.' All works are published in both Japanese and English (translations by our staff if necessary). The most important criteria is artistic level. We look for works that reflect simply 'being human.' Stories on intercultural (not international) relations are desired. *The Plaza* is devoted to offering a spiritual *Plaza* where people around the world can share their creative work. We introduce contemporary writers and artists as our generation's contribution to the continuing human heritage." Length: Less than 1,000 words, minimalist short stories are welcomed. Send complete ms with cover letter. Sample copy and guidelines free.

PREMONITIONS, Pigasus Press, 13 Hazely Combe, Arreton, Isle of Wight PO30 3AJ England. Fiction Editor: Tony Lee. Semiannually. Publishes 12 stories/issue. "Digest-sized magazine-anthology of science fictional horror stories and genre poetry." (Also publishes *The Zone* listed in this section.) Length: 1,000 words minimum; 5,000 words maximum. Pays contributor's copies. "Send SAE/IRC for free contributor's guidelines. Study recent issues of the magazine. Unsolicited submissions are always welcome but writers must enclose SAE/IRC for reply, plus adequate postage to return 'ms' if unsuitable." Sample copies available for $7 (cash, US Dollars) or 7 IRCs. For UK and EC countries: £2.50 cheques/eurocheques, International Money Order, etc. should be made payable to: Tony Lee.

QUADRANT, Box 1495, Collingwood, Victoria 3066 Australia. Fiction Editor: Mr. Les Murray. Monthly. Circ. 6,000. Publishes 1-2 stories/issue. "Magazine of current affairs, culture, politics, economics, the arts, literature, ideas; stories: general and varied." Length: 5,000 words maximum. Pays contributor's copies and a minimum of $90 (Australian). For sample copy "write to us, enclosing cheque (or equivalent) for $8 (Australian)."

‡REDOUBT, Faculty of Communication, University of Canberra, P.O. Box 1, Belconnen, ACT 2616, Australia. Fiction Editor: Ruth Sless. Circ. 300. Publishes 10 stories/issue. "Literary magazine—short poems, stories, reviews, articles, graphics. All types of fiction welcome—quality is the main criterion." Length: 2,000 words maximum. "Must enclose SAE; must not send original (if you do, we can't be responsible if it gets lost)." Pays 20-30 Australian dollars "according to how much we've got in the bank. Read the magazine to get a feel for the kind of thing we publish. Read the guidelines. Provide a short biography, a SAE, and your name on every page of the ms. Be prepared to wait for an answer—it can take months. We make no distinction between local and distant mss. The SAE is always a problem—international postal coupons are the answer." A sample copy is available for A$5 (or three back issues for A$12). Guidelines are printed in the magazine, or can be sent separately on application to the above address.

ROMANIAN REVIEW, Redactia Publicatiilor Pentru Strainatate, Piata Presei Libere NR1, 71341 Bucuresti Romania. Fiction Editor: Mrs. Andreea Ionescu. Monthly. Fiction 40%. "Our review is scanning the Romanian history and cultural realities, the cooperation with other countries in the cultural field and it is also a mean of acquaintance with Romanian and overseas writers. We publish the *Romanian Review* in six languages (English, German, French, Spanish, Russian, Chinese). Fiction related to Romanian civilization may enter the pages of the *Review*." Length: 2,000 words minimum; 5,000 words maximum. "As we do not have the possibility of payment in foreign currency, we can only offer "lei" 800-2,000/story, depending on its length and qualities. The exchange may be done on the writer's account." Sample copies available; write for information.

SEPIA, Poetry & Prose Magazine, (I), Kawabata Press, Knill Cross House, Knill Cross, Millbrook, Nr Torpoint, Cornwall England. Editor-in-Chief: Colin David Webb. Published 3 times/year. "Magazine for those interested in modern un-clichéd work." Contains 32 pages/issue. Length: 200-4,000 words (for short stories). Pays 1 contributor's copy. Always include SAE with IRCs. Send $1 for sample copy and guidelines.

STAND MAGAZINE, 179 Wingrove Rd., Newcastle Upon Tyne, NE4 9DA England. Fiction Editor: Lorna Tracy. Circ. 4,500. Quarterly. Averages 16-20 stories/year. "*Stand* is an international quarterly publishing poetry, short stories, reviews, criticism and translations." Length: 5,000 words maximum. Payment: £30 per 1,000 words of prose on publication (or in US dollars); contributor's copies. "Read copies of the magazine before submitting. Enclose sufficient IRCs for return of mss/reply. No more than 6 poems or 2 short stories at any one time. Avoid specific genre writing—e.g. science fiction, travel, etc. Should not be under consideration elsewhere." Sponsors biennial short competition: First prize, $1,500. Send 2 IRCs for information. Sample copy: $6.50. Guidelines on receipt of 2 IRCs/SASE (U.K. stamps).

STAPLE, Tor Cottage 81, Cavendish Rd., Matlock DE4 3HD U.K.. Fiction Editor: Don Measham. Published 3 times/year. Circ. up to 600. Publishes up to 50% fiction. *Staple* is "90+ pages, perfect-bound; beautifully designed and produced. Stories used by *Staple* have ranged from social realism (through autobiography, parody, prequel, parable) to visions and hallucinations. We don't use unmodified genre fiction, i.e. adventure, crime or westerns. We are interested in extracts from larger works—provided author does the extraction." Length: 200 words minimum; 5,000 words maximum. Adequate IRCs and large envelope for return, if return is required. Otherwise IRC for decision only. Pays complimentary copy plus subscription for US contributors. Get a specimen copy of one of the issues with strong prose representation. Send $10 for airmail dispatch, $5 for surface mail. The monograph series *Staple First Editions* has been re-launched. IRC for details. Please note that *Staple* requires stories to be previously unpublished world-wide.

STUDIO: A JOURNAL OF CHRISTIANS WRITING, (II), 727 Peel St., Albury 2640 Australia. Managing Editor: Paul Grover. Circ. 300. Quarterly. Averages 20-30 stories/year. "*Studio* publishes prose and poetry of literary merit, offers a venue for new and aspiring writers, and seeks to create a sense of community among Christians writing." Length: 500-5,000 words. Pays in copies. Sample copy available for $8 (Australian). Subscription $40 (Australian) for 4 issues (1 year). International draft in Australian dollars and IRC required.

SUNK ISLAND REVIEW, P.O. Box 74, Lincoln LN1 1QG England. Fiction Editor: Michael Blackburn. Biannual. "A biannual magazine of new fiction, poetry, translations. Articles and graphics. Short stories, science fiction and excerpts from novels, novellas are all welcome. No romance, historical fiction etc." Length: Open. Send cover letter and no more than 2 short stories at a time. Pays on publication. "Read the magazine first. We prefer disposable mss. All mss must be accompanied by adequate number of IRCs for reply or return."

TEARS IN THE FENCE, (II), 38 Hod View, Stourpaine, Nr. Blandford Forum, Dorset DT11 8TN England. Editor: David Caddy. Triannual. A magazine of poetry, fiction and graphics and reviews, open to a variety of contemporary voices from around the world. Publishes short and long fiction. Publishes 1-2 stories/issue. Pays £7.50 per story plus complimentary copy of the magazine. Sample copy for $5 (US).

TERRIBLE WORK, 21 Overton Gardens, Mannamead, Plymouth, Devon PL3 5BX UK. Fiction Editor: Tim Allen. Triannually. Circ. 300. Publishes 1 story/issue. "Modern poetry with art, articles, reviews and some fiction/prose poetry. Slipstream fiction." Length: 1 word minimum; 2,000 words maximum. "Always include SASE or SAE and IRC, short bios and publication lists also help." Pays in copies. "Always best to see a copy first unless you know the publication by repute." *Terrible Work* costs £3 or £8 for 3 issue subscription in sterling, but will accept $7 for 1 or $20 for 3 issue subscription (including p&h). On an individual basis offers trade for a chapbook or mag, as it is good to see what is being published across the water."

THE THIRD ALTERNATIVE, 5 Martins Lane, Witcham, Ely, Cambs CB6 2LB England. Phone: 01353 777931. Fiction Editor: Andy Cox. Quarterly. Publishes 10 stories/issue. "A5, 60 pages, lithographed, glossy. Innovative, quality science fiction/fantasy/horror and slipstream material (cross-genre)." Length: No minimum; 7,000-8,000 words maximum. No simultaneous submissions. Reprints only in exceptional circumstances (will read unsolicited reprint material anyway). Standard ms format and SAE (overseas: disposable ms and 2 IRCs). Pays in copies. "Include a covering letter! Make an effort to ascertain editorial requirements, or better still, study the magazine. Be original and/or daring. Quality is the main criterion here. If in doubt, send it anyway." Guidelines, ad rates, etc. all available for SAE or 2 IRCs.

THE THIRD HALF MAGAZINE, "Amikeco," 16, Fane Close, Stamford, Lincolnshire PE9 1H9 England. Fiction Editor: Kevin Troop. Published irregularly (when possible). "*The Third Half* literary magazine publishes mostly poetry, but editorial policy is to publish as much *short* short story writing as possible in each issue. Short stories especially for children, for use in the classroom, with 'questions' and 'work to do' are occasionally produced, along with poetry books, as separate editions. I wish to expand on this." Length: 1,800 words maximum. Pays in contributor's copies.

VIGIL, (II), Vigil Publications, 12 Priory Mead, Bruton, Somerset BA10 ODZ England. Editor: John Howard Greaves. Estab. 1979. Circ. 250. "Simply the enjoyment of varied forms of poetry and literature with an informed view of poetic technique." Plans special fiction issue. Needs: experimental, literary, regional. Length: 500-1,500 words. Pays in contributor's copies. "Most of the stories we receive are work in progress rather than finished pieces. Well structured, vibrantly expressed work is a delight when it arrives. Freshness and originality must always find an audience." Contributor guidelines available for IRC.

WESTERLY, English Dept., University of Western Australia, Nedlands, 6009 Australia. Caroline Horobin, Administrator. Quarterly. Circ. 1,000. "A quarterly of poetry, prose, reviews and articles of a literary and cultural kind, giving special attention to Australia and Southeast Asia." Pays $50 (AUS) minimum and 1 contributor's copy. Sample copy for $6 (AUS).

WORKS, 12 Blakestones Rd., Slaithwaite, Huddersfield HD7 5UQ England. Fiction Editor: D. W. Hughes. Circ. 1,000. 70% of content is fiction. "A4, 40 pages speculative and imaginative fiction (science fiction) with poetry, illustrated." Quarterly. Price: £5 *cash only or cheque in sterling* for 1 issue, £20 *cash* or check in pounds sterling for 4 issues; enclose IRC. Member of the New Science Fiction Alliance. Pays in copies. "All manuscripts should be accompanied by a SASE (in the UK). USA send 2 IRC's with ms, if disposable or 4 IRCs, if not. Usual maximum is 4,500 words."

‡XENOS, 29 Prebend St., Bedford MK40 1QN England. Fiction Editor: S.U. Copestake. Bimonthly. Circ. 250. Publishes 7-8 stories/issue. "*Xenos* is a glossly-cover story magazine. (No nonfiction, advertisements, captions or illustrations). We consider science fiction fantasy, horror, occult. humor, detective, ripping yarns, etc. We do not consider purely romantic stories, pornography, explicit sex, blood and gore, etc. We hold an annual short story competition (closing date usually May 31) for which cash prizes and complimentary copies of the magazine (totalling £100) are given. Read our guidelines and/or a copy of *Xenos* before considering submission. This is very important. Sufficient IRCs for return postage is essential. Submissions must meet our guidelines, be written in good English, and be suitable for the English market." Sample copy £3.45 plus £1-00 (£4.45 total). We can only accept sterling, i.e., sterling cheques or sterling IRC. Guidelines only require an address or envelope and 1 IRC.

THE ZONE, Pigasus Press, 13 Hazely Combe, Arreton, Isle of Wight, PO30 3AJ England. Fiction Editor: Tony Lee. Published 5 times a year. Publishes 3 stories/issue. "*The Zone*: A4-size magazine of quality science fiction plus articles and reviews." (Also publishes *Premonitions* listed in this section.) Length: 1,000 words minimum; 5,000 words maximum. Pays in copies. "Token payment for stories and articles of 2,000 words and over. Send SAE/IRC for free contributor's guidelines. Study recent issues of the magazine. Unsolicited submissions are always welcome but writers must enclose SAE/IRC for reply, plus adequate postage to return ms if unsuitable." Sample copies available for $7 (cash, US dollars) or 7 IRCs. For UK and EC countries: £2.25 (cheques/eurocheques, International Money Order, etc. should be made payable to: Tony Lee).

Literary and small circulation magazines/'95-'96 changes

The following literary magazines appeared in the 1995 edition but are not in the 1996 edition. Those publications whose editors did not respond to our request for an update of their listings may not have done so for a variety of reasons—they may have ceased publication, or be overstocked with submissions.

Animal Trails
Ansuda Magazine
Apalachee Quarterly
Argonaut (suspended publication)
Area of Operations
Array (requested deletion)
Art's Garbage Gazzette
(requested deletion)
As If
Ascent
The Atlantean Press Review
Avalon Rising
Bakunin
Ball Magazine
bare wire
Best of the Midwest's Science
Fiction, Fantasy & Horror
Bloodreams Magazine
Bluff City

Both Sides Now
The Caribbean Writer
Catalyst (no longer accepting
mss)
Chips Off the Writer's Block
Colorado Review
Compost Newsletter (ceased pub-
lication)
Cottonwood
Dance
Dance Connection
Dancing Shadow Review
Dark Tome
Daughters of Sarah
The Dexter Review
Drop Forge
Earth's Daughters
Eulogy
Evil Dog Magazine (overstocked)

eXpErImENtAL (bAsEemEnT)
(requested deletion)
Fame Magazine
Fayrdaw (no unsolicited mss)
Fighting Woman News
Fireweed (requested deletion)
Free Worlds Magazine
Frontiers
Furious Fictions
Gaia
The Galactic Bard & Grill
Garm Lu
Gaslight
Golden Isis Magazine
Great River Review
Herspectives (ceased publication)
Hyphen Magazine
Hysteria (ceased publication)
The Idiot

In Darkness Eternal II
Infinity Forum Magazine
Interim
Iris (GA)
The Journal (OH)
Journal of Regional Criticism
Kairos
Kansas Quarterly (reorganizing)
Karamu
Keltic Fringe
Kokopelli Notes (ceased publication)
Kumquat Meringue
Language Bridges Quarterly
The Leading Edge
Linington Lineup
Lizard's Eyelid Magazine
Long Shot
The Long Story (funding cut)
Lords of the Abyss
The Madison Review
Medley of Pens
Mississippi Valley Review (ceased publication)
Mixed Media
The Moocher's Periodical
Moving Out
Muse Portfolio
Mystery Notebook
The National Gay & Lesbian Reader (ceased publication)
Negative Capability
The New Crucible
The New Jersey Review of Literature (ceased publication)
New Writing

Night Owl's Newsletter (ceased publication)
Noir Stories
Nostoc Magazine
Notable Novellettes
Now & Then
Object Lesson
Offworld
Out Your Backdoor (no longer publishing fiction)
Over My Dead Body
Palace Corbie
Paper Rainbow
Passages North
Pennsylvania Review
The Pikestaff Forum (ceased publication)
Poetic Space
Prolific Writer's Magazine (requested deletion)
Prophetic Voices (backlogged)
A Quiet Cup (with feet up)
Rajah
Reach Magazine
Rebel Yell Magazine
Romantic Expressions
Room 4 Insanity
San Gabriel Valley Magazine
San Jose Studies (ceased publication)
San Miguel Writer
Scifant
Scream of the Buddha
Shapeshifter!
Shockbox
Skull (ceased publication)

Snake River Reflections (requested deletion)
Southeastern Front
Spectrum●txt (requested deletion)
Spellbound
Spilled Ink
The Squib
Starquest S.F. Magazine (ceased publication)
Starry Nights
The Steelhead Special
Stiletto III
Studio One
Surreal
Swoon (requested deletion)
Tales of the Heart
Tertesticulopolis (ceased publication)
Thin Ice (ceased publication)
13th Moon
The Threepenny Review
Turnstile
Two-Ton Santa
Undiscovered Countries Journal
The Unsilenced Voice (requested deletion)
A Very Small Magazine
Wagons of Steel Magazine
Washington Review
Willow Review
Witness
Woman's Way
WonderDisk
Young Voices Magazine
Zoiks! (ceased publication)

International literary and small circulation magazines/"95-'96 changes

Acumen
Cencrastus
Cobweb (ceased publication)
Diliman Review
First Word Bulletin
Foolscap
Global Tapestry Journal
Grotesque
Idiom 23
Indian Writer
Island

Linq
Massacre
The Mower
New Europa
Night Dreams
Paris/Atlantic
Perceptions
Plurilingual Europe/Europe Plurilingue
Purple Patch
Quartos

Rashi
Scarp
Shoggoth
Social Alternatives
Takahe, Quarterly Literary Magazine
10th Muse
Verandah
Wasafiri

For information on entering the **Novel & Short Story Writer's Market** *Cover Letter Contest, see page 19.*

Commercial Periodicals

In this section of *Novel & Short Story Writer's Market* are nearly 200 magazines with circulations of more than 10,000. Many of them, in fact, have circulations in the hundreds of thousands or millions. Among the oldest magazines listed here are ones not only familiar to us, but also to our parents, grandparents and even great-grandparents: *The Atlantic Monthly* (1857); *Capper's* (1879); *Christian Century* (1900); *Redbook* (1903); *The New Yorker* (1925); *Analog Science Fiction & Fact* (1930); *Esquire* (1933); and *Jack and Jill* (1938).

Commercial periodicals make excellent markets for fiction in terms of exposure, prestige and payment. Because these magazines are well-known, however, competition is great. Even the largest commercial publications buy only one or two stories an issue, yet thousands of writers submit to these popular magazines. Last year, *Harper's Magazine*, one of the top but also toughest markets for contemporary fiction, reported that they received 300 unsolicited manuscripts a month. This year, editors at *Harper's* say they are receiving over 600 unsolicited manuscripts a month but, from among those, still only finding one manuscript a year they can publish. Other top publications have followed *McCall's* lead and no longer publish fiction. *Cosmopolitan Magazine*, for instance, has ceased publishing short stories, but plans to still occasionally print excerpts from published novels. And, although *First* no longer publishes fiction, its sister publication, *Woman's World Magazine*, remains one of the top-paying fiction markets listed in this section.

Despite the odds, it is possible for talented new writers to break into print in the magazines listed here. Editors at *Redbook*, a top fiction market which receives up to 600 unsolicited submissions a month, say, "We are interested in new voices and buy up to a quarter of our stories from unsolicited submissions." The fact that *Redbook* and other well-respected publications such as *The Atlantic Monthly* and *The New Yorker* continue to list their fiction needs in *Novel & Short Story Writer's Market* year to year indicates that they are open to both new and established writers. Your keys to breaking into these markets are careful research, professional presentation and, of course, top-quality prose.

Types of magazines

In this section you will find a number of popular publications, some for a broad-based, general-interest readership and others for large but select groups of readers—children, women, men, seniors and teenagers. You'll also find regional publications such as *Northeast*, publishing stories for their Connecticut audience; *Northwest Journal*, "the magazine of the interior Northwest"; and city magazines that include *Boston Review* and *Portland Magazine*.

You'll find religious and church-affiliated magazines, including *The Friend Magazine*, *Home Life* and *Guideposts for Kids*. Other magazines are devoted to the interests of particular cultures and outlooks such as *African Voices*, publishing "enlightening and entertaining literature on the varied lifestyles of people of color," and *Spirit Talk*, featuring themes on American Indian culture.

This section also includes the top markets for genre fiction; many of these have excellent records for publishing new writers. For example, mystery markets include

Ellery Queen's Mystery Magazine, *Alfred Hitchcock Mystery Magazine* and *New Mystery*. For science fiction, you'll find *Asimov's Science Fiction*, *Omni*, *Amazing Stories* and several others. Other genre magazines include *Dragon® Magazine* (fantasy), *Louis L'Amour Western Magazine* (western). These magazines are known to book publishers as fertile ground for budding novelists.

Special interest magazines are another possible market for fiction, but only if your story involves a particular magazine's theme. Some of the highly specialized magazines in this section are *Balloon Life* (hot air ballooning); *Beckett Baseball Card Monthly*; *Easyriders Magazine* (biker-oriented); and *Juggler's World*.

Choosing your market

Unlike smaller journals and publications, most of the magazines listed are available at newsstands and bookstores. Many can also be found in the library, and guidelines and sample copies are almost always available by mail. Start your search, then, by familiarizing yourself with the fiction included in the magazines that interest you.

Don't make the mistake of thinking, just because you are familiar with a magazine, that their fiction isn't any different today than when you first saw it. Nothing could be further from the truth—commercial magazines, no matter how well established, are constantly revising their fiction needs as they strive to reach new readers and expand their audience base.

In a magazine that uses only one or two stories an issue, take a look at the nonfiction articles and features as well. These can give you a better idea of the audience for the publication and clues to the type of fiction that might appeal to them.

If you write a particular type of fiction, such as children's stories or mysteries, you may want to look that subject up in the Category Index at the back of this book. There you will find a list of markets that say they are looking for a particular subject. Check also the subcategories given within each listing. For example, a magazine may be in the Category Index as needing mystery fiction, but check the listing to find out if only a particular subcategory interests them such as hard-boiled detective stories or police procedurals or English-style cozies.

You may want to use our ranking codes as a guide, especially if you are a new writer. At the end of this introduction is a list of the Roman numeral codes we use and what they mean.

About the listings

See How to Get the Most Out of This Book (page 3) for information about the material common to all listings in this book. In this section in particular, pay close attention to the number of submissions a magazine receives in a given period and how many they publish in the same period. This will give you a clear picture of how stiff your competition can be.

While many of the magazines listed here publish one or two pieces of fiction in each issue, some also publish special fiction issues once or twice a year. We have indicated this in the listing information. We also note if the magazine is open to novel excerpts as well as short fiction and we advise novelists to query first before submitting long work.

The Business of Fiction Writing, beginning on page 9, covers the basics of submitting your work. Professional presentation is a must for all markets listed. Editors at commercial magazines are especially busy, and anything you can do to make your manuscript easy to read and accessible will help your chances of being published. Most magazines want to see complete manuscripts, but watch for publications in this section that require a query first.

More about the listings

As in the previous section, we've included our own comments in many of the listings, set off by a bullet (●). Whenever possible, we list the publication's recent awards and honors. We've also included any special information we feel will help you in determining whether a particular publication interests you.

Some of the publishers whose magazines are in this section publish more than one publication. We've cross-referenced these so you can easily find sister magazines as well as contests sponsored by magazines.

Also, you may notice in the case of many of the top-name mystery, romance and science fiction markets, we have included a notation that more information is available in one of our other books. The *Mystery Writer's Sourcebook*, *The Romance Writer's Sourcebook* and the *Science Fiction Writer's Marketplace and Sourcebook*, new titles in our Marketplace Series, are specialized books devoted to these subjects. They contain longer, more in-depth interviews with editors at many mystery, romance and science fiction publications. Also included in these books are articles on various aspects of mystery, romance or science fiction; lists of conventions; awards; and bookstores specializing in these topics.

The maple leaf symbol (❦) identifies our Canadian listings. All North American listings are grouped together first, and you'll find a list of commercial publications from other countries following the main section. Remember to use International Reply Coupons rather than stamps when you want a reply from a country other than your own.

For more information

For more on trends in commercial fiction, see our Commercial Fiction Trends Report starting on page 33. For more on commercial magazines in general, see issues of *Writer's Digest* and industry trade publications such as *Folio*, available in larger libraries.

For news about some of the genre publications listed here and information about a particular field, there are a number of magazines devoted to genre topics, including *Mystery Scene*, *Locus* (for science fiction) and *Science Fiction Chronicle*. Addresses for these and other industry magazines can be found in the section, Publications of Interest to Fiction Writers.

Membership in the national groups devoted to specific genre fields is not restricted to novelists and can be valuable to writers of short fiction in these fields. Many include awards for "Best Short Story" in their annual contests. For information on groups such as the Mystery Writers of America, the Romance Writers of America and the Science fiction and Fantasy Writers of America see the Organizations and Resources section.

The ranking system we've used in this section is as follows:

I **Periodical encourages beginning or unpublished writers to submit work for consideration and publishes new writers regularly.**

II **Periodical publishes work by established writers and by new writers of exceptional talent.**

III **Magazine does not encourage beginning writers; prints mostly writers with previous publication credits and very few new writers.**

IV **Special-interest or regional magazine, open only to writers on certain topics or from certain geographical areas.**

‡**ABORIGINAL SCIENCE FICTION, (II, IV)**, Box 2449, Woburn MA 01888-0849. Editor: Charles C. Ryan. Magazine: 8½×11; 100-116 pages; 40 lb. paper; 60 lb. cover; 4-color cover and b&w interior illustrations;

photos. "*Aboriginal Science Fiction* is looking for good science fiction stories. While 'hard' science fiction will get the most favorable attention, *Aboriginal Science Fiction* also wants good action-adventure stories, *good* space opera, humor and science fantasy for adult science fiction readers." Quarterly. Estab. 1986. Circ. 21,000.

Needs: Science fiction. Original, previously unpublished work only. "No fantasy, sword and sorcery, horror, or Twilight-Zone type stories." Receives 250 unsolicited mss/week. Buys 12 mss/issue; 48 mss/year. Publishes ms 1 year after acceptance. Agented fiction 5%. Published work by Larry Niven, David Brin and Walter Jon Williams; published many new writers within the last year. Length: 2,500 words minimum; 6,000 words maximum. Some shorter material accepted, but "no shorter than 1,500-2,000 words for fiction. Jokes may be 50-150 words." Always comments on rejected mss.

How to Contact: Send complete ms. Reports in 2-3 months. SASE. Sample copy for $4.95 (double issue) plus $1.05 postage and handling. Fiction guidelines for #10 SASE. Reviews novels and short story collections. Send books to Janice M. Eisen, 225 State St., Apt. 454, Schenectady NY 12305 or Darrell Schweitzer, 113 Deepdale Rd., Strafford PA 19087.

Payment/Terms: Pays "$250 flat" and 2 contributor's copies on publication for first North American serial rights and non-exclusive reprint and foreign options.

Advice: "Stories with the best chance of acceptance will make unique use of the latest scientific theories; science ideas; have lively, convincing characters; an ingenious plot; a powerful and well integrated theme, and use an imaginative setting. Read all the science fiction classics and current magazines to understand the field and to avoid clichés."

ADVENTURE CYCLIST, (I, IV), (formerly *Bike Report*), The Adventure Cycling Assn., Box 8308, Missoula MT 59807. (406)721-1776. Editor: Daniel D'Ambrosio. Magazine on bicycle touring: 8⅜ × 10⅞; 24 pages; coated paper; self cover; illustrations and b&w photos. Published 9 times annually. Estab. 1974. Circ. 30,000.

Needs: Adventure, fantasy, historical (general), humor/satire and regional and with a bicycling theme. Buys variable number of mss/year. Published new writers within the last year. Length: 2,000 words average; 1,000 words minimum; 2,500 words maximum. Publishes short shorts. Occasionally comments on rejected ms.

How to Contact: Send complete ms with SASE. Reports in 6 weeks. Simultaneous and previously published submissions OK. Accepts electronic submissions; prefers hard copy with disk submission. Sample copy for $1, 9 × 12 SAE and 60¢ postage. Fiction guidelines for #10 SASE.

Payment/Terms: Pays $25-65/published page on publication for first North American serial rights.

AFRICAN VOICES, The Art and Literary Publication With Class & Soul, (I, II), African Voices Communications, Inc., 270 W. 96th St., New York NY 10025. (212)865-2982. Editor: Carolyn A. Butts. Fiction Editor: Gail Sharbaan. Tabloid: 11 × 15; 24 pages; 30 lb. newsprint; illustrations and photos. "*AV* publishes enlightening and entertaining literature on the varied lifestyles of people of color." Bimonthly. Estab. 1993. Circ. 20,000.

Needs: African-American: children's/juvenile (10-12 years), condensed/excerpted novel, erotica, ethnic/multicultural, gay, historical (general), horror, humor/satire, literary, mystery/suspense, psychic/supernatural/occult, religious/inspirational, science fiction (hard science), young adult/teen (adventure, romance). List of upcoming themes available for SASE. Publishes special fiction issue. Receives 20-50 unsolicited mss/month. Buys 20 mss/issue. Publishes ms 3-6 months after acceptance. Agented fiction 5%. Published work by Darcey Amos, Leslie Pietrzyk and Carol Dixon. Length: 2,000 words average; 500 words minimum; 3,000 words maximum. Occasionally publishes short shorts. Also publishes literary essays and poetry.

How to Contact: Query with clips of published work. Should include short bio. Reports in 4-6 weeks on queries; 2-3 months on mss. Send SASE for return of ms. Simultaneous, reprint and electonic submissions OK. Sample copy for $2 and 9 × 12 SAE. Free fiction guidelines. Reviews novels and short story collections. Send books to Book Editor.

Payment/Terms: Pays $25 maximum on publication for first North American serial rights, free subscription and 5 contributor's copies.

Advice: "A manuscript stands out if it is neatly typed with a well-written and interesting story line or plot. Originality encouraged. We are interested in more horror, erotic and drama pieces. *AV* wants to highlight the diversity in our culture. Stories must go beyond being 'black' and touch the humanity in us all."

AIM MAGAZINE, (I, II), 7308 S. Eberhart Ave., Chicago IL 60619. (312)874-6184. Editor: Ruth Apilado. Fiction Editor: Mark Boone. Newspaper: 8½ × 11; 48 pages; slick paper; photos and illustrations. "Material of social significance: down-to-earth gut. Personal experience, inspirational." For "high school, college and general public." Quarterly. Estab. 1973. Circ. 10,000.

• *Aim* sponsors an annual short story contest listed in this book.

Needs: Open. No "religious" mss. Published special fiction issue last year; plans another. Receives 25 unsolicited mss/month. Buys 15 mss/issue; 60 mss/year. Published work by Thomas J. Cottle, Karl Damgaard, Richie Zeiler; published new writers within the last year. Length: 800-1,000 words average. Publishes short shorts. Sometimes comments on rejected mss.

How to Contact: Send complete ms. SASE with cover letter and author's photograph. Simultaneous submissions OK. Reports in 1 month. Sample copy for $4 with SAE (9×12) and $1.35 postage. Fiction guidelines for #10 SASE.
Payment/Terms: Pays $15-25 on publication for first rights.
Advice: "Search for those who are making unselfish contributions to their community and write about them. Our objective is to purge racism from the human bloodstream. Write about your own experiences. Be familiar with the background of your characters." Known for "stories with social significance, proving that people from different ethnic, racial backgrounds are more alike than they are different."

ALOHA, The Magazine of Hawaii and the Pacific, (IV), Davick Publications, 1240 Ala Moana Blvd., #320, Honolulu HI 96814. (808)593-1191. Fax: (808)593-1327. Editorial Director: Cheryl Tsutsumi. Magazine about the 50th state. Upscale demographics. Bimonthly. Estab. 1977. Circ. 65,000.
● The publisher of *ALOHA* has published a coffee table book, *The Best of ALOHA*. Note *Aloha* has a new address.
Needs: "Only fiction that illuminates the true Hawaiian experience. No stories about tourists in Waikiki or contrived pidgin dialogue." Receives 6 unsolicited mss/month. Publishes ms up to 1 year after acceptance. Length: 1,000-2,500 words average.
How to Contact: Send complete ms. No simultaneous submissions. Reports in 2 months. SASE. Sample copy for $2.95—include SASE (postage is $2.90).
Payment/Terms: Pays between $200-500 on publication for first-time rights.
Advice: "Submit only fiction that is truly local in character. Do not try to write anything about Hawaii if you have not experienced this culturally different part of America."

THE AMERICAN CITIZEN ITALIAN PRESS, 13681 "V" St., Omaha NE 68137. (402)896-0403. Fax: (402)895-7820. Editor: Diana C. Failla. Magazine. Quarterly.
Needs: Ethnic, historical (general), sports, celebrity, human interest, mainstream and translations. "Will assign stories to corresponding writers." Buys 1-2 mss/issue. Length: 80 words minimum; 1,200 words maximum. Publishes short shorts.
How to Contact: Send complete ms with cover letter. Reports in 2 months on queries. Simultaneous submissions OK. "Send photo(s) to accompany story if possible. Pays $5/photo. Poetry also welcome." Sample copy and fiction guidelines for 9×12 SAE.
Payment/Terms: Pays $20-25 on publication for one-time rights.

AMERICAN GIRL, (III), Pleasant Company Publications, 8400 Fairway Place, Middleton WI 53562. (608)836-4848. Editor: Judith Woodburn. Magazine: 8½×11; 52 pages; illustrations and photos. "Four-color bimonthly magazine for girls age 8-12." Estab. 1991.
● Pleasant Company is known for its series of books featuring girls from different periods of American history.
Needs: Children's/juvenile (girls 8-12 years): "contemporary, realistic fiction, adventure, historical, problem stories." Receives 100 unsolicited mss/month. Buys 1 ms/issue; 6 mss/year. Length: 2,500 words average. Publishes short shorts. Also publishes literary essays and poetry (if age appropriate).
How to Contact: Send complete ms with a cover letter. Should include bio (1 paragraph). Send SASE for reply, return of ms or send a disposable copy of ms. Simultaneous submissions OK. Sample copy for $3.95 plus $1.93 postage.
Payment/Terms: Pays in cash; amount negotiable. Pays on acceptance for first North American serial rights. Sends galleys to author.

THE AMERICAN NEWSPAPER CARRIER, (II), Box 2225, Kernersville NC 27285. (910)788-4336. Editor: Will H. Lowry. Newsletter: 9×12; 4 pages; slick paper; b&w illustrations and photos. "A motivational newsletter publishing upbeat articles—mystery, humor, adventure and inspirational material for newspaper carriers (younger teenagers, male and female; also adults)." Monthly. Estab. 1927.
Needs: Adventure, comics, humor/satire, inspirational, suspense/mystery and young adult/teen. No erotica, fantasy, feminist, gay, juvenile, lesbian, preschool, psychic/supernatural or serialized/excerpted novel. Receives approximately 12 unsolicited mss/month. Buys 1 ms/issue; 12 mss/year. Publishes ms 3-6 months after acceptance. "About all" of fiction is agented. Published new writers within the last year. Length: 1,000 words average; 800 words minimum; 1,200 words maximum. Rarely critiques rejected mss.

‡ ***The double dagger before a listing indicates that the listing is new in this edition. New markets are often the most receptive to submissions by new writers.***

How to Contact: Send complete ms. Reports in 1 month. SASE. Free sample copy and fiction guidelines with #10 SASE for each.
Payment/Terms: Pays $25 on acceptance for all rights.
Advice: "We could use some stories dealing with motor route carriers and adult carriers."

ANALOG SCIENCE FICTION & FACT, (II), Doubleday Dell Magazines, 1540 Broadway, New York NY 10036. (212)782-8532. Editor: Stanley Schmidt. Magazine: $5\frac{3}{16} \times 7\frac{3}{8}$; 178 pages; illustrations (drawings); photos. "Well-written science fiction based on speculative ideas and fact articles on topics on the present and future frontiers of research. Our readership includes intelligent laymen and/or those professionally active in science and technology." Thirteen times yearly. Estab. 1930. Circ. 85,000.
- *Analog* is considered one of the leading science fiction publications. The magazine has won a number of Hugos, Chesleys and Nebula Awards. *Asimov's* (also listed in this book) is Doubleday Dell Magazines' other science fiction publication. For an interview with Stanley Schmidt see the first edition of *Science Fiction Writer's Marketplace and Sourcebook* (Writer's Digest Books).

Needs: Science fiction (hard science, soft sociological) and serialized novels. "No stories which are not truly science fiction in the sense of having a plausible speculative idea *integral to the story*. We do two double-size issues per year (January and July)." Receives 300-500 unsolicited fiction mss/month. Buys 4-8 mss/issue. Agented fiction 20%. Published work by Jerry Oltion, Spider Robinson, Geoffrey A. Landis, Ben Bova and Charles Sheffield; published new writers within the last year. Length: 2,000-80,000 words. Publishes short shorts. Critiques rejected mss "when there is time." Sometimes recommends other markets.
How to Contact: Send complete ms with SASE. Cover letter with "anything that I need to know before reading the story, e.g. that it's a rewrite I suggested or that it incorporates copyrighted material. Otherwise, no cover letter is needed." Query with SASE only on serials. Reports in 1 month on both query and ms. No simultaneous submissions. E-mail address: 71154.662@compuserve.com. Fiction guidelines for SASE. Sample copy for $3.50. Reviews novels and short story collections. Send books to Tom Easton.
Payment/Terms: Pays 5-8¢/word on acceptance for first North American serial rights and nonexclusive foreign rights. Sends galleys to author.
Advice: Mss are rejected because of "inaccurate science; poor plotting, characterization or writing in general. We literally only have room for 1-2% of what we get. Many stories are rejected not because of anything conspicuously *wrong*, but because they lack anything sufficiently *special*. What we buy must stand out from the crowd. Fresh, thought-provoking ideas are important. Familiarize yourself with the magazine—but don't try to imitate what we've already published."

✿**THE ANNALS OF ST. ANNE DE BEAUPRÉ, (II)**, Redemptorist Fathers, P.O. Box 1000, St. Anne de Beaupré, Quebec G0A 3C0 Canada. (418)827-4538. Fax: (418)827-4530. Editor: Roch Achard, C.Ss.R. Magazine: 8×11; 32 pages; glossy paper; photos. "Our aim is to promote devotion to St. Anne and Catholic family values." Monthly. Estab. 1878. Circ. 50,000.
Needs: Religious/inspirational. "We only wish to see something inspirational, educational, objective, uplifting. Reporting rather than analysis is simply not remarkable." Receives 50-60 unsolicited mss/month. Published work by Beverly Sheresh, Eugene Miller and Aubrey Haines. Publishes short stories. Length: 1,500 maximum. Always critiques or comments on rejected ms.
How to Contact: Send complete ms with a cover letter. Should include estimated word count. Reports in 3 weeks. Send SASE for reply or return of ms. No simultaneous submissions. Free sample copy and guidelines.
Payment/Terms: Pays 3-4¢/word on acceptance and 3 contributor's copies on publication for first North American serial rights.

ARIZONA COAST, (II), Hale Communications, Inc., 1212 Fourth St., Parker AZ 85344. (602)669-6464. Editor: Jerry Hale. Magazine: $5\frac{1}{2} \times 8\frac{1}{2}$; 40 pages; 70 lb. gloss; illustrations; photos. Publication prints stories about tourism, old West, lifestyle for young travel-oriented family audiences, snowbirds and senior citizens. Bimonthly. Estab. 1988. Circ. 15,000.
Needs: Condensed/excerpted novel, historical (general), senior citizen/retirement, serialized novel, western. Receives 1 unsolicited ms/month. Accepts 1 ms/issue; 6 mss/year. Publishes ms 6 months after acceptance. Publishes short shorts. Sometimes critiques rejected mss.
How to Contact: Send complete ms with cover letter. Reports in 2 months. Simultaneous submissions OK. Accepts electronic submissions. Sample copy free. Reviews novels and short story collections.
Payment/Terms: Pays free subscription to magazine. Acquires one-time rights.
Advice: "Don't give up!"

ART TIMES, (II), A Literary Journal and Resource for All the Arts, P.O. Box 730, Mt. Marion NY 12456. Phone/fax: (914)246-6944. Editor: Raymond J. Steiner. Magazine: 12×15; 20 pages; Jet paper and cover; illustrations; photos. "Arts magazine covering the disciplines for an over 40, affluent, arts-conscious and literate audience." Monthly. Estab. 1984. Circ. 15,000.
- *Art Times* received a citation for "dedication and commitment to the arts" in 1994 from the governor of New York.

Needs: Adventure, contemporary, ethnic, fantasy, feminist, gay, historical, humor/satire, lesbian, literary, mainstream and science fiction. "We seek quality literary pieces. Nothing violent, sexist, erotic, juvenile, racist, romantic, political, etc." Receives 30-50 mss/month. Buys 1 ms/issue; 11 mss/year. Publishes ms within 18-24 months of acceptance. Length: 1,500 words maximum. Publishes short shorts.

How to Contact: Send complete ms with cover letter. Simultaneous submissions OK. Reports in 6 months. SASE. Sample copy for $1.75, 9 × 12 SAE and 3 first-class stamps. Fiction guidelines for #10 SASE.

Payment/Terms: Pays $25, free subscription to magazine (one year) and 6 contributor's copies on publication for first North American serial rights.

Advice: "Competition is greater (more submissions received), but keep trying. We print new as well as published writers."

ASIMOV'S SCIENCE FICTION, (II), Doubleday Dell Magazines, 380 Lexington Ave., New York NY 10168-0035. (212)782-8200. Editor: Gardner Dozois. Executive Editor: Sheila Williams. Magazine: 5³⁄₁₆ × 7⅜ (trim size); 192 pages; 29 lb. newspaper; 70 lb. to 8 pt. C1S cover stock; illustrations; rarely photos. Magazine consists of science fiction and fantasy stories for adults and young adults. Publishes 13 issues/year. Estab. 1977. Circ. 120,000.

• Named for a science fiction "legend," *Asimov's* regularly receives Hugo and Nebula Awards. Editor Gardner Dozois has received several awards for editing including Hugos and those from *Locus* and *Science Fiction Chronicle* magazines. *Locus* also named *Asimov's* "Best Magazine" in 1993, 1994 and 1995. For more, see the interview with Dozois in the first edition of *Science Fiction Writer's Marketplace and Sourcebook*. Doubleday Dell Magazine's other science fiction magazine is *Analog*, also listed in this book.

Needs: Science fiction (hard science, soft sociological) and fantasy. No horror or psychic/supernatural. "We have two double-issues per year (April and November)." Receives approximately 800 unsolicited fiction mss each month. Buys 10 mss/issue. Publishes ms 6-12 months after acceptance. Agented fiction 10%. Published work by George Alec Effinger, Connie Willis, Walter Jon Williams, Gregory Benford and Judith Moffett; published new writers in the last year. Length: up to 20,000 words. Publishes short shorts. Critiques rejected mss "when there is time."

How to Contact: Send complete ms with SASE. No simultaneous submissions. Reports in 2-3 months. Fiction guidelines for #10 SASE. Sample copy for $3.50 and 9 × 12 SASE. Reviews novels and short story collections. Send books to book reviewer.

Payment/Terms: Pays 6-8¢/word for stories up to 7,500 words; 5¢/word for stories over 12,500; $450 for stories between those limits. Pays on acceptance for first North American serial rights plus specified foreign rights, as explained in contract. Very rarely buys reprints. Sends galleys to author.

Advice: "We are looking for character stories rather than those emphasizing technology or science. New writers will do best with a story under 10,000 words. Every new science fiction or fantasy film seems to 'inspire' writers—and this is not a desirable trend. Be sure to be familiar with our magazine and the type of story we like; workshops and lots of practice help. Try to stay away from trite, cliched themes. Start in the middle of the action, starting as close to the end of the story as you possibly can."

THE ASSOCIATE REFORMED PRESBYTERIAN, (II, IV), The Associate Reformed Presbyterian, Inc., 1 Cleveland St., Greenville SC 29601. (803)232-8297. Editor: Ben Johnston. Magazine: 8½ × 11; 32-48 pages; 50 lb. offset paper; illustrations; photos. "We are the official magazine of our denomination. Articles generally relate to activities within the denomination—conferences, department work, etc., with a few special articles that would be of general interest to readers." Monthly. Estab. 1976. Circ. 6,200.

Needs: Contemporary, juvenile, religious/inspirational, spiritual and young adult/teen. "Stories should portray Christian values. No retelling of Bible stories or 'talking animal' stories. Stories for youth should deal with resolving real issues for young people." Receives 30-40 unsolicited fiction mss/month. Buys 1 ms/some months; 10-12 mss/year. Publishes ms within 1 year after acceptance. Recently published work by Lawrence Dorr, Jan Johnson and Deborah Christensen. Length: 300-750 words (children); 1,250 words maximum (youth). Sometimes critiques rejected mss.

How to Contact: Include cover letter. Reports in 6 weeks on queries and mss. Simultaneous submissions OK. Sample copy for $1.50; fiction guidelines for #10 SASE.

Payment/Terms: Pays $20-75 for first rights and contributor's copies.

Advice: "Currently we are seeking stories aimed at the 10 to 15 age group. We have an oversupply of stories for younger children."

THE ATLANTIC MONTHLY, (II), 745 Boylston St., Boston MA 02116. (617)536-9500. Editor: William Whitworth. Senior Editors: Michael Curtis and Jack Beatty. Managing Editor: Cullen Murphy. General magazine for the college educated with broad cultural interests. Monthly. Estab. 1857. Circ. 500,000.

• Work published in *The Atlantic Monthly* has been selected for inclusion in Best American Short Stories and O. Henry Prize anthologies for 1995. The magazine was also a finalist for the National Magazine Awards.

Needs: Literary and contemporary. "Seeks fiction that is clear, tightly written with strong sense of 'story' and well-defined characters." Buys 15-18 stories/year. Receives 1,000 unsolicited fiction mss each month.

Published work by Alice Munro, E.S. Goldman, Charles Baxter and T.C. Boyle; published new writers within the last year. Preferred length: 2,000-6,000 words.

How to Contact: Send cover letter and complete ms with SASE. Reports in 2 months on mss.

Payment/Terms: Pays $2,500/story on acceptance for first North American serial rights.

Advice: When making first contact, "cover letters are sometimes helpful, particularly if they cite prior publications or involvement in writing programs. Common mistakes: melodrama, inconclusiveness, lack of development, unpersuasive characters and/or dialogue."

THE BABY CONNECTION NEWS JOURNAL, (IV), Parent Education for Infant Development, P.O. Drawer 13320, San Antonio TX 78213. Editor: G. Morris-Boyd. Newspaper: 35″ web press; 10¾×16; 24 pages; newsprint paper; newsprint cover; illustrations and photographs. "Material on pregnancy, infant sensory development, birthing and breastfeeding for new and expectant parents, midwives, nurses, ob/gyn's." Quarterly. Estab. 1986. Circ. 45,000.

Needs: Humor/satire, mainstream, parenting, pregnancy, romance (contemporary). Receives 40-60 unsolicited mss/month. Accepts 40-50 mss/quarter; 200 mss/year. Publishes ms 6-9 months after acceptance. Published work by Susan Ludington and Vicki Lansky. Length: 800 words average; 800 words minimum; 1,100 words maximum. Publishes short shorts.

How to Contact: Query with clips of published work. Send complete manuscript with cover letter. "Always include a brief personal bio—not all about works published but info on the writer personally. Married? Children? Hobbies? Our readers like to feel they know the writers personally." Simultaneous submissions OK. Reports in 6-9 months. Sample copy for 10×13 SAE with 3 first-class stamps and $3. Fiction guidelines for #10 SASE and $1.50.

Payment/Terms: Pays in contributor's copies; acquires first rights. Charges for extras.

Advice: "Our needs are definitely more focused. We need fiction based on human experience and prefer writing which allows our readers a window to view humanity clearly. Never call an editor to see if work is received. Always send a letter with a SASE if you have any questions regarding your submission. Remember, thousands of reviews are being catalogued at any given time. A phone call shuts down systems."

BALLOON LIFE, The Magazine for Hot Air Ballooning, (II,IV), 2145 Dale Ave., Sacramento CA 95815. (916)922-9648. Editor: Tom Hamilton. Magazine: 8½×11; 48 pages; color, b&w photos. "Sport of hot air ballooning. Readers participate in hot air ballooning as pilots, crew, official observers at events and spectators."

Needs: Humor/satire, related to hot air ballooning. "Manuscripts should involve the sport of hot air ballooning in any aspect." Buys 4-6 mss/year. Publishes ms within 3-4 months after acceptance. Length: 800 words minimum; 1,500 words maximum; 1,200 words average. Publishes 400-500 word shorts. Sometimes critiques rejected mss and recommends other markets.

How to Contact: Send complete ms with cover letter that includes Social Security number. Reports in 3 weeks on queries; 2 weeks on mss. SASE. Simultaneous and reprint submissions OK. E-mail address: blnlife@scn.org. Sample copy for 9×12 SAE and $1.90 postage. Guidelines for #10 SASE.

Payment/Terms: Pays $25-75 and contributor's copies on publication for first North American serial, one-time or other rights.

Advice: "Generally the magazine looks for humor pieces that can provide a light-hearted change of pace from the technical and current event articles. An example of a work we used was titled 'Balloon Astrology' and dealt with the character of a hot air balloon based on what sign it was born (made) under."

‡THE BEAR ESSENTIAL, (I, II), ORLO, 2516 NW 29th, P.O. Box 10342, Portland OR 97210. (503)242-2330. Fax: (503)243-2645. Editor: Thomas L. Webb. Magazine: 11×14; 72 pages; newsprint paper; Kraft paper cover; illustrations and photos. "*The Bear Essential* has an environmental focus, combining all forms and styles. Fiction should have environmental theme or thread to it, and should be engaging to a cross-section of audiences. The more street-level, the better." Semiannually. Estab. 1993. Circ. 15,000.

• *The Bear Essential* was a finalist in the 1995 Readers' Alternative Media Awards.

Needs: Environmentally focused: children's/juvenile, historical (general), horror, humor/satire, literary, science fiction. Upcoming themes: "Travel" (winter 1995). List of upcoming themes available for SASE. Receives 5-10 unsolicited mss/month. Accepts 2-3 mss/issue; 4-6 mss/year. Publishes ms 6 weeks after acceptance. Agented fiction 10%. Recently published work by David James Duncan, Hannah Hinchman and Gerald Vizenor. Length: 2,500 words average; 900 words minimum; 4,500 words maximum. Publishes short shorts. Also publishes literary essays, literary criticism, poetry, reviews, opinion, investigative journalism, interviews and creative nonfiction. Sometimes critiques or comments on rejected ms.

How to Contact: Send complete ms with a cover letter, or call and discuss with editor. Should include estimated word count, 10-15 word bio, list of publications, copy on disk, if possible. Reports in 1 month on queries; 3 months on mss. Send a disposable copy of mss. Simultaneous, electronic submissions OK. E-mail address: orlo@teleport.com. Sample copy for $2, 7½×11 envelope and 5 first-class stamps. Fiction guidelines for #10 SASE. Reviews novels and short story collections.

Payment/Terms: Pays free subscription to the magazine, 10 contributor's copies; additional copies for postage. Acquires first or one-time rights. Sends galleys to author. Not copyrighted. Sponsors contests, awards or grants for fiction writers.

Advice: "Keep sending work. Write actively and focus on the connections of man, animals, nature, etc., not just flowery descriptions. Urban and suburban environments are grist for the mill as well. Have not seen enough quality humor and irony writing. Juxtaposition of place most welcome. Action and hands-on great. Not all that interested in environmental ranting and simple 'walks through the park.' Make it powerful, yet accessible to a wide audience."

BECKETT BASEBALL CARD MONTHLY, (IV), Statabase, 15850 Dallas Parkway, Dallas TX 75244. (214)991-6657. Editor: Mike Payne. Magazine: 8½ × 11; 128 pages; coated glossy paper; 8 pt. Sterling cover; 12 illustrations; 100 photographs. "Collecting baseball cards is a leisure-time avocation. It's wholesome and something the entire family can do together. We emphasize its positive aspects. For card collectors and sports enthusiasts, 6-60." Monthly. Estab. 1984. Circ. 500,000 paid.

Needs: Humor/satire, sports, young adult/teen (10-18 years). "Sports hero worship; historical fiction involving real baseball figures; fictionalizing specific franchises of national interest such as the Yankees, Dodgers or Mets." No fiction that is "unrealistic sportswise." Publishes ms 4-6 months after acceptance. Length: 1,500 words average; 2,500 words maximum. Publishes short shorts. Sometimes comments on rejected mss or recommends other markets "if we feel we can help the reader close the gap between rejection and acceptance."

How to Contact: Send complete ms with cover letter. Include Social Security number. Reports in 6 weeks. SASE. Will consider reprints "if prior publication is in a very obscure or very prestigious publication." Sample copy for $3. Fiction guidelines free.

Payment/Terms: Pays $80-400 on acceptance for first rights.

Advice: "Fiction must be baseball oriented and accessible to both pre-teenagers and adults; fiction must stress redeeming social values; fictionalization must involve the heroes of the game (past or present) or a major-league baseball franchise with significant national following. The writer must have a healthy regard for standard English usage. A prospective writer must examine several issues of our publication prior to submission. Our publication is extremely successful in our genre, and our writers must respect the sensitivities of our readers. We are different from other sports publications, and a prospective writer must understand our distinctiveness to make a sale here. Especially desirable at this time are action-fiction narratives that can be adapted to comic book treatments. These pieces should be directed to the attention of Fred Reed, Vice President Publishing."

BEPUZZLED, (II, IV), Lombard Marketing, Inc., 22 E. Newberry Rd., Bloomfield CT 06002. (203)769-5700. Editor: Sue Tyska. "Mystery jigsaw puzzles . . . includes short mystery story with clues contained in puzzle picture to solve the mystery for preschool, 8-12 year olds, adults." Estab. 1987.

● Most of the large bookstore chains and specialty shops carry *bePuzzled* and other mystery puzzles.

Needs: Mystery: Adventure, juvenile, mainstream, preschool, suspense, young adult—all with mystery theme. Receives 3 unsolicited fiction mss/month. Buys 20 mss/year. Publishes ms 6-18 months after acceptance. Published work by John Lutz, Matt Christopher, Alan Robbins, Henry Slesar, Katherine Hall Page. Length: 4,000 words preferred; 3,000 words minimum; 4,000 words maximum. Sometimes recommends other markets.

How to Contact: Query for submission guidelines. Reports in 2 months. SASE. Simultaneous submissions OK. Fiction guidelines free.

Payment/Terms: Pays $200 minimum on delivery of final ms. Buys all rights.

Advice: "Thoughtful, challenging mysteries that can be concluded with the visual element of a puzzle. Many times we select certain subject matter and then send out these specifics to our pool of writers . . . List clues and red herrings. Then write the story containing supporting information. Play one of our mystery thrillers so you understand the relationship between the story and the picture."

BLACK BELT, (II), Rainbow Publications, Inc., 24715 Ave. Rockefeller, Valencia CA 91355. (805)257-4066. Executive Editor: Jim Coleman. Magazine: 154 pages. Emphasizes "martial arts for both practitioner and layman." Monthly. Circ. 100,000.

● Note *Black Belt* has increased its maximum payment from $200 to $300.

Needs: Martial arts-related, historical and modern-day. Buys 1-2 fiction mss/year. Publishes ms 3 months to 1 year after acceptance. Published work by Glenn Yancey.

How to Contact: Query first. Reports in 2-3 weeks.

Payment/Terms: Pays $100-300 on publication for first North American serial rights; retains right to republish.

BOMB MAGAZINE, (II), New Art Publications, 594 Broadway, Suite 1002A, New York NY 10012. (212)431-3943. Editor: Betsy Sussler. Magazine: 11 × 14; 100 pages; 70 lb. gloss cover; illustrations and photographs. "Artist-and-writer-edited magazine." Quarterly. Estab. 1981.

Needs: Contemporary, experimental, serialized novel. "We are starting *First Proof*, a special literary supplement to *Bomb*." Publishes "Summer Reading" issue. Receives 40 unsolicited mss/week. Buys 6 mss/issue; 24 mss/year. Publishes ms 3-6 months after acceptance. Agented fiction 80%. Published work by Jim Lewis, AM Homes, Sandra Cisneros and Leslie Dick. Length: 10-12 pages average. Publishes interviews.

How to Contact: Send complete manuscript with cover letter. Reports in 4 months on mss. SASE. Sample copy for $4 with $1.67 postage.

Payment/Terms: Pays $100 and contributor's copies on publication for first or one-time rights. Sends galleys to author.

Advice: "We are committed to publishing new work that commercial publishers often deem too dangerous or difficult. The problem is, a lot of young writers confuse difficult with dreadful. Read the magazine before you even think of submitting something."

BOSTON REVIEW, (II), Boston Critic Inc., E53-407, MIT, Cambridge MA 02139. (617)253-3642. Publisher/Editor: Joshua Cohen. "A bimonthly magazine of politics, arts and culture." Tabloid: 11×17; 40 pages; jet paper. Estab. 1975. Circ. 20,000.

• *Boston Review* sponsors a fiction contest listed in Contests and Awards. Note their new address.

Needs: Contemporary, ethnic, experimental, literary, prose poem, regional, and translations. Publishes an annual Christmas issue. Receives 100 unsolicited fiction mss/month. Buys 4-6 mss/year. Publishes ms an average of 4 months after acceptance. Published work by Joyce Carol Oates, Yasunari Kawabata, Stephen Dixon, Heidi Jon Schmidt and Alice Mattison. Length: 4,000 words maximum; 2,000 words average. Publishes short shorts. Occasionally critiques rejected ms.

How to Contact: Send complete ms with cover letter and SASE. "You can almost always tell professional writers by the very thought-out way they present themselves in cover letters. But even a beginning writer should find some link between the work (its style, subject, etc.) and the publication—some reason why the editor should consider publishing it." Reports in 2-4 months. Simultaneous submissions OK (if noted). E-mail address: bostonreview@mit.edu. Sample copy for $4.50. Reviews novels and short story collections. Send books to John Thompson, managing editor.

Payment/Terms: Pays $50-100 and 5 contributor's copies after publication for first rights.

Advice: "We believe that original fiction is an important part of our culture—and that this should be represented by the *Boston Review*."

BOWHUNTER MAGAZINE, The Number One Bowhunting Magazine, (IV), Cowles Magazines, Inc., Box 8200, Harrisburg PA 17105. (717)657-9555. Fax: (717)657-9526. Editor: M.R. James. Publisher: Dave Canfield. Managing Editor: Richard Cochran. Magazine: $8 \times 10\frac{1}{2}$; 150 pages; 75 lb. glossy paper; 150 lb. glossy cover stock; illustrations and photographs. "We are a special interest publication for people who hunt with the bow and arrow. We publish hunting adventure and how-to stories. Our audience is predominantly male, 30-50, middle income." Bimonthly. Circ. 200,000.

• Themes included in most fiction considered for *Bowhunter* are pro-conservation as well as pro-hunting.

Needs: Bowhunting, outdoor adventure. "Writers must expect a very limited market. We buy only one or two fiction pieces a year. Writers must know the market—bowhunting—and let that be the theme of their work. No 'me and my dog' types of stories; no stories by people who have obviously never held a bow in their hands." Receives 1-2 unsolicited fiction mss/month. Buys 1-2 mss/year. Publishes ms 3 months to 2 years after acceptance. Length: 1,500 words average; 500 words minimum; 2,000 words maximum. Publishes short shorts. Length: 500 words. Sometimes critiques rejected mss and recommends other markets.

How to Contact: Query first or send complete ms with cover letter. Reports in 2 weeks on queries; 4 weeks on mss. Sample copy for $2 and $8\frac{1}{2} \times 11$ SAE with appropriate postage. Fiction guidelines for #10 SASE.

Payment/Terms: Pays $100-350 on acceptance for first North American serial rights.

Advice: "We have a resident humorist who supplies us with most of the 'fiction' we need. But if a story comes through the door which captures the essence of bowhunting and we feel it will reach out to our readers, we will buy it. Despite our macho outdoor magazine status, we are a bunch of English majors who love to read. You can't bull your way around real outdoor people—they can spot a phony at 20 paces. If you've never camped out under the stars and listened to an elk bugle and try to relate that experience without really experiencing it, someone's going to know. We are very specialized; we don't want stories about shooting apples off people's heads or of Cupid's arrow finding its mark. James Dickey's *Deliverance* used bowhunting metaphorically, very effectively . . . while we don't expect that type of writing from everyone, that's the kind of feeling that characterizes a good piece of outdoor fiction."

BOYS' LIFE, For All Boys, (II), Boy Scouts of America, Magazine Division, Box 152079, 1325 W. Walnut Hill Lane, Irving TX 75015-2079. (214)580-2366. Fiction Editor: Shannon Lowry. Magazine: 8×11; 68 pages; slick cover stock; illustrations; photos. "*Boys' Life* covers Boy Scout activities and general interest subjects for ages 8 to 18, Boy Scouts, Cub Scouts and others of that age group." Monthly. Estab. 1911. Circ. 1,300,000.

• *Boys' Life* has received numerous awards including the 1994 EdPress Distinguished Achievement In Fiction Award.

Needs: Adventure, humor/satire, mystery/suspense (young adult), science fiction, sports and western (young adult). "We publish short stories aimed at a young adult audience and frequently written from the viewpoint of a 10- to 16-year-old boy protagonist." Receives approximately 150 unsolicited mss/month. Buys 12-18 mss/year. Published work by Donald J. Sobol, Geoffrey Norman, G. Clifton Wisler and Marlys Stapelbroek; published new writers within the last year. Length: 500 words minimum; 1,500 words maximum; 1,200 words average. "Very rarely" critiques rejected ms.

How to Contact: Send complete ms with SASE. "We'd much rather see manuscripts than queries." Reports in 6-8 weeks. Simultaneous submissions OK. For sample copy "check your local library." Writer's guidelines available; send SASE.

Payment/Terms: Pays $500 and up ("depending on length and writer's experience with us") on acceptance for one-time rights.

Advice: "*Boys' Life* writers understand the readers. They treat them as intelligent human beings with a thirst for knowledge and entertainment. We tend to use some of the same authors repeatedly because their characters, themes, etc., develop a following among our readers. Read at least a year's worth of the magazine. You will get a feeling for what our readers are interested in and what kind of fiction we buy."

BUFFALO SPREE MAGAZINE, (II, IV), Spree Publishing Co., Inc., 4511 Harlem Rd., Buffalo NY 14226. (716)839-3405. Editor: Johanna Van De Mark. "City magazine for professional, educated and above-average income people." Quarterly. Estab. 1967. Circ. 21,000.

Needs: Literary, contemporary, feminist, mystery, adventure, humor and ethnic. No pornographic or religious. Buys about 15 mss/issue; 60 mss/year. Length: 2,500 words maximum.

How to Contact: Send complete ms with SASE. Reports within 3-6 months. Sample copy for $2, 9×12 SASE and $2.40 postage.

Payment/Terms: Pays $80-150 and 1 contributor's copy on publication for first rights.

BUGLE, Journal of Elk and the Hunt, (II, IV), Rocky Mountain Elk Foundation, P.O. Box 8249, Missoula MT 59807-8249. (406)523-4568. Fax: (406)523-4550. Editor: Dan Crockett. Magazine: 8½×11; 114-172 pages; 55 lb. Escanaba paper; 80 lb. sterling cover; b&w, 4-color illustrations and photographs. "The Rocky Mountain Elk Foundation is a nonprofit conservation organization, established in 1984 to help conserve critical habitat for elk and other wildlife. *BUGLE*, the Foundation's quarterly magazine specializes in articles, research, stories (fiction and nonfiction), art and photography pertaining to the world of elk and elk hunting." Quarterly. Estab. 1984.

Needs: Elk-related adventure, children's/juvenile (5-9 years, 10-12 years), historical, human interest, natural history, scientific. Receives 10-15 unsolicited mss/month. Buys 5 mss/issue; 18-20 mss/year. Publishes ms 6 months after acceptance. Published work by Don Burgess and Mike Logan. Length: 2,500 words preferred; 1,500 words minimum; 5,000 words maximum. Publishes short shorts. Also publishes literary essays and poetry.

How to Contact: Query first or send complete ms with a cover letter. Should include estimated word count and bio (100 words). Reports in 2-4 weeks on queries; 4-6 weeks on ms. Send SASE for reply, return of ms or send a disposable copy of ms. Sample copy for $5. Writers guidelines free.

Payment/Terms: Pays 15¢/word maximum on acceptance for one-time rights.

Advice: "We accept fiction and nonfiction stories about elk that show originality, and respect for the animal and its habitat. No 'formula' outdoor writing. No how-to writing."

BUZZ, The Talk of Los Angeles, (II, IV), Buzz Inc., 11835 W. Olympic #450, Los Angeles CA 90064. (310)473-2721. Fax: (310)473-2876. Editor: Allan Mayer. Fiction Editor: Renée Vogel. Magazine: 9×10⅞; 96-120 pages; coated paper. Published 10 times/year. Estab. 1990. Circ. 125,000.

Needs: Literary, mainstream/contemporary, regional. Receives 75-100 unsolicited mss/month. Buys 1 ms/issue; 10 mss/year. Published work by Thom Jones, Charles Bukowski, Barbara Kingsolver and Walter Mosley. Length: 2,000 words minimum; 5,000 words maximum. Sometimes critiques or comments on rejected mss.

How to Contact: Send complete ms with a cover letter. Reports on mss in 2 months. SASE for return of ms. Simultaneous and electronic submissions OK. E-mail addresses: buzzmag@aol.com; buzz@earthlink.net. Sample copy for $2.50, 11×14 SAE and $3 postage. Fiction guidelines for SASE. Send books to Renée Vogel.

Market categories: (I) Open to new writers; (II) Open to both new and established writers; (III) Interested mostly in established writers; (IV) Open to writers whose work is specialized.

Payment/Terms: Pays $1,000-2,300 and contributor's copies for first North American serial rights. Sends galleys to author.
Advice: "Only interested in fiction by L.A. writers or about L.A."

CAMPUS LIFE MAGAZINE, (II), Christianity Today, Inc., 465 Gundersen Drive, Carol Stream IL 60188. (708)260-6200. Fax: (708)260-0114. Managing Editor: Christopher Lutes. Magazine: 8¼ × 11¼; 100 pages; 4-color and b&w illustrations; 4-color and b&w photos. "General interest magazine with a Christian point of view." Articles "vary from serious to humorous to current trends and issues, for high school and college age readers." Monthly except combined May-June and July-August issues. Estab. 1942. Circ. 130,000.
• *Campus Life* regularly receives awards from the Evangelical Press Association.
Needs: Condensed novel, humor/satire, prose poem, serialized/excerpted novel. "All submissions must be contemporary, reflecting the teen experience in the '90s. We are a Christian magazine but are *not* interested in sappy, formulaic, sentimentally religious stories. We *are* interested in well crafted stories that portray life realistically, stories high school and college youth relate to. Nothing contradictory of Christian values. If you don't understand our market and style, don't submit." Buys 5 mss/year. Reading and response time slower in summer. Published work by Barbara Durkin and Tracy Dalton; published new writers within the last year. Length: 1,000-3,000 words average, "possibly longer." Publishes short shorts.
How to Contact: Query with short synopsis of work, published samples and SASE. Does not accept unsolicited manuscripts. Reports in 4-6 weeks on queries. Sample copy for $2 and 9½ × 11 envelope.
Payment/Terms: Pays "generally" $250-400; 2 contributor's copies on acceptance for one-time rights.
Advice: "We print finely crafted fiction that carries a contemporary teen (older teen) theme. First person fiction often works best. Ask us for sample copy with fiction story. Fiction communicates to our reader. We want experienced fiction writers who have something to say to or about young people without getting propagandistic."

CAPPER'S, (II), Stauffer Magazine Group, 1503 S.W. 42nd St., Topeka KS 66609-1265. (913)274-4300. Fax: (913)274-4305. Editor: Nancy Peavler. Magazine: 24-48 pages; newsprint paper and cover stock; photos. A "clean, uplifting and nonsensational newspaper for families from children to grandparents." Biweekly. Estab. 1879. Circ. 375,000.
• Stauffer Communications also publishes *Grit* listed in this book. See the interview with Nancy Peavler in the 1995 edition. *Capper's* is interested in longer works, 7,000 words or more.
Needs: Serialized novels. "We accept novel-length stories for serialization. No fiction containing violence, sexual references or obscenity." Receives 2-3 unsolicited fiction mss each month. Buys 4-6 stories/year. Published work by Juanita Urbach, Colleen L. Reece and John E. Stolberg; published new writers within the last year. Length: 7,000 words minimum; 40,000 words maximum.
How to Contact: Send complete ms with SASE. Cover letter and/or synopsis helpful. Reports in 6-8 months on ms. Sample copy for $1.50.
Payment/Terms: Pays $75-400 for one-time serialization and contributor's copies (1-2 copies as needed for copyright) on acceptance for second serial (reprint) rights and one-time rights.
Advice: "Please proofread and edit carefully. We've seen major characters change names partway through the manuscript."

CAREER FOCUS, COLLEGE PREVIEW, DIRECT AIM, JOURNEY, VISIONS, (IV), Communications Publishing Group, Inc., 106 W. 11th St., #250, Kansas City MO 64105-1806. (816)221-4404. Editor: Michelle Paige. Magazines: 70 pages; 50 lb. paper; gloss enamel cover; 8 × 10 or 5 × 7 (preferred) illustrations; camera ready photographs. *Career Focus*, "For Today's Professionals" includes career preparation, continuing education and upward mobility skills for advanced Black and Hispanic college students and college graduates. Bimonthly. *College Preview*, "For College-Bound Students" is designed to inform and motivate Black and Hispanic high school students on college preparation and career planning. *Direct Aim*, "A Resource for Career Strategies," is designed for Black and Hispanic college students. Discusses career preparation advancement and management strategies as well as life-enhancement skills. Quarterly. Circ. 600,000. *Journey*, "A Success Guide for College and Career-Bound Students" is for Asian American high school and college students who have indicated a desire to pursue higher education through college, vocational/technical or proprietary schools. Semiannually. *Visions*, "A Success Guide for Career-Bound Students" is designed for Native American students who want to pursue a higher education through college, vocational/technical or proprietary schools. Semiannually. Specialized publication limited to certain subjects or themes.
Needs: Adventure, condensed/excerpted novel, contemporary, ethnic, experimental, historical (general), humor/satire, prose poem, romance (contemporary, historical, young adult), science fiction, sports, suspense/mystery. Receives 2-3 unsolicited mss/month. Buys 2-4 mss/year. After acceptance of ms, time varies before it is published. Length: 1,000 words minimum; 4,000 words maximum. Publishes short shorts. Does not usually comment on rejected ms.
How to Contact: Query with clips of published work (include Social Security number) or send copy of resume and when available to perform. Reports in 4-6 weeks. SASE. Simultaneous and reprint submissions OK. Sample copy and fiction guidelines for 9 × 10 SASE.

Payment/Terms: Pays 10¢ per word on acceptance for first rights and second serial (reprint) rights.

Advice: "Today's fiction market is geared toward stories that are generated from real-life events because readers are more sophisticated and aware of current affairs. But because everyday life is quite stressful nowadays, even young adults want to escape into science fiction and fairytales. Fiction should be entertaining and easy to read. Be aware of reader audience. Material should be designed for status-conscious young adults searching for quality and excellence. Do not assume readers are totally unsophisticated and avoid casual mention of drug use, alcohol abuse or sex. Avoid overly ponderous, overly cute writing styles. We are an ethnic market so fiction cannot be obviously Anglo. Query describing the topic and length of proposed article. Include samples of published work if possible. Must be typed, double spaced on white bond paper (clean copy only)."

CATS MAGAZINE, (IV), CATS Magazine Inc., P.O. Box 290037, Port Orange FL 32129. (904)788-2770. Editor: Tracey Copeland. Magazine: 8×11; 76-100 pages; 40 lb. paper; 60 lb. cover; illustrations and photos. "*CATS Magazine* provides articles that appeal to average cat owners, as well as breeders, on a broad range of topics." Monthly. Estab. 1945. Circ. 150,000.

● *CATS Magazine* received four bronze awards from the Florida Magazine Association in 1994.

Needs: Inspirational. "No reformed cat haters or anything with cats in a bad light (occult ties, etc.)." Receives 50 unsolicited mss/month. Buys 3-4 ms/issue; 36-48 mss/year. Publishes ms 6-18 months after acceptance. Length: 1,000 words average; 350 words minimum; 1,200 words maximum. Publishes short shorts.

How to Contact: Send complete ms with a cover letter. Should include estimated word count and list of publications. Reports in 1-3 months on queries; 2-4 months on mss. SASE for return of ms. Simultaneous and electronic (with hard copy) submissions OK. Sample copy for $3 or send 9×12 SAE with $1.70 postage. Fiction guidelines for #10 SASE. "Please state if it is a simultaneous submission."

Payment/Terms: Pays $20-50 and 1 contributor's copy on publication for first rights or one-time rights.

Advice: "Our short story section, Tails & Tales, is subtitled 'Short stories from our readers about special cats in their lives.' Stories should be believable. No stories are accepted from the cats point of view. Know the basics. Study the cat market. To get the best idea of what a magazine's fiction needs are, read several of their back issues. Also, don't force yourself to write on a certain topic. Write what you know and are comfortable with and then submit to appropriate publications."

✤CHICKADEE, The Magazine for Young Children from OWL, (II), Owl Communications, Suite 500, 179 John St., Toronto, Ontario M5T 3G5 Canada. (416)971-5275. Fax: (416)971-5294. Managing Editor: Carolyn Meredith. Editor: Lizann Flatt. Magazine: 8½×11¾; 32 pages; glossy paper and cover stock; illustrations and photographs. "*Chickadee* is created to give children under eight a lively, fun-filled look at the world around them. Each issue has a mix of activities, puzzles, games and stories." Monthly except July and August. Estab. 1979. Circ. 110,000.

● *Chickadee* has won several awards including the EDPRESS Golden Lamp Honor award and the Parents' Choice Golden Seal awards.

Needs: Juvenile. No religious or anthropomorphic material. Buys 1 ms/issue; 10 mss/year. Publishes ms an average of 1 year after acceptance. Published new writers within the last year. Length: 900 words maximum.

How to Contact: Send complete ms and cover letter with $1 to cover postage and handling. Simultaneous submissions OK. Reports in 2 months. Sample copy for $4.50. Fiction guidelines for SASE.

Payment/Terms: Pays $25-250 (Canadian); 2 contributor's copies on acceptance for all rights. Occasionally buys reprints.

Advice: "Read back issues to see what types of fiction we publish. Common mistakes include: loose, rambling, and boring prose; stories that lack a clear beginning, middle and end; unbelievable characters; and overwriting."

CHILD LIFE, (IV), Children's Better Health Institute, Box 567, 1100 Waterway Blvd., Indianapolis IN 46206. (317)636-8881. Editor: Lise Hoffman. Juvenile magazine for kids aged 9-11. Looking for "nonfiction stories on health, sports, fitness, exercise, nutrition and safety; fiction stories using contemporary kids and situations involving health, humor or adventure."

● The Children's Better Health Institute also publishes *Children's Digest, Children's Playmate, Humpty Dumpty, Jack and Jill* and *Turtle* magazines listed in this book.

Needs: Juvenile. No book manuscripts or adult or adolescent fiction. Recently published work by Eileen Spinelli, Ellen Senisi, Charles Ghigna and Pete Garvey. "Will publish new writers if they demonstrate knowledge of and ability to meed editorial needs." Length: 900 words maximum.

How to Contact: Send complete ms with SASE. No queries. Reports in 12 weeks. Sample copy for $1.25. Writer's guidelines for SASE.

Payment/Terms: Approximately 12¢/word on publication for all rights. One-time rights for photos.

Advice: "Don't guess at what kids like—hang out with them. What interests or concerns them? What do their conversations sound like? Use dialogue to elaborate on contemporary situations in fiction stories. Nonfiction stories with professional-quality, color slides and factual, current information with a sports/health angle will receive preference. Tell your readers (and your editors) something they don't already know. Avoid tired themes of underachiever turns hero, child rescues adult or pet, and animal main characters."

CHILDREN'S DIGEST, (II, IV), Children's Better Health Institute, P.O. Box 567, 1100 Waterway Blvd., Indianapolis IN 46206. Editor: Layne Cameron. Magazine: 6½×9; 48 pages; reflective and preseparated illustrations; color and b&w photos. Magazine with special emphasis on health, nutrition, exercise and safety for preteens.
   • Other magazines published by Children's Better Health Institute and listed in this book are *Child Life, Children's Playmate, Humpty Dumpty, Jack and Jill* and *Turtle.* The magazine has become known for stories featuring contemporary situations and sports/fitness stories.
Needs: "Realistic stories, short plays, adventure and mysteries. We would like to see more stories that reflect today's society: concern for the environment, single-parent families and children from diverse backgrounds. Humorous stories are highly desirable. We especially need stories that *subtly* encourage readers to develop better health or safety habits. Stories should not exceed 1,500 words." Receives 40-50 unsolicited fiction mss each month. Published work by Judith Josephson, Pat McCarthy, Sharen Liddell; published new writers within the last year.
How to Contact: Send complete ms with SASE. "A cover letter isn't necessary unless an author wishes to include publishing credits and special knowledge of the subject matter." Reports in 10 weeks. Sample copy for $1.25. Guidelines with SASE.
Payment/Terms: Pays 12¢/word minimum with up to 10 contributor's copies on publication for all rights.
Advice: "We try to present our health-related material in a positive—not a negative—light, and we try to incorporate humor and a light approach wherever possible without minimizing the seriousness of what we are saying. Fiction stories that deal with a health theme need not have health as the primary subject but should include it in some way in the course of events. Most rejected health-related manuscripts are too preachy or they lack substance. Children's magazines are not training grounds where authors learn to write 'real' material for 'real' readers. Because our readers frequently have limited attention spans, it is very important that we offer them well-written stories."

CHILDREN'S PLAYMATE, (IV), Children's Better Health Institute, P.O. Box 567, 1100 Waterway Blvd., Indianapolis IN 46206. (317)636-8881. Editor: Terry Harshman. Magazine: 6½×9; 48 pages; preseparated and reflective art; b&w and color illustrations. Juvenile magazine for children ages 6-8 years. Published 8 times/year.
   • *Child Life, Children's Digest, Humpty Dumpty Jack and Jill* and *Turtle* magazines are also published by Children's Better Health Institute and listed in this book.
Needs: Juvenile with special emphasis on health, nutrition, safety and exercise. "Our present needs are for short, entertaining stories with a subtle health angle. Seasonal material is also always welcome." No adult or adolescent fiction. Receives approximately 150 unsolicited fiction mss each month. Published work by Batta Killion, Ericka Northrop, Elizabeth Murphy-Melas; published new writers within the last year. Length: 625 words or less.
How to Contact: Send complete ms with SASE. Indicate word count on material and date sent. Reports in 8-10 weeks. Sample copy for $1.25.
Payment/Terms: Pays up to 17¢/word and 10 contributor's copies on publication for *all* rights.
Advice: "Stories should be kept simple and entertaining. Study past issues of the magazine—be aware of vocabulary limitations of the readers."

THE CHRISTIAN CENTURY, An Ecumenical Weekly, (I, IV), 407 S. Dearborn St., Chicago IL 60605. (312)427-5380. Fax: (312)427-1302. Editor: James Wall. Magazine: 8¼×10⅞; 24-40 pages; illustrations and photos. "A liberal Protestant magazine interested in the public meaning of Christian faith as it applies to social issues, and in the individual appropriation of faith in modern circumstances." Weekly (sometimes biweekly). Estab. 1900. Circ. 37,000.
   • *Christian Century* has received several awards each year from the Associated Church Press, including: best critical review, best written humor, best feature article, etc.
Needs: Religious/inspirational: feminist, mainstream/contemporary. "We are interested in articles that touch on religious themes in a sophisticated way; we are not interested in simplistic pietistic pieces." Receives 80 unsolicited mss/month. Buys 10% of unsolicited mss. Publishes ms 1-3 months after acceptance. Published work by Robert Drake and Madeleine Mysko. Length: 2,500 words average; 1,500 words minimum; 3,000 words maximum. Also publishes literary essays and poetry.
How to Contact: Send complete ms with a cover letter. Should include bio (100 words). Reports in 1 week on queries; 1 month on mss. Send a disposable copy of ms. No simultaneous submissions. Sample copy for $2. Reviews novels and short story collections.
Payment/Terms: Pays $200 maximum and 1 contributor's copy (additional copies for $1) on publication for all rights. Sends galleys to author.

CHRISTIAN SINGLE, (II), Lifeway Press, 127 Ninth Ave. N., MSN 140, Nashville TN 37234. (615)251-2228. Editor-in-Chief: Stephen Felts. Magazine: 8½×11; 50 pages; illustrations; photographs. "We reflect the doctrine and beliefs of evangelical Christian single adults. We prefer positive, uplifting, encouraging

Avoid the Sermon When Writing Religious Fiction

Although *The Christian Century* magazine has been in print since 1884, it's only just begun to start publishing fiction in the last year. Fiction Editor Trudy Bush says she's anxious to be flooded with "really good writing" from writers who are both well-published or have yet to see their name in print. "We'd like to publish people with the potential to become the John Updikes of the future," says Bush.

Trudy Bush

A Protestant weekly publication, *The Christian Century* is read primarily by religious professionals of all denominations, as well as educated lay people of all ages (particularly in the 30- to 55-year-old age group) and covers religion, society, politics and the arts from a Christian perspective. Although the magazine may be spiritual in its focus, it does not run fiction which has the intention of conveying a specific message or that mimics a sermon. Like editors at similar publications, Bush is not interested in preachy material.

"We want submissions to our publication to be broadly marked by some kind of concern with the religious dimensions of life, by which we mean with moral and ethical issues, but we want pieces with real literary merit," says Bush. "We are not looking for very pious, sentimental religious stuff. We're not like that at all," she adds.

Contemporary religious publications look for fiction dealing with current social and ethical issues. "One recent story in our magazine was about a middle-aged mother coming to terms with the death of her daughter," says Bush. The magazine also recently ran a story written by a man who has been in prison for a long time. "He wrote a beautiful story narrated by a brother who tells of his sister's severe depression and its effects on the family as she returns to a sense of balance," says Bush.

Readers of religious fiction want to come away with more than just a simple life lesson. They want "the aesthetic satisfaction that always comes from encountering a good work of art," says Bush, "along with an increased understanding of themselves and of human relationships."

Bush was a professor of English at the University of Wisconsin before joining the editorial staff of *The Christian Century* two years ago. As the wife of a United Methodist pastor, she's had to change jobs a number of times. Bush finds she's particularly happy in her role as a fiction editor. "I always thought journalism would be fun. As someone who is very immersed in the church, I like working for a religious publication. I feel I work on something which makes a worthwhile contribution to the world, and I particularly like finding talented writers and helping them develop their talent." In addition to working with well-established writers, Bush says she hopes to have the opportunity to discover and work with many beginning writers as well.

Still, finding well-written stories remains a challenge. "We reject almost all of the manuscripts we receive because people misunderstand the type of religious fiction we want." All too often, says Bush, the manuscripts which she receives lack a plot. "They're very much just a slice of life such as 'My Afternoon at the Soup Kitchen' where nothing happens at all," she says with a laugh. "The stories we print don't have to have a conventional plot but we want something to happen; we want some kind of resolution." Bush would also like to make it clear that the magazine is not a New Age publication nor is she interested in science fiction.

Any advice for the new fiction writer interested in selling to religious publications? "I would say not to underestimate readers by making the message too obvious," says Bush. "Make your stories accessible and touching, but remember you're writing for intelligent and discriminating people." For those just getting started as writers, Bush says flexibility will serve them well. "Writers will often treasure every word and bristle at change; be willing to listen to literary criticism and revise if necessary."

—*Kathleen M. Heins*

fiction written from the single perspective." Monthly. Estab. 1979. Circ. 75,000.
Needs: Religious/inspirational. Receives 100 unsolicited ms/month. Buys 1 ms/issue; 4-5 mss/year. Length: 600-1,200 words average. Publishes short shorts and poetry.
How to Contact: Send query with SASE. Should include estimated word count and opening paragraph. Reports in 1-2 weeks on queries; 3-6 weeks on mss. Send SASE for reply, return of ms or send a disposable copy of the ms. No simultaneous submissions. Accepts reprint and electronic submissions. Sample copy for 9×12 SAE and 4 first-class stamps.
Payment/Terms: Payment is "negotiable." Pays on acceptance. Buys all rights, first rights, first North American serial rights or one-time rights.
Advice: Looks for "mss that are not preachy and intended for a single audience. Write to evoke an emotion. No Pollyanna stories please. I want stories of 'real' life with 'real' people finding real answers using biblical principles. Take a lot of time to draft a well-written query letter that includes a paragraph or two of the actual piece. I can feel by the query letter what quality of an article I can expect to receive."

✦**COMPANION MAGAZINE, (II)**, Conventual Franciscan Friars, Box 535, Postal Station F, Toronto, Ontario M4Y 2L8 Canada. (416)690-5611. Editor: Fr. Rick Riccioli, OFM. Conv. Managing Editor: Betty McCrimmon. Publishes material "emphasizing religious and human values and stressing Franciscan virtues— peace, simplicity, joy." Monthly. Estab. 1936. Circ. 5,000.
 • *Companion* received three awards from the Canadian Church Press in 1994.
Needs: Adventure, humor, mainstream, religious. Canadian settings preferred. Receives 50 unsolicited fiction mss/month. Buys 2 mss/issue. Time varies between acceptance and publication. Length: 1,200 words maximum. Publishes short shorts.
How to Contact: Send complete mss. Reports in 3 weeks to 1 month on mss. SAE with "cash to buy stamps" or IRC. Sample copy and fiction guidelines free.
Payment/Terms: Pays 6¢/word (Canadian funds) on publication for first North American serial rights.

COMPUTOREDGE, San Diego's Free Weekly Computer Magazine, (IV), The Byte Buyer, Inc., Box 83086, San Diego CA 92138. (619)573-0315. Fax: (619)573-0205. Editor: Leah Steward. Magazine: $8\frac{1}{2} \times 11$; 60-80 pages; newsprint; 50 lb. bookwrap cover; illustrations. Publishes material relating to "personal computers from a human point of view. For new users/shoppers." Weekly. Estab. 1983. Circ. 90,000.
Needs: Fiction that includes computers. "Keep it short! Can be science fiction including computers or 'future' stories." Receives up to 3 unsolicited fiction mss/month. Buys 10 fiction mss/year. Publishes ms 1-4 months after acceptance. Length: 800 words minimum; 1,200 words maximum.

How to Contact: Send complete ms with cover letter. Include Social Security number and phone number. Reports in 2 months. SASE. Electronic submission of *accepted* mss *only*. Sample copy for 9 × 12 SAE and $1.50 postage; writer's guidelines for #10 SASE.
Payment/Terms: Pays 8-10¢/word on publication for first rights or first North American serial rights. Offers $15 kill fee.
Advice: Magazine fiction today is "too trendy. Reader should be able to come away moved, enlightened, edified."

CONTACT ADVERTISING, (IV), Box 3431, Ft. Pierce FL 34948. (407)464-5447. Editor: Herman Nietzche. Magazines and newspapers. Publications vary in size, 56-80 pages. "Group of 26 erotica, soft core publications for swingers, single males, married males, gay males, transgendered and bisexual persons." Bimonthly, quarterly and monthly. Estab. 1975. Circ. combined is 2,000,000.
  ● This a group of regional publications with *very* explicit sexual content, graphic personal ads, etc. Not for the easily offended.
Needs: Erotica, fantasy, feminist, fetish, gay and lesbian. Receives 8-10 unsolicited mss/month. Buys 1-2 mss/issue; 40-50 mss/year. Publishes ms 1-3 months after acceptance. Length: 2,000 words minimum; 3,500 words maximum; 2,500-3,000 words average. Sometimes critiques rejected mss.
How to Contact: Query first, query with clips of published work or send complete ms with cover letter. Reports in 1-2 weeks on queries; 3-4 weeks on mss. SASE. Simultaneous and reprint submissions OK. Sample copy for $6. Fiction guidelines with SASE.
Payment/Terms: First submission, free subscription to magazine; subsequent submissions $25-75 on publication for all rights or first rights; all receive three contributor's copies.
Advice: "Know your grammar! Content must be of an adult nature but well within guidelines of the law. Fantasy, unusual sexual encounters, swinging stories or editorials of a sexual bend are acceptable. Read Henry Miller!"

CORNERSTONE MAGAZINE, (I, II), Cornerstone Communications, Inc., 939 W. Wilson Ave., Chicago IL 60640. (312)561-2450 ext. 2394. Fax (312)989-2076. Editor: Dawn Herrin Mortimer. Fiction Editor: Jean Erickson. Magazine: 8½ × 11; 64 pages; 35 lb. coated matie paper; self cover; illustrations and photos. "For young adults, 18-35. We publish nonfiction (essays, personal experience, religious), music interviews, current events, film and book reviews, fiction, poetry. *Cornerstone* challenges readers to look through the window of biblical reality. Known as avant-garde, yet attempts to express orthodox belief in the language of the nineties." Approx. quarterly. Estab. 1972. Circ. 40,000.
  ● *Cornerstone Magazine* has won numerous awards from the Evangelical Press Association.
Needs: Ethnic/multicultural, fantasy (science fantasy), humor/satire, literary, mainstream/contemporary, religious/inspirational. Special interest in "issues pertinent to contemporary society, seen with a biblical worldview." No "pornography, cheap shots at non-Christians, unrealistic or syrupy articles." Upcoming theme: "Racism." Receives 60 unsolicited mss/month. Buys 1 mss/issue; 3-4 mss/year. Does not read mss during Christmas/New Year's week and the first week of July. Published work by Dave Cheadle, C.S. Lewis and J.B. Simmonds. Length: 1,200 words average; 250 words minimum; 2,500 words maximum. Publishes short shorts. Length: 250-450 words. Also publishes literary essays, literary criticism and poetry.
How to Contact: Send complete ms. Should include estimated word count, bio (50-100 words), list of publications, and name, address, phone and fax number on every item submitted. Send disposable copy of the ms. Will consider simultaneous submissions, reprints and electronic (disk or modem) submissions. Reports in up to 3 months. Sample copy for 8½ × 11 SAE and 6 first-class stamps. Reviews novels and short story collections.
Payment/Terms: Pays 8-10¢/word maximum; also 6 contributor's copies on publication. Purchases first serial rights.
Advice: "Articles may express Christian world view but shouldn't be unrealistic or syrupy. We're looking for high-quality fiction with skillful characterization and plot development and imaginative symbolism." Looks for "mature Christian short stories, as opposed to those more fit for church bulletins. We want fiction with bite and an edge but with a Christian worldview."

COSMOPOLITAN MAGAZINE, (III), The Hearst Corp., 224 W. 57th St., New York NY 10019. (212)649-2000. Editor: Helen Gurley Brown. Fiction Editor: Betty Kelly. Associate Fiction Editor: Alison Brower. Most stories include male-female relationships, traditional plots, characterizations. Single career women (ages 18-34). Monthly. Circ. just under 3 million.
Needs: Adventure, contemporary, mystery and romance. "Stories should include a romantic relationship and usually a female protagonist. The characters should be in their 20s or 30s (i.e., same ages as our readers). No highly experimental pieces. Upbeat endings." Buys novel or book excerpts occasionally; but "only if the novel or book has been published." Agented fiction 98%. Published excerpts by Danielle Steel, Pat Booth and Belva Plain; published new writers within the last year. Occasionally recommends other markets.
How to Contact: Send complete ms with SASE. Guidelines for #10 SASE. Reports in 8-10 weeks. "We cannot contact you unless you enclose a #10 SASE." Publishes ms 6-18 months after acceptance.
Payment/Terms: Pays $750-2,000 on acceptance for first North American serial rights. Buys reprints.

COUNTRY WOMAN, (IV), Reiman Publications, Box 643, Milwaukee WI 53201. (414)423-0100. Editor: Ann Kaiser. Managing Editor: Kathleen Pohl. Magazine: 8½ × 11; 68 pages; excellent quality paper; excellent cover stock; illustrations and photographs. "Articles should have a rural theme and be of specific interest to women who live on a farm or ranch, or in a small town or country home, and/or are simply interested in country-oriented topics." Bimonthly. Estab. 1971.

Needs: Fiction must be upbeat, heartwarming and focus on a country woman as central character. "Many of our stories and articles are written by our readers!" Published work by Lori Ness, Wanda Luttrell and Dixie Laslett Thompson; published new writers within last year. Publishes 1 fiction story/issue. Length: 750-1,000 words.

How to Contact: All manuscripts should be sent to Kathy Pohl, Managing Editor. Reports in 2-3 months. Include cover letter and SASE. Simultaneous and reprint submissions OK. Sample copy and writer's guidelines for $2 and SASE. Guidelines for #10 SASE.

Payment/Terms: Pays $90-125 on acceptance for one-time rights.

Advice: "Read the magazine to get to know our audience. Send us country-to-the-core fiction, not yuppie-country stories—our readers know the difference! Very traditional fiction—with a definite beginning, middle and end, some kind of conflict/resolution, etc."

CRICKET MAGAZINE, (II), Carus Corporation, P.O. Box 300, Peru IL 61354. (815)224-6656. Editor-in-Chief: Marianne Carus. Magazine: 8 × 10; 64 pages; illustrations; photos. Magazine for children, ages 9-14. Monthly. Estab. 1973. Circ. 100,000.

- *Cricket* has received a Parents Choice Award, a Paul A. Witty Short Story Award and awards from Edpress. Carus Corp. also publishes *Ladybug*, *Spider* and a new publication for infants and toddlers, *Babybug*.

Needs: Adventure, contemporary, ethnic, fantasy, historic fiction, folk and fairytales, humorous, juvenile, mystery, science fiction and translations. No adult articles. All issues have different "mini-themes." Receives approximately 1,100 unsolicited fiction mss each month. Publishes 6-24 months or longer after acceptance. Buys 180 mss/year. Agented fiction 1-2%. Published work by Peter Dickinson, Mary Stolz and Jane Yolen; published new writers within the last year. Length: 500-2,000 words.

How to Contact: Do not query first. Send complete ms with SASE. List previous publications. Reports in 3 months on mss. Sample copy for $4; Guidelines for SASE.

Payment/Terms: Pays up to 25¢/word; 2 contributor's copies; $2 charge for extras on publication for first rights. Sends edited mss for approval. Buys reprints.

Advice: "Do not write *down* to children. Write about well-researched subjects you are familiar with and interested in, or about something that concerns you deeply. Children *need* fiction and fantasy. Carefully study several issues of *Cricket* before you submit your manuscript." Sponsors contests for readers of all ages.

CRUSADER MAGAZINE, (II), Calvinist Cadet Corps, Box 7259, Grand Rapids MI 49510. (616)241-5616. Fax: (616)241-5558. Editor: G. Richard Broene. Magazine: 8½ × 11; 24 pages; 50 lb. white paper and cover stock; illustrations; photos. Magazine to help boys ages 9-14 discover how God is at work in their lives and in the world around them. 7 issues/year. Estab. 1958. Circ. 12,000.

- *Crusader Magazine* won an Award of Merit in the Youth Category from the Evangelical Press Association in 1995. The magazine is noted for getting the message across with humor.

Needs: Adventure, comics, juvenile, religious/inspirational, spiritual and sports. Receives 60 unsolicited fiction mss/month. Buys 3 mss/issue; 18 mss/year. Publishes ms 4-11 months after acceptance. Published work by Sigmund Brouwer, Alan Cliburn and Betty Lou Mell. Length: 800 words minimum; 1,500 words maximum; 1,200 words average. Publishes short shorts.

How to Contact: Send complete ms and SASE with cover letter including theme of story. Reports in 4-8 weeks. Simultaneous and previously published submissions OK. Sample copy with a 9 × 12 SAE and 3 first-class stamps. Fiction guidelines for #10 SASE.

Payment/Terms: Pays 2-5¢/word and 1 contributor's copy. Pays on acceptance for one-time rights. Buys reprints.

Advice: "On a cover sheet list the point your story is trying to make. Our magazine has a theme for each issue, and we try to fit the fiction to the theme."

DRAGON® MAGAZINE, The Monthly Adventure Role-Playing Aid, (IV), TSR, Inc., 201 Sheridan Springs Rd., Lake Geneva WI 53147. (414)248-3625. Fiction Editor: Barbara G. Young. Magazine: 8½ × 11; 120 pages; 50 penn. plus paper; 80 lb. northcote cover stock; illustrations; rarely photos. "*Dragon Magazine* contains primarily nonfiction—articles and essays on various aspects of the hobby of role-playing games. One short fantasy story is published per issue. Readers are mature teens and young adults; over half our

---

Read the Business of Fiction Writing section to learn the correct way to prepare and submit a manuscript.

readers are under 18 years of age. The majority are male." Monthly. Estab. 1976. Circ. 85,000.

• TSR also has a listing in the Commercial Publishers section of this book. For more on *Dragon* and TSR, see the first edition of *Science Fiction Writer's Marketplace and Sourcebook* (Writer's Digest Books).

Needs: "We are looking for all types of fantasy (not horror) stories. We are *not* interested in fictionalized accounts of actual role-playing sessions. Upcoming themes: "fantasy humor" (April); "dragons" (June); "gothic horror" (October). Receives 50-60 unsolicited fiction mss/month. Buys 12 mss/year. Publishes ms 3-12 months after acceptance. Published work by Lois Tilton, Heather Lynn Sarik and Jean Lorrah; published new writers within the last year. Length: 1,500 words minimum; 8,000 words maximum; 3,000-5,000 words average. Occasionally critiques rejected mss.

How to Contact: Send complete ms, estimated word length, SASE. List only credits of professionally published materials within genre. No simultaneous submissions. Reports in 6-8 weeks. Sample copy for $4.50. Fiction guidelines for #10 SASE. Reviews fantasy and science fiction novels for their application to role-playing games.

Payment/Terms: Pays 5-8¢/word; 2 free contributor's copies on acceptance for fiction only for first world-wide English language rights; $2.50 charge for extras.

Advice: "It is *essential* that you actually see a copy (better, several copies) of the magazine to which you are submitting your work. Do not rely solely on market reports, as stories submitted to the wrong publication waste both your time and the editor's. Stories need not be set in a pseudo-medieval fantasy world, but should still have fantasy or magical elements."

DRUMMER, (II, IV), Desmodus, Inc., Box 410390, San Francisco CA 94141. (415)252-1195. Editor: Wickie Stamp. Magazine: 8½×11; 84 pages; glossy full-color cover; illustrations and photos. "Gay male erotica, fantasy and mystery with a leather, SM or other fetish twist." Monthly. Estab. 1975. Circ. 45,000.

Needs: "Fiction must have an appeal to gay men." Adventure, erotica, fantasy, gay, horror, humor/satire, mystery/suspense, science fiction and western. Receives 20-30 unsolicited fiction mss/month. Accepts 3 mss/issue. Publishes ms 6-8 months after acceptance.

How to Contact: Send complete ms with cover letter. SASE. Simultaneous submissions OK. Reprints OK "only if previously in foreign or very local publications." Accepts electronic submissions compatible with IBM PC. Reports in approximately 3 months. Sample copy for $6.95. Fiction guidelines for #10 SASE. Reviews novels and short collections.

Payment/Terms: Pays $100 and contributor's copies on publication for first North American serial rights.

EASYRIDERS MAGAZINE, (II), Entertainment for Adult Riders, Box 3000, Aurora Hills CA 91301. Fiction Editor: Keith R. Ball. Magazine: 7¾×10½; 50 lb. coated paper; 70 lb. coated cover stock; illustrations; photos. Men's magazine with bike-related material: how-to's, travel, new equipment information, and fiction for adult men who own or desire to own expensive custom motorcycles, and rugged individualists who own and enjoy their choppers and the good times derived from them. Monthly. Circ. 370,000.

• *Easyriders* is now taking longer stories, changing their maximum length requirements from 1,560 to 4,500 words.

Needs: Adventure. Should be bike-oriented, but doesn't have to dwell on the fact. "We are only interested in hard-hitting, rugged fiction that depicts bikers in a favorable light, and we're strongly inclined to favor material with a humorous bent." Published work by John D. Kenworthy, Mark Petterson and J.J. Solari; published new writers within the last year. Length: 3,500-4,500 words.

How to Contact: Send complete ms with SASE and cover letter. Reports in 6 weeks on mss. Sample copy for $4.50.

Payment/Terms: Pays 15-25¢/word on publication for first rights; payment depends on quality, length and use in magazine.

Advice: "Gut level language accepted; sex scenes OK but are not to be graphically described. As long as the material is directly aimed at our macho intelligent male audience, there should be no great problem breaking into our magazine. Before submitting material, however, we strongly recommend that the writer observe our requirements and study a sample copy."

EMERGE MAGAZINE, Black America's News Magazine, (III), 1 Bet Plaza, 1900 W. Place St. NE, Washington DC 20018-1211. (202)608-2093. Editor: George E. Curry. Managing Editor: Ms. Florestine Purnell. 8⅛×10⅞; 84 pages; 40 lb. paper; 70 lb. cover stock; 5-6 illustrations; 45 photographs. "*Emerge* is an African-American news monthly that covers news, politics, arts and lifestyles for the college educated, middle class African American audience." Published 10 times/year. Estab. 1989.

Needs: Ethnic, fantasy, humor/satire, literary. "*Emerge* is looking for humorous, tightly written fiction and nonfiction no longer than 2,000 words about African-Americans."

How to Contact: Submit complete ms. Reviews novels and short story collections.

Payment/Terms: Pays $1,000-2,000 and contributor's copies for first North American serial rights. Pays 25% kill fee.

Advice: "*Emerge* stories must accomplish with a fine economy of style what all good fiction must do: make the unusual familiar. The ability to script a compelling story is what has been missing from most of our submissions."

EMPHASIS ON FAITH AND LIVING, (IV), Missionary Church, Inc., P.O. Box 9127, Fort Wayne IN 46899-9127. (219)747-2027. Fax: (219)747-5331. Editor: Robert L. Ransom. Magazine: 8½×11; 16 pages; offset paper; illustrations and photos. "Religious/church oriented for the 45 and up age group." Bimonthly. Estab. 1969. Circ. 12,000.
Needs: Religious/inspirational. Receives 10-15 unsolicited mss/month. Buys 2 mss/year. Publishes ms 3-6 months after acceptance. Published work by Debra Wood and Denise George. Length: 500 words average; 200 words minimum; 1,000 words maximum. Publishes short shorts. Length: 200-250 words.
How to Contact: Send complete ms with a cover letter. Should include estimated word count, bio and Social Security number. Reports in 2-3 months on mss. Send SASE for reply, return of ms or send a disposable copy of ms. Simultaneous reprint and electronic submissions OK. Sample copy for 9×12 SAE.
Payment/Terms: Pays $10-50 and 5 contributor's copies on publication.

ESQUIRE, The Magazine for Men, (III), Hearst Corp., 250 W. 55th St., New York NY 10019. (212)649-4020. Editor: Ed Kosner. Fiction Editors: Will Blythe and Rust Hills. Magazine. Monthly. Estab. 1933. Circ. 750,000.
 • *Esquire* is well-respected for its fiction and has received several National Magazine Awards. Work published in *Esquire* has been selected for inclusion in the *Best American Short Stories* anthology.
Needs: No "pornography, science fiction or 'true romance' stories." Publishes special fiction issue in July. Receives "thousands" of unsolicited mss/month. Rarely accepts unsolicited fiction. Published work by Cormac McCarthy, Richard Ford, Mark Richard, Jayne Ann Phillips, James Salter, Jim Harrison and Will Self.
How to Contact: Send complete ms with cover letter or submit through an agent. Simultaneous submissions OK. Fiction guidelines for SASE.
Payment/Terms: Pays in cash on acceptance, amount undisclosed.
Advice: "Submit one story at a time. Worry a little less about publication, a little more about the work itself."

EVANGEL, (IV), Light & Life Press, P.O. Box 535002, Indianapolis IN 46253-5002. (317)244-3660. Editor: Carolyn B. Smith. Sunday school take-home paper for distribution to adults who attend church. Fiction involves couples and singles coping with everyday crises, making decisions that show growth. Magazine: 5½×8½; 8 pages; 2-color illustrations; b&w photos. Weekly. Estab. 1896. Circ. 35,000.
Needs: Religious/inspirational. "No fiction without any semblance of Christian message or where the message clobbers the reader." Receives approximately 75 unsolicited fiction mss/month. Buys 1 ms/issue, 52 mss/year. Published work by C. Ellen Watts, Jeanne Zornes and Betty Steele Everett. Length: 1,000-1,200 words.
How to Contact: Send complete ms with SASE. Reports in 1 month. Sample copy and writer's guidelines with #10 SASE.
Payment/Terms: Pays 4¢/word on publication for first rights; 3¢/word for reprints and 2 contributor's copies; charge for extras.
Advice: "Choose a contemporary situation or conflict and create a good mix for the characters (not all-good or all-bad heroes and villains). Don't spell out everything in detail; let the reader fill in some blanks in the story. Keep him guessing." Rejects mss because of "unbelievable characters and predictable events in the story."

EXPANSE® MAGAZINE, (II), Suite 49, 7982 Honeygo Blvd., Baltimore MD 21236. Fiction Editor: Steven E. Fick. Magazine: 8½×11; 80-112 pages; 50 lb. paper; 80 lb. gloss enamel cover stock; illustrations. "We strive to publish the best in speculative fiction and publish it in the best possible way for an intelligent readership with developed tastes. Seeing ourselves as a kind of gallery of fine literature, we use innovative design to 'frame' each story and best present its unique style." Quarterly. Estab. 1993. Circ. 13,000.
 • An interview with Steven Fick appears in the first edition of *Science Fiction Writer's Marketplace and Sourcebook* (Writer's Digest Books).
Needs: Receives 100 unsolicited mss/month. Buys 8-10 mss/issue; 40 mss/year. Publishes ms 18 months after acceptance. Agented fiction 5%. Published work by L. Sprague DeCamp, Mark Rich, John Brunner, Darrell Schweitzer and T. Jackson King. Accepts serialized novels. Length: 6,500 words average; 2,500 words minimum; 10,000 words maximum. Publishes short shorts. Length: 1,500 words or less. Also publishes interviews. Sometimes critiques or comments on rejected mss.
How to Contact: Send complete ms with cover letter. Should include estimated word count, one page bio, list of publications and phone number. Reports on mss in 2-3 months. Serialized novels in up to 6 months. SASE. E-mail address: sfzine@aol.com. Sample copy for $5 (overseas: add $2) payable in US funds only. Fiction guidelines for #10 SASE.

Payment/Terms: Pays 5-8¢/word; additional copies at 50% discount. Pays on acceptance. Buys first North American serial rights and non-exclusive world English-language serial rights. Sometimes buys anthology or other rights.

Advice: "*EXPANSE ® Magazine* has E-X-P-A-N-D-E-D! We now publish more fiction than ever before, and much of it is longer. Serialized novels are appearing with growing regularity, often published a full year or so before their release as paperbacks. We also publish a greater variety of fiction than ever before. Science fiction, in its myriad of forms, remains our mainstay. But we do now accept fantasy, horror and, indeed, anything that could be considered 'speculative fiction.' As always, only *excellence* is our requirement. Think in terms of plot, not wordplay. More than ever in history, your writing must be immediate and speak directly to the soul. No one will endure your soliloquies. You're competing with a lot of other media. And remember: The opening is more than the start of your story. It's the promotional copy for the rest of your tale. Each word should drag me on to the next."

THE FAMILY, (II, IV), Daughters of St. Paul, 50 St. Paul's Ave., Boston MA 02130. (617)522-8911. Managing Editor: Sr. Theresa Frances FSP. Magazine: 8½×11; 32 pages; matte paper; self-cover; illustrations and photos. Family life—themes include parenting issues, human and spiritual development, marital situations, for teen-adult popular audience predominantly Catholic. Monthly, except July-Aug. Estab. 1953. Circ. 10,000.
• Another magazine published by the Daughters of St. Paul is *My Friend*, listed in this book.
Needs: Religious/inspirational. "We favor upbeat stories with some sort of practical or moral message." No sex, romance, science fiction, horror, western. Receives about 100 unsolicited mss/month. Buys 3-4 mss/issue; 30-40 mss/year. Publishes ms 4-6 months after acceptance. Length: 800 words minimum; 1,500 words maximum; 1,200 words average.
How to Contact: Send complete ms with cover letter that includes Social Security number and list of previously published works. Reports in 2 months on mss. SASE. No simultaneous submissions. Reprint submissions OK. Sample copy for $3, 9×12 SAE and 5 first-class stamps. Guidelines for #10 SASE.
Payment/Terms: Pays $50-100 on publication for first North American serial or one-time rights (reprints). Sends galleys to author "only if substantive editing was required."
Advice: "We look for 1) message; 2) clarity of writing; 3) realism of plot and character development. If seasonal material, send at least 7 months in advance. We're eager to receive submissions on family topics. And we love stories that include humor."

FIRST HAND, Experiences for Loving Men, (II, IV), First Hand Ltd., Box 1314, Teaneck NJ 07666. (201)836-9177. Fax: (201)836-5055. Editor: Bob Harris. Magazine: digest size; 130 pages; illustrations. "Half of the magazine is made up of our readers' own gay sexual experiences. Rest is fiction and columns devoted to health, travel, books, etc." Monthly. Estab. 1980. Circ. 60,000.
• First Hand Ltd. also publishes *Guys* and *Manscape*, listed in this book.
Needs: Erotica, gay. "Should be written in first person." No science fiction or fantasy. Erotica should detail experiences based in reality. Receives 75-100 unsolicited mss/month. Buys 6 mss/issue; 72 mss/year. Publishes ms 9-18 months after acceptance. Published work by John Hoff, Rick Jackson and Jack Sofelot; published new writers within the last year. Length: 3,000 words preferred; 2,000 words minimum; 3,750 words maximum. Sometimes critiques rejected mss.
How to Contact: Send complete ms with cover letter which should include writer's name, address, telephone and Social Security number and "should advise on use of pseudonym if any. Also whether selling all rights or first North American rights." No simultaneous submissions. E-mail address: firsthand3@aol.com. Reports in 1-2 months. SASE. Sample copy for $5. Fiction guidelines for #10 SASE.
Payment/Terms: Pays $100-150 on publication for all rights or first North American serial rights.
Advice: "Avoid the hackneyed situations. Be original. We like strong plots."

FLORIDA WILDLIFE, (IV), Florida Game & Fresh Water Fish Commission, 620 S. Meridian St., Tallahassee FL 32399-1600. (904)488-5563. Editor: Dick Sublette. Associate Editor: Frank Adams. Magazine: 8½×11; 32 pages. "Conservation-oriented material for an 'outdoor' audience." Bimonthly. Estab. 1947. Circ. 26,000.
• *Florida Wildlife* received the Governor's Environmental Communication Award in 1994.
Needs: Adventure, sports. "Florida-related adventure or natural history only. We rarely publish fiction." Buys 18 ms/year. Length: 1,200 words average; 500 words minimum; 1,500 words maximum.
How to Contact: Send complete ms with cover letter including Social Security number. "We prefer to review article. Response time varies with amount of material on hand." Sample copy for $2.95.
Payment/Terms: Pays minimum of $50 per published page on publication for one-time rights.
Advice: "Send your best work. It must *directly* concern Florida wildlife."

THE FRIEND MAGAZINE, (II), The Church of Jesus Christ of Latter-day Saints, 23rd Floor, 50 E. North Temple, Salt Lake City UT 84150. (801)240-2210. Editor: Vivian Paulsen. Magazine: 8½×10½; 50 pages; 40 lb. coated paper; 70 lb. coated cover stock; illustrations; photos. Publishes for 3-11 year-olds. Monthly. Estab. 1971. Circ. 275,000.
• The Church of Jesus Christ of Latter-Day Saints also publishes *New Era*, listed in this book.

Needs: Adventure, ethnic, some historical, humor, mainstream, religious/inspirational, nature. Length: 1,000 words maximum. Publishes short shorts. Length: 250 words.

How to Contact: Send complete ms. "No query letters please." Reports in 6-8 weeks. SASE. Sample copy for $1.50 with 9½×11 SAE and $1 postage.

Payment/Terms: Pays 11-13¢/word on acceptance for all rights.

Advice: "The *Friend* is particularly interested in stories with substance for tiny tots. Stories should focus on character-building qualities and should be wholesome without moralizing or preaching. Boys and girls resolving conflicts is a theme of particular merit. Since the magazine is circulated worldwide, the *Friend* is interested in stories and articles with universal settings, conflicts, and character. Other suggestions include rebus, picture, holiday, sports, and photo stories, or manuscripts that portray various cultures. Very short pieces (up to 250 words) are desired for younger readers and preschool children. Appropriate humor is a constant need."

GALLERY MAGAZINE, (I), Montcalm Publishing Corporation, 401 Park Avenue South, New York NY 10016. (212)779-8900. Editor: Barry Janoff. Fiction Editor: Rose Rubin Rivera. Magazine: 170 pages; illustrations and photographs. Magazine for men, 18-45. Monthly. Estab. 1972. Circ. 425,000.

Needs: Adventure, erotica, humor/satire, literary, mainstream, suspense/mystery. Receives 100 unsolicited fiction mss/month. Buys 13 mss/year. Publishes ms 5 months after acceptance. Less than 10% of fiction is agented. Length: 1,500-3,000 words average; 1,000 words minimum; 3,500 words maximum. Sometimes critiques rejected mss and recommends other markets.

How to Contact: Send complete ms. Reports in 2 months. SASE. Accepts electronic submissions, if Mac or compatible disk available. Sample copy for $7.95. Fiction guidelines for #10 SASE.

Payment/Terms: Pays $500 and contributor's copies on publication. Buys first North American serial rights.

Advice: Fiction is "slightly off-beat, but always reflecting some aspect of life that our readers can relate to. We reject all manuscripts regarding UFOs, sci-fi, horror, and prostitution. All of the manuscripts that we publish are extremely well written, but not overly polished—we prefer pieces that are rough around the edges. We also give special consideration to writers who have never been published or only have minor publishing credits. Don't assume anything. *Gallery* is a men's magazine, but we do not publish the 'typical' men's magazine fiction. Check each market carefully by reading several issues of each particular magazine, always ask for fiction guidelines before submitting a manuscript, and never send a cover letter that has the line, 'My friends loved this piece and I know it is perfect for your magazine.' Also, we are not impressed if someone submitting a manuscript tells us that his professor in college called him 'a future Hemingway.' "

THE GEM, (II), Churches of God, General Conference, Box 926, Findlay OH 45839. (419)424-1961. Editor: Evelyn Sloat. Magazine: 6×9; 8 pages; 50 lb. uncoated paper; illustrations (clip art). "True-to-life stories of healed relationships and growing maturity in the Christian faith for senior high students through senior citizens who attend Churches of God, General Conference Sunday Schools." Weekly. Estab. 1865. Circ. 8,000.

Needs: Adventure, humor, mainstream, religious/inspirational, senior citizen/retirement. Nothing that denies or ridicules standard Christian values. Prefers personal testimony or nonfiction short stories. Receives 30 unsolicited fiction mss/month. Buys 1 ms every 2-3 issues; 20-25 mss/year. Publishes ms 4-12 months after submission. Published work by Betty Steele Everett, Todd Lee and Betty Lou Mell. Length: 1,500 words average; 1,000 words minimum; 1,700 words maximum.

How to Contact: Send complete ms with cover letter ("letter not essential, unless there is information about author's background which enhances story's credibility or verifies details as being authentic"). Reports in 6 months. SASE. Simultaneous and reprint submissions OK. Sample copy and fiction guidelines for #10 SASE. "If more than one sample copy is desired along with the guidelines, will need 2 oz. postage."

Payment/Terms: Pays $10-15 and contributor's copies on publication for one-time rights. Charge for extras (postage for mailing more than one).

Advice: "Competition at the mediocre level is fierce. There is a dearth of well-written, relevant fiction which wrestles with real problems involving Christian values applied to the crisis times and 'passages' of life. Humor which puts the daily grind into a fresh perspective and which promises hope for survival is also in short supply. Write from your own experience. Avoid religious jargon and stereotypes. Conclusion must be believable in terms of the story—don't force a 'Christian' ending. Avoid simplistic solutions to complex problems. Listen to the storytelling art of Garrison Keillor. Feel how very particular experiences of small town life in Minnesota become universal."

GENT, (II), Dugent Publishing Corp., Suite 600, 2600 Douglas Rd., Coral Gables FL 33134. (305)443-2378. Editor: Bruce Arthur. "Men's magazine designed to have erotic appeal for the reader. Our publications are directed to a male audience, but we do have a certain percentage of female readers. For the most part, our audience is interested in erotically stimulating material, but not exclusively." Monthly. Estab. 1959. Circ. 175,000.

● Dugent Publishing also publishes *Nugget* listed in this section.

Needs: Erotica: contemporary, science fiction, horror, mystery, adventure and humor. *Gent* specializes in "D-Cup cheesecake," and fiction should be slanted accordingly. "Most of the fiction published includes several sex scenes. No fiction that concerns children, religious subjects or anything that might be libelous." Receives 30-50 unsolicited fiction mss/month. Buys 2 mss/issue; 26 mss/year. Publishes ms an average of 3 months after acceptance. Agented fiction 10%. Published new writers within the last year. Length: 2,000-3,500 words. Critiques rejected mss "when there is time."

How to Contact: Send complete ms with SASE. Reports in 1 month. Sample copy for $5. Fiction guidelines for #10 SASE.

Payment/Terms: Pay starts at $200; 1 contributor's copy. Pays on publication for first North American serial rights.

Advice: "Since *Gent* magazine is the 'Home of the D-Cups,' stories and articles containing either characters or themes with a major emphasis on large breasts will have the best chance for consideration. Study a sample copy first." Mss are rejected because "there are not enough or ineffective erotic sequences, plot is not plausible, wrong length, or not slanted specifically for us."

GOLD AND TREASURE HUNTER, (II), 27 Davis Rd., P.O. Box 47, Happy Camp CA 96039. (916)493-2029. Editor: Dave McCracken. Fiction Editor: Janice Trombetta. Magazine: 8×10⅞; 72 pages; 40 lb. coated #5 paper; 70 lb. Westvaco Marva cover; pen-and-ink illustrations; photographs. "Recreational and small-scale gold mining, treasure and relic hunting. All stories must be related to these topics. For recreational hobbyists, adventure loving, outdoor people." Bimonthly. Estab. 1988. Circ. 50,000.

Needs: Adventure, experimental, historical, humor, mystery/suspense, senior citizen/retirement. "Subject-related futuristic stories OK, but not sci-fi. No erotica, gay, lesbian--absolutely no 'cussing!'" Buys 1-2 mss/issue; 6-16 mss/year. Publishes ms 6-8 months after acceptance. Published work by Ken Hodgson and Michael Clark. Length: 1,500 words preferred; 500 words minimum; 2,000 words maximum. Publishes short shorts. Length: 400-500 words. Sometimes critiques or comments on rejected mss.

How to Contact: Send complete ms with cover letter. Include Social Security number, "brief outline of the story and something about the author." Reports in 4-6 weeks on queries; 8-10 weeks on mss. SASE for mss. "When submitting fiction material, please include any photos or illustrations available to enhance the story." Macintosh formatted 3.5 and IBM compatible 5.25 or 3.5 disks, along with computer printout, are also acceptable. E-mail address: goldgold@snowcrest.net. Sample copy for $3.50 (U.S.), $4.50 (Canada). Free fiction guidelines.

Payment/Terms: Pays 3¢/word and contributor's copy on publication for all rights. "We reserve the right to republish any of our previously-published and paid for material inside our Internet publication, *Wonderful World of Gold and Treasure Hunting*. Any material which we publish on the Internet that has not yet been printed in our magazine will be paid at a rate of 2¢/word and $10/photo used, with the balance of magazine rates to be paid if and when the same material, or a portion of it, is published in the printed magazine."

Advice: Looks for "as always, quality writing. We can edit small changes but the story has to grab us. Our readers love 'real life' fiction. They love exploring the 'that could happen' realm of a good fiction story. Keep your story geared to gold mining or treasure hunting. Know something about your subject so the story doesn't appear ridiculous. Don't try to dazzle readers with outlandish adjectives and keep slang to a minimum." Sponsors fiction contest—look for rules in upcoming issues.

GOOD HOUSEKEEPING, (II), 959 Eighth Ave., New York NY 10019. Contact: Fiction Editor. "It is now our policy that all submissions of unsolicited fiction received in our offices will be read and, if found to be unsuitable for us, destroyed by recycling. If you wish to introduce your work to us, you will be submitting material that will not be critiqued or returned. The odds are long that we will contact you to inquire about publishing your submission or to invite you to correspond with us directly, so please be sure before you take the time and expense to submit it that it is our type of material."

GRAND TIMES, Exclusively for Active Retirees, (II), P.O. Box 9493, Berkeley CA 94709. (510)848-0456. Editor: Kira Albin. Magazine: 8½×11; 32 pages; illustrations and photographs. "All items must be upbeat in tone and written on subjects of interest to an older audience, i.e. active retirees. The style of writing must be entertaining, succint and clear; comparable with that in *Reader's Digest*." Bimonthly. Estab. 1992. Circ. 20,000.

Needs: Senior citizen/retirement: adventure, historical (general), humor/satire, mainstream/contemporary, mystery/suspense (mature adult), romance (mature adult), sports. "All pieces should be of special interest to reader's aged 65 + ." Receives 15-30 unsolicited mss/month. Accepts 1 ms/issue; 6-8 mss/year. Publishes ms 1-12 months after acceptance. Published work by Jane Bosworth and Ted Carroll. Length: 800-1,200 average; 250 words minimum; 1,700 words maximum. Publishes short shorts. Length: 250-500 words.

How to Contact: "It is recommended that manuscripts be submitted only after obtaining Writers' Guidelines." Send complete ms with a cover letter. Should include estimated word count and very short bio. Reports in 1-4 weeks on queries; 2-3 months on mss. SASE for return of ms or send a disposable copy of ms. Simultaneous and reprint submissions OK. Sample copy for $2. Writers' guidelines for #10 SASE.

Payment/Terms: Pays 1 contributor's copy. "The amount of additional payment is dependent on subject matter, quality and length. Average payment is $15-35/ms." Pays on acceptance for one-time rights.

Advice: "The characters or plot need to have some relevance to active retirees. Don't lose the focus/theme of the story by bringing in too many ideas. Make sure characters are really developed and bring meaning to the story. *Please* obtain Writers' Guidelines before making a submission. Remember that *Grand Times* is for active retirees—stories should be geared specifically. Beware of any condescension, ageism or stereotyping."

GUIDE MAGAZINE, (I, II, IV), Review & Herald Publishing Association, 55 W. Oak Ridge Dr., Hagerstown MD 21740. (301)791-7000. Fax: (301)790-9734. Editor: Carolyn Rathbun. Magazine: 6×9; 32 pages; glossy (coated) paper; illustrations; photographs. "*Guide* is a weekly Christian journal geared toward 10- to 14-year-olds. Stories and other features presented are relevant to the needs of today's young person, and emphasize positive aspects of Christian living." Weekly. Estab. 1953. Circ. 34,000.
 • Affiliated with the Seventh-day Adventist Church, *Guide* has won awards from the Protestant Church Publishing Association, Associated Church Press, Evangelical Church Press and the Christian Magazine Publishers.
Needs: Religious/inspirational: adventure (10-14 years), humor, sports. No romance, science fiction, horror, etc. "We use four general categories in each issue: spiritual/devotional; personal growth; adventure/nature; humor. We need more true stories. No stories that lack clear spiritual application." Receives 80-100 unsolicited mss/month. Buys 2-3 mss/issue; 150 mss/year. Publishes ms 3-12 months after acceptance. Length: 1,000-1,200 words average. Publishes short shorts. Often critiques or comments on rejected mss.
How to Contact: Send complete ms. Should include estimated word count, Social Security number. Reports in 2 weeks. SASE for return of ms or send disposable copy. Simultaneous and reprint submissions OK. Sample copy for #10 SAE and 2 first-class stamps. Writer's guidelines for #10 SASE.
Payment/Terms: Pays 3¢/word and 3 contributor's copies. Additional copies 50¢ each. Buys first, first North American serial, one-time, reprint or simultaneous rights.
Advice: "The aim of *Guide* magazine is to reflect in creative yet concrete ways the unconditional love of God to young people 10 to 14 years of age. Believing that an accurate picture of God is a prerequisite for wholeness, our efforts editorially and in design will be focused on accurately portraying His attributes and expectations."

GUIDEPOSTS FOR KIDS, (III), P.O. Box 538A, Chesterton IN 46304. Assistant Fiction Editor: Tracey Dils. Magazine: 8¼×10¾; 32 pages. "Value-centered bimonthly for kids 7-12 years old. Bible-based; not preachy, concerned with contemporary issues." Bimonthly. Estab. 1990. Circ. 200,000.
 • Although the main office of the magazine is in New York, submissions should go to the assistant editor who will send them on to Fiction Editor Lurlene McDaniel. McDaniel says her magazine publishes many new writers but is primarily a market for writers who have already been published. *Guideposts for Kids* received an Award of Excellence from the Ed Press Association in 1995.
Needs: Children's/juvenile: Fantasy, historical (general), humor, mystery/suspense, religious/inspirational, westerns. "No 'adult as hero' or 'I-prayed-I-got' stories." Upcoming themes: Choices, Animals, Humor, Courage. Receives 200+ unsolicited mss/month. Buys 1-2 mss/issue; 6-10 mss/year. Published work by Judy Baer, Pam Zollman and Cameron Judd. Length: 1,300 words preferred; 1,200 words minimum; 1,400 words maximum. Publishes short shorts. Also publishes small amount of poetry. Sometimes critiques rejected mss; "only what shows promise."
How to Contact: Send complete ms with cover letter. Should include estimated word count, Social Security number, phone number and SASE. Reports in 6-8 weeks. Send SASE for reply, return of ms or send disposable copy of ms. Simultaneous submissions OK. Sample copy for $3.25 with 10×13 SAE and $1.21 postage (in US). Fiction guidelines for #10 SASE.
Payment/Terms: $250-450 on acceptance for all rights; 2 contributor's copies. Additional copies available.

GUYS, FirstHand Ltd., Box 1314, Teaneck NJ 07666. (201)836-9177. Fax: (201)836-5055. Editor: William Spencer. Magazine: digest size; 160 pages; illustrations; photos. "Fiction and informative departments for today's gay man. Fiction is of an erotic nature, and we especially need short shorts and novella-length stories." Published 10 times/year. Estab. 1988.
 • *FirstHand* and *Manscape*, other magazines by this publisher, also are listed in this book.
Needs: Gay. "Should be written in first person. No science fiction or fantasy. No four-legged animals. All characters must be over 18. Stories including members of ethnic groups or the disabled are especially welcome. Erotica should be based on reality." Upcoming special issues: "Jock Tales," "Seafood Tales," "Prison Tales," "Campus Tales," "Uniform Tales." Buys 6 mss/issue; 66 mss/year. Publishes ms 6-12

months after acceptance. Published work by Rick Jackson, Kenn Richie and Jay Shaffer; published new writers within the last year. Length: 3,000 words average; 2,000 words minimum; 3,750 words maximum. For novellas: 7,500-8,600 words. Publishes short shorts. Length: 750-1,250 words. Sometimes critiques rejected mss and recommends other markets.

How to Contact: Send complete ms with cover letter, which should include writer's name, address, telephone and Social Security number and whether selling all rights or first North American serial rights. Reports in 6-8 weeks on ms. SASE. Accepts computer printout submissions. Sample copy for $5. Fiction guidelines for #10 SASE. Reviews novels and short story collections.

Payment/Terms: Pays $100-150; $75 for short shorts (all rights); $250 for novellas (all rights). Pays on publication or in 180 days, whichever comes first, for all rights or first North American serial rights.

Advice: "Use language you'd normally use. Don't get poetic or rhapsodic. Sex is a basic act. Use basic language."

HADASSAH MAGAZINE, (IV), 50 W. 58th St., New York NY 10019. Executive Editor: Alan M. Tigay. Senior Editor: Zelda Shluker. Jewish general interest magazine: 8½×11; 48-70 pages; coated and uncoated paper; slick, medium weight coated cover; drawings and cartoons; photos. Primarily concerned with Israel, the American Jewish community, Jewish communities around the world and American current affairs. Monthly except combined June/July and August/September issues. Circ. 300,000.

●*Hadassah* has been nominated for a National Magazine Award and has received numerous Rockower Awards for Excellence in Jewish Journalism.

Needs: Ethnic (Jewish). Receives 20-25 unsolicited fiction mss each month. Published fiction by Joanne Greenberg, Anita Desai and Lori Ubell; published new writers within the last year. Length: 1,500-2,000 words.

How to Contact: Query first with writing samples. Reports in 3-4 months on mss. "Not interested in multiple submissions or previously published articles." Must submit appropriate size SASE.

Payment/Terms: Pays $300 minimum on publication for U.S. publication rights.

Advice: "Stories on a Jewish theme should be neither self-hating nor schmaltzy."

HARPER'S MAGAZINE, (II, III), 666 Broadway, 11th Floor, New York NY 10012. (212)614-6500. Editor: Lewis H. Lapham. Magazine: 8×10¾; 80 pages; illustrations. Magazine for well-educated, widely read and socially concerned readers, college-aged and older, those active in political and community affairs. Monthly. Circ. 218,000.

●This is considered a top but tough market for contemporary fiction.

Needs: Contemporary and humor. Stories on contemporary life and its problems. Does a summer reading issue usually in August. Receives 600 unsolicited fiction mss/month. Buys 1 ms/year. Published new writers within the last year. Length: 1,000-5,000 words.

How to Contact: Query to managing editor, or through agent. Reports in 6 weeks on queries.

Payment/Terms: Pays $500-1,000 on acceptance for rights, which vary on each author and material. Negotiable kill fee. Sends galleys to author.

Advice: Buys very little fiction but *Harper's* has published short stories traditionally.

HIGH ADVENTURE, (II), General Council Assemblies of God (Gospel Publishing Co.), 1445 Boonville, Springfield MO 65802-1894. (417)862-2781, ext. 4178. Editor: Marshall Bruner. Magazine: 8×11; 16 pages; lancer paper; self cover; illustrations; photos. Magazine for adolescent boys. "Designed to provide boys with worthwhile, enjoyable, leisure reading; to challenge them in narrative form to higher ideals and greater spiritual dedication; and to perpetuate the spirit of the Royal Rangers program through stories, ideas and illustrations." Quarterly. Estab. 1971. Circ. 86,000.

Needs: Adventure, historical (general), religious/inspirational, suspense/mystery. Published new writers within the last year. Length: 1,000 words maximum. Publishes short shorts to 1,000 words. Occasionally critiques rejected mss.

How to Contact: Send ms with SASE. Include Social Security number. Reports in 2 months. Simultaneous and reprint submissions OK. Free sample copy, theme list and fiction guidelines for 9×12 SASE.

Payment/Terms: Pays 2-3¢/word (base) and 3 contributor's copies on acceptance for first rights and one-time rights.

Advice: "Ask for list of upcoming themes."

HIGHLIGHTS FOR CHILDREN, 803 Church St., Honesdale PA 18431. (717)253-1080. Editor: Kent L. Brown, Jr. Address fiction to: Beth Troop, Manuscript Coordinator. Magazine: 8½×11; 42 pages; uncoated paper; coated cover stock; illustrations; photos. Monthly. Circ. 2.8 million.

●*Highlights* is very supportive of writers. The magazine sponsors a contest and a workshop each year at Chautauqua (New York). See the listings for these and for their press, Boyds Mills Press, in other sections of this book. Several authors published in *Highlights* have received SCBWI Magazine Merit Awards.

Needs: Juvenile (ages 2-12). Unusual stories appealing to both girls and boys; stories with good characterization, strong emotional appeal, vivid, full of action. "Begin with action rather than description, have strong plot, believable setting, suspense from start to finish." Length: 400-900 words. "We also need easy stories for very young readers (100-400 words)." No war, crime or violence. Receives 600-800 unsolicited fiction mss/month. Buys 6-7 mss/issue. Also publishes rebus (picture) stories of 125 words or under for the 3- to 7-year-old child. Published work by Laurie Knowlton, Harriett Diller and Vashanti Rahaman; published new writers within the last year. Critiques rejected mss occasionally, "especially when editors see possibilities in story."

How to Contact: Send complete ms with SASE and include a rough word count and cover letter "with any previous acceptances by our magazine; any other published work anywhere." No simultaneous submissions. Reports in 1 month. Free guidelines on request.

Payment/Terms: Pays 14¢ and up/word on acceptance for all rights. Sends galleys to author.

Advice: "We accept a story on its merit whether written by an unpublished or an experienced writer. Mss are rejected because of poor writing, lack of plot, trite or worn-out plot, or poor characterization. Children *like* stories and learn about life from stories. Children learn to become lifelong fiction readers by enjoying stories. Feel passion for your subject. Create vivid images. Write a child-centered story; leave adults in the background."

ALFRED HITCHCOCK MYSTERY MAGAZINE, (I, II), Doubleday Dell Magazines, 1540 Broadway., New York NY 10036. (212)782-8532. Editor: Cathleen Jordan. Mystery fiction magazine: 5¹⁄₁₆×7³⁄₈; 160 pages; 28 lb. newsprint paper; 60 lb. machine-/coated cover stock; illustrations; photos. Published 13 times/year. Estab. 1956. Circ. 215,000; 615,000 readers.

- Stories published in *Alfred Hitchcock Mystery Magazine* have won Edgar Awards for "Best Mystery Story of the Year," Shamus Awards for "Best Private Eye Story of the Year" and Robert L. Fish Awards for "Best First Mystery Short Story of the Year." See *Ellery Queen's Mystery Magazine* also listed in this book. For more, see the interview with Cathleen Jordan in the *Mystery Writer's Sourcebook* (Writer's Digest Books.)

Needs: Mystery and detection (amateur sleuth, private eye, police procedural, suspense, etc.). No sensationalism. Number of mss/issue varies with length of mss. Length: up to 14,000 words. Also publishes short shorts.

How to Contact: Send complete ms and SASE. Reports in 2 months. Guideline sheet for SASE.

Payment/Terms: Pays 8¢/word on acceptance.

HOME LIFE, (II, IV), A magazine for Today's Christian Family, Sunday School Board of Southern Baptist Convention, 127 Ninth Ave. N., Nashville TN 37234. Fax: (615)251-3866. Editor: Charlie Warren. Magazine: 8×10³⁄₄; 66 pages; illustrations and photos. "Ours is a Christian family magazine." Monthly. Estab. 1947. Circ. 560,000.

- *Home Life* has received awards for its design and contents including a First Place Award from the Baptist Public Relations Association. The magazine is noted for fiction about family relationships.

Needs: Religious/inspirational. No fictionized Bible stories. Receives 10-15 mss/month. Buys 1 ms/issue; 12 mss/year. Published work by Geo. A. Cruz, Barbara L. Weston, Janet F. Ford and Paul Wieland. Length: 1,400 words minimum; 2,000 words maximum.

How to Contact: Query first. Should include estimated word count and short bio. Reports in 1 month on queries; 3 months on mss. Send SASE for reply, return of ms or send a disposable copy of ms. Simultaneous submissions OK. Sample copy for $1, 9×12 SAE and 2 first-class stamps. Fiction guidelines for #10 SASE.

Payment/Terms: Pays $100-275 and 3 contributor's copies on acceptance for first rights or first North American serial rights.

Advice: "Stories related to marriage, parenting and family situations fit our mag best."

HOME TIMES, (I, II, IV), Neighbor News, Inc., P.O. Box 16096, West Palm Beach FL 33416. (407)439-3509. Editor: Dennis Lombard. Newspaper: tabloid; 20-32 pages; newsprint; illustrations and photographs. "Conservative news, views, fiction, poetry, sold to general public." Weekly. Estab. 1980. Circ. 5,000.

- The publisher offers "101 Reasons Why I Reject Your Manuscript," a 120-page report for a cost of $15.

Needs: Adventure, historical (general), humor/satire, literary, mainstream, religious/inspirational, romance, sports. "All fiction needs to be related to the publication's focus on current events and conservative perspective—we feel you must examine a sample issue because *Home Times* is *different*." Nothing "preachy or doctrinal, but Biblical worldview needed." Receives 50 unsolicited mss/month. Buys 10 mss/issue. Publishes ms 1-6 months after acceptance. Recently published work by Cal Thomas, Mona Charen and Don Leder. Length: 700 words average; 500 words minimum; 1,000 words maximum.

How to Contact: Send complete manuscript with cover letter including Social Security number and word count. "Absolutely no queries." Include in cover letter "1-2 sentences on what the piece is and on who you are." Reports on mss in 1 month. SASE. Simultaneous and reprint submissions OK. Sample copy for $1, 9×12 SAE and 4 first-class stamps ($3 for 3 samples). Guidelines for #10 SASE.

Payment/Terms: Pays $5-35 for one-time rights.

Advice: "We are very open to new writers, but read our newspaper—get the drift of our rather unusual conservative, pro-Christian, pro-Jewish but non-religious content. Looks for "historical, issues, or family orientation; also like creative nonfiction on historical and issues subjects." Send $10 for a writer's 1-year subscription (12 issues plus 3 samples).

‡HOT SHOTS, (IV), Sunshine Publishing Company, Inc., 7060 Convoy Court, San Diego CA 92111. (619)278-9080. Editor: Ralph Cobar. Magazine; digest sized; 100 pages; Dombrite paper; 4-color cover; color centerfold and photographs. "Adult erotica, real life fantasies, and true reader experience. Explicit fiction about 18-50 year old males only. For gay males." Monthly. Plans special fiction issue. Estab. 1986. Circ. 35,000.
Needs: Confession, erotica, gay. No subjugation, rape, heavy s&m, beastiality, incest, unless characters are of consenting age. Accepts 100-150 mss/year. Length: 3,000 words average; 2,500 words minimum; 3,500 words maximum. Sometimes critiques rejected mss.
How to Contact: Send complete ms with cover letter. Reports in 1-2 months. Accepts electronic submissions via disk convertable to ASCII format or WP5.1. Requires hard copy when sending disk submissions. Sample copy for $5. Fiction guidelines free.
Payment/Terms: Pays $100 on publication for all rights plus contributor's copies.
Advice: "Keep all sexual activity between fictional characters within the realm of possibility. Do not overexaggerate physical characteristics. We want stimulating fiction, not comedy. The overall tone of *Hot Shots* is always exciting, up beat, compassionate."

HUMPTY DUMPTY'S MAGAZINE, (II), Children's Better Health Institute, Box 567, 1100 Waterway Blvd., Indianapolis IN 46206. Editor: Sandy Grieshop. Magazine: 6½×9⅛; 48 pages; 35 lb. paper; coated cover; illustrations; some photos. Children's magazine stressing health, nutrition, hygiene, exercise and safety for children ages 4-6. Publishes 8 issues/year.
• Children's Better Health Institute also publishes *Child Life*, *Children's Digest*, *Children's Playmate*, *Jack and Jill* and *Turtle* listed in this book.
Needs: Juvenile health-related material and material of a more general nature. No inanimate talking objects. Rhyming stories should flow easily with no contrived rhymes. Receives 250-300 unsolicited fiction mss/month. Buys 3-5 mss/issue. Length: 500 words maximum.
How to Contact: Send complete ms with SASE. No queries. Reports in 8-10 weeks. Sample copy for $1.25. Editorial guidelines for SASE.
Payment/Terms: Pays up to 22¢/word for stories plus 10 contributor's copies on publication for all rights. (One-time book rights returned when requested for specific publication.)
Advice: "In contemporary stories, characters should be up-to-date, with realistic dialogue. We're looking for health-related stories with unusual twists or surprise endings. We want to avoid stories and poems that 'preach.' We try to present the health material in a positive way, utilizing a light humorous approach wherever possible." Most rejected mss "are too wordy. Need short, short nonfiction."

HUSTLER, Larry Flynt Publications, 9171 Wilshire Blvd., Suite 300, Beverly Hills CA 90210. Does not accept outside fiction; all fiction is staff written.

HUSTLER BUSTY BEAUTIES, (I, IV), HG Publications, Inc., 8484 Wilshire Blvd., Suite 900, Beverly Hills CA 90211. (213)651-5400. Editor: N. Morgen Hagen. Magazine: 8×11; 100 pages; 60 lb. paper; 80 lb. cover; illustrations and photographs. "Adult entertainment and reading centered around large-breasted women for an over-18 audience, mostly male." Published 13 times/year. Estab. 1988. Circ. 150,000.
Needs: Adventure, erotica, fantasy, mystery/suspense. All must have erotic theme. Receives 25 unsolicited fiction mss/month. Buys 1 ms/issue; 6-12 mss/year. Publishes mss 3-6 months after acceptance. Published work by Mike Dillon and H.H. Morris. Length: 1,600 words preferred; 1,000 words minimum; 2,000 words maximum.
How to Contact: Query first. Then send complete ms with cover letter. Reports in 2 weeks on queries; in 2-4 weeks on mss. SASE. Sample copy for $5. Fiction guidelines free.
Payment/Terms: Pays $80-500 on publication for all rights.
Advice: Looks for "1. plausible plot, well-defined characters, literary ingenuity; 2. hot sex scenes; 3. readable, coherent, grammatically sound prose."

IN TOUCH FOR MEN, (IV), 13122 Saticoy St., North Hollywood CA 91605. (818)764-2288. Editor: Allan W. Mills. Magazine: 8×10¾; 100 pages; glossy paper; coated cover; illustrations and photographs. "*In Touch* is a magazine for gay men. It features five to six nude male centerfolds in each issue, but is erotic rather than pornographic. We include fiction." Monthly. Estab. 1973. Circ. 70,000.
Needs: Confession, gay, erotica, romance (contemporary, historical). All characters must be over 18 years old. Stories must have an explicit erotic content. No heterosexual or internalized homophobic fiction. Buys 3 mss/month; 36 mss/year. Publishes ms 3 months after acceptance. Length: 2,500 words average; up to 3,500 words maximum. Sometimes critiques rejected mss and recommends other markets.
How to Contact: Send complete ms with cover letter, name, address and Social Security number. Reports in 2 weeks on queries; 2 months on mss. SASE. Simultaneous and reprint submissions, if from local publication, OK. Sample copy for $5.95. Fiction guidelines free. Reviews novels and short story collections.

Payment/Terms: Pays $25-75 (except on rare occasions for a longer piece) on publication for one-time rights.

Advice: Publishes "primarily erotic material geared toward gay men. Periodically (but very seldom) we will run fiction of a non-erotic nature (but still gay-related), but that's not the norm. I personally prefer (and accept) manuscripts that are not only erotic/hardcore, but show a developed story, plot and concise ending (as opposed to just sexual vignettes that basically lead nowhere). If it's got a little romance, too, that's even better. Emphasis still on erotic, though. We're starting to fuse more 'safe sex' depictions in fiction, hoping that it becomes the standard for male erotica. Hopefully portraying responsible activity will prompt people to act responsibly, as well."

INDIA CURRENTS, (II,IV), The Complete Indian American Magazine, Box 21285, San Jose CA 95151. (408)274-6966. Fax: (408)274-2733. Editor: Arvind Kumar. Magazine: 8½ × 11; 104 pages; newsprint paper; illustrations and photographs. "The arts and culture of India as seen in America for Indians and non-Indians with a common interest in India." Monthly. Estab. 1987. Circ. 25,000.

  • Editor Arvind Kumar was honored by KQED Channel 9, the local PBS affiliate, as an "Unsung Hero" during Lesbian and Gay Pride Month of June 1995.

Needs: All Indian content: contemporary, ethnic, feminist, historical (general), humor/satire, literary, mainstream, prose poem, regional, religious/inspirational, romance, translations (from Indian languages). "We seek material with insight into Indian culture, American culture and the crossing from one to another." Receives 12 unsolicited mss/month. Buys 1 ms/issue; 12 mss/year. Publishes ms 2-6 months after acceptance. Published work by Chitra Divakaruni, Jyotsna Sreenivasan and Mathew Chacko; published new writers within the last year. Length: 1,500 words average; 1,000 words minimum; 2,000 words maximum. Publishes short shorts. Length: 500 words.

How to Contact: Send complete ms with cover letter and clips of published work. Reports in 2-3 months on mss. SASE. Simultaneous and reprint submissions OK. Accepts electronic submissions. E-mail address: editor@indiacur.com. Sample copy for $3.

Payment/Terms: Pays in subscriptions on publication for one-time rights.

Advice: "Story must be related to India and subcontinent in some meaningful way. The best stories are those which document some deep transformation as a result of an Indian experience, or those which show the humanity of Indians as the world's most ancient citizens."

✦**INDIAN LIFE MAGAZINE, (II, IV)**, Indian Life Ministries, P.O. Box 3765, RPO, Red Wood Center, Station B, Winnipeg, Manitoba R2W 3R6 Canada. (204)661-9333 or (800)665-9275 in Canada only. Fax: (204)661-3982. Contact: Editor. Magazine: 8½ × 11; 24 pages; newsprint paper and cover stock; illustrations; full cover; photos. A nondenominational Christian magazine written and read mostly by Native Americans. Bimonthly. Estab. 1979. Circ. 30,000.

  • *Indian Life Magazine* has won several awards for "Higher Goals in Christian Journalism" and "Excellence" from the Evangelical Press Association. The magazine also won awards from the Native American Press Association.

Needs: Ethnic (Indian), historical (general), juvenile, religious/inspirational, young adult/teen, native testimonies, bible teaching articles. Length: 1,000-1,200 words average.

How to Contact: Query letter preferred. Simultaneous submissions OK. Reports in 1 month on queries. IRC or SASE ("U.S. stamps no good up here"). Sample copy for $1 and 8½ × 11 SAE. Fiction guidelines for $1 and #10 SAE.

Advice: "Keep it simple with an Indian viewpoint at about a 7th grade reading level. Read story out loud. Have someone else read it to you. If it doesn't come across smoothly and naturally, it needs work."

INSIDE, The Magazine of the Jewish Exponent, (II), Jewish Federation, 226 S. 16th St., Philadelphia PA 19102. (215)893-5700. Editor-in-Chief: Jane Biberman. Magazine: 175-225 pages; glossy paper; illustrations; photos. Aimed at middle- and upper-middle-class audience, Jewish-oriented articles and fiction. Quarterly. Estab. 1980. Circ. 80,000.

Needs: Contemporary, ethnic, humor/satire, literary and translations. No erotica. Receives approximately 10 unsolicited fiction mss/month. Buys 1-2 mss/issue; 4-8 mss/year. Published new writers within the last year. Length: 1,500 words minimum; 3,000 words maximum; 2,000 words average. Occasionally critiques rejected mss.

How to Contact: Query first with clips of published work. Reports on queries in 3 weeks. SASE. Simultaneous submissions OK. Sample copy for $4. Fiction guidelines for SASE.

Payment/Terms: Pays $100-600 on acceptance for first rights. Sometimes buys reprints. Sends galleys to author.

Advice: "We're looking for original, avant-garde, stylish writing but we buy very little."

INTERRACE MAGAZINE, The Source for Interracial Living, (I, II, IV), P.O. Box 12048, Atlanta GA 30355-2048. (404)364-9690. Editor: Candy Mills. Magazine: 8½ × 11; 40 pages; gloss paper; 60 lb. gloss cover; illustrations and photos. "All submissions must have an interracial theme as this is a national magazine serving interracial couples/families, biracial/multiracial people and those who have transracially adopted." Published 6 times/year.

Needs: All submissions must have an interracial/multiracial theme!!! Adventure, condensed novel, fantasy (science fiction), humor/satire, literary, mainstream/contemporary, mystery/suspense, romance (contemporary), serialized novel, westerns (traditional), young adult. List of upcoming themes available for SASE. Publishes annual special fiction issue or anthology. Receives 5-10 unsolicited mss/month. Publishes 1 ms/issue; 6 mss/year. Publishes ms 4 months-1 year after acceptance. Published work by Christopher Conlon, Frances Parker and Bob Slaymaker. Length: 2,400 words average; 1,600 words minimum; 4,000 words maximum. Publishes short shorts. Also publishes literary essays, literary criticism, poetry. Sometimes critiques or comments on rejected mss.

How to Contact: Send complete ms with cover letter and synopsis. Should include estimated word count, bio, Social Security number and list of publications. Reports in 2-4 weeks on queries; 1-2 months on mss. Send a disposable copy of ms. Simultaneous, reprint and electronic submissions OK. Sample copy for $2 and 9 × 12 SASE. Fiction and nonfiction guidelines for #10 SASE. Reviews novel and short story collections.

Payment/Terms: Pays $20-50, free subscription to magazine and up to 5 contributor's copies on publication. Buys one-time rights.

Advice: "It's not so much how well-written the piece is but how 'smart' it is. In other words, the characters are continually evolving, the story holds your attention from start to finish and the storyline has a beginning, middle and end, always with a multicultural/interracial focus."

JACK AND JILL, (IV), The Children's Better Health Institute, Box 567, 1100 Waterway Blvd., Indianapolis IN 46206. (317)636-8881. Editor: Daniel Lee. Children's magazine of articles, stories and activities, many with a health, safety, exercise or nutritional-oriented theme, ages 7-10 years. Monthly except January/February, March/April, May/June, July/August. Estab. 1938.

- Other publications by this publisher listed in this book include *Child Life, Children's Digest, Children's Playmate, Humpty Dumpty* and *Turtle.*

Needs: Science fiction, mystery, sports, adventure, historical fiction and humor. Health-related stories with a subtle lesson. Published work by Peter Fernandez, Adriana Devoy and Myra Schomberg; published new writers within the last year. Length: 500-800 words.

How to Contact: Send complete ms with SASE. Reports in 3 months on mss. Sample copy for $1.25. Fiction guidelines for SASE.

Payment/Terms: Pays up to 20¢/word on publication for all rights.

Advice: "Try to present health material in a positive—not a negative—light. Use humor and a light approach wherever possible without minimizing the seriousness of the subject. We need more humor and adventure stories."

JIVE, BLACK CONFESSIONS, BLACK ROMANCE, BRONZE THRILLS, BLACK SECRETS, (I, II), Sterling/Mcfadden, 233 Park Ave. S., Fifth Floor, New York NY 10003. (212)780-3500. Editor: Marcia Mahan. Magazine: 8½ × 11; 72 pages; newsprint paper; glossy cover; 8 × 10 photographs. "We publish stories that are romantic and have romantic lovemaking scenes in them. Our audience is basically young. However, we have a significant audience base of housewives. The age range is from 18-49." Bimonthly (*Jive* and *Black Romance* in odd-numbered months; *Black Confessions* and *Bronze Thrills* in even-numbered months). 6 issues per year. Estab. 1962. Circ. 100,000.

Needs: Confession, romance (contemporary, young adult). No "stories that are stereotypical to black people, ones that do not follow the basic rules of writing, or ones that are too graphic in content and lack a romantic element." Receives 20 or more unsolicited fiction mss/month. Buys 6 mss/issue (2 issues/month); 144 mss/year. Publishes ms an average of 2-3 months after acceptance. Published work by Linda Smith; published new writers within the last year. Length: 18-24 pages.

How to Contact: Query with clips of published work or send complete ms with cover letter. "A cover letter should include an author's bio and what he or she proposes to do. Of course, address and phone number." Reports in 3 months. SASE. Simultaneous submissions OK. "Please contact me if simultaneously submitted work has been accepted elsewhere." Sample copy for 9 × 12 SAE and 5 first-class stamps; fiction guidelines for #10 SAE and 2 first-class stamps.

Payment/Terms: Pays $75-100 on publication for all rights.

Advice: "Our five magazines are a great starting point for new writers. We accept work from beginners as well as established writers. Please study and research black culture and lifestyles if you are not a black writer. Stereotypical stories are not acceptable. Set the stories all over the world and all over the USA—not just down south. We are not looking for 'the runaway who gets turned out by a sweet-talking pimp' stories. We are looking for stories about all types of female characters. Any writer should not be afraid to communicate with us if he or she is having some difficulty with writing a story. We are available to help at any stage of the submission process. Also, writers should practice patience. If we do not contact the writer, that means that the story is being read or is being held on file for future publication. If we get in touch with the writer, it usually means a request for revision and resubmission. Do the best work possible and don't let rejection slips send you off 'the deep end.' Don't take everything that is said about your work so personally. We are buying all of our work from freelance writers."

JUGGLER'S WORLD, (IV), International Juggler's Association, Box 443, Davidson NC 28036. (704)892-1296. Editor: Bill Giduz. Fiction Editor: Ken Letko. Magazine: 8½×11; 40 pages; 70 lb. paper and cover stock; illustrations and photos. For and about jugglers and juggling. Quarterly.

Needs: Historical (general), humor/satire, science fiction. No stories "that don't include juggling as a central theme." Receives "very few" unsolicited mss/month. Buys 2 mss/year. Publishes ms an average of 6-12 months to 1 year after acceptance. Length: 2,000 words average; 1,000 words minimum; 2,500 words maximum. Sometimes critiques rejected mss.

How to Contact: Query first. Reports in 1 week. Simultaneous submissions OK. Prefers electronic submissions via IBM or Macintosh compatible disk. E-mail address: bigiduz@davidson.edu. Sample copy for $2.50.

Payment/Terms: Pays $25-50, free subscription to magazine and 3 contributor's copies on acceptance for first rights.

Advice: "Submit a brief story outline to the editor before writing the whole piece."

JUNIOR TRAILS, (I, II), Gospel Publishing House, 1445 Boonville Ave., Springfield MO 65802. (417)862-2781. Elementary Editor: Sinda S. Zinn. Magazine: 5¼×8; 8 pages; 36 lb. coated offset paper; art illustrations; photos. "A Sunday school take-home paper of nature articles and fictional stories that apply Christian principles to everyday living for 10-to 12-year-old children." Weekly. Estab. 1954. Circ. 70,000.

Needs: Contemporary, juvenile, religious/inspirational, spiritual and sports. Adventure stories are welcome. No Biblical fiction or science fiction. Buys 2 mss/issue. Published work by Betty Lou Mell, Mason M. Smith and Nanette L. Dunford; published new writers within the last year. Length: 1,200-1,500 words. Publishes short shorts.

How to Contact: Send complete ms with SASE. Reports in 4-6 weeks. Free sample copy and guidelines with SASE.

Payment/Terms: Pays 5¢/word and 3 contributor's copies on acceptance for first rights.

Advice: "Know the age level and direct stories relevant to that age group. Since junior-age children (grades 5 and 6) enjoy action, fiction provides a vehicle for communicating moral/spiritual principles in a dramatic framework. Fiction, if well done, can be a powerful tool for relating Christian principles. It must, however, be realistic and believable in its development. Make your children be children, not overly mature for their age. We would like more stories with a *city* setting. Write for contemporary children, using setting and background that includes various ethnic groups."

LADIES' HOME JOURNAL, (III), Published by Meredith Corporation, 100 Park Ave., New York NY 10017. (212)953-7070. Editor-in-Chief: Myrna Blyth. Fiction/Articles Editor: Mary Mohler. Magazine: 190 pages; 34-38 lb. coated paper; 65 lb. coated cover; illustrations and photos.

• *Ladies' Home Journal* has won several awards for journalism.

Needs: Book mss and short stories, *accepted only through an agent.* Return of unsolicited material cannot be guaranteed. Published work by Fay Weldon, Anita Shreve, Jane Shapiro, Anne Rivers Siddons. Length: approximately 2,000-2,500 words.

How to Contact: Send complete ms with cover letter (credits). Simultaneous submissions OK. Publishes ms 4-12 months after acceptance.

Payment/Terms: Buys First North American rights.

Advice: "Our readers like stories, especially those that have emotional impact. Stories about relationships between people—husband/wife—mother/son—seem to be subjects that can be explored effectively in short stories. Our reader's mail and surveys attest to this fact: Readers enjoy our fiction, and are most keenly tuned to stories dealing with children. Fiction today is stronger than ever. Beginners can be optimistic; if they have talent, I do believe that talent will be discovered. It is best to read the magazine before submitting."

LADYBUG, (II, IV), The Cricket Magazine Group, P.O. Box 300, Peru IL 61354. (815)224-6643. Editor-in-Chief: Marianne Carus. Contact: Paula Morrow. Magazine: 8×10; 36 pages plus 4-page pullout section; illustrations. "*Ladybug* publishes original stories and poems and reprints written by the world's best children's authors. For young children, ages 2-6." Monthly. Estab. 1990. Circ. 130,000.

• The Cricket Magazine Group's magazines include *Cricket*, *Spider* and *Babybug*. *Ladybug* has received the Parents Choice Award; the Golden Lamp Honor Award and the Golden Lamp Award (1994) from the Educational Press Association, and Magazine Merit awards from the Society of Children's Book Writers and Illustrators.

Needs: Fairy tales, fantasy (children's), folk tales, juvenile, picture stories, preschool, read-out-loud stories. Length: 300-750 words preferred. Publishes short shorts.

Check the Category Indexes, located at the back of the book, for publishers interested in specific fiction subjects.

The Old West Lures New Voices

"I like to be surprised," says Elana Lore, editor of *Louis L'Amour Western Magazine*, when asked what sparks her interest in a story. "I like a story that just grabs me on the first page and makes me feel compelled to read it to the end. It helps if the story's real, if there's some detail—a different point of view, an unusual fact—that makes it come to life."

The name Louis L'Amour brings with it a set of standards. Profanity, unnecessary violence and sex are not found in the well-known western writer's works and readers expect the same of a magazine which bears his name. Yet, the days of the standard horse opera, shoot-'em-ups are over. Lore says, "A lot of new voices are being heard. The genre is no longer predominantly male, white voices. The stories of women, Indians, Mexicans and African-Americans are being told. Their voices are being heard, not only as characters, but as writers."

Elana Lore

© Photo by Camera 1

What makes a good western story? "Good writing is essential—more than anything else," she says. "The other thing that's really important to this magazine is the genre's big trend now toward historical accuracy. I, personally, like to learn something. I don't want to hear the same stuff over and over again."

In the spirit of L'Amour, whose stories ranged from the earliest frontier days to the modern era, no constraints are placed upon a story's period setting—though Lore would like to see more "traditional" stories, meaning those generally accepted as occurring from approximately 1860 through the 1880s.

Genre mixing has become popular in recent years. Lore says enthusiastically, "Western mysteries work well and . . . I bought a really good ghost story." However, she discourages submissions of westerns which feature supernatural, fantasy or science fiction elements, and the magazine does not accept poetry, reprints or novel-length submissions for serialization or excerpting.

One crucial piece of advice Lore has for all fiction writers: "Never submit more than one story at a time. If you submit three stories and the first one isn't very good, I can't really greet the next two with the same enthusiasm, so it works against you. I've talked to a lot of editors and I think it's true—reading more than one story at a time from a writer is very hard to do, and it's not fair to the writer either. If you have three stories, put them in three separate envelopes and mail one Monday, one Tuesday and one Wednesday so there's a little separation and I come to each story fresh."

Lore assures that new writers need not fear getting lost in the shuffle. "We have a policy here in the Dell Magazine Fiction Group [publishers of the magazine] of reading all submissions. You don't need an agent. You don't need prior publishing credit—just send the manuscript and we'll read it."

She has this encouraging final thought: "The magazine won the Golden Spur award this year for best short fiction and it was a first story. It beat out Elmore Leonard and Gordon D. Shirreffs." The author has also been approached for a possible motion picture option. First stories, she says, can do just as well as those written by established authors.

—*Glenn Marcum*

How to Contact: Send complete ms with cover letter. Include word count on ms (do not count title). Reports in 3 months. SASE. Reprints are OK. Fiction guidelines for SASE. Sample copy for $4. For guidelines *and* sample send 9×12 SAE (no stamps required) and $4.
Payment/Terms: Pays up to 25¢/word (less for reprints) on publication for first publication rights or second serial (reprint) rights. For recurring features, pays flat fee and copyright becomes property of The Cricket Magazine Group.
Advice: Looks for "well-written stories for preschoolers: age-appropriate, not condescending. We look for rich, evocative language and sense of joy or wonder."

LADY'S CIRCLE, (II), GCR Publishing, 1700 Broadway, 34th Floor, New York NY 10019. (212)541-7100. Managing Editor: Sandra Kosherick. Magazine. "A lot of our readers are in Midwestern states." Bimonthly. Estab. 1963. Circ. 100,000.
● *Lady's Circle* has recently been sold to GCR Publishing. The publisher is not sure when or if they will publish the magazine again. Query first.
Needs: Historical, humor/satire, mainstream, religious/inspirational, senior citizen/retirement. Receives 100 unsolicited fiction mss/month. Buys about 3-4 fiction mss/year. Time between acceptance and publication "varies, usually works 6 months ahead." Length: 1,000 words minimum; 1,200 words maximum. Accepts short shorts "for fillers." Sometimes critiques rejected ms.
How to Contact: Query first. Reports in 3 months on queries. SASE. Simultaneous and reprint submissions OK. Accepts electronic submissions via disk or modem. Sample copy for $3.95; fiction guidelines for SAE.
Payment/Terms: Pay varies, depending on ms.
Terms: Pays on publication for first North American serial rights.

LOUIS L'AMOUR WESTERN MAGAZINE, (I, II, IV), Doubleday Dell Magazines, 1540 Broadway, 15th Floor, New York NY 10036. (212)782-8532. Fax: (212)782-8338. Editor: Elana Lore. Magazine: 8×10¾; 104 pages; coated stock; 100 lb. Sterling cover with UV coating; illustrations and photographs. "We publish western short stories for an audience that is about 70 percent male, 35-64 years old, largely non-urban, with a minimum household income of $35,000." Bimonthly. Estab. 1993.
● Dell's magazine group also includes *Ellery Queen's Mystery Magazine, Alfred Hitchcock Mystery Magazine, Analog Science Fiction & Fact* and *Asimov's Science Fiction.*
Needs: Westerns (frontier, traditional). "We will also consider modern, mystery-oriented, Native American and other types of western fiction." Receives 250 unsolicited mss/month. Buys 6-9 mss/issue. Publishes ms 6 months after acceptance. Agented fiction 5%. Length: 5,000-7,000 preferred; 12,000 words maximum.
How to Contact: Send complete ms with a cover letter. Should include Social Security number and list of publications. Reports in 2-3 months. Send SASE for reply, return of ms or send a disposable copy of ms. Sample copy for $4.50, make check out to LLWM and send to Meshan Germinder, Subscription Department at the above address. Fiction guidelines for #10 SASE.
Payment/Terms: Pays 8¢/word on acceptance for first rights.
Advice: "Get a copy of our writers' guidelines and read the magazine before you submit to see what kinds of things we're looking for." Looking for "original ideas that bring to life the people and places of the West. We don't want any shoot-em-ups, any reworked Saturday morning TV show western stories."

LIGUORIAN, (I, IV), "A Leading Catholic Magazine," Liguori Publications, 1 Liguori Dr., Liguori MO 63057. (314)464-2500. Editor-in-Chief: Allan Weinert, CSS.R. Magazine: 5×8½; 72 pages; b&w illustrations and photographs. "*Liguorian* is a Catholic magazine aimed at helping our readers to live a full Christian life. We publish articles for families, young people, children, religious and singles—all with the same aim." Monthly. Estab. 1913. Circ. 400,000.

• *Liguorian* received Catholic Press Association awards for 1994 including Best Cover and Second Place for General Excellence.

Needs: Religious/inspirational, young adult and senior citizen/retirement (with moral Christian thrust), spiritual. "Stories submitted to *Liguorian* must have as their goal the lifting up of the reader to a higher Christian view of values and goals. We are not interested in contemporary works that lack purpose or are of questionable moral value." Receives approximately 25 unsolicited fiction mss/month. Buys 12 mss/year. Published work by Sharon Helgens, Kathleen Choi, Shirley Anne Morgan and Beverly Sheresh; published new writers within the last year. Length: 1,500-2,000 words preferred. Also publishes short shorts. Occasionally critiques rejected mss "if we feel the author is capable of giving us something we need even though this story did not suit us."

How to Contact: Send complete ms with SASE. Accepts disk submissions compatible with IBM or Macintosh, using a DOS program; prefers hard copy with disk submission. Reports in 10-12 weeks on mss. Sample copy and fiction guidelines for #10 SASE.

Payment/Terms: Pays 10-12¢/word and 5 contributor's copies on acceptance for all rights. Offers 50% kill fee for assigned mss not published.

Advice: "First read several issues containing short stories. We look for originality and creative input in each story we read. Since most editors must wade through mounds of manuscripts each month, consideration for the editor requires that the market be studied, the manuscript be carefully presented and polished before submitting. Our publication uses only one story a month. Compare this with the 25 or more we receive over the transom each month. Also, many fiction mss are written without a specific goal or thrust, i.e., an interesting incident that goes nowhere is *not a story*. We believe fiction is a highly effective mode for transmitting the Christian message and also provides a good balance in an unusually heavy issue."

LILITH MAGAZINE, The Independent Jewish Women's Magazine, (I, II, IV), 250 W. 57th St., Suite 2432, New York NY 10107. (212)757-0818. Editor: Susan Weidman Schneider. Fiction Editor: Faye Moskowitz. Magazine: 8½×11; 40 pages; 80 lb. cover; b&w illustrations; b&w and color photos. Publishes work relating to Jewish feminism, for Jewish feminists, feminists and Jewish households. Quarterly. Estab. 1975. Circ. 25,000.

Needs: Ethnic, feminist, lesbian, literary, prose poem, psychic/supernatural/occult, religious/inspirational, senior citizen/retirement, spiritual, translation, young adult. "Nothing that does not in any way relate to Jews, women or Jewish women." Receives 15 unsolicited mss/month. Accepts 1 ms/issue; 3 mss/year. Publishes ms 2-10 months after acceptance. Published work by Lesléa Newman and Gloria Goldreich. Publishes short shorts.

How to Contact: Send complete ms with cover letter, which should include a 2-line bio. Reports in 2 months on queries; 2-6 months on mss. SASE. Simultaneous and reprint submissions OK. E-mail address: lilithmag@aol.com. Sample copy for $5. Fiction guidelines for #10 SASE. Reviews novels and short story collections. Send books to Robin Beth Schaer.

Payment/Terms: Varies. Acquires first rights.

Advice: "A clear, concise cover letter is important."

LIVE, (IV), Assemblies of God, 1445 Boonville, Springfield MO 65802-1894. (417)862-2781. Editor: Paul W. Smith. "A take-home story paper distributed weekly in young adult/adult Sunday school classes. *Live* is a fictional story paper primarily. True stories in narrative style are welcome. Poems, first-person anecdotes and humor are used as fillers. The purpose of *Live* is to present in short story form realistic characters who utilize biblical principles. We hope to challenge readers to take risks for God and to resolve their problems scripturally." Weekly. Circ. 155,000.

Needs: Religious/inspirational, prose poem and spiritual. "Inner city, ethnic, racial settings." No controversial stories about such subjects as feminism, war or capital punishment. Buys 2 mss/issue. Published work by Maxine F. Dennis, E. Ruth Glover and Larry Clark; published new writers within the last year. Length: 500-1,700 words.

How to Contact: Send complete ms. Social Security number and word count must be included. Simultaneous submissions OK. Reports in 12-18 months. Sample copy and guidelines for SASE.

Payment/Terms: Pays 5¢/word (first rights); 3¢/word (second rights) on acceptance.

Advice: "Stories should go somewhere! Action, not just thought-life; interaction, not just insights. Heroes and heroines, suspense and conflict. Avoid simplistic, pietistic conclusions, preachy, critical or moralizing. We don't accept science or Bible fiction. Stories should be encouraging, challenging, humorous. Even problem-centered stories should be upbeat." Reserves the right to change titles, abbreviate length and clarify flashbacks for publication.

‡LOOKING AHEAD—NAPA, A Monthly Publication for Active Retirees, (IV), Professional Salutations, 100 Coombs, Napa CA 94559. (707)226-2474. Fax: (707)226-2491. Editor: Ronda Rhoads. Tabloid: 10×13; 40 pages; Electro Brite paper; illustrations and photos. "*Looking Ahead* publishes upbeat features of interest to readers 50 and over." Monthly. Estab. 1994. Circ. 10,000.

Needs: Humor/satire, mainstream/contemporary, senior citizen/retirement. Receives 30 unpublished mss/month. Accepts 3 mss/issue; 36 mss/year. Recently published work by June King, Vern Harden and Beatrice

Davis. Length: 500 words minimum; 1,000 words maximum. Also publishes literary essays.

How to Contact: Send complete ms with a cover letter. Should include estimated word count. Send SASE for reply, return of ms or send a disposable copy of ms. Simultaneous, reprint, electronic submissions OK. Sample copy for $2, legal SAE and 5 first-class stamps.

Payment/Terms: Pays $25 and 1 contributor's copy on publication for one-time rights.

Advice: "We love humor." Does not wish to see "disease-of-the-week articles, or downbeat pieces on aging."

THE LOOKOUT, (II), Standard Publishing, 8121 Hamilton Ave., Cincinnati OH 45231. (513)931-4050. Fax: (513)931-0904. Editor: Simon J. Dahlman. Magazine: 8½×11; 16 pages; newsprint paper; newsprint cover stock; illustrations; photos. "Conservative Christian magazine for adults." Weekly. Estab. 1894. Circ. 120,000.

 • *The Lookout* has won awards from the Evangelical Press Association. Standard Publishing also publishes *Radar* and *Seek* listed in this book. Note *The Lookout* is buying less stories now, so competition is greater. The magazine is using less fiction—they've cut their needs in half.

Needs: Religious/inspirational. No predictable, preachy material. Taboos are blatant sex and swear words. Receives 60 unsolicited mss/month. Buys 15-20 mss/year. Publishes ms 2-12 months after acceptance. Published work by Bob Hartman, Myrna J. Stone, Dave Cheadle and Daniel Schantz; published new writers within the last year. Length: 1,200-2,000 words.

How to Contact: Send complete ms with SASE. Reports in 3-4 months on ms. Simultaneous and reprint submissions OK. Sample copy for 75¢. Guidelines for #10 SASE.

Payment/Terms: Pays 6-9¢/word on acceptance for first rights; 5-6¢/word for other rights and contributor's copies. Buys reprints.

Advice: "We would like to see a better balance between stories that focus on external struggles (our usual fare in the past) and those that focus on internal (spiritual, emotional, psychological) struggles. Send us good stories—not good sermons dressed up as stories. Keep stories in a contemporary setting with an adult's point of view. Many writers with a Christian viewpoint try to 'preach' in their stories. That is as deadly for our purposes as for anyone. Tell the story, and let the 'message' take care of itself."

THE LUTHERAN JOURNAL, (II), Macalester Park Publishing, 7317 Cahill Rd., Minneapolis MN 55439. (612)941-6830. Editor: Rev. A.U. Deye. "A family magazine providing wholesome and inspirational reading material for the enjoyment and enrichment of Lutherans." Quarterly. Estab. 1936. Circ. 125,000.

Needs: Literary, contemporary, religious/inspirational, romance (historical), senior citizen/retirement and young adult. Must be appropriate for distribution in the churches. Buys 3-6 mss/issue. Length: 1,000-1,500 words.

How to Contact: Send complete ms with SASE. Sample copy for SAE with 59¢ postage.

Payment/Terms: Pays $10-25 and 6 contributor's copies on publication for all and first rights.

McCALL'S, 110 5th Ave., New York NY 10011-5603. No longer publishes fiction.

MADEMOISELLE MAGAZINE, Condé Nast Publications, Inc., 350 Madison Ave., New York NY 10017. No longer publishes fiction.

MANSCAPE, (II, IV), First Hand Ltd., Box 1314, Teaneck NJ 07666. (201)836-9177. Editor: Bill Jaeger. Magazine: digest sized; 130 pages; illustrations. "Magazine is devoted to gay male sexual fetishes; publishes fiction and readers' letters devoted to this theme." Monthly. Estab. 1985. Circ. 60,000.

 • This publisher also publishes *First Hand* and *Guys* listed in this section as well as *Mantalk and Manshots*.

Needs: Erotica, gay. Should be written in first person. No science fiction or fantasy. Erotica must be based on real life. Receives 25 unsolicited fiction mss/month. Buys 5 mss/issue; 60 mss/year. Publishes ms an average of 12-18 months after acceptance. Published new writers within the last year. Length: 3,000 words average; 2,000 words minimum; 3,750 words maximum. Sometimes critiques rejected ms.

How to Contact: Send complete ms with cover letter. SASE. Sample copy for $5; guidelines for #10 SASE.

Payment/Terms: Pays $100-150 on publication or in 180 days, whichever comes first, for all rights or first North American serial rights.

MASSAGE, Keeping You—In Touch, (IV), Noah Publishing Inc., P.O. Box 1500, Davis CA 95617. (916)757-6033. Fax: (916)757-6041. Managing Editor: Karen Menehan. Magazine: 8¼×11; 130 pages; 70 lb. gloss paper; 80 lb. gloss cover; illustrations and photographs. "The philosophy is to spread the good word about massage therapy and other healing arts. Material published includes pieces on technique, business advice, experiential pieces and interviews/profiles on pioneers/leaders in the field. Intended audience is those who practice massage and other allied healing arts." Bimonthly. Estab. 1985. Circ. 20,000.

Needs: "We only accept fiction that places massage or bodywork in a positive light." Receives 10 unsolicited ms/month. Buys 1 ms/issue; 6 mss/year. Publishes ms within 1 year after acceptance. Published work by

Erik Lee and Mary Bond. Length: 2,000 words preferred; 1,500 words minimum; 2,500 words maximum. Always critiques or comments on rejected mss.

How to Contact: Query first. Should include bio (2-3 sentences). Reports in 2 months. Send SASE for reply or send a disposable copy of ms. Writer's guidelines and sample copy free.

Payment/Terms: Pays $250 maximum and 2 contributor's copies 30 days after publication for first rights; additional copies for $3.

Advice: "Looking for stories that will touch the reader emotionally by showing the importance of human contact—which doesn't mean they have to be melodramatic. Humor is appreciated, as are descriptive detail and vibrant characterizations."

MATURE LIVING, (II), Sunday School Board of the Southern Baptist Convention, MSN 140, 127 Ninth Ave. North, Nashville TN 37234. (615)251-2191. Fax: (615)251-5008. Editor: Al Shackleford. Magazine: 8½×11; 52 pages; non-glare paper; slick cover stock; full color illustrations and photos. "Our magazine is Christian in content and the material required is what would appeal to 55 and over age group: inspirational, informational, nostalgic, humorous. Our magazine is distributed mainly through churches (especially Southern Baptist churches) that buy the magazine in bulk and distribute it to members in this age group." Monthly. Estab. 1977. Circ. 360,000.

Needs: Humor, religious/inspirational and senior citizen/retirement. Avoid all types of pornography, drugs, liquor, horror, science fiction and stories demeaning to the elderly. Receives 10 mss/month. Buys 1-2 mss/ issue. Publishes ms an average of 1 year after acceptance. Published work by Burndean N. Sheffy, Pearl E. Trigg, Joyce M. Sixberry; published new writers within the last year. Length: 600-1,200 words (prefers 1,000).

How to Contact: Send complete ms with SASE. Include estimated word count and Social Security number. Reports in 2 months. Sample copy for $1. Guidelines for SASE.

Payment/Terms: Pays $75 on acceptance; 3 contributor's copies. $1 charge for extras. First rights only.

Advice: Mss are rejected because they are too long or subject matter unsuitable. "Our readers seem to enjoy an occasional short piece of fiction. It must be believable, however, and present senior adults in a favorable light."

MATURE YEARS, (II), United Methodist Publishing House, 201 Eighth Ave. S., Nashville TN 37202. (615)749-6292. Editor: Marvin W. Cropsey. Magazine: 8½×11; 112 pages; illustrations and photos. Magazine "helps persons in and nearing retirement to appropriate the resources of the Christian faith as they seek to face the problems and opportunities related to aging." Quarterly. Estab. 1953.

Needs: Humor, integrational relationships, nostalgia, older adult issues, religious/inspirational, spiritual (for older adults). "We don't want anything poking fun at old age, saccharine stories or anything not for older adults." Buys 1 ms/issue, 4 mss/year. Publishes ms 1 year after acceptance. Published new writers within the last year. Length: 1,000-1,800 words.

How to Contact: Send complete ms with SASE and Social Security number. No simultaneous submissions. Reports in 2 months. Sample copy for 10½×11 SAE and $3.50 postage.

Payment/Terms: Pays 5¢/word on acceptance.

Advice: "Practice writing dialogue! Listen to people talk; take notes; master dialogue writing! Not easy, but well worth it! Most inquiry letters are far too long. If you can't sell me an idea in a brief paragraph, you're not going to sell the reader on reading your finished article or story."

✤MESSENGER OF THE SACRED HEART, (II), Apostleship of Prayer, 661 Greenwood Ave., Toronto, Ontario M4J 4B3 Canada. (416)466-1195. Editors: Rev. F.J. Power, S.J. and Alfred DeManche. Magazine: 7×10; 32 pages; coated paper; self-cover; illustrations; photos. Magazine for "Canadian and U.S. Catholics interested in developing a life of prayer and spirituality; stresses the great value of our ordinary actions and lives." Monthly. Estab. 1891. Circ. 16,000.

Needs: Religious/inspirational. Stories about people, adventure, heroism, humor, drama. No poetry. Buys 1 ms/issue. Length: 750-1,500 words. Recommends other markets.

How to Contact: Send complete ms with SAE. No simultaneous submissions. Reports in 1 month. Sample copy for $1.50 (Canadian).

Payment/Terms: Pays 4¢/word, 3 contributor's copies on acceptance for first North American serial rights. Rarely buys reprints.

Advice: "Develop a story that sustains interest to the end. Do not preach, but use plot and characters to convey the message or theme. Aim to move the heart as well as the mind. If you can, add a light touch or a sense of humor to the story. Your ending should have impact, leaving a moral or faith message for the reader."

METRO SINGLES LIFESTYLES, (I), Metro Publications, Box 28203, Kansas City MO 64118. (816)436-8424. Editor: Robert L. Huffstutter. Fiction Editor: Earl R. Stonebridge. Tabloid: 36 pages; 30. lb newspaper stock; 30 lb. cover; illustrations; photos. "Positive, uplifting, original, semi-literary material for all singles: widowed, divorced, never-married, of all ages 18 and over." Bimonthly. Estab. 1984. Circ. 25,000.

Needs: Humor/satire, literary, prose poem, religious/inspirational, romance (contemporary), special interest, spiritual, single parents. Receives 2-3 unsolicited mss/month. Buys 1-2 mss/issue; 12-18 mss/year. Publishes ms 2 months after acceptance. Length: 1,500 words average; 1,200 words minimum; 4,000 words maximum. Publishes short shorts. Published work by Patricia Castle, Libby Floyd, Donald G. Smith; published new writers within the last year. Length: 1,200. Occasionally critiques rejected mss. Recommends other markets.

How to Contact: Send complete ms with cover letter. Include short paragraph/bio listing credits (if any), current profession or job. Reports in 2 months on queries. SASE. Sample copy for $3.

Payment/Terms: Pays $25-50 on publication, free subscription to magazine and contributor's copies.

Advice: Looks for "singular way of life, problems and blessings of single parent families, the eternal search for the right mate—or the right date. Forget what society and the media says, write exactly how you feel about a certain subject and never worry about the negative responses . . . If you can imagine it, it's probably possible."

MIDSTREAM, A Monthly Jewish Review, (II, IV), Theodor Herzl Foundation, 110 E. 59th St., New York NY 10022. (212)339-6021. Editor: Joel Carmichael. Magazine: 8½×11; 48 pages; 50 lb. paper; 65 lb. white smooth cover stock. "We are a Zionist journal; we publish material with Jewish themes or that would appeal to a Jewish readership." Published 9 times/year. Estab. 1955. Circ. 10,000.

• Work published in *Midstream* was included in the *O. Henry Award* prize anthology.

Needs: Historical (general), humor/satire, literary, mainstream, translations. Receives 15-20 unsolicited mss/ month. Accepts 1 mss/issue; 10 mss/year. Publishes ms 6-18 months after acceptance. Agented fiction 10%. Published work by I. B. Singer, Anita Jackson and Enid Shomer. Length: 2,500 words average; 1,500 words minimum; 4,500 words maximum. Sometimes critiques rejected mss.

How to Contact: Send complete ms with cover letter, which should include "address, telephone, or affiliation of author; state that the ms is fiction." Reports in "up to 6 months." SASE.

Payment/Terms: Pays 5¢/word and contributor's copies on publication for first rights.

Advice: "Be patient—we publish only one piece of fiction per issue and we have a backlog."

MONTANA SENIOR CITIZENS NEWS, (II,IV), Barrett-Whitman Co., Box 3363, Great Falls MT 59403. (406)761-0305. Editor: Jack Love. Tabloid: 11×17; 60-80 pages; newsprint paper and cover; illustrations; photos. Publishes "everything of interest to seniors, except most day-to-day political items like Social Security and topics covered in the daily news. Personal profiles of seniors, their lives, times and reminiscences." Bimonthly. Estab. 1984. Circ. 25,000.

Needs: Historical, senior citizen/retirement, western (historical or contemporary). No fiction "unrelated to experiences to which seniors can relate." Buys 1 or fewer mss/issue; 4-5 mss/year. Publishes ms within 6 months of acceptance. Published work by Anne Norris, Helen Clark, Juni Dunklin. Length: 500-800 words preferred. Publishes short stories. Length: under 500 words.

How to Contact: Send complete ms with cover letter and phone number. Only responds to selected mss. SASE. Simultaneous and reprint submissions OK. Accepts electronic submission via WordPerfect disk. Sample copy for 9×12 SAE and $2 postage and handling.

Payment/Terms: Pays 4¢/word on publication for first rights or one-time rights.

MS, 230 Park Ave., 7th Floor, New York NY 10169-0799. No unsolicited fiction.

MY FRIEND, The Catholic Magazine for Kids, (II), Pauline Books & Media, 50 St. Paul's Ave., Boston MA 02130. (617)522-8911. Editor: Sister Anne Joan. Magazine: 8½×11; 32 pages; smooth, glossy paper and cover stock; illustrations; photos. Magazine of "religious truths and positive values for children in a format which is enjoyable and attractive. Each issue contains Bible stories, lives of saints and famous people, short stories, science corner, contests, projects, etc." Monthly during school year (September-June). Estab. 1979. Circ. 10,000.

• *My Friend* was honored by Catholic Press Association for General Excellence, Best Short Story and Best Illustration in 1995. Pauline Books & Media also publish *The Family* listed in this book.

Needs: Juvenile, religious/inspirational, spiritual (children), sports (children). Receives 60 unsolicited fiction mss/month. Buys 3-4 mss/issue; 30-40 mss/year. Published work by Eileen Spinelli, Bob Hartman and M. Donaleen Howitt; published new writers within the past year. Length: 200 words minimum; 900 words maximum; 600 words average.

How to Contact: Send complete ms with SASE. Reports in 1-2 months on mss. Publishes ms an average of 1 year after acceptance. Sample copy for $2 and 9×12 SASE ($1 postage).

A bullet introduces comments by the editor of Novel & Short Story Writer's Market *indicating special information about the listing.*

Payment/Terms: Pays $20-150 (stories, articles).
Advice: "We prefer child-centered stories in a real-world setting. We are particularly interested in media-related articles and stories that involve healthy choices regarding media use. Try to write visually—be 'graphics-friendly.' "

NEW ERA MAGAZINE, (II, IV), The Church of Jesus Christ of Latter-day Saints, 50 E. North Temple St., Salt Lake City UT 84150. (801)532-2951. Editor: Richard M. Romney. Magazine: 8×10½; 51 pages; 40 lb. coated paper; illustrations and photos. "We will publish fiction on any theme that strengthens and builds the standards and convictions of teenage Latter-day Saints ('Mormons')." Monthly. Estab. 1971. Circ. 200,000.
● This publisher also publishes *The Friend* listed in this book. *New Era* is a recipient of the Focus on Excellence Award from Brigham Young University. The magazine also sponsors a writing contest.
Needs: Stories on family relationships, self-esteem, dealing with loneliness, resisting peer pressure and all aspects of maintaining Christian values in the modern world. "All material must be written from a Latter-day Saint ('Mormon') point of view—or at least from a generally Christian point of view, reflecting LDS life and values." Receives 30-35 unsolicited mss/month. Buys 1 ms/issue; 12 mss/year. Publishes ms 3 months to 3 years after acceptance. Length: 1,500 words average; 250 words minimum; 2,000 words maximum.
How to Contact: Query letter preferred; send complete ms. Reports in 6-8 weeks. SASE. Sample copy for $1 and 9×12 SAE with 2 first-class stamps. Fiction guidelines for #10 SASE.
Payment/Terms: Pays $50-375 and contributor's copies on acceptance for all rights (reassign to author on request).
Advice: "Each magazine has its own personality—you wouldn't write the same style of fiction for *Seventeen* that you would write for *Omni*. Very few writers who are not of our faith have been able to write for us successfully, and the reason usually is that they don't know what it's like to be a member of our church. You must study and research and know those you are writing about. We love to work with beginning authors, and we're a great place to break in if you can understand us." Sponsors contests and awards for LDS fiction writers. "We have an annual contest; entry forms are in each September issue. Deadline is January; winners published in August."

NEW MYSTERY, (III), The Best New Mystery Stories, 175 Fifth Ave., #2001, New York NY 10010. (212)353-1582. Editor: Charles Raisch III. Magazine: 8½×11; 96 pages; illustrations and photographs. "Mystery, suspense and crime." Quarterly. Estab. 1990. Circ. 50,000.
● Response time for this magazine seems to be slower in summer months. The mystery included here is gritty and realistic. See the interview with Charles Raisch in the *Mystery Writer's Sourcebook* (Writer's Digest Books).
Needs: Mystery/suspense (cozy to hardboiled). Plans special annual anthology. Receives 350 unsolicited mss/month. Buys 6-10 ms/issue. Agented fiction 50%. Published work by Josh Pachter, Henry Slesar and Lawrence Block. Length: 3,000-5,000 words preferred. Also buys short book reviews 500-3,000 words. Sometimes critiques rejected mss.
How to Contact: Send complete ms with cover letter. Reports on ms in 1 month. SASE. Accepts electronic submissions. Sample copy for $5, 9×12 SAE and 4 first-class stamps.
Payment/Terms: Pays $25-1,000 on publication for all rights.
Advice: Stories should have "believable characters in trouble; sympathetic lead; visual language." Sponsors "Annual First Story Contest."

THE NEW YORKER, (III), The New Yorker, Inc., 20 W. 43rd St., New York NY 10036. (212)536-5972. Fiction Department. A quality magazine of interesting, well-written stories, articles, essays and poems for a literate audience. Weekly. Estab. 1925. Circ. 750,000.
How to Contact: Send complete ms with SASE. Reports in 10-12 weeks on mss. Publishes 1 ms/issue.
Payment/Terms: Varies. Pays on acceptance.
Advice: "Be lively, original, not overly literary. Write what you want to write, not what you think the editor would like. Send poetry to Poetry Department."

NORTHEAST, the Sunday Magazine of the Hartford Courant, (IV), 285 Broad St., Hartford CT 06115. (203)241-3700. Editor: Lary Bloom. Magazine: 10×11½; 20-40 pages; illustrations; photos. "A regional (New England, specifically Connecticut) magazine, we publish stories of varied subjects of interest to our Connecticut audience" for a general audience. Weekly. Published special fiction issue and a special college writing issue for fiction and poetry. Estab. 1981. Circ. 325,000.
Needs: Contemporary and regional. No children's stories or stories with distinct setting outside Connecticut. Receives 150 unsolicited mss/month. Buys 1 ms/issue; 2 mss/month. Publishes short shorts. Length: 750 words minimum; 3,000 words maximum.
How to Contact: Send complete ms with 10×12 SASE. Reports in 8-10 weeks. Simultaneous submissions OK. No reprints or previously published work. Sample copy and fiction guidelines for 10×12 or larger SASE.
Payment/Terms: Pays $250-1,000 on acceptance for one-time rights.

NUGGET, (II), Dugent Publishing Corp., Suite 600, 2600 Douglas Rd., Coral Gables FL 33134. (305)443-2378. Editor-in-Chief: Christopher James. A newsstand magazine designed to have erotic appeal for a fetish-oriented audience. Published 9 times a year. Estab. 1956. Circ. 100,000.

● Dugent Publishing also publishes *Gent* listed in this section.

Needs: Offbeat, fetish-oriented material encompassing a variety of subjects (B&D, TV, TS, spanking, amputeeism, infantalism, catfighting, etc.). Most of fiction includes several sex scenes. No fiction that concerns children or religious subjects. Buys 2 mss/issue. Agented fiction 5%. Length: 2,000-3,500 words.

How to Contact: Send complete ms with SASE. Reports in 1 month. Sample copy for $3.50. Guidelines for legal-sized SASE.

Payment/Terms: Pay starts at $200 and 1 contributor's copy on publication for first rights.

Advice: "Keep in mind the nature of the publication, which is fetish erotica. Subject matter can vary, but we prefer fetish themes."

‡NU*REAL, The Electronic Magazine of Art & Technology, (I, II), Mindset, P.O. Box 7000-822, Redondo Beach CA 90277. (310)793-4590. Editor: Christopher Simmons. Digital Magazine: 28-36 pages; illustrations and photos. "*Nu*Real* publishes new technology, art and fiction." Estab. 1995. Circ. 20,000.

● *Nu*Real* is produced in digital paper format which can be read on any computer. It's distributed on disk, online and on CD-ROM. Check with them for details.

Needs: Adventure, fantasy (science fantasy), horror, mystery/suspense (romantic suspense), psychic/supernatural/occult, romance (futuristic/time travel), science fiction. Publishes annual special fiction issue or anthology. Receives 20-30 mss/month. Accepts 2 mss/issue; 15-30 mss/year. Does not read mss between Christmas and mid-January. Publishes ms 30-60 days after acceptance. Recently published work by Paula Simmons and Judy Klass. Length: 9,500 words average; 5,000 words minimum; 15,000 words maximum. Also publishes literary essays, literary criticism, poetry. Sometimes critiques or comments on rejected ms.

How to Contact: Send complete ms with a cover letter or via electronic mail. Should include estimated word count, 100 word bio, list of publications. Reports in 3 weeks. Send a disposable copy of mss. E-mail address: simchris@aol.com. Sample copy for $3. Fiction guidelines for #10 SASE. Reviews novels and short story collections.

Payment/Terms: Pays $10-25 and contributor's copies on publication for one-time rights; additional copies $1.

Advice: "Read as many of the masters of science fiction as possible. They are the best of all possible teachers."

ODYSSEY, Science That's Out of this World, Cobblestone Publishing, Inc., 7 School St., Peterborough NH 03458. Editor: Elizabeth E. Lindstrom. Magazine. "Scientific accuracy, original approaches to the subject are primary concerns of the editors in choosing material. For 8-14 year olds." Monthly (except July and August). Estab. 1991. Circ. 30,000.

● Cobblestone Publications also publishes *Calliope*, *Cobblestone* and *Faces*.

Needs: Material must match theme; send for theme list and deadlines. Children's/juvenile (8-14 years), "authentic historical and biographical fiction, science fiction, retold legends, etc., relating to theme." List of upcoming themes available for SASE. Length: 750 words maximum.

How to Contact: Query first or query with clips of published work (if new to *Odyssey*). "Should include estimated word count and a detailed 1-page outline explaining the information to be presented; an extensive bibliography of materials authors plan to use." Reports in several months. Send SASE for reply or send stamped postcard to find out if ms has been received. Sample copy for $3.95, 7½ × 10½ SAE and $1.05 postage. Fiction guidelines for SASE.

Payment/Terms: Pays 10-17¢/word on publication for all rights.

Advice: "We also include in-depth nonfiction, plays and biographies."

OMNI, (II), General Media, 277 Park Ave. 4th Fl, New York NY 10172-0003. Fiction Editor: Ellen Datlow. Magazine: 8½ × 11; 114-182 pages; 40-50 lb. stock paper; 100 lb. Mead off cover stock; illustrations; photos. "Magazine of science and science fiction with an interest in near future; stories of what science holds, what life and lifestyles will be like in areas affected by science for a young, bright and well-educated audience between ages 18-45." Quarterly (print); monthly (online). Estab. 1978. Circ. 1,000,000.

● *Omni* has won numerous awards (see "Advice" below). Datlow also edits *The Year's Best Fantasy and Horror* (a reprint anthology). For more about the editor, see the interview with her in the first edition of *Science Fiction Writer's Marketplace and Sourcebook*. (Writer's Digest Books). Note *Omni* has a new address. The magazine is very active online and has a series of original novellas only on online.

Needs: Science fiction, contemporary fantasy and technological horror. No sword and sorcery or space opera. Buys 20 mss/year. Receives approximately 400 unsolicited fiction mss/month. Agented fiction 5%. Recently published work by John Kessel, Terry Bisson, Ray Bradbury, M. John Harrison, Kathe Koja and Pat Cadigan. Length: 2,000 words minimum, 10,000 words maximum. Critiques rejected mss that interest me "when there is time." Sometimes recommends other markets.

How to Contact: Send complete ms with SASE. No simultaneous submissions. E-mail address: ellendat@a ol.com. Reports within 8 weeks. Publishes ms 3 months to 1 year after acceptance.

Payment/Terms: Pays $1,250-2,500; 3 free contributor's copies on acceptance for first North American serial rights with exclusive worldwide English language periodical rights and nonexclusive anthology rights.

Advice: "Beginning writers should read a lot of the best science fiction short stories today to get a feeling for what is being done. Also, they should read outside the field and nonfiction for inspiration. We are looking for strong, well-written stories dealing with the next 100 years. When submitting your stories, don't be cute, don't be negative. Keep it simple. If you have credentials (writing or workshopping or whatever may be relevant), mention them in your cover letter. Never tell the plot of your story in a cover letter. Send the full story. I don't know any editor of short fiction who wants a query letter. Rewrite and learn to be your own editor. Don't ever call an editor on the phone and ask why he/she rejected a story. You'll either find out in a personal rejection letter (which means the editor liked it or thought enough of your writing to comment) or you won't find out at all (most likely the editor won't remember a form-rejected story)." Recent award winners and nominees: Harlan Ellison's story "The Man Who Rowed Christopher Columbus Ashore" was chosen for inclusion in *The Best American Short Stories 1993* and his novella "Mefisto in Onyx" was nominated for the Edgar Award, the Bram Stoker Award and the Hugo Award for 1993. Terry Bisson's novelette "England Underway" was nominated for the Nebula and Hugo Award. Ellen Datlow has been nominated in Best Professional editor category of the Hugos 6 years running.

ON THE LINE, (II), Mennonite Publishing House, 616 Walnut Ave., Scottdale PA 15683-1999. (412)887-8500. Editor: Mary Meyer. Magazine: 7×10; 8 pages; illustrations; b&w photos. "A religious take-home paper with the goal of helping children grow in their understanding and appreciation of God, the created world, themselves and other people." For children ages 10-14. Weekly. Estab. 1970. Circ. 6,500.
- *Purpose, Story Friends* and *With* are also published by the Mennonite Publishing House.

Needs: Adventure and problem solving stories with Christian values for older children and young teens (10-14 years). Receives 50-100 unsolicited mss/month. Buys 1 ms/issue; 52 mss/year. Recently published work by O.B. Comer, Eileen Spinelli and Linda Peavy; published new writers within the last year. Length: 800-1,500 words.

How to Contact: Send complete ms noting whether author is offering first-time or reprint rights. Reports in 1 month. SASE. Simultaneous and previously published work OK. Free sample copy and fiction guidelines.

Payment/Terms: Pays on acceptance for one-time rights.

Advice: "We believe in the power of story to entertain, inspire and challenge the reader to new growth. Know children and their thoughts, feelings and interests. Be realistic with characters and events in the fiction. Stories do not need to be true, but need to *feel* true."

OPTIONS, The *Bi*-Monthly, (I, II, IV), AJA Publishing, Box 470, Port Chester NY 10573. Associate Editor: Diana Sheridan. Magazine: digest-sized; 114 pages; newsprint paper; glossy cover stock; illustrations and photos. Sexually explicit magazine for and about bisexuals. "Please read our Advice subhead." 10 issues/year. Estab. 1982. Circ. 100,000.
- AJA Publishing also publishes *Beau* but it is not listed in this book.

Needs: Erotica, bisexual, gay, lesbian. "First person as-if-true experiences." Buys 6 unsolicited fiction mss/issue. "Very little" of fiction is agented. Published new writers within the last year. Length: 2,000-3,000 words average; 2,000 words minimum. Sometimes critiques rejected mss.

How to Contact: Send complete ms with or without cover letter. No simultaneous submissions. Reports in approximately 3 weeks. SASE. "Submissions on Macintosh disk welcome and can often use IBM submissions in ASCII (text only) format, but please include hard copy too." E-mail address: dianaeditr@aol.com. Sample copy for $2.95 and 6×9 SAE with 5 first-class stamps. Fiction guidelines for SASE.

Payment/Terms: Pays $100 on publication for all rights.

Advice: "Read a copy of *Options* carefully and look at our spec sheet before writing anything for us. That's not new advice, but to judge from some of what we get in the mail, it's necessary to repeat. We only buy 2 bi/lesbian pieces per issue; need is greater for bi/gay male mss. Though we're a bi rather than gay magazine, the emphasis is on same-sex relationships. If the readers want to read about a male/female couple, they'll buy another magazine. Gay male stories sent to *Options* will also be considered for publication in *Beau*, our gay male magazine. *Most important:* We *only* publish male/male stories that feature 'safe sex' practices unless the story is clearly something that took place pre-AIDS."

ORANGE COAST MAGAZINE, The Magazine of Orange County, (III), 245-D Fischer Ave., Suite 8, Costa Mesa CA 92626. (714)545-1900. Editor: Martin V. Smith. Managing Editor: Allison Joyce. Magazine: 8½×11; 175 pages; 50 lb. Sonoma gloss paper; Warrenflo cover; illustrations and photographs. *Orange Coast* publishes articles offering insight into the community for its affluent, well-educated Orange County readers. Monthly. Estab. 1974. Circ. 38,000.

Needs: Open to most subjects. No science fiction or fantasy; mystery only if well written. Fiction submissions need not have Orange County setting or characters. Receives 30 unsolicited mss/month. Buys 2 mss/year. Publishes ms 4-6 months after acceptance. Published work by Robert Ray. Length: 2,500 words average; 1,500 words minimum; 3,000 words maximum.

How to Contact: Send complete ms with cover letter that includes Social Security number. Reports in 3 months. SASE. Simultaneous submissions OK. Sample copy for 9×12 SASE.
Payment/Terms: Pays $250 on acceptance for first North American serial rights.

PARABOLA, The Magazine of Myth and Tradition, (IV), Society for the Study of Myth and Tradition, 656 Broadway, New York NY 10012. (212)505-9037. Fax: (212)979-7325. Magazine: 6½×10; 128 pages; illustrations and photos. "The exploration of the quest for meaning as expressed in the myths, symbols and tales of the world's religious/spiritual traditions. Mostly we publish essays and retellings of traditional stories." Quarterly. Estab. 1976. Circ. 40,000.
Needs: Religious/inspirational, translations, mythology, folklore. "No experimental, no genre fiction. Nothing preachy or sentimental. Must relate to an upcoming theme." Upcoming themes: "Prophecy" (February 96); "The Soul" (May 96). List of upcoming themes available for SASE. Receives 8-12 unsolicited mss/ month. Accepts 1-2 mss/year. Publishes ms 3 months after acceptance. Length: 750 words minimum; 3,000 words maximum.
How to Contact: Query first or send complete ms with a cover letter. Should include estimated word count, bio (2-3 sentences), Social Security number and availability of disk or e-mail transmission. Reports in 3-4 weeks on queries; 1-3 months on mss. SASE for reply or return of ms. Simultaneous and reprint submissions OK. "Queries accepted by e-mail. No unsolicited e-mail submissions." E-Mail address: parabola@panix.c om. Sample copy for $6. Fiction guidelines for SASE. Reviews novels and short story collections.
Payment/Terms: Pays $75-200 and 2 contributor's copies for first North American serial rights or one-time rights. Sends galleys to author.
Advice: "We almost never publish fiction, so it takes an exceptional manuscript which explores our theme from a mythological, symbolic, or spiritual perspective. Don't send stories just vaguely related to a theme. Stories should explore some universal meaning underlying the theme."

PLAYBOY MAGAZINE, 680 N. Lake Shore Dr., Chicago IL 60611. Prefers not to share information.

POCKETS, Devotional Magazine for Children, (II), The Upper Room, Box 189, 1908 Grand Ave., Nashville TN 37202. (615)340-7333. Editor-in-Chief: Janet R. Knight. Magazine: 7×9; 48 pages; 50 lb. white econowrite paper; 80 lb. white coated, heavy cover stock; color and 2-color illustrations; some photos. Magazine for children ages 6-12, with articles specifically geared for ages 8 to 11. "The magazine offers stories, activities, prayers, poems—all geared to giving children a better understanding of themselves as children of God." Published monthly except for January. Estab. 1981. Estimated circ. 99,000.
• *Pockets* has received honors from the Educational Press Association of America. The magazine's fiction tends to feature children dealing with real-life situations "from a faith perspective."
Needs: Adventure, contemporary, ethnic, historical (general), juvenile, religious/inspirational and suspense/ mystery. "All submissions should address the broad theme of the magazine. Each issue will be built around several themes with material which can be used by children in a variety of ways. Scripture stories, fiction, poetry, prayers, art, graphics, puzzles and activities will all be included. Submissions do not need to be overtly religious. They should help children experience a Christian lifestyle that is not always a neatly wrapped moral package, but is open to the continuing revelation of God's will. Seasonal material, both secular and liturgical, is desired. No violence, horror, sexual and racial stereotyping or fiction containing heavy moralizing." No talking animal stories. Receives approximately 200 unsolicited fiction mss/month. Buys 4-5 mss/issue; 44-60 mss/year. Publishes short shorts. A peace-with-justice theme will run throughout the magazine. Published work by Peggy King Anderson, Angela Gibson and John Steptoe; published new writers last year. Length: 600 words minimum; 1,600 words maximum; 1,200 words average.
How to Contact: Send complete ms with SASE. Previously published submissions OK, but no simultaneous or faxed submissions. Reports in 1 month on mss. Publishes ms 1 year to 18 months after acceptance. Sample copy free with SASE and 4 first-class stamps. Fiction guidelines and themes with SASE. "Strongly advise sending for themes before submitting."
Payment/Terms: Pays 12¢/word and up and 2-5 contributor's copies on acceptance for first North American serial rights. $1.95 charge for extras; $1 each for 10 or more.
Advice: "Listen to children as they talk with each other. Please send for a sample copy as well as guidelines and themes. Many mss we receive are simply inappropriate. Each issue is theme-related. Please send for list of themes. New themes published in December of each year. Include SASE." Sponsors annual fiction writing contest. Deadline: Aug. 15. Send for guidelines. $1,000 award and publication.

PORTLAND MAGAZINE, Maine's City Magazine, (I, II), 578 Congress St., Portland ME 04101. (207)775-4339. Editor: Colin Sargent. Magazine: 48 pages; 60 lb. paper; 80 lb. cover stock; illustrations and photographs. "City lifestyle magazine—style, business, real estate, controversy, fashion, cuisine, interviews and art relating to the Maine area." Monthly. Estab. 1986. Circ. 100,000.
Needs: Contemporary, historical, literary. Receives 20 unsolicited fiction mss/month. Buys 1 mss/issue; 10 mss/year. Publishes short shorts. Published work by Janwillem Vande Wetering, Sanford Phippen and Mamene Medwood. Length: 3 double-spaced typed pages.

How to Contact: Query first. "Fiction below 700 words, please." Send complete ms with cover letter. Reports in 6 months. SASE. Accepts electronic submissions.

Payment/Terms: Pays on publication for first North American serial rights.

Advice: "We publish ambitious short fiction featuring everyone from Frederick Barthelme to newly discovered fiction by Edna St. Vincent Millay."

POWER AND LIGHT, (I, II), Word Action Publishing Company, 6401 The Paseo, Kansas City MO 64131. (816)333-7000. Fax: (816)333-4439. Editor: Beula J. Postlewait. Associate Editor: Melissa Hammer. Story paper: 5×8; 8 pages; storypaper and newsprint; illustrations and photos. "Relates Sunday School learning to preteens' lives. Must reflect theology of the Church of the Nazarene." Weekly. Estab. 1993. Circ. 30,000.
• Word Action Publishing also publishes *Discoveries* and *Standard* listed in this section.

Needs: Children's/juvenile (10-12 years): adventure, fantasy (children's fantasy), religious/inspirational. Receives 10-15 mss/month. Buys 1 ms/month. Publishes ms 1 year after acceptance. Length: 700 words average; 500 words minimum; 800 words maximum. Always critiques or comments on rejected mss.

How to Contact: Query first. Should include estimated word count and Social Security number. Reports in 1 month on queries; 3 months on mss. SASE for reply or return or ms. Simultaneous, reprint and electronic (disk) submissions OK. Sample copy for #10 SASE. Fiction guidelines for #10 SASE.

Payment/Terms: Pays ½¢/word and 4 contributor's copies on publication for multi-use rights.

Advice: Looks for "creativity—situations relating to preteens that are not trite such as shoplifting, etc."

‡POWERPLAY MAGAZINE, (II, IV), Brush Creek Media, Inc., 2215R Market St., #148, San Francisco CA 94114. (415)552-1506. Fax: (415)552-3244. Editor: Alec Wagner. Magazine: 8 ½×11; 64 pages; white husky paper; gloss cover; b&w photos. "Geared toward gay men. *Powerplay* is kink-oriented." Quarterly. Estab. 1992. Circ. 38,000.
• This publisher also publishes *Bear.*

Needs: Gay: erotica, humor/satire. Receives 5-10 unsolicited mss/month. Buys 2-3 mss/issue; 15-20 mss/year. Length: Open. Sometimes critiques or comments on reject mss.

How To Contact: Send complete ms with cover letter. Should include bio and social security number with submission. Send SASE for return or send disposable copy of the ms. Will consider simultaneous submissions and electronic (disk or modem) submissions. Sample copy for $6.50. Fiction guidelines free.

Payment/Terms: Pays $75 minimum; $125 maximum on publication. Purchases first North American serial rights. Also pays 2-3 contributor's copies.

PRIME TIME SPORTS AND FITNESS, (I, IV), Prime Time Publishing, P.O. Box 6097, Evanston IL 60204. (708)864-8113. Editor: Dennis Dorner. Fiction Editor: Linda Jefferson. Magazine; 8½×11; 40-80 pages; coated enamel paper and cover stock; 10 illustrations; 42 photographs. "For active sports participants." Estab. 1975. Circ. 67,000.
• *Prime Time Sports and Fitness* has won several awards for "recreational and sports reporting."

Needs: Adventure, contemporary, erotica, fantasy, historical, humor/satire, mainstream, mystery/suspense (romantic suspense), sports, young adult/teen (10-18 years). No gay, lesbian. Receives 30-40 unsolicited mss/month. Buys 1-2 mss/issue; 20/year. Publishes ms 3-8 months after acceptance. Agented fiction 10%. Published work by Dennis Dorner and Sally Hammill. Length: 2,000 words preferred; 250 words minimum; 3,000 words maximum. Publishes short shorts. Length: 250-500 words. Sometimes critiques rejected ms and recommends other markets.

How to Contact: Send complete ms with cover letter, include Social Security number. "Do *not* include credits and history. We buy articles, not people." Reports in 1-3 months on queries; 1 week - 3 months on mss. SASE. Simultaneous and reprint submissions OK. Sample copy for 10×12 SAE and $1.40 postage. Fiction guidelines free for SAE.

Payment/Terms: Pays $25-500 on publication for all rights, first rights, first North American serial rights, one-time rights; "depends on manuscript."

Advice: Looks for "short, funny, humorous 'I Can Do It' type of stories. Be funny, ahead of particular sports season, and enjoy your story. Bring out some human touch that would relate to our readers."

PURPOSE, (II), Mennonite Publishing House, 616 Walnut Ave., Scottdale PA 15683-1999. (412)887-8500. Editor: James E. Horsch. Magazine: 5⅜×8⅜; 8 pages; illustrations; photos. "Magazine focuses on Christian discipleship—how to be a faithful Christian in the midst of tough everyday life complexities. Uses story form to present models and examples to encourage Christians in living a life of faithful discipleship." Weekly. Estab. 1968. Circ. 16,000.
• Mennonite Publishing House also publishes *On the Line* and *Story Friends* listed in this book.

Needs: Historical, religious/inspirational. No militaristic/narrow patriotism or racism. Receives 100 unsolicited mss/month. Buys 3 mss/issue; 140 mss/year. Recently published work by J. Grant Swank, Hope Douglas and James Pecquet. Length: 600 words average; 900 words maximum. Occasionally comments on rejected mss.

How to Contact: Send complete ms only. Reports in 2 months. Simultaneous and previously published work OK. Sample copy for 6×9 SAE and 2 first-class stamps. Writer's guidelines free with sample copy only.

Payment/Terms: Pays up to 5¢/word for stories and 2 contributor's copies on acceptance for one-time rights.

Advice: Many stories are "situational—how to respond to dilemmas. Write crisp, action moving, personal style, focused upon an individual, a group of people, or an organization. The story form is an excellent literary device to use in exploring discipleship issues. There are many issues to explore. Each writer brings a unique solution. Let's hear them. The first two paragraphs are crucial in establishing the mood/issue to be resolved in the story. Work hard on developing these."

ELLERY QUEEN'S MYSTERY MAGAZINE, (II), Doubleday Dell Magazines, 1540 Broadway, New York NY 10036. (212)782-8546. Editor: Janet Hutchings. Magazine: digest-sized; 160 pages with special 288-page issues in March and October. Magazine for lovers of mystery fiction. Published 13 times/year. Estab. 1941. Circ. 500,000 readers.

• Doubleday Dell Magazines other mystery publication is *Alfred Hitchcock Mystery Magazine* listed in this book. Stories submitted to *EQMM* are *not* considered for AHMM. Submissions must be made for each separately. The magazine has won numerous awards and sponsors its own award for Best Stories of the Year, nominated by its readership.

Needs: "We accept only mystery, crime, suspense and detective fiction." Receives approximately 400 unsolicited fiction mss each month. Buys 10-15 mss/issue. Publishes ms 6-12 months after acceptance. Agented fiction 50%. Published work by Peter Lovesey, Clark Howard, Robert Barnard and Ruth Rendell; published new writers within the last year. Length: up to 7,000 words, occasionally longer. Publishes 2-3 short novels of up to 17,000 words/year by established authors; minute mysteries of 250 words; short mystery verse. Critiques rejected mss "only when a story might be a possibility for us if revised." Sometimes recommends other markets.

How to Contact: Send complete ms with SASE. Cover letter should include publishing credits and brief biographical sketch. Simultaneous submissions OK. Reports in 3 months or sooner on mss. Fiction guidelines with SASE. Sample copy for $2.75.

Payment/Terms: Pays 3¢/word and up on acceptance for first North American serial rights. Occasionally buys reprints.

Advice: "We have a Department of First Stories and usually publish at least one first story an issue—i.e., the author's first published fiction. We select stories that are fresh and of the kind our readers have expressed a liking for. In writing a detective story, you must play fair with the reader re clues and necessary information. Otherwise you have a better chance of publishing if you avoid writing to formula."

R-A-D-A-R, (II), Standard Publishing, 8121 Hamilton Ave., Cincinnati OH 45231. (513)931-4050. Editor: Elaina Meyers. Magazine: 12 pages; newsprint; illustrations; a few photos. "*R-A-D-A-R* is a take-home paper, distributed in Sunday school classes for children in grades 3-6. The stories and other features reinforce the Bible lesson taught in class. Boys and girls who attend Sunday school make up the audience. The fiction stories, Bible picture stories and other special features appeal to their interests." Weekly. Estab. 1978.

• *Seek* and *The Lookout* also are published by Standard.

Needs: Fiction—The hero of the story should be an 11- or 12-year-old in a situation involving one or more of the following: history, mystery, animals, sports, adventure, school, travel, relationships with parents, friends and others. Stories should have believable plots and be wholesome, Christian character-building, but not "preachy." No science fiction. Receives approximately 75-100 unsolicited mss/month. Published new writers within the last year. Length: 900-1,000 words average; 400 words minimum; 1,200 words maximum.

How to Contact: Send complete ms. Reports in 6-8 weeks on mss. SASE for ms. Simultaneous submissions permitted if noted as such; reprint submissions OK. Sample copy and guidelines with SASE.

Payment/Terms: Pays 3-7¢/word on acceptance for first rights, reprints, etc.; 2 contributor's copies sent on publication.

Advice: "Send SASE for sample copy, guidelines and theme list. Follow the specifics of guidelines. Keep your writing current with the times and happenings of our world. Our needs change as the needs of middlers (3rd-4th graders) and juniors (5th and 6th graders) change. Writers must keep current."

RADIANCE, The Magazine for Large Women, (II), Box 30246, Oakland CA 94604. (510)482-0680. Editor: Alice Ansfield. Fiction Editors: Alice Ansfield and Catherine Taylor. Magazine: 8½×11; 56 pages;

The maple leaf symbol before a listing indicates a Canadian publisher, magazine, conference or contest.

glossy/coated paper; 70 lb. cover stock; illustrations; photos. "Theme is to encourage women to live fully now, whatever their body size. To stop waiting to live or feel good about themselves until they lose weight." Quarterly. Estab. 1984. Circ. 8,000. Readership: 30,000.

Needs: Adventure, contemporary, erotica, ethnic, fantasy, feminist, historical, humor/satire, mainstream, mystery/suspense, prose poem, science fiction, spiritual, sports, young adult/teen. "Want fiction to have a larger-bodied character; living in a positive, upbeat way. Our goal is to empower women." Receives 150 mss/month. Buys 40 mss/year. Publishes ms within 1 year of acceptance. Published work by Marla Zarrow, Sallie Tisdale and Mary Kay Blakely. Length: 2,000 words average; 800 words minimum; 3,500 words maximum. Publishes short shorts. Sometimes critiques rejected mss.

How to Contact: Query with clips of published work and send complete mss with cover letter. Reports in 3-4 months. SASE. Reprint submissions OK. Sample copy for $3.50. Guidelines for #10 SASE. Reviews novels and short story collections ("with at least 1 large-size heroine.")

Payment/Terms: Pays $35-100 and contributor's copies on publication for one-time rights. Sends galleys to the author if requested.

Advice: "Read our magazine before sending anything to us. Know what our philosophy and points of view are before sending a manuscript. Look around within your community for inspiring, successful and unique large women doing things worth writing about. At this time, prefer fiction having to do with a larger woman (man, child). *Radiance* is one of the leading resources in the size acceptance movement. Each issue profiles dynamic large women from all walks of life, along with articles on health, media, fashion and politics. Our audience is the 30 million American women who wear a size 16 or over. Feminist, emotionally-supportive, quarterly magazine."

RANGER RICK MAGAZINE, (II), National Wildlife Federation, 1400 16th St. NW, Washington DC 20036-2266. (703)790-4274. Editor: Gerald Bishop. Fiction Editor: Deborah Churchman. Magazine: 8×10; 48 pages; glossy paper; 60 lb. cover stock; illustrations; photos. "*Ranger Rick* emphasizes conservation and the enjoyment of nature through full-color photos and art, fiction and nonfiction articles, games and puzzles, and special columns. Our audience ranges in ages from 6-12, with the greatest number in the 7 to 10 group. We aim for a fourth grade reading level. They read for fun and information." Monthly. Estab. 1967. Circ. 850,000.

● *Ranger Rick* has won several Ed Press awards. The editors say the magazine has had a backlog of stories recently, yet they would like to see more *good* mystery and science fiction stories (with nature themes).

Needs: Adventure, fantasy, humor, mystery (amateur sleuth), science fiction and sports. "Interesting stories for kids focusing directly on nature or related subjects. Fiction that carries a conservation message is always needed, as are adventure stories involving kids with nature or the outdoors. Moralistic 'lessons' taught children by parents or teachers are not accepted. Human qualities are attributed to animals only in our regular feature, 'Adventures of Ranger Rick.' " Receives about 150-200 unsolicited fiction mss each month. Buys about 6 mss/year. Published fiction by Leslie Dendy. Length: 900 words maximum. Critiques rejected mss "when there is time."

How to Contact: Query with sample lead and any clips of published work with SASE. May consider simultaneous submissions. Reports in 3 months on queries and mss. Publishes ms 8 months to 1 year after acceptance, but sometimes longer. Sample copy for $2. Guidelines for legal-sized SASE.

Payment/Terms: Pays $550 maximum/full-length ms on acceptance for all rights. Very rarely buys reprints. Sends galleys to author.

Advice: "For our magazine, the writer needs to understand kids and that aspect of nature he or she is writing about—a difficult combination! Mss are rejected because they are contrived and/or condescending—often overwritten. Some mss are anthropomorphic, others are above our readers' level. We find that fiction stories help children understand the natural world and the environmental problems it faces. Beginning writers have a chance equal to that of established authors *provided* the quality is there. Would love to see more science fiction and fantasy, as well as mysteries."

REDBOOK, (II), The Hearst Corporation, 224 W. 57th St., New York NY 10019. (212)649-2000. Fiction Editor: Dawn Raffel. Magazine: 8×10¾; 150-250 pages; 34 lb. paper; 70 lb. cover; illustrations; photos. "*Redbook*'s readership consists of American women, ages 25-44. Most are well-educated, married, have children and also work outside the home." Monthly. Estab. 1903. Circ. 3,200,000.

Needs: "*Redbook* generally publishes one or two short stories per issue. Stories need not be about women exclusively; but must appeal to a female audience. We are interested in new voices and buy up to a quarter of our stories from unsolicited submissions. Standards are high: Stories must be fresh, felt and intelligent; no formula fiction." Receives up to 600 unsolicited fiction mss each month; published new writers within the last year. Length: up to 22 ms pages.

How to Contact: Send complete ms with SASE. No queries, please. Simultaneous submissions OK. Reports in 8-12 weeks.

Payment/Terms: Pays on acceptance for first North American serial rights.

Advice: "Superior craftsmanship is of paramount importance: We look for emotional complexity, dramatic tension, precision of language. Note that we don't run stories that look back on the experiences of childhood or adolescence. Please read a few issues to get a sense of what we're looking for."

REFORM JUDAISM, (II, IV), Union of American Hebrew Congregations, 838 5th Ave., New York NY 10021. (212)650-4240. Editor: Aron Hirt-Manheimer. Managing Editor: Joy Weinberg. Magazine: 8 × 10¾; 80 pages; illustrations; photos. "We cover subjects of Jewish interest in general and Reform Jewish in particular, for members of Reform Jewish congregations in the United States and Canada." Quarterly. Estab. 1972. Circ. 295,000.
 • Recipient of The Simon Rockower Award for Excellence in Jewish Journalism for feature writing, graphic design, and photography. The editor says they would publish more stories if they could find excellent, sophisticated, contemporary Jewish fiction.
Needs: Humor/satire, religious/inspirational. Receives 75 unsolicited mss/month. Buys 3 mss/year. Publishes ms 6 months after acceptance. Length: 1,200 words average; 600 words minimum; 3,000 words maximum.
How to Contact: Send complete ms with cover letter. Reports in 6 weeks. SASE for ms. Simultaneous submissions OK. Sample copy for $3.50.
Payment/Terms: Pays 25¢/word on publication for first North American serial rights.

ST. ANTHONY MESSENGER, (II), 1615 Republic St., Cincinnati OH 45210-1298. Editor: Norman Perry, O.F.M. Magazine: 8 × 10¾; 56 pages; illustrations; photos. "*St. Anthony Messenger* is a Catholic family magazine which aims to help its readers lead more fully human and Christian lives. We publish articles which report on a changing church and world, opinion pieces written from the perspective of Christian faith and values, personality profiles, and fiction which entertains and informs." Monthly. Estab. 1893. Circ. 325,000.
 • This is a leading Catholic magazine, but has won awards for both religious and secular journalism and writing from the Catholic Press Association, the International Association of Business Communicators and the Cincinnati Editors Association.
Needs: Contemporary, religious/inspirational, romance, senior citizen/retirement and spiritual. "We do not want mawkishly sentimental or preachy fiction. Stories are most often rejected for poor plotting and characterization; bad dialogue—listen to how people talk; inadequate motivation. Many stories say nothing, are 'happenings' rather than stories." No fetal journals, no rewritten Bible stories. Receives 70-80 unsolicited fiction mss/month. Buys 1 ms/issue; 12 mss/year. Publishes ms up to 1 year after acceptance. Published work by Marjorie Franco, Joseph Pici, Joan Savro and Philip Gambone. Length: 2,000-2,500 words. Critiques rejected mss "when there is time." Sometimes recommends other markets.
How to Contact: Send complete ms with SASE. No simultaneous submissions. Reports in 6-8 weeks. Sample copy and guidelines for #10 SASE. Reviews novels and short story collections. Send books to Barbara Beckwith, book review editor.
Payment/Terms: Pays 14¢/word maximum and 2 contributor's copies on acceptance for first North American serial rights; $1 charge for extras.
Advice: "We publish one story a month and we get up to 1,000 a year. Too many offer simplistic 'solutions' or answers. Pay attention to endings. Easy, simplistic, deus ex machina endings don't work. People have to feel characters in the stories are real and have a reason to care about them and what happens to them. Fiction entertains but can also convey a point in a very telling way just as the Bible uses stories to teach."

ST. JOSEPH'S MESSENGER AND ADVOCATE OF THE BLIND, (II), Sisters of St. Joseph of Peace, 541 Pavonia Ave., Jersey City NJ 07306. (201)798-4141. Magazine: 8½ × 11; 16 pages; illustrations; photos. For Catholics generally but not exclusively. Theme is "religious—relevant—real." Quarterly. Estab. 1903. Circ. 20,000.
Needs: Contemporary, humor/satire, mainstream, religious/inspirational, romance and senior citizen/retirement. Receives 30-40 unsolicited fiction mss/month. Buys 3 mss/issue; 20 mss/year. Publishes ms an average of 1 year after acceptance. Published work by Eileen W. Strauch; published new writers within the last year. Length: 800 words minimum; 1,800 words maximum; 1,500 words average. Occasionally critiques rejected mss.
How to Contact: Send complete ms with SASE. Simultaneous and previously published submissions OK. Sample copy for #10 SASE. Fiction guidelines for SASE.
Payment/Terms: Pays $15-40 and 2 contributor's copies on acceptance for one-time rights.
Advice: Rejects mss because of "vague focus or theme. Write to be read—keep material current and of interest. *Do not preach*—the story will tell the message. Keep the ending from being too obvious. Fiction is the greatest area of interest to our particular reading public."

SASSY MAGAZINE, (I, II, IV), Lang Communications, 230 Park Ave., New York NY 10169. (212)551-9500. Editor: Christina Kelly. Managing Editor: Virginia O'Brien. Magazine: 9½ × 11; 100-130 pages; glossy 40 lb. stock paper and cover; illustrations and photographs. "Lifestyle magazine for girls, ages 14-19, covering entertainment, fashion as well as serious subjects." Monthly. Estab. 1988. Circ. 650,000.
 • *Sassy*, known for its gutsy approach to writing for young women, received a *MagazineWeek* Award for Editorial Excellence in 1992 and was a finalist again in 1993. Look for the interview with editor Christina Kelly in the 1994 *Novel & Short Story Writer's Market*.

Needs: Contemporary, ethnic, experimental, feminist, gay, humor/satire, literary, mainstream, prose poem, young adult/teen (10-18 years). "No typical teenage romance." Publishes annual special fiction issue. Receives 300 unsolicited mss/month. Buys 1 ms/issue; 12 mss/year. Publishes ms 3-6 months after publication. Published Christina Kelly, John Elder, Elizabeth Mosier. Length: 2,000 words; 1,000 words minimum; 3,500 words maximum. Sometimes critiques rejected mss and recommends other markets.

How to Contact: Send complete manuscript with cover letter. Include social security number and address, brief background, perhaps one sentence on what story is about or like. Reports in 3 months. SASE (or IRC). Simultaneous submissions OK. Sample copy for $2. Fiction guidelines are free.

Payment/Terms: Pays $1,000 and contributor's copies on acceptance. Offers 20% kill fee. Buys all rights or first North American serial righs. Send galleys to author (if requested and if time permits).

Advice: "We look for unusual new ways to write for teenagers. It helps if the story has a quirky, vernacular style that we use throughout the magazine. Generally our stories have to have a teenage protagonist but they are not typical teen fiction. In the end, our only real criterion is that a story is original, intelligent, well-crafted and moves us."

SEEK, (II), Standard Publishing, 8121 Hamilton Ave., Cincinnati OH 45231. Editor: Eileen H. Wilmoth. Magazine: 5½×8½; 8 pages; newsprint paper; art and photos in each issue. "Inspirational stories of faith-in-action for Christian young adults; a Sunday School take-home paper." Weekly. Estab. 1970. Circ. 40,000.

● Standard Publishing also publishes *R-A-D-A-R* and *The Lookout* listed in this book.

Needs: Religious/inspirational. Buys 150 mss/year. Publishes ms an average of 1 year after acceptance. Published new writers within the last year. Length: 500-1,200 words.

How to Contact: Send complete ms with SASE. No simultaneous submissions. Reports in 2-3 months. Free sample copy and guidelines.

Payment/Terms: Pays 5-7¢/word on acceptance. Buys reprints.

Advice: "Write a credible story with Christian slant—no preachments; avoid overworked themes such as joy in suffering, generation gaps, etc. Most mss are rejected by us because of irrelevant topic or message, unrealistic story, or poor character and/or plot development. We use fiction stories that are believable."

SEVENTEEN, (II), III Magazine Corp., 850 3rd Ave., New York NY 10022. (212)407-9700. Fiction Editor: Joe Bargmann. Magazine: 8½×11; 125-400 pages; 40 lb. coated paper; 80 lb. coated cover stock; illustrations; photos. A general interest magazine with fashion, beauty care, pertinent topics such as current issues, attitudes, experiences and concerns of teenagers. Monthly. Estab. 1944. Circ. 1.9 million.

● *Seventeen* sponsors an annual fiction contest for writers age 13-21. See the listing for this in the Contests and Awards section.

Needs: High-quality literary fiction. Receives 350 unsolicited fiction mss/month. Buys 1 mss/issue. Agented fiction 50%. Published work by Margaret Atwood, Joyce Carol Oates and Ellen Gilchrist; published new writers within the last year. Length: approximately 1,500-3,500 words.

How to Contact: Send complete ms with SASE and cover letter with relevant credits. Reports in 3 months on mss. Guidelines for submissions with SASE.

Payment/Terms: Pays $700-2,500 on acceptance for one-time rights.

Advice: "Respect the intelligence and sophistication of teenagers. *Seventeen* remains open to the surprise of new voices. Our commitment to publishing the work of new writers remains strong; we continue to read every submission we receive. We believe that good fiction can move the reader toward thoughtful examination of her own life as well as the lives of others—providing her ultimately with a fuller appreciation of what it means to be human. While stories that focus on female teenage experience continue to be of interest, the less obvious possibilities are equally welcome. We encourage writers to submit literary short stories concerning subjects that may not be immediately identifiable as 'teenage,' with narrative styles that are experimental and challenging. Too often, unsolicited submissions possess voices and themes condescending and unsophisticated. Also, writers hesitate to send stories to *Seventeen* which they think too violent or risqué. Good writing holds the imaginable and then some, and if it doesn't find its home here, we're always grateful for the introduction to a writer's work."

SHOFAR, For Jewish Kids On The Move, (I, II, IV), 43 Northcote Dr., Melville NY 11747. (516)643-4598. Editor: Gerald H. Grayson, Ph.D. Magazine: 8½×11; 32-48 pages; 60 lb. paper; 80 lb. cover; illustration; photos. Audience: Jewish children in fourth through eighth grades. Monthly (October-May). Estab. 1984. Circ. 10,000.

Needs: Children's/juvenile (middle reader): cartoons, contemporary, humorous, poetry, puzzles, religious, sports. "All material must be on a Jewish theme. Receives 12-24 unsolicited mss/month. Buys 3-5 mss/issue; 24-40 mss/year. Published work by Caryn Huberman, Diane Claerbout and Rabbi Sheldon Lewis. Length: 500-700 words. Occasionally critiques rejected mss. Recommends other markets.

How to Contact: Send complete ms with cover letter. Reports in 6-8 weeks. SASE. Simultaneous and reprint submissions OK. Sample copy for 9×12 SAE and $1.04 first-class postage. Fiction guidelines for 3½×6½ SASE.

Payment/Terms: Pays 10¢/word and 5 contributor's copies on publication for first North American serial rights.

Advice: "Know the magazine and the religious-education needs of Jewish elementary-school-age children. If you are a Jewish educator, what has worked for you in the classroom? Write it out; send it on to me; I'll help you develop the idea into a short piece of fiction. A beginning fiction writer eager to break into *Shofar* will find an eager editor willing to help."

SOJOURNER, A Women's Forum, (I, IV), 42 Seaverns, Jamaica Plain MA 02130. (617)524-0415. Editor: Karen Kahn. Magazine: 11×17; 48 pages; newsprint; illustrations; photos. "Feminist journal publishing interviews, nonfiction features, news, viewpoints, poetry, reviews (music, cinema, books) and fiction for women." Published monthly. Estab. 1975. Circ. 40,000.
Needs: Contemporary, ethnic, experimental, fantasy, feminist, lesbian, humor/satire, literary, prose poem and women's. Upcoming themes: "Fiction/Poetry Issue" (February); "Annual Health Supplement" (March). Receives 20 unsolicited fiction mss/month. Accepts 10 mss/year. Agented fiction 10%. Published new writers within the last year. Length: 1,000 words minimum; 4,000 words maximum; 2,500 words average.
How to Contact: Send complete ms with SASE and cover letter with description of previous publications; current works. Simultaneous submissions OK. Reports in 6-8 months. Publishes ms an average of 6 months after acceptance. Sample copy for $3 with 10×13 SASE. Fiction guidelines for SASE.
Payment/Terms: Pays subscription to magazine and 2 contributor's copies, $15 for first rights. No extra charge up to 5 contributor's copies; $1 charge each thereafter.
Advice: "Pay attention to appearance of manuscript! Very difficult to wade through sloppily presented fiction, however good. Do write a cover letter. If not cute, it can't hurt and may help. Mention previous publication(s)."

SPIDER, The Magazine for Children, (II), Carus Publishing Co./The Cricket Magazine Group, P.O. Box 300, Peru IL 61354. Editor-in-Chief: Marianne Carus. Associate Editor: Christine Walske. Magazine: 8×10; 33 pages; illustrations and photos. "*Spider* publishes high-quality literature for beginning readers, mostly children ages 6 to 9." Monthly. Estab. 1994. Circ. 73,400.
● Carus Publishing also publishes *Ladybug, Cricket* and *Babybug*.
Needs: Children's/juvenile (6-9 years), fantasy (children's fantasy). "No religious, didactic, or violent stories, or anything that talks down to children." Buys 4 mss/issue. Publishes ms 1-2 years after acceptance. Agented fiction 2%. Published work by Lissa Rovetch, Ursula K. LeGuin and Eric Kimmel. Length: 775 words average; 300 words minimum; 1,000 words maximum. Publishes short shorts. Also publishes poetry. Often critiques or comments on rejected ms.
How to Contact: Send complete ms with a cover letter. Should include estimated word count. Reports in 3 months. Send SASE for return of ms. Simultaneous and reprint submissions OK. Sample copy for $4. Fiction guidelines for #10 SASE.
Payment/Terms: Pays 25¢/word and 2 contributor's copies on publication for first rights or one-time rights; additional copies for $2.
Advice: "Read back issues of *Spider*." Looks for "quality writing, good characterization, lively style, humor. We would like to see more multicultural fiction."

SPIRIT TALK, A Publication in Celebration of Indian Culture, (IV), Drawer V, 1992 Bear Chief's Lodge, Browning MT 59417. (406)338-2882. Editor: Long Standing Bear Chief. Periodic Book: 8½×11; 44-64 pages; glossy 80 lb. paper; illustrations and photos. "We publish themes based upon American Indian culture." Estab. 1994. Circ. 50,000.
Needs: North and South American Indian: ethnic/multicultural, fantasy (children's fantasy), historical (general), humor/satire, literary, religious/inspirational, young adult (adventure). List of upcoming themes available for SASE. Receives 3 unsolicited mss/month. Publishes ms 6-12 months after acceptance. Length: 1,500 words average; 2,500 words maximum. Publishes short shorts. Also publishes literary essays. Often critiques or comments on rejected mss.
How to Contact: Query first. Should include estimated word count, bio (1 page), Social Security number and list of publications. Reports in 2 weeks on queries; 1 month on mss. SASE for return of ms. Simultaneous submissions OK. Sample copy for $7.95 and SAE. Fiction guidelines for SAE. Reviews novels and short story collections.
Payment/Terms: Pays 10¢/word and 2 contributor's copies on publication for one-time rights; additional copies for 20% off cover price. Sends galleys to author.
Advice: "We tend to give preference to Native American authors."

STANDARD, (I, II, IV), Nazarene International Headquarters, 6401 The Paseo, Kansas City MO 64131. (816)333-7000. Editor: Everett Leadingham. Magazine: 8½×11; 8 pages; illustrations; photos. Inspirational reading for adults. Weekly. Estab. 1936. Circ. 165,000.
● Other magazines listed in this book associated with the Nazarene are *Discoveries* and *Power & Light*.
Needs: Religious/inspirational, spiritual. Receives 350 unsolicited mss/month (both fiction and nonfiction). Accepts 240 mss/year. Publishes ms 14-18 months after acceptance. Published new writers within the last

INSIDER VIEWPOINT

Magazine Growth Offers Opportunities and Challenges

While making money should be a goal for aspiring writers, it shouldn't be the main focus, according to Sy Safransky, editor of the North Carolina-based magazine, *The Sun.* "There are advantages to submitting to lesser-known magazines," Safransky says, "not the least of which is their interest in lesser-known writers."

Publishing a small magazine is usually a labor of love and the writers published in these magazines should understand what goes into the process. As editor of a 40-page monthly magazine, Safransky is aware of the space and financial crunches smaller publications can face. When he and a friend began publishing *The Sun* in 1974, money was tight. Safransky borrowed $50 to get the magazine printed

Sy Safransky

on a photocopier, then peddled it himself on the streets. For many years, *The Sun* couldn't pay writers anything.

Today the magazine is able to pay writers up to $300 for fiction and up to $500 for nonfiction and essays, thanks to a growth in circulation. During the magazine's first ten years, it had a base of 1,000 subscribers. Now, more than 25,000 subscribers receive the magazine. A grant from the National Endowment for the Arts also helps, but Safransky says it represents less than five percent of the magazine's budget. *The Sun* thrives due to the support of its subscribers.

For writers published in the magazine, this growth has brought with it additional exposure and prestige, as well as financial gain, but not without some sacrifice. As magazines grow, editors have less time and competition increases. The surge in readership and number of submissions over the years have meant a change in Safransky's editing style. In the publication's early years, he read every submission and answered each with a personal reply. Eventually the load became too heavy, and today *The Sun* employs two part-time readers to sift through the 600 to 700 poetry, fiction and nonfiction submissions received each month. They are read and categorized, but even those rejected by the staff land on Safransky's desk. "I look at them, but I tend to look rather quickly," he says.

And the personal reply is also a thing of the past, replaced by the standard rejection letter. "It broke my heart" when the publication began using the letters, Safransky says. However, if he sees something that he thinks has merit, he writes a personal comment on the letter.

From the avalanche of submissions, *The Sun* staff selects two or three each month. "It's a narrow gate," Safransky says. Interested writers should be as prepared as possible, honing their writing skills and studying the market.

The best way to get Safransky's attention, he says, is "to do nothing in particular except send me a really good story." He admits, he's "bored with writing that seems to be done for the sake of writing, rather than a passion."

He refrains from trying to define *The Sun*, "partly because it doesn't want to be defined. While we tend to favor personal writing, we're open to just about everything—even experimental writing, if it doesn't make us feel stupid." He calls his publication "quirky, offbeat, nontraditional. I don't know of any other magazine quite like *The Sun*."

Safransky's advice to writers applies equally to other publications: Read the publication first before sending something. Writers should "at least be able to find out whether they resonate more or less from the tone of the publication."

When a story is accepted, Safransky says, "we probably edit more aggressively than other publications, but all of our edits are approved by the writers." This, he notes, is sometimes a lengthy process, but "almost always, writers end up feeling respected."

That leads to another piece of advice: Don't be afraid of rejection, but even more, don't be afraid of rewriting. Safransky says "most beginning writers don't spend enough time rewriting. Then they should rewrite what they've rewritten. Writing is hard work."

Safransky encourages writers "not to measure their success by comparing themselves to media heavyweights. The only real success is in what you do on the blank page in front of you."

—*Bob Beckstead*

---

year. Length: 1,200-1,500 words average; 300 words minimum; 1,700 words maximum. Also publishes short shorts of 300-350 words.
How to Contact: Send complete ms with name, address and phone number. Reports in 2-3 months on mss. SASE. Simultaneous submissions OK but will pay only reprint rates. Sample copy and guidelines for SAE and 2 first-class stamps.
Payment/Terms: Pays 3½¢/word; 2¢/word (reprint); contributor's copies on acceptance for one-time rights.

STORY FRIENDS, (II), Mennonite Publishing House, 616 Walnut Ave., Scottdale PA 15683. (412)887-8500. Editor: Rose Mary Stutzman. Sunday school publication which portrays Jesus as a friend and helper. Nonfiction and fiction for children 4-9 years of age. Weekly.
● The Mennonite Publishing House also publishes *On the Line*, *Purpose* and *With* magazines.
Needs: Juvenile. Stories of everyday experiences at home, in church, in school or at play, which provide models of Christian values. Length: 300-800 words.
How to Contact: Send complete ms with SASE. Seasonal or holiday material should be submitted 6 months in advance. Free sample copy.
Payment/Terms: Pays 3-5¢/word on acceptance for one-time rights. Buys reprints. Not copyrighted.
Advice: "It is important to include relationships, patterns of forgiveness, respect, honesty, trust and caring. Prefer exciting yet plausible short stories which offer different settings, introduce children to wide ranges of friends and demonstrate joys, fears, temptations and successes of the readers."

STRAIGHT, (II), Standard Publishing Co., 8121 Hamilton Ave., Cincinnati OH 45231. (513)931-4050. Editor: Carla Crane. "Publication helping and encouraging teens to live a victorious, fulfilling Christian life. Distributed through churches and some private subscriptions." Magazine: 6½×7½; 12 pages; newsprint paper and cover; illustrations (color); photos. Quarterly in weekly parts. Estab. 1951. Circ. 40,000.
Needs: Contemporary, religious/inspirational, romance, spiritual, mystery, adventure and humor—all with Christian emphasis. "Stories dealing with teens and teen life, with a positive message or theme. Topics that interest teenagers include school, family life, recreation, friends, church, part-time jobs, dating and music.

Main character should be a 15- or 16-year-old boy or girl, a Christian and regular churchgoer, who faces situations using Bible principles." Receives approximately 100 unsolicited fiction mss/month. Buys 1-2 mss/issue; 75-100 mss/year. Publishes ms an average of 1 year after acceptance. Less than 1% of fiction is agented. Published work by Alan Cliburn, Marian Bray and Teresa Cleary; published new writers within the last year. Length: 800-1,200 words. Recommends other markets.

How to Contact: Send complete ms with SASE and cover letter (experience with teens especially preferred from new writers). Reports in 1-2 months. Sample copy and guidelines for SASE.

Payment/Terms: Pays 3-7¢/word on acceptance for first and one-time rights. Buys reprints.

Advice: "Get to know us before submitting, through guidelines and sample issues (SASE). And get to know teenagers. A writer must know what today's teens are like, and what kinds of conflicts they experience. In writing a short fiction piece for the teen reader, don't try to accomplish too much. If your character is dealing with the problem of prejudice, don't also deal with his/her fights with sister, desire for a bicycle, or anything else that is not absolutely essential to the reader's understanding of the major conflict."

STUDENT LEADERSHIP JOURNAL, (IV), InterVarsity Christian Fellowship, P.O. Box 7895, 6400 Schroeder Rd., Madison WI 53707-7895. (608)274-9001. Editor: Jeff Yourison. "The journal is a networking and leadership development tool for audience described below. We publish articles on leadership, spiritual growth and evangelism. We publish occasional poetry, short stories and allegories. The audience is Christian student leaders on secular college campuses." Quarterly. Estab. 1988. Circ. 8,000.

• *Student Leadership Journal* has received awards from the Evangelical Press Association.

Needs: Religious/inspirational, prose poem. "The form of fiction is not nearly as important as its quality and content. Fiction published by *Student Leadership* will always reflect a Christian worldview." No romance, teen, or children's fiction. Receives 10-15 unsolicited fiction mss/month. Buys up to 1 ms/issue; 4 ms/year. Publishes ms up to 2 years after acceptance. Length: 2,000 words preferred; 200 words minimum; 2,500 words maximum.

How to Contact: Query first with clips of published work. "A good cover letter will demonstrate familiarity with the magazine and its needs and will briefly describe the submission and any relevant information." Reports in up to 3 months on queries; up to 6 months on mss. SASE. Simultaneous and reprint submissions OK. Sample copy for $3, 9×12 SAE and $1 postage. Fiction guidelines for #10 SASE. Reviews novels and short story collections "if they address our audience *and* contemporary cultures."

Payment/Terms: Pays $25-125 on acceptance for first or one-time rights. Sends galleys to author.

Advice: "Read! Read! Read! The short story author must be an *artist* with words in so short a space. *Read* the best work of others. Observe it; get it into your bones. Just like a picture, a story must be vivid, colorful, well-balanced and eye-catching. Write! Write! Write! Don't be afraid to have at it! Picasso pitched many of his sketches. You'll pitch most of yours. But it's good practice, and it keeps your creative mind flowing."

THE SUN, (II), The Sun Publishing Company, Inc., 107 N. Roberson St., Chapel Hill NC 27516. (919)942-5282. Editor: Sy Safransky. Magazine: 8½×11; 40 pages; offset paper; glossy cover stock; illustrations; photos. "*The Sun* is a magazine of ideas. We publish all kinds of writing—fiction, articles, poetry. Our only criteria are that the writing make sense and enrich our common space. We direct *The Sun* toward interests which move us, and we trust our readers will respond." Monthly. Estab. 1974. Circ. 30,000.

Needs: Open to all fiction. Accepts 3 ms/issue. Receives approximately 400 unsolicited fiction mss each month. Recently published work by Josip Novakovich, Gillian Kendall and William Penrod; published new writers within the last year. Length: 7,000 words maximum. Also publishes poetry.

How to Contact: Send complete ms with SASE. Reports in 3 months. Publishes ms an average of 6-12 months after acceptance. Sample copy for $3.50

Payment/Terms: Pays up to $300 on publication, plus 2 contributor's copies and a complimentary one-year subscription for one-time rights. Publishes reprints.

‡SURFING MAGAZINE, (IV), Western Empire, Box 3010, San Clemente CA 92673. (714)492-7873. Editor-in-chief: Nick Carroll. Magazine: 8×11; 140 pages; 45 lb. free sheet paper; 80 lb. cover stock; photos. Magazine covering "all aspects of the sport of surfing for young, active surfing enthusiasts." Monthly. Estab. 1964. Circ. 102,000.

Needs: Surfing-related fiction. Receives 2 unsolicited mss/month. Buys 3 mss/year. Length: 2,000-3,000 words average. Occasionally critiques rejected mss. Also publishes short shorts.

How to Contact: Cover letter with background on surfing. Query first. Reports in 2 weeks. SASE. E-mail address: surfing@netcom.com. Free sample copy and fiction guidelines.

Payment/Terms: Pays 15-20¢/word on publication for one-time rights.

Advice: "Establish yourself as a *Surfing* general contributor before tackling fiction."

SWANK MAGAZINE, (II, IV), Swank Publication, 210 Route 4 East, Suite 401, Paramus NJ 07652. Editor: Paul Gambino. Magazine: 8½×11; 116 pages; 20 lb. paper; 60 lb. coated stock; illustrations; photos. "Men's sophisticated format. Sexually-oriented material. Our readers are after erotic material." Published 13 times a year. Estab. 1952. Circ. 350,000.

Needs: High-caliber erotica. "Fiction always has an erotic or other male-oriented theme; also eligible would be mystery or suspense with a very erotic scene. Writers should try to avoid the clichés of the genre." Buys 1 ms/issue, 18 mss/year. Receives approximately 80 unsolicited fiction mss each month. Published new writers within the last year. Length: 1,500-2,750 words.

How to Contact: Send complete ms with SASE and cover letter, which should list previous publishing credits. No simultaneous submissions. Reports in 3 weeks on mss. Sample copy for $5.95 with SASE.

Payment/Terms: Pays $300-500. Buys first North American serial rights. Offers 25% kill fee for assigned ms not published.

Advice: "Research the men's magazine market." Mss are rejected because of "typical, overly simple story-lines and poor execution. We're looking for interesting stories—whether erotic in theme or not—that break the mold of the usual men's magazine fiction. We're not only just considering strict erotica. Mystery, adventure, etc. with erotica passages will be considered."

TATTOO REVUE, (I, IV), Outlaw Biker Enterprises, Inc., Box 447, Voorhees NJ 08043. Editorial Director: J.C. Miller. Magazine: 8½×11, 96 pages; 50 lb. coated paper; 80 lb. cover stock; illustrations and photos. "Art magazine devoted to showcasing the very best of modern tattooing." Published 10 times/year. Estab. 1988. Circ. 180,000.

● The publisher of *Tattoo Revue* also publishes *Outlaw Biker* and *Skin Art.*

Needs: Fiction pertaining to subject matter (tattooing). Receives 20 unsolicited mss/month. Publishes 1 fiction ms/issue. Publishes ms 2-8 months after acceptance. Length: 1,000-2,500 words. "Very open to freelance writers and unpublished writers. Freelance photographers also needed."

How to Contact: Send complete ms with cover letter and SASE. Sample copy for $5 and 8½×11 SAE with 2 first-class stamps.

Payment/Terms: Payment varies according to length and quality of work; pays on publication. Buys all rights.

Advice: "Very targeted market, strongly suggest you read magazine before submitting work."

TEEN LIFE, (II), Gospel Publishing House, 1445 Boonville Ave., Springfield MO 65802-1894. (417)862-2781. Editor: Tammy Bicket. Take-home Sunday school paper for teenagers (ages 12-17). Weekly. Estab. 1936. Circ. 60,000.

Needs: Religious/inspirational, mystery/suspense, adventure, humor, spiritual and young adult, "with a strong but not preachy Biblical emphasis." Receives 100 unsolicited fiction mss/month. Published work by Betty Steele Everett, Alan Cliburn and Michelle Starr. Published new writers within the last year. Length: up to 1,500 words.

How to Contact: Send complete ms with SASE. "We want mss that reflect our upcoming themes. Please send for guidelines before sending ms." Reports in 1-3 months. Simultaneous and reprint submissions OK. Free sample copy and guidelines.

Payment/Terms: Varies. Pays on acceptance for one-time rights.

Advice: "Most manuscripts are rejected because of shallow characters, shallow or predictable plots, and/or a lack of spiritual emphasis. Send seasonal material approximately 18 months in advance."

'TEEN MAGAZINE, (II), Petersen Publishing Co., 6420 Wilshire Blvd., Los Angeles CA 90048-5515. (213)782-2000. Fax: (213)782-2660. Editor: Roxanne Camron. Magazine: 100-150 pages; 34 lb. paper; 60 lb. cover; illustrations and photos. "The magazine contains fashion, beauty and features for the young teenage girl. The median age of our readers is 16. Our success stems from our dealing with relevant issues teens face." Monthly. Estab. 1957. Circ. 1.1 million.

Needs: Adventure, humor, mystery, romance and young adult. Every story, whether romance, mystery, humor, etc., must be aimed at teenage girls. The protagonist should be a teenage girl. No experimental, science fiction, fantasy or horror. Buys 1 ms/issue; 12 mss/year. Generally publishes ms 3-5 months after acceptance. Length: 2,500-4,000 words. Publishes short shorts.

How to Contact: Send complete ms and short cover letter with SASE. Reports in 10 weeks on mss. Sample copy for $2.50. Guidelines for SASE.

Payment/Terms: Pays $200 and up on acceptance for all rights.

Advice: "Try to find themes that suit the modern teen. We need innovative ways of looking at the age-old problems of young love, parental pressures, making friends, being left out, etc. Subject matter and vocabulary should be appropriate for an average 16-year-old reader. 'TEEN would prefer to have romance balanced with a plot, re: a girl's inner development and search for self. Handwritten mss will not be read."

TEEN POWER, (IV), Scripture Press Publications, Inc., Box 632, Glen Ellyn IL 60138. (708)668-6000. Editor: Amy Cox. Magazine: 5⅜×8⅜; 8 pages; glossy paper and cover; illustrations and photographs. "*Teen Power* publishes true stories and fiction with a conservative Christian slant—must help readers see how principles for Christian living can be applied to everyday life; for young teens (11-16 years); many small town and rural; includes large readerships in Canada, England and other countries in addition to U.S." Estab. 1966.

● Another magazine by this publisher, *Zelos*, is listed in this book. *Teen Power* won an Award of

Merit in 1992 and a Higher Goals Award for redesign in 1994 from the Evangelical Press Association.
Needs: Adventure, humor/satire, religious/inspirational, young adult/teen (11-16 years). "All must have spiritual emphasis of some sort." Receives approximately 75-100 unsolicited mss/month. Buys 2 mss/issue; about 100 mss/year. Publishes ms at least 1 year after acceptance. Published work by Alan Cliburn, Betty Steele Everett and Marlys G. Stapelbroek; published new writers within the last year. Length: 1,000 words preferred; 250 words minimum; 1,100 words maximum. Publishes short shorts. Length: 300-500 words. Sometimes critiques rejected mss and recommends other markets.
How to Contact: Send complete ms with cover letter. Include Social Security number. Reports in 2-3 months. SASE. Simultaneous and reprint submissions OK. Sample copy and fiction guidelines for #10 SASE.
Payment/Terms: Pays $20 minimum; $120 maximum on acceptance for one-time rights; contributor's copies.
Advice: "We are looking for fresh, creative true stories, true-to-life, and nonfiction articles. All must show how God and the Bible are relevant in the lives of today's teens. All manuscripts must have a clear, spiritual emphasis or 'take away value.' We don't use stories which merely have a good moral. Be careful not to preach or talk down to kids. Also, be realistic. Dialogue should be natural. Resolutions should not be too easy or tacked on. We are a specialized market with a distinct niche, but we do rely heavily on freelance writers. We are open to any new writer who grasps the purpose of our publication."

‡TEXAS CONNECTION MAGAZINE, (IV), Box 541805, Dallas TX 75220. (214)951-0316. Editor: Alan Miles. Magazine: 8½×11; 168 pages; book offset paper; 100 lb. enamel cover; illustrations and photographs. "Adult erotica, for adults only." Monthly. Estab. 1985. Circ. 50,000.
Needs: Erotica, erotic cartooning, sexual fantasy, feminist, gay, humor/satire and lesbian. "Publishes new quarterly digest—100% fiction." Receives 20-30 unsolicited mss/month. Buys 2-3 mss/issue. Publishes ms 2-3 months after acceptance. Length: 1,750 words preferred; 1,000 words minimum; 2,500 words maximum.
How to Contact: Send complete ms with cover letter. Cover letter must state writer/author's age (18 yrs. minimum). Reports in 4-6 weeks. SASE for ms, not needed for query. Simultaneous and reprint submissions OK. Sample copy for $8.50. Free fiction guidelines. Reviews erotic fiction only.
Payment/Terms: Pays $25-200, free subscription to magazine and contributor's copies on publication. Purchases all rights on some, first rights on most.
Advice: "We publish an adult, alternative lifestyle magazine that is (uniquely) distributed both in the adult store market and mass-market outlets (convenience stores) throughout 5 states: Texas (main), Oklahoma, Arkansas, Louisiana, New Mexico. We are, of course, interested in fresh, erotic fiction only."

TOUCH, (II), Calvinettes, Box 7259, Grand Rapids MI 49510. (616)241-5616. Editor: Jan Boone. Magazine: 8½×11; 24 pages; 50 lb. paper; 50 lb. cover stock; illustrations and photos. "Our purpose is to lead girls into a living relationship with Jesus Christ and to help them see how God is at work in their lives and the world around them. Puzzles, poetry, crafts, stories, articles, and club input for girls ages 9-14." Monthly. Circ. 16,000.
 • *Touch* has received awards for fiction and illustration from the Evangelical Press Association. Each year *Touch* selects a theme. The theme for 1995-1996 is "Do You Know the Way?" While writers should not write for this theme, the editors say they should keep it in the back of their minds as they write.
Needs: Adventure, ethnic, juvenile and religious/inspirational. Write for upcoming themes. Receives 50 unsolicited fiction mss/month. Buys 3 mss/issue; 30 mss/year. Published work by A.J. Schut; published new writers within the last year. Length: 400 words minimum; 1,000 words maximum; 800 words average.
How to Contact: Send complete ms with 8×10 SASE. Cover letter with short description of the manuscript. Reports in 2 months. Simultaneous and previously published submissions OK. Sample copy for 8×10 SASE. Free guidelines.
Payment/Terms: Pays 3-5¢/word on acceptance for simultaneous, first or second serial rights.
Advice: "Try new and refreshing approaches. The one-parent, new girl at school is a bit overdone in our market. We have been dealing with issues like AIDS, abuse, drugs, and family relationships in our stories—more awareness-type articles."

TURTLE MAGAZINE FOR PRESCHOOL KIDS, (I, II), Children's Better Health Institute, Benjamin Franklin Literary & Medical Society, Inc., Box 567, 1100 Waterway Blvd., Indianapolis IN 46206. (317)636-8881. Editor: Nancy S. Axelrod. Magazine of picture stories and articles for preschool children 2-5 years old.
 • Children's Better Health Institute also publishes magazines for older children including *Child Life*,

---

‡ *The double dagger before a listing indicates that the listing is new in this edition. New markets are often the most receptive to submissions by new writers.*

Children's Digest, Children's Playmate, Jack and Jill and *Humpty Dumpty* listed in this book.
Needs: Juvenile (preschool). Special emphasis on health, nutrition, exercise and safety. Also has need for "action rhymes to foster creative movement, very simple science experiments, and simple food activities." Receives approximately 100 unsolicited fiction mss/month. Published work by Ginny Winter, Robin Kraut-bauer and Ann Devendorf; published new writers within the last year. Length: 8-24 lines for picture stories; 500 words for bedtime or naptime stories.
How to Contact: Send complete mss with SASE. No queries. Reports in 8-10 weeks. Send SASE for Editorial Guidelines. Sample copy for $1.25.
Payment/Terms: Pays up to 22¢/word (approximate); varies for poetry and activities; includes 10 complimentary copies of issue in which work appears. Pays on publication for all rights. (One-time book rights may be returned when requested for specific publication.)
Advice: "Become familiar with past issues of the magazine and have a thorough understanding of the preschool child. You'll find we are catering more to our youngest readers, so think simply. Also, avoid being too heavy-handed with health-related material. First and foremost, health features should be fun! Because we have developed our own turtle character ('PokeyToes'), we are not interested in fiction stories featuring other turtles."

‡UPSTATE NEW YORKER MAGAZINE, (I, II), JRH Communications, 401 N. Salina St., 3rd Floor, Syracuse NY 13203-1773. (315)422-0194. Fax: (315)422-0197. Editor: Stephanie DeJoseph. Fiction Editor: Deborah Clarke. Magazine: 8½×11; 48 pages; glossy paper; UV coated Fortuna Brilliant White cover; illustrations and photos. Bimonthly. Estab. 1994. Circ. 10,000.
Needs: Adventure, condensed/excerpted novel, ethnic/multicultural, historical, horror, humor/satire, literary, mainstream/contemporary, mystery/suspense, regional, religious/inspirational, romance, science fiction (soft), sports. List of upcoming themes available for SASE. Receives several unsolicited mss/month. Accepts 1 ms/issue; 6 mss/year. Publishes ms 3-6 months after acceptance. Recently published work by Deborah Clarke and Michael Langan. Length: 1,500-2,000 words average. Publishes short shorts. Length: 750-1,200 words. Also publishes literary essays, literary criticism, poetry. Often critiques or comments on rejected ms.
How to Contact: Query first. Should include estimated word count, 2-3 line bio, Social Security number. Reports in 3 weeks on queries. Send a disposable copy of ms. Simultaneous submissions OK. Reviews novels and short story collections.

VENTURE, (II, IV), Christian Service Brigade, P.O. Box 150, Wheaton IL 60189. (708)665-0630. Fax: (708)665-0372. Editor: Deborah Christensen. Magazine: 8¼×10⅞; 16 pages; self-cover; illustrations and photos. "We publish entertaining stories for boys 8-11 years old. All stories are from a Christian perspective." Bimonthly. Estab. 1960. Circ. 18,000.
● *Venture* won an Award for Excellence for the Youth Category from the Evangelical Press Association.
Needs: Children's/juvenile (8-11 years): adventure, humor/satire, mystery/suspense (amateur sleuth), religious/inspirational, sports. No "fantasy, science fiction, horror, fiction for girls. We will ask female writers to provide a male pen name." Receives 100-120 unsolicited mss/month. Buys 2 mss/issue; 12 mss/year. Publishes ms within "several" months after acceptance. Recently published work by Teresa Cleary and Patricia Wyman. Length: 750 words average; 500 words minimum; 1,000 words maximum. Publishes short shorts. Always critiques or comments on rejected mss.
How to Contact: Send complete ms with a cover letter. Should include estimated word count and Social Security number. Reports in 1 week. Send SASE for reply, return of ms or send disposable copy of ms. Simultaneous and reprint submissions OK. Sample copy for $1.85, 9×12 SAE and 4 first-class stamps. Fiction guidelines for #10 SASE.
Payment/Terms: Pays 5-10¢/word and 2 contributor's copies on publication for first rights or reprint rights.
Advice: Looks for work that "is well written, active verbs, weaves Christianity naturally through story. I want to see humor. Don't send non-Christian stories or stories for girls."

VISTA, (II), Wesleyan Publishing House, Box 50434, Indianapolis IN 46953. (317)595-4144. Editor: Kelly Trennespohl. Magazine: 8½×11; 8 pages; offset paper and cover; illustrations and photos. "*Vista* is our adult take-home paper." Weekly. Estab. 1906. Circ. 40,000.
Needs: Religious/inspirational, convictional. Receives 100 unsolicited mss/month. Buys 4 mss/issue. Publishes ms 10 months after acceptance. Length: 500 words minimum; 1,300 words maximum.
How to Contact: Send complete ms with cover letter. Reports in 6-8 weeks. SASE. Simultaneous and reprint submissions OK. Sample copy for 9×12 SAE.
Payment/Terms: Pays 2-4¢/word on acceptance for first or reprint.
Advice: "Manuscripts for all publications must be in keeping with early Methodist teachings that people have a free will to personally accept or reject Christ. Wesleyanism also stresses a transformed life, holiness of heart and social responsibility. Obtain a writers' guidelines before submitting ms."

‡THE WEEKLY SYNTHESIS, (II), Apartment 8 Productions, P.O. Box 3223, Chico CA 95927-3223. Phone/fax: (916)899-7708. Editor: Bill Fishkin. Fiction Editor: Jesse Jackson. Magazine: 11½×14; 28-40 pages;

newsprint paper; newsprint cover; illustrations and photos. "*The Weekly Synthesis* is an entertaining alternative to informative news and views for readers 15-35." Weekly. Estab. 1994. Circ. 10,000.

Needs: Adventure, condensed/excerpted novel, erotica, ethnic/multicultural, experimental, fantasy (science fantasy), historical (general), horror, humor/satire, literary, mainstream/contemporary, mystery/suspense (amateur sleuth, police procedural, private eye/hardboiled, romance suspense), psychic/supernatural/occult, romance (contemporary, futuristic/time travel), science fiction (soft/sociological), sports, westerns (traditional), young adult/teen (western). "No cliché ridden, tired old retread formula stories with cardboard characters and see-through plotting." Publishes annual special fiction issue or anthology. Receives 7-8 unsolicited mss/month. Buys 1-2 mss/issue; 52-70 mss/year. Recently published work by Mike Bagwell, R. Eirik Ott and Jesse Jackson. Length: 1,200 words average; 900 words minimum; 1,500 words maximum. Publishes short shorts. Also publishes poetry. Sometimes critiques or comments on rejected ms.

How to Contact: Send complete ms with a cover letter. Should include estimated word count. Reports in 6-8 weeks on queries; 2-5 months on mss. Send a disposable copy of ms. Reprint, electronic submissions OK. E-mail address: synthesis8@aol.com. Sample copy for $1, 11×14 SAE. Fiction guidelines for 8×11 SASE.

Payment/Terms: Pays $5-50 on publication for first North American serial rights. Sponsors contests, awards or grants for fiction writers.

Advice: "Be honest. Write about what you know, don't be esoteric or gaudy. We publish stuff for regular people, not the New York Art Society. No 'Dick and Jane' dialogue—realism, flow important. Strong characters in a show-don't-tell method."

WITH: The Magazine for Radical Christian Youth (II, IV), Faith & Life Press, Box 347, Newton KS 67114. (316)283-5100. Editors: Corel Duerksen and Eddy Hall. Editorial Assistant: Delia Graber. Magazine: 8½×11; 32 pages; 60 lb. coated paper and cover; illustrations and photos. "Our purpose is to help teenagers understand the issues that impact them and to help them make choices that reflect Mennonite-Anabaptist understandings of living by the Spirit of Christ. We publish all types of material—fiction, nonfiction, poetry, teen personal experience, etc." Published 8 times/year. Estab. 1968. Circ. 5,700.

• *With* won several awards from the Associated Church Press and the Evangelical Press Association.

Needs: Contemporary, ethnic, humor/satire, mainstream, religious, young adult/teen (15-18 years). "We accept issue-oriented pieces as well as religious pieces. No religious fiction that gives 'pat' answers to serious situations." Receives about 50 unsolicited mss/month. Buys 1-2 mss/issue; 10-12 mss/year. Publishes ms up to 1 year after acceptance. Published new writers within the last year. Length: 1,500 words preferred; 400 words minimum; 2,000 words maximum. Rarely critiques rejected mss.

How to Contact: Send complete ms with cover letter, which should include short summary of author's credits and what rights they are selling. Reports in 1-2 months on mss. SASE. Simultaneous and reprint submissions OK. Sample copy for 9×12 SAE and $1.21 postage. Fiction guidelines for #10 SASE.

Payment/Terms: Pays 3¢/word for reprints; 5¢/word for simultaneous rights (one-time rights to an unpublished story); 5¢ to 7¢/word for assigned stories (first rights). Supplies contributor's copies; charge for extras.

Advice: "Except for humorous fiction (which can be just for laughs) each story should make a single point that our readers will find helpful through applying it in their own lives. Request our theme list and detailed fiction guidelines (enclose SASE). All our stories are theme-related, so writing to our themes greatly improves your odds."

WOMAN'S DAY, 1633 Broadway, New York NY 10019. No longer accepts fiction.

WOMAN'S WORLD MAGAZINE, The Woman's Weekly, (II), 270 Sylvan Ave., Englewood Cliffs NJ 07632. Fiction Editor: Brooke Comer. Magazine; 9½×11; 54 pages; newspaper quality. "The magazine for 'Mrs. Middle America.' We publish short romances and mini-mysteries for all women, ages 18-68." Weekly. Estab. 1980. Circ. 1.5 million.

Needs: Romance (contemporary), suspense/mystery. No humor, erotica or holiday stories. "Romance stories must be light and upbeat. No death or disease. Let your characters tell the story through detail and dialogue. Avoid prolonged descriptive passages in third person. The trick to selling a mystery is to weave a clever plot full of clues that don't stand out as such until the end. If we can guess what's going to happen, we probably won't buy it." Receives 2,500 unsolicited mss/month. Buys 2 mss/issue; 104 mss/year. Publishes mss 6-10 weeks after acceptance. Agented fiction 2%. Published work by Tima Smith, Carin Ford, Gloria Rosenthal and Fay Thompson. Length: romances—1,800 words; mysteries—1,200 words. Sometimes critiques rejected mss and recommends other markets.

How to Contact: "*No queries.*" Send complete ms, double spaced and typed in number 12 font." Cover letter not necessary. Include name, address and phone number on first page of mss. Reports in 6-8 weeks. SASE. Sample copy for $1. Fiction guidelines free.

Payment/Terms: Romances—$1,000, mysteries—$500. Pays on acceptance for first North American serial rights only.

‡**WONDER TIME, (II)**, World Action Publications, 6401 The Paseo, Kansas City MO 64131. (816)333-7000. Editor: Lois Perrigo. Magazine: 8¼×11; 4 pages; self cover; color illustrations. Hand-out story paper

published through WordAction Publications; stories should follow outline of Sunday School lessons for 6-8 year-olds. Weekly. Circ. 45,000.

Needs: Religious/inspirational and juvenile. Stories must have first- to second-grade readability. No fairy tales or science fiction. Receives 50-75 unsolicited fiction mss/month. Buys 1 ms/issue. Length: 200-350 words.

How to Contact: Send complete ms with SASE. Reports in 6 weeks. Sample copy and curriculum guide with SASE.

Payment/Terms: Pays $25 minimum on production (about 1 year before publication) for multi-use rights.

Advice: "We are looking for shorter stories (200-350 words) with a 1-2 grade readability. The stories need to apply to the weekly Sunday School lesson truths."

WRITER'S WORLD, (I, II), Mar-Jon Publishing Co., 204 E. 19th St., Big Stone Gap VA 24219. (703)523-0830. Fax: (703)523-5757. Editor: Gainelle Murray. Magazine: 8½×11; 24 pages; 60 lb. paper; 80 lb. glossy cover; illustrations and photos. Publishes "writing-related material: technical and personal aspect of writing well." Bimonthly. Estab. 1990. Circ. 10,000.

• Work submitted to *Writer's World* is automatically entered in their fiction contest.

Needs: Adventure, children's/juvenile (10-12 years), condensed/excerpted novel, ethnic/multicultural/ historical (general), humor/satire, literary, mainstream/contemporary, mystery/suspense (romantic suspense), religious/inspirational, romance (contemporary, futuristic/time travel, historical), senior citizen/retirement, westerns, young adult/teen (adventure, mystery, romance). "No stories dealing with drugs, sex and violence." Receives 10-15 unsolicited mss/month. Accepts 1-3 mss/issue; 12-15 mss/year. Publishes ms 6-9 months afer acceptance. Published work by Sandy Whelchel, Debra Purdy Kong and Florencia F. Haines. Length: 1,950 words average; 1,500 words minimum; 2,000 words maximum. Also publishes literary essays, literary criticism and poetry. Often critiques or comments on rejected ms.

How to Contact: Send complete ms with a cover letter. Should include estimated word count, 1-page bio, Social Security number and list of publication; publication history on reprints. Reports in 1 month. Send SASE for reply, return of ms or send a disposable copy of ms. Simultaneous and reprint submissions OK. Sample copy for $4.50, 9×12 SAE and $1.01 postage. Fiction guidelines for #10 SASE.

Payment/Terms: Pays 2 contributor's copies; additional copies for $3. Acquires one-time rights.

Advice: "We want stories that the entire family can enjoy, a polished manuscript that doesn't rely on profanity to get the story told." Looks for "a neat well-crafted, professional looking manuscript that has been fine tuned to the best of the writer's ability. Send for a sample copy to familiarize yourself with our publication. We would like to see more nostalgia/historical fiction. No anti-religious, pornographic, distasteful or offensive material."

WY'EAST HISTORICAL JOURNAL, (II), Crumb Elbow Publishing, P.O. Box 294, Rhododendron OR 97049. (503)622-4798. Editor: Michael P. Jones. Journal: 5½×8½; 60 pages; top-notch paper; hardcover and soft-bound; illustrations and photographs. "The journal is published for Cascade Georgraphic Society, a nonprofit educational organization. Publishes historical or contemporary articles on the history of Oregon's Mt. Hood, the Columbia River, the Pacific NW, or the Old Oregon Country that includes Oregon, Washington, Idaho, Wyoming, Montana, Alaska, Northern California and British Columbia and sometimes other areas. For young adults to elderly." Quarterly. Estab. 1992. Circ. 5,000.

Needs: Open. Special interests include wildlife and fisheries, history of fur trade in Pacific Northwest, the Oregon Trail and Indians. "All materials should relate—somehow—to the region the publication is interested in." Publishes annual special fiction issue in winter. Receives 10 unsolicited mss/month. Accepts 1-2 mss/ issue; 22-24 mss/year. Publishes ms up to one year after acceptance. Published work by Joel Palmer. Publishes short shorts. Recommends other markets. "We have several other publications through Crumb Elbow Publishing where we can redirect the material."

How to Contact: Query with clips of published work or send complete ms with cover letter. Reports in 2 months "depending upon work load." SASE (required or material will *not* be returned). Simultaneous and reprint submissions OK. Sample copy for $7. Fiction guidelines for #10 SASE.

Payment/Terms: Pays contributor's copies on publication. Acquires one-time rights.

Advice: "A ms has to have a historical or contemporary tie to the Old Oregon Country, which was the lands that lay west of the Rocky Mountains to the Pacific Ocean, south to and including Northern California, and north to and including Alaska. It has to be about such things as nature, fish and wildlife, the Oregon Trail, pioneer settlement and homesteading, the Indian wars, gold mining, wild horses—which are only a few ideas. It has to be written in a non-offensive style, meaning please remove all four-letter words or passages dealing with loose sex. Do not be afraid to try something a little different. No prima donnas, please! Will not return long-distance calls. We wish to work with writers who are professionals, even if they haven't had any of their works published before. This is a great place to break into the publishing world as long as you are an adult who acts like an adult. Send copies only! And please note that we cannot be responsible for the U.S. Postal Service once you mail something to us, or we mail something to you. We are looking forward to working with those who love history and nature as much as we do. Be sure to send a SASE (with proper postage) with all correspondence."

YOUNG SALVATIONIST, (II, IV), The Salvation Army, P.O. Box 269, 615 Slaters Lane, Alexandria VA 22313. (703)684-5500. Production Manager: Lesa Davis. Magazine: 8×11; 16 pages; illustrations and photos. Christian emphasis articles for youth members of The Salvation Army. 10 issues/year. Estab. 1984. Circ. 50,000.

Needs: Religious/inspirational, young adult/teen. Receives 150 unsolicited mss/month. Buys 9-10 ms/issue; 90-100 mss/year. Publishes ms 3-4 months after acceptance. Length: 1,000 words preferred; 750 words minimum; 1,200 words maximum. Publishes short shorts. Sometimes critiques rejected mss and recommends other markets.

How to Contact: Send complete ms. Reports in 1-2 weeks on queries; 2-4 weeks on mss. SASE. Simultaneous and reprint submissions OK. Sample copy for 9×12 SAE and 3 first-class stamps. Fiction guidelines and theme list for #10 SASE. Address submissions to Lesa Davis.

Payment/Terms: Pays 10¢/word on acceptance for all rights, first rights, first North American serial rights and one-time rights.

Advice: "Don't write about your high school experience. Write about teens now."

ZELOS, (II), (formerly *Freeway*), Scripture Press Publications, Inc., Box 632, Glen Ellyn IL 60138. (708)668-6000 (ext. 3210). Weekly Sunday school paper "specializing in first-person true stories about how God has worked in teens' lives," for Christian teens ages 15-21.

● Another magazine for teens by this publisher, *Teen Power*, is listed in this book.

Needs: Comics, humor/satire, spiritual, allegories and parables. Length: 400-1,000 words average. Occasionally critiques rejected mss.

How to Contact: Send complete ms with SASE. Reports in 2-3 months. Simultaneous submissions OK. Sample copy or fiction guidelines available for SASE.

Payment/Terms: Pays $30-120 for stories on acceptance for one-time rights.

Advice: "Send us humorous fiction with a clever twist and new insight on Christian principles. Do *not* send us typical teenage short stories. Watch out for cliché topics and approaches." Looks for "true-to-life, contemporary. Our fiction must have a 'take-away value'—a biblical principle for Christian living the reader can apply to his or her life."

International commercial periodicals

The following commercial magazines, all located outside the United States and Canada, also accept work in English from fiction writers. Countries represented here range from England, Ireland and Scotland to Germany and Italy. Also included are Australia and China.

As with other publications, try to read sample copies. While some of these may be available at large newsstands, most can be obtained directly from the publishers. Write for guidelines as well. Whereas one editor may want fiction with some connection to his or her own country, another may seek more universal settings and themes. Watch, too, for payment policies. Many publications pay only in their own currencies.

In all correspondence, use self-addressed envelopes (SAEs) with International Reply Coupons (IRCs) for magazines outside your own country. IRCs may be purchased at the main branch of your local post office. In general, send IRCs in amounts roughly equivalent to return postage. When submitting work to these international publications, you may find it easier to include a disposable copy of your manuscript and only one IRC with a self-addressed postcard for a reply. This is preferred by many editors, and it saves you the added cost of having your work returned.

BELLA MAGAZINE, 25 Camden Road, London, England. Fiction Editor: Linda O'Byrne. Weekly. Circ. 1 million. Publishes 2 short stories/issue. "Women's magazine using one general and one twist-ending story in each issue." Length: 1,200-2,500 words. Pays for published fiction and provides contributor's copies. "Read and study the magazine." Send SAE for guidelines.

‡CHAT, King's Reach Tower, Stamford St., London SE1 9LS England. Fiction Editor: Shelley Silas. Weekly. Circ. 550,000. Publishes 1 story/issue; 2/Christmas issue; 4-8/Summer special. "We look for a twist in the tale, a surprise ending, quick pace, and relationship-based pieces. Humor welcome!" Length: 700 words minimum; 1,000 words maximum. Payment "negotiated with the fiction editor and made by cheque. I accept and buy fiction from anyone, anywhere. Send material with reply coupons if you want your story returned." Call or write editor for sample copy. Writer's guidelines available for SAE and IRCs.

EROTIC STORIES, (IV), 4 Selsdon Way, City Harbour, London E14 9GL England. Editor: Joanna Payne. Commissioning Editor: Mary Tofts. Published 6 times/year. Buys 200 stories/year. "*Erotic Stories* is Britain's only magazine devoted to short erotic fiction. We are looking for erotic stories in which plot and characterization are as important as erotic content." Length: 2,000-3,500 words. "Slightly longer stories are also acceptable. For guidelines send SAE with IRC." Pays 1 contributor copy.

FORUM, Northern and Shell Tower, Box 381, City Harbour, London E14 9GL England. Fiction Editor: Elizabeth Coldwell. Circ. 30,000. Publishes 13 stories/year. "*Forum* is the international magazine of human relations, dealing with all aspects of relationships, sexuality and sexual health. We are looking for erotic stories in which the plot and characterisation are as important as the erotic content." Length: 2,000-3,000 words. Pays contributor's copy. "Try not to ask for the ms to be returned, just a letter of acceptance/rejection as this saves on your return postage. Anything which is very 'American' in language or content might not be as interesting to readers outside America. Writers can obtain a sample copy by saying they saw our listing."

‡INTERZONE: Science Fiction and Fantasy, (IV), 217 Preston Drove, Brighton BN1 6FL England. Editor: David Pringle. Monthly. Circ. 10,000. Publishes 5-6 stories/issue. "We're looking for intelligent science fiction in the 2,000-7,000 word range. Send 2 IRCs with 'overseas' submissions and a *disposable* ms." Pays £30 per 1,000 words on publication and 2 contributor's copies. "Please *read the magazine*—available through specialist science-fiction dealers or direct by subscription." Sample copies to USA: $5. Write for guidelines.

‡IRELAND'S OWN, (IV), 1 North Main St., Wexford Ireland. Editors: Austin Channing and Margaret Galvin. Weekly. Circ. 50,000. Publishes 3 stories/issue. "*Ireland's Own* is a homey family-oriented weekly magazine with a story emphasis on the traditional values of Irish society. Short stories must be written in a straightforward nonexperimental manner with an Irish orientation." Length: 1,800-3,000 words. Pays £30-40 on publication and contributor's copies. "Study and know the magazine's requirements, orientation and target market. Guidelines and copies sent out on request."

LONDON REVIEW OF BOOKS, 28 Little Russell St., London WC1A England. Editor: Mary-Kay Wilmers. Circ. 16,000. Publishes 3-6 stories annually. Publishes "book reviews with long essay-length reviews. Also publishes the occasional short story." Pays £200 per story and 6 contributor's copies.

NOVA SF, (IV), Perseo Libri srl, Box 1240, I-40100 Bologna Italy. Fiction Editor: Ugo Malaguti. Bimonthly. Circ. 5,000. "Science fiction and fantasy short stories and short novels." Pays $100-600, depending on length, and 2 contributor's copies on publication. "No formalities required, we read all submissions and give an answer in about 20 weeks. Buys first Italian serial rights on stories."

PEOPLE'S FRIEND, 80 Kingsway East, Dundee DD4 8SL Scotland. Fiction Editor: W. Balnave. Weekly. Circ. 500,000. Publishes 5 stories/issue. Length: 1,000-3,000 words. Pays $75-85 and contributor's copies. "British backgrounds preferred (but not essential) by our readership." Sample copy and guidelines available on application.

REALITY MAGAZINE, 75 Orwell Rd., Rathgar, Dublin 6 Ireland. Editor: Fr. Gerard R. Moloney, C.Ss.R. Monthly. Circ. 20,000. Publishes an average of 5 short stories annually. Length: 900-1,200 words. Pays £25-£35 (Ireland)/1,000 words and 2 contributor's copies. "Be clear, brief, to the point and practical. Write only about your own country. Sample copies supplied on request."

SCHOOL MAGAZINE, Private Bag 3, Ryde NSW 2112 Australia. Fiction Editor: Jonathan Shaw. Circ. 200,000. Publishes 40 stories/year. "Literary magazine for 8-11 year olds (much like *Cricket*). All types of stories—real life, fantasy, sci-fi, folk tales." Pays $146.75 (Aust.)/1,000 words on acceptance—one use only. Two free copies.

‡THE SCOTS MAGAZINE, (IV), 2 Albert Square, Dundee DD1 9QJ Scotland. Editor: Alan Halley. Monthly. Circ. 75,000. "One of the world's oldest popular periodicals. We use well-written fiction in a Scottish setting with a specific Scottish content." Length: 1,000-4,000 words. Payment made in pounds sterling, also contributor's copies. "No ghosts of Culloden or Glen Coe, no haggis and no phoney Scots dialogue." Guidelines available on request.

Sending to a country other than your own? Be sure to send International Reply Coupons instead of stamps for replies or return of your manuscript.

‡TEENAGERS IN CHINA & ABROAD, 9 Yuanhu Rd., Jieli Publishing House, 530022, Nanning Guangxi P.R. China. Fiction Editor: Xia Pei. Monthly. Circ. 300,000. Publishes 10-15 stories/issue. "*TICA* is a popular magazine for Chinese high school students; it reflects the life, study or amusement of teenagers in different countries. We use fiction about teenagers." Length: 1,000-4,000 words. "We hope that our writers will kindly give us a brief introduction about themselves when they write for us." Pays $15-20 (US) for 1,000 words. "Please type your manuscript so that we can read without any difficulty. And please don't submit your manuscript to other publishers within three months when you submit to us. You can write letters to publishers in different countries and ask for advice. If you are willing write for Chinese readers, we will recommend you to different publishers."

‡WOMAN'S DAY, G.P.O. Box 5245, Sydney NSW 2001 Australia. "*Woman's Day* looks for two types of short stories: first for Five Minute Fiction page at the back of the magazine, around 1,000 words long; longer short stories, between 2,500 and 4,000 words in length, are used less frequently. Manuscripts should be typed with double spacing and sufficient margins on either side of the text for notes and editing. They should be sent to the Fiction Editor with SAE and IRC." Payment is usually about $250 (Australian) for the Five Minute Fiction, from $350 for longer stories. *Woman's Day* purchases the first Australian and New Zealand rights. After publication, these revert to the author. "We accept unsolicited manuscripts, but must point out that we receive around 100 of these in the fiction department each week, and obviously, are limited in the number we can accept."

WOMAN'S WEEKLY, IPC Magazines, King's Reach, Stamford St., London SE1 9LS England. Fiction Editor: Gaynor Davies. Circ. 800,000. Publishes 1 serial and at least 2 short stories/week. "Short stories can be on any theme, but must have love as the central core of the plot, whether in a specific romantic context, within the family or mankind in general. Serials need not be written in installments. They are submitted as complete manuscripts and we split them up. Send first installment of serial (7,000 words) and synopsis of the rest." Length: 1,000-3,500 words for short stories; 14,000-42,000 words for serials. Short story payment starts at £230 and rises as writer becomes a more regular contributor. Serial payments start at around £500/installment. Writers also receive contributor's copies. "Read the magazine concerned and try to understand who the publication is aimed at." Writers' guidelines available. Write to "fiction department."

THE WORLD OF ENGLISH, P.O. Box 1504, Beijing China. Chief Editor: Chen Yu-lun. Monthly. Circ. 300,000. "We welcome contributions of short and pithy articles that would cater to the interest of our reading public, new and knowledgeable writings on technological finds, especially interesting stories and novels, etc. As our currency is regrettably inconvertible, we send copies of our magazines as the compensation for contributions. Aside from literary works, we put our emphasis on the provision of articles that cover various fields in order to help readers expand their vocabulary rapidly and enhance their reading level effectively, and concurrently to raise their level in writing. Another motive of us is to render assistance to those who, while learning English, are able also to enrich their knowledge and enlarge their field of vision."

Commercial periodicals/'95-'96 changes

The following commercial magazines appeared in the 1995 edition of *Novel & Short Story Writer's Market* but are not in the 1996 edition. Those publications whose editors did not respond this year to our request for an update are listed below without further explanation. They may have done so for a variety of reasons—they may have ceased publication, are no longer taking fiction or may be overstocked with submissions. They may have responded too late for inclusion in this edition. If we received information about why a publication would not appear, we included the explanation next to its name below.

AMAZING® Stories
American Atheist
American Bowhunter (selling magazine)
Appalachia Journal
Baltimore Jewish Times
Bear
The Black Scholar
Bowbender
Calliope
Cat Fancy (no unsolicited mss)
Changes (ceased publication)
Chic
Clubhouse (CO) (requested deletion)

Clubhouse (MI) (overstocked)
Cobblestone
Creative Kids
Detroit Jewish News
Dialogue
Discoveries
Faces
Feedback
Fifty Something Magazine
First (no longer publishes fiction)
Golf Journal
Grit
Ideals Magazine (requested deletion)
Kid City

Lethbridge Magazine
Lollipops Magazine
The Magazine for Christian Youth! (ceased publication)
Magazine of Fantasy and Science Fiction
Military Lifestyle (ceased publication)
NA'AMAT Woman
Northwest Journal
On Our Backs
The Other Side (requested deletion)
Oui Magazine (requested deletion)

Outlaw Biker
Realms of Fantasy (requested
   deletion)
The Rhode Islander Magazine
   (ceased publication)
Romantic Interludes
Science Fiction Age
Skin Art
Teen Power

Teenage Christian
Thrasher
TWN, South Florida's Weekly
   Gay Alternative
Valley Journal (ceased publica-
   tion)
Virtue
The Washingtonian (no fiction)
Women's American ORT Re-

porter
Women's Glib (suspended publi-
   cation)
Xtra Magazine
Yankee Magazine
The Young Crusader (ceased pub-
   lication)

International commercial periodicals/'95-'96 changes

Loving Magazine
Overseas!

For information on entering the Novel & Short Story Writer's Market Cover Letter Contest, see page 19.

Small Press

In this section we use the term "small press" in the broadest sense. Under this heading are more than 200 presses including one- and two-person operations, small or mid-size independent presses, university presses and other nonprofit publishers. Although most publish only a handful of books each year, a few publish 25 or more titles annually.

Introducing new writers to the reading public has become the most important role played by the small press today. Increasingly, too, small press publishers have devoted themselves to keeping accessible the work of talented fiction writers who are not currently in the limelight or whose work has had limited exposure. Many of the more successful small presses listed in this section, including Coffee House, Four Walls Eight Windows and Zoland Books, have built their reputations and their businesses in this way and have become known for publishing prize-winning literary fiction.

Today, small press publishers have better technology, distribution, marketing and business savvy than ever before. Despite their size, they've become big competition for their larger counterparts. More and more readers looking for good literary or experimental fiction and new, talented writers are turning to the small press to find them.

The benefits of working with the small press

Despite the growth and success of several small presses, even the most successful are unable to afford the six-figure advances, lavish promotional budgets and huge press runs possible in the large, commercial houses. Yet, there are some very tangible benefits to working with the small press.

For one thing, small presses tend to keep books in print a lot longer than larger houses. And, as Lane Stiles, editor of Mid-List Press points out in the Insider Viewpoint on page 402, small presses tend to treat every book they publish as a frontlist title. Since small presses publish a small number of books, each one is equally important to the publisher and each one is promoted in much the same way and with the same commitment.

Small presses also offer a much closer and more personal relationship between author and editor. In the Insider Viewpoint with Jeff Putnam on page 376, Putnam, editor at Baskerville Publishers, says, "There's a lot of interaction with our authors. Many of them become our friends."

Another advantage of small presses is that many are owned by one or just a few people. Editors stay longer because they have more of a stake in the business—often they own the business. Many small press publishers are writers themselves and know first-hand the importance of this type of editor-author or publisher-author relationship.

Curtis White, editor of the author-administered press FC2, notes in the Insider Viewpoint on page 390 that "Nonprofit presses like FC2 take risks profit-driven presses can't." This means small presses are more open to the avant-garde and what White calls "edgy" fiction often ignored by larger publishers.

Types of small presses

The very small presses are sometimes called micropresses and are owned or operated by one to three people, usually friends or family members. Some are cooperatives of writers and most of these presses started out publishing their staff members' books or books by their friends. These presses can easily be swamped with submissions, but writers published by them are usually treated as "one of the family."

Nonprofit presses depend on grants and donations to help meet operating costs. Keep in mind, too, some of these presses are funded by private organizations such as churches or clubs, and books that reflect the backer's views or beliefs are most likely to be considered for publication.

Funding for university presses is often tied to government or private grants as well. Traditionally, universities tend to publish writers who are either affiliated with the university or whose work is representative of the region in which the school is located. Recently, however, university presses are trying their hand at publishing books without university connections aimed at the same readership as other publishers. This is mostly happening in nonfiction, but chances are university presses may start to publish more general fiction as well.

Many publishers in this section are independent literary and regional presses. Several have become highly sophisticated about competing in the marketplace and in carving out their own niche.

Selecting a small press

As with magazines, reading the listing should be just your first step in finding markets that interest you. It's best to familiarize yourself with a press's focus and line. Most produce catalogs or at least fliers advertising their books. Whenever possible, obtain these and writers' guidelines.

If possible, read some of the books published by a press that interests you. It is sometimes difficult to locate books published by a small press (especially by micropress publishers). Some very small presses sell only through the mail. Literary and larger independent press books can be found at most independent bookstores, and the number of books from these presses that make it into the large chain super stores is growing. Also try university bookstores and libraries.

In How to Get the Most Out of This Book we discuss how to use the Category Index located near the end of this book. If you've written a particular type of novel, look in the Small Press section of the Category Index under the appropriate heading to find presses interested in your specific subject.

We've also included Roman numeral ranking codes placed at the start of each listing to help you determine how open the press is to new writers. The explanations of these codes appear at the end of this introduction.

In addition to the double dagger (‡) indicating new listings, we include other symbols to help you in narrowing your search. The maple leaf symbol (❦) identifies Canadian presses. If you are not a Canadian writer, but are interested in a Canadian press, check the listing carefully. Many small presses in Canada receive grants and other funds from their provincial or national government and are, therefore, restricted to publishing Canadian authors.

Book packagers are marked with a box symbol (■). A packager, also known as a book producer, creates books and then sells them to a publisher. Normally, they buy all rights and the writer may or may not get credit for it. Work is paid for by a flat sum rather than royalties.

You may also see an asterisk (*) at the start of a listing. This lets you know the press sometimes funds the publication of its books through a subsidy arrangement. By our definition, a subsidy press is one that requires writers to pay some or all of the costs of producing, marketing and distributing their books. Approach subsidy arrangements with caution. Find out exactly what type of production is involved and how many books will be produced. Check with a printer to find out how much it would cost to have this type and amount of books printed yourself. If the subsidy cost is more, find out what the extra money will pay for—how much and what type of marketing and distribution will be done? Don't hesitate to ask for a full accounting of any money to be spent, for copies of their other books (or information on where you can obtain them) and for any other information that will help you make an informed decision before you part with your money. Also when special circumstances require payment from the writer (for example, critiques), we have highlighted this information by putting it in italics.

In the listings

Again, How to Get the Most Out of This Book outlines the material common to all listings and how it will help you determine the right market for your work. Keep in mind many small presses do fewer than ten books a year and have very small staffs. We asked them to give themselves a generous amount of response time in their listing, but note it is not unusual for a small press to get behind. Add three or four weeks to the reporting time listed before checking on the status of your submission.

As with commercial book publishers, we ask small presses to give us a list of recent titles each year. If they did not change their title list from last year, it may be that, because they do so few fiction titles, they have not published any or they may be particularly proud of certain titles published earlier. If the recent titles are unchanged, we've altered the sentence to read "Published" rather than "Recently published."

The Business of Fiction Writing gives the fundamentals of approaching book publishers. The listings include information on what the publisher wishes to see in a submission package: sample chapters, an entire manuscript or other material.

Our editorial comments are set off by a bullet (●) within the listing. We use this feature to include additional information on the type of work published by the press, the awards and honors received by presses and other information we feel will help you make an informed marketing decision.

There are a number of publishing awards open to small presses or to their books. Many books published by the small press have received the Abby, a special award given by booksellers (the American Booksellers Association) to books they most enjoyed selling over the last year. The Lambda Literary Awards, given to books published by gay and lesbian presses, is another award often given to small press books. The Beyond Columbus Foundation awards the American Book Awards, given to books by American authors that reflect cultural diversity in American Writing, and the National Book Foundation honors one fiction book by an American author each year. Although most of these awards are open to all book publishers, books published by the small press have received several.

In addition to grants by states and national agencies, a few private and nonprofit organizations have stepped in to help fledgling small presses by providing funding and even guidance with the business side of their operations. We asked presses to give us this information and it sometimes appears in the editorial comments. One organization frequently mentioned was the Council of Literary Magazines and Presses (CLMP) with its Lila Wallace-Readers Digest Literary Publishers Marketing Development Program. Also mentioned is COSMEP, the International Association of Independent Publishers, one of the oldest organizations devoted to supporting the small press.

For more information

For more small presses see the *International Directory of Little Magazines and Small Presses* published by Dustbooks (P.O. Box 100, Paradise CA 95967). To keep up with changes in the industry throughout the year, check issues of two small press trade publications: *Small Press Review* (also published by Dustbooks) and *Small Press* (Small Press Inc., Kymbolde Way, Wakefield RI 02879).

The ranking codes used in this section are as follows:

I **Publisher encourages beginning or unpublished writers to submit work for consideration and publishes new writers frequently.**

II **Publisher accepts work by established writers and by new writers of exceptional talent.**

III **Publisher does not encourage beginning writers; publishes mostly writers with extensive previous publication credits or agented writers.**

IV **Special-interest or regional publisher, open only to writers on certain topics or from certain geographical areas.**

ACADIA PRESS, (IV), Acadia Publishing Co., P.O. Box 170, Bar Harbor ME 04609. (207)288-9025. Assistant to the President: Julie Savage. Estab. 1982. Small regional publisher. Publishes hardcover and paperback originals. Average print order: 3,000. Published new writers within the last year. Plans 1 first novel this year. Averages 2-3 total titles each year. Sometimes comments on rejected ms.
Needs: "We only publish books dealing directly with Acadia National Park and Mt. Desert Island (Maine)." Recently published *Parasols of Fern*, by Jack Perkins.
How to Contact: Does not accept unsolicited mss. Query first. Include bio and list of publishing credits. SASE for reply or send disposable copy of ms. Reports in 2 weeks on queries; 3 months on mss. Simultaneous submissions OK.
Terms: Pays royalties of 8% minimum; 15% maximum. Sends galleys to author. Publishes ms 18 months after acceptance. Writer's guidelines for #10 SASE. Book catalog for #10 SASE.

‡ACME PRESS, (I, II), P.O. Box 1702, Westminster MD 21158. (410)848-7577. Managing Editor: Ms. E.G. Johnston. Estab. 1991. "We operate on a part-time basis and publish 1-2 novels/year." Publishes hardcover and paperback originals. Average print order: 2,000; first novel print order: 2,000. Published new writers within the last year. Averages 1-2 novels/year. Always comments on rejected ms.
● Acme Press received the 1993 Benjamin Franklin Award for Humor.
Needs: Humor/satire. "We publish only humor novels. So we don't want to see anything that's not funny." Recently published *She-Crab Soup*, by Dawn Langly Simmons (fictional memoir/humor); and *Biting the Wall*, by J. M. Johnston (humor/mystery).
How to Contact: Accepts unsolicited mss. Query first, submit outline/synopsis and first 50 pages or submit complete ms with cover letter. Include estimated word count with submission. SASE for reply, return of ms or send a disposable copy of ms. Agented fiction 25%. Reports in 1-2 weeks on queries; 4-6 weeks on mss. Simultaneous submissions OK.
Terms: Provides 25 author's copies; pays 50% of profits. Sends galleys to author. Publishes ms 1 year after acceptance. Writer's guidelines and book catalog for #10 SASE.

ADVOCACY PRESS, (IV), Box 236, Santa Barbara CA 93102. Executive Director: Barbara Fierro Lang. Estab. 1983. Small publisher with 3-5 titles/year. Hardcover and paperback originals. Books: perfect or Smyth-sewn binding; illustrations; average print order: 5,000-10,000 copies; first novel print order: 5,000-10,000. Averages 2 children's fiction (32-48 pg.) titles per year.
● Advocacy Press books have won the Ben Franklin Award (*My Way Sally*) and the Friends of American Writers Award (*Tonia the Tree*). The press also received the Eleanor Roosevelt Research and Development Award from the American Association of University Women for its significant contribution to equitable education.
Needs: Juvenile. Wants only feminist/nontraditional messages to boys or girls—picture books; self-esteem issues. Published *Minou*, by Mindy Bingham (picture book); *Kylie's Song*, by Patty Sheehan (picture book); *Nature's Wonderful World in Rhyme*, by William Sheehan. Publishes the World of Work Series (real life stories about work).
How to Contact: Submit complete manuscript with SASE for return. Reports in 10 weeks on queries. Simultaneous submissions OK.
Terms: Pays in royalties of 5-10%. Book catalog for SASE.
Advice: Wants "only fictional stories for children 4-12-years-old that give messages of self-sufficiency for little girls; little boys can nurture and little girls can be anything they want to be, etc. Please review some of our publications *before* you submit to us. *Because of our limited focus, most of our titles have been written inhouse.*"

*AEGINA PRESS, INC., (I,II), 59 Oak Lane, Spring Valley, Huntington WV 25704. (304)429-7204. Imprint is University Editions, Inc. Managing Editor: Ira Herman. Estab. 1984. Independent small press. Publishes paperback and hardcover originals and reprints. Books: 50 lb. white text/10 point high gloss covers; photo-offset printing; perfect binding; illustrations; average print order: 500-1,000. Plans 5-10 first novels this year. Averages 30 total titles, 15 fiction titles each year. Sometimes comments on rejected ms.
• See also the listing for University Editions in this book.
Needs: Adventure, contemporary, experimental, fantasy, historical, horror, literary, mainstream, regional, romance (gothic), science fiction (hard science, soft sociological), short story collections, mystery/suspense (romantic suspense, young adult), thriller/espionage. No racist, sexist, or obscene materials. Recently published *Object of Desire*, by Susan Ann Moore (novel); *Linda Stories*, by Judith Robinson (short story collection); *The Incident at Crystal Lake*, by Richard C. Nelson (novel); and *Du Quesne*, by Richard C. Ashton (historical novel). Published new writers within the last year.
How to Contact: Accepts unsolicited mss. Send outline/synopsis and 3 sample chapters or complete ms with cover letter. SASE. Agented fiction 5%. Reports in 1 week on queries; 1 month on mss. Simultaneous submissions OK.
Terms: Pays 15% royalties. *Subsidy publishes most new authors.* "If the manuscript meets our quality standards but is financially high risk, self-publishing through the University Editions imprint is offered. All sales proceeds go to the author until the subsidy is repaid. The author receives a 40% royalty thereafter. Remaining unsold copies belong to the author." Sends galleys to author. Publishes ms 6-9 months after acceptance. Writer's guidelines for #10 SASE. Book catalog for 9×12 SAE, 4 first-class stamps and $2.

AGELESS PRESS, (II, IV), P.O. Box 5915, Sarasota FL 34277-5915. Phone/fax: (941)952-0576. Editor: Iris Forrest. Estab. 1992. Independent publisher. Publishes paperback originals. Books: acid-free paper; notched perfect binding; no illustrations; average print order: 5,000; first novel print order: 5,000. Published new writers within the last year. Averages 1 title each year. Sometimes comments on rejected ms.
Needs: Experimental, fantasy, humor/satire, literary, mainstream/contemporary, mystery/suspense, New Age/mystic/spiritual, science fiction, short story collections and thriller/espionage. Looking for material "based on personal computer experiences." Stories selected by editor. Published *Computer Legends, Lies & Lore*, by various (anthology); and *Computer Tales of Fact & Fantasy*, by various (anthology).
How to Contact: Does not accept unsolicited mss. Query first. Send SASE for reply, return of ms or send a disposable copy of ms. Reports in 1 week. Simultaneous and disk submissions (5¼ or 3.5 IBM) OK. E-mail address: Compuserve irisf@aol.com
Terms: Offers negotiable advance. Publishes ms 6-12 months after acceptance.

ALASKA NATIVE LANGUAGE CENTER, (IV), University of Alaska, P.O. Box 757680, Fairbanks AK 99775-0120. (907)474-7680. Editor: Tom Alton. Estab. 1972. Small education publisher limited to books in and about Alaska native languages. Generally nonfiction. Publishes hardcover and paperback originals. Books: 60 lb. book paper; offset printing; perfect binding; photos, line art illustrations; average print order: 500-1,000 copies. Averages 6-8 total titles each year.
Needs: Ethnic. Publishes original fiction only in native language and English by Alaska native writers. Recently published *A Practical Grammar of the Central Alaskan Yup'ik Eskimo Language*, by Steven A. Jacobson; *One Must Arrive With a Story to Tell*, by the Elders of Tununak, Alaska.
How to Contact: Does not accept unsolicited mss.
Terms: Does not pay. Sends galleys to author.

ALYSON PUBLICATIONS, INC., (II), 6922 Hollywood Blvd., Suite 1000, Los Angeles CA 90028. (213)871-1788. Fiction Editor: Helen Eisenbach. Estab. 1977. Medium-sized publisher specializing in lesbian- and gay-related material. Publishes paperback originals and reprints. Books: paper and printing varies; trade paper, perfect-bound; average print order: 8,000; first novel print order: 6,000. Published new writers within the last year. Plans 4 first novels this year. Plans 49 total titles, 15 fiction titles each year.
• Alyson Publications was recently bought and moved from Boston to Los Angeles. In addition to adult titles, Alyson Publications is known for its line of young adult and children's books. It is not yet known how much they will be dealing with children's books in the future.
Needs: "We are interested in all categories; *all* materials must be geared toward lesbian and/or gay readers." Recently published *B-Boy Blues*, by James Earl Hardy; *Amnesty*, by Louise A. Blum; and *Small Favors*, by James Russell Mayes (stories). Publishes anthologies. Authors may submit to them directly.

 The asterisk indicates a publisher who sometimes offers subsidy arrangements. Authors are asked to subsidize part of the cost of book production. See the introduction for more information.

How to Contact: Query first with SASE. Reports in 3 weeks on queries; 2 months on mss.
Terms: "We prefer to discuss terms with the author." Sends galleys to author. Book catalog for SAE and 3 first-class stamps.

❦**ANNICK PRESS LTD., (IV)**, 15 Patricia Ave., Willowdale, Ontario M2M 1H9 Canada. (416)221-4802. Publisher of children's books. Publishes hardcover and paperback originals. Books: offset paper; full-color offset printing; perfect and library bound; full-color illustrations; average print order: 9,000; first novel print order: 7,000. Plans 18 first picture books this year. Averages approximately 20 titles each year, all fiction. Average first picture book print order 2,000 cloth, 12,000 paper copies. Occasionally critiques rejected ms.
Needs: Children's books only.
How to Contact: "Annick Press publishes only work by Canadian citizens or residents." Does not accept unsolicited mss. Query with SASE. Free book catalog.
Terms: No terms disclosed.
Advice: "Publishing more fiction this year, because our company is growing. But our publishing program is currently full."

ANOTHER CHICAGO PRESS, (II), Box 11223, Chicago IL 60611. Senior Editor: Lee Webster. Estab 1976. Small literary press, non-profit. Books: offset printing; perfect-bound, occasional illustrations; average print order 2,000. Averages 4 total titles, 2 fiction titles each year. Occasionally critiques or comments on rejected ms.
Needs: Literary. No inspirational religious fiction. Recently published *Jack's Universe*, by Robert Pope; *Divine Days*, by Leon Forest; and *The Empty Lot*, by Mary Gray Hughes.
How to Contact: Does not accept or return unsolicited mss. Queries only. SASE. Agented fiction 10%. Reports in 6 months. Simultaneous submissions OK.
Terms: Advance negotiable; pays royalties of 10%. Sends galleys to author.
Advice: "We publish novels and collections of short stories and poetry as our funds and time permit—and then probably only by solicitation. We have not published an unsolicited manuscript in many, many years! We publish literary fiction and poetry of substance and quality. We publish books that will entertain, enlighten or disturb. Our books, our authors will be read well into the 21st Century."

❦**ANVIL PRESS, (I, II)**, Bentall Centre, P.O. Box 1575, Vancouver, British Columbia V6C 2P7 Canada; or Lee Building, #204-A, 175 E. Broadway, Vancouver, British Columbia V5T 1W2 Canada. (604)876-8710. Managing Editor: Brian Kaufman. Fiction Editors: Brian Kaufman and Dennis E. Bolen. Estab. 1988. "1½ person operation with volunteer editorial board." Publishes paperback originals. Books: offset or web printing; perfect-bound; average print order: 1,000-1,500; first novel print order: 1,000. Plans 2 first novels this year. Averages 1-2 fiction titles each year. Often comments on rejected ms. Also offers a critique service for a fee.
● Anvil Press publishes *Sub-Terrain* listed in the Literary and Small Circulation Section of this edition.
Needs: Experimental, literary, short story collections. Published *Stupid Crimes*, by Dennis E. Bolen (literary novel); *A Circle of Birds*, by Hayden Trenholm (literary novella); and *Stolen Voices/Vacant Rooms*, by Steve Lundin and Mitch Parry (2 novellas in one volume). Published new writers within the last year. Publishes the Anvil Pamphlet series: shorter works (essays, political tracts, polemics, treatises and works of fiction that are shorter than novel or novella form).
How to Contact: Canadian writers only. Accepts unsolicited mss. Query first or submit outline/synopsis and 1-2 sample chapters. Include estimated word count and bio with submission. Send SASE for reply, return of ms or a disposable copy of ms. Reports in 1 month on queries; 2-4 months on mss. Simultaneous submissions OK (please note in query letter that manuscript is a simultaneous submission).
Terms: Pays royalties of 15% (of final sales). Average advance: $100-200. Sends galleys to author. Publishes ms within contract year. Book catalog for 9 × 12 SASE and 2 first-class stamps.
Advice: "We are only interested in writing that is progressive in some way—form, content. We want contemporary fiction from serious writers who intend to be around for awhile and be a name people will know in years to come."

ARIADNE PRESS, (I), 4817 Tallahassee Ave., Rockville MD 20853. (301)949-2514. President: Carol Hoover. Estab. 1976. Shoestring operation—corporation with 4 directors who also act as editors. Publishes hardcover and paperback originals. Books: 50 lb. alkaline paper; offset printing; Smyth-sewn binding; average print order 1,000; first novel print order 1,000. Plans 1 first novel this year. Averages 1 total title each year; only fiction. Sometimes critiques rejected ms. "We comment on selected mss of superior writing quality, even when rejected."
Needs: Adventure, contemporary, feminist, historical, humor/satire, literary, mainstream, psychological, family relations and marital, war. Looking for "literary-mainstream" fiction. No short stories or fictionalized biographies; no science fiction, horror or mystery. Recently published *Walking West*, by Noelle Sickels; *The Greener Grass*, by Paul Bourguignon; and *A Rumor of Distant Tribes*, by Eugene Jeffers.
How to Contact: *Query first.* SASE. Agented fiction 5%. Reports in 1 month on queries; 2 months on mss. Simultaneous submissions OK.

Terms: Pays royalties of 10%. No advance. Sends galleys to author. Writer's guidelines and list of books in stock for #10 SASE.
Advice: "We exist primarily for nonestablished writers. Try large, commercial presses first. Characters and story must fit together so well that it is hard to tell which grew out of the other."

ARJUNA LIBRARY PRESS, (II), Subsidiaries include: The Journal of Regional Criticism, 1025 Garner St., D, Space 18, Colorado Springs CO 80905-1774. Director: Dr. Joseph A. Uphoff, Jr.. Estab. 1979. "The Arjuna Library is an artist's prototype press." Publishes paperback originals. Books: 20 lb. paper; photocopied printing; perfect bound; b&w illustrations; average print order: 20. Averages 6 total titles, 3 fiction titles each year. Sometimes comments on rejected ms.
● Arjuna Press has had exhibits at the Colorado Springs Fine Arts Center, KTSC Public Television (academic), University of Southern Colorado and The Poets House, New York. The press is known for its surrealism and science fiction titles.
Needs: Adventure, childrens/juvenile (fantasy), erotica, experimental, fantasy (surrealist), horror (supernatural), lesbian, romance (futuristic/time travel), science fiction (hard science/technological, soft/sociological poetry), young adult/teen (fantasy/science fiction). Nothing obscene or profane. Recently published *Deep Ellum*, by Robert W. Howington (surrealist); poetry broadsides by Toni Ortner, B.Z. Niditch and Neal Michael Dwyer; and the anthology, *English Is A Second Language*.
How to Contact: Accepts unsolicited mss. Submit complete ms with cover letter, resume. Include list of publishing credits, a disposable copy of the ms to be filed; will return samples in envelopes. Simultaneous and electronic submissions OK.
Terms: Pays 1 author's copy, plus potential for royalties. Writer's guidelines for SASE.
Advice: "Sometimes, ideas are not popular specifically because they refer to matters of necessity. In fact, entertainment is often an escape from reality. Writers often find it appropriate to simplify the social problems created by philosophy and speculation by dissolving ideology into the universe of fiction. Why is so much contemporary poetry in the first person? This individual of reference may not be an actual subjective expression yet, abstractly, ideas speak for themselves. This is the basis for the poetic novel as well."

♣ARSENAL PULP PRESS, (II), 103-1014 Homer St., Vancouver, British Columbia V6B 2W9 Canada. (604)687-4233. Fax: (604)669-8250. Editor: Linda Field. Literary press. Publishes paperback originals. Average print order: 1,500-3,000; first novel print order: 1,500. Published new writers within the last year. Plans 1 first novel this year. Averages 12-15 total titles; 2 fiction titles each year. Sometimes comments on rejected ms.
Needs: Ethnic/multicultural (general), feminist, gay, lesbian, literary and short story collections. No genre fiction, i.e. westerns, romance, horror, mystery, etc. Recently published *Time of the Kingfishers*, by David Watmough (novel); *Wigger*, by Lawrence Braithwaite; and *Lovely in Her Bones*, by J. Jill Robinson (short stories).
How to Contact: Accepts unsolicited mss. Query with outline/synopsis and 2 sample chapters. Include list of publishing credits. Send SASE for reply, return of ms or send a disposable copy of ms. Agented fiction 10%. Reports in 1 month on queries; 3-4 months on mss. Simultaneous submissions OK.
Terms: Pays royalties of 10% minimum; 10% maximum. Negotiable advance. Sends galleys to author. Publishes ms 1 year after acceptance. Writer's guidelines and book catalog free.
Advice: "We very rarely publish American writers."

ARTE PUBLICO PRESS, (II, IV), University of Houston, Houston TX 77204-2090. (713)743-2841. Publisher: Dr. Nicolas Kanellos. Estab. 1979. "Small press devoted to the publication of contemporary U.S.-Hispanic literature. Mostly trade paper; publishes 4-6 clothbound books/year. Publishes fiction and belles lettres." Publishes paperback originals and occasionally reprints. Average print order 2,000-5,000; first novel print order 2,500-5,000. Sometimes critiques rejected ms.
● Arte Publico Press has started the Piñata Books imprint featuring children's and young adult literature by U.S.-Hispanic authors. The press received the 1994 American Book Award for *In Search of Bernabé*, by Graciela Limón; the Thorpe Menn Award for Literary Achievement; the Southwest Book Award and others.
Needs: Contemporary, ethnic, feminist, literary, short story collections written by US-Hispanic authors. Published *Rain of Gold*, by Victor Villaseñor (autobiography); *Happy Birthday Jesús*, by Ronald Ruiz; *To a Widow with Children*, by Lionel Garcia; and *The Candy Vendor's Boy and Other Stories*, by Beatriz de la Garza.
How to Contact: Accepts unsolicited mss. Submit outline/synopsis and sample chapters or complete ms with cover letter and SASE. Agented fiction 1%.
Terms: Average advance: $1,000. Provides 20 author's copies; 40% discount on subsequent copies. Sends galleys to author. Book catalog free on request.
Advice: "Include cover letter in which you 'sell' your book—why should we publish the book, who will want to read it, why does it matter, etc."

BAGMAN PRESS, (I), P.O. Box 81166, Chicago IL 60681-0166. Fiction Editor: Carl Rudorf. Estab. 1989. Small independent publisher. Publishes paperback originals. Books: acid free paper; first novel print order: 1,000. Published new writers within the last year. Plans 1 first novel this year. Averages 1-2 total titles, 1 fiction title each year. Sometimes comments on rejected ms.
Needs: Children's/juvenile, feminist, gay, historical, lesbian, literary, mainstream/contemporary, science fiction, short story collections and translations. Published *Playing Soldiers in the Dark*, by Stephen Dueweke (gay fiction).
How to Contact: Accepts unsolicited mss (as long as SASE enclosed). Query with outline/synopsis and 1 sample chapter. Include bio and list of publishing credits. Send SASE. Reports in 1 month on queries; 4-6 months on mss. No simultaneous submissions.
Terms: Pays royalties of 5% minimum; 10% maximum. "Royalty statements/payment every 6 months." Publishes ms 1 year after acceptance. Writer's guidelines for SASE and 2 first-class stamps. Book catalog for SASE and 2 first-class stamps.

BAMBOO RIDGE PRESS, (IV), P.O. Box 61781, Honolulu HI 96839-1781. (808)599-4823. Editors: Darrell Lum and Eric Chock. Estab. 1978. "Bamboo Ridge Press publishes *Bamboo Ridge: The Hawaii Writers' Quarterly*, a journal of fiction and poetry with special issues devoted to the work of one writer—fiction or poetry." Publishes paperback originals and reprints. Books: 60 lb. natural; perfect-bound; illustrations; average print order: 2,000. Published new writers within the last year. Averages 2-4 total titles.
● Bamboo Ridge Press received an Excellence in Literature award from the Hawaii Book Publishers Association for its anthology, *The Best of Bamboo Ridge* and Book of the Year from the National Asian American Studies Association for a book of poetry.
Needs: Ethnic, literary and short story collections. "Interested in writing that reflects Hawaii's multicultural ethnic mix. No psuedo-Hawaiiana myths or Hawaii-Five-O type of mentality—stereotypical portrayals of Hawaii and its people." Published *The Watcher of Waipuna*, by Gary Pak.
How to Contact: Accepts unsolicited mss. Query first. SASE. Reports in 4-6 weeks on queries; 3-6 months on mss. Simultaneous submissions OK.
Terms: Payment depends on grant/award money. Sends galleys to author. Publishes ms 6 months-1 year after acceptance. Writer's guidelines for #10 SASE. Book catalog for #10 SASE and 52¢ postage.
Advice: Ask yourself these questions before submitting: "Does the writing have a unique perspective? What does it contribute to the developing tradition of literature by and about Hawaii's people?"

BASKERVILLE PUBLISHERS, INC., (III), 7616 LBJ Freeway, Suite 220, Dallas TX 75251. (214)934-3451. Fax: (214)239-4023. Imprint: Basset Books. Acquisitions Editor: Sam Chase. Publishes hardcover and paperback originals. Books: offset printing; average print order: 3,000-10,000; first novel print order: 3,000. Published new writers within the last year. Plans 3 first novels this year. Averages 14 total titles, mostly fiction, each year. Sometimes comments on rejected ms.
Needs: Literary, humor/satire. Recently published *Fata Morgana*, by Lynn Stegner; *Playing The Game*, by Alan Lelchuk; and *The Stolen Child*, by Paul Cody.
How to Contact: Accepts unsolicited mss. Query with outline/synopsis and 2 sample chapters. Include estimated word count, bio and list of publishing credits. SASE. Agented fiction 50%. Simultaneous submissions OK.
Terms: Pays royalties of 10% minimum; 15% maximum. Average advance: $3,000. Sends galleys to author. Publishes ms 6-12 months after acceptance. Writer's guidelines free for SASE. Book catalog for 8½×11 SASE and $1.25 postage.

FREDERIC C. BEIL, PUBLISHER, INC., (II), 609 Whitaker St., Savannah GA 31401. Imprints include The Sandstone Press. President: Frederic C. Beil III. Estab. 1983. General trade publisher. Publishes hardcover originals and reprints. Books: acid-free paper; letterpress and offset printing; Smyth-sewn, hardcover binding; illustrations; average print order: 3,000; first novel print order: 3,000. Plans 2 first novels this year. Averages 14 total titles, 4 fiction titles each year.
Needs: Historical, literary, regional, short story collections, translations. Recently published *A Woman of Means*, by Peter Taylor; *An Exile*, by Madison Jones; and *Priceless Souls*, by Desmond Tarrant.
How to Contact: Does not accept unsolicited mss. Query first. Reports in 1 week on queries. E-mail address: beilbook@delphi.com.
Terms: Payment "all negotiable." Sends galleys to author. Book catalog free on request.

 A bullet introduces comments by the editor of Novel & Short Story Writer's Market *indicating special information about the listing.*

Striving to Challenge Readers

"I can speak for almost all the small presses in saying that their goal is to keep really high-quality, challenging, exciting, intellectually-stimulating work out there," says Jeff Putnam, editor at Baskerville Publishers.

"Somehow good, original work of low economic impact has to be available to readers who want to be challenged, who read out of love and artistic appreciation."

And that's precisely what Putnam and his press strive to do—keep publishing good literary fiction by writers "who don't have high commercial expectations, who write for the love of it, who write seriously, who are real masters of their craft. Quite a different goal, he says, from that of commercial publishers.

Jeff Putnam

"As opposed to the commercial presses, there is much more satisfaction in what small presses do," he says. "There's more of a sense of a life reward; you really feel like you're doing something valuable, earnest and good."

Putnam believes "good stuff is going to bubble to the top for the small presses, and it will be an influence to make the bestseller kind of book a little more literary, a little more intelligent."

Small presses also differ from larger, commercial publishers in their relationships with authors. "We don't go to lunches. We don't waste our time courting authors. We don't waste our time coddling them. We don't have to. The expectations of authors are routinely much lower [working with a small press], which helps us to get a better book."

In fact, he's been known to send a 20- or 30-page critique of a manuscript to an author. "There's a lot of interaction with our authors. Many of them have become our friends. We work a long time and in-depth on their books, and really care about their books. We don't work on the 'star system' and don't have authors who expect that. There's a tremendous personal satisfaction in our books."

Baskerville Publishers routinely receives more than 70 queries and about 40 full-length requested manuscripts in a week. The editors have definite ideas about what makes good writing—and good writing comes first. Their books must be strongly grounded in experience; authors must have paid their dues.

Good literary fiction also needs solid characters with experience of their own, says Putnam, "not just a brief description that calls to mind a stock television type. As soon as the recognizable types appear, I turn off, no matter how imaginative the story."

Putnam also warns that "comparison to other writers is perilous. People have to care enough about the artistic side of their writing to have a style of their own.

"I would say to beginning writers, respect your means. Putting words together is powerful magic. Create some magic before you start comparing yourself to the sorcerers of the past. And don't compare yourself to the quick-buck artists of today unless you don't want to grow as an artist."

Another thing Putnam cautions against is formulaic fiction. For example, he says Baskerville is not interested in love stories, "but we're tremendously interested in the pain and passion of love. When you say 'love story' you bring in expectations, because love stories tend to follow a certain formula in spite of themselves; so do mysteries and so do a lot of other so-called genre books.

The stories Baskerville accepts must hinge on the unexpected. "Maybe the best surprises in the books we read are those that surprised the author when they were written," says Putnam. "I don't care where a particular relationship in a story goes, as long as it's authentic, as long as I get the feeling the author is hanging out there with me, discovering things, exploring, and is just as surprised as I in the direction the story takes. The closer we as readers get to the creative process, the more we are rewarded. That's the ideal I'm looking for."

Baskerville does not publish what Putnam calls "escape fiction." He says, "if our books are read as an escape, they should be an escape from cyberspace, an excursion into real life, however imaginative the author's approach. Life is the teacher."

Above all, Putnam wants Baskerville's books to be a challenge. "We don't care how disturbing they are, how much sleep is lost because of them," he says. "We want our readers to really care about the outcome for the people in the stories we've published—that's all." Authors who make that happen, Putnam says, are heroes.
—*Alice P. Buening*

66. . . good stuff is going to bubble to the top for the small presses, and it will be an influence to make the bestseller kind of book a little more literary, a little more intelligent. **99**
—**Jeff Putnam**

BETHEL PUBLISHING, (IV), 1819 S. Main, Elkhart IN 46516.(219)293-8585. Contact: Senior Editor. Estab. 1903. Mid-size Christian book publisher. Publishes paperback originals and reprints. Averages 3-5 total titles per year. Occasionally critiques or comments on rejected manuscripts.
Needs: Religious/inspirational, young adult/teen. No "workbooks, cookbooks, coloring books, theological studies, pre-school or elementary-age stories."
How to Contact: Accepts unsolicited complete mss. 30,000 words maximum. Query first. Enclose 8½ × 11 SAE and 3 first-class stamps. Reports in 2 weeks on queries; 3 months on mss. Accepts simultaneous submissions. Publishes mss 8-16 months after acceptance.
Terms: Pays royalties of 5-10% and 12 author's copies. Writer's guidelines and book catalog on request.

BILINGUAL PRESS/EDITORIAL BILINGÜE, (II, IV), Hispanic Research Center, Arizona State University, Tempe AZ 85287-2702. (602)965-3867. Editor: Gary Keller. Estab. 1973. "University affiliated." Publishes hardcover and paperback originals, and reprints. Books: 60 lb. acid-free paper; single sheet or web press printing; case-bound and perfect-bound; illustrations sometimes; average print order: 4,000 copies (1,000 case-bound, 3,000 soft cover). Published new writers within the last year. Plans 2 first novels this year. Averages 12 total titles, 6 fiction each year. Sometimes comments on rejected ms.
● A book published by Bilingual Press received the 1995 PEN Oakland Josephine Miles Award.
Needs: Ethnic, literary, short story collections, translations. "We are always on the lookout for Chicano, Puerto Rican, Cuban-American or other U.S.-Hispanic themes with strong and serious literary qualities and distinctive and intellectually important themes. We have been receiving a lot of fiction set in Latin America (usually Mexico or Central America) where the main character is either an ingenue to the culture or a spy, adventurer or mercenary. We don't publish this sort of 'Look, I'm in an exotic land' type of thing. Also, novels about the Aztecs or other pre-Columbians are very iffy." Recently published *MotherTongue*, by Demetria Martinez (novel); *Rita and Los Angeles*, by Leo Romero (short stories); and *Sanctuary Stories*, by Michael Smith (stories and essays).
How to Contact: Query first. SASE. Reports in 3 weeks on queries; 2 months on mss. Simultaneous submissions OK.
Terms: Pays royalties of 10%. Average advance $300. Provides 10 author's copies. Sends galleys to author. Publishes ms 1 year after acceptance. Writer's guidelines available. Book catalog free.
Advice: "Writers should take the utmost care in assuring that their manuscripts are clean, grammatically impeccable, and have perfect spelling. This is true not only of the English but the Spanish as well. All accent marks need to be in place as well as other diacritical marks. When these are missing it's an immediate first indication that the author does not really know Hispanic culture and is not equipped to write about it. We are interested in publishing creative literature that treats the U.S.-Hispanic experience in a distinctive, creative, revealing way. The kinds of books that we publish we keep in print for a very long time irrespective of sales. We are busy establishing and preserving a U.S.-Hispanic canon of creative literature."

BIRCH BROOK PRESS, (IV), P.O. Box 81, Delhi NY 13753. (212)353-3326. Publisher: Tom Tolnay. Estab. 1982. Small publisher of popular culture and literary titles in handcrafted letterpress editions. Plans 1 first novel this year. Averages 4 total titles, 2 fiction titles each year. Sometimes critiques or comments on rejected ms.
Needs: "We make specific calls for fiction when we are doing an anthology." Plans to publish anthology in the future. Will call for submissions at that time. Recently published *El Dorado: Lament for the Gold Double Eagle*, by William Oppenheimer and *Fiction, Flyfishing & The Search for Innocence*, by Lyons/McGuane/Enger, et al.
How to Contact: Does not accept unsolicited mss. Query first. SASE.
Terms: Modest flat fee.

BLACK HERON PRESS, (I, II), P.O. Box 95676, Seattle WA 98145. Publisher: Jerry Gold. Estab. 1984. One-person operation; no immediate plans to expand. Publishes paperback and hardback originals. Average print order: 2,000; first novel print order: 1,500. Averages 4 fiction titles each year.
● Three books published by Black Heron Press have won awards from King County Arts Commission.
Needs: Adventure, contemporary, experimental, humor/satire, literary, science fiction. Vietnam war novel—literary. "We don't want to see fiction written for the mass market. If it sells to the mass market, fine, but we don't see ourselves as a commercial press." Recently published *Renderings*, by James Sallis; *The War Against Gravity*, by Kristine Rosemary; and *Terminal Weird*, by Jack Remick.
How to Contact: Query and sample chapters only. Reports in 3 months on queries. Simultaneous submissions OK.
Terms: Pays standard royalty rates. No advance.
Advice: "A query letter should tell me: 1) number of words; 2) number of pages; 3) if ms is available on floppy disk; 4) if parts of novel been published; 5) if so, where?"

♣BLACK MOSS PRESS, (II), Box 143 Station A, Windsor ON N9A-6L7 Canada. (519)252-2551. Fiction Editor: Marty Gervais. Estab. 1969. "Small independent publisher assisted by government grants." Publishes paperback originals. Books: Zephyr paper; offset printing; perfect binding; 4-color cover, b&w interior illustrations; average print order: 500. Averages 10-14 total titles, 7 fiction titles each year.

Needs: Humor/satire, literary, short story collections. "Usually open to adult poetry. Nothing religious, moralistic, romantic." Published *The Failure of Love*, by Paul Vasey; *Ethel on Fire*, by Helen Humphreys; *Priest's Boy*, by Clive Doucet.

How to Contact: Accepts unsolicited mss. Submit outline/synopsis and 2 sample chapters with cover letter. SASE. Reports in 1-3 months. *Canadian authors only.*

Terms: Pays in author's copies. Sends galleys to author. Publishes ms 1-2 years after acceptance. Book catalog for SASE.

Advice: "Generally, originality, well-developed plots, strong, multi-dimensional characters and some unusual element catch my interest. It's rare that we publish new authors' works, but when we do, that's what we want. (We do publish short story collections of authors who have had some stories in lit mags.) Because we are assisted by government grants which place certain restrictions on us, we are unable to publish any material by anyone other than a Canadian citizen or immigrant landed in Canada."

BOOKS FOR ALL TIMES, INC., (III), Box 2, Alexandria VA 22313. Publisher/Editor: Joe David. Estab. 1981. One-man operation. Publishes hardcover and paperback originals. Books: 60 lb. paper; offset printing; perfect binding; average print order: 1,000. "No plans for new writers at present." Has published 1 fiction title to date. Occasionally critiques rejected ms.

Needs: Contemporary, literary, short story collections. "No novels at the moment; hopeful, though, of someday soon publishing a collection of quality short stories. No popular fiction or material easily published by the major or minor houses specializing in mindless entertainment. Only interested in stories of the Victor Hugo or Sinclair Lewis quality."

How to Contact: Query first with SASE. Simultaneous submissions OK. Reports in 1 month on queries.

Terms: Pays negotiable advance. "Publishing/payment arrangement will depend on plans for the book." Book catalog free on request.

Advice: Interested in "controversial, honest books which satisfy the reader's curiosity to know. Read Victor Hugo, Fyodor Dostoyevsky and Sinclair Lewis, for example. I am actively looking for short articles (up to 5,000 words) on contemporary education. I prefer material critical of the public schools when documented and convincing."

✤**BOREALIS PRESS, (I, IV)**, 9 Ashburn Dr., Nepean, Ontario K2E 6N4 Canada. Imprint includes *Journal of Canadian Poetry*. Editor: Frank Tierney. Fiction Editor: Glenn Clever. Estab. 1970. Publishes hardcover and paperback originals and reprints. Books: standard book-quality paper; offset printing; perfect and cloth binding; average print order: 1,000. Buys juvenile mss with b&w illustrations. Average number of titles: 4.
- Borealis Press has a series, "New Canadian Drama," with six books in print. The series won Ontario Arts Council and Canada Council grants.

Needs: Contemporary, literary, juvenile, young adult. "Must have a Canadian content or author; query first." Published *The Untempered Wind*, by Joanna E. Wood; *Our Little Life*, by J.G. Sime; *Armand Durand*, by Rosanna Leprohon; and *Cousin Cinderella*, by Sara Veannette Duncan.

How to Contact: Submit query with SASE (Canadian postage). No simultaneous submissions. Reports in 2 weeks on queries, 3-4 months on mss. Publishes ms 1-2 years after acceptance.

Terms: Pays 10% royalties and 3 free author's copies; no advance. Sends galleys to author. Free book catalog with SASE.

Advice: " Have your work professionally edited. Our greatest challenge is finding good authors, i.e., those who do not fit the popular mode."

*****BROWNELL & CARROLL, INC., (II)**, Imprints include Publishers Group and Military Literary Guild, 3901 MacArthur Blvd., Suite 200, Newport Beach CA 92660. (714)252-5451. (800)643-6604. Fax: (714)851-8725. Senior Editor: Lynne A. Lewis. Estab. 1983. Midsize independent publisher specializing in trade paperback originals. Average print order 2,000. Published new writers within the last year. Plans 15 first novels this year. Averages 30 total titles, 15 fiction titles each year.
- The publisher is actively seeking work from gay and lesbian authors.

Needs: Adventure, contemporary, ethnic, fantasy, feminist, gay, glitz, historical, horror, humor/satire, lesbian, literary, mainstream, military/war, mystery/suspense (amateur sleuth, police procedural), private eye, psychic/supernatural/occult, regional, religious/inspirational, romance, science fiction, short story collections, spiritual, thriller/espionage, western. Recently published *Mindset*, by Fred J. Kruger; *Squattin' Pigeon*, by Oscar Smith; and *A Legacy For Our Children*, by Steven J. Bolen.

How to Contact: Accepts unsolicited mss. Submit complete ms with cover letter. SASE. Reports in 1 month. Simultaneous submissions OK.

Terms: *Subsidy publishes 10% of books* (cooperative terms, approx. 60/40%). No advance. Provides 50 author's copies. Sends galleys to author. Publishes ms 9 months after acceptance. Writer's guidelines/book catalog for 9×12 SAE and $1.25 postage.

Advice: "New Authors should keep the action of the story moving constantly; do not let story drag or become repetitious; resolve the plot in a clear and concise way quickly; do not have too many sub-plots running through manuscript. Character development and style are as important as plot line."

BURNING GATE PRESS, (I, II), Burningate, Inc., 3333 Wilshire Blvd., Suite 607, Los Angeles CA 90010. (213)383-3144. Fax: (213)383-8038. Publisher: Mark Kelly. Estab. 1990. "Small independent general trade publisher." Publishes hardcover and paperback originals and paperback reprints. Average print order: 7,500; first novel print order: 3,000-5,000. Published new writers within the last year. Plans 2 first novels this year. Averages 4-5 total titles, 2-3 fiction titles each year. Sometimes comments on rejected ms.

Needs: Adventure, experimental, horror (psychological), literary, mainstream/contemporary, military/war, mystery/suspense (amateur sleuth, malice domestic, police procedural, private eye/hardboiled), thriller/espionage, western (frontier saga, traditional). "No short story collections. No WWII stories." Published *The Gentle Infantryman*, by W.Y. Boyd (military); and *The Dignity of Danger*, by E. Meade (military).

How to Contact: Does not accept unsolicited mss. Query with outline/synopsis and 3 sample chapters. Include list of publishing credits. Send SASE for reply, return of ms or send a disposable copy of ms. Agented fiction 100%. Reports in 2 months. Simultaneous submissions OK. Accepts disk submissions (Macintosh). E-mail address: GAISUN@netcom.com.

Terms: Pays royalties, amount varies per contract. Sends galleys to author. Publishes ms 6-12 months after acceptance.

Advice: "We do not publish any more World War II-based military titles, but will consider other military fiction and all contemporary fiction. Get a good critical review from a professional before submitting."

BUTTERNUT PUBLICATIONS, (II, IV), P.O. Box 1851, Martinsburg WV 25401. (304)267-0635. Publisher: Easther A. Watson. Estab. 1991. Midsize independent publisher. Publishes hardcover and paperback originals. Average print order: 5,000; first novel print order: 2,500. Published new writers within the last year. Plans 3 first novels this year. Averages 15 total titles, 7 fiction titles each year. Always critiques or comments on rejected ms.

Needs: Accepts work by West Virginians or about West Virginia only: children's/juvenile (historical, mystery), historical, mystery/suspense (cozy), new age/mystic/spiritual, psychic/supernatural/occult, regional (West Virginia themes), young adult/teen (historical). Especially looking for "young adult/teen and historical/ Civil War. Do not want to see anything that is unsuitable for family reading. No excessive violence, profanity, etc." Published *Reflections*, by Odessa Snyder (regional); *Murder At Confederate Headquarters*, by Susan Crites (mystery); and *Architecture of Berkeley County*, by Don Woods (regional).

How to Contact: Accepts unsolicited mss. Query with outline/synopsis and 3 sample chapters. Include estimated word count with submission. "We want the author's perspective on who will want the book." Send SASE for reply and disposable copy of ms. Reports in 2 weeks on queries; 1 month on mss. Simultaneous submissions OK.

Terms: Pays royalties, offers advance. "Specifics are proprietary information." Sends galleys to author. Publishes ms 6-12 months after acceptance. Writer's guidelines for SAE and 2 first-class stamps. Book catalog for 5½×8½ SAE and 3 first-class stamps.

Advice: "There seems to be a growing market for family reading. Large-print requests are skyrocketing; easy-to-read has become highly lucrative. We aren't interested in boring, high-brow, literary magazine writing. We want a delightful 'story.' We would like to see more manuscripts with family values, solid entertainment, less blood and guts (a good mystery doesn't need it)."

CADMUS EDITIONS, (III), Box 126, Tiburon CA 94920. (707)431-8527. Editor: Jeffrey Miller. Estab. 1979. Emphasis on quality literature. Publishes hardcover and paperback originals. Books: Approximately 25% letterpress; 75% offset printing; perfect and case binding; average print order: 2,000; first novel print order: 2,000. Averages 1-3 total titles.

Needs: Literary. Published *The Wandering Fool*, by Yunus Emre, translated by Edouard Roditi and Guzin Dino; *The Hungry Girls*, by Patricia Eakins; *Zig-Zag*, by Richard Thornley.

How to Contact: *Does not accept or return unsolicited mss.* Query first. SASE.

CALYX BOOKS, (II,IV), P.O. Box B, Corvallis OR 97339. (503)753-9384. Editor: M. Donnelly. Fiction Editor: Micki Reaman. Estab. 1986. "We publish fine literature and art by women." Publishes hardcover and paperback originals. Books: offset printing; paper and cloth binding; average print order: 5,000-10,000 copies; first novel print order: 5,000. Published new writers within the last year. Averages 2-4 total titles each year.

　● *Calyx*, a literary journal by this publisher, is also listed in this book. Books published by Calyx have received the American Book Award, GLCA Fiction Award, Bumbershoot and other awards.

Market categories: (I) Open to new writers; (II) Open to both new and established writers; (III) Interested mostly in established writers; (IV) Open to writers whose work is specialized.

Past anthologies include *Forbidden Stitch: An Asian American Women's Anthology* and *Women and Aging*. See the interview with Margarita Donnelly in the 1995 edition of *Novel & Short Story Writer's Market*.

Needs: Contemporary, ethnic, experimental, feminist, lesbian, literary, short story collections, translations. Published *The Violet Shyness of Their Eyes: Notes from Nepal*, by Barbara J. Scot; *Light in the Crevice Never Seen*, by Haunani-Kay Trook; and *The Adventures of Mona Pinsky*, by Harriet Ziskin. Published new writers within the last year.

How to Contact: Query first. Send SASE for reply. Reports in 1 month on queries.

Terms: Pays royalties of 10% minimum, author's copies, (depends on grant/award money). Sends galleys to author. Publishes ms 2 years after acceptance. Writer's guidelines for #10 SASE. Book catalog free on request.

Advice: "Read our book catalog and journal. Be familiar with our publications. Also, be patient—our collective process is lengthy."

*CAROLINA WREN PRESS, (II), 120 Morris St., Durham NC 27701. (919)560-2738. Imprints include Lollipop Power Books. "Small non-profit independent publishing company which specializes in women's and minority work and non-sexist, multi-racial children's books." Publishes paperback originals. Books: offset printing; perfect and saddle-stitched binding; illustrations mainly in children's; average print run: 1,000 adult titles, 3,000 children's. Published new authors within the last year. Averages 1 total title each year.

Needs: Contemporary, ethnic, experimental, feminist, gay, juvenile (contemporary, easy-to-read), lesbian, literary, preschool/picture book, regional, short story collections, translations. No standard clichéd stuff, romances, etc. No animals (children's books). "Women and minority authors encouraged to reply." Recently published *In the Arms of Our Elders*, by William Henry Lewis (short story collection).

How to Contact: Query for guidelines (SASE) and to inquire if currently accepting unsolicited mss.

Terms: Pays in copies (10% of print run for adult titles, 5% for children's books).

CATBIRD PRESS, (II), 16 Windsor Rd., North Haven CT 06473. Publisher: Robert Wechsler. Estab. 1987. Small independent trade publisher. Publishes paperback originals and reprints. Books: acid-free paper; offset printing; paper binding; illustrations (where relevant). Average print order: 4,000; first novel print order: 3,000. Averages 4 total titles, 1-2 fiction titles each year.

Needs: Humor (specialty); literary, translations (specialty Czech, French and German read in-house). No thriller, historical, science fiction, or other genre writing; only writing with a fresh style and approach. Recently published *Human Resources*, by Floyd Kemske; *Diplomatic Pursuits*, by Joseph von Westphalen; and *Tales from Two Pockets*, by Karel Čapek.

How to Contact: Accepts unsolicited mss but no queries. Submit outline/synopsis with sample chapter. SASE. Reports in 2-4 weeks on mss. Simultaneous submissions OK, but let us know if simultaneous.

Terms: Pays royalties of 7½-10%. Average advance: $2,000; offers negotiable advance. Sends galleys to author. Publishes ms approximately 1 year after acceptance. Terms depend on particular book. Writer's guidelines for #10 SASE.

Advice: "Book publishing is a business. If you're not willing to learn the business and research the publishers, as well as learn the craft, you should not expect much from publishers. They simply will have no respect for you. If you send genre or other derivative writing to a quality literary press, they won't even bother to look at it. If you can't write a decent cover letter, keep your fiction in your drawer. We are interested in unpublished novelists who combine a sense of humor with a true knowledge of and love for language, a lack of ideology, care for craft and self-criticism."

CAVE BOOKS, (IV), Subsidiary of Cave Research Foundation, 756 Harvard Ave., St. Louis MO 63130. (314)862-7646. Editor: Richard A. Watson. Estab. 1957. Small press. Publishes hardcover and paperback originals and reprints. Books: acid-free paper; various printing methods; binding sewn in signatures; illustrations; average print order: 1,500; first novel print order: 1,500. Averages 4 total titles each year. number of fiction titles varies. Critiques or comments on rejected ms.

● For years now Cave Books has been looking for realistic adventure novels involving caves. A writer with a *quality* novel along these lines would have an excellent chance for publication.

Needs: Adventure (cave exploration). Needs any realistic novel with caves as central theme. "No gothic, romance, fantasy or science fiction. Mystery and detective OK if the action in the cave is central and realistic. (What I mean by 'realistic' is that the author must know what he or she is talking about.)"

How to Contact: Accepts unsolicited mss. Submit complete ms with cover letter. Reports in 1 week on queries; 1 month on mss. Simultaneous submissions OK.

Terms: Pays in royalties of 10%. Sends galleys to author. Book catalog free on request.

Advice: Encourages first novelists. "We would like to publish more fiction, but we get very few submissions. Why doesn't someone write a historical novel about Mammoth Cave or Carlsbad Caverns?"

CENTER PRESS, (III), P.O. Box 16452, Encino CA 91416-6452. (818)377-4301. Managing Editor: Gabriella Stone. Estab. 1979. "Small three-person publisher with expansion goals." Publishes hardcover and paperback originals, especially poetry collections. Plans 1-2 novels this year. Averages 6 total titles. Occasionally critiques or comments on rejected ms; fee varies.

● Center Press sponsors the Masters Literary Awards listed in the Conference and Awards section.

Needs: Erotica, historical, humor/satire, literary, short story collections. *List for novels filled for next year or two.*

How to Contact: Does not accepting unsolicited mss. Query through agent only. SASE. Agented fiction 90%. Reports in 2 months on queries. Simultaneous submissions OK.

Terms: Payment rate is "very variable." Sends galleys to author.

Advice: "Be competent, be solvent. Know who you are. Target your market."

*CHINA BOOKS, (IV), 2929 24th St., San Francisco CA 94110. (415)282-2994. Editor: James Wang. Estab. 1959. "Publishes books about China or things Chinese." Publishes hardcover and paperback originals. Books: letterpress, offset printing; perfect-bound; b&w illustrations; average print order: 5,000. Published new writers within the past year. Averages 6 total titles, 2 fiction titles each year. Sometimes critiques rejected mss.

Needs: Ethnic, subjects relating to China and translations from Chinese. Recently published *Mutant Mandarin*, by James Wong.

How to Contact: Query first or submit outline/synopsis and 2 sample chapters. Reports in 2 weeks on queries; in 1 month on mss. Simultaneous submissions OK.

Terms: Pays royalties of 5-8%. Sends galleys to author. Publishes ms 1 year after acceptance. *Subsidy publishes 1%/year.* Writer's guidelines and book catalog free on request.

CIRCLET PRESS, (IV), 1770 Massachusetts Ave., #278, Cambridge MA 02140. Phone/fax: (617)864-0492, call before faxing. Publisher: Cecilia Tan. Estab. 1992. Small, independent specialty book publisher. Publishes paperback originals. Books: perfect binding; illustrations sometimes; average print order: 2,000. Published new writers within the last year. Averages 6-8 anthologies each year. Always critiques or comments on rejected ms.

Needs: "We publish only short stories of erotic science fiction/fantasy, of all persuasions (gay, straight, bi, feminist, lesbian, etc.). No horror! No exploitative sex, murder or rape. No degradation." No novels. All books are anthologies of short stories. Recently published *Selling Venus*, edited by C. Tan; *Blood Kiss*, edited by C. Tan (vampire erotica).

How to Contact: Accepts unsolicited mss between April 1 and August 31. "Any manuscript sent other than this time period will be held." Submit complete short story with cover letter. Include estimated word count, 50-100 word bio, list of publishing credits. Send SASE for reply, return of ms or send a disposable copy of ms. Agented fiction 5%. Reports in 1-3 months. Simultaneous submissions OK.

Terms: Pays ½¢/word for 1-time anthology rights only, plus 2 copies; author is free to sell other rights. Sends galleys to author. Publishes ms 1-12 months after acceptance. Writer's guidelines for #10 SASE. Book catalog for #10 SAE and 2 first-class stamps.

Advice: "Would like to see more depth of character, internal monologue and psychological introspection, less stereotypical science fiction/fantasy heroes. Most manuscripts that we reject either have not enough sex in them, or sex that is degrading or harmful." Note: "We do *not* publish novels."

COFFEE HOUSE PRESS, (II), 27 N. Fourth St., Minneapolis MN 55401. (612)338-0125. Editor: Allan Kornblum. Estab. 1984. "Nonprofit publisher with a small staff. We publish literary titles: fiction and poetry." Publishes paperback originals. Books: acid-free paper; Smyth-sewn binding; cover illustrations; average print order: 2,500; first novel print order: 3,000-4,000. Published new writers within the last year. Plans 2 first novels this year. Averages 12 total titles, 5-6 fiction titles each year. Sometimes critiques rejected ms.

● This successful nonprofit small press has received numerous grants from various organizations including NEA, the Mellon Foundation and Lila Wallace/Readers Digest. Recent award-winning books include: *A Place Where the Sea Remembers*, by Sandra Benitez, the Discover Great New Writers Award for 1994 and the Minnesota Book Award for 1994; *Losing Absalom*, the First Novelist Award from the Black Caucus of the American Library Association.

Needs: Contemporary, ethnic, experimental, satire, literary, short story collections. Looking for "non-genre, contemporary, high quality, unique material." No westerns, romance, erotica, mainstream, science fiction, mystery. Publishes anthologies, but they are closed to unsolicited submissions. Also publishes a series of short-short collections called "Coffee-to-Go." Recently published *Ex Utero*, by Laurie Foos (first novel); *Gunga Din Highway*, by Frank Chin (novel); and *A .38 Special & a Broken Heart*, by Jonis Agee (short short stories).

How to Contact: Accepts unsolicited mss. Submit samples with cover letter. SASE. Agented fiction 10%. Reports in 3 months on queries; 9 months on mss.

Terms: Pays royalties of 8%. Average advance: $1,000. Provides 15 author's copies. Writer's guidelines for #10 SASE with 55¢ postage.

CONFLUENCE PRESS INC., (II), 500 Eighth Ave., Lewis-Clark State College, Lewiston ID 83501. (208)799-2336. Imprints: James R. Hepworth Books and Blue Moon Press. Fiction Editor: James R. Hepworth. Estab. 1976. Small trade publisher. Publishes hardcover and paperback originals and reprints. Books: 60 lb. paper;

photo offset printing; Smyth-sewn binding; average print order: 1,500-5,000 copies. Published new writers within the last year. Averages 5 total titles each year. *Critiques rejected mss for $25/hour.*

• Books published by Confluence Press have received Western States Book Awards and awards from the Pacific Northwest Booksellers Association.

Needs: Contemporary, literary, mainstream, short story collections, translations. "Our needs favor serious fiction, 1 novel and 1 short fiction collection a year, with preference going to work set in the contemporary western United States." Published *Cheerleaders From Gomorrah*, by John Rember; and *Gifts and Other Stories*, by Charlotte Holmes

How to Contact: Query first. SASE for query and ms. Agented fiction 50%. Reports in 6-8 weeks on queries and mss. Simultaneous submissions OK.

Terms: Pays royalties of 10%. Advance is negotiable. Provides 10 author's copies; payment depends on grant/award money. Sends galleys to author. Book catalog for 6×9 SASE.

Advice: "We are very interested in seeing first novels from promising writers who wish to break into serious print. We are also particularly keen to publish the best short story writers we can find. We are also interested in finding volume editors for our American authors series. Prospective editors should send proposals."

COOL HAND COMMUNICATIONS, INC., (II), 1098 NW Boca Raton Blvd., Boca Raton FL 33432. (407)750-9826. Fax: (407)750-9869. Editor: Peter Ackerman. Estab. 1992. Imprint: Cool Kids Press. Editor: Lisa McCourt. Estab. 1995. "Mid-size independent publisher." Publishes hardcover and trade paperback originals. Averages 15 total titles, 1-3 fiction titles and 6 children's titles each year. Sometimes comments on rejected ms.

Needs: Mainstream/contemporary, how-to, children's. No science fiction, fantasy, religious or romance fiction. Recently published *Bobby Joe: In the Mind of a Monster*, by Bernie Ward.

How to Contact: Accepts unsolicited mss. Query with outline/synopsis and 3 sample chapters. Include estimated word count, bio (1 page), Social Security number, and list of publishing credits. Send SASE for reply, return of ms or send a disposable copy of ms. Agented fiction 1%. Reports in 3 months. Simultaneous submissions OK. Accepts disk submissions (Mac/PC Word; Mac Quark).

Terms: Pays royalties of 3% minimum; 10% maximum. Offers negotiable advance. Sends galleys to author. Publishes ms 6-18 months after acceptance. Writer's guidelines for #10 SASE and 1 first-class stamp.

Advice: Looks for "quality writing, with professional workmanship. Neatness counts. Will consider first-time authors. Children's book illustrators must be highest quality."

✿COTEAU BOOKS, (IV), Thunder Creek Publishing Co-operative Ltd., 401-2206 Dewdney Ave., Regina, Saskatchewan S4R 1H3 Canada. (306)777-0170. Managing Editor: Shelley Sopher. Estab. 1975. Small, independent publisher. Publishes hardcover and paperback originals. Books: #2 offset or 60 lb. hi-bulk paper; offset printing; perfect and Smyth-sewn binding; 4-color illustrations; average print order: 1,500-3,000; first novel print order: approx. 1,500. Published new writers within the last year. Plans 1 first novel this year. Publishes 12 total titles, 5-6 fiction titles each year. Sometimes comments on rejected mss.

• Books published by Coteau Books have received awards including Smith Books/Books in Canada First Novel Award nomination for *The Crew*, Saskatchewan Publishers' Prize for *Sun Angel*, Saskatchewan Book of the Year for *Bad Luck Dog* and The Gerald Lampert Award for *The Night You Called Me a Shadow*. The publisher does anthologies and these are announced when open to submissions.

Needs: Middle years and young adult fiction. No science fiction. No children's picture books. Published *The Crew*, by Don Dickinson (novel); *Cut-Out*, by Wilma Riley (novel); and *Bad Luck Dog*, by Dianne Warren (short story).

How to Contact: *Canadian writers only.* Query first, then submit complete ms with cover letter. SASE. No simultaneous or multiple submissions. Agented fiction 10%. Reports on queries in 3 weeks; 4 months on mss.

Terms: "We're a co-operative and receive subsidies from the Canadian, provincial and local governments. We do not accept payments from authors to publish their works." Sends galleys to author. Publishes ms 1-2 years after acceptance. Book catalog for 8½×11 SASE.

Advice: "We publish short-story collections, novels and poetry collections, as well as literary interviews and children's books. This is part of our mandate."

CREATIVE ARTS BOOK CO., (II), 833 Bancroft Way, Berkeley CA 94710. (415)848-4777. Imprints: Creative Arts Communications Books, Creative Arts Life and Health Books and Saturday Night Specials. Editorial Production Manager: Donald Ellis. Estab. 1975. Small independent trade publisher. Publishes hardcover originals and paperback originals and reprints. Average print order: 2,500-10,000; average first novel print order: 2,500-10,000. Published new writers within the last year. Plans 3 first novels this year. Averages 10-20 titles each year.

• Books published by Creative Arts have been finalists for the American Book Award. They've published fiction by William Saroyan, Allen Ginsberg, Aldous Huxley, Nikos Kazantzakis, Barry Gifford and Al Young.

Needs: Contemporary, erotica (literary), feminist, historical, literary, mystery/suspense (Saturday night specials), regional, short story collections, translations, music, western. Publishes anthologies, *Black Lizard*

Crime Fiction (Vols. I & II) and *Stolen Moments*, a collection of love stories. Recently published *Heaven*, by Al Young; *Miss Coffin & Mrs. Blood*, by Sandy Diamond; *The Art of Seeing*, by Aldous Huxley; and *Just Being at the Piano*, by Mildred Chase. Publishes the Childhood (growing up) series.

How to Contact: Accepts unsolicited ms. Submit outline/synopsis and 3 sample chapters (approximately 50 pages). SASE. Agented fiction 50%. Reports in 1 month on queries; 6 weeks on mss. Simultaneous submissions OK.

Terms: Pays royalties of 7½-15%; average advance of $1,000-10,000; 10 author's copies. Sends galleys to author. Writers guidelines and book catalog for SASE.

‡CREATIVE WITH WORDS PUBLICATIONS, (I), Box 223226, Carmel CA 93922. Editor-in-Chief: Brigitta Geltrich. Estab. 1975. One-woman operation on part-time basis "with guest editors, artists and readers from throughout the U.S." Books: bond and stock paper; mimeographed printing; saddle-stitched binding; illustrations; average print order varies. Publishes paperback anthologies of new and established writers. Averages 6 anthologies each year. *Critiques rejected mss; $10 for short stories; $20 for longer stories, folklore items; $5 for poetry.*

Needs: Humor/satire, juvenile (animal, easy-to-read, fantasy), nature. "Editorial needs center on folkloristic items (according to themes): tall tales and such for annual anthologies." Needs seasonal short stories appealing to general public; "tales" of folklore nature, appealing to all ages, poetry and prose written by children. Recently published anthologies, *Colors: The Spectrum of the Rainbow* and *Mankind*.

How to Contact: Accepts unsolicited mss. Query first; submit complete ms (prose no more than 1,000 words) with SASE and cover letter. Reports in 1 month on queries; 2 months on mss. Publishes ms 1-2 months after deadline. Writer's guidelines (1 oz.) for SASE. No simultaneous submissions.

Terms: Pays in 20% reduced author copies.

Advice: "Our fiction appeals to general public: children-senior citizens. Follow guidelines and rules of Creative With Words Publications and not those the writer feels CWW should have. We only consider fiction along the lines of folklore, seasonal genres and themes set by CWW. We set our themes twice a year: July 1 and January 1. Be brief, sincere, well-informed and proficient!"

CREATIVITY UNLIMITED PRESS, (II), 30819 Casilina, Rancho Palos Verdes CA 90274. (310)377-7908. Contact: Rochelle Stockwell. Estab. 1980. One-person operation with plans to expand. Publishes paperback originals and self-hypnosis cassette tapes. Books: perfect binding; illustrations; average print order: 1,000; first novel print order 1,000. Averages 1 title (fiction or nonfiction) each year.

Needs: Published *Insides Out*, by Shelley Stockwell (plain talk poetry); *Sex and Other Touchy Subjects*, (poetry and short stories); *Timetravel: Do-It Yourself Past Life Regression Handbook*; *Denial is Not a River in Egypt* and *Overcome Denial, Depression, Addiction and Compulsion.*

Advice: Write for more information.

CROSS-CULTURAL COMMUNICATIONS, (I, IV), 239 Wynsum Ave., Merrick NY 11566-4725. (516)868-5635. Fax: (516)379-1901. Editorial Director: Stanley H. Barkan. Estab. 1971. "Small/alternative literary arts publisher focusing on the traditionally neglected languages and cultures in bilingual and multimedia format." Publishes chapbooks, magazines, anthologies, novels, audio cassettes (talking books) and video cassettes (video books, video mags); hardcover and paperback originals. Publishes new women writers series, Holocaust series, Israeli writers series, Dutch writers series, Asian-, African- and Italian-American heritage writers series, Native American writers series, Latin American writers series.

● Authors published by this press have received international awards including Nat Scammacca who won the National Poetry Prize of Italy and Gabriel Preil who won the Bialik Prize of Israel.

Needs: Contemporary, literary, experimental, ethnic, humor/satire, juvenile and young adult folktales, and translations. "Main interests: bilingual short stories and children's folktales, parts of novels of authors of other cultures, translations; some American fiction. No fiction that is not directed toward other cultures. For an annual anthology of authors writing in other languages (primarily), we will be seeking very short stories with original-language copy (other than Latin script should be print quality 10/12) on good paper. Title: *Cross-Cultural Review Anthology: International Fiction 1.* We expect to extend our *CCR* series to include 10 fiction issues: *Five Contemporary* (Dutch, Swedish, Yiddish, Norwegian, Danish, Sicilian, Greek, Israeli, etc.) *Fiction Writers.*" Recently published *Sicilian Origin of the Odyssey*, by L.G. Pocock (bilingual English-Italian translation by Nat Scammacca); *Sikano L'Americano!—Bye Bye America*, by Nat Scammacca; and *Milkrun*, by Robert J. Gress.

✝ The double dagger before a listing indicates that the listing is new in this edition. New markets are often the most receptive to submissions by new writers.

How to Contact: Accepts unsolicited mss. Query with SAE with $1 postage to include book catalog. "Note: Original language ms should accompany translations." Simultaneous and photocopied submissions OK. Reports in 1 month.

Terms: Pays "sometimes" 10-25% in royalties and "occasionally" by outright purchase, in author's copies— "10% of run for chapbook series," and "by arrangement for other publications." No advance.

Advice: "Write because you want to or you must; satisfy yourself. If you've done the best you can, then you've succeeded. You will find a publisher and an audience eventually. Generally, we have a greater interest in nonfiction novels and translations. Short stories and excerpts from novels written in one of the traditional neglected languages are preferred—with the original version (i.e., bilingual). Our kinderbook series will soon be in production with a similar bilingual emphasis, especially for folktales, fairy tales, and fables."

‡CROWBAR PRESS, (I), P.O. Box 8815, Madison WI 53708. (608)258-8814. President: Craig Froelich. Estab. 1994. "Small regional press." Publishes hardcover and paperback originals. Books: 50 lb. paper; offset printing; perfect binding; illustrations; average print order: 1,000; first novel print order: 1,000. Published new writers within the last year. Plans 2 first novels this year. Averages 6 total titles, 6 fiction titles each year. Sometimes critiques or comments on rejected ms.

Needs: Regional (midwest): adventure, ethnic/multicultural (general), historical, humor/satire, literary, mainstream/contemporary, military/war, short story collections. Looking for "novels, short stories for Illinois, Michigan, Minnesota and Wisconsin collections." Plans anthologies in the next year or two on collections of Minnesota, Wisconsin, Michigan and Illinois writers (4 separate books). Recently published *Anthology of Wisconsin Writers 1995* and *Anthology of Minnesota Writers 1995*.

How to Contact: Accepts unsolicited mss. Query first for novels, complete ms for stories. Should include estimated word count. Send SASE for reply, return of ms or send a disposable copy of ms. Agented fiction 5%. Reports in 2 weeks on queries; 2 months on mss. Simultaneous submissions OK.

Terms: Pays royalties of 10-15% (novels only); provides 25 contributor's copies (novels only). Sends galleys to author. Publishes ms 6-12 months after acceptance. Writer's guidelines for #10 SASE. Book catalog not available.

Advice: "Please type all query letters and any letters. Never send any manuscript without a cover letter. Always include SASE. A professional appearance goes a long way, even if you've never published anything before. We're open to anything well written."

*DAN RIVER PRESS, (I,II), Conservatory of American Letters, Box 298, Thomaston ME 04861. (207)354-0998. President: Robert Olmsted. Fiction Editor: R.S. Danbury III. Estab. 1976. Publishes hardcover and paperback originals. Books: 60 lb. offset paper; offset printing; perfect (paperback); hardcover binding; illustrations; average print order: 1,000; first novel print order: 1,000. Published new writers within the last year. Averages 4-5 total titles; 3 fiction titles last year.

● Dan River Press publishes *Dan River Anthology* listed in this book.

Needs: Adventure, contemporary, experimental, fantasy, historical, horror, humor/satire, literary, mainstream, military/war, psychic/supernatural/occult, regional, science fiction, short story collections, western. "We want good fiction that can't find a home in the big press world. No mindless stuff written flawlessly." Recently published *Blue Collar and Other Stories*, by Tom Laird (short story collection); *Tropical Fugue*, by A.T. Allan; and *Moses Rose*, by William Rainbolt.

How to Contact: Accepts unsolicited mss, "but we accept nothing until the author has read our guidelines. Send #10 SASE before submitting anything."

Terms: Pays $250 cash advance (minimum) on acceptance; 10% royalties on 1,000 copies, then 15%. Sends galleys to author. After acceptance, publication "depends on many things (funding, etc.). Probably in six months once funding is achieved." Writer's guidelines for #10 SAE and 2 first-class stamps. Book catalog for 6×9 SAE and 2 first-class stamps.

Advice: "Submit to us (and any other small press) when you have exhausted all hope for big press publication. Then, do not expect the small press to be a big press. We lack the resources to do things like 'promotion,' 'author's tours.' These things either go undone or are done by the author. When you give up on marketability of any novel submitted to small press, adopt a different attitude. Become humble, as you get to work on your second/next novel, grow, correct mistakes and create an audience. Remember . . . logic dictates that a small press can *not* market successfully. If they could, they'd be a large press, with no time for unknowns."

JOHN DANIEL AND COMPANY, PUBLISHERS, (I, II), Division of Daniel & Daniel, Publishers, Inc., Box 21922, Santa Barbara CA 93121. (805)962-1780. Fiction Editor: John Daniel. Estab. 1980; reestablished 1985. Small publisher with plans to expand. Publishes paperback originals. Books: 55-65 lb. book text paper; offset printing; perfect-bound paperbacks; illustrations sometimes; average print order: 2,000; first novel print order: 2,000. Published new writers within the last year. Plans 2 short story collections this year. Averages 5 total titles, 2-3 fiction titles each year. Sometimes critiques rejected ms.

● This press has become known for belles-lettres and literary fiction, and work that addresses social issues.

Needs: "I'm open to all subjects (including nonfiction)." Literary, mainstream, short story collections. No pornographic, exploitive, illegal or badly written fiction. Recently published *The Palmer Method*, by E.S.

Goldman (stories); *Talking to the World*, by Dennis Lynds (stories); *Brick*, by William Thompson (novel); and *Ru$$ia*, by David Evan Kaun (novel).

How to Contact: Accepts unsolicited mss. Query first. SASE. Submit outline/synopsis and 2 sample chapters. Reports in 3 weeks on queries; 2 months on mss. Simultaneous submissions OK.

Terms: Pays in royalties of 10% of net minimum. Sends galleys to author.

Advice: "As an acquiring editor, I would never sign a book unless I were willing to publish it in its present state. Once the book is signed, though, I, as a developmental editor, would do hard labor to make the book everything it could become. Read a lot, write a lot, and stay in contact with other artists so you won't burn out from this, the loneliest profession in the world. We are small and therefore cautious, and therefore very selective. So the odds are long-shot at best."

*MAY DAVENPORT PUBLISHERS, (I, II, IV), 26313 Purissima Rd., Los Altos Hills CA 94022. (415)948-6499. Editor/Publisher: May Davenport. Estab. 1975. One-person operation with independent sub-contractors. Publishes hardcover and paperback originals. Books: 65-80 lb. paper; off-set printing; perfect binding/saddle-stitched/plastic spirals; line drawing; average print order 500-3,000; average first novel print order: 3,000. Plans 1-3 first novels this year. Averages 3-5 total titles/year (including coloring books/reprints); 2-5 fiction titles/year. Sometimes critiques rejected ms.

Needs: "Overstocked with picture book mss. Prefer novels for junior and senior high students. Don't preach. Entertain!" Recently published *Mickey Steals the Show*, by Diane Harris-Filderman; *Driver's Ed is Dead*, by Pat Delgado; and *The History of Papa Frog*, by William Meisburger (children's story).

How to Contact: Query first with SASE. Agented fiction 2%. Reports in 2-3 weeks.

Terms: Pays royalties of 10-15%; no advance. Sends galleys to author. "*Partial subsidy whenever possible in advance sales of 3,000 copies, which usually covers the printing and binding costs only.* The authors are usually teachers in school districts who have a special book of fiction or textbook relating to literature." Writer's guidelines free with SASE.

Advice: "Personal tip: Combat illiteracy by creating material which will motivate children/young adults to enjoy words and actions. Try writing third person perspective humorous novels for young adults. Create youthful characters and make them come alive on the pages. If you can write fiction like the goose who laid the gold eggs, your descriptive adjectives, poetic dialogue and imaginative plots will be evident in your literature. If you just color your eggs for the Easter bunny, forget it."

‡DELPHINIUM BOOKS, (II, III), 127 W. 24th St., New York NY 10011. Phone/fax: (212)255-6098. Editor-in-Chief: William G. Thompson. Executive Editor: Noah T. Lukeman. Estab. 1989/1995. Midsize independent publisher. Publishes hardcover originals. Books: 60 lb. heavy stock; offset printing; sewn binding; average print order: 5,000; first novel print order: 5,000. Published new writers within the last year. Plans 3 first novels this year. Averages 6 total titles, 5-6 fiction titles each year. Sometimes comments on rejected ms.

● *Absent Without Leave*, written by Jessica Treadway, won a *Ploughshares* First Book Award; *Snares* won a 1993 American Insitute of Graphic Arts Award of Excellence; and numerous Delphinium titles have won Society of Illustrators Certificates of Merit.

Needs: Literary, short story collections. Publishes anthologies. Writers may submit directly to Noah T. Lukeman, anthology editor. "We also solicit submissions from select authors." Recently published *Absent Without Leave*, by Jessica Treadway (literary short story collection); *Christopher Park*, by Rosemary Clement (literary); and *Delphinium Blossoms* (literary anthology).

How to Contact: Does not accept unsolicited mss. Query first or submit through agent. Include 1-paragraph bio and list of publishing credits. Send a disposable copy of ms. Agented fiction 90%. Reports in 2 weeks on queries; 2-3 months on mss. Simultaneous submissions OK.

Terms: Pays royalties of 6% minimum; 15% maximum. Offers negotiable advance. Sends galleys to author. Publishes ms 6-12 months after acceptance. Book catalog for 9 × 12 SAE and 8 first-class stamps.

‡DEPTH CHARGE, (II), P.O. Box 7037, Evanston IL 60201. (708)733-9554. Fax: (708)733-0928. Editor: Eckhard Gerdes. Estab. 1986. "We are a small independent publisher." Publishes paperback originals. Books: 24 lb. paper; offset printing; perfect binding; average print order: 500; first novel print order: 500. Plans 2 first novels this year. Averages 2-4 fiction titles each year. Often comments on rejected ms.

Needs: Experimental. Looking for "subterficial fiction." No conventional fiction. Recently published *The Darkness Starts Up Where You Stand*, by Arthur Winfield Knight; *Openings*, by Richard Kostelanetz; and *Ring in a River*, by Eckhard Gerdes. Publishes *The Journal of Experimental Fiction* series.

How to Contact: Accepts unsolicited mss. Query first. Include bio and list of publishing credits with submission. Send SASE for reply, return of ms or send a disposable copy of ms. Agented fiction 10%. Reports in 3 months. Disk submissions OK.

Terms: Pays royalties of 8% minimum; 8% maximum. Sends galleys to author. Publishes ms 18 months after acceptance. Writer's guidelines for #10 SASE. Book catalog for 9 × 12 SASE and 4 first-class stamps.

Advice: "Much of the work claiming to be experimental' or 'innovative' is actually very conventional. Learn all the conventions, then violate them meaningfully. Familiarize yourself with subterficial fiction as well as the earlier movements of experimental fiction (the Noveau Roman, metafiction, etc.)."

*DISTINCTIVE PUBLISHING CORP., (I), P.O. Box 17868, Plantation FL 33318-7868. (305)975-2413. Fax: (305)972-3949. Editorial Assistant: C. Pierson. Estab. 1986. Midsize independent publisher. Publishes hardcover and paperback originals. Books: 50-60 lb. paper; offset printing; casebound or perfect binding; b&w and color illustrations; average print order: 2,000; first novel print order: 2,000. Plans 1-2 first novels this year. Averages 25-30 total titles, 1-2 fiction titles each year. Always comments on rejected ms; *$50 charge for critiques.*
Needs: Children's/juvenile (adventure, easy-to-read, preschool/picture book, series, sports), horror, mainstream/contemporary, military/war, new age/mystic/spiritual, religious/inspirational, thriller/espionage.
How to Contact: Accepts unsolicited mss. Submit complete ms with cover letter. Include estimated word count, bio, Social Security number and list of publishing credits. Reports in 1 month on queries; 3 months on mss. Simultaneous submissions OK.
Terms: Pays royalties of 6% minimum; 10% maximum. Offers negotiable advance. Also cooperative and individual publishing/payment arrangement. Subsidy publishes 25% of books. Sends galleys to author. Publishes ms 1 year after acceptance. Writer's guidelines for #10 SASE. Book catalog for $2 and 9×12 SAE.

♣DUNDURN PRESS, (II), 2181 Queen St. E., #301, Toronto, Ontario M4E 1E5 Canada. (416)698-0454. Editorial Contact Person: Kirk Howard. Estab. 1972. Subsidiaries include Hounslow Press, Simon & Pierre, Boardwalk Books and Umbrella Press. Midsize independent publisher with plans to expand. Publishes hardcover and paperback originals.
Needs: Contemporary, literary. Recently published *Love Minus One*, by Norma Harrs; *Grave Deeds*, by Betsy Struthers; and *Sherlock Holmes: Travels in the Canadian West*, by Ronald Weyman.
How to Contact: Accepts unsolicited mss. Submit outline/synopsis and sample chapters. SASE for ms. Simultaneous submissions OK. Accepts electronic submissions. E-mail address: editorial@dundurn.com (unsolicited mss *not* accepted by e-mail).
Terms: Pays royalties of 10%; 10 author's copies. Sends galleys to author. Publishes ms 6-9 months after acceptance. Writer's guidelines available for SASE. Book catalog free on request for SASE.

E.M. PRESS, INC., (I,II), P.O. Box 4057, Manassas VA 22110. (703)439-0304. Editor: Beth Miller. Estab. 1991. "Small, traditional publishing company." Publishes paperback and hardcover originals. Books: 50 lb. text paper; offset printing; perfect binding; illustrations; average print order: 1,200-5,000. Averages 6 total titles, fiction, poetry and nonfiction, each year.
Needs: Adventure, children's/juvenile, family saga, fantasy, humor/satire, literary, mainstream/contemporary, military/war, mystery/suspense, thriller/espionage. Recently published *Mournful Numbers*, by Frank Goldstein; *All The Way Home*, by Jim Hanyen; *Recalling August*, by H.R. Coursen.
How to Contact: Accepts unsolicited mss. Submit outline/synopsis and sample chapters or complete ms with cover letter. Include estimated word count. Send a SASE for reply, return of ms or send a disposable copy of the ms. Agented fiction 10%. Reports in 2 months on queries; 2 months on mss. Simultaneous submissions OK.
Terms: Amount of royalties and advances varies. Sends galleys to author. Publishes ms 1 year after acceptance. Writer's guidelines for SASE.
Advice: "Write, rewrite and have patience."

EARTH-LOVE PUBLISHING HOUSE LTD., (IV), 3440 Youngfield St., Suite 353, Wheatridge CO 80033. (303)233-9354. Fax: (303)233-9354. Director: Laodeciae Augustine. Estab. 1989. Small publisher. Publishes paperback originals and reprints. Books: 60 lb. paper; offset printing; sew and wrap binding; halftone illustrations; average print order: 5,000; first novel print order: 5,000. Averages 2 total titles, 1 fiction title each year. Often comments on rejected ms.
Needs: Metaphysical adventure, mystery/suspense (English amateur sleuth), new age/mystic/spiritual.
How to Contact: Does not accept unsolicited mss. Query first. Include estimated word count and list of publishing credits with submission. SASE. Reports in 3 weeks on queries; 5 weeks on mss. Simultaneous submissions OK. Accepts electronic (disk) submissions.
Terms: Pays royalties of 8% minimum; 12% maximum or 10% of run for author's copies. Publishes ms 6-10 months after acceptance.

THE ECCO PRESS, (II), 100 W. Broad St., Hopewell NJ 08525. (609)466-4748. Editor-in-Chief: Daniel Halpern. Estab. 1970. Small publisher. Publishes hardcover and paperback originals and reprints. Books: acid-free paper; offset printing; Smythe-sewn binding; occasional illustrations. Averages 50 total titles, 10 fiction titles each year. Average first novel print order 3,000 copies.
Needs: Literary and short story collections. "We can publish possibly one or two original novels a year." No science fiction, romantic novels, western (cowboy). Published *Where Is Here*, by Joyce Carol Oates; *Have You Seen Me*, by Elizabeth Graver; *Coming Up Down Home*, by Cecil Brown.
How to Contact: Accepts unsolicited mss. Query first, especially on novels, with SASE. Reports in 2 to 3 months, depending on the season.

Terms: Pays in royalties. Advance is negotiable. Writer's guidelines for SASE. Book catalog free on request.
Advice: "We are always interested in first novels and feel it's important they be brought to the attention of the reading public."

‡**ECOPRESS, (IV)**, 1029 N.E. Kirsten Place, Corvallis OR 97330. (503)758-7545. Editor/Art Director: Chris Beatty. Estab. 1993. Publishes "books and art that enhance environmental awareness." Publishes hardcover and paperback originals. Books: recycled paper; offset printing; perfect binding; illustrations; average print order 2,000; first novel print order: 1,000. Averages 2 total titles, 1 fiction title each year. Often comments on rejected ms.
Needs: Adventure, literary, mainstream/contemporary, mystery/suspense, science fiction, short story collections, thriller/espionage, young adult/teen. Fiction "must have an environmental aspect." Recently published *Journey of the Tern*, by Robert Beatty.
How to Contact: Accepts unsolicited mss. Query with outline/synopsis and 3 sample chapters. Include estimated word count, half-page bio and list of publishing credits with submission. Send SASE for reply, return of ms or send a disposable copy of ms. Agented fiction 10%. Reports in 1 month on queries; 4 months on mss. Simultaneous, disk (ASCII text) and electronic submissions OK. E-mail address: 74451.74@compuserve.com.
Terms: Pays royalties; offers negotiable advance. Sends galleys to author. Publishes ms 1 year after acceptance. Writer's guidelines for SASE.

THE EIGHTH MT. PRESS, (II, IV), 624 SE 29th Ave., Portland OR 97214. (503)233-3936. Publisher: Ruth Gundle. Estab. 1984. One-person operation on full-time basis. Publishes paperback originals. Books: acid-free paper; perfect-bound; average print order: 5,000. Averages 2 total titles, 1 fiction title every few years.
Needs: Books written only by women. Feminist, lesbian, literary, short story collections. Published *Cows and Horses*, by Barbara Wilson (feminist/literary); and *Minimax*, by Anna Livia.
How to Contact: Accepts unsolicited mss. Query first. SASE (or IRC). Reports in 1 month.
Terms: Pays royalties of 8-10%. Sends galleys to author. Publishes ms within 1 year of acceptance.
Advice: "Query first! And present a clear and concise description of the project along with your publication credits, if any."

‡✽**EKSTASIS EDITIONS, (IV)**, Box 8474, Main P.O., Victoria, British Columbia V8W 3S1 Canada. Phone/fax: (604)385-3378. Publisher: Richard Olafson. Estab. 1982. Independent publisher. Publishes paperback originals. Books: acid free paper; offset printing; perfect/Smyth binding; average print order: 1,000-3,000; first novel print order: 1,000-2,000. Published new writers within the last year. Plans 3 first novels this year. Averages 14 total titles, 5 fiction titles each year.
Needs: Erotica, experimental, literary, mainstream/contemporary, New Age/mystic/spiritual, short story collections, translations. Recently published *Bread of the Birds*, by André Carpentier.
How to Contact: Accepts unsolicited mss. Submit complete ms with cover letter. Should include estimated word count, bio, list of publishing credits. SASE for reply. Reports in 5 months on queries; 4 months on mss.
Terms: Pays royalties of 6%. Pays 75 author's copies. Sends galleys to author. Book catalog available for $2.

FABER AND FABER, INC., (II), 50 Cross St., Winchester MA 01890. Small trade house which publishes literary fiction and collections. Averages 4-6 fiction titles each year.
Needs: Literary. "No romances, juvenile, please." Allow 2 months for response. Recently published *Coconuts for the Saint*, by Debra Spask; *The Legend of the Barefoot Mailman*, by John Henry Fleming.
How to Contact: Send query and 1 or 2 sample chapters with SASE for reply. Requires synopsis/description—cannot consider ms without this. Address to Publishing Assistant.

FASA CORPORATION, (II, IV), 1100 W. Cermac, B305, Chicago IL 60608. Editor: Donna Ippolito. "Company responsible for science fiction, adventure games, fantasy, to include adventures, scenarios, game designs and novels, for an audience high school age and up." Published new writers within the last year. Publishes 12 novels/year and 30 game products/year.
Needs: Novels set in our three game universes: Battle Tech® (military SF), Shadowrun® (technofantasy), Earthdawn® (high fantasy). Publishes ms an average of 12-18 months after acceptance. Recently published *Who Hunts the Hunter*, by Nyx Smith; *Malicious Intent*, by Michael A. Stackpole; and *Tactics of Duty*, by William H. Keith.
How to Contact: Query first. Send SASE for guidelines before submitting. Reports in 6-12 weeks. Simultaneous submissions OK.
Terms: Pays on publication for all rights. Sends galleys to author.
Advice: "Must be familiar with our product and always ask about suitability before plunging into a big piece of work that I may not be able to use. Writers *must* write to spec. Interested in writers for line of fiction and in writing for game products."

‡FC2/BLACK ICE BOOKS, (I), Unit for Contemporary Literature, Illinois State University, Normal IL 61790-4241. (309)438-3582. Fax: (309)438-3523. Co-director: Curtis White. Estab. 1974. "Publisher of innovative fiction." Publishes hardcover and paperback originals. Books: perfect/Smyth binding; illustrations; average print order: 2,200; first novel print order: 2,200. Published new writers within the last year. Plans 2 first novels this year. Averages 10 total titles, 10 fiction titles each year. Often critiques or comments on rejected ms.
Needs: Feminist, gay, literary, science fiction (cyberpunk), short story collections. Plans future anthologies written by women and selected by editors. Recently published *Cares of the Day*, by Ivan Webster (minority); *Angry Nights*, by Larry Fondation (literary); and *Little Sisters of the Apocalypse*, by Kit Reed (science fiction).
How to Contact: Accepts unsolicited mss. Query with outline/synopsis. Should include 1 page bio, list of publishing credits. SASE. Agented fiction 5%. Reports on queries in 3 weeks. Simultaneous submissions OK. E-mail address: ckwhite@rs6000.cmp.ilstu.edu.
Terms: Pays royalties of 8-10%; offers $100 advance. Sends galleys to author. Publishes ms 1 year after acceptance. Writer's guidelines for SASE.
Advice: "Be familiar with our list."

THE FEMINIST PRESS AT THE CITY UNIVERSITY OF NEW YORK, 311 E. 94th St., New York NY 10128. (212)360-5790. Publisher: Florence Howe. Estab. 1970. "Nonprofit, tax-exempt, education organization interested in changing the curriculum, the classroom and consciousness." Publishes hardcover and paperback reprints. "We use a fine quality paper, perfect-bind our books, four color covers; and some cloth for library sales if the book has been out of print for some time; we shoot from the original text when possible. We always include a scholarly and literary afterword, since we are introducing a text to a new audience; average print run: 4,000." Publishes no original fiction. Averages 8-10 total titles/year; 3-5 fiction titles/year (reprints of feminist classics only).
 ● Publisher Florence Howe received a LMP Certificate of Excellence in scholarly editorial in 1994 and the press has received two (1992 and 1993) Indian Book Review Book awards for *Women Writing in India*.
Needs: Children's, contemporary, ethnic, feminist, gay, lesbian, literary, regional, science fiction, translations, women's. Published *Songs My Mother Taught Me: Stories, Plays, and Memoir*, by Wakako Yamauchi; *Folly*, by Maureen Brady; and *Changes*, by Ama Ata Aidoo.
How to Contact: Accepts unsolicited mss. Query first. Submit outline/synopsis and 1 sample chapter. SASE. Reports in 2 weeks on queries; 2 months on mss. Simultaneous submissions OK.
Terms: Pays royalties of 10% of net sales; $100 advance; 10 author's copies. Sends galleys to author. Book catalog free on request.

FIREBRAND BOOKS, (II), 141 The Commons, Ithaca NY 14850. (607)272-0000. Contact: Nancy K. Bereano. Estab. 1985. Publishes quality trade paperback originals. Averages 8-10 total titles each year.
Needs: Feminist, lesbian. Recently published *The Gilda Stories*, by Jewelle Gomez (novel); and *Stone Butch Blues*, by Leslie Feinberg (novel).
How to Contact: Accepts unsolicited mss. Submit outline/synopsis and sample chapters or send complete ms with cover letter. SASE. Reports in 2 weeks on queries; 2 months on mss. Simultaneous submissions OK with notification.
Terms: Pays royalties.

*FLORIDA LITERARY FOUNDATION PRESS, (II), distributed by Woldt Corp., 2516 Ridge Ave., Sarasota FL 34235. (813)957-1281. Chairman: Virginia G. McClintock. Fiction Editor: Patrick J. Powers. Estab. 1989. "Nonprofit literary foundation." Publishes paperback originals. Books: quality trade paper. Averages 4-5 total titles each year. Sometimes comments on rejected ms.
 ● Woldt Corp. also distributes books by Starbooks listed in this book.
Needs: Literary. "Quality work on any subject—nothing clichéd." Published *The Princess' Lover*, by Elizabeth Clough (novel); and *Whores from Samarkand*, by Arpine K. Grenier (poetry).
How to Contact: Submit outline/synopsis and sample chapters. SASE. Reports in 1 month on queries; 6 weeks on mss. Simultaneous submissions OK. Accepts electronic submissions.
Terms: Provides 10-50 author's copies, honorarium; payment depends on grant/award money. Individual arrangement with author depending on the book. *Specialists in subsidy publishing*. Sends galleys to author. Writer's guidelines for SASE.

‡FORT DEARBORN PRESS, (I), 245 Bluff Ct., (LBS), Barrington IL 60010. Contact: G. Ahrens, President. Estab. 1993. "We are a midsize independent publisher." Publishes hardcover and paperback originals and paperback reprints. Books: "normal" paper; "best" printing; "best" binding; average print order: 100,000; first novel print order: 50,000. Published new writer within the last year. Averages 10 total titles, 9 fiction titles each year.
Needs: Open to all categories of fiction. Published *God and Sex Too, The Novel*, by Dean C. Dauw (general). Publishes the God and Sex series.

INSIDER VIEWPOINT

A Place for "Edgy" Fiction

It might seem strange that radical fiction has found a safe haven in a small prairie town named Normal. But Normal, Illinois, is also a university town— a place where avant-garde poetry readings are as common as weekly bingo games. Normal is also home base to a number of thriving nonprofit publishing ventures, including FC2, an author-administered press specializing in work that is, according to co-director Curtis White, "too edgy, too difficult, or too iconoclastic for establishment presses.

Curtis White

"Nonprofit presses like FC2 take risks profit driven publishers can't take," says White. "There are some wonderful writers out there and some are published by commercial presses. But if we had to depend on commercial publishers for the entirety of our literary culture, we would be impoverished. There just isn't enough breadth to represent a literary culture the size of ours."

Originally called the Fiction Collective (FC), the press was born in Brooklyn in 1974 when four writers, whose avant-garde work was ignored by the mainstream, banded together to publish their own work. FC thrived in the 1970s but nearly succumbed to growing pains and inertia in the mid-80s. In 1988, writers White and Ronald Sukenick staged a revival, rechristened the press FC2, and co-ran it from their respective locations in Normal, Illinois, and Boulder, Colorado. In 1995 the press consolidated its offices, settling in Normal, where White is a faculty member in the Unit for Contemporary Literature at Illinois State. ISU provides office space, graduate students and support staff, and gives White release time from his teaching duties to work on the press.

White says work FC2 chooses to publish must be "edgy. That could mean edgy in the sense that the writer is doing something unusual with language, or edgy in that the novel introduces unsettling political and cultural ideas." White cites *The Lost Scrapbook*, by Evan Dara, an American novelist living in Paris, as an example of edgy fiction. "Dara deals with a difficult and urgent subject," says White. "It's about an ecological disaster. And it's a legitimately great book."

White also points to Samuel Delany's *Hogg* as a novel that went unpublished for years until FC2 found it. Told from the point of view of its main character, a self described rapist-for-hire, "the story places the reader inside a thoroughly disgusting brain for the entire novel," says White. "It is all the more disturbing because that brain is sort of charming. We think it's an important book and a smart book and one that ultimately condemns violence."

Reviewers call FC2's books "experimental," but White isn't happy with the label, "Experimental doesn't mean self-indulgent," he says. "The trite, self-referential avant-garde novel is common and we see a lot of those. The writers we publish know exactly what they are doing. Their work is only experimental in that it tests the parameters of what is possible and permissable in writing."

White also points out, however, that even the best novel manuscript might need editorial help to make it better. "If parts of a brilliant novel are boring, it's time to cut. Writers respect our suggestions because we are writers, too. They know we won't cut words to save money on printing."

Writers won't get rich on alternative press books but, when a title creates a stir, its author becomes visible and viable to commercial publishers. *I Smell Esther Williams & Other Stories*, by Mark Leyner, is a typical small press success story. Leyner couldn't find a publisher until the original FC published his kaleidoscopic collection. The resulting buzz brought Leyner's work to the attention of Michael Pietsch, then an editor at Crown. Harmony Books, a Crown imprint, published Leyner's next book, *My Cousin, My Gastroenterologist*. Now Leyner regularly turns up on TV, plugging his imaginatively titled books (most recently, *Tooth Imprints on a Corn Dog*) on late night talk shows.

FC2 accepts work over-the-transom, but not out-of-the-blue. White advises writers to read FC2's guidelines and catalog to understand the avant-pop nature of the works it seeks. For example, FC2's Black Ice Books imprint publishes science fiction, but only if it has an avant-garde edge. FC2 would not publish a mystery or a detective novel, but it published *New Noir*, a book that plays with noir conventions. Writers who submit conventional fiction to FC2 "just aren't paying attention," says White.

White's own luxuriously bizarre fiction includes *The Idea of Home*, published by Sun and Moon, *Anarcho-Hindu*, published by Black Ice Books in 1995, and a surrealistic memoir he's writing now about "watching TV with my dad in the sixties." As a writer and publisher, he is convinced of the advantages a small press can offer beginning as well as established authors: "There is just enough old hippie in me to think that working for something that has its roots in the idea of cooperative ventures is a good thing. And I love the idea of authors controlling their own fate."

—*Mary Cox*

How to Contact: Does not accept unsolicited mss. Query first. When given permission to submit, include estimated word count, bio, Social Security number and list of publishing credits with submission. Send SASE for reply, return of ms or send a disposable copy of ms. Simultaneous, disk and electronic submissions OK. E-mail address: deandauw@aol.com.
Terms: Pays royalties of 16% maximum; offers negotiable advance; provides author's copies. Sends galleys to author. Publishes ms 6 months after acceptance. Writer's guidelines and book catalog free.

FOUR WALLS EIGHT WINDOWS, (II), 39 W. 14th St., #503, New York NY 10011. (212)206-8965. Co-Publishers: John Oakes/Dan Simon. Estab. 1986. "We are a small independent publisher." Publishes hardcover and paperback originals and paperback reprints. Books: quality paper; paper or cloth binding; illustrations sometimes; average print order: 3,000-7,000; first novel print order: 3,000-5,000. Averages 18 total titles/year; approximately 5-6 fiction titles/year.
• Four Walls Eight Windows' books have received mention from the *New York Times* as "Notable Books of the Year" and have been nominated for *L.A. Times* fiction prizes.
Needs: Literary. Published *Flan*, by Stephen Tunney; *The Bodhran Makers*, by John B. Keane; and *Simple Passion*, by Annie Ernaux.

How to Contact: Does not accept unsolicited submissions. "Query letter accompanied by sample chapter and SASE is best. Useful to know if writer has published elsewhere, and if so, where." Agented fiction 70%. Reports in 2 months. Simultaneous submissions OK.

Terms: Pays standard royalties; advance varies. Sends galleys to author. Book catalog free on request.

Advice: "We get 2,000 or so submissions a year: 1. Learn what our taste is, first; 2. Be patient."

GAY SUNSHINE PRESS AND LEYLAND PUBLICATIONS, (IV), P.O. Box 410690, San Francisco CA 94141. (707)996-6082. Editor: Winston Leyland. Estab. 1970. Publishes hardcover and paperback originals. Books: natural paper; perfect-bound; illustrations; average print order: 5,000-10,000.

   • Gay Sunshine Press has received a Lambda Book Award for *Gay Roots* (volume 1), named "Best Book by a Gay or Lesbian Press."

Needs: Literary, experimental, translations—all gay male material only. "We desire fiction on gay themes of *high* literary quality and prefer writers who have already had work published in literary magazines. We also publish erotica—short stories and novels." Recently published *Partings at Dawn: An Anthology of Japanese Gay Literature from the 12th to the 20th Centuries.*

How to Contact: "Do not send an unsolicited manuscript." Query with SASE. Reports in 3 weeks on queries; 2 months on mss. Send $1 for catalog.

Terms: Negotiates terms with author. Sends galleys to author. Pays royalties or by outright purchase.

Advice: "We continue to be interested in receiving queries from authors who have book-length manuscripts of high literary quality. We feel it is important that an author know exactly what to expect from our press (promotion, distribution, etc.) before a contract is signed. Before submitting a query or manuscript to a particular press, obtain critical feedback from knowledgeable people on your manuscript. If you alienate a publisher by submitting a manuscript shoddily prepared/typed, or one needing very extensive rewriting, or one which is not in the area of the publisher's specialty, you will surely not get a second chance with that press."

✦GOOSE LANE EDITIONS, (I, II, IV), 469 King St., Fredericton, New Brunswick E3B 1E5 Canada. (506)450-4251. Acquisitions Editor: Laurel Boone. Estab. 1957. Publishes hardcover and paperback originals and occasional reprints. Books: some illustrations; average print run: 2,000; first novel print order: 1,500. Averages 12 total titles, 2-4 fiction titles each year.

Needs: Contemporary, historical, literary, short story collections. "Not suitable for mainstream or mass-market submissions." Recently published *The Republic of Nothing*, by Lesley Choyce; *Sleeping With the Insane*, by Jennifer Mitton.

How to Contact: Considers unsolicited mss; complete work, or "samples." Query first. SASE "with Canadian stamps, International Reply Coupons, cash, check or money order. No U.S. stamps please." Reports in 6 months. Simultaneous submissions OK.

Terms: Pays royalties of 8% minimum; 12% maximum. Average advance: $100-200, negotiable. Sends galleys to author. Writers guidelines for 9 × 12 SAE and IRC.

Advice: "We consider submissions from outside Canada only when they have a strong Canadian connection and exhibit outstanding literary skill."

GRAYWOLF PRESS, (III), 2402 University Ave., St. Paul MN 55114. (612)641-0077. Publisher: Fiona McCrae. Estab. 1974. Growing small press, nonprofit corporation. Publishes hardcover and paperback originals and paperback reprints. Books: acid-free quality paper; offset printing; hardcover and soft binding; illustrations occasionally; average print order: 3,000-10,000; first novel print order: 2,000-6,000. Averages 18-20 total titles, 6-8 fiction titles each year. Occasionally critiques rejected ms. No genre books (romance, western, suspense).

   • Graywolf Press books have won numerous awards. Most recently, *Cloud Street*, by Tim Winton received the Australian Miles Franklin Award; *Licorice*, by Abby Frucht received Quality Paperback Book's New Voices Award and *Skywater*, by Melinda Worth Popham received *Buzzworm*'s Edward Abbey Award. The press has recently started the Graywolf Discovery Series featuring reprint paperbacks of out-of-print "gems."

Needs: Literary, and short story collections. Published *The Last Studebaker*, by Robin Hemley (novel); *The Secret of Cartwheels*, by Patricia Henley (short stories); *Cloudstreet*, by Tim Winton (novel).

How to Contact: Query with SASE. Reports in 2 weeks. Simultaneous submissions OK.

Terms: Pays in royalties of 7½-10%; negotiates advance and number of author's copies. Sends galleys to author. Free book catalog.

GRIFFON HOUSE PUBLICATIONS, Box 81, Whitestone NY 11357. (718)767-8380. President: Frank D. Grande. Estab. 1976. Small press. Publishes paperback originals and reprints.

Needs: Contemporary, drama, ethnic (open), experimental, literary, multinational theory, poetry, reprints, theory and translations.

How to Contact: Query with SASE. No simultaneous submissions. Reports in 1 month.

Terms: Pays in 6 free author's copies. No advance.

‡GRYPHON PUBLICATIONS, (I, II), Imprints include Gryphon Books, Gryphon Doubles, P.O. Box 209, Brooklyn NY 11228. (718)646-6126 (after 6 pm EST). Owner/Editor: Gary Lovisi. Estab. 1983. Publishes hardcover and paperback originals and trade paperback reprints. Books: bond paper; offset printing; perfect binding; average print order: 500-1,000. Published new writers within the last year. Plans 2 first novels this year. Averages 5-10 total titles, 4 fiction titles each year. Often comments on rejected ms.
Needs: Mystery/suspense (private eye/hardboiled, crime and true crime), science fiction (hard science/technological, soft/sociological), short story collections, thriller/espionage. No horror, romance or westerns. Plans anthology of hardboiled crime fiction. Authors may submit story. Published *The Dreaming Detective*, by Ralph Vaughn (mystery-fantasy-horror); *The Woman in the Dugout*, by Gary Lovisi and T. Arnone (baseball novel); and *A Mate for Murder*, by Bruno Fischer (hardboiled pulp). Publishes Gryphon Double novel series.
How to Contact: "I am not looking for novels now and *only* want to see a *1 page synopsis* with SASE for anything longer than 3,000 words." Include estimated word count, 50-word bio, short list of publishing credits, "how you heard about us." Send SASE for reply, return of ms or send a disposable copy of the ms. Agented fiction 5-10%. Reports in 2-4 weeks on queries; 2-6 weeks on mss. Simultaneous and electronic submissions OK (with hard copy—disk in ASCII).
Terms: For magazines, $5-45 on publication plus 2 contributor's copies; for novels/collections payment varies and is much more. Usually sends galleys to author. Publishes ms 1-3 years after acceptance. Writers guidelines and book catalog for SASE.
Advice: "I am looking for better and better writing, more cutting-edge material with *impact*! Keep it lean and focused."

‡❀GUERNICA EDITIONS, (III, IV), P.O. Box 117, Toronto, Ontario M5S 2S6 Canada. Editor: Antonio D'Alfonso. Fiction Editor: Umberto Claudio. Estab. 1978. Publishes paperback originals. Books: offset printing; perfect/sewn binding; average print order: 1,000; average first novel print order: 1,000. Plans to publish 1 first novel this year. Publishes 16-20 total titles each year.
- The press has recently won the American Booksellers Association Award for *Benedetha in Guysterland*, by Giose Rimanelli and the Governor General Award for *Aknos*, by Fulvio Caccia.
Needs: Contemporary, ethnic, literary, translations of foreign novels. Looking for novels about women and ethnic subjects. No unsolicited works. Recently published *The World at Noon*, by Eugene Mirabelli; *Surface Tension*, by Marisa De Franceschi; *Fabrizio's Passion*, by Antonio D'Alfonso; and *The Voices We Carry: New Fiction by Italian/American Women*, edited by Mary Jo Bona.
How to Contact: Does not accept or return unsolicited mss. Query first. IRCs. 100% of fiction is agented. Reports in 6 months. Electronic submissions via IBM WordPerfect disks. E-mail address: 102026.1331@compuserve.com.
Terms: Pays royalties of 7-10% and 10 author's copies. Book catalog for SAE and $2 postage. (Canadian stamps only).
Advice: Publishing "more pocket books."

*HEAVEN BONE PRESS, (II), 86 Whispering Hills Dr., Chester NY 10918. (914)469-9018. Editor: Steve Hirsch. Estab. 1986. "Literary publisher." Publishes paperback originals. Books: paper varies; saddle or perfect binding; average print order: 2,000. Averages 4 total titles, 1 fiction title each year. Sometimes comments on rejected ms.
- See the listing for *Heaven Bone* magazine in this book.
Needs: Experimental, literary, new age/mystic/spiritual, psychic/supernatural, science fiction (hard science/technological, soft/sociological).
How to Contact: Accepts unsolicited mss. Query first. Include estimated word count, short bio, list of publishing credits. SASE. Agented fiction 10%. Reports in 1 month on queries; 6 months on mss. No simultaneous submissions. Accepts electronic submissions.
Terms: Pays author's copies (10% of press run); depends on grant/award money. "We also do cooperative arrangements or individual arrangement with author." Sends galleys to author. Publishes ms up to 18 months after acceptance. Writer's guidelines or book catalog for #10 SAE and 2 first-class stamps.
Advice: "Know our magazine, *Heaven Bone*, very well before attempting to be published by us. Looking for more experimental, surreal work—less workshop exercises."

*HERITAGE PRESS, (II, IV), Box 18625, Baltimore MD 21216. (410)728-8521. President: Wilbert L. Walker. Estab. 1979. One-man operation, full-time basis; uses contractual staff as needed. Publishes hardcover originals. Books: 60 lb. white offset paper; offset printing; sewn hardcover binding; average print order: 2,000; first novel print order: 1,000. Averages 2 total titles, 1-2 fiction titles each year.
Needs: Ethnic (African-American). Interested in "fiction that presents a balanced portrayal of the black experience in America, from the black perspective. No fiction not dealing with African-Americans, or which views blacks as inferior." Published *Stalemate at Panmunjon* (the Korean War), and *Servants of All*, both by Wilbert L. Walker.
How to Contact: Does not accept unsolicited mss. Query first with SASE. Simultaneous submissions OK. Reports in 2 weeks on queries; 2 months on mss. Publishes ms an average of 9 months after acceptance.

Individual Attention Benefits Writers

Fiona McCrae, the director and publisher of Minnesota-based Graywolf Press, believes that many beginning writers get frustrated by trying to hit the market too quickly. "Once you've been turned down, you lose your appetite," says McCrae. "So don't send out your book until you're sure it's ready. Don't even start thinking about book publication until you've revised the manuscript. Revise, revise, revise!"

Novices also make the mistake of not properly researching their markets. "It's a question of getting a match," says McCrae. "People will send us murder mysteries, for example, even though we don't publish mysteries. We wouldn't be very good at publishing Scott Turow, for instance. The important thing is finding the right company for you."

Since its founding by Scott Walker in 1974, Graywolf Press has been known as "the right company" for poets and literary novelists who don't write for the mass market. And yet Graywolf has the almost uncanny ability to get its titles stocked by mainstream booksellers. Among the many writers who have called Graywolf home are Tess Gallagher, John Haines, Jane Kenyon, and Brenda Euland (whose book *If You Want to Write* remains the company's bestseller at over 100,000 copies).

Since 1984, Graywolf has been a nonprofit operation. The company annually receives a generous $30,000 grant from the NEA and additional funding from the Minnesota State Arts Board, United Arts, and other Minnesota foundations.

But nonprofit doesn't mean the press is isolated from the concerns of the marketplace. Like other small presses, Graywolf must deal with issues such as rising paper costs and increasing return rates from booksellers wanting a more immediate return on their investments. "Because the big houses are searching for instant bestsellers, we're taking on more and more books that were submitted to and rejected by major publishers," says McCrae. "That's what we're here for, to try and catch these books that otherwise would be neglected and bring them into print."

Many writers turn to small presses because they offer a closer writer-press relationship and this in turn benefits both. "We often now have authors who had one book published by a mainstream press and can't get the kind of individual attention from them that we can offer," McCrae says . "We're the door that opens when other doors close. Because of that, the quality of our list improves."

Since the publishing world moves much quicker than it used to, McCrae stresses the importance of targeting your submissions. "The best thing to do is to walk into a bookstore and find out which imprints publish books that are like what you've written," she says. "If you see one of the big names on the spine, that's where you belong. If you see a small press on the spine, try them."

An inquisitive mind doesn't hurt either. "If you get an offer from a publisher, ask for a list of titles that company has produced. If you're approached by an agent, find out what authors he represents. Ask questions of whoever you approach."

McCrae also recommends that aspiring writers enroll in a creative writing program. "Some of these creative writing programs are quite a good resource in terms of getting your work criticized by a group of your peers," she says. "They're also helpful just in getting good contacts."

But for Graywolf Press, the only real measurement that matters in the end is quality. "We're looking for a distinct voice and a distinct imagination," says McCraw. "Be bold in the writing. Follow your heart."

—Dave Edelman

Terms: Must return advance if book is not completed or is unacceptable. *"We plan to subsidy publish only those works that meet our standards for approval.* No more than 1 or 2 a year. Payment for publication is based on individual arrangement with author." Book catalog free on request.

Advice: "Write what you know about. No one else can know and feel what it is like to be black in America better than one who has experienced our dichotomy on race." Would like to see new ideas with broad appeal. "First novels must contain previously unexplored areas on the black experience in America. We regard the author/editor relationship as open, one of mutual respect. Editor has final decision, but listens to author's views."

‡HOLLOW EARTH PUBLISHING, (II), P.O. Box 1355, Boston MA 02205-1355. Phone/fax: (603)433-8735. Publisher: Helian Grimes. Estab. 1983. "Small independent publisher." Publishes hardcover and paperback originals and reprints. Books: acid-free paper; offset printing; Smythe binding.

Needs: Comics/graphic novels, fantasy (sword and sorcery), feminist, gay, lesbian, literary, New Age/mystic/spiritual, translations. Looking for "computers, Internet, Norse mythology, magic." Publishes various computer application series.

How to Contact: Does not accept unsolicited mss. Query letter only first. Should include estimated word count, 1-2 page bio, list of publishing credits. Send SASE for reply, return of ms or send disposable copy of ms. Agented fiction 90%. Reports in 2 months. Accepts disk submissions.

Terms: Pays in royalties. Sends galleys to author. Publishes ms as soon as possible after acceptance.

Advice: Looking for "less fiction, more computer information."

*HOMESTEAD PUBLISHING, (I, II), Box 227, Moose WY 83012. (307)733-6248. Editor: Carl Schreier. Estab. 1980. Midsize firm. Publishes hardcover and paperback originals and reprints. Books: natural stock to enamel paper; web, sheet-feed printing; perfect or Smythe-sewn binding; b&w or color illustrations; average print order: 10,000; first novel print order: 2,000-5,000. Plans 3-4 first novels this year. Averages 16-20 total titles; 1-2 fiction titles each year. Sometimes critiques rejected ms.

Needs: Murder mystery, literary, preschool/picture book, short story collection, western, young adult/teen (10-18 years, historical). Looking for "good quality, well written and contemporary" fiction. Recently published *A Grizzly Death in Yellowstone*, by Cal Glover; and *Never too Late for Love*, by Warren Adler.

How to Contact: Accepts unsolicited mss. Query first. SASE. Reports in 1 month. Sends galleys to author. Simultaneous submissions OK.

Terms: Pays royalties of 6% minimum; 10% maximum. Provides 6 author's copies. *Subsidy publishes "occasionally, depending on project."*

‡*HUNTINGTON HOUSE PUBLISHERS, (II), Prescott Press, P.O. Box 53788, Lafayette LA 70505. (318)237-7049. Editor-in-Chief: Mark Anthony. "Midsize independent publisher." Publishes hardcover and paperback originals. Books: average print order: 3,000-15,000; first novel print order: 3,000-15,000. Averages 30-35 total titles.

Needs: Childrens/juvenile (adventure, historical), family saga, historical (general), literary, mainstream/contemporary, religious/inspirational (general, children's religious), young adult/teen.

How to Contact: Accepts unsolicited mss. Query with outline/synopsis. Should include estimated word count, 1-2 page bio, list of publishing credits. SASE for reply. Reports in 6-8 weeks. Simultaneous submissions OK.

Terms: Pays royalties. Subsidy publishes. Sends galleys to author. Publishes ms 6 months after acceptance. Writer's guidelines free.

Advice: "We will always consider fiction for publication, but choose a limited amount depending on its marketability for us. Our market is geared more toward nonfiction (religious, political, philosophical, academic). Novels that are related to current events or have a political and/or religious nature will be considered more seriously."

INVERTED-A, INC., (II), 401 Forrest Hill, Grand Prairie TX 75052. (214)264-0066. Editors: Amnon and Aya Katz. Estab. 1977. A small press which evolved from publishing technical manuals for other products. "Publishing is a small part of our business." Publishes paperback originals. Books: bond paper; offset printing; illustrations; average print order: 250; first novel print order: 250. Publishes 1 title a year, "in recent years mostly poetry; fiction is now about every other year." Also publishes a periodical *Inverted-A, Horn*, which appears irregularly and is open to very short fiction as well as excerpts from unpublished longer fiction.
Needs: "We are interested in justice, freedom and honor approached from a positive and romantic perspective." Published *Damned in Hell*, by A.A. Wilson (novella); *Inverted Blake* (collection); *Inverted Blake #2* (collection); *Undimmed by Tears* (collection); and *Tested Positive*, by John D. Collins.
How to Contact: Submit query with sample. SASE. Reports in 6 weeks on queries; 3 months on mss. Simultaneous submissions OK. Accepts electronic submissions via modem or ASCII file on a pc MS-DOS diskette. Electronic submission mandatory for final ms of accepted work.
Terms: "We do not pay except for author's copies." Sends galleys to author. For current list send SASE.
Advice: "Our volume is very small. You must hit home with subject and execution that are exceptional. We do not care about your credentials. We judge only by what we read. Study a sample and learn about us before you submit."

♣JESPERSON PRESS LTD., (I), 39 James Lane, St. John's, Newfoundland A1E 3H3 Canada. (709)753-0633. Trade Editor: John Symonds. Midsize independent publisher. Publishes hardcover and paperback originals. Averages 7-10 total titles, 1-2 fiction titles each year. Sometimes comments on rejected ms.
Needs: Adventure, fantasy, humor/satire, juvenile (5-9 yrs. including: animal, contemporary, easy-to-read, fantasy, historical, sports, spy/adventure). Published *Daddy's Back*, by Barbara Ann Lane; *Fables, Fairies & Folklore of Newfoundland*, by Miké McCarthy and Alice Lannon; and *Justice for Julie*, by Barbara Ann Lane. Published new writers within the last year.
How to Contact: Accepts unsolicited mss. Submit complete ms with cover letter. SASE. Reports in 3 months on mss.
Terms: Pays negotiable royalties. Sends galleys to author. Book catalog free.

BOB JONES UNIVERSITY PRESS, (I, II), Greenville SC 29614. (803)242-5100, ext. 4315. Fax: (803)370-1800, ext. 4357. Acquisitions Editor: Mrs. Gloria Repp. Estab. 1974. "Small independent publisher." Publishes paperback originals and reprints. Books: 50 lb. white paper; Webb lithography printing; perfect-bound binding; average print order: 5,000; first novel print order: 5,000. Published new writers within the last year. Plans 3 first novels this year. Averages 12 total titles, 10 fiction titles each year. Sometimes comments on rejected ms.
Needs: Children's/juvenile (adventure, animal, easy-to-read, historical, mystery, series, sports), young adults (adventure, historical, mystery/suspense, series, sports, western). Published *Mice of the Herringbone*, by Tim Davis (animal fantasy easy-reader); *Mystery of Pelican Cove*, by Milly Howard (adventure ages 7-9); and *Mountain Born*, by Elizabeth Yates (historical fiction ages 9-12).
How to Contact: Accepts unsolicited mss. Query with outline and 5 sample chapters. Submit complete ms with cover letter. Include estimated word count, short bio, Social Security number and list of publishing credits. Send SASE for reply, return of ms or send a disposable copy of ms. Reports in 3 weeks on queries; 6 weeks on mss. Simultaneous and disk submissions (IBM compatible preferred) OK.
Terms: "Pay flat fee for all rights plus complimentary copies." Sends galleys to author. Publishes ms 12-18 months after acceptance. Writer's guidelines and book catalog free.
Advice: Needs "more upper-elementary adventure/mystery or a good series. Fewer picture books. Fewer didactic stories. Read guidelines carefully. Send SASE if you wish to have ms returned."

‡KAR-BEN COPIES INC., (IV), 6800 Tildenwood Lane, Rockville MD 20852. (800)452-7236. Executive Editor: Madeline Wikler. Estab. 1975. "Publisher of books and tapes on Jewish themes for young children." Publishes hardcover and paperback originals. Books: 100 lb. coated paper; offset printing; Smythe/perfect binding; full color illustrations; average print order: 10,000. Published new writers within the last year. Plans 1-2 first novels this year (picture books only). Averages 5-6 total titles, 4-5 fiction titles each year.
   ● Kar-Ben Copies, Inc. has received honors from the National Jewish Book Awards.
Needs: Childrens/juvenile (easy-to-read, preschool/picture book), ethnic/multicultural (Jewish). Recently published *Sammy Spider's First Passover*, by Sylvia Russ (holiday fiction); and *Northern Lights—A Hanukkah Story*, by Diana Conway (holiday fiction).
How to Contact: Accepts unsolicited mss with SASE only. Submit complete ms with cover letter. SASE for reply. Reports in 4-6 weeks. Simultaneous submissions OK.

Terms: Pays royalties of 5-8%; offers negotiable advance. Sends galleys to author. Publishes ms 6-12 months after acceptance. Writer's guidelines for 9×12 SAE and 2 first-class stamps. Book catalog for 9×12 SAE and 2 first-class stamps.

‡*■**LAREDO PUBLISHING CO., (I, IV),** 8907 Wilshire Blvd., Beverly Hills CA 90211. (310)358-5288. Fax: (310)358-5282. President: S. Laredo. "Book packager, juvenile Spanish and bilingual publisher." Publishes hardcover originals. Books: 70 lb. matte paper; offset printing; hard binding; 4-color illustrations; average print order: 2,000. Published new writers within the last year. Plans 3 first novels this year. Averages 15-20 total titles. Sometimes critiques or comments on rejected ms.
Needs: Adventure, childrens/juvenile (adventure, animal, easy-to-read, fantasy, mystery, preschool/picture book). Plans anthology. Recently published *El Circo*, by Alma Flor Ada; *Pin Pin Sarabin*; and *Barriletes*. Publishes Cuentos Con Alma series.
How to Contact: Accepts unsolicited mss. Submit complete ms with cover letter. Send SASE for reply, return of ms or send a disposable copy of ms. Reports in 5 weeks on queries. Simultaneous submissions OK.
Terms: Pays royalties of 6-10%; offers negotiable advance. Provides 100-500 author's copies. Subsidy publishes 40%. Sends galleys to author. Publishes ms 6 weeks after acceptance.

LEE & LOW BOOKS, (I, II), 95 Madison Ave., 14th Floor, New York NY 10016. (212)779-4400. Fax: (212)683-1894. Editor-in-Chief: Elizabeth Szabla. Estab. 1991. "Independent multicultural children's book publisher." Publishes hardcover originals. Averages 6 total titles, 4-6 fiction titles each year. Sometimes comments on rejected mss.
Needs: Children's/juvenile (historical, multicultural, preschool/picture book). Published *Abuela's Weave*, by Omar Castañeda (hardcover picture book); *Baseball Saved Us*, by Ken Mochizuki (hardcover picture book); and *Zora Hurston and the Chinaberry Tree*, by William Miller (hardcover picture book).
How to Contact: Accepts unsolicited mss. Send complete ms with cover letter or through an agent. Send SASE for reply, return of ms or send a disposable ms. Agented fiction 30%. Reports in 3-5 weeks on queries; 1-3 months on mss. Simultaneous submissions OK.
Terms: Pays royalties. Offers advance. Sends galleys to author. Publishes ms 18 months after acceptance. Writer's guidelines for #10 SASE. Book catalog for SASE with 78¢ postage.
Advice: "Writers should familiarize themselves with the styles and formats of recently published children's books. Lee & Low Books is a multicultural children's book publisher. We would like to see more contemporary stories set in the U.S. Animal stories and folktales are discouraged."

‡❖**LEMEAC EDITEUR INC., (I, II),** 1124 Marie Anne Est, Montreal, Québec H2J 2B7 Canada. (514)524-5558. Fax: (514)524-3145. Directeur Litteraire: Pierre Filion. Estab. 1957. Publishes paperback originals. Books: offset #2 paper; offset printing; allemand binding; color/cover illustration; average print order: 1,000; first novel print order: 1,000. Published new writers within the last year. Plans 1 first novel this year. Averages 25 total titles, 20 fiction titles each year. Often critiques or comments on rejected ms.
Needs: Literary, romance (contemporary, futuristic/time travel, historical), short story collections, translations. Plans anthology on "désires et réalités." Writers submit to editor. Recently published *Un Ange Cornu . . .*, by Michele Tremblay (novel); *Rendez-moi Ma Mére*, by Daniel Gagnon (novel); and *La Vievolte*, by Nancy Huston (novel). Publishes L'Oiseau de feu series.
How to Contact: Accepts unsolicited mss. Submit complete ms with cover letter. Send a disposable copy of ms. Agented fiction 10%. Reports in 3 months on queries; 6 months on mss. No simultaneous submissions.
Terms: Pays royalties of 10%. Sends galleys to author. Publishes ms 1-2 years after acceptance.

❖**LESTER PUBLISHING LIMITED, (II),** 56 The Esplanade, 507A, Toronto, Ontario M5E 1A7 Canada. (416)362-1032. Fax: (416)362-1647. Editor: Ann Schoen. Estab. 1991. Small independent publisher. Publishes hardcover and paperback originals. Published new writers within the last year. Plans 2 first novels this year. Averages 20 total titles, 3-5 fiction titles each year. Sometimes comments on rejected mss.
• Lester Publishing published *Hero of Lesser Causes* which received the Governor General's Award for Text in Children's Literature, Best Book Award from *School Library Journal* and the 10DE Violet Downey Book Award.
Needs: Children's/juvenile (preschool/picture book), historical (general), humor/satire, literary, mainstream/contemporary, short story collections, young adult/teen (adventure, historical, mystery/suspense, problem novels). No romance or science fiction. Recently published *A Gift of Rags*, by Abraham Boyarsky; *Adam and Eve*, by Julie Johnston.

 Listings marked with a solid box are book packagers. See the introduction for more information.

How to Contact: Accepts unsolicited mss. Submit outline/synopsis and 2-3 sample chapters. Should include estimated word count and cover letter. Send SASE (or IRC) for reply, return of ms or send a disposable copy of the ms. Agented fiction 60-75%. Reports in 1 month on queries; 6 months on manuscripts.

Terms: Pays royalties, negotiable advance and 6-10 author's copies. Sends galleys to author. Publishes ms 6-18 months after acceptance. Writer's guidelines and catalog free.

Advice: "Fiction is a risky venture, especially in Canada. We publish very little and all in trade paperback (with the exception of young adult fiction, which we do as hardcover originals). We receive hundreds of manuscripts a year. I would simply advise writers to be patient; we will get to their work eventually and we do read everything that is submitted to us."

*LIBRA PUBLISHERS, INC., (II), 3089C Clairemont Dr., Suite 383, San Diego CA 92117. (619)571-1414. President: William Kroll. Estab. 1960. Small independent publisher. Hardcover and paperback originals. Books: 60 lb. offset paper; offset printing; hardcover—Smyth-sewn binding; paperback—perfect binding; illustrations occasionally; average print order 3,000; first novel print order 1,000. Plans to publish 3 first novels this year. Averages approximately 15 total titles, 3-4 fiction titles each year.

Needs: "We consider all categories." Published *All God's Children*, by Alex LaPerchia (inspirational); *Seed of the Divine Fruit*, by Enrico Rinaldi (multi-generational about founding of Atlantic City); and *Caveat Emptor*, by William Attias (racist takeover of a city).

How to Contact: Accepts unsolicited mss. Send complete ms with cover letter. SASE. Reports on queries in 1 week; on mss in 2-3 weeks. Simultaneous submissions OK.

Terms: Pays 10-40% royalties. Sends galleys to author. Publishes ms an average of 6-12 months after acceptance. Book catalog for SAE with 5 first-class stamps.

Advice: "Libra publishes nonfiction books in all fields, specializing in the behavioral sciences. We also publish two professional journals: *Adolescence* and *Family Therapy*. We have published fiction on a royalty basis but because of the difficulty in marketing works by unknown writers, we are not optimistic about the chances of offering a standard contract. However, we shall continue to consider fiction in the hope of publishing on a standard basis books that we like and believe have good marketing potential. In addition, our procedure is as follows: Manuscripts we do not consider publishable are returned to the author. When we receive manuscripts which we feel are publishable but are uncertain of the marketability, we suggest that the author continue to try other houses. If they have already done so and are interested in self-publishing, we offer two types of services: (1) we provide editing, proofreading, book and cover design, copyrighting and production of the book; copies are then shipped to the author. (2) We provide these services plus suggestions for promotion and distribution. In all cases, the problems and risks are spelled out."

LINCOLN SPRINGS PRESS, (II), 32 Oak Place, Hawthorne NJ 07506. Editor: M. Gabrielle. Estab. 1987. Small, independent press. Publishes poetry, fiction, photography, high quality. Publishes paperback originals. Books: 65 lb paper; offset printing; perfect binding; average print order: 1,000. "Prefers short stories, but will publish first novels if quality high enough." Averages 4 total titles, 2 fiction titles each year.

Needs: Contemporary, ethnic, experimental, feminist, historical, literary, short story collections. No "romance, Janet Dailey variety." Published *Maybe It's My Heart*, by Abigail Stone (novel); and *Subway Home*, by Justin Vitiello.

How to Contact: Accepts unsolicited mss. Query first with 1 sample chapter. SASE. Reports in 2 weeks-3 months. Simultaneous submissions OK.

Terms: Authors receive royalties of 5% minimum; 15% maximum "after all costs are met." Provides 10 author's copies. Sends galleys to author.

‡LIVINGSTON PRESS, (II), Station 22, University of Alabama, Livingston AL 35470. Imprint: Swallows Tale Press. Director: Joe Taylor. Estab. 1982. "Literary press." Publishes hardcover and paperback originals. Books: acid-free paper; offset printing; perfect binding; average print order: 1,500; first novel print order: 1,000. Published new writers within the last year. Plans 2 first novels this year. Averages 4-6 total titles, 5 fiction titles each year. Sometimes critiques or comments on rejected ms.

Needs: Literary, short story collections. No genre. Recently published *Sideshows*, by B.K. Smith; *A Bad Piece of Luck*, by Tom Abrams; and *Alabama Bound*, by Colquitt.

How to Contact: Does not accept unsolicited mss. Query first. Should include bio, list of publishing credits. Send SASE for reply, return of ms or send a disposable copy of ms. Agented fiction 10%. Reports in 3 weeks on queries; 6 months on mss. Simultaneous submissions OK.

Terms: Pays royalties of 6% minimum; 7½% maximum. Provides 12 author's copies. Sends galleys to author. Publishes ms 1-2 years after acceptance. Book catalog free.

‡LOLLIPOP POWER BOOKS, (II), 120 Morris St., Durham NC 27701. (919)560-2738. Editor: Ruth A. Smullin. Estab. 1970. "Children's imprint of the Carolina Wren Press, a small, nonprofit press which publishes non-sexist, multi-racial picture books." Publishes paperback originals. Averages 1 title (fiction) each year. Average first book run 3,000 copies.

Needs: Juvenile. "Picture books only. Our current publishing priorities are: books with African American, Hispanic/Latino or Native American characters; bilingual (English/Spanish) books. Recently published *Maria*

Teresa, by Mary Atkinson (bilingual); *In Christina's Toolbox*, by Diane Homan; and *Grownups Cry Too*, by Nancy Hazen (bilingual).
How to Contact: Send complete manuscript with SASE. Do not send illustrations. Reports in 3 months on mss. Simultaneous submissions OK. Publishes ms from 1-2 years after acceptance. Guidelines for SASE.
Terms: Pays royalties of 10%.
Advice: "Lollipop Power Books must be well-written stories that will appeal to children. We are not interested in preachy tales where 'message' overpowers plot and character. We are looking for good stories told from a child's point of view. Our books present a child's perspective and feelings honestly and without condescension."

HENDRICK LONG PUBLISHING CO., (II, IV), Box 25123, Dallas TX 75225. (214)358-4677. Vice President: Joann Long. Estab. 1969. Independent publisher focusing on Texas and Southwest material geared primarily to a young audience. (K through high school). Publishes hardcover and paperback originals and hardcover reprints. Books: average print order: 3,000. Published new writers within the last year. Averages 8 total titles, 4 fiction titles each year. Sometimes comments on rejected ms.
Needs: Texas themes: historical, regional, for juvenile, young adult, teen. "No material not suitable for junior high/high school audience." Recently published *Baxter Badgen's Home*, by Doris McClellan; *I Love You, Daisy Phew*, by Ruby C. Tolliver; and *New Medicine*, by Jeanne Williams (reprint).
How to Contact: Query first or submit outline/synopsis and sample chapters (at least 2—no more than 3). SASE. Reports in 2 weeks on queries; 2 months on ms.
Terms: Offers advance. Sends galleys to author. Publishes ms 18 months after acceptance. Writer's guidelines for SASE. Book catalog for $1.

LONGSTREET PRESS, (III), 2140 Newmarket Pkwy., Suite 118, Marietta GA 30067. (404)980-1488. Senior Editor: John Yow. Editor: Suzanne Comer Bell. Estab. 1988. Publishes hardcover and paperback originals. Published new writers within the last year. Averages 40-45 total titles, 2-3 fiction titles each year. Sometimes comments on rejected ms.
• Longstreet Press has become known for publishing literary and humorous work, as well as some Southern fiction (but not exclusively, says the editor.)
Needs: Literary, humorous, mainstream. "Quality fiction." No "genre fiction, highly experimental work, ya, juvenile." Recently published *Lizzie*, by Dorothy Shawhan; and *The Heat of the Sun*, by Louis D. Rubin, Jr.
How to Contact: Agented or solicited mss only. Submit outline/synopsis and sample chapters. SASE. Reports on queries in 6 weeks; on mss in 3 months. Simultaneous submissions OK (if told).
Terms: Pays in royalties; advance is negotiable; provides author's copies. Sends galleys to author. Publishes ms 6-12 months after acceptance. Writer's guidelines for #10 SASE. Book catalog for 9 × 12 envelope with 4 first-class stamps.
Advice: "Only a few slots for fiction here. We seek novels with a good story, good characters and superb writing. Send samples of writing rather than plot summaries. Need agent or good credentials as previously published author."

LOONFEATHER PRESS, (II), P.O. Box 1212, Bemidji MN 56601. (218)751-4869. Editor/Publisher: Betty Rossi. Estab. 1979. "One-person staff with working board, also publish a literary magazine." Publishes paperback originals. Books: text paper; offset printing; perfect binding; illustrations; average print order: 500-3,000. Plans are for 2 fiction and 1 poetry title this year. Often comments on rejected ms.
• Loonfeather Press also publishes *Loonfeather* listed in the Literary/Small Circulation section.
Needs: Ethnic/multicultural (Ojibwa, Native American), regional (upper midwest), short story collections. No science fiction, western, romance. Publishes anthology. Writers may submit to anthology editor.
How to Contact: Accepts unsolicited mss. Query first. Include estimated word count and bio (maximum 1 page), Social Security number, list of publishing credits with submission. Send SASE for reply, return of ms or send a disposable copy of ms. Reports in 3 weeks on queries; 3 months on mss. No simultaneous submissions.
Terms: Pays royalties of 10%. Advance is negotiable. Provides 15 author's copies. Sends galleys to author. Time between acceptance of the ms and publication is dependent on funding. Writer's guidelines free for #10 SASE. Book catalog for #10 SASE.
Advice: "We have just started publishing and have done some anthologies which include fiction, and some poetry and creative nonfiction. As publisher of a literary magazine, we see a lot of bad fiction. Our publishing plans for the future are to do one anthology and one fiction (novel or short story collection) every two years."

LUCKY HEART BOOKS, (I), Subsidiary of Salt Lick Press, Salt Lick Foundation, Inc., 3530 SE Madison St., Portland OR 97214-4255. (503)249-1014. Editor/Publisher: James Haining. Estab. 1969. Small press with significant work reviews in several national publications. Publishes paperback originals and reprints. Books: offset/bond paper; offset printing; hand-sewn or perfect-bound; illustrations; average print order: 500; first novel print order: 500. Sometimes comments on rejected ms.

Needs: Open to all fiction categories. Recently published *Catch My Breath*, by Michael Lally.
How to Contact: Accepts unsolicited mss. SASE. Agented fiction 1%. Reports in 2-16 weeks on mss.
Terms: Pays 10 author's copies. Sends galleys to author.
Advice: "Follow your heart. Use the head, but follow the heart."

MACMURRAY & BECK, INC., (II), 400 W. Hopkins, #5, Aspen CO 81611. (970)925-5284. Fax: (970)925-6198. Fiction Editor: Greg Michalson. Estab. 1990. Publishes hardcover and paperback originals. Books: average print order: 6,000; first novel print order: 6,000. Published new writers within the last year. Plans 3-4 novels this year. Averages 8 total titles, 2-3 fiction titles each year. Sometimes critiques or comments on rejected ms.
Needs: Contemporary, literary, western (urban west, western writers geog.). Looking for "eccentric, reflective fiction with high literary quality and commercial potential. No plot-driven, traditional, frontier western or mainstream." Recently published *Rocket City*, by Cathryn Alpert (literary); *Stygo*, by Laura Hendrie (literary); and *Summer of Rescue*, by Barbara Nelson (literary).
How to Contact: Accepts unsolicited mss. Query with outline/synopsis and 3 sample chapters. Include 1-page bio, list of publishing credits, any writing awards or grants. SASE for reply. Agented fiction 75%. Reports in 1 month on queries; 2 months on mss. Simultaneous submissions OK.
Terms: Pays royalties; offers negotiable advance. Sends galleys to author (usually at author's request). Book catalog free.
Advice: "We publish a very limited number of novels each year and base our selection on literary quality first. Submit a concise, saleable proposal. Tell us why we should publish the book, not just what it is about."

MADWOMAN PRESS, (I, IV), P.O. Box 690, Northboro MA 01532. (508)393-3447. Editor/Publisher: Diane Benison. Estab. 1991. Independent small press publishing lesbian fiction. Publishes paperback originals. Books: perfect binding; average print order: 4,000-6,000. Averages 2-4 total titles, 2 fiction titles each year. Sometimes comments on rejected ms.
   • Madwoman Press published *Thin Fire* and *Lesbians in the Military Speak Out*, which were nominated for American Library Association Gay and Lesbian Book awards. This press is becoming known for its lesbian mysteries.
Needs: "All must have lesbian themes: adventure, erotica, ethnic, feminist, mystery/suspense (amateur sleuth, police procedure, private eye), romance, science fiction (hard science, soft sociological), thriller/espionage, western. Especially looking for lesbian detective stories." No horror. No gratuitous violence. Recently published *Fertile Betrayal*, by Becky Bohan; and *Fool Me Once*, by Katherine Kreuter.
How to Contact: Query first. Include brief statement of name, address, phone, previous publication and a 1-2 page precis of the plot. SASE. Reports in 2 months on queries; 3 months on solicited mss. Simultaneous submissions OK. E-mail address: 76620.460@compuserve.com.
Terms: Pays royalties of 8-15% "after recovery of publications costs." Provides 20 author's copies. Sends galleys to author. Publishes ms 1-2 years after acceptance. Writer's guidelines for #10 SASE.
Advice: "Your query letter will often cause your manuscript to be rejected before it's even read. Write clearly, succinctly, tell the publisher how the book ends and save the hype for the jacket copy. We're looking to form long-term relationships with writers, so talented first novelists are ideal for us. We want to publish an author regularly over the years, build an audience for her and keep her in print. We publish books by, for and about lesbians, books that are affirming for lesbian readers and authors."

MAGE PUBLISHERS, (IV), 1032 29th St. NW, Washington DC 20007. (202)342-1642. Editorial Contact: Amin Sepehri. Estab. 1985. "Small independent publisher." Publishes hardcover originals. Averages 4 total titles, 1 fiction title each year.
Needs: "We publish *mainly* books on Iran and translations of Iranian fiction writers." Ethnic (Iran) fiction. Recently published *Sutra & Other Stories*, by Simin Daneshvar and *King of the Benighted*, by Manvchehr Irani.
How to Contact: Query first. SASE. Reports in 3 months on queries. Simultaneous submissions OK. E-mail address: mage1@access.digex.net.
Terms: Pays royalties. Publishes ms 6-9 months after acceptance. Writer's guidelines for SASE. Book catalog free.
Advice: "If it isn't related to Persia/Iran, forget it!"

Market conditions are constantly changing! If you're still using this book and it is 1997 or later, buy the newest edition of Novel & Short Story Writer's Market *at your favorite bookstore or order from* Writer's Digest Books.

*MAYHAVEN PUBLISHING, (I, II), P.O. Box 557, Mahomet IL 61853. (217)586-4493. Fax: (217)586-6330. Publisher: Doris R. Wenzel. "Fulltime trade publisher." Hardcover and paperback originals and reprints. Books: offset printing; illustrations; average print order: 2,000-5,000; first novel print order: 2,000. Plans 4-6 first novels this year. Averages 5-12 total titles. Sometimes comments on rejected ms; *$100 charge for critiques.*
Needs: Children's/juvenile (all types), historical (general), mystery/suspense, young adult. Recently published *Yats in Movieland*, by Michael Russ.
How to Contact: Accepts unsolicited mss. Submit outline/synopsis and 3 sample chapters. Include ½-page bio and listing of publishing credits. Send SASE for reply, return of ms or send a disposable copy of ms. Reports in 3 months. No simultaneous submissions.
Terms: Pays royalties of 6-10%; offers $100 advance; provides 10 author's copies. Also individual arrangement with author depending on the book. "Because of many requests, we will be doing a few subsidy books/co-operative books under alternate imprint, Wild Rose Publishing. Authors will pay for production but receive expanded royalties on first 400-600 books sold." Sends galleys to author. Publishes ms 6 months-2 years after acceptance. Book catalogs are free.

♣THE MERCURY PRESS, (IV), 137 Birmingham St., Stratford, Ontario N5A 2T1 Canada. Editor: Beverley Daurio. Estab. 1978. "Literary publisher." Publishes paperback originals. Books: offset printing; perfect binding; average print order: 1,500; first novel print order: 1,000. Published new writers within the last year. Averages 10 total titles, 5 fiction titles each year.
● Books published by The Mercury Press have received awards for design and content, including awards from The Crime Writers of Canada and the Commonwealth Writers Prize.
Needs: Regional (Canadian only). Looking for "murder mysteries set in Canada." Publishes Midnight Originals (murder mysteries).
How to Contact: Accepts unsolicited mss if SASE is included. Submit complete ms with cover letter. Include estimated word count, bio (1 page) and list of publishing credits. SASE for return of ms. Agented fiction 1%. Reports in 2-4 months on mss. No simultaneous submissions.
Terms: Pays royalties of 10%. Sends galleys to author. Publishes ms 1 year after acceptance. Book catalog for SASE.
Advice: "Please have a look at our books or a catalog before submitting. Please note we only publish work by Canadians."

*MEY-HOUSE BOOKS, (II), Box 794, Stroudsburg PA 18360. (717)646-9556. Editorial contact: Ted Meyer. Estab. 1983. One-person, part-time operation with plans for at least 2 novels shortly. Publishes hardcover and paperback originals. Averages 1 title each year. Occasionally critiques or comments on rejected ms, "cost varies."
Needs: Adventure, contemporary, ethnic, science fiction. "No gay, erotic or lesbian fiction."
How to Contact: Accepts unsolicited mss. Query first. SASE. Reports in 1 month on queries. Simultaneous submissions OK.
Terms: Payment "varies." Sends galleys to author. *Subsidy publishes "on an individual basis."*

MID-LIST PRESS, (I), Jackson, Hart & Leslie, Inc., 4324-12th Ave. S., Minneapolis MN 55407-3218. (612)822-3733. Associate Publisher: Marianne Nora. Senior Editor: Lane Stiles. Estab. 1989. Nonprofit literary small press. Publishes hardcover originals and paperback originals and hardcover reprints. Books: acid-free paper; offset printing; perfect or Smyth-sewn binding; average print order: 2,000. Plans 1 first novel this year. Averages 4-5 total titles, 2-3 fiction titles each year. Rarely comments on rejected ms.
● The publisher's philosophy is to nurture "mid-list" titles—books of literary merit that may not fit "promotional pigeonholes."
Needs: General fiction. No children's/juvenile, romance, young adult, religious. Recently published *16 Bananas*, by Hugh Gross; *Jump*, by John Prendergast; and *The Hemingway Sabbatical*, by Allan Conan (1994 First Series Award for the Novel winner). Publishes First Series Award for the Novel and First Series Award for Short Fiction.
How to Contact: Accepts unsolicited mss. Query first for guidelines. Include #10 SASE. Send SASE for reply, return of ms or send a disposable copy of the ms. Agented fiction less than 10%. Reports in 1-3 weeks on queries; 1-3 months on mss. Simultaneous submissions OK.
Terms: Pays royalty of 40% minimum; 50% maximum of profits. Average advance: $1,000. Sends galleys to author. Publishes ms 6-12 months after acceptance. Writer's guidelines for #10 SASE.
Advice: "Take the time to read some of the books the publisher you're submitting to has put out. And remember that first impressions are very important. If a query, cover letter, or first page is sloppily or ineptly written, an editor has little hope for the manuscript as a whole."

MILKWEED EDITIONS, 430 First Ave. N., Suite 400, Minneapolis MN 55401. (612)332-3192. Publisher: Emilie Buchwald. Estab. 1984. Nonprofit publisher with the intention of transforming society through literature. Publishes hardcover and paperback originals. Books: book text quality—acid-free paper; offset printing;

INSIDER VIEWPOINT

With Small Presses, Every Book is Frontlist

© Photo by Marianne Nora

Lane Stiles

Mid-List Press was founded in 1989 with a mission. A small group of established publishing professionals, including editor Lane Stiles, believed that the publishing industry's focus on blockbuster books and books by proven authors (those they consider "frontlist" titles) had led to an exclusion of quality fiction from publication. Many of the books excluded were considered "midlist" titles—books by newer authors or those with limited audiences such as literary and experimental novels. Because midlist titles often become perennial backlist titles (books that sell in small, but steady, quantities each year), or even the classics of the future, authors and works of great and long-lasting merit were being lost forever. Stiles speaks with unabashed pride when he says, "Our mission is to preserve the midlist and to locate and nurture emerging writers."

Indeed, for most authors, says Stiles, "small presses are really the way to go. There is something for everyone in the small press world, and about 75 percent of all books published come from small presses." Small presses generally do not require the work of an agent, either; the lack of the right agent can be a formidable barrier to the emerging writer interested in large, commercial publishers.

If authors want to be involved in the production of their manuscripts, they had best seek out a small press, says Stiles. He develops a close relationship with his authors and their work. An editor at Mid-List handles every editorial task, from acceptance of a manuscript to editing the dust jacket copy. The author is a full participant at every step along the way.

"The great thing is, at a small press you see the publication process from beginning to end. It is hands-on; you're intimately involved in it. There's tremendous satisfaction after the one- or two- or even three-year process, of having this artifact, this complete book, come into your hands."

Stiles speaks of Mid-List Press's books with a touch of wonder. Each book is given the attention and care it earned upon its acceptance for publication. Every book, in other words, is frontlist. Mid-List's commitment to their books is as lasting as it is strong: "We won't take a book out of print."

Mid-List is currently publishing five books a year, and seeks to add one additional book each year. The emphasis in their selection of books for publication is their "First Series" awards, one award each for a first novel, a first collection of poetry, and (new in 1995) a first collection of short fiction. It is an extraordinarily competitive process—there were about 1,000 submissions in the most recent First Novel competition.

Stiles says Mid-List Press strives to maintain open and democratic submission processes. At Mid-List, synopses and proposals are not required, simultaneous submissions are okay, and an agent is wholly unnecessary. This is the type of freedom small presses can offer to new authors.

Like many small presses, Mid-List is nonprofit, having recently changed its status. Because Midlist has always been motivated by its mission rather than by profit, they are free to publish the books they want. "We don't have a set idea of a book we're going to choose . . . We look for just the best book we can find," says Stiles.

At Mid-List Press, the best book is by an author who has something significant to say. There is a tendency toward the more "literary" author, but the book has to be able to find its audience among the general public. For this reason, experimental or more obtuse fiction is less likely to be considered. While they don't rule out genre fiction—mystery, romance, western, etc.—"The author's going to have to do something special with it."

With a small press chances are your work will be judged by its merits rather than by its marketability or the prestige of a high-powered agent. The editors at Mid-List look for technically-adroit, well-written work. One of the most common reasons for rejection is uncontrolled language—unexplained shifts of tense or point of view, grammatical errors, and inconsistencies of character or plot. But if an author has something important to say, and says it very well, there is a good possibility the manuscript will advance a step closer to publication.

There is no such thing as the typical small press, so it is especially important for an author to examine a press closely before submitting. For example: Mid-List might shy away from experimental fiction, but other small publishers make it their specialty; and some small presses specialize in regional fiction, while Mid-List routinely considers international submissions. Stiles advises authors to read the type of books they would like to write, and see who publishes them. He urges people always to query, follow guidelines, and send a self-addressed stamped envelope (SASE).

According to Stiles, if your book finds a home with a small press it will be nurtured and even pampered. And, because a small press publishes fewer titles, yours will always be one of the most important books in the catalog. You will have the opportunity to be more closely involved in the publication of your manuscript, and you will develop a closer working relationship with your editors. In other words, books considered midlist by large houses, will be treated as frontlist titles in the small press.

—*Greta Ode*

perfect or hardcover binding; average print order: 4,000; first novel print order depends on book. Averages 14 total titles/year. Number of fiction titles "depends on manuscripts."

● Milkweed Editions books have received numerous awards, including Finalist, *LMP* Individual Achievement Award for Editor Emilie Buchwald, awards from the American Library Association, and several Pushcarts.

Needs: For adult readers: literary fiction, nonfiction, poetry, essays; for children (ages 8-12): fiction and biographies. Translations welcome for both audiences. No legends or folktales for children. No romance, mysteries, science fiction.

How to Contact: Accepts unsolicited mss, send to the attention of Elisabeth Fitz, First Reader. Submit outline/synopsis with 2 sample chapters and SASE. Reports in 1 month on queries; 6 months on mss.

Simultaneous submissions OK. "Send for guidelines. Must enclose SASE."

Terms: Authors are paid in royalties of 7%; offers negotiable advance; 10 author's copies. Sends galleys to author. Book catalog for $1.50 postage.

Advice: "Read good contemporary literary fiction, find your own voice, and persist. Familiarize yourself with our list before submitting."

MOYER BELL LIMITED, Kymbolde Way, Wakefield RI 02879. (401)789-0074. President: Jennifer Moyer. Fiction Editor: Britt Bell. Estab. 1984. "Small publisher established to publish literature, poetry, reference and art books." Publishes hardcover and paperback originals and reprints. Books: Average print order 3,000; first novel print order: 3,000. Averages 18 total titles, 6 fiction titles each year. Sometimes comments on rejected ms.

Needs: Serious literary fiction. No genre fiction. Published *The Other Garden*, by Francis Wyndham.

How to Contact: Accepts unsolicited mss. Submit outline/synopsis and 2 sample chapters. SASE. Reports in 2 weeks on queries; 2 months on mss. Simultaneous and electronic submissions OK.

Terms: Pays royalties of 10% minimum. Average advance $1,000. Sends galleys to author. Publishes ms 9-18 months after acceptance. Book catalog free.

THE NAIAD PRESS, INC., (I, II, IV), Box 10543, Tallahassee FL 32302. (904)539-5965. Fax: (904)539-9731. Editorial Director: Barbara Grier. Estab. 1973. Books: 55 lb. offset paper; sheet-fed offset; perfect-bound; average print order: 12,000; first novel print order: 12,000. Publishes 24 total titles each year.

• The Naiad Press is one of the most successful and well-known lesbian publishers. Barbara Grier and Donna J. McBride received a Publisher's Service Award from the Lambda Literary Awards for 20 years of service and were featured speakers at the 1993 Gay Pride Rally in New York City. The publisher has also produced eight of their books on audio cassette.

Needs: Lesbian fiction, all genres. Recently published *Getting to the Point*, by Teresa Stores; *The First Time Ever; Love Stories by Naiad Press Authors*, edited by Barbara Grier and Christine Cassidy; and *Double Bluff: a Carol Ashton Mystery*, by Claire McNab.

How to Contact: Query first only. SASE. Reports in 3 weeks on queries; 3 months on mss. No simultaneous submissions.

Terms: Pays 15% royalties using a standard recovery contract. Occasionally pays 7½% royalties against cover price. "Seldom gives advances and has never seen a first novel worthy of one. Believes authors are investments in their own and the company's future—that the best author is the author who produces a book every 12-18 months forever and knows that there is a *home* for that book." Publishes ms 1-2 years after acceptance. Book catalog for legal-sized SASE.

Advice: "We publish lesbian fiction primarily and prefer honest work (i.e., positive, upbeat lesbian characters). Lesbian content must be accurate . . . a lot of earlier lesbian novels were less than honest. No breast beating or complaining. Our fiction titles are becoming increasingly *genre* fiction, which we encourage. Original fiction in paperback is our main field, and its popularity increases. We publish books BY, FOR AND ABOUT lesbians. We are not interested in books that are unrealistic. You know and we know what the real world of lesbian interest is like. Don't even try to fool us. Short, well written books do best. Authors who want to succeed and will work to do so have the best shot."

THE NAUTICAL & AVIATION PUBLISHING CO. OF AMERICA INC., (IV), 8 W. Madison St., Baltimore MD 21201. (410)659-0220. President: Jan Snouck-Hurgronje. Estab. 1979. Small publisher interested in quality military history and literature. Publishes hardcover originals and reprints. Averages 10 total titles, 1-4 fiction titles each year. Sometimes comments on rejected mss.

Needs: Military/war (especially military history and Civil War). Looks for "novels with a strong military history orientation." Published *New Guinea*, and *Checkfire*, by VADM William P. Mack.

How to Contact: Accepts unsolicited mss. Query first or submit complete mss with cover letter. SASE necessary for return of mss. Agented fiction "miniscule." Reports on queries in 2-3 weeks; on mss in 3 weeks. Simultaneous submissions OK.

Terms: Pays royalties of 14%. Advance negotiable. After acceptance publishes ms "as quickly as possible—next season." Book catalog free on request.

Advice: Publishing more fiction. Encourages first novelists. "We're interested in good writing—first novel or last novel. Keep it historical, put characters in a historical context. Professionalism counts. Know your subject. *Convice us.*"

NEW RIVERS PRESS, 420 N. Fifth St., Suite 910, Minneapolis MN 55401. Publisher: C.W. Truesdale. Estab. 1968.

• See also the Minnesota Voices Project, sponsored by New Rivers Press, listed in the Contests and Awards section of this book. An interview with C.W. Truesdale appeared in the 1994 edition of this book.

Needs: Contemporary, literary, experimental, translations. "No popular fantasy/romance. Nothing pious, polemical (unless other very good redeeming qualities). We are interested in only quality literature and always have been (though our concentration in the past has been poetry)." Published *Out Far, in Deep*, by

Alvin Handleman (short stories); *Borrowed Voices*, by Roger Sheffer (short stories); *Suburban Metaphysics*, by Ronald J. Rindo (short stories).

How to Contact: Query. SASE. Reports in 4-6 months on queries; within 4-6 months of query approval on mss. "No multiple submissions tolerated."

Terms: Pays 100 author's copies; also pays royalties; no advance. Minnesota Voices Series pays authors $500 plus 15% royalties on list price for second and subsequent printings. Free book catalog.

Advice: "We are not really concerned with trends. We read for quality, which experience has taught can be very eclectic and can come sometimes from out of nowhere. We are interested in publishing short fiction (as well as poetry and translations) because it is and has been a great indigenous American form and is almost completely ignored by the commercial houses. Find a *real* subject, something that belongs to you and not what you think or surmise that you should be doing by current standards and fads."

NEW VICTORIA PUBLISHERS, (I), Box 27, Norwich VT 05055. (802)649-5297. Editor: Claudia Lamperti. Publishes trade paperback originals. Averages 8-10 titles/year.
  • Books published by New Victoria Publishers have been nominated for Lambda Literary Awards and the Vermont Book Publishers Special Merit Award.

Needs: Lesbian/feminist: adventure, fantasy, historical, humor, mystery (amateur sleuth), romance, science fiction (soft sociological), thriller, western. Looking for "strong feminist characters, also strong plot and action. We will consider most anything if it is well written and appeals to a lesbian/feminist audience." Publishes anthologies or special editions. Query for guidelines. Recently published *Bad Company* (6th Stoner McTavish Mystery), by Sarah Dreher; *Give My Secrets Back*, by Kate Allen; and *All The Ways Home: Parenting and Children in the Lesbian and Gay Communities* (collection of short fiction).

How to Contact: Submit outline/synopsis and sample chapters. SASE. Reports in 2 weeks on queries; 1 month on mss. E-mail address: newvic@telecomp.com.

Terms: Pays royalties of 10%.

Advice: "Be sure you fit our guidelines before sending a query. We prefer unagented work."

✦**NEWEST PUBLISHERS LTD., (IV)**, 10359 Whyte Ave., #310, Edmonton, Alberta T6E 1Z9 Canada. General Manager: Liz Grieve. Editorial Coordinator: Eva Radford. Estab. 1977. Publishes trade paperback originals. Published new writers within the last year. Averages 8 total titles, fiction and nonfiction. Rarely offers comments on rejected ms.
  • NeWest received the Writers' Guild of Alberta Award for Short Fiction in 1994 for *The Cock's Egg*, by Rosemary Nixon and the Commonwealth Writers Prize for Best First Published Book in the Caribbean and Canadian Region for *Chorus of Mushrooms*, by Hiromi Goto. The publisher is continuing its Nunatak New Fiction Series featuring first novels by western Canadian writers.

Needs: Literary. "Our press is interested in western Canadian writing." Recently published *Icefields*, by Thomas Wharton (novel); *The Cock's Egg*, by Rosemary Nixon (short story collection); and *Chorus of Mushrooms*, by Hiromi Goto (novel). Publishes the New Fiction Series.

How to Contact: Accepts unsolicited mss. Query first or submit outline/synopsis and 3 sample chapters. SASE necessary for return of manuscript. Reports in 2 months on queries; 4 months on mss.

Terms: Pays royalties of 10% minimum. Sends galleys to author. Publishes ms at least 1 year after acceptance. Book catalog for 9×12 SASE.

Advice: "We publish western Canadian writers only or books about western Canada. We are looking for excellent quality and originality."

NIGHTSHADE PRESS, (II), Ward Hill, Troy ME 04987. (207)948-3427. Contact: Carolyn Page or Roy Zarucchi. Estab. 1988. "Fulltime small press publishing literary magazine, poetry chapbooks, 1 or 2 short story collections, plus 1 or 2 nonfiction projects. per year. Short stories *only, no novels please.*" Publishes paperback originals. Books: 60 lb. paper; offset printing; saddle-stitched or perfect-bound; illustrations; average print order: 400. Published new writers within the last year. Averages 10 total titles, 1 or more fiction titles each year, plus 19th century history collection. Sometimes comments on rejected ms.
  • Nightshade Press also publishes *Potato Eyes* listed in this book.

Needs: Contemporary, feminist humor/satire, literary, mainstream, regional. No religious, romance, preschool, juvenile, young adult, psychic/occult. Recently published *Wood Head: Stories from up North*, by Rebecca Rule; *Grass Creek Chronicles*, by Pat Carr; and *Nightshade Nightstand Short Story Reader*, by Fred Chappell.

How to Contact: Accepts unsolicited mss—short stories only. "Willing to read agented material." Reports in 1 month on queries; 3-4 months on mss.

Terms: Pays 2 author's copies. Publishes ms about 1 year after acceptance. Writer's guidelines and book catalog for SASE. Individual contracts negotiated with authors.

Advice: "Would like to see more real humor; less gratuitous violence—the opposite of TV. We have overdosed on heavily dialected southern stories which treat country people with a mixture of ridicule and exaggeration. We prefer treatment of characterization which offers dignity and respect for folks who make do with little and who respect their environment. We are also interested in social criticism, in writers who take chances and who color outside the lines." We also invite experimental forms. Read us first. An invesetment of $5 may save the writer twice that in postage."

OBELESK BOOKS, (I, II, IV), P.O. Box 1118, Elkton MD 21922-1118. Publisher: S.G. Johnson. Editor: Gary Bowen. Estab. 1993. "Small but professional press." Publishes paperback originals and reprints. Books: 50 lb. paper; perfect binding. Published new writers within the last year. Averages 5 total titles, all fiction, each year. Sometimes comments on rejected ms.
Needs: Science fiction, fantasy, horror: adventure, erotica, ethnic/multicultural, feminist, gay, historical, humor/satire, lesbian, military/war and romance. "We are especially interested in historical, ethnic, and alternative science fiction/fantasy, horror for mature readers." Recently published *Green Echo: Ecological Science Fiction*, edited by Gary Bowen (anthology); *Winter of the Soul: Gay Vampire*, by Gary Bowen; *Dangerous Women*, edited by S.G. Johnson (chapbook anthology).
How to Contact: Accepts unsolicited mss. Submit complete ms with cover letter. Include estimated word count, bio (50 words) and list of publishing credits. Always send SASE for reply; prefer disposable copy of ms. Reports in 1 month on queries; 1 week on mss. Simultaneous and reprint submissions OK. E-mail address: obelesk@tantalus.dark.net.
Terms: Pays $10 flat fee plus author's copy. Sends galleys to author. Publishes ms 2-12 months after acceptance. Writer's guidelines for #10 SASE. Book catalog for #10 SASE. Sample copy for $6.
Advice: "We publish short fiction only, 5,000 words maximum. No novels. Know your subject thoroughly, our readers are educated and sophisticated. Immature, underdeveloped, and ignorant fiction will not fly here. Always review samples first, we have a unique editorial perspective. Do not submit blind. We are always looking for fiction by and about women, sexual and ethnic, and differently-abled people. We are an alternative press, traditional anything is not what we publish. Push the envelope."

ONTARIO REVIEW PRESS, (III), 9 Honeybrook Dr., Princeton NJ 08540. Generally does not accept unsolicited ms. Query first. Send SASE with query.

♥ORCA BOOK PUBLISHERS LTD., (I, IV), P.O. Box 5626, Station B, Victoria, British Columbia V8R 6S4 Canada. (604)380-1229. Publisher: R.J. Tyrrell. Estab. 1984. "Regional publisher of West Coast-oriented titles." Publishes hardcover and paperback originals. Books: quality 60 lb. book stock paper; illustrations; average print order: 3,000-5,000; first novel print order: 2,000-3,000. Plans 1-2 first novels this year. Averages 12 total titles, 1-2 fiction titles each year. Sometimes comments on rejected ms.
Needs: Contemporary, juvenile (5-9 years), literary, mainstream, young adult/teen (10-18 years). Looking for "contemporary fiction." No "romance, science fiction."
How to Contact: Query first, then submit outline/synopsis and 1 or 2 sample chapters. SASE. Agented fiction 20%. Reports in 2 weeks on queries; 1-2 months on mss. Publishes Canadian authors only.
Terms: Pays royalties of 10%; $500 average advance. Sends galleys to author. Publishes ms 6 months-1 year after acceptance. Writer's guidelines for SASE. Book catalog for 8½×11 SASE.
Advice: "We are looking to promote and publish new West Coast writers, especially Canadians."

OUR CHILD PRESS, 800 Maple Glen Lane, Wayne PA 19087. (610)964-0606. CEO: Carol Hallenbeck. Estab. 1984. Publishes hardcover and paperback originals and reprints. Plans 2 first novels this year. Plans 2 titles this year. Sometimes comments on rejected ms.
   ● An Our Child Press book, *Don't Call Me Marda*, received the Benjamin Franklin Award in 1993.
Needs: Adventure, contemporary, fantasy, juvenile (5-9 yrs.), preschool/picture book and young adult/teen (10-18 years). Especially interested in books on adoption or learning disabilities. Published *Don't Call Me Marda*, by Sheila Welch (juvenile); *Oliver—An Adoption Story*, by Lois Wickstrom; and *Blue Ridge*, by Jon Patrick Harper.
How to Contact: Does not accept unsolicited mss. Query first. Reports in 2 weeks on queries; 2 months on mss. Simultaneous submissions OK.
Terms: Pays royalties of 5% minimum. Publishes ms up to 6 months after acceptance. Book catalog free.

OUTRIDER PRESS, (I), 1004 E. Steger Rd., Suite C-3, Crete IL 60417. (708)672-6630. Fax: (708)672-6630. President: Phyllis Nelson. Fiction Editor: Whitney Scott. Estab. 1988. "Small operation." Publishes paperback originals. Books: offset printing; perfect binding; average print order: under 5,000. Averages 1-2 total titles, 1 fiction title each year. Sometimes comments on rejected ms; *charges $2 double-spaced pages with 10-page minimum, prepaid and SASE for return*.
Needs: Feminist, gay, lesbian, literary, New Age/mystic/spiritual, short story collection. No Christian/religious work. Publishes anthologies. Scheduled for 1996 publication: *Prairie Hearts— An Anthology of Writings on the Midwest*. Published *Dancing to the End of the Shining Bar*, by Whitney Scott.
How to Contact: Accepts unsolicited mss with SASE. Submit complete ms with cover letter (with short stories). Include estimated word count and list of publishing credits. SASE for return of ms. Reports in 1 month on queries; 2 months on mss. Simultaneous submissions OK. Accepts electronic submissions (3.5 IBM compatible—WordPerfect 5.1).

Terms: Payment depends on award money. Sends galleys to author.

Advice: "We have a need for short and super-short fiction with pace and flair."

THE OVERLOOK PRESS, 149 Wooster St., New York NY 10012. (212)477-7162. Estab. 1972. Small-staffed, fulltime operation. Publishes hardcover and paperback originals and reprints. Averages 30 total titles, 7 fiction titles each year. Occasionally critiques rejected mss.

Needs: Fantasy, juvenile (contemporary, fantasy, historical), literary, psychic/supernatural/occult, regional (Hudson Valley), science fiction, translations. No romance or horror. No short story collections. Published *Divina Trace*, by Robert Antoni (novel); *Cafe Berlin*, by Harold Nebenzal (novel); *The Museum of Love*, by Steve Weiner (novel); and *The Food Chain*, by Geoff Nicholson (novel).

How to Contact: Query first or submit outline/synopsis. SASE. Allow up to 6 months for reports on queries. Simultaneous submissions OK.

Terms: Vary.

PAPIER-MACHE PRESS, (IV), 135 Aviation Way, #14, Watsonville CA 95076. (408)763-1420. Editor/Publisher: Sandra Martz. Acquisitions Editor: Shirley Coe. Estab. 1984. "Specializes in women's issues; the art of growing older for both men and women." Publishes anthologies novels, short story. Books: 60-70 lb. offset paper; perfect-bound or case-bound. Average print order: 6,000-10,000. Publishes 6-10 total titles/year.

- Papier-Mache Press publishes a number of well-received themed anthologies. Their anthology, *I Am Becoming the Woman I've Wanted*, received a 1995 American Book Award.

Needs: Contemporary, feminist, short story collections, women's. Recently published *Late Summer Break*, by Ann Knox; *Maud's House*, by Sherry Roberts; and *Milkweed*, by Mary Gardner. Published new writers within the last year.

How to Contact: Query first. SASE. Reports in 2 months on queries; 6 months on mss. Simultaneous and photocopied submissions OK. Accepts computer printouts.

Terms: Standard royalty agreements and complimentary copy.

Advice: "Absolutely essential to query first with only sample chapters. Send complete manuscript upon request only. Please note on the query whether it's a simultaneous submission."

‡PAPYRUS PUBLISHERS & LETTERBOX LITERARY SERVICE, (II), P.O. Box 27383, Las Vegas NV 89126. (702)256-3838. Editor-in-Chief: Geoffrey Hutchison-Cleaves. Fiction Editor: Jessie Rosé. Estab. London 1946; USA 1982. Small publisher. Publishes hardcover originals and reprints. Audio books; average print order 2,500. Averages 3 total titles each year.

Needs: Mystery/suspense. "No erotica, gay, feminist, children's, spiritual, lesbian, political. Recently published *Wilderness*, by Tony Dawson (suspense); *Curse of the Painted Cats*, by Heather Latimer (romantic suspense); *Is Forever Too Long?*, by Heather Latimer (romantic fiction); and *Violet*, by Joan Griffith.

How to Contact: "Not accepting right now." Fully stocked.

Terms: Pays royalties of 10% minimum. Advance varies. Publishes ms 1 year after acceptance.

PATH PRESS, INC., (II), 53 W. Jackson, Suite 724, Chicago IL 60604. (312)663-0167. Fax: (312)663-5318. Editorial Director: Herman C. Gilbert. "Small independent publisher which specializes in books by, for and about African-Americans and Third World Peoples." Published new writers within the last year. Averages 6 total titles, 3 fiction titles each year. Occasionally critiques rejected ms.

Needs: Ethnic, historical, sports, and short story collections. Needs for novels include "black or minority-oriented novels of any genre, style or subject." Recently published *The Negotiations*, by Herman C. Gilbert (political thriller).

How to Contact: Accepts unsolicited mss. Query first or submit synopsis and 5 sample chapters with SASE. Reports in 2 months on queries; 4 months on mss. Simultaneous submissions OK.

Terms: Pays in royalties.

Advice: "Deal honestly with your subject matter and with your characters. Dig deeply into the motivations of your characters, regardless how painful it might be to you personally."

PEACHTREE PUBLISHERS, LTD., (II), 494 Armour Circle NE, Atlanta GA 30324. (404)876-8761. President: Margaret Quinlin. Estab. 1977. Small, independent publisher specializing in general interest publications, particularly of Southern origin. Publishes hardcover and paperback originals and hardcover reprints. Averages 12-15 total titles, 1-2 fiction titles each year. Average first novel print run 5,000-8,000.

- Peachtree recently put a stronger emphasis on books for children and young adults.

Check the Category Indexes, located at the back of the book, for publishers interested in specific fiction subjects.

Needs: Contemporary, literary, mainstream, regional, short story collections. "We are primarily seeking Southern fiction: Southern themes, characters, and/or locales, and children's books." No science fiction/fantasy, horror, religious, romance, historical or mystery/suspense. Published *The Blue Valleys*, by Robert Morgan (stories); *The Song of Daniel*, by Philip Lee Williams; *To Dance with the White Dog*, by Terry Kay; *Out to Pasture*, by Effie Wilder.

How to Contact: Accepts unsolicited mss. Query, submit outline/synopsis and 50 pages, or submit complete ms with SASE. Reports in 1 month on queries; 3 months on mss. Simultaneous submissions OK.

Terms: Pays in royalties. Sends galleys to author. Free writer's guidelines. Book catalog for 2 first-class stamps.

Advice: "We encourage original efforts in first novels."

♣**PEMMICAN PUBLICATIONS, (II, IV)**, 1635 Burrows Ave., Unit 2, Winnipeg, Manitoba R3T 0H6 Canada. (204)589-6346. Fax: (204)589-2063. Managing Editor: Sue Maclean. Estab. 1980. Metis and Aboriginal children's books, some adult. Publishes paperback originals. Books: stapled binding and perfect-bound; 4-color illustrations; average print order: 2,500; first novel print order: 1,000. Published new writers within the last year. Averages 9 total titles each year.

Needs: Children's/juvenile (American Indian, easy-to-read, preschool/picture book); ethnic/multicultural (Native American). Publishes the Builders of Canada series.

How to Contact: Accepts unsolicited mss. Submit complete ms with cover letter. Send SASE (or IRC) for reply, return of ms or send a disposable copy of ms. Reports in 1 year. Simultaneous and disk submissions OK.

Terms: Pays royalties of 5% minimum; 10% maximum. Average advance: $350. Provides 10 author's copies.

PERMEABLE PRESS, (II), 47 Noe St., #4, San Francisco CA 94114-1017. (415)648-2175. Imprint: Puck. Publisher: Brian Clark. Editor: Kurt Putnam. Estab. 1984. "Small literary press with inhouse design and typesetting." Publishes hardcover and paperback originals and paperback reprints. Books: 60 lb. paper; offset printing; perfect-bound; illustrations; average print order: 3,500. Published new writers within the last year. Plans 1 first novel this year. Averages 3 total titles, all fiction, each year. Sometimes comments on rejected ms.

• Permeable Press has a new imprint, Pocket Rockets™, novellas in small-format paperback editions.

Needs: Erotica, experimental, feminist, gay, lesbian, literary, psychic/supernatural/occult, science fiction (hard science, soft sociological), short story collections. Looking for "cyberpunk; conspiracy. Should be challenging to read." No romance. Recently published *Three-Hand Jax & Other Spells*, by Staszek; *The Naughty Yard*, by Michael Hemmingson; and *The Final Dream & Other Fictions*, by Daniel Pearlman.

How to Contact: Query first or submit outline/synopsis and 3 sample chapters. SASE. Reports in 4-6 weeks on queries; 3 months on mss. Accepts electronic submissions. E-mail address: bcclark@igc.apc.org.

Terms: Pays royalties of 5-20%. Author's copies vary. Honorarium depends on grant/award money. Sends galleys to author. Writer's guidelines and book catalog for 9 × 12 SAE and 2 first-class stamps.

Advice: "You should be familiar with the Press—our novels and our magazine—before submitting. Keep in mind that we want fiction that bites the reader in the neocortex and sends an illuminating shock down the spine. Bear in mind, Permeable is not a genre publisher. We are extremely picky and are only interested in seeing manuscripts of very high quality."

‡**PIEPER PUBLISHING, (I, II)**, P.O. Box 9136, Virginia Beach VA 23450-9136. Publisher/Editor: Ron Pieper. Estab. 1995. "We are a small recently-established company offering a personal touch on an international basis." Publishes hardcover and paperback originals and reprints. Plans to publish 10-20 books/year, including several anthologies. Often comments on rejected ms.

Needs: Adventure, children's/juvenile, erotica, ethnic/multicultural, family saga, fantasy, feminist, gay, historical, horror, humor/satire, lesbian, literary, mainstream/contemporary, military/war, mystery/suspense/ psychic/supernatural, regional, romance, science fiction, short story collections, thriller/espionage, translations, western, young adult/teen. "We warmly entertain all submissions. During the next year, we are preparing anthologies of short stories and poems among other publishing efforts."

How to Contact: Query with outline/synopsis and available sample chapters or submit complete ms with cover letter. "In the cover letter, discuss your manuscript's potential and other issues pertinent to yourself." Reports in 1 week on queries; 1-2 months on novel mss; 1-2 weeks on short stories and poems. Simultaneous submissions OK. Accepts disk submissions (MicroSoft Works or WordPerfect).

Terms: Pays royalties of 7% minimum; 12% maximum. "If your manuscript becomes part of an anthology, payment is prorated on the size of the publication." Sends galleys to author. "We encourage author involvement in finalizing the product to ensure author satisfaction." Publishes ms 6 months after acceptance. Writer's guidelines for SASE.

Advice: "Fiction manuscripts should present a situation or environment which is imaginative, yet so enticing it's believable. Go beyond that which is already on the book shelf; otherwise you do nothing more than offer readers what they already have."

PINEAPPLE PRESS, (II, IV), P.O. Drawer 16008, Southside Station, Sarasota FL 34239. (941)952-1085. Executive Editor: June Cussen. Estab. 1982. Small independent trade publisher. Publishes hardcover and paperback originals and paperback reprints. Books: quality paper; offset printing; Smyth-sewn or perfect-bound; illustrations occasionally; average print order: 5,000; first novel print order: 2,000-5,000. Published new writers within the last year. Averages 12 total titles each year.
Needs: "In 1996 we prefer to see only Florida-related novels." Recently published two "Cracker Westerns" *Death in Bloodhound Red*, by Virginia Lanier; and *Guns of the Palmetto Plains*, by Rick Tonyan.
How to Contact: Prefers query, outline or one-page synopsis with sample chapters (including the first) and SASE. Then if requested, submit complete ms with SASE. Reports in 2 months. Simultaneous submissions OK.
Terms: Pays royalties of 7½-15%. Advance is not usually offered. "Basically, it is an individual agreement with each author depending on the book." Sends galleys to author. Book catalog sent if label and 52¢ postage enclosed.
Advice: "Quality first novels will be published, though we usually only do one or two novels per year. We regard the author/editor relationship as a trusting relationship with communication open both ways. Learn all you can about the publishing process and about how to promote your book once it is published."

‡PIPPIN PRESS, 229 E. 85th Street, Gracie Station Box 1347, New York NY 10028. (212)288-4920. Publisher: Barbara Francis. Estab. 1987. "Small, independent children's book company, formed by the former editor-in-chief of Prentice Hall's juvenile book division." Publishes hardcover originals. Books: 135-150 GSM offset-semi-matte paper (for picture books); offset, sheet-fed printing; Smythe-sewn binding; full color, black and white line illustrations and half tone, b&w and full color photographs. Averages 5-6 titles each year. Sometimes comments on rejected mss.
Needs: Juvenile only (5-9 yrs. including animal, easy-to-read, fantasy, science, humorous, spy/adventure). "I am interested in humorous novels for children of about 7-12 and in picture books with the focus on humor. Also interested in autobiographical novels for 8-12 year olds and selected historical fiction for the same age group."
How to Contact: No unsolicited mss. Query first. SASE. Reports in 2-3 weeks on queries. Simultaneous submissions OK.
Terms: Pays royalties. Sends galleys to author. Publication time after ms is accepted "depends on the amount of revision required, type of illustration, etc."

*POCAHONTAS PRESS, INC., (I, IV), Manuscript Memories, P.O. Drawer F, Blacksburg VA 24063-1020. (540)951-0467. Editorial contact person: Mary C. Holliman. Estab. 1984. "One-person operation on part-time basis, with several part-time colleagues. Subjects not limited, but stories about real people are almost always required." Books: 70 lb. white offset paper; offset litho printing; perfect binding; illustrations; average print order: 3,000-5,000. Averages 5 total titles each year. Usually critiques or comments on rejected mss.
• This press uses very little fiction. The publisher may consider making a short story into a short book, but does not generally publish novels or collections.
Needs: "Stories based on historical facts about real people." Contemporary, ethnic, historical, regional, sports, translations, western. "I will treat a short story as a book, with illustrations and a translation into Spanish or French and also Chinese someday." No fantasy or horror. Published *From Lions to Lincoln*, by Fran Hartman; and *Mountain Summer*, by Bill Mashburn.
How to Contact: Accepts unsolicited mss. Query first. "I don't expect to be considering *any* new material for at least a year. I need to complete current projects first." Reports in 1 month on queries; 1-2 months on mss. "I try to meet these deadlines but seldom succeed." Simultaneous submissions OK. "If simultaneous, I would need to know up front what other options the author is considering."
Terms: Pays royalties of 10% maximum. Sends galleys or page proofs to author. "I will subsidy publish—but expect book and author to meet the same qualifications as a regular author, and will pay royalties on all copies sold as well as pay back the author's investment as books are sold."
Advice: "Tell a *story*—don't tell what happened, show it happening. Let your characters be real, squirm in their chairs, look out windows. Don't let them be so caught up in your idea or theme that you don't let the character be a person. And don't 'preach.' If you have to state your theme or the point you want to make, you haven't succeeded in making the point."

THE POST-APOLLO PRESS, (I), 35 Marie St., Sausalito CA 94965. (415)332-1458. Publisher: Simone Fattal. Estab. 1982. Publishes paperback originals. Book: acid-free paper; lithography printing; perfect-bound; average print order: 3,000; first novel print order: 3,000. Published new writers within the last year. Averages 2 total titles, 1 fiction title each year. Sometimes comments on rejected ms.
Needs: Feminist, lesbian, literary, spiritual and translations. No juvenile, horror, sports or romance. Recently published *Home For The Summer*, by Georgina Kleege; *A Beggar at Damascus Gate*, by Yasmine Zahran; and *Agatha/Savanna Bay*, by Marguerite Duras.
How to Contact: Send query or sample chapters with SASE. Reports in 3 months. E-mail address: tpapress @crl.com.

Terms: Pays royalties of 6½% minimum or by individual arrangement. Sends galleys to author. Publishes ms 1½ years after acceptance. Book catalog free.

‡♣PRAIRIE JOURNAL PRESS, (I, IV), Prairie Journal Trust, P.O. Box 61203, Brentwood Postal Services, Calgary, Alberta T2L 2K6 Canada. Estab. 1983. Small-press, noncommercial literary publisher. Publishes paperback originals. Books: bond paper; offset printing; stapled binding; b&w line drawings. Averages 2 total titles or anthologies each year. Occasionally critiques or comments on rejected ms if requested.
- See the listing for *The Prairie Journal of Canadian Literature* in the Literary/Small Circulation section of this book.

Needs: Literary, short stories. No romance, horror, pulp, erotica, magazine type, children's, adventure, formula, western. Published *Prairie Journal Fiction*, *Prairie Journal Fiction II* (anthologies of short stories) and *Solstice* (short fiction on the theme of aging).

How to Contact: Accepts unsolicited mss. Query first and send Canadian postage or IRCs and $3 for sample copy, then submit outline/synopsis and 1-2 stories with SASE. Reports in 6 months.

Terms: Pays 1 author's copy; honorarium depends on grant/award provided by the government or private/corporate donations. Sends galleys to author. Book catalog free on request to institutions; SAE with IRC for individuals. "No U.S. stamps!"

Advice: "We wish we had the means to promote more new writers. We often are seeking theme-related stories. We look for something different each time and try not to repeat types of stories."

♣THE PRAIRIE PUBLISHING COMPANY, Box 2997, Winnipeg, Manitoba R3C 4B5 Canada. (204)885-6496. Publisher: Ralph Watkins. Estab. 1969. Buys juvenile mss with illustrations. Books: 60 lb. high-bulk paper; offset printing; perfect-bound; line-drawings; average print order: 2,000; first novel print order: 2,000.

Needs: Open. Published: *The Homeplace*, (historical novel); *My Name is Marie Anne Gaboury*, (first French-Canadian woman in the Northwest); and *The Tale of Jonathan Thimblemouse*. Published work by previously unpublished writers within the last year.

How to Contact: Query with SASE or IRC. No simultaneous submissions. Reports in 1 month on queries, 6 weeks on mss. Publishes ms 4-6 months after acceptance. Free book catalog.

Terms: Pays 10% in royalties. No advance.

Advice: "We work on a manuscript with the intensity of a Max Perkins. A clean, well-prepared manuscript can go a long way toward making an editor's job easier. On the other hand, the author should not attempt to anticipate the format of the book, which is a decision for the publisher to make. In order to succeed in today's market, the story must be tight, well written and to the point. Do not be discouraged by rejections."

PREP PUBLISHING, (I, II), PREP Inc., 1110½ Hay St., Fayetteville NC 28305. (910)483-6611. Editor: Anne McKinney. Estab. 1994. New publishing division affiliated with a 13-year-old company. Publishes hardcover and paperback originals. Books: acid free paper; offset printing; perfect binding; illustrations; average print order: 5,000; first novel print order: 5,000. Plans 1 first novel this year. Averages up to 15 total titles, 10 fiction titles each year. Often comments on rejected ms.

Needs: Children's/juvenile (adventure, mystery), religious/inspirational, romance (contemporary, romantic suspense), thriller/espionage, young adult (adventure, mystery/suspense, romance, sports). "Spiritual/inspirational novels are most welcome." Recently published *Second Time Around*.

How to Contact: Accepts unsolicited mss. Submit complete ms with cover letter and brief synopsis/summary. Include bio (1 page) and list of publishing credits. SASE for return of ms. Reports in 3 weeks on queries; 2 months on mss. Simultaneous submissions OK.

Terms: Pays negotiable royalties. Advance is negotiable. Individual arrangement with author depending on the book. Sends galleys to author. Publishes ms 1-2 years after acceptance.

Advice: "Rewrite and edit carefully before sending manuscript."

♣PRESS GANG PUBLISHERS, (II, IV), 225 E. 17 Ave., Suite 101, Vancouver, British Columbia V5V 1A6 Canada. (604)876-7787. Fax: (604)876-7892. Estab. 1974. Feminist press, 3 full-time staff. Publishes paperback originals and reprints. Books: paperback; offset printing; perfect-bound; average print order: 3,500; first novel print order: 2,000. Plans 3 novels this year.
- Press Gang Publishers received the 1995 Small Press Award from the Lambda Literary Awards for *Her Tongue on My Theory*, by Kiss & Tell.

Needs: Looking for "feminist, mystery/suspense, short stories." Also accepts contemporary, erotica, ethnic (native women especially), humor/satire, lesbian, literary. No children's/young adult/teen. Priority given to

The maple leaf symbol before a listing indicates a Canadian publisher, magazine, conference or contest.

Canadian writers. Recently published *Choral*, by Karen McLaughlin (novel); *Bellydancer*, by SKY Lee; and *Her Head a Village*, by Makeda Silvera (stories).

How to Contact: Accepts unsolicited mss. Query first. SASE. Reports in 2 months on queries; 3-4 months on mss. Simultaneous submissions OK.

Terms: Pays 8-10% royalties. Sends galleys to author. Book catalog free on request.

PUCKERBRUSH PRESS, (I,II), 76 Main St., Orono ME 04473. (207)581-3832. Publisher/Editor: Constance Hunting. Estab. 1971. One-person operation on part-time basis. Publishes paperback originals. Books: laser printing; perfect-bound; sometimes illustrations; average print order: 1,000. Published new writers within the last year. Averages 3 total titles each year. Sometimes comments on rejected ms. *If detailed comment, $500.*

● The publisher has been concentrating on poetry lately, but may consider fiction. See the listing for *Puckerbrush Review* in this book.

Needs: Contemporary, experimental, literary, high-quality work. Published *An Old Pub Near the Angel*, by James Kelman.

How to Contact: Accepts unsolicited mss. Submit complete ms with cover letter. SASE. Reports in 2 weeks on queries; 2 months on mss.

Terms: Pays royalties of 10%; 20 author's copies. Sends galleys to author. Publishes ms usually 1 year after acceptance. Writer's guidelines for #10 SASE. "I have a book list and flyers."

PURPLE FINCH PRESS, (I, II), P.O. Box 758, Dewitt NY 13214. (315)445-8087. Publisher: Mrs. Nancy Benson. Estab. 1992. One-person operation. Publishes hardcover and paperback originals. Books: 60-70 lb. paper; from laser printer to commercial printer; perfect or hardcover bound; illustrations; average print order: 250-500; first novel print order: 500. Plans 1 first novel this year. Averages 1 total fiction title each year. Sometimes critiques or comments on rejected ms.

Needs: Children's/juvenile (adventure, mystery), literary, short story collections. "No erotica, violence."

How to Contact: Accepts unsolicited mss. Query first. Include estimated word count and list of publishing credits. Send SASE for reply, return of ms or send a disposable copy of ms. Reports in 3 months on queries; 4 months on mss. Simultaneous submissions OK. Accepts disk submissions (Macintosh).

Terms: Pays royalties of 6% minimum; 10% maximum. Provides 20 author's copies. Sends galleys to author. Publishes ms 1-2 years after acceptance ("could be less"). Writer's guidelines for 9×4 SASE. Book catalog for 9×4 SASE.

Advice: "We would like to see more literary poetry, stories—less vulgar language, curse words, erotica and violence."

‡*PYX PRESS, (III, IV), P.O. Box 922648, Sylmar CA 91392-2648. Editor-in-Chief: C. Darren Butler. Fiction Editors: Julie Thomas, Patricia Hatch. Estab. 1990. Publishes hardcover and paperback originals and reprints. Books: offset or xerography printing; binding varies from saddle-stitched to hand-sewn; average print order: 100-2,500; first novel order: 200-1,000. Plans 0-2 first novels this year. Averages 5-12 total titles, 2-5 fiction titles each year. Sometimes comments on rejected ms.

● See *Magic Realism* and *A Theatre of Blood* listings in the Literary/Small Circulation section of this book.

Needs: Experimental, fantasy (magic realism, glib fantasy, folktales, literary fantasy, fables, fairy tales, exaggerated realism), horror (dark fantasy), literary, religious/inspirational (religious fantasy), science fiction (soft/sociological) short story collections. Plans to publish *A Theater of Blood*, limited edition dark fantasy anthology and a fiction anthology by and about lawyers/law to include literary fantasy and humor. "We have expanded our operation from publishing two little magazines to include three chapbooks series, one serial anthology *A Theater of Blood*, and 2-6 book projects per year." Chapbook series includes "North-American Magic Realism," "Strike Through the Mask" and "Avatar."

How to Contact: Accepts unsolicited mss. Query first with 2 paragraph bio, list of credits and first 3 pages of ms. SASE for reply. Reports in 1 months on queries; 6-12 months on mss.

Terms: Pays royalties of 6% minimum; 15% maximum (after we have broken even on the project). Provides 20 author's copies. *Subsidy publishes 10%.* Sends galleys to author. Publishes ms 2-18 months after acceptance. Writer's guidelines for #10 SASE. Book catalog for #10 SASE.

Advice: "Most authors who have placed book-length or chapbook collections with us have previously appeared in *Magic Realism* Magazine. 95% of all books/chapbooks are by invitation."

‡*QED PRESS, (I), 155 Cypress St., Ft. Bragg CA 95437. (707)964-9520. Senior Editor: John Fremont. Estab. 1985. "Small press publisher subsidiary of mid-size production house." Publishes hardcover and paperback originals. Books: acid-free recycled 60 lb. paper; offset, Cameron Belt or Web press printing; perfect or Smyth-sewn binding; average print order: 3,000; first novel print order: 1,000. Plans 1 first novel this year. Averages 10 total titles, 2-3 fiction titles each year.

● The publisher received a 1994 Western States Book award for creative nonfiction for publishing *Iron House*, by Jerome Washington (a Quality Paperback Book Club New Visions selection in 1995).

Needs: Experimental, literary, mystery/suspense, translations. "Our needs are minimal, but we'll jump on something we think is hot. No formula anything." Recently published *Iron House*, by Jerome Washington (creative nonfiction); *Malmmd*, by Ivan Laslo (science fiction); and *Bats in the Belfry*, by Titus Stauffer (techno-thriller).

How to Contact: Accepts unsolicited mss. Submit outline/synopsis with 3 sample chapters. SASE. Agented fiction 10%. Reports in 5-6 weeks.

Terms: Pays royalties of 8-15%. *Subsidy publishes under another imprint.* Publishes ms 6 months - 2 years after acceptance. Writer's guidelines call for laser or typed double-spaced mss/queries. No disk submissions.

Advice: "Frequently, we bypass publishable manuscripts because we're not currently looking for a particular genre. Persist."

✦**QUARRY PRESS, (I,II)**, Box 1061, Kingston, Ontario, K7L 4Y5 Canada. (613)548-8429. Estab. 1965. Small independent publisher with plans to expand. Publishes paperback originals. Books: 1 lb. paper offset sheet; perfect-bound; illustrations; average print order: 1,200; first novel print order: 1,200. Published new writers within the past year. Plans 1 first novel this year. Averages 20 total titles, 4 fiction titles each year. Sometimes comments on rejected mss.

Needs: Children's folklore and poetry, experimental, feminist, historical, literary, short story collections. Published *Ritual Slaughter,* by Sharon Drache; *Engaged Elsewhere,* edited by Kent Thompson (includes work by Mavis Gallant, Margaret Laurence, Dougles Glover, Ray Smitz, Keath Fraser and others); published fiction by previously unpublished writers within the last year.

How to Contact: Query first. SASE for query and ms. Reports in 4 months. Simultaneous submissions OK.

Terms: Pays royalties of 7-10%. Advance: negotiable. Provides 5-10 author's copies. Sends galleys to author. Publishes ms 6-8 months after acceptance. Book catalog free on request.

Advice: "Publishing more fiction than in the past. Encourages first novelists. Canadian authors only."

✦**RAGWEED PRESS INC./gynergy books, (IV)**, P.O. Box 2023, Charlottetown, Prince Edward Island C1A 7N7 Canada. (902)566-5750. Fax: (902)566-4473. Contact: Senior Editor. Estab. 1980. "Independent Canadian-owned press." Publishes paperback originals. Books: 60 lb. paper; perfect binding; average print order: 3,000. Averages 12 total titles, 3 fiction titles each year.

Needs: *Canadian-authors only.* Children's/juvenile (adventure, preschool/picture book, girl-positive), feminist, lesbian, young adult. Plans *Lesbian Parenting, Lesbian Sisters* anthology; writers submit to Anthology Editor; editor selects stories. "We do accept submissions to anthologies from U.S. writers." Recently published *Dancing at the Club Holocaust*, by J.J. Steinfeld (short stories about Holocaust survivors); *Friends I Never Knew*, by Tanya Lester (feminist); *A House Not Her Own*, by Emily Nasrallah (translation); *Next Teller* (book of Canadian story telling), includes 31 contributors. Published new writers within the last year.

How to Contact: Does not accept unsolicited mss. Query first. Include estimated word count, brief bio, list of publishing credits. SASE (or IRC) for reply. Reports in 16 weeks on queries. Simultaneous submissions OK.

Terms: Pays royalties of 10% minimum; offers negotiable advance. Provides 10 author's copies. Sends galleys to author. Publishes ms 12-18 months after acceptance. Writer's guidelines for #10 SAE and 1 first-class stamp. Book catalog for large SAE and 2 first-class stamps.

Advice: "Specialized market—lesbian novels especially. Be brief, give good outline, give resume."

*READ 'N RUN BOOKS, (I), Subsidiary of Crumb Elbow Publishing, Box 294, Rhododendron OR 97049. (503)622-4798. Imprints are Elbow Books, Research Centrex, Wind Dancer Press, Silhouette Imprints, Tyee Press, Oregon Fever Books and Trillium Art Productions. Publisher: Michael P. Jones. Estab. 1978. Small independent publisher with three on staff. Publishes hardcover and paperback originals and reprints. Books: special order paper; offset printing; "usually a lot" of illustrations; average print order: varies. Published new writers within the last year. Averages 30 titles, 5 fiction titles each year. Sometimes comments on rejected ms; *$25-75 charge for critiques depending upon length.*

● Read'N Run has started the Wind Dancer Press imprint for poetry and sponsors several poetry awards.

Needs: Adventure, contemporary, ethnic, experimental, fantasy, feminist, historical, horror, humor/satire, juvenile (animal, easy-to-read, fantasy, historical, sports, spy/adventure, contemporary), literary, mainstream, military/war, multicultural, preschool/picture book, psychic/supernatural/occult, regional, religious/inspirational, romance (contemporary, historical), science fiction, short story collections, spiritual, suspense/mystery, technical and professional translations, western, young adult/teen (easy-to-read, fantasy/science fiction, historical, problem novels, romance, sports, spy/adventure). Looking for fiction on "historical and wildlife" subjects. "Also, some creative short stories would be nice to see for a change. No pornography." Publishes anthologies. Send SASE for details. Published *Umpqua Agriculture, 1851*, by Jesse Applegate; *Bone to His Bone*, by E.G. Swain; and *The Confession of Charles Linkworth*, by E.F. Benson. This year starting anthology. Interested writers should query with SASE.

How to Contact: Accepts unsolicited ms. Query first. Submit outline/synopsis (*copies only*, no originals) and complete ms with cover letter. SASE. Reports in 1 month on queries; 1-2 months on mss. Simultaneous submissions OK. Send SASE for reply or return of ms. "If SASE with adequate return postage does not accompany manuscript, it will be discarded immediately."

Terms: Provides 5 author's copies (negotiated). Sends galleys to author. Publishes ms 10-12 months after acceptance. *Subsidy publishes two books or more/year.* Terms vary from book to book. Writer's guidelines for SASE. Book catalog for SASE and $3 postage.

Advice: Publishing "more hardcover fiction books based on real-life events. They are in demand by libraries. Submit everything you have—even artwork. Also, if you have ideas for layout, provide those also. If you have an illustrator that you're working with, be sure to get them in touch with us. Do not be pushy! We are very busy and deal with a lot of people, which means you and your needs are equal to everyone else's. Phone calls are fine, but we cannot return calls due to overwhelming volume. We are a great place for writers to get started if they have a professional working attitude and manner. Be sure to send a SASE with every correspondence."

‡READER'S BREAK, (I), (formerly *Just a Moment*), Pine Grove Press, P.O. Box 40, Jamesville NY 13078. (315)423-9268. Editor: Gertrude S. Eiler. Annual anthology with an "emphasis on short stories written with style and ability. Our aim has always been to publish work of quality by authors with talent, whether previously published or not."

Needs: "We welcome stories about relationships, tales of action, adventure, science fiction and fantasy, romance, suspense and futuristic. No "pornography, sexual perversion, incest or stories for children." Length: 3,500 words maximum. Also publishes "poems to 75 lines in any style or form and on any subject with the above exceptions."

How to Contact: Accepts unsolicited mss. Include SASE. Reports in 3-5 months "since the stories are considered by a number of editorial readers."

Terms: Pays 1 contributor's copy for one-time rights.

Advice: "We prefer fiction with a well-constructed plot and well-defined characters of any age or socio-economic group. Upbeat endings are not required. Please check the sequence of events, their cause-and-effect relationship, the motivation of your characters, and the resolution of plot."

♣RED DEER COLLEGE PRESS, (II, IV), Box 5005, Red Deer, Alberta T4N 5H5 Canada. (403)342-3321. Managing Editor: Dennis Johnson. Estab. 1975. Publishes adult and young adult hardcover and paperback originals. Books: offset paper; offset printing; hardcover/perfect-bound; average print order: 1,000-4,000; first novel print order: 2,500. Averages 14-16 total titles, 2 fiction titles each year. Sometimes comments on rejected mss.

• Red Deer College Press has received honors and awards from the Alberta Book Publishers Association and the Canadian Children's Book Centre (designations for individual books). They recently received awards from the Writers Guild of Alberta for *Beneath the Faceless Mountain*, by Roberta Rees (adult fiction) and *Mission Impossible*, by Teth Goobie (young adult novel).

Needs: Contemporary, experimental, literary, short story collections, young adult. No romance, science fiction. Published anthologies under Roundup Books imprint focusing on stories/poetry of the Canadian and American West. Recently published *100 Years of Cowboy Stories*, by Ted Done; *Beneath the Faceless Mountain*, by Roberta Rees; and *Yellow Pages*, by Nicole Markotié. New series for young and/or reluctant readers under series imprint—The Carny Kids.

How to Contact: *Canadian authors only.* Does not accept unsolicited mss. Query first or submit outline/synopsis and 2 sample chapters. SASE. Agented fiction 10%. Reports in 3 months on queries; in 6 months on mss. Simultaneous submissions OK. Final manuscripts must be submitted on Mac disk in MS Word.

Terms: Pays royalties of 8-10%. Advance is negotiable. Sends galleys to author. Publishes ms 1 year after acceptance. Book catalog for 9×12 SASE.

Advice: "We tend to look for authors with a proven track record (either published books or widely published in established magazines or journals) and for manuscripts with regional themes and/or a distinctive voice. We publish Canadian authors almost exclusively."

RIO GRANDE PRESS, (I), Imprints include *Se La Vie Writer's Journal*, P.O. Box 71745, Las Vegas NV 89170. (702)736-8833. Publisher: Rosalie Avara. Estab. 1989. "One-person operation on a half-time basis." Publishes paperback originals. Books: offset printing; saddle-stitched binding; average print order: 100. Published new writers within the last year. Averages 10 total titles, 2 fiction titles each year. Sometimes comments on rejected ms.

• Look for the *Se La Vie Writer's Journal* contest listing in this book. The publisher also sponsors a short short story contest quarterly.

Needs: Adventure, contemporary, ethnic, family saga, fantasy, humor/satire, literary, mystery/suspense (amateur sleuth, private eye, romantic suspense), regional. Looking for "general interest, slice of life stories; good, clean, wholesome stories about everyday people. No sex, nor porn, no science fiction (although I may consider flights of fantasy, day dreams, etc.), no religious. Any subject within the 'wholesome' limits. No experimental styles, just good conventional plot, characters, dialogue." Published *The Story Shop* I & II & III (short story anthologies; 13 stories by individual authors). "Currently we are only accepting short stories for *The Story Shop IV*. Limit: 1,500 words. Send up to two only; one or both will be selected."

How to Contact: Submit story after August 1. SASE. Reports in 2 weeks on queries or acceptance.
Terms: Pays, if contest is involved, up to $15 + $5 on honorable mentions.
Advice: "I enjoy working with writers new to fiction, especially when I see that they have really worked hard on their craft, i.e., cutting out all unnecessary words, using action dialogue, interesting descriptive scenes, thought-out plots and well rounded characters that are believable. Please read listing carefully noting what type and subject of fiction is desired."

RISING TIDE PRESS, (II), 5 Kivy St., Huntington Station NY 11746. (516)427-1289. Editor: Lee Boojamra. Estab. 1988. "Small, independent press, publishing lesbian nonfiction and fiction—novels only—no short stories." Publishes paperback trade originals. Books: 60 lb. vellum paper; sheet fed and/or web printing; perfect-bound; average print order: 5,000; first novel print order: 4,000-6,000. Plans 6 first novels this year. Averages 4-6 total titles. Comments on rejected ms.
Needs: Lesbian adventure, contemporary, erotica, fantasy, feminist, romance, science fiction, suspense/mystery, western. Looking for romance and mystery. "Minimal heterosexual content." Published *Deadly Rendezvous*, by Diane Davidson; *Danger! Crosscurrents*, by Sharon Gilligan; and *Heartstone and Saber*, by Jacqui Singleton. Developing a dark fantasy line.
How to Contact: Accepts unsolicited mss with SASE. Reports in 1 week on queries; 2-3 months on mss.
Terms: Pays 10-15% royalties. *"We will assist writers who wish to self-publish for a nominal fee."* Sends galleys to author. Publishes ms 6-18 months after acceptance. Writer's guidelines for #10 SASE.
Advice: "Our greatest challenge is finding quality manuscripts."

*RIVERCROSS PUBLISHING, INC., (I, II), Dept. WM, 127 E. 59th St., New York NY 10022. (212)421-1950. Editor-in-Chief: Josh Furman. Estab. 1945. "Small, independent publisher." Publishes hardcover and paperback originals. Books: book paper; offset printing. Published new writers within the last year. Sometimes comments on rejected ms.
Needs: Open. Published *Fools Gold*, by Charles Knickerbocker (novel); *The Consortium*, by David Stone (novel); and *Uninvited Memories*, by Ina Smith (poetry).
How to Contact: Accepts unsolicited mss. Query first, submit outline/synopsis and sample chapters or complete ms with cover letter. SASE for reply. Reports in 3 weeks. Simultaneous and electronic submissions OK.
Terms: Pays royalties of 40% maximum. *Subsidy publishes 80%.* Sends galleys to author. Publishes ms 6-12 months after acceptance. Writer's guidelines and book catalog free.

♣RONSDALE PRESS/CACANADADADA, (II, IV), 3350 W. 21 Ave., Vancouver, British Columbia V6S 1G7 Canada. (604)738-1195. President: Ronald B. Hatch. Estab. 1988. Publishes paperback originals. Books: 60 lb. paper; photo offset printing; perfect binding; average print order: 1,000; first novel print order: 1,000. Plans 2 first novels this year. Averages 3 fiction titles each year. Sometimes comments on rejected ms.
• See the interview with Ronald Hatch in the 1994 edition of this book.
Needs: Experimental and literary. Recently published *Home from the Party*, by Robert McLean; *Nicolette*, by Robert Zend (experimental novel); *Blackouts to Bright Lights*, by Barbara Ladouceur (personal stories); *Out of the Interior*, by Harold Rhenisch (stories/memoir); and *Frankie Zapper and the Disappearing Teacher*, by Linda Rogers, illustrations by Rick Van Krugel (children's novel).
How to Contact: *Canadian authors only.* Accepts unsolicited mss. Submit outline/synopsis and 2 sample chapters (60-100 pgs.). SASE. Short story collections must have some magazine publication. Reports in 2 weeks on queries; 2 months on mss.
Terms: Pays royalties of 10%. Provides author's copies. Sends galleys to author. Publishes ms 6 months after acceptance.
Advice: "We publish both fiction and poetry. Authors *must* be Canadian."

‡ROSE CREEK PUBLISHING, (I, II), 41 W. Arlington Ave., #201, St. Paul MN 55117. Imprints are Rose Creek SoftBooks and Rose Creek SoftClassics. Publisher: Craig Hansen. Estab. 1995. "One-person operation publishing electronic book originals and reprints." Books on floppy disks and CD-ROMs. Published new writers within the last year. Averages 4-12 total titles, 2-6 fiction titles each year. Sometimes comments on rejected ms.
Needs: Adventure, fantasy (space), horror (dark fantasy, futuristic, psychological, supernatural), literary, mainstream/contemporary, mystery/suspense (amateur sleuth), private eye/hardboiled), religious/inspirational (general, religious fantasy), romance (contemporary, romantic suspense), science fiction (soft/sociological,

---

Sending to a country other than your own? Be sure to send International Reply Coupons instead of stamps for replies or return of your manuscript.

time travel), short story collections, thriller/espionage, young adult/teen (horror, mystery/suspense, problem novels). "Mostly, I need *big*, mass-market ideas, intelligently written and character-driven. No gay/lesbian, New Age, sword and sorcery or agenda- or message-based politically correct fiction." Publishes anthologies. "Our anthology editor, Paula Gavan, selects from contest entries on America Online's Dark Fiction/Horror Writer's Workshop." Recently published *Laughter of Spirits* (SoftBooks), by Julia Nunnaly Duncan (poetry collection); *Mary Shelley's Frankenstein* (SoftClassic), by Mary Shelley (classic fiction reprint); and *Year of Horror*, edited by Paula Gavan (short story collection).

How to Contact: Accepts unsolicited mss. Query with outline/synopsis and 3 sample chapters (e-mail queries OK). Include 1-page bio and list of publishing credits with submission. SASE for reply, return of ms or send a disposable copy of ms. Agented fiction 0-25%. Reports in 1-2 months on queries; 2-5 months on mss. Simultaneous and disk submissions (ASCII-text on Windows or Mac floppy disk and hard copy) OK. E-mail address: wpinesq@winternet.com, World Wide Web URL:http://www.winternet.com/wpinesq/.

Terms: Pays royalties of 15% minimum; 20% maximum and 1-10 author's copies "We are a commercial publisher paying author on royalty basis only; no cash advance." Sends galleys to author, "time permitting." Publishes ms 1-2 years after acceptance. Writer's guidelines for SAE and 2 first-class stamps.

Advice: "Fiction needs to become more concise to retain appeal as an electronic experience. Read great writers and never stop writing. Be open to rewrites. Be flexible. I'd like to see more writers who are computer- and online-literate, who are open to new avenues of publicity like online interviews and Web pages."

SAND RIVER PRESS, (I), 1319 14th St., Los Osos CA 93402. (805)543-3591. Editor: Bruce Miller. Estab. 1987. "Small press." Publishes paperback originals. Books: offset printing; b&w or color illustrations; average print order: 3,000; first novel print order: 2,000. Averages 2-3 total titles, 1 fiction title each year. Sometimes comments on rejected ms.

Needs: Native American, lesbian, literary, regional (west).

How to Contact: Accepts unsolicited mss. Submit outline/synopsis and 3 sample chapters. Include list of publishing credits. SASE for return of ms or a disposable copy of the ms. Reports in 3 weeks on queries; 6 weeks on mss. Simultaneous submissions OK.

Terms: Pays royalties of 8% minimum; 15% maximum. Average advance: $500-1,000. Provides 10 author's copies. Sends galleys to author. Publishes ms 1 year after acceptance. Book catalog for SASE.

‡SANDPIPER PRESS, (IV), Box 286, Brookings OR 97415. (503)469-5588. Owner: Marilyn Reed Riddle. Estab. 1979. One-person operation specializing in low-cost large-print 18 pt. books. Publishes paperback originals. Books: 70 lb. paper; saddle-stitched binding, perfect-bound; 84 pgs. maximum; leatherette cover; b&w sketches or photos; average print order 2,000; no novels. Averages 1 title every 2 years. Occasionally comments on rejected ms.

Needs: From Native-American "Indian" writers only, *true* visions and prophesies; from general public writers, unusual quotations, sayings.

How to Contact: Does not accept unsolicited mss. Query first or submit outline/synopsis. SASE. Reports in 1 month on queries; 1 month on mss. Simultaneous submissions OK.

Terms: Pays 2 author's copies and $10 Native-American. Publisher buys true story and owns copyright. Author may buy any number of copies at 40% discount and postage. Book catalog for #10 SASE.

Advice: Send SASE for more information.

‡SARABANDE BOOKS, INC., (II), 2234 Dundee Rd., Suite 200, Louisville KY 40205. Editor-in-Chief: Sarah Gorham. Estab. 1994. "Small literary press." Publishes hardcover and paperback originals. Averages 6 total titles, 2-3 fiction titles each year.

● Sarabande Books sponsors the Mary McCarthy Prize in Short Fiction listed in the Contests and Awards section.

Needs: Short story collections, 300 pages maximum (or collections of novellas, or single novellas of 150 pages). "Short fiction *only*. We do not publish full length novels."

How to Contact: Submit (in September only.) Query with outline/synopsis and 1 sample story or ten-page sample. Should include 1 page bio, listing of publishing credits. SASE for reply. Reports in 3 months on queries; 6 months on mss. Simultaneous submissions OK.

Terms: Pays in royalties, author's copies. Sends galleys to author. Writer's guidelines available for contest only. Send #10 SASE. Book catalog not available.

THE SAVANT GARDE WORKSHOP, (II, IV), a privately-owned affiliate of The Savant Garde Institute, Ltd., P.O. Box 1650, Sag Harbor NY 11963. (516)725-1414. Publisher: Vilna Jorgen II. Estab. 1953. "Midsize multiple-media publisher." Publishes hardcover and paperback originals and reprints. Averages 8 total titles. Sometimes comments on rejected ms.

● Be sure to look at this publishers' guidelines first. Works could best be described as avant-garde/ post modern, experimental.

Needs: Contemporary, futuristic, humanist, literary, philosophical. "We are open to the best, whatever it is." No "mediocrity or pot boilers." Published *01 or a Machine Called SKEETS*, by Artemis Smith (avant-garde); and *Bottomfeeder*, by Mark Spitzer. Series include "On-Demand Desktop Collectors' Editions,"

"Artists' Limited Editions," "Monographs of The Savant Garde Institute."

How to Contact: Do not send unsolicited mss. Query first with SASE and biographical statement. Agented fiction 1%. Reports in 6 weeks on queries ("during academic year"); 2 months on mss.

Terms: Average advance: $500, provides author's copies, honorarium (depends on grant/award money). Terms set by individual arrangement with author depending on the book and previous professional experience. Sends galleys to author. Publishes ms 18 months after acceptance. Writer's guidelines free.

Advice: "Most of the time we recommend authors to literary agents who can get better deals for them with other publishers, since we are looking for extremely rare offerings. We are not interested in the usual commercial submissions. Convince us you are a real artist, not a hacker." Would like to see more "thinking for the 21st Century of Nobel Prize calibre. We're expanding into multimedia CD-ROM co-publishing and seek multitalented authors who can produce and perform their own multimedia work for CD-ROM release. We are overbought and underfunded—don't expect a quick reply or fast publication date."

‡SEAL PRESS, (I, IV), 3131 Western Ave., Seattle WA 98121. (206)283-7844. President: Faith Conlon. Estab. 1976. "Midsize independent publisher of fiction and nonfiction by women." Publishes hardcover and paperback originals. Books: 55 lb. natural paper; Cameron Belt, Web or offset printing; perfect binding; illustrations occasionally; average print order: 6,500; first novel print order: 4,000-5,000. Averages 15 total titles, 6 fiction titles each year. Sometimes critiques rejected ms "very briefly."
- Seal has received numerous awards including Lambda Literary Awards for mysteries, humor and translation.

Needs: Ethnic, feminist, humor/satire, lesbian, literary, mystery (amateur sleuth, cozy, private eye/hardboiled), young adult (easy-to-read, historical, sports). "We publish women only. Work must be feminist, non-racist, non-homophobic." Publishes anthologies. Send SASE for list of upcoming projects. Recently published *An Open Weave*, by Devorah Major (literary novel); *Faint Praise*, by Ellen Hart (mystery novel); and *The Lesbian Parenting Book*, by D. Menlee Clunis and G. Dorsey Green.

How to Contact: Query with outline/synopsis and 2 sample chapters. SASE. Reports in 2 months.

Terms: Pays royalties; offers negotiable advance. Publishes ms 1-2 years after acceptance. Writer's guidelines and book catalog are free.

SECOND CHANCE PRESS AND THE PERMANENT PRESS, (II), RD 2 Noyac Rd., Sag Harbor NY 11963. (516)725-1101. Publishers: Judith and Martin Shepard. Estab. 1977. Mid-size, independent publisher. Publishes hardcover originals and reprints. Books: hardcover; average print order: 1,500-2,000; first novel print order: 1,500-2,000. Published new writers within the last year. Averages 12 total titles, all fiction, each year.
- *Lead Us Not Into Penn Station*, by Bruce Dickens and published by Second Chance Press, received the Colorado Award for the Book in 1995.

Needs: Contemporary, erotica, ethnic/multicultural, experimental, family saga, literary, mainstream/contemporary, mystery/suspense. "We like novels that have a unique point of view and have a high quality of writing." No genre novels. Recently published *Flesh*, by David Galef; *The Alibi Breakfast*, by Larry Duberstein; and *Résumé with Monsters*, by William Browning Spencer.

How to Contact: Query with outline and no more than 2 chapters. SASE. Agented fiction 35%. Reports in 1 month on queries; 4 months on mss. Simultaneous submissions OK.

Terms: Pays royalties of 10-15%. Advance: $1,000. Sends galleys to author. Book catalog for $3.

Advice: "We are looking for good books, be they tenth novels or first novels, it makes little difference. The fiction is more important than the track record."

SERENDIPITY SYSTEMS, (I, II, IV), P.O. Box 140, San Simeon CA 93452. (805)927-5259. Imprints include Books on Disks™ and Bookware.™ Publisher: John Galuszka. Estab. 1985. "Electronic publishing for IBM-PC compatible systems." Publishes "electronic editions originals and reprints." Books on disk. Published new writers within the last year. Averages 36 total titles, 15 fiction titles each year (either publish or distribute). Often comments on rejected ms.

Needs: "Works of fiction which use, or have the potential to use, hypertext, multimedia or other computer-enhanced features. We cannot use on-paper manuscripts." No romance, religion, occult. Recently published *Costa Azul*, by C.J. Newton (humor); *Sideshow*, by Marian Allan (science fiction); and *Silicon Karma*, by Tom Easton (science fiction).

How to Contact: Submit complete ms with cover letter. *IBM-pc compatible disk required.* ASCII files required unless the work is hypertext or multimedia. Send SASE for reply, return of ms or send disposable copy of ms. Reports in 2 weeks on queries; 1 month on mss. E-mail address: j.galuszka@genie.geis.com.

Terms: Pays royalties of 25%. "We distribute the works of self-published authors and have a cooperative program for authors who don't have the skills to electronically self-publish. We also distribute shareware electronic editions." Publishes ms 1 month after acceptance. Writer's guidelines for SASE. Book catalog for $1 (on IBM-PC 360K or 720K disk).

Advice: "A number of new tools have recently become available, Hypertext publishing programs DART and ORPHEUS, for example, and we look forward to selling works which can take advantage of the features of these and other programs. Would like to see: more works of serious literature—novels, short stories, plays, etc. Would like to not see: right wing adventure fantasies from 'Tom Clancy' wanna-be's."

SEVEN BUFFALOES PRESS, (II), Box 249, Big Timber MT 59011. Editor/Publisher: Art Cuelho. Estab. 1975. Publishes paperback originals. Averages 4-5 total titles each year.

● The Seven Buffaloes Press also publishes a number of magazines including *Azorean Express*, *Black Jack*, *Hill and Holler* and *Valley Grapevine*.

Needs: Contemporary, short story collections, "rural, American Hobo, Okies, Native-American, Southern Appalachia, Arkansas and the Ozarks. Wants farm- and ranch-based stories." Published *Rig Nine*, by William Rintoul (collection of oilfield short stories).

How to Contact: Query first with SASE. Reports in 1 week on queries; 2 weeks on mss.

Terms: Pays royalties of 10% minimum; 15% on second edition or in author's copies (10% of edition). No advance. Writer's guidelines and book catalog for SASE.

Advice: "There's too much influence from TV and Hollywood, media writing I call it. We need to get back to the people, to those who built and are still building this nation with sweat, blood and brains. More people are into it for the money, instead of for the good writing that is still to be cranked out by isolated writers. Remember, I was a writer for ten years before I became a publisher."

HAROLD SHAW PUBLISHERS, (II), Box 567, 388 Gundersen Dr., Wheaton IL 60189. (708)665-6700. Managing Editor: Joan Guest. Literary Editor: Lil Copan. Estab. 1968. "Small, independent religious publisher with expanding fiction line." Publishes paperback originals and reprints. Books: 35 lb. Mando Supreme paper; sheet-fed printing; perfect-bound; average print order: 5,000. Plans 1 novel per year in Northcote Books (literary/academic fiction subsidiary). Averages 38 total titles, 1-2 fiction titles each year. Sometimes critiques rejected mss.

Needs: Literary, religious/inspirational. Looking for religious literary novels. No short stories, romances, children's fiction. Published *Starts Over East L.A.*, by Marian Flandrick Bray (novel); *The Sioux Society*, by Jeffrey Asher Nesbitt; *The Northcote Anthology of Short Stories*. Published new writers within the last year. Also publishes under OMF imprint: books published in conjunction with Overseas Missionary Fellowship.

How to Contact: Accepts unsolicited mss. Query first. Submit outline/synopsis and 2-3 sample chapters. SASE. Reports in 4-6 weeks on queries; 3-4 months on mss. No simultaneous submissions.

Terms: Pays royalties of 10%. Provides 10 author's copies. Sends pages to author. Publishes ms 12-18 months after acceptance. Free writer's guidelines. Book catalog for 9 × 12 SAE and $1.32 postage.

Advice: "Character and plot development are important to us. We look for quality writing in word and in thought. 'Sappiness' and 'pop-writing' don't go over well at all with our editorial department."

‡SHIELDS PUBLISHING, (I, II), NEO Press, 301 E. Liberty, Suite 120, Ann Arbor MI 48104. (313)996-9229. Fax: (313)996-4544. Editor: Ms. Joanna Henning. "Two-person operation on part-time basis." Publishes hardcover and paperback originals. Plans 1 first novel this year. Averages 1 fiction title each year. Sometimes comments on rejected ms.

Needs: Adventure, children's/juvenile, ethnic/multicultural, experimental, family saga, fantasy, feminist, gay, historical, horror, humor/satire, lesbian, literary, mainstream/contemporary, military/war, mystery/suspense, new age/mystic/spiritual, psychic/supernatural, regional, religious/inspirational, romance, science fiction, short story collections, thriller/espionage, translations, western, young adult/teen.

How to Contact: Accepts unsolicited mss. Query with outline/synopsis and 2 sample chapters. Include list of publishing credits with submission. Send SASE for reply, return of ms or send a disposable copy of ms.

Terms: Pays "variable" royalties. Offers negotiable advance.

SILVER MOUNTAIN PRESS, (II), P.O. Box 12994, Tucson AZ 85732. (520)790-1561. Fax: (520)790-1561. Editor: Jon Owens. Estab. 1993. "Small independent publisher of quality fiction and poetry." Publishes paperback originals. Books: offset printing; perfect binding; average print order: 3,000-5,000; first novel print order: 3,000-5,000. Published new writers within the last year. Plans 3 novels this year. Averages 3 total titles, 1-2 fiction titles each year. Sometimes comments on rejected ms.

Needs: Literary, mainstream/contemporary. Published *Isla Grande*, by Richard Hughes (literary adventure-thriller).

How to Contact: Query first. Include a one or two paragraph synopsis of the novel within the query letter. SASE for reply. Agented fiction 50-75%. Reports in 2 weeks on queries; 2 months on mss. Simultaneous submissions OK.

Terms: Pays royalties of 10% minimum; 15% maximum. Offers negotiable advance. Sends galleys to author. Publishes ms 8-12 months after acceptance. Books catalog for #10 SASE.

Advice: "Spend a great deal of care and thought on your query letter, make it an excellent representation of the quality of your writing."

‡✤SIMON & PIERRE PUBLISHING CO. LTD., (IV), A member of the Dundurn Group, 2181 Queen St. E., Suite 301, Toronto, Ontario M4E 1E5 Canada. (416)698-0454. Fax: (416)698-1102. Publisher: Jean Paton. Estab. 1972. "Small literary press." Publishes paperback originals. Books: Hi Bulk paper; book printer printing; perfect binding; b&w illustrations; average print order: 2,000; first novel print order: 1,000. Averages 10 total titles, 2 fiction titles each year.

Needs: Literary, mainstream/contemporary, mystery/suspense (amateur sleuth, cozy). Plans Canadian mystery anthologies. Recently published *Grave Deeds*, by B. Struthers (mystery-cozy); and *Crime in a Cold Climate*, by D. Shene-Melvin (mystery-anthology).
How to Contact: Accepts unsolicited mss. Query first or query with outline/synopsis. Should include estimated word count; 1 page bio; list of publishing credits. Send SASE for reply, return of ms or send a disposable copy of ms. Reports in 2 months on queries; 3 months on mss. Simultaneous submissions OK.
Terms: Pays royalties of 10%. Average advance $750. Provides 10 author's copies. Sends galleys to author. Publishes ms 8-12 months after acceptance. Writer's guidelines free. Book catalog for 9×12 SASE and $1 postage.

THE SMITH, (I), 69 Joralemon St., Brooklyn NY 11201. Editor: Harry Smith. Estab. 1964. Books: 70 lb. vellum paper for offset and 80 lb. vellum for letterpress printing; perfect binding; often uses illustrations; average print order: 1,000; first novel print order: 1,000. Plans 2 fiction titles this year.
● The Poor Richard Award was presented to publisher Harry Smith for his "three decades of independent literary publishing activities."
Needs: *Extremely limited* book publishing market—currently doing only 3-5 books annually, and these are of a literary nature, usually fiction or poetry. Recently published *The Cleveland Indian* (novel) and *Blue Eden* (connected long stories), both by Luke Salisbury; and *Bodo*, by John Bennett (novel).
Advice: "We find most synopses are stupid. Send one or two chapters, or one to three stories, depending on length. Complete manuscripts may not be read. Our list is our only guide and our motto is: Anything goes as long as it's good. Remember that we publish outside the mainstream, and do not publish any self-help, recovery or inspirational books. And SASE, please! Because of unusual working hours, we are unable to accept registered or certified mail. Also, packages that are bulky will not fit through our mail slot and the post office is not conveniently located for us to pick up mail."

SOHO PRESS, (I, II), 853 Broadway, New York NY 10003. (212)260-1900. Publisher: Juris Jurjevics. Publishes hardcover originals and trade paperback reprints. Published new writers within the last year. Averages 20 titles/year.
Needs: Adventure, ethnic, historical, literary, mainstream, mystery/espionage, suspense. "We do novels that are the very best of their kind." Published *The Sixteen Pleasures*, by Robert R. Hellenga; *Breath, Eyes, Memory*, by Edwidge Danticat; and *Adrian Mole: The Lost Years*, by Sue Townsend. Also publishes the Hera series (serious historical fiction with strong female leads).
How to Contact: Submit query or complete ms with SASE. Reports in 1 month on queries; 6 weeks on mss. Simultaneous submissions OK.
Terms: Pays royalties of 10-15% on retail price. For trade paperbacks pays 7½% royalties on first 10,000 copies; 10% after. Offers advance. Book catalog plus $1 for SASE.
Advice: Greatest challenge is "introducing brand new, untested writers. We do not care if they are agented or not. Half the books we publish come directly from authors. We look for a distinctive writing style, strong writing skills and compelling plots. We are not interested in trite expression of mass market formulae."

SOUTHERN METHODIST UNIVERSITY PRESS, (I), P.O. Box 415, Dallas TX 75275. (214)768-1433. Senior Editor: Kathryn M. Lang. Estab. 1936. "Small university press publishing in areas of film/theater, Southwest life and letters, religion/medical ethics and contemporary fiction." Publishes hardcover and paperback originals and reprints. Books: acid-free paper; perfect-bound; some illustrations; average print order 2,000. Published new writers within the last year. Plans 2 first novels this year. Averages 10-12 total titles; 3-4 fiction titles each year. Sometimes comments on rejected ms.
● Five of this press's seven fall (1994) books were reviewed in the *New York Times Book Review*.
Needs: Contemporary, ethnic, literary, regional, short story collections. "We are always willing to look at 'serious' or 'literary' fiction." No "mass market, science fiction, formula, thriller, romance." Published *Alligator Dance*, by Janet Peery (collection); and *The 23rd Dream*, by Kathy Egbert (novel).
How to Contact: Accepts unsolicited mss. Query first. Submit outline/synopsis and 3 sample chapters. SASE. Reports in 3 weeks on queries; 6 months on mss. No simultaneous submissions.
Terms: Pays royalties of 10% net, negotiable advance, 10 author's copies. Publishes ms 1 year after acceptance. Book catalog free.
Advice: "We view encouraging first time authors as part of the mission of a university press. Send query describing the project and your own background. Research the press before you submit—don't send us the kinds of things we don't publish." Looks for "quality fiction from new or established writers."

SPECTRUM PRESS, (I), Box 109, 3023 N. Clark St., Chicago IL 60657. (312)281-1419. Editor D.P. Agin. Estab. 1991. "Small independent electronic publisher." Publishes computer disks only. Published new writers within the last year. Plans 5 first novels this year. Averages 50 total titles, 35 fiction titles each year. Sometimes comments on rejected ms.
Needs: Avant-garde, contemporary, erotica, experimental, feminist, gay, lesbian, literary, mainstream, short story collections, translations. "Quality lesbian fiction of all kinds, feminist writing, literary novels." No juvenile or young adult. Recently published *Kippo's World*, by Jean Erhardt; *Tools of the Trade*, by K.T.

Butler; and *The Algebra of Snow*, by Virginia A.K. Moran. "We now have five lines: Spectrum Classics (classic literature and nonfiction); Contemporary Fiction and Poetry; Spectrum Obelisk Library (erotica); Artemis Books (lesbian/feminist fiction and nonfiction); Sheridan Square Library (gay fiction and nonfiction).
How to Contact: Accepts unsolicited mss. Query first. Submit outline/synopsis and sample chapters or complete ms with cover letter. Reports in 2 weeks on queries; 1 month on mss. Simultaneous submissions OK. Accepts electronic submissions on disk only. Prefers submissions on IBM/MS-DOS or Mac computer disk. Mac disk must be 3.5″ HD (1.44M). E-mail address: specpress@aol.com (for correspondence only, no online submissions).
Terms: Pays royalties of 10-15%. Sends copies to author. Publishes within 2 months after acceptance. Writer's guidelines available. Book catalog free.
Advice: "We are interested in new voices and new attitudes. For the coming year, we are most interested in lesbian fiction and quality erotica. We will publish 25 titles in these categories. We prefer disk submissions in ASCII code or WordPerfect 5.1 format. Contact us first for other formats."

THE SPEECH BIN, INC., (IV), 1965 25th Ave., Vero Beach FL 32960. (407)770-0007. Fax: (407)770-0006. Senior Editor: Jan J. Binney. Estab. 1984. Small independent publisher and major national and international distributor of books and material for speech-language pathologists, audiologists, special educators and caregivers. Publishes hardcover and paperback originals. Averages 15-20 total titles/year. "No fiction at present time, but we are very interested in publishing fiction relevant to our specialties."
Needs: "We are most interested in seeing fiction, including books for children, dealing with individuals experiencing communication disorders, other handicaps, and their families and caregivers, particularly their parents, or family members dealing with individuals who have strokes, physical disability, hearing loss, Alzheimer's and so forth."
How to Contact: Accepts unsolicited mss. Query first. SASE. Agented fiction 10%. Reports in 4-6 weeks on queries; 1-3 months on mss. Simultaneous submissions OK, but only if notified by author.
Terms: Pays royalties. Sends galleys to author. Writer's guidelines for #10 SASE. Book catalog for 9 × 12 SAE with 4 first-class stamps.
Advice: "We are most interested in publishing fiction about individuals who have speech, hearing and other handicaps."

SPINSTERS INK, (IV), 32 E. First St., #330, Duluth MN 55802. Acquisitions: Jami Snyder. Estab. 1978. Moderate size women's publishing company growing steadily. Publishes paperback originals and reprints. Books: 55 lb. acid-free natural paper; photo offset printing; perfect-bound; illustrations when appropriate; average print order: 5,000. Published new writers within the last year. Plans 3 first novels this year. Averages 6 total titles, 3-5 fiction titles each year. Occasionally critiques rejected ms.
  • Spinsters Ink published *The Two-Bit Tango*, by Elizabeth Pincus, which received a Lambda Award and *Vital Ties*, by Karen Kringle, a finalist for the ALA Gay and Lesbian Book Awards.
Needs: Feminist, lesbian. Wants "full-length quality fiction—thoroughly revised novels which display deep characterization, theme and style. We *only* consider books by women. No books by men, or books with sexist, racist or ageist content." Recently published *Martha Moody*, by Susan Stinson (feminist western); *The Hangdog Hustle*, by Elizabeth Pincus (mystery); and *Common Murder*, by Val McDermid (mystery). Publishes anthologies. Writers may submit directly. Series include: "Coming of Age Series" and "Forgotten Women's Series."
How to Contact: Query or submit outline/synopsis and 2-5 sample chapters not to exceed 50 pages with SASE. Reports in 1 month on queries; 2 months on mss. Simultaneous submissions discouraged. Disk submissions OK (DOS or Macintosh format—MS Word 4.0). Prefers hard copy with disk submission.
Terms: Pays royalties of 7-10%, plus 25 author's copies; unlimited extra copies at 45% discount. Free book catalog.
Advice: "In the past, lesbian fiction has been largely 'escape fiction' with sex and romance as the only required ingredients; however, we encourage more complex work that treats the lesbian lifestyle with the honesty it deserves."

*STARBOOKS PRESS, Subsidiary of Woldt Corp., P.O. Box 2737, Sarasota FL 34230-2737. (813)957-1281. President/Publisher: Patrick J. Powers. Estab. 1978. "Niche press specializing in mature adult fiction and nonfiction, including mainly titles of gay orientation." Publishes paperback originals. Averages 10-12 total titles, 3 anthologies each year. Comments on rejected ms.

Market conditions are constantly changing! If you're still using this book and it is 1997 or later, buy the newest edition of Novel & Short Story Writer's Market *at your favorite bookstore or order from Writer's Digest Books.*

• Woldt Corp. also distributes books by the Florida Literary Foundation Press, listed in this book.

Needs: Gay fiction and nonfiction. Published *Boys of Spring*, *Boy Toy* and *Heartthrobs*, by John Patrick; and *The Boy on the Bicycle*, by Thom Nickels.

How to Contact: Accepts unsolicited mss. Submit outline/synopsis and sample chapters. SASE. Reports in 1 month on queries; 6 weeks on mss. Simultaneous submissions OK.

Terms: Provides 5-25 contributor's copies on short stories or direct payment depending on author's publishing credits. Individual arrangement with author depending on the book. *Will consider subsidy publishing; offers co-op program.* Sends galleys to author. Publishes ms 6-8 months after acceptance. Writers guidelines for SASE. Book catalog free.

STARBURST PUBLISHERS, (II), P.O. Box 4123, Lancaster PA 17604. (717)293-0939. Editorial Director: Ellen Hake. Estab. 1982. Publishes trade paperback and hardcover originals and trade paperback reprints. Receives 1,000 submission/year. 60% of books by first-time authors. Averages 10-15 total titles each year.

Needs: Religious/inspirational: Adventure, contemporary, fantasy, historical, horror, military/war, psychic/supernatural/occult (with Judeo-Christian solution), romance (contemporary, historical), spiritual, suspense/mystery, western. Wants "inspirational material." Recently published *The Remnant*, by Gilbert Morris (historical/fantasy).

How to Contact: Submit outline/synopsis, 3 sample chapters, bio, photo and SASE. Agented fiction less than 25%. Reports in 6-8 weeks on manuscripts; 1 month on queries. Accepts electronic submissions via disk and modem, "but also wants clean double-spaced typewritten or computer printout manuscript."

Terms: Pays royalties of 6% minimum; 16% maximum. "Individual arrangement with writer depending on the manuscript as well as writer's experience as a published author." Publishes ms up to one year after acceptance. Writer's guidelines for #10 SASE. Book catalog for 9×12 SAE and 5 first-class stamps.

Advice: "50% of our line goes into the Christian marketplace; 50% into the general marketplace. We are one of the few publishers that has direct sales representation into both the Christian and general marketplace."

STERLING HOUSE PUBLISHER, (I, II), Subsidiary of Lee Shore Agency, Sterling Bldg., 440 Friday Rd., Pittsburgh PA 15209. (412)821-6211. Imprint: One Foot on the Mountain Press. Estab. 1988. Publishes paperback originals. Books: offset printing; perfect-bound; illustrations; average print order: 750. Published new writers within the last year. Plans 4 first novels this year. Averages 30 total titles, 2 fiction titles each year. Sometimes comments on rejected ms.

Needs: Contemporary, erotica, short story collections. No "historical romances, experimental fiction, anything over 65,000 words."

How to Contact: Accepts unsolicited mss. Query first. SASE. Reports in 2 weeks on queries; 3 months on mss. Simultaneous submissions OK.

Terms: Pays royalties of 7% maximum. "We make individual arrangements with authors depending on the book. We do straight publishing and cooperative publishing. We send out press releases, include books in catalog, market mainly through mail and book conventions." Sends galleys to author. Publishes ms 6-9 months after acceptance. Writer's guidelines and book catalog for 4×9 SASE.

Advice: "When submitting a manuscript do not send us your first draft. We will reject it. Work on your story, give it time to evolve. Read fiction and how-to books. Please type, double space and use healthy margins."

STONE BRIDGE PRESS, (IV), P.O. Box 8208, Berkeley CA 94707. (510)524-8732. Fax: (510)524-8711. Publisher: Peter Goodman. Estab. 1989. "Independent press focusing on books about Japan in English (business, language, culture, literature)." Publishes paperback originals and reprints. Books: 60-70 lb. offset paper; web and sheet paper; perfect-bound; some illustrations; average print order: 3,000; first novel print order: 2,000-2,500. Averages 6 total titles, 2 fiction titles, each year. Sometimes comments on rejected ms.

• Stone Bridge Press received a PEN West Literary Award for Translation and a Japan-U.S. Friendship Prize for *Still Life*, by Junzo Shono, translated by Wayne P. Lammers. Another book, *A Long Rainy Season* received the 1995 Benjamin Franklin Award for Fiction/Poetry from PMA.

Needs: Japan-themed. If not translation, interested in the expatriate experience—all categories welcome: contemporary, erotica, ethnic, experimental, literary, science fiction, short story collections, translations (from Japanese). "Primarily looking at material relating to Japan. Mostly translations, but we'd like to see samples of work dealing with the expatriate experience. Also Asian- and Japanese-American. Published *Wind and Stone*, by Masaaki Tachihara; *Still Life and Other Stories*, by Junzo Shono; *One Hot Summer in Kyoto*, by John Haylock.

How to Contact: Accepts unsolicited mss. Query first. Submit outline/synopsis and 3 sample chapters. SASE. Agented fiction 25%. Reports in 1 month on queries; 3-4 months on mss. Simultaneous submissions OK. E-mail address: sbp@netcom.com.

Terms: Pays royalties, offers negotiable advance. Publishes ms 18-24 months after acceptance. Catalog for 1 first-class stamp.

Advice: "As we focus on Japan-related material there is no point in approaching us unless you are very familiar with Japan. We'd especially like to see submissions dealing with the expatriate experience and fantasy and science fiction on Japanese themes as well, but with a decided literary tone, not mass market. Please, no commercial fiction."

STORMLINE PRESS, (I, II), P.O. Box 593, Urbana IL 61801. Publisher: Raymond Bial. Estab. 1985. "Small independent literary press operated by one person on a part-time basis, publishing one or two books annually." Publishes hardcover and paperback originals. Books: acid-free paper; paper and cloth binding; b&w illustrations; average print order: 1,000-2,000; first novel print order: 1,000-2,000. Published new writers within the last year. Averages 1-2 total titles, all fiction each year.
   • Stormline's title, *First Frost*, was selected for a *Pushcart Prize*.
Needs: Literary. Looks for "serious literary works, especially those which accurately and sensitively reflect rural and small town life." Published *Silent Friends: A Quaker Quilt*, by Margaret Lacey (short story collection).
How to Contact: Accepts unsolicited mss. Query (with SASE), preferably during November or December. Include estimated word count, bio, list of publishing credits. SASE for reply or return of ms. Reports in 2 weeks on queries; 1 month on mss. Simultaneous submissions OK.
Terms: Pays royalties of 10% maximum. Provides author's copies. Sends galleys to author. Publishes ms 6-12 months after acceptance. Writer's guidelines for SASE. Book catalog free.
Advice: "We look for a distinctive voice and writing style. We are always interested in looking at manuscripts of exceptional literary merit. We are not interested in popular fiction or experimental writing. Please review other titles published by the press, notably *Silent Friends: A Quaker Quilt*, to get an idea of the type of books published by our press."

STORY LINE PRESS, (II), Three Oaks Farm, Brownsville OR 97327-9718. (503)466-5352. Fax: (503)466-3200. Editor: Robert McDowell. Estab. 1985. "Nonprofit literary press." Publishes hardcover and paperback originals and hardcover and paperback reprints. Published new writers within the last year. Plans 1 first novel this year. Averages 10 total titles, 3 fiction titles each year.
   • Story Line Press books have received awards including the Oregon Book Award.
Needs: Adventure, ethnic/multicultural, literary, mystery/suspense, regional, short story collections and translations. Published *Among the Immortals*, by Paul Lake (vampire mystery); *Second Story Theatre*, by James Brown (literary); and *The Raquet*, by George Hitchcock (picaresque). Publishes Stuart Mallory Mystery series.
How to Contact: Accepts unsolicited mss. Returns mss "if postage is included." Query with outline. Include bio and list of publishing credits. Send SASE for reply, return of ms or send a disposable copy of ms. Agented fiction 2.7%. Reports in 9-12 weeks on queries; 6-9 months on mss. Simultaneous submissions OK.
Terms: Provides author's copies; payment depends on grant/award money. Sends galleys to author. Publishes ms 1-3 years after acceptance. Book catalog for 7×10 SASE.
Advice: "Patience . . . understanding of a nonprofit literary presses' limitations."

SUNSTONE PRESS, (IV), Box 2321, Santa Fe NM 87504-2321. (505)988-4418. Contact: James C. Smith, Jr. Estab. 1971. Midsize publisher. Publishes paperback originals. Average first novel print order: 2,000. Published new writers within the last year. Plans 2 first novels this year. Averages 16 total titles, 2-3 fiction titles, each year.
   • Sunstone Press published *Ninez*, by Virginia Nylander Ebinger which received the Southwest Book Award from the Border Regional Library Association.
Needs: Western. "We have a Southwestern theme emphasis. Sometimes buys juvenile mss with illustrations." No science fiction, romance or occult. Recently published *Apache: The Long Ride Home*, by Grant Gall (Indian/Western); *Sorrel*, by Rita Cleary; and *To Die in Dinetah*, by John Truitt.
How to Contact: Accepts unsolicited mss. Query first or submit outline/synopsis and 2 sample chapters with SASE. Reports in 2 weeks. Simultaneous submissions OK. Publishes ms 9-12 months after acceptance.
Terms: Pays royalties, 10% maximum, and 10 author's copies.

THIRD SIDE PRESS, INC., (II), 2250 W. Farragut, Chicago IL 60625-1802. (312)271-3029. Fax: (312)271-0459. Publisher: Midge Stocker. Estab. 1991. "Small press, feminist." Publishes paperback originals. Books: 50 lb. recycled, acid-free paper; offset-web or sheet printing; perfect binding; average print order: 3,000; first novel print order: 3,000. Published new writers within the last year. Averages 4 total titles, 2 fiction titles each year. Sometimes comments on rejected ms.
   • Third Side Press Inc., published *Hawkings*, by Karen Lee Osborne, an ALA Gay & Lesbian Literature Award finalist and *Aftershocks*, by Jess Wells, a nominee for this award. Another book, *She's Always Liked Girls Best*, by Claudia Allen was a finalist for the ALA Gay & Lesbian Literature and the Lambda Literary Awards.
Needs: Lesbian: erotica (lesbian only), feminist, historical, literary, mainstream/contemporary, mystery/suspense (amateur sleuth). No "collections of stories; horror; homophobic" material. Recently published *The Sensual Thread*, by Beatrice Stone (first novel); *Out for Blood: Tales of Mystery and Suspense by Women*,

edited by Victoria A. Brownworth; and *Aftershocks*, by Jess Wells (first novel). Series include Royce Madison mysteries; Women/Cancer/Fear/Power series.

How to Contact: Query first. Include bio (1-2 paragraphs) and synopsis. Send SASE for reply, return of ms or send a disposable copy of ms. Reports in 2-3 weeks on queries; 3-6 months on mss. Simultaneous submissions OK with notice.

Terms: Pays royalties (varies). Provides 10 author's copies. Publishes ms 6-18 months after acceptance. Writer's guidelines for #10 SAE and 2 first-class stamps. Book catalog for 2 first-class stamps.

Advice: "Look at our catalog and read one or two of our other books to get a feel for how your work will fit with what we've been publishing. Plan to book readings and other appearances to help your book sell. And don't quit your day job."

THIRD WORLD PRESS, P.O. Box 19730, Chicago IL 60619. (312)651-0700. Publisher/Editor: Haki Madhubuti. Estab. 1967. Black-owned and operated independent publisher of fiction and nonfiction books about the black experience throughout the Diaspora. Publishes paperback originals. Plans 1 first novel this year, as well as short story collections. Averages 10 total titles, 3 fiction titles each year. Average first novel print order 15,000 copies.

Needs: Ethnic, historical, juvenile (animal, easy-to-read, fantasy, historical, contemporary), preschool/picture book, short story collections, and young adult/teen (easy-to-read/teen, folktales, historical). "We primarily publish nonfiction, but will consider fiction by and about blacks."

How to Contact: Accepts unsolicited mss October-May each year. Query or submit outline/synopsis and 1 sample chapter with SASE. Reports in 6 weeks on queries; 5 months on mss. Simultaneous submissions OK. Accepts computer printout submissions.

Terms: Individual arrangement with author depending on the book, etc.

♣THISTLEDOWN PRESS, (II, IV), 633 Main St., Saskatoon, Saskatchewan S7H 0J8 Canada. (306)244-1722. Editor-in-Chief: Patrick O'Rourke. Estab. 1975. Publishes paperback originals. Books: Quality stock paper; offset printing; perfect-bound; occasional illustrations; average print order 1,500-2,000; first novel print order: 1,000-1,500. Publishes 12 titles, 6 or 7 fiction, each year.

- A story included in the press's *The Blue Jean Collection* received a Vicky Metcalf Award, and books published by Thistledown have been selected as "Our Choice" by the Canadian Children's Book Centre and the Arthur Ellis Crime Writers Award (Best Juvenile Story).

Needs: Literary, experimental, short story collections, novels.

How to Contact: "We *only* want to see Canadian-authored submissions. We will *not* consider multiple submissions." No unsolicited mss. Query first with SASE. Photocopied submissions OK. Reports in 2 months on queries. Publishes anthologies. "Stories are nominated." Published *It's A Hard Cow*, by Terry Jordan (short stories); *Soldier Boys*, by David Richards; *The Woman on the Bridge*, by Mel Dagg (short stories); and *The Blue Camaro*, by R.P. MacIntyre. Also publishes The Mayer Mystery Series (mystery novels for young adults) and The New Leaf Series (first books for poetry and fiction).

Advice: "We are primarily looking for quality writing that is original and innovative in its perspective and/or use of language. Thistledown would like to receive queries first before submission—perhaps with novel outline, some indication of previous publications, periodicals your work has appeared in. *We publish Canadian authors only.* We are continuing to publish more fiction and are looking for new fiction writers to add to our list. New Leaf Editions line is first books of poetry or fiction by emerging Western Canadian authors. Familiarize yourself with some of our books before submitting a query or manuscript to the press."

THREE CONTINENTS PRESS, (III, IV), P.O. Box 38009, Colorado Springs CO 80937-8009. Fiction Editor: Donald Herdeck. Estab. 1973. Small independent publisher with expanding list. Publishes hardcover and paperback originals and reprints. Books: library binding; illustrations; average print order: 1,000-1,500; first novel print order: 1,000. Averages 15 total titles, 6-8 fiction titles each year. Occasionally critiques ("a few sentences") rejected mss.

Needs: "We publish original fiction only by writers from Africa, the Caribbean, the Middle East, Asia and the Pacific. No fiction by writers from North America or Western Europe." Recently published *Lina: Portrait of a Damascene Girl*, by Samar Altar; *The Native Informant*, by Ramzi Salti (stories); and *Repudiation*, by Rachid Boudjedra.

How to Contact: Query with outline/synopsis and sample pages with SASE. State "origins (non-Western), education and previous publications." Reports in 1 month on queries; 2 months on mss. Simultaneous submissions OK.

Terms: "Send inquiry letter first and ms only if so requested by us. We are not a subsidy publisher, but do a few specialized titles a year with grants. In those cases we accept institutional subventions. Foundation or institution receives 20-30 copies of book and at times royalty on first printing. We pay royalties twice yearly (against advance) as a percentage of net paid receipts." Royalties of 5% minimum; 10% maximum. Offers negotiable advance, $300 average. Provides 10 author's copies. Sends galleys to author. Free book catalog available; inquiry letter first and ms only if so requested by us.

Advice: "Submit professional work (within our parameters of interest) with well worked-over language and clean manuscripts prepared to exacting standards."

THRESHOLD BOOKS, RD 4, Box 600, Dusty Ridge Rd., Putney VT 05346. (802)254-8300. Director: Edmund Helminski. Estab. 1981. Small independent publisher with plans for gradual expansion. Books: 60 lb. natural paper; offset litho printing; sew-wrap binding; average print order: 2,500. Averages 2-3 total titles each year.
Needs: Spiritual literature and translations of sacred texts. Published *Awakened Dreams*, by Ahmet Hilmi, translated by Camille Helminski and Refik Algan.
How to Contact: Accepts unsolicited mss. Query first, submit outline/synopsis and sample chapters or complete ms with SASE. Reports in 2 months. Simultaneous submissions OK. Publishes ms an average of 18 months after acceptance.
Terms: Pays in royalties of 7% of gross. Sometimes sends galleys to author. Book catalog free on request.
Advice: "We are still small and publishing little fiction." Publishing "less fiction, more paperbacks due to our particular area of concentration and our size."

‡*TIDE BOOK PUBLISHING COMPANY, Box 101, York Harbor ME 03911. Subsidiary of Tide Media. President: Rose Safran. Estab. 1979. Independent, small publisher. Publishes paperback originals. Averages 1 title each year. Occasionally critiques rejected mss.
Needs: Contemporary, feminist, historical, humor/satire, literary, mainstream, regional. Needs "women's novels with a social service thrust. No gothic, trash."
How to Contact: Query first or submit outline/synopsis and 1-2 sample chapters with SASE. Reports in 1 month. Simultaneous submissions OK. Accepts computer printout submissions.
Terms: Pays 100 author's copies. *Considering cost plus subsidy arrangements*—will advertise.

‡TIMES EAGLE BOOKS, (IV), Box 2441, Berkeley CA 94702. Fiction Editor: Mark Hurst. Estab. 1971. "Small operation on part-time basis." Specialized publisher limited to contributors from West Coast region. First novel print order: 2,500. Plans 2 first novels this year. Averages 2 titles each year, all fiction.
Needs: Contemporary. "Graphic descriptions of teenage life by West Coast youth, such as Bret Easton Ellis's *Less than Zero*." Recently published *Sunbelt Stories*, by V.O. Blum (erotic/metaphysical novella collection).
How to Contact: Does not accept or return unsolicited mss. Query first in one paragraph. Typically reports in 3 weeks.
Terms: Pays in royalties of 10%.

TUDOR PUBLISHERS, INC., (II), P.O. Box 38366, Greensboro NC 27438. (919)282-5907. Editor: Pam Cox. Estab. 1986. Small independent press. Publishes hardcover and paperback originals. Book: offset; Smyth-sewn hardcover/trade paperback; occasional illustrations; average print order: 3,000; first novel print order: 1,000-2,000. Published new writers within the last year. Plans 1 first novel this year. Averages 3-5 total titles, 1-2 fiction titles each year. Sometimes comments on rejected ms.
  ● *The Mean Lean Weightlifting Queen* has been named to the Sunshine State Reader's List by the Florida Library Association and to the Books for the Teen Age List by the New York City Public Library.
Needs: Literary, multicultural, thriller (adult and young adult), regional (Southeast), young adult/teen (10-18 years). "No romance, western." Currently not accepting mystery submissions. Recently published *The Mean Lean Weightlifting Queen*, by Mark Emerson (young adult novel); *Locked Out*, by Margaret Yang; and *Chemo*, by Carol Hazelwood.
How to Contact: Accepts unsolicited mss. "Outline and query first, please." Submit outline/synopsis and 3 sample chapters. SASE. Reports in 2 weeks on queries; 6 weeks on mss.
Terms: Pays royalties of 10%. Sends galleys to author. Publishes ms 12-18 months after acceptance. Book catalog for #10 SASE.
Advice: "Tell us of any publishing done previously. Send a clear summary or outline of the book with a cover letter and SASE. Interested in suspense in both adult and young adult; also literary fiction of high quality. Send only your best work. No romance, science fiction, western; no multigenerational sagas unless of extremely high quality. Prefer work by previously-published author."

✦TURNSTONE PRESS, (II), 607-100 Arthur St., Winnipeg, Manitoba R3B 1H3 Canada. (204)947-1555. Managing Editor: Jamie Hutchinson. Estab. 1976. Books: Offset paper; perfect-bound; average first novel print order: 1,500. Published new writers within the last year. Averages 8 total titles/year. Occasionally critiques rejected ms.

✝ **The double dagger before a listing indicates that the listing is new in this edition. New markets are often the most receptive to submissions by new writers.**

Needs: Experimental and literary. "We will be doing only 2-3 fiction titles a year. Interested in new work exploring new narrative/fiction forms. We publish some anthologies (e.g. *Made in Manitoba*, edited by Wayne Tefs). Stories are nominated." Published *Raised by the River*, by Jake MacDonald; *Some Great Thing*, by Lawrence Hill; and *Touch the Dragon*, by Karen Connelly.

How to Contact: *Canadian authors only.* Send SASE. Reports in 1 month on queries; 2-4 months on mss.

Terms: Pays royalties of 10%; 10 author's copies. Book catalog free on request.

Advice: "Like most Canadian literary presses, we depend heavily on government grants which are not available for books by non-Canadians. Do some homework before submitting work to make sure your subject matter/genre/writing style falls within the publishers area of interest. Specializes in experimental literary, and prairie writing."

TURTLE POINT PRESS, (II), 103 Hog Hill, Chappaqua NY 10514. (800)453-2992. President: J.D. Rabinowitz. Estab. 1990. "Small press publishing mostly lost literary fiction in quality paperback editions. Beginning in 1994 doing contemporary fiction as well." Publishes paperback originals and reprints. Books: recycled 60 lb. stock paper; sewn binding; occasional illustrations; average print order: 1,500; first novel print order 800-1,500. Plans 2 first novels this year. Averages 4-5 fiction titles each year. Sometimes comments on rejected ms.

Needs: Literary, novels, translations. "Literary fiction, *tranlations* particularly from French, Spanish and Italian." Published *The Toys of Princes*, by Ghislain de Diesbach (Richard Howard, translator) (short stories); *Clovis*, by Michael Ferrier (social-satire fiction); and *The Diary of a Forty-Niner*, edited by Jackson/Carfield (journal).

How to Contact: Submit outline/synopsis and sample chapters. Include estimated word count, short bio, list of publishing credits. Send SASE for reply, return of ms or send a disposable copy of ms. Reports in 1 month.

Terms: Pays royalty (varies), negotiable advance or honorarium. Publishes ms 4-12 months after acceptance. Book catalogs are free.

Advice: "We are publishers of lost fiction with a keen interest in doing contemporary writing and contemporary translation."

ULTRAMARINE PUBLISHING CO., INC., (III), Box 303, Hastings-on-the-Hudson NY 10706. (914)478-1339. Fax: (914)478-1365. Publisher: Christopher P. Stephens. Estab. 1973. Small publisher. "We have 200 titles in print. We also distribute for authors where a major publisher has dropped a title." Encourages new writers. Averages 15 total titles, 12 fiction titles each year. Buys 90% agented fiction. Occasionally critiques rejected ms.

Needs: Experimental, fantasy, mainstream, science fiction, short story collections. No romance, westerns, mysteries.

How to Contact: Prefers agented ms. Does not accept unsolicited mss. Submit outline/synopsis and 2 sample chapters with SASE. Reports in 6 weeks. Simultaneous submissions OK.

Terms: Pays royalties of 10% minimum; advance is negotiable. Publishes ms an average of 8 months after acceptance. Free book catalog.

*UNIVERSITY EDITIONS, (I, II), 59 Oak Lane, Spring Valley, Huntington WV 25704. Imprint of Aegina Press. Managing Editor: Ira Herman. Estab. 1983. Independent publisher presently expanding. Publishes hardcover and paperback originals and reprints. Books: 50 lb. library-weight paper; litho offset printing; most are perfect-bound; illustrations; average print order: 500-1,000; first novel print order: 500-1,000. Plans 20 first novels this year. "We strongly encourage new writers." Averages 35 total titles, approximately 25 fiction titles each year. Often critiques rejected ms.

● See also the listing for Aegina Press in this section.

Needs: Adventure, contemporary, ethnic, experimental, fantasy, feminist, historical, romance (gothic), horror, humor/satire, juvenile (all types), literary, mainstream, mystery/suspense (private eye, romantic suspense, young adult), regional, science fiction (hard science, soft sociological), short story collections, translations, war. "Historical, literary and regional fiction are our main areas of emphasis." Recently published *Voice of the Vanquished*, by Helen Heightsman Gordan (novel); *Denise, and Other Stories*, by Claude H. Rolle (short story collection); and *Sepulchral House*, by Richard J. Johnson (novel)

How to Contact: Accepts unsolicited mss. "We depend upon manuscripts that arrive unsolicited." Query or submit outline/synopsis and 3 or more sample chapters or complete ms. "We prefer to see entire manuscripts; we will consider queries and partials as well." SASE. Reports in 1 week on queries; 1 month on mss. Simultaneous submissions OK.

Terms: Payment is negotiated individually for each book. Depends upon author and subject. *Subsidy publishes most new titles.* Sends galleys to author.

Advice: "We attempt to encourage and establish new authors. Editorial tastes in fiction are eclectic. We try to be open to any type of fiction that is well written. We are publishing more fiction now that the very large publishers are getting harder to break into. We publish softcovers primarily, in order to keep books affordable."

THE UNIVERSITY OF ARKANSAS PRESS, (I), Fayetteville AR 72701. (501)575-3246. Director: Miller Williams. Acquisitions Editor: Kevin Brock. Estab. 1980. Small university press. Publishes hardcover and paperback originals. Average print order: 750 cloth and 2,000 paper copies. Averages 30 total titles, 2 short fiction titles (a novel only in translation or reprint) each year.
Needs: Literary, mainstream, short story collections and translations. Publishes anthologies or special editions. Stories are usually selected by the editor. Recently published *Augustus*, by John Williams (novel); *Horses into the Night*, by Baltasar Porcel, translated by John Gatman (novel); *Overgrown with Love*, by Scott Ely (short story collection); and *Atomic Love*, by Joe David Bellamy (novella and short stories).
How to Contact: Accepts unsolicited mss. Query first with SASE. Reports in 2 weeks. Simultaneous submissions OK.
Terms: Pays royalties of 10% on hardback, 6% on paperback; 10 author's copies. Publishes ms an average of 1 year after acceptance. Writer's guidelines and book catalog for 9×12 SASE.
Advice: "We are looking for fiction—primarily short fiction—written with energy, clarity and economy. Apart from this, we have no predisposition concerning style or subject matter. The University of Arkansas Press does not respond to queries or proposals not accompanied by SASE."

UNIVERSITY OF MISSOURI PRESS, (II), 2910 LeMone Blvd., Columbia MO 65201. (314)882-7641. Fax: (314)884-4498. Fiction Editor: Clair Willcox. Estab. 1958. "University press." Publishes paperback originals (short story collections only). Published new writers within the last year. Averages story collections each year. Sometimes comments on rejected ms.
• A University of Missouri Press book, *From Hunger*, by Gerald Shapiro, received the Edward Lewis Wallant Award in 1994.
Needs: Short story collections. No children's fiction. Recently published *Goodnight Silky Sullivan*, by Laurie Alberts (stories); *Kneeling On Rice*, by Elizabeth Denton (stories); and *Mississippi History*, by Steve Yarbrough (stories).
How to Contact: Query first. Submit cover letter and sample story or two. Include estimated word count. "Bio/publishing credits optional." SASE for reply. Simultaneous submissions OK.
Terms: Pays in royalties. Sends galleys to author. Book catalogs are free.

VANDAMERE PRESS, (II), P.O. Box 5243, Arlington VA 22205. Editor: Jerry Frank. Estab. press 1984; firm 1976. "Small press, independent publisher of quality hard and softcover books." Publishes hardcover and paperback originals. Published new writers within the last year. Averages 6 total titles, 1 fiction title each year. Sometimes comments on rejected ms.
Needs: Adventure, erotica, humor/satire, military/war. No children's/juvenile/young adult. Published *War That Never Was*, by Michael Palmer; and *Ancestral Voices*, by Hugh Fitzgerald Ryan.
How to Contact: Accepts unsolicited mss. Submit outline/synopsis and 3-4 sample chapters or complete ms with cover letter. Include bio (1-2 pages), list of publishing credits. Send SASE for reply, return of ms or send a disposable copy of the ms. Reporting time varies with work load. Simultaneous submissions OK.
Terms: Pays royalties; negotiable small advance. Sends galleys to author. Publishes ms 3 months-2 years after acceptance.
Advice: "Submissions must be neat, clean and double spaced. Author should include a résumé. Manuscript package should not take ten minutes to unwrap. And do not send registered or certified."

♣VÉHICULE PRESS, (IV), Box 125, Place du Parc Station, Montreal, Quebec H2W 2M9 Canada. Imprint: Signal Editions for poetry. Publisher/Editor: Simon Dardick. Estab. 1973. Small publisher of scholarly, literary and cultural books. Publishes hardcover and paperback originals. Books: good quality paper; offset printing; perfect and cloth binding; illustrations; average print order: 1,000-3,000. Averages 13 total titles each year.
• A Véhicule Press book, *Evil Eye* received the QSPELL Prize for Fiction.
Needs: Feminist, literary, regional, short story collections, translations—"*by Canadian residents only.*" No romance or formula writing. Recently published *Evil Eye*, by Ann Diamond; *Snow Over Judaea*, by Kenneth Radu; *Friends & Marriages*, by George Szonto; and *The Book & The Veil*, by Yeshim Ternar.
How to Contact: Query first or send sample chapters. SASE ("no U.S. stamps, please"). Reports in 3 months on mss.
Terms: Pays in royalties of 10% minimum; 12% maximum. "Depends on press run and sales." Sends galleys to author. "Translators of fiction can receive Canada Council funding, which publisher applies for." Book catalog for 9×12 SASE.
Advice: "Quality in almost any style is acceptable. We believe in the editing process."

VINE BOOKS IMPRINT, (II), Servant Publications, P.O. Box 8617, Ann Arbor MI 48107. Managing Editor: Heidi Hess. Estab. 1973. "Midsize independent publisher." Publishes paperback originals. Published new writers within the last year. Plans 1 first novel this year. Averages 25 total titles, 2 fiction titles each year.
Needs: Religious/inspirational (general), romance (historical, romantic suspense), western (frontier saga). "All published manuscripts have a strong moral theme, as we are a Christian publishing house and publish primarily for the religious (CBA) market." Published *Strike Midnight*, by Matera (apocalyptic); *Bloodlines*,

by Weaver/Jenkins (supernatural); and *Theodosia*, by McMath (historical). Publishes The American Woman series.

How to Contact: Accepts unsolicited mss ("only from published authors"). Query with outline/synopsis and 2 sample chapters. Include estimated word count, bio (2 pages) and list of publishing credits. Send a disposable copy of ms. Reports in 2 months on queries. Simultaneous submissions OK.

Terms: Pays royalties of 10% minimum. Offers negotiable advance. Publishes ms 6 months to 1 year after acceptance.

‡*THE VIRTUAL PRESS, (II), 408 Division St., Shawano WI 54166. Imprints are Virtual Fantasy, Virtual Mystery, Virtual Science Fiction, Virtual Truth. Publisher: William Stanck. Estab. 1994. "Nontraditional publisher (small press)." Publishes electronic novels. Books: on floppy/CD. Published new writers within the last year. Plans 1-2 first novels this year. Averages 20 total titles, 18-20 fiction titles each year. Sometimes critiques or comments on rejected ms.

Needs: Fantasy (sword and sorcery, high fantasy), horror (dark fantasy), mystery/suspense (cozy, malice domestic), science fiction, thriller/espionage, young adult/teen (fantasy/science fiction, mystery/suspense, series, sports). Looking for fantasy, science fiction and mystery. "No erotica, overly violent." Plans anthologies on fantasy, mystery, science fiction. Stories are chosen from contest winners and submissions. Recently published *At Dream's End: A Kingdom in the Balance* (fantasy). Publishes The Destiny Chronicles (fantasy) and The Myndstar Novels (science fiction) series.

How to Contact: No unsolicited submissions. Query letter first. Should include estimated word count, list of publishing credits. SASE for reply. Reports in 2-3 months on queries. Accepts disk submissions (3½, 5¼, DOS, MAC, Amiga). E-mail address: william@tvp.com.

Terms: Pays royalties of 8% minimum; 25% maximum. Subsidy publishes 25%. "We offer electronic publishing services to authors who want 100% control over their works, only when requested." Publishes ms 6-9 months after acceptance.

Advice: "Our press will continue to grow and need new books. We are a nontraditional press doing some dynamic things. We prefer serial fiction. In the electronic marketplace second sales are the key to success. While electronic publishing allows us to offer higher royalties and give our books longer lives, we don't sell at high volume. Our e-books sell slowly over a long period of time."

VISTA PUBLICATIONS, (II), P.O. Box 661447, 107 Westward Dr., Miami Springs FL 33166. Owner: Helen Brose. Estab. 1988. One-person operation. Publishes paperback originals. Books: bond paper; offset printing; perfect binding; average print order: 1,000-1,200; first novel print order: 1,000. Averages 2 total titles, 1-2 fiction titles each year. Sometimes comments on rejected ms.

Needs: Adventure, ethnic/multicultural, historical, mystery/suspense, regional (Guatemala and Central America), romance, short story collections. "We publish books about Guatemala and/or Central America in English or Spanish." Published *El Salvador de Buques*, by Rodrigo Rey Rosa (novel).

How to Contact: Accepts unsolicited mss. Query first. Include bio, list of publishing credits. SASE for reply. Agented fiction 30%. Reports in 1 month on queries; 3 months on mss. Simultaneous submissions OK. Accepts electronic submissions.

Terms: Pays royalties of 10% minimum; 15% maximum. Sends galleys to author. Publishes ms 6-12 months after acceptance. Writer's guidelines free. Book catalog free.

Advice: "We publish fiction and nonfiction in English and/or Spanish which relate to Guatemala or the Central America area. Each book is judged on its own merit; category is not important. However, you should keep in mind the guidelines of interest of our publishing house. We appreciate good writing."

W.W. PUBLICATIONS, (IV), Subsidiary of A.T.S., Box 373, Highland MI 48357-0373. (813)585-0985. Also publishes *Minas Tirith Evening Star*. Editor: Philip Helms. Estab. 1967. One-man operation on part-time basis. Publishes paperback originals and reprints. Books: typing paper; offset printing; staple-bound; black ink illustrations; average print order: 500; first novel print order: 500. Averages 1 title (fiction) each year. Occasionally critiques rejected ms.

• *Minas Tirith Evening Star* is also listed in this book. The publisher is an arm of the American Tolkien Society.

Needs: Fantasy, science fiction, and young adult/teen (fantasy/science fiction). "Specializes in Tolkien-related or middle-earth fiction." Published *The Adventures of Fungo Hafwirse*, by Philip W. Helms and David L. Dettman.

How to Contact: Accepts unsolicited mss. Submit complete ms with SASE. Reports in 1 month. Simultaneous submissions OK.

Terms: Individual arrangement with author depending on book, etc.; provides 5 author's copies. Free book catalog.

Advice: "We are publishing more fiction and more paperbacks. The author/editor relationship: a friend and helper."

WHITE PINE PRESS, (I), 10 Village Square, Fredonia NY 14063. (716)672-5743. Fax: (716)672-5743. Director: Dennis Maloney. Fiction Editor: Elaine La Mattina. Estab. 1973. Independent literary publisher.

Publishes paperback originals and reprints. Books: 60 lb. natural paper; offset; perfect binding; average print order: 2,000-3,000; first novel print order: 2,000. Averages 8-10 total titles, 6-7 fiction titles each year.

● See the interview with Fiction Editor Elaine La Mattina in the 1995 edition of *Novel & Short Story Writer's Market*.

Needs: Ethnic/multicultural, literary, short story collections. Looking for "strong novels." No romance, science fiction. Publishes anthologies. Editors select stories. Recently published *Limbo*, by Dixie Salazar (novel); *Happy Days, Uncle Sergio*, by Margali Garcia Ramis (novel); and *Remaking A Lost Harmony—Stories from the Hispanic Caribbean*, edited by Lizabeth P. Gebert and Margarite Fernandez-Olmos. Publishes Dispatches series (international fiction), a Human Rights series, and Secret Weavers series (writing by Latin American Women).

How to Contact: Accepts unsolicited mss. Query letter with outline/synopsis and 2 sample chapters. Should include estimated word count and list of publishing credits. SASE for reply or return of ms. Agented fiction 10%. Reports in 2 weeks on queries; 3 months on mss. Simultaneous submissions OK.

Terms: Pays royalties of 5% minimum; 10% maximum. Offers negotiable advance. Pays in author's copies; payment depends on grant/award money. Sends galleys to author. Publishes 1-2 years after acceptance. Book catalog free.

WILLOWISP PRESS, (II), Division of PAGES, Inc., 801 94th Ave. N., St. Petersburg FL 33702-2426. (813)578-7600. Imprints include Worthington Press, Hamburger Press, Riverbank Press. Address material to Acquisitions Editor. Estab. 1984. Publishes paperback originals for children. Published new writers within the last year.

Needs: "Children's fiction and nonfiction, K-middle school." Adventure, contemporary and romance, for grades 5-8; preschool/picture book. No "violence, sex; romance must be very lightly treated." Recently published *Corey's Fire*, by Lee Wardlaw; *Johnny Appleseed and the Bears*, by David Novak; and *For the Love of Chimps: The Jane Goodall Story*, by Martha E. Kendall.

How to Contact: Accepts unsolicited mss. Query (except picture books) with outline/synopsis and 2 sample chapters. Must send SASE. Reporting time on queries varies; 2 months on mss. Simultaneous submissions OK. "Prefer hard copy for original submissions; prefer disk for publication."

Terms: Pay "varies." Publishes ms 6-12 months after acceptance. Writer's guidelines for #10 SASE. Book catalog for 9×12 SAE with 5 first-class stamps.

Advice: "We publish what *kids* want to read, so tell your story in a straightforward way with 'kid-like' language that doesn't convey an adult tone or sentence structure. When possible and natural, consider incorporating multicultural themes and characters. Give us your *best* shot; one story or proposal per envelope."

WOMAN IN THE MOON PUBLICATIONS, (I, IV), P.O. Box 2087, Cupertino CA 95015-2087. (408)738-4623 or (408)864-8212. Publisher: Dr. SDiane A. Bogus. Editor-in-Chief: Mario Zelaya. Estab. 1979. "We are a small press with a primary publishing agenda for poetry, New Age and reference books of no more than 1,000 words biannually. We accept short story manuscripts." Averages 2-4 total titles each year. Comments on rejected mss.

Needs: Contemporary, ethnic, fantasy, gay, lesbian, psychic/supernatural/occult, prisoner's stories, short story collections.

How to Contact: Accepts unsolicited mss between January 1-April 30 only up to 100 mss. Query first or submit outline/synopsis and sample chapters. Query by letter, phone, fax or e-mail. SASE for query. Acknowledges in 1 week; reports during or at end of season. Simultaneous submissions OK. E-mail address: 5b02701@mercury.fhda.edu.

Terms: *$30 reading fee required.* Pays royalties of 5% minimum; 10% maximum. Pays $25 plus 2 copies for short stories in quarterly newsletter. Publishes ms within 2 years after acceptance. Writer's guidelines for #10 SASE. Book catalog for 6×9 SAE and $2.01 postage.

Advice: "To the short story writer, write us a real life lesbian gay set of stories. Tell us how life is for a Black person in an enlightened world. Create a possibility, an ideal that humanity can live toward. Write a set of stories that will free, redeem and instruct humanity. The trends in fiction by women have to do with the heroine as physical and capable and not necessarily defended by or romantically linked to a male." Sponsors fiction and nonfiction prose contest in the name of Audre Lorde. Awards two $250 prizes. Contest runs from September 1 to November 30. Winners announced in February.

✱WOMEN'S PRESS, (I, II, IV), 517 College St., Suite 233, Toronto, Ontario M6G 4A2 Canada. (416)921-2425. Estab. 1972. Publishes paperback originals. Books: web coat paper; web printing; perfect-bound; average print order: 2,000; first novel print order: 1,500. Published new writers within the last year. Plans 2 novels this year. Averages 9 total titles each year. Sometimes "briefly" critiques rejected ms.

Needs: Prefers Canadian material. Contemporary, feminist, lesbian, juvenile, adolescent (contemporary, fantasy, historical), literary, multicultural, preschool/picture book, short story collections, mysteries, women's and young adult/teen (problem novels). Recently published *S.P. Likes A.D.*, by Catherine Brett; *Harriet's Daughter*, by Marlene Nourbese Philip; *The Shrunken Dream*, by Jane Tapsubei Creider; and *Division of Surgery*, by Donna McFarlane.

How to Contact: Send query letter with SAE and "Canadian stamps or a check. Our mandate is to publish Canadian women or landed immigrants." Reports in 3 months.

Terms: Pays in royalties of 10% maximum; small advance. Sends galleys to author. Free book catalog.

Advice: "We publish feminist, lesbian and adolescent novels, anthologies of short stories and single-author story collections. We encourage women of all races and ethnicities to submit work and we support the work of writers of color, disabled writers and others facing barriers to publishing."

WOODLEY MEMORIAL PRESS, (IV), English Dept., Washburn University, Topeka KS 66621. (913)234-1032. Editor: Robert N. Lawson. Estab. 1980. "Woodley Memorial Press is a small press which publishes book-length poetry and fiction collections by Kansas writers only; by 'Kansas writers' we mean writers who reside in Kansas or have a Kansas connection." Publishes paperback originals. Averages 2 titles each year. Sometimes comments on rejected ms.

• Check for next short story collection contest. Work must be by a Kansas resident only. Most of the fiction the press publishes comes from its short story competition.

Needs: Contemporary, experimental, literary, mainstream, short story collection. "We do not want to see genre fiction, juvenile, or young adult." Recently published *The Monday-Wednesday-Friday Girl and Other Stories*, by Stuart Levine (short stories).

How to Contact: *Charges $5 reading fee.* Accepts unsolicited mss. Send complete ms. SASE. Reports in 2 weeks on queries; 2 months on mss. E-mail address: zzlaws@acc.wuacc.edu.

Terms: "Terms are individually arranged with author after acceptance of manuscript." Publishes ms one year after acceptance. Writer's guidelines for #10 SASE.

Advice: "We only publish one work of fiction a year, on average, and definitely want it to be by a Kansas author. We are more likely to do a collection of short stories by a single author."

WRITE WAY PUBLISHING, (II), 3806 S. Fraser, Aurora CO 80014. (303)680-1493. Fax: (303)680-2181. Owner/Editor: Dorrie O'Brien. Estab. 1993. Small press. Publishes hardcover and paperback originals. Average print order: 2,500; first novel print order: 1,000. Published new writers within the last year. Averages 10-12 total titles, all fiction, each year. Often comments on rejected ms.

Needs: Adventure, family saga, fantasy, glitz, historical (general), horror, humor/satire, military/war, mystery/suspense (amateur sleuth, cozy, police procedural, private eye/hardboiled), psychic/supernatural, science fiction (soft/sociological, space trilogy/series), thriller/espionage. Recently published *Death of A DJ*, by Jane Rubino; *Roadkill*, by Richard Sanford; *The Sherman Letter*, by Leonard Palmer; and *Unprotected Witness*, by Guy Slaughter.

How to Contact: Query with short outline/synopsis and 1-2 sample chapters. Include estimated word count, bio (reasonably short) and list of publishing credits. Send SASE for reply, return of ms or send a disposable copy of ms. Agented fiction 10%. Reports in 2-4 weeks on queries; 6-8 months on mss. Simultaneous submissions OK.

Terms: Pays royalties of 8% minimum; 10% maximum. Does not pay advances. Sends galleys to author. Writer's guidelines for SASE.

Advice: "Always have the query letter, synopsis and the first chapters edited by an unbiased party prior to submitting them to us. Remember: first impressions are just as important to a publisher as they might be a prospective employer."

ZEPHYR PRESS, (III), 13 Robinson St., Somerville MA 02145. Subsidiary of Aspect, Inc. Editorial Directors: Ed Hogan and Leora Zeitlin. Estab. 1980. Publishes hardcover and paperback originals. Books: acid-free paper; offset printing; Smyth-sewn binding; some illustrations; average print order: 1,500-2,000; first novel print order: 1,000-1,500. Averages 5 total titles, 1-2 fiction titles each year.

Needs: Contemporary, ethnic, feminist/lesbian, historical, literary, mainstream, regional, short story collections, translations (Russian, Eastern European fiction). Published *The Shoemaker's Tale*, by Mark Ari; and *Sleeper at Harvest Time*, by Leonid Latynin.

How to Contact: "We no longer read unsolicited mss. Our focus in fiction is now on contemporary Russian writers in translation. We accept queries from agents, and from authors whose previous publications and professional credits (you must include a summary of these) evince work of exceptional talent and vision. Queries should include vita, list of publications, and up to 10 sample pages, photocopies only. If we are interested, we will request the full manuscript. Otherwise, we will make no response."

Terms: Pays royalties of approximately 12% of publisher's net for first edition. Occasional flexibility of terms." Sends galleys to author. Book catalog for SASE.

Advice: "Seek well qualified feedback from literary magazine editors or agents and/or professionally established writers before submitting manuscripts to publishers. We regard the author/editor relationship as one of close cooperation, from editing through promotion."

ZOLAND BOOKS, INC., (III), 384 Huron Ave., Cambridge MA 02138. (617)864-6252. Publisher: Roland Pease. Associate Editor: Michael Lindgren. Marketing Associate: Sonig MacNeil. Estab. 1987. "We are a literary press, publishing poetry, fiction, nonfiction, photography, and other titles of literary interest." Publishes hardcover and paperback originals. Books: acid-free paper; sewn binding; some with illustrations; average print order: 2,000-5,000. Averages 10 total titles each year.

- *An Altogether Different Language*, by Ann Porlee and published by Zoland Books, was a finalist for the 1995 National Book Award.

Needs: Contemporary, feminist, literary, short story collections. Recently published *Offspring*, by Jonathan Strong; *Seeing Eye*, by Michael Martore; and *The Country Road*, by James Loughlin.

How to Contact: Accepts unsolicited mss. Query first, then send complete ms with cover letter. SASE. Reports in 4-6 weeks on queries; 3-6 months on mss.

Terms: Pays royalties of 5-8%. Average advance: $1,500; negotiable (also pays author's copies). Sends galleys to author. Publishes ms 1-2 years after acceptance. Book catalog for 6×9 SAE and 2 first-class stamps.

International small press

The following small presses from countries outside the U.S. and Canada will consider novels or short stories in English. Some of the countries represented here include Australia, England, France, India, Ireland, Italy, Ghana, New Zealand, South Africa, Sweden, Germany and Zimbabwe. Many of these markets do not pay in cash, but may provide author copies. Always include a self-addressed envelope with International Reply Coupons to ensure a response or the return of your manuscript. International Reply Coupons are available at the main branch of your local post office. To save the cost of return postage on your manuscript, you may want to send a copy of your manuscript for the publisher to keep or throw away and enclose a self-addressed postcard with one IRC for a reply.

ADAEX EDUCATIONAL PUBLICATIONS, P.O. Box AK188, Kumasi, Ghana. Publisher/Fiction Editor: Asare Konadu Yamoah. Average 5-10 fiction titles/year. "Publication development organization for Ghanaian, African and world literature: novels, workbooks, language development, etc." Length: 8-250 typed pages. Send brief summary and first and last chapter. Pays advance and royalties. Looks for cultural development, romance, literary translators and copyright brokers.

AFRICA CHRISTIAN PRESS, P.O. Box 30, Achimota, Ghana, West Africa. Editorial Assistant: Mrs. Margaret Saah. Averages 6 fiction titles/year. "We are a Christian publishing house specializing in Christian fiction works by Africans or expariates with a long association with Africa." Length: 15,000 words minimum. Send: Cover letter, synopsis, brief summary, sample chapter/s and/or entire manuscript. Pays royalties. Mss should be "typewritten, double spaced, with generous margins." Send 2 copies and a SAE with IRCs for response/return. Write for catalog and/or writer's guidelines.

‡THE AMERICAN UNIVERSITY IN CAIRO PRESS, 113 Kasr El Aini St., Cairo Egypt. Director: Werner Mark Linz. Averages 2-4 fiction titles/year. "Egyptology, Middle East studies, Islamic art and architecture, social anthropology, Arabic literature in translation. The press publishes the journal *Cario Papers*, a quarterly monograph series in social studies. Special series, joint imprints, and/or copublishing programs: Numerous copublishing programs with U.S. and U.K. university presses and other U.S. and European publishers." Length: 30,000 words minimum; 75,000 words maximum. Send a cover letter and entire ms. "Manuscripts should deal with Egypt and/or Middle East."

ATTIC PRESS, (IV), 4 Upper Mount St., Dublin 2, Ireland. Contact: Managing Editor. Averages 6-8 fiction titles/year. "Attic Press is an independent, export-oriented, Irish-owned publishing house with a strong international profile. The press specializes in the publication of fiction and nonfiction books by and about women by Irish and international authors." Publishes a series of teenage fiction, Bright Sparks. Send cover letter, synopsis, brief summary, sample chapters. Pays advance on signing contract and royalties. Write for catalog.

BASEMENT PRESS, 4 Upper Mount St., Dublin 2, Ireland. Contact: Managing Editor. "Basement Press is the general division of Attic Press (see listing in this section), publishing fiction and nonfiction by both men and women, specializing in biography, business and political exposé. Basement Press aims to be fresh, irreverent, controversial and entertaining, and publishes a series of Gay and Lesbian fiction and nonfiction entitled Queer Views." Send cover letter, synopsis, brief summary and sample chapters. Pays advance on signing contract and royalties.

Sending to a country other than your own? Be sure to send International Reply Coupons instead of stamps for replies or return of your manuscript.

BIBLIOTECA DI NOVA SF, FUTURO, GREAT WORKS OF SF, (IV), Perseo Libri srl, Box 1240, I-40100 Bologna, Italy. Fiction Editor: Ugo Malaguti. "Science fiction and fantasy; novels and/or collections of stories." Pays 7% royalties on cover price; advance: $800-1,000 on signing contract. Buys Italian book rights; other rights remain with author. "While preferring published writers, we also consider new writers."

CANONGATE BOOKS LTD., 14 High St., Edinburgh EH1 1TE Scotland, UK. Fiction Editor: Jamie Byng. Averages 2-8 fiction titles/year. "Cultural contribution rather than just hedonistic exuberance provides the flavor of novels published by Canongate in the past, but this criterion is not inflexible if the exuberance has, in our view, genuine quality." Length: 40,000 words minimum; 500,000 words maximum. Send cover letter, synopsis and 3 sample chapters. Pays advance and 10% royalty. Submitting writers should be sure ms "possesses literary merit and commercial potential." Canongate's new imprint, Payback Press, publishes African-American and Jamaican culture work. Write for information and guidelines.

‡CHRISTCHURCH PUBLISHERS LTD., 2 Caversham St., London S.W.3, 4AH UK. Fiction Editor: James Hughes. Averages 25 fiction titles/year. "Miscellaneous fiction, also poetry. More 'literary' style of fiction, but also thrillers, crime fiction etc." Length: 30,000 words minimum. Send a cover letter, synopsis, brief summary. "Preliminary letter and *brief* synopsis favored." Pays advance and royalties. "We have contacts and agents worldwide."

‡GERALD DUCKWORTH & CO. LTD., 48 Hoxton Square, London N1 6PB U.K. Publisher and Managing Director: Robin Baird-Smith. Averages 10 titles/year. Estab. 1898. Literary fiction only (Alice Thomas Ellis, Beryl Bainbridge, John Bayley). Length: 50,000 words minimum; 100,000 words maximum. Send a cover letter, synopsis and 2 sample chapters. Pays advance—½ on signature of agreement; ½ on first hardback publication. "Please only submit if work is of excellent literary standard."

HANDSHAKE EDITIONS, Atelier A2, 83 rue de la Tombe Issoire, 75014 Paris France. Editor: Jim Haynes. Publishes 4 story collections or novels/year. "Only face-to-face submissions accepted. More interested in 'faction' and autobiographical writing." Pays in copies. Writers interested in submitting a manscript should "have lunch or dinner with me in Paris."

HEMKUNT, Publishers A-78 Naraina Industrial Area Ph.I, New Delhi India 110028. Managing Director: G.P. Singh. Export Directors: Deepinder Singh/Arvinder Singh. "We would be interested in novels, preferably by authors with a published work. Would like to have distribution rights for US, Canada and UK beside India." Send a cover letter, brief summary, 3 sample chapters (first, last and one other chapter). "Writer should have at least 1-2 published novels to his/her credit." Catalog on request.

KAWABATA PRESS, (II), Knill Cross House, Knill Cross, Millbrook, Torpoint, Cornwall PL10 1DX England. Fiction Editor: C. Webb. "Mostly poetry—but prose should be realistic, free of genre writing and clichés and above all original in ideas and content." Length: 200-4,000 words (for stories). "Don't forget return postage (or IRC)." Writers receive half of profits after print costs are covered. Write for guidelines and book list.

‡THE LILLIPUT PRESS, 4 Rosemount Terrace, Arbour Hill, Dublin 7 Ireland. Fiction Editor: Antony Farrell. Averages 2-3 fiction titles/year. Length: 50,000 words minimum. Send a cover letter, brief summary and 1 sample chapter. Pays small advance and royalties. "Send double-spaced hard copy." Write for catalog.

THE LITERATURE BUREAU, P.O. Box CY749 Causeway, Harare Zimbabwe. Fiction Editor: B.C. Chitsike. Averages 12 fiction titles/year. "All types of fiction from the old world novels to the modern ones with current issues. We publish these books in association with commercial publishers but we also publish in our own right. We specialize in Shona and Ndebele, our local languages in Zimbabwe. Manuscripts in English are not our priority." Length: 7,000-30,000 words. Send entire manuscript. Pays royalties. "Send the complete manuscript for assessment. If it is a good one it is either published by the Bureau or sponsored for publication. If it needs any correction, a full report will be sent to the author." Obtain guidelines by writing to the Bureau. "We have 'Hints to New Authors,' a pamphlet for aspiring authors. These can be obtained on request."

THE LUTTERWORTH PRESS, P.O. Box 60, Cambridge CB1 2NT England. Editorial Director: Colin Lester. "Almost 200-year-old small press publishing wide range of adult nonfiction, religious and children's books. The only fiction we publish is for children: picture books (with text from 0-10,000 words), educational, young novels, story collections. Also nonfiction as well as religious children's books." Send synopsis and sample chapter. Pays advance plus royalty. "Send IRCs. English language is universal, i.e., mid-Atlantic English."

MAROVERLAG, Riedingerstrasse 24, D-86153, Augsburg Germany. Editor: Benno Käsmayr. Publishes 4-6 novels or story collections/year. Publishes "exciting American authors in excellent translations; e.g. Charles Bukowski, Jack Kerouac, William Burroughs, Paul Bowles, Gerald Locklin, Keith Abbott, Raymond Federman and Gilbert Sorrentino." Send a cover letter, synopsis, brief summary and 2 sample chapters. Writers paid for published fiction. "Please include SAE and postage. Our books and catalogs can be ordered at every German bookstore. Most of them send to the U.S. too."

DAVID PHILIP PUBLISHERS, P.O. Box 23408, Claremont 7735 Cape Province South Africa. "Fiction with Southern African concern or focus. Progressive, often suitable for school or university prescription, literary, serious." Send synopsis and 1 sample chapter. Pays royalties. "Familiarize yourself with list of publisher to which you wish to submit work." Write for guidelines.

‡**VIRAGO PRESS LIMITED**, 20 Vauxhall Bridge Rd., London SWIV 2SA England. Fiction Editors: Lennie Goodings, Lynn Knight, Melanie Silgardo. Averages approximately 20 fiction titles/year. "Women's press—romance wanted. Anything top quality." Length: 60,000-120,000 words. Send cover letter with brief summary and 3 sample chapters with return postage. Pays advance and royalty."Be original and interesting!"

Small press/'95-'96 changes

The following small presses appeared in the 1995 edition of *Novel & Short Story Writer's Market* but are not in the 1996 edition. Those presses whose editors did not respond to our request for an update are listed below without explanation. If an explanation was given, it is next to the listing.

Acclaim Publishing Company
Accord Communications Ltd.
American Atheist Press
Asylum Arts (selling business)
The Atlantean Press
Audio Entertainment, Inc.
Audiozine Press
BkMk Press
Blind Beggar Press
Clothespin Fever Press (out of business)
Crystal River Press

Harry Cuff Publications Ltd.
Dare to Dream Books
Dawnwood Press
Diva Press
Frog in the Well
Helicon Nine Editions
Hermes House Press (out of business)
HMS Press
Italica Press
Left Bank Distribution
Les éditions de L'instant même

Lintel
Mercury House (requested deletion)
Pikestaff Publications, Inc. (retiring)
Senior Press
Slough Press
Sound Publications
The Spirit That Moves Us Press
Textile Bridge Press (not accepting new mss)
Wonder Digital Press

International small press/'95-'96 changes

Ashton Scholastic Ltd. (requested deletion)
Aidan Ellis Publishing
Karnak House

The Malvern Publishing Company, Ltd.
Millennium
Renditions

Serpent's Tail
Sheba Feminist Press
Shiksha Bharati
Sinclair-Stevenson Ltd.

For information on entering the **Novel & Short Story Writer's Market** *Cover Letter Contest, see page 19.*

Commercial Book Publishers

The Commercial Book Publishers section includes many of the "big-name" publishers—Avon Books; The Berkley Publishing Group; Harcourt Brace & Company; Harlequin; Alfred A. Knopf; Little, Brown and Company . . . the list goes on and on. Here is where you will find the publishers who are known for blockbuster fiction, well-known authors and billion-dollar sales figures.

This remains a tough market for new writers or for those whose work might be considered literary or experimental. All the publishers listed here publish at least several fiction titles each year, but most are novels by established authors. And, although book sales have continued to rise through the nineties, some predictions are for a slowing of growth and tightening of the market in 1996 and perhaps for the remainder of the century. (For more information on industry trends, see the Commercial Fiction Trends Report beginning on page 33.)

Although breaking into the commercial publishing market is difficult, it is not impossible. The trade magazine *Publishers Weekly* routinely features interviews with writers whose first novels are being released by top publishers. Whitney Otto's first novel, *How to Make an American Quilt*, is now a movie by Steven Spielberg.

Many editors find great satisfaction in publishing a writer's first novel. In the Insider Viewpoint with Jay Schaefer on page 440, Schaefer, senior editor at Chronicle Books, says, "Nothing excites an editor more than to be the first to publish a writer, to develop that writer and establish a relationship that will last for years. It's not a negative if you haven't been published before. It's a positive in our eyes." And Jessica Lichtenstein, senior editor for HarperPaperbacks which publishes 15 to 20 paperback titles a month, says in her Insider Viewpoint on page 448, "Every year we publish first-time writers; it's a big part of what we do, trying to discover new people. I'm constantly buying books by writers who have never been published before."

Types of commercial publishers

The publishers in this section publish books "for the trade." That is, unlike textbook, technical or scholarly publishers, trade publishers publish books to be sold to the general consumer through bookstores, chain stores or other retail outlets. Within the trade book field, however, there are a number of different types of books.

The easiest way to categorize books is by their physical appearance and the way they are marketed. Hardcover books are the more expensive editions of a book, sold through bookstores and carrying a price tag of around $20 and up. Trade paperbacks are soft-bound books, also sold mostly in bookstores, but they carry a more modest price tag of usually around $10 to $20. Today a lot of fiction is published in this form because it means a lower financial risk than hardcover.

Mass market paperbacks are another animal altogether. These are the smaller "pocket-size" books available at bookstores, grocery stores, drug stores, chain retail outlets, etc. Much genre or category fiction is published in this format. This area of the publishing industry is very open to the work of talented new writers who write in specific genres such as science fiction, romance and mystery.

At one time publishers could be easily identified and grouped by the type of books they do. Today, however, the lines between hardcover and paperback books are blurred.

Many publishers known for publishing hardcover books also publish trade paperbacks and have paperback imprints. This enables them to offer established authors (and a very few lucky newcomers) hard-soft deals in which their book comes out in both versions. Thanks to the mergers of the past decade, too, the same company may own several hardcover and paperback subsidiaries and imprints, even though their editorial focuses may remain separate.

Choosing a commercial publisher

In addition to checking the bookstores and libraries for books by publishers that interest you, you may want to refer to the Commercial Publisher section of the Category Index to find publishers divided by specific subject categories. The subjects listed in the Index are general. Read the individual listings to find which subcategories interest a publisher. For example, you will find several romance publishers listed under that heading in the Category Index, but read the listings to find which type of romance is considered—gothic, contemporary, Regency or futuristic. See How to Get the Most Out of This Book for more on how to refine your list of potential markets.

The Roman numeral ranking codes appearing after the names of the publishers will also help you in selecting a publisher. These codes are especially important in this section, because many of the publishing houses listed here require writers to submit through an agent. A numeral **III** identifies those that mostly publish established and agented authors, while a numeral **I** points to publishers most open to new writers. See the end of this introduction for a complete list of ranking codes.

In the listings

As with other sections in this book, we identify new listings with a double-dagger symbol (‡). In this section, many of these are not new publishers, but instead are established publishers who decided to list this year in the hope of finding promising new writers

We use a maple leaf symbol (✹) to identify the Canadian publishers. North American commercial publishers are grouped together and are followed by a group of publishers from around the world. Remember, self-addressed envelopes for replies from countries other than your own should include International Reply Coupons rather than stamps.

Book packagers, companies who produce books for publishers, are identified by a box symbol (■). Most book packagers pay writers a flat fee rather than royalties and buy all rights. Writers may not even get credit for the books they do for packagers, but they are very open to working with new writers.

You may also see an asterisk (*) at the start of a listing. This lets you know a press sometimes funds the publications of its books through a subsidy arrangement. By subsidy, we mean any arrangement in which the writer is expected to pay all or part of the cost of producing, distributing and marketing his book. Approach subsidy publishers with caution. Find out exactly how many books they plan to produce and what paper and binding will be used. Check with a printer to find out how much those books would cost to be printed. If the subsidy amount is more, ask what specific marketing and distribution will be done for the additional money. As with any business arrangement, feel free to ask any questions about the arrangement that concern you.

We're continuing to include editorial comments this year, set off by a bullet symbol (●) within the listing. This is where we can tell you of any honors or awards received by publishers or their books. We include information about any special requirements or circumstances that will help you know even more about the publisher's needs and policies.

A note about agents

The Business of Fiction Writing outlines how to prepare work to submit directly to a publisher. Many publishers are willing to look at unsolicited submissions, but most feel having an agent is to the writer's best advantage. In this section more than any other, you'll find a number of publishers who prefer submissions from agents.

Because the commercial fiction field has become so competitive, and publishers have so little time, more and more are relying on agents. For publishers, agents act as "first readers," wading through the deluge of submissions from writers to find the very best. For writers, a good agent can be a foot in the door—someone willing to do the necessary work to put your manuscript in the right editor's hands.

Because it is almost as hard to find a good agent as it is to find a publisher, many writers see agents as just one more roadblock to publication. Yet those who have agents say they are invaluable. Not only can a good agent help you make your work more marketable, an agent acts as your business manager and adviser, keeping your interests up front during contract negotiations.

Still, finding an agent can be very difficult for a new writer. Those already published in magazines or other periodicals have a better chance than someone with no publishing credits. Although many agents will read queries, packages and manuscripts from unpublished authors without introduction, referrals from other clients can be a big help. If you don't know any published authors, you may want to try to meet an agent at a conference before approaching them with your manuscript. Some agents even set aside time at conferences to meet new writers.

For listings of agents and more information on how to approach and deal with them, see the 1996 *Guide to Literary Agents*, published by Writer's Digest Books. The book separates nonfee- and fee-charging agents. While many agents do not charge any fees up front, a few charge writers to cover the costs of using outside readers. Be wary of those who charge large sums of money for reading a manuscript. Reading fees do not guarantee representation. Think of an agent as a potential business partner and feel free to ask tough questions about his or her credentials, experience and business practices.

For more . . .

Several of the mystery, romance and science fiction publishers included in this section are also included in *Mystery Writer's Sourcebook*, *Romance Writer's Sourcebook* or *Science Fiction Writer's Marketplace and Sourcebook* (all published by Writer's Digest Books). These books, published in alternate years, include in-depth interviews with editors and publishers. Also check issues of *Publishers Weekly* for publishing industry trade news in the U.S. and around the world or *Quill & Quire* for book publishing news in the Canadian book industry.

The ranking system we've used for listings in this section is as follows:

    I **Publisher encourages beginning or unpublished writers to submit work for consideration and publishes new writers frequently.**

    II **Publisher accepts work by established writers and by new writers of exceptional talent.**

    III **Publisher does not encourage beginning writers; publishes mostly writers with extensive previous publication credits or agented writers.**

    IV **Special-interest or regional publisher, open only to writers on certain topics or from certain geographical areas.**

ACADEMY CHICAGO PUBLISHERS, (I), 363 W. Erie St., Chicago IL 60610. (312)751-7302. Senior Editor: Anita Miller. Estab. 1975. Midsize independent publisher. Publishes hardcover and paperback originals and paperback reprints.

• Senior Editor Anita Miller received the 1994 "Publisher of the Year" award from Chicago Women in Publishing.

Needs: Biography, history, feminist, academic and anthologies. Only the most unusual mysteries, no private-eyes or thrillers. No explicit sex or violence. Serious fiction, not romance/adventure. "We will consider historical fiction that is well researched. No science fiction/fantasy, no religious/inspirational, no how-to, no cookbooks. In general, we are very conscious of women's roles. We publish very few children's books." Recently published *Circling Eden*, by Carol Magren; *Sam & His Brother Len*, by John Manderino; and *Blond Relations*, by Carlos Montgomery.

How to Contact: Accepts unsolicited mss. Query and submit first three chapters, triple spaced, with SASE and a cover letter briefly describing the content of your work. No simultaneous submissions. "Manuscripts without envelopes will be discarded. *Mailers* are a *must*."

Terms: Pays 5-10% on net in royalties; no advance. Sends galleys to author.

Advice: "At the moment we are swamped with manuscripts and anything under consideration can be under consideration for months."

ACE SCIENCE FICTION, Berkley Publishing Group, 200 Madison Ave., New York NY 10016. (212)951-8800. Estab. 1977. Publishes paperback originals and reprints. See Berkley/Ace Science Fiction.

ALGONQUIN BOOKS OF CHAPEL HILL, 708 Broadway, New York NY 10003. Prefers not to share information at this time.

ARCHWAY PAPERBACKS/MINSTREL BOOKS, 1230 Avenue of the Americas, New York NY 10020. (212)698-7268. Vice President/Editorial Director: Patricia MacDonald. Published by Pocket Books. Imprints: Minstrel Books (ages 7-11); and Archway (ages 11 and up). Publishes paperback originals and reprints.

Needs: Young adult: mystery, suspense/adventure, thrillers. Young readers (80 pages and up): adventure, animals, humor, family, fantasy, friends, mystery, school, etc. No picture books. Published *Fear Street: The New Boy*, by R.L. Stine; and *Aliens Ate My Homework*, by Bruce Coville. Published new writers this year.

How to Contact: Submit query first with outline; SASE "mandatory. If SASE not attached, query letter will not be answered."

ASPECT, (III), Imprint of Warner Books, 1271 Avenue of the Americas, New York NY 10020. (212)522-5320. Fax: (212)522-7990. Editor-in-Chief: Betsy Mitchell. Estab. 1994. Science fiction/fantasy imprint of Warner Books. Publishes hardcover and paperback originals and hardcover reprints. Published new writers within the last year. Plans 2 first novels this year. Averages 32 total fiction titles this year. Often critiques or comments on rejected ms.

Needs: Fantasy, science fiction. "No humorous fantasy or short story collections." Recently published *The Sword of Bedwyr*, R.A. Salvatore (fantasy hardcover); *Tripoint*, by C.J. Cherryh (science fiction paperback); and *Challenger's Hope*, by David Feintuch (science fiction paperback). Plans to publish ongoing series in the future.

How to Contact: No unsolicited mss. Query first or submit through agent. Include estimated word count, ½-page bio and list of publishing credits with submission. Send SASE for reply, return of ms or send a disposable copy of ms. Agented fiction 98%. Reports in 3 weeks on queries; 2 months on mss. E-mail address: 72662.2617@compuserve.com.

Terms: Offers negotiable advance. Sends galleys to author. Publishes ms approximately 1 year after acceptance.

Advice: "We are a new market because Warner has decided to revamp its science fiction and fantasy publishing program. We are publishing more titles per month across the board—hardcovers, trade paper, and mass market."

ATHENEUM BOOKS FOR YOUNG READERS, (II), Imprint of the Simon & Schuster Children's Publishing Division, 1230 Avenue of the Americas, New York NY 10022. (212)698-2716. Vice President/Editorial Director: Jonathan J. Lanman. Fiction Editors: Marcia Marshall, Sarah Caguiat, Ana Cerro, Anne Schwartz. Second largest imprint of large publisher/corporation. Publishes hardcover originals. Books: Illustrations for picture books, some illustrated short novels; average print order: 6,000-7,500; first novel print order: 5,000. Averages 60 total titles, 30 middle grade and YA fiction titles each year. Very rarely critiques rejected mss.

• Books published by Atheneum Books for Children have received the Newbery Medal (*Shiloh*, by Phyllis Reynolds Naylor) and the Christopher Award (*The Gold Coin*, by Alma Flor Ada, illustrated by Neal Waldman). Because of the merger of Macmillan and Simon & Schuster, Atheneum Books has absorbed the Scribners imprint of Macmillan.

Needs: Juvenile (adventure, animal, contemporary, fantasy, historical, sports), preschool/picture book, young adult/teen (fantasy/science fiction, historical, mystery, problem novels, sports, spy/adventure). No "paperback romance type" fiction. Recently published books include *Albert's Thanksgiving*, by Lesle Tryon (3-6, picture book); *Downriver*, by Will Hobbs (3-6, picture book); *Alice the Brave*, by Phyllis Reynolds Naylor (8-12, middle grade novel); *Uncle Vampire*, by Cynthia Grant (12 & up young adult novel).

How to Contact: Accepts unsolicited mss "if novel length, please query first." SASE. Agented fiction 40%. Reports in 4-6 weeks on queries; 8-10 weeks on mss. Simultaneous submissions OK "if we are so informed and author is unpublished."

Terms: Pays in royalties of 10%. Average advance: $3,000 "along with advance and royalties, authors standardly receive ten free copies of their book and can purchase more at a special discount." Sends galleys to author. Writer's guidelines for #10 SASE.

Advice: "We publish all hardcover originals, occasionally an American edition of a British publication. Our fiction needs have not varied in terms of quantity—of the 60-70 titles we do each year, 30 are fiction in different age levels. We are less interested in specific topics or subject matter than in overall quality of craftsmanship. First, know your market thoroughly. We publish only children's books, so caring for and *respecting* children is of utmost importance. Also, fad topics are dangerous, as are works you haven't polished to the best of your ability. (Why should we choose a 'jewel in the rough' when we can get a manuscript a professional has polished to be ready for publication.) The juvenile market is not one in which a writer can 'practice' to become an adult writer. In general, be professional. We appreciate the writers who take the time to find out what type of books we publish by visiting the libraries and reading the books. Neatness is a pleasure, too."

AVALON BOOKS, (I, II, IV), 401 Lafayette St., New York NY 10003. (212)598-0222. Vice President/ Publisher: Marcia Markland. Imprint of Thomas Bouregy Company, Inc. Publishes hardcover originals. Average print order for all books (including first novels): 2,100. Averages 60 titles/year.

Needs: "Avalon Books publishes wholesome romances, mysteries, westerns and interesting love stories. Intended for family reading, our books are read by adults as well as teenagers, and their characters are all adults. There is no graphic sex in any of our novels; kisses and embraces are as far as our characters go. Currently, we publish five books a month: two romances, one mystery romance, one career romance and one western. All the romances are contemporary; all the westerns are historical." Published *Mountain Love Song*, by Georgette Livingston (career romance); *Bachelor for Rent*, by Karen Morrell (career romance); *Night Run*, by Alice Sharpe (mystery); *Valley of the Lawless*, by Lee Martin (western). Books range in length from a minimum of 40,000 words to a maximum of 50,000 words.

How to Contact: Submit the first three chapters. "We'll contact you if we're interested." Publishes many first novels. Enclose ms-size SASE. "Will not return without a SASE." Reports in about 3 months. "Send SASE for a copy of our tip sheet."

Terms: The first half of the advance is paid upon signing of the contract; the second within 30 days after publication. Usually publishes within 6 to 8 months.

AVON BOOKS, (II), The Hearst Corporation, 1350 Avenue of the Americas, New York NY 10019. (212)261-6800. Imprints include Avon, Camelot and Flare. Senior Vice-President/Publisher: Lou Aronica. Estab. 1941. Large paperback publisher. Publishes paperback originals and reprints. Averages 300 titles a year.

● Avon will begin to publish hardcovers in September, 1996.

Needs: Fantasy, historical romance, mainstream, science fiction, medical thrillers, intrigue, war, western and young adult/teen. No poetry, short story collections, religious, limited literary or esoteric nonfiction. Published *Butterfly*, by Kathryn Harvey; *So Worthy My Love*, by Kathleen Woodiwiss.

How to Contact: Query letters only. SASE to insure response.

Terms: Vary. Sponsors Flare Novel competition.

BAEN BOOKS, (II), P.O. Box 1403, Riverdale NY 10471. (718)548-3100. Imprints are Baen Science Fiction and Baen Fantasy. Publisher and Editor: Jim Baen. Executive Editor: Toni Weisskopf. Estab. 1983. Independent publisher; books are distributed by Simon & Schuster. Publishes hardcover and paperback originals and paperback reprints. Published new writers within the last year. Plans 6-10 first novels this year. Averages 60 fiction titles each year. Occasionally critiques rejected mss.

Needs: Fantasy and science fiction. Interested in science fiction novels (generally "hard" science fiction) and fantasy novels "that at least strive for originality." Recently published *The Ship Who Won*, by Anne McCaffrey and Jody Lynn Nye (science fiction); *Oath of Swords*, by David Webe (fantasy); and *Mirro Dance*, by Lois McMaste Bujold. Published new writers within the last year.

Market categories: (I) Open to new writers; (II) Open to both new and established writers; (III) Interested mostly in established writers; (IV) Open to writers whose work is specialized.

How to Contact: Accepts unsolicited mss. Submit ms or outline/synopsis and 3 consecutive sample chapters with SASE (or IRC). Reports in 3-4 weeks on partials; 4-8 weeks on mss. Will consider simultaneous submissions, "but grudgingly and not as seriously as exclusives."

Terms: Pays in royalties; offers advance. Sends galleys to author. Writer's guidelines for SASE.

Advice: "Keep an eye and a firm hand on the overall story you are telling. Style is important but less important than plot. Good style, like good breeding, never calls attention to itself. Read *Writing to the Point*, by Algis Budrys. We like to maintain long-term relationships with authors."

BAKER BOOK HOUSE, (II), P.O. Box 6287, Grand Rapids MI 49516. (616)676-9185. Assistant Editor, Trade Books: Jane Schrier. Estab. 1939. "Midsize Evangelical publisher." Publishes hardcover and paperback originals. Books: web offset print; average print order: 5,000-10,000; first novel print order: 5,000. Averages 130 total titles. Sometimes comments on rejected ms.

Needs: "We are mainly seeking Christian fiction of two genres: Contemporary women's fiction and mystery." No fiction that is not written from a Christian perspective or of a genre not specified. Published *A Multitude of Sins*, by Virginia Stem Owens; *Familiar Darkness*, by Evelyn Minshull; and *In The Silence There Are Ghosts*, by James Schaap.

How to Contact: Does not accept unsolicited mss. Submit query letter, outline/synopsis and 3 sample chapters. SASE. Agented fiction 80% (so far). Reports in 3-4 weeks on queries. Simultaneous submissions OK.

Terms: Pays royalties of 14% (of net). Sometimes offers advance. Sends galleys to author. Publishes ms 1 year after acceptance. Writer's guidelines for #10 SASE. Book catalog for 9½ × 12½ SAE and 3 first-class stamps.

Advice: "We are not interested in historical fiction, romances, science fiction, Biblical narratives, or spiritual warfare novels. Please write for further information regarding our fiction lines. Do not send complete manuscripts."

BALLANTINE BOOKS, 201 E. 50th St., New York NY 10022. Subsidiary of Random House. Assistant Editor: Betsy Flagler. Publishes originals (general fiction, mass-market, trade paperback and hardcover). Published new writers this year. Averages over 120 total titles each year.

Needs: Major historical fiction, women's mainstream and general fiction.

How to Contact: Submit query letter or brief synopsis and first 100 pages of ms. SASE required. Reports in 2 months on queries; 4-5 months on mss.

Terms: Pays in royalties and advance.

BANTAM BOOKS, Division of Bantam Doubleday Dell Publishing Group, Inc. 1540 Broadway, New York NY 10036. Did not respond.

BANTAM SPECTRA BOOKS, (II, IV), Subsidiary of Bantam Doubleday Dell Publishing Group, 1540 Broadway, New York NY 10036. (212)765-6500. Executive Editor: Jennifer Hershey. Senior Editor: Tom Dupree. Associate Editor: Anne Groell. Estab. 1985. Large science fiction, fantasy and speculative fiction line. Publishes hardcover originals, paperback originals and trade paperbacks. Averages 60 total titles, all fiction.

● Many Bantam Spectra Books have received Hugos and Nebulas including Connie Willis's *Doomsday Book*, which won both in 1993.

Needs: Fantasy, literary, science fiction. Needs include novels that attempt to broaden the traditional range of science fiction and fantasy. Strong emphasis on characterization. Especially well written traditional science fiction and fantasy will be considered. No fiction that doesn't have at least some element of speculation or the fantastic. Published *Star Wars: The Courtship of Princess Leia*, by Dave Wolverton; *Green Mars*, Kim Stanley Robinson; and *The Seventh Gate*, by Margaret Weis and Tracy Hickman.

How to Contact: Query first with 3 chapters and a short (no more than 3 pages double-spaced) synopsis. SASE. Agented fiction 90%. Reports in 6-8 weeks on queries.

Terms: Pays in royalties; negotiable advance. Sends galleys to author.

Advice: "Please follow our guidelines carefully and type neatly."

BANTAM/DOUBLEDAY/DELL BOOKS FOR YOUNG READERS DIVISION, (III), Bantam/Doubleday/Dell, 1540 Broadway, New York NY 10036. Imprints include Delacort Hardcover, Doubleday Picture Books; Paperback line: Dell Yearling, Laurel-Leaf, Skylark, Star Fire, Little Rooster, Sweet Dreams, Sweet Valley High. President: Georg Richiter. Editor-in-Chief to the Young Readers Division: Beverly Horowitz. Estab. 1945. Complete publishing: hardcover, trade, mass market.

● The Young Readers Division offers two contests, the Delacorte Press Annual Prize for a First Young Adult Novel and the Marguerite DeAngeli Prize. Both are listed in the Contests and Awards section.

Needs: Childrens/juvenile, young adult/teen. Published *Baby*, by Patricia MacLachlan; *Whatever Happened to Janie*, by Caroline Cooney; *Nate the Great and the Pillowcase*, by Marjorie Sharmat.

How to Contact: Does not accept unsolicited mss. Submit through agent. Agented fiction 100%. Reports on queries "as soon as possible." Simultaneous submissions OK.

Terms: Individually negotiated; offers advance.

THE BERKLEY PUBLISHING GROUP, (III), Subsidiary of G.P. Putnam's Sons, 200 Madison Ave., New York NY 10016. (212)951-8800. Imprints are Berkley, Jove, Boulevard, Ace Science Fiction. Editor-in-Chief: Leslie Gelbman. Fiction Editors: Natalee Rosenstein, Judith Stern, John Talbot, Gail Fortune, Susan Allison, Ginjer Buchanan, Laura Anne Gilman, Gary Goldstein and Hillary Cige. Nonfiction: Elizabeth Beier, Denise Silvestro and Hillary Cige. Large commercial category line. Publishes paperback originals, trade paperbacks and hardcover and paperback reprints. Books: Paperbound printing; perfect binding; average print order: "depends on position in list." Plans approx. 10 first novels this year. Averages 1,180 total titles, 1,000 fiction titles each year. Sometimes critiques rejected mss.
Needs: Fantasy, mainstream, mystery/suspense, romance (contemporary, historical), science fiction.
How to Contact: Accepts no unsolicited mss. Submit through agent only. Agented fiction 98%. Reports in 6-8 weeks on mss. Simultaneous submissions OK.
Terms: Pays royalties of 4-10%. Provides 25 author's copies. Writer's guidelines and book catalog not available.
Advice: "Aspiring novelists should keep abreast of the current trends in publishing by reading *The New York Times* Bestseller Lists, trade magazines for their desired genre and *Publishers Weekly*."

BERKLEY/ACE SCIENCE FICTION, (II), Berkley Publishing Group, 200 Madison Ave., New York NY 10016. (212)951-8800. Editor-in-Chief: Susan Allison. Estab. 1948. Publishes paperback originals and reprints and 6-10 hardcovers per year. Number of titles: 8/month. Buys 85-95% agented fiction.
Needs: Science fiction and fantasy. No other genre accepted. No short stories. Published *The Cat Who Walks Through Walls*, by Robert Heinlein; and *Neuromancer*, by William Gibson.
How to Contact: Submit outline/synopsis and 3 sample chapters with SASE. No simultaneous submissions. Reports in 2 months minimum on mss. "Queries answered immediately if SASE enclosed." Publishes ms an average of 18 months after acceptance.
Terms: Standard for the field. Sends galleys to author.
Advice: "Good science fiction and fantasy are almost always written by people who have read and loved a lot of it. We are looking for knowledgeable science or magic, as well as sympathetic characters with recognizable motivation. We are looking for solid, well-plotted science fiction: good action adventure, well-researched hard science with good characterization and books that emphasize characterization without sacrificing plot. In fantasy we are looking for all types of work, from high fantasy to sword and sorcery." Submit fantasy and science fiction to Susan Allison, Ginjer Buchanan and Laura Anne Gilman.

JOHN F. BLAIR, PUBLISHER, (III, IV), 1406 Plaza Dr., Winston-Salem NC 27103. (919)768-1374. President: Carolyn Sakowski. Estab. 1954. Small independent publisher. Publishes hardcover and paperback originals. Books: Acid-free paper; offset printing; illustrations; average print order: 2,500-5,000. Number of titles: 8 in 1992, 12 in 1993, 15 in 1994. "Among our 12-15 books, we do one novel a year."
Needs: Prefers regional material dealing with southeastern U.S. No confessions or erotica. "Our editorial focus concentrates mostly on nonfiction." Recently published works include *The Big Ear*, by Robin Hemley (short story collection); and *Touring the Middle Tennessee Backroads*, by Robert Brandt.
How to Contact: Query or submit with SASE. Simultaneous submissions OK. Reports in 1 month. Publishes ms 1-2 years after acceptance. Free book catalog.
Terms: Negotiable.
Advice: "We are primarily interested in nonfiction titles. Most of our titles have a tie-in with North Carolina or the southeastern United States. Please enclose a cover letter and outline with the manuscript. We prefer to review queries before we are sent complete manuscripts. Queries should include an approximate word count."

BOOKS IN MOTION, (I), 9212 E. Montgomery, Suite #501, Spokane WA 99206. (509)922-1646. President: Gary Challender. Estab. 1980. "Audiobook company, national marketer. Publishes novels, novellas and short stories in audiobook form *only*." Published new writers within the last year. Plans 12 first novels this year. Averages 70 total titles, 65 fiction titles each year.
● Books in Motion is known for its audio westerns. The publisher has received favorable reviews from *Library Journal*, *Kliatt Magazine* and *Audio-File* magazine.
Needs: Published *Dead Man's Mine*, by Orville Johnson (mystery, 4 full-length tapes); *Bless The Children*, by Robert Guenzel (fiction, 6 full-length tapes); and *To A Promise True*, by Barbara Francis (sequel, historical drama).
How to Contact: Accepts unsolicted mss. Submit outline/synopsis and 4 sample chapters. SASE for ms. Reports within 3 weeks to 3 months. Simultaneous submissions OK.
Terms: Pays royalties of 10%. "We pay royalties every 6 months. Royalties that are received are based on the gross sales that any given title generates during the 6-month interval. Authors must be patient since it usually takes a minimum of one year before new titles will have significant sales." Publishes ms 6-12 months after acceptance. Book catalog free on request.

Advice: "We prefer light cuss words and sex scenes, or none at all. We want novels with a strong plot. The fewer the characters, the better it will work on tape. Six-tape audiobooks sell and rent better than any other size in the unabridged format. One hour of tape is equal to 40 pages of double-spaced, 12 pitch, normal margin, typed pages."

THOMAS BOUREGY & COMPANY, INC., 401 Lafayette St., New York NY 10003. Small category line. See Avalon Books.

BOYDS MILLS PRESS, (II), Subsidiary of Highlights for Children, 815 Church St., Honesdale PA 18431. (800)949-7777. Manuscript Coordinator: Beth Troop. Estab. 1990. "Independent publisher of quality books for children of all ages." Publishes hardcover. Books: Coated paper; offset printing; case binding; 4-color illustrations; average print order varies. Plans 4 fiction titles (novels).
• Boyd Mills Press is the publishing arm of *Highlights for Children*. See listings for the related magazine, a contest and a conference in this book.
Needs: Juvenile, young adult (adventure, animal, contemporary, ethnic, historical, sports). Recently published *Cowgirl Dreams*, by Jennifer Owings Dewey; *The Bells of Lake Superior*, by Dayton O. Hyde; and *Water Ghost*, by Ching Yeung Russell.
How to Contact: Accepts unsolicited mss. Send first three chapters and synopsis. Reports in 1 month. Simultaneous submissions OK.
Terms: Pays standard rates. Sends pre-publication galleys to author. Time between acceptance and publication depends on "what season it is scheduled for." Writer's guidelines for #10 SASE.
Advice: "We're interested in young adult novels of real literary quality as well as middle grade fiction that's imaginative with fresh ideas. Getting into the mode of thinking like a child is important. We publish very few novels each year, so make sure your story is as strong and as polished as possible before submitting to us. We do not deal with romance or fantasy novels, so please do not submit those genres."

BRANDEN PUBLISHING CO., (I, II), Subsidiary of Branden Press, Box 843, 17 Station St., Brookline Village MA 02147. Imprint: I.P.L. Estab. 1967. Publishes hardcover and paperback originals and reprints. Books: 55-60 lb. acid-free paper; case- or perfect-bound; illustrations; average print order: 5,000. Plans 5 first novels this year. Averages 15 total titles, 5 fiction titles each year.
Needs: Ethnic, historical, literary, military/war, short story collections and translations. Looking for "contemporary, fast pace, modern society." No porno, experimental or horror. Recently published *I, Morgain*, by Harry Robin; *The Bell Keeper*, by Marilyn Seguin; and *The Straw Obelisk*, by Adolph Caso.
How to Contact: Does not accept unsolicited mss. Query *only* with SASE. Reports in 1 week on queries.
Terms: Pays royalties of 5-10% minimum. Advance negotiable. Provides 10 author's copies. Sends galleys to author. Publishes ms "several months" after acceptance.
Advice: "Publishing more fiction because of demand. *Do not make phone inquiries.* Do not oversubmit; single submissions only; do not procrastinate if contract is offered."

*GEORGE BRAZILLER, INC., (III), 60 Madison Ave., New York NY 10010. (212)889-0909. Fax: (212)689-5405. President: George Braziller. Manuscript submissions: Adrienne Baxter. Estab. 1955. Publishes hardcover originals and paperback reprints. Books: Cloth binding; illustrations sometimes; average print order: 4,000. Average first novel print order: 3,000. Buys 10% agented fiction. Averages 25 total titles, 6 fiction titles each year. Occasionally critiques rejected mss.
Needs: Art, feminist, literary, short story collections and translations. Published *The Laws*, by Connie Palmen (literary); *There Is No Borges*, by Gerhard Köpf (literary); and *The African in Me*, by Howard Gordon (African-American/literary).
How to Contact: Query first with SASE. Reports in 2 weeks on queries. Publishes ms an average of 1 year after acceptance.
Terms: *Some subsidy publishing.* Negotiates advance. Must return advance if book is not completed or is not acceptable. Sends galleys to author. Free book catalog on request with oversized SASE.
Advice: "Only send work which, in your eyes, is *completely* finished—in other words, don't send it until you are 100% certain that you've submitted the best manuscript you can."

*BRIDGE PUBLISHING, INC., (II, IV), 2500 Hamilton Blvd., South Plainfield NJ 07080. (908)754-0745. Editor: Catherine J. Barrier. Estab. 1981. Midsize independent publisher of Christian literature. Publishes hardback and paperback originals and reprints. Averages 25 total titles/year.
Needs: "We want quality, literary Christian fiction, written in styles such as those of Frederick Buechner, John Cheever, and John Updike. We want well-written fiction that shows believable characters struggling to 'work out their salvations' in believable situations, books that exhibit real human drama and stylistic craftsmanship." Recently published *A Darkness Over Covenant*, by William J. Eyer; and *Jacob of Canaan*, by Helen Wood.
How to Contact: Accepts complete unsolicited mss (with cover letter), but *prefers proposals* (including cover letter, detailed outline of the books' chapters—a 500-600 word synopsis of the plot and the first 3-4 chapters). SASE. Reports in 2-3 months. Simultaneous submissions OK.

Writers and Editors Are On the Same Side

Many writers assume editors aren't interested in unpublished authors. The reverse is often true. "Every editor dreams of discovering a new voice," says Jay Schaefer, senior editor at Chronicle Books. "Nothing excites an editor more than to be the first to publish a writer, to develop that writer and establish a relationship that will last for years. It's not a negative if you haven't been published before. It's a positive in our eyes."

When Chronicle added literary fiction to its already successful list, the literary world applauded the San Francisco publisher's lofty goals. But more than a few observers kept their fingers crossed. Championing literary fiction is risky business. After *A Parallel Life and Other Stories*, Chronicle's

Jay Schaefer

first original fiction title, achieved commercial success, everybody was surprised except Jay Schaefer, the editor who discovered author Robin Beeman's remarkable prose.

Schaefer never doubted readers would respond to Beeman's work. "The experiences she wrote about struck a chord and led to insight," says Schaefer. Three years after the line's debut, he continues to choose first-time authors for more than half the fiction he acquires. Schaefer is betting the world will always welcome good new writers who have interesting things to say in compelling ways.

"Every time I open an envelope, I am hoping to find a great manuscript and a new writer. My assumption is that every manuscript is good enough until an author does something to get ruled out." Yet too often Schaefer is let down by what he sees. "Too many writers rule out their own fiction by displaying nothing more than a facility with words. They know how to write, the words are put together nicely on the page, but their work is a series of well-rendered moments without a purpose, with no illumination at the end. There is no epiphany. The story doesn't resonate with a larger audience."

The fiction Schaefer looks for must speak to people and lead them toward some understanding about the world and about themselves. "Writing without a purpose can be therapy," he says, "a way of processing experience and coming to self-understanding. But when writing is too personal, all it does is speak to the author—a perfectly good reason to write, but not a good enough reason for a publisher to publish."

Unacceptable, too, says Schaefer, "is prose that is all technique, all voice, all carefully studied workshop devices—works which place more emphasis on rendering a particular voice or character than on the overall meaning of the piece." Schaefer sees style as important, "but it needs to be in service of something larger. It can't be an end in itself."

To make sure your fiction reaches beyond yourself and out to readers, Schaefer suggests you ask others to read it. "But if you give it only to admirers, they probably will admire it. You have to be brave and give it to your writer's group, or to people who are a little distanced from you personally."

Schaefer also notes that writers too often finish a manuscript and rush it to the post office. "Then, before an editor even has the chance to read it, the writer is on the phone with second thoughts, asking the editor to change something. That can be the kiss of death to a manuscript." Instead, he says, "let your manuscript simmer. Place your final draft in a drawer, close it, and leave it alone for a month. You'll be amazed at the changes you'll make after returning to it with fresh eyes."

Once your manuscript is as good as it can possibly be, says Schaefer, do your homework carefully and find out which publishers to approach. Every publisher focuses on certain types of writing. Chronicle's fiction line, for instance, is made up of novels, short stories, novellas and illustrated fiction such as its best-selling *Griffin & Sabine* trilogy by Nick Bantock. Schaefer looks for the sort of literary fiction found in *The New Yorker*, *The Atlantic*, *Story* and *The Gettysburg Review*. When a manuscript comes in fitting that description, Schaefer reads it thoroughly with time and care.

Yet, he says, no matter how carefully he words his listings in market books, specifying "literary fiction only," the mail is filled with inappropriate manuscripts—"mysteries, romances, historical novels, science fiction, and 500-page 'blockbuster' novels" which he summarily rejects. "Even novels by popular authors like Danielle Steel, Stephen King or Tom Clancy would not be right for Chronicle's list," says Schaefer. "That's not to say that type of fiction is not good, or that it doesn't make millions of dollars for its publishers—it's just not what we publish."

Schaefer recommends *Novel & Short Story Writer's Market* and *Writer's Market* as good places to begin your search for publishers. But, he says, don't stop there. Take it to the next level. "I can't emphasize enough that you won't get a feel for a publisher's needs until you read a few of the books it publishes, or at the very least, examine a catalog. It's so easy, I'm astonished more writers don't catch on."

If, after reading a few of the titles on a publisher's list, you find their fiction is the type you strive to create, submit your manuscript. But, says Schaefer, submit it in a professional manner. "Include a brief business-like letter describing the type of work enclosed, but don't brag or get overly chatty. Efforts to impress can turn editors against your work. It is also helpful to include a short summary of your novel on a separate sheet of paper. This helps editors determine whether you have succeeded in what you set out to do."

Finally, says Schaefer, remember that writers and editors are on the same side. "We'll try to do our part by continuing to publish new writers. You can help us by writing the best book you can, making sure it gets into the right hands, and by buying and reading books of publishers you want to submit to. After all, if writers won't support fiction, who will?"

—*Mary Cox*

Terms: *Offers self/cooperative publishing services.* Writer's guidelines for #10 SASE. Book catalog for $1.95.

Advice: "While we have not generally accepted fiction much in the recent past, we are now open to consider manuscripts of exceptional merit. Authors must already have material published and/or other books published by reputable publishers. Only mss that have already been completed will be considered. The fictional piece must contain a strong Christian (evangelical) message and/or give glory to the Lord Jesus Christ and encourage and build up the body of Christ."

BROADMAN & HOLMAN PUBLISHERS, (II), 127 Ninth Ave. N., Nashville TN 37234. (615)251-2000. Editorial Director: Richard P. Rosenbaum, Jr. Religious publisher associated with the Southern Baptist Convention. Publishes hardcover and paperback originals. Books: Offset paper stock; offset printing; perfect or Smythe sewn binding; illustrations possible; average print order depends on forecast. Averages 3 total titles each year.

Needs: Christian living, religious/inspirational, humor/satire, juvenile, and young adult. Will accept no other genre. Recently published *Recovery of the Lost Sword*, by L.L. Chaikin; *Mary of Magdala*, by Anne C. Williman; *Journey to Amanah: The Beginning*, by Colleen K. Snyder; *What Would Jesus Do?*, by Garrett W. Sheldon; and *The Fallen*, by Robert Don Hughes.

How to Contact: Query first. Simultaneous submissions OK. Reports in 2 months on queries and mss.

Terms: Pays 12% in royalties; offers advance.

Advice: "We publish very few fiction works. We encourage a close working relationship with the author to develop the best possible product."

CARROLL & GRAF PUBLISHERS, INC., (III), 260 Fifth Ave., New York NY 10001. (212)889-8772. Editor: Kent Carroll. Estab. 1983. Publishes hardcover and paperback originals and paperback reprints. Plans 5 first novels this year. Averages 120 total titles, 75 fiction titles each year. Average first novel print order 7,500 copies. Occasionally critiques rejected mss.

Needs: Contemporary, erotica, fantasy, science fiction, literary, mainstream and mystery/suspense. No romance.

How to Contact: Does not accept unsolicited mss. Query first or submit outline/synopsis and sample chapters. SASE. Reports in 2 weeks.

Terms: Pays in royalties of 6% minimum; 15% maximum; advance negotiable. Sends galleys to author. Free book catalog on request.

CHRONICLE BOOKS, (II), 275 Fifth St., San Francisco CA 94103. (415)777-7240. Fiction Editor: Jay Schaefer. Estab. 1966. "Full-line publisher of 150 books per year." Publishes hardcover and paperback originals. Averages 150 total titles, 10 fiction this year. Sometimes comments on rejected ms.

Needs: Open. Looking for novellas, collections and novels. No romances, science fiction, or any genre fiction: no category fiction. Publishes anthologies. Recently published *Griffin & Sabine*, by Bantock; *Dancer with Bruised Knees*, by McFall; *Loving Wanda Beaver*, by Baker.

How to Contact: Accepts unsolicited mss. Submit complete ms with cover letter. "No queries, please." Send SASE for reply and return of ms. Agented fiction 50%. Prefers no simultaneous submissions.

Terms: Standard rates. Sends galleys to author. Publishes ms 9-12 months after acceptance. No writer's guidelines available.

CONTEMPORARY BOOKS, 2 Prudential Plaza, 180 N. Stetson Ave., Suite 1200, Chicago IL 60601-6790. Mostly nonfiction. Prefers not to share information.

COOK COMMUNICATIONS MINISTRY, (formerly David C. Cook Publishing Co.), 4050 Lee Vance View, Colorado Springs CO 80918. (719)536-3280. Imprints: Chariot Books, Life Journey Books. Editorial Director: Karl Schaller. Send mss to Julie Smith, managing editor. Estab. 1875. Publishes hardcover and paperback originals. Number of fiction titles: 35-40 juvenile, 4-6 adult. Encourages new writers.

Needs: Religious/inspirational, juvenile, young adult and adult; sports, animal, spy/adventure, historical, Biblical, fantasy/science fiction, picture book and easy-to-read. Published *With Wings as Eagles*, by Elaine Schulte; *Mystery of the Laughing Cat*, by Elspeth Campbell Murphy; *Mystery Rider at Thunder Ridge*, by David Gillett. Published new writers within the last year.

The asterisk indicates a publisher who sometimes offers subsidy arrangements. Authors are asked to subsidize part of the cost of book production. See the introduction for more information.

How to Contact: All unsolicited mss are returned unopened. Query with SASE. Simultaneous submissions OK.

Terms: Royalties vary ("depending on whether it is trade, mass market or cloth" and whether picture book or novel). Offers advance. Writer's guidelines with SASE.

Advice: "Chariot Books publishes books for toddlers through teens which help children better understand their relationship with God, and/or the message of God's book, the Bible. Interested in seeing contemporary novels (*not* Harlequin-type) adventure, romance, suspense with Christian perspective."

CROSSWAY BOOKS, (II, IV), Division of Good News Publishers, 1300 Crescent, Wheaton IL 60187. Vice President/Editorial Director: Leonard G. Goss. Estab. 1938. Midsize independent religious publisher with plans to expand. Publishes paperback originals. Average print order 5,000-10,000 copies. Averages 50-60 total titles, 20-25 fiction titles each year.
• Crossway Books is known as a leader in Christian fiction. Several of their books have received "Gold Medallion" awards from the Evangelical Christian Publishers Association.

Needs: Contemporary, adventure, historical, literary, religious/inspirational and young adult. "All fiction published by Crossway Books must be written from the perspective of evangelical Christianity. It must understand and view the world through a Christian worldview." No sentimental, didactic, "inspirational" religious fiction; heavy-handed allegorical or derivative (of C.S. Lewis or J.R.R. Tolkien) fantasy. Recently published *Sunset Coast*, by Susan DeVore Williams; *The Lost Manuscript of Martin Taylor Hamson*, by Stephen Bly; and *The Vienna Passage*, by David Porter.

How to Contact: Does not accept unsolicited mss. Send query with synopsis and sample chapters only. Reports in 6-8 weeks on queries. Publishes ms 1-2 years after acceptance.

Terms: Pays in royalties and negotiates advance. Writer's guidelines for SASE. Book catalog for 9×12 SAE and 6 first-class stamps.

Advice: "We feel called to publish fiction in the following categories: Supernatural fiction, fantasy, Christian realism, historical fiction, mystery fiction, intrigue, western fiction and children's fiction. All fiction should include explicit Christian content, artfully woven into the plot, and must be consistent with our statements of vision, purpose and commitment. Crossway can successfully publish and market *quality* Christian novelists. Also read John Gardner's *On Moral Fiction*. We require a minimum word count of 25,000 words."

DARK HORSE COMICS, INC., (I, IV), 10956 SE Main St., Milwaukie OR 97222. (503)652-8815. Contact: Submissions Editor. Estab. 1986. "Dark Horse publishes all kinds of comics material, and we try not to limit ourselves to any one genre or any one philosophy. Most of our comics are intended for readers 15-40, though we also publish material that is accessible to younger readers." Comic books: newsprint or glossy paper, each title 24-28 pages. Averages 10-30 total titles each year.
• Dark Horse Press's comics have won several awards including the Eisner and Harvey awards. See the interview with Submissions Editor Edward Martin in the 1995 *Novel & Short Story Writer's Market*.

Needs: Comics: adventure, childrens/juvenile, fantasy (space fantasy, super hero, sword and sorcery), horror, humor/satire, mystery/suspense (private eye/hardboiled), psychic/supernatural, romance (contemporary), science fiction (hard science, soft/sociological), western (traditional). Proposals or scripts for comic books only. Plans anthology. Recently published comics by Andrew Vachss, Frank Miller, Clive Barker, Steven Grant, Eric Luke and Adam Hughes. Published short story comic anthologies: *Dark Horse Presents*.

How to Contact: Does not accept unsolicited mss. Query letter first. Should include one-page bio, list of publishing credits. SASE or disposable copy of ms. Reports in 1-2 months. Simultaneous submissions OK.

Terms: Pays $25-100/page and 5-25 author's copies. "We usually buy first and second rights, other rights on publication." Writer's guidelines free for #10 SASE.

Advice: "Obtain copies of our Writer's Guidelines before making a submission." Looks for "originality, a sense of fun. No concept too wild or mundane. Creativity is the only essential."

DAW BOOKS, INC., (I), 375 Hudson St., New York NY 10014. Publishers: Elizabeth R. Wollheim and Sheila E. Gilbert. Executive VP/Secretary-Treasurer: Elsie B. Wollheim. Submissions Editor: Peter Stampfel. Estab. 1971. Publishes paperback originals and hardcover originals. Books: Illustrations sometimes; average print and first novel order vary widely. May publish as many as 6 or more first novels a year. Averages 36 new titles plus 40 or more reissues, all fiction, each year. Occasionally critiques rejected mss.

Needs: Science fiction (hard science, soft sociological) and fantasy only. Recently published *Exiles*, by Melanie Rawn (novel); *Storm Warning*, by Mercedes Lackey (novel); *Invader*, by C.J. Cherryh; *Death Watch*, by Elizabeth Forrest. Publishes many original and reprint anthologies including *Sword & Sorceress* (edited by Marion Zimmer Bradley); *Cat Fantastic* (edited by Martin H. Greenberg); *Tales From the Twilight Zone* (edited by Carol Serling). "You may write to the editors (after looking at the anthology) for guidelines % DAW."

How to Contact: Submit complete ms with return postage and SASE. Usually reports in 3-5 months on mss, but in special cases may take longer. "No agent required."

Terms: Pays an advance against royalties. Sends galleys to author (if there is time).

Advice: "We strongly encourage new writers. To unpublished authors: Try to make an educated submission and don't give up; write for our guidelines."

DEL REY BOOKS, Subsidiary of Ballantine Books, 201 E. 50 St., New York NY 10022. (212)572-2677. Estab. 1977. Publishes hardcover originals and paperback originals and reprints. Plans 6-7 first novels this year. Publishes 60 titles each year, all fiction. Sometimes critiques rejected mss.

Needs: Fantasy and science fiction. Fantasy must have magic as an intrinsic element to the plot. No flying-saucer, Atlantis or occult novels. Published *The Chronicles of Pern*, by Anne McCaffrey (science fiction/hardcover original); *The Shining Ones*, by David Eddings (fantasy/hardcover original); and *Jack the Bodiless*, by Julian May (science fiction/paperback reprint).

How to Contact: Accepts unsolicited mss. Submit cover letter with complete manuscript or brief outline/synopsis and *first* 3 chapters. Prefers complete ms. Address science fiction to SF editor; fantasy to fantasy editor. Reports in 2 weeks on queries; 2-10 months on mss.

Terms: Pays in royalties; "advance is competitive." Sends galleys to author. Writer's guidelines for #10 SASE.

Advice: Has been publishing "more fiction and more hardcovers, because the market is there for them. Read a lot of science fiction and fantasy, such as works by Anne McCaffrey, David Eddings, Larry Niven, Arthur C. Clarke, Terry Brooks, Frederik Pohl, Barbara Hambly. When writing, pay particular attention to plotting (and a satisfactory conclusion) and characters (sympathetic and well-rounded)—because those are what readers look for."

DELACORTE/DELL BOOKS FOR YOUNG READERS/DOUBLEDAY, (II, III, IV), Division of Bantam Doubleday Dell Publishing Group, Inc., 1540 Broadway, New York NY 10036. See listing for Bantam/Doubleday/Dell Books for Young Readers.

DELL PUBLISHING, 1540 Broadway, New York NY 10036. (212)354-6500. Imprints include Delacorte Press, Delta, Dell, Dial Press, Laurel. Estab. 1922. Publishes hardcover and paperback originals and paperback reprints.

Needs: See below for individual imprint requirements.

How to Contact: Reports in 3 months. Simultaneous submissions OK. "Please adhere strictly to the following procedures: 1. Send *only* a 4-page synopsis or outline with a cover letter stating previous work published or relevant experience. Enclose SASE. 2. *Do not* send ms, sample chapters or artwork. 3. *Do not* register, certify or insure your letter. Dell is comprised of several imprints, each with its own editorial department. Please review carefully the following information and direct your submissions to the appropriate department. Your envelope must be marked: Attention: (One of the following names of imprints), Editorial Department—Proposal."

DELACORTE: Publishes in hardcover; looks for top-notch commercial fiction and nonfiction; 35 titles/year.

DELTA: Publishes trade paperbacks including original fiction and nonfiction; 20 titles/year.

DELL: Publishes mass-market and trade paperbacks; looks for family sagas, historical romances, sexy modern romances, adventure and suspense thrillers, mysteries, psychic/supernatural, horror, war novels, fiction and nonfiction. 200 titles/year.

DIAL PRESS: Publishes literary fiction and high-end nonfiction 2 titles/year.

Terms: Pays 6-15% in royalties; offers advance. Sends galleys to author.

Advice: "Don't get your hopes up. Query first only with 4-page synopsis plus SASE. Study the paperback racks in your local drugstore. We encourage first novelists. We also encourage all authors to seek agents."

DIAL BOOKS FOR YOUNG READERS, (II), Division of Penguin Books U.S.A. Inc., 375 Hudson St., New York NY 10014. (212)366-2000. Imprints include Pied Piper Books, Easy-to-Read Books. Editor-in-Chief/Pres./Publisher: Phyllis Fogelman. Estab. 1961. Trade children's book publisher, "looking for picture book mss and novels." Publishes hardcover originals. Plans 1 first novel this year. Averages 100 titles, mainly fiction. Occasionally critiques or comments on rejected ms.

Needs: Juvenile (1-9 yrs.) including: animal, fantasy, spy/adventure, contemporary and easy-to-read; young adult/teen (10-16 years) including: fantasy/science fiction, literary and commercial mystery and fiction. Published *Waiting for the Evening Star*, by Rosemary Wells and Susan Jeffers; *Soul Looks Back in Wonder*, by Tom Feelings, Maya Angelou, Langston Hughes and others; *Parents in the Pigpen and Pigs in the Tub*, by Steven Kellogg and Amy Ehrlich.

How to Contact: Does not accept unsolicited mss. Query. "Please include SASE for reply."

Terms: Pays advance against royalties. Writer's guidelines for #10 SASE. Book catalog for 9 × 12 SAE and $1.92 postage.

Advice: "We are publishing more fiction books than in the past, and we publish only hardcover originals, most of which are fiction. At this time we are particularly interested in both fiction and nonfiction for the middle grades, and innovative picture book manuscripts. We also are looking for easy-to-reads for first and second graders. Plays, collections of games and riddles, and counting and alphabet books are generally discouraged. Before submitting a manuscript to a publisher, it is a good idea to request a catalog to see what the publisher is currently publishing. As the 'Sweet Valley High' phenomenon has loosened its stranglehold on YA fiction, we are seeing more writers able to translate traditional values of literary excellence and contemporary innovation into the genre. Make your cover letters read like jacket flaps—short and compelling. Don't spend a lot of time apologizing for a lack of qualifications. In fact, don't mention them at all unless you have publishing credits, or your background is directly relevant to the story: 'I found this folktale during a return trip to the Tibetan village where I spent the first ten years of my life.' "

DOUBLEDAY, (III), a division of Bantam Doubleday Dell Publishing Group, Inc., 1540 Broadway., New York NY 10036. (212)354-6500. Estab. 1897. Publishes hardcover and paperback originals and paperback reprints.
Needs: "Doubleday is not able to consider unsolicited queries, proposals or manuscripts unless submitted through a bona fide literary agent, except that we will consider fiction for Perfect Crime line, romance and western imprints."
How to Contact: Send copy of complete ms (60,000-80,000 words) to Perfect Crime Editor, Loveswept Editor or Western Editor as appropriate. Sufficient postage (or IRC) for return via fourth class mail must accompany ms. Reports in 2-6 months.
Terms: Pays in royalties; offers advance.

DOUBLEDAY CANADA LIMITED, 105 Bond St., Toronto, Ontario M5B 1Y3 Canada. No unsolicited submissions. Prefers not to share information.

DUTTON SIGNET, (III), (formerly NAL/Dutton), A division of Penguin USA, Inc., 375 Hudson St., New York NY 10014. (212)366-2000. Imprints include Dutton, Onyx, Signet, Topaz, Mentor, Signet Classic, Plume, Plume Fiction, Meridian, Roc. Contact: Michaela Hamilton, vice president/publisher, Signet and Onyx; Arnold Dolin, associate publisher, Dutton, publisher, Plume; Amy Stout, editorial director, Roc. Estab. 1948. Publishes hardcover and paperback originals and paperback reprints. Published new writers within the last year.
Needs: "All kinds of commercial and literary fiction, including mainstream, historical, Regency, New Age, western, thriller, science fiction, fantasy, gay. Full length novels and collections." Recently published *Insomnia*, by Stephen King; *Trial by Fire*, by Nancy Taylor Rosenberg; *Black Cross*, by Greg Iles; and *The Takeover*, by Stephen Frey.
How to Contact: Agented mss only. Queries accepted with SASE. "State type of book and past publishing projects." Simultaneous submissions OK. Reports in 3 months.
Terms: Pays in royalties and author's copies; offers advance. Sends galleys to author. Book catalog for SASE.
Advice: "Write the complete manuscript and submit it to an agent or agents. We publish The Trailsman, Battletech and other western and science fiction series—all by ongoing authors. Would be receptive to ideas for new series in commercial fiction."

EAKIN PRESS, (II, IV), Box 90159, Austin TX 78709-0159. (512)288-1771. Imprint: Nortex. Editor: Edwin M. Eakin. Estab. 1978. Publishes hardcover originals. Books: Old style (acid-free); offset printing; case binding; illustrations; average print order 2,000; first novel print order 5,000. Published new writers within the last year. Plans 2 first novels this year. Averages 80 total titles each year.
Needs: Juvenile. Specifically needs historical fiction for school market, juveniles set in Texas for Texas grade schoolers. Published *Wall Street Wives*, by Ande Ellen Winkler; *Jericho Day*, by Warren Murphy; and *Blood Red Sun*, by Stephen Mertz.
How to Contact: Prefers queries, but accepts unsolicited mss. Send SASE for guidelines. Agented fiction 5%. Simultaneous submissions OK. Reports in 3 months on queries.
Terms: Pays royalties; average advance: $1,000. Sends galleys to author. Publishes ms 1-1½ years after acceptance. Writers guidelines for #10 SASE. Book catalog for 75¢.
Advice: "Juvenile fiction only with strong Texas theme. We receive around 600 queries or unsolicited mss a year."

PAUL S. ERIKSSON, PUBLISHER, (II), P.O. Box 62, Forest Dale VT 05745. (802)247-4210. Editor: Paul S. Eriksson. Estab. 1960. Publishes hardcover and paperback originals.
Needs: Mainstream. Published *The Headmaster's Papers*, by Richard A. Hawley; and *Hand in Hand*, by Tauno Yliruusi.
How to Contact: Query first. Publishes ms an average of 6 months after acceptance.
Terms: Pays 10-15% in royalties; advance offered if necessary. Free book catalog.
Advice: "Our taste runs to serious fiction."

M. EVANS & CO., INC., (II), 216 E. 49th St., New York NY 10017. (212)688-2810. Publishes hardcover and trade paper fiction and nonfiction. Publishes 40-50 titles each year.
How to Contact: Query first with outline/synopsis and 3 sample chapters. SASE. Agented fiction: 100%. Simultaneous submissions OK.

Terms: Pays in royalties and offers advance; amounts vary. Sends galleys to author. Publishes ms 6-12 months after acceptance.

FANTAGRAPHICS BOOKS, (II, IV), 7563 Lake City Way NE, Seattle WA 98115. (206)524-1967. Publisher: Gary Groth. Estab. 1976. Publishes comic books, comics series and graphic novels. Books: offset printing; saddle-stitched periodicals and Smythe-sewn books; heavily illustrated. Publishes originals and reprints. Publishes 15 titles each month.
Needs: Comic books and graphic novels (adventure, fantasy, horror, mystery, romance, science, social parodies). "We look for subject matter that is more or less the same as you would find in mainstream fiction." Published *Blood of Palomar*, by Gilbert Hernandez; *The Dragon Bellows Saga*, by Stan Sakai; *Death of Speedy*; *Housebound with Rick Geary*; *Little Nemo in Slumberland*.
How to Contact: Send a plot summary, pages of completed art (photocopies only) and character sketches. May send completed script if the author is willing to work with an artist of the publisher's choosing. Include cover letter and SASE. Reports in 1 month.
Terms: Pays in royalties of 8% (but must be split with artist) and advance.

FARRAR, STRAUS & GIROUX, (III), 19 Union Square W., New York NY 10003. (212)741-6900. Imprints include Hill & Wang, The Noonday Press and North Point Press. Editor-in-Chief: Jonathan Galassi. Midsized, independent publisher of fiction, nonfiction, poetry. Publishes hardcover originals. Published new writers within the last year. Plans 2 first novels this year. Averages 100 total titles, 30 fiction titles each year.
Needs: Open. No genre material. Published *The Mambo Kings Play Songs of Love*, by Oscar Hijuelos; *My Son's Story*, by Nadine Gordimer; *The Burden of Proof*, by Scott Turow.
How to Contact: Does not accept unsolicited mss. Query first. "Vast majority of fiction is agented." Reports in 2 months. Simultaneous submissions OK.
Terms: Pays royalties (standard, subject to negotiation). Advance. Sends galleys to author. Publishes ms one year after acceptance. Writer's guidelines for #10 SASE.

FARRAR, STRAUS & GIROUX/CHILDREN'S BOOKS, (II), 19 Union Square W., New York NY 10003. Children's Books Editorial Director: Margaret Ferguson. Number of titles: 40. Published new writers within the last year. Buys juvenile mss with illustrations. Buys 25% agented fiction.
Needs: Children's picture books, juvenile novels, nonfiction. Recently published *The Library*, by Sarah Stewart and David Small; *Jack's New Power*, by Jack Gantos; and *Working River*, by Fred Powledge.
How to Contact: Submit outline/synopsis and 3 sample chapters, summary of ms and any pertinent information about author, author's writing, etc. Reports in 2 months on queries, 3 months on mss. Publishes ms 18 months to 2 years after acceptance.
Terms: Pays in royalties; offers advance. Book catalog with 9×12 SASE.
Advice: "Study our list before sending something inappropriate."

FAWCETT, (I, II, III), Division of Random House/Ballantine, 201 E. 50th St., New York NY 10022. (212)751-2600. Imprints include Ivy, Crest, Gold Medal, Columbine and Juniper. Executive Editor: Barbara Dicks. Editor-in-Chief: Leona Nevler. Estab. 1955. Major publisher of mass market and trade paperbacks. Publishes paperback originals and reprints. Prints 160 titles annually. Encourages new writers. "Always looking for *great* first novels."
Needs: Mysteries. Recently published *Noelle*, by Diana Palmer; *Writing for the Moon*, by Kristin Hannah.
How to Contact: Query with SASE. Send outline and sample chapters for adult mass market. If ms is requested, simultaneous submissions OK. Prefers letter-quality. Reports in 2-4 months.
Terms: Pays usual advance and royalties.
Advice: "Gold Medal list consists of four paperbacks per month—usually three are originals."

DONALD I. FINE, INC., (III), 375 Hudson St., New York NY 10014. Imprint of Penguin USA. President/Publisher: Don Fine. Associate Editor: Jason Poston. Estab. 1983. "Mini-major book publisher." Publishes hardcover originals. Published new writers within the last year. Plans 6 first novels this year. Averages 50 total titles, 30 fiction titles each year.
Needs: Adventure, historical, horror (dark fantasy, psychological), literary, military/war, mystery/suspense, thriller/espionage, western. Upcoming anthology themes include western, mystery, sports/literary. Recently published *A Certain Justice*, by John T. Lescroart (trial novel/mystery); *Collected Short Fiction of Bruce Jay Friedman* (literary fiction); and *Grand Jury*, by Philip Friedman (novel).
How to Contact: No unsolicited mss. Submit through agent only. Agented fiction 100%. Simultaneous submissions OK.
Terms: Pays royalties; offers negotiable advance.

Read the Business of Fiction Writing section to learn the correct way to prepare and submit a manuscript.

FLARE BOOKS, (II), Imprint of Avon Books, Div. of the Hearst Corp., 1350 Avenue of the Americas, New York NY 10019. (212)261-6816. Editorial Director: Gwen Montgomery. Estab. 1981. Small, young adult line. Publishes paperback originals and reprints. Plans 2-3 first novels this year. Averages 24 titles, all fiction each year.

Needs: Young adult (easy-to-read [hi-lo], problem novels, historical romance, spy/adventure), "very selective." Looking for contemporary fiction. No science fiction/fantasy, heavy problem novels, poetry. Published *Nothing But the Truth, A Documentary Novel*, by Avi; *Night Cries*, by Barbara Steiner; and *The Weirdo*, by Theodore Taylor.

How to Contact: Accepts unsolicited mss. Submit complete ms with cover letter (preferred) or outline/synopsis and 3 sample chapters. Agented fiction 75%. Reports in 3-4 weeks on queries; 3-4 months on mss. Simultaneous submissions OK.

Terms: Royalties and advance negotiable. Sends galleys to author. Writer's guidelines for #10 SASE. Book catalog for 9 × 12 SAE with 98¢ postage. "We run a young adult novel competition each year."

GESSLER PUBLISHING COMPANY, 10 E. Church Ave., Roanoke VA 24011. (703)345-1429. Contact: Richard Kurshan. Estab. 1932. "Publisher/distributor of foreign language educational materials (primary/secondary schools)." Publishes paperback originals and reprints, videos and software. Averages 75 total titles each year. Sometimes comments on rejected ms.

Needs: "Foreign language or English as a Second Language." Needs juvenile, literary, preschool/picture book, short story collections, translations. Published *Don Quixote de la Mancha*, (cartoon version of classic, in Spanish); *El Cid*, (prose and poetry version of the classic, In Spanish); and *Les Miserables* (simplified version of Victor Hugo classic, in French).

How to Contact: Query first, then send outline/synopsis and 2-3 sample chapters; complete ms with cover letter. Agented fiction 40%. Reports on queries in 1 month; on mss in 6 weeks. Simultaneous submissions OK.

Terms: Pay varies with each author and contract. Sends galleys to author. "Varies on time of submission and acceptance relating to our catalog publication date." Writer's guidelines not available. Book catalog free on request.

Advice: "We specialize in the foreign language market directed to teachers and schools. A book that would interest us has to be attractive to the market. A teacher would be most likely to create a book for us."

GLOBE FEARON, (II), Subsidiary of Simon & Schuster, Secondary Education Group, 1 Lake St., Upper Saddle River NJ 07458. (201)236-5850. Associate Publisher: Virginia Seeley. Estab. 1954. Publisher of multicultural, remedial and special education products. Publishes paperback originals and reprints. Books: 3 lb. book set paper; offset printing; perfect or saddle-wired binding; line art illustrations; average print order: 5,000.

Needs: "All materials are written to specification. It's a hard market to crack without some experience writing at low reading levels. Manuscripts for specific series of fiction are solicited from time to time, and unsolicited manuscripts are accepted occasionally." Published *A Question of Freedom*, by Lucy Jane Bledsoe (adventure novella—one of series of eight); *Just for Today*, by Tana Reiff (one novella of series of seven life-issues stories); and *The Everett Eyes*, by Bernard Jackson & Susie Quintanilla (one of 20 in a series of extra-short thrillers).

How to Contact: Submit outline/synopsis and sample chapters. SASE. Reports in 3 months. Simultaneous submissions OK.

Terms: Authors usually receive a predetermined project fee. Book catalog for 9 × 12 SAE with 4 first-class stamps.

DAVID R. GODINE, PUBLISHER, INC., (III), P.O. Box 9103, 9 Lewis St., Lincoln MA 01773. (617)259-0700. Imprints: Nonpareil Books (trade paperbacks), Verba Mundi (literature in translation), Imago Mundi (photography). President: David R. Godine. Editorial Director: Mark Polizzotti. Estab. 1970. Books: acid free paper; sewn binding; illustrations; average print order: 4,000-5,000; first novel print order: 3,500-6,500. Small independent publisher (6-person staff). Publishes hardcover and paperback originals and reprints.

Needs: Literary, mystery, historical, children's and young adult. Recently published *Great Topics of the World*, by Albert Goldbarth; *The Stonecutter's Hand*, by Richard Tillinghast; *No Effect*, by Daniel Hayes; and *The Journalist*, by Harry Mathews.

How to Contact: Does not accept unsolicited mss.

Terms: Standard royalties; offers advance. Sends galleys to author.

GROSSET & DUNLAP, INC., (III), A Division of the Putnam & Grosset Group, 200 Madison Ave., 11th Floor, New York NY 10016. (212)951-8700. Publisher/Vice President: Jane O'Connor. Editor-in-Chief: Judy Donnelly.

Needs: Juvenile, preschool/picture book.

How to Contact: Queries only. "Include such details as length and intended age group and any other information that you think will help us to understand the nature of your material. Be sure to enclose a

Editors Look for Strong Voices

"I think it's important to write from the heart, to really write the book that you want to write, and you might just find that if you do, that will be the next bandwagon that everybody else is jumping on," says Jessica Lichtenstein, senior editor for HarperPaperbacks, an imprint of HarperCollins. "It's important to not just be a follower because even though publishers have to be sort of cautious, at the same time we're always looking for something fresh and wonderful. We want that thrill of discovery; we don't want writers to just follow instructions or write a book in the same vein as one already on the bestseller list."

Lichtenstein says writers who are hoping to land their first book deal should put their energy into making their manuscript the best it can be and not worry so much about the networking that some writers feel is necessary. "I think that networking at conferences and writer workshops can be very worthwhile for writers, but I also believe that writers should not feel pressured to hand-sell their project," she says. "If you're a writer who is more the stay-at-home type, there's nothing wrong with relying on sending in your manuscript or proposal because I think ultimately at the end of the day, we make the decision based on the text itself. Of course, it's very important to be current, educate yourself about the field, learn what house publishes what, but basically the writing itself is still the most important thing."

HarperPaperbacks publishes 15 to 20 paperback titles a month, originals and reprints. Categories published under the imprint include inspirational, children's, mysteries, romance and westerns. Lichtenstein is responsible for nonfiction such as true crime, celebrity biographies and general interest, but most of her work is with fiction titles, including mainstream material, western and frontier fiction, and books for children and young adults.

What's Lichtenstein's top criterion when reviewing a fiction manuscript? "I look for strong characterization," she says. "No matter what the plot is, or no matter how compelling the story might sound when it's described, the difference between something that we would or would not buy is characterization. If there's somebody you can root for and really get behind it can make the difference between something that's possible for paperback and something that might be limited to a smaller audience. You have to have a character the reader can really believe in for the book to reach a mass audience."

Humor can be a plus in some cases, but it can also be very tricky. "It's a very individual thing," Lichtenstein says. "In women's fiction, for instance, humor is a nice, refreshing change. A lot of our best authors have the ability to write humorous love stories. But a humor book, or a book of jokes is very tough for us to sell in mass market. It would have to be a very special project; it's not something that we have every month in our list."

Unlike some editors at large publishing houses, Lichtenstein will consider unsolicited manuscripts, if they are addressed to her. A number of beginning novelists and nonfiction writers, in fact, have made their first publishing deals with HarperPaperbacks. "Every year we publish first-time writers; it's a big part of what we do, trying to discover new people," Lichtenstein says. "I'm constantly buying books by writers who have never been published before."

Lichtenstein confesses that she doesn't go out and actually look for new authors because "a lot of people just find you." The longer you've been at a publishing house, she says, the easier it becomes for new writers to recognize what you specialize in." She sometimes does research for nonfiction titles, but not for fiction. "For me, it's more likely that I'll find something in the manuscripts coming in to me from the outside, either from agents, or directly from the author. Once the authors find out that you handle certain categories, you really have no shortage of submissions."

Lichtenstein doesn't see the market getting tighter for writers in the future, but she does see it getting more complex. "There are a lot of issues related to new technology—CD-ROM and multi-media projects—and these are causing some anxiety," says Lichtenstein. "There are also a lot of different formats out there for writers to be published in, everything from mass market paperbacks, which I do, traditional hardcovers, trade paperbacks, and now, books on disk. And so there is a lot of uncertainty about the ways books will be published in the future, and I think it's just going to continue to get more complicated."

Writers can't help but feel cynical at times about how hard it is to get their manuscript in the door and looked at, but they should never give up, Lichtenstein says. "I'm sure people hear horror stories about the slush pile and how hard it is to get somebody to actually read your manuscript, but I think a strong manuscript will eventually get published. I really believe that. Somebody will find it. It might bounce from house to house and it may take a long time, but ultimately, if there is a strong voice it will spark someone's interest. I think writers really need to concentrate on that part and not throw up their hands and say it's too hard unless I know somebody at a particular house or unless my brother's a literary agent. That's again the kind of thing that can make you lose confidence. And I think the hardest thing is keeping your confidence up."

—Dorothy Maxwell Goepel

stamped, self-addressed envelope for our reply. We can no longer review manuscripts that we have not asked to see, and they will be returned unread."

HARCOURT BRACE & CO., (III), 525 B St., Suite 1900, San Diego CA 92101. (619)699-6810. Fax: (619)699-6777. Imprints include Harcourt Brace Children's Books, Gulliver Books, Jane Yolen Books and Browndeer Press. Director: Louise Howton. Senior Editor: Diane D'Andrade. Executive Editor: Allyn Johnston. Editor: Karen Grove. Editorial Director of Browndeer Press: Linda Zuckerman. Executive Editor of Gulliver Books: Elizabeth Van Doren. Publishes hardcover originals and paperback reprints. Averages 150 titles/year. Published new writers within the last year.
- Books published by Harcourt Brace & Co. have received numerous awards including the Caldecott and Newbery medals and selections as the American Library Association's "Best Books for Young Adults." Note that the publisher now only accepts manuscripts through an agent. Unagented writers may query only.

Needs: Nonfiction for all ages, picture books for very young children, historical, mystery. Published *Coyote*, by Gerald McDermott; *Stellaluna*, by Janell Cannon; *The Car*, by Gary Paulsen; and *Mole's Hill*, by Lois Ehlert.

How to Contact: No unsolicited mss. Query first. Submit through agent only.

Terms: Terms vary according to individual books; pays on royalty basis. Catalog for 9×12 SASE.

Advice: "Read as much current fiction as you can; familiarize yourself with the type of fiction published by a particular house; interact with young people to obtain a realistic picture of their concerns, interests and speech patterns."

❦**HARLEQUIN ENTERPRISES, LTD., (II, IV)**, 225 Duncan Mill Rd., Don Mills, Ontario M3B 3K9 Canada. (416)445-5860. Imprints include Harlequin Romances, Harlequin Presents, Harlequin American Romances, Superromances, Temptation, Intrigue and Regency, Silhouette, Worldwide Mysteries, Gold Eagle. Editorial Director Harlequin: Randall Toye; Silhouette: Isabel Swift; Gold Eagle: Randall Toye. Estab. 1949. Publishes paperback originals and reprints. Books: Newsprint paper; web printing; perfect-bound. Published new writers within the last year. Number of titles: Averages 700/year. Buys agented and unagented fiction.
- Harlequin recently introduced a new imprint, Mira for single-title women's fiction. Query for more information/guidelines.

Needs: Romance, glitz, heroic adventure, mystery/suspense (romantic suspense *only*). Will accept nothing that is not related to the desired categories.

How to Contact: Send query letter or send outline and first 50 pages (2 or 3 chapters) or submit through agent with SASE (Canadian). Absolutely no simultaneous submissions. Reports in 1 month on queries; 2 months on mss.

Terms: Offers royalties, advance. Must return advance if book is not completed or is unacceptable. Sends galleys to author. Guidelines available.

Advice: "The quickest route to success is to follow directions for submissions: Query first. We encourage first novelists. Before sending a manuscript, read as many current Harlequin titles as you can. It's very important to know the genre and the series most appropriate for your submission." Submissions for Harlequin Romance and Harlequin Presents should go to: Mills & Boon Limited Eton House, 18-24 Paradise Road, Richmond, Surrey TW9 1SR United Kingdom, Attn: Karin Stoecker; Superromances: Paula Eykelhof, senior editor; Temptation: Birgit Davis-Todd, senior editor; Regencies: Maureen Stonehouse, editor. American Romances and Intrigue: Debra Matteucci, senior editor and editorial coordinator, Harlequin Books, 6th Floor, 300 E. 42 Street, New York, NY 10017. Silhouette submissions should also be sent to the New York office, attention Isabel Swift. "The relationship between the novelist and editor is regarded highly and treated with professionalism."

HARMONY BOOKS, (II), Subsidiary of Crown Publishers, 201 E. 50th St., New York NY 10022. (212)572-6179. Contact: General Editorial Department. Publishes hardcover and paperback originals.

Needs: Literary fiction. Also publishes serious nonfiction, history, biography, personal growth, media and music fields.

How to Contact: Accepts unsolicited mss. Query first with outline/synopsis and 2-3 sample chapters. SASE. Agented fiction: 75%. Simultaneous submissions OK.

Terms: Pays royalties and advance; amounts negotiable. Sends galleys to authors.

HARPERCOLLINS, 10 E. 53rd St., New York NY 10022. See listing for HarperPaperbacks.

‡**HARPERCOLLINS CHILDREN'S BOOKS, (II)**, 10 E. 53rd St., New York NY 10022. (212)207-7044. Senior Vice President/Publisher: Marilyn Kriney. Vice President/Associate Publisher/Editor-in-Chief: Lisa Holton. Vice President/Editorial Director, Joanna Cotler Books: Joanna Cotler. Vice President/Publisher, Michael di Capua Books: Michael di Capua. Vice President/Editorial Director, Laura Geringer Books: Laura Geringer. Vice President/Editorial Director, Harper Trophy: Stephanie Spinner. Editorial Director, HarperFestival: Mary Alice Moore. Executive Editors: Sally Doherty, Kate M. Jackson, Ginee Seo, Katherine B. Tegen, and Robert O. Warren. Publishes hardcover trade titles and paperbacks.

Needs: Picture books, easy-to-read, middle-grade, teenage and young adult novels; fiction, fantasy, animal, sports, spy/adventure, historical, science fiction, problem novels and contemporary. Recently published Harper: *Walk Two Moons*, by Sharon Creech (ages 8-12); *The Best School Year Ever*, by Barbara Robinson (ages 8 up); Harper Trophy (paperbacks): *Catherine, Called Birdy*, by Karen Cushman (ages 12 and up). Also publishes The Danger Guys series by Tony Abbott (ages 7-10).

How to Contact: Query; submit complete ms; submit outline/synopsis and sample chapters; submit through agent. SASE for query, ms. Please identify simultaneous submissions. Reports in 2-3 months.

Terms: Average 10% in royalties. Royalties on picture books shared with illustrators. Offers advance. Writer's guidelines and book catalog for SASE.

Advice: "Write from your own experience and the child you once were. Read widely in the field of adult and children's literature. Realize that writing for children is a difficult challenge. Read other young adult novelists as well as adult novelists. Pay attention to styles, approaches, topics. Be willing to rewrite, perhaps many times. We have no rules for subject matter, length or vocabulary but look instead for ideas that are fresh and imaginative. Good writing that involves the reader in a story or subject that has appeal for young readers is also essential. One submission is considered by all imprints."

HARPERPAPERBACKS, (II), 10 E. 53rd St., New York NY 10022. (212)207-7752. Fax: (212)207-7759. Imprints include HarperPaperbacks, Monogram, Spotlight, Prism. Editor: Carolyn Marino. Independent publisher. Publishes paperback originals and reprints. Published new writers within the last year.

Needs: Children's/juvenile, fantasy, historical (romance), horror, mainstream/contemporary, mystery/suspense, romance (contemporary, futuristic/time travel, historical, regency/period, romantic suspense), science fiction, thriller/espionage, western, young adult/teen.

How to Contact: Accepts unsolicited mss. Query with outline/synopsis and 3 sample chapters. Include estimated word count, brief bio and list of publishing credits with submission. Send SASE for reply. Reports in 1 month on queries; 2 months on mss. Simultaneous submissions OK.
Terms: Pays advance and royalties.

HARPERPRISM, imprint of HarperCollins, 10 E. 53rd St., New York NY 10022. New HarperCollins imprint for science fiction and fantasy. Query for more information.

HARVEST HOUSE PUBLISHERS, (II, IV), 1075 Arrowsmith, Eugene OR 97402. (503)343-0123. Editorial Manager: LaRae Weikert. Editorial Director: Carolyn McCready. Estab. 1974. Midsize independent publisher with plans to expand. Publishes hardcover and paperback originals and reprints. Books: 40 lb. ground wood paper; offset printing; perfect binding; average print order: 10,000; first novel print order: 10,000-15,000. Averages 80 total titles, 6 fiction titles each year.
Needs: Christian living, contemporary issues, family saga, humor, Christian mystery (romantic suspense), religious/inspirational and Christian romance (historical). Especially seeks inspirational, romance/historical and mystery. Recently published *Jerusalem—The City of God*, by Ellen Traylor; *The Legend of Robin Brodie*, by Lisa Samson; and *Sophie's Heart*, by Lori Wick and *Samson*, by Ellen Gunderson Traylor. New fiction series for youth: "Addie McCormick Adventures," by Leanne Lucas.
How to Contact: Accepts unsolicited mss. Query first or submit outline/synopsis and 2 sample chapters with SASE. Reports on queries in 2-8 weeks; on mss in 6-8 weeks. Simultaneous submissions OK.
Terms: Pays in royalties of 14-18%; 10 author's copies. Sends galleys to author. Writer's guidelines for SASE. Book catalog for 8½×11 SASE.
Advice: "Contact us to get a copy of our guidelines. We seek exceptional manuscripts which are original, relevant, well-written, and grounded in the teachings of scripture."

HERALD PRESS, (II), Division of Mennonite Publishing House, 616 Walnut Ave., Scottdale PA 15683. (412)887-8500. Imprints include Congregational Literature Division; Herald Press. Book Editor: S. David Garber. Fiction Editor: Michael A. King. Estab. 1908. "Church-related midsize publisher." Publishes paperback originals. Books: Recycled, acid-free Glatfelter thor paper; offset printing; adhesive binding; illustrations for children; average print order: 4,000; first novel print order: 3,500. Published new writers in the last year. Company publishes 30 titles/year. Number of fiction titles: 5/year. Sometimes critiques rejected mss.
  ● Several Herald Press books have received Silver Angel Awards from Excellence in Media.
Needs: Adventure, family saga, historical, juvenile (contemporary, historical, spy/adventure), literary, religious/inspirational, young adult/teen (historical, mystery, problem novels and spy/adventure). "Does not want to see fantasy, talking animals." Recently published *Abiquil*, by James R Shott; *Katie and the Lemon Tree*, by Esther Bender; *Polly*, by Mary Borntrager; and *A Winding Path*, by Carrie Bender.
How to Contact: Accepts unsolicited mss. Submit outline/synopsis and 2 sample chapters with SASE. Agented fiction 2%. Reports in 1 month on queries, 2 months on mss. Accepts electronic submissions (only *with* paper copy).
Terms: Pays 10-12% in royalties; 12 free author's copies. Pays after first 3 months, then once/year. Sends galleys to author. Publishes ms 1 year after acceptance. Writer's guidelines free. Book catalog for 50¢.
Advice: "Need more stories with Christian faith integrated smoothly and not as a tacked-on element."

HOLIDAY HOUSE, INC., (I, II), 425 Madison, New York NY 10017. (212)688-0085. Editor-in-Chief: Margery Cuyler. Estab. 1935. Independent publisher of children's books. Books: high quality printing; occasionally reinforced binding; illustrations sometimes. Publishes hardcover originals and paperback reprints. Published new writers within the last year. Number of titles: Approximately 50 hardcovers and 15 paperbacks each year.
  ● *The Wright Brothers: How They Invented the Airplane* by Russell Freedman and published by Holiday House is a Newbery Honor Book.
Needs: Children's books only: contemporary, Judaica and holiday, literary, adventure, humor and animal stories for young readers—preschool through middle grade. Recently published *I Am an Artichoke*, by Lucy Frank; *Maizie*, by Linda Oatman High; and *Tarantula Shoes*, by Tom Birdseye. "We're not in a position to be too encouraging, as our list is tight, but we're always open to good 'family' novels and humor."
How to Contact: "We prefer query letters and three sample chapters for novels; complete manuscripts for shorter books and picture books." Simultaneous submissions OK as long as a cover letter mentions that other publishers are looking at the same material. Reports in 1 month on queries, 6-8 weeks on mss. "No phone calls, please."
Terms: Advance and royalties are flexible, depending upon whether the book is illustrated.
Advice: "We have received an increasing number of manuscripts, but the quality has not improved vastly. This appears to be a decade in which publishers are interested in reviving the type of good, solid story that was popular in the '50s. Certainly there's a trend toward humor, family novels, novels with school settings, biographies and historical novels. Problem-type novels and romances seem to be on the wane. We are always

open to well-written manuscripts, whether by a published or nonpublished author. Submit only one project at a time."

HENRY HOLT & COMPANY, (II), 115 W. 18th St., 6th Floor, New York NY 10011. (212)886-9200. Imprint includes Owl (paper). Publishes hardcover and paperback originals and reprints. Averages 80-100 total original titles, 35% of total is fiction each year.
  ● Henry Holt is publishing more titles and more fiction.
How to Contact: Accepts queries; no unsolicited mss. Agented fiction 95%.
Terms: Pays in royalties of 10% minimum; 15% maximum; advance. Sends galleys to author.

HOUGHTON MIFFLIN COMPANY, (III), 222 Berkeley St., Boston MA 02116. (617)351-0000. Managing Editor: Christina Coffin. Publishes hardcover and paperback originals and paperback reprints. Averages 100 total titles, 50 fiction titles each year.
Needs: None at present. Published *The Translator*, by Ward Just.
How to Contact: Does not accept unsolicited mss. Buys virtually 100% agented fiction.

HYPERION, (III), Walt Disney Co., 114 Fifth Ave., New York NY 10011. (212)633-4400. Fax: (212)633-4811. Editorial Contacts: Pat Mulcahy/Leslie Wells. Estab. 1990. "Mainstream commercial publisher." Publishes hardcover and paperback originals. Published new writers within the last year. Plans 2 first novels this year. Averages 110 total titles, 20 fiction titles each year.
Needs: Ethnic/multicultural, gay, literary, mainstream/contemporary, mystery/suspense, religious/inspirational, thriller/espionage. Recently published *Burning Angel*, by James Lee Burke; *Bone*, by Fae Mynne Ng (literary); and *No Witnesses*, by Ridley Pearson (suspense).
How to Contact: Does not accepted unsolicited mss. Query first. Include bio (1 page) and list of publishing credits. Send SASE for reply, return of ms or send a disposable copy of ms. Agented fiction 100%. Reports in 2 weeks on queries; 1 month on mss. Simultaneous submissions OK.
Terms: Pays royalties; offers negotiable advance. Sends galleys to author. Publishes ms 6 months after acceptance.

INTERLINK PUBLISHING GROUP, INC., (IV), 46 Crosby St., Northampton MA 01060. (413)582-7054. Fax: (413)582-7057. Imprints include: Interlink Books, Olive Branch Press and Crocodile Books USA. Contemporary fiction in translation published under Emerging Voices: New International Fiction. Publisher: Michel Moushabeck. Fiction Editor: Phyllis Bennis. Estab. 1987. "Midsize independent publisher." Publishes hardcover and paperback originals. Books: 55 lb. Warren Sebago Cream white paper; web offset printing; perfect binding; average print order: 5,000; first novel print order: 5,000. Published new writers within the last year. Plans 5-8 first novels this year. Averages 30 total titles, 5-8 fiction titles each year.
Needs: "Adult fiction from around the world." Published *A Woman of Nazareth*, by Hala Deeb Jabbour; *The Children Who Sleep by the River*, by Debbie Taylor; *Prairies of Fever*, by Ibrahim Nasrallah; and *The Silencer*, by Simon Louvish. Publishes the International Folk Tales series.
How to Contact: Does not accept unsolicited mss. Submit outline/synopsis only. SASE. Reports in 2 weeks on queries. E-mail address: interpg@aol.com.
Terms: Pays royalties of 5% minimum; 8% maximum. Sends galleys to author. Publishes ms 1-1½ years after acceptance.
Advice: "Our Emerging Voices Series is designed to bring to North American readers the once-unheard voices of writers who have achieved wide acclaim at home, but were not recognized beyond the borders of their native lands. We are also looking for folktale collections (for adults) from around the world that fit in our International Folk Tale Series."

JAMESON BOOKS, (I, II, IV), Jameson Books, Inc., The Frontier Library, 722 Columbus St., Ottawa IL 61350. (815)434-7905. Editor: Jameson G. Campaigne, Jr. Estab. 1986. Publishes hardcover and paperback originals and reprints. Books: free sheet paper; offset printing; average print order: 10,000; first novel print order: 5,000. Plans 6-8 novels this year. Averages 12-16 total titles, 4-8 fiction titles each year. Occasionally critiques or comments on rejected mss.
Needs: Very well-researched western (frontier pre-1850). No cowboys, no science fiction, mystery, poetry, et al. Recently published *Yellowstone Kelly*, by Peter Bowen; *Wister Trace*, by Loren Estelman; and *One-Eyed Dream*, by Terry Johnston.

Market conditions are constantly changing! If you're still using this book and it is 1997 or later, buy the newest edition of Novel & Short Story Writer's Market at your favorite bookstore or order from Writer's Digest Books.

How to Contact: Does not accepted unsolicited mss. Submit outline/synopsis and 3 consecutive sample chapters. SASE. Agented fiction 50%. Reports in 2 weeks on queries; 2-5 months on mss. Simultaneous submissions OK.
Terms: Pays royalties of 5% minimum; 15% maximum. Average advance: $1,500. Sends galleys to author. Book catalog for 6×9 SASE.

KENSINGTON PUBLISHING CORP., (II), 850 Third Ave., New York NY 10022. (212)407-1500. Editor, Arabesque: Monica Harris. Executive Editor, Denise Little Presents: Denise Little. Executive Editor, Kensington Books: Sarah Gallick. Executive Editor, Kensington Trade Paperbacks: Tracy Bernstein. Executive Editor, Pinnacle Books: Paul Dinas. Executive Editor, Zebra Books and Kensington Mass Market: Ann La Farge. Estab. 1975. Publishes hardcover originals, trade paperbacks and mass market originals and reprints. Averages 400 total titles/year.
Needs: Contemporary, adventure, mysteries, romance (contemporary, historical, regency, multicultural), true crime, nonfiction, women's, erotica, thrillers and horror. No science fiction. Recently published *Destiny Mine*, by Janelle Taylor; *The Fall Line*, by Mark T. Sullivan; and *Cemetary of Angels*, by Noel Hynd. Ms length ranges from 100,000 to 125,000 words.
How to Contact: Query or submit complete ms or outline/synopsis and sample chapters with SASE. Simultaneous submissions OK. Reports in 3-5 months.
Terms: Pays royalties and advances. Free book catalog.
Advice: "We want fiction that will appeal to the mass market and we want writers who want to make a career."

ALFRED A. KNOPF, (II), Division of Random House, 201 E. 50th St., New York NY 10022. Contact: The Editors. Estab. 1915. Publishes hardcover originals. Number of titles: approximately 46 each year. Buys 75% agented fiction. Published new writers in the last year.
Needs: Contemporary, literary, suspense and spy. No western, gothic, romance, erotica, religious or science fiction. Published *Mystery Ride*, by Robert Boswell; *The Night Manager*, by John Le Carre; *Lasher*, by Anne Rice. Published new writers within the last year.
How to Contact: Submit outline or synopsis with SASE. Reports within 1 month on mss. Publishes ms an average of 1 year after acceptance.
Terms: Pays 10-15% in royalties; offers advance. Must return advance if book is not completed or is unacceptable.
Advice: Publishes book-length fiction of literary merit by known and unknown writers.

KNOPF BOOKS FOR YOUNG READERS, (II), Division of Random House, 201 E. 50th St., New York NY 10022. Editor-in-Chief: Arthur Levine. Publishes hardcover and paperback originals and reprints. New paperback imprint includes Dragonfly Books (picture books). Averages 50 total titles, approximately 20 fiction titles each year.
Needs: "High-quality contemporary, humor, picture books, middle grade novels." Published *No Star Nights*, by Anna Smucker; *Mirandy and Brother Wind*, by Patricia McKissoch; *The Boy Who Lost His Face*, by Lewis Sachar.
How to Contact: Query with outline/synopsis and 2 sample chapters with SASE. Simultaneous submissions OK. Reports in 6-8 weeks on mss.
Terms: Sends galleys to author.

LEISURE BOOKS, (II), Division of Dorchester Publishing Co., Inc., 276 Fifth Ave., Suite 1008, New York NY 10001. (212)725-8811. Address submissions to Jennifer Eaton, editorial assistant. Mass-market paperback publisher—originals and reprints. Books: Newsprint paper; offset printing; perfect-bound; average print order: variable; first novel print order: variable. Plans 25 first novels this year. Averages 150 total titles, 145 fiction titles each year. Comments on rejected ms "only if requested ms requires it."
   ● See the listing for Leisure Books' imprint, Love Spell, in this section.
Needs: Romance (Love Spell), horror. Looking for "historical romance (90,000-115,000 words)." Recently published *Broken Vows*, by Shirl Henke; *Lakota Renegade*, by Madeline Baker.
How to Contact: Accepts unsolicited mss. Query first. SASE. Agented fiction 70%. Reports in 1 month on queries; 2 months on mss. "All mss must be typed, double-spaced on one side and left unbound."
Terms: Offers negotiable advance. Payment depends "on category and track record of author." Sends galleys to author. Publishes ms within 2 years after acceptance. Romance guidelines for #10 SASE.
Advice: Encourages first novelists "if they are talented and willing to take direction, *and* write the kind of category fiction we publish. Please include a brief synopsis if sample chapters are requested."

LERNER PUBLICATIONS COMPANY, (II), 241 First Ave. N., Minneapolis MN 55401. Imprints include First Avenue Editions. Editor: Jennifer Martin. (612)332-3344. Estab. 1959. "Midsize independent *children's* publisher." Publishes hardcover originals and paperback reprints. Books: Offset printing; reinforced library binding; perfect binding; average print order: 5,000-7,500; first novel print order: 5,000. Averages 70 total titles, 1-2 fiction titles each year. Sometimes comments on rejected ms.

• Lerner Publication's joke book series is recommended by "Reading Rainbow" (associated with the popular television show of the same name).

Needs: Young adult: general, problem novels, sports, adventure, mystery (young adult). Looking for "well-written middle grade and young adult. No *adult fiction* or single short stories." Published *Ransom for a River Dolphin*, by Sarita Kendall.

How to Contact: Accepts unsolicited mss. Query first or submit outline/synopsis and 2 sample chapters. Reports in 1 month on queries; 2 months on mss. Simultaneous submissions OK.

Terms: Pays royalties. Offers advance. Provides author's copies. Sends galleys to author. Publishes ms 12-18 months after acceptance. Writer's guidelines for #10 SASE. Book catalog for 9×12 SAE with $1.90 postage.

Advice: Would like to see "less gender and racial stereotyping; protagonists from many cultures."

LION PUBLISHING, (II), 4005 Lee Vance View, Colorado Springs CO 80916. (800)708-5550. Attention: Editorial. Estab. 1984. "Christian book publisher publishing books for the *general* market." Publishes hardcover and paperback originals and paperback reprints. Books: Average print order 7,500; first novel print order 5,000. Plans 1-2 first novels this year. Averages 10 total titles, 2-3 fiction titles each year. Often comments on rejected ms.

• Lion Publishing's books *The Paradise War* and *The Silver Hand*, both by Stephen Lawhead, won the Critics' Choice Award by *Christianity Today* and Book of the Year awards from *Cornerstone* magazine. Another book, *Midnight Blue*, by Pauline Fisk received England's Smarties Award, the largest cash prize for children's literature.

Needs: Open. "Because we are a Christian publisher, all books should be written from a Christian perspective." Published *The Silver Hand*, by Stephen Lawhead (fantasy); *An Ordinary Exodus*, by Roger Bichelberger (literary); *Bury Her Sweetly*, by Linda Amey (mystery).

How to Contact: Accepts unsolicited mss. Submit first two chapters with a synopsis and cover letter. SASE *required*. Agented fiction 5%. Reports in 1-4 weeks on queries; 1-3 months on mss.

Terms: Pays negotiable royalties. Sends galleys to author. Publishes ms 18 months after acceptance. Writer's guidelines and book catalog free.

Advice: "We are interested in concentrating on the children's area and phasing out adult titles. We are also open to additional titles in our fantasy line, but the ideas presented need to be fresh, informed by what's currently marketable. We are not satisfied with work in the 'tradition' of J.R.R. Tolkien and C.S. Lewis. Lion books are written by Christians, but Lion is a *general-market* house. Compare your work with similar books currently selling in your local bookstore. Too many Christian writers seem out of touch with current books and genres, as if Christian imaginative writing ended with Tolkien, Lewis, etc. Read widely and write for the world at large, not fellow churchgoers."

LITTLE, BROWN AND COMPANY CHILDREN'S BOOKS, (III), Trade Division; Children's Books, 34 Beacon St., Boston MA 02108. (617)227-0730. Fax: (617)227-8344. Editorial Department. Contact: John G. Keller, publisher; Maria Modugno, editor-in-chief. Books: 70 lb. paper; sheet-fed printing; illustrations. Sometimes buys juvenile mss with illustrations "if by professional artist." Published new writers within the last year.

• *Maniac Magee*, by Jerry Spinelli and published by Little, Brown and Company Children's Books, received a Newbery Award.

Needs: Middle grade fiction and young adult. Recently published *Yang the Youngest*, by Lensey Namiko; *Take Care of My Girl*, by Patricia Hermes; and *For the Love of Pete*, by Jan Marino.

How to Contact: No unsolicited mss. Submit through agent only.

Terms: Pays on royalty basis. Sends galleys to author. Publishes ms 1-2 years after acceptance.

Advice: "We are looking for trade books with bookstore appeal. We are especially looking for young children's (ages 3-5) picture books. We encourage first novelists. New authors should be aware of what is currently being published. We recommend they spend time at the local library and bookstore familiarizing themselves with new publications." Known for "humorous middle grade fiction with lots of kid appeal. Literary, multi-layered young adult fiction with distinctive characters and complex plots."

LITTLE, BROWN AND COMPANY, INC., (II, III), 1271 Avenue of the Americas, New York NY 10020 and 34 Beacon St., Boston MA 02108. (212)522-8700 and (617)227-0730. Imprints include Little, Brown; Back Bay; Bulfinch Press. Medium-size house. Publishes adult and juvenile hardcover and paperback originals. Averages 200-225 total adult titles/year. Number of fiction titles varies.

• Send children's submissions to Submissions Editor, Children's Books, at Boston address. Include SASE.

Needs: Open. No science fiction. Published *Along Came a Spider*, by James Patterson; *The Poet*, by Michael Connelly; *The Pugilist at Rest: Stories*, by Thom Jones. Published new writers within the last year.

How to Contact: Does not accept unsolicited adult mss. Query editorial department first; "we accept submissions from authors who have published before, in book form, magazines, newspapers or journals. No submissions from unpublished writers." Reports in 4-6 months on queries. Simultaneous and photocopied submissions OK.

Terms: "We publish on a royalty basis, with advance."

LITTLE SIMON, Imprint of Simon & Schuster Children's Publishing Division, 866 Third Ave., New York NY 10022. This imprint publishes novelty books only (pop-ups, lift-the-flaps board books, etc). Query for more information.

LODESTAR BOOKS, (II), An affiliate of Dutton Children's Books; A division of Penguin Books USA, Inc., 375 Hudson St., New York NY 10014. (212)366-2627. Editorial Director: Virginia Buckley. Executive Editor: Rosemary Brosnan. Books: 50 or 55 lb. antique cream paper; offset printing; printing from Syquest disk; hardcover binding; illustrations sometimes; average print order: 5,000-6,500; first novel print order 5,000. Published new writers within the last year. Averages 20 total titles, 12-15 fiction titles each year.
● Books published by Lodestar have won numerous awards including the American Library Association's "Notable Children's Books" and "Best Books for Young Adults," the New England Book Award for Children's Books and the Scott O'Dell Award for Historical Fiction.
Needs: Contemporary, family saga, humorous, sports, mystery, adventure, for middle-grade and young adult. Recently published *Flip-Flop Girl*, by Katherine Paterson (ages 8-12); *Mr. Lincoln's Drummer*, by G. Clifton Wisler (ages 10-14); and *Imagining Isabel*, by Omar Castaneda (ages 12 up).
How to Contact: Does not accept unsolicited mss. Send query letter plus first three chapters. SASE. Simultaneous submissions OK. Agented fiction 50%. Reports in 2-4 months. Publishes ms an average of 18 months after acceptance.
Terms: Pays 8-10% in royalties; offers negotiable advance. Sends galleys to author. Free book catalog.
Advice: "A strong individual is important. It is also important to know the needs of each publisher. We are still looking for more books about contemporary African American, Hispanic, Native American, and Asian children, but the market has become tighter and excellent writing is more important than ever."

LOTHROP, LEE & SHEPARD BOOKS, (III), William Morrow & Co., 1350 Sixth Ave., New York NY 10019. (212)261-6641. Fax: (212)261-6648. Imprints: Tambourine Books (Contact: Chris Geisel), Morrow Junior Books (Contact: Diana Capriotti), and Greenwillow Books (Contact: Barbara Trueson). Vice President/Editor-in-Chief: Susan Pearson. Senior Editor: Melanie Donovan. Estab. mid 19th century. "We publish children's books for all ages—about 25 books a year—primarily picture books." Publishes hardcover originals. Published new writers within the last year. Averages 25 total titles, 2-3 fiction titles each year. Sometimes comments on rejected ms.
● The press has recently received the Coretta Scott King Award for Illustration for *Meet Danitra Brown*, Mildred L. Batchelder Honor Award for Translation for *Sister Shako & Kolo the Goat*, and the Archer/Eckblad Children's Picture Book Award for *Circus of the Wolves*.
Needs: "Our needs are not by category but by quality—we are interested only in fiction of a superlative quality." Recently published *Sister Shako & Kolo the Goat*, by Vedat Dalokay; *What Kind of Love?*, by Shelia Cole; and *Dreamtime*, by Oodgeroo (anthology of Aboriginal stories).
How to Contact: Does not accept unsolicited mss. Submit through agent only. SASE for return of ms. Agented fiction 100%. Reports in 3-6 months on mss.
Terms: Pays royalties of 10% minimum; negotiable advance. Sends galleys to author.
Advice: "I'd like to see more quality. More mss that move me to out-loud laughter or real tears—i.e. mss that touch my heart. Find an agent. Work on the craft. We are less able to work with beginners with an eye to the future; mss must be of a higher quality than ever before in order to be accepted."

LOVE SPELL, (II), Division of Dorchester Publishing Co., Inc., 276 Fifth Ave., Suite 1008, New York NY 10001. (212)725-8811. Editorial Assistant: Sharon Morey. Mass market paperback publisher—originals and reprints. Books: newsprint paper; offset printing; perfect-bound; average print order: varies; first novel print order: varies. Plans 15 first novels this year. Comments "only if requested ms requires it."
● See also the listing in this book for Leisure Books. An interview with Sharon Morey appears in the 1995 *Novel & Short Story Writer's Market*.
Needs: Romance (futuristic time travel, historical). Looking for romances of 90,000-115,000 words. Published *A Time to Love Again*, by Flora Speer (time-travel romance); *Heart of the Wolf*, by Saranne Dawson (futuristic romance).
How to Contact: Accepts unsolicited mss. Query first. "All mss must be typed, double-spaced on one side and left unbound." SASE for return of ms. Agented fiction 70%. Reports in 1 month on queries; 2 months on mss.
Terms: Offers negotiable advance. "Payment depends on category and track record of author." Sends galleys to author. Publishes ms within 2 years after acceptance. Writer's guidelines for #10 SASE.
Advice: Encourages first novelists "if they are talented and willing to take direction, *and* write the kind of category fiction we publish. Please include a brief synopsis if sample chapters are requested."

LOVESWEPT, (I, II), Bantam Books, 1540 Broadway, New York NY 10036. (212)354-6500. Associate Publisher: Nita Taublib. Senior Editors: Wendy McCurdy and Beth de Guzman. Imprint estab. 1982. Publishes paperback originals. Plans several first novels this year. Averages 72 total titles each year.

Needs: "Contemporary romance, highly sensual, believable primary characters, fresh and vibrant approaches to plot. No gothics, regencies or suspense."
How to Contact: Query with SASE; no unsolicited mss or partial mss. "Query letters should be no more than two to three pages. Content should be a brief description of the plot and the two main characters."
Terms: Pays in royalties of 6%; negotiates advance.
Advice: "Read extensively in the genre. Rewrite, polish and edit your own work until it is the best it can be—before submitting."

MACMILLAN BOOKS FOR YOUNG READERS, (I, II), Simon and Schuster Children's Publishing Division, 1230 Avenue of the Americas, New York NY 10020. (212)698-2850. Vice President and Editorial Director: Stephanie Laurie. Publishes juvenile hardcover originals. Books: Excellent quality paper printing and binding; full-color or black-and-white illustrations—depends on what the book needs. Seldom comments on rejected mss.
● With the merger of Macmillan and Simon & Schuster, Macmillan books for Young Readers now includes Bradbury Press.
Needs: Juvenile and young adult: adventure, contemporary, mystery. Published *Weasel*, by Cynthia de Felice; *Windcatcher*, by Avi; and *Cricket and the Crackerbox Kid*, by Alane Ferguson.
How to Contact: Query first on novels. Send complete picture book ms with SASE. Specify simultaneous submissions. Reports in 3 months on mss.
Terms: Pays royalty based on retail price. Advance negotiable.

MACMILLAN PUBLISHING CO, INC., 866 3rd Ave., New York NY 10022. Does not accept fiction mss.

WILLIAM MORROW AND COMPANY, INC., (II), 1350 Avenue of the Americas, New York NY 10019. (212)261-6500. Imprints include Beech Tree Books, Fielding Publications (travel books); Greenwillow Books; Hearst Books; Hearst Marine Books; Lothrop; Lee & Shepard; Morrow; Morrow Junior Books; Mulberry Books; Quill Trade Paperbacks; Tambourine Books; and Tupels Books. Estab. 1926. Approximately one fourth of books published are fiction.
Needs: "Morrow accepts only the highest quality submissions" in contemporary, literary, experimental, adventure, mystery/suspense, spy, historical, war, feminist, gay/lesbian, science fiction, horror, humor/satire and translations. Juvenile and young adult divisions are separate.
How to Contact: Submit through agent. All unsolicited mss are returned unopened. "We will accept queries, proposals or mss only when submitted through a literary agent." Simultaneous submissions OK. Reports in 2-3 months.
Terms: Pays in royalties; offers advance. Sends galleys to author. Free book catalog.
Advice: "The Morrow divisions of Beech Tree Books, Greenwillow Books, Lee & Shepard, Lothrop, Mulberry Books and Morrow Junior Books handle juvenile books. We do five to ten first novels every year, and about one-fourth of the titles are fiction. Having an agent helps to find a publisher."

MORROW JUNIOR BOOKS, (III), 1350 Avenue of the Americas, New York NY 10019. (212)261-6691. Editor-In-Chief: David L. Reuther. Plans 1 first novel this year. Averages 55 total titles each year.
Needs: Juvenile (5-9 years) including animal, easy-to-read, fantasy (little), spy/adventure (very little), pre-school/picture book, young adult/teen (10-18 years) including historical, sports.
How to Contact: Does not accept unsolicited mss. Recently published *Birthday Surprises*, edited by Johanna Horwitz; *My Own Two Feet*, by Beverly Cleary; and *The White Deer*, by John Bierhoust.
Terms: Authors paid in royalties. Books published 12-18 months after acceptance. Book catalog free on request.
Advice: "Our list is very full at this time. No unsolicited manuscripts."

MULTNOMAH BOOKS, (II), Questar Publishers, Inc. P.O. Box 1720, Sisters OR 97759. (503)549-1144. Fax: (503)549-2044. Contact: Editorial Dept. Estab. 1987. Midsize independent publisher of evangelical fiction and nonfiction. Publishes paperback originals. Books: perfect binding; average print order: 12,000. Averages 75 total titles, 6-7 fiction titles each year.
● Multnomah Books has received several Gold Medallion Book Awards from the Evangelical Christian Publishers Association.
Needs: Literary, religious/inspirational (children's religious, general, religious fantasy). Published *Deadline*, by Randy Alcorn (contemporary); *A Promise Unbroken*, by Al Lacy (historical/romance); and *Jordan's Crossing*, by Randall Arthur (religious/adventure). Publishes "Battles of Destiny" (Civil War series).

Check the Category Indexes, located at the back of the book, for publishers interested in specific fiction subjects.

How to Contact: Submit outline/synopsis and 2 sample chapters. "Include a cover letter with any additional information that might help us in our review." Send SASE for reply, return of ms or send a disposable copy of ms. Reports in 10 weeks. Simultaneous submissions OK.

Terms: Pays royalties. Provides 100 author's copies. Sends galleys to author. Publishes ms 1-2 years after acceptance. Writer's guidelines for SASE.

Advice: "Looking for clean, moral, uplifting fiction—not necessarily religious. We're particularly interested in contemporary women's fiction, gift fiction, superior romance, and Grisham-type big fiction."

THE MYSTERIOUS PRESS, (III), 1271 Avenue of the Americas, New York NY 10120. (212)522-7200. Crime and mystery fiction imprint for Warner Books. Editor-in-Chief: William Malloy. Editor: Sara Ann Freed. Estab. 1976. Publishes hardcover originals and paperback reprints. Books: Hardcover (some Smythe-sewn) and paperback binding; illustrations rarely. Average first novel print order 5,000 copies. Published new writers within the last year. Critiques "only those rejected writers we wish particularly to encourage."

Needs: Mystery/suspense. Recently published *The Yellow Room Conspiracy*, by Peter Dickinson; *A Wild and Lonely Place*, by Marcia Muller; and *Ah, Treachery*, by Ross Thomas.

How to Contact: Agented material only.

Terms: Pays in royalties of 10% minimum; offers negotiable advance. Sends galleys to author. Buys hard and softcover rights. Book catalog for SASE.

Advice: "Write a strong and memorable novel, and with the help of a good literary agent, you'll find the right publishing house. Don't despair if your manuscript is rejected by several houses. All publishing houses are looking for new and exciting crime novels, but it may not be at the time your novel is submitted. Hang in there, keep the faith—and good luck."

W.W. NORTON & COMPANY, INC., (II), 500 Fifth Ave., New York NY 10110. (212)354-5500. For unsolicited mss contact: Liz Malcolm. Estab. 1924. Midsize independent publisher of trade books and college textbooks. Publishes hardcover originals. Occasionally comments on rejected mss.

• See the interview with Editor Gerald Howard in the 1995 edition of this book.

Needs: High-quality fiction (preferably literary). No occult, science fiction, religious, gothic, romances, experimental, confession, erotica, psychic/supernatural, fantasy, horror, juvenile or young adult. Recently published *Seduction Theory*, by Thomas Beller; *Come and Go, Molly Snow*, by Mary Ann Taylor-Hall; and *The Book of Knowledge*, by Doris Grumbach.

How to Contact: Submit outline/synopsis and first 50 pages. SASE. Simultaneous submissions OK. Reports in 8-10 weeks. Packaging and postage must be enclosed to ensure safe return of materials.

Terms: Graduated royalty scale starting at 7½% or 10% of list price, in addition to 15 author's copies; offers advance. Free book catalog.

Advice: "We will occasionally encourage writers of promise whom we do not immediately publish. We are principally interested in the literary quality of fiction manuscripts. A familiarity with our current list of titles will give you an idea of what we're looking for. Chances are, if your book is good and you have no agent you will eventually succeed; but the road to success will be easier and shorter if you have an agent backing the book. We encourage the submission of first novels."

PANTHEON BOOKS, (III), Subsidiary of Random House, 201 E. 50th St., New York NY 10022. (212)572-2404. Estab. 1942. "Small but well-established imprint of well-known large house." Publishes hardcover and trade paperback originals and trade paperback reprints. Averages 75 total titles, about one-third fiction, each year.

Needs: Quality fiction and nonfiction.

How to Contact: Query letter and sample material. SASE. Attention: Editorial Department.

PELICAN PUBLISHING COMPANY, (IV), Box 3110, Gretna LA 70054. Editor: Nina Kooij. Estab. 1926. Publishes hardcover reprints and originals. Books: Hardcover and paperback binding; illustrations sometimes. Buys juvenile mss with illustrations. Published new writers within the last year. Comments on rejected mss "infrequently."

Needs: Juvenile fiction, especially with a regional and/or historical focus. No contemporary fiction or fiction containing graphic language, violence or sex. Also no "psychological" novels. Recently published *Little Freddie's Legacy*, by Kathryn Cocquyt (juvenile novel); *The Calling of Dan Matthews*, by Harold Bell Wright (novel); and *Why Cowboys Sleep With Their Boots On*, by Laurie Lazzaro Knowlton (picture book).

How to Contact: Prefers query. May submit outline/synopsis and 2 sample chapters with SASE. No simultaneous submissions. "Not responsible if writer's only copy is sent." Reports in 1 month on queries; 3 months on mss. Publishes ms 12-18 months after acceptance.

Terms: Pays 10% in royalties; 10 contributor's copies; advance considered. Sends galleys to author. Catalog of titles and writer's guidelines for SASE.

Advice: "Research the market carefully. Order and look through publishing catalogs to see if your work is consistent with our list. For ages 8 and up, story must be planned in chapters that will fill at least 150 double-spaced manuscript pages. Topic should be historical and, preferably, linked to a particular region or culture. We look for stories that illuminate a particular place and time in history and that are clean entertainment."

PENGUIN USA, 375 Hudson St., New York NY 10014. See the listing for Dutton Signet.

PHILOMEL BOOKS, (II), The Putnam & Grosset Book Group, 200 Madison Ave., New York NY 10016. (212)951-8722. Editorial Director: Patricia Gauch. Associate Editor: Michael Green. "A high-quality oriented imprint focused on stimulating picture books, middle-grade novels, and young adult novels." Publishes hardcover originals and paperback reprints. Averages 40 total titles, 35 fiction titles/year. Sometimes comments on rejected ms.
  • Books published by Philomel have won numerous awards. Their book, *Seven Blind Mice*, by Ed Young, was a Caldecott Honor book.
Needs: Adventure, ethnic, family saga, fantasy, historical, juvenile (5-9 years), literary, preschool/picture book, regional, short story collections, translations, western (young adult), young adult/teen (10-18 years). Looking for "story-driven novels with a strong cultural voice but which speak universally." No "generic, mass-market oriented fiction." Recently published *The Bellmaker*, by Brian Jacques; *The Merlin Effect*, by T.A. Barron; *The Dandelion Garden*, by Budge Wilson.
How to Contact: Accepts unsolicited mss. Query first or submit outline/synopsis and first 3 chapters. SASE. Agented fiction 40%. Reports in 6-8 weeks on queries; 6-10 weeks on mss. Simultaneous submissions OK.
Terms: Pays royalties, negotiable advance and author's copies. Sends galleys to author. Publishes ms anywhere from 1-3 years after acceptance. Writer's guidelines for #10 SASE. Book catalog for 9×12 SASE.
Advice: "We are not a mass-market publisher and do not publish short stories independently. In addition, we do just a few novels a year."

PINNACLE BOOKS, 850 Third Ave., New York NY 10022. See Kensington Publishing Corp.

POCKET BOOKS, (II), Division of Simon & Schuster, 1230 Avenue of the Americas, New York NY 10020. (212)698-7000. Imprints include Washington Square Press and Star Trek. Executive Vice President/Editorial Director: William Grose. Publishes paperback and hardcover originals and reprints. Averages 300 titles each year. Buys 90% agented fiction. Sometimes critiques rejected mss.
Needs: Contemporary, literary, adventure, spy, historical, western, gothic, romance, military/war, mainstream, suspense/mystery, feminist, ethnic, erotica, psychic/supernatural, fantasy, horror and humor/satire. Published *Waiting to Exhale*, by Terry McMillan; *The Way Things Ought To Be*, by Rush Limbaugh (hardcover and paperback); *Perfect*, by Judith McNaught (hardcover and paperback); and *The Red Horseman*, by Stephen Coonts (hardcover and paperback); published new writers within the last year.
How to Contact: Query with SASE (or IRC). No unsolicited mss. Reports in 6 months on queries only. Publishes ms 12-18 months after acceptance.
Terms: Pays in royalties and offers advance. Sends galleys to author. Writer must return advance if book is not completed or is not acceptable. Free book catalog.

PRESIDIO PRESS, (IV), 505B San Marin Dr., Room 300, Novato CA 94945. (415)898-1081. Editor-in-Chief: E.J. McCarthy (ext. 125). Estab. 1976. Small independent general trade—specialist in military. Publishes hardcover originals. Publishes an average of 2 works of fiction per list under its Lyford Books imprint. Averages 24 new titles each year. Critiques or comments on rejected ms.
Needs: Historical with military background, war. Also mystery/suspense (police procedural, private eye), thriller/espionage. Published *Synbat*, by Bob Mayer; *Hawks*, by Ray Rosenbaum; and *Fenwick Travers and the Years of Empire*, by Raymond Saunders. Regularly publishes new writers.
How to Contact: Accepts unsolicited mss. Query first. SASE. Reports in 2 weeks on queries; 2-3 months on mss. Simultaneous submissions OK.
Terms: Pays in royalties of 15% of net minimum; advance: $1,000 average. Sends edited manuscripts and page proofs to author. Book catalog and guidelines free on request. Send 9×12 SASE with $1.30 postage.
Advice: "Think twice before entering any highly competitive genre; don't imitate; do your best. Have faith in your writing and don't let the market disappoint or discourage you."

G.P. PUTNAM'S SONS, (III), The Putnam Publishing Group, 200 Madison Ave., New York NY 10016. (212)951-8400. Imprints include Perigee, Philomel and Grosset. Publishes hardcover originals.
Needs: Published fiction by Stephen King, Lawrence Sanders, Alice Hoffman; published new writers within the last year.
How to Contact: Does not accept unsolicited mss.

RANDOM HOUSE, INC., 201 E. 50th St., New York NY 10022. (212)751-2600. Imprints include Pantheon Books, Panache Press at Random House, Vintage Books, Times Books, Villard Books and Knopf. Contact: Adult Trade Division. Publishes hardcover and paperback originals. Encourages new writers. Rarely comments on rejected mss.
Needs: Adventure, contemporary, historical, literary, mainstream, short story collections, mystery/suspense. "We publish fiction of the highest standards." Authors include James Michener, Robert Ludlum, Mary Gordon.

How to Contact: Query with SASE. Simultaneous submissions OK. Reports in 4-6 weeks on queries, 2 months on mss.

Terms: Payment as per standard minimum book contracts. Free writer's guidelines.

Advice: "Please try to get an agent because of the large volume of manuscripts received, agented work is looked at first."

✿**RANDOM HOUSE OF CANADA, (III)**, Division of Random House, Inc., 33 Yonge St., Suite 210, Toronto, Ontario M5E 1G4 Canada. Prefers not to share information.

‡**RESOURCE PUBLICATIONS, INC., (I, IV)**, 160 E. Virginia St., Suite 290, San Jose CA 95112. (408)286-8505. Book Editor: Kenneth Guentert. Estab. 1973. "Independent book and magazine publisher focusing on imaginative resources for professionals in ministry, education and counseling." Publishes paperback originals. Averages 12-14 total titles, 2-3 fiction titles each year.

Needs: Story collections for storytellers, "not short stories in the usual literary sense." Recently published *Morgan's Baby Sister: A Read-Aloud Book For Families Who Have Experienced the Death of a Newborn*, by Patricia Polin Johnson and Donna Reilly Williams; and *Dream Catcher: Lectionary-based stories for Preaching and Teaching*, by James Henderschedt. Occasionally publishes book-length stories that meet some need (*The Cure: The Hero's Journey with Cancer*). No novels in the literary sense.

How to Contact: Query first or submit outline/synopsis and 1 sample chapter with SASE. Reports in 2 weeks on queries; 6 weeks on mss. No simultaneous submissions. Accepts disk submissions compatible with CP/M, IBM system. Prefers hard copy with disk submissions.

Terms: Pays in royalties of 8% minimum, 10% maximum; 10 author's copies. "We do not subsidy publish under the Resource Publications imprint. However, our graphics department will help author's self-publish for a fee."

REVELL PUBLISHING, (III), Subsidiary of Baker Book House, P.O. Box 6287, Grand Rapids MI 49516-6287. (616)676-9185. Fax: (616)676-9573. Imprints include Spire Books. Editorial Director: Wm. J. Petersen. Estab. 1870. "Midsize evangelical book publishers." Publishes paperback originals. Average print order: 7,500. Published new writers within the last year. Plans 1 first novel this year. Averages 60 total titles, 8 fiction titles each year. Sometimes comments on rejected ms.

Needs: Religious/inspirational (general). Recently published *Ordeal at Iron Mountain*, by Linda Rae Rao (historical); *A Time to Weep*, by Gilbert Morris (historical); and *The End of the Age*, by David Dolan (suspense).

How to Contact: Query with outline/synopsis. Include estimated word count, bio and list of publishing credits. Send SASE for reply, return of ms or send a disposable copy of ms. Agented fiction 20%. Reports in 3 weeks on queries; 2 weeks on mss. Simultaneous submissions OK.

Terms: Pays royalties. Sends galleys to author. Publishes ms 1 year after acceptance. Writer's guidelines for SASE.

ROC, (II, III), Imprint of Dutton Signet, a division of Penguin USA, Inc., 375 Hudson St., New York NY 10014. (212)366-2000. Fax: (212)366-2888. Executive Editor: Amy Stout. Publishes hardcover, trade paperback and mass market originals and hardcover, trade paperback (and mass market) reprints. Published new writers within the last year. Averages 40 (all fiction) titles each year. Sometimes comments on rejected ms.

● A Roc book, *The Inn Keeper's Song* won a Locus Award and was nominated for a World Fantasy Award.

Needs: Fantasy, horror (dark fantasy) and science fiction. Publishes science fiction, horror and fantasy anthologies. Anthologies by invitation only. Published *The Innkeeper's Song*, by Peter S. Beagle (fantasy); *The Hollowing*; by Robert Hordstock (fantasy); *Star Gate: Rebellion*, by Bill McCay (science fiction). Publishes the Battletech® and Shadowrun® series.

How to Contact: Accepts unsolicited mss. Query with outline/synopsis and 3 sample chapters. Include list of publishing credits. Send SASE for reply, return of ms or send a disposable copy of ms. Agented fiction 99%. Reports in 2 weeks on queries; 3-4 months on mss. Simultaneous submissions OK.

Terms: Offers negotiable advance. Sends galleys to author. Publishes ms 1-2 years after acceptance.

ST. MARTIN'S PRESS, 175 Fifth Ave., New York NY 10010. (212)674-5151. Imprint: Thomas Dunne. Chairman and CEO: Thomas J. McCormack. President: Roy Gainsburg. Publishes hardcover and paperback reprints and originals.

The maple leaf symbol before a listing indicates a Canadian publisher, magazine, conference or contest.

Needs: Contemporary, literary, experimental, adventure, mystery/suspense, spy, historical, war, gothic, romance, confession, feminist, gay, lesbian, ethnic, erotica, psychic/supernatural, religious/inspirational, science fiction, fantasy, horror and humor/satire. No plays, children's literature or short fiction. Published *The Silence of the Lambs*, by Thomas Harris; *The Shell Seekers* and *September* by Rosamunde Pilcher.
How to Contact: Query or submit complete ms with SASE. Simultaneous submissions OK (if declared as such). Reports in 2-3 weeks on queries, 4-6 weeks on mss.
Terms: Pays standard advance and royalties.

ST. PAUL BOOKS AND MEDIA, (I), Subsidiary of Daughters of St. Paul, 50 St. Paul's Ave., Jamaica Plain, Boston MA 02130. (617)522-8911. Children's Editor: Sister Mary Mark, fsp. Estab. 1934. Roman Catholic publishing house. Publishes hardcover and paperback originals. Averages 20 total titles, 5 fiction titles each year.
Needs: Juvenile (easy-to-read, historical, religion, contemporary), preschool/picture book. All fiction must communicate high moral and family values. "Our fiction needs are entirely in the area of children's literature. We are looking for bedtime stories, historical and contemporary novels for children. Would like to see characters who manifest faith and trust in God." Does not want "characters whose lifestyles are not in conformity with Catholic teachings."
How to Contact: Does not accept unsolicited mss. Query first. SASE. Reports in 2 weeks.
Terms: Pays royalties of 8% minimum; 12% maximum. Provides negotiable number of author's copies. Publishes ms 2 or 3 years after acceptance. Writer's guidelines for #10 SASE.
Advice: "There is a dearth of juvenile fiction appropriate for Catholics and other Christians."

SCRIBNER, 1230 Avenue of the Americas, New York NY 10020. Prefers not to share information.

SCRIBNER'S BOOKS FOR YOUNG READERS, 1230 Avenue of the Americas, New York NY 10020. Has been absorbed by Atheneum Books for Young Readers. The Editorial Director for Atheneum is Jonathan Lanman.

SIERRA CLUB BOOKS, 100 Bush St., San Francisco CA 94104. (415)291-1617. Fax: (415)291-1600. Senior Editor: Jim Cohee. Estab. 1892. Midsize independent publisher. Publishes hardcover and paperback originals and paperback reprints. Averages 30 titles, 1-2 fiction titles each year.
Needs: Contemporary (conservation, environment).
How to Contact: Submit complete ms. Simultaneous submissions OK. Reports in 6 weeks on queries.
Terms: Pays in royalties. Book catalog for SASE.
Advice: "We publish one or two novels per year. We will consider novels on their quality and on the basis of their relevance to our organization's environmentalist aims."

SIGNAL HILL PUBLICATIONS, (IV), (formerly New Readers Press), Publishing imprint of Laubach Literacy International, Box 131, Syracuse NY 13210. (315)422-9121. Estab. 1959. Publishes paperback originals. Books: offset printing; paper binding; 6-12 illustrations per fiction book; average print order: 7,500; first novel print order: 5,000. Fiction titles may be published both in book form and as read-along audio tapes. Averages 30 total titles, 8-12 fiction titles each year.
Needs: High-interest, low-reading-level materials for adults with limited reading skills. Short novels of 12,000-15,000 words, written on 2nd-5th grade level. "Can be mystery, romance, adventure, science fiction, sports or humor. Characters are well-developed, situations realistic, and plot developments believable." Accepts short stories only in collections of 8-20 very short stories of same genre. Will accept collections of one-act plays that can be performed in a single class period (45-50 min.) with settings than can be created within a classroom. Short stories and plays can be at 3rd-5th grade reading level. All material must be suitable for classroom use in public education, i.e., little violence and no explicit sex. "We will not accept anything at all for readers under 16 years of age." Published *The Orange Grove & Other Stories*, by Rosanne Keller; *The Kite Flyer & Other Stories* by Rosanne Keller.
How to Contact: Accepts unsolicited mss. Query first or submit outline/synopsis and 3 sample chapters. SASE. Reports in 1 month on queries; 3 months on mss.
Terms: Pays royalties of 5% minimum, 7.5% maximum on gross sales. Average advance: $200. "We may offer authors a choice of a royalty or flat fee. The fee would vary depending on the type of work." Book catalog, authors' brochure and guidelines for short novels free.
Advice: "Many of our fiction authors are being published for the first time. It is necessary to have a sympathetic attitude toward adults with limited reading skills and an understanding of their life situation. Direct experience with them is helpful."

SILHOUETTE BOOKS, (I, II, IV), 300 E. 42nd St., 6th Floor, New York NY 10017. (212)682-6080. Imprints include Silhouette Romance, Silhouette Special Edition, Silhouette Desire, Silhouette Intimate Moments, Silhouette Yours Truly, Harlequin Historicals; also Silhouette and Harlequin Historicals' short story collections. Editorial Director: Isabel Swift. Senior Editor and Editorial Coordinator (SIM): Leslie J. Wainger. Seniors Editors: (SE) Tara Hughes Gavin, (SD) Lucia Macro, (SR) Anne Canadeo. Editors (SYT): Melissa Senate, Gail Chasan, Marcia Adirim. Historicals: Senior Editor: Tracy Farrell. Estab. 1979. Publishes paperback originals. Published 10-20 new writers within the last year. Buys agented and unagented adult romances. Averages 360 total titles each year.360/year. Occasionally comments on rejected mss.

● Books published by Silhouette Books have received numerous awards including Romance Writers of America's Rita Award, awards from Romantic Times and best selling awards from Walden and B. Dalton bookstores.

Needs: Contemporary romances, historical romances. Recently published *Sheik Daddy*, by Barbara McMahon (SR); *Saddle Up*, by Mary Lynn Baxter (SD); *New Year's Daddy*, by Lora Jackson (SE); *Nighthawk*, by Rachel Lee (IM); *Blackguard*, by Evelyn Vaughn (SS); *Wanted: Perfect Partner*, by Debbie Macumber (SYT); and *The Wedding Promise*, by Cheryl Reams (HH).

How to Contact: Submit query letter with brief synopsis and SASE. No unsolicited or simultaneous submissions. Publishes ms 9-24 months after acceptance.

Terms: Pays in royalties; offers advance (negotiated on an individual basis). Must return advance if book is not completed or is unacceptable.

Advice: "You are competing with writers that love the genre and know what our readers want—because many of them started as readers. Please note that the fact that our novels are fun to read doesn't make them easy to write. Storytelling ability, clean compelling writing and love of the genre are necessary."

SIMON & SCHUSTER, 1230 Avenue of the Americas, New York NY 10020. (212)698-7000. Imprints include Pocket Books, Poseidon Press.

Needs: General adult fiction, mostly commercial fiction.

How to Contact: Agented material 100%.

SIMON & SCHUSTER BOOKS FOR YOUNG READERS, (II), (formerly Four Winds Press, Green Tiger Press), Subsidiary of Simon & Schuster Children's Publishing Division, 1230 Avenue of the Americas, New York NY 10020. (212)698-2851. Fax: (212)698-2796. Vice President/Editorial Director: Stephanie Owens Lurie. Large children's imprint of enormous children's publishing firm. Publishes hardcover originals. Published new writers within the last year. Plans 2 first novels this year. Averages 75 total titles, 18 fiction titles each year.

Needs: Children's/juvenile (adventure, historical, mystery, picture book, contemporary fiction). No chapter books. No problem novels. No anthropomorphic characters. Publishes anthologies. Editor solicits from established writers. Published *The Crying for a Vision*, by Walter Wangerin (YA novel); *Juliet's Story*, by William Trevor (middle-grade novel); *Fire on the Mountain*, by Jane Kurtz/Earl Lewis (picture book).

How to Contact: Accepts unsolicited mss. Submit complete ms with cover letter. Include estimated word count, list of publishing credits. SASE for return of ms. Agented fiction 90%. Reports in 3 months on mss. Simultaneous submissions OK (not for novels).

Terms: Pays royalties. Offers negotiable advance. Sends galleys to author. Publishes ms within 2 years of acceptance. Writer's guidelines for #10 SASE. Book catalog free from Marketing Department.

■SINGER MEDIA CORP., (III, IV), Unit 106, Seaview Business Park, 1030 Calle Cordillera, San Clemente CA 92673. (714)498-7227. Fiction Editor: Janis Hawkridge. "Book packagers based on our newspaper/syndicates production. License books to foreign publishers; co-production, co-financing." Publishes paperback originals and hardcover and paperback reprints. Averages 100 total titles, 35 fiction titles each year. Often comments on rejected ms; $350 charge for critiques.

● This packager licenses books to foreign publishers (usually books *already* published in North America). They will work with agents or directly with authors.

Needs: *Previously published novels for licensing to foreign language publishers:* childrens/juvenile (fantasy, mystery, series, sports), comics/graphic novels, erotica, fantasy (space fantasy), horror (psychological, supernatural), mystery/suspense (amateur sleuth), New Age/mystic/spiritual, religious/inspirational (general), romance (contemporary, gothic, historical, regency/period, romantic suspense), science fiction (hard science/techno), thriller espionage, translations, western, young adult/teen (horror, mystery/suspense, romance), computer and business/fiction. "Nothing of local interest. Overloaded with westerns. No porno." Published *Jade Princess*, by W.E.D. Ross (historical romance); *Cerissa*, by B. Woodword (romance); and *Amy*, by Jane Edward (suspense/romance). Publishes modern romance series.

How to Contact: Query first. Include list of publishing credits. Send SASE for reply, return of ms or send disposable copy of ms. Agented fiction 15% US, 20% foreign. Reports on queries in 2 weeks; 1 months on mss. Simultaneous, disk (IBM Compatible Windows, WordPerfect 6.0), electronic submissions OK.

Terms: Pays royalties plus advance (varies from country to country and book). Publishes ms 3-18 months after acceptance. Guidelines for $2.

Listings marked with a solid box are book packagers. See the introduction for more information.

STANDARD PUBLISHING, (II, IV), 8121 Hamilton Ave., Cincinnati OH 45231. (513)931-4050. Director: Mark Plunkett. Estab. 1866. Independent religious publisher. Publishes paperback originals and reprints. Books: offset printing; paper binding; b&w line art; average print order: 7,500; first novel print order: 5,000-7,500. Rarely buys juvenile mss with illustrations. Occasionally comments on rejected mss.

● Standard publishes *The Lookout, R-A-D-A-R* and *Seek*, listed in the Commercial Periodicals section.

Needs: Religious/inspirational and easy-to-read. "We do not accept adult fiction at this time; some fiction for very young children accepted. Should have some relation to moral values or Biblical concepts and principles."

How to Contact: Query or submit outline/synopsis and 2-3 sample chapters with SASE. Reports in 1 month on queries, 3 months on mss. Publishes ms 1-2 years after acceptance.

Terms: Pays varied royalties and by outright purchase; offers varied advance. Sends galleys to author. Writer's guidelines and catalog with SASE.

STODDART, 34 Lesmill Rd., Toronto, Ontario M3B 2T6 Canada. No American authors. Prefers not to share information.

THORNDIKE PRESS, (IV), Division of Simon & Schuster, Inc., Box 159, Thorndike ME 04986. (800)223-6121. Contact: Diane Hull. Estab. 1979. Midsize publisher of hardcover and paperback large print *reprints*. Books: alkaline paper; offset printing; Smythe-sewn library binding; average print order: 2,000. Publishes 500 total titles each year.

Needs: *No fiction that has not been previously published.*

How to Contact: Does not accept unsolicited mss. Query.

Terms: Pays 10% in royalties.

Advice: "We do not accept unpublished works."

TOR BOOKS, (II), 175 Fifth Ave., New York NY 10010. (212)388-0100. Editor-in-Chief: Robert Gleason. Estab. 1980. Publishes hardcover and paperback originals, plus some paperback reprints. Books: 5 point Dombook paper; offset printing; Bursel and perfect binding; few illustrations. Averages 200 total titles, mostly fiction, each year. Some nonfiction titles.

Needs: Fantasy, mainstream, science fiction, suspense and westerns. Published *Xenocide*, by Orson Scott Card; *Midnight Sun*, by Ramsey Campbell; *The Nemesis Mission*, by Dean Ing; and *The Dragon Reborn*, by Robert Jordan.

How to Contact: Agented mss preferred. Buys 90% agented fiction. No simultaneous submissions. Address manuscripts to "Editorial," *not* to the Managing Editor's office.

Terms: Pays in royalties and advance. Writer must return advance if book is not completed or is unacceptable. Sends galleys to author. Free book catalog on request.

TROLL ASSOCIATES, (II), Watermill Press, 100 Corporate Dr., Mahwah NJ 07430. (201)529-4000. Editorial Contact Person: M. Frances. Estab. 1968. Midsize independent publisher. Publishes hardcover originals, paperback originals and reprints. Averages 100-300 total titles each year.

Needs: Adventure, historical, juvenile (5-9 yrs. including: animal, easy-to-read, fantasy), preschool/picture book, young adult/teen (10-18 years) including: easy-to-read, fantasy/science fiction, historical, romance (young adult), sports, spy/adventure. Published new writers within the last year.

How to Contact: Accepts and returns unsolicited mss. Query first. SASE. Submit outline/synopsis and sample chapters. Reports in 2-3 weeks on queries.

Terms: Pays royalties. Sometimes sends galleys to author. Publishes ms 6-18 months after acceptance.

TYNDALE HOUSE PUBLISHERS, (II, IV), P.O. Box 80, 351 Executive Drive, Wheaton IL 60189. (708)668-8300. Vice President of Editorial: Ron Beers. Acquisition Director: Ken Petersen. Estab. 1962. Privately owned religious press. Publishes hardcover and trade paperback originals and paperback reprints. Plans 2 first novels this year. Averages 100 total titles, 10-15 fiction titles each year. Average first novel print order: 5,000-15,000 copies.

● Three books published by Tyndale House have received the Gold Medallion Book Award. They include *An Echo in the Darkness*, by Francine Rivers; *The Sword of Truth*, by Gilbert Morris; and *A Rose Remembered*, by Michael Phillips.

Needs: Religious/inspirational. Published *A Voice in the Wind*, by Francine Rivers (historical romance); *The Eleventh Hour*, by Michael Phillips; *Gate of His Enemies*, by Gil Morris. Series include "Grace Livingston Hill," "Appomattax Saga," "Mark of the Lion," "Secret of the Rose" and "Wakefield Dynasty."

How to Contact: Does not accept unsolicited mss. Queries only. Reports in 6-10 weeks. Publishes ms an average of 1-2 years after acceptance.

Terms: Pays in royalties of 10% minimum; negotiable advance. Writer's guidelines and book catalog for 9×12 SAE and $2.40 for postage.

Advice: "We are a religious publishing house with a primarily evangelical Christian market. We are looking for spiritual themes and content within established genres."

✦*VESTA PUBLICATIONS, LTD, (I),** Box 1641, Cornwall, Ontario K6H 5V6 Canada. (613)932-2135. Fax: (613)932-7735. Editor: Stephen Gill. Estab. 1974. Midsize publisher with plans to expand. Publishes hardcover and paperback originals. Books: bond paper; offset printing; paperback and sewn hardcover binding; illustrations; average print order: 1,200; first novel print order: 1,000. Plans 4 first novels this year. Averages 18 total titles, 5 fiction titles each year. *Negotiable charge for critiquing rejected mss.*

Needs: Adventure, contemporary, ethnic, experimental, fantasy, feminist, historical, literary, mainstream, mystery/suspense, psychic/supernatural/occult, regional, religious/inspirational, romance, science fiction, short story collections, translations, war and young adult/teen. Recently published *House Eternal*, by Margery King (religious); *The Blessings of a Bird*, by Stephen Gill (juvenile); and *Whistle Stop and Other Stories*, by Ordrach.

How to Contact: Submit 2-3 sample chapters with SASE or SAE and IRC. Reports in 1 month. Simultaneous submissions OK. Disk submissions OK with CPM/Kaypro 2 and IBM compatible systems.

Terms: Pays in royalties of 10% minimum. Sends galleys to author. *"For first novel we usually ask authors from outside of Canada to pay half of our printing cost."* Free book catalog.

WALKER AND COMPANY, (I), 435 Hudson St., New York NY 10014. Editors: Michael Seidman (mystery), Jacqueline Johnson (western), Emily Easton (young adult). Midsize independent publisher with plans to expand. Publishes hardcover and trade paperback originals. Average first novel print order: 2,500-3,500. Number of titles: 120/year. Published many new writers within the last year. Occasionally comments on rejected mss.

- Books published by Walker and Company have received numerous awards including the Spur Award (for westerns) and the Shamus Awards for Best First Private Eye Novel and Best Novel.

Needs: Nonfiction, sophisticated, quality mystery (amateur sleuth, cozy, private eye, police procedural), traditional western and children's and young adult nonfiction. Recently published *The Killing of Monday Brown*, by Sandra West Prowell; *Murder in the Place of Anubis*, by Lynda S. Robinson; and *Who In Hell Is Wanda Fuca*, by G.M. Ford.

How to Contact: Submit outline and chapters as preliminary. Query letter should include "a concise description of the story line, including its outcome, word length of story (we prefer 70,000 words), writing experience, publishing credits, particular expertise on this subject and in this genre. Common mistakes: Sounding unprofessional (i.e. too chatty, too braggardly). Forgetting SASE." Agented fiction 50%. Notify if multiple or simultaneous submissions. Reports in 3-5 months. Publishes ms an average of 1 year after acceptance.

Terms: Negotiable (usually advance against royalty). Must return advance if book is not completed or is unacceptable.

Advice: "As for mysteries, we are open to all types, including suspense novels and offbeat books that maintain a 'play fair' puzzle. We are always looking for well-written western novels that are offbeat and strong on characterization. Character development is most important in all Walker fiction. We expect the author to be expert in the categories, to know the background and foundations of the genre. To realize that just because some subgenre is hot it doesn't mean that that is the area to mine—after all, if everyone is doing female p.i.s, doesn't it make more sense to do something that isn't crowded, something that might serve to balance a list, rather than make it top heavy? Finally, don't tell us why your book is going to be a success; instead, show me that you can write and write well. It is your writing, and not your hype that interests us."

WARNER BOOKS, 1271 Avenue of the Americas, New York NY 10020. Prefers not to share information. See also listing for Aspect.

WASHINGTON SQUARE PRESS, (III), Subsidiary of Pocket Books/Simon & Schuster, 1230 Avenue of the Americas, New York NY 10020. Fiction Editor: Amy Einhorn. Estab. 1959. Quality imprint of mass-market publisher. Publishes very few paperback originals, mostly reprints. Averages 15 titles, mostly fiction, each year.

Needs: Literary, high quality novels; serious nonfiction. Published *Pizza Face*, by Ken Siman; *Montana 1948*, by Larry Watson; and novels by Susan Minot and Stephen McCauley.

How to Contact: Query first. Publishes mostly agented fiction. Simultaneous submissions OK. "We cannot promise an individual response to unsolicited mss."

■**DANIEL WEISS ASSOCIATES, INC., (II),** 33 W. 17th St., New York NY 10011. (212)645-3865. Fax: (212)633-1236. Estab. 1987. "Packager of 140 titles a year including juvenile and young adult fiction as well as nonfiction titles. We package for a range of publishers within their specifications." Publishes paperback originals. All titles by first-time writers are commissioned for established series.

Needs: Juvenile (ballet, friendship, horse, mystery), mainstream, preschool/picture book, young adult (continuity series, romance, romantic suspense, thriller). Publishes Sweet Valley Kids, Sweet Valley Twins, Sweet Valley High and Sweet Valley University series. "We cannot acquire single-title manuscripts that are not part of a series the author is proposing or submitted specifically according to our guidelines for an established series." Published *Sweet Valley High*, by Francine Pascal (young adult series); *Thoroughbred*, by Joanna

Campbell (juvenile horse series); and *Boyfriends & Girlfriends*, by Katherine Applegate (young adult continuity series).

How to Contact: Accepts unsolicited mss. Query first with synopsis/outline and 2 sample chapters. SASE. Agented fiction 60%. Reports in 2 months. Simultaneous submissions OK.

Terms: Pays flat fee plus royalty. Advance is negotiable. Publishes ms 1 year after acceptance. Writer's guidelines for #10 SASE.

Advice: "We are always happy to work with and encourage first-time novelists. Being packagers, we often create and outline books by committee. This system is quite beneficial to writers who may be less experienced. Usually we are contacted by the agent rather than the writer directly. Occasionally, however, we do work with writers who send in unsolicited material. I think that a professionally presented manuscript is of great importance."

WESTERN PUBLISHING COMPANY, INC., 850 Third Ave., New York NY 10022. (212)753-8500. Imprint: Golden Books. Juvenile Senior Editor: Marilyn Salomon. Estab. 1907. High-volume mass market and trade publisher. Publishes hardcover and paperback originals. Number of titles: Averages 160/year. Buys 20-30% agented fiction.

Needs: Juvenile: Adventure, mystery, humor, sports, animal, easy-to-read picture books, and "a few" nonfiction titles. Published *Little Critter's Bedtime Story*, by Mercer Mayer; *Cyndy Szekeres' Mother Goose Rhymes*; and *Spaghetti Manners*, by Stephanie Calmenson, illustrated by Lisa MaCue Karsten.

How to Contact: Unsolicited mss are returned unread. Publishes ms an average of 1 year after acceptance.

Terms: Pays by outright purchase or royalty.

Advice: "Read our books to see what we do. If you do illustrations, call for appointment to show your work. Do not send illustrations. Illustrations are not necessary; if your book is what we are looking for, we can use one of our artists."

ALBERT WHITMAN & COMPANY, (I), 6340 Oakton St., Morton Grove IL 60053. (708)581-0033. Associate Editor: Christy Grant. Senior Editors: Judith Mathews and Abby Levine. Editor-in-Chief: Kathleen Tucker. Estab. 1919. Small independent juvenile publisher. Publishes hardcover originals and paperback reprints. Books: paper varies; printing varies; library binding; most books illustrated; average print order: 7,500. Published new writers within the last year. Averages 30 total titles each year. Number of fiction titles varies.

Needs: Juvenile (2-12 years including easy-to-read, fantasy, historical, adventure, contemporary, mysteries, picture-book stories). Primarily interested in picture book manuscripts and nonfiction for ages 2-8. Recently published *Walking the Edge*, by Alice Mead; and *Dark Starry Morning*, by David Patneaude.

How to Contact: Accepts unsolicited mss. Submit complete ms; if not possible, send 3 sample chapters and outline; complete ms for picture books. "Queries don't seem to work for us." SASE. "Half or more fiction is not agented." Reports in 4-6 weeks on queries; 2-3 months on mss. Simultaneous submissions OK. ("We must be told.")

Terms: Payment varies. Royalties, advance; number of author's copies varies. Some flat fees. Sends galleys to author. Writer's guidelines for SASE. Book catalog for 9×12 SAE and $1.35 postage.

Advice: "Writers need only to send a manuscript; artwork does not need to be included. If we decide to buy the story, *we* will find an artist. Though it's *okay* to send a whole package, it's not necessary."

*WINSTON-DEREK PUBLISHERS, (II), Box 90883, Nashville TN 37209. (615)321-0535, 329-1319. Imprint: Scythe. Senior Editor: Marjorie Staton. Estab. 1978. Midsize publisher. Publishes hardcover and paperback originals and reprints. Books: 60 lb. old Warren style paper; litho press; perfect and/or sewn binding; illustrations sometimes; average print order: 3,000-5,000 copies; first novel print order: 2,000 copies. Plans 10 first novels this year. Averages 55-65 total titles, 20 fiction titles each year; "90% of material is from freelance writers; each year we add 15 more titles."

Needs: Historical, juvenile (historical), religious/inspirational, and young adult (easy-to-read, historical, romance) and programmed reading material for middle and high school students. "Must be 65,000 words or less. Novels strong with human interest. Characters overcoming a weakness or working through a difficulty. Prefer plots related to a historical event but not necessary. No science fiction, explicit eroticism, minorities in conflict without working out a solution to the problem. Downplay on religious ideal and values." Recently published *Tomorrow*, by Lou Berry; *West of Sheba*, by Joanne Homstad; and *Sashone*, by Bernadine Bayer-Synder. Published new writers within the last year.

How to Contact: Submit outline/synopsis and 3-4 sample chapters with SASE. Simultaneous submissions OK. Reports in 4-6 weeks on queries; 6-8 weeks on mss. Must query first. Do not send complete ms.

Terms: Pays in royalties of 10% minimum, 15% maximum; negotiates advance. *Offers some subsidy arrangements.* Book catalog on request for $1 postage.

Advice: "We need highly plotted fiction relative to African-American and other ethnic minorities. The public is reading contemplative literature. Authors should strive for originality and a clear writing style, depicting universal themes which portray character building and are beneficial to mankind. Consider the historical novel; there is always room for one more."

❖**WORLDWIDE LIBRARY, (II)**, Division of Harlequin Books, 225 Duncan Mill Rd., Don Mills, Ontario M3B 3K9 Canada. (416)445-5860. Imprints are Worldwide Mystery; Gold Eagle Books. Senior Editor/ Editorial Coordinator: Feroze Mohammed. Estab. 1979. Large commercial category line. Publishes paperback originals and reprints. Published new writers within the last year. Averages 72 titles, all fiction, each year. Sometimes critiques rejected ms. "Mystery program is reprint; no originals please."
Needs: "We are looking for action-adventure series; future fiction." Recently published *Omega*; *Stakeout Squad*, *Black Ops* and *Destroyer*.
How to Contact: Query first or submit outline/synopsis/series concept or overview and sample chapters. SAE. U.S. stamps do not work in Canada; use International Reply Coupons or money order. Agented fiction 95%. Reports in 10 weeks on queries. Simultaneous submissions OK.
Terms: Advance and sometimes royalties; copyright buyout. Publishes ms 1-2 years after acceptance.
Advice: "Publishing fiction in very selective areas. As a genre publisher we are always on the lookout for innovative series ideas, especially in the men's adventure area."

ZONDERVAN, (III, IV), 5300 Patterson SE, Grand Rapids MI 49530. (616)698-6900. Contact: Manuscript Submissions. Large evangelical Christian publishing house. Publishes hardcover and paperback originals and reprints, though fiction is generally in paper only. Published new writers in the last year. Averages 150 total titles, 5-10 fiction titles each year. Average first novel: 5,000 copies.
Needs: Adult fiction, (mainstream, biblical, historical, adventure, sci-fi, fantasy, mystery), "Inklings-style" fiction of high literary quality and juvenile fiction (primarily mystery/adventure novels for 8-12-year-olds). Christian relevance necessary in all cases. Will *not* consider collections of short stories or inspirational romances. Published *McKinney High, 1946*, by Ken Gire.
How to Contact: Accepts unsolicited mss. Write for writer's guidelines first. Include #10 SASE. Query or submit outline/synopsis and 2 sample chapters. Reports in 4-6 weeks on queries; 3-4 months on mss.
Terms: "Standard contract provides for a percentage of the net price received by publisher for each copy sold, usually 14-17% of net."
Advice: "Almost no unsolicited fiction is published. Send plot outline and one or two sample chapters. Most editors will *not* read entire mss. Your proposal and opening chapter will make or break you."

International commercial book publishers

The following commercial publishers, all located outside the United States and Canada, also accept work from fiction writers. The majority are from England, a few are from Scotland and even India. As with other publishers, obtain catalogs and writer's guidelines from those that interest you to determine the types of fiction published and how well your work might fit alongside other offerings.

Remember to use self-addressed envelopes (SAEs) with International Reply Coupons (IRCs) in all correspondence with publishers outside your own country. IRCs may be purchased at the main branch of your local post office. In general, send IRCs in amounts roughly equivalent to return postage. When submitting work to international publishers, you may want to send a disposable copy of your manuscript and only one IRC along with a self-addressed postcard for a reply.

THE BLACKSTAFF PRESS, (I), 3 Galway Park, Dundonald BT16 0AN Northern Ireland. Editor: Hilary Bell. Midsize publisher, wide range of subjects. Publishes hardcover and paperback originals and reprints. Contemporary, ethnic (Irish), historical, politics, humor/satire, literary, short story collections, political thrillers, educational and feminist.

MARION BOYARS PUBLISHERS INC., 237 E. 39th St., New York NY 10016. Editorial Office (all submissions): 24 Lacy Road, London SW15 1NL England. Fiction Editor: Marion Boyars. Publishes 15 novels or story collections/year. "A lot of American fiction. Authors include Ken Kesey, Eudora Welty, Stephen Koch, Samuel Charters, Page Edwards, Viatia Spiegelman, Kenneth Gangemi, Tim O'Brien, Julian Green. British and Irish fiction. Translations from the French, German, Turkish, Arabic, Italian, Spanish." Send cover letter and entire manuscript "always with sufficient return postage by check." Pays advance against royalties. "Most fiction working *well* in one country does well in another. We usually have world rights, i.e. world English plus translation rights." Enclose return postage by check, minimum $3, for catalog.

‡**GHANA PUBLISHING CORPORATION, PUBLISHING DIVISION**, Private Post Bag, Tema, Accra, 1001 Ghana. Fiction Editor: Muhammed, Amuda Iddi. Ghana Publishing "is the largest publishing house in Ghana; owned by the government, but run independently in the main. We publish all types of fiction but are biased towards classics, the sort that the Ministry of Education may prescribe to students. In general, the merit of a book lends itself to publication however." Length: 40,000-80,000 words. Send cover letter, synopsis, brief

summary, 3 sample chapters or entire manuscript. Pays royalties of 10%. "Research the area of concern and market. Material could be contemporary and relevent. Technique must be clear and accessible to target readership. We prefer novels to short stories, which must be around 60 to 80,000 words. Novella's should be about 40,000. Materials must deal with relations affecting Ghanaian (African) culture under transition—clash of cultures, clash of old and new, personalities, young and aged, socio-economic conventions and morals. Treatment could have humorous bent. Ghanaians love to be relaxed and entertained; and they admire adventure and success worn through hard work—against corruption and indirection." Write for guidelines.

‡**ROBERT HALE LIMITED, (II)**, Clerkenwell House, 45/47 Clerkenwell Green, London EC1R 0HT England. Publishes hardcover and trade paperback originals and hardcover reprints. Historical, mainstream and western. Length: 40,000-150,000 words. Send cover letter, synopsis or brief summary and 2 sample chapters.

HARPERCOLLINS PUBLISHERS (NEW ZEALAND) LIMITED, (IV), P.O. Box 1, Auckland, New Zealand. Publisher: Paul Bradwell. Averages 20-24 fiction titles/year (15-20 nonfiction). Teen fiction: 12 years plus: Tui imprint; Junior fiction: 8-11 years: Tui Junior imprint. Tui Turbo imprint, 6-10 years and slow readers. Length: Tui: 20-35,000 words; Tui Junior: 15-17,000 words. Tui Turbo: 2-3,000 words and line drawings. Full ms preferred. Pays royalties. "It helps if the author and story have New Zealand connections/content. Write and ask for guidelines."

JULIA MACRAE BOOKS, Random House, 20 Vauxhall Bridge Road, London SW1V 2SA England. Editors: Julia MacRae, Delia Huddy, Anne Tothill. Children's books: Board books, picture books, fiction for juniors and teenagers, nonfiction. Adult titles: biography, history, music, religion. Send cover letter and entire manuscript. Writers are paid by royalties. Julia MacRae Books is an imprint of Random House.

MILLENNIUM, Orion Publishing Group, Orion House, 5 Upper St. Martin's Lane, London WC2H 9EA England. Editorial Director: Caroline Oakley. Averages 12-15 fiction titles/year. "Midsize commercial genre imprint. Hardcover and paperback originals and paperback reprints. Science fiction, fantasy and horror." Novel-length material only. Accepts 90% agented submissions. Send cover letter (including estimated word count and list of publishing credits), synopsis and first 50 sample pages. Pays advance plus royalties.

‡**MILLS & BOON, (IV)**, Eton House, 18-24 Paradise Road, Richmond, Surrey TW9 1SR England. Publishes 250 fiction titles/year. Contemporary romance fiction, historical romances and medical romances. "We are happy to see the whole manuscript or 3 sample chapters and synopsis."

MY WEEKLY STORY LIBRARY, (IV), D.C. Thomson and Co., Ltd., 22 Meadowside, Dundee DD19QJ, Scotland. Fiction Editor: Mrs. D. Hunter. Publishes 48, 35,000-word romantic novels/year. "Cheap paperback story library with full-colour cover. Material should not be violent, controversial or sexually explicit." Length: 35,000-45,000 words. Writers are paid on acceptance. "Send the opening 3 chapters and a synopsis. Avoid too many colloquialisms/Americanisms. Stories can be set anywhere but local colour not too 'local' as to be alien." Both contemporary and historical novels considered. Guidelines available on request.

ORIENT PAPERBACKS, A division of Vision Books Pvt Ltd., Madarsa Rd., Kashmere Gate, Delhi 110 006 India. Editor: Sudhir Malhotra. Publishes 10-15 novels or story collections/year. "We are one of the largest paperback publishers in S.E. Asia and publish English fiction by authors from this part of the world." Length: 40,000 words minimum. Pays royalty on copies sold. Send cover letter, brief summary, 1 sample chapter and author's bio data. "We send writers' guidelines on accepting a proposal."

PETER OWEN PUBLISHERS, 73 Kenway Rd., London SW5 0RE England. Fiction Editor: Jill Foulston. Averages 25 fiction titles/year. "Independent publishing house now 45 years old. Publish fiction from around the world, from Russia to Japan. Publishers of Shusaku Endo, Paul and Jane Bowles, Hermann Hesse, Octavio Paz, Colette, etc." Send cover letter, synopsis and/or sample chapter. Please include SASE (or IRC). Pays advance and standard royalty. "Be concise. Always include SASE and/or international reply coupon. Best to work through agent. Writers can obtain copy of our catalogue by sending SASE, and/or international reply coupon. It would help greatly if author was familiar with the list."

‡**RANDOM HOUSE PTY. LTD.**, 20 Alfred St., Milson's Point, New South Wales 2061 Australia. Contact: Roberta Ivers. Publishes 30 novels/year. "We like to publish a broad cross section of crime, 'new fiction,' romance, historical genres, etc. We really like to keep our options open in terms of what is submitted. Short stories are not a preferred option, although we do publish anthologies. Poetry is not accepted." Length: 60,000 words minimum; 200,000 words maximum. Send 3 sample chapters (typed, double-spaced), cover letter and return postage. Pays individually-negotiated advances plus royalty. "Be very patient. We receive up to 2,000 manuscripts a year."

REED PUBLISHING (NZ) LTD., (IV), Private Bag 34901, Birkenhead, Auckland 10, New Zealand. Fiction Editor: Ian Watt. Averages 5 or 6 fiction titles/year. "Reed Publishing NZ has two divisions: Reed Consumer

Books (trade publishing); and Heinemann Education. We publish literary fiction and children's books, with a strong bias towards writing by New Zealanders or about New Zealand and the Pacific." Length: 40,000 words minimum. Send a cover letter with synopsis and 3 sample chapters. SASE (SAE and IRC). "Authors are paid a royalty. Advances are negotiable. It is unlikely that we would accept fiction not written by a New Zealander or Pacific Islander or without some content that relates to New Zealand." Catalog available on request.

SINCLAIR-STEVENSON, (II), Reed Consumer Books Ltd., Michelin House, 81 Fulham Road, London SW3 6RB England. Fiction Editors: Penelope Hoare, Neil Taylor. Averages 30 fiction titles/year. "Trade hardbacks of quality fiction from new and established authors: Jane Gardam, Rose Tremain, Susan Hill, William Boyd, Peter Ackroyd." Length: open. Send a cover letter. Pays advance and royalties. Contact sales manager for catalog. No guidelines available.

VISION BOOKS PVT LTD., Madarsa Rd., Kashmere Gate, Delhi 110006 India. Fiction Editor: Sudhir Malhotra. Publishes 25 titles/year. "We are a large multilingual publishing house publishing fiction and other trade books." Pays royalties. "A brief synopsis should be submitted initially. Subsequently, upon hearing from the editor, a typescript may be sent."

THE WOMEN'S PRESS, (IV), 34 Great Sutton St., London EC1V 0DX England. Publishes approximately 50 titles/year. "Women's fiction, written by women. Centered on women. Theme can be anything—all themes may be women's concern—but we look for political/feminist awareness, originality, wit, fiction of ideas. Includes literary fiction, crime, and teenage list *Livewire*." Writers receive royalty, including advance. Writers should ask themselves, "Is this a manuscript which would interest a feminist/political press?"

Commercial book publishers/'95-'96 changes

The following commercial publishers appeared in the 1995 edition of *Novel & Short Story Writer's Market* but do not appear in the 1996 edition. Those listings that did not respond to our request for an update are listed without further explanation below. There could be several reasons why a publisher did not respond—they could be overstocked, no longer taking fiction or have been recently sold—or they may have responded too late for inclusion. If a reason for omission is known, it is included next to the publisher's name.

Aladdin Paperbacks
Arcade Publishing
Avon Nova
The Bookcraft
Christian Publications, Inc.
Citadel Press
Horizon Publishers and Dist., Inc.

(requested deletion)
Lucas/Evans Books Inc.
Margaret K. McElderry Books
Macmillan Canada (no longer
 publishes fiction)
Modern Publishing
Thomas Nelson Publishers

Quill
Tab Book Club
Ticknor & Fields (out of business)
Trillium
TSR, Inc.

International commercial book publishers/'95-'96 changes

Constable and Company
Headline Book Publishing Ltd.
Picador
Touchstone Publishing, Pvt. Lim-
 ited

For information on entering the Novel & Short Story Writer's Market *Cover Letter Contest, see page 19.*

Contests and Awards

In addition to honors and, quite often, cash awards, contests and awards programs offer writers the opportunity to be judged on the basis of quality alone without the outside factors that sometimes influence publishing decisions. New writers who win contests may be published for the first time, while more experienced writers may gain public recognition of an entire body of work.

There are nearly 600 contest listings in this section. Those include literary magazines and small presses that have developed award programs to garner attention and to promote writers. Grant programs that lost funding in the past are starting to bounce back with renewed commitment. All this represents increased opportunities for writers.

There are contests for almost every type of fiction writing. Some focus on form, such as *Story*'s Short Short Fiction Contest, for stories up to 1,500 words. Others feature writing on particular themes or topics including The Isaac Asimov Award for science fiction, the ASF Translation Prize and the Arthur Ellis Awards for crime fiction. Still others are prestigious prizes or awards for work that must be nominated such as the Pulitzer Prize in Fiction and the Whiting Writers' Awards. Chances are no matter what type of fiction you write, there is a contest or award program that may interest you.

Selecting and submitting to a contest

Use the same care in submitting to contests as you would sending your manuscript to a publication or book publisher. Deadlines are very important and where possible we've included this information. At times contest deadlines were only approximate at our press deadline, so be sure to write or call for complete information.

Follow the rules to the letter. If, for instance, contest rules require your name on a cover sheet only, you will be disqualified if you ignore this and put your name on every page. Find out how many copies to send. If you don't send the correct amount, by the time you are contacted to send more it may be past the submission deadline.

One note of caution: Beware of contests that charge entry fees that are disproportionate to the amount of the prize. Contests offering a $10 prize, but charging $7 in entry fees, are a waste of your time and money.

If you are interested in a contest or award that requires your publisher to nominate your work, it's acceptable to make your interest known. Be sure to leave them plenty of time, however, to make the nomination deadline.

The Roman numeral coding we use to rank listings in this section is different than that used in previous sections. The following is our ranking system:

- **I** Contest for unpublished fiction, usually open to both new and experienced writers.
- **II** Contest for published (usually including self-published) fiction, which may be entered by the author.
- **III** Contest for fiction, which must be nominated by an editor, publisher or other nominating body.
- **IV** Contest limited to residents of a certain region, of a certain age or to writing on certain themes or subjects.

ABIKO QUARTERLY INTERNATIONAL FICTION CONTEST/TSUJINAKA AWARD (I), 8-1-8 Namiki, Abiko-shi, Chiba-ken 270-11 Japan. Editor: Laurel Sicks. Award to "best short story in English of up to 5,000 words." Award: 100,000 yen. Entry fee $7. Previously unpublished submissions. Word length: up to 5,000 words. "Include SAE with 2 IRCs for notification. No American postage."

‡JANE ADDAMS CHILDREN'S BOOK AWARD, (II), Jane Addams Peace Association/Women's International League for Peace and Freedom, 2015 Bluebell Ave., Boulder CO 80302. Chair: Judith Volc. "To honor the writer of the children's book that most effectively promotes peace, social justice, world community and the equality of the sexes and all races." Annual competition for short stories, novels and translations. Award: certificate. Competition receives approximately 200 submissions. Judges: committee. Guidelines for SASE. Deadline April 1, for books published during previous year.

‡AFRICAN VOICES SHORT STORY CONTEST (I, IV), *African Voices*, 270 W. 96th St., New York NY 10025. (212)865-2982. Contact: Fiction Editor. Award to "give exposure to talented, young writers." Annual award for short stories. Award: Free admission to an intermediate or beginner's workshop (1st prize); $75 book certificate for a New York City bookstore (2nd prize); free copy of *Writer's Market* (3rd prize). Judges: Prominent authors and literary agents. Entry fee $10. Guidelines for SASE. Deadline July 31. Unpublished submissions (with a publication of less than 50,000 circulation). Limited to writers within the New York area. Word length: 2,500 words. "All winners will be published in upcoming issue of *AV* and be included in our publicity campaign."

AIM MAGAZINE SHORT STORY CONTEST, (I), P.O. Box 20554, Chicago IL 60620. (312)874-6184. Contact: Ruth Apilado and Mark Boone, publisher and fiction editor. Estab. 1984. "To encourage and reward good writing in the short story form. The contest is particularly for new writers." Contest offered annually if money available. Award: $100 plus publication in fall issue. "Judged by *Aim*'s editorial staff." Sample copy for $4. Contest rules for SASE. Unpublished submissions. "We're looking for compelling, well-written stories with lasting social significance."

❤AIR CANADA AWARD, (IV), Canadian Authors Association and Air Canada, 27 Doxsee Ave. N., Campbellford Ontario K0L 1L0 Canada. (705)653-0323. Fax: (705)653-0593. Contact: Awards Chairperson. "It takes many years for a Canadian writer to achieve national (and, increasingly, international) recogniton, but Air Canada believes the signs of greatness can usually be detected before the writer reaches 30. That is why the airline offers a trip for two to the winner of the annual Canadian Author Association competition. The Air Canada Award goes to the writer under age 30 deemed to show the most promise in the field of literary creation." Annual competition for "body of work." Award: 2 tickets to any destination on Air Canada route. Judges: the Awards chairperson/Canadian Authors Association. Guidelines for SASE. Deadline April 30. Writers must be Canadian and 30 years old or under by the deadline. The nomination can be in any form but the recommended approach is to submit a 1-page outline of why the writer shows promise and attach samples of the writer's work or reviews of that work. Full-length works need not be sent; copies of a few pages are sufficient. Note date of birth of writer on submitted samples. Nominations are made through CAA branches or other writing organizations to the Canadian Authors Association. The nominee need not be a CAA member.

AKC GAZETTE, (formerly *Pure Bred Dogs/American Kennel Gazette*), 51 Madison Ave., New York NY 10010. (212)696-8333. Executive Editor: Beth Adelman. Annual contest for short stories under 2,000 words. Award: Prizes of $350, $250 and $150 for top three entries. Top entry published in magazine. Judges: Panel. Contest requirements available for SASE. "The *Gazette* sponsors an annual fiction contest for short short stories on some subject relating to purebred dogs. Fiction for our magazine needs a slant toward the serious fancier with real insight into the human/dog bond and breed-specific purebred behavior."

‡AKRON MANUSCRIPT CLUB ANNUAL FICTION CONTEST (I), Akron Manuscript Club and A.U., Falls Writer's Workshop, and Taylor Memorial Library, P.O. Box 1101, Cuyahoga Falls OH 44223-0101. (216)923-2094. Contest Director: M.M. LoPiccolo. Award to "encourage writers with cash prizes and certificates and to provide in-depth critique that most writers have never had the benefit of seeing." Annual competition for short stories. Award: $50 (first prize in three fiction categories); certificates for second and third prizes. Competition receives approx. 20-50 submissions per category. Judge: M.M. LoPiccolo. Guidelines for SASE. Deadline March-April. Unpublished submissions. Word length: 2,500 words (12-13 pages).

The double dagger before a listing indicates that the listing is new in this edition. New markets are often the most receptive to submissions by new writers.

ALABAMA STATE COUNCIL ON THE ARTS INDIVIDUAL ARTIST FELLOWSHIP, (II, IV), 1 Dexter Ave., Montgomery AL 36130. (205)242-4076. Contact: Becky Mullen. "To provide assistance to an individual artist." Semiannual awards: $5,000 and $10,000 grants awarded in even-numbered years ('96-'98). Competition receives approx. 30 submissions annually. Judges: Independent peer panel. Entry forms or rules for SASE. Deadline May 1. Two-year Alabama residency required.

‡❧ALBERTA FOUNDATION FOR THE ARTS/WRITERS GUILD OF ALBERTA NEW FICTION COMPETITION, (I, IV), 10158-1035 St., 5th Floor/Beaver House, Edmonton, Alberta T5J 0X6 Canada. (403)427-6515. Fax: (403)422-9132. Arts Development Officer: Scott Morison. Award "to encourage and publicize Albertan fiction writers." Biannual competition for novels. Award: $4,500 including a 12 month option for motion picture and TV rights. Competition receives approx. 50 submissions. Judges: A jury of respected writers. Entry fee $25. Guidelines for SASE. Deadline Dec. 1, 1997. Unpublished submissions. The writer must have been a resident of the province of Alberta for 12 of the last 18 months. Word length: approx. 60,000 words. "On alternate years there is the *Write for Youth* competition. This competition is for children's literature."

‡❧ALBERTA FOUNDATION FOR THE ARTS/WRITERS GUILD OF ALBERTA WRITING FOR YOUTH COMPETITION, (I, IV), 10158-103 St., 5th Floor/Beaver House, Edmonton, Alberta T5J 0X6 Canada. (403)427-6515. Fax: (403)422-9132. Arts Development Officer: Scot Morison. Award "to encourage and publicize writing for children in Alberta." Biannual competion for novels. Award: $4,500 including a publishing contract. Competition receives approx. 50 submissions. Judges: A jury of respected writers. Entry fee $25. Guidelines for SASE. Deadline Dec. 1, 1996. Unpublished submissions. The writer must have been a resident of Alberta for 12 of the last 18 months. Word length: approx. 40,000 words.

THE NELSON ALGREN AWARD FOR SHORT FICTION, (I), *Chicago Tribune*, 435 N. Michigan Ave., Chicago IL 60611. Annual award to recognize an outstanding, unpublished short story, minimum 2,500 words, maximum 10,000 words. Awards: $5,000 first prize; 3 runners-up receive $1,000 awards. Publication of 4 winning stories in the *Chicago Tribune*. No entry fee. "All entries must be from 'the Heartland,' typed, double spaced and accompanied by SASE." For guidelines, send business-size SASE. Guidelines mailed in the fall. Deadline: Entries are accepted only from November 31-February 1.

***AMELIA* MAGAZINE AWARDS, (I)**, 329 "E" St., Bakersfield CA 93304. (805)323-4064. Contact: Frederick A. Raborg, Jr., editor. The Reed Smith Fiction Prize; The Willie Lee Martin Short Story Award; The Cassie Wade Short Fiction Award; The Patrick T. T. Bradshaw Fiction Award; and four annual genre awards in science fiction, romance, western and fantasy/horror. Estab. 1984. Annual. "To publish the finest fiction possible and reward the writer; to allow good writers to earn some money in small press publication. *Amelia* strives to fill that gap between major circulation magazines and quality university journals." Unpublished submissions. Length: The Reed Smith—3,000 words maximum; The Willie Lee Martin—3,500-5,000 words; The Cassie Wade—4,500 words maximum; The Patrick T. T. Bradshaw—10,000 words; the genre awards— science fiction, 5,000 words; romance, 3,000 words; western, 5,000 words; fantasy/horror, 5,000 words. Award: "Each prize consists of $200 plus publication and two copies of issue containing winner's work." The Reed Smith Fiction Prize offers two additional awards when quality merits of $100 and $50, and publication; Bradshaw Book Award: $250 plus serialization in 4 issues of *Amelia*, 2 copies. Deadlines: The Reed Smith Prize—September 1; The Willie Lee Martin—March 1; The Cassie Wade—June 1; The Patrick T. T. Bradshaw—February 15; *Amelia* fantasy/horror—February 1; *Amelia* western—April 1; *Amelia* romance—October 1; *Amelia* science fiction—December 15. Entry fee: $5. Bradshaw Award fee: $10. Contest rules for SASE. Looking for "high quality work equal to finest fiction being published today."

***AMERICAN FICTION* AWARDS, (I)**, New Rivers Press, Moorehead State University, P.O. Box 229, Moorhead MN 56563. (218)236-4681. Editor: Alan Davis. "To find and publish short fiction by emerging writers." Annual award for short stories. Award: $1,000 (1st prize), $500 (2nd prize), $250 (3rd prize). Competition receives approx. 1,000 submissions. Editor chooses finalists; guest judge chooses winners; past judges have included Tim O'Brien and Wallace Stegner. Entry fee $7.50. Guidelines for SASE. Deadline May 1. Unpublished submissions. Word length: up to 10,000 words. "We are looking for quality literary or mainstream fiction—all subjects and styles. No genre fiction. For a sample copy, contact your bookstore or New Rivers Press, N. Fifth St., Suite 910, Minneapolis MN 55401. Send ms and cover letter with bio "after reading our ads in *AWP* and *Poets and Writers* each spring." (Previous editions published by Birch Lane Press/Carol Publishing Groups.)

‡AMERICAN SHORT FICTION CONTEST, English Dept., Parlin 108, University of Texas at Austin, Austin TX 78712-1164. (512)471-1772. Contact: Joseph Kruppa, editor. Annual competition for short stories. Award: $1,000 and publication (1st prize); $500 (2nd prize); $300 (3rd prize). Entry fee: $20 (includes subscription to *ASF*). Guidelines in *ASF*. Deadline May 15. Unpublished submissions. Word length: 4,000 words or less.

***ANALECTA* COLLEGE FICTION CONTEST, (I, IV)**, The Liberal Arts Council, FAC 17, Austin TX 78712. (512)471-6563. Awards Coordinator: Jennifer Conwell. Award to "give student writers, at the University of

Texas and universities across the country, a forum for publication. We believe that publication in a magazine with the quality and reputation of *Analecta* will benefit student writers." Annual competition for short stories. Award: $100. Competition receives approximately 80 submissions. Judges: Student editorial board of approximately 25 people. No entry fee. Guidelines for SASE. Deadline: October 6. Unpublished submissions. Limited to college students. Length: 15 pages or less. "We also accept poetry, drama and art submissions."

SHERWOOD ANDERSON SHORT FICTION PRIZE, (I), *Mid-American Review*, Dept. of English, Bowling Green State University, Bowling Green OH 43403. (419)372-2725. Contact: Rebecca Meacham, fiction editor. Award frequency is subject to availability of funds. "To encourage the writer of quality short fiction." No entry fee. No deadline. Unpublished material. "Winners are selected from stories published by the magazine, so submission for publication is the first step."

ANDREAS-GRYPHIUS-PREIS (LITERATURPREIS DER KÜNSTLERGILDE), (II, IV), Die Kunstlergilde e.V., Hafenmarkt 2, D-73728 Esslingen a.N., Germany. 0711/39 69 01-0. "The prize is awarded for the best piece of writing or for complete literary works." Annual competition for short stories, novels, story collections, translations. Award: 1 prize of DM 15,000; 3 prizes of DM 7,000. Competition receives 30-50 entries. Judges: Jury members (8 persons). Fiction should be published in the last 5 years. "The prize is awarded to writers who are dealing with the particular problems of the German culture in eastern Europe."

✣**THE ANNUAL/ATLANTIC WRITING COMPETITIONS, (I, IV)**, Writers' Federation of Nova Scotia, 1809 Barrington St., Suite 901, Halifax, Nova Scotia B3J 3K8 Canada. (902)423-8116. Executive Director: Jane Buss. "To recognize and encourage unpublished writers in the region of Atlantic Canada. (Competition only open to residents of Nova Scotia, Newfoundland, Prince Edward Island and New Brunswick, the four Atlantic Provinces.)" Annual competition for short stories, novels, poetry, nonfiction, children's writing and drama. Award: Various cash awards. Competition receives approximately 10-12 submissions for novels; 75 for poetry; 75 for children's; 75 for short stories; 10 for nonfiction. Judges: Professional writers, librarians, booksellers. Entry fee $15/entry. Guidelines for SASE. Unpublished submissions.

***ANTIETAM REVIEW* LITERARY AWARD, (I, IV)**, *Antietam Review*, 7 W. Franklin St., Hagerstown MD 21740. (301)791-3132. Executive Editor: Susanne Kass. Annual award to encourage and give recognition to excellence in short fiction. Open to writers from Maryland, Pennsylvania, Virginia, West Virginia, Washington DC and Delaware. "We consider only previously unpublished work. We read manuscripts between September 1 and February 1." Award: $100 for the story; the story is printed as lead in the magazine. "We consider all fiction mss sent to *Antietam Review* as entries for the prize. We look for well-crafted, serious literary prose fiction under 5,000 words." Award dependent on funding situation. Send #10 SASE for guidelines.

✣**ANVIL PRESS 3-DAY NOVEL WRITING CONTEST, (I)**, Anvil Press, Box 1575, Bentall Centre, Vancouver, British Columbia V6C 2P7 Canada. (604)876-8710. Fax: (604)879-2667. Editor: Brian Kaufman. Annual contest to write the best novel in 3 days, held every Labor Day weekend. "Prize is publication plus 15% royalties on sales." Receives approx. 500 entries for each award. Judges: Anvil Press editorial board. Entry fee $25. Guidelines for SASE. Deadline Friday before Labor Day weekend. "Entrants must register with Anvil Press. Winner is announced October 31."

ARIZONA AUTHORS' ASSOCIATION NATIONAL LITERARY CONTEST, (I), 3509 E. Shea Blvd., Suite 117, Phoenix AZ 85028. (602)867-9001. Contact: Iva Martin. Estab. 1981. Annual award "to encourage AAA members and all other writers in the country to write regularly for competition and publication." Award: "Cash prizes totalling $1,000 for winners and honorable mentions in short stories, essays and poetry. Winning entries are published in the *Arizona Literary Magazine*." Entry fee: $5 for poetry, $7 for essays and short stories. Contest rules for SASE. Deadline July 29. Unpublished submissions. Looking for "strong concept; good, effective writing, with emphasis on the subject/story."

ARIZONA COMMISSION ON THE ARTS CREATIVE WRITING FELLOWSHIPS, (I, IV), 417 W. Roosevelt St., Phoenix AZ 85003. (602)255-5882. Literature Director: Tonda Gorton. Fellowships awarded in alternate years to fiction writers and poets. Award: $5,000-7,500. Judges: Out-of-state writers/editors. Arizona resident poets and writers over 18 years of age only.

ARTIST TRUST ARTIST FELLOWSHIPS; GAP GRANTS, (I, II, IV), Artist Trust, 1402 Third Ave., #415, Seattle WA 98101-2118. (206)467-8734. Program Coordinator: Christina De Paolo. Artist Trust has 2 grant programs for generative artists in Washington State; the GAP and Fellowships. The GAP (Grants for Artist's Projects) is an annual award of up to $1,000 for a project proposal. The program is open to artists in all disciplines. The Fellowship grant is an award of $5,000 in unrestricted funding. Fellowships for Craft, Media, Literature and Music will be awarded in 1997, and Fellowships for Dance, Design, Theater and Visual Art will be awarded in 1996. Competition receives approximately 200-300 submissions. Judges: Fellowship— Peer panel of 3 professional artists and arts professionals in each discipline; GAP—Interdisciplinary peer panel of 6-8 artists and arts professionals. Deadlines: Fellowship—summer; GAP—late winter. Call or write for more information with SASE.

ASF TRANSLATION PRIZE, (II, IV), American-Scandinavian Foundation, 725 Park Ave., New York NY 10021. (212)879-9779. Contact: Publishing office. Estab. 1980. "To encourage the translation and publication of the best of contemporary Scandinavian poetry and fiction and to make it available to a wider American audience." Annual competition for poetry, drama, literary prose and fiction translations. Award: $2,000, a bronze medallion and publication in *Scandinavian Review*. Competition rules and entry forms available with SASE. Deadline June 1. Submissions must have been previously published in the original Scandinavian language. No previously translated material. Original authors should have been born within past 200 years.

THE ISAAC ASIMOV AWARD, (I, IV), International Association for the Fantastic in the Arts and *Asimov's* magazine, USF 3177, 4202 E. Fowler, Tampa FL 33620-3177. (813)974-6792. Awards Administrator: Rick Wilber. "The award honors the legacy of one of science fiction's most distinguished authors through an award aimed at undergraduate writers." Annual award for short stories. Award: $500 and consideration for publication in *Asimov's*. Judges: *Asimov's* editors. No entry fee. Guidelines available for SASE. Deadline December 15. Unpublished submissions. Full-time college undergraduates only.

✤ASTED/GRAND PRIX DE LITTERATURE JEUNESSE DU QUEBEC-ALVINE-BELISLE, (III, IV), Association pour l'avancement des sciences et des techniques de la documentation, 3414 Avenue du Parc, Bureau 202, Montreal, Quebec H2X 2H5 Canada. (514)281-5012. Fax: (514)281-8219. President: Vesna Dell'Olio. "Prize granted for the best work in youth literature edited in French in the Quebec Province. Authors and editors can participate in the contest." Annual competition for fiction and nonfiction for children and young adults. Award: $500. Deadline June 1. Contest entry limited to editors of books published during the preceding year. French translations of other languages are not accepted.

THE ATHENAEUM LITERARY AWARD, (II, IV), The Athenaeum of Philadelphia, 219 S. Sixth St., Philadelphia PA 19106. (215)925-2688. Contact: Literary Award Committee. Annual award to recognize and encourage outstanding literary achievement in Philadelphia and its vicinity. Award: A bronze medal bearing the name of the award, the seal of the Athenaeum, the title of the book, the name of the author and the year. Judged by committee appointed by Board of Directors. Deadline December. Submissions must have been published during the preceding year. Nominations shall be made in writing to the Literary Award Committee by the author, the publisher or a member of the Athenaeum, accompanied by a copy of the book. The Athenaeum Literary Award is granted for a work of general literature, not exclusively for fiction. Juvenile fiction is not included.

AUTHORS IN THE PARK/*FINE PRINT* CONTEST, (I), P.O. Box 85, Winter Park FL 32790-0085. (407)658-4520. Fax: (407)898-4075. Contact: David Foley. Annual competition. Award: $500 (1st prize), $250 (2nd prize), $125 (3rd prize). Competition receives approx. 200 submissions. Entry fee $8 (includes copy of *Fine Print*). Guidelines for SASE. Deadline March 31. Word length: 5,000 words maximum.

AWP AWARD SERIES IN THE NOVEL AND SHORT FICTION, (I), The Associated Writing Programs, Tallwood House, Mail Stop 1E3, George Mason University, Fairfax VA 22030. Annual award. The AWP Award Series was established in cooperation with several university presses in order to publish and make fine fiction available to a wide audience. Awards: $2,000 honorarium and publication with a university press. In addition, AWP tries to place mss of finalists with participating presses. Judges: Distinguished writers in each genre. Entry fee $15 nonmembers, $10 AWP members. Contest/award rules and guidelines for SASE. No phone calls please. Mss must be postmarked between January 1-February 29. Only book-length mss in the novel and short story collections are eligible. Manuscripts previously published in their entirety, including self-publishing, are not eligible. No mss returned.

AWP INTRO JOURNALS PROJECT, (I, IV), Tallwood House, Mail Stop 1E3, George Mason University, Fairfax VA 22030. Contact: Charles Fort. "This is a prize for students in AWP member university creative writing programs only. Authors are nominated by the head of the creative writing department. Each school may send 2 nominated short stories." Annual competition for short stories. Award: $50 plus publication in participating journal. 1993 journals included *Puerto del Sol*, *Indiana Review*, *Quarterly West*, *Mid-American Review*, *Willow Springs* and *Hayden's Ferry Review*. Judges: AWP. Deadline December. Unpublished submissions only.

EMILY CLARK BALCH AWARDS, (I), *The Virginia Quarterly Review*, One West Range, Charlottesville VA 22903. Editor: Staige D. Blackford. Annual award "to recognize distinguished short fiction by American writers." For stories published in *The Virginia Quarterly Review* during the calendar year. Award: $500.

MILDRED L. BATCHELDER AWARD, (II), Association for Library Service to Children/American Library Association, 50 E. Huron St., Chicago IL 60611. (312)944-6780, ext. 2164. To encourage international

"WE WANT TO PUBLISH YOUR WORK."

You would give anything to hear an editor speak those 6 magic words. So you work hard for weeks, months, even years to make that happen. You create a brilliant piece of work and a knock-out presentation, but there's still one vital step to ensure publication. You still need to submit your work to the right buyers. With rapid changes in the publishing industry it's not always easy to know who those buyers are. That's why each year thousands of writers, just like you, turn to the most current edition of this indispensable market guide.

Keep ahead of the changes by ordering *1997 Novel & Short Story Writer's Market* today! You'll save the frustration of getting manuscripts returned in the mail stamped MOVED: ADDRESS UNKNOWN. And of NOT submitting your work to new listings because you don't know they exist. All you have to do to order the upcoming 1997 edition is complete the attached order card and return it with your payment. Order now and you'll get the 1997 edition at the 1996 price—just $22.99—no matter how much the regular price may increase! *1997 Novel & Short Story Writer's Market* will be published and ready for shipment in January 1997.

Keep on top of the ever-changing industry and get a jump on selling your work with help from the *1997 Novel & Short Story Writer's Market*. Order today—you deserve it!

Turn Over for More Great Books to Help Get Your Fiction Published!

Get Your Fiction Published with help from these Writer's Digest Books!

Totally Updated!
1996 Guide to Literary Agents
Literary agents can open doors for you in the publishing industry. This invaluable directory (now in its 5th year) gives you 500 agent listings, plus answers the most-often-asked questions about working with agents. #10443/$21.99/available 2-96

Writer's Digest Sourcebook for Building Believable Characters
Learn how to create vivid characters who think, hope, love, laugh, cry, and cause or feel pain. You'll artfully construct their human characteristics—physical and psychological—to make them so real they'll climb right off the page. #10463/$17.99/288 pages

The ABCs of Writing Fiction
Author/instructor Ann Copeland combines penetrating advice with intelligent and practical fiction-writing instruction culled from her 15 years of teaching. These 300 mini-lessons help you unstick your imagination, sustain your writing spirit and cast fresh light on puzzling technical problems. #48017/$18.99/256 pages/available 3-25-96

Writing to Sell
Let Scott Meredith guide you along the professional writing path, as he has for so many others. You'll find help creating characters, plotting your novel and placing it, formatting your manuscript, deciphering your contract—even combating a slump. #10476/$17.99/240 pages

The Writer's Guide to Everyday Life from Prohibition through World War II
Add color, depth, and a ring of truth to your work using this slice of life reference. You'll get a glimpse of what life was like back then, including popular slang, music and dance, fashion, transportation, and Prohibition and the Depression. #10450/$18.99/272 pages

Fill out order card on reverse side and mail today!

exchange of quality children's books by recognizing US publishers of such books in translation. Annual competition for translations. Award: Citation. Judge: Mildred L. Batchelder award committee. Guidelines for SASE. Deadline: December. Books should be US trade publications for which children, up to and including age 14, are potential audience.

BAUHINIA LITERARY AWARDS, (I, IV), *Idiom 23 Literary Magazine*, Regional Centre of the Arts, Central Queensland University, Rockhampton, Queensland 4702 Australia. (079)309336. Contact: Contest Director. "To promote the work of students under age 25 and writers from Central Queensland." Annual competition for short stories. Open Award: $600 (Australian); Student Award: $250 (Australian); Regional Award: $250 (Australian). Judges: the editors. Guidelines for SASE. Deadline June 24. Unpublished submissions. Student Award is open to full-time students, under age 25. Regional Award open to writers living in Central Queensland. Word length: 2,000 words; 3 story limit. "Outstanding entries will be published in *The Morning Bulletin* and *Idiom 23*."

BELLETRIST REVIEW ANNUAL FICTION CONTEST, (I), Belletrist Review, 17 Farmington Ave,. Suite 290, Plainville CT 06062. Editor: Marlene Dube. "To provide an incentive for writers to submit quality fiction for consideration and recognition." Annual competition for short stories. Award: $200. Competition receives approx. 350-400 submissions. Judges: Editorial panel of *Belletrist Review*. Entry fee $5. Guidelines for SASE. Deadline July 1. Unpublished submissions. Word length: 2,500-5,000 words. "An interview with the winning author will also be published with the winning story in the September issue."

GEORGE BENNETT FELLOWSHIP, (I), Phillips Exeter Academy, Exeter NH 03833. Coordinator, Selection Committee: Charles Pratt. "To provide time and freedom from monetary concerns to a person contemplating or pursuing a career as a professional writer." Annual award of writing residency. Award: A stipend ($5,000 at present), plus room and board for academic year. Competition receives approximately 150 submissions. Judges are a committee of the English department. Entry fee $5. SASE for application form and guidelines. Deadline December 1.

BEST FIRST MALICE DOMESTIC NOVEL, (I, IV), Thomas Dunne Books, St. Martin's Press, 175 Fifth Ave., New York NY 10010. (212)674-5151, ext. 596. "To publish a writer's first 'malice domestic novel.' " Annual competition for novels. Award: Publication by St. Martin's Press in the US. Advance: $10,000 (and standard royalties). Judges are selected by sponsors. Guidelines for SASE. Accepts mss from May 15 to October 15. Unpublished submissions. "Open to any professional or nonprofessional writer who has never published a malice domestic mystery novel and who is not under contract with a publisher to publish one. Malice domestic is a traditional mystery novel that is not hardboiled; emphasis is on the solution rather than the details of the crime. Suspects and victims know one another. In marginal cases, judges will decide whether entry qualifies."

BEST FIRST NEW MYSTERY AWARD, (I, IV), *New Mystery Magazine*, 175 Fifth Ave., Suite 2001, New York NY 10010. (212)353-1582. Awards coordinator: Miss Linda Wong. Award to "find the best new mystery, crime or suspense writer, and promote high standards in the short story form. For writers who have never been paid for their writing." Annual award for short stories. Award: publication in *New Mystery Magazine*. Competition receives approx. 800 submissions. Judges: editorial panel of veteran mystery writers. No entry fee. No guidelines available. Deadline July 4. Unpublished submissions. Word length: 1,000-5,000 words. "Please mark ms 'First Mystery Award.' Study back issues of *New Mystery* for style. Sample copy: $7 plus 9×12 SAE with $1.24 postage.

BEST FIRST PRIVATE EYE NOVEL CONTEST, (I, IV), Private Eye Writers of America, Thomas Dunne Books, St. Martin's Press, 175 Fifth Ave., New York NY 10010. Annual award. To publish a writer's first "private eye" novel. Award: Publication of novel by St. Martin's Press. Advance: $10,000 against royalties (standard contract). Judges are selected by sponsors. Guidelines for SASE. Deadline August 1. Unpublished submissions. "Open to any professional or nonprofessional writer who has never published a 'private eye' novel and who is not under contract with a publisher for the publication of a 'private eye' novel. As used in the rules, 'private eye' novel means: a novel in which the main character is an independent investigator who is not a member of any law enforcement or government agency."

‡BEST OF SOFT SCIENCE FICTION CONTEST, (II, IV), Soft SF Writers Assoc., 1277 Joan Dr., Merritt Island FL 32952. (407)454-2424. Contest Director: Lela E. Buis. Award to "encourage the publication of science fiction styles in which values, emotional content and artistic effect are emphasized rather than plot and deterministic science. Adult issues are encouraged, but gratuitous violence and graphic sex are not the emotional impacts we want." Annual award for short stories. Awards: $100 (1st prize), $50 (2nd prize), $25 (3rd prize). Received 100 entries in 1993 (first year of contest). Judges: members of the Soft SF Writers Association. No entry fee. Guidelines for SASE. Entries accepted October 1 through December 15. Entries must have been submitted for publication or published between January 1 and December 15. Word length: 7,000 words. Story must have elements of science fiction, though cross-genre stories are acceptable. Judging criteria: emotional impact, artistic style, clarity, originality, characterization, theme weight, imagery, sensuality; violence or sex added for shock value are discouraged. Format: Send disposable manuscript in standard format. Securely attach name and address.

❧THE GEOFFREY BILSON AWARD FOR HISTORICAL FICTION FOR YOUNG PEOPLE, (II, IV), The Canadian Children's Book Centre, 35 Spadina Rd., Toronto, Ontario M5R 2S9 Canada. (416)975-0010. Fax: (416)975-1839. Program Director: Jeffrey Canton. "Award given for best piece of historical fiction for young people." Annual competition for novels. Award: $1,000 (Canadian). Competition receives approximately 12 submissions. Judged by a jury of five people from the children's literature community. Previously published submissions. Canadian authors only. "Publishers of Canadian children's books regularly submit copies of their books to the Centre for our library collection. From those books, selections are made for inclusion in the Our Choice list of recommended Canadian children's books each year. The shortlist for the Bilson Award is created after the selections have been made for Our Choice, as the book must first be selected for Our Choice to be part of the Bilson shortlist."

IRMA S. AND JAMES H. BLACK CHILDREN'S BOOK AWARD, (II), Bank Street College, 610 W. 112th St., New York NY 10025. (212)875-4452. Children's Librarian: Linda Greengrass. Annual award "to honor the young children's book published in the preceding year judged the most outstanding in text as well as in art. Book must be published the year preceding the May award." Award: Press function at Harvard Club, a scroll and seals by Maurice Sendak for attaching to award book's run. No entry fee. Deadline January 15. "Write to address above. Usually publishers submit books they want considered, but individuals can too. No entries are returned."

***THE BLACK WARRIOR REVIEW* LITERARY AWARD, (II, III)**, P.O. Box 2936, Tuscaloosa AL 35486. (205)348-4518. Editor: Mindy Wilson. "Award is to recognize the best fiction published in *BWR* in a volume year. Only fiction accepted for publication is considered for the award." Competition is for short stories and novel chapters. Award: $500. Competition receives approximately 3,000 submissions. Prize awarded by an outside judge.

BOARDMAN TASKER PRIZE, (III, IV), 14 Pine Lodge, Dairyground Rd., Bramhall, Stockport, Cheshire SK7 2HS United Kingdom. Contact: Mrs. D. Boardman. "To reward a book which has made an outstanding contribution to mountain literature. A memorial to Peter Boardman and Joe Tasker, who disappeared on Everest in 1982." Award: £2,000. Competition receives approx. 15 submissions. Judges: A panel of 3 judges elected by trustees. Guidelines for SASE. Deadline August 1. Limited to works published or distributed in the UK for the first time between November 1 and October 31. Publisher's entry only. "May be fiction, nonfiction, poetry or drama. Not an anthology. The prize is not primarily for fiction though that is not excluded. Subject must be concerned with a mountain environment. Previous winners have been books on expeditions, climbing experiences; a biography of a mountaineer; novels."

‡BOOK PUBLISHERS OF TEXAS AWARD, (II, IV), The Texas Institute of Letters, TCU Press, P.O. Box 30783, Fort Worth TX 76129. (817)921-7822. Secretary: Judy Alter. "Award to honor the best book written for children or young people that was published the year prior to that in which the award is given." Annual competition for children's literature. Award: $250. Competition receives approx. 15 submissions. Judges: Committee selected by TIL. Guidelines for SASE. Deadline January 2, 1997. Previously published submissions from January 1, 1996-December 31, 1996. "To be eligible, the writer must have been born in Texas or have lived in the state for two years at some time, or the subject matter of the work must be associated with Texas."

***BOSTON GLOBE-HORN BOOK* AWARDS, (II)**, *Boston Globe* Newspaper, *Horn Book Magazine*, 11 Beacon St., Suite 1000, Boston MA 02108. Annual award. "To honor most outstanding children's fiction or poetry, picture and nonfiction books published within the US." Award: $500 and engraved silver bowl first prize in each category; engraved silver plate for the 2 honor books in each category. No entry fee. Entry forms or rules for SASE. Deadline May 15. Previously published material from July 1-June 30 of previous year. Books must be submitted by publisher, not individuals.

BOSTON REVIEW SHORT STORY CONTEST, (II), *Boston Review*, E53-407, MIT, Cambridge MA 02139. Annual award for short stories. Award: $300. Processing fee $10. Deadline October 1. Unpublished submissions. No restrictions on subject matter. Word length: 4,000 words. Winning entry published in December issue. All entrants receive a 1-year subscription to the *Boston Review* beginning with the December issue. Stories not returned. Winner notified by mail.

BRAZOS BOOKSTORE (HOUSTON) AWARD (SINGLE SHORT STORY), (II, IV), The Texas Institute of Letters, % TCU Press, P.O. Box 30783, Ft. Worth TX 76129. (817)921-7822. Awards Coordinator: Judy Alter. Award to "honor the writer of the best short story published for the first time during the calendar year before the award is given." Annual competition for short stories. Award: $500. Competition receives approx.

40-50 submissions. Judges: Panel selected by TIL Council. Guidelines for SASE. Deadline January 2. Previously published submissions. Entries must have appeared in print between January 1 and December 31 of the year prior to the award. "Award available to writers who, at some time, have lived in Texas at least two years consecutively or whose work has a significant Texas theme. Entries must be sent directly to the three judges. Their names and addresses are available from the TIL office. Include SASE."

‡**BREVILOQUENCE, (I, IV)**, Media Weavers, 1738 NE 24th, Portland OR 97212. (503)771-5166. Contact: J. Colombo. "To create—with 99 words or less—a story with all the important elements of the form. Only open to writers in the Northwest—Oregon, Washington, Alaska, Idaho, Montana, Alberta and British Columbia." Annual competition for short stories. Award: Books—usually reference. Judges: Editors of newspaper. Entry fee $5. Deadline May 1. Unpublished submissions.

BRODY ARTS FUND LITERARY FELLOWSHIP, (I, II, IV), California Community Foundation, 606 S. Olive St., Suite 2400, Los Angeles CA 90014. (213)413-4042. Contact: Senior Program Secretary. "To recognize and support the work of emerging writers resident in Los Angeles County, California, whose work reflects the ethnic and cultural diversity of the region." Award granted every 3 years for short stories, novels, potry, plays and screenplays. Award: $2,500 unrestricted fellowship (approximately 5-7 awarded once every 3 years). Competition receives approximately 40-60 submissions. Judges: A peer panel of local writers and editors. No deadline/applications possible until after January 1, 1997. Probable deadline in mid-March 1997. Previously published or unpublished submissions. All applicants must be based in Los Angeles County, California. Guidelines and application forms can be requested by phone or letter, but not until December, 1996 or January, 1997.

BRONX RECOGNIZES ITS OWN (B.R.I.O.), (I, IV), Bronx Council on the Arts, 1738 Hone Ave., New York NY 10461. (718)931-9500. Fax: (718)409-6445. Arts Services Associate: Ben Spierman. Award "To recognize local artistic talent in Bronx County." Annual competition for novels. Award: $1,500 fellowship (awards 10/year in visual, performing and literary arts). Competition receives approximately 160 submissions. Judges: A collective of non-Bronx based artists to avoid conflict. Guidelines for SASE. Deadline March. Unpublished submissions. Only Bronx-based individual artists may apply. Proof of Bronx residency required. Word length: 20 typed pages of ms.

✤**GEORGES BUGNET AWARD FOR THE NOVEL, (II, IV)**, Writers Guild of Alberta, 3rd Floor, Percy Page Centre, 11759 Groat Rd., Edmonton, Alberta T5M 3K6 Canada. (403)422-8174. Fax: (403)422-2663. Assistant Director: Darlene Diver. "To recognize outstanding books published by Alberta authors each year." Annual competition for novels. Award: $500 (Canadian) and leather-bound book. Competition receives approx. 20-30 submissions. Judges: selected published writers across Canada. Guidelines for SASE. Deadline December 31. Previously published submissions. Must have appeared in print between January 1 and December 31. Open to Alberta authors only.

✤**BURNABY WRITERS' SOCIETY ANNUAL COMPETITION, (I, IV)**, 6584 Deer Lake Ave., British Columbia V5G 2J3 Canada. (604)435-6500. Annual competition to encourage creative writing in British Columbia. "Category varies from year to year." Award: $200, $100 and $50 (Canadian) prizes. Receives 400-600 entries for each award. Judge: "independent recognized professional in the field." Entry fee $5. Contest requirements for SASE. Deadline: May 31. Open to British Columbia authors only.

BUSH ARTIST FELLOWSHIPS, (I, IV), The Bush Foundation, E-900 First Nat'l Bank Building, 332 Minnesota St., St. Paul MN 55101. (612)227-5222. Contact: Sally Dixon, Program Director. "To provide support for artists to work in their chosen art forms." Annual grant. Award: $36,000 for 12-18 months. Competition receives approx. 500 submissions. Judges are writers, critics and editors from outside Minnesota, South Dakota, North Dakota or Wisconsin. Applicants must be at least 25 years old, and Minnesota, South Dakota, North Dakota or Western Wisconsin residents. Students not eligible.

BYLINE **MAGAZINE LITERARY AWARDS, (I, IV)**, PO Box 130596, Edmond OK 73013. (405)348-5591. Executive editor/publisher: Marcia Preston. "To encourage our subscribers in striving for high quality writing." Annual awards for short stories and poetry. Award: $250 in each category. Judges are published writers not on the *Byline* staff. Entry fee $5 for stories; $3 for poems. Postmark deadline: November 1. "Entries should be unpublished and not have won money in any previous contest. Winners announced in February issue and published February or March issue with photo and short bio. Open to subscribers only."

CACHH GRANTS/CREATIVE ARTIST PROGRAM, (I, II, IV), Cultural Arts Council of Houston/Harris County, P.O. Box 131027, Houston TX 77219-1027. (713)527-9330. Fax: (713)630-5210. Grants Coordinator: Trina Finley. "To recognize the significant accomplishments of local artists and their contributions to the community." Annual competition for creative nonfiction, fiction, poetry, playwriting. Award: $5,000 unrestricted grant. Competition receives approximately 100-130 submissions. Judges: jury panel of literary professionals. Guidelines for SASE. Deadline fall of every year. "Applicants must reside in Houston and have been a resident for past two years."

CALIFORNIA WRITERS' CLUB CONTEST, (I), California Writers' Club, 1090 Cambridge St., Novato CA 94947-4963. Cash awards "to encourage writing." Competition is held biennially in odd-numbered years. Competition receives varying number of submissions. Judges: Professional writers, members of California Writers' Club. Entry fee to be determined. For the contest rules, write to the Secretary between February 1 and April 30, 1997. Unpublished submissions. "Open to all."

CALIFORNIA WRITERS' ROUNDTABLE ANNUAL WRITING CONTESTS, (I), The Los Angeles Chapter, Women's National Book Association, 11684 Ventura Blvd., Suite 807, Studio City CA 91604-2652. Contact: Lou Carter Keay. Annual competition for short stories. Award: $150 first prize; $75 second prize; $25 third prize. Entry fee $5 to nonmembers of Women's National Book Association. Guidelines for SASE. Deadline September 30. Previously unpublished submissions. 3,000 word limit. "Manuscripts must be typed, on standard paper, 8½x11 inches. Margins of one inch on all sides. The title of short story must appear on each page, all pages numbered. Send 3 copies of the short story. Include in a small envelope a card containing the author's name, address and phone number, along with the title of short story. Do not put the name of author on the manuscript itself. If you wish one copy of your manuscript returned, include a SASE."

JOHN W. CAMPBELL MEMORIAL AWARD FOR THE BEST SCIENCE-FICTION NOVEL OF THE YEAR; THEODORE STURGEON MEMORIAL AWARD FOR THE BEST SF SHORT FICTION, (II, III), Center for the Study of Science Fiction, English Dept., University of Kansas, Lawrence KS 66045. (913)864-3380. Professor and Director: James Gunn. "To honor the best novel and short science fiction of the year." Annual competition for short stories and novels. Award: Certificate. "Winners' names are engraved on a trophy." Competition receives approx. 50-100 submissions. Judges: 2 separate juries. Deadline May 1. For previously published submissions. "Ordinarily publishers should submit work, but authors have done so when publishers would not. Send for list of jurors."

✤**CANADA COUNCIL AWARDS, (III, IV)**, Canada Council, P.O. Box 1047, 350 Albert St., Ottawa, Ontario K1P 5V8 Canada. (613)566-4376. The Canada Council sponsors the following awards, for which no applications are accepted. *Canada-Australia Literary Prize*: 1 prize of $3,000 (Canadian), awarded in alternate years to an Australian or Canadian writer for the author's complete work; *Canada-French Community of Belgium Literary Prize*: 1 prize of $5,000 (Canadian), awarded in alternate years to a Canadian or Belgian writer on the basis of the complete works of the writer; *Canada-Switzerland Literary Prize*: 1 prize of $2,500 (Canadian), awarded in alternate years to a Canadian or Swiss writer for a work published in French during the preceding 8 years.

✤**CANADA COUNCIL GOVERNOR GENERAL'S LITERARY AWARDS, (III, IV)**, Canada Council, 350 Albert St., P.O. Box 1047, Ottawa, Ontario K1P 5V8 Canada. (613)566-4376. Contact: Writing and Publishing Section. "Awards of $10,000 each are given annually to the best English-language and best French-language Canadian work in each of seven categories: children's literature (text) and children's literature (illustration), drama, fiction, poetry, nonfiction and translation." All literary works published by Canadians between October 1 and September 30 the following year are considered. Canadian authors, illustrators and translators only. Books must be submitted by publishers (4 copies must be sent to the Canada Council) and accompanied by a Publisher's Submissions Form, available from the Writing and Publishing Section. All entries (books or bound galleys) must be received by August 31. (If the submission is in the form of bound galleys, the actual book must be published and received at the Canada Council no later than September 30.)

✤**CANADIAN AUTHORS ASSOCIATION LITERARY AWARDS, (FICTION), (II, IV)**, Canadian Authors Association, 27 Doxsee Ave. N., Campbellford, Ontario K0L 1L0 Canada. (705)653-0323. Fax: (705)653-0593. President: Cora Taylor. Annual award "to honor writing that achieves literary excellence without sacrificing popular appeal." For novels published during the previous calendar year. Award: $5,000 plus silver medal. No entry fee. Entry forms or rules for SASE. Deadline December 15. Restricted to *full-length* English language novels. Author must be Canadian or Canadian landed immigrant. CAA also sponsors the Air Canada Award, literary awards in poetry, nonfiction and drama, and the Vicky Metcalf Awards for children's literature.

✤**CANADIAN AUTHORS ASSOCIATION STUDENTS' CREATIVE WRITING CONTEST, (I, IV)**, 27 Doxsee Ave. N., Campbellford, Ontario K0l 1L0 Canada. (705)653-0323. Fax: (705)653-0593. Contact: Bernice Lever-Farrar. Annual competition for short stories, articles and poems. Awards $500 for best short story, $500 for best article, $500 for best poem, 4 honorable mentions in each category. All 15 winners will receive *Canadian Author* magazine for 1 year; first-place winners will be published in *Canadian Author*. "Entry form in winter and spring issues of *Canadian Author*." Entry fees $5/short story of 2,000 words or less; $5/article of 2,000 words of less; $5/2 to 3 poems of not more than 30 lines each. Deadline March. Unpublished submissions except in a student class anthology, newspaper or yearbook. Writers must be enrolled in secondary schools, colleges or universities and must be Canadian residents or citizens.

THE CAPRICORN AWARD, (I), The Writer's Voice, 5 W. 63rd St., New York NY 10023. (212)875-4124. Fax: (212)875-4177. Annual competition for novels or story collections. Award: $1,000, plus featured reading. Entry fee $15. Deadline December 31. Applicants may submit excerpts of work that have been previously published, however complete work cannot have been previously published elsewhere. Submit first 150 pgs. of novel/story collection.

RAYMOND CARVER SHORT STORY CONTEST, (I, IV), Dept. of English, Humboldt State University, Arcata CA 95521-4957. Contact: Coordinator. Annual award for previously unpublished short stories. First prize: $500 and publication in *Toyon*. Second Prize: $250. Entry fee $10/story. SASE for rules. Deadline November 1. For authors living in United States only. Send 2 copies of story; author's name, address, phone number and title of story on separate cover page only. Story must be no more than 6,000 words. Title must appear on first page. For notification of receipt of ms, include self-addressed, stamped postcard. For Winners List include SASE. For a copy of the *Toyon*, send $2.

‡❋CAVENDISH TOURIST ASSOCIATION CREATIVE WRITING AWARD, (I, IV), PEI Council of the Arts, P.O. Box 2234, Charlottetown, P.E.I., C1A 8B9 Canada. (902)368-4410. Fax: (902)368-4418. Awarded annually to students at the Elementary, Junior and Senior High levels. Students may write on the topic of their choice. Annual competition for short stories. Award: $75 (first prize); $50 (second prize); $25 (third prize). Deadline February 15. Unpublished submissions. Open to students in PEI who have been residents for 6 of the last 12 months. Word length: 5 pages. "Entries may be either typed or printed, double-spaced and should be submitted with name and address on a separate cover sheet for anonymous judging. Enclose SASE for return of manuscript."

THE *CHELSEA* AWARDS, (II), P.O. Box 773, Cooper Station, New York NY 10276. *Mail entries to*: Richard Foerster, Editor, P.O. Box 1040, York Beach ME 03910. Annual competition for short stories. Prize: $500 and publication in *Chelsea* (all entries are considered for publication). Judges: the editors. Entry fee $10 (for which entrants also receive a subscription). Guidelines available for SASE. Deadline June 15. Unpublished submissions. Manuscripts may not exceed 30 typed pages or about 7,500 words. The stories must not be under consideration elsewhere or scheduled for book publication within 6 months of the competition deadline.

CHEVRON AWARD AND WRITERS UNLIMITED AWARD, Writers Unlimited, 910 Grant Ave., Pascagoula MS 39567-7222. (601)762-4230. Contest Chairman: Nina Mason. "Part of an annual contest to encourage first-class writing of poetry and prose." Annual competition for short stories. Prize amounts vary with $50 being the maximum. Deadline September 1. Send SASE for guidelines.

‡CHICANO/LATINO LITERARY CONTEST, (I, IV), Dept. of Spanish & Portuguese, University of California-Irvine, Irvine CA 92714. (714)824-5702. Fax: (714)824-2803. Coordinator: Ruth M. Gratzer. Annual award for novels, short stories (different genre every year). Award: Usually $1,000. Guidelines for SASE. Deadline April 1996. Unpublished submissions.

CHILD STUDY CHILDREN'S BOOK AWARD, (III, IV), Child Study Children's Book Committee at Bank St. College, 610 W. 112th St., New York NY 10025. (212)875-4540. Contact: Anita Wilkes Dore, Committee Chair. Annual award. "To honor a book for children or young people which deals realistically with problems in their world. It may concern social, individual and ethical problems." Only books sent by publishers for review are considered. No personal submissions. Books must have been published within current calendar year. Award: Certificate and cash prize.

THE CHRISTOPHER AWARD, (II), The Christophers, 12 E. 48th St., New York NY 10017. (212)759-4050. Contact: Ms. Peggy Flanagan, awards coordinator. Annual award "to encourage creative people to continue to produce works which affirm the highest values of the human spirit in adult and children's books." Published submissions only. Award: Bronze medallion. "Award judged by a grassroots panel and a final panel of experts. Juvenile works are 'children tested.' " Examples of books awarded: *Dear Mr. Henshaw*, by Beverly Cleary (ages 8-10); *Sarah, Plain and Tall*, by Patricia MacLachlan (ages 10-12).

CINTAS FELLOWSHIP, (I, II, IV), Cintas Foundation/Arts International Program of I.I.E., 809 U.N. Plaza, New York NY 10017. (212)984-5370. Contact: Program Coordinator. "To foster and encourage the profes-

The maple leaf symbol before a listing indicates a Canadian publisher, magazine, conference or contest.

sional development and recognition of talented Cuban creative artists. *Not* intended for furtherance of academic or professional study, nor for research or writings of a scholarly nature." Annual competition for authors of short stories, novels, story collections and poetry. 5 awards of $10,000 each. Fellowship receives approximately 40 literature applicants/year. Judges: Selection committee. Guidelines for SASE. Deadline: March 1. Previously published or unpublished submissions. Limited to artists of Cuban lineage *only*. "Awards are given to artists in the following fields: visual arts, literature, music composition and architecture."

COMMONWEALTH CLUB OF CALIFORNIA, (II, IV), California Book Awards, 595 Market St., San Francisco CA 94105. (415)597-6700. Director of Member Services: James L. Coplan. Main contest established in 1931. Annual. "To encourage California writers and honor literary merit." Awards: Gold and silver medals. Judges: Jury of literary experts. For books published during the year preceding the particular contest. Three copies of book and a completed entry form required. "Write or phone asking for the forms. Either an author or publisher may enter a book. We usually receive over 300 entries."

‡CONNECTICUT COMMISSION ON THE ARTS ARTIST FELLOWSHIPS, (I, II, IV), 227 Lawrence St., Hartford CT 06106. (203)566-4770. Program Manager: Linda Dente. "To support the creation of new work by a creative artist *living in Connecticut*." Biennial competition for the creation or completion of new works in literature, i.e. short stories, novels, story collections, poetry and playwriting. Awards: $5,000 and $2,500. Judges: Peer professionals (writers, editors). Guidelines available in August. Deadline January. Writers may send either previously published or unpublished submissions—up to 10 pages of material. Connecticut residents only.

COUNCIL FOR WISCONSIN WRITERS ANNUAL WRITING CONTEST, (II, IV), Box 55322, Madison WI 53705. President: Russell King. "To recognize excellence in Wisconsin writing published during the year in 11 categories." Annual competition for short stories and novels. Award: $500 for 9 categories, $1,000 for 2 categories. Competition receives between 5 and 80 entries, depending on category. Judges: qualified judges from other states. Entry fee $25 for nonmembers and $10 for members. Guidelines for SASE. Previously published submissions. Wisconsin residents only. Official entry form (available in November) required. Deadline mid-January.

‡CREATIVE CHALLENGES LITERARY WRITING COMPETITIONS (I), 1131 Manzanita Dr., Pacifica CA 94044. (415)359-1581. Fax: (415)359-1581. Owner: Gerri Smith. Award "to reach many persons who have to write, enjoy challenge and competition, and to show off their writing skill(s)." Award granted when money is available (if enough entries are received) for short stories. Award: $150. Judge: Gerri Smith. Entry fee $15. Guidelines for SASE. Deadline March 15, July 15 and November 15. Unpublished submissions. Word length: 2,500 words. "If less than two entries are received in any of three categories: short-story—romance; short-story—humorous; article or essay on one of two topics, that category is cancelled and fee refunded. All participants receive a certificate and information on writing and contests."

CRIME WRITERS' ASSOCIATION AWARDS, (III, IV), Box 172, Tring Herts HP23 5LP England. Six awards. Annual awards for crime novels and nonfiction. Deadline October 1. Published submissions in UK in current year. Book must be nominated by UK publishers.

THE *CRUCIBLE* POETRY AND FICTION COMPETITION, (I), *Crucible*, Barton College, College Station, Wilson NC 27893. Annual competition for short stories. Award: $150 (1st prize); $100 (2nd prize) and publication in *Crucible*. Judges: The editors. Guidelines for SASE. Deadline April. Unpublished submissions. Fiction should be 8,000 words or less.

DALY CITY POETRY AND SHORT STORY CONTEST, (I), Daly City History, Arts, and Science Commission, % Serramonte Library, 40 Wembley Dr., Daly City CA 94015. (415)991-8025. Contest coordinator: Ruth Hoppin. "To encourage poets and writers and to recognize and reward excellence." Annual competition for short stories. Awards: $40, $25, $10 and $5. Competition receives approx. 50 submissions. Judges are usually teachers of creative writing. Entry fee: $2/story. Guidelines for SASE. Deadline January 4. Unpublished submissions. Length: 3,000 words maximum. "No profanity."

MARGUERITE DE ANGELI PRIZE, (I), Bantam Doubleday Dell Books for Young Readers, 1540 Broadway, New York NY 10036. "To encourage the writing of fiction that examines the diversity of the American experience (either contemporary or historical) in the same spirit as the works of Marguerite de Angeli." Open to US and Canadian writers. Annual competition for first novels for middle-grade readers (ages 7-10). Award: One BDD hardcover and paperback book contract, with $1,500 cash prize and $3,500 advance against royalties. Judges: Editors of BDD Books for Young Readers. Guidelines for SASE. Deadline: Submissions must be postmarked between April 1 and June 30. Previously unpublished (middle-grade) fiction.

DEEP SOUTH WRITERS CONFERENCE ANNUAL COMPETITION, (I), DSWC Inc., English Dept., University of Louisiana at Lafayette, P.O. Box 44691, Lafayette LA 70504. (318)482-6908. Contact: director or contest clerk. Annual awards "to encourage aspiring, unpublished writers." Categories: Novels, short stories, nonfiction, poetry, plays, and French language literature. Awards: Certificates and cash plus possible publication of shorter works. Contest rules for SASE and addition to mailing list. Deadline July 15. Unpublished submissions.

DELACORTE PRESS ANNUAL PRIZE FOR A FIRST YOUNG ADULT NOVEL, (I), Delacorte Press, Department BFYR, 1540 Broadway, New York NY 10036. (212)354-6500. Estab. 1983. Annual award "to encourage the writing of contemporary young adult fiction." Award: Contract for publication of book; $1,500 cash prize and a $6,000 advance against royalties. Judges are the editors of Delacorte Press Books for Young Readers. Contest rules for SASE. Unpublished submissions; fiction with a contemporary setting that will be suitable for ages 12-18. Deadline: December 30 (no submissions accepted prior to Labor Day). Writers may be previously published, but cannot have published a young adult novel before.

DELAWARE DIVISION OF THE ARTS, (I, IV), 820 N. French St., Wilmington DE 19801. (302)577-3540. Coordinator: Barbara R. King. "To help further careers of emerging and established professional artists." Annual awards for Delaware residents only. Awards: $5,000 for established professionals; $2,000 for emerging professionals. Judges are out-of-state professionals in each division. Entry forms or rules for SASE. Deadline March 1.

***THE DEXTER REVIEW* WRITING COMPETITION, (I)**, *The Dexter Review*, P.O. Box 8418, Ann Arbor MI 48107. (313)426-0420. Editor: R. Farrington Sharp. Annual competition for short stories. Award: $150 (1st place), $75 (2nd place), plus publication in *The Dexter Review*. Entry fee $7. Unpublished submissions. Word length: 2,500 words. "Keep in mind that this is a literary magazine when submitting your work."

JOHN DOS PASSOS PRIZE FOR LITERATURE, (III, IV), Longwood College, Farmville VA 23909. (804)395-2155. "The John Dos Passos Prize for Literature annually commemorates one of the greatest of 20th-century American authors by honoring other writers in his name." Award: A medal and $1,000. "The winner, announced each fall in ceremonies at the college, is chosen by an independent jury charged especially to seek out American creative writers in the middle stages of their careers—men and women who have established a substantial body of significant publication, and particularly those whose work demonstrates one or more of the following qualities: all characteristics of the art of the man for whom the prize is named; an intense and original exploration of specifically American themes; an experimental tone; and/or writing in a wide range of literature forms." Application for prize is by nomination only.
 • This competition is celebrating its 15th anniversary.

EATON LITERARY ASSOCIATES' LITERARY AWARDS PROGRAM, (I), Eaton Literary Associates, P.O. Box 49795, Sarasota FL 34230. (813)366-6589. Vice President: Richard Lawrence. Biannual award for short stories and novels. Award: $2,500 for best book-length ms, $500 for best short story. Competition receives approx. 2,000 submissions annually. Judges are 2 staff members in conjunction with an independent agency. Entry forms or rules for SASE. Deadline March 31 for short stories; August 31 for book-length mss.

✤**ARTHUR ELLIS AWARDS, (II, IV)**, Crime Writers of Canada, Box 113, 3007 Kingston Rd., Scarborough, Ontario M1M 1P1 Canada. Contact: Secretary-Treasurer. "To recognize excellence in all aspects of crime-writing." Annual competition for short stories and novels. Award: statuette (plus *maybe* cash or goods). Judges: panels of members and experts. Guidelines for SASE. Deadline December 31 for published submissions that appeared in print between January 1 and December 31 of that year. Open to Canadian residents (any citizenship) or Canadian citizens living abroad. Four complete copies of each work must be submitted. Every entry must state category entered. Categories include Best Novel, Best First Novel, Best Short Story, Best Nonfiction, Best Play and Best Juvenile.

‡**EMERGING LESBIAN WRITERS FUND AWARDS, (II)**, Astraea National Lesbian Action Foundation, 116 E. 16th St., 7th Floor, New York NY 10003. (212)529-8021. Fax: (212)982-3321. Program Director: Ivy Young. Award to "recognize and encourage new/emerging writers and poets." Annual competition for fiction and poetry. Award: $11,000 (one time only grantees). Competition receives approx. 600-700 submissions. Judges: Established writers/poets (2 each category). Entry fee $5. Guidelines for SASE (application form required). Deadline March 8. Previously published submissions. U.S. residents only. Write for guidelines. "Must have at least one published work. No submissions accepted without application form."

EYSTER PRIZES, (II), *The New Delta Review*, LSU/Dept. of English, Baton Rouge LA 70803. (504)388-4079. Contact: Editors. "To honor author and teacher Warren Eyster, who served as advisor to *New Delta Review* predecessors *Manchac* and *Delta*." Semiannual awards for best short story and best poem in each issue. Award: $50 and 2 free copies of publication. Competition receives approximately 400 submissions/issue. Judges are published authors. Deadlines: September 1 for fall, February 15 for spring.

‡**FAMILY CIRCLE MYSTERY/SUSPENSE SHORT STORY CONTEST, (I)**, *Family Circle Magazine*, 110 Fifth Ave., New York NY 10011. (212)463-1240. Fax: (212)463-1808. Senior Editor: Kathy Sagan. Annual

competition for mystery/suspense short stories. Award: $3,000 (1st prize, $2,000 award, $1,000 to publish) $1,000 (runner-up). Competition receives approx. 3,000 submissions. Judge: Mary Higgins Clark. Guidelines for SASE. Unpublished submissions. Word length: no longer than 3,000 words.

JOAN FASSLER MEMORIAL BOOK AWARD, (II, IV), Association for the Care of Children's Health, 7910 Woodmont Ave., #300, Bethesda MD 20814. (301)654-6549. Fax: (301)986-4553. Membership Manager: Trish McClean. "Recognizes outstanding literature that makes a distinguished contribution to a child's or young person's understanding of hospitalization, illness, disabling conditions, dying and death, and preventive care." Annual competition for short stories and novels. Award: $1,000 honorarium and plaque. Competition receives approximately 50-70 submissions. Judges: multidisciplinary committee of 8 ACCH members. Deadline December 31. Previously published submissions must have appeared in print within previous year.

VIRGINIA FAULKNER AWARD FOR EXCELLENCE IN WRITING, (II), Prairie Schooner, 201 Andrews Hall, University of Nebraska, Lincoln NE 68588-0334. (402)472-0911. Editor: Hilda Raz. "An award for writing published in *Prairie Schooner* in the previous year." Annual competition for short stories, novel excerpts and translations. Award: $1,000. Judges: Editorial Board. Guidelines for SASE. "We only read mss from September through May." Work must have been published in *Prairie Schooner* in the previous year.

WILLIAM FAULKNER COMPETITION IN FICTION, (I), The Pirate's Alley Faulkner Society Inc., 632 Pirate's Alley, New Orleans LA 70116-3254. (504)586-1609. Fax: (504)522-9725. Contest Director: Joseph J. DeSalvo, Jr. "To encourage publisher interest in writers with potential." Annual competition for short stories, novels and novellas. Award: $7,500 for novel, $2,500 for novella, $1,500 for short story and gold medals, plus trip to New Orleans for presentation. Competition receives approximately 200-300 submissions. Judges: professional writers, academics. Entry fee $25 for short story; $30 for novella; $35 for novel. Guidelines for SASE. Deadline April 1. Unpublished submissions. Word length: for novels, over 50,000; for novellas, under 20,000; for short stories, under 20,000. "All entries must be accompanied by official entry form which is provided with guidelines."

‡FC2/ILLINOIS STATE UNIVERSITY NATIONAL FICTION COMPETITION (I), Illinois State University, Unit for Contemporary Literature, Normal IL 61790-4241. (309)438-3582. Fax: (309)438-3523. Director: Curtis White. Annual competition for novels, story collections. Award: Publication, trip to university, standard royalties. Competition receives approx. 300 submissions. Judges: Fiction writers of national note. Entry fee $15. Guidelines for SASE. Unpublished submissions. Word length: 400 pages. "Contest winners include: Gerald Vizenor, Richard Grossman, Eurudice and Don Webb. Contest judges include: Robert Coover, Toby Olsen, William Vollmann, Paul Auster."

FELLOWSHIPS/WRITER-IN-RESIDENCE, (IV), Idaho Commission on the Arts, Box 83720, Boise ID 83720-0008. (208)334-2119 or (800)ART-FUND. "Fellowships awarded to Idaho writers for artistic excellence. Writer-in-Residence awarded to one Idaho writer for distinguished work and artistic excellence." Biennial competition for fiction, creative nonfiction and poetry. Award: $5,000 fellowship, $10,000 writer-in-residence. Competition receives approximately 85 submissions. Judges: nationally-known panel of poets and writers from outside Idaho. Guidelines for SASE. All work must have been completed within the last 5 years. Idaho authors only.

FEMINIST WRITER'S CONTEST, Des Plaines/Park Ridge NOW Chapter, 648 N. Northwest Hwy., #258, Park Ridge IL 60068. (708)696-1817. Contest Director: Pamela Sims. "To encourage and reward feminist writers, to give them an opportunity to be read by competent judges, and to be published in our chapter newsletter." Annual competition for short stories and essays. Award: $100 (1st place), $50 (2nd place). Competition receives approx. 50 submissions. Judges are feminist professors, teachers, writers, political activists, social workers and entrepeneurs. Entry fee $10. Guidelines for SASE. Deadline August 31. May be either published or unpublished. "We accept both foreign or domestic entries. Stories/essays may be on any subject, but should reflect feminist awareness." Word length: 5,000 words or less.

ROBERT L. FISH MEMORIAL AWARD, (II, IV), Mystery Writers of America, Inc., 17 E. 47th St., 6th Floor, New York NY 10017. Estab. 1984. Annual award "to encourage new writers in the mystery/detective/suspense short story—and, subsequently, larger work in the genre." Award: $500 and plaque. Judges: The MWA committee for best short story of the year in the mystery genre. Deadline December 1. Previously published submissions published the year prior to the award. Looking for "a story with a crime that is central to the plot that is well written and distinctive."

‡*FISH STORIES* BEST FICTION CONTEST, (I), 5412 N. Clark, South Suite, Chicago IL 60640. Editor-in-Chief: Amy Davis. Award to "honor a previously unpublished story that stands out consistently to the editorial board with payment to that writer." Annual competition for short stories, poetry. Award: $50-200 depending on place. Judges: a national editorial board. Entry fee $5 for up to 5,000 words; $10 for 5,000 to 10,000 words. Guidelines for SASE. Deadline October 1 to January 1. Unpublished submissions. "We are not looking for genre fiction. We are open to poetry and literary fiction." Word length: poetry (no more than 3 pgs.), short-shorts and stories (up to 10,000 words). "The contest winners are published along with the standard submissions selected for *Fish Stories*. Writers can read a sample copy to preview what we may be looking for regarding quality and range of work."

DOROTHY CANFIELD FISHER AWARD, (III), Vermont Dept. of Libraries and Vermont PTA, % Southwest Regional Library, Pierpoint Avenue, Rutland VT 05701. (802)828-3261. Contact: Grace Greene. Estab. 1957. Annual award. "To encourage Vermont schoolchildren to become enthusiastic and discriminating readers and to honor the memory of one of Vermont's most distinguished and beloved literary figures." Award: Illuminated scroll. Publishers send the committee review copies of books to consider. Only books of the current publishing year can be considered for next year's award. Master list of titles is drawn up in March each year. Children vote each year in the spring and the award is given before the school year ends. Submissions must be "written by living American authors, be suitable for children in grades 4-8, and have literary merit. Can be nonfiction also."

FLORIDA ARTS COUNCIL/LITERATURE FELLOWSHIPS, (I, IV), Division of Cultural Affairs, Dept. of State, The Capitol, Tallahassee FL 32399-0250. (904)487-2980. Director: Ms. Peyton C. Fearington. "To allow Florida artists time to develop their artistic skills and enhance their careers." Annual awards for fiction, poetry or children's literature. Award: $5,000; approximately 7 fellowships awarded/year. Competition receives approx. 150 submissions/year. Judges are review panels made up of individuals with a demonstrated interest in literature. Deadline January. Entry restricted to practicing, professional writers who are legal residents of Florida and have been living in the state for 12 consecutive months at the time of the deadline. Graduate or undergraduate students enrolled in any degree-seeking programs are not eligible.

‡FLORIDA FIRST COAST WRITERS' FESTIVAL NOVEL, SHORT FICTION & POETRY AWARDS, Writers' Festival & Florida Community College at Jacksonville, FCCJ North Campus, 4501 Capper Rd., Jacksonville FL 32218. (904)766-6559. Fax: (904)766-6554. Festival Coordinator/Contest Director: Howard Denson. Conference and contest "to create a healthy writing environment, honor writers of merit, select some stories for *The State Street Review* (a literary magazine) and find a novel manuscript to recommend to St. Martin's Press for 'serious consideration.' " Annual competition for short stories and novels. Competition receives 60 novel, 150-200 short fiction and 300-600 poetry submissions. Judges: university faculty and freelance and professional writers. Entry fee $75 plus $25/person for banquet tickets. Deadlines: October 1 (novels) and November 1 (short fiction and poetry). Winners announced at the Florida First Coast Writers' Festival held in April. Unpublished submissions. Word length: none for novel; short fiction, 6,000 words.

FLORIDA STATE WRITING COMPETITION, (I), Florida Freelance Writers Association, P.O. Box A, Stratford NH 03590. (603)922-8338. "To offer additional opportunities for writers to earn income from their stories." Annual competition for short stories and novels. Award: varies from $50-150. Competition receives approximately 300 short stories; 125 novels. Judges: authors, editors and teachers. Entry fee from $5-15. Guidelines for SASE. Deadline: March 15. Unpublished submissions. Categories include literary, science fiction/fantasy, genre and novel chapter. Length: 7,500 words maximum. "Guidelines are revised each year and subject to change. New guidelines are available in fall of each year."

‡FOSTER CITY INTERNATIONAL WRITERS' CONTEST, (I), Foster City Arts & Culture Committee, 650 Shell Blvd., Foster City CA 94404. (415)345-3751. Chairman: Clarke N. Simm. Award "to encourage and support new writers." Annual competition for short stories. Award: $250 (first); certificate of merit (second-fifth). Competition receives approx. 2,500 submissions. Judges: Peninsula Press Club. Entry fee $10. Guidelines for SASE. Deadline November 1st each year. Unpublished submissions. Word length: no more than 3,000 words.

♣FOUNDATION FOR THE ADVANCEMENT OF CANADIAN LETTERS AUTHOR'S AWARDS, (II, IV), In conjunction with Periodical Marketers of Canada (PMC), South Tower, 175 Bloor St., E., Suite 1007, Toronto, Ontario M4W 3R8 Canada. (416)968-7218. Award Coordinator: Janette Hatcher. "To recognize outstanding Canadian writing in English-language mass market magazines and paperback books." Annual award for short stories, novels. Special recognition is given to Book of the Year, as well as Author of the Year. "Must be published in a Canadian 'mass market' publication." Write for details.

‡H.E. FRANCIS SHORT STORY AWARD, (I), Ruth Hindman Foundation, 2007 Gallatin St., Huntsville AL 35801. (205)539-3320. Fax: (205)533-6893. Chairperson: Patricia Sammon. Annual short story competition to honor H.E. Francis, retired professor of English at the University of Alabama in Huntsville. Award: $1,000. Competition receives approx. 1,000 submissions. Judges: distinguished writers. Entry fee. Guidelines for SASE. Unpublished submissions.

MILES FRANKLIN LITERARY AWARD, (II, IV), Arts Management Pty. Ltd., 180 Goulburn St., Darlinghurst NSW 2010 Australia. Associate Director Projects & Artists: Hanne Larsen. "For the advancement, improvement and betterment of Australian literature." Annual award for novels. Award: AUS $25,000, to the author. Competition receives approx. 60 submissions. Guidelines for SASE. Deadline January 31. Previously published submissions. "The novel must have been published in the year of competition entry, and must present Australian life in any of its phases."

SOUERETTE DIEHL FRASER AWARD, (II, IV), The Texas Institute of Letters, P.O. Box 30783-TCU, Fort Worth TX 76129. (817)921-7822. Secretary: Judy Alter. "To recognize the best literary translation of a book into English, the translation published between January 1 and December 30 of the year prior to the award's announcement in the spring." Annual competition for translations. Award: $1,000. Judges: committee of three. Guidelines for SASE. Deadline January 4. "Award available to translators who were born in Texas, or who have lived in the state at some time for two consecutive years."

‡FUNNIEST WOMEN IN THE WORLD CONTEST, (I), *Women's HARPOON*/Women's Free Press, 8 Ilene Court, #7, Belle Meade NJ 08502. Annual competition for short stories, novels, story collections. "Seven finalists will be published in a special edition of *Women's HARPOON* magazine. The winner of each category (articles or stories, cartoons, and photos) will be flown to the Bahamas and receive a 4-day barefoot cruise with the staff of *Women's HARPOON*." Entry fee $35. Guidelines for SASE. Deadline September 30, 1996. Unpublished submissions. "You must be a woman and you must be funny!" Word length: 2,000 words.

GEORGETOWN REVIEW SHORT STORY AND POETRY CONTEST, (I), Georgetown Review, Box 227, 400 E. College St., Georgetown KY 40324-1696. (502)863-8308. Fax: (502)868-8888. Editor: Steve Carter. "To reward excellent fiction." Annual competition for short stories. Award: $150 to the winning story. Runner-up stories receive publication and authors receive free subscription. Competition receives approximately 300-350 submissions. Judges: *GR* editors. Entry fee $5/story. Guidelines for SASE. Deadline August 1, 1996. Unpublished submissions. Word length: no requirement. "Must include SASE for return of work."

GEORGIA COUNCIL FOR THE ARTS INDIVIDUAL ARTIST GRANTS, (I, IV), 530 Means St. NW, Suite 115, Atlanta GA 30318. (404)651-7920. Contact: Ann Davis. Annual award for "artist's option for creation of new work." Award: $5,000 maximum. Competition receives approximately 125 submissions. Judges: Professional advisory panel. Guidelines for SASE. Deadline April 1. "Support material must be current within past two years; application must be for new work. Artist must be resident of Georgia for at least one year prior to application date."

GLIMMER TRAIN'S SHORT-STORY AWARD FOR NEW WRITERS, (I), Glimmer Train Press, Inc., 812 S.W. Washington St., Suite 1205, Portland OR 97205. (503)221-0836. Fax: (503)221-0837. Contest Director: Linda Davies. Contest offered 2 times/year for any writer whose fiction hasn't appeared in a nationally-distributed publication with a circulation over 5,000. "Send original, unpublished short (1,200-8,000 words) story with $11 reading fee (covers up to two stories sent together in same envelope) during the months of February/March and August/September. Title page must include name, address, phone and Short Story Award for New Writers must be written on outside of envelope. No need for SASE as materials will not be returned. We cannot acknowledge receipt or provide status of any particular manuscript. Winners notified by July 1 (for February/March entrants) and January 1 (for August/September entrants). Winner receives $1,200 and publication in *Glimmer Train Stories*. First/second runners-up receive $500/$300, respectively, and honorable mention. All applicants receive a copy of the issue in which winning entry is published and runners-up announced."

GOLD MEDALLION BOOK AWARDS, (III, IV), Evangelical Christian Publishers Association, 3225 S. Hardy Dr., Suite 101, Tempe AZ 85282. (602)966-3998. Executive Director of ECPA: Doug Ross. Annual award to "encourage excellence in evangelical Christian book publishing in 22 categories." Judges: "At least eight judges for each category chosen from among the ranks of evangelical leaders and book-review editors." Entry fee $110 for ECPA member publishers; $250 for non-member publishers. Deadline December 1. For books published the previous year: Publishers submit entries.

‡JEANNE CHARPIOT GOODHEART PRIZE FOR FICTION, (I), Shenandoah, 2nd Floor, Troubadour Theater, Washington & Lee University, Lexington VA 24450. (203)463-8765. Editor: R.T. Smith. Award to "recognize the best story from a calendar year of *Shenandoah*." Annual competition for short stories. Award: $1,000. Competition receives approx. 800 submissions. Judge: previous winner. Guidelines for SASE. Deadline on-going. Unpublished submissions.

‡GOVERNMENT OF NEWFOUNDLAND AND LABRADOR ARTS AND LETTERS COMPETITION (I, IV), Government of Newfoundland and Labrador Dept. of Tourism and Culture, P.O. Box 1854, St. John's, Newfoundland A1C SP7. (709)729-5253. Fax: (709)729-5952. Secretary: Regina Best. Award "to encourage the creative talent of people of the Province of Newfoundland and Labrador." Annual competition for short stories. Award: $600 (1st prize), $300 (2nd prize), $150 (3rd prize). Competition receives approx. 800-900 submissions. Judges: Outside people who are professionals in their field. Guidelines for SASE. Unpublished submissions. Competition is only open to residents of this province. "There are two divisions in this competition: Junior (12-17 years) and Senior (18-on). There are prizes in several categories; fiction; nonfiction; poetry; dramatic script, painting and 3-D art; drawing and graphic art, photography."

GREAT LAKES COLLEGES ASSOCIATION NEW WRITERS AWARD, Great Lakes Colleges Association, 2929 Plymouth Rd., Suite 207, Ann Arbor MI 48105-3206. Director of New Writers Award: Mark Andrew Clark. Annual award. Winners are invited to tour the GLCA colleges. An honorarium of at least $300 will be guaranteed the author by each of the GLCA colleges they visit. Receives 30-40 entries annually. Judges: Professors from member colleges. No entry fee. Deadline February 28. Unpublished submissions. First publication in fiction or poetry. Writer must be nominated by publisher. Four copies of the book should be sent to: Mark Andrew Clark, Director, New Writers Award, GLCA Philadelphia Center, North American Bldg., 121 South Broad St., Seventh Floor, Philadelphia PA 19107.

GREAT PLAINS STORYTELLING & POETRY READING CONTEST, (I,II), P.O. Box 438, Walnut IA 51577. (712)784-3001. Director: Robert Everhart. Estab. 1976. Annual award "to provide an outlet for writers to present not only their works, but also to provide a large audience for their presentation *live* by the writer. Attendance at the event, which takes place annually in Avoca, Iowa, is *required*." Award: 1st prize $75; 2nd prize $50; 3rd prize $25; 4th prize $15; and 5th prize $10. Entry fee: $5. Entry forms available at contest only. Deadline is day of contest, which takes place over Labor Day Weekend. Previously published or unpublished submissions.

GREEN RIVER WRITERS CONTEST, (I, II), Green River Writer, 1043 Thornfield, Cincinnati OH 45224. (513)522-2493. Contact: Linda Frisa. Annual competition for short stories and novels. Award: for short stories up to 2,000 words, $150; 2,000-3,000 words $150, first chapter of novel, $50. Competition receives approx. 30-75 submissions. Judges are appointed by sponsors. Entry fee $5 each, $25 total. Guidelines for SASE. Deadline October 31. Unpublished submissions. Word length: up to 3,000 words, depends on category.

THE GREENSBORO REVIEW LITERARY AWARDS, (I), Dept. of English, UNC-Greensboro, Greensboro NC 27412. (910)334-5459. Editor: Jim Clark. Annual award. Award: $250. Contest rules for SASE. Deadline September 15. Unpublished submissions.

HACKNEY LITERARY AWARDS, (I), Box A-3, Birmingham Southern College, Birmingham AL 35254. (205)226-4921. Fax: (205)226-4931. Director of Special Events: Martha Andrews. Annual award for previously unpublished short stories, poetry and novels. Award: $2,000 (novel); $2,000 (poetry and short stories; 6 prizes). Competition receives approx. 700 submissions. Entry fee: $20 novel; $5 poetry and short story. Rules/entry form for SASE. Novel submissions must be postmarked on or before September 30. Short stories and poetry submissions must be postmarked on or before December 31.

HAMMETT PRIZE (NORTH AMERICAN), (II, IV), International Association of Crime Writers, North American Branch, JAF Box 1500, New York NY 10116. (212)757-3915. Award to promote "excellence in the field of crime writing as reflected in a book published in the English language in the US and/or Canada." Annual competition for novels or nonfiction. Award: trophy. Competition receives approx. 150 submissions. Judges: Nominations committee made up of IACW members screens titles and selects 3-5 nominated books. These go to three outside judges, who choose the winner. Guidelines for SASE. Deadline December 1. Previously published submissions. Published entries must have appeared in print between January 1 and December 31 (of contest year). "Writers must be US or Canadian citizens or permanent residents working in the field of crime writing (either fiction or nonfiction). No word-length requirement."

BAXTER HATHAWAY PRIZE, (I), *Epoch Magazine*, 251 Goldwin Smith, Cornell University, Ithaca NY 14853-3201. (607)255-3385. Contact: Michael Koch. Award "to honor the memory of Baxter Hathaway, founder of *Epoch*, and to encourage new poets and fiction writers." Biennial award for a novella or long poem, depending on the year (1996, novella; 1997, long poem). Award: $1,000 and publication in *Epoch*. Competition receives 400 submissions. Judge: A distinguished outsider. "Submissions accepted October 1-30, 1996." Guidelines for SASE. Sample copies with past winners for $5 each. Unpublished submissions. "Limited to writers who have published not more than one book of fiction or poetry (chapbooks excluded)."

THE HEARTLAND PRIZES, (II), *The Chicago Tribune*, 435 N. Michigan Ave., Chicago IL 60611-4041. "The Heartland Prizes are for nonfiction and the novel. To honor a novel and a book of nonfiction embodying the spirit of the nation's Heartland." Annual award for novels. Award: $5,000. Winners are notified in August.

DRUE HEINZ LITERATURE PRIZE, (II), University of Pittsburgh Press, 127 N. Bellefield Ave., Pittsburgh PA 15260. (412)624-4111. Annual award "to support the writer of short fiction at a time when the economics of commercial publishing make it more and more difficult for the serious literary artist working in the short story and novella to find publication." Award: $10,000 and publication by the University of Pittsburgh Press. Request complete rules of the competition before submitting a manuscript. Submissions will be received only during the months of July and August. Deadline August 31. Manuscripts must be unpublished in book form. The award is open to writers who have published a book-length collection of fiction or a minimum of three short stories or novellas in commercial magazines or literary journals of national distribution.

HEMINGWAY DAYS SHORT STORY COMPETITION, (I), Hemingway Days Festival, P.O. Box 4045, Key West FL 33041. (305)294-4440. "To honor Nobel laureate Ernest Hemingway, who was often pursued during his lifetime by young writers hoping to learn the secrets of his success." Annual competition for short stories. Awards: $1,000—1st; $500—2nd; $500—3rd. Competition receives approx. 900 submissions. Judges: Panel lead by Lorian Hemingway, granddaughter of Ernest Hemingway and novelist based out of Seattle, WA. Entry fee $10/story. Deadline postmarked June 1. "Open to writers who have not been published in national magazines with circulations over 5,000. No longer than 3,000 words." Send SASE for guidelines.

ERNEST HEMINGWAY FOUNDATION/PEN AWARD FOR FIRST FICTION, (II), PEN American Center, 568 Broadway, New York NY 10012. Awards Coordinator: John Morrone. Annual award "to give beginning writers recognition and encouragement and to stimulate interest in first novels among publishers and readers." Award: $7,500. Novels or short story collections must have been published during calendar year under consideration. Entry form or rules for SASE. Deadline December 20. "The Ernest Hemingway Foundation/ Pen Award For First Fiction is given to an American author of the best first-published book-length work of fiction published by an established publishing house in the US each calendar year."

THE O. HENRY AWARDS, (III), Doubleday, 1540 Broadway, New York NY 10036. Annual award "to honor the memory of O. Henry with a sampling of outstanding short stories and to make these stories better known to the public." These awards are published by Doubleday in hardcover and by Anchor Books in paperback every spring. Previously published submissions. "All selections are made by the editor of the volume, William Abrahams. No stories may be submitted."

HIGHLIGHTS FOR CHILDREN, **(I, IV)**, 803 Church St., Honesdale PA 18431. Editor: Kent L. Brown, Jr. "To honor quality stories (previously unpublished) for young readers." Three $1,000 awards. Stories: up to 500 words for beginning readers (to age 8) and 900 words for more advanced readers (ages 9 to 12). No minimum word length. No entry form necessary. To be submitted between January 1 and February 29 to "Fiction Contest" at address above. "No violence, crime or derogatory humor." Nonwinning entries returned in June if SASE is included with ms. "This year's category is stories about children in today's world." Send SASE for information.

THE ALFRED HODDER FELLOWSHIP, (II), The Council of the Humanities, Princeton University, 122 E. Pyne, Princeton NJ 08544. Executive Director: Carol Rigolot. "This fellowship is awarded for the pursuit of independent work in the humanities. The recipient is usually a writer or scholar in the early stages of his or her career, a person 'with more than ordinary learning' and with 'much more than ordinary intellectual and literary gifts.' " Traditionally, the Hodder Fellow has been a humanist outside of academia. Candidates for the Ph.D. are not eligible. Award: $42,000. The Hodder Fellow spends an academic year in residence at Princeton working independently. Judges: Princeton Committee on Humanistic Studies. Deadline November 15. Applicants must submit a résumé, a sample of previous work (10 page maximum, not returnable), and a project proposal of 2 to 3 pages. Letters of recommendation are not required.

THEODORE CHRISTIAN HOEPFNER AWARD, (I), *Southern Humanities Review*, 9088 Haley Center, Auburn University AL 36849. Contact: Dan R. Latimer or Virginia M. Kouidis, co-editors. Annual. "To award the authors of the best essay, the best short story and the best poem published in *SHR* each year." Award: $100 for the best short story. Judges: Editorial staff. Only published work in the current volume (4 issues) will be judged.

PEARL HOGREFE FELLOWSHIP, (I, II, IV), The Pearl Hogrefe Fund and Department of English, 203 Ross Hall, Iowa State University, Ames IA 50011. (515)294-8753. Professor: Dr. Neal Bowers. "To provide new M.A. students with writing time." Annual competition for manuscript sample of 25 pages, any genre. Award: $825/month for 9 months and full payment of tuition and fees. Competition receives approximately 75 submissions. Judges: the creative writing staff at Iowa State University. Guidelines for SASE. Deadline January 31. Either published or unpublished submissions. "No restrictions, except the applicant cannot hold or expect to receive a masters in English or creative writing during the current year."

HONOLULU **MAGAZINE/BORDERS BOOKS & MUSIC FICTION CONTEST, (I, IV)**, *Honolulu* Magazine, 36 Merchant St., Honolulu HI 96813. (808)524-7400. Editor: John Heckathorn. "We do not accept fiction except during our annual contest, at which time we welcome it." Annual award for short stories. Award: $1,000 and publication in the April issue of *Honolulu* Magazine. Competition receives approx. 400 submissions. Judges: Panel of well-known Hawaii-based writers. Rules for SASE. Deadline early December. "Stories must have a Hawaii theme, setting and/or characters. Author should enclose name and address in separate small envelope. Do not put name on story."

‡HOUSEWIFE WRITER'S FORUM SHORT STORY CONTEST, (I), *Housewife Writer's Forum*, P.O. Box 780, Lyman WY 82937. (307)782-7003. "To give new fiction writers a chance to have their work recognized." Annual contest for short stories. Awards: $30, $20, $10. Competition receives approx. 75 submissions. Judges: Fiction Editor Edward Wahl and Editor Emma Bluemel. Entry fee $4. Guidelines for SASE. Unpublished submissions. Any genre except risqué; 2,000 words maximum.

L. RON HUBBARD'S WRITERS OF THE FUTURE CONTEST, (I, IV), P.O. Box 1630N, Los Angeles CA 90078. Contest Administrator: Leslie Potter. Estab. 1984. Quarterly. "Foremost contest for new writers of science fiction, fantasy and horror. Awards $2,250 in quarterly prizes, annual $4,000 Grand Prize, five-day Writer's Workshop with major authors, publication in leading international anthology. Outstanding professional judges panel. No entry fee. Entrants retain all rights. For explicit instructions on how to enter send SASE to the above address."

THE 'HUGO' AWARD (Science Fiction Achievement Award), (III, IV), The World Science Fiction Convention, L.A. Con III/World Con, % SCIFI, Box 8442, Van Nuys CA 91409. E-mail: lacon3info@netcom .com. Temporary; address changes each year. "To recognize the best writing in various categories related to science fiction and fantasy." Award: Metal spaceship 15 inches high. "Winning the award almost always results in reprints of the original material and increased payment. Winning a 'Hugo' in the novel category frequently results in additional payment of $10,000-20,000 from future publishers." The award is voted on by ballot by the members of the World Science Fiction Convention from previously published material of professional publications. Writers may not nominate their own work.

ZORA NEALE HURSTON/RICHARD WRIGHT AWARD, (I, IV), Zora Neale Hurston/Richard Wright Foundation, English Dept., Virginia Commonwealth University, Richmond VA 23284-2005. (804)828-1331. President: Marita Golden. "Awards best fiction written by African-American college students enrolled full- or part-time in a U.S. college or university." Annual award for short stories and novels. Award: $1,000 first prize and publication in *Catalyst Magazine*; $500 second prize. Competition receives 50-75 submissions. Judges: published writers. Guidelines for SASE. Deadline: December 7. Unpublished submissions. Word length: 25 pages maximum.

ILLINOIS ARTS COUNCIL ARTISTS FELLOWSHIPS, (I, IV), Illinois Arts Council, #10-500, James R. Thompson Center, 100 W. Randolph, Chicago IL 60601. (312)814-4990. Contact: Richard Gage. Award "to enable Illinois artists of exceptional talent to pursue their artistic goals." Biannual for short stories, novels, story collections and creative nonfiction (essays, memoirs) completed within four years prior to the deadline. Awards: $500, $5,000 and $10,000. Competition receives approx. 200 prose submissions and 140 poetry submissions. Judges: non-Illinois writers/editors of exceptional talent. Deadline September 1. Recipients must have been Illinois residents for at least 1 year prior to deadline. Prose applicants limited to 30 pages; poetry limited to 15 pages.

INTERNATIONAL JANUSZ KORCZAK LITERARY COMPETITION, (II, IV), Joseph H. and Belle R. Braun Center for Holocaust Studies Anti-Defamation League of B'nai B'rith, 823 United Nations Plaza, New York NY 10017. (212)490-2525. Contact: Mark A. Edelman. Biennial award for published novels, novellas, translations, short story collections. "Books for or about children which best reflect the humanitarianism and leadership of Janusz Korczak, a Jewish and Polish physician, educator and author." Inquire for details and deadline.

INTERNATIONAL READING ASSOCIATION CHILDREN'S BOOK AWARDS, (II), Sponsored by IRA, P.O. Box 8139, 800 Barksdale Rd., Newark DE 19714-8139. (302)731-1600. Annual awards given for a first or second book in three categories (younger readers: ages 4-10; older readers: ages 10-16 and up; informational book) to authors who show unusual promise in the children's book field. Books from any country and in any language copyrighted during the previous calendar year will be considered. Entries in a language other than English must include a one-page abstract in English and a translation into English of one chapter or similar selection that in the submitter's estimation is representative of the book. The awards each carry a

---

Market categories: (I) Unpublished entries; (II) Published entries nominated by the author; (III) Published entries nominated by the editor, publisher or nominating body; (IV) Specialized entries.

US $500 stipend. Entries must be received by December 1. To submit a book for consideration by the selection committee, send 10 copies to Katharine G. Fralick, 6 Batchelder St., Plymouth NH 03264, USA.

INTERNATIONAL WRITERS CONTEST, (I), Foster City Arts and Culture Committee, 650 Shell Blvd., Foster City CA 94404. (415)345-5731. Contact: Contest chairman. Annual. "To foster and encourage aspiring writers." Unpublished submissions. Award: 1st prize in each of 5 categories $250. The 5 categories are: Best Fiction, Best Nonfiction, Best Humor, Best Story for Children, Best Poem. Deadline November 1. Winners announced December 31. English language entries only. Entry fee $10. Contest rules for SASE.

IOWA SCHOOL OF LETTERS AWARD FOR SHORT FICTION, THE JOHN SIMMONS SHORT FICTION AWARD, (I), Iowa Writers' Workshop, 436 English-Philosophy Building, The University of Iowa, Iowa City IA 52242. Annual awards for short story collections. To encourage writers of short fiction. Award: publication of winning collections by University of Iowa Press the following fall. Entries must be at least 150 pages, typewritten, and submitted between August 1 and September 30. Stamped, self-addressed return packaging must accompany manuscript. Rules for SASE. Iowa Writer's Workshop does initial screening of entries; finalists (about 6) sent to outside judge for final selection. "A different well-known writer is chosen each year as judge. Any writer who has not previously published a volume of prose fiction is eligible to enter the competition for these prizes. Revised manuscripts which have been previously entered may be resubmitted."

‡IOWA WOMAN CONTEST, INTERNATIONAL WRITING CONTEST, (I, IV), P.O. Box 680, Iowa City IA 52244-0680. Annual award for short fiction, poetry and essays. Awards first place of $500; second place $250, in each category. Judges: anonymous, women writers who have published work in the category. Entry fee $15 for one story, essay or up to 3 poems; $5 for each additional story, essay, or group of 3 poems. Guidelines available for SASE. Deadline December 30. Previously unpublished submissions *only*. Entries may not be simultaneously under consideration elsewhere in *any* form. Limited to women writers, with a 6,500 word limit on fiction and essays. "Submit typed or computer printed manuscripts with a cover sheet listing category, title, name, address and phone number. A single cover sheet per category is sufficient. Identify actual entry by title only. Do not identify author on the manuscript. Manuscripts cannot be returned; do not send SASE for return."

JOSEPH HENRY JACKSON AWARD, (I, IV), Intersection for the Arts/The San Francisco Foundation, 446 Valencia St., San Francisco CA 94103. (415)626-2787. Literary Program Director: Charles Wilmoth. Award "to encourage young, unpublished writers." Annual award for short stories, novels and story collections. Award: $2,000. Competition receives approx. 200 submissions. Entry form and rules available for SASE. Deadline January 31. Unpublished submissions only. Applicant must be resident of northern California or Nevada for 3 consecutive years immediately prior to the deadline date. Age of applicant must be 20 through 35. Work cannot exceed 100 double-spaced, typed pages.

JAMES FELLOWSHIP FOR THE NOVEL IN PROGRESS, (I), The Heekin Group Foundation, P.O. Box 1534, Sisters OR 97759. (503)548-4147. Fiction Director: Sarah Heekin Redfield. Award to "support unpublished writers in their writing projects." Two annual awards for novels in progress. Awards: $10,000 and $3,000. Receives approx. 500 applications. Judges: Invitation of publisher: past judges, Graywolf Press, SOHO Press, Dalkey Archive Press. Application fee $20. Guidelines for SASE. Deadline December 1. Unpublished submissions. Word length: Submit first 50-75 pages only.

JAPAN FOUNDATION ARTISTS FELLOWSHIP PROGRAM, (IV), 152 W. 57th St., 39th Floor, New York NY 10019. (212)489-0299. Fax: (212)489-0409. Program Assistant: Maki Uchiyama. "This program provides artists and specialists in the arts with the opportunity to pursue creative projects in Japan and to meet and consult with their Japanese counterparts." Annual competition. Several artists fellowships of from two to six months' duration during the 1996 Japanese fiscal year (April 1-March 31) are available to artists, such as writers, musicians, painters, sculptors, stage artists, movie directors, etc.; and specialists in the arts, such as scenario writers, curators, etc. Benefits include transportation to and from Japan; settling-in, research, activities and other allowances and a monthly stipend. See brochure for more details. Competition receives approx. 30-40 submissions. Judges: foundation staff in Japan. Deadline December 1. "Work should be related substantially to Japan. Applicants must be accredited artists or specialists. Affiliation with a Japanese artist or institution is required. Three letters of reference, including one from the Japanese affiliate must accompany all applications.

JAPANOPHILE SHORT STORY CONTEST, (I, II, IV), *Japanophile*, P.O. Box 223, Okemos MI 48864. (517)669-2109. Editor: Earl R. Snodgrass. Estab. 1974. Annual award "to encourage quality writing on Japan-America understanding." Award: $100 plus possible publication. Entry fee: $5. Send $4 for sample copy of magazine. Contest rules for SASE. Deadline December 31. Prefers unpublished submissions. Stories should involve Japanese and non-Japanese characters.

‡JEFFERSON CUP, (III, IV), Virginia Library Association, 669 S. Washington St., Alexandria VA 22314. (703)519-7853. Fax: (703)519-7732. Annual competition for U.S. history, historical fiction or biography for young people. Award: cup and $500. Judges: Jefferson Cup Committee. Previously published one year prior to selection. Writer must be nominated by publisher.

JESSE JONES AWARD FOR FICTION (BOOK), (II, IV), The Texas Institute of Letters, % TCU Press, P.O. Box 30783, Fort Worth TX 76129. (817)921-7822. Awards Coordinator: Judy Alter. "To honor the writer of the best novel or collection of short fiction published during the calendar year before the award is given." Annual award for novels or story collections. Award: $6,000. Competition receives approx. 30-40 entries per year. Judges: Panel selected by TIL Council. Guidelines for SASE. Deadline January 4. Previously published fiction, which must have appeared in print between January 1 and December 31 of the prior year. "Award available to writers who, at some time, have lived in Texas at least two years consecutively or whose work has a significant Texas theme."

JAMES JONES FIRST NOVEL FELLOWSHIP, (I), James Jones Society, Wilkes University, Wilkes-Barre PA 18766. (717)831-4520. Chair, English Department: Patricia B. Heaman. Award to "honor the spirit of unblinking honesty, determination, and insight into modern culture exemplified by the late James Jones by encouraging the work of an American writer who has not published a book-length work of fiction." Annual award for unpublished novel, novella, or collection of related short stories in progress. Award: $2,500. Receives approx. 400 applications. Judges: Kaylie Jones, J. Michael Lennon, Patricia Heaman, Kevin Heisler, Don Sackrider. Application fee $10. Guidelines for SASE. Deadline March 1. Unpublished submissions. "Award is open to American writers." Word length: 50 opening pages and a two-page thematic outline.

‡THE JANET HEIDINGER KAFKA PRIZE FOR FICTION BY AN AMERICAN WOMAN, (III, IV), University of Rochester, Susan B. Anthony Institute for Women's Studies, 538 Lattimore Hall, Rochester NY 14627. Award for fiction by a "woman who is a US citizen, and who has written the best, recently published, book-length work of prose fiction, whether novel, short stories, or experimental writing." Annual competition for short stories, story collections and novels. Award: Cash prizes to be announced. Guidelines for SASE. Deadline May 31, 1996. Recently published submissions. American women only. Writer must be nominated by publisher.

ROBERT F. KENNEDY BOOK AWARDS, (II, IV), 1206 30th St. NW, Washington DC 20007. (202)333-1880. Endowed by Arthur Schlesinger, Jr., from proceeds of his biography, *Robert Kennedy and His Times*. Annual. "To award the author of a book which most faithfully and forcefully reflects Robert Kennedy's purposes." For books published during the calendar year. Award: $2,500 cash prize awarded in the spring. Deadline: January 2. Looking for "a work of literary merit in fact or fiction that shows compassion for the poor or powerless or those suffering from injustice." Four copies of each book submitted should be sent, along with a $25 entry fee.

KENTUCKY ARTS COUNCIL, KENTUCKY ARTISTS FELLOWSHIPS, (I, IV), 31 Fountain Place, Frankfort KY 40601. (502)564-3757. "To encourage and assist the professional development of Kentucky artists." 10-15 writing fellowships offered every other (or even-numbered) year in fiction, poetry, playwriting. Award: $5,000. Competition received approx. "250 submissions in 1994 in all writing categories." Judges are out-of-state panelists (writers, editors, playwrights, etc.) of distinction. Open only to Kentucky residents (minimum one year). Entry forms available for *Kentucky residents in July 1996.*" Deadline September 1996.

‡JACK KEROUAC LITERARY PRIZE, (I), P.O. Box 8788, Lowell MA 01853-8788. Sponsored by Middlesex Community College, the University of Massachusetts at Lowell, Lowell Celebrates Kerouac!, and the Estate of Jack & Stella (Sampas) Kerouac. Annual award for short stories, poems and essays. Award: $500 honorarium and invitation to read at the annual Lowell Celebrates Kerouac! Festival in Lowell, MA. Competition receives approximately 200 submissions. Judges: Professional authors. Guidelines available for SASE. Deadline August 1. Unpublished submissions. Limited to: fiction—30 pages or less; nonfiction—30 pages or less; poetry—15 pages or less.

AGA KHAN PRIZE FOR FICTION, *The Paris Review*, 541 E. 72nd St., New York NY 10021. (212)861-0016. Editor: George Plimpton. Best previously unpublished short story. Annual competition for short stories. Award: $1,000. Competition receives approximately 1,000 submissions/month. Guidelines with SASE. Unpublished submissions. Word length: approximately 1,000-10,000 words.

KILLER FROG CONTEST, (I, II, IV), *Scavenger's Newsletter*, 519 Ellinwood, Osage City KS 66523. (913)528-3538. Contact: Janet Fox. Competition "to see who can write the funniest/most overdone horror story, or poem, or produce the most outrageous artwork on a horror theme." Annual award for short stories, poems and art. Award: $25 for each of 4 categories and "coveted froggie statuette." Winners also receive complimentary copies of *The Killer Frog* Anthology. Judge: Editor of *Scavenger*, Janet Fox. Guidelines available for SASE. Submissions must be postmarked between April 1 and July 1. Published or previously unpublished submissions. Limited to horror/humor. Length: up to 4,000 words.

‡KOREAN LITERATURE TRANSLATION AWARD, (IV), The Korean Culture and Arts Foundation, 1-130 Dongsoong-Dong, Chongro-Ku, Seoul South Korea 110-510. Fax: (0)2-760-4700. Biannual competition for translations (of Korean Literature). Award: $50,000 (grand prize), two work-of-merit prizes of $10,000. (If it is decided that there is no work of sufficient merit for the grand prize, the finest entry will be awarded $30,000.) Competition receives approx. 35 submissions. Judges: Translators. Unpublished submissions. Only translations in Korean Literature previously published. (Translators or publishers may submit their works in book.)

LATINO LITERATURE PRIZE, (II, IV), Latin American Writers Institute, % Hostos Community College, 500 Grand Concourse, Bronx NY 10451. (718)518-4195. Fax: (718)518-4294. Director: Isaac Goldemberg. "To recognize the work of Latino writers in the U.S. The competition is for books published in English or Spanish." Annual competition for novels and poetry. Award: $1,000 in each category (fiction and poetry). Competition receives approximately 125 submissions. Judges: recognized critics and writers. Guidelines for SASE. Deadline February 28, 1996. Previously published submissions published between January 1994 and December 1995. Open only to Latino writers who live in the United States. Publishers may also submit books for competition. "A special issue of our bilingual literary journal, *Brújula/Compass*, is devoted to the winning authors."

LAWRENCE FOUNDATION PRIZE, (I), *Michigan Quarterly Review*, 3032 Rackham Bldg., Ann Arbor MI 48109-1070. (313)764-9265. Editor: Laurence Goldstein. "An annual cash prize awarded to the author of the best short story published in *Michigan Quarterly Review* each year—chosen from both solicited and unsolicited submissions. Approximately eight short stories are published each year." Annual competition for short stories. Award: $1,000. The Review receives approximately 2,000 mss/year. Judges: Editorial Board. Guidelines for SASE. Deadline August 15. Unpublished submissions.

✦STEPHEN LEACOCK MEDAL FOR HUMOUR, (II, IV), Stephen Leacock Associates, P.O. Box 854, Orillia, Ontario L3V 6K8 Canada. (705)325-6546. Award "to encourage writing of humour by Canadians." Annual competition for short stories, novels and story collections. Award: Stephen Leacock (silver) medal for humour and Manulife Bank of Canada cash award of $5,000 (Canadian). Receives 25-40 entries. Five judges selected across Canada. Entry fee $25 (Canadian). Guidelines for SASE. Deadline December 30. Submissions should have been published in the previous year. Open to Canadian citizens or landed immigrants only.

LETRAS DE ORO SPANISH LITERARY PRIZES, (I, IV), The Graduate School of International Studies, University of Miami, P.O. Box 248123, Coral Gables FL 33124. (305)284-3266. Director: Joaquin-Roy. "The *Letras de Oro* Spanish Literary Prizes were created in order to reward creative excellence in the Spanish language and to promote Spanish literary production in this country. *Letras de Oro* also serves to recognize the importance of Hispanic culture in the United States." Annual award for novels, story collections, drama, essays and poetry. The prizes are $2,500 cash and book publication in the *Letras de Oro* literary collection. Competition receives approx. 325 submissions. Deadline October 12.

LINES IN THE SAND SHORT FICTION CONTEST, Le Sand Publications, 1252 Terra Nova Blvd., Pacifica CA 94044-4340. (415)355-9069. Associate Editor: Barbara J. Less. "To encourage the writing of good short fiction, any genre." Annual competition for short stories. Award: $50, $25, or $10 and publication in *Lines in the Sand*. January/February awards edition. Honorable mentions will be published as space allows. Competition receives approx. 80 submissions. Judges: the editors. Entry fee $5. Guidelines for SASE. Deadline October 31. Previously published or unpublished submissions. Word length: 2,000 words maximum.

‡LITERATURE AND BELIEF WRITING CONTEST, (I, IV), Center for the Study of Christian Values in Literature, 3076-E JKHB, Brigham Young University, Provo UT 84602. (801)378-3073. Director: Richard H. Cracroft. Award to "encourage affirmative literature in the Judeo-Christian tradition." Annual competition for short stories. Award $150 (1st place); $100 (2nd place). Competition receives 200-300 entries. Judges: BYU faculty. Guidelines for SASE. Deadline May 15. Unpublished submissions, up to 30 pages. All winning entries are considered for publication in the annual journal *Literature and Belief*.

LOFT-MCKNIGHT WRITERS AWARDS, (I, IV), The Loft, Pratt Community Center, 66 Malcolm Ave. SE, Minneapolis MN 55414. (612)379-8999. Program Coordinator: Debbie Pope. "To give Minnesota writers of demonstrated ability an opportunity to work for a concentrated period of time on their writing." Annual awards of $7,500; 3 in poetry and 5 in creative prose; 2 awards of distinction of $10,500. Competition receives approx. 525 submissions/year. Judges are from out-of-state. Entry forms or rules for SASE. Deadline November. "Applicants must be Minnesota residents and must send for and observe guidelines."

LONG FICTION CONTEST, (I), White Eagle Coffee Store Press, P.O. Box 383, Fox River Grove IL 60021-0383. (708)639-9200. Contact: Publisher. To promote and support the long fiction form. Annual award for short stories. Winning story receives A.E. Coppard Award—publication as chapbook plus $200, 25 contributor's copies; 40 additional copies sent to book publishers/agents and 10 press kits. Entry fee $10. SASE for best results. Deadline December 15. Accepts previously unpublished submissions, but previous publication of small parts with acknowledgements is okay. Simultaneous submissions okay. No limits on style or subject matter. Length: 8,000-14,000 words (30-50 pages double spaced) single story; may have multiparts or be a self-contained novel segment. Send cover with title, name, address, phone; second title page with title only. Submissions are not returned; they are recycled.

LOS ANGELES TIMES BOOK PRIZES, (III), *L.A. Times*, Times Mirror Square, Los Angeles CA 90053. Contact: Jack Miles, director. Annual award. "To recognize finest books published each year." For books published between August 1 and July 31. Award: $1,000 cash prize. Entry is by nomination. Juries appointed by the *Times*. No entry fee.

LOUISIANA LITERARY AWARD, (II, IV), Louisiana Library Association (LLA), PO Box 3058, Baton Rouge LA 70821. (504)342-4928. Contact: Chair, Louisiana Literary Award Committee. Annual award "to promote interest in books related to Louisiana and to encourage their production." Submissions must have been published during the calendar year prior to presentation of the award (the award is presented in March or April). Award: Bronze medallion and $250. No entry fee. Books must be published by December 31 to be eligible. "All Louisiana-related books which committee members can locate are considered, whether submitted or not. Interested parties may correspond with the committee chair at the address above. All books considered *must* be on subject(s) related to Louisiana or be written by a Louisiana author. Each year, there may be a fiction *and/or* nonfiction award. Most often, however, there is only one award recipient."

‡LSU/SOUTHERN REVIEW SHORT FICTION AWARD (I), *The Southern Review*, 43 Allen Hall, LSU, Baton Rouge LA 70803. (504)388-5108. Fax: (504)388-5098. Contact: Michael Griffith. Award "to recognize the best first collection of short stories published in the U.S. in the past year." Annual competition for story collections. Award: $500. Competition receives approx. 35-40 submissions. Judges: A committee of 4 faculty members at LSU. Guidelines for SASE. Submissions must have been published between January 1, 1995 and December 31, 1995. Only books published in the U.S.

‡MARY MCCARTHY PRIZE IN SHORT FICTION, (I, IV), Sarabande Books, Inc., P.O. Box 4999, Louisville KY 40204. Editor-in-Chief: Sarah Gorham. "To award publication and $2,000 to an outstanding collection of short stories or novellas or single novella of 150-300 pages." Annual competition for story collections. Award: $2,000 and publication. Competition receives approx. 700 submissions. Judge: Barry Hannah. Entry fee $15. Guidelines for SASE. Unpublished submissions. US citizens. Word length: 150-300 pages. "Writers must submit a required entry form and follow contest guildelines for ms submission. Writers must include a #10 SASE."

THE JOHN H. MCGINNIS MEMORIAL AWARD, (I), *Southwest Review*, Box 374, 307 Fondren Library West, Southern Methodist University, Dallas TX 75275. (214)768-1037. Contact: Elizabeth Mills, senior editor. Annual awards (fiction and nonfiction). Stories or essays must have been published in the *Southwest Review* prior to the announcement of the award. Awards: $1,000. Pieces are not submitted directly for the award, but simply for publication in the magazine.

JENNY MCKEAN MOORE WRITER IN WASHINGTON, (II), Jenny McKean Moore Fund & The George Washington University, Dept. of English, George Washington University, Washington DC 20052. (202)994-6180. Fax: (202)994-7915. Associate Professor of English: Faye Moskowitz. Annual award "of a teaching residency for a different genre each year." Award: $40,000 and an "attractive benefits package." Receives approx. 90-100 applications. Judges: George Washington University English faculty and members of the J.M. Moore Fund. Guidelines for SASE. Deadline November 15. Previously published submissions.

THE ENID MCLEOD LITERARY PRIZE, (II, IV), Franco-British Society, Room 623, Linen Hall, 162-168 Regent St., London W1R 5TB England. Executive Secretary: Mrs. Marian Clarke. "To recognize the work of the author published in the UK which in the opinion of the judges has contributed most to Franco-British understanding." Annual competition for short stories, novels and story collections. Award: Monetary sum. Competition receives approx. 6-12 submissions. Judges: The Marquis of Lansdowne (FBS President), Martyn Goff and Professor Douglas Johnson. Guidelines for SASE. Deadline December 31. Previously published submissions. "Writers, or their publishers, may submit 4 copies to the London Office. No nominations are necessary."

MAGGIE AWARD, (I, IV), Georgia Romance Writers, Inc., P.O. Box 142, Acworth GA 30101. (404)974-6678. Contact: Marian Oaks. "To encourage and instruct unpublished writers in the romance genre." Annual competition for novels. Award: Silver pendant (1st place), certificates (2nd-4th). 4 categories—short contemporary romance, long contemporary romance, historical romance, mainstream. Judges: Published romance authors. Entry fee $25. Guidelines for SASE. Deadline is on or about May 1 (deadline not yet final).

Unpublished submissions. Writers must be members of Romance Writers of America. Entries consist of 3 chapters plus synopsis.

‡*MAGIC-REALISM MAGAZINE* SHORT-FICTION AWARD, (II), Magic Realism/Pyx Press, P.O. Box 922648, Sylmar CA 91392-2648. Editor and Publisher: C. Darren Butler. Annual short story competition "to honor original works of magic realism in English published in the previous year." Author receives $25 and chapbook publication; publisher also receives $25. Judges: the editors of *Magic Realism*. Guidelines for SASE. Deadline February 15. Previously published submissions. Published entries must have appeared in print between January and December of previous year. Reprint rights must be available. Length: 20,000 words maximum.

‡MALICE DOMESTIC GRANT, (I, IV), Malice Domestic Bookstore, 27 W. Washington St., Hagerstown MD 21740. (301)797-8896. Fax (301)797-9453. Grants Chair: Paul Reed. Given "to encourage unpublished writers in their pursuit—grant may be used to offset registration, travel or other expenses relating to attending writers' conferences, etc., within one year of award." Annual competition for novels and nonfiction. Award: $500. Competition receives 8-10 submissions. Judges: the Malice Domestic Board. Guidelines for SASE. Unpublished submissions. "Our genre is loosely translated as mystery stories of the Agatha Christie type, that is 'mysteries of manners.' These works usually feature amateur detective characters who know each other. No excessive gore or violence." Submit plot synopsis and 3 chapters of work in progress. Include resume, a letter of reference from someone familiar with your work, a typed letter of application explaining qualifications for the grant, and the workshop/conference to be attended or the research to be funded.

❤MANITOBA ARTS COUNCIL SUPPORT TO INDIVIDUAL ARTISTS, (II, IV), Manitoba Arts Council, 525-93 Lombard Ave., Winnipeg, Manitoba R3B 3B1 Canada. (204)945-2237. Grants "to encourage and support Manitoba writers." Five awards: Major Arts Grant ($25,000 Canadian) for writers of national or international reputation. Writers Grants "A" ($10,000 Canadian) for writers who have published 2 books or had a full-length script produced. Writers Grants "B" for writers who have published a book. Writers Grants "C" for writers with modest publication history, research and travel. Deadlines: April 15 and September 15. Open only to Manitoba writers.

‡MARIN ARTS COUNCIL INDIVIDUAL ARTIST GRANTS, (I, II, IV), 251 N. San Pedro Rd., San Rafael CA 94903. (415)499-8350. Fax: (415)499-8537. Grants Coordinator: Beky Carter. "For Marin County residents only. Award to provide unrestricted grants of $5,000 to individual artists in a variety of media." Every other year competition for short stories, novels, plays, screenplays. Award: $5,000. Competition receives approx. 15-90 submissions. Judges: Professionals in the field. Guidelines for SASE. Previously published submissions and unpublished submissions. Marin County residents only.

THE MARTEN BEQUEST AWARD, (I, IV), Arts Management Pty. Ltd., 180 Goulburn St., Darlinghurst NSW 2010 Australia. Awards Coordinator: Aimee Said. "For the furtherance of culture and the advancement of education in Australia by means of the provision of travelling scholarships as numerous as income will permit, to be awarded entrants who have been born in Australia, and awarded to candidates of either sex between the ages of 21 years and 35 years, who shall be adjudged of outstanding ability and promise." Award granted to writers every 2 years (next in 1996). Competition for writers of short stories, novels and story collections. Award: AUS $15,000 payable in two installments of $7,500 per annum. Guidelines for SASE. Deadline Oct. 31.

WALTER RUMSEY MARVIN GRANT, (I, IV), Ohioana Library Association, 65 S. Front St., Room 1105, Columbus OH 43215. (614)466-3831. Contact: Linda Hengst. "To encourage young unpublished writers (under age 30)." Biennial competition for short stories. Award: $1,000. Guidelines for SASE. Deadline January 31. Open to unpublished authors born in Ohio or who have lived in Ohio for a minimum of five years. Must be under 30 years of age. Up to six pieces of prose may be submitted; maximum 60 pages, minimum 10 pages.

MASSACHUSETTS CULTURAL COUNCIL ARTIST GRANTS, (IV), 120 Boylston St., 2nd Floor, Boston MA 02116. (617)727-3668. Fax: (617)727-0044. Program Coordinator: Richard Barreto. "The Artist Grants Program provides direct support to artists in recognition of exceptional work." Biennial competition for short stories and novels. Grant: $7,500. "In fiscal year 1994, we received 156 applications; 3 awards were granted. The number of awards is dependent on panel recommendations." The judges are people actively involved in the literary world. Guidelines for SASE. Previously published or unpublished submissions. This award is only available to writers who have been residents of Massachusetts for at least three years, who are 18 years or older, and who are not enrolled in a related degree-granting program.

MASTERS LITERARY AWARD, (I), Center Press, Box 16452, Encino CA 91416-6452. "One yearly Grand Prize of $1,000, and four quarterly awards of "Honorable Mention" each in either 1) fiction; 2) poetry and song lyrics; 3) nonfiction." Judges: Three anonymous literary professionals. Entry fee $10. Awards are given on March 15, June 15, September 15 and December 15. Any submission received prior to an award date is eligible for the subsequent award. Submissions accepted throughout the year. Fiction and nonfiction must be no more than 20 pages (5,000 words); poetry no more than 150 lines. All entries must be in the English language. #10 SASE required for guidelines.

‡**THE MENTOR AWARD, (IV)**, *Mentor Magazine*, P.O. Box 4382, Overland Park KS 66204. (913)362-7889. Editor: Maureen Waters. "The Mentor Award is given for supporting and promoting the art and practice of mentoring through the written word, and thereby helping to create a new sense of community." Quarterly and annually: Grand Prize ($100) will be awarded each January to the 1 best submission from all quarterly first-prize winners in all categories from the previous year. Competition for short stories (1,000-3,000 words); essay (700-1,500 words); feature article (1,500-3,000 words); interview (1,000-3,000 words); book review (500-1,000 words); and movie review (500-1,000 words). Entry fee $5. Guidelines for SASE. Deadlines for quarterly competitions: March 31, June 30, September 30, December 31. Previously published and unpublished submissions. Submissions must be about "a mentor or a mentoring relationship."

❧**THE VICKY METCALF BODY OF WORK AWARD, (II, IV)**, Canadian Authors Association, 27 Doxsee Ave. N., Campbellford, Ontario K0L 1L0 Canada. (705)653-0323. Fax: (705)653-0593. President: Cora Taylor. Annual award. "The prize is given solely to stimulate writing for children, written by Canadians, for a *number* of strictly children's books—fiction, nonfiction or even picture books. No set formula." To be considered, a writer must have published at least 4 books. Award: $10,000 for a body of work inspirational to Canadian youth. Deadline December 31. No entry fee. "Nominations may be made by any individual or association by letter *in triplicate* listing the published works of the nominee and providing biographical information. The books are usually considered in regard to their inspirational value for children. Entry forms or rules for SASE."

❧**VICKY METCALF SHORT STORY AWARD, (II, IV)**, Canadian Authors Association, 27 Doxsee Ave. N., Campbellford, Ontario K0L 1L0 Canada. (705)653-0323. Fax: (705)653-0593. President: Cora Taylor. "To encourage Canadian writing for children (open only to Canadian citizens)." Submissions must have been published during previous calendar year in Canadian children's magazine or anthology. Award: $3,000 (Canadian). Award of $1,000 to editor of winning story if published in a Canadian journal or anthology. No entry fee. Entry forms or rules for #10 SASE. Deadline December 15. Looking for "stories with originality, literary quality for ages 7-17."

‡**MICHIGAN AUTHOR AWARD, (II, IV)**, Michigan Library Association/Michigan Center for the Book, 6810 S. Cedar, Suite 6, Lansing MI 48911. (517)694-6615. Fax: (517)694-4330. Executive Director: Marianne Hartzell. "Award to recognize an outstanding published body of fiction, nonfiction, poetry and/or playscript, by a Michigan author." Annual competition for short stories, novels, story collections. Award: $1,000. Competition receives approx. 30 submissions. Judges: Panel members represent a broad spectrum of expertise in writing, publishing and book collecting. Guidelines for SASE. Previously published submissions. Michigan authors only. "Nominee must have three published works."

MIDLAND AUTHORS' AWARD, (II, IV), Society of Midland Authors, P.O. Box 10419, Fort Dearborn Station, Chicago IL 60610. "To honor outstanding books published during the previous year by Midwestern authors and professionally produced plays." Award: Monetary sum and plaque. Competition receives approximately 400-500 book and play submissions. Judges are librarians, book reviewers, radio network program reviewers, bookstore executives and university faculty members. Entry forms or rules for SASE. Authors must be residents of Illinois, Indiana, Iowa, Kansas, Michigan, Minnesota, Missouri, Nebraska, Ohio, South Dakota, North Dakota or Wisconsin. Send for entry form.

MID-LIST PRESS FIRST SERIES AWARD FOR SHORT FICTION, (I, II), Mid-List Press, 4324-12th Ave. South, Minneapolis MN 55407-3218. (612)822-3733. Senior Editor: Lane Stiles. To encourage and nurture short fiction writers who have never published a collection of fiction. Annual competition for fiction collections. Award: $1,000 advance and publication. Judges: manuscript readers and the editors of Mid-List Press. Entry fee $10. Deadline July 1. Previously published or unpublished submissions. Word length: 50,000 words minimum. "Application forms and guidelines are available after September 1 for a #10 SASE."

MID-LIST PRESS FIRST SERIES AWARD FOR THE NOVEL , (I), Mid-List Press, 4324-12th Ave. South, Minneapolis MN 55407-3218. (612)822-3733. Senior Editor: Lane Stiles. To encourage and nurture first-time novelists. Annual competition for novels. Award: $1,000 advance and publication. Competition receives approx. 400-500 submissions. Judges: manuscript readers and the editors of Mid-List Press. Entry fee $10. Deadline February 1. Unpublished submissions. Word length: minimum 50,000 words. "Application forms and guidelines are available after September 1 for a #10 SASE."

MILKWEED EDITIONS NATIONAL FICTION PRIZE, (II), Milkweed Editions, 430 First Ave. N., Suite 400, Minneapolis MN 55401. (612)332-3192. Publisher: Emilie Buchwald. Annual award for a novel, a short story collection, one or more novellas, or a combination of short stories and novellas. The prize will be awarded to the best work of fiction that Milkweed accepts for publication during each calendar year by a writer not previously published by Milkweed Editions. The winner will receive $2,000 cash over and above any payment agreed upon at the time of acceptance. Must request guidelines; send SASE. There is no deadline. Judged by Milkweed Editions. "Please look at previous winners: *Confidence of the Heart*, by David Schweidel; *Montana 1948*, by Larry Watson; *Aquaboogie*, by Susan Straight; and *Larabi's Ox*, by Tony Ardizzone—this is the caliber of fiction we are searching for. Catalog available for $1.50 postage, if people need a sense of our list."

MILKWEED EDITIONS PRIZE FOR CHILDREN'S LITERATURE, (II), Milkweed Editions, 430 First Ave. N., Suite 400, Minneapolis MN 55401. (612)332-3192. Publisher: Emilie Buchwald. "Our goal is to encourage writers to create books for the important age range of middle readers." Annual award for novels and biographies for children ages 8 to 12. The prize will be awarded to the best work for children ages 8 to 12 that Milkweed accepts for publication during each calendar year by a writer not previously published by Milkweed. The winner will receive $2,000 cash over and above any advances, royalties, or other payment agreed upon at the time of acceptance. There is no deadline. Judges: Milkweed Editions. Guidelines for SASE. Unpublished in book form. Page length: 110-350 pages.

THE MILNER AWARD, (III, IV), Friends of the Atlanta-Fulton Public Library, 1 Margaret Mitchell Square, Atlanta GA 30303. (404)730-1710. Susie Click, Milner chair. Award to a living American author of children's books. Annual competition for authors of children's books. Award: $1,000 honorarium and specially commissioned glass sculpture by Hans Frabel. Judges: Children of Atlanta vote during children's book week. Prior winners not eligible. Children vote at will—no list from which to select. Winner must be able to appear personally in Atlanta to receive the award at a formal program.

MIND BOOK OF THE YEAR—THE ALLEN LANE AWARD, (II, IV), MIND, Granta House, 15-19 Broadway, London E15 4BQ Great Britain. Contact: Ms. A. Brackx. "To award a prize to the work of fiction or nonfiction which outstandingly furthers public understanding of the causes, experience or treatment of mental health problems." Annual competition for novels and works of nonfiction. Award: £1,000. Competition receives approximately 50-100 submissions. Judges: A panel drawn from MIND's Council of Management. Deadline: December. Previously published submissions. Author's nomination is accepted. All books must be published in English in the UK.

MINNESOTA VOICES PROJECT, (IV), New Rivers Press, 420 N. Fifth St., #910, Minneapolis MN 55401. (612)339-7114. Contact: C.W. Truesdale, editor/publisher. Annual award "to foster and encourage new and emerging regional writers of short fiction, novellas, personal essays and poetry." Requires entry form. Awards: $500 to each author published in the series plus "a generous royalty agreement if book goes into second printing." No entry fee. Send request with SASE for guidelines in October. Deadline: April 1. Restricted to new and emerging writers from Minnesota, Wisconsin, North and South Dakota and Iowa.

MISSISSIPPI ARTS COMMISSION ARTIST FELLOWSHIP GRANT, (I, IV), 239 N. Lamar St., Suite 207, Jackson MS 39201. (601)359-6030. Contact: Program Administrator. "To support the creation of new work and recognize the contributions made by artists of exceptional talent to Mississippi's culture. Awards are based on mastery of artistic discipline and originality of prior art work; and evidence that new work of significant value and originality be produced during the grant period." Award granted every 2 years on a rotating basis. Award for writers of short stories, novels and story collections. Grant: $5,000. Judges: Peer panel. Guidelines for SASE. "The next available grants for creative writing, including fiction, nonfiction and poetry will be in 1997-98." Deadline: March 1. Applicants must be Mississippi residents. The Mississippi Arts Commission's Art in Education Program contains a creative writing component. For more information, contact the AIE Coordinator. The Mississippi Touring Arts program offers writers the opportunity to give readings and workshops. For more information, contact the Program Administrator.

THE MISSOURI REVIEW EDITORS' PRIZE CONTEST, 1507 Hillcrest Hall, Columbia MO 65211. (314)882-4474. Annual competition for short stories, poetry and essays. Award: Cash and publication in *The Missouri Review*. Competition receives approximately 1,200 submissions. Judges: *The Missouri Review* staff. Page restrictions: 25 typed, double-spaced, for fiction and essays, 10 for poetry. Entry fee $15 for each entry

Market conditions are constantly changing! If you're still using this book and it is 1997 or later, buy the newest edition of Novel & Short Story Writer's Market *at your favorite bookstore or order from* Writer's Digest Books.

(checks payable to The Missouri Review). Each fee entitles entrant to a one-year subscription to MR, an extension of a current subscription, or a gift. Outside of envelope should be marked "Fiction," "Essay," or "Poetry." Enclose an index card with author's name, address, and telephone number in the left corner and, for fiction and essay entries only, the work's title in the center. Entries must be previously unpublished and will not be returned. Enclose SASE for notification of winners. No further guidelines necessary.

♣**MR. CHRISTIE'S BOOK AWARD, (II, IV)**, Christie Brown & Co., 2150 Lakeshore Blvd. W., Toronto, Ontario M8V 1A3 Canada. (416)503-6050. Fax: (416)503-6010. Program Coordinator: Marlene Yustin. Award to "honor excellence in the writing and illustration of Canadian children's literature and to encourage the development and publishing of high quality children's books." Annual competition for short stories and novels. Award: Six awards of $7,500 (Canadian) each given in 3 categories to works published in English and French. Competition receives approx. 300 submissions. Judges: Two judging panels, one English and one French. Guidelines for SASE. Submissions must published within the year prior to the award ceremony. The author/illustrator must be a Canadian resident. A Canadian is defined as a person having Canadian citizenship or having landed immigrant status at the time of his/her book's publication. Books will be judged based on their ability to: inspire the imagination of the reader; recognize the importance of play; represent the highest standard of integrity; bring delight and edification; help children understand the world both intellectually and emotionally.

MONEY FOR WOMEN, Money for Woman/Barbara Deming Memorial Fund, Inc., Box 40-1043, Brooklyn NY 11240-1043. "Small grants to individual feminists in the arts." Biannual competition. Award: $200-1,000. Competition receives approximately 200 submissions. Judges: Board of Directors. Guidelines for SASE. Deadline December 31, June 30. Limited to U.S. and Canadian citizens. Word length: 6-25 pages. May submit own fiction. "Only for feminists in the arts. Subject matter must be feminist-related. Fund includes two additional awards: the Gerty, Gerty, Gerty in the Arts, Arts Arts award for works by lesbians and The Fanny Lou Hamer Award for work which combats racism and celebrates women of color."

MONTANA ARTS COUNCIL FIRST BOOK AWARD, (IV), 316 N. Park Ave., Room 252, Helena MT 59620. (406)444-6430. Director of Artist Services-Programs: Fran Morrow. Biennial award for publication of a book of poetry or fiction—the best work in Montana. Submissions may be short stories, novellas, story collections or poetry. Award: Publication. Competition receives about 35 submissions/year. Judges are professional writers. Entry forms or rules for SASE. Deadline is early April (1996). Restricted to residents of Montana; not open to degree-seeking students.

MONTANA ARTS COUNCIL INDIVIDUAL ARTIST FELLOWSHIP, (IV), 316 N. Park Ave., Room 252, Helena MT 59620. (406)444-6430. Director of Artist Services-Programs: Fran Morrow. Annual award of $2,000. Competition receives about 80-200 submissions/year. Panelists are professional artists. Contest requirements available for SASE. Deadline spring 1996. Restricted to residents of Montana; not open to degree-seeking students.

‡**MONTANA BOOK AWARDS, (III, IV)**, (formerly Wattie Book Award), Montana Wines Ltd., Book Publishers Association of New Zealand (BPANZ), Box 10127, Northshore Mail Centre, Auckland, New Zealand. Contact: Tony Hawkins, BPANZ, Committee. "To recognize excellence in writing and publishing books by New Zealanders. This is not a category award. Fiction/nonfiction/children's etc. are all included." Award: 1st: NZ$20,000; 2nd: NZ$10,000; 3rd: NZ$5,000. Competition receives approx. 90-100 submissions. Judges: Panel of 3 selected annually by the BPANZ—1 writer, 1 book trade person and 1 other. Entry fee NZ$100. Guidelines for SASE. Deadline April 5. "Writer must be New Zealander or resident of New Zealand and its former Pacific territories. Must be submitted by publisher. Fuller details available from BPANZ."

‡♣**L.M. MONTGOMERY PEI CHILDREN'S LITERATURE AWARD, (I, IV)**, Lucy Maud Montgomery Memorial, The Bookmark, Friends of the Confederation Centre/PEI Council of the Arts, 115 Richmond St., Charlottetown, P.E.I., C1A 1H7 Canada. (902)368-4410. Fax: (902)368-4418. "Awarded by Island Literary Awards to the author of a manuscript written for children within the age range of 5-12." Annual competition for children's stories. Award: $500 (first prize); $200 (second prize); $100 (third prize). Entry fee $6. Deadline February 15. Unpublished submissions. "Open to authors who have been Island residents for six of the last twelve months." Page length: maximum 60 pages. "Must be original and unpublished, submitted with name and address on separate cover sheet for anonymous judging. Entry should be typed, double spaced, one side page only. Work may not have won any other prize competition. SASE will ensure return of manuscript."

‡**"MY FAVORITE HOLIDAY STORY" COMPETITION, (I)**, Fortney Publishing, P.O. Box 1564, Centreville VA 22020. (703)612-5501. Contact: Daniel R. Fortney. "Fortney Publishing's mission is to generate profitable markets for writers." Annual competition for short stories. Awards: $500, $250, $125, $75, $50. "In addition, the authors of the top 40 stories will be offered a royalty contract for publication in the book, *My Favorite Holiday Stories*." Entry fee $7. Guidelines for SASE. Deadline November 15. Unpublished submissions.

Word length: 500-5,000 words. "Holidays can be real or fictitious. All entries will be judged on originality and creativity demonstrating the true spirit of holiday celebrations."

‡MYSTERY MAYHEM CONTEST, (I), *Mystery Time*/Hutton Publications, P.O. Box 2907, Decatur IL 62524. Editor: Linda Hutton. Award "to encourage writers to have fun writing a mystery spoof." Annual competition for short stories. Award: $10 cash and publication in *Mystery Time*. Competition receives approx. 90-100 submissions. Judge: Linda Hutton, editor of *Mystery Time*. Guidelines for SASE. Deadline September 15 annually. Unpublished submissions. Word length: Must be one sentence of any length. "One entry per person, of one sentence which can be any length, which is the opening of a mystery spoof. Must include SASE. Entry form not required."

‡NATIONAL BOOK COUNCIL/BANJO AWARDS, (III, IV), National Book Council, 21 Drummond Place, Suite 3, Carlton, Victoria 3053 Australia. "For a book of highest literary merit which makes an outstanding contribution to Australian literature." Annual competition for creative writing. Award: $20,000 each for a work of fiction and nonfiction. Competition receives approx. 100-140 submissions. Judges: 4 judges chosen by the National Book Council. Entry fee $65. Guidelines for SASE. Deadline March 20. Previously published submissions. For works "written by Australian citizens or permanent residents and first published in Australia during the qualifying period." Books must be nominated by the publisher.

‡NATIONAL BOOK FOUNDATION, INC., (III), 260 Fifth Ave., Room 904, New York NY 10001. (212)685-0261. Executive Director: Neil Baldwin. Program Officer: Margaret Kearney. Program Associate: Ken LaFollette. Annual award to honor distinguished literary achievement in 3 categories: nonfiction, fiction and poetry. Books published December 1 through November 30 are eligible. Award: $10,000 to each winner; $1,000 to 4 runners-up in each category. Awards judged by panels of critics and writers. Entry fee $100 per title. Deadline July 15. November ceremony. Selections are submitted by publishers only, or may be called in by judges. Read *Publishers Weekly* for additional information.

‡❦THE NATIONAL CHAPTER OF CANADA IODE VIOLET DOWNEY BOOK AWARD, (I, IV), The National Chapter of Canada IODE, 254-40 Orchard View Blvd., Toronto, Ontario M4R 1B9 Canada. (416)487-4416. Fax: (416)487-4417. Chairman, Book Award Committee: Marty Dalton. "The award is given to a Canadian author for an English language book suitable for children 13 years of age and under, published in Canada during the previous calendar year. Fairy tales, anthologies and books adapted from another source are not eligible." Annual competition for novels, children's literature. Award: $3,000. Competition receives approx. 80-100 submissions. Judges: A six-member panel of judges including four National IODE officers and two non-members who are recognized specialists in the field of children's literature. Guidelines for SASE. Deadline January 31, 1996. Previously published January 1, 1995 and December 31, 1995. "The book must have been written by a Canadian citizen and must have been published in Canada during the calendar year." Word length: Must have at least 500 words of text preferably with Canadian content.

NATIONAL ENDOWMENT FOR THE ARTS CREATIVE WRITING FELLOWSHIP, (I), Literature Program, Room 722, Pennsylvania Ave. NW, Washington DC 20506. (202)682-5451. "The mission of the NEA is to foster the excellence, diversity and vitality of the arts in the United States, and to help broaden the availability and appreciation of such excellence, diversity and vitality." The purpose of the fellowship is to enable creative writers "to set aside time for writing, research or travel and generally to advance their careers." Competition open to fiction writers who have published a novel or novella, a collection of stories or at least 5 stories in 2 or more magazines since January 1, 1986. Annual award: $20,000. All mss are judged anonymously. Application and guidelines available upon request.

‡NATIONAL FEDERATION OF THE BLIND WRITER'S DIVISION FICTION CONTEST, (I), National Federation of the Blind Writer's Division, 2704 Beach Dr., Merrick NY 11566. (516)868-8718. Fax: (516)868-9076. First Vice President, Writer's Division: Lori Stayer. "To promote good writing for blind writers and Division members, blind or sighted." Annual competition for short stories. Award: $40, $25, $15. Entry fee $5/story. Guidelines for SASE. Deadline May 1, 1996 (contest opens 9/1/95). Unpublished submissions. "You don't have to be blind, but it helps. Story must be in English, and typed. SASE necessary." Critique on request, $5. Word length: 2,000 max.

NATIONAL FICTION COMPETITION, (I), FC2, Illinois State University, Campus Box 4241, Normal IL 61790-4241. (309)438-3025. Director: Curtis White. Award to "publish new authors in the experimental, avant-garde, post-modern genre." Annual competition for novels. Awards publication to winning ms. Competition receives 350 submissions. "Final judging done by a prose writer of national prominence." Entry fee $15. Guidelines available for SASE. Deadline: November 15. (Fliers are sent in August/September.) Unpublished submissions. Open to mss of the experimental, avant-garde, post-modern genres only. Word length: 400 double-spaced, typewritten pages maximum.

NATIONAL FOUNDATION FOR ADVANCEMENT IN THE ARTS, ARTS RECOGNITION AND TALENT SEARCH (ARTS), (I, IV), 800 Brickell Ave., #500, Miami FL 33131. (305)377-1140. President: William H.

Banchs. "To encourage 17- and 18-year-old writers and put them in touch with institutions which offer scholarships." Annual award for short stories, novels, "fiction, essay, poetry, scriptwriting." Awards: $3,000, $1,500, $1,000, $500, and $100. Judges: Nationally selected panel. Entry fee $25 before June 1, $35 until October 1. Guidelines for SASE. 17- and 18-year-old writers only. Applicants must be US citizens or permanent residents of the US.

NATIONAL JEWISH BOOK AWARDS, (II, IV), JWB Jewish Book Council, 45 E. 33rd St., New York NY 10016. Executive Director: Steve Dowling. Annual awards "to promote greater awareness of Jewish-American literary creativity." Previously published submissions in English only by a US or Canadian author/translator. Awards judged by authors/scholars. Award: $750 to the author/translator plus citation to publisher. Over 100 entries received for each award. Contest requirements available for SASE. Awards made in these categories: Autobiography/Memoir (autobiography or memoir of life of Jewish person); Children's Literature (children's book on Jewish theme); Children's Picture Book (author and illustrator of a picture book on Jewish theme); Fiction (fiction of Jewish interest); Yiddish Literature (book of literary merit in Yiddish language); also nonfiction awards in Jewish Thought, Jewish Education, Jewish History, the Holocaust, Israel, Scholarship, Sephardic Studies, Folklore/Anthropology and Visual Arts.

NATIONAL WRITERS ASSOCIATION ANNUAL NOVEL WRITING CONTEST, (I), National Writers Association, 1450 S. Havana, Suite 424, Aurora CO 80012. (303)751-7844. Contact: Sandy Whelchel, director. Annual award to "recognize and reward outstanding ability and to increase the opportunity for publication." Award: $500 first prize; $300 second prize; $100 third prize. Award judged by successful writers. Charges $35 entry fee. Judges evaluation sheets sent to each entry. Contest rules and entry forms available with SASE. Opens December 1. Deadline April 1. Unpublished submissions, any genre or category. Length: 20,000-100,000 words.

NATIONAL WRITERS ASSOCIATION ANNUAL SHORT STORY CONTEST, (I), National Writers Association, 1450 S. Havana, Suite 424, Aurora CO 80012. (303)751-7844. Contact: Sandy Whelchel, executive director. Annual award to encourage and recognize writing by freelancers in the short story field. Award: $200 first prize; $100 second prize; $50 third prize. Opens April 1. Charges $15 entry fee. Write for entry form and rule sheet. All entries must be postmarked by July 1. Evaluation sheets sent to each entrant if SASE provided. Unpublished submissions. Length: No more than 5,000 words.

THE NATIONAL WRITTEN & ILLUSTRATED BY ... AWARDS CONTEST FOR STUDENTS, (I, IV), Landmark Editions, Inc., P.O. Box 4469, Kansas City MO 64127. (816)241-4919. Contact: Nan Thatch. "Contest initiated to encourage students to write and illustrate original books and to inspire them to become published authors and illustrators." Annual competition. "Each student whose book is selected for publication will be offered a complete publishing contract. To insure that students benefit from the proceeds, royalties from the sale of their books will be placed in an individual trust fund, set up for each student by his or her parents or legal guardians, at a bank of their choice. Funds may be withdrawn when a student becomes of age, or withdrawn earlier (either in whole or in part) for educational purposes or in case of proof of specific needs due to unusual hardship. Reports of book sales and royalties will be sent to the student and the parents or guardians annually." Winners also receive an all-expense-paid trip to Kansas City to oversee final reproduction phases of their books. Books by students may be entered in one of three age categories: A—6 to 9 years old; B—10 to 13 years old; C—14 to 19 years old. Each book submitted must be both written and illustrated by the same student. "Any books that are written by one student and illustrated by another will be automatically disqualified." Book entries must be submitted by a teacher or librarian. Entry fee $1. For rules and guidelines, send a #10 SAE with 64¢ postage. Deadline May 1 of each year.

***NEGATIVE CAPABILITY* SHORT FICTION COMPETITION, (I, IV)**, *Negative Capability*, 62 Ridgelawn Dr. E., Mobile AL 36608. (205)343-6163. Contact: Sue Walker. "To promote and publish excellent fiction and to promote the ideals of human rights and dignity." Annual award for short stories. Award: $1,000 best story. Judge: Eugene Walter. Reading fee $10, "includes copy of journal publishing the award." Guidelines for SASE. Deadline December 15. Length: 1,500-4,500 words.

NEUSTADT INTERNATIONAL PRIZE FOR LITERATURE, (III), *World Literature Today*, 110 Monnet Hall, University of Oklahoma, Norman OK 73019-0375. Contact: Djelal Kadir, director. Biennial award to recognize distinguished and continuing achievement in fiction, poetry or drama. Awards: $40,000, an eagle feather cast in silver, an award certificate and a special issue of *WLT* devoted to the laureate. "We are looking for outstanding accomplishment in world literature. The Neustadt Prize is not open to application. Nominations are made only by members of the international jury, which changes for each award. Jury meetings are held in March of even-numbered years. Unsolicited manuscripts, whether published or unpublished, cannot be considered."

‡NEVADA STATE COUNCIL ON THE ARTS ARTISTS' FELLOWSHIPS, (I, IV), 602 N. Curry St., Carson City NV 89710. (702)687-6680. Fax: (702)687-6688. Director of Artists' Services: Sharon Rosse. Award "to honor individual artists and their artistic achievements to support artists' efforts in advancing their careers." Annual competition for fiction, nonfiction, poetry, playwriting. Award: $5,000 ($4,500 immediately, $500 after public service component completed). Competition receives approx. 12 submissions. Judges: Peer panels of professional artists. Guidelines available, no SASE required. Deadline August 15. "Only available to Nevada writers." Word length: 25 pages.

THE NEW ERA WRITING, ART, PHOTOGRAPHY AND MUSIC CONTEST, (I, IV), *New Era Magazine* (LDS Church), 50 E. North Temple, Salt Lake City UT 84150. (801)240-2951. Managing Editor: Richard M. Romney. "To encourage young Mormon writers and artists." Annual competition for short stories. Award: partial scholarship to Brigham Young University or Ricks College or cash awards. Competition receives approx. 300 submissions. Judges: *New Era* editors. Guidelines for SASE. Deadline December 31. Unpublished submissions. Contest open only to 12-23-year-old members of the Church of Jesus Christ of Latter-Day Saints.

NEW HAMPSHIRE STATE COUNCIL ON THE ARTS INDIVIDUAL ARTIST FELLOWSHIP, (I, II, IV), 40 N. Main St., Concord NH 03301-4974. (603)271-2789. Artist Services Coordinator: Audrey V. Sylvester. Fellowship "for career development to professional artists who are legal/permanent residents of the state of New Hampshire." Award: Up to $3,000. Competition gives 8 awards in disciplines such as crafts, literature, music, dance, etc. Judges: Panels of in-state and out-of-state experts review work samples. Guidelines for SASE. Postmark deadline July 1. Submissions may be either previously published or unpublished. Applicants must be over 18 years of age; not enrolled as fulltime students; permanent, legal residents of New Hampshire 1 year prior to application. Application form required.

NEW JERSEY STATE COUNCIL ON THE ARTS PROSE FELLOWSHIP, (I, IV), CN306, Trenton NJ 08625. (609)292-6130. Annual grants for writers of short stories, novels, story collections. Award: Maximum is $12,000; other awards are $5,000, $7,000 and $12,000. Judges: Peer panel. Guidelines for SASE. Deadline: December 15. For either previously published or unpublished submissions. "Previously published work must be submitted as a manuscript." Applicants must be New Jersey residents. Submit several copies of short fiction, short stories or prose not exceeding 15 pages and no less than 10 pages. For novels in progress, a synopsis and sample chapter should be submitted.

NEW LETTERS LITERARY AWARD, (I), UMKC, 5101 Rockhill Rd., Kansas City MO 64110-2499. (816)235-1168. Awards Coordinator: Glenda McCrary. Award to "discover and reward unpublished work by new and established writers." Annual competition for short stories. Award: $750 and publication. Competition receives 600 entries/year. Entry fee $10. Guidelines for SASE. Deadline May 15. Submissions must be unpublished. Length requirement: 5,000 words or less.

‡NEW VOICES IN POETRY AND PROSE SPRING AND FALL COMPETITION, (I), *New Voices in Poetry and Prose Magazine*, P.O. Box 52196, Shreveport LA 71135. (318)797-8243. Publisher: Cheryl White. "To recognize and publish a previously unpublished work of outstanding short fiction." Biannual award for short stories. Award: $50 (first place) and publication in *New Voices*. Competition receives approx. 50 submissions. Judges: Panel. Entry fee $10/short story. Guidelines for SASE. Deadlines April 30 and September 30. Unpublished submissions. "All writers welcome. There is no line limit, but as a general rule, works under 5,000 words are preferred."

NEW YORK FOUNDATION FOR THE ARTS FELLOWSHIP, (I, II, IV), New York Foundation for the Arts, 14th Floor, 155 Avenue of the Americas, New York NY 10013. Contact: Penelope Dannenberg. Biennial competition for short stories, plays, screenplays, nonfiction literature and novels. Approximately 15 awards of $7,000 each. Competition receives approximately 700 submissions. Judges: Fiction writers from New York State. Call for guidelines or send SASE. Manuscript sample (20 pp maximum) may be drawn from published or unpublished work. Applicants must be over 18; must have lived in New York state at least 2 years immediately prior to application deadline; and may not be currently enrolled in any degree program.

NEW YORK STATE EDITH WHARTON CITATION OF MERIT, (State Author), (III, IV), NYS Writers Institute, Humanities 355, University at Albany, Albany NY 12222. (518)442-5620. Associate Director: Donald Faulkner. Awarded biennially to honor a New York State fiction writer for a lifetime of works of distinction. Fiction writers living in New York State are nominated by an advisory panel. Recipients receive an honorarium of $10,000 and must give two public readings a year.

JOHN NEWBERY AWARD, (III, IV), American Library Association (ALA) Awards and Citations Program, Association for Library Service to Children, 50 E. Huron St., Chicago IL 60611. Executive Director: S. Roman. Annual award. Only books for children published in the US during the preceding year are eligible. Award: Medal. Entry restricted to US citizens-residents.

NFB WRITERS' FICTION CONTEST, (I), The Writers' Division of the National Federation of the Blind, 1203 Fairview Rd., Columbia MO 65203. (Send submission to: Loraine Stayer, 2704 Beach Dr., Merrick

NY 11566.) (314)445-6091. President: Tom Stevens. Award to "encourage members and other blind writers to write fiction." Annual competition for short stories. Three prizes of $40, $25, $15, plus two honorable mentions and possible publication in *Slate & Style*. Competition receives approx. 20 submissions. Entry fee $5 per story. For guidelines send SASE to Loraine Stayer at above address. Deadline May 1, 1996. Unpublished submissions. Word length: 2,000 words (maximum). "Send a 150 word bio with each entry. Please, no erotica."

THE NOMA AWARD FOR PUBLISHING IN AFRICA, (III, IV), % Hans Zell Associates, P.O. Box 56, Oxford OX1 2SJ England. Sponsored by Kodansha Ltd. Administered by *The African Book Publishing Record*. Award "to encourage publication of works by African writers and scholars in Africa, instead of abroad as is still too often the case at present." Annual competition for a new book in any of these categories: Scholarly or academic; books for children; literature and creative writing, including fiction, drama and poetry. Award: $5,000. Competition receives approximately 140 submissions. Judges: A committee of African scholars and book experts and representatives of the international book community. Chairman: Walter Bgoya. Guidelines for SASE. Previously published submissions. Submissions are through publishers only.

NORTH AMERICAN NATIVE AUTHORS FIRST BOOK AWARD, (I, II, IV), *The Greenfield Review* Literary Center, P.O. Box 308, Greenfield Center NY 12833. (518)584-1728. Fax: (518)583-9741. Editor: Joe Bruchac. "To recognize and encourage writing by Native American authors (American Indian)." Annual award for fiction. Award: $500 and recommendation of ms to a press (publication is *not* guaranteed). Competition receives 50-100 submissions. Judges: Anonymous. Guidelines for SASE. Deadline May 1. Published or unpublished (as a book) submissions. Native American authors only. Word length: prose mss no longer than 240 typed double-spaced pages.

NORTH CAROLINA ARTS COUNCIL FELLOWSHIP, (IV), 221 E. Lane St., Raleigh NC 27611. (919)733-2111. Literature Director: Deborah McGill. Grants program "to encourage the continued achievements of North Carolina's writers of fiction, poetry, literary nonfiction and literary translation." Annual award: Up to $8,000 each. Council receives approx. 200 submissions. Judges are a panel of editors and published writers from outside the state. Writers must be over 18 years old, not currently enrolled in degree-granting program, and must have been a resident of North Carolina for 1 full year prior to applying. Deadline February 1.

NORTH CAROLINA ARTS COUNCIL RESIDENCIES, (IV), 407 N. Person St., Raleigh NC 27601-2807. (919)733-7897. Literature Director: Deborah McGill. "To recognize and encourage North Carolina's finest creative writers." "We offer a two- to three-month residency at the LaNapoule Foundation in southern France every two years, an annual two- to three-month residency at the Headlands Center for the Arts (California), and an annual one-month residency at The MacDowell Colony (New Hampshire)." Judges: Editors and published writers from outside the state. Deadline for France, February 1, 1997; for US residencies, early June, 1996. Writers must be over 18 years old, not currently enrolled in degree-granting program on undergraduate or graduate level and *must have been a resident of North Carolina for 1 full year prior to applying*.

NORTH CAROLINA WRITERS' NETWORK SCHOLARSHIPS, (IV), P.O. Box 954, Carrboro NC 27510. Executive Director: Marsha Warren. "To provide North Carolina writers of fiction, poetry, and literary nonfiction (including children's literature) with opportunities for research or enrichment. Available on a minimum of three weeks' notice throughout the year." Award up to $500 (with $4,500 budgeted for the category). "To be eligible writers *must have lived in the state for at least a year*." Send SASE for application.

‡NORWEGIAN LITERATURE ABROAD GRANT (NORLA), (I), Bygdoy Allè 21, 0262 Oslo Norway. (47)22 43 48 70. Fax: (47)22 44 52 42. Manager: Kristin Brudevoll. Award to "help Norwegian fiction to be published outside Scandinavia and ensure that the tranlator will be paid for his/her work." Annual compensation for translations, 50-60% of the translation's cost. Receives approx. 40-50 submissions. Judges: an advisory (literary) board of 5 persons. Guidelines for SASE. Deadline December 15. Previously published submissions. "Application form can be obtained from NORLA. Foreign (non-Scandanavian) publishers may apply for the award."

THE FLANNERY O'CONNOR AWARD FOR SHORT FICTION, (I), The University of Georgia Press, 330 Research Dr., Athens GA 30602. (706)369-6140. Fax: (708)369-6131. Contact: Award coordinator. Annual award "to recognize outstanding collections of short fiction. Published and unpublished authors are welcome." Award: $1,000 and publication by the University of Georgia Press. Deadline June 1-July 31. "Manuscripts cannot be accepted at any other time." Entry fee $10. Contest rules for SASE. Ms will not be returned.

FRANK O'CONNOR FICTION AWARD, (I), *descant*, Dept. of English, Texas Christian University, Fort Worth TX 76129. (817)921-7240. Managing Editor: Claudia Knott. Estab. 1979 with *descant*; earlier awarded through *Quartet*. Annual award to honor achievement in short fiction. Submissions must be published in the magazine during its current volume. Award: $500 prize. No entry fee. "About 12 to 15 stories are published annually in *descant*. Winning story is selected from this group."

❤**HOWARD O'HAGAN AWARD FOR SHORT FICTION, (II, IV)**, Writers Guild of Alberta, 3rd Floor, Percy Page Centre, 11759 Groat Rd., Edmonton, Alberta T5M 3K6. (403)422-8174. Fax: (403)422-2663. Assistant Director: Darlene Diver. "To recognize outstanding books published by Alberta authors each year." Annual competition for short stories. Award: $500 (Canadian) cash and leather bound book. Competition receives approx. 20-30 submissions. Judges: selected published writers across Canada. Guidelines for SASE. Deadline December 31. Previously published submissions published between January and December 31. Open to Alberta authors only.

OHIOANA AWARD FOR CHILDREN'S LITERATURE, ALICE WOOD MEMORIAL, (IV), Ohioana Library Association, 65 S. Front St., Room 1105, Columbus OH 43215. (614)466-3831. Director: Linda Hengst. Competition "to honor an individual whose body of work has made, and continues to make, a significant contribution to literature for children or young adults." Annual award for body of work. Amount of award varies (approximately $500-1,000). Guidelines for SASE. Deadline December 31 prior to year award is given. "Open to authors born in Ohio or who have lived in Ohio for a minimum of five years."

OHIOANA BOOK AWARDS, (II, IV), Ohioana Library Association, 65 S. Front St., Room 1105, Columbus OH 43215. Contact: Linda R. Hengst, director. Annual awards granted (only if the judges believe a book of sufficiently high quality has been submitted) to bring recognition to outstanding books by Ohioans or about Ohio. Five categories: Fiction, Nonfiction, Juvenile, Poetry and About Ohio or an Ohioan. Criteria: Books written or edited by a native Ohioan or resident of the state for at least 5 years; two copies of the book MUST be received by the Ohioana Library by December 31 prior to the year the award is given; literary quality of the book must be outstanding. Awards: Certificate and glass sculpture (up to 6 awards given annually). Each spring a jury considers all books received since the previous jury. Award judged by a jury selected from librarians, book reviewers, writers and other knowledgeable people. No entry forms are needed, but they are available. "We will be glad to answer letters asking specific questions."

❤**THE OKANAGAN SHORT FICTION AWARD, (I, IV)**, *Canadian Author*, 27 Doxsee Ave. N., Campbellford, Ontario K0L 1L0 Canada. (705)653-0323. Fax: (705)653-0593. Contact: Bill Valgardson, fiction editor. Award offered 4 times a year. To present good fiction "in which the writing surpasses all else" to an appreciative literary readership, and in turn help Canadian writers retain an interest in good fiction. Award: $125 to each author whose story is accepted for publication. Entries are invited in each issue of the quarterly *CA*. Sample copy for $5.50. "Our award regulations stipulate that writers must be Canadian, stories must not have been previously published, and be under 3,000 words. Mss should be typed double-spaced on 8½×11 bond. SASE with Canadian postage or mss will not be returned. Looking for superior writing ability, stories with good plot, movement, dialogue and characterization. A selection of winning stories has been anthologized as *Pure Fiction: The Okanagan Award Winners*, and is essential reading for prospective contributors."

OMMATION PRESS BOOK AWARD, (I, II), Ommation Press, 5548 N. Sawyer, Chicago IL 60625. (312)539-5745. Annual competition for short stories, novels, story collections and poetry. Award: Book publication, 100 copies of book. Competition receives approx. 60 submissions. Judge: Effie Mihopoulos, editor. Entry fee $15, includes copy of former award-winning book. Guidelines for SASE. Deadline December 30. Either previously published or unpublished submissions. Submit no more than 50 pages.

OOPS AWARD, (I, IV), Oops Foundation, P.O. Box 6606, Huntington Beach, CA 92615. (714)968-5162. Contact: Dr. Oops. Award to "motivate people to write science fiction and science fiction satire." Annual competition for short stories. Award: first prize: $25; second prize: $10. Competition receives approx. 100 submissions. Guidelines available for SASE. Deadline June 13. Unpublished submissions. Open to amateur writers with less than 3 published short stories and no published books. Word length: 600 words minimum; 3,000 words maximum. "All submissions must be science fiction satire or science fiction. Please, no dungeons and dragons, fantasy, horror, sword and sorcery, vampire or werewolf stories. They won't be accepted."

‡**OPEN VOICE AWARDS, (I)**, Westside YMCA—Writer's Voice, 5 W. 63rd St., New York NY 10023. (212)875-4124. Competition for fiction or poetry. Award: $500 honorarium and featured reading. Deadline December 31. "Submit 10 double-spaced pages in a single genre. Enclose $10 entry fee."

‡**OPUS MAGNUM DISCOVERY AWARDS, (I)**, C.C.S. Entertainment Group, 433 N. Camden Dr., #600, Beverly Hills CA 90210. (310)288-1881. Fax: (310)288-0257. President: Carlos Abreu. Award "to discover new unpublished manuscripts." Annual competition for novels. Award: Film rights options up to $10,000. Judges: Industry professionals. Entry fee $75. Deadline December 1 of each year. Unpublished submissions.

ORANGE BLOSSOM FICTION CONTEST, (I), *The Oak*, 1530 Seventh St., Rock Island IL 61201. (309)788-3980. Editor: Betty Mowery. "To build up circulation of publication and give new authors a chance for competition and publication along with seasoned writers." Award given every 6 months for short stories. Award: $10 (first prize); $5 (second prize); 1-year subscription to *The Oak* (third prize). Competition receives approx. 75 submissions. Judges: various editors from other publications, some published authors and previous contest winners. Entry fee $2. Guidelines for SASE. Deadline February 1. Word length: 500 words maximum. "May be on any subject, but avoid gore and killing of humans or animals."

DOBIE PAISANO FELLOWSHIPS, (IV), Office of Graduate Studies, University of Texas at Austin, Austin TX 78712. (512)471-7213. Coordinator: Audrey N. Slate. Annual fellowships for creative writing (includes short stories, novels and story collections). Award: 6 months residence at ranch; $7,200 stipend. Competition receives approximately 100 submissions. Judges: faculty of University of Texas and members of Texas Institute of Letters. Entry fee: $10. Application and guidelines on request. "Open to writers with a Texas connection—native Texans, people who have lived in Texas at least two years or writers with published work on Texas and Southwest." Deadline is the third week in January.

KENNETH PATCHEN COMPETITION, (I, II), Pig Iron Press, P.O. Box 237, Youngstown OH 44501. (216)747-6932. Contact: Jim Villani. Awards works of fiction and poetry in alternating years. Award: publication; $100; 50 copies. Judge with national visibility selected annually. Entry fee $10. Guidelines available for SASE. Reading period: January 1 to December 31. Award for fiction: 1996, 1998; fiction award for novel or short story collection, either form eligible. Previous publication of individual stories, poems or parts of novel OK. Ms should not exceed 500 typed pages.

PEARL SHORT STORY CONTEST, (I), *Pearl* Magazine, 3030 E. Second St., Long Beach CA 90803. (310)434-4523. Editor: Marilyn Johnson. Award to "provide a larger forum and help widen publishing opportunities for fiction writers in the small press; and to help support the continuing publication of *Pearl*." Annual competition for short stories. Award: $50, publication in *Pearl* and 10 copies. Competition receives approx. 100 submissions. Judges: Editors of *Pearl* (Marilyn Johnson, Joan Jobe Smith, Barbara Hauk). Entry fee $7 per story. Guidelines for SASE. Deadline December 1-March 15. Unpublished submissions. Length: 4,000 words maximum. Include a brief biographical note and SASE for reply or return of manuscript. Accepts simultaneous submissions, but asks to be notified if story is accepted elsewhere. All submissions are considered for publication in *Pearl*. "Although we are open to all types of fiction, we look most favorably upon coherent, well-crafted narratives, containing interesting, believable characters and meaningful situations."

JUDITH SIEGEL PEARSON AWARD, (I, IV), Wayne State University, Detroit MI 48202. Contact: Chair, English Dept. Competition "to honor writing about women." Annual award. Short stories up to 20 pages considered every third year (poetry and drama/nonfiction in alternate years). Award: Up to $400. Competition receives up to 100 submissions/year. Submissions are internally screened; then a noted writer does final reading. Entry forms for SASE.

WILLIAM PEDEN PRIZE IN FICTION, (I), *The Missouri Review*, 1507 Hillcrest Hall, University of Missouri, Columbia MO 65211. (314)882-4474. Contact: Speer Morgan, Greg Michalson, editors. Annual award "to honor the best short story published in *The Missouri Review* each year." Submissions are to be previously published in the volume year for which the prize is awarded. Award: $1,000. No entry deadline or fee. No rules; all fiction published in *MR* is automatically entered.

PEGASUS PRIZE, (III), Mobil Corporation, (Room 3C916), 3225 Gallows Rd., Fairfax VA 22037-0001. (703)846-2375. Contact: Director. To recognize distinguished works from literature not normally translated into English. Award for novels. "Prize is given on a country-by-country basis and does not involve submissions unless requested by national juries."

PEN CENTER USA WEST LITERARY AWARD IN FICTION, (II, IV), PEN Center USA West, 672 S. LaFayette Park Place, #41, Los Angeles CA 90057. (213)365-8500. Fax: (213)365-9616. Program Coordinator: Rachel Howzell. To recognize fiction writers who live in the western United States. Annual competition for novels and story collections. Award: $500, plaque, and honored at a ceremony in Los Angeles. Competition receives approximately 100-125 submissions. Judges: panel of writers, booksellers, editors. Guidelines for SASE. Previously published submissions published between January 1, 1995 and December 31, 1995. Open only to writers living west of the Mississippi.

PEN/BOOK-OF-THE-MONTH CLUB TRANSLATION PRIZE, (II, IV), PEN American Center, 568 Broadway, New York NY 10012. (212)334-1660, Awards Coordinator: John Morrone. Award "to recognize the art of the literary translator." Annual competition for translations. Award: $3,000. Deadline December 20. Previously published submissions within the calendar year. "Translators may be of any nationality, but book must have been published in the US and must be a book-length literary translation." Books may be submitted by publishers, agents or translators. No application form. Send three copies. "Early submissions are strongly recommended."

THE PEN/FAULKNER AWARD FOR FICTION, (II, III, IV), c/o The Folger Shakespeare Library, 201 E. Capitol St. SE, Washington DC 20003. (202)544-7077. Attention: Janice Delaney, PEN/Faulkner Foundation

Executive Director. Annual award. "To award the most distinguished book-length work of fiction published by an American writer." Award: $15,000 for winner; $5,000 for nominees. Judges: Three writers chosen by the Trustees of the Award. Deadline December 31. Published submissions only. Writers and publishers submit four copies of eligible titles published the current year. No juvenile. Authors must be American citizens.

PEN/NORMA KLEIN AWARD, (III), PEN American Center, 568 Broadway, New York NY 10012. (212)334-1660. Award Director: John Morrone. "Established in 1990 in memory of the late PEN member and distinguished children's book author, the biennial prize recognizes an emerging voice of literary merit among American writers of children's fiction. Candidates for the award are new authors whose books (for elementary school to young adult readers) demonstrate the adventuresome and innovative spirit that characterizes the best children's literature and Norma Klein's own work (but need not resemble her novels stylistically)." Award: $3,000. Judges: a panel of three distinguished children's authors. Guidelines for SASE. Previously published submissions. Writer must be nominated by other authors or editors of children's books. Next award: 1997.

PENNSYLVANIA COUNCIL ON THE ARTS, FELLOWSHIP PROGRAM, (I, IV), 216 Finance Bldg., Harrisburg PA 17101. (717)787-6883. Director, Literature and Theatre Programs: Marcia D. Salvatore. Award "to enable Pennsylvania creative writers of exceptional talent to set aside time to write." Biennial fellowships for fiction and poetry. Award: Up to $10,000. Competition receives approx. 300 submissions for 20 to 30 awards/year. Judges: Out-of-state jurors with credentials in the art form. Guidelines for SASE. Deadline August 1. Applicants must be Pennsylvania residents for 2 years preceding deadline. Word length: 6,250 words maximum (fiction); 10 pages maximum (poetry).

✿PENNY DREADFUL ANNUAL SHORT STORY CONTEST, (I), *sub-TERRAIN Magazine*, P.O. Box 1575, Bentall Center, Vancouver, British Columbia V6C 2P7 Canada. (604)876-8710. Fax: (604)879-2667. Contact: Brian Kaufman. "To inspire writers to get down to it and struggle with a form that is condensed and difficult. To encourage clean, powerful writing." Annual award for short stories. Prize: $200 and publication. Runners-up also receive publication. Competition receives about 300 submissions. Judges: An editorial collective. Entry fee $15 (includes 4-issue subscription). Guidelines for SASE in November. "Contest kicks off in November." Deadline May 15. Unpublished submissions. Length: 2,000 words maximum. "We are looking for work that is trying to do something unique/new in form or content. Radical as opposed to the standard short story format. Experiment, take risks."

JAMES D. PHELAN AWARD, (I, IV), Intersection for the Arts/The San Francisco Foundation, 446 Valencia St., San Francisco CA 94103. (415)626-2787. Literary Program Director: Charles Wilmoth. Annual award "to author of an unpublished work-in-progress of fiction (novel or short story), nonfictional prose, poetry or drama." Award: $2,000 and certificate. Rules and entry forms available after November 1 for SASE. Deadline January 31. Unpublished submissions. Applicant must have been born in the state of California, but need not be a current resident, and be 20-35 years old.

PLAYBOY COLLEGE FICTION CONTEST, (I, IV), *Playboy* Magazine, 680 N. Lake Shore Dr., Chicago IL 60611. (312)751-8000. Fiction Editor: Alice K. Turner. Award "to foster young writing talent." Annual competition for short stories. Award: $3,000 plus publication in the magazine. Judges: Staff. Guidelines available for SASE. Deadline: January 1. Submissions should be unpublished. No age limit; college affiliation required. Stories should be 25 pages or fewer. "Manuscripts are not returned. Results of the contest will be sent via SASE."

POCKETS FICTION WRITING CONTEST, (I), *Pockets Magazine*, Upper Room Publications, P.O. Box 189, Nashville TN 37202-0189. (615)340-7333. Fax: (615)340-7006. (Do not send submissions via fax.) Associate Editor: Lynn Gilliam. To "find new freelance writers for the magazine." Annual competition for short stories. Award: $1,000 and publication. Competition receives approx. 450 submissions. Judged by *Pockets* editors and editors of other Upper Room publications. Guidelines for SASE. Deadline August 15, 1996. Former winners may not enter. Unpublished submissions. Word length: 1,000-1,600 words. "No historical fiction."

EDGAR ALLAN POE AWARDS, (II, IV), Mystery Writers of America, Inc., 17 E. 47th St., Sixth Floor, New York NY 10017. Executive Director: Priscilla Ridgway. Annual awards to enhance the prestige of the mystery. For mystery works published or produced during the calendar year. Award: Ceramic bust of Poe. Awards for best mystery novel, best first novel by an American author, best softcover original novel, best short story, best critical/biographical work, best fact crime, best young adult, best juvenile novel, best screenplay, best television feature and best episode in a series. Contact above address for specifics. Deadline December 1.

KATHERINE ANNE PORTER PRIZE FOR FICTION, (I), *Nimrod*, Arts and Humanities Council of Tulsa, 2210 S. Main St., Tulsa OK 74114. (918)584-3333. Editor: Francine Ringold. "To award promising young writers and to increase the quality of manuscripts submitted to *Nimrod*." Annual award for short stories.

Award: $1,000 first prize, $500 second prize plus publication, two contributors copies and $5/page up to $25 total. Receives approx. 700 entries/year. Judge varies each year. Past judges: Ron Carlson, Rosellen Brown, Alison Lurie, Gordon Lish, George Garrett, Toby Olson, John Leonard and Gladys Swan. Entry fee: $15. Guidelines for #10 SASE. Deadline for submissions April 15. Previously unpublished manuscripts. Length: 7,500 words maximum. "Must be typed, double-spaced. Our contest is judged anonymously, so we ask that writers take their names off of their manuscripts (need 2 copies total). Include a cover sheet containing your name, full address, phone and the title of your work. Include a SASE for notification of the results. We encourage writers to read *Nimrod* before submission to discern whether or not their work is compatible with the style of our journal. Back awards issues are $6 (book rate postage included), current issue is $8."

PRAIRIE SCHOONER THE LAWRENCE FOUNDATION AWARD, (II), 201 Andrews Hall, University of Nebraska, Lincoln NE 68588-0334. (402)472-0911. Contact: Hilda Raz, editor. Annual award "given to the author of the best short story published in *Prairie Schooner* during the preceding year." Award: $1,000. "Only short fiction published in *Prairie Schooner* is eligible for consideration. Manuscripts are read September-May."

‡THE PRESIDIO LA BAHIA AWARD, (II, IV), The Sons of the Republic of Texas, 5942 Abrams Rd., #222, Dallas TX 75231. (214)343-2145. "To promote suitable preservation of relics, appropriate dissemination of data, and research into our Texas heritage, with particular attention to the Spanish Colonial period." Annual competition for novels. Award: "A total of $2,000 is available annually for winning participants, with a minimum first place prize of $1,200 for the best published book. At its discretion, the SRT may award a second place book prize or a prize for the best published paper, article published in a periodical or project of a nonliterary nature." Judges: recognized authorities on Texas history. Entries will be accepted from June 1 to September 30. Previously published submissions and completed projects. Competition is open to any person interested in the Spanish Colonial influence on Texas culture.

♣PRISM INTERNATIONAL SHORT FICTION CONTEST, (I), *Prism International*, Dept. of Creative Writing, University of British Columbia, E462-1866 Main Mall, Vancouver, British Columbia V6T 1Z1 Canada. (604)822-2514. E-mail address: prism@unixg.ubc.ca. Contact: Publicity Manager. Award: $2,000 first prize and five $200 consolation prizes. Deadline December 1 of each year. Entry fee $15 plus $5 reading fee for each story (includes a 1 year subscription). SASE for rules/entry forms.

♣PRIX LITTÉRAIRE CHAMPLAIN, (IV), Conseil De La Vie Francaise En Amérique, 56, Rue Saint-Pierre, 1, Le Étage, Quebec G1K 4A1 Canada. (418)692-1150. Fax: (418)692-4578. Director: Esther Taillon. Annual competition. Judges: jury. Guidelines for SASE. Deadline December 31. Previously published submissions. French-speaking Americans only.

PULITZER PRIZE IN FICTION, (III, IV), Columbia University, 702 Journalism Bldg., New York NY 10027. (212)854-3841. Annual award for distinguished short stories, novels and story collections *first* published in America in book form during the year by an American author, preferably dealing with American life. Award: $3,000 and certificate. Guidelines available for SASE. Deadline: Books published between January 1 and June 30 must be submitted by July 1. Books published between July 1 and December 31 must be submitted by November 1; books published between November 1 and December 31 must be submitted in galleys or page proofs by November 1. Submit 4 copies of the book, entry form, biography and photo of author and $20 handling fee. Open to American authors.

PUSHCART PRIZE, (III), Pushcart Press, P.O. Box 380, Wainscott NY 11975. (516)324-9300. President: Bill Henderson. Annual award "to publish and recognize the best of small press literary work." Previously published submissions, short stories, poetry or essays on any subject. Must have been published during the current calendar year. Award: Publication in *Pushcart Prize: Best of the Small Presses*. Deadline: December 1. Nomination by small press publishers/editors only.

♣QSPELL BOOK AWARDS/HUGH MCLENNAN FICTION AWARD, (II, IV), Quebec Society for the Promotion of English Language Literature, 1200 Atwater, Montreal, Quebec H3Z 1X4 Canada. Phone/fax: (514)933-0878. Secretary: Jeanne Randle. "To honor excellence in writing in English in Quebec." Annual competition for short stories, novels, poetry and nonfiction. Award: $2,000 (Canadian) in each category. Competition receives approx. 10-30 submissions. Judges: panel of 3 jurors, different each year. Entry fee $10 (Canadian) per title. Guidelines for SASE. Previously published submissions published in previous year from May 15 to May 15. "Writer must have resided in Quebec for 3 of the past 5 years." Books may be published anywhere. Page length: more than 48 pages.

QUARTERLY WEST NOVELLA COMPETITION, (I), University of Utah, 317 Olpin Union, Salt Lake City UT 84112. (801)581-3938. Biennial award for novellas. Award: 2 prizes of $500 and publication in *Quarterly West*. Send SASE for contest rules. Deadline: Postmarked by December 31.

‡QUINCY WRITERS GUILD ANNUAL CREATIVE WRITING CONTEST, (I), P.O. Box 433, Quincy IL 62306-0433. (217)222-2898. Contest Chairperson: Michael Barrett. "Award to promote writing." Annual competition for short stories, nonfiction, poetry. Award: Cash based on dollar amount of entry fees received. Competition receives approx. 100 submissions. Judges: Independent panel of writing professionals not affiliated with Quincy Writers Guild. Entry fee: $4 (Fiction and nonfiction, each entry); $2 (poetry each entry). Guidelines for SASE. Deadline April 15, 1996. Unpublished submissions. Word length: Fiction: 3,500 words; Nonfiction: 2,000 words. Poetry: any length, any style. "Guidelines are very important and available for SASE. No entry form is required. Entries accepted after January 1. Awards and certificate for first, second, third places each category."

SIR WALTER RALEIGH AWARD, (II, IV), North Carolina Literary and Historical Association, 109 E. Jones St., Raleigh NC 27601-2807. (919)733-7305. Secretary-Treasurer: Jeffrey J. Crow. "To promote among the people of North Carolina an interest in their own literature." Annual award for novels. Award: Statue of Sir Walter Raleigh. Judges: University English and history professors. Guidelines for SASE. Book must be an original work published during the 12 months ending June 30 of the year for which the award is given. Writer must be a legal or physical resident of North Carolina for the three years preceding the close of the contest period. Authors or publishers may submit 3 copies of their book to the above address.

‡*RAMBUNCTIOUS REVIEW*, ANNUAL FICTION CONTEST, (I), 1221 W. Pratt, Chicago IL 60626. Editor: M. Alberts. Award to "publish high-quality fiction." Annual award for short stories. Award: $100 (1st prize), $75 (2nd prize), $50 (3rd prize). Competition receives approx. 100 submissions. Judges: editors and writers. Entry fee $3 per story. Guidelines for SASE. Unpublished submissions. Requirements: Typed, double-spaced, maximum 12 pages. SASE for deadline, rules/entry forms.

***READ* WRITING & ART AWARDS, (I, IV)**, *Read* Magazine & Weekly Reader Corp., 245 Long Hill Rd., Middletown CT 06457. (203)638-2406. Fax: (203)346-5826. Associate Editor: Kate Davis. "To recognize and publish outstanding writing and art by students in grades 6-12." Annual award for short stories. Award: $100 (first prize), $75 (second prize), $50 (third prize); publication of first prize winner, certificates of excellence. Competition receives approx. 1,000 submissions. Judges: editors of Weekly Reader Corp. Guidelines for SASE. Unpublished submissions. Word length: 5 pages typed double-space. "Fiction category includes short stories and play formats."

REGINA MEDAL AWARD, (III), Catholic Library Association, St. Joseph Central High School Library, 22 Maplewood Ave., Pittsfield MA 01201. Contact: Jean R. Bostley, SSJ Chair, CLA Awards Committee. Annual award. To honor a continued distinguished contribution to children's literature. Award: silver medal. Award given during Easter week. Selection by a special committee; nominees are suggested by the Catholic Library Association Membership.

RHODE ISLAND STATE COUNCIL ON THE ARTS, (I, IV), Individual Artist's Fellowship in Literature, 95 Cedar St., Suite 103, Providence RI 02903-1062. (401)277-3880. Contact: Individual Artist Program. Biennial fellowship. Award: $5,000. Competition receives approximately 50 submissions. In-state panel makes recommendations to an out-of-state judge, who recommends finalist to the council. Entry forms for SASE. Deadline: April 1, 1997. Artists must be Rhode Island residents and not undergraduate or graduate students. "Program guidelines may change. Prospective applicants should contact RISCA prior to deadline."

HAROLD U. RIBALOW PRIZE, (II, IV), *Hadassah Magazine*, 50 W. 58th St., New York NY 10019. (212)688-0227. Contact: Alan M. Tigay, Executive Editor. Estab. 1983. Annual award "for a book of fiction on a Jewish theme. Harold U. Ribalow was a noted writer and editor who devoted his time to the discovery and encouragement of young Jewish writers." Book should have been published the year preceding the award. Award: $1,000 and excerpt of book in *Hadassah Magazine*. Deadline is April of the year following publication.

THE MARY ROBERTS RINEHART FUND, (III), Mail Stop Number 3E4, English Dept., 4400 University Dr., Fairfax VA 22030-4444. (703)993-1185. Director: William Miller. Biennial award for short stories, novels, novellas and story collections by unpublished writers (that is, writers ineligible to apply for NEA grants). Award: Two grants whose amount varies depending upon income the fund generates. Competition receives approx. 75-100 submissions annually. Rules for SASE. Next fiction deadline November 30. Writers must be nominated by a sponsoring writer, writing teacher, editor or agent.

RITE OF SPRING FICTION CONTEST, (I), *Phantasm*, 1530 Seventh St., Rock Island IL 61201. (309)788-3980. Editor: Betty Mowery. "To build up circulation of publication and provide new authors a home for work along with seasoned authors." Award given every 6 months from March 31 to September 31. Competition for short stories. Awards: $10 (first place), $5 (second place), 1-year subscription to *Phantasm* (third place). Entry fee $2. Guidelines for SASE. Deadline September 31. "Writers must submit their own fiction of no more than 500 words. We are looking for fiction of quiet horror, mystery or fantasy."

RIVER CITY WRITING AWARDS IN FICTION, (I), *River City*, Dept. of English, The University of Memphis, Memphis TN 38152. (901)678-4509. Awards Coordinator: Paul Naylor. "Annual award to reward the best short stories." Award: $2,000 first prize; $500 second; $300 third. Judge: To be announced. Entry fee $12 which begins or extends a subscription to *River City*. Guidelines available with SASE. Deadline December 8. Unpublished fiction. Open to all writers. Word length: 7,500 maximum.

‡**SUMMERFIELD G. ROBERTS AWARD, (I, II, IV)**, The Sons of the Republic of Texas, 5942 Abrams Rd., Suite 222, Dallas TX 75231. Executive Secretary: Maydee J. Scurlock. "Given for the best book or manuscript of biography, essay, fiction, nonfiction, novel, poetry or short story that describes or represents the Republic of Texas, 1836-1846." Annual award of $2,500. Deadline January 15. "The manuscripts must be written or published during the calendar year for which the award is given. Entries are to be submitted in quintuplicate and will not be returned."

BRUCE P. ROSSLEY LITERARY AWARDS, (I, II, III, IV), 96 Inc., P.O. Box 15559, Boston MA 02215. (617)267-0543. Fax: (617)267-6725. Associate Director: Nancy Mehegan. "To increase the attention for writers of merit who have received little recognition." Annual award for short stories, novels and story collections. Award: $1,000 for the literary award and $100 for Bruce P. Rossley New Voice Award. Competition receives approx. 75 submissions. Judges: professionals in the fields of writing, journalism and publishing. Entry fee $10. Guidelines for SASE. Deadline September 30. Published or unpublished submissions. "In addition to writing, the writer's accomplishments in the fields of teaching and community service will also be considered." Open to writers from Massachusetts. Work must be nominated by "someone familiar with the writer's work."

CARL SANDBURG AWARDS, (I, IV), Friends of the Chicago Public Library, Harold Washington Library Center, 400 S. State St., Chicago IL 60605. (312)747-4905. Administrator: Thea Ellesin-Janus. Annual. To honor excellence in Chicago or Chicago area authors (including 6 counties). Books published between May 31 (the following year) and June 1. $1,000 honorarium for fiction, nonfiction, poetry and children's literature. Medal awarded also. Deadline August 1. All entries become the property of the Friends.

SASSY **FICTION CONTEST, (I, IV)**, *Sassy*, 437 Madison Ave., New York NY 10022. (212)935-9150. Competition "to recognize promise in fiction writers aged 13-19 and to encourage teenagers to write." Annual award for short stories. Award: 3 prizes, changes each year. Competition receives approximately 5,000 submissions. Judges: Christina Kelly and Virginia O'Brien. No entry fee. Guidelines available for SASE. Information in June issue of magazine; winners published in January issue. Unpublished fiction. Only for writers aged 13-19.

THE SCHOLASTIC WRITING AWARDS, (I, IV), 555 Broadway, New York NY 10012. Program Coordinator: Evelyn Guzman. To provide opportunity for recognition of young writers. Annual award for short stories and other categories. Award: Cash awards and grants. Competition receives 25,000 submissions/year. Judges vary each year. Deadline: mid-January. Unpublished submissions. Contest limited to junior high and senior high students; grades 7-12. Entry blank must be signed by teacher. "Program is run through school and is only open to students in grades 7 through 12, regularly and currently enrolled in public and non-public schools in the United States and its territories, U.S.-sponsored schools abroad or any schools in Canada."

SCIENCE FICTION WRITERS OF EARTH (SFWoE) SHORT STORY CONTEST, (I, IV), Science Fiction Writers of Earth, P.O. Box 121293, Fort Worth TX 76121. (817)451-8674. SFWoE Administrator: Gilbert Gordon Reis. Purpose "to promote the art of science fiction/fantasy short story writing." Annual award for short stories. Award: $200 (first prize); $100 (second prize); $50 (third prize). Competition receives approx. 75 submissions/year. Judge: Author Edward Bryant. Entry fee $5 for 1st entry; $2 for additional entries. Guidelines for SASE. Deadline October 30. Submissions must be unpublished. Stories should be science fiction or fantasy, 2,000-7,500 words. "Although many of our past winners are now published authors, there is still room for improvement. The odds are good for a well-written story."

SE LA VIE WRITER'S JOURNAL **CONTEST, (I, IV)**, Rio Grande Press, P.O. Box 71745, Las Vegas NV 89170. (702)736-8833. Contact: Rosalie Avara, editor. Competition offered quarterly for short stories. Award: Publication in the *Se La Vie Writer's Journal* plus up to $10 and contributor's copy. Judge: Editor. Entry fee $4 for each or $7 for two. Guidelines for SASE. Deadlines: March 31, June 30, September 30, December 31. Unpublished submissions. Themes: slice-of-life, mystery, adventure, social. Length: 500 words maximum.

‡**SEATTLE ARTISTS PROGRAM, (IV)**, Seattle Arts Commission, 221 First Ave. W., #100, Seattle WA 98119-4223. (206)687-7306. Fax: (206)684-7172. Public Information Officer: Daria DeCooman. "Award to support development of new works by Seattle's independent, generative writers." Biannual competition for short stories, novels. Award: $2,000 or $7,500. Competition receives approx. 150 submissions. Judges: peer review panels. Guidelines for SASE. Deadline May 30, 1996. Previously published submissions or unpub-

lished submissions. Only Seattle residents may apply. Word length: Word-length requirements vary; the guidelines must be read.

‡❉CARL SENTNER SHORT STORY AWARD, (I, IV), P.E.I. Council of the Arts/C. Sentner Memorial, 115 Richmond St., Charlottetown, P.E.I. C1A 1H7 Canada. (902)368-4417. Fax: (902)368-4418. Administrative Assistant: Brenda Larter. "Awarded by Island Literary Awards to the author of a short story." Annual competition for short stories. Award: $500 (first prize); $200 (second prize), $100 (third prize). Entry fee $6. Deadline February 15. Unpublished submissions. "Competition is open to individuals who have been residents of Prince Edward Island at least six of the last twelve months. Not open to authors with one or more books published in the last five years. Enclose SASE for return of manuscript."

SEVENTEEN MAGAZINE FICTION CONTEST, (I, IV), *Seventeen Magazine*, 850 Third Ave., New York NY 10022. Contact: Joe Bargmann. To honor best short fiction by a young writer. Rules published in the November issue. Contest for 13-21 year olds. Deadline April 30. Submissions judged by a panel of outside readers and *Seventeen*'s editors. Cash awarded to winners. First-place story considered for publication.

SFWA NEBULA® AWARDS, (III, IV), Science fiction and Fantasy Writers of America, Inc., 5 Winding Brook Dr., #1B, Guilderland NY 12084. (518)869-5361. Executive Secretary: Peter Dennis Pautz. Annual awards for previously published short stories, novels, novellas, novelettes. Science fiction/fantasy only. "No submissions; nominees upon recommendation of members only." Deadline December 31. "Works are nominated throughout the year by active members of the SFWA."

‡SHORT AND SWEET CONTEST, (II, IV), Perry Terrell Publishing, M.A. Green Shopping Center, Inc., Metairie Bank Bldg., 7809 Airline Hwy., Suite 215-A, Metairie LA 70003. (504)737-7781. "The purpose is to inspire and encourage creativity in humor. (My personal purpose is to see who has a sense of humor and who doesn't.)" Monthly competition, 1 to 2 months after deadline, for short stories. Award: $5. Receives approximately 15 to 47/month. Judges: Perry Terrell. Entry fee 50¢/entry. Guidelines for SASE. "Each month has a theme and begins with an open-ended sentence. Send SASE for details."

SHORT GRAIN CONTEST, (I), Box 1154, Regina, Saskatchewan S4P 3B4 Canada. E-mail address: grain@b ailey2.unibase.com. ("E-mail entries not accepted.") Contact: J. Jill Robinson. Annual competition for post-card stories, prose poems and dramatic monologues. Awards $500 (first prize), $300 (second prize) and $200 (third prize) in each category. "All winners and Honourable Mentions will also receive regular payment for publication in *Grain*." Competition receives approximately 800 submissions. Judges: Canadian writers with national and international reputations. Entry fee $20 for 2 entries in one category (includes one-year subscription); each additional entry in the same category $5. Guidelines for SASE or SAE and IRC. Deadline January 31. Unpublished submissions. Contest entries must be either an original postcard story (a work of narrative fiction written in 500 words or less) or a prose poem (a lyric poem written as a prose paragraph or paragraphs in 500 words or less).

SIDE SHOW ANNUAL SHORT STORY CONTEST, (II), Somersault Press, P.O. Box 1428, El Cerrito CA 94530-1428. (510)215-2207. Editors: Shelley Anderson, M.K. Jacobs and Kathe Stolz. "To attract quality writers for our 300-odd page paperback fiction annual." Awards: first: $30; second: $25; third: $20; $5/ printed page extra to all accepted writers (on publication). Judges: The editors of *Side Show*. Entry fee $10 (includes subscription). Leaflet available but no guidelines or restrictions on length, subject or style. Sample copy for $10 plus $2 postage. Deadline June 30. Multiple submissions encouraged (only one entry fee required for each writer). All mss with SASE critiqued, if requested. "A story from *Side Show* was selected for inclusion in *Pushcart Prize XVIII: Best of the Small Presses*."

CHARLIE MAY SIMON BOOK AWARD, (III, IV), Arkansas Department of Education, Elementary School Council, State Education Building, Capitol Mall, Technical Assistance, Room 302-B, Little Rock AR 72201. (501)682-4371. Contact: James A. Hester, Secretary/Treasurer, Arkansas Elementary School Council. Annual award "to encourage reading by children of Arkansas, to promote book discussions of books read, and to bring before children of Arkansas examples of quality children's literature they would not normally read or would have heard read." Award: Medallion (first prize); plaque (Honor Book). No entry fee. Previously published submissions. "The committee doesn't accept requests from authors. They will look at booklists produced during the previous year and check recommendations from the following sources: *Booklist, Bulletin of the Center for Children's Books, Children's Catalog, Elementary School Library Collection, Hornbook, Library of Congress Children's Books, School Library Journal*."

BERNICE SLOTE AWARD, (II), *Prairie Schooner*, 201 Andrews Hall, University of Nebraska, Lincoln NE 68588-0334. (402)472-0911. Editor: Hilda Raz. "An award for the best work by a beginning writer published in *Prairie Schooner* during the previous year." Annual award for short stories, novel excerpts and translations. Award: $500. Judges: editorial board. Guidelines for SASE. Unpublished submissions. Must be beginning writers (not have a book published). "We only read mss September through May."

❖SMITHBOOKS/BOOKS IN CANADA FIRST NOVEL AWARD, (III, IV), Books in Canada, 130 Spadina Ave., #603, Toronto, Ontario M5V 2L4 Canada. (416)703-9880. Contact: Barbara Carey, editor. Annual award "to promote and recognize Canadian writing." Award: $5,000. No entry fee. Submissions are made by publishers. Contest is restricted to published first novels in English, intended for adults, written by Canadian citizens or residents.

KAY SNOW CONTEST, (I, IV), Willamette Writers, 9045 SW Barbur Blvd., Suite 5-A, Portland OR 97219. (503)452-1592. Contact: Contest Coordinator. Award "to create a showcase for writers of all fields of literature." Annual competition for short stories; also poetry (structured and nonstructured), nonfiction, juvenile and student writers. Award: $200 first prize in each category, second and third prizes, honorable mentions. Competition receives approximately 500 submissions. Judges: nationally recognized writers and teachers. Entry fee $15, nonmembers; $10, members; $5, students. Guidelines for #10 SASE. Deadline July 1 postmark. Unpublished submissions. Maximum 5 double-spaced pages or up to 3 poems per entry fee with maximum 5 double-spaced pages. Prize winners will be honored at the December monthly Willamette writers meeting. Press releases will be sent to local and national media announcing the winners, and excerpts from winning entries will run in the January newsletter.

SOCIETY OF CHILDREN'S BOOK WRITERS AND ILLUSTRATORS GOLDEN KITE AWARDS, (II, IV), Society of Children's Book Writers and Illustrators, 22736 Vanowen St., Suite 106, West Hills CA 91307. (818)888-8760. Contact: Sue Alexander, chairperson. Annual award. "To recognize outstanding works of fiction, nonfiction and picture illustration for children by members of the Society of Children's Book Writers and published in the award year." Published submissions should be submitted from January to December of publication year. Deadline December 15. Rules for SASE. Award: Statuette and plaque. Looking for quality material for children. Individual "must be member of the SCBWI to submit books."

SOCIETY OF CHILDREN'S BOOK WRITERS AND ILLUSTRATORS WORK-IN-PROGRESS GRANTS, (I, IV), 22736 Vanowen St., Suite 106, West Hills CA 91307. (818)888-8760. Contact: SCBWI. Annual grant for any genre or contemporary novel for young people; also nonfiction research grant and grant for work whose author has never been published. Award: First-$1,000, second-$500 (work-in-progress). Competition receives approx. 180 submissions. Judges: Members of children's book field—editors, authors, etc. Guidelines for SASE. Deadline February 1-May 1. Unpublished submissions. Applicants must be SCBWI members.

SONORA REVIEW SHORT STORY CONTEST, (I, II), (formerly *Sonora Review* Fiction Contest), Dept. of English, University of Arizona, Tucson AZ 85721. (520)626-8383. Contact: Fiction Editor. Annual contest to encourage and support quality short fiction. $500 first prize plus publication in *Sonora Review*. All entrants receive copy of the magazine. Entry fee. Send SASE for contest rules and deadlines.

SOUTH CAROLINA ARTS COMMISSION AND *THE POST AND COURIER* NEWSPAPER (CHARLESTON, SC) SOUTH CAROLINA FICTION PROJECT, (I, IV), 1800 Gervais St., Columbia SC 29201. (803)734-8696. Steve Lewis, director, Literary Arts Program. The purpose of the award is "to get money to fiction writers and to get their work published and read." Annual award for short stories. Award: $500 and publication in *The Post and Courier*. Competition receives between 300 and 400 submissions for 12 awards (up to 12 stories chosen). Judges are a panel of professional writers and Book Editor/Features writer for *The Post and Courier*. Entry forms or rules for SASE. *South Carolina residents only.*

SOUTH CAROLINA ARTS COMMISSION LITERATURE FELLOWSHIPS AND LITERATURE GRANTS, (I, IV), 1800 Gervais St., Columbia SC 29201. (803)734-8696. Steve Lewis, director, Literary Arts Program. "The purpose of the fellowships is to give a cash award to two deserving writers (one in poetry, one in creative prose) whose works are of the highest caliber." Award: $7,500 fellowship. Matching project grants up to $7,500. Competition receives approximately 100 submissions/fellowship. Judges are out-of-state panel of professional writers and editors for fellowships, and panels and SCAC staff for grants. Entry forms or rules for SASE. Fellowship deadline September 15. Grants deadline November 15. *South Carolina residents only.*

SOUTH DAKOTA ARTS COUNCIL, ARTIST FELLOWSHIP, (I, II, IV), 230 S. Phillips Ave., Suite 204, Sioux Falls SD 57102-0720. (605)339-6646. Award "to assist artists with career development. Grant can be used for supplies or to set aside time to work, but cannot be used for academic research or formal study toward a degree." Annual competition for writers. Award: Artist Career Development grant, $1,000; Artist Fellowship, $5,000. Competition receives approx. 80 submissions. "Grants are awarded on artists' work and *not* on financial need." Judges: Panels of in-state and out-of-state experts in each discipline. Guidelines for SASE. Deadline February 1. Previously published or unpublished submissions. Fellowships are open only to residents of South Dakota.

SOUTHERN ARTS LITERATURE PRIZE, (II, IV), 13 St. Clement St., Winchester, Hampshire S023 9DQ England. Award "to recognize good works by authors (known or unknown) in the southern region of the

U.K." Annual competition run on 3-year cycle alternating fiction, poetry and nonfiction. Award £1,000 (plus winner commissions piece of work; value to £600). Competition receives approximately 20-30 submissions. Judges: 3 people involved in literature or authors themselves; different each year. Guidelines for SASE. Southern arts region covers Hampshire, Berkshire, Wiltshire, Oxfordshire, Buckinghamshire, Isle of Wight and East Dorset. Write for information.

‡THE SOUTHERN PRIZE, (I), *The Southern Anthology*, 2851 Johnston St., #123, Lafayette LA 70503. Managing Editor: Dr. R. Sebastian Bennett. Award to "promote and reward outstanding writing; to encourage both traditional and avant-garde forms." Annual competition for short stories, novel excerpts and poetry. Award: $600 Grand Prize and publication; six finalists are also published. Judges: Editorial Panel. Entry fee $10. Guidelines for SASE. Postmark deadline: May 30, 1996. Unpublished submissions. "Available to all authors writing in English, regardless of citizenship. There are no form or genre restrictions. Submissions need not address 'Southern' themes. *The Southern Anthology* encourages both traditional and avant-garde writing." Word length: 7,500 words. "*The Southern Anthology* has no restrictions on style. However, we tend to prefer work which is oppositional or formally innovative in nature; which destablilizes established institutions or genres; or which portrays often-overlooked elements of society, avoiding or mimicking stereotypes. We do not subscribe to any political, aesthetic, or moral agenda; and detest conformance to 'political correctness' for its own sake. Often, we publish work which has been deemed 'too risky' for other journals. We also publish a variety of traditional forms."

THE SOUTHERN REVIEW/LOUISIANA STATE UNIVERSITY ANNUAL SHORT FICTION AWARD, (II), *The Southern Review*, 43 Allen Hall, Louisiana State University, Baton Rouge LA 70803. (504)388-5108. Contact: Editors, *The Southern Review*. Annual award "to encourage publication of good fiction." For a first collection of short stories by an American writer appearing during calendar year. Award: $500 to author. Possible campus reading. Deadline a month after close of each calendar year. The book of short stories must be released by a US publisher. Two copies to be submitted by publisher or author. Looking for "style, sense of craft, plot, in-depth characters."

STAND MAGAZINE SHORT STORY COMPETITION, (I), *Stand Magazine*, 179 Wingrove Road, Newcastle upon Tyne NE4 9DA England. Biennial award for short stories. Award: First prize £1,500; second prize £500; third prize £250; fourth prize £150; fifth prize £100 (or US $ equivalent). Entry fee $8. Guidelines and entry form on receipt of UK SAE or 2 IRCs. Deadline March 31, 1997.

WALLACE E. STEGNER FELLOWSHIP, (I, IV), Creative Writing Program, Stanford University, Stanford CA 94305-2087. (415)723-2637. Fax: (415)725-0755. Program Administrator: Gay Pierce. Annual award for short stories, novels, poetry and story collections. Five fellowships in fiction ($13,000 stipend plus required tuition of $5,000 annually). Entry fee $25. Guidelines for SASE. Deadline: the first working day following January 1st. For unpublished or previously published fiction writers. Residency required. Word length: 9,000 words or 40 pages.

STORY'S SHORT SHORT STORY COMPETITION, *Story* Magazine, 1507 Dana Ave., Cincinnati OH 45207. (513)531-2222. Editor: Lois Rosenthal. Award to "encourage the form of the short short and to find stories for possible publication in the magazine." Contest begins June 1 and closes October 31. Award: $1,000 (first prize); $500 (second prize); $250 (third prize); plus other prizes that change annually. Entry fee $10. Guidelines are published in the magazine. Word length: 1,500 words or less.

‡SUGAR MILL PRESS CONTESTS, (I, II), Perry Terrell Publishing, M.A. Green Shopping Center, Inc., Metairie Bank Bldg., 7809 Airline Hwy., Suite 215-A, Metairie LA 70003. (504)737-7781. "The purpose is to draw manuscripts from all writers, especially new writers, pay the winners first and reserve the right to print all (acceptable) material that is sent to Perry Terrell Publishing in *The Ultimate Writer*, *The Bracelet Charm*, *Amulet* or *The Veneration Quarterly*; also, to choose manuscripts of unique and outstanding quality to recommend to a small movie production company I have been invited to work with in California. (Writers will be notified before recommendation is made.)" Award is granted monthly, 4 to 6 months after contest deadlines. For short stories. Award: $100, $75, $50, $25 and 2 honorable mentions ($5). Competition receives approximately 25 to 75/deadline. Judges: Perry Terrell, Editor; Jonathan Everett, Associate Editor; Julie D. Terrell, Features Editor. Entry fee $5. Guidelines for SASE. Deadlines are throughout each month. Previously published or unpublished submissions. "Please specify which deadline and/or contest being entered. If not specified, the editor will read, when time permits, and place the entry the next month." Send SASE for theme list.

THE JOAN G. SUGARMAN CHILDREN'S BOOK AWARD, (II, IV), Washington Independent Writers Legal and Educational Fund, Inc., 220 Woodward Bldg. 733 Fifteenth St. NW, Washington DC 20005 (202)347-4973. The Joan G. Sugarman Children's Book Award was established in 1987 to recognize excellence in children's literature. Biennial competition for novels "children's literature, both fiction and nonfiction, geared for children ages 15 and under." Award: $1,000. Competition receives approximately 100 submissions. Judges are selected by the WIW Legal and Educational Fund, Inc. They have included librarians, professors of children's literature and children's bookstore owners. Guidelines for SASE. For the 1996-1997 Award, the expected deadline is the end of January 1998. Previously published submissions. The authors must reside in Washington DC, Maryland or Virginia. There is no word length requirement.

TARA FELLOWSHIP FOR SHORT FICTION, (I), The Heekin Group Foundation, P.O. Box 1534, Sisters OR 97759. (503)548-4147. Fiction Director: Sarah Heekin Redfield. "To support unpublished, beginning career writers in their writing projects." Two annual awards for completed short stories. Awards: $5,000 and $1,500. Receives approx. 500 applications. Judges: Invitation of Publisher judge. Past judges: Graywolf Press, SOHO Press, Dalkey Archive Press. Application fee $20. Guidelines for SASE. Deadline December 1. Unpublished submissions. Word length: 2,500-10,000 words.

‡TENNESSEE ARTS COMMISSION LITERARY FELLOWSHIP, (I, II, IV), 404 James Robertson Pkwy., Suite 160, Nashville TN 37243-0780. (615)741-1701. Fax: (615)741-8559. Contact: Alice Swanson, director of literary arts. Award to "honor promising writers." Annual award for fiction. Award: at least $2,500. Competition receives approx. 30 submissions. Judges are out-of-state jurors. Previously published and unpublished submissions. Writers must be residents of Tennessee. Word length: 20 ms pages. Write for guidelines.

THURBER HOUSE RESIDENCIES, (II), The Thurber House, 77 Jefferson Ave., Columbus OH 43215. (614)464-1032. Literary Director: Michael J. Rosen. "Four writers/year are chosen as writers-in-residence, one for each quarter." Award for writers of novels and story collections. $5,000 stipend and housing for a quarter in the furnished third-floor apartment of James Thurber's boyhood home. Judges: Advisory panel. To apply send letter of interest and curriculum vitae. Deadline: December 15. "The James Thurber Writer-in-Residence will teach a class in the Creative Writing Program at The Ohio State University in either fiction or poetry, and will offer one public reading and a short workshop for writers in the community. Significant time outside of teaching is reserved for the writer's own work in progress. Candidates should have published at least one book with a major publisher, in any area of fiction, nonfiction or poetry, and should possess some experience in teaching."

♥*TICKLED BY THUNDER* ANNUAL FICTION CONTEST, Tickled By Thunder, 7385-129 St., Surrey, British Columbia V3W 7B8 Canada. Phone/fax: (604)591-6095. Editor: Larry Lindner. "To encourage new writers." Annual competition for short stories. Award: $25 (Canadian), 1 year's (4-issue) subscription plus publication. Competition receives approx. 25 submissions. Judges: the editor and other writers. Entry fee $5 (Canadian) per entry (free for subscribers but more than one story requires $2 per entry.) Deadline February 15. Unpublished submissions. Word length: 2,000 words or less. "Chances of winning this contest are high (if only because last year we received so few entries). We would love to hear from you!"

♥TILDEN CANADIAN LITERARY AWARDS, (I, IV), (formerly CBC Radio/Saturday Night Literary Competition), CBC Radio/Saturday Night Magazine, Box 500, Station A, Toronto, Ontario M5W 1E6 Canada. (416)205-6001. Contact: Robert Weaver. Offers major award and encouragement to Canadian writers. Annual competition for short stories, poetry and personal essays. Award: $10,000 (Canadian) for each winner of the 3 categories. Competition receives approximately 5,000 total submissions for the 3 categories. Judged by a 3-person panel changing each year for each category: writers, book publishers, editors, etc. Unpublished submissions. Open to all residents of Canada and Canadian citizens living abroad. Word length: 2,000-3,500 words.

TOWSON STATE UNIVERSITY PRIZE FOR LITERATURE, (II, IV), Towson State University Foundation, Towson State University, Towson MD 21204. (410)830-2128. Contact: Dan L. Jones, Acting Dean, College of Liberal Arts. Annual award for novels or short story collections, previously published. Award: $1,000. Requirements: Writer must not be over 40; must be a Maryland resident. SASE for rules/entry forms. Deadline May 15.

TRI-STATE FAIR LITERARY AWARDS, (I), % Marianne McNeil Logan, 2700 S. Roosevelt, Amarillo TX 79103. (806)374-4354. Annual competition for short stories and poetry. Award: small cash awards, Best of Show Awards. Judges: Different each year. Entry fee $7 prose, $5 poetry. Guidelines for SASE. Deadline: August 1. Unpublished submissions. Length: 3,500 words maximum. "Categories may change a bit from year to year. Guidelines required. Open. Entries are displayed at Literary Booth at Tri-State Fair during Fair Week."

STEVEN TURNER AWARD, (II, IV), The Texas Institute of Letters, TCU, P.O. Box 30783, Fort Worth TX 76129. (817)921-7822. Secretary: Judy Alter. "To honor the best first book of fiction published by a writer who was born in Texas or who has lived in the state for two years at some time, or whose work concerns the state." Annual award for novels and story collections. Award: $1,000. Judges: committee. Guidelines for SASE. Previously published submissions appearing in print between January 1 and December 31.

MARK TWAIN AWARD, (III, IV), Missouri Association of School Librarians, 8049 Highway E, Bonne Terre MO 63628-3771. Estab. 1970. Annual award to introduce children to the best of current literature for children and to stimulate reading. Award: A bronze bust of Mark Twain, created by Barbara Shanklin, a Missouri sculptor. A committee selects pre-list of the books nominated for the award; statewide reader/selectors review and rate the books, and then children throughout the state vote to choose a winner from the final list. Books must be published two years prior to nomination for the award list. Publishers may send books they wish to nominate for the list to the committee members. 1) Books should be of interest to children in grades 4 through 8; 2) written by an author living in the US; 3) of literary value which may enrich children's personal lives.

UPC SCIENCE FICTION AWARD, (I, IV), Universitat Politècnica de Catalunya Board of Trustees, gran capità 2-4, Edifici NEXUS, 08034 Barcelona, Spain. (93)401 43 63. "The award is based on the desire for integral education at UPC. The literary genre of science fiction is undoubtedly the most suitable for a university such as UPC, since it unifies the concepts of science and literature." Annual award for short stories; 1,000,000 pesetas (about 10,000 US $). Judges: professors of the university and science fiction writers. Deadline: September 12. Previously unpublished entries. Length: 70-115 pages, double-spaced, 30 lines/page, 70 characters/line. Submissions may be made in Spanish, English, Catalan or French. The author must sign his work with a pseudonym and enclose a sealed envelope with full name, a personal ID number, address and phone. The pseudonym and title of work must appear on the envelope. Write for more details.

UTAH ORIGINAL WRITING COMPETITION, (I, IV), Utah Arts Council, 617 E. South Temple, Salt Lake City UT 84102-1177. (801)533-5895. Fax: (801)533-6196. Literary Arts Coordinator: Guy Lebeda. Annual competition for poetry, essays, nonfiction books, short stories, novels and story collections. Awards: Vary; last year between $200-1,000. Competition receives 700 entries. Judges: "Published and award-winning judges from across America." Guidelines available, no SASE necessary. Deadline: Mid-June or later. Submissions should be unpublished. Limited to Utah residents. "Some limitation on word-length. See guidelines for details."
● This writing competition is celebrating its 37th anniversary.

‡VIOLET CROWN BOOK AWARD, (I, IV), Austin Writers' League, 1501 W. Fifth St., Suite E-2, Austin TX 78703. (512)499-8914. Fax: (512)499-0441. Executive Director: Angela Smith. Award "to recognize the best books published by Austin Writers' League members over the period Sept. 1 to Aug. 31 in fiction, nonfiction and literary (poetry, short story collections, etc.) categories." Annual competition for novels, story collections, translations. Award: Three $1,000 cash awards and trophies. Competition receives approx. 100 submissions. Judges: A panel of judges who are not affiliated with the Austin Writers' League. Entry fee $10. Guidelines for SASE. Deadline August 31. Previously published submissions between Sept. 1 and Aug. 31. "Entrants must be Austin Writers' League members. League members reside all over the U.S. and some foreign countries. Persons may join the League when they send in entries." Publisher may also submit entry in writer's name. "Awards are co-sponsored by the University Co-op Bookstore. Special citations are presented to finalists."

‡THE VIRTUAL PRESS ANNUAL WRITER'S CONTEST (I), The Virtual Press, 408 Division St., Shawano WI 54166. Publisher: William Stanek. "Award to promote writing of quality short fiction." Annual competition for short stories. Award: $75 (1st prize); $50 (2nd prize); $25 (3rd prize); $10 (4th prize) in categories of fantasy, mystery and science fiction, plus publication in anthology. Competition receives approx. 50-200 submissions. Judges: Panel of judges. Entry fee $10/submission. Guidelines for SASE. Deadline Nov. 1. Unpublished submissions. Mystery, fantasy and science fiction writers. Word-length: 5,000. "Winners will be published in one of three anthologies featuring winning entries. Runners up in 5th-10th place will be considered for publication."

‡VOGELSTEIN FOUNDATION GRANTS, (II), The Ludwig Vogelstein Foundation, Inc., P.O. Box 277, Hancock ME 04640-0277. Executive Director: Frances Pishny. "A small foundation awarding grants to individuals in the arts and humanities. Criteria are merit and need. No student aid given." Send SASE for complete information after January 1.

WALDEN FELLOWSHIP, (I, IV), Coordinated by: Extended Campus Programs, Southern Oregon State College, 1250 Siskifou Blvd., Ashland OR 97520. (503)552-6331. Award "to give Oregon writers the opportunity to pursue their work at a quiet, beautiful farm in southern Oregon." Annual competition for all types of writing. Award: 3-6 week residencies. Competition receives approx. 30 submissions. Judges: committee judges selected by the sponsor. Guidelines for SASE. Deadline end of November. Oregon writers only. Word length: maximum 30 pages prose, 8-10 poems.

EDWARD LEWIS WALLANT MEMORIAL BOOK AWARD, (II, IV), 3 Brighton Rd., West Hartford CT 06117. Sponsored by Dr. and Mrs. Irving Waltman. Contact: Mrs. Irving Waltman. Annual award. Memorial to Edward Lewis Wallant offering incentive and encouragement to beginning writers, for books published the year before the award is conferred in the spring. Award: $300 plus award certificate. Books may be submitted for consideration to Dr. Sanford Pinsker, Department of English, Franklin & Marshall College, P.O. Box 3003, Lancaster PA 17604-3003. "Looking for creative work of fiction by an American which has significance for the American Jew. The novel (or collection of short stories) should preferably bear a kinship to the writing of Wallant. The award will seek out the writer who has not yet achieved literary prominence."

WASHINGTON PRIZE FOR FICTION, (I), 1301 S. Scott St., #424, Arlington VA 22204. (703)920-3771. Director: Larry Kaltman. Awards: $5,000 (first prize), $2,500 (second prize), $1,000 (third prize). The judges are English Department professors of Washington-area universities. The submission may be a novel, several novellas or a collection of short stories. There are no restrictions as to setting or theme. Contestants may reside anywhere. Length: 65,000 words minimum, previously unpublished. Entry fee: $30. Deadline November 30 annually.

WATERS SOUTHWEST WRITING AWARD FOR THE NOVEL, (I, IV), The Frank Waters Foundation of Taos and the Martin Foundation for the Creative Arts of San Francisco and Taos, P.O. Box 1357, Ranchos de Taos NM 87529. (505)758-9869. Contact: Mag Dimond. Award "to honor Frank Waters who died June 3, 1995, and to recognize novel writers from the following six western states: New Mexico, Arizona, Nevada, Utah, Colorado and Texas." Annual competition. Awards: $2,000 plus publication by University of New Mexico Press (1st prize); and 2 honorable mentions with awards of $2,000 each. Reading fee $25. Deadline August 31, 1996. Winners "will be announced in May of 1997 with a special awards ceremony at the Waters's Taos home."

WELLSPRING SHORT FICTION CONTEST, *Wellspring Magazine*, 770 Tonkawa Rd., Long Lake MN 55356-9233. (612)471-9259. Award "to select well-crafted short fiction with interesting story lines." Biannual competition for short stories. Awards: $100, $75, $25 and publication. Competition receives approx. 80 submissions. Judges: writers and readers. Entry fee $10. Guidelines for SASE. Deadlines July 1, January 1. Unpublished submissions. Word length: 2,000 words maximum.

♣**WESTERN CANADIAN MAGAZINE AWARDS, (II, IV)**, 3898 Hillcrest Ave., North Vancouver, British Columbia V7R 4B6 Canada. (604)984-7525. "To honour and encourage editorial excellence." Annual competition for short stories (fiction articles in magazines). Award: $500. Entry fee: $18-24 (depending on circulation of magazine). Deadline: January. Previously published submissions (between January and December). "Must be Canadian or have earned immigrant status or be a full-time Canadian resident, and the fiction article must have appeared in a publication (magazine) that has its main editorial offices located in the 4 Western provinces, the Yukon or Northwest territories."

WESTERN HERITAGE AWARDS, (II, IV), National Cowboy Hall of Fame, 1700 NE 63rd St., Oklahoma City OK 73111. (405)478-2250. Contact: Dana Sullivant, public relations director. Annual award "to honor outstanding quality in fiction, nonfiction and art literature." Submissions are to have been published during the previous calendar year. Award: The Wrangler, a replica of a C.M. Russell Bronze. No entry fee. Entry forms and rules available October 1 for SASE. Deadline November 30. Looking for "stories that best capture the spirit of the West."

WESTERN STATES BOOK AWARDS, (III, IV), Western States Arts Federation, 236 Montezuma, Santa Fe NM 87501. (505)988-1166. Literature Coordinator: Robert Sheldon. Annual award "to recognize writers living in the West; encouragement of effective production and marketing of quality books published in the West; increase of sales and critical attention." For unpublished manuscripts submitted by publisher. Award: $5,000 for authors; $5,000 for publishers. Contest rules for SASE. Write for information on deadline.

WHITING WRITERS' AWARDS, (III), Mrs. Giles Whiting Foundation, 1133 Avenue of the Americas, New York NY 10036-6710. Director: Dr. Gerald Freund. Annual award for writers of fiction, poetry, nonfiction and plays with an emphasis on emerging writers. Award: $30,000 (10 awards). Candidates are submitted by appointed nominators and chosen for awards by an appointed selection committee. Direct applications and informal nominations not accepted by the foundation.

‡**WISCONSIN ARTS BOARD INDIVIDUAL ARTIST PROGRAM, (II, IV)**, 101 E. Wilson St., First Floor, Madison WI 53702. (608)266-0190. Contact: Elizabeth Malner. Biennial awards for short stories, poetry,

---

Market categories: (I) Unpublished entries; (II) Published entries nominated by the author; (III) Published entries nominated by the editor, publisher or nominating body; (IV) Specialized entries.

novels, novellas, drama, essay/criticism. Awards: 5 awards of $8,000. Competition receives approx. 175 submissions. Judges are 3 out-of-state jurors. Entry forms or rules upon request. Deadline September 15 of even-numbered years (1996, 1998 etc.). Wisconsin residents only. Students are ineligible.

WISCONSIN INSTITUTE FOR CREATIVE WRITING FELLOWSHIP, (I, II, IV), University of Wisconsin— Creative Writing, English Department, 600 N. Park St., Madison WI 53706. Director: Ron Wallace. Competition "to provide time, space and an intellectual community for writers working on first books." Annual award for short stories, novels and story collections. Award: $20,000/9-month appointment. Competition receives approx. 400 submissions. Judges: English Department faculty. Required guidelines available for SASE; write to Ron Kuka. Deadline is month of February. Published or unpublished submissions. Applicants must have received an M.F.A. or comparable graduate degree in creative writing. Limit one story up to 30 pages in length. Two letters of recommendation required.

‡PAUL A. WITTY SHORT STORY AWARD, (II), International Reading Association, P.O. Box 8139, 800 Barksdale Rd., Newark DE 19714-8139. (302)731-1600. Annual award "given to the author of an original short story published for the first time in 1995 in a periodical for children." Award: $1,000. Judges: International Reading Association committees. For guidelines write to: Debra Gail Herrera, 111 E. Conner, Eastland, TX 76448. Deadline December 1. Published submissions.

THOMAS WOLFE FICTION PRIZE, (I), North Carolina Writers' Network, 3501 Hwy. 54 W., Studio C, Chapel Hlll NC 27516. "Our international literary prizes seek to recognize the best in today's writing." Annual award for fiction. Award: $500 and publication. Competition receives approx. 1,000 submissions. Entry fee $5. Guidelines for SASE. Deadline August 31. Unpublished submissions. Word length: 3,000 words maximum.

WORLD'S BEST SHORT SHORT STORY CONTEST, (I), English Department Writing Program, Florida State University, Tallahassee FL 32306-1036. (904)644-4230. Director, Writing Program: Jerome Stern. Annual award for short-short stories, unpublished, under 250 words. Prizewinning story gets $100 and a crate of Florida oranges; winner and finalists are published in *Sun Dog: The Southeast Review*. Competition receives approx. 3,000 submissions. Entry fee $1. SASE for rules. Deadline February 15. Open to all.Word-length: 250 words.

WRITERS AT WORK FELLOWSHIP COMPETITION, Writers at Work (W@W), P.O. Box 1146, Centerville, UT 84014-5146. (801)292-9285. Vice President: Dawn Marano. Administrative Assistant: Niquie Love. "Through the recognition of excellence in fiction and poetry, we hope to foster the growth of the supportive literary community which characterizes our annual conference in Park City, Utah." Annual competition for short stories, novels (novel excerpts) and poetry. Award: $1,500, a featured reading at and tuition for the afternoon sessions at 1996 conference, and publication in both *Quarterly West* literary magazine and *The Best of Writers at Work*, an annual anthology (first prize); $500, tuition for the afternoon sessions at the 1996 conference and publication in the anthology (second prize). Competition receives 1,500 submissions. Judges: Faculty of Writers at Work Conference. Entry fee $12. Guidelines available for SASE. Deadline March 15. Unpublished submissions. Open to any writer who has not yet published a book-length volume of original work. Word length: 20 double-spaced pages, one story (or excerpt) only; 6 poems, up to 10 total pages. "The 12th Annual Writers At Work Conference is scheduled for July 7-12, 1996."

THE WRITERS COMMUNITY RESIDENCY AWARDS, (II), The National Writer's Voice Project of the YMCA of the USA. 5 W. 63rd St., New York NY 10023. (212)875-4276. Program Director: Jennifer O'Grady. Offers semester-long residencies to mid-career writers at YMCAs nationwide. Biannual award for novels and story collections. Award: A semester-long residency. Residents conduct a master-level workshop and give a public reading at their host Writer's Voice center. Honoraria currently range from $6,000-$7,500. Judges: A committee at each Writer's Voice center. Deadlines vary. Previously published submissions in book form. "There is currently little money available for transporation costs. Writers should live near the Writer's Voice center at which they wish to hold a residency. Writers should apply directly to the Writer's Voice center, as application procedures vary. For a list of Writer's Voice center addresses, send SASE to The Writers Community, The National Writer's Voice Project, 5 W. 63rd St., New York NY 10023."

WRITER'S DIGEST **ANNUAL WRITING COMPETITION, (Short Story Division), (I)**, *Writer's Digest*, 1507 Dana Ave., Cincinnati OH 45207. (513)531-2222. Contact: Contest Director. Grand Prize is an expenses-paid trip to New York City with arrangements to meet editors/agents in writer's field. Other awards include cash, reference books and certificates of recognition. Names of grand prize winner and top 100 winners are announced in the October issue of *Writer's Digest*. Top entry published in booklet ($5.75). Send SASE to *WD* Writing Competition for rules and entry form, or see January-May issues of *Writer's Digest*. Deadline May 31. Entry fee $7 per manuscript. All entries must be original, unpublished and not previously submitted to a *Writer's Digest* contest. Length: 2,000 words maximum. No acknowledgment will be made of receipt of mss nor will mss be returned. Contest now includes 2 short fiction categories: literary and genre/mainstream.

♣**WRITERS GUILD OF ALBERTA LITERARY AWARD, (II, IV)**, Writers Guild of Alberta, 3rd Floor, Percy Page Centre, 11759 Groat Rd., Edmonton, Alberta T5M 3K6 Canada. (403)422-8174. Fax: (403)422-2663. Executive Director: Miki Andrejevic. "To recognize, reward and foster writing excellence." Annual competition for novels and story collections. Award: $500, plus leather-bound copy of winning work. Short story competition receives 5-10 submissions; novel competition receives about 20; children's literature category up to 40. Judges: 3 published writers. Guidelines for SASE. Deadline December 31. Previously published submissions (between January and December). Open to Alberta authors, resident for previous 18 months. Entries must be book-length and published within the current year.

WRITERS' INTERNATIONAL FORUM WRITING CONTEST, (I), *Writers' International Forum*, P.O. Box 516, Tracyton WA 98393. Editorial Director: Sandra E. Haven. Award "to encourage strong storyline in a tight package." One or more contests per year for short stories. Awards: Cash prizes and certificates (amounts vary per contest). Competitions receive approx. 150 entries. Judges: *Writers' International Forum* staff. No entry fee for subscribers; entry fee for nonsubscribers. Guidelines available for SASE. Previously unpublished submissions. "Length, theme, prizes, deadline, fee and other requirements vary for each contest. Send for guidelines. Entries are judged on creativity, technique, mechanics and appeal."

WRITERS' JOURNAL ANNUAL FICTION CONTEST, (I), Val-Tech Publishing, Inc., P.O. Box 25376, St. Paul MN 55125-0376. Publisher/Managing Editor: Valerie Hockert. Annual award for short stories. Award: first place, $50; second place, $25; third place, $15. Also gives honorable mentions. Competition receives approximately 500 submissions/year. Judges are Valerie Hockert, Glenda Olsen and others. Entry fee $5 each. Maximum of 3 entries/person. Entry forms or rules for SASE. Maximum length is 2,000 words. Two copies of each entry are required—one *without* name or address of writer.

WRITERS' JOURNAL ROMANCE CONTEST, (I), *Writers' Journal*, Val-Tech Publishing, Inc., P.O. Box 25376, St. Paul MN 55125-0376. Competition for short stories. Award: $50 (first prize), $25 (second prize), $15 (third prize), plus honorable mentions. Entry fee $5/entry. Guidelines for SASE (4 entries/person). Unpublished submissions. Word length: 2,000 words maximum. "Enclose #10 SASE for winner's list."

WRITERS' JOURNAL SCIENCE FICTION CONTEST, (I), *Writers' Journal*, Val-Tech Publishing, Inc., P.O. Box 25376, St. Paul MN 55125-0376. Competition for short stories. Award: $50 (first prize), $25 (second prize), $15 (third prize) plus honorable mentions. Entry fee $5/entry (4 entries/person). Guidelines for SASE. Unpublished submissions. Word length: 2,000 words maximum. "If you need some tips, make sure to check out our recent issues. Enclose #10 SASE for winner's list."

THE WRITERS' WORKSHOP INTERNATIONAL FICTION CONTEST, (I), The Writers' Workshop, P.O. Box 696, Asheville NC 28802. (704)254-8111. Executive Director: Karen Tager. Annual awards for fiction. Awards: $500 (1st prize), $250 (2nd prize), $100 (3rd prize). Competition receives approximately 350 submissions. Past judges have been D.M. Thomas, Mark Mathabane and Robert Creely. Entry fee $18/$15 members. Guidelines for SASE. Deadline: February 1. Unpublished submissions. Length: 20 typed, double-spaced pages per story. Multiple submissions are accepted.

WRITING COMPETITION FOR WRITERS OVER 50, (I, IV), Yachats Literary Festival, 124 NE California, Yachats OR 97498. (503)547-3271. Director: Frena Bloomfield. "For writers over 50." Annual competition for various categories. Award: cash prizes plus attendance at the Yachats Literary Festival. Judges: panel of writers, academics and editors. Guidelines for SASE. Previously unpublished submissions. Contest closes end of April.

WYOMING ARTS COUNCIL LITERARY FELLOWSHIPS, (I, IV), Wyoming Arts Council, 2320 Capitol Ave., Cheyenne WY 82002. (307)777-7742. Contact: Literature consultant. Annual awards to "honor the most outstanding new work of Wyoming writers—fiction, nonfiction, drama, poetry." Award: 4 awards of $2,000 each. Competition receives approx. 70-90 submissions. Judges: Panel of three writers selected each year from outside Wyoming. Guidelines for SASE. Deadline: June 15. Applicant "must be Wyoming resident for two years prior to application deadline. Must not be a full-time student." No genre exclusions; combined genres acceptable. 25 pages double-spaced maximum; 10 pages maximum for poetry. Winners may not apply for 4 years after receiving fellowships.

YOUNG READER'S CHOICE AWARD, (III), Pacific Northwest Library Association, Graduate School of Library and Information Sciences, P.O. Box 352930, FM-30, University of Washington, Seattle WA 98195. (206)543-1897. Contact: Carol A. Doll. Annual award "to promote reading as an enjoyable activity and to provide children an opportunity to endorse a book they consider an excellent story." Award: silver medal. Judges: children's librarians and teachers nominate; children in grades 4-8 vote for their favorite book on the list. Guidelines for SASE. Deadline February 1. Previously published submissions. Writers must be nominated by children's librarians and teachers.

Contests and awards/'95-'96 changes

The following contests, grants and awards appeared in the 1995 edition of *Novel & Short Story Writer's Market* but do not appear in the 1996 edition. Those contests, grants and awards that did not respond to our request for an update appear below without further explanation. If a reason was given, it is included next to the listing.

The American Way Faux Faulkner Contest

B.C.L.A. Translation Competition

Brandeis University Creative Arts Awards (discontinued)

Ann Connor Brimer Award

Bumbershoot Written Works Competition (discontinued)

The Children's Book Award

City of Regina Writing Award

Conseil de la Vie Francaise en Amérique/Prix Champlain

Dreams & Visions: Best Short Story of the Year (discontinued)

Essence's Short-Short Story Contest (no longer sponsors contest)

Excalibur Book Award (requested deletion)

Friends of American Writers

Awards

Kansas Quarterly/Kansas Arts Commission Awards (discontinued)

Ezra Jack Keats/Kerlan Collection Memorial Fellowship

Latin American and Caribbean Literture Award Juan Rulfo

Le Prix Molson de l'Académie des Lettres du Québec

Les Grands Prix Du Journal de Montréal

Michigan Creative Artist Grant

Military Lifestyle Short Story Contest

Minnesota State Arts Board/Artists Assistance Fellowship

Missouri Writers' Biennial (discontinued)

The Nene Award

New Writing Award

The Scott O'dell Award for His-

torical Fiction

Chris O'Malley Prize in Fiction

Oregon Individual Artist Fellowship

The Regina Book Award

Romantic Novelists' Association Romantic Novel of the Year Award

San Jose Studies Best Story Award

Saskatchewan Book Awards

The Seaton Awards (discontinued)

Snake Nation Press Annual Fall Contest

So To Speak Voices Fiction and Poetry Contest

SWG Literary Awards

Takeshi Kaiko Award

Vermont Council on the Arts Fellowship

Laura Ingalls Wilder Award

For information on entering the Novel & Short Story Writer's Market *Cover Letter Contest, see page 19.*

Resources

Resources

Conferences and Workshops

Why are conferences so popular? Writers and conference directors alike tell us it's because writing can be such a lonely business otherwise—that at conferences writers have the opportunity to meet (and commiserate) with fellow writers, as well as meet and network with publishers, editors and agents. Conferences and workshops provide some of the best opportunities for writers to make publishing contacts and pick up valuable information on the business, as well as the craft, of writing.

The bulk of the listings in this section are for conferences. Most conferences last from one day to one week and offer a combination of workshop-type writing sessions, panel discussions, and a variety of guest speakers. Topics may include all aspects of writing from fiction to poetry to scriptwriting, or they may focus on a specific area such as those sponsored by the Romance Writers of America for writers specializing in romance or the SCBWI conferences on writing for children's books.

Workshops, however, tend to run longer—usually one to two weeks. Designed to operate like writing classes, most require writers to be prepared to work on and discuss their work-in-progress while attending. An important benefit of workshops is the opportunity they provide writers for an intensive critique of their work, often by professional writing teachers and established writers.

Each of the listings here includes information on the specific focus of an event as well as planned panels, guest speakers and workshop topics. It is important to note, however, some conference directors were still in the planning stages for 1996 when we contacted them. If it was not possible to include 1996 dates, fees or topics, we have provided information from 1995 so you can get an idea of what to expect. For the most current information, it's best to send a self-addressed, stamped envelope to the director in question about three months before the date(s) listed.

Finding a conference

Many writers try to make it to at least one conference a year, but cost and location count as much as subject matter or other considerations, when determining which conference to attend. There are conferences in almost every state and province and even some in Europe open to North Americans.

To make it easier for you to find a conference close to home—or to find one in an exotic locale to fit into your vacation plans—we've divided this section into geographic regions. The conferences appear in alphabetical order under the appropriate regional heading.

Note that conferences appear under the regional heading according to where they will be held, which is sometimes different than the address given as the place to register or send for information. For example, the Women's Wilderness Canoe Trips Writing Retreat is held in Mexico and is listed under the International heading, although writers are instructed to write to Sante Fe, New Mexico, for information.

The regions are as follows:

Northeast: Connecticut, Maine, Massachusetts, New Hampshire, New York, Rhode Island, Vermont

Midatlantic: Washington DC, Delaware, Maryland, New Jersey, Pennsylvania

Midsouth: North Carolina, South Carolina, Tennessee, Virginia, West Virginia

Southeast: Alabama, Arkansas, Florida, Georgia, Louisiana, Mississippi, Puerto Rico

Midwest: Illinois, Indiana, Kentucky, Michigan, Ohio

North Central: Iowa, Minnesota, Nebraska, North Dakota, South Dakota, Wisconsin

South Central: Colorado, Kansas, Missouri, New Mexico, Oklahoma, Texas

West: Arizona, California, Hawaii, Nevada, Utah

Northwest: Alaska, Idaho, Montana, Oregon, Washington, Wyoming

Canada

International

Learning and networking

Besides learning from workshop leaders and panelists in formal sessions, writers at conferences also benefit from conversations with other attendees. Writers on all levels enjoy sharing insights. Often, a conversation over lunch can reveal a new market for your work or let you know which editors are most receptive to the work of new writers. You can find out about recent editor changes and about specific agents. A casual chat could lead to a new contact or resource in your area.

Many editors and agents make visiting conferences a part of their regular search for new writers. A cover letter or query that starts with "I met you at the National Writers Association Conference," or "I found your talk on your company's new romance line at the Cape Cod Writers Conference most interesting . . . " may give you a small leg up on the competition.

While a few writers have been successful in selling their manuscripts at a conference, the availability of editors and agents does not usually mean these folks will have the time there to read your novel or six best short stories (unless, of course, you've scheduled an individual meeting with them ahead of time). While editors and agents are glad to meet writers and discuss work in general terms, usually they don't have the time (or energy) to give an extensive critique during a conference. In other words, use the conference as a way to make a first, brief contact.

Selecting a conference

Besides the obvious considerations of time, place and cost, choose your conference based on your writing goals. If, for example, your goal is to improve the quality of your writing, it will be more helpful to you to choose a hands-on craft workshop rather than a conference offering a series of panels on marketing and promotion. If, on the other hand, you are a science fiction novelist who would like to meet your fans, try one of the many science fiction conferences or "cons" held throughout the country and the world.

Look for panelists and workshop instructors whose work you admire and who seem to be writing in your general area. Check for specific panels or discussions of topics relevant to what you are writing now. Think about the size—would you feel more comfortable with a small workshop of eight people or a large group of 100 or more attendees?

If your funds are limited, start by looking for conferences close to home, but you may want to explore those that offer contests with cash prizes—and a chance to recoup your expenses. A few conferences and workshops also offer scholarships, but the competition is stiff and writers interested in these should find out the requirements early. Finally, students may want to look for conferences and workshops that offer college credit. You will find these options included in the listings here. Again, send a self-addressed, stamped envelope for the most current details.

The science fiction field in particular offers hundreds of conventions each year for writers, illustrators and fans. To find additional listings for these, see *Locus* (P.O. Box 13305, Oakland CA 94661) or the *Science Fiction Convention Register* (101 S. Whiting St., Alexandria VA 22304). For more information on conferences and even more conferences from which to choose, check the May issue of *Writer's Digest. The Guide to Writers Conferences* (ShawGuides, 10 W. 66th St., Suite 30H, New York NY 10023) is another helpful resource.

Northeast (CT, MA, ME, NH, NY, RI, VT)

BECOME A MORE PRODUCTIVE WRITER, (formerly Writing With Your Whole Self), P.O. Box 1310, Boston MA 02117. (617)266-1613. Director: Marcia Yudkin. Estab. 1991. Workshop held approximately 3 times/year. Workshop held on one Saturday in April, September, February. Average attendance 15. "Creativity workshop for fiction writers and others. Based on latest discoveries about the creative process, participants learn to access their unconscious wisdom, find their own voice, utilize kinesthetic, visual and auditory methods of writing, and bypass longstanding blocks and obstacles. Held at a hotel in central Boston."
Costs: $99.
Accommodations: List of area hotels and bed & breakfasts provided.
Additional Information: "Audiotapes of seminar information also available."

BREAD LOAF WRITERS' CONFERENCE, Middlebury College, Middlebury VT 05753. (802)388-3711 ext. 5286. Administrative Coordinator: Carol Knauss. Estab. 1926. Annual. Conference held in late August. Conference duration: 12 days. Average attendance: 230. For fiction, nonfiction and poetry. Held at the summer campus in Ripton Vermont (belongs to Middlebury College).
Costs: $1,585 (includes room/board) (1995).
Accommodations: Accommodations are at Ripton. Onsite accommodations $545 (1995).

CAPE COD WRITERS' CONFERENCE of Cape Cod Writers Center, Inc., % Cape Cod Conservatory, Route 132, West Barnstable MA 02668. (508)775-4811. Executive Director: Marion Vuilleumier. Estab. 1963. Annual. Conference held: August 20-25. Conference duration: one week. Average attendance: 125. For fiction, nonfiction, poetry, juvenile writing and mystery/suspense. Held at Craigville Conference Center, a campus arrangement on shore of Cape's south side. Guest speakers and panelists for 1995 were Christine Tomasino, agent; Denise Little, editor; Art Buchwald; Bernard Cornwell, novelist and Sandra Goroff-Mailley, publicist.
Costs: $80 registration and $90 per course; housing and meals separate, paid to the Conference Center.
Accommodations: Information on overnight accommodations made available. On-site accommodations at Craigville Conference Center plus 3 meals, approx. $70/day.
Additional Information: Conference brochures/guidelines are available for SASE.

CAPE WRITING WORKSHOP, sponsored by Cape Cod Writers Center, Inc., % Cape Cod Conservatory, Route 132, West Barnstable MA 02668. (508)775-4811. Executive Director: Marion Vuilleumier. Estab. 1985. Annual. Workshops held in 6 sessions, simultaneously. Workshop duration: 6 days. Average attendance: limit to 10/workshop. Concentrations include mystery/suspense, scriptwriting, children's book writing, poetry, memoirs, and magazine article writing. August workshop held at Parish House St. Mary's Church in Barnstable (Cape Cod)."
Costs: $75 registration; $335 tuition.
Accommodations: Information on overnight accommodations is made available. Accommodations are made at nearby bed and breakfast establishments.
Additional Information: Brochures are available for SASE.

> *Can't find a conference? Conferences are listed by region. Check the introduction to this section for a list of regional categories.*

‡**DOWNEAST MAINE WRITER'S WORKSHOPS**, P.O. Box 446, Stockton Springs ME 04981. (207)567-4317. Fax: (207)567-3023. Director: Janet J. Barron. E-mail address: 6249304@mcimail.com. Estab. 1994. Held periodically throughout the year. Workshop held in spring. Workshops last 1-5 days. Average attendance: 3-15. 1996 workshops will be held on: Creative Writing, Writing for the Juvenile Market, and How to Get Your Writing Published. Workshops held "in the studio of a 275 year-old historic building on the beautiful coast of Maine. Our workshops have one professional veteran teacher. Our next scheduled teacher is Janet J. Barron, a publishing industry author/editor, publisher and instructor."
Costs: $95-495, depending on length of workshop. "Accomodations and meals at area locations are extremely reasonable."
Accommodations: Attendees must make their own transportation arrangements. Discounts and a list of area hotels are available.
Additional Information: "DEMWW has a 'Writer's Clinic' for those who seek feedback on their work. We do not require writers to submit work before or during. Our workshops are for beginning writers who want to learn practical, inside-the-industry-information on how to write for publication. Each of our workshops concentrates on only one aspect of writing and has only one professional author/editor/publisher instructor." Conference brochures/guidelines are available for SASE.

‡**EASTERN WRITERS' CONFERENCE**, English Dept., Salem State College, Salem MA 01970. (508)741-6330. Conference Director: Rod Kessler. Estab. 1977. Annual. Conference held over a weekend in late June. Average attendance: 60. Conference to "provide a sense of community and support for area poets and fiction writers. We try to present speakers and programs of interest, changing our format from time to time. Conference-goers usually have an opportunity to read to an audience or have manuscripts professionally critiqued. We tend to draw regionally." Previous speakers have included Nancy Mairs, Susanna Kaysen, Katha Pollitt, Bill Littlefield.
Costs: "Under $100."
Accommodations: Information on overnight accommodations is made available.
Additional Information: "Optional ms critiques are available for an additional fee." Conference brochures/guidelines available for SASE.

FEMINIST WOMEN'S WRITING WORKSHOPS, INC., P.O. Box 6583, Ithaca NY 14851. Directors: Mary Beth O'Connor and Margo Gumosky. Estab. 1975. Workshop held every summer. Workshop duration: 8 days. Average attendance: 20-40 women writers. "Workshops provide a women-centered community for writers of all levels and genres. Workshops are held on the campuses of Hobart/William Smith Colleges in Geneva, NY. Geneva is approximately mid-way between Rochester and Syracuse. Each writer has a private room and 3 meals daily. College facilities such as pool, tennis courts and weight room are available. Public reading by guest writer held in Ionoca, NY on the Cornell University campus. FWWW invites all interests. Past speakers include Nancy Bereano, publisher of Firebrand Books, Ithaca, NY; Dorothy Allison, National Book Award Finalist for *Bastard Out of Carolina*, and Ruth Stone, author of *Second-Hand Coat*, *Who Is The Widow's Muse?* and *Simplicity*.
Costs: $495 for tuition, room, board.
Accommodations: Shuttle service from airports available for a small fee.
Additional Information: "Writers may submit manuscripts up to 10 pages with application." Brochures/guidelines available for SASE.

THE FIGURATIVE LANGUAGE MASTER CLASS, (formerly The Creative Writing Master Class), 441 E. 20 St., Suite 11B, New York NY 10010-7515. (212)674-1143. Director: Sheila Davis. Estab. 1993. 3 times a year. Workshop held in March. Workshop duration: 8 weeks. Average attendance: limited to 10. "A unique enrichment for all writers of: fiction, ad copy, cartoons, lyrics, editorials, press releases, newsletters and brochures. This course will expand and enhance your usual ways of thinking and expressing ideas through the practice of figurative language. You'll also acquire new skills in structuring your thoughts to make your writing more forceful and thus—more marketable." The conference is held at the New York headquarters of the Songwriters Guild of America.
Costs: $295.
Additional Information: Application form available for SASE.

‡**FINE ARTS WORK CENTER IN PROVINCETOWN**, 24 Pearl St., Provincetown MA 02657. (508)487-9960. Contact: Writing Coordinator. Conference "located on the grounds of the former Days Lumberyard complex. The facility has offered studio space to artists and writers since 1914." Offers 1-week open enrollment workshops in fiction, poetry and nonfiction, June 23-August 31. Faculty includes Grace Paley, Michael Cunningham, Gerald Stern and Robert Pinsky.
Costs: Catalog available January 1996.
Additional Information: Writers' apartments are in "several houses and a refurbished Victorian barn."

DOROTHY CANFIELD FISHER WRITERS CONFERENCE, P.O. Box 1058, Waitsfield VT 05673-1058. (802)496-3271. Fax: (802)496-7271. E-mail address: kwerner@aol.com; Compuserve 73562,1150. Director:

Kitty Werner. Estab. 1990. Annually, fourth weekend in June. Conference duration: 2 days. Average attendance: 100-116. For "fiction, nonfiction, marketing, children's, occasionally screenplays. Emphasis on improving writing skills and marketing." Conference held at the Sheraton-Burlington Hotel in Burlington VT. Jackie Cantor (Dell), Nancy Yost (Lowenstein Agency), Eamon Dolan (HarperCollins) and Damares Rowland (agent) are scheduled to speak at the next conference. Workshop leaders come from NY and have included: Dawn Raffel (Redbook); Margaret Daly (BH&G); Meg Ruley (agent); and Agent in Residence: Bobbe Siegel.
Costs: $100-160 registration includes snacks and lunch, two dinners are separate.
Accommodations: Burlington airport is 2 miles away—Sheraton has free shuttle service. Our brochure has all the information for registration and staying at the Sheraton at special rates. Costs are from $177 quad to $324 single; includes conference registration.
Additional Information: Conference brochures/guidelines are available for SASE.

HOFSTRA UNIVERSITY SUMMER WRITERS' CONFERENCE, 110 Hofstra University, UCCE, 205 Davison Hall, Hempstead NY 11550-1090. (516)463-5016. Assistant Dean, Liberal Arts: Lewis Shena. Estab. 1972. Annual (every summer, starting week after July 4). Conference to be held July 8 to July 19, 1996. Average attendance: 50. Conference offers workshops in fiction, nonfiction, poetry, juvenile fiction, stage/screenwriting and, on occasion, one other genre such as detective fiction or science fiction. Site is the university campus, a suburban setting, 25 miles from NYC. Guest speakers are not yet known. "We have had the likes of Oscar Hijuelos, Robert Olen Butler, Hilma and Meg Wolitzer, Budd Schulberg and Cynthia Ozick."
Costs: Non-credit (no meals, no room): approximately $300 per workshop. Credit: Approximately $850/workshop (2 credits).
Accommodations: Free bus operates between Hempstead Train Station and campus for those commuting from NYC. Dormitory rooms are available for approximately $450. Those who request area hotels will receive a list. Hotels are approximately $75 and above/night.
Additional Information: "All workshops include critiquing. Each participant is given one-on-one time of ½ hour with workshop leader. Only credit students must submit manuscripts when registering. We submit work to the Shaw Guides Contest and other Writer's Conferences and Retreats contests when appropriate."

THE INTERNATIONAL FILM WORKSHOPS, 2 Central St., Rockport ME 04856. (207)236-8581. Director: David Lyman. Estab. 1973. Workshops held weekly throughout summer and fall. Average attendance: Maximum of 16/workshop. The workshops include screenwriting, feature film scripts, television documentaries, TV episodes. "The workshop is located in old Town Hall in the small harbor village of Rockport, Maine—facilities include library, gallery, theater, darkrooms, studios, feature film production center, accommodations for 150, dining room." Themes planned for next workshops include the feature film script, the TV doc script, writing drama, the mystery writer, the scene writing workshop, comedy writing, writing horror, the first novel. Faculty include Christopher Keane, Stanley Ralph Ross, Janet Roach.
Costs: Course tuition, one week: starts at $695. Meals and accommodations: $355-625.
Accommodations: Discount airline ticket, airport van service, housing available.
Additional Information: "Writing samples and professional résumé must accompany application." Workshop brochures are available: call (207)236-2093 or fax (207)236-2558.

IWWG MEET THE AGENTS AND EDITORS: THE BIG APPLE WORKSHOPS, % International Women's Writing Guild, P.O. Box 810, Gracie Station, New York NY 10028. (212)737-7536. Executive Director: Hannelore Hahn. Estab. 1980. Biannual. 1996 workshops: April 20-21 and October 19-20. Average attendance: 200. Workshops to promote creative writing and professional success. Site: Private meeting space of the New York Genealogical Society, mid-town New York City. Sunday afternoon openhouse with agents and editors.
Costs: $100 for the weekend.
Accommodations: Information on transportation arrangements and overnight accommodations made available.
Additional Information: Workshop brochures/guidelines are available for SASE.

IWWG SUMMER CONFERENCE, % International Women's Writing Guild, P.O. Box 810, Gracie Station, New York NY 10028. (212)737-7536. Execuive Director: Hannelore Hahn. Estab. 1977. Annual. 1996 conference: August 9-16. Average attendance: 400, including international attendees. Conference to promote writing in all genres, personal growth and professional success. Conference is held "on the tranquil campus of Skidmore College in Saratoga Springs, NY, where the serene Hudson Valley meets the North Country of the Adirondacks." Fifty different workshops are offered. Overall theme: "Writing Towards Personal and Professional Growth."
Costs: $300 for week-long program, plus room and board.
Accommodations: Transportation by air to Albany, New York, or Amtrak train available from New York City. Conference attendees stay on campus.
Additional Information: Features "lots of critiquing sessions and contacts with literary agents." Conference brochures/guidelines available for SASE.

‡**MANHATTANVILLE COLLEGE WRITERS' WEEK**, 2900 Purchase St., Purchase NY 10577. (914)694-3425. Dean of Adult and Special Programs: Ruth Dowd, R.S.C.J. Estab. 1982. Annual. Conference held last week in June. Average attendance: 90. "The Conference is designed not only for writers but for teachers of writing. Each workshop is attended by a Master teacher who works with the writers/teachers in the afternoon to help them to translate their writing skills for classroom use. Workshops include children's literature, journal writing, creative nonfiction, personal essay, poetry, fiction, travel writing and short fiction. Manhattanville is a suburban campus 30 miles from New York City. The campus centers around Reid Castle, the administration building, the former home of Whitelaw Reid. Workshops are conducted in Reid Castle. We usually feature a major author as guest lecturer during the Conference. Past speakers have included such authors as Toni Morrison, Mary Gordon, Gail Godwin, Pete Hamill."

Costs: Conference cost was $690 in 1995 for 2 graduate credits plus $40 fee. Noncredit fee in 1995 was $560.

Accommodations: Students may rent rooms in the college residence halls. More luxurious accommodations are available at neighboring hotels. In the summer of 1995 the cost of renting a room in the residence halls was $21 per night.

Additional Information: Conference brochures/guidelines are available for SASE.

‡**MOHONK'S WRITERS RETREAT**, Lake Mohonk, New Paltz NY 12561. (914)255-1000. Fax: (914)256-2161. Contact: Helen Dorsey. Estab. 1993. Annual. Conference held March 14-17, 1996. Conference duration: 4 nights and 3 days. Average attendance: 80. "The conference is held at Mohonk Mountain House, a 127-year-old National Historic Landmark, featuring 275 guest rooms, situated on mountaintop and lakeside resort property." Conference includes hands-on writing workshops and individual ms consultations. Retreat leaders have included Cynthia Blair, Andrea Blaugrund, Jim Defelice, Priscilla Dunhill and Bill Henderson.

Costs: "The cost of the workshop is included in the overnight room rate of $171-287/day plus $25 program fee; service charge and tax are additional."

Accommodations: "Transportation from Stewart airport and the Poughkeepsie train station can be arranged through our transporation desk."

Additional Information: Critiques mss; should be 4 pages, double-spaced, mailed at least 1 month prior to the event. A private consultation is available during the workshop. Conference brochures/guidelines are available for SASE.

NEW ENGLAND WRITERS' WORKSHOP AT SIMMONS COLLEGE, 300 The Fenway, Boston MA 02115. (617)521-2090. Assistant Director: Jean Chaput Welch. Estab. 1977. Annually in summer. Workshop held 1st week of June. Workshop lasts one week. Average attendance: 45. "Adult fiction: novel or short story." "Boston and its literary heritage provide a stimulating environment for a workshop of writers. Simmons College is located in the Fenway area near the Museum of Fine Arts, Symphony Hall, the Isabella Stewart Gardner Museum, and many other places of educational, cultural, and social interest. Our theme is usually fiction (novel or short story) with the workshops in the morning and then the afternoon speakers either talk about their own work or talk about the 'business' of publishing." Past speakers and workshop leaders have included John Updike, Anne Beattie and Stephen King as well as editors from *The New Yorker*, *The Atlantic* and Houghton Mifflin.

Costs: $525 (1995 included full week of workshops and speakers, individual consultations, refreshments and 2 receptions).

Accommodations: Cost is $150 for Sunday to Sunday on-campus housing. A list of local hotels is also available.

Additional Information: "Up to 30 pages of manuscript may be sent in prior to workshop to be reviewed privately with workshop leader during the week."

NEWPORT WRITERS CONFERENCE, P.O. Box 12, Newport RI 02840. (401)846-9884. Fax: (401)846-1649. E-mail address: ascreengem@aol.com. Executive Director: Eleyne Austen Sharp. Estab. 1992. Annual. Conference held in October. Conference duration: 3 days. For fiction, magazine writing, screenwriting, writing for children, hypertext fiction and getting your book published. Held at The Inn at Shadow Lawn, a beautiful Victorian home with a pleasant view of rolling lawns and gardens. Guest rooms are named for female Victorian writers; some have kitchens and working fireplaces. Writing workshops are located in the downstairs parlor and library. Speakers for 1995 were Robert B. Parker (*Spenser* detective series author), Marci Coyote Rose (comedy writer and performer), John G. McDaid (science fiction author), James Gabriel Berman (author of *Uninvited*), Jennifer Moyer (editor), Britt Bell (publisher of *Small Press Magazine*), and Cynthia Sterling (literary agent at Lee Shore Agency).

Costs: (1995) full tuition, $195 plus $50 non-refundable registration fee.

Accommodations: Accommodations available at The Inn at Shadow Lawn (conference site). Ranges from $95 per night.

Additional Information: Offers evaluations on manuscripts (short stories, essays and novel chapters). Sponsors the annual CWA Writing Competition. Poetry and short story submissions accepted. Entries judged by panel of qualified writing professionals. Conference brochures/guidelines are available for #10 SASE.

‡**OLD CHATHAM FICTION WORKSHOP**, P.O. Box 211, Old Chatham NY 12136. Director: Jeff Seroy. Estab. 1994. Annual. Workshop usually held in the summer. Workshop duration: 1 week. Average attendance: 30. Workshop concentrates on fiction. "Faculty is drawn from publishing (editors and agents) as opposed to writers or writing teachers." Held at the "New York State Society of Friends Retreat—old, rambling house on 57 acres." Manuscript workshops are held in the morning. Panels on various aspects of publishing (editing, getting an agent, marketing, rights, sales, publicity) are held in the afternoon. "We also run a class to coach writers on how to read and present their own work in public."
Costs: $650 (commuters); $1,100 (regular); $1,350 (single room).
Accommodations: Transportation provided to and from the local airport and train station. "Accomodations are at the Quaker retreat. Also, arrangements can be made at local Bed and Breakfasts."
Additional Information: "We select participants based on 25-page manuscript; two 25-page manuscripts must be sent in to be workshopped, also. Admission is selective." Conference brochures/guidelines are available for SASE. "We have a high success rate of placing writers with agents and publishers."

ROMANCE WRITERS OF AMERICA/NEW YORK CITY CHAPTER/FROM DREAM TO REALITY WORKSHOP, P.O. Box 3722, Grand Central Station, New York NY 10163. (212)781-0067. President, RWA/NYC: Rita Madole. Estab. 1986. Annual. Workshop held March 8-10, 1996. Duration of conference: 3 days. Average attendence: 80. For those interested in writing and selling a romance novel. The conference is held at the Long Island Marriott, Mellville NY. "The workshop will include writing basics, the business of writing, editors panel, one-on-one conference sessions with published authors, and much more. Speakers will include leading romance authors and professional editors from major romance publishing houses."
Costs: "Registration fee is *less than* $100 (not including meals and accommodations)."
Additional Information: "Our Love and Laughter contest is opened to all unpublished writers. Fee is $15. Deadline: early December. Winner is announced at the workshop. Grand prize is $50 and a critique by an editor." Send SASE for contest brochure.

S.U.N.Y. COLLEGE WRITING ARTS FESTIVALS, State University of New York at Oswego, Oswego NY 13126. (315)341-2609. Director of the Program in Writing Arts: Leigh Allison Wilson. Estab. 1968. Biannual. Conferences held October and April. "The theme of the April conference will be 'The Year of the Child.' " Conference duration: 4 days, Monday-Thursday. Average attendance: 40-60. For writers of fiction, poetry and drama. Conference held at the Student Union facilities. Past themes have included gay and lesbian writing, Afro-American writing.
Costs: All sessions free and open to public.
Accommodations: Attendees must make their own arrangements for board and accommodations. May be given information through the Office of Continuing Education at Swetmen Hall, State University College, Oswego NY 13126.
Additional Information: Information poster available for SASE.

SCBWI/HOFSTRA CHILDREN'S LITERATURE CONFERENCE, Hofstra University, University College of Continuing Education, 205 Davison Hall, Hempstead NY 11550. (516)463-5016. Co-organizers: Connie C. Epstein, Adrienne Betz and Lewis Shena. Estab. 1985. Annual. Conference to be held April 20. Average attendance: 175. Conference to encourage good writing for children. "Purpose is to bring together various professional groups—writers, illustrators, librarians, teachers—who are interested in writing for children. Each year we organize program around a theme. One year it was Style and Substance, and another was The Global Village." The conference takes place at the Student Center Building of Hofstra University, located in Hempstead, Long Island. "We have two general sessions and five or six break-out groups that we hold in rooms in the Center or nearby classrooms. Lunch is provided." Last year's conference featured Vera B. Williams and Anne Pellowski as general speakers and offered special-interest groups in nonfiction (Fran Nankin), picture books (Steven Kroll), fiction (Pat Hermes), photo essay (Susan Kuklin), writing for packagers (Ellise Howard), submission procedures (George Nicholson).
Cost: $51 (previous year) for SCBWI members; $58 for nonmembers. Lunch included.

‡**SEACOAST WRITER'S ASSOCIATION SPRING MEETING AND FALL CONFERENCE**, P.O. Box 6553, Portsmouth NH 03802-6553. Membership Director: Paula Flanders. Annual. Conferences held in May and October. Conference duration: 1 day. Average attendance: 50. "At our spring meeting, we choose the topic of interest to our members. The fall conference offers workshops covering fiction, nonfiction and poetry, and has included a workshop on plotting science fiction novels."
Costs: $50.
Additional Information: "We sometimes include critiques. It is up to the speaker." Spring meeting includes a contest. Categories are fiction, nonfiction (essays) and poetry. Judges vary from year to year. Conference brochures/guidelines are available for SASE.

STATE OF MAINE WRITERS' CONFERENCE, P.O. Box 7146, Ocean Park ME 04063. (207)934-9806 June-August; (413)596-6734 September-May. Chairman: Richard F. Burns. Estab. 1941. Annual. Conference held August 20-23, 1996. Conference duration: 4 days. Average attendance: 70-75. "We try to present a

balanced as well as eclectic conference. There is quite a bit of time and attention given to poetry but we also have children's literature, mystery writing, travel, novels/fiction and lots of items and issues of interest to writers such as speakers who are: publishers, editors, illustrators and the like. Our concentration is, by intention, a general view of writing to publish. We are located in Ocean Park, a small seashore village 14 miles south of Portland. Ours is a summer assembly center with many buildings from the Victorian Age. The conference meets in Porter Hall, one of the assembly buildings which is listed on the National Register of Historic Places. Within recent years our guest list has included Lewis Turco, Bob Anderson, David McCord, Dorothy Clarke Wilson, Dennis LeDoux, Will Anderson, Christopher Keane and many others. We usually have about 10 guest presenters a year."
Costs: $85 includes the conference banquet. There is a reduced fee, $40, for students ages 21 and under. The fee does not include housing or meals which must be arranged separately by the conferees.
Accommodations: An accommodations list is available. "We are in a summer resort area and motels, guest houses and restaurants abound."
Additional Information: "We have a contest announcement which comes out in January-March and has about 15 contests on various genres. The prizes, all modest, are awarded at the end of the conference and only to those who are registered." Program guide comes out in April-June.

‡STONECOAST WRITERS' CONFERENCE, Summer Session Office, University of Southern Maine, 96 Falmouth St., Portland ME 04103. (207)280-4076. Contact: Barbara Hope, Director. Estab. 1977. Annual. Conference held late July or early August. Conference duration: 10 days. Average attendance: over 100. "Stonecoast is a teaching conference emphasizing short fiction, the novel, creative nonfiction, poetry and genre writing. The conference is held at the University of Southern Maine's Shore House on Casco Bay. Guest speakers have included Carolyn Chute, Joyce Johnson, Gerald Stern, Robley Wilson, Alix Kates Shulman, David Bradley.
Costs: $399 (tuition only).
Accommodations: Attendees must make their own transporation arrangements. Dormitory accommodations (including private bath) available at Boudoin College.
Additional Information: Activities include "daily workshops—work is submitted prior to conference." Also includes lectures, panels and readings. Offers 2 scholarships for participants. Brochures available for SASE.

VASSAR COLLEGE INSTITUTE OF PUBLISHING AND WRITING: CHILDREN'S BOOKS IN THE MARKETPLACE, Vassar College, Box 300, Poughkeepsie NY 12601. (914)437-5903. Associate Director of College Relations: Maryann Bruno. Estab. 1983. Annual. Conference held in second week of June or July. Conference duration: 1 week. Average attendance: 40. Writing and publishing children's literature. The conference is held at Vassar College, a 1,000-acre campus located in the mid-Hudson valley. The campus is self-contained, with residence halls, dining facilities, and classroom and meeting facilities. Vassar is located 90 miles north of New York City, and is accessible by car, train and air. Participants have use of Vassar's athletic facilities, including swimming, squash, tennis and jogging. Vassar is known for the beauty of its campus. "The Institute is directed by Barbara Lucas of Lucas-Evans Books and features top working professionals from the field of publishing."
Costs: $800, includes full tuition, room and three meals a day.
Accommodations: Special conference attendee accommodations are in campus residence halls.
Additional Information: Writers may submit a 10-page sample of their writing for critique, which occurs during the week of the conference. Conference brochures/guidelines are available upon request.

WELLS WRITERS' WORKSHOPS, 69 Broadway, Concord NH 03301. (603)225-9162. Director: Victor A. Levine. Estab. 1988. Held: 2 times/year in Wells, Maine. Conferences held from May 20 to May 25; September 9 to September 14. Maximum attendance: 5. "Workshop concentrates on short and long fiction, especially the novel. Focus is on the rational structuring of a story, using Aristotelian and scriptwriting insights. Throughout, the workshop balances direct instruction with the actual plotting and writing of the basic scenes of a novel or short story." Conference located in a "large, airy and light house overlooking the ocean with ample individual space for writers and group conferences. While the purposes of the workshop is to teach the process of plotting as it applies across the board—to all kinds of fiction, including novels, short stories, movies—it strives to meet the specific needs of participants, especially through individual conferences with the instructors."
Costs: "The cost of $950 covers tuition, room and board. Registration cost is $95 (nonrefundable). Payment may be in two or three installments."
Accommodations: Workshop supplies transportation from/to Portland International Airport—or other places, by arrangement. Workshop supplies accommodations.
Additional Information: Conference brochures/guidelines available for SASE. "Workshop has a scholarship fund which can, as it has in the past, defray part of the total expense of $950."

WESLEYAN WRITERS CONFERENCE, Wesleyan University, Middletown CT 06459. (860)685-3604. Director: Anne Greene. Estab. 1956. Annual. Conference held from June 23-28. Average attendance: 100. For novel, short story, poetry, screenwriting, nonfiction, literary journalism. The conference is held on the campus of Wesleyan University, in the hills overlooking the Connecticut River. Meals and lodging are provided on campus. Features readings of new fiction and guest lectures on a range of topics including the art of memoir. **Costs:** In 1995, tuition $430; meals $173; room $95.

Accommodations: "Participants can fly to Hartford or take Amtrak to Meriden, CT. We are happy to help participants make travel arrangements." Overnight participants stay on campus.

Additional Information: Ms critiques are available as part of the program but are not required. "We sponsor several scholarship competitions and award teaching fellowships. Application information is in conference brochure." Brochures/guidelines are available for SASE.

‡WESTCHESTER WRITERS' CONFERENCE, P.O. Box 294, White Plains NY 10603. (914)472-8438. Conference Director: Linda Simone. Estab. 1985. Annual. Conference held April 13. Average attendance: 200. Conference includes fiction, journalism, poetry, writing for children, enhancing creativity, writers and computers; writers' rights. Conference held on private college campus. Panels include: meet the agents; the young adult market; the short story.

Costs: $75 includes all workshops and luncheon.

Additional Information: Conference brochures/guidelines are available for SASE.

THE WRITERS' CENTER AT CHAUTAUQUA, P.O. Box 408, Chautauqua NY 14722. (716)357-2445 or (717)872-8337. Director: Mary Jean Irion. Estab. 1987. Annual. Workshops held late June through August "are offered in combination with a vacation at historic Chautauqua Institution, a large cultural resort in western New York for families and singles. Workshops are 2 hours, Monday-Friday; average attendance is 12." Past workshop leaders: Kristin Kovacic, short story; Nina da Vinci Nichols, novel; David McKain, Writing the Stories of Your Life; Susan Rowan Masters, writers 6-12 years old and 13-18 years old; Carol H. Behrman and Margery Facklam, Writing for Children.

Costs: In 1995, $60/week. Meals, housing, gate ticket (about $150 per week), parking ($20) are in addition.

Accommodations: Information is available; but no special rates have been offered.

Additional Information: Each leader specifies the kind of workshop offered. Most accept submissions in advance; information is made available in March on request. Conference brochures/guidelines are available for 55¢ SASE.

WRITERS RETREAT WORKSHOP, % Write It/Sell It, P.O. Box 139, South Lancaster MA 01561-0139. Phone/fax: (508)368-0287. Manager: Gail Provost. Estab. 1987. May 1996 workshop held in Erlanger, KY (just south of Cincinnati, OH). Workshop duration: 10 days. Average attendance: 12-25. "Focus on fiction and narrative nonfiction books in progress. All genres. "The Writers Retreat Workshop is an intensive learning experience for small groups of serious-minded writers. Founded by the late Gary Provost, one of the country's leading writing instructors and his wife Gail, an award-winning author, the WRW is a challenging and enriching adventure. Conducting workshop classes in 1996 is Alice Orr, nationally known author, agent and editor. Also participating is Robin Hardy, author of nonfiction and young adult fiction, and a former editor at Cloverdale Press. He will work one-on-one with students and their manuscripts with emphasis on plotting. WRW graduates and published novelists Jean Stone and Frank Strunk will participate as authors-in-residence, working with small groups of students to develop editing skills and individual style. Several WRW graduates will be available as mentors for private consultation with students. The goal of the WRW staff is for students to leave with a new understanding of the marketplace and the craft of writing. In the heart of a supportive and spirited community of fellow writers, students are able to make remarkable creative leaps over the course of the 10-day workshop."

Costs: Costs vary (discount for past participants), but average about $1,595 for ten days which include all food and lodging. "Workshop participants are responsible for arranging their own transportation but WRW helps to coordinate taxis, etc. from the airport."

Additional Information: Participants are asked to submit a brief overview and synopsis before the workshop and are given assignments and feedback during the 10-day workshop. Brochures/guidelines are available for SASE.

Midatlantic (DC, DE, MD, NJ, PA)

BALTIMORE SCIENCE FICTION SOCIETY WRITER'S WORKSHOP, P.O. Box 686, Baltimore MD 21203-0686. (301)563-2737. Contact: Steve Lubs. Estab. 1983. Conference/workshop held: roughly, 2 times/year. "Conference dates vary, please write for next date held and deadline information." Conference duration: 1 day. Average attendance: 7. Conference concentration is science fiction and fantasy. "Conference is held in a former movie theater (small) in the process of being renovated."

Costs: Manuscripts are submitted in advance; cost 75¢/page.

Additional Information: "Manuscripts are submitted in advance, by a particular deadline. A copy of every submission is mailed to each participant, to read and critique before the workshop. We are an amateur writer's group, attempting to help anyone interested in writing better science fiction and/or fantasy. This workshop is sponsored by a nonprofit group who promotes science fiction and fantasy in the Baltimore-Washington DC area."

‡**BLUEGRASS WRITERS WORKSHOP**, P.O. Box 3098, Princeton NJ 08543-3098. (609)275-2947. Fax: (609)275-1243. National Director: Karl G. Garson. Estab. 1994. Annual. Workshop held in June. Workshop duration: 2 weeks. Average attendance: 15. "Workshop concentrates on all genres using the horse and/or horse racing as the subject." Held at Churchill Downs racetrack, Louisville, Kenturky. Guest speakers for 1996 will include Gerald Costanzo, founder/director, Carnegie Mellon University Press; Lee K. Abbott, Ohio State University; and Jana Harris, University of Washington.
Costs: Fee for 1995 was $750 (included tuition and daily lunches).
Accommodations: Transportation to workshop site and field trip locations is furnished. Participants are responsible for their travel to and from Louisville. On-campus housing and hotel information is furnished. On-campus housing: $18/single; $13/double, per person, per night. Hotel (Holiday Inn): $35/single or double, per night.
Additional Information: "A representative sample of writing is requested with the workshop application." Conference brochures/guidelines are available for SASE.

‡**CUMBERLAND VALLEY FICTION WRITERS WORKSHOP**, Dickinson College, Carlisle PA 17013-2896. (717)245-1291. Director: Judy Gill. Estab. 1990. Annual. Workshop held in late June. Average attendance: 30-40. "5-day fiction workshop. Workshop is held on the campus of Dickinson College, a small liberal arts college, in Carlisle, PA." Panel: "Writers Roundtable"—faculty respond to wide variety of questions submitted by participants.
Costs: Tuition for 5-day workshop: $300; Room (optional): $125.
Accommodations: Special accommodations made. A residence hall on campus is reserved for workshop participants. Cost is $25 per night.
Additional Information: Applicants must submit a 10-page manuscript for evaluation prior to the workshop. Conference brochures/guidelines are available for SASE.

FAIRVIEW SUMMIT CENTER WRITER'S WORKSHOPS, 10800 Mt. Fairview Rd. S.E., Cumberland MD 21502. (301)724-6842. Director: Petrina Aubol. Estab. 1992. "In conjunction with the local Tri-State Writer's Guild we plan to hold a summer (second weekend in July) and fall (second weekend in October) two day retreat, limit 30. One day will be devoted to fiction, one to nonfiction with participants welcome to attend for one day. Fairview Summit is located on a dead end road on top of Irons Mountain. The retreat center, located in the middle of a 100 acre forest, is equipped to provide meals, indoor and outdoor meeting space, work stations and comfortable lodging for 20. Our 1995 speakers included Jo Gilbert, associate editor of *Writer's Digest Magazine*; Gail Adams, West Virginia University short story writer and novelist; and Jim Ralston, Charleston, West Virginia columnist and essayist." A local computer expert updates authors on latest electronic aids at each retreat.
Costs: Two-day weekend retreat $100 includes one night lodging, 5 meals (breakfast Saturday-lunch Sunday). $25 including breakfast per day for extra lodging.
Additional Information: In addition to the two sponsored retreats, writer's groups reserve space for retreats year round, some open to the public. Write for schedules, or to reserve space for group retreat. Group rates (minimum 10) $20 per person. Meals: breakfast/snack $3, lunch $6, dinner $8.

HIGHLIGHTS FOUNDATION WRITERS WORKSHOP AT CHAUTAUQUA, Dept. NM, 814 Court St., Honesdale PA 18431. (717)253-1192. Conference Director: Jan Keen. Estab. 1985. Annual. Workshop held July 13 to July 20. Average attendance: 100. "Writer workshops geared toward those who write for children—beginner, intermediate, advanced levels. Small group workshops, one-to-one interaction between faculty and participants plus panel sessions, lectures and large group meetings. Workshop site is the picturesque community of Chautauqua, New York." Classes offered include Children's Interests, Writing Dialogue, Outline for the Novel, Conflict and Developing Plot. Past faculty has included Eve Bunting, Pam Conrad, James Cross Giblin, Walter Dean Myers, Laurence Pringle, Jerry Spinelli and Ed Young.
Accommodations: "We coordinate ground transportation to and from airports, trains and bus stations in the Erie, Pennsylvania and Jamestown/Buffalo, New York area. We also coordinate accommodations for conference attendees."
Additional Information: "We offer the opportunity for attendees to submit a manuscript for review at the conference." Workshop brochures/guidelines are available for SASE.

Market conditions are constantly changing! If you're still using this book and it is 1997 or later, buy the newest edition of Novel & Short Story Writer's Market *at your favorite bookstore or order from* Writer's Digest Books.

LIGONIER VALLEY WRITERS CONFERENCE, RR4, Box 8, Ligonier PA 15658. (412)238-6397 or (412)238-5749. Director: Tina Thoburn. Estab. 1986. Annual. Conference held from July 13 to 15. Average attendance: 100. Conference concentrates on fiction, nonfiction and poetry. The conference is centered in a scenic small town with classrooms in the town hall and several nearby inns, hotels and restaurants. Included are a picnic and brunch featuring faculty readings and a noon garden luncheon. This year's conference may include more on marketing with a literary agent and/or an editor on the faculty or available to offer one-on-one critiques of pre-submitted work. David McCullough; Ralph Bennett, senior editor of *Reader's Digest* and humorist Jeffrey E. O'Brien have been keynote speakers.

Accommodations: All registrants are provided with a list of motels, inns and bed and breakfasts. Last year's special rates began at $65 per night.

Additional Information: "Work to be critiqued must be submitted by June 1." Participants are invited to submit work to our literary journal—*Loyalhanna Review*. Brochures/guidelines available for SASE after March 1.

‡METROPOLITAN WRITERS CONFERENCE, Seton Hall University, South Orange NJ 07079. (201)761-9430. Fax: (201)761-9794. Contact: Jane Degnan. Estab. 1987. Annual. Conference duration: 1-3 days (varies). Average attendance: 100. Conference to help writers get their fiction and writing for children published. Held on the campus of Seton Hall University. Workshop topics focus on helping writers improve their use of plot, characterization, setting, point of view, etc., as well as a discussion on how to get an agent. Speakers have included Belva Plain, Meredith Sue Willis, Stefanie Matteson and Thomas William Simpson.

Costs: $59 (meals not included).

Accommodations: On-site dorm rooms available for $20/night.

Additional Information: Maximum 10-page submissions critiqued for $20. Conference brochures/guidelines are available for SASE.

MID-ATLANTIC MYSTERY BOOK FAIR & CONVENTION, Detecto Mysterioso Books at Society Hill Playhouse, 507 South 8th St., Philadelphia PA 19147. Contact: Deen Kogan, chairperson. Estab. 1991. Annual. Convention held in early November. 1996: November 8-10; 1997: November 3-5. Average attendance: 350-400. Focus is on mystery, suspense, thriller, true crime novels. "An examination of the genre from many points of view." The convention is held at the Holiday Inn-Independence Mall, located in the historic area of Philadelphia. Speakers at 1995 convention included Lawrence Block, Jeremiah Healy, Neil Albert, Michael Connelly, Paul Levine, Eileen Dreyer, Earl Emerson, Wendy Hornsby.

Costs: $45 registration fee.

Accommodations: Attendees must make their own transportation arrangements. Special room rate available at convention hotel.

Additional Information: "The Bookroom is a focal point of the convention. Twenty-five specialty dealers are expected to exhibit and collectables range from hot-off-the-press bestsellers to 1930's pulp; from fine editions to reading copies."

MONTROSE CHRISTIAN WRITER'S CONFERENCE, 5 Locust St., Montrose Bible Conference, Montrose PA 18801. (717)278-1001. (800)598-5030. Bible Conference Director: Jim Fahringer. Conference Co-Director: Jill Renich-Meyers. (717)766-1100. Estab. 1990. Annual. Conference held July 8-12, 1996. Average attendance: 65. "We try to meet a cross-section of writing needs, for beginners and advanced, covering fiction, poetry and writing for children. We meet in the beautiful village of Montrose, Pennsylvania, situated in the mountains. The Bible Conference provides motel-like accommodations and good food. The main sessions are held in the chapel with rooms available for other classes. Fiction writing has been taught each year." 1995 speakers were Leslie Stobbe, editor; Sandra Brooks, editor and freelance writer; Rebecca Price Janney, author of 8 volumes in a mystery series; and Frank Andrews, news director of a television station.

Costs: In 1995 registration was $70.

Accommodations: Will meet planes in Binghamton NY and Scranton PA; will meet bus in Binghamton. Information on overnight accommodations is available. On-site accommodations: room and board $192-$276/week; $32-$46/day including food.

Additional Information: "Writers can send work ahead and have it critiqued for $20." Brochures/guidelines are available for SASE. "The attendees are usually church related (interchurch). The writing has a Christian emphasis."

‡NEW JERSEY ROMANCE WRITERS PUT YOUR HEART IN A BOOK CONFERENCE, P.O. Box 513, Plainsboro NJ 08536. (201)263-8477. President: Elaine Charton. Estab. 1984. Annual. Conference held October 4 and October 5. Average attendance: 250. Conference concentrating on romance fiction. "Workshops offered on various topics for all writers of romance, from beginner to multi-published." Held at the Holiday Inn in Jamesburg, New Jersey. Offers workshops with a panel of editors and a panel of agents. Speakers have included Diana Gabaldon, Andrea Kane, Nora Roberts and Alice Orr.

Costs: $120 (New Jersey Romance Writers members) and $135 (nonmembers).
Accommodations: Special hotel rate available for conference attendees.
Additional Information: Sponsors Put Your Heart in a Book Contest for unpublished writers and the Golden Leaf Contest for published members of RWA Regional. Conference brochures, guidelines and membership information are available for SASE. "Appointments offered for conference attendees, both published and unpublished, with editors and/or agents in the genre."

‡OUTDOOR WRITERS ASSOCIATION OF AMERICA ANNUAL CONFERENCE, 2017 Cato Ave., Suite 101, State College PA 16801-2768. (814)234-1011. Meeting Planner: Eileen King. Estab. 1927. Annual. Conference held from June 16 to June 20. Average attendance: 800-950. Conference concentrates on outdoor communications (all forms of media). Held at the Duluth Entertainment Convention Center. Featured speakers have included Don Ranley, University of Missouri, Columbia; US Forest Service Chief Jack Ward Thomas; USFWS Secretary, Mollie Beattie; Secretary of the Interior, Bruce Babbitt; and Director, Bureau of Land Management, Michael Dombeck.
Costs: $130 for nonmembers; "applicants must have prior approval from executive director." Registration fee includes cost of most meals.
Accommodations: List of accommodations available after April. Special room rate for attendees.
Additional Information: Sponsors contests, "but all is done prior to the conference and you must be a member to enter them." Conference brochures/guidelines are available for SASE.

ST. DAVIDS CHRISTIAN WRITERS CONFERENCE, 1775 Eden Rd., Lancaster PA 17601-3523. (717)394-6758. Registrar: Shirley Eaby. Estab. 1957. Annual. Conference held June 25-30. Average attendance: 85. Conference "to prepare writers to be published in both religious and general markets. Major workshops: fiction, nonfiction, beginners, advanced, poetry, writing for children, devotional." Held on eastern college campus, west of Philadelphia, picturesque with ponds and swans, retreat atmosphere. Fiction workshop leaders have included Barbara Robinson, author of *The Best Christmas Pageant Ever*. Previous guest speakers include poet David Page.
Costs: Tuition is $250-295 (1994); room and board is $192-227/week; optional tutorials are $35-175.
Accommodations: "We provide transportation from local train station/hotel to the campus (must make prior arrangements). Limo ($18); (you make reservation) from airport to local hotel where we will pick you up. Let us know your arrival time at train station or hotel." Overnight accommodations in dormatories on campus.
Additional Information: Critiques do not require pre-conference submission of manuscript. Informal group discussion led by a professional. Usually small groups. Sponsors a contest for short fiction. Several contests are held. Deadline for submission is usually late May. Judges are usually faculty members, editors or agents. You must attend conference to enter. Conference brochures/guidelines are available for SASE. "We have many successful published fiction writers on staff available for teaching, critiquing, encouraging or just being a friend."

SANDY COVE CHRISTIAN WRITERS CONFERENCE, Sandy Cove Bible Conference, North East MD 21901. (800)287-4843. Director: Gayle Roper. Estab. 1991. Annual. Conference held October 7-11. Conference duration: 4 days (Sunday dinner to Thursday breakfast). Average attendance: 100. "There are major, continuing workshops in fiction, article writing, nonfiction books and beginner's and advanced workshops. Twenty-eight one-hour classes touch many topics. While Sandy Cove has a strong emphasis on available markets in Christian publishing, all writers are more than welcome. Sandy Cove is a full-service conference center located on the Chesapeake Bay. All the facilities are first class with suites, single or double rooms available." Past faculty has included Judith Couchman, editor, *Clarity*; William Petersen, editor, Revell; Ken Petersen, editor, Tyndale House; Linda Tomblin, editor, *Guideposts* and Col. Henry Gariepy, editor-in-chief, The Salvation Army.
Costs: Tuition is $225.
Accommodations: "If one flies into Philadelphia International Airport, we will transport them the one hour drive to Sandy Cove. Accommodations are available at Sandy Cove. Information available upon request." Cost is $200 double occupancy room and board, $250 single occupancy room and board for 4 nights and meals.
Additional Information: Special critiques are available—a one-time critique for $30 and a continuing critique for $75 (one time is 30-minute appointment and written critique; continuing is 3 30-minute appointments). Conference brochures/guidelines are available for SASE.

TRENTON STATE COLLEGE WRITERS' CONFERENCE, English Dept., Trenton State College, Hillwood Lakes CN 4700, Trenton NJ 08650-4700. (609)771-3254. Director: Jean Hollander. Estab. 1980. Annual. Conference held every spring. Conference duration: 9 a.m. to 10:30 p.m. Average attendance: 600-1,000. "Conference concentrates on fiction (the largest number of participants), poetry, children's literature, play and screenwriting, magazine and newspaper journalism, overcoming writer's block, nonfiction books. Conference is held at the student center at the college in two auditoriums and workshop rooms; also Kendall Theatre on campus." We focus on various genres: romance, detective, mystery, TV writing, etc. Topics have included

"How to Get Happily Published," "How to Get an Agent" and "Earning a Living as a Writer." The conference usually presents twenty or so authors, plus two featured speakers, who have included Arthur Miller, Saul Bellow, Toni Morrison, Joyce Carol Oates, Erica Jong. Alice Walker will be a featured speaker at the 1996 conference.

Costs: General registration $45, plus $10 for each workshop. Lower rates for students.

Additional Information: Brochures/guidelines available.

‡**WASHINGTON INDEPENDENT WRITERS (WIW) SPRING WRITERS CONFERENCE**, #220, 733 15th St. NW, Washington DC 20005. (202)347-4973. Executive Director: Isolde Chapin. Estab. 1975. Annual. Conference held in May. Conference duration: Friday evening and Saturday. Average attendance: approximately 350. "Gives participants a chance to hear from and talk with dozens of experts on book and magazine publishing as well as on the craft, tools and business of writing." Past keynote speakers include Erica Jong, Haynes Johnson and Diane Rehm.

Costs: $85 members; $110 nonmembers; $150 membership and conference.

Additional Information: Brochures/guidelines available for SASE in mid-March.

WRITING FOR PUBLICATION, Pittsburgh Theological Seminary, 616 N. Highland Ave., Pittsburgh PA 15206. Director of Continuing Education: The Rev. Mary Lee Talbot. Estab. 1983. Annual. Conference held April 16-17, 1996. Average attendance: 20. To teach techniques for getting published. "Pittsburgh Theological Seminary is located in the East End of Pittsburgh. The 13-acre campus is in the middle of an urban center." Dr. Roland Tapp is the leader.

Costs: $75 registration plus room ($19 single, $13.50 double per person per night) and meals (breakfast and lunch served on campus).

Accommodations: On-campus housing is available.

Additional Information: Critiques are available. Manuscripts sent to Dr. Tapp one month before conference. Dr. Tapp also does individual sessions during the conference. Conference brochures/guidelines are available for SASE.

‡**WRITING FOR PUBLICATION**, Villanova University, Villanova PA 19085. (215)645-4620. Director: Wm. Ray Heitzmann, Ph.D. Estab. 1975. Semiannual. Conference dates vary, held fall, spring. Next session: March 1-2, 1996. Average attendance: 15-20 (seminar style). Conference covers marketing one's manuscript (fiction, nonfiction, book, article, etc.); strong emphasis on marketing. Conference held in a seminar room at a university (easy access, parking, etc.). Panels include "Advanced Writing for Publication," "Part-time Writing," "Working With Editors." Panelists include Ray Heitzman, and others.

Costs: $345 (graduate credit); $100 (non-credit) plus $10 registration fee.

Accommodations: List of motels/hotels available, but most people live in area and commute. Special arrangements made on an individual basis.

Additional Information: Critiques available. Voluntary submission of manuscripts. Brochures/guidelines are available. "Workshop graduates have been very successful."

Midsouth (NC, SC, TN, VA, WV)

‡**THE CHARLESTON WRITERS' CONFERENCE**, Lightsey Conference Center, College of Charleston, Charleston SC 29424. (803)953-5822. Conference Coordinator: Judy Sawyer. Estab. 1990. Annual. Conference held in March. Conference duration: 3½ days. Average attendance: 165. "Conference concentrates on fiction, poetry and nonfiction. The conference is held at conference center on urban campus in historic setting." Themes are different each year and varied within confines of each conference. 1995 faculty included Yusef Komunyakaa, Jill McCorkle, Kelly Cherry, Bret Lott, Sydney Lea, Carol Houck Smith, Martha Bennett Stiles, Paul Hoover, Franklin Ashley, Alexa Self.

Costs: Under $125. Includes receptions and breaks.

Accommodations: Special rates available at hotels within walking distance.

Additional Information: "Critiques are available for an extra fee—not a requirement." Those making inquiries are placed on mailing list.

CHRISTOPHER NEWPORT UNIVERSITY WRITERS' CONFERENCE, 50 Shoe Lane, Newport News VA 23606-2998. (804)594-7158. Coordinator: Terry Cox-Joseph. Estab. 1981. Annual. Conference held April 12-13. Average attendance: 100. "Our workshop is for both published and unpublished writers in all genres. It provides a network for area writers, connecting them with markets, literary agents, editors and printers." The conference is held on the campus of Christopher Newport University in Newport News, VA. "We have a good food service, a bookstore, adequate meeting rooms and total access for the handicapped." Workshop presenters have included Kathryn Hammer (humor), author of *And How Are We Feeling Today?*; Joseph Bosco (nonfiction), author of *Blood Will Tell*, published by Wm. Morrow; and other literary experts.

Costs: $69, includes pre-conference presenters reception on Friday evening in "Celebration of the Arts," coffee and pastries and lunch on Saturday.
Accommodations: Adequate parking available. "Our staff could help with arrangements for overnight accommodations."
Additional Information: "We have a literary contest in four areas: poetry, fiction, nonfiction and juvenile fiction. Each entry is critiqued by a judge who is a published writer in the field." Conference brochures/ guidelines available for SASE.

DUKE UNIVERSITY WRITERS' WORKSHOP, Box 90703, Durham NC 27708. (919)684-3255. Director: Georgann Eubanks. Estab. 1978. Annual. Workshop held in June. Average attendance: 50. To promote "creative writing: beginning, intermediate and advanced fiction; short story; scriptwriting; children's writing; poetry; creative nonfiction." Workshop held at "Duke University campus classrooms and meeting facilities. Gothic architecture, rolling green hills. Nationally recognized for its academic excellence, Duke sponsors this workshop annually for creative writers of various genres."
Costs: $350 for conference (meals not included).
Accommodations: Hotel rooms available near campus.
Additional Information: Critiques available. "Works-in-progress requested 3 weeks before workshop. Each participant gets *private* consult plus small-group in-class critiques." Brochures/guidelines are available. "No 'big' names, no mammoth lectures; simply *excellent*, concentrated instruction plus time to work. No glitz. Hard work. Great results."

‡FRANCIS MARION WRITERS' CONFERENCE, Francis Marion University, Florence SC 29501. (803)661-1500. Director: David Starkey. Estab. 1982. Conference held annually in June. Conference duration: 3 days. Average attendance: 40-50. Conference for "fiction, poetry, nonfiction and drama." Held in classrooms/ college auditorium at Francis Marion University.
Costs: $85.
Accommodations: Information on overnight accommodations made available through directors.
Additional Information: Some workshops for fiction writers are included. Sponsors a chapbook competition for participants. Brochures or guidelines available for SASE.

HIGHLAND SUMMER CONFERENCE, Box 7014, Radford University, Radford VA 24142. (703)831-5366. Chair, Appalachian Studies Program: Dr. Grace Toney Edwards. Estab. 1978. Annual. Conference held in mid-June. Conference duration: 12 days. Average attendance: 25. "The HSC features one (two weeks) or two (one week each) guest leaders each year. As a rule, our leaders are well known writers who have connections, either thematic, or personal, or both, to the Appalachian region. The genre(s) of emphasis depends upon the workshop leader(s). In the past we have had as our leaders Jim Wayne Miller, poet, novelist, teacher; and Wilma Dykemen, novelist, journalist, social critic, author of *Tall Woman* among others. The Highland Summer Conference is held at Radford University, a school of about 9,000 students. Radford is in the Blue Ridge Mountains of southwest Virginia about 45 miles south of Roanoke, VA."
Costs: "The cost is based on current Radford tuition for 3 credit hours plus an additional conference fee. On-campus meals and housing are available at additional cost. In 1995 conference tuition was $406 for undergraduates, $424 for graduate students."
Accommodations: We do not have special rate arrangements with local hotels. We do offer accommodations on the Radford University Campus in a recently refurbished residence hall. (In 1995 cost was $16-25 per night.)
Additional Information: "Conference leaders do typically critique work done during the two-week conference, but do not ask to have any writing submitted prior to the conference beginning." Conference brochures/ guidelines are available for SASE.

‡MID SOUTH WRITERS FESTIVAL, 5858 Sweet Oak Cove, Bartlett TN 38134-5545. (901)377-8250. Festival Director: Michael Denington. Estab. 1994. Annual. Usually held the second Saturday in May. Average attendance: 80. "To support, encourage and praise writers is our reason for being. The areas of concentration are fiction, poetry, nonfiction, playwriting, and children's literature." Festival held at local hotel. Panelists have included: editors, a theater director and professor of theater, poets, an author of children's books, and an agent.
Costs: Registration fee was $7. Awards Banquet was $17.50.
Accommodations: "We try to get reduced rates if people want to stay overnight."
Additional Information: Sponsors a contest as part of conference. Fee is charged. Judges are professional writers. Conference brochures/guidelines are available around January 1 for SASE.

‡NATIONAL LEAGUE OF AMERICAN PEN WOMEN, Richmond Branch, P.O. Box 35935, Richmond VA 23235. (804)323-0417. Director: Sara Bird Wright. Estab. 1970. Biennial. Next conference will be held "probably in fall 1997." Conference duration: 1 day. Average attendance: 100. "The purpose of our conference is to reach out to the writing community with a conference geared to a wide range of interests except poetry. We meet in the lovely Fort Magruder Inn in Williamsburg, Virginia." Past speakers include: David

Baldacci, "Writing & Publishing a First Novel"; Claudine Wirths and Mary Bowman-Kruhm, "Online for Research and Networking"; and Rebecca Greer, "Freelancing for Major Magazines."
Costs: $70 members and $80 nonmembers plus $10 contest fee.
Accommodations: Discounts available for attendees at Fort Magruder Inn for Friday through Sunday.
Additional Information: Conference brochures/guidelines are available for SASE.

‡NORTH CAROLINA WRITERS' NETWORK FALL CONFERENCE, P.O. Box 954, Carrboro NC 27510. (919)967-9540. Executive Director: Marsha Warren. Estab. 1985. Annual. "Conference will be held in Durham NC, November 15-17." Average attendance: 350. "The conference is a weekend full of workshops, panels, readings and discussion groups. We try to have *all* genres represented. In the past we have had novelists, poets, journalists, editors, children's writers, young adult writers, storytellers, puppetry, screenwriters, etc. We take the conference to a different location in North Carolina each year in order to best serve our entire state. We hold the conference at a conference center with hotel rooms available."
Costs: "Conference cost is approximately $95 and includes three to four meals."
Accommodations: "Special conference hotel rates are obtained, but the individual makes his/her own reservations. If requested, we will help the individual find a roommate."
Additional Information: Conference brochures/guidelines are available for 2 first-class stamps.

‡SCBWI/MID-ATLANTIC, 616 Old Dominion Rd., Yorktown VA 23692. (804)898-4679. Regional Advisor: Linda Wirkner. Estab. 1984. Annual. Conference held in the fall. Conference duration: one day. Average attendance: 100. Writing for children. Usually held at a conference center of a well-known hotel chain. Past themes include "Marketing," fiction workshops for writers and "How-to" for illustrators. Past guest speakers include Connie Epstein, Jim Giblin, Norm Bomor, editors and writers.
Costs: $55 members, $60 non-members, includes continental breakfast and lunch.
Accommodations: Special conference rate on-site.
Additional Information: Sponsors writer's contest, illustrator's display and critique of contest entries. Entry requirements: Paid registration; 1,500 word ms, typed, double-spaced; limited to one manuscript per person. Conference brochures/guidelines are available for SASE.

‡SEWANEE WRITERS' CONFERENCE, 310 St. Luke's Hall, Sewanee TN 37383-1000. (615)598-1141. Fax: (615)598-1145. Conference Administrator: Cheri B. Peters. Estab. 1990. Annual. Conference held July 16-28, 1996. Conference duration: 12 days. Average attendance: 110. "We offer genre-based workshops (in fiction, poetry, and playwriting), not theme-based workshops. The Sewanee Writers' Conference uses the facilities of the University of the South. Physically, the University is a collection of ivy-covered Gothic-style buildings, located on the Cumberland Plateau in mid-Tennessee. We allow invited editors, publishers, and agents to structure their own presentations, but there is always opportunity for questions from the audience." The 1995 faculty included Russell Banks, James Gordon Bennett, Ellen Douglas, Ann Hood and Stephen Wright.
Costs: Full conference fee (tuition, board, and basic room) is $1,150; a single room costs an additional $50.
Accommodations: Complimentary chartered bus service is available, on a limited basis, on the first and last days of the conference. Participants are housed in University dormitory rooms. Motel or B&B housing is available but not abundantly so. Dormitory housing costs are included in the full conference fee.
Additional Information: "We offer each participant (excluding auditors) the opportunity for a private manuscript conference with a member of the faculty. These manuscripts are due one month before the conference begins." Conference brochures/guidelines are available, "but no SASE is necessary. The conference has available a limited number of fellowships and scholarships; these are awarded on a competitive basis."

‡THE WRITERS' WORKSHOP, P.O. Box 696, Asheville NC 28802. (704)254-8111. Executive Director: Karen Tager. Estab. 1984. Held throughout the year. Conference duration: varies from 1 day to 20 weeks. Average attendance: 10. "All areas, for adults and children. We do not offer workshops dealing with romance or religion, however." Sites are throughout the South, especially North Carolina. Past guest speakers include John Le Carré, Peter Matthiessen and D.M. Thomas. Retreat locations have included the Florida Keys and Nice, France.
Costs: Vary. Financial assistance available to low-income writers. Information on overnight accommodations is made available.

Southeast (AL, AR, FL, GA, LA, MS, PR [Puerto Rico])

‡ALABAMA WRITERS' CONCLAVE, P.O. Box 230787, Montgomery AL 36123-0787. President: Donna Tennis. Estab. 1923. Annual. Conference held August 3 to August 5. Average attendance: 85-120. Conference

to promote "all phases" of writing. Held at the Ramsay Conference Center (University of Montevallo). "We attempt to contain all workshops under this roof. Some functions take place at other campus buildings."
Costs: In 1993 fees for 3 days were $35 for members; $45 for nonmembers. Lower rates for one- or two-day attendence.
Accommodations: Accommodations available on campus (charged separately).
Additional Information: "We have had a works-in-progress group with members helping members." Sponsors a contest. Conference brochures/guidelines available for SASE. Membership dues are $15. Membership information from Harriette Dawkins, 117 Hanover Rd., Homewood AL 35209.

ARKANSAS WRITERS' CONFERENCE, 1115 Gillette Dr., Little Rock AR 72227. (501)225-0166. Director: Clovita Rice. Estab. 1944. Annual. Conference held: first weekend in June. Average attendence: 225. "We have a variety of subjects related to writing—we have some general sessions, some more specific, but try to vary each year's subjects."
Costs: Registration: $10; luncheon: $11; banquet: $13.
Accommodations: "We meet at a Holiday Inn—rooms available at reasonable rate." Holiday Inn has a bus to bring anyone from airport. Rooms average $56/single.
Additional Information: "We have 36 contest categories. Some are open only to Arkansans, most are open to all writers. Our judges are not announced before conference, but are qualified, many from out of state." Conference brochures are available for SASE after February 1. "We have had 226 attending from 12 states—over 3,000 contest entries from 43 states and New Zealand, Mexico and Canada. We have a get acquainted party at my home on Thursday evening for early arrivers."

‡DEEP SOUTH WRITERS CONFERENCE, P.O. Drawer 44691, Lafayette LA 70504. (318)231-6908. Contact: Director. Estab. 1960. Annual. Conference held third weekend in September. Average attendance: 200. Conference focuses on "workshops and readings with an emphasis on poetry and fiction, secondarily on drama and nonfiction. Workshops may be how-to-do-it craft lectures, but they have varied tremendously over the years. Special, extra-fee, intensive workshops include critical evaluation and peer review of participants' writing. Sites include a building housing the English department on the University of Louisiana at Lafayette and off-campus at Vermillionville, a reconstructured Acadian village and museum. Readers and workshop leaders have not been finalized. "Last year's conference featured Alan Cheuse, Ernest Gaines, Wendell Mayo, Tim O'Brien, Burton Raffel and Patricia Smith."
Costs: Pre-registration is $40; registration at the conference is $50, students pay $25 all times; intensive workshops are an additional $40 each. Extra fee for dinner/reception.
Accommodations: "We have provided a shuttle service for participants in the past. Some information regarding local restaurants and local attractions is given out at the conference. Local per diem expenses in Lafayette for room and board range between $50 and $150."
Additional Information: Sponsors contest. Prize-winning works in select categories published in annual chapbook. Send SASE for rules and entry requirements. Send name and address for addition to newsletter mailing list. E-mail queries can be made to jwfiero@aol.com or jwf4516@usl.edu.

FLORIDA FIRST COAST WRITERS' FESTIVAL, 3939 Roosevelt Blvd., FCCJ Kent Campus, Box 109, Jacksonville FL 32205. (904)766-6559. Fax: (904)766-6554. Director: Howard Denson. Estab. 1985. Annual. 1996 Festival: April 12-13. Average attendance: 150-250. All areas: mainstream plus genre. Held on Kent Campus of Florida Community College at Jacksonville.
Costs: Maximum of $75 for 2 days, plus $25 for banquet tickets.
Accommodations: Orange Park Holiday Inn, (904)264-9513, has a special festival rate.
Additional Information: Conference brochures/guidelines are available for SASE. Sponsors a contest for short fiction, poetry and novels. Novel judges are David Poyer and Elisabeth Graves. Entry fees: $30, novels; $10, short fiction; $5, poetry. Deadline: Nov. 1 in each year.

‡FLORIDA ROMANCE WRITERS' CONFERENCE, 9630 NW 25th St., Sunrise FL 33324. (305)749-3736. Fax: (305)749-2724. Procurement Chairman: Barry Glusky. Estab. 1986. Annual. Conference held last weekend in February. Average attendance: 200. Conference covering "all areas of writing but mainly romance. Our membership includes published authors in mystery, science fiction and nonfiction areas." Conference is held at the Hilton Hotel where there are conference and meeting rooms and adequate facilities for parking. Conference concentration is on romance writing and guest speakers include editors and agents from the romance field.
Costs: Charge for upcoming conference being determined; will include a Saturday night awards dinner plus luncheons.
Accommodations: Special conference rates available at Hilton Hotel for conference attendees.
Additional Information: Conference brochures/guidelines are available for SASE.

‡FLORIDA SUNCOAST WRITERS' CONFERENCE, University of South Florida, Division of Lifelong Learning, 4202 E. Fowler Ave., MGZ144, Tampa FL 33620-6610. (813)974-2403. Fax: (813)974-5732.

Directors: Steve Rubin and Ed Hirshberg. Estab. 1970. Annual. Held in February. Conference duration: 3 days. Average attendance: 450. Conference covering poetry, short story, novel and nonfiction, including science fiction, detective, travel writing, drama, TV scripts, photojournalism and juvenile. "We do not focus on any one particular aspect of the writing profession. The conference is held on the picturesque university campus fronting on the bay in St. Petersburg, Florida." Features panels with agents and editors. Guest speakers have included Lady P.D. James, Carolyn Forche and Marge Piercy.

Costs: Early registration $115; $95 for students/teachers; late registration (after January 26) is $135.

Accommodations: Special rates available at area motels. "All information is contained in our brochure."

Additional Information: Participants may submit work for critiquing. Extra fee charged for this service. Conference brochures/guidelines are available for SASE.

HEMINGWAY DAYS WRITER'S WORKSHOP AND CONFERENCE, P.O. Box 4045, Key West FL 33041. (305)294-4440. Director of Workshop: Dr. James Plath. Festival Director: Michael Whalton. Estab. 1988. Annual. Conference/workshop held July 15 to July 17. Average attendance: 75. "The Hemingway Days Writer's Workshop and Conference focuses on fiction, poetry and Ernest Hemingway and his work. The workshop and conference is but one event in a week-long festival which honors Ernest Hemingway."

Costs: $120. Guaranteed admission on a space-available basis includes admission to all sessions, workshop t-shirt and two socials.

Accommodations: "As the time draws nearer, Hemingway Days packages will be available through Ocean Key House, Pier House, Southernmost Motel and Holiday Inn LaConcha. Last year the cost for 3 nights ranged from $60/2 in room per night plus tax; $160/3 in room per night suite, plus tax."

Additional Information: Brochures/guidelines are available for SASE. "The conference/workshop is unique in that it combines studies in craft with studies in literature, and serious literary-minded events to celebrate Hemingway the writer in a week-long festival celebrating 'papa' the myth."

KEY WEST LITERARY SEMINAR, 419 Petronia St., Key West FL 33040. (305)293-9291. Executive Director: Miles Frieden. Estab. 1983. Annual. Conference held second week in January. Conference duration: 3-5 days. Average attendance: 450. "Each year a different topic of literary interest is examined. Writers, scholars, editors, publishers, critics, and the public meet for panel discussions and dialogue. The agenda also includes readings, performances, question and answer sessions, book sales, a writers' workshop, social receptions, and a literary walking tour of Key West. The sessions are held at various locations in Key West, Florida, including the San Carlos Institute, 516 Duval Street and the Key West Art and Historical Society's East Martello Museum. Upcoming theme for 1996 is American Writers and the Natural World. Past speakers include William Goldman, Elmore Leonard, Jan Morris, Octavio Paz, Russell Banks, Mary Higgins Clark, James Merrill, John Wideman, Anna Quindlen, David Halberstam, Ellen Hume.

Costs: Seminar $295 and workshop $200 plus tax.

Accommodations: Catalogs detailing the seminar schedule, guest speakers, registration, and accommodations are available. Special room rates are available at participating hotels, motels, guest houses and inns. Room rates usually begin around $100.

Additional Information: Manuscript critique is an optional component of the writers' workshop. No more than 10 typewritten, double spaced pages may be submitted with workshop registration.

‡MOONLIGHT AND MAGNOLIAS WRITER'S CONFERENCE, 530 Saddle Creek Circle, Roswell GA 30076. (770)594-1854. President, Georgia Romance Writers: Ellen Taber. Estab. 1982. Annual. Conference held 3rd weekend in September. Average attendance: 300. "Conference concentrates on writing of women's fiction with emphasis on romance. The conference site is the Doubletree Hotel located just off I-285, the perimeter highway which circles Atlanta. There is limo service to Atlanta International Airport." Themes include Hands-on Learning for the Beginner, Crossing Genres, Promotion Networking, Self-Help for the Published. Past speakers include approximately 10 editors from major publishing houses and 3-5 agents, along with published writers who make up 25-30% of attendees.

Costs: Hotel $70/day (1995) single or double, conference; non GRW members $135 (1995), includes continental breakfast, lunch and banquet.

Additional Information: Maggie Awards are presented to unpublished writers. Synopsis and first 3 chapters must be submitted in early June. Please check with president for new dates. Published writers judge first round: Editors in category judge finals. Brochures/guidelines available for SASE in spring. The Maggie Award for published writers is an award limited to members of Region III Romance Writers of America.

OZARK CREATIVE WRITERS, INC., 511 Perry Rd., Springdale AR 72764. (501)751-7246. President: Dusty Richards. Estab. 1973. Annual. Conference always held 2nd weekend in October. Conference duration: 2½ days. Average attendance: 250. "All types of writing. Main speaker for workshop in morning sessions—usually a novelist. Satellite speakers—afternoon—various types, including a Poetry Seminar. Conference site is the convention center. Very nice for a small group setting. Reserve early prior to September 1 to insure place."

Costs: $50 plus approximately $30 for 2 banquets. Rooms are approximately $65/night; meals extra. Registration fee allows you to enter the writing contests.

Accommodations: Chamber of Commerce will send list; 60 rooms are blocked off for OCW prior to August 15th. Accommodations vary at hotels. Many campsites also available. "Eureka Springs is a resort town near Branson, Missouri, the foothills of the beautiful Ozark Mountains."
Additional Information: We have approximately 20 various categories of writing contests. Selling writers are our judges. Entry fee required to enter. Brochures are available for SASE after May 1. "OCWI Conference is 22 years old."

RICE UNIVERSITY WRITER'S CONFERENCE, Rice University Continuing Studies, MS 550, 6100 Main St., Houston TX 77005-1892. (713)520-6022. Fax: (713)285-5213. E-mail address: scs@rice.edu. Co-director: Susan Vallhonrat. Estab. 1992. Annual. Conference held June 7-8. Average attendance: 250. "Conference on children's books, mysteries, novels, poetry, plays, screenplays, short stories." Held at Wyndham Greenspoint Hotel. In 1995 speakers (43 total) included: Jeff Abbott, Robert Crais, Carolyn Hart, D.R. Meredith (mysteries); Carol Farley, Sherry Garland, Pat Mora, Jeanne Titherington (children's books); and Peggy Moss Fielding, Isabelle Holland, Clay Reynolds (novels).
Costs: Conference fee, $195; Friday luncheon fee, $6; Saturday Luncheon fee, $8; Manuscript Contest & Critique fee, $30.
Accommodations: Shuttle transportation free from Houston Intercontinental Airport to conference site. Overnight accommodations available at hotel for conference registrants at special room rate of $75/night.
Additional Information: "A critique and brief one-on-one meeting is provided in conjunction with the Manuscript Contest. For conference brochure/contest guidelines, please call in, fax, or e-mail a request."

‡ROMANCE & MORE, P.O. Box 52505, Shreveport LA 71115. Contact: K. Sue Morgan, President. Estab. 1985. Annual. Conference held first Saturday of March. Average attendance: 60-70. Conference focuses on fiction. Held at the Holiday Inn-Riverfront. Past themes include "Writing the Bestseller." Guest speakers have included published authors Jennifer Blake, Tami Hoagg and Betina Krohn, and editors Shauna Summers (Bantam) and Cristine Nussner (Silhouette Books).
Costs: $70 (members) and $80 (nonmembers). Includes light breakfast and lunch.
Accommodations: Available at Holiday Inn where conference is held ($60/night for 2).
Additional Information: Sponsors contest for novels. Submit first 3 chapters plus synopsis. First-round judges are published authors; final-round judges are editors. Conference and contest brochures/guidelines are available for SASE.

‡SCBWI/FLORIDA ANNUAL FALL CONFERENCE, 2158 Portland Ave., Wellington FL 33414. (407)798-4824. Florida Regional Advisor: Barbara Casey. Estab. 1985. Annual. Conference held Saturday, September 14, 1996. Conference duration: one-half day. Average attendance: 70. Conference to promote "all aspects of writing and illustrating for children. The facilities include the meeting rooms of the Library and Town Hall of Palm Springs, Florida (near West Palm Beach)." 1995 title theme: Everything Secret and Not So Secret about Writing for Young People. 1995 guest speakers: Stephanie Gordon Tessler and Judith Ross Enderle, authors and editors for Boyds Mills Press.
Costs: $45 for SCBWI members, $50 for non-SCBWI members.
Accommodations: Special conference rates at Airport Hilton, West Palm Beach FL.
Additional Information: Conference brochures/guidelines are available for SASE.

‡SEA OATS WRITER'S CONFERENCE, P.O. Box 16463, Mobile AL 36616. (334)343-8235. Annual. Held in April. "The conference stimulates writers with new ideas through a day-long series of workshops and speakers (including authors, publishers, editors, agents)." Most recent subjects include: "Priming the Fiction Pump," "Computers and Other Research Technology for the Writer," "Nonfiction and the Current Market," "Sales Boost with Self-Promotion," "Working With an Agent," "Impact of Regional Magazines." The conference is held on the Fairhope AL campus of Faulkner State Community College, on the eastern shore of Mobile Bay.
Costs: Fees will be approximately $50, and include a reception the night before the conference.
Accommodations: Fairhope is about a 45-minute drive from the Mobile Municipal Airport, and has quick access to the Gulf Coast beaches. A choice of motels and hotels, in all price ranges, exist a short drive from the conference site.
Additional Information: "Each participant may submit a synopsis of a completed project or work in progress for a critique with an editor from a major publishing house." The conference is sponsored by the Metropolitan Writers Guild. Brochures/guidelines are available for #10 SASE.

SOUTHEASTERN WRITERS ASSOCIATION ANNUAL WORKSHOP, 4021 Gladesworth Lane, Decatur GA 30035. (404)288-2064. Director: Nancy Knight. Estab. 1976. Annual. Workshop held the third week in June. Average attendance: 75. "For poetry, short story, mass market fiction, novel, playwriting, children's literature, nonfiction, inspiration. The workshop is held at Epworth-by-the-Sea on St. Simon's Island, Georgia. The immaculate grounds are expansive and inspirational for writers. Several historical buildings are located on the site. Housing is reasonable and includes all meals."

Costs: $225 nonmembers, $185 members, $175 seniors.

Accommodations: 1995 rates for on-site, handicap-accessible lodging: approximately $212-297 (double), $277-414 (single); includes *all* meals and banquet.

Additional Information: Three mss may be submitted for critique and private consultation. Sponsors a contest. All categories of mss are judged for contests by the instructor. Workshop attendance is the requirement. Workshop brochures/guidelines are available for SASE. "We stress interaction between students and staff. Teachers are housed in the same area and available to students at almost any time. We are a hands-on kind of workshop—students are assigned work to be completed during free time which is usually read in class."

SOUTHEASTERN WRITERS CONFERENCE, Rt. 1, Box 102, Cuthbert GA 31740. (912)679-5445. Advertising Director: Pat Laye. Estab. 1975. Annual. Conference held June 16 to June 22, 1996. Conference duration: 1 week. Average attendence: 100 (limited to 100 participants). Concentration is on fiction, poetry and juvenile—plus nonfiction and playwriting." Site is "St. Simons Island, Georgia. Conference held at Epworth-by-the-Sea Conference Center—tropical setting, beaches. Each year we offer market advice, agent updates. All our instructors are professional writers presently selling in New York."

Costs: $235. Meals and lodging are separate. Senior citizen discount.

Accommodations: Information on overnight accommodations is made available. "On-site-facilities at a remarkably low cost. Facilities are motel style of excellent quality. Other hotels are available on the island."

Additional Information: Three manuscripts of one chapter each are allowed in three different categories. Sponsors a contest, many cash prizes. Brochures are available for SASE.

SOUTHWEST FLORIDA WRITERS' CONFERENCE, P.O. Box 60210, Ft. Myers FL 33906-6210. (813)489-9226. Conference Director: Joanne Hartke. Estab. 1980. Annual. Conference held Feb. 23-24 (always the 4th Friday and Saturday of February). Average attendance: 150. "This year's conference will include fiction, poetry, nonfiction, an agent and others. The purpose is to serve the local writing community, whether they are novice or published writers." The conference is held on the Edison Community College campus.

Costs: "Reasonable." Call or write for conference brochures/guidelines and to be put on mailing list.

Additional Information: "We do sponsor a contest annually, with the prizes being gift certificates to local bookstores. Local, published writers offer volunteer critique/judging services."

WRITE FOR SUCCESS WORKSHOP: CHILDREN'S BOOKS, 3748 Harbor Heights Dr., Largo FL 34644. (813)581-2484. Speaker/Coordinator: Theo Carroll. Estab. 1988. Held irregularly. Conference duration: 1 day. Average attendance: 110. Concentration is writing for children. Site is the Belleview Mido Resort Hotel, a Victorian landmark built in 1896 in Clearwater FL; or the Don CeSar Beach Resort Hotel in St. Petersburg Beach FL.

Costs: $85 includes breakfast, lunch and materials. Limo available from Tampa airport. Information on special conference attendee accommodations available.

Additional Information: Brochures for latest seminar are available for SASE.

WRITING STRATEGIES FOR THE CHRISTIAN MARKET, 2712 S. Peninsula Dr., Daytona Beach FL 32118. (904)322-1111. Instructor: Rosemary Upton. Estab. 1991. Seminars given approximately 4 times a year. Conference duration: 3 hours. Average attendance: 10-20. Seminars include Basics I, Marketing II, Business III, Building the novel. Held in a conference room: three to four persons seated at each table; instructor teaches from a podium. Question and answer session provided. Critique shop included once a month, except summer (July and August). Instructors include Rosemary Upton, novelist; Kistler London, editor; Jeanne Bader, agent/publicist.

Costs: $30 for each 3-hour seminar.

Additional Information: Those who have taken Writing Strategies instruction are able to attend an ongoing monthly critiqueshop where their peers critique their work. Manual provided with each seminar. Conference brochures/guidelines are available for SASE. Independent study by mail also available.

‡WRITING TODAY—BIRMINGHAM-SOUTHERN COLLEGE, Box A-3, Birmingham AL 35254. (205)226-4921. Contact: Martha Andrews, Director of Special Events. Estab. 1978. Annual. Conference held April 12 and 13. Average attendance: 400-500. "This is a two day conference with approximately 18 workshops, lectures and readings. We try to offer workshops in short fiction, novels, poetry, children's literature, magazine writing, and general information of concern to aspiring writers such as publishing, agents, markets and research. The conference is sponsored by Birmingham-Southern College and is held on the campus in classrooms and lecture halls." The 1995 conference featured award-winning novelist Ray Bradbury. Mark Childress, Dori Sanders, Sharon Dennis Wyeth, and Peter Hellman were some of the workshop presenters.

Costs: $85 for both days. This includes lunches, reception and morning coffee and rolls.

Accommodations: Attendees must arrange own transporation. Local hotels and motels offer special rates, but participants make their own reservations.

Additional Information: "We usually offer a critique for interested writers. We have had poetry and short story critiques. There is an additional charge for these critiques." Sponsors the Hackney Literary Competition Awards for poetry, short story and novels. Brochures available for SASE.

Midwest (IL, IN, KY, MI, OH)

ANTIOCH WRITERS' WORKSHOP, P.O. Box 494, Yellow Springs OH 45387. Director: Susan Carpenter. Estab. 1984. Annual. Average attendance: 80. Workshop concentration: poetry, nonfiction and fiction. Workshop located on Antioch College campus in the Village of Yellow Springs. Speakers have included Sue Grafton, Imogene Bolls, George Ella Lyon and Herbert Martin.
Costs: Tuition is $450—lower for local and repeat—plus meals.
Accommodations: "We pick up attendees free at the airport." Accommodations made at dorms and area hotels. Cost is $16-26/night (for dorms).
Additional Information: Offers free critique sessions. Conference brochures/guidelines are available for SASE.

AUTUMN AUTHORS' AFFAIR, 1507 Burnham Ave., Calumet City IL 60409. (708)862-9797. President: Nancy McCann. Estab. 1983. Annual. Conference held in late October. Begins with Friday night dinner and ends with Sunday brunch. Average attendence: 300. "Focused on romance, contemporary and historical, but also features poetry, short story, mystery, young adult, childrens, screenplay writing and journalism." Site: Hyatt Regency, Lisle. Panels planned include "everything from the basics, to getting started, to how to handle the business aspects of your writing. Out of 25 workshops, 23 focus on 'fiction' writing."
Costs: 1995 cost was $120, which included Friday night dinner, Saturday continental breakfast, Saturday night dessert buffet and luncheon and Sunday brunch. Saturday only package available for $75.
Accommodations: Information on overnight accommodations is made available with a "special" room rate for those attending conference.
Additional Information: Brochures/guidelines available for SASE.

‡CHRISTIAN WRITERS CONFERENCE, 600 Rinehart Rd., Lake Mary FL 32746. (407)333-4618. Fax: (407)333-4675. Conference Director: Dottie McBroom. Estab. 1945. Annual. Conference in Chicago area on June 6-8, 1996. Average attendance: 150. For fiction, writing for children, nonfiction. In 1994 guest speaker was Gilbert Morris.
Costs: $199 (Early Bird) for tuition; then $239 (meals and room are not included).
Accommodations: United Airlines conference rates available.
Additional Information: Sponsors 2 contests: 1. Must register for entire conference; 2. Editors on staff judge the entries. Conference brochures/guidelines are available for SASE. Also holds a conference for advanced and beginning writers in February in Orlando FL featuring Dr. Dennis Hensley. For free brochure: Write Christian Writers' Institute at the above address, or call (800)233-1757.

‡CLARION SCIENCE FICTION & FANTASY WRITING WORKSHOP, Lyman Briggs School, E—185 Holmes Hall, Michigan State University, East Lansing MI 48825-1107. (517)355-9598. E-mail address: 22323mes@msu.edu. Administrative Assistant: Mary Sheridan. Estab. 1968. Workshop held annually for six weeks in the summer. Average attendance: 17-20. "Workshop concentrates on science fiction and fantasy writing. The workshop is held at Michigan State University and is sponsored by Lyman Briggs School, a residential program linking the sciences and humanities. Participants are housed in single rooms in a graduate residence hall adjoining the workshop site. Facilities are handicapped accessible." Writers in residence during the summer of 1996 will be Maureen McHugh, Judith Tarr, Spider Robinson, Elizabeth Hand, John Kessel and James Patrick Kelly.
Costs: Course fees for the 1995 Clarion workshop were $786. Students will be enrolled as Life-Long Education students and will receive four undergraduate semester credits and a transcript from MSU.
Accommodations: Rates for a single room and meals in a graduate residence hall on the MSU campus are being negotiated; 1995 costs were approximately $700.
Additional Information: Admission to the workshop is based on submission of a writing sample of two complete short stories between 10 and 25 pages long and a completed application form with a $25 application fee. A $100 enrollment fee is required upon acceptance. For brochures/guidelines, send SASE.

Can't find a conference? Conferences are listed by region. Check the introduction to this section for a list of regional categories.

‡THE COLUMBUS WRITERS CONFERENCE, P.O. Box 20548, Columbus OH 43220. (614)451-3075. Fax: (614)451-0174. Director: Angela Palazzolo. Estab. 1993. Annual. Conference held September 28, 1996. Average attendance: 200. The conference is held in the Fawcett Center for Tomorrow, 2400 Olentangy River Road, Columbus, OH. "The conference covers a wide variety of fiction and nonfiction topics. Fiction topics have included novel, short story, children's, science fiction, fantasy, humor, and mystery writing; playwriting and screenwriting. Nonfiction writing topics have included travel, humor, technical, query letter, corporate, educational, and greeting card writing. Other topics: finding and working with an agent, targeting markets, research, time management, obtaining grants, and writers colonies. Speakers have included Lee K. Abbott, Mike Harden, Stephanie S. Tolan, Dennis L. McKiernan, Karen Harper, Melvin Helitzer, Susan Porter, Les Roberts, Tracey E. Dils, and many other professionals in the writing field.
Costs: $75 includes morning and afternoon refreshments and lunch (cost is $75 if registration postmarked by September 14; after September 14, $89).
Additional Information: Call or write to obtain a conference brochure, available mid-summer.

‡EASTERN KENTUCKY UNIVERSITY CREATIVE WRITING CONFERENCE, Eastern Kentucky University, Richmond KY 40475. (606)622-5861. Conference Director: Dorothy Sutton. Estab. 1962. Annual. Conference held June 17-21 (usually 3rd week in June). Average attendance: 15. Conference to promote poetry, fiction and creative nonfiction, including lectures, workshops, private conferences and peer group manuscript evaluation. The conference is held on the campus of Eastern Kentucky University "in the rolling hills of Eastern Kentucky, between the horse farms of the Bluegrass and the scenic mountains of the Appalachian chain." Three distinguished visiting writers will teach at the conference. Past speakers have included Donald Justice, Maggie Anderson, Maura Stanton, Richard Marius, Gregory Orr, David Citino. Also helping with workshops will be EKU faculty Harry Brown, Hal Blythe, Charlie Sweet.
Costs: $75 for undergraduates ($207 if out-of-state); $109 for graduates ($302 if out-of-state). Cost includes 1 hour of credit in creative writing and is subject to change (please check brochure for changes). Auditors welcome at same price. Dining in the cafeteria is approximately $6-8/day.
Accommodations: Air-conditioned dormitory rooms are available for $39 (double) or $55 (single) per week. "Linens furnished. Bring your own blankets, pillow and telephone, if desired. Subject to change. Check brochure."
Additional Information: "Participants are asked to submit manuscript by May 15 to be approved before June 1." For conference brochure, send SASE to English Department (attn: Creative Writing Conference).

CHARLENE FARIS SEMINARS FOR BEGINNERS, 610 W. Poplar St., Zionsville IN 46077. (317)873-0738. Director: Charlene Faris. Estab. 1985. Held 2 or 3 times/year in various locations in spring, summer and fall. Conference duration: 2 days. Average attendance: 10. Concentration on all areas of publishing and writing, particularly marketing and working with editors. Locations have included Phoenix, Los Angeles, Madison WI, and Indianapolis.
Costs: $150, tuition only; may attend only one day for $75.
Accommodations: "We can assist attendees with information on overnight accommodations."
Additional Information: Guidelines available for SASE.

GREEN RIVER WRITERS NOVELS-IN-PROGRESS WORKSHOP, 11906 Locust Rd., Middletown KY 40243. (502)245-4902. President: Mary E. O'Dell. Director: Mary E. O'Dell. Estab. 1991. Annual. Conference held from in early January. Conference duration: 1 week. Average attendance: 40. Open to persons, college age and above, who have approximately 3 chapters (60 pages) or more of a novel. Mainstream and genre novels handled by individual instructors. Short fiction collections welcome. Each novelist instructor works with a small group (5-7 people) for five days; then agents/editors are there for panels and appointments on the weekend." Site is The University of Louisville's Shelby Campus, suburban setting, graduate dorm housing (private rooms available w/shared bath for each 2 rooms). Meetings and classes held in nearby classroom building. Grounds available for walking, etc. Lovely setting, restaurants and shopping available nearby. Participants carpool to restaurants, etc." This year we are covering mystery, romance, mainstream/literary, young adult, suspense. Guest speakers are Gary Devon (suspense); Sara Hoskinson Frommer (mystery); Elaine Fowler Palencia (mainstream/literary); Liz Bevarly (romance); Beth Henderson (young adult); and Ruth Moose (mainstream/literary).
Costs: Tuition—$275, housing $20 per night private, $16 shared. Does not include meals.
Accommodations: "We do meet participants' planes and see that participants without cars have transportation to meals, etc. If participants would rather stay in hotel, we will make that information available."
Additional Information: Participants send 60 pages/3 chapters with synopsis $25 reading fee which applies to tuition. Deadline will be in late November. Conference brochures/guidelines are available for SASE.

THE HEIGHTS WRITERS CONFERENCE, P.O. Box 24684, Cleveland OH 44124-0684. Coordinator: Lavern Hall. Estab. 1991. Annual. Conference held first Saturday in May. Average attendance: 100. "Fiction, nonfiction, science fiction, poetry, children's, marketing, etc." The conference is sponsored by Writer's World Press and held at the Cleveland Marriott East, Beachwood OH. Offers seminars on the craft, business, and legal

aspects of writing plus two teaching, hands-on workshops. "No theme, published authors and experts in their field sharing their secrets and networking for success."
Additional Information: Conference brochure available for SASE.

‡IMAGINATION, Cleveland State University, Division of Continuing Education, 2344 Euclid Ave., Cleveland OH 44115. (216)687-4522. Contact: Neal Chandler. Estab. 1990. Annual. Conference lasts 5 days and is held in mid-July. Average attendance: 60. "Conference concentrates on fiction and poetry. Held at Mather Mansion, a restored 19th Century Euclid Blvd. Mansion on the campus of Cleveland State University." 1995 themes included Writing Beyond Realism and Business of Writing. For more information send for brochure.

INDIANA UNIVERSITY WRITERS' CONFERENCE, 464 Ballantine Hall, Bloomington IN 47405. (812)855-1877. Fax: (812)855-9535. Director: Maura Stanton. Estab. 1940. Annual. Conference/workshops held from June 23-28. Average attendance: 100. "Conference to promote poetry, fiction and nonfiction (emphasis on poetry and fiction)." Located on the campus of Indiana University, Bloomington. "We do not have themes, although we do have panels that discuss issues such as how to publish. We also have classes that tackle just about every subject of writing. Ralph Burns, Gerald Stern, David Wojahn and Brigit Pegeen Kelly are scheduled to speak and teach workshops at the 1996 conference.
Costs: Approximately $200; does not include food or housing. This price does *not* reflect the cost of taking the conference for credit. "We supply conferees with options for overnight accommodations. We offer special conference rates for both the hotel and dorm facilities on site.
Additional Information: "In order to be accepted in a workshop, the writer must submit the work they would like critiqued. Work is evaluated before accepting applicant. Scholarships are available determined by an outside reader/writer, based on the quality of the manuscript." Conference brochures/guidelines available for SASE in February. "We are the second oldest writer's conference in the country. We are in our 56th year."

LAKELAND WRITERS MINI CONFERENCE, 34200 Ridge Rd., #110, Willoughby OH 44094. (800)OLD-HAM1. E-mail address: fa837@cleveland.freenet.edu. Coordinator: Lea Leever Oldham Estab. 1992. Annual. Conference held March 30, 1996. Average attendance: 100. "Fiction, nonfiction, scifi, poetry, childrens." Held "Lakeland Community College, Kirtland, Ohio. Classrooms, wheelchair accessible—right off I90, east of Cleveland." Panels include "no theme, just published authors sharing their secrets." Conference brochures/guidelines are available for SASE.
Costs: $29.

MEDINA-WAYNE WRITERS CONFERENCE, 311 W. Washington St., Medina OH 44256. (216)723-2633. Coordinator: Betty Wetzel. Estab. 1976. Held every two years. Conference held September, 1996. Conference duration: 2 days (Friday evening and all day Saturday) Average attendance: 30-35. "To provide information on writing and publishing and to promote contacts between writers and speakers. Speakers are professionals in each area (fiction, nonfiction, poetry and juvenile). Sometimes editor is included. 6 sessions are presented on Saturday. Since each speaker conducts only 3 sessions, opportunity is available for informal conversation with participants during the other sessions. We also offer a class in basics (how to get started, etc.) Conference is held at Wayne College of the University of Akron. The college is in Orrville, Ohio, in a rural area easily accessible from main highways. Individual classrooms are provided for classes and a main room for general meeting and for informal 'coffee and conversation' periods. The building is handicapped-accessible." Past guest speakers or panelists have included Les Roberts (fiction), Eileen Kindig (nonfiction), Bonnie Pryor (juvenile), Judy Totts (poetry).
Costs: In 1994: $40 pre-registration; $45 if paid at the door. Lunch is provided on Saturday, as well as coffee/tea and donuts in morning. Light reception on Friday evening, between keynote and panel discussion.
Accommodations: List of area motels is available.
Additional Information: Manuscripts submitted for contest are critiqued in writing by judges. Sponsors contest for each category. No restrictions except length. One ms may be submitted with registration; additional mss may be submitted for fee of $5 each. Cash prizes for 1st and 2nd place. Brochure and guidelines available for SASE.

MIDLAND WRITERS CONFERENCE, Grace A. Dow Memorial Library, 1710 W. St. Andrews, Midland MI 48640. (517)835-7151. Conference Chair: Katherine Redwine. Estab. 1980. Annual. Conference held June 8. Average attendance: 100. "The Conference is composed of a well-known keynote speaker and six workshops on a variety of subjects including poetry, children's writing, freelancing, agents, etc. The attendees are both published and unpublished authors. The Conference is held at the Grace A. Dow Memorial Library in the auditorium and conference rooms. Keynoters in the past have included Andrew Greeley, Kurt Vonnegut, David Halberstam."
Costs: Adult - $45 before May 17, $55 after May 17; students, senior citizens and handicapped - $35 before May 17, $45 after May 17. A box lunch is available for $7. Costs are approximate until plans for upcoming conference are finalized.

Accommodations: A list of area hotels is available.
Additional Information: Conference brochures/guidelines are available for SASE.

MIDWEST WRITERS' CONFERENCE, 6000 Frank Ave. NW, Canton OH 44720 (216)499-9600. Conference Coordinator: Debbie Ruhe. Estab. 1968. Annual. Conference held in early October. Conference duration: 2 days. Average attendance: 350. "The conference provides an atmosphere in which aspiring writers can meet with and learn from experienced and established writers through lectures, workshops, competitive contest, personal interviews and informal group discussions. The areas of concentration include fiction, nonfiction, juvenile literature and poetry. The Midwest Writers' Conference is held on Kent State University Stark Campus in Canton, Ohio. This two-day conference is held in Main Hall, a four-story building and wheel chair accessible." Past topics have included "Writing and Selling Nonfiction," "(Almost) Anything Can Be Funny: Humor Writing," "Stories in the Song: How to use Narrative Elements in a Lyric Poem," "Forty + Years of Writing Together for Children," "Contracts for Dummies: An Introduction to the Book Publishing Agreement," "Performance Poetry," "Plotting is Murder: Every Good Mystery Starts with a Skeleton," "Plot: The Little Engine That Wants." 1995 presenters included: Kirk Polking, freelance writer and author; Sandra Gurvis, author, editor; David Baker, associate professor of English, Denison University; Arnold and Jeanne Cheyney, writers, teachers; Andrew Zack, literary agent, Scovil Chichak Galen Literary Agency, Inc.; Kat Snider Blackbird, instructor, Kent State University; William Pomidor, freelance writer, author; Steven Bauer, associate professor, director of creative writing, Miami University.
Costs: $65 includes Friday workshops, keynote address, Saturday workshops, box luncheon and manuscript entry fee (limited to two submissions); $40 for contest only (includes two manuscripts).
Accommodations: Arrangements are made with a local hotel which is near Kent Stark, and offers a special reduced rate for conference attendees. Conferees must make their own reservations 3 weeks before the conference to be guaranteed this special conference rate.
Additional Information: Each manuscript entered in the contest will receive a critique. If the manuscript is selected for final judging, it will receive an additional critique from the final judge. Conference attendees are not required to submit manuscripts to the writing contest. Manuscript deadline is early August. For contest: A maximum of 1 entry for each category is permitted. Entries must be typed on $8\frac{1}{2} \times 11$ paper, double-spaced. A separate page must accompany each entry bearing the author's name, address, phone, category and title of the work. Entries are not to exceed 3,000 words in length. Work must be original, unpublished and not a winner in any contest at the time of entry. Conference brochures and guidelines are available for SASE.

‡MIDWEST WRITERS WORKSHOP, Dept. of Journalism, Ball State University, Muncie IN 47306. (317)285-8200. Co-Director: Earl L. Conn. Estab. 1974. Annual. Workshop to be held July 31-Aug. 3, 1996. Average attendance: 130. For fiction, nonfiction, poetry. Conference held at Hotel Roberts in downtown Muncie.
Costs: In 1995, cost was $175 including opening reception, hospitality room and closing banquet.
Accommodations: Special hotel rates offered.
Additional Information: Critiques available. $25 for individual critiquing. Conference brochures/guidelines are available for SASE.

MISSISSIPPI VALLEY WRITERS CONFERENCE, 3403 45th St., Moline IL 61265. (309)762-8985. Conference Founder/Director: David R. Collins. Estab. 1973. Annual. Conference held June 2 to June 7, 1996. Average attendance: 80. "Conference for all areas of writing for publication." Conference held at Augustana College, a liberal arts school along the Mississippi River. 1995 guest speakers included Evelyn Witter, Connie Heckert, Max Collins, David McFarland, Karl Largent, Roald Tweet, Rich Johnson.
Costs: $25 for registration; $40 for 1 workshop; $75 for two; plus $30 for each additional workshops; $20 to audit.
Accommodations: On-campus facitilites available. Accommodations are available at Westerlin Hall on the Augustana College campus. Cost for 6 nights is $100; cost for 15 meals is $90.
Additional Information: Conferees may submit manuscripts to workshop leaders for personal conferences during the week. Cash awards are given at the end of the conference week by workshop leaders based on manuscripts submitted. Conference brochures/guidelines are available for SASE. "Conference is open to the beginner as well as the polished professional—all are welcome."

‡OF DARK & STORMY NIGHTS, Mystery Writers of America—Midwest Chapter, %200 S. Garden Ave., Roselle IL 60172. (708)231-3131. Fax: (708)231-8594. Workshop Director: Marilyn Nelson. Estab. 1982. Annual. Workshop held June. Workshop duration: 1 day. Average attendance: 200. Dedicated to "writing *mystery* fiction and crime related nonfiction. Workshops and panels presented on techniques of mystery writing from ideas to revision, marketing, investigative techniques and more by published writers, law enforcement experts and publishing professionals. 1994 luncheon speaker was Deanie Francis Mills." Site is Holiday Inn, Rolling Meadows IL.

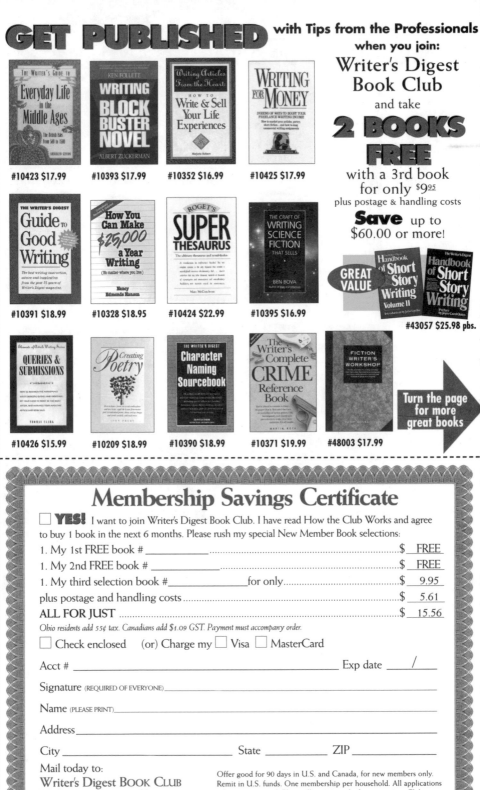

Costs: $85 for MWA members; $110 for non-members; $50 for manuscript critique.
Accommodations: Easily accessible by car or train (from Chicago) Holiday Inn, Rolling Meadows $65 per night + tax; free airport bus and previously arranged rides from train.
Additional Information: "We accept manuscripts for critique (first 25 pages maximum); $50 cost. Writers meet with critiquer during one of the sessions for one-on-one discussion." Brochures available for SASE after March 30.

OHIO WRITERS' HOLIDAY, P.O. Box 24247, Columbus OH 43224. Newsletter Editor: Judie Hershner. Estab. 1990. Annual. Conference held May 4. Average attendance: 120. "Womens' fiction, particularly romance fiction." Held in 1995 at the Radisson, Columbus, Ohio. Offers published authors roundtable—anyone can ask a questions of published author present. Guest speakers have included Susan Wiggs (historical romance author) and Shauna Summers (editor, Bantam/Doubleday/Dell).
Costs: $35 (includes meal/lunch and seminar).
Additional Information: Conference brochures/guidelines are available for SASE.

‡ROPEWALK WRITERS' RETREAT, 8600 University Blvd., Evansville IN 47712. (812)464-1863. E-mail address: ucs@smtp.usi.edu. Conference Coordinator: Linda Cleek. Estab. 1989. Annual. Conference held June 9-15, 1996. Average attendance: 42. "The week-long RopeWalk Writers' Retreat gives participants an opportunity to attend workshops and to confer privately with one of five prominent writers. Historic New Harmony, Indiana, site of two nineteenth century utopian experiments, provides an ideal setting for this event with its retreat-like atmosphere and its history of creative and intellectual achievement. At RopeWalk you will be encouraged to write—not simply listen to others talks about writing. Each workshop will be limited to twelve participants. The New Harmony Inn and Conference Center will be headquarters for the RopeWalk Writers' Retreat. Please note that reservations at the Inn should be confirmed by May 1." 1995 faculty were Andrew Hudgins, Barry Hannah, Bob Shacochis, Margaret McMullan and Ellen Bryant Voigt.
Costs: $375 (1995), includes breakfasts and lunches.
Accommodations: Information on overnight accommodations is made available. "Room-sharing assistance; some low-cost accommodations."
Additional Information: For critiques submit mss approx. 6 weeks ahead. Brochures are available after January 15.

‡SELF PUBLISHING YOUR OWN BOOK, 34200 Ridge Rd., #110, Willoughby OH 44094. (216)943-3047 or (800)653-4261. E-mail address: fa837@cleveland.freenet.edu. Teacher: Lea Leever Oldham. Estab. 1989. Quarterly. Conferences usually held in February, April, August and October. Conference duration: 2½ hours. Average attendance: up to 25. Conference covers copyright, marketing, pricing, ISBN number, Library of Congress catalog number, reaching the right customers and picking a printer. Held at Lakeland Community College, Kirtland, OH (east of Cleveland off I-90). Classrooms are wheelchair accessible. Conference guidelines are available for SASE.

WESTERN RESERVE WRITERS & FREELANCE CONFERENCE, 34200 Ridge Rd., #110, Willoughby OH 44094. (216)943-3047 or (800)653-4261. E-mail address: fa837@cleveland.freenet.edu. Coordinator: Lea Leever Oldham. Estab. 1984. Annual. Conference held every September. Conference duration: 1 day. Average attendance: 150. "Fiction, nonfiction, inspirational, children's, poetry, humor, scifi, copyright and tax information, etc." Held "at Lakeland Community College, Kirtland, OH. Classrooms wheelchair accessible. Accessible from I-90, east of Cleveland." Panels include "no themes, simply published authors and other experts sharing their secrets." Conference brochures/guidelines are available for SASE.
Costs: $55 plus lunch.

‡WESTERN RESERVE WRITERS MINI CONFERENCE, 34200 Ridge Rd., #110, Willoughby OH 44094. (216)943-3047 or (800)653-4261. E-mail address: fa837@cleveland.freenet.edu. Coordinator: Lea Leever Oldham. Estab. 1991. Annual. Conference held in March. Conference duration: ½ day. Average attendance: 125. Conference to promote "fiction, nonfiction, children's, poetry, science fiction, etc." Held at Lakeland Community College, Kirtland, OH (east of Cleveland off I-90). Classrooms are wheelchair accessible. "Conference is for beginners, intermediate and advanced writers." Past speakers have included Mary Grimm, Nick Bade, James Martin and Mary Ryan. Conference brochures/guidelines are available for SASE.
Costs: $29.

‡WRITING FOR MONEY WORKSHOP, 34200 Ridge Rd., #110, Willoughby OH 44094. (216)943-3047 or (800)653-4261. E-mail address: fa837@cleveland.freenet.edu. Contact: Lea Leever Oldham. Conference held several times during the year. 1996 dates: January 20, April 27, July 13, October 19. Conference duration: One day. "Covers query letters, characterization for fiction, editing grammar, manuscript preparation and marketing salable manuscripts." Held at Lakeland Community College, Kirtland, OH. Right off I-90, east of Cleveland.
Costs: $39/day.

North Central (IA, MN, NE, ND, SD, WI)

‡**BLACK HILLS WRITERS GROUP WORKSHOP**, P.O. Box 1539, Rapid City SD 55709-1539. (605)343-7130. Workshop Chair: Renie Smith. One-day conference held every other odd-numbered year; next conference Spring 1997. Average attendance: 75-100. Conference concentrates on "elements of successful writing leading to publication. All genres are covered." Held in a motel/hotel with individual rooms for seminars and large room for main speaking event. Themes planned for next conference include "What do editors want?"; various fiction genres, article writing, beginners' tips, various poetry types and book-length nonfiction. "Our main speaker at the 1995 conference was Denise Little, editor at Kensington. Seminars and panels have featured published authors from several genres."
Costs: $35 includes lunch.
Accommodations: "For those traveling a long distance to attend our workshop, the host motel/hotel offers a special conference rate."
Additional Information: "Critiquing of manuscripts usually offered for a small extra fee. In even-numbered years, we offer the Laura Bower Van Nuys Writing Contest." Conference brochures/guidelines are available for SASE.

‡**COPYRIGHT WORKSHOP**, 610 Langdon St., Madison WI 53703. (608)262-3447. Director: Christine DeSmet. Offered 2 times/year. Average attendance: 50. "Copyright law for writers, publishers, teachers, designers." Conference held at Wisconsin Center, University of Wisconsin—Madison.
Costs: $145.
Additional Information: Conference brochures/guidelines are available.

PETER DAVIDSON'S WRITER'S SEMINAR, 12 Orchard Lane, Estherville IA 51334. (712)362-2604. Seminar Presenter: Peter Davidson. Estab. 1985. Seminars held about 30 times annually, in various sites. Offered year round. Seminars last 1 day, usually 9 a.m.-4 p.m. Average attendance: 35. "All writing areas including books of fiction and nonfiction, children's works, short stories, magazine articles, poetry, songs, scripts, religious works, personal experiences and romance fiction. All seminars are sponsored by community colleges or colleges across the U.S. Covers many topics including developing your idea, writing the manuscript, copyrighting, and marketing your work. A practical approach is taken."
Costs: Each sponsoring college sets own fees, ranging from $35-55, depending on location, etc.
Accommodations: "Participants make their own arrangements. Usually, no special arrangements are available."
Additional Information: "Participants are encouraged to bring their ideas and/or manuscripts for a short, informal evaluation by seminar presenter, Peter Davidson." Conference brochures/guidelines are available for SASE. "On even-numbered years, usually present seminars in Colorado, Wyoming, Nebraska, Kansas, Iowa, Minnesota, and South Dakota. On odd-numbered years, usually present seminars in Illinois, Iowa, Minnesota, Arkansas, Missouri, South Dakota, and Nebraska."

GREAT LAKES WRITER'S WORKSHOP, Alverno College, 3401 S. 39 St., P.O. Box 343922, Milwaukee WI 53234-3922. (414)382-6176. Contact: Debra Pass, Director, Telesis Institute. Estab. 1985. Annual. Workshop held during second week in July (Friday through Thursday). Average attendance: 250. "Workshop focuses on a variety of subjects including fiction, writing for magazines, freelance writing, writing for children, poetry, marketing, etc. Participants may select individual workshops or opt to attend the entire week-long session. Classes are held during evenings and weekends. The workshop is held in Milwaukee, Wisconsin at Alverno College."
Costs: In 1995, cost was $99 for entire workshop. "Individual classes are priced as posted in the brochure with the majority costing $20 each."
Accommodations: Attendees must make their own travel arrangments. Accommodations are available on campus; rooms are in residence halls and are not air-conditioned. Cost in 1995 was $25 for single, $20 per person for double. There are also hotels in the surrounding area. Call (414)382-6040 for information regarding overnight accommodations.
Additional Information: "Some workshop instructors may provide critiques, but this changes depending upon the workshop and speaker. This would be indicated in the workshop brochure." Brochures available for SASE.

GREEN LAKE CHRISTIAN WRITERS CONFERENCE, Green Lake Conference Center/American Baptist Assembly, Green Lake WI 54941-9300. (800)558-8898. Estab. 1948. Annual. 1996 conference date is July 13-20. Average attendance: 75. "This conference provides quality instructors who are published authors and experienced at being both friend and coach. Held annually at this 1,000 acre conference center located on a lake offering a wide range of recreational and creative craft opportunities in a hospitable accepting environment. This ecumenical conference attracts participants from across the country." Conference speakers have included Marion Dane Bauer, Ben Logan and many excellent workshop leaders.

Costs: Tuition is $80/person.
Accommodations: "We can provide ground transportation from Appleton and Oshkosh airports; the Amtrak station in Columbus and Greyhound Bus Stop in Fond du Lac for a modest fee. Room costs vary depending on facilities. All rooms are on the American Food Plan. Campground and cabin facilities also available." Conference brochures are available upon request.

‡**INTERNATIONAL MUSIC CAMP CREATIVE WRITING WORKSHOP**, 1725 11th St. S.W., Minot ND 58701. (701)838-8472. Camp Director: Joseph T. Alme. Estab. 1970. Annual. Conference usually held in July. Conference duration: 6 days. Average attendance: 20. "Conference to promote fiction, poetry, children's writing, plays and mystery stories including feedback from the professionals. The conference is held in the Frances Leach Library at the International Music Camp. The summer Arts camp is located at the International Peace Garden on the border between Manitoba and North Dakota. 3,000 acres of hand-planted flowers, fountains and natural beauty create a perfect setting for a creative writing workshop."
Costs: $185 including room, board and tuition. "The food in the spacious new cafeteria is excellent. Housing in the spacious new dormitories provide privacy and comfort."
Accommodations: Northwest and Frontier Airlines fly to Minot, ND. AMTRAK goes to Rugby, ND. A shuttle service is available from both terminals. "Area motels vary in rates. However, the accommodations located on sight are excellent and at no additional cost."
Additional Information: No auditions are required. Critiques are given throughout the week. Conference brochures/guidelines are available for SASE. "A $50 deposit is required. It is refundable until June 1st, 1996. When an application is received, a list of materials needed for the workshop is sent to the student. A promotional video is available upon request."

IOWA SUMMER WRITING FESTIVAL, 116 International Center, University of Iowa, Iowa City IA 52242. (319)335-2534. Director: Peggy Houston. Assistant Director: Amy Margolis. Estab. 1987. Annual. Festival held in June and July. Workshops are one week, two weeks or a weekend. Average attendance: limited to 12/class—over 1,000 participants throughout the summer. "We offer courses in most areas of writing: novel, short story, essay, poetry, playwriting, screenwriting, freelance, nonfiction, writing for children, memoirs, women's writing, romance and mystery." Site is the University of Iowa campus. Guest speakers are undetermined at this time. Readers and instructors have included W.P. Kinsella, Elizabeth Benedict, Joy Harjo, Gish Jen, Abraham Verghese, Robert Olen Butler, Ethan Canin, Clark Blaise, Robert Waller, Gerald Stern, Donald Justice, Michael Dennis Browne.
Costs: $360/week; $150, weekend workshop (1995 rates). Discounts available for early registration. Housing and meals are separate.
Accommodations: Shuttle service from the Cedar Rapids airport to the university is available for a reasonable fee. "We offer participants a choice of accommodations: Dormitory, $25/night; Iowa House, $56/night; Holiday Inn, $58/night (rates subject to changes)."
Additional Information: Brochure/guidelines are available.

LAKEWOOD COMMUNITY COLLEGE WRITERS' SEMINAR, 3401 Century Avenue, White Bear Lake MN 55110. (612)779-3259. Director Continuing Education: Pat Lockyear. Estab. 1990. Held quarterly in fall and spring. Workshop duration: 1 day. Average attendance: 30-50. "Workshops concentrate on either fiction or writing for children. Held on campus in college conference room with tables for individuals." Guest speakers have included Peter Davidson.
Costs: $57.
Additional Information: Brochures/guidelines available for SASE.

‡**SCBWI/MINNESOTA CHAPTER CONFERENCES**, 7080 Coachwood Rd., Woodbury MN 55125. (612)739-0119. Conferences held 1 day in spring and 1 day in fall. Average Attendance: 100. Features authors, illustrators and/or editors of children's books and periodicals. Spring 1995 featured motivational speaker, Jerry Allen; author/illustrator Debra Frasier; editor Gwenyth Swain of Carolrhoda Books; and Mike Palmquist, software designer with MECC. Fall 1995 conference featured author Mary Casanova and editor Andrea Cascardi of Hyperion Books for Children; author Marsh Qualey and editor Laura Hornik of Bantam/Doubleday/Dell; author Alice McLerran presenting a workshop on school visits; and author Cris Peterson doing a workshop on self-promotion.
Costs: Around $75, with discounts given for SCBWI members and early registration.
Accommodations: No accommodations available. Information and hotel names for SASE.
Additional Information: Workshop brochure available 6 weeks prior to conference for SASE. Portfolio review and ms critiques will be available for an additional fee.

SCBWI/WISCONSIN FALL RETREAT, 26 Lancaster Ct., Madison WI 53719-1433. (608)271-0433. Regional Advisor: Sheri Cooper Sinykin. Estab. 1991. Annual. Conference held in late September or early October. Average attendance: 60. Writing for children. In 1993 (and odd years) held at Siena Center in Racine, in even years, if available, held at St. Benedict Center in Madison. Speakers in 1994 were editors Patricia Gauch and Sharyn November; authors Bruce Coville and Marion Dane Bauer.

Costs: In 1995 cost was $215 for SCBWI members ($235 non-members), includes room, board, program.
Accommodations: We try to have volunteers assist with airport transportation. Overnights are on-site and included. On-site housing runs about $25/night.
Additional Information: Critiques were offered in 1993 for an extra fee of $25. Conference brochures/guidelines are available in June for SASE.

SINIPEE WRITERS' WORKSHOP, P.O. Box 902, Dubuque IA 52004-0902. (319)556-0366. Director: John Tigges. Estab. 1985. Annual conference held in April. Average attendance: 50-75. To promote "primarily fiction although we do include a poet and a nonfiction writer on each program. The two mentioned areas are treated in such a way that fiction writers can learn new ways to expand their abilities and writing techniques." The workshop is held on the campus of Loras College in Dubuque. "This campus holds a unique atmosphere and everyone seems to love the relaxed and restful mood it inspires. This in turn carries over to the workshop and friendships are made that last in addition to learning and experiencing what other writers have gone through to attain success in their chosen field." Speakers for the Eleventh Annual Workshop will be: Paul Polansky, research expert and geneologist; Kasandra McNeil, freelance photographer and writer; Shirley Schirz, poetry; Marshall Cook, nonfiction and romance novelist.
Costs: $60 early registration/$65 at the door. Includes all handouts, necessary materials for the workshop, coffee/snack break, lunch, drinks and snacks at autograph party following workshop.
Accommodations: Information is available for out-of-town participants, concerning motels, etc., even though the workshop is one day long.
Additional Information: Sponsors fiction, nonfiction and poetry contests: limit 1,500 words (fiction), 40 lines (poetry). 1st prize in both categories: $100 plus publication in an area newspaper or magazine; 2nd prize in both categories: $50; 3rd prize in both categories: $20. Written critique service available for contest entries, $15 extra.

SPLIT ROCK ARTS PROGRAM, University of Minnesota, 306 Wesbrook Hall, 77 Pleasant St. SE, Minneapolis MN 55455. (612)624-6800. Fax: (612)625-2568. Estab. 1982. Annual. Workshops held in July and August. Over 45 one-week intensive residential workshops held. "The Split Rock Arts Program is offered through the University of Minnesota on its Duluth campus. Over 45 one-week intensive residential workshops in writing, visual arts, fine crafts and the process of creativity are held for 5 weeks in July and August. This unique arts community provides a nurturing environment in a beautiful setting overlooking Lake Superior and the cool summer port city of Duluth. Courses, which can be taken for credit, are offered in long and short fiction, nonfiction, poetry and children's literature." Instructors in 1995 included Christina Baldwin, Sandra Benitez, Carol Bly, Michael Dennis Browne, Sharon Doubiago, Kate Green, Phebe Hanson, Alexs Pate, Jane Resh Thomas, Dan Coffey (Dr. Science of NPR), Jane Hirshfield, Mary LaChapelle and Gayle Pemberton.
Costs: $360, tuition (may vary with options). Moderately priced housing available for additional cost.
Accommodations: Campus apartments available.
Additional Information: A limited number of scholarships are available based on qualification and need. Call for catalog.

‡UNIVERSITY OF WISCONSIN AT MADISON SCHOOL OF THE ARTS AT RHINELANDER, 726 Lowell Hall, 610 Langdon St., Madison WI 53703. Administrative Coordinator: Kathy Berigan. Estab. 1964. Annual. Conference duration: 1 week. Conference held in late July. Average attendance: 300. Courses offered in writing, visual arts, drama, photography, music, folk arts, folk dancing. Conference held in junior high school in the city of Rhinelander in northern Wisconsin (James Williams Junior High School).
Costs: Tuition only—ranges from $110-235. Some courses require materials or lab fee.
Accommodations: Information on overnight accommodations (cabins, motels, camping) made available.
Additional Information: Ms critique workshop available. Request to be put on mailing list.

‡UNIVERSITY OF WISCONSIN AT MADISON WRITERS INSTITUTE, 610 Langdon St., Madison WI 53703. (608)262-3447. Director: Christine DeSmet. Estab. 1990. Annual. Conference held in July. Average attendance: 175. "Day 2 is fiction—genre writing; Day 1 is nonfiction—journalism freelance writing." Conference held at Wisconsin Center, University of Wisconsin at Madison. Themes: Mystery, suspense, science fiction, romance, mainstream for fiction. Guest speakers are published authors, editors and agents.
Costs: $125/day or $175 for 2 days; critique fees.
Accommodations: Info on accommodations sent with registration confirmation. Critiques available Conference brochures/guidelines are available for SASE.

WRITING WORKSHOP, P.O. Box 65, Ellison Bay WI 54210. (414)854-4088. Resident Manager: Don Buchholz. Estab. 1935. Annual. Conference held in June. Average attendance: 16. "General writing journal, poetry as well as fiction and nonfiction." Held in a "quiet, residential setting in deep woods on the shore of Green Bay. Past guest speakers include Lowell B. Komie (short story), T.V. Olsen (novelist) and Barbara Vroman (novelist).

Costs: In 1995, cost was $525 (twin bed) or $480 (dormitory).

Accommodations: "Two to a room with private bath in rustic log and stone buildings. Great hall type of classroom for the conference."

Additional Information: Catalog (8½ × 11) available upon request.

South Central (CO, KS, MO, NM, OK, TX)

AUSTIN WRITERS' LEAGUE WORKSHOPS/CONFERENCES/CLASSES, E-2, 1501 W. Fifth, Austin TX 78703. (512)499-8914. Fax: (512)499-0441. Executive Director: Angela Smith. Estab. 1982. Programs ongoing through the year. Duration: varies according to program. Average attendance from 15 to 150. To promote "all genres, fiction and nonfiction, poetry, writing for children, screenwriting, playwriting, legal and tax information for writers, also writing workshops for children and youth." Programs held at "St. Edward's University, AWL Resource Center/Library, other sites in Austin and Texas. Topics include: Finding and working with agents and publishers; writing and marketing short fiction; dialogue; characterization; voice; research; basic and advanced fiction writing/focus on the novel; business of writing; also workshops for genres. Past speakers have included Dwight Swain, Natalie Goldberg, David Lindsey, Shelby Hearon, Gabriele Rico, Benjamin Saenz, Rosellen Brown, Sandra Scofield, Reginald Gibbons, Anne Lamott and Sterling Lord.

Costs: Vary from free to $185, depending on program. Most classes, $20-50; workshops $35-75; conferences: $125-185.

Accommodations: Austin Writers' League will provide assistance with transportation arrangements on request. List of hotels is available for SASE. Special rates given at some hotels for program participants.

Additional Information: Critique sessions offered at some programs. Individual presenters determine critique requirements. Those requirements are then made available through Austin Writers' League office and in workshop promotion. Contests and awards programs are offered separately. Brochures/guidelines are available on request.

‡COLORADO CHRISTIAN WRITERS CONFERENCE, 67 Seminole Court, Lyons CO 80540. (303)823-5718. Director: Debbie Barker. Estab. 1984. Annual. Conference held the first Thursday, Friday and Saturday of March. Average attendance: 250. Conference designed "to train writers to excellence in fiction, nonfiction and poetry. We always have a fiction track and sessions on marketing. Also have sessions, if not an entire track for children/youth."

Costs: $100-130/3 days; includes 2 lunches, 1 dinner, breaks, 56-64 workshops to choose from, 3-4 plenaries, meetings with editors, etc.

Accommodations: Shuttles to and from hotel. Information on overnight accommodations is available.

Additional Information: "We have paid critiques, $25-30 for ½ hour/written critique. Also, 15-minute appointments with editors and freelancers." Sponsors a contest as part of conference. Conference brochures/guidelines are available for SASE.

‡CRAFT OF WRITING, UTD Box 830688, CN 1.1, Richardson TX 75083. (214)883-2204. Director: Janet Harris. Estab. 1983. Annual. Conference held September (check for exact dates). Average attendance: 150. "To provide information to accomplished and aspiring writers on how to write and how to get published. All genres are included. Areas of writing covered include characterization and dialogue to working with an agent." Workshops in 1995 included a panel of editors and agents (both national and local), "How To Write a Query Letter That Gets Your Work Read," "Finding The Right Agent for You," "How the Publisher Looks at Your Writing," "Make Their Hearts Race: Using Suspense in Fiction," and "Show and Tell: How to Balance and Pace Your Fiction."

Costs: $195; includes a lunch and a banquet.

Accommodations: A block of rooms is held at the OMNI Richardson Hotel for $59/night. Call (214)231-9600 for reservations.

Additional Information: Critiques available. "There are no requirements. Participants may have manuscripts critiqued by members of the Greater Dallas Writers Association. Two manuscript critique sessions are scheduled. A manuscript contest is held prior to the conference. The deadline for submissions is July. Judges are specialists in the areas they are critiquing. There are 11 categories with several cash prizes. Conference brochures/guidelines are available. Twenty-eight workshops are scheduled on a wide range of topics. Presenters include nationally known authors, agents, editors and publishers."

Market conditions are constantly changing! If you're still using this book and it is 1997 or later, buy the newest edition of Novel & Short Story Writer's Market *at your favorite bookstore or order from* Writer's Digest Books.

FORT CONCHO MUSEUM PRESS LITERARY FESTIVAL, 630 S. Oakes St., San Angelo TX 76903. (915)481-2646. Contact: Cora Pugmire. Estab. 1988. Annual. Conference held the first weekend in August. Average attendance: 450. "The purposes of the festival are to showcase writers—from beginners to professionals—of Texas and the southwest through public readings, book displays and informal gatherings; to offer help for writers through writing workshops and informal gatherings with other writers, editors and publishers; and, generally, to support and encourage the literary arts in Texas and the Southwest." Location: A 22-building, 40-acre historic site. The festival is held in the oldest, fully restored building (1865). Several of the other buildings are also used for workshops. Free tours are offered to all participants. "Current festival plans include no special topic, but we will have at least one fiction workshop. Guest speakers will be published Texas writers and publishers/editors of Texas journals of books."
Costs: All events except the banquet are free. Banquet fee is between $8-12.
Accommodations: Transportation arrangements are made on an informal basis only. ("That is, people who need a ride can always find one.") Special accommodations are made at our motel; a list of other area motels and hotels is available.
Additional Information: Current contests are "literary performance" contests. Of those who read from their works during the festival, one poet and one prose writer receive an award. Conference brochures/guidelines are available for SASE.

‡GOLDEN TRIANGLE WRITERS GUILD, 4245 Calder, Beaumont TX 77706. (409)898-4894. Administrative Assistant: Becky Blanchard. Estab. 1984. Annual. Conference held during third weekend in October. Attendance limited to 450. Held at the Holiday Inn on Walden Road in Beaumont, Texas.
Costs: $195 before September 20th; $220 after September 20th. Cost covers conference only; room not included.
Accommodations: Special conference rates available at Holiday Inn (Beaumont).
Additional Information: Sponsors a contest. Attendance required. Preliminary judging done by published authors and/or specialists in each specific genre. Final judging done by editors and/or agents specializing in each specific area.

‡GULF COAST WRITERS CONFERENCE AT THE UNIVERSITY OF HOUSTON-CLEAR LAKE, 2700 Bay Area Blvd., Box 198, Houston TX 77058. (713)283-2560. Fax: (713)283-2566. E-mail address: glendenning@cl4.cl.uh.edu. Graduate Asst. of Cultural Arts: Joanie Glendenning. Coordinator, UHCL Cultural Arts: Mark Dolney. Estab. 1995. Annual. Conference held in March. Conference duration: 2½ days. Average attendance: 50. "The overall purpose of the conference is to examine how literature is affected by multiculturalism—how has the divergence of culture enriched the way writers perceive society, and therefore, the way in which these new perceptions speak through their writing. We welcome those from all genres to participate in using theme. The Gulf Coast Writers Conference is held on the UHCL campus. Workshops and presentations are held on university grounds. However, some entertainment and meals are held off campus. For instance, in 1995, we held an International Banquet at a hotel ballroom." Lorenzo Thomas, writer in residence and professor of literature at the UH-Downtown campus spoke on "Virtual Literacy" at the International Banquet held as part of the conference. In addition, a multicultural panel discussed "Cultural Diversity in the Southwest."
Costs: "First year fees were $15 general public and $10 student fee. This will rise in the second year as we determine the overall cost of the event."
Accommodations: "Arrangements can be made for transportation to and from William P. Hobby Airport if we are given advanced notice prior to the event. Two to three weeks advance notice is appreciated and preferred. We publicize the area hotel that gives us the most competitive hotel rate for festival participants."
Additional Information: "We hold a competition for readers, workshop leaders, and lecturers. Individuals submit their work which goes through a jury process. From that process, individuals are selected and invited to come. We also hold a juried poetry and prose competition. In 1995, we awarded the first place of poetry and prose with $100 each." Entrants may submit in two categories: poetry and prose. A jury panel of writers and faculty judges the entries according to craft excellence and compliance with theme. For guidelines and brochures, interested individuals can write or call (713)283-2560 and ask for Joanie Glendenning, organizer of the conference. "We encourage writers from everywhere to examine multiculturalism and how it is bringing a new voice to contemporary literature. We do not limit writers to this theme; however, we welcome a diversity of theme in addition to culture."

‡HEART OF AMERICA WRITERS' CONFERENCE, Johnson County Community College, 12345 College Blvd., Overland Park KS 66210. Program Director: Judith Choice. Estab. 1984. Annual. Conference held April 12-13, 1996. Average attendance: 110-160. "The conference features a choice of 16 plus sections focusing on nonfiction, children's market, fiction, journaling, essay, poetry and genre writing." Conference held in state-of-the-art conference center in suburban Kansas City. Individual sessions with agents and editors are available. Manuscript critiques are offered for $40. Past keynote speakers have included Natalie Goldberg, Ellen Gilchrist, Linda Hogan, David Ray, Stanley Elkin, David Shields, Luisa Valenzuela.
Costs: $100 includes lunch, reception, breaks.
Accommodations: "We provide lists of area hotels."

NATIONAL WRITERS ASSOCIATION CONFERENCE, 1450 S. Havana, Suite 424, Aurora CO 80012. (303)751-7844. Fax: (303)751-8593. E-mail address: sandy.nwa@genie.geis.com. Executive Director: Sandy Whelchel. Estab. 1926. Annual. Conference held in June. Conference duration: 3 days. Average attendance: 200-300. General writing and marketing. 1996 conference in Denver, CO.
Costs: $300 (approx.).
Accommodations: All accommodations are included.
Additional Information: Awards for previous contests will be presented at the conference. Conference brochures/guidelines are available for SASE.

THE NEW LETTERS WEEKEND WRITERS CONFERENCE, University of Missouri-Kansas City, College of Arts and Sciences Continuing Ed. Division, 215 SSB, 5100 Rockhill Rd., Kansas City MO 64110-2499. (816)235-2736. Estab. in the mid-70s as The Longboat Key Writers Conference. Annual. Runs during June. Conference duration is 3 days. Average attendance: 75. "The New Letters Weekend Writers Conference brings together talented writers in many genres for lectures, seminars, readings, workshops and individual conferences. The emphasis is on craft and the creative process in poetry, fiction, screenwriting, playwriting and journalism; but the program also deals with matters of psychology, publications and marketing. The conference is appropriate for both advanced and beginning writers. The conference meets on the beautiful campus of The University of Missouri-Kansas City."
Costs: Several options are available. Participants may choose to attend as a non-credit student or they may attend for 1-3 hours of college credit from the University of Missouri. Conference registration includes continental breakfasts. For complete information, contact the University of Missouri-Kansas City.
Accommodations: Registrants are responsible for their own transportation, but information on area accommodations is made available. Also, special arrangements are made with the dormitory located on the University of Missouri-Kansas City campus. "On-campus rates are very reasonable."
Additional Information: Those registering for college credit are required to submit a manuscript in advance. Manuscript reading and critique is included in the credit fee. Those attending the conference for non-credit also have the option of having their manuscript critiqued for an additional fee. Conference brochures/guidelines are available for SASE.

‡NORTHWEST OKLAHOMA WORKSHOP, P.O. Box 1308, Enid OK 73702. (405)234-4562. Workshop Chairman: Earl Mabry. Estab. 1991. Annual. Conference held in Spring. Conference duration: 6 hours. Average attendance: 20-30. "Usually fiction is the concentration area. The purpose is to help writers learn more about the craft of writing and encouraging writers 'to step out in faith' and submit." Held in the Community Room at Oakwood Mall. "The room is a store site that is not being rented." Past speakers have been Norma Jean Lutz, inspirational and magazine writing; Deborah Bouziden, fiction and magazine writing; Anna Meyers, children's writing—fiction, nonfiction, poetry; Sondra Soli, poetry.
Costs: $40; does not include meal. "However, the food court and a cafeteria are nearby."
Additional Information: Conference brochures/guidelines are available for SASE. "A contest is sponsored by the Enid Writers Club. Waldenbooks is located next door to the Community Room and the manager has been very cooperative in getting books for the workshop."

OKLAHOMA FALL ARTS INSTITUTES, P.O. Box 18154, Oklahoma City OK 73154. (405)842-0890. Contact: Associate Director of Programs. Estab. 1983. Annual. Conference held in late October. Conference duration: 4 days. Average attendance 100. 1995 workshops included: The Art of Teaching Poetry (Robin Behn); Poetry (Peggy Shumaker); Fiction (Diane Glancy); Writing for Children (Joyce Carol Thomas); and Biography/Autobiography (Diane Middlebrook). Held at "Quartz Mountain Arts and Conference Center, an Oklahoma state lodge located in Southwest Oklahoma at the edge of Lake Altus/Lugert in the Quartz Mountains. Workshop participants are housed either in the lodge itself (in hotel-room accommodations) or in cabins or duplexes with kitchens. Classes are held in special pavilions built expressly for the Arts Institute. Pavilions offer a view of the lake and mountains." No featured panelists. Classes are taught by nationally recognized writers. Evenings include presentations and readings by faculty members, and a Friday night chamber music concert.
Costs: $450, which includes double-occupancy lodging, meals, tuition and registration fee.
Accommodations: The Oklahoma Arts Institute leases all facilities at Quartz Mountain Arts and Conference Center for the exclusive use of the Fall Arts Institutes participants. Lodging is included in workshop cost.
Additional Information: Critique is usually done in class. Writers will need to bring completed works with them. 1996 Course Catalog is available. The Institutes are open to anyone.

ROMANCE WRITERS OF AMERICA NATIONAL CONFERENCE, Suite 315, 13700 Veteran Memorial Dr., Houston TX 77014. (713)440-6885. Executive Manager: Allison Kelley. Estab. 1981. Annual. Conference held in July or August. Average attendance: 1,500. "Popular fiction, emphasis on all forms of romance and women's fiction. 1996 conference will be held at Wyndham, Anatole, Dallas TX; 1997 conference will be held at Marriott World Hotel, Orlando FL. Our conference always focuses on selling romantic fiction with special workshops from publishers telling attendees how, specifically to sell to their houses." Past keynote and special speakers have included Sandra Canfield and Sandra Brown.

Costs: Fee for 1995 was $260 and included a reception, four meals plus two continental breakfasts. Room rates are separate.

Additional Information: Annual RITA awards are presented for romance authors. Annual Golden Heart awards are presented for unpublished writers. Entry is restricted to RWA members. Conference brochures/guidelines are available for SASE.

SCBWI/DRURY COLLEGE WRITING FOR CHILDREN WORKSHOP, 900 N. Benton, Springfield MO 65802. (417)873-7313. Directors: Lynn Doke or Sandy Asher. Estab. 1986. Annual. One-day workshop held in October. Average attendance: 65. Workshop to promote writing and illustrating fiction and nonfiction for young readers, held at Drury College. Topics for 1994 included Writing and Illustrating Picture Books, Marketing Your Work, and Writing for Middle Grade and Young Adult Readers. Faculty includes an editor from a major publishing house (i.e. Bantam, Scholastic) and invited authors. 1994 guest speakers included author P.J. Petersen and illustrator Bobette McCarthy.

Costs: $50, includes continental breakfast and luncheon. Discount for SCBWI members and early registrants.

Accommodations: Hotel information is made available.

Additional Information: Faculty will meet with individuals to discuss manuscripts and/or illustrations, $25 fee. Workshop brochures/guidelines are available for SASE.

‡SOUTHWEST CHRISTIAN WRITERS ASSOCIATION, P.O. Box 2635, Farmington NM 87499-2635. (505)334-2258. President: Patti Cordell. Estab. 1980. Annual. Conference held September 16. Average attendance: 30. For "fiction (novel), short stories, writing for teens." Conference held at the First Presbyterian Church, 865 N. Dustin, Farmington, NM 87401. Panels for 1995 included: "Making Leap from Novice to Professional"; "Confronting Issues, Addressing Hurts"; and "Know Your Characters." 1995 guest speaker was Joy P. Gage. Guest speaker for 1996 will be Dr. Dan Montgomery.

Costs: $47 (meals are "Dutch" at a local restaurant); $5 off early registration and additional $5 off for members.

Additional Information: Sponsors a contest. "One additional speaker invited (not decided yet). Freebies and a booktable available (authors may bring books to sell if attending conference)."

SOUTHWEST WRITERS WORKSHOP CONFERENCE, Suite B, 1338 Wyoming, NE, Albuquerque NM 87112-5000. (505)293-0303. Fax: (505)237-2665. Estab. 1983. Annual. Conference held in August. Average attendance: 500-600. "Conference concentrates on all areas of writing." Workshops and speakers include writers and editors of all genres for all levels from beginners to advanced. 1995 theme was "From Inspiration to Publication." Keynote speaker was Dr. David Morrell, award-winning author of *First Blood*. Featured speakers: Bill Buchanan and Deanne Stillman.

Costs: $240 (members) and $295 (nonmembers); includes conference sessions, 2 luncheons, 2 banquets, and 2 breakfasts.

Accommodations: Usually have official airline and discount rates. Special conference rates are available at hotel. A list of other area hotels and motels is available.

Additional Information: Sponsors a contest judged by editors and agents from New York, Los Angeles, etc., and from major publishing houses. Sixteen categories. Deadline: May 15. Entry fee is $24 (members) or $34 (nonmembers). Brochures/guidelines available for SASE. "An appointment (15 minutes, one-on-one) may be set up at the conference with editor or agent of your choice on a first-registered/first-served basis."

STEAMBOAT SPRINGS WRITERS GROUP, P.O. Box 774284, Steamboat Springs CO 80477. (970)879-9008. Chairperson: Harriet Freiberger. Estab. 1982. Annual. Conference held July 20. Conference duration: 1 day. Average attendance: 30. "Our conference emphasizes instruction within the seminar format. Novices and polished professionals benefit from the individual attention and the camaraderie which can be established within small groups. A pleasurable and memorable learning experience is guaranteed by the relaxed and friendly atmosphere of the old train depot. Registration is limited." Steamboat Arts Council sponsors the group at the restored Train Depot.

Costs: $25 for members; $35 for nonmembers. Fee covers all conference activities, including lunch. Lodging available at Steamboat Resorts; 10% discount for participants."

‡TAOS SCHOOL OF WRITING, P.O. Box 20496, Albuquerque NM 87154. (505)294-4601. Administrator: Suzanne Spletzer. Estab. 1993. Annual. Conference held in July. Conference duration: 1 week. Average attendance: 40. "All fiction and nonfiction. No poetry or screenwriting. Purpose—to promote good writing skills. We meet at the Thunderbird Lodge in the Taos Ski Valley, NM. (We are the only ones there.) No telephones or televisions in rooms. No elevator. Slightly rustic landscape. Quiet mountain setting at 9,000 feet." Conference focuses on writing fiction and nonfiction and publishing. Guest speakers for 1995 were David Morrell, Suzy McKee Charnas, Stephen R. Donaldson, Norman Zollinger, Denise Chavez and Richard S. Wheeler.

Costs: $950, includes tuition, room and board.

Accommodations: "Travel agent arranges rental cars or shuttle rides to Ski Valley from Albuquerque Sunport."

Additional Information: "Acceptance to school is determined by evaluation of submitted manuscript. Manuscripts are critiqued by faculty and students in the class during the sessions." Conference brochures/ guidelines are available for SASE.

MARK TWAIN WRITERS CONFERENCE, Suite A, 921 Center, Hannibal MO 63401. (800)747-0738. Contact: Cyndi Allison. Estab. 1985. Annual. Conference held in June. Conference duration: 5 days. Average attendance: 75-125. "Concentration in fiction and nonfiction with specialization in humor, children's writing, Mark Twain, poetry, etc." Site is the "Hannibal-LaGrange College campus. Excellent classroom and dining facilities near Mark Twain museum and other historical sites."
Costs: Approximately $395; includes meal, lodging, all program fees, trips to Mark Twain sites.
Accommodations: Free pickup at Quincy, IL airport and Amtrak station. Accommodations made available in college residence hall.
Additional Information: Brochures are available by calling or writing.

WRITERS' CONFERENCE AT SANTA FE, P.O. Box 4187, Santa Fe NM 87502. (505)438-1251. Fax: (505)438-1302. Contact: Rita Martinez-Purson. Estab. 1989. Annual. Conference held in February. Average attendance: 150. Held at Santa Fe Community College. Robin Moore was the keynote speaker for 1995.
Costs: $168 (before February 1); $198 (after February 1). Includes meals.
Accommodations: Shuttle from airport available. Attendees have special conference accommodations at Ramada Inn. Cost is $60-70.
Additional Information: Conference brochures/guidelines are available for SASE. Preconference session also offered.

WRITERS WORKSHOP IN SCIENCE FICTION, English Department/University of Kansas, Lawrence KS 66045. (913)864-3380. Professor: James Gunn. Estab. 1985. Annual. Conference held July 1-14, 1996. Average attendance: 15. Conference for writing and marketing science fiction. "Housing is provided and classes meet in university housing on the University of Kansas campus. Workshop sessions operate informally in an lounge." 1995 guest writers: Frederik Pohl, SF writer and former editor and agent; Kij Johnson, writer and editor; John Ordover, writer and editor.
Costs: Tuition: $400. Housing and meals are additional.
Accommodations: Several airport shuttle services offer reasonable transportation from the Kansas City International Airport to Lawrence. In 1995 students were housed in a student dormitory at $12/day single, $17.50/day double.
Additional Information: "Admission to the workshop is by submission of an acceptable story. Two additional stories should be submitted by the end of June. These three stories are copied and distributed to other participants for critiquing and are the basis for the first week of the workshop; one story is rewritten for the second week." Brochures/guidelines are available for SASE. "The Writers Workshop in Science Fiction is intended for writers who have just started to sell their work or need that extra bit of understanding or skill to become a published writer."

West (AZ, CA, HI, NV, UT)

AMERICAN CHRISTIAN WRITERS CONFERENCES, P.O. Box 5168, Phoenix AZ 85010. (800)21-WRITE. Director: Reg Forder. Estab. 1981. Annual. Conference duration: 3 days. Average attendance: 200. To promote all forms of Christian writing. Conferences held throughout the year in cities such as Houston, Dallas, Minneapolis, St. Louis, Detroit, Atlanta, Washington DC, San Diego, Seattle, Ft. Lauderdale and Phoenix. Usually located at a major hotel chain like Holiday Inn.
Costs: Approximately $199 plus meals and accommodation.
Accommodations: Special rates available at host hotel.
Additional Information: Conference brochures/guidelines are available for SASE.

‡BAY AREA WRITERS WORKSHOP, 1450 Fourth St., #4, Berkeley CA 94710. (510)525-5476. Co-Directors: Jennifer Rodrigue, Katy Kennedy. Estab. 1988. Annual. Offers 4-5 separate weekend intensive workshops and a biennial 1-day conference, "Literary Publishing Day." Average attendance for 1-day conference: 250; each weekend workshop: 15. Workshops are offered in fiction and poetry, "both with a strong literary bent and a master class format." Sites: San Francisco, Berkeley and Oakland. "Literary Publishing & Resources" features agents and editors from large and small presses. Workshop leaders for the last three years included Robert Hass, Li-Young Lee, Wanda Coleman, Olga Broumas, Larry Heinemann, Robert Olmstead, Carolyn Forché, Jessica Hagedorn, Jack Gilbert, Joy Williams, David Shields and Clarence Major."
Costs: $250/weekend workshop plus $15 application fee. Scholarships are available for writers based on the quality of the application manuscript. Cost for Literary Publishing & Resources: $50.
Additional Information: Weekend workshops include 15 hours of in-class time. No individual consultations. Brochures are available for SASE.

BE THE WRITER YOU WANT TO BE MANUSCRIPT CLINIC, 23350 Sereno Ct., Villa 30, Cupertino CA 95014. (415)691-0300. Contact: Louise Purwin Zobel. Estab. 1969. Workshop held irregularly—usually semiannually at several locations. Workshop duration: 1-2 days. Average attendance: 20-30. "This manuscript clinic enables writers of any type of material to turn in their work-in-progress—at any stage of development—to receive help with structure and style, as well as marketing advice." It is held on about 40 campuses at different times, including University of California and other university and college campuses throughout the west.

Costs: Usually $45-65/day, "depending on campus."

Additional Information: Brochures/guidelines available for SASE.

‡CALIFORNIA WRITER'S CLUB CONFERENCE, 4913 Marlborough Way, Carmichael CA 95608. Phone/fax: (916)488-7094. Contact: Nancy Elliott. Estab. 1941. Biennial. Next conference will be held in June, 1997. Conference duration: 2 days. Average attendance: 500-600. Conference to promote "all forms of writing, nonfiction, fiction, articles, books, self-publishing, screenplays and television scripts." Conference is held at Asilomar which is near Carmel and Monterey on the California coast. "This is a convention center that can accommodate up to 700 people. Speakers and panelists are editors and agents from major publishing houses."

Costs: "Cost averages between $350 and $450 and includes all meals and lodging beginning with dinner on Friday through lunch on Sunday."

Accommodations: "Asilomar has full hotel services available. There is an airport to Monterey with good taxi service, but CWC makes no arrangements for travel."

Additional Information: Critique service available for a separate fee. Sponsors contest for unpublished authors only. Judges are members of CWC who each specialize in a particular type of writing. Complete brochure is available 6-8 months prior to the conference. This brochure covers information on cost, services available, and contest and critique information.

DESERT WRITERS WORKSHOP/CANYONLANDS FIELD INSTITUTE, P.O. Box 68, Moab UT 84532. (801)259-7750 or (800)860-5262. Executive Director and Conference Coordinator: Karla Vanderzanden. Estab. 1984. Annual. Held November 2-5. Conference duration: 3 days. Average attendance: 30. Concentrations include fiction, nonfiction, poetry. Site is the Pack Creek Ranch, Moab, Utah. "Theme is oriented towards understanding the vital connection between the natural world and human communities." Faculty panel in 1995 included Mary Sojourner for fiction.

Costs: $400 (members of CFI, $385); $150 deposit required by September 22, which includes meals Friday-Sunday, instruction, field trip, lodging.

Accommodations: At Pack Creek Ranch, included in cost.

Additional Information: Brochures are available for SASE. "Participants may submit work in advance, but it is not required. Student readings, evaluations and consultations with guest instructors/faculty are part of the workshop. Desert Writers Workshop is supported in part by grants from the Utah Arts Council and National Endowment for the Arts. A scholarship is available. College credit is also available for an additional fee."

‡GILA WRITERS' CONFERENCE, 11012 E. Crescent Ave., Apache Junction AZ 85220. (602)986-1399. Contact: Meg Files. Estab. 1994. Annual. Conference held in August, 1996. Conference duration: 5 days. Average attendance: 60. Conference on fiction, nonfiction, poetry, screenwriting, writing for children, and publishing. The conference is held on the campus of Western New Mexico University, Silver City. Speakers have included writers Frank Gaspar, Joanne Greenberg, Simon Hawke, Sharman Russell, Allen Woodman, Edward Bryant, John Legg, Maurya Simon and Ron Querry as well as editors and agents.

Costs: $200 (includes manuscript critique). Meals and accommodations additional.

Accommodations: Travel information and airport pickup are provided. Ride-sharing arrangements are coordinated. On-site dormitory rooms are available for $10/night. Motel and campground information is provided.

Additional Information: Optional critiques are included in the conference fee. Manuscripts (20-pages maximum) must be submitted 3 weeks in advance. Conference brochures/guidelines are available for SASE.

INLAND EMPIRE CHRISTIAN WRITERS GUILD, 10653 Ridgefield Terrace, Moreno Valley CA 92557. (909)924-0610. Founders: Bill Page and Carole Gift. Page. President: Bill Page. Estab. 1990. Workshops in February and September. Conference lasts one day, Saturday, 9 a.m.-4:30 p.m. Average attendance: 75. "Conference to promote all areas of writing with Christian emphasis. Held in hotel conference room with extra room(s) for small groups.

Costs: Early registration, $45; $60 at door; breakfast and lunch included.

Accommodations: "One-day conference, but if overnight stay is desired, hotel gives special rate."

Additional Information: Conference brochure/guidelines are available for SASE or by phone.

I'VE ALWAYS WANTED TO WRITE BUT . . ., 23350 Sereno Ct., Villa 30, Cupertino CA 95014. (415)691-0300. Contact: Louise Purwin Zobel. Estab. 1969. Workshop held irregularly, several times a year at different

locations. Workshop duration: 1-2 days. Average attendance: 30-50. Workshop "encourages real beginners to get started on a lifelong dream. Focuses on the basics of writing." Workshops held at about 40 college and university campuses in the west, including University of California.
Costs: Usually $45-65/day "depending on college or university."
Additional Information: Brochures/guidelines available for SASE.

IWWG EARLY SPRING IN CALIFORNIA CONFERENCE, International Women's Writing Guild, P.O. Box 810, Gracie Station, New York NY 10028. (212)737-7536. Executive Director: Hannelore Hahn. Estab. 1982. Annual. Conference held March 15 to March 17. Average attendance: 50. Conference to promote "creative writing, personal growth and empowerment." Site is a redwood forest mountain retreat in Santa Cruz, California.
Costs: $100 for weekend program, plus room and board.
Accommodations: Accommodations are all at conference site; $110 for room and board.
Additional Information: Conference brochures/guidelines are available for SASE.

JACK LONDON WRITERS' CONFERENCE, 135 Clark Dr., San Mateo CA 94402-1002. (415)342-9123. Coordinator: Marlo Faulkner. Estab. 1987. Annual. Conference held March 9 from 8:30-4:30. Average attendance: 200. "Our purpose is to provide access to professional writers. Workshops have covered genre fiction, nonfiction, marketing, poetry and children's. Held at the San Francisco Airport Holiday Inn. Panelists have included Richard North Patterson, Joanne Meschery, Max Byrd and Barnaby Conrad. Isabel Allende is one of the 1996 keynote speakers."
Costs: $75; includes continental breakfast, lunch and all sessions.
Additional Information: "Special rates on accommodations available at Holiday Inn." Sponsors a contest judged by the California Writers Club (requirements in brochure). Brochures/guidelines available for SASE. The Jack London Conference has had over 80 professional writers speak and 800 participants. It's sponsored by the California Writers' Club.

MENDOCINO COAST WRITERS CONFERENCE, 1211 Del Mar Dr., Fort Bragg CA 95437. (707)961-1001. Director: Marlis Manley Broadhead. Estab. 1990. Annual. Conference held in June. Conference duration: 2 days. Average attendance: 120. "Inclusive—poetry, long and short fiction, science fiction, mystery, food, travel, personal histories, screenplay, publishing and marketing, advertising, writing for children, self-publishing, etc." Workshops and individual editing sessions. Held at "College of the Redwoods at the south edge of Fort Bragg, CA, a small mill town/tourist and retirees center. The tiny campus overlooks the Pacific and is 8 miles north of Mendocino Village, a preserved Victorian town. Over 25 movies and TV shows have been filmed in this area."
Costs: $100.
Accommodations: Information on overnight accommodations made available. Local rooms go from $42 to $125 (elegant B&Bs)."
Additional Information: Conference brochures/guidelines are available for SASE. "The purpose of this conference is to study and celebrate writing in a supportive atmosphere. In the past, we've gotten high marks from attendees and presentors alike on the substance and atmosphere of the conferences."

MOUNT HERMON CHRISTIAN WRITERS CONFERENCE, P.O. Box 413, Mount Hermon CA 95041. (408)335-4466. Fax: (408)335-9218. Director of Specialized Programs: David R. Talbott. Estab. 1970. Annual. Conference held Friday-Tuesday over Palm Sunday weekend, March 29-April 2. Average attendance: 175. "We are a broad-ranging conference for all areas of Christian writing, including fiction, children's, poetry, nonfiction, magazines, books, educational curriculum and radio and TV script writing. This is a working, how-to conference, with many workshops within the conference involving on-site writing assignments. The conference is sponsored by and held at the 440-acre Mount Hermon Christian Conference Center near San Jose, California, in the heart of the coastal redwoods. Registrants stay in hotel-style accommodations, and full board is provided as part of conference fees. Meals are taken family style, with faculty joining registrants. The faculty/student ratio is about 1:6 or 7. The bulk of our faculty are editors and publisher representatives from major Christian publishing houses nationwide."
Costs: Registration fees include tuition, conference sessions, resource notebook, refreshment breaks, room and board and vary from $485 (economy) to $650 (deluxe), double occupancy.
Accommodations: Airport shuttles are available from the San Jose International Airport. Housing is not required of registrants, but about 95% of our registrants use Mount Hermon's own housing facilities (hotel style double-occupancy rooms). Meals with the conference are required, and are included in all fees.
Additional Information: Registrants may submit 2 works for critique in advance of the conference, then have personal interviews with critiquers during the conference. No advance work is required, however. Conference brochures/guidelines are available for SASE. "The residential nature of our conference makes this a unique setting for one-on-one interaction with faculty/staff. There is also a decided inspirational flavor to the conference, and general sessions with well-known speakers are a highlight."

NAPA VALLEY WRITERS' CONFERENCE, Napa Valley College, 1088 College Ave., St. Helena CA 94574. (707)967-2900. Program Director: John Leggett. Managing Director: Sherri Hallgren. Estab. 1980. Annual.

Conference held first week of August. Average attendance: 70-80. Conference to promote literary fiction and poetry. "No real work in genres and an emphasis on craft rather than marketing. Poets spend the week writing new poems, though there is also a critique of already finished work." Workshops are held on the upper Valley campus of Napa Valley College, in the heart of the famed wine growing region of California. Evenings feature readings hosted by valley wineries. "We have visiting agents and publishers on panels. Each faculty writer gives a craft talk and a public reading."

Costs: Approximately $450. Scholarships available.

Accommodations: Attendees are mailed a list of Napa Valley motels, many of which offer a package rate. "We also offer some community housing (guest rooms or spare sofas in the homes of Napa residents) for a charge of $20 for the week."

Additional Information: "We require a qualifying manuscript of ten pages of fiction or five pages of poetry as well as a letter describing applicant's background as a writer. In workshops we critique a 25-page ms of fiction." Conference brochures/guidelines are available for SASE. Application deadline: June 1.

‡PALM SPRINGS WRITERS' CONFERENCE, 646 Morongo Rd., Palm Springs CA 92264. (619)864-9760. Fax: (619)322-1833. Co-director: Arthur Lyons. Estab. 1993. Annual. Conference held in May. Average attendance: 225. Conference to promote "the writing and selling of marketable fiction and nonfiction." The conference is held at "Riviera Resort, a first-class hotel in Palm Springs." Panels planned include mystery, short story, nonfiction, travel writing, mainstream novel, romance novel, woman's novel, TV writing, screenwriting, CD-ROM. Guest speakers or panelists will include Olivia Goldsmith, Dean Koontz (tentative), Sue Grafton (tentative), Ray Bradbury, Roderick Thorp, Elda Minger, Jerry Hulse, Gerald Petievich, Tom and Marilyn Ross.

Costs: $299-349; includes 1 lunch and 1 dinner; rolls and coffee in the morning; does not include hotel. Free one-on-one meetings with agents' and editors'. Scholarships will be available for special cases.

Accommodations: Provides transport to hotel from airport if attendees stay at hotel. Information available on overnight accommodations. Special hotel rate of $89 per night for conference attendees.

Additional Information: Critiques available from faculty writers for a charge. Also, 10-page ms must be submitted early for agents'/editors' meetings.

PASADENA WRITERS' FORUM, P.C.C. Community Education Dept., 1570 E. Colorado Blvd., Pasadena CA 91106-2003. (818)585-7608. Coordinator: Meredith Brucker. Estab. 1954. Annual. Conference held March 9. Average attendance: 225. "For the novice as well as the professional writer in any field of interest: fiction or nonfiction, including scripts, children's, humor and poetry." Conference held on the campus of Pasadena City College. A panel discussion by agents, editors or authors is featured at the end of the day.

Costs: $100, including box lunch and coffee hour.

Additional Information: Brochure upon request, no SASE necessary. "Pasadena City College also periodically offers an eight-week class 'Writing for Publication.' "

PIMA WRITERS' WORKSHOP, Pima College, 2202 W. Anklam Rd., Tucson AZ 85709. (520)884-6974. Fax: (520)884-6975. Director: Meg Files. Estab. 1988. Annual. Conference held in May. Conference duration 3 days. Average attendance 200. "For anyone interested in writing—beginning or experienced writer. The workshop offers sessions on writing short stories, novels, nonfiction articles and books, children's and juvenile stories, poetry and screenplays." Sessions are held in the Center for the Arts on Pima Community College's West Campus. Past speakers include Michael Blake, Ron Carlson, Greg Levoy, Nancy Mairs, Linda McCarriston, Sam Smiley, Jerome Stern, Connie Willis and literary agents Judith Riven and Fred Hill.

Costs: $65 (can include ms critique). Participants may attend for college credit, in which case fees are $68 for Arizona residents and $310 for out-of-state residents. Meals and accommodations not included.

Accommodations: Information on local accommodations is made available, and special workshop rates are available at a specified motel close to the workshop site (about $50/night).

Additional Information: Participants may have up to 20 pages critiqued by the author of their choice. Manuscripts must be submitted 2 weeks before the workshop. Conference brochure/guidelines available for SASE. "The workshop atmosphere is casual, friendly, and supportive, and guest authors are very accessible. Readings, films and panel discussions are offered as well as talks and manuscript sessions."

‡SAN DIEGO STATE UNIVERSITY WRITERS CONFERENCE, SDSU-Aztec Center, San Diego CA 92182-0723. (619)594-2517. E-mail address: ealcaraz@mail.sdsu.edu. Assistant to Director of Extension: Erin Grady Alcaraz. Estab. 1984. Annual. Conference held on 3rd weekend in January. Conference duration: 2 days. Average attendance: Approx. 350. "This conference is held on the San Diego State University campus at the Aztec Center. The Aztec Center is conveniently located near parking. The meeting rooms are spacious and comfortable. All sessions meet in the same general area. Each year the SDSU Writers Conference offers a variety of workshops for the beginner and the advanced writer. This conference allows the individual writer to choose which workshop best suits his/her needs. In addition, read and critique and office hours are provided so attendees may meet with speakers, editors and agents in small, personal groups to discuss specific questions. A wine-and-cheese reception is offered Saturday immediately following the workshops where attendees may socialize with the faculty in a relaxed atmosphere. Keynote speaker is to be determined."

Costs: Not to exceed $225. This includes all conference workshops and office hours, coffee and pastries in the morning, lunch and wine-and-cheese reception Saturday evening.
Accommodations: The Howard Johnson offers conference attendees a reduced rate, $45/night. Attendees must say they are with the SDSU Writers Conference.
Additional Information: A critique session will be offered in addition to the research emporium where experts will lecture and answer questions about various topics such as forensics, police procedures, historical clothing and customs, weapons, etc. To receive a brochure, call or send a postcard with address to: SDSU Writers Conference, College of Extended Studies, San Diego State University, San Diego CA 92182-1920. No SASE required.

SCBWI/NATIONAL CONFERENCE ON WRITING & ILLUSTRATING FOR CHILDREN, 22736 Vanowen St., Suite 106, West Hills CA 91307-2650. (818)888-8760. Executive Director: Lin Oliver. Estab. 1972. Annual. Conference held in August. Conference duration: 4 days. Average attendance: 350. Writing and illustrating for children. Site: Doubletree Inn in the Marina Del Rey area (at the beach) in Los Angeles. Theme: "The Business of Writing."
Costs: $250 (members), $275 (nonmembers). Cost does not include hotel room.
Accommodations: Information on overnight accommodations made available. Conference rates at the hotel about $100/night.
Additional Information: Ms and illustration critiques are available. Conference brochures/guidelines are available (after June) for SASE.

SCBWI/NORCAL CHAPTER RETREAT AT ASILOMAR, 1316 Rebecca Dr., Suisun CA 94585-3603. (707)426-6776. Contact: Bobi Martin, Regional Advisor. Estab. 1984. Annual. Conference held during last weekend in February. Attendance limited to 65. "The retreat is designed to refresh and encourage writers and illustrators for children. Speakers have been published writers, illustrators and editors. Topics vary year to year and have included writing techniques, understanding marketing, plotting, pacing, etc. The retreat is held at the Asilomar conference grounds in Monterey. There is time for walking on the beach or strolling through the woods. Rooms have private baths and two beds. Meals are served semi-cafeteria style and the group eats together. Vegetarian meals also available.
Costs: $200 for SCBWI members; $235 for nonmembers.
Accommodations: "All accommodations are on-site and are included in the cost. All rooms are double occupancy and disabled-accessible. Those insisting on a private room may stay off grounds." Attendees must make their own transportation arrangements.
Additional Information: Scholarships available to SCBWI members. "Applicants for scholarships should write a letter explaining their financial need and describing how attending the retreat will help further their career. All applications are kept fully confidential." Brochures available for SASE. "Registration begins in October of previous year and fills quickly, but a waiting list is always formed and late applicants frequently do get in."

‡SCBWI/SOUTHERN CALIFORNIA SCBWI WRITERS' DAY, 1937 Pelham Ave. #2, Los Angeles CA 90025. (310)446-4799. Contact: Judy or Stephanie, Regional Advisors. Annual. Conference held April 13. Average attendance: 80-100. Conference to promote writing and marketing of children's books. Held on private school grounds. Themes for 1996 are picture books, young adult fiction, nonfiction.
Costs: $60-70 (discount for early registration). "Bring your own lunch or eat nearby."
Additional Information: Sponsors contests for picture books, middle grade and young adult fiction, nonfiction, poetry. Contests open to attendees only. Submit up to 10 pages plus synopsis. Brochures available for SASE. "This one-day conference is popular and growing. A good place to network with other children's book writers, both published and unpublished."

SOCIETY OF SOUTHWESTERN AUTHORS WRITERS' CONFERENCE, P.O. Box 30355, Tucson AZ 85751-0355. (520)296-5299. Fax: (520)296-0409. Conference Chair: Penny Porter. Estab. 1972. Annual. Conference held in January. Average attendance: 300. Conference "covers a spectrum of practical topics for writers. Each year varies, but there is a minimum of 12 different classes during the day, plus the keynote speaker." Recent keynote speaker was Ray Bradbury. Conference held at University of Arizona.
Costs: $60 general.
Additional Information: Conference brochures/guidelines are available for SASE.

SOUTHERN CALIFORNIA WRITERS CONFERENCE/SAN DIEGO, 2596 Escondido Ave., San Diego CA 92123. (619)278-4099. Director: Michael Steven Gregory. Estab. 1987. Annual. Conference held in January over the Martin Luther King birthday weekend. Conference duration: 4 days. Average attendence: 200. "Our purpose is to provide expertise in helping writers fine-tune and prepare their manuscripts for market." Site is the Sheraton Inn, Four Points Hotel, Montgomery Field, San Diego, CA. Conference emphasis is on fiction and screen writing. Workshops also cover genre-specific fiction, nonfiction, travel writing, the writing business etc. and poetry. "We also have two agents' panels." Past speakers have included Nancy Taylor

Rosenberg (*Interest of Justice*), Elizabeth George (*A Suitable Vengeance*), T. Jefferson Parker (*Summer of Fear*) and D.C. Fontana ("Star Trek: Deep Space Nine").

Costs: Send for brochure with current information on programs and cost.

Accommodations: Hotel has shuttle service from airport. Special conference attendee accommodations made. Conferees register for hotel and conference through the conference.

Additional Information: "Work may be submitted for advance critique, followed by one-on-one discussion with the SCWC/SD readers during conference. Work may be read aloud and critiqued with designated workshops. No requirements for submission of work. Awards are given for work heard or read at conference. A special award is given for topic writing done at the conference. Judges are working, published writers or editors."

‡SQUAW VALLEY COMMUNITY OF WRITERS, 10626 Banner Lava Cap Rd., Nevada City CA 96146. (916)274-8551. (September-June address). P.O. Box 2352, Olympic Valley CA 96146. (916)583-5200. (June-September address). Programs Director: Brett Hall Jones. Estab. 1969. Annual. Conference held in July and August. Each program is one week. Average attendance approximately 120. "Squaw Valley Workshops include four separate one-week programs—Art of the Wild, Poetry, Fiction and Screenwriting. Each concentrates on its particular discipline except the Art of the Wild which includes poetry, fiction and nonfiction about nature, the environment and the ecological crisis. The workshops are conducted in the Olympic House, a large ski lodge built for the 1960 Winter Olympics. The environment includes pine trees, alpine lakes, rivers and streams; the elevation is 6200 feet, and we have cool mornings and sunny, warm afternoons."

Costs: Tuition is $550 for the week. Scholarships are available.

Accommodations: "We have vans which will pick up participants at the Reno airport and at the Truckee Bus and train stations. The Community of Writers rents large ski houses in the Valley to house the attendees. This fosters the community atmosphere which makes our experience unique, as well as allowing us to keep the weekly rate reasonable: $160 multi, 220 double and 320 single."

Additional Information: "Acceptance is based on submitted work. Each participant's manuscript is critiqued in depth during the week of the workshop. A written critique is not available for each work submitted. Brochures/guidelines available. Each participant will have an opportunity to have an additional manuscript read by a staff member who will then meet with them for a private conference."

‡UCI EXTENSION ANNUAL WRITERS' CONFERENCE, Pereira & Berkeley, P.O. Box 6050, Irvine CA 92716-6050. (714)824-5990. Fax: (714)824-3651. Director, Arts & Humanities: Nancy Warzer-Brady. Estab. 1994. Conference held in July. Conference duration: 2 days. Average attendance: 100. Conference to promote "screenwriting, fiction writing." Conference held in UCI Extension classroom facility equipped for conference-type meetings. "In addition to the annual summer writers' conference, we offer approximately ten short courses and workshops on fiction, nonfiction, poetry, and screenwriting on a quarterly basis. We are planning a one-day Poetry Conference in Spring 1996. Details available."

Costs: $230 for 2-day conference; $130 for 1-day; meals not included. "Schedules and fees are subject to change."

Accommodations: Accommodations available for out of town participants if requested. Special University rates at Holiday Inn, $64.80/night including breakfast.

Additional Information: Conference brochures/guidelines available for SASE.

UCLA EXTENSION WRITERS' PROGRAM, 10995 Le Conte Ave., #440, Los Angeles CA 90024. (310)825-9416 or (800)388-UCLA. E-mail address: writers@unex.ucla.edu. Estab. 1891. Courses held year-round with one-day or intensive weekend workshops to 12-week courses. "The diverse offerings span introductory seminars to professional novel and script completion workshops. A number of 1, 2 and 4-day intensive workshops are popular with out-of-town students due to their specific focus and the chance to work with industry professionals. The most comprehensive and diverse continuing education writing program in the country, offering over 400 courses a year including: screenwriting, fiction, writing for young people, poetry, nonfiction, playwriting, publishing and writing for interactive multimedia. Courses are offered in Los Angeles on the UCLA campus, Santa Monica and Universal City as well as online over the internet. Adult learners in the UCLA Extension Writers' Program study with professional screenwriters, fiction writers, playwrights, poets, nonfiction writers, and interactive multimedia writers, who bring practical experience, theoretical knowledge, and a wide variety of teaching styles and philosophies to their classes." Online courses are also available. Call for details.

Costs: Vary from $75-425.

Accommodations: Students make own arrangements. The program can provide assistance in locating local accommodations.

Additional Information: "Some advanced-level classes have manuscript submittal requirements; instructions are always detailed in the quarterly UCLA Extension course catalog. The Writers' Program publishes an annual literary journal, *West/Word*. Work can be submitted by current and former Writers' Program students. An annual fiction prize, The James Kirkwood Prize in Creative Writing, has been established and is given annually to one fiction writer who was published that year in *WEST/WORD*."

WRITE TO SELL WRITER'S CONFERENCE, 8465 Jane St., San Diego CA 92129. (619)484-8575. Director: Diane Dunaway. Estab. 1989. Annual. Conference held in May. Conference duration: 1 day. Average attendance: 300. Concentration includes general fiction and nonfiction; screenwriting to include mystery, romance, children's, television, movies; special novel writing workshop, contacts with top NY agents and editors. Site is the campus of San Diego State University. Panelists include NY editors and agents, bestselling authors and screenwriters.
Costs: $95, includes lunch both days.
Accommodations: Write for details.

WRITE YOUR LIFE STORY FOR PAY, 23350 Sereno Ct., Villa 30, Cupertino CA 95014. (415)691-0300. Contact: Louise Purwin Zobel. Estab. 1969. Workshop held irregularly, usually semiannually at several locations. Workshop duration: 1-2 days. Average attendance: 30-50. "Because every adult has a story worth telling, this conference helps participants to write fiction and nonfiction in books and short forms, using their own life stories as a base." This workshop is held on about 40 campuses at different times, inluding University of California and other university and college campuses in the west.
Costs: Usually $45-65/day, "depending on campus."
Additional Information: Brochures/guidelines available for SASE.

WRITERS CONNECTION SELLING TO HOLLYWOOD, P.O. Box 24770, San Jose CA 95154-4770. (408)445-3600. Fax: (408)445-3609. Directors: Steve and Meera Lester. Estab. 1988. Annual. Conference held second week in August in L.A. area. Conference duration: 3 days. Average attendance: 275. "Conference targets scriptwriters and fiction writers, whose short stories, books, or plays have strong cinematic potential, and who want to make valuable contacts in the film industry. Full conference registrants receive a private consultation with the film industry producer or professional of his/her choice who make up the faculty. Panels, workshops, and 'Ask a Pro' discussion groups include agents, professional film and TV scriptwriters, and independent as well as studio and TV and feature film producers.
Costs: In 1995: full conference by June, $475 members, $500 nonmembers; after June 10, $495 (members), $520 (nonmembers). Includes meals. Partial registration available.
Accommodations: Discount with designated conference airline. "Special rate if we make hotel reservations: $100/night (in L.A.) for private room; $50/shared room."
Additional Information: "This is the premier screenwriting conference of its kind in the country, unique in its offering of an industry-wide perspective from pros working in all echelons of the film industry. Great for making contacts." Conference brochure/guidelines available.

‡WRITER'S CONSORTIUM, P.O. Box 234112, Encinitas CA 92023-4112. (619)414-1004. Fax: (619)631-1303. Director: Carol Roper. Estab. 1990. Annual. Conference held in May or June. Conference duration: 2 days. Average attendance: 100. "Emphasis is on the writer's process primarily for beginning to mid-level screenwriters and fiction writers. Attention is given to craft and the market place." Held in "rustic cabins and conference rooms at Camp Cedar Glen in Julian County, 50 miles east of San Diego in the mountains. Altitude 4,000 feet." Panels planned include "Writing for the 21st Century—What's Ahead for Writers and Are You Prepared?" Guests for 1995 included Diane Drake, screenwriter ("Only You"); Mollie Gregory, novelist ("Triplets," "Private Lies") and President of P.E.N. West, Michael MacCarthy ("The Celestial Bar").
Costs: $175, includes dormitory room, meals and workshops. Some scholarships available. Write for details.
Accommodations: "Conference includes overnight accommodations, but Julian has several hotels and B&Bs for those who prefer more luxury than the cottages. Hotels cost $68-160 per night."
Additional Information: Seven pages of a novel or 10 pages of a screenplay must be submitted 30 days prior to the conference and include final or full payment for conference.

Northwest (AK, ID, MT, OR, WA, WY)

ARTS AT MENUCHA, P.O. Box 4958, Portland OR 97208. (503)234-6827. Board Member: Connie Cheifetz. Estab. 1966. Annual. Conference held first two full weeks in August. Conference duration: Each class lasts 1 week. Average attendance: 60 overall (6-10 per class). Conference held at a "residential private estate with dorm rooms, most with private bath. 100-acre wooded grounds overlooking the Columbia River. A beautiful, relaxing place with pool, tennis, volleyball and walking trails. Meals provided (family-style). 1995 offered Doug Marx, poet, essayist, freelance journalist and teacher, focusing on craft as a process of revision and critical, creative reading; and Maggie Chula, who taught haiku and creative writing at universities in Japan and has won national and international awards for her haiku and tanka. Also offered are 5 different visual arts classes.
Costs: 1994 rates $475 for 1 week; $875 for 2 weeks; includes room and board, tuition and membership.
Accommodations: "We will pick folks up from Portland Airport, bus or train depot." Everyone, including instructors, stays at "Menucha" overnight Sunday-Saturday a.m.

Additional Information: Conference brochures/guidelines are available (no SASE needed).

CLARION WEST WRITERS' WORKSHOP, 340 15th Ave. E., Suite 350, Seattle WA 98112. (206)322-9083. Contact: Admissions Department. Estab. 1983. Annual. Workshop held June 16-July 26. Workshop duration 6 weeks. Average attendance: 20. "Conference to prepare students for professional careers in science fiction and fantasy writing. Held at Seattle Central Community College on Seattle's Capitol Hill. An urban site close to restaurants and cafes, not too far from downtown." Deadline for applications: April 1.
Costs: Workshop: $1,100 ($100 discount if application received by March 1). Dormitory housing: $750, meals not included.
Accommodations: Students are strongly encouraged to stay on-site, in dormitory housing at Seattle University. Cost: $750, meals not included, for 6-week stay.
Additional Information: "This is a critique-based workshop. Students are encouraged to write a story a week; the critique of student material produced at the workshop forms the principle activity of the workshop. Students and instructors critique mss as a group." Conference guidelines available for SASE. "Limited scholarships are available, based on financial need. Students must submit 20-30 pages of ms to qualify for admission. Dormitory and classrooms are handicapped accessible."

FISHTRAP GATHERING: WRITING IN THE WEST WINTER AND SUMMER, P.O. Box 38, Enterprise OR 97828. (503)426-3623. Fax: (503)426-3281. Executive Director: Rich Wandschneider. Estab. summer 1988, winter 1992. Annual. Conference held winter: February 23-25; summer: July 8-14. Average attendance: winter: 50; summer: 150. Winter theme: "Fire." Summer theme: "Eros and Nature." In winter, held at the Eagle Cap Chalet which has a conference room and rooms for rent. Meals are catered or in nearby restaurants. In summer held at the Wallowa Lake Methodist Camp, rooms and meals available. Winter guest speaker: Stephen J. Pyne, author of *World Fire*. Summer guest speakers: Terry Tempest Williams and other major writers and teachers.
Costs: Winter: $290 single occupancy, six meals and two nights lodging. Summer: $175 registration fee; workshops, meals, lodging variable.
Accommodations: We give attendees an option for lodging. Sites range from tenting, to dormitory, to motel suites. Prices vary from $4/day to $80/day.
Additional Information: "There are five full fellowships given annually for the summer session." Write or call for details.

FLIGHT OF THE MIND—SUMMER WRITING WORKSHOP FOR WOMEN, 622 SE 29th Ave., Portland OR 97214. (503)236-9862. Director: Judith Barrington. Estab. 1984. Annual. Workshops held June 16-23 and June 25-July 2. Conference duration: Each workshop lasts 1 week. Average attendance: 65. "Conference held at an old retreat center on the Mackenzie River in the foothills of the Oregon Cascades. Right on the river—hiking trails, hot springs nearby. Most students accommodated in single dorm rooms; a few private cabins available. We have our own cooks and provide spectacular food." Five classes—topics vary year to year. 1995 included "Storytelling" taught by Grace Paley.
Costs: Approximately $700 for tuition, board and single dorm room. Extra for private cabin.
Accommodations: Special arrangements for transportation: "We charter a bus to pick up participants in Eugene, OR, at airport, train station and bus station." Accommodations are included in cost.
Additional Information: "Critiquing is part of most classes; no individual critiques. We require manuscript submissions for acceptance into workshop. (Receive about twice as many applications as spaces)." Workshop brochures/guidelines are available for 1 first-class stamp (no envelope). "This is a feminist-oriented workshop with an emphasis on the work, literature and problems of women writers."

HAYSTACK WRITING PROGRAM, PSU School of Extended Studies, P.O. Box 1491, Portland OR 97207. (503)725-8500. Contact: Maggie Herrington. Estab. 1968. Annual. Program runs from last week of June through first week of August. Workshop duration varies; one-week and weekend workshops are available throughout the six-week program. Average attendance: 10-15/workshop; total program: 325. "The program features a broad range of writing courses for writers at all skill levels. Classes are held in Cannon Beach, Oregon." Past instructors have included William Stafford, Ursula K. LeGuin, Craig Lesley, Molly Gloss, Mark Medoff, Tom Spanbauer, Sallie Tisdale.
Costs: Approximately $310/course. Does not include room and board.
Accommodations: Attendees must make their own transportation arrangements. Various accommodations available including: B&B, motel, hotel, private rooms, camping, etc. A list of specific accommodations is provided.

Can't find a conference? Conferences are listed by region. Check the introduction to this section for a list of regional categories.

Additional Information: Free brochure available. University credit (graduate or undergraduate) is available.

‡**MAKING WAVES WITH WRITERS, (II)**, AHRRC, P.O. Box 6024, Flagstaff AZ 86011-6024. (520)523-3559. Fax: (520)523-5233. Director: Ray Newton. Estab. 1994. Biennial. Conference held from September 22 to September 29, 1996. Conference duration: 8 days. Average attendance: 50-60. Conference concentrating on "both fiction and nonfiction for all levels of writers—beginners through established. We place lots of emphasis upon marketing and publishing." Conference held aboard the MS Ryndam cruise ship to Alaska, with stops at various ports along the Inland Passage to Alaska from Vancouver. 1996 speakers include Tom Clark, editor, *Writer's Digest*; Caroll Shreeve, editor, Gibbs-Smith Publishing; Robert Early, editor, *Arizona Highways*; Ray Newton, professor-writing; Bud Gardner, professor-writing and speaking; Nancy Elliott, award-winning novelist/writer; and Carol O'Hara, award-winning editor-publisher, Cat-Tales Press.
Costs: $995-2,515; includes shipboard accommodations, meals and workshop. Does not include airfare to Anchorage from home city.
Accommodations: Handicapped facilities are available. Rooms are also available in Vancouver and Anchorage for early or late arrivals.
Additional Information: "A special feature will be the addition of a 'Learn to Speak Publicly' workshop, taught by Bud Gardner."

‡**THE MENTORS—THE WRITERS' CONFERENCE IN EUGENE**, % Stephen Bruno Publishing, Inc., P.O. Box 466, Eugene OR 97440. (503)683-5855. Fax: (503)683-7349. Director: Joyce M. Hart. Estab. 1995. Annual. Conference held June 16-22, June 23-29. Conference duration: 1 week. Average attendance: 250. Conference for writers of fiction, creative nonfiction, poetry and screenwriting. Conference is held on the campus of the University of Oregon, housing and classrooms. 1995 Theme: "Revving Up the Muse." 1995 panel: "Life of a Writer." Stephen Bruno, publisher of *Beyond Essence Magazine*, is scheduled to speak at the 1996 conference.
Costs: $325 includes tuition and reception (dessert).
Accommodations: Discount airline tickets available, as well as discount car rental while in town. Housing available on campus; discount hotel rates. $26/night/person—double, $35/night/person—single (on campus).
Additional Information: Workshop—submissions required. Classes—no submissions required. Sponsors a contest. Send fiction and creative nonfiction—no more than 20 pgs., double spaced. Conference brochures/guidelines are available for SASE. "Conference is sponsored by Stephen Bruno Publishing, Inc. Every night during conference, staff members from *Beyond Essence Magazine* are on hand to listen to readings of fiction and poetry and accept submissions."

NORTHWEST CHRISTIAN WRITERS CONFERENCE, P.O. Box 1754, Post Falls ID 83854. Phone/fax: (208)667-9730. Director: Sheri Stone. Estab. 1988. Annual conference held in September. Conference duration: 3 days. Average attendance: 200. "The mission of the conference is to help writers develop their own potential. Covers all areas including music, plays, screenwriting, journalism, novels, children's fiction and nonfiction, marketing, poetry, short stories, fiction and nonfiction, etc." Held at Templins Resort at the Spokane River Conference Center. Past speakers have included Chuck Missler (internationally known author, speaker), Woody Young (publisher/owner Joy Publishing) and Frank Peretti.
Costs: $150 includes all workshops, banquet and all plenaries.
Accommodations: A shuttle bus is available from Spokane International Airport. "We list not only Templins Resort but also all area accommodations. Templins Resort's special conference rates are: between $60-70 for up to four persons. Other local hotel/motels run close to the same rate $40-60."
Additional Information: Included in registration fee: 3 manuscript evaluations/critiques sent 2 weeks prior to conference. Sponsors a contest for short fiction. NWCWC Writer's Contest: Subject dictated prior to conference via brochure. Conference brochures/guidelines are available for SASE.

PACIFIC NORTHWEST WRITERS SUMMER CONFERENCE, 2033 6th Ave., #804, Seattle WA 98121. (206)443-3807. E-mail address: sbinc@halcyon.com. Contact: Shirley Bishop. Estab. 1955. Annual. Conference held last weekend in July. Average attendance: 700. Conference focuses on "fiction, nonfiction, poetry, film, drama, self-publishing, the creative process, critiques, core groups, advice from pros and networking." Site is Doubletree Suites Hotel, Seattle WA. "Editors and agents come from both coasts. They bring lore from the world of publishing. The PNWC provides opportunities for writers to get to know editors and agents. The literary contest provides feedback from professionals and possible fame for the winners." The 1994 guest speakers were John Nichols, Betty Eadie and Colleen McElroy.
Costs: $90-110/day. Meals and lodging are available at hotel.
Additional Information: On-site critiques are available in small groups. Literary contest in these categories: adult article/essay, adult genre novel, adult mainstream novel, adult genre short story, adult mainstream short story, juvenile article or short story, juvenile novel, nonfiction book, picture books for children, playwriting and poetry. Deadline: March 15. Up to $7,000 awarded in prizes. Send SASE for guidelines.

PORT TOWNSEND WRITERS' CONFERENCE, Centrum, Box 1158, Port Townsend WA 98368. (360)385-3102. Director: Carol Jane Bangs. Estab. 1974. Annual. Conference held mid-July. Average attendance: 180.

Conference to promote poetry, fiction, creative nonfiction, writing for children. The conference is held at a 700-acre state park on the strait of Juan de Fuca. "The site is a Victorian-era military fort with miles of beaches, wooded trails and recreation facilities. The park is within the limits of Port Townsend, a historic seaport and arts community, approximately 80 miles northwest of Seattle, on the Olympic Peninsula." Panels include "Writing About Nature," "Journal Writing," "Literary Translation." There will be 5-10 guest speakers in addition to 10 fulltime faculty.
Costs: Approximately $400 tuition and $200 room and board. Less expensive option available.
Accommodations: "Modest room and board facilities on site." Also list of hotels/motels/inns/bed & breakfasts/private rentals available.
Additional Information: "Admission to workshops is selective, based on manuscript submissions." Brochures/guidelines available for SASE. "The conference focus is on the craft of writing and the writing life, not on marketing."

‡PORTLAND STATE UNIVERSITY HAYSTACK WRITING PROGRAM, PSU Summer Session, P.O. Box 1491, Portland OR 97207. (503)725-4186. Contact: Maggie Herrington. Estab. 1968. Annual. Conference held from late June to early August in one-week sessions meeting Monday through Friday; some weekend workshops. Average attendance: 10-15/class. Conference offers a selection of writing courses including fiction, nonfiction, poetry, essay and memoir—taught by well-known writers in small-group sessions. Classes are held in the local school with supplemental activities at the beach, community lecture hall, and other areas of the resort town. University credit available.
Costs: $185 (weekend)-$305 (weeklong). Participants locate their own housing and meals.
Accommodations: Housing costs are $50-400/week. Camping, bed and breakfasts and hotels are available.

SEATTLE PACIFIC UNIVERSITY CHRISTIAN WRITERS CONFERENCE, Seattle Pacific University School of Humanities, Seattle WA 98119. (206)281-2109. Director: Linda Wagner. Estab. 1980. Annual. Conference held in June. Conference duration: 3 days. Average attendence: 160. Concentration is both fiction and nonfiction writing for Christian writers. Site is on a college campus; dining room and dorms available for meals and boarding. 1995 guest speaker was Madeleine L' Engle and several other writers and editors.
Costs: $200 (pre-registration $160); meals and dorm separate.
Accommodations: Dorms available on campus.
Additional Information: Critiques available; send SASE for guidelines. "Available sessions include both lecture and writing workshops."

‡SITKA SYMPOSIUM ON HUMAN VALUES & THE WRITTEN WORD, P.O. Box 2420, Sitka AK 99835. (907)747-3794. Fax: (907)747-6554. Director: Carolyn Servid. Estab. 1984. Annual. Conference held in June. Conference duration: 1 week. Average attendance: 50. Conference "to consider the relationship between writing and the ideas of a selected theme focusing on social and cultural issues. The Symposium is held on Sheldon Jackson College campus, a small, older private school in Sitka. It is located within walking distance of downtown Sitka and many points of visitor interest. The campus also looks out over the water and mountains that surround Sitka." Themes have included "Landscape and Community: Imagining Common Ground." Guest speakers have included poet and essayist Alison Deming, author and mayor Daniel Kemmis, Tlingit Indian community leader Ken Grant, essayist and novelist Scott Russell Sanders and Santa Clara Pueblo architect and artist Rina Swentzell.
Costs: $220 before May 1; $250 after May 1.
Accommodations: Accommodations are available on Sheldon Jackson College campus; rates are listed on Symposium brochure.
Additional Information: Manuscript critiques (individually with faculty) are available for people submitting work before May 20. Conference brochures/guidelines are available for SASE.

WILLAMETTE WRITERS CONFERENCE, 9045 SW Barbur, Suite 5-A, Portland OR 97219. Contact: Conference Director Estab. 1968. Annual. Conference held in August. Average attendance: 220. "Willamette Writers is open to all writers, and we plan our conference accordingly. We offer workshops on all aspects of fiction, nonfiction, marketing, the creative process, etc. Also we invite top notch inspirational speakers for key note addresses. Most often the conference is held on a local college campus which offers a scholarly atmosphere and allows us to keep conference prices down. Recent theme was 'Craft and Creativity.' We always include at least one agent or editor panel and offer a variety of topics of interest to both fiction and nonfiction writers." Past editors and agents in attendance have included: Marc Aronson, Senior Editor, Henry Holt & Co.; Tom Colgan, Senior Editor, Avon Books; Charles Spicer, Senior Editor, St. Martin's Press; Sheree Bykofsky, Sheree Bykofsky Associates; Laurie Harper, Sebastian Agency; F. Joseph Spieler, The Spieler Agency; Robert Tabian and Ruth Nathan.
Costs: Cost for full conference including meals is $195.
Accomodations: If necessary, these can be made on an individual basis. Some years special rates are available.
Additional Information: Conference brochures/guidelines are available for SASE.

WRITE ON THE SOUND WRITERS' CONFERENCE, 700 Main St., Edmonds WA 98020. (206)771-0228. Arts Coordinator: Christine Sidwell. Estab. 1986. Annual. Conference held second weekend in October. Conference duration: 2 days. Average attendance: 160. "We try to offer something in all writing disciplines. Large sessions are held in the Plaza Room of the Edmonds Library. Classes are held in the Frances Anderson Center next door."
Costs: $75 for 2 days, $40 for 1 day; includes tuition and continental breakfast. Box lunches available at additional cost.
Additional Information: Brochures available in August for SASE.

‡WRITERS WEEKEND AT BEACH, P.O. Box 877, Ocean Park WA 98640. (360)665-6576. Co-Director: Birdie Etchison. Estab. 1992. Annual. Conference held last weekend in February. Average attendance: 60. Conference covers fiction, nonfiction, writing for children, poetry and photography. Held at a location "with a fantastic view of the Pacific Ocean. The new conference center provides all workshops, sleeping and eating on one floor." 1995 guest keynote speaker was Michael Whelan, screenwriter.
Costs: $110, includes meals, lodging and workshop fees.
Additional Information: Conference brochures/guidelines are available for SASE.

YACHATS LITERARY FESTIVAL, 124 NE California, Yachats OR 97498. (503)547-3271. Contact: Frena Gray-Davidson, Director. Estab. 1993. Annual. Conference held in September. Topics include "all classifications" of writing. Conference activities are "held at various sites in the extraordinarily beautiful setting of ancient forest, agate beaches, spectacular rocky promontaries of the Oregon Coast." Workshops have included short story, life story, writing over 50, journalism and poetry. Speakers have included Robert Sheckley, Sharon Donbiago and Jan Mitchell.
Costs: In 1995, $275 for the week. Accommodations extra.
Accommodations: Conference organizers will assist with transporation arrangements "if asked." Accommodation information available with brochure request.
Additional Information: Sponsors 3 chapbook competitions. Prize for each is $500 plus publication. Contest closes at end of March. Brochures available for SASE.

YELLOW BAY WRITERS' WORKSHOP, Center for Continuing Education, University of Montana, Missoula MT 59812. (406)243-6486. Contact: Program Manager. Estab. 1988. Annual. Conference held from mid to late August. Average attendance: 50-60. Includes four workshops: 2 fiction; 1 poetry; 1 creative nonfiction/personal essay. Conference "held at the University of Montana's Flathead Lake Biological Station, a research station with informal educational facilities and rustic cabin living. Located in northwestern Montana on Flathead Lake, the largest natural freshwater lake west of the Mississippi River. All faculty are requested to present a craft lecture—usually also have an editor leading a panel discussion." 1995 faculty included Andrea Barrett, Robert Hass, William Kittredge, Melanie Rae Thon and publisher Fiona McCrae.
Costs: In 1995, for all workshops, lodging (single occupancy) and meals $725; $695 with double occupancy; $425 for commuters.
Accommodations: Shuttle is available from Missoula to Yellow Bay for those flying to Montana. Cost of shuttle is $40 (1995).
Additional Information: Brochures/guidelines are available for SASE.

Canada

✤CANADIAN AUTHORS ASSOCIATION CONFERENCE, 27 Doxsee Ave. N., Campbellford, Ontario K0L 1L0 Canada. (705)653-0323. Fax: (705)653-0593. President: Cora Taylor. Estab. 1921. Annual conference held June 23-28 (approximately). Average attendance: 150. To promote "all genres—varies from year to year." 1996 conference to be held at the University of Manitoba, Winnipeg, Manitoba.
Costs: To be announced; all expenses included in convention center price. Special early-bird discounts.
Accommodations: Special accommodations available on request, but registrants using this option will be asked to pay daily rates.
Additional Information: Conference brochures/registration forms are available for SAE and IRC.

✤FESTIVAL OF THE WRITTEN ARTS, Writers-in-Residence Program, Box 2299, Sechelt, British Columbia V0N 3A0 Canada. (604)885-9631. Registrar: Gail Bull. Estab. 1985. Three times/year (spring, summer, fall). Average attendance: 21. "Each set of workshops features different genres, but usually fiction at each season. All workshop leaders are qualified, published Canadian writers. Conference site is the "Rockwood Centre overlooking the town of Sechelt on the beautiful Sunshine Coast. The Lodge around which the Centre is organized was built in 1937 as a destination for holidayers arriving on the Old Union Steamship Line. A new twelve-bedroom annex was added in 1982, and in 1989 the Festival of the Written Arts constructed a pavilion for outdoor performances next to the annex."

Costs: "To be announced."

Accommodations: "Writers-in-Residence participants are accommodated two (and in a few cases three) to a room with a private bathroom. Simple but nutritious meals are served in the dining room of the old Lodge." Students make their own transportation arrangements, including ferry transportation. Accommodation is provided as above.

Additional information: "Students must submit a sample of their work before being accepted for the program—usually 2,000 words are asked for fiction classes. Each instructor has a chance to preview these submissions so that he/she may design the workshop appropriately." Conference brochures/guidelines are available for SASE. "We keep our classes small for optimum benefit to the student. Many students return for further workshops but we are now getting applications from all over Canada and parts of the US."

♣THE FESTIVAL OF THE WRITTEN ARTS, Box 2299, Sechelt, British Columbia V0N 3A0 Canada. (800)565-9631 or (604)885-9631. Fax: (604)885-3967. Producer: Michael Barnholden. Estab. 1983. Annual. Festival held: August 8-11. Average attendance: 2,500. To promote "all writing genres." Festival held at the Rockwood Centre. "The Centre overlooks the town of Sechelt on the Sunshine Coast. The lodge around which the Centre was organized was built in 1937 as a destination for holidayers arriving on the old Union Steamship Line; it has been preserved very much as it was in its heyday. A new twelve-bedroom annex was added in 1982, and in 1989 the Festival of the Written Arts constructed a Pavilion for outdoor performances next to the annex. The festival does not have a theme. Instead, it showcases 20 or more Canadian writers in a wide variety of genres each year."

Costs: In 1995, costs were $10 per event or $120 for a four-day pass (Canadian funds).

Accommodations: Lists of hotels and bed/breakfast available.

Additional Information: The festival runs contests during the 4½ days of the event. Prizes are books donated by publishers. Brochures/guidelines are available.

♣MARITIME WRITERS' WORKSHOP, Extension & Summer Session, UNB Box 4400, Fredericton, New Brunswick E3B 5A3 Canada. (506)453-4646. Coordinator: Glenda Turner. Estab. 1976. Annual. Conference held in July. Conference duration: 1 week. Average attendance: 50. "Workshops in four areas: fiction, poetry, nonfiction, writing for children." Site is University of New Brunswick, Fredericton campus.

Costs: $300, tuition; $135 meals; $115/double room; $130/single room (Canadian funds).

Accommodations: On-campus accommodations and meals.

Additional Information: "Participants must submit 10-20 manuscript pages which form a focus for workshop discussions." Brochures are available. No SASE necessary.

♣MEMORIES INTO STORIES, Hollyhock Box 127, Mansons Landing, British Columbia V0P 1K0 Canada. (800)933-6339. E-mail address: hollyhock1@aol.com. Program Director: Oriane Lee Johnston. Estab. 1993. Conference held irregularly. Conference duration: 5 days. Average attendance: 15-30. "We use memory to tap into creativity and write stories through individual and group exercises. Held at Hollyhock Seminar and Holiday Centre on Cortes Island, British Columbia, 48 acres of forest trails, sandy beaches, hot tub, central dining lodge and individual cabins and meeting rooms." Workshop led by Christine Cohen Park and Joan Logghe.

Costs: Tuition is $395 (Canadian), meals and accommodations are extra and vary depending on the type of accommodation selected.

Accommodations: "We have a 32-page catalog available listing all Hollyhock Programs, accommodations, travel, etc. Costs from $54-119 (Canadian)/person/night, depending on the type of accommodation selected. Hollyhock has everything from tenting, to dorm rooms, to shared and private rooms with shared or private bath. Above prices include 3 meals/day. Brochures/guidelines available for SASE.

♣SAGE HILL WRITING EXPERIENCE, Box 1731, Saskatoon, Saskatchewan S7K 3S1 Canada. Executive Director: Steven Smith. Annual. Workshops held in August and October. Workshop duration 7-21 days. Attendance: limited to 36-40. "Sage Hill Writing Experience offers a special working and learning opportunity to writers at different stages of development. Top quality instruction, low instructor-student ratio and the beautiful Sage Hill setting offer conditions ideal for the pursuit of excellence in the arts of fiction, poetry and playwriting." The Sage Hill location features "individual accommodation, in-room writing area, lounges, meeting rooms, healthy meals, walking woods and vistas in several directions." Six classes are held: Introduction to Writing Fiction & Poetry; Fiction Workshop, Poetry Workshop, Intermediate; Poetry Colloquium, Advanced; Fiction Colloquium, Advanced; Playwriting Lab. 1995 faculty included Tim Lilburn, Janice Kulyk Keefer, Ven Begamudré, Di Brandt, William Robertson, Rosemary Nixon, John Murrell.

Costs: $475 (Canadian) includes instruction, accommodation, meals and all facilities. Fall Poetry Colloquium: $700.

Accommodations: On-site individual accommodations located at Lumsden 45 kilometers outside Regina. Fall Colloquium is at Muenster, Saskatchewan.

Additional Information: For Introduction to Creative Writing: A five-page sample of your writing or a statement of your interest in creative writing; list of courses taken required. For intermediate and colloquium program: A resume of your writing career and a 12-page sample of your work plus 5 pages of published work required. Application deadline is May 1. Guidelines are available for SASE. Scholarships and bursaries are available.

❦**THE VANCOUVER INTERNATIONAL WRITERS FESTIVAL**, 1243 Cartwright St., Vancouver, British Columbia V6H 4B7 Canada. (604)681-6330. Estab. 1988. Annual. Held during the 3rd week of October. Average attendance: 8,000. "This is a festival for readers and writers. The program of events is diverse and includes readings, panel discussions, seminars. Lots of opportunities to interact with the writers who attend." Held on Granville Island—in the heart of Vancouver. Two professional theaters are used as well as Performance Works (an open space). "We try to avoid specific themes. Programming takes place between February and June each year and is by invitation."
Costs: Tickets are $10-15 (Canadian).
Accommodations: Local tourist info can be provided when necessary and requested.
Additional Information: Brochures/guidelines are available for SASE. "A reminder—this is a festival, a celebration, not a conference or workshop."

❦**WRITERS IN RESIDENCE PROGRAMS**, Festival of the Written Arts, Box 2299, Sechelt, British Columbia V0N 3A0 Canada. (800)565-9631 or (604)885-9631. Fax: (604)885-3967. Producer: Michael Barnholden. Estab. 1986. Mentor/writer workshops held throughout the year. Three and five day sessions. Average attendance: 6-7 per workshop. "The Rockwood Centre overlooks the town of Sechelt on the Sunshine Coast. The Lodge around which the Centre was organized was built in 1937 as a destination for holidayers arriving on the old Union Steamship Line; it has been preserved very much as it was in its heyday. A new twelve-bedroom annex was added in 1982, and in 1989 the Festival of the Written Arts constructed a Pavilion for outdoor performances next to the annex. The whole complex is managed by the Rockwood Society and reserved exclusively for the arts, recreation and learning. Writers-in-residence participants are accommodated two (and in a few cases three) to a room with a private bathroom."
Costs: $100/day (Canadian) includes tuition, accommodation and meals.
Additional Information: Brochures/guidelines are available for SASE.

International

‡**AKUMAL WRITERS CONFERENCE**, % Daniel & Daniel, P.O. Box 21922, Santa Barbara CA 93121. (805)962-1780. Fax: (805)962-8835. Director: John Daniel. Estab. 1995. Annual. Conference held November 11-15, 1996. Average attendance: 17. To promote "fiction, poetry, creative nonfiction. The conference is held at Hotel Villas Mayas, a modest beach resort about 60 miles south of Cancun, in Southern Mexico. The 1995 faculty included Pete Fromm, Mary Jane Moffat, Toby Tompkins, and Susan and John Daniel.
Costs: 1995: $1,400, includes lodging and two meals a day.
Accommodations: Travel costs not included. Participants make their own travel arrangements. Lodging is provided, and cost is included in enrollment fee.
Additional Information: Applicants must submit writing samples: prose between 2,000-3,000 words. Conference brochures/guidelines are available for SASE.

ART WORKSHOP INTERNATIONAL, 463 West St. 1028H, New York NY 10014. (212)691-1159. Contact: Bea Kreloff, Co-director. Estab. 1977. Annual. Workshop held in summer. Workshop lasts 1 month. Average attendance: 20-25. Held in Assisi, Italy. Instructional program plus independent program for professional writers and artists. Panels planned for next workshop include Creative Writing Workshop with instructor, publisher, editor and poet, Beatrix Gates.
Costs: Fee $2,790. Includes room, board and tuition. Attendees must make their own travel arrangements.
Additional Information: For independent programs, submission of written work and curriculum vita is required. Conference brochures/guidelines are available for SASE. Writing workshop is combined with an art workshop. Send for brochure for details on additional workshops.

EDINBURGH UNIVERSITY CENTRE FOR CONTINUING EDUCATION CREATIVE WRITING WORK-SHOPS, 11 Buccleuch Place, Edinburgh Scotland EH8 9LW. (31)650-4400. E-mail address: b.stevens@ed.ac. uk. Administrative Director of International Summer Schools: Bridget M. Stevens. Estab. 1990. Introductory course held July 9-15; short story course held July 16-22; playwriting course held July 23-29. Average attendance: 15. Courses cover "basic techniques of creative writing, the short story and playwriting. The University of Edinburgh Centre for Continuing Education occupies traditional 18th century premises near the George Square Campus. Located nearby are libraries, banks, recreational facilities and the university faculty club which workshop participants are invited to use."
Costs: In 1995 cost was £190 per one-week course (tuition only).
Accommodations: Information on overnight accommodations is available. Accommodations include student dormitories, self-catering apartment and local homes.

Additional Information: Participants are encouraged to submit work in advance, but this is not obligatory. Conference brochures/guidelines available for SASE.

‡**FICTION WRITING RETREAT IN ACAPULCO**, 3584 Kirkwood Place, Boulder CO 80304. (303)444-0086. Conference Director: Barbara Steiner. Estab. 1991. Annual. Conference held in November. Conference duration: 1 week. Average attendance: 10. Conference concentrates on creativity and fiction technique/any market. Oceanfront accommodations on private estate of Mexican artist Nora Beteta. Rooms in villa have bath (private) but usually dual occupancy. Swimming in pool or ocean/bay. Classes held on large porches with ocean breeze and views."
Costs: $595 for 1 week includes room, meals, classes.
Accommodations: Airfare separate. Travel agent books flights for groups from Denver. Will book from anyplace in US.
Additional Information: "Writers submit one short fiction piece in advance of workshop. Classes include writing, lecture and assignments." Brochures/guidelines available for SASE.

SUMMER IN FRANCE WRITING WORKSHOPS, HCOI, Box 102, Plainview TX 79072. (806)889-3533. Director: Bettye Givens. Annual. Conference: 27 days. Average attendance: 10-15. For fiction, poetry. The classrooms are in the Val de Grace 277 Rue St. Jacques in the heart of the Latin Quarter near Luxeumbourg Park in Paris. Guest speakers include Paris poets, professors and editors (lectures in English).
Costs: Costs vary. Costs includes literature classes, art history and the writing workshop.
Accommodations: Some accommodations with a French family.
Additional Information: Conference brochures/guidelines are available for SASE. "Enroll early. Side trips out of Paris are planned as are poetry readings at the Paris American Academy and at Shakespeare & Co."

TŶ NEWYDD WRITER'S CENTRE, Llanystumdwy, Cricieth Gwynedd LL52 OLW, 01766-522811 United Kingdom. Administrator: Sally Baker. Estab. 1990. Regular courses held throughout the year. Every course held Monday-Saturday. Average attendance: 14. "To give people the opportunity to work side by side with professional writers." Site is Ty Newydd. Large manor house. Last home of the prime minister, David Lloyd George. Situated in North Wales, Great Britain-between mountains and sea." Featured tutors in 1995 were novelists Beryl Bainbridge and Bernice Rubens.
Costs: £250 for Monday-Saturday (includes full board, tuition).
Accommodations: Transportation from railway stations arranged. Accommodation in TyNewydd (onsite).
Additional Information: "We have had several people from US on courses here in the past three years."

WOMEN'S WILDERNESS CANOE TRIPS WRITING RETREAT, P.O. Box 9109, Santa Fe NM 87504. (505)984-2268. Owner and Guide: Beverly Antaeus. Estab. 1985. Annual. Conference held in October or November. Conference duration: 8 days. Average attendance: 20. Writing retreat with Deena Metzger. "All genres welcome as the means to bring forth something truer and newer than ever before." Held "on the beach, Sea of Cortez, Baja California, Mexico. Living under sun and moon; tents and palapas available for sleeping."
Costs: For 1995 cost was $1,495; land costs, tuition and food included in fee.
Accommodations: All transportation details are provided upon enrollment. "We live outdoors throughout the workshop—all rendezvous and departure details provided in full."
Additional Information: Brochures/guidelines available upon request.

THE WRITERS' SUMMER SCHOOL, SWANWICK, The New Vicarage, Woodford Halse, Daventry, NN11 3RE England. Secretary: Brenda Courtie. Estab. 1949. Annual. Conference held August 12-18. Average attendance: 300 plus. "Conference concentrates on all fields of writing." In 1995 courses included: The Novel, The Historical Novel, Writing & Selling Articles, Writing for Children, Writing Biography, Religious Markets, Short Stories, Starting Out. Speakers in 1995 included Dannie Abse, Roy Hattersley, Cathy MacPhail, Sheila Watson, Susan Curran, Tim Waterstone, Robin Lloyd-Jones, Joyce Begg.
Costs: £185 inclusive.
Accommodations: Buses from main line station to conference centre provided.
Additional Information: "Course Leaders will accept mss prior to the conference. The Writers' Summer School is a nonprofit-making organization."

Conferences and workshops/'95-'96 changes

The following conferences and workshops appeared in the 1995 edition of *Novel & Short Story Writer's Market* but do not appear in the 1996 edition. Those conferences and workshops that did not respond to our request for an update appear below without further explanation. If a reason for the omission is available, it is included next to the listing name. There are several reasons why a conference or workshop may not appear— it may not be an annual event, for example, or it may no longer be held.

Blue Ridge Writers Conference
Cedar Hills Christian Writers' Weekend
Central Arizona Christian Writers Workshop
Children's Reading Roundtable/ Writers & Illustrators Summer Seminar
Fiction From the Heartland Conference
Florida Christian Writers Conference
IWWG Midwestern Conference

(requested deletion)
IWWG New Jersey Conference
IWWG San Diego Conference (requested deletion)
IWWG Write Your Own Story Conference (requested deletion)
Maple Woods Community College Writer's Conference
Novelist, Inc. Annual National Conference
Professionalism in Writing School

Robert Quackenbush's Children's Book Writing & Illustrating Workshops
SCBWI/Rocky Mountain Chapter Summer Retreat
Taste of Chicago Writing Conference
Thunder Bay Literary Conference (discontinued)
Writing By The Sea (requested deletion)
Young Writers at Penn Conference (program discontinued)

International conferences/'95-'96 changes

The Arvon Foundation Ltd. Workshops
Paris Writers' Workshop/WICE

For information on entering the Novel & Short Story Writer's Market *Cover Letter Contest, see page 19.*

Retreats and Colonies

If you are looking for a quiet place to start or complete your novel or short story collection, a retreat or writers' colony may offer just what you need. Often located in tranquil settings, these are places for writers to find solitude and concentrated time to focus solely on their writing. Unlike conferences or workshop settings, communal meals may be the only scheduled activities. Also, a writer's stay at a retreat or colony is typically anywhere from one to twelve weeks (sometimes longer), while time spent at a conference or workshop is generally anywhere from one day to two weeks (perhaps a month at most).

Like conferences and workshops, however, retreats and colonies span a wide range. Some, such as Yaddo offer residencies for established writers, while others, such as Dorset Colony House for Writers, are open to writers on all levels. Other programs are restricted to writers from certain areas or who write on certain subjects such as the Camargo Foundation retreat for a writer working on a project relating to French culture. And you'll find retreats and colonies located in Pahoa, Hawaii; County Monaghan, Ireland; Cape Cod, Massachusetts; and Taos, New Mexico. Accommodations vary from a restored antebellum home in Mississippi to a castle in Scotland to wood-frame cottages on an island off the coast of Washington state.

Despite different focuses and/or locations, all retreats and colonies have one thing in common: They are places where writers may work undisturbed, usually in nature-oriented and secluded settings. A retreat or colony serves as a place for rejuvenation; a writer can find new ideas, rework old ones or put the finishing touches to works-in-progress.

Arrangements at retreats and colonies differ dramatically so it may help to determine your own work habits before you begin searching through these pages. While some retreats house writers in one main building, others provide separate cottages. In both cases, residents are generally given private work space, although they usually must bring along their own typewriters or personal computers. Some colonies offer communal, family-style meals at set times; some prepare meals for each resident individually and still others require residents to prepare meals themselves. If you tend to work straight through meals now, you might want to consider a retreat or colony that offers the last option.

A related consideration for most folks is cost. Again, the types of arrangements vary. A good number of residencies are available at no cost or only a minimal daily cost, sometimes including the cost of meals, sometimes not. The Ragdale Foundation charges a mere $15 a day and offers scholarships, for example, and the Millay Colony for the Arts charges no fees. Other residencies, such as those through the Ucross Foundation, are "awards," resulting from competitive applications. Finally, for those residencies that are fairly expensive, scholarships or fee waivers are often available.

In general, residencies at retreats and colonies are competitive because only a handful of spots are available at each place. Writers must often apply at least six months in advance for the time period they desire. While some locations are open year-round, others are available only during certain seasons. Planning to go during the "off-season" may lessen your competition. Also, most places will want to see a writing sample with your application, so be prepared to show your best work—whether you are a beginning or established writer. In addition, it will help to have an idea of the project you'll work on while in residence, since some places request this information with their applications as well.

Each listing in this section provides information about the type of writers the retreat or colony accepts; the location, accommodations and meal plan available; the costs; and, finally, the application process. As with markets and conferences and workshops, changes in policies may be made after this edition has gone to press. Send a self-addressed, stamped envelope to the places that interest you to receive the most up-to-date details.

For other listings of retreats and colonies, you may want to see *The Guide to Writers Conferences* (ShawGuides, 10 W. 66th St., Suite 30H, New York NY 10023), which not only provides information about conferences, workshops and seminars but also residencies, retreats and organizations. An exceptional resource is *Havens for Creatives*, available from ACTS Institute, Inc. (c/o Charlotte Plotsky, P.O. Box 30854, Palm Beach Gardens FL 33420), which features almost 400 retreats, colonies, art programs and creative vacation opportunities for writers, artists, photographers and other creative types. This directory also includes a bibliography of works written about art and writing colonies and a selection of creative work written during residencies.

EDWARD F. ALBEE FOUNDATION, (THE BARN), 14 Harrison St., New York NY 10013. (212)226-2020. Foundation Secretary: David Briggs. For writers (fiction, nonfiction, playwrights, etc.) and visual artists (painters, sculptors, etc.). " 'The Barn' is located in Montauk, NY." Available for 1 month residencies from June-September. Provisions for the writer include private rooms. Accommodates 2-3 writers at one time. Residencies supported by the Edward F. Albee Foundation Fellowship.
Costs: No cost, but residents are responsible for their food, travel and supplies.
To Apply: Write or call for information and applications (accepted January 1 to April 1). Brochures or guidelines are available for SASE.

BELLAGIO STUDY AND CONFERENCE CENTER, Rockefeller Foundation, 420 Fifth Ave., New York NY 10018-2702. (212)852-8468. Manager: Susan Garfield. Estab. 1960. "Scholars and artists from any country and in any discipline are invited to apply. Successful applicants will be individuals of achievement with significant publications, exhibitions or shows to their credit. Bellagio Study and Conference Center, also known as Villa Serbelloni, occupies a wooded promontory . . . Includes main house and seven other buildings. Set in the foothills of the Italian Alps." Residencies are approximately 4 weeks long. Offered February through mid-December. Each scholar and artist is provided with a private room and bath and with a study in which to work. IBM and Apple PCs and printers available. Accommodates 130 residents. Deadlines: January 8 and June 1.
Costs: "The center does not provide financial assistance to scholars in residence nor does it ordinarily contribute to travel expenses. Once at the center, all scholars and spouses are guests of the foundation."
To Apply: Send for application. Application must include form, half-page abstract describing purpose of project, detailed project description, brief curriculum vitae, one sample of published work, reviews. Brochure/guidelines available. Do not send SASE.

THE BLUE MOUNTAIN CENTER, Blue Mountain Lake, New York NY 12812. (518)352-7391. Director: Harriet Barlow. Residencies for established writers. "Provides a peaceful environment where residents may work free from distractions and demands of normal daily life." Residencies awarded for 1 month between June 15 and October 30 (approx.). For more information, send SASE for brochure.
To Apply: Application deadline: February 1.

THE MARY INGRAHAM BUNTING INSTITUTE, 34 Concord Ave., Cambridge MA 02138. (617)495-8212. Fellowships Coordinator: Linda Roach. Estab. 1960. For women scholars, researchers, creative writers, and visual and performing artists. "The Institute occupies three recently renovated 19th century buildings which house staff and fellows' offices, art and music studios, a colloquium room, a common room, a library/conference room, and a small exhibition gallery." Eleven-month appointments available for the Bunting Fellowship Program: September 15, 1996-August 15, 1997. Office space, auditing privileges, and access to most other resources of Radcliffe College and Harvard University are provided. Eleven-month to six-month appointments available for the Affiliation Program: fall (September 15, 1996-January 31, 1997); spring (February 1, 1997-August 15, 1997); or 11-month (September 15, 1996-August 15, 1997). Accommodates multiple writers.

Costs: Fellowships are available. "Applications are judged on the quality and significance of the proposed project, the applicant's record of accomplishment, and the potential importance of the fellowship at this stage in the applicant's career."
To Apply: Applications by nomination only; no unsolicited applications accepted. Brochure/guidelines available for SASE.

CAMARGO FOUNDATION, W-1050 First National Bank Bldg., 332 Minnesota St., St. Paul MN 55101-1312. Administrative Assistant: Ricardo Bloch. Estab. 1971. For one artist, one writer, one musician; and graduate students and scholars working on projects relating to French and Francophone culture. There are facilities for 12 grantees each semester. "Grantees are given a furnished apartment, rent free, on an estate on the Mediterranean about twenty miles east of Marseilles. Families may accompany grantee, but must remain the entire period of the grant." Grant period is from early September to mid-December or from mid-January to May 31. Minimum residency is three months. "A workroom is available and computer facilities, though it is suggested that writers bring their own equipment; space and scheduling may be tight."
Costs: None. There is no stipend.
To Apply: "There is no fee. Write to Administrative Assistant giving name and address to request application materials. Packet will be mailed upon request. All application materials requested must be received in this ofice by February 1. Applicants will be notified of selection decisions by April 1."

CHÂTEAU DE LESVAULT, Onlay 58370 France. (33)86-84-32-91 Fax: (33)86-84-35-78. Director: Bibbi Lee. Estab. 1984. Open to writers of fiction and nonfiction, poets, playwrights, researchers. Located in "Burgundy within the National Park 'Le Morvan,' the Château de Lesvault is a classic French manor with fully furnished rooms including a salon, dining room and library. The château is surrounded by a large private park and there is a lake on the property." Available in 4-week sessions from October through April. Provisions for the writer include a large private room for sleeping and working, complete use of the château facility. Accommodates 5.
Costs: Cost for a 4-week session is 4,500 French francs (approx. US \$900). Included is all lodging and all meals.
To Apply: Send a letter to the Selection Committee briefly describing the writing project, two references and a sample of work (max. 3 pages). Specify the 4-week session requested. No application fee required. Brochure/guidelines available for SASE.

CURRY HILL PLANTATION WRITER'S RETREAT, 404 Cresmont Ave., Hattiesburg MS 39401. (601)264-7034. Director: Elizabeth Bowne. Estab. 1977. Open to all fiction and nonfiction writing, except poetry and technical writing. This workshop is held at an antebellum home, located on 400-acres of land. It is limited to only eight guests who live in, all of whom receive individual help with their writing, plus a 3-hour workshop each evening when the group meets together. The location is six miles east of Bainbridge, Georgia. Offered March 31-April 6 and April 14-20, 1996. "The date of the retreat is different every year but always in the spring—March/April." Provisions for the writer include room and board. Accommodates 8 writers.
Costs: \$500 for the week; includes room and board and individual help, one hour per guest each day.
To Apply: Interested persons should apply *early* January. Brochure/guidelines available for SASE.

DJERASSI RESIDENT ARTISTS PROGRAM, 2325 Bear Gulch Rd., Woodside CA 94062-4405. Executive Director: Charles Amirkhanian. "The Djerassi Program appoints approximately 50 artists a year to spend 1 to 2 months working on independent or collaborative projects in a setting of unusual beauty and privacy. The facility is located on a former cattle ranch 1 hour south of San Francisco in the Santa Cruz Mountains above Stanford University, facing the Pacific Ocean. We are seeking applications at all levels." Provisions for the writer include living/studio accommodations with balcony or garden access, as well as meals. Accommodates 10 artists of various disciplines at one time. Open April 1-October 31.
Costs: The Djerassi Program award is strictly a residential grant. All accommodations are provided at no cost.
To Apply: Send SASE to: Djerassi Resident Artists Program at above address and request application packet. Deadline for 1997 season is February 15, 1996.

DORLAND MOUNTAIN ARTS COLONY, P.O. Box #6, Temecula CA 92593. (909)676-5039. Director of Operations: Karen Parrott. Estab. 1978. Open to visual artists, composers, writers, playwrights, theater artists. Provides uninterrupted time in a natural environment. The colony is located on a 300-acre nature preserve. No electricity, rustic single wall constructed cabins; large oak grove; 2 ponds; trails. Available for 1 to 2-month residencies year round. Provisions for the writer include private cabins with living and work space. Manual (older) typewriters provided. Responsible for own meals. There are a total of 6 cabins.
Costs: \$150/month.
To Apply: Application deadlines: March 1 and September 1. Brochure/guidelines available for SASE.

DORSET COLONY HOUSE FOR WRITERS, Box 519, Dorset VT 05251. (802)867-5777. Director: John Nassivera. Estab. 1980. Colony is open to all writers. Facility and grounds include large 19th century house

in New England village setting; national historic landmark house and village. Available in spring and fall. Accommodates 8 writers.
Costs: $95/week; meals not included; fully functional kitchen in house and restaurants easy walk away.
To Apply: No fees to apply; send inquiry anytime. Brochures are available for SASE.

FAIRVIEW SUMMIT RETREAT HOUSE, 10800 Mt. Fairview Rd. SE, Cumberland MD 21502. (301)724-6842. Director: Petrina Aubol. Estab. 1991. For writers and artists. "Anyone wishing to get away to a creative environment. Group rates available for those wishing to hold their own retreat." The retreat center is located on a dead end road on top of Irons Mountain in the middle of a 100-acre forest. Available year-round. Provisions for the writer include private room, workspace throughout both houses, meals on request, meeting space indoors and out, indoor pool, hiking trails, scenic vistas, only 6½ miles from town. Accommodates 20 writers.
Costs: $25/day includes breakfast; group rate available (10 person minimum); meals provided at extra cost. Barter available for room and board costs.
To Apply: Send reservation form plus 25% deposit on full cost to hold space.

FINE ARTS WORK CENTER IN PROVINCETOWN, 24 Pearl St., Provincetown MA 02657. (508)487-9960. Contact: Writing Coordinator. Estab. 1968. Open to emerging writers and visual artists. "Located on the grounds of the former Days Lumberyard complex, the facility has offered studio space to artists and writers since 1914. Renovated coal bins provide artist studios; several houses and a refurbished Victorian Barn offer apartments for writers. The complex encircles the Stanley Kunitz Common Room where fellows and visiting artists offer readings to the public." A 7-month residency offered from October 1 to May 1 each year. "Each writer is awarded his/her own apartment with kitchen and bath. All apartments are furnished and equipped with kitchen supplies. A monthly stipend of $375 is also provided." Accommodates 10 writers (four fiction, four poets).
Costs: No fees other than application fee ($35).
To Apply: Application deadline: February 1. Writing sample: Send 1 or 2 short stories. If novel, excerpt including opening section and synopsis. Limit: 35 pages. Send up to 15 pages of poetry. Send six copies. Check guidelines for details. Brochure/guidelines available for SASE.

THE GELL WRITERS CENTER OF THE FINGER LAKES, % Writers & Books, 740 University Ave., Rochester NY 14607. (716)473-2590. Fax: (716)729-0982. Executive Director: Joseph Flaherty. Estab. 1989. For active writers. "A two-bedroom house located on 25 acres of wooded hillside in New York's Finger Lakes area." Offered year-round for periods of time from 1-4 weeks. Provisions for the writer include private room with bathroom, shared kitchen, dining and living room areas. Accommodates 2 writers.
Costs: $35 per day. Does not include meals.
To Apply: Call or write for application. "Must send résumé showing a publication history or a writing sample." Brochure/guidelines available for SASE.

THE TYRONE GUTHRIE CENTRE AT ANNAGHMAKERRIG, Newbliss, County Monaghan, Ireland. Tel: 047-54003. Resident Director: Bernard Loughlin. Estab. 1981. Open to writers, painters, sculptors, composers, directors, artists. There are "11 work rooms in house, generally with private bathroom. Also 5 new houses which are self-contained. 400-acres, large lake and gardens. Sitting room, library, kitchen, dining room." Closed for 2-week period at Christmas only. Provisions for the writer include private room and meals. Accommodates 16 writers and other artists.
Costs: IR £1,200-£1,600, depending on season, per month in Big House, all meals included. IR £300/week for self-contained houses—also have to pay food, heating, electricity and outgoings.
To Apply: Write for application form. Considered at bimonthly board meeting. Brochure/guidelines available for SASE.

‡THE HAMBIDGE CENTER, P.O. Box 339, Rabun Gap GA 30568. Estab. 1934. Open to artists from all fields. Includes "600 acres of wooded, rural property serenely set in north Georgia mountains; traversed by streams and waterfalls." 2-week to 6-week stays from May to October, with limited winter residencies also. Provisions for writers include private cottages and studios. Accommodates 8 artists.
Costs: $125/week with dinner provided Monday-Friday. Some scholarships available (very limited and reviewed individually).
To Apply: Deadline for reviews is January 31. Application fee is $20. Application form mailed upon request. Brochure/guidelines available for SASE.

HEDGEBROOK, (formerly Cottages at Hedgebrook), 2197 E. Millman Rd., Langley WA 98260. (360)321-4786. Director: Linda Bowers. Estab. 1988. For "women writers, published or not, of all ages and from all cultural backgrounds." Located on "30-acres on Whidbey Island one hour north of Seattle WA. Six individual cottages, a bathhouse for showers and a farmhouse where dinner is served. The cottages are wood frame, wood heat, electricity, no TV or phone." Applicants request a stay of 1 week to 3 months (may attend only once). Two application periods a year: mid-January-May; mid-June-early December. "Writers must provide

their writing equipment. Very good writing space and relaxing space in each cottage; sleeping loft, down comforters. Lunch delivered, small kitchen facility—dinner in the farmhouse." Accommodates 6 writers.
Costs: No charge for food or housing. Meals are nutritious, diet conscious. There is a travel scholarship fund.
To Apply: Deadlines are October 1 and April 1. Application form—5 copies needed for committee review. Approximately 25 writers are invited each of 2 sessions a year. Limited facility for a differently-abled person. Application available for SASE.

ISLE ROYALE ARTIST-IN-RESIDENCE PROGRAM, 800 E. Lakeshore Dr., Houghton MI 49931-1895. (906)482-0986. Fax: (906)482-8753. Coordinator: Greg Blust. Estab. 1991. For writers, journalists, visual artists, musicians, composers, dancers and other performing artists. "Isle Royale is an island wilderness in Lake Superior and is 45 miles long and 8.5 miles wide. It is a roadless area with transportation either by boat or by foot. There are wave-washed shores, boreal forests of spruce and fir, miles of ridge and valley topography, fascinating mammals and colorful birds." Available for 2-3 weeks from early June to mid-September. A rustic cabin with pit toilet, no electricity or running water and a canoe for transportation. Basic cooking equipment, bedding and fuel are provided. Accommodates 1 artist.
Costs: None. However, artists are asked to contribute a piece of work representative of their stay at Isle Royale National Park and to share their experience with the public by demonstrations, talks or other means.
To Apply: Send for application. Deadline February 15. Brochure/guidelines available for SASE.

KALANI HONUA, RR2, Box 4500, Pahoa HI 96778. (808)965-7828. Director: Richard Koob. Estab. 1980. Open to all education interests. "Kalani Honua, the 'harmony of heaven and earth,' provides an environment where the spirit of Aloha flourishes. Located on 20 secluded acres bordered by lush jungle and rugged coastline forged by ancient lava flows, Kalani Honua offers an authentic experience of rural Hawaii. The surrounding area, including sacred sites and state and national parks, is rich with the island's history and magic." Available year-round, although greatest availability is May and June and September, October, November, December. Provisions for the writer include "comfortable, private room/workspace. 3 meals offered/day, beautiful coastal surroundings and recreation facilities (pool, sauna, jacuzzi, tennis, volleyball, biking) near beaches and Volcanoes National Park. (Qualifying writers receive stipend to help with costs.)" Accommodates usually 1-5 as artists-in-residence.
Costs: $85/night depending on choice of lodging (varying from private room with shared bath to private cottage with private bath). Meals are approximately $24/day or may be self-provided in lodge kitchen. Scholarships available. Professional career documentation and assurance the residency will be successfully completed.
To Apply: Application fee $10. Brochure/guidelines available for SASE. College credit may be arranged through University of Hawaii.

‡❀**LEIGHTON STUDIOS, THE BANFF CENTRE**, (formerly Leighton Artist Colony), Box 1020 Station 22, Banff, Alberta T0L 0C0 Canada. (403)762-6180. Assistant Registrar: Theresa Boychuck. Estab. 1984. "The Leighton Studios provide a year-round working retreat for professional artists. Set in a mountainside pine grove slightly apart from the Centre's main buildings and above the town of Banff, Alberta, the eight studios are part of the Banff Centre for the Arts within The Banff Centre for Continuing Education. Available for one week to three month residencies. Apply at anytime. Adjudications are three times a year. Space is limited and artists are encouraged to apply at least six months in advance of start date. Provisions include private room, studio and flexible meal. Accommodates 3 professional artists at one time.
Costs: Approximately $86/day (Canadian). Financial assistance provided in the form of a studio fee discount which varies according to need and will be indicated at the time of acceptance.
To Apply: Send completed application form, resume, press releases, reviews and a selection of published work or manuscripts in progress to The Banff Centre. Brochures or guidelines available for free.

THE MACDOWELL COLONY, 100 High St., Peterborough NH 03458. (603)924-3886 or (212)535-9690. Admissions Coordinator: Pat Dodge. Estab. 1907. Open to writers, composers, visual artists, film/video artists, interdisciplinary artists and architects. Includes main building, library, 3 residence halls and 32 individual studios on over 450 mostly wooded acres, one mile from center of small town in southern New Hampshire. Available up to 8 weeks year-round. Provisions for the writer include meals, private sleeping room, individual secluded studio. Accommodates variable number of writers, 10 to 20 at a time.
Costs: Artists are asked to contribute toward the cost of their residency according to their financial resources.
To Apply: Application forms available. Application deadline: January 15 for summer, April 15 for fall/winter, September 15 for winter/spring. Writing sample required. For novel, send a chapter or section. For short stories, send 2-3. Send 6 copies. Brochure/guidelines available; SASE appreciated.

MILLAY COLONY FOR THE ARTS, P.O. Box 3, Austerlitz NY 12017-0003. (518)392-3103. Executive Director: Ann-Ellen Lesser. Assistant Director: Gail Giles. Estab. 1973. Open to professional writers, composers, visual artists. Includes "600-acres—mostly wooded, fields, old farm. Two buildings house artists—

separate studios (14×20) and bedrooms." Available year round. Accommodates 5 people at a time for one month residencies.

Costs: No fees.

To Apply: Requires sample of work and 1 professional reference. Application deadlines: February 1 for June-September; May 1 for October-January; September 1 for February-May. Brochure/guidelines available for SASE.

MY RETREAT, P.O. Box 1077, Lincoln Rd., South Fallsburg NY 12779. (914)436-7455. Owner: Cora Schwartz. Estab. 1993. For writers, poets, "artists of life." "Retreat is situated in the foothills of the Catskill Mountains, 90 miles from Albany or New York City. The colony consists of one main house and two summer cottages." A "room of one's own" offered year-round. Provisions for the writer include private room, breakfast foods, kitchen facilities for own cooking. Accommodates 12 writers.

Costs: $45/night per person; $65/night per couple. Reduced rates for longer stays.

To Apply: Brochure/guidelines available for SASE.

N.A.L.L. ASSOCIATION, 232, Blvd. de Lattre, 06140 Vence France. (33)93 58 13 26. Fax: (33)93 58 09 00. Contact: N.A.L.L. founder. Estab. 1993. "The N.A.L.L. is open to artists of all vocations—painters, sculptors, writers, playwrights, musicians—regardless of race, religion or age. There are 9 houses available on 8 acres of grounds between Saint Paul and Vence." Available in "minimal seasonal three-month terms. Yearly sabbatical programs are also available." Provisions for the artist include housing only; meals not included. Accommodates 10 writers at a time.

Costs: Range from 1,500-6,000 FF/month, depending on type of accommodation and season.

To Apply: "The artist is to send a curriculum vitae of accomplishments and future projects."

NEW YORK MILLS ARTS RETREAT, P.O. Box 246, New York Mills MN 56567. (218)385-3339. Founder: John Davis. Estab. 1989. For any visual, performing, or literary artists; especially looking for playwrights. "The retreat is a small, old farm in a rural, agricultural area of north central Minnesota. The barn loft forms the studio space. The farm house provides shared living space." Residencies available year-round lasting from 1-8 weeks, with 1 month or less as the typical case. Provisions for the writer include living space, writing space; "artist provides his own meals and transportation."

Costs: Offers stipends ($250-1,500) to each artist. "Fellowships are often available by special request, based on artistic excellence, quality of application materials, and the value or uniqueness the proposed community impact or involvement." Send SASE for application packet. Brochure/guidelines available for SASE.

NORTHWOOD UNIVERSITY ALDEN B. DOW CREATIVITY CENTER, 3225 Cook Rd., Midland MI 48640-2398. (517)837-4478. Executive Director: Carol B. Coppage. Estab. 1979. "The Fellowship Program welcomes project ideas from all disciplines: the arts, humanities and sciences. Individuals must be able to work independently. Project ideas are evaluated on the basis of uniqueness, creativity and innovation. Northwood University is a business college located in the central part of the lower peninsula. Fellows are in residence on the campus for 8 weeks. The campus is surrounded by lovely woods and is close to lakes." Available 8 weeks during the summer— early June- early August. Provisions for the writer include large furnished apartments for living quarters and work space. Lunches are provided during the weekday at the Creativity Center. Accommodates 4 Fellows/year.

Costs: Application fee: $10. The Creativity Center provides room and board, plus a stipend of $750 to be applied to project costs and/or personal needs. No accommodations for family or pets.

To Apply: Send for a brochure/application to be submitted and postmarked no later than December 31 of the year preceding the summer's program. Brochure/guidelines available for SASE.

OREGON WRITERS COLONY, P.O. Box 15200, Portland OR 97215. (503)771-0428. Contact: Marlene Howard, property manager. Estab. 1986. The Oregon Writers Colony is open to members only ($25 annual dues). The colony is located in a large log house containing 4 bedrooms and 2 baths. Available from September through May only. Accommodates a maximum of 3 writers.

Costs: $350/week; during second week of month, $100/week.

To Apply: Brochure/guidelines available for SASE.

PENDLE HILL, Box G, 338 Plush Mill Rd., Wallingford PA 19086-6099. (800)742-3150. Information Services Associate: Mary Gabel. Estab. 1930. "Grounded in the social and spiritual values of the Religious Society of Friends (Quakers), Pendle Hill welcomes people of all faiths who seek a time of spiritual renewal through reading, writing, study, solitude, or time in community. It is an adult inter-faith center for study and contemplation, set on 23 acres of beautiful trees and gardens 12 miles southwest of Philadelphia. Its 16 buildings include a conference center, crafts studio, library, bookstore, meeting room, dining room, classrooms and dormitories." The Resident Study Program offers three 10-week terms between October and June. "People may also come to 'sojourn' or come for a short stay for a self-directed retreat. Sojourning is an ideal way to come and have time for writing." The Extension Program offers weekend conferences on topics of interest to writers. The conference center is also available for groups wishing to rent it for their own

program. Provisions for the writer include private room, meals, a library, crafts studio, and bookstore. Accommodates 30 in Resident Study program; 12 sojourners; 30 conferees. The cost of sojourning is $55.75 per day; $51.50 per day after one week. Conferences range from $165 for a weekend to $340 for one week in the summer. The cost of the Resident Study Program is $3,780 per term; $11,030 for three. All rates include room and board. Please call for rental rates. Scholarships and financial aid available for Resident Study Program.
To Apply: Call 1-800-742-3150, or write for more information. Applications for Resident Study Program are accepted throughout the year. Those interested in sojourning or conferences may call the registrar at the toll-free number to make arrangements.

PUDDING HOUSE WRITERS RESOURCE CENTER, 60 N. Main St., Johnstown OH 43031. (614)967-6060. Director/Owner: Jennifer Bosveld. Estab. 1987. For writers. Located in "historical old downtown of small Ohio village only 30 minutes from Columbus." Available 1 night to 1 month year-round. Provisions for writers include private room and workspace; kitchen priviledges negotiable; copier, fax, library and computer.
Costs: $65/night includes full breakfast (1-5 nights); 10% discount for working writers; longer stay negotiable. Scholarship availability is individually based. Some work programs available for all services.
To Apply: Phone to discuss or to make reservations. Brochure/guidelines available for inquiry and SASE; however Pudding House recommends a phone call instead.

RAGDALE FOUNDATION, 1260 N. Green Bay Rd., Lake Forest IL 60045. (708)234-1063. Estab. 1976. For qualified writers, artists and composers. Ragdale, located 30 miles north of Chicago near Lake Michigan, is "the grounds of acclaimed Chicago architect Howard Van Doren Shaw's historic family home." Accommodations include the Ragdale House, the Barnhouse and the new Friends Studio. Available in 2 week to 2 month sessions year-round, except for 2 weeks in early summer and 2 weeks in December. Provisions for the writer include room, linens laundered by Ragdale and meals. "Breakfast and lunch supplies are stocked in communal kitchens, enabling residents to work throughout the day uninterrupted by scheduled meals. The evening meal is the only exception: wholesome, well-prepared dinners are served six nights a week. The Ragdale House and Barnhouse both contain informal libraries, and the property overlooks a large nature preserve." Accommodates 12.
Costs: $12/day. Fee waivers based on financial need are available. "Fee waiver application and decision process is separate from artistic admission process."
To Apply: "Residents are chosen by a selection committee composed of professionals in their artistic discipline." Application fee: $20. Deadlines: January 15 for June-December 15; June 1 for January-May 31. Brochure/guidelines available for SASE or call.

‡✿SASKATCHEWAN WRITERS'/ARTISTS' COLONIES, Box 3986, Regina, Saskatchewan S4P 3R9 Canada. (306)757-6310. Program Director: Paul Wilson. Estab. 1979. For all writers and artists, "although priority is given to Saskatchewan residents." St. Peter's College is "a Benedictine Abbey in the serene location just outside the village of Muenster. Emma Lake is located in a forest region approximately 25 miles north of Prince Albert." A 6-week summer colony and year-round individual retreats are held at St. Peter's. A 2-week colony is held in August at Emma Lake. St. Peter's provides private rooms and "home-grown meals" served in the college facility. Residents at Emma Lake "are housed in separate cabins or in single rooms in a one-story unit. The dining room and lounge are located in a central building." The 6-week summer colony at St. Peter's accommodates 8 people a week, "but applicants may request as much time as they need." The individual retreats accommodate no more than 3 at one time.
Costs: $100 (Canadian)/week, includes meals and accommodation.
To Apply: Applications should be typewritten and include a check for length of stay as well as 10 ms pages or slides of artwork, a brief resume, a project description and 2 references. Deadline for 6-week summer colony April 15. Deadline for individual retreats 1 month before preferred date of attendance. Brochure/guidelines available for SASE.

UCROSS FOUNDATION, 2836 U.S. Hwy. 14-16 East, Clearmont WY 82835. (307)737-2291. Executive Director: Elizabeth Guheen. Estab. 1982. For "artists of *all* disciplines. We are in rural Wyoming, in a town with a very small population. The facilities are part of a renovated ranch. Residencies are available for two weeks to two months. Each artist is provided a private studio, private bedroom, common living area and meals. We have the potential of accommodating four writers and four visual artists at one time."
Costs: Room, board and studio space provided without charge.
To Apply: Residents are selected through biannual competition, judged by a 3-member committee. Deadlines: March 1 for August-December; October 1 for February-June. Brochure/guidelines available for SASE.

‡VERMONT STUDIO CENTER, P.O. Box 613NW, Johnson VT 05656. (802)635-2727. Fax: (802)635-2730. Estab. 1984. "The Vermont Studio Center now offers six 2-week Writing Studio Sessions in fiction, nonfiction and poetry during February, March and April. These are limited to 12 writers and feature individual conferences and readings by prominent visiting and staff writers. We invite serious writers to participate in

workshops, readings and private conferences focusing on the craft of writing. Independent Writers' Retreats are also available year-round for 2-12 weeks for those wishing more solitude. Room/private studio and excellent meals are included in all our programs. Generous work-exchange Fellowships are available."
Costs: All-inclusive fees are $1,200 per 2-week Writing Studio Session and $1,400 per 4-week Writing Residency ($750 for 2 weeks). Financial assistance up to 50% is available for Writing Studio Sessions. Write for application.

VILLA MONTALVO ARTIST RESIDENCY PROGRAM, P.O. Box 158, Saratoga CA 95071. Artist Residency Program Director: Lori A. Wood. Estab. 1942. For "writers, visual artists, musicians and composers. Villa Montalvo is a 1912 Mediterranean-style villa on 176 acres. There are extensive formal gardens and miles of redwood trails. Residencies are from 1-3 months, year-round. Each writer is given a private apartment with kitchen. Apartments for writers have either 2 rooms or a unique balcony or veranda. All apartments are fully-stocked (dishes, linens, etc.), except for food. Artists provide their own food." Accommodates 3 writers (5 artists in total).
Costs: "There are no costs for residency. We require a $100 security deposit, which is returned at end of residency. There are four fellowships available each year. These are awarded on the basis of merit to the four most highly-rated applicants. One of these must be a writer, and one a woman artist or writer."
To Apply: Application form, résumé, statement of proposed project, 3 professional recommendations, $20 application fee. Brochure/guidelines available for SASE.

‡WALKER WOODS, 1397 LaVista Rd. Northeast, Atlanta GA 30324. (404)634-3309. Founder: Dalian Moore. Walker Woods "offers four to eight month residencies to writers completing their first book (novels, short stories, poetry, etc.), and to foreign authors writing or translating a first book in the English language. Writers yet to publish a full-length book in the English language are eligible for residency." Situated on 1½ acres of prime real estate in North Atlanta. Property features a waterfall into a pond stocked with fish, a stone-lined stream, hot tub, inspiration garden and a three-story treehouse currently in design. Eight writers may live here at any given time. Writers may share a room or have one of their own, and all meals are taken commonly with residents cooking for each other. Three private suites (two with bathrooms), shared, and convertible rooms. Kitchen and library are shared. There is a NEC MultiSync 3V computer system with a laser printer and fax machine, but writers are encouraged to bring lap-tops and journals for portability and privacy.
Costs: Writers pay what they can ($300-600) per month depending upon accommodation and needs. Residents selected for support live at Walker Woods free, but pay for food, phone calls and office time. Everyone in residence takes up small projects on the property. Full or partial scholarship residencies are available on a competitive basis, and writers must submit two chapters of a novel or nonfiction book or 20 poems for a collection in progress. Deadlines vary, and are usually two or three months in advance of desired residency. A once in a lifetime fee of $20 is required, and writers may reapply at any time throughout their lives.
To Apply: Call or write for information or send SASE with 96¢ postage for application.

THE WOODSTOCK GUILD'S BYRDCLIFFE ARTIST RESIDENCY PROGRAM, 34 Tinker St., Woodstock NY 12498. (914)679-2079. Interim Executive Director: Kathryn McCullough. Estab. 1902. For writers, playwrights and visual artists. "The historic 600-acre Byrdcliffe Arts Colony is in Woodstock, one and a half miles from the village center. The residency program takes place in the Villetta Inn and Annex and includes a large community living room and common kitchen. Available for four one-month periods starting in June. Provisions for writer include a private room and studio space. Meals are not provided; residents share a large fully-equipped communal kitchen." Accommodates 10 writers.
Costs: $400-500 per month. Fee reductions available for writers staying for more than 1 period. Financial aid is available. "Potential residents are asked to include a list of savings and holdings, a list of income from the last two years (photocopied tax forms), and a projection of income and expenses for the current year."
To Apply: Submit application with $5 handling fee. Literary artists must submit no more than 12 pages of poetry, 1 chapter or story-length prose piece, professional résumé, reviews of articles (if available) and 2 references. Residents are selected by a committee of professionals in the arts. Brochure and application available for SASE.

HELENE WURLITZER FOUNDATION OF NEW MEXICO, Box 545, Taos NM 87571. (505)758-2413. President: Henry A. Sauerwein, Jr. Estab. 1953. "No restrictions. 12 separate houses, studios." Available April 1-September 30 annually. Provisions for the writer include single house/studio dwelling. "Presently booked into 1998, for all media."
Costs: No charge. (Must supply own food.) Rent-free and utility-free housing.
To Apply: Write to the Foundation.

YADDO, Box 395, Saratoga Springs NY 12866-0395. Contact: Admissions Committee. Estab. 1926. "Those qualified for invitations to Yaddo are highly qualified writers, visual artists, composers, choreographers, performance artists and film and video artists who are working at the professional level in their fields. Artists who wish to work collaboratively are encouraged to apply. An abiding principle at Yaddo is that applications for residencies are judged on the quality of the artists' work and professional promise." Provisions include room, board and studio space. No stipends are offered. Site includes four small lakes, a rose garden, woodland. Two seasons: large season is mid-May-Labor Day; small season is October-May (stays from 2 weeks to 2 months; average stay is 5 weeks). Accommodates approximately 16 writers in large season.

Costs: Voluntary payment of $20/day encouraged. "No artist who is deemed qualified for a residency will be denied admission because of inability to contribute."

To Apply: Filing fee is $20 (checks to Corporation of Yaddo). Applications are considerd by the Admissions Committee and invitations are issued by April (deadline: January 15) and September (deadline: August 1).

Retreats and colonies/'95-'96 changes

The following retreats and colonies appeared in the 1995 edition of *Novel & Short Story Writer's Market* but do not appear in the 1996 edition. Those that did not respond to our request for an update appear below without further explanation. If a reason for the omission is available, it is included next to the listing name. There are several reasons why a retreat or colony may not appear—it may not have room for fiction writers this year or it may no longer be open.

Act I Creativity Center
The Clearing
Hawthornden Castle
Hilai Residencies

Organizations and Resources

When you write, you write alone. It's just you and the typewriter or computer screen. Yet the writing life does not need to be a lonely one. Joining a writing group or organization can be an important step in your writing career. By meeting other writers, discussing your common problems and sharing ideas, you can enrich your writing and increase your understanding of this sometimes difficult, but rewarding life.

The variety of writers' organizations seems endless—encompassing every type of writing and writer—from small, informal groups that gather regularly at a local coffee house for critique sessions to regional groups that hold annual conferences to share technique and marketing tips. National organizations and unions fight for writers' rights and higher wages for freelancers, and international groups monitor the treatment of writers around the world.

We're pleased this year to include listings for several large writers' organizations. In this section you will find state-, province- and regional-based groups such as the Arizona Authors Association and the Writers Federation of Nova Scotia. You'll also find national organizations including the National Writers Association and the Canadian Authors Association. The Mystery Writers of America, Western Writers of America and the Small Press Genre Association (formerly the Small Press Writers and Artists Organization) are examples of groups devoted to a particular type of writing. Whatever your needs or goals, you're likely to find a group listed here to interest you.

A few organizations helpful to writers are not clubs or groups and they do not fit neatly into any one category. We've included a few of these here, too, as "resources" that are gathering places or helpful services available to writers. The Writer's Center in Bethesda, Maryland, and the Just Buffalo Literary Center are two examples of those resources featured here.

Selecting a writers' organization

To help you make an informed decision, we've provided information on the scope, membership and goals of the organizations listed on these pages. We asked groups to outline the types of memberships available and the benefits members can expect. Most groups will provide additional information for a self-addressed, stamped envelope and you may be able to get a sample copy of their newsletter for a modest fee.

Keep in mind joining a writers' organization is a two-way street. When you join an organization, you become a part of it and, in addition to membership fees, most groups need and want your help. If you want to get involved, opportunities can include everything from chairing a committee to writing for the newsletter to helping set up an annual conference. The level of your involvement is up to you and almost all organizations welcome contributions of time and effort.

Selecting a group to join depends on a number of factors. As a first step, you must determine what you want from membership in a writers' organization. Then send away for more information on the groups that seem to fit your needs. Start, however, by asking yourself:

- Would I like to meet writers in my city? Am I more interested in making contacts with other writers across the country or around the world?
- Am I interested in a group that will critique and give me feedback on work-in-progress?

- Do I want marketing information and tips on dealing with editors?
- Would I like to meet other writers who write the same type of work I do or am I interested in meeting writers from a variety of fields?
- How much time can I devote to meetings and are regular meetings important to me? How much can I afford to pay in dues?
- Would I like to get involved in running the group, working on the group's newsletters, planning a conference?
- Am I interested in a group devoted to writers' rights and treatment or would I rather concentrate on the business of writing?

For more information

Because they do not usually have the resources or inclination to promote themselves widely, finding a local writers' group is usually a word-of-mouth process. If you think you'd like to join a local writer's group and do not know of any in your area, check notices at your library or contact a local college English department. You might also try contacting a group based in your state, province or region listed here for information on smaller groups in your area.

If you have a computer and would like to meet with writers in other areas of the country, you will find many commercial online services, such as GEnie and America Online, have writers' sections and "clubs" online. Many free online services available through Internet also have writers' "boards."

For more information on writers' organizations, check *The Writer's Essential Desk Reference: A Companion to Writer's Market*, 2nd edition (Writer's Digest Books, 1507 Dana Ave., Cincinnati OH 45207). Other directories listing organizations for writers include the *Literary Market Place* or *International Literary Market Place* (R.R. Bowker, 245 W. 17th St., New York NY 10011). The National Writers Association also maintains a list of writers' organizations.

ARIZONA AUTHORS ASSOCIATION, 3509 E. Shea Blvd., Suite 117, Phoenix AZ 85028. (602)867-9001. President: Iva Martin. Estab. 1978. Number of Members: 500. Type of Memberships: Professional, writers with published work; associate, writers working toward publication; affiliate, professionals in the publishing industry. "Primarily an Arizona organization but open to writers nationally." Benefits include bimonthly newsletter, discount rates on seminars, workshops and newsletter ads, discounts on writing books, discounts at bookstores, copy shops, critique groups and networking events. "Sponsors workshops on a variety of topics of interest to writers (e.g. publishing, marketing, structure, genres)." Publishes *Authors Newsletter*, bimonthly ($25/yr.). Dues: Professional and associate, $40/year; affiliate: $45/year; student: $25/year. Holds monthly critique group, quarterly networking events and annual literary contest. Send SASE for information.

ASSOCIATED WRITING PROGRAMS, Tallwood House, Mail Stop 1E3, George Mason University, Fairfax VA 22030. (703)993-4301. Publications Editor: D.W. Fenza. Estab. 1967. Number of Members: 4,300 (individual members). Types of Membership: Institutional (universities); graduate students; *Chronicle* subscribers. Open to any person interested in writing; most members are students or faculty of university writing programs (worldwide). Benefits include information on creative writing programs; grants and awards to writers; a job placement service for writers in academe and beyond. AWP holds an Annual Conference in a different US city every spring; also conducts an annual Award Series in poetry, short story collections, novel and creative nonfiction, in which winner receives $2,000 honorarium and publication by a participating press. AWP acts as agent for finalists in Award Series and tries to place their manuscript with publishers throughout the year. Manuscripts accepted January 1-February 28 only. SASE for guidelines. Publishes *AWP Chronicle* 6 times/year; 3 times/academic semester. Available to members for free. Nonmembers may order a subscription for $18/yr. Also publishes the *AWP Official Guide to Writing Programs* which lists about 330 creative writing programs in universities across the country and in Canada. *Guide* is updated every 2 years; cost is $18.95 plus $5 for first-class mail. Dues: $45 for individual membership and an additional $37 for our placement service. AWP keeps dossiers on file and sends them to school or organization of person's request. Holds two meetings per year for the Board of Directors. Send SASE for information.

AUSTIN WRITERS' LEAGUE RESOURCE CENTER, Austin Writers' League, 1501 W. Fifth, E-2, Austin TX 78703. (512)499-8914. Fax: (512)499-0441. Executive Director: Angela Smith. Estab. 1981. Number of

Members: 1,600. Types of Memberships: Regular, student/senior citizen, family. Monthly meetings and use of resource center/library is open to the public. "Membership includes both aspiring and professional writers, all ages and all ethnic groups." Job bank is also open to the public. Public also has access to technical assistance. Partial and full scholarships offered for some programs. Of 1,600 members, 800 reside in Austin. Remaining 800 live all over the US and in other countries. Benefits include monthly newsletter, monthly meetings, study groups, resource center/library-checkout privileges, discounts on workshops, seminars, classes, job bank, discounts on books and tapes, participation in awards programs, technical/marketing assistance, copyright forms and information, access to computers and printers. Center has 5 rooms plus 2 offices and storage area. Public space includes reception and job bank area; conference/classroom; library/computer room; and copy/mail room. Library includes 1,000 titles. Two computers and printers are available for member use. Sponsors fall and spring workshops, weekend seminars, informal classes, sponsorships for special events such as readings, production of original plays, media conferences, creative writing programs for children and youth; Violet Crown Book Awards, newsletter writing awards, Young Texas Writers awards, contests for various anthologies. Publishes *Austin Writer* (monthly newsletter), sponsors with Texas Commission on the Arts Texas Literary Touring Program. Membership/subscription: $40, $35-students, senior citizens, $60 family membership. Monthly meetings. Study groups set their own regular meeting schedules. Send SASE for information.

THE AUTHORS GUILD, 330 W. 42nd St., 29th Floor, New York NY 10036. (212)563-5904. Executive Director: Robin Davis Miller. Purpose of organization: membership organization of 6,700 members offers services and information materials intended to help authors with the business and legal aspects of their work, including contract problems, copyright matters, freedom of expression and taxation. Qualifications for membership: book author published by an established American publisher within 7 years or any author who has had 3 works, fiction or nonfiction, published by a magazine or magazines of general circulation in the last 18 months. Associate membership also available. Annual dues: $90. Different levels of membership include: associate membership with all rights except voting available to an author who has a firm contract offer from an American publisher. Workshops/conferences: "The Guild and Authors League of America conduct several symposia each year at which experts provide information, offer advice, and answer questions on subjects of interest and concern to authors. Typical subjects have been the rights of privacy and publicity, libel, wills and estates, taxation, copyright, editors and editing, the art of interviewing, standards of criticism and book reviewing. Transcripts of these symposia are published and circulated to members." Symposia open to members only. "The *Author's Guild Bulletin*, a quarterly journal, contains articles on matters of interest to writers, reports of Guild activities, contract surveys, advice on problem clauses in contracts, transcripts of Guild and League symposia, and information on a variety of professional topics. Subscription included in the cost of the annual dues."

THE BRITISH FANTASY SOCIETY, 2 Harwood St., Stockport SK4 1JJ U.K. Secretary: Robert Parkinson. Estab. 1971. Open to: "Anyone interested in fantasy. The British Fantasy Society was formed to provide coverage of the fantasy, science fiction and horror fields. To achieve this, the Society publishes its *Newsletter*, packed with information and reviews of new books and films, plus a number of other booklets of fiction and articles: *Winter Chills*, *Mystique*, *Masters of Fantasy* and *Dark Horizons*. The BFS also organises an annual Fantasy Conference at which the British Fantasy Awards are presented for categories such as Best Novel, Best Short Story and Best Film." Dues and subscription is £15 (UK); $32 (US); £18 (Europe), £23 (elsewhere). Payment in sterling or US dollars only. Send SASE or IRC for information.

❧**BURNABY WRITERS' SOCIETY**, 6584 Deer Lake Ave., Burnaby, British Columbia V5G 2J3. (604)435-6500. Corresponding Secretary: Eileen Kernaghan. Estab. 1967. Number of members: 300. "Membership is regional, but open to anyone interested in writing." Benefits include monthly market newsletter; workshops/ critiques; guest speakers; information on contests, events, reading venues, etc.; opportunity to participate in public reading series. Sponsors annual competition open to all British Columbia residents; monthly readings at Burnaby Art Gallery; Canada Council sponsored readings; workshops. Publishes *Burnaby Writers Newsletter* monthly (except July/August), available to anyone for $20/year subscription. Dues: $20/year (includes newsletter subscription). Meets second Thursday of each month. Send SASE for information.

CALIFORNIA WRITERS' CLUB, 1090 Cambridge St., Novato CA 94947-4963. Estab. 1909. Number of Members: 900. Type of Memberships: Associate and active. Open to: "All published writers and those deemed able to publish within five years." Benefits include: speakers—authors, editors, agents, anyone connected with writing—heard at monthly meetings; marketing information; workshops; camaraderie of fellow writers. Sponsors workshops, conferences, awards programs/contests. Publishes a monthly newsletter at state level, monthly newsletter at branch level. Available to members only. Dues: $35/year. Meets monthly. Send SASE for information.

❧**CANADIAN AUTHORS ASSOCIATION**, 27 Doxsee Ave. N., Campbellford, Ontario K0L 1L0 Canada. (705)653-0323. Fax: (705)653-0593. President: Cora Taylor. Estab. 1921. Number of Members: 800. Type of Memberships: Member (voting); associate (non-voting). "Member must have minimum sales to commercial publications. Associates need not have published yet." National scope (Canada) with 17 regional branches. Benefits include networking, marketing advice, legal advice, several publications, annual conference, awards programs. Sponsors workshops, conferences, awards programs/contests. Publishes *Canadian Author*, quarterly $15 (Canadian)/year; $20 (Canadian) for foreign and *National Newsline* (to members only). Dues: $123.05 (Canadian). "Each branch meets monthly." Send SASE for information.

‡✿CANADIAN SOCIETY OF CHILDREN'S AUTHORS, ILLUSTRATORS AND PERFORMERS (CANS-CAIP), 35 Spadina Rd., Toronto, Ontario M5R 2S9 Canada. (416)654-0903. Executive Secretary: Nancy Prasad. Estab. 1977. Number of Members: 1,100. Types of membership: Full professional member and friend (associate member). Open to professional active writers, illustrators and performers in the field of children's culture (full members); beginners and all other interested persons and institutions (friends). International scope, but emphasis on Canada. Benefits include quarterly newsletter, marketing opportunities, publicity via our membership directory and our "members available" list, jobs (school visits, readings, workshops, residencies, etc.) through our "members available" list, mutual support through monthly meetings. Sponsors annual workshop, "Packaging Your Imagination," held every October for beginners. Publishes *CANSCAIP News*, quarterly, available to all (free with membership, otherwise $20 Canadian). Dues: professional fees: $50 Canadian/year; friend fees: institutional $25/year; individual $20/year. "Professionals must have written, illustrated or performed work for children commercially, sufficient to satisfy the membership committee (more details on request)." CANSCAIP National has open meetings from September to June, monthly in Toronto. CANSCAIP West holds bimonthly meetings in Vancouver. Send SASE for information.

FAIRBANKS ARTS ASSOCIATION, P.O. Box 72786, Fairbanks AK 99707-2786. (907)456-6485. Program Director: Tawney Barnebey. Estab. 1966. Members: 400. "Membership is open to anyone interested in supporting Fairbanks's arts and cultural community." Scope: Regional (interior Alaska) although a number of members are scattered throughout Alaska and the lower 48 states. Benefits include reduced fees for technical and professional workshops; assistance in all of art (or technique, great writing, resumes, etc.); invitations to all association events (including gallery openings, political forums, workshops, etc.); group medical insurance (including studio insurance); discount on all items purchased through gallery store; subscription to *Fairbanks Arts*. Sponsors several art-related events. "We publish *Fairbanks Arts*, a bimonthly newsletter that is also sent to 100 subscribers and sold in local retail outlets throughout interior Alaska." Subscriptions are $15/year. Membership $25/year (includes newsletter, etc.). Board of Directors meets 1st Thursday every month, plus monthly visual, literary and community arts meetings. Send SASE for information.

✿FEDERATION OF BRITISH COLUMBIA WRITERS, MPO Box 2206, Vancouver, British Columbia V6B 3W2 Canada. Manager: Corey Van't Haaff. Estab. 1982. Number of Members: 650. Types of Membership: regular. "Open to established and emerging writers in any genre, province-wide." Benefits include newsletter, liaison with funding bodies, publications, workshops, readings, literary contests, various retail and educational discounts. Sponsors readings and workshops. Publishes a newsletter 4 times/year, included in membership. Dues: $50 regular; $25 for those with limited income. Send SASE for information.

GARDEN STATE HORROR WRITERS, Manalapan Library, P.O. Box 696, Matawan NJ 07747. (609)778-2159. President: Dina Leacock. Estab. 1991. Number of Members: 50. Membership levels: active and associate. Open to "anyone interested in pursuing a career in fiction writing." Scope is national. Benefits include "latest market news, use of library meeting rooms, free copies of guidelines for magazine and book publishers, free in-house critique service in person and by mail." Sponsors monthly guest speakers and/or workshops, annual short fiction contest. A future conference/convention is being planned. A free sample of monthly newsletter *The Graveline* is available for SASE. Subscription is included in the cost of any membership. Dues: $30 active; $20 associate/annually. Active members must be 16 years of age. Holds regular monthly meetings. Send SASE for information.

INTERNATIONAL ASSOCIATION OF CRIME WRITERS (NORTH AMERICAN BRANCH), JAF Box 1500, New York NY 10116. (212)757-3915. Executive Director: Mary A. Frisque. Estab. 1987. Number of Members: 225. Open to: "Published authors of crime fiction, nonfiction, screenplays and professionals in the mystery field (agents, editors, booksellers). Our branch covers the US and Canada, there are other branches world-wide." Benefits include information about crime-writing world-wide and publishing opportunities in other countries. "We sponsor annual members' receptions during the Edgar awards week in New York and in the spring and in the fall we host a reception at the Bouchercon. We also have occasional receptions for visiting authors/publishers. We give an annual award, the North American Hammett Prize, for the best work (fiction or nonfiction) of literary excellence in the crime writing field. We publish a quarterly newsletter, *Border Patrol*, available to members only." Dues: $50 year. Send SASE for information.

JUST BUFFALO LITERARY CENTER, INC., 493 Franklin St., Buffalo NY 14202-1109. (716)881-3211. Executive Director: Debora Ott. "Just Buffalo is a community-based literary center that recognizes the contemporary writer as a cultural bridge among peoples and supports the development, the study, and the appreciation of contemporary writing in its cultural and ethnic diversity, through performance, instruction and promotion. Just Buffalo seeks to amplify voices not always heard in the mainstream, and brings contemporary literature to people of all ages, ethnic, educational and economic backgrounds to help them appreciate the lives, experiences and communicative arts of others. Just Buffalo's programs include: readings, lectures, performances, residencies and workshops by prominent and emerging writers; a Writers-in-Education component in the Buffalo schools, whose purpose is to enrich the lives of children through language arts; Spoken Arts Radio, a biweekly literary arts broadcast, and interdisciplinary programs in music and poetry with writers, composers and musicians of African American and Latin American descent." Send SASE for information.

MYSTERY WRITERS OF AMERICA (MWA), 17 E. 47th St., 6th Floor, New York NY 10017. Executive Director: Priscilla Ridgway. Estab. 1945. Number of Members: 2,500. Type of memberships: Active (professional, published writers of fiction or nonfiction crime/mystery/suspense); associate (professionals in allied fields, i.e. editor, publisher, writer, critic, news reporter, publicist, librarian, bookseller, etc.); corresponding (writers qualified for active membership who live outside the US). Unpublished writers may petition for Affiliate member status. Benefits include promotion and protection of writers' rights and interests, including counsel and advice on contracts, MWA courses and workshops, a national office, an annual conference featuring the Edgar Allan Poe Awards, the *MWA Anthology*, a national newsletter, regional conferences, meetings and newsletters. Newsletter, *The Third Degree*, is published 10 times/year for members. Annual dues: $65 for US members; $32.50 for Corresponding members.

‡THE NATIONAL LEAGUE OF AMERICAN PEN WOMEN, INC., Headquarters: The Pen Arts Building, 1300 17th St., NW, Washington DC 20036. Phone/fax: (202)785-1997. Contact: National President. Estab. 1897. Number of Members: 5,000. Types of Membership: Three classifications: Art, Letters, Music. Open to: Professional women. "Professional to us means our membership is only open to women who sell their art, writings or music compositions. We have 200 branches in the continental US, Hawaii and the Republic of Panama. Some branches have as many as 100 members, some as few as 10 or 12. It is necessary to have 5 members to form a new branch." Benefits include marketing advice, use of a facility, critiques and competitions. Our facility is The Pen Arts Building. It is a 20-room Victorian mansion. It's most distinguished resident was President Abraham Lincoln's son, Robert Todd Lincoln, the former Secretary of War and Minister of Great Britain. It has a few rooms available for Pen Women visiting the D.C. area, and for Board members in session 3 times a year. Branch and State Association competitions, as well as biennial convention competitions. Offers a research library of books and histories of our organization only. Sponsors awards biennially to Pen Women in each classification: Art, Letters, Music, and $1,000 award biennially to non-Pen Women in each classification for women over 35 years of age who wish to pursue special work in her field. *The Pen Woman* is our membership magazine, published 6 times a year, free to members, $18 a year for nonmember subscribers. Dues: $30/year for national organization, from $5-10/year for branch membership and from $1-5 for state association dues. Branches hold regular meeting each month, September through May except in northern states which meet usually March through September (for travel convenience). Send SASE for information.

NATIONAL WRITERS ASSOCIATION, 1450 S. Havana, Suite 424, Aurora CO 80012. (303)751-7844. Executive Director: Sandy Whelchel. Estab. 1937. Number of Members: 4,000. Types of Memberships: Regular membership for those without published credits; professional membership for those with published credits. Open to: Any interested writer. National/International plus we have 16 chapters in various states. Benefits include critiques, marketing advice, editing, literary agency, complaint service, chapbook publishing service, research reports on various aspects of writing, 4 contests, National Writers Press—self-publishing operation, computer bulletin board service, regular newsletter with updates on marketing, bimonthly magazine on writing related subjects, discounts on supplies, magazines and some services. Sponsors periodic conferences and workshops: short story contest opens April, closes July 1; novel contest opens December, closes April 28. Publishes *Flash Market News* (monthly publication for professional members only); *Authorship Magazine* (bimonthly publication available by subscription $18 to nonmembers). Dues: $50 regular; $60 professional. For professional membership requirement is equivalent of 3 articles or stories in a national or regional magazine; a book published by a royalty publisher, a play, TV script, or movie produced. Send SASE for information. Chapters hold meetings on a monthly basis.

NEW HAMPSHIRE WRITERS AND PUBLISHERS PROJECT, P.O. Box 2693, Concord NH 03302-2693. (603)226-6649. Executive Director: Patricia Scholz-Cohen. Estab. 1988. Number of Members: 600. Type of Memberships: Senior/student; individual; business. Open to anyone interested in the literary arts—writers (fiction, nonfiction, journalists, poets, scriptwriters, etc.), teachers, librarians, publishers and *readers*. Statewide scope. Benefits include a bimonthly publication featuring articles about NH writers and publishers; leads for writers, new books listings; and NH literary news. Also—use of resource library and discounts on workshops, readings, conferences. Dues: $35 for individuals; $15 for seniors, students; $50 for businesses. Send SASE for information.

NORTH CAROLINA WRITERS' NETWORK, P.O. Box 954, Carrboro NC 27510. (919)967-9540. Fax: (919)929-0535. Executive Director: Marsha Warren. Estab. 1985. Number of Members: 1,600. Open to: All writers, all levels of skill and friends of literature. Membership is approximately 1,400 in North Carolina and 200 in 28 other states. Benefits include bimonthly newsletter, reduced rates for competition entry fees, fall conference, workshops, etc., use of critiquing service, use of library and resource center, press release and publicity service, information database(s). Sponsors annual Fall Conference, Creative Nonfiction Competition, statewide workshops, Writers & Readers Series, Randall Jarrell Poetry Prize, Poetry Chapbook Competition, Thomas Wolfe Fiction Prize, Fiction Competition, Paul Green Playwright Prize. Publishes *The Network News*, 28-pages, bimonthly, and North Carolina's Literary Resource Guide. Subscription included in dues. Dues: $35/year, $20/year (students to age 23, seniors 65+ and disabled). Events scheduled throughout the year. Send SASE for information.

PHILADELPHIA WRITERS ORGANIZATION, P.O. Box 42497, Philadelphia PA 19101. (215)649-8918. Administrative Coordinator: Jane Brooks: Estab. 1981. Number of Members: 250. Types of Memberships: Full (voting), associate, student. Open to any writer, published or unpublished. Scope is tri-state area—Pennsylvania, Delaware, New Jersey, but mostly Philadelphia area. Benefits include medical insurance (for full members only), monthly meetings with guest panelists, spring workshop (full day) plus Editors Marketplace. Publishes a monthly newsletter for members only. Dues: $50 (full and associate); $25 (student). Proof of publication required for full members (minimum of 2,000 words). Meets monthly throughout year except July and August. Send SASE for information.

PIG IRON LITERARY & ART WORKS, INC., Pig Iron Press, 26 North Phelps St., Youngstown OH 44503. (216)747-6932. Director: Jim Villani. Estab. 1980. Number of Members: 75. Open to: Writers, readers, artists, musicians and dancers living in northeast Ohio and western Pennsylvania. Benefits include use of Independent Press research library, museum and gallery, copy center, meeting spaces and discounts on publishing services. Sponsors workshops and conferences. Publishes *Out of the Pen*, a quarterly newsletter; subscriptions are $10/year. Dues: $25/year. Send SASE for information.

ROMANCE WRITERS OF AMERICA (RWA), 13700 Veterans Memorial, Suite 315, Houston TX 77014. (713)440-6885. Fax: (713)440-7510. Executive Manager: Allison Kelley. Estab. 1981. Number of members: over 7,500. Type of Memberships: General and associate. Open to: "Any person actively pursuing a writing career in the romance field." Membership is international. Benefits include annual conference, contests and awards, magazine, forums with publishing representatives, network for published authors, group insurance, regional newsletters and more. Dues: $70/new members; $60/renewal fee. Send SASE for information.

SCIENCE FICTION AND FANTASY WRITERS OF AMERICA, INC., 5 Winding Brook Drive #1B, Guilderland NY 12084. (518)869-5361. Executive Secretary: Peter Dennis Pautz. Estab. 1965. Number of Members: 1,200. Type of Memberships: Active, associate, affiliate, institutional, estate. Open to: "Professional writers, editors, anthologists, artists in the science fiction/fantasy genres and allied professional individuals and institutions. Our membership is international; we currently have members throughout Europe, Australia, Central and South America, Canada and some in Asia." We produce a variety of journals for our members, annual membership directory and provide a grievance committee, publicity committee, circulating book plan and access to medical/life/disability insurance. We award the SFWA Nebula Awards each year for outstanding achievement in the genre at novel, novella, novelet and short story lengths." Quarterly *SFWA Bulletin* to members; nonmembers may subscribe at $15/4 issues within US/Canada; $18.50 overseas. Bimonthly *SFWA Forum* for active and associate members only. Annual *SFWA Membership Directory* for members; available to professional organizations for $60. Active membership requires professional sale in the US of at least 3 short stories or 1 full-length book. Affiliate or associate membership requires at least 1 professional sale in the US or other professional sale in the US or other professional involvement in the field. Dues are pro-rated quarterly; info available upon request. Business meetings are held during Annual Nebula Awards weekend and usually during the annual World SF Convention. Send SASE for information.

SCIENCE FICTION WRITERS OF EARTH, P.O. Box 121293, Fort Worth TX 76121. (817)451-8674. Administrator: Gilbert Gordon Reis. Estab. 1980. Number of Members: 64-100. Open to: Unpublished writers of science fiction and fantasy short stories. "We have a few writers in Europe, Canada and Australia, but the majority are from the US. Writers compete in our annual contest. This allows the writer to find out where he/she stands in writing ability. Winners often receive requests for their story from publishers. Many winners have told us that they believe that placing in the top ten of our contest gives them recognition and has assisted in getting their first story published." Dues: One must submit a science fiction or fantasy short story to our annual contest to be a member. Cost is $5 for membership and first story. $2 for each additional ms. The nominating committee meets several times a year to select the top ten stories of the annual contest. Author Edward Bryant selects the winners from the top ten stories. Information about the organization is available for SASE.

SMALL PRESS GENRE ASSOCIATION (SPGA), P.O. Box 6301, Concord CA 94514. (510)254-7442. President: Joe Morey. Open to all members (anyone who paid dues for current year). "An international service organization whose purpose is the promotion of excellence in writing (all manner of writing including poetry), illustration (including comics), editing and publication of material related to the genres of science fiction, fantasy, horror, western, mystery and their related genres and sub-genres, in publications with limited distribution." Publishes *The Genre Press Digest*, 6 issues a year, with market news section, reviews, articles, poetry, art and a short story (as space allows). Sample copy $3.95. Free benefits to all members include critiquing services (art, poetry, fiction), grievance arbitration, editor-mentor program, info-swap/collaboration, newsletters on tape, membership in COSMEP. Will sponsor awards. Dues: $25 US and Canada, new and renewable; $30 International. Send SASE for information.

SOCIETY OF MIDLAND AUTHORS, P.O. Box 10419, Fort Dearborn Station, Chicago IL 60610. President: Stella Pevsner. Estab. 1915. Number of Members: 260. Type of memberships: Regular, published authors and performed playwrights; Associate, librarians, editors, etc., others involved in publishing. Open to: Residents or natives of 12 midland states: Illinois, Iowa, Indiana, Michigan, Wisconsin, Nebraska, S. Dakota, N. Dakota, Ohio, Kansas, Missouri and Minnesota. Benefits include newsletter, listing in directory. Sponsors annual awards in 7 categories, with upwards of $300 prizes. Awards dinner in May at 410 Club (Wrigley Bldg.), Chicago. Publishes newsletter several times/year. Dues: $25/year. Holds "5 program meetings/year, open to public at 410 Club, Chicago, featuring writers, editors, etc. on bookwriting subjects, theatrical subjects etc." Brochures are available for SASE.

SOCIETY OF SOUTHWESTERN AUTHORS, P.O. Box 30355, Tucson AZ 85751-0355. (520)296-5299. Fax:(520)296-0409. President/Chairman: Penny Porter. Estab. 1972. Number of Members: 170. Memberships: Professional, Associate and Honorary. Professional: published authors of books, articles, poetry, etc.; Associate: aspiring writers not yet published; Honorary: one whose contribution to the writing profession or to SSA warrants such regonition. Benefits include conference, short story writing contest, critiques, marketing advice. Sponsors annual conference in January and annual short story writing contest. Publishes *The Write Word* which appears 6 times/year. Dues: $20/year. Meets monthly. Send SASE for information.

WASHINGTON CHRISTIAN WRITERS FELLOWSHIP, P.O. Box 11337, Bainbridge Island WA 98110. (206)842-9103. Director: Elaine Wright Colvin. Estab. 1982. Number of Members: 300. Open to: All writers. Scope is state-wide. Benefits include meetings, speakers, how-to critiques, private consultation. Sponsors a monthly seminar; date, time and place varies. Ask to be put on the mailing list. Publishes a bimonthly newsletter, *W.I.N.* Dues: $25. Meets monthly in Seattle. Brochures are available for SASE.

WASHINGTON INDEPENDENT WRITERS, 733 15th St. NW, #220, Washington DC 20005. (202)347-4973. Executive Director: Isolde Chapin. Estab. 1975. Number of Members: 2,500. Type of Memberships: Full, associate, senior, student, dual. Open to any writer or person who has an interest in writing. Regional scope. Benefits include group health insurance, grievance committee, job bank, social events, workshops, small groups, networking, etc. Sponsors monthly workshops, spring conference. Publishes *The Independent Writer* newsletter, published 11 times/year. Newsletter subscription $45/year, must live outside metropolitan area. Dues: $95/year full and associate members; $55 senior and student members; $80 current renewing members. Holds monthly workshops and small group meetings. Send SASE for information.

WESTERN WRITERS OF AMERICA, Office of the Secretary Treasurer, 1012 Fair St., Franklin TN 37064. (615)791-1444. Secretary Treasurer: James A. Crutchfield. Estab. 1953. Number of Members: 528. Type of Membership: Active, associate, patron. Open to: Professional, published writers who have multiple publications of fiction or nonfiction (usually at least three) about the West. Associate membership open to those with one book, a lesser number of short stories or publications or participation in the field such as editors, agents, reviewers, librarians, television producers, directors (dealing with the West). Patron memberships open to corporations, organizations and individuals with an interest in the West. Scope is international. Benefits: "By way of publications and conventions, members are kept abreast of developments in the field of Western literature and the publishing field, marketing requirements, income tax problems, copyright law, research facilities and techniques, and new publications. At conventions members have the opportunity for one-on-one conferences with editors, publishers and agents." Sponsors an annual four-day conference during fourth week of June featuring panels, lectures and seminars on publishing, writing and research. Includes the Spur Awards to honor authors of the best Western literature of the previous year. Publishes *Roundup Magazine* (6 times/year) for members. Available to nonmembers for $30. Publishes membership directory. Dues: $60 for active membership, $60 for associate membership, $250 for patron. For information on Spur Awards, send SASE.

WILLAMETTE WRITERS, 9045 SW Barbur Blvd., Suite 5A, Portland OR 97219. Phone/fax: (503)452-1592. Office Manager: Linda McClain. Estab. 1965. Number of members: 700. "Willamette Writers is a nonprofit, tax exempt corporation staffed by volunteers. Membership is open to both published and aspiring writers. WW provides support, encouragement and interaction for all genres of writers." Open to national membership, but serves primarily the Pacific Northwest. Benefits include a writers' referral service, critique groups, membership discounts, youth programs (4th-12th grades), monthly meetings with guest authors, intern program, annual writing contest, community projects, library and research services, as well as networking with other writing groups, office with writing reference and screenplay library. Sponsors annual conference held the second weekend in August; quarterly workshops; annual Kay Snow Writing Contest; and the Distinguished Northwest Writer Award. Publishes *The Willamette Writer* monthly: a 12-page newsletter for members and complimentary subscriptions. Information consists of features, how-to's, mechanics of writing, profile of featured monthly speaker, markets, workshops, conferences and benefits available to writers. Dues: $36/year; includes subscription to newsletter. Meets first Tuesday of each month; board meeting held last Tuesday of each month. Send SASE for information.

THE WRITERS ALLIANCE, 12 Skylark Lane, Stony Brook NY 11790. Executive Director: Kiel Stuart. Estab. 1979. Number of Members: 125. Open to all writers: Professional, aspiring, those who have to write business memos or brochures; those interested in desktop publishing. National scope. Benefits: Members can run one classified or display ad in each issue of membership newsletter, *Keystrokes*; which also provides software and hardware reviews, how-to articles, market information and general support. Sponsors local writer's workshops. Publishes *Keystrokes*, quarterly, $15/year (payable to Kiel Stuart) covers both the cost of membership and newsletter. Local writer's critique group meets every two weeks. Send SASE for information.

THE WRITER'S CENTER, 4508 Walsh St., Bethesda MD 20815. (301)654-8664. Director: Jane Fox. Estab. 1977. Number of Members: 2,200. Open to: Anyone interested in writing. Scope is regional DC, Maryland, Virginia, West Virginia, Pennsylvania. Benefits include newsletter, discounts in bookstore, workshops, public events, subscriptions to *Poet Lore*, use of equipment and library, computer BBS (301)656-1638, annual small press book fair. Center offers workshops, reading series, research library, equipment, newsletter and limited workspace. Sponsors workshops, conferences, award for narrative poem. Publishes *Writer's Carousel*, bimonthly. Nonmembers can pick it up at the Center. Dues: $30/year. Fees vary with service, see publications. Brochures are available for SASE.

✤**WRITERS' FEDERATION OF NEW BRUNSWICK**, P.O. Box 37, Station A, Fredericton, New Brunswick E3B 4Y2 Canada. (902)423-8116. Project Coordinator: Anna Mae Snider. Estab. 1983. Number of Members: 230. Membership is open to anyone interested in writing. "This a provincial organization. Benefits include promotion of members' works through newsletter announcements and readings and launchings held at fall festival and annual general meeting. Services provided by WFNB include a Writers-in-Schools Program and manuscript reading. The WFNB sponsors a fall festival and an annual general meeting which feature workshops, readings and book launchings." There is also an annual literary competition, open to residents of New Brunswick only, which has prizes of $200, $100 and $30 in four categories: Fiction, nonfiction, children's literature and poetry; two $400 prizes for the best manuscript of poems (48 pgs.); and the best short novel or collection of short stories. Publishes a quarterly newsletter. Dues: $25/year. Board of Directors meets approximately 5 times a year. Annual General Meeting is held in the spring of each year. Send SASE for information.

✤**WRITERS GUILD OF ALBERTA**, Percy Page Centre, 11759 Groat Rd., 3rd Floor, Edmonton, Alberta T5M 3K6 Canada. (403)422-8174. Fax: (403)426-2663. Executive Director: Miki Andrejevic. Estab. 1980. Number of Members: 700. Membership open to current and past residents of Alberta. Regional (provincial) scope. Benefits include discounts on programs offered; manuscript evaluation service available; bimonthly newsletter; contacts; info on workshops, retreats, readings, etc. Sponsors workshops 2 times/year, retreats 3 times/year, annual conference, annual book awards program (Alberta writers only). Publishes *WestWord* 6 times/year; available for $55/year (Canadian) to nonmembers. Dues: $55/year for regular membership; $20/ year senior/students/limited income; $100/year donating membership—charitable receipt issued (Canadian funds). Organized monthly meetings. Send SASE for information.

WRITERS INFORMATION NETWORK, P.O. Box 11337, Bainbridge Island WA 98110. (206)842-9103. Director: Elaine Wright Colvin. Estab. 1980. Number of Members: 1,000. Open to: All interested in writing for religious publications/publishers. Scope is national and several foreign countries. Benefits include bimonthly newsletter, market news, advocacy/grievance procedures, professional advice, writers conferences, press cards, author referral, free consultation. Sponsors workshops, conferences throughout the country each year—mailing list and advertised in *W.I.N.* newsletter. Bimonthly newsletter: $25 US; $35 foreign/year. Dues: $25 US (newsletter subscription included). Holds monthly meetings in Seattle, WA. Brochures are available for SASE.

‡**WRITERS OF KERN**, P.O. Box 6694, Bakersfield CA 93386-6694. (805)871-5834. President: Debbie Bailey. Estab. 1993. Number of members: 100. Types of memberships: Professional, writers with published work; writers working toward publication, students. Open to published writers and any person interested in writing. Benefits of membership: Monthly meetings on the third Saturday of every month, except September which is our conference month, with speakers who are authors, agents, etc., on topics pertaining to writing; critique groups for several fiction genres, nonfiction and screenwriting which meet weekly or biweekly; several of our members are successfully published and full-time writers; members receive a monthly newsletter with marketing tips, conferences and contests; access to club library; discount to annual conference.

Annual conference held the third Saturday in September; annual writing contest held May-June with winners announced at the conference. Dues: $18/year, discount for students. Send SASE for information.

THE WRITERS ROOM, INC., 10 Astor Place, 6th Floor, New York NY 10003. (212)254-6995. Executive Director: Donna Brodie. Estab. 1978. Number of Members: 185. Open to: Any writer who shows a serious commitment to writing. "We serve a diverse population of writers, but most of our residents live in or around the NYC area. We encourage writers from around the country (and world!) to apply for residency if they plan to visit NYC for a while." Benefits include 24-hour access to the facility. "We provide desk space, storage areas for computers, typewriters, etc., a kitchen where coffee and tea are always available, bathrooms and a lounge. We also offer in-house workshops on topics of practical importance to writers and monthly readings of work-in-progress." Dues: $165 per quarter/year. Send SASE for application and background information.

‡**THE WRITERS' WORKSHOP**, P.O. Box 696, Asheville NC 28802. (704)254-8111. Executive Director: Karen Tager. Estab. 1984. Number of Members: 1,250. Types of Memberships: Student/low income $25; family/organization $55; individual $30. Open to all writers. Scope is national and international. Benefits include discounts on workshops, quarterly newsletter, admission to Annual Celebration every summer, critiquing services through the mail. Center offers reading room, assistance with editing your work, contacts with NY writers and agents. Publishes a newsletter. Available to nonmembers. Offers workshops year-round in NC and the South; 6 retreats a year, 25 readings with nationally awarded authors. Contests and classes for children and teens as well. Advisory board includes Kurt Vonnegut, E.L. Doctorow, Peter Matthiessen and Eudora Welty. Also sponsors international contests in fiction, poetry and creative nonfiction. Brochures are available for SASE.

Organizations and resources/'95-'96 changes

The following organizations and resources appeared in the 1995 edition of *Novel & Short Story Writer's Market* but do not appear in the 1996 edition. Those that did not respond to our request for an update appear below without further explanation. There are several reasons why an organization may not appear—its membership may be too full or the group may have disbanded.

Horror Writers Association (HWA)
National Writers Union

Ozarks Writers League
Science Fiction and Fantasy Workshop

Women Who Write, Inc.
Writers' Fed. of Nova Scotia
Writer's Helpline (discontinued)

Publications of Interest to Fiction Writers

This section features listings for magazines and newsletters that focus on writing or the publishing industry. While many of these are not markets for fiction, they do offer articles, marketing advice or other information valuable to the fiction writer. Several magazines in this section offer actual market listings while others feature reviews of books in the field and news on the industry.

The timeliness factor is a primary reason most writers read periodicals. Changes in publishing happen very quickly and magazines can help you keep up with the latest news. Some magazines listed here, including *Writer's Digest*, *The Writers' Nook News* and the *Canadian Writer's Journal* cover the entire field of writing, while others such as *Gothic Journal* and *Children's Book Insider* focus on a particular type of writing. We've also added publications which focus on a particular segment of the publishing industry, including *Locus* and *The Small Press Book Review*.

Information on some publications for writers can be found in the introductions to other sections in this book. In addition, many of the literary and commercial magazines for writers listed in the markets sections are helpful to the fiction writer. Keep an eye on the newsstand and the library shelves for others and let us know if you've found a publication particularly useful.

AWP CHRONICLE, Associated Writing Programs, George Mason University, Tallwood House, Mail Stop 1E3, Fairfax VA 22030. (703)993-4305. Editor: D.W. Fenza. 6 times/year. Essays on contemporary literature and articles on the teaching of creative writing only. Does *not* publish fiction. Lists fiction markets (back pages for "Submit"). Sample copies available; single copy price $3.95. Subscription: $20/year; $25/year Canada; $35/year overseas.

✿**CANADIAN CHILDREN'S LITERATURE/LITTÉRATURE CANADIENNE POUR LA JEUNESSE**, Department of English, University of Guelph, Guelph, Ontario N1G 2W1 Canada. (519)824-4120, ext. 3189. Editors: Mary Rubio and Daniel Chouinard. Associate Editor: Marie Davis. Administrator: Gay Christofides. Quarterly. "In-depth criticism of English and French Canadian literature for young people. Scholarly articles and reviews are supplemented by illustrations, photographs, and interviews with authors of children's books. The main themes and genres of children's literature are covered in special issues." Reviews novels and short story collections. Send review copies to the editors. Sample copies available; single copy price is $10 (Canadian). Subscriptions: $29 (Canadian), plus $10 for non-Canadian addresses.

✿**CANADIAN WRITER'S JOURNAL**, Box 6618, STN LCD 1, Victoria, British Columbia V8P 5N7 Canada. (604)477-8807. Editor: Gordon M. Smart. Quarterly. "Mainly short how-to and motivational articles related to all types of writing and of interest to both new and established writers. Sponsors annual short fiction contest." Lists markets for fiction. Sample copies available for $4 ($C for Canadian orders, $US for US orders). Subscription price: $15/year; $25/2 years ($C for Canadian orders, $US for US orders).

CHILDREN'S BOOK INSIDER, P.O. Box 1030, Fairplay CO 80440-1030. E-mail address: cbinsider@aol.com. Editor/Publisher: Laura Backes. Monthly. "Publication is devoted solely to children's book writers and illustrators. 'At Presstime' section gives current market information each month for fiction, nonfiction and illustration submissions to publishers. Other articles include writing and illustration tips for fiction and nonfiction, interviews with published authors and illustrators, features on alternative publishing methods (self-publishing, co-op publishing, etc.), how to submit work to publishers, industry trends. Also publishes books and writing tools for both beginning and experienced children's book writers." Sample copy and catalog for SASE (no charge). Single copy price: $3.25. Subscription price: $29.95/year (US); $35/year (Canadian).

CROW QUARTERLY REVIEW, 147 Vera Marie Lane, Box 170, Rollinsville CO 80474. (303)258-3851. E-mail address: kpmc@indra.com. Editor: Kevin McCarthy. Quarterly. "A review of *unpublished* and self-published work—sent to writers, editors, agents and producers. Helps writers market their work. Also serves to bridge the gap between the professions with writer's Crow Bar columns; writer's, editor's, agent's, producer's POV columns, Good Words column, profiles of various professionals and feature articles and classified ads. Send 9×12 SASE for more info." Critiques and reviews unpublished and self-published novels and short story collections. Sample copies available for 9×12 SASE. Also available on the World Wide Web: http://www.boms.com/crow/crow.html. "Writers should write for info before sending anything.'

FEMINIST BOOKSTORE NEWS, P.O. Box 882554, San Francisco CA 94188. (415)626-1556. Fax: (415)626-8970. Editor: Carol Seajay. Bimonthly. "*FBN* is a 124-page bimonthly magazine with reviews of more than 300 new feminist and lesbian titles and articles on the world of women and books. Regular columns include a 'Writing Wanted' section featuring calls for submission from various publishers." Reviews novels and short story collections. Send review copies to Beth Morgan. Sample copies available; single copy price is $6. Subscriptions: $70/year ($9 Canadian postage/$19 international postage). *Note: As with other listings in this section, this is not a "market;" do not send mss.*

FICTION WRITER'S GUIDELINE, P.O. Box 4065, Deerfield Beach, FL 33442. Editor: Blythe Camenson. Bimonthly. Our publication is "a 10-12 page newsletter with agent/editor/author interviews, how-to articles on writing fiction and getting it published, fiction markets, conference listings, Q&A column, success stories and more." Sample copies available for $3.50. Subscriptions: $39/year; free to members of the Fiction Writer's Connection. "Membership in FWC is $59/year includes a free newsletter, free critiquing, and a toll-free hotline for questions and free advice. Send SASE for information."

GOTHIC JOURNAL, 19210 Forest Rd. North, Forest Lake MN 55025-9766. (612)464-1119. Fax: (612)464-1331. Publisher: Kristi Lyn Glass. Bimonthly. "*Gothic Journal* is a news and review magazine for readers, writers and publishers of romantic suspense, romantic mysteries, and supernatural, gothic, and woman-in-jeopardy romance novels. It contains articles; reviews; letters; author, editor and agent profiles; market news; book lists and more." Lists fiction markets. Reviews novels and short story collections. Sample copies available for $3 plus $1 postage and handling. Subscriptions: $24/year (6 issues); $30/year (Canada); $36/year (foreign).

‡**HAVENS FOR CREATIVES**, ACT I Creativity Center, P.O. Box 30854, Palm Beach Gardens FL 33420. Editor: Char Plotsky. Annual directory of information on retreats and colonies for artists of all disciplines, including writers. Send SASE for information.

LAMBDA BOOK REPORT, 1625 Connecticut Ave. NW, Washington DC 20009-1013. (202)462-7924. Editor: Jim Marks. Bimonthly. "This review journal of contemporary gay and lesbian literature appeals to both readers and writers. Fiction queries published regularly." Lists fiction markets. Reviews novels and short story collections. Send review copies to Attn: Book Review Editor. Single copy price is $3.95/US. Subscriptions: $19.95/year (US); international rate: $31.95 (US $).

LOCUS, The Newspaper of the Science Fiction Field, P.O. Box 13305, Oakland CA 94661. Editor: Charles N. Brown. Monthly. "Professional newsletter of science fiction, fantasy and horror; has news, interviews of authors, book reviews, column on electronic publishing, forthcoming books listings, monthly books-received listings, etc." Lists markets for fiction. Reviews novels or short story collections. Sample copies available. Single copy price: $4.50. Subscription price: $43/year, (2nd class mail) for US, $48 (US)/year, (2nd class) for Canada; $48 (US)/year (2nd class) for overseas.

❖**THE MYSTERY REVIEW, A Quarterly Publication for Mystery & Suspense Readers**, P.O. Box 233, Colborne, Ontario K0K 1S0 Canada. (613)475-4440. Editor: Barbara Davey. Quarterly. "Book reviews, information on new releases, interviews with authors and other people involved in mystery, 'real life' mysteries, out-of-print mysteries, mystery/suspense films, word games and puzzles with a mystery theme." Reviews mystery/suspense novels and short story collections. Send review copies to editor. Single copy price is $5.95 CDN in Canada/$5.95 US in the United States. Subscriptions: $21.50 CDN (includes GST) in Canada; $20 US in the US and $28 US elsewhere.

NEW WRITER'S MAGAZINE, P.O. Box 5976, Sarasota FL 34277. E-mail address: newriters@aol.com. (941)953-7903. Editor: George J. Haborak. Bimonthly. "*New Writer's Magazine* is a publication for aspiring writers. It features 'how-to' articles, news and interviews with published and recently published authors. Will use fiction that has a tie-in with the world of the writer." Lists markets for fiction. Reviews novels and short story collections. Send review copies to Editor. Send #10 SASE for guidelines. Sample copies available; single copy price is $3. Subscriptions: $15/year, $25/two years. Canadian $20 (US funds). International $35/year (US funds).

THE NIGHTMARE EXPRESS, 11 W. Winona St., St. Paul MN 55107. Editor: Donald L. Miller. Bimonthly. *"The Nightmare Express* was established in 1986 as a vehicle for horror writers (both published/unpublished). Its purpose is to give market information, ideas, how-to information to help the author further advance their career." Recent articles included "One Way to Write Your Novel," "Cover Letters and Their Friends." Articles include "Dark Windows," NightTime Selections, etc." Lists markets for horror (12-24 markets) each issue. Reviews novels or short story collections. Sample copy available for $2. Subscription price: $10/year; $8 renewals; foreign orders add $4. Please remit in U.S. funds.

‡OHIO WRITER, P.O. Box 528, Willoughby OH 44094. (216)257-6410. Editor: Linda Rome. Bimonthly. "Interviews with Ohio writers of fiction and nonfiction; current fiction markets in Ohio." Lists fiction markets. Reviews novels and short story collections. Sample copies available for $2. Subscriptions: $12/year; $30/3 years; $18/institutional rate.

POETS & WRITERS, 72 Spring St., New York NY 10012. Covers primarily poetry and fiction writing. Bimonthly. "Keeps writers in touch with the news they need. Reports on grants and awards, including deadlines for applications; publishes manuscript requests from editors and publishers; covers topics such as book contracts, taxes, writers' colonies and publishing trends; features essays by and interviews with poets and fiction writers. Lists markets for fiction. Sample copies available; single copy price is $3.95. Subscriptions: $18/year; $32/2 years; $46/3 years.

PROSETRY, Newsletter For, By, About Writers, P.O. Box 117727, Burlingame CA 94011-7727. Editor: P.D. Steele. Monthly. Estab. 1986. "A newsletter for writers, offering markets, conferences, exercises, information, workshops, and a monthly guest writer column with tips to the fiction writer." Reviews short story collections. Send review copies to P.D. Steele or E. B. Maynard. Sample copy available for 3 first-class stamps. Subscriptions: $12/year. Guidelines for #10 SASE.

THE REGENCY PLUME, 711 D. St. N.W., Ardmore OK 73401. Editor: Marilyn Clay. Bimonthly. "The newsletter focus is on providing accurate historical facts relating to the Regency period: customs, clothes, entertainment, the wars, historical figures, etc. I stay in touch with New York editors who acquire Regency romance novels. Current market info appears regularly in newsletter—see Bits & Scraps." Current Regency romances are "Previewed." Sample copy available for $3; single copy price is $3, $4 outside States. Subscriptions: $12/year for 6 issues; $16 Canada; $22 foreign. ("Check must be drawn on a US bank. Postal money order okay.") Back issues available. Send SASE for subscription information, article guidelines or list of research and writing aids available, such as audiotapes, historical maps, books on Regency period furniture, etc.

‡RISING STAR, 47 Byledge Rd., Manchester NH 03104. (603)623-9796. Editor: Scott E. Green. Published every 5-7 weeks. "A newsletter which covers new markets for writers and artists in the science fiction/fantasy/horror genres." Lists markets for fiction. Reviews novels and short story collections. Send review copies to Scott E. Green. Sample copies available. Single copy price: $1.50. Subscription price: $7.50 for 6 issues (checks payable to Scott E. Green), $10 for overseas subscribers.

SCAVENGER'S NEWSLETTER, 519 Ellinwood, Osage City KS 66523. (913)528-3538. Editor: Janet Fox. Monthly. "A market newsletter for SF/fantasy/horror/mystery writers with an interest in the small press. Articles about SF/fantasy/horror/mystery writing/marketing. Now using Flash fiction to 1,200 words, genres as above. No writing-related material for fiction. Payment for articles and fiction is $4 on acceptance." Lists markets for fiction. Sample copies available. Single copy price: $2. Subscription price: $15.50/year, $7.75/6 months. Canada: $18.50, $9.25 overseas $24.50, $12.25 (US funds only).

SCIENCE FICTION CHRONICLE, P.O. Box 022730, Brooklyn NY 11202-0056. (718)643-9011. Editor: Andrew Porter. Monthly. "Monthly newsmagazine for professional writers, editors, readers of SF, fantasy, horror." Lists markets for fiction "updated every 4 months." Reviews novels, small press publications, audiotapes, software, and short story collections. Send review copies to SFC and to Don D'Ammassa, 323 Dodge St., E. Providence RI 02914. Sample copies available with 9×12 SAE with $1.24 postage; single copy price is $2.95 (US) or £3 (UK). Subscriptions: $30 bulk, $36 first class US and Canada; $45 overseas. *Note: As with other listings in this section, this is not a "market"—Do not send mss or artwork.*

SCIENCE FICTION CONVENTION REGISTER, 101 S. Whiting St., Alexandria VA 22304. (703)461-8645. Editor: Erwin S. Strauss. 3 issues/year. "Directory of over 500 upcoming science fiction and related conventions." Sample copies available; single copy price is $4. Subscriptions: $10/year.

‡THE SMALL PRESS BOOK REVIEW, P.O. Box 176, Southport CT 06490. (203)332-7629. Editor: Henry Berry. Quarterly. "Brief reviews of all sorts of books from small presses/independent publishers." Addresses of publishers are given in reviews. Reviews novels and short story collections. Send review copies to editor. Published electronically via the Internet and America Online.

SMALL PRESS REVIEW/SMALL MAGAZINE REVIEW, P.O. Box 100, Paradise CA 95967. (916)877-6110. Editor: Len Fulton. Monthly. "Publishes news and reviews about small publishers, books and magazines." Lists markets for fiction and poetry. Reviews novels, short story and poetry collections. Sample copies available. Subscription price: $25/year.

A VIEW FROM THE LOFT, 66 Malcolm Ave. SE, Minneapolis MN 55414. (612)379-8999. Editor: Ellen Hawley. Monthly. "Publishes articles on writing and list of markets for fiction, poetry and creative nonfiction." Sample copies available; single copy price is $4 US. Subscriptions: $40 in Twin Cities metro area; $25 elsewhere in US; $35 international, $20 low income student. (Subscription available only as part of Loft membership; rates are membership rates.)

THE WRITER, 120 Boylston St., Boston MA 02116-4615. Editor: Sylvia K. Burack. Monthly. Contains articles on improving writing techniques and getting published. Includes market lists of magazine and book publishers. Subscription price: $27/year, $50/2 years. Canadian and foreign at additional $8 (US) per year. Also publishes *The Writer's Handbook*, an annual book on all fields of writing plus market lists of magazine and book publishers.

WRITERS BLOC MAGAZINE, A Collection of Collaborative Literature, 1278 Morgan St., Santa Rosa CA 95401. (800)544-7033. Editor: Bernie Hamilton-Lee. Semi-annually. "We publish only collaborative writing of Writers Bloc members." Annual membership is $25 which enables members to participate in stories in the genre of their choice (mystery, science fiction, romance, etc.). Sample copies available for $2.95. Subscriptions: $10.50 for one year.

WRITER'S CAROUSEL, (formerly *Carousel*), The Writer's Center, 4508 Walsh St., Bethesda MD 20815. (301)654-8664. Editors: Allan Lefcowitz and Jeff Minerd. Bimonthly. "*Writer's Carousel* publishes book reviews and articles about writing and the writing scene." Lists fiction markets. Reviews novels and short story collections. Sample copies available. Subscriptions: $30 Writer's Center Membership.

WRITERS CONNECTION, P.O. Box 24770, San Jose CA 95154-4770. (408)445-3600. Fax: (408)445-3609. Editor: Jan Stiles. Monthly. "How-to articles for writers, editors and self-publishers. Topics cover all types of writing, from fiction to technical writing. Columns include markets, contests and writing events and conferences for fiction, nonfiction and scriptwriting." Lists markets for fiction. Sample copies for $3. Single copy price: $3. Subscription: $25/year. "We do not publish fiction or poetry."

WRITER'S DIGEST, 1507 Dana Ave., Cincinnati OH 45207. (513)531-2222. Editor: Thomas Clark. Monthly. "*Writer's Digest* is a magazine of techniques and markets. We *inspire* the writer to write, *instruct* him or her on how to improve that work, and *direct* him or her toward appropriate markets." Lists markets for fiction, nonfiction, poetry. Single copy price: $2.99. Subscription price: $27.

WRITER'S DIGEST BOOKS–MARKET BOOKS, 1507 Dana Ave., Cincinnati OH 45207. (513)531-2222. Annual. In addition to *Novel & Short Story Writer's Market*, Writer's Digest Books also publishes *Writer's Market, Poet's Market, Children's Writer's and Illustrator's Market, Mystery Writer's Sourcebook, Science Fiction Writer's Sourcebook, Romance Writer's Sourcebook* and the *Guide to Literary Agents*. All include articles and listings of interest to writers. All are available at bookstores, libraries or through the publisher. (Request catalog.)

WRITER'S GUIDELINES, HC77 Box 608, Pittsburg MO 65724. Fax: (417)993-5544. Editor: Susan Salaki. Bimonthly. "Fiction writers are welcome to submit material for our Roundtable Discussions, a section devoted to the grassroots approach to getting your work published. Our magazine also assists writers in obtaining guidelines from over 500 different magazine and book editors through our Guidelines Service." Lists markets for fiction. Reviews novels and short story collections of subscribers. Send SASE for guidelines. Single copy price: $4. Subscription price: $18; Canada, $26; Overseas, $36.

WRITERS' JOURNAL, (Minnesota Ink section), Val-Tech Publishing, Inc., P.O. Box 25376, St. Paul MN 55125-0376. Managing Editor: Valerie Hockert. Bimonthly. "Provides a creative outlet for writers of fiction." Sample copies available. Single copy price: $3.25; $4 (Canadian). Subscription price: $14.97; $18.97 Canada.

WRITERS NEWS, P.O. Box 4, Nairn 1V12 4HU Scotland. "Practical advice for established and aspiring writers. How-to articles, news, markets and competitions." Overseas subscribers are now automatically enrolled in the British Overseas Writers Circle, which includes a newsletter of specialized information for writers outside Britain. Lists markets for fiction. Free trial issue available. Subscriptions: £41.60 (UK), £48.60 (Europe/Eire), £53.60 (elsewhere).

WRITER'S YEARBOOK, 1507 Dana Ave., Cincinnati OH 45207. (513)531-2222. Editor: Thomas Clark. Annual. "A collection of the best writing *about* writing, with an exclusive survey of the year's 100 top markets for freelancers." Single copy price: $4.99.

THE WRITING SELF, P.O. Box 245, Lenox Hill Station, New York NY 10021. Editor: Scot Nourok. Quarterly. *"The Writing Self* is devoted to the act of writing. The goal of this publication is to create a network and support for creative writers: poets, novelists, short story writers, as well as playwrights and journalists. We publish personal essays that describe what it is like to be a writer. Each issue includes an interview, little magazine review, book review, contest, and special columns, Inner Voices, Short Shorts, The Workshop Beat, Short Fiction, First Novels." Reviews novels, short story collections and books on writing. Send review copies to editor. Sample copies available; single copy price is $3. Subscriptions: $10 (US), $15 in Canada and $22 overseas.

ZENE, 5 Martins Lane, Witcham Ely, Cambs CB6 2LB England. Editor: Andy Cox. Quarterly (but may be monthly soon). *Zene* is a guide to independent literary markets worldwide. We list complete contributors' guidelines, including subscription details, plus updates, news and feedback from writers. Every issue contains wide-ranging articles by leading small press writers, editors, publishers, ER, plus interviews, letters, market info, etc. We are international, with correspondents and guidelines from all over the world." Lists fiction markets. Reviews novels, magazines and short story collections. Sample copies available for $4.50 (AIR)(US). Subscriptions: $16.60 (AIR) US checks OK.

Publications of interest to fiction writers/'95-'96 changes

The following publications appeared in the 1995 edition of *Novel & Short Story Writer's Market* but do not appear in the 1996 edition. Those that did not respond to our request for an update appear below without further explanation. If a reason for the omission is available, it is included next to the listing name.

Afraid (ceased publication)
Factsheet Five (requested
    deletion)
Fairbanks Arts
Gila Queen's Guide to Markets

The Nook News Conferences &
    Klatches Bulletin
The Nook News Contests &
    Awards Bulletin
The Nook News Market Bulletin

The Nook News Review of
    Writer's Publications
The Writer's Nook News

Glossary

Advance. Payment by a publisher to an author prior to the publication of a book, to be deducted from the author's future royalties.

All rights. The rights contracted to a publisher permitting a manuscript's use anywhere and in any form, including movie and book-club sales, without additional payment to the writer.

Anthology. A collection of selected writings by various authors.

Auction. Publishers sometimes bid against each other for the acquisition of a manuscript that has excellent sales prospects.

Backlist. A publisher's books not published during the current season but still in print.

Belles lettres. A term used to describe fine or literary writing more to entertain than to inform or instruct.

Book producer/packager. An organization that may develop a book for a publisher based upon the publisher's idea or may plan all elements of a book, from its initial concept to writing and marketing strategies, and then sell the package to a book publisher and/or movie producer.

Category fiction. See Genre.

Chapbook. A booklet of 15-30 pages of fiction or poetry.

Cliffhanger. Fictional event in which the reader is left in suspense at the end of a chapter or episode, so that interest in the story's outcome will be sustained.

Clip. Sample, usually from newspaper or magazine, of a writer's published work.

Cloak-and-dagger. A melodramatic, romantic type of fiction dealing with espionage and intrigue.

Commercial. Publishers whose concern is salability, profit and success with a large readership.

Contemporary. Material dealing with popular current trends, themes or topics.

Contributor's copy. Copy of an issue of a magazine or published book sent to an author whose work is included.

Copublishing. An arrangement in which the author and publisher share costs and profits.

Copyediting. Editing a manuscript for writing style, grammar, punctuation and factual accuracy.

Copyright. The legal right to exclusive publication, sale or distribution of a literary work.

Cover letter. A brief letter sent with a complete manuscript submitted to an editor.

"Cozy" (or "teacup") mystery. Mystery usually set in a small British town, in a bygone era, featuring a somewhat genteel, intellectual protagonist.

Cyberpunk. Type of science fiction, usually concerned with computer networks and human-computer combinations, involving young, sophisticated protagonists.

Division. An unincorporated branch of a company (e.g. Viking Penguin, a division of Penguin USA).

Elf punk. Type of fantasy involving magical creatures such as elves who behave like urban punks and live on the fringe of society in a bleak, urban setting.

E-mail. Mail that has been sent electronically using a computer and modem.

Experimental fiction. Fiction that is innovative in subject matter and style; avant-garde, non-formulaic, usually literary material.

Exposition. The portion of the storyline, usually the beginning, where background information about character and setting is related.

Fair use. A provision in the copyright law that says short passages from copyrighted material may be used without infringing on the owner's rights.

Fanzine. A noncommercial, small-circulation magazine usually dealing with fantasy, horror or science-fiction literature and art.

First North American serial rights. The right to publish material in a periodical before it appears in book form, for the first time, in the United States or Canada.

Formula. A fixed and conventional method of plot development, which varies little from one book to another in a particular genre.

Frontier novel. Novel that has all the basic elements of a traditional western but is based upon the frontier history of "unwestern" places like Florida or East Tennessee.

Galleys. The first typeset version of a manuscript that has not yet been divided into pages.

Genre. A formulaic type of fiction such as romance, western or horror.

Gothic. A genre in which the central character is usually a beautiful young woman and the setting an old mansion or castle, involving a handsome hero and real danger, either natural or supernatural.

Graphic novel. An adaptation of a novel into a long comic strip or heavily illustrated story of 40 pages or more, produced in paperback.

Hard-boiled detective novel. Mystery novel featuring a private eye or police detective as the protagonist; usually involves a murder. The emphasis is on the details of the crime.

Honorarium. A small, token payment for published work.

Horror. A genre stressing fear, death and other aspects of the macabre.

Imprint. Name applied to a publisher's specific line (e.g. Owl, an imprint of Henry Holt).

Interactive fiction. Fiction in book or computer-software format where the reader determines the path the story will take by choosing from several alternatives at the end of each chapter or episode.

International Reply Coupon (IRC). A form purchased at a post office and enclosed with a letter or manuscript to a international publisher, to cover return postage costs.

Juvenile. Fiction intended for children 2-12.

Libel. Written or printed words that defame, malign or damagingly misrepresent a living person.

Literary. The general category of serious, non-formulaic, intelligent fiction, sometimes experimental, that most frequently appears in little magazines.

Literary agent. A person who acts for an author in finding a publisher or arranging contract terms on a literary project.

Mainstream. Traditionally written fiction on subjects or trends that transcend experimental or genre fiction categories.

Malice domestic novel. A traditional mystery novel that is not hard-boiled; emphasis is on the solution. Suspects and victims know one another.

Manuscript. The author's unpublished copy of a work, usually typewritten, used as the basis for typesetting.

Mass market paperback. Softcover book on a popular subject, usually around 4×7, directed to a general audience and sold in drugstores and groceries as well as in bookstores.

Ms(s). Abbreviation for manuscript(s).

Multiple submission. Submission of more than one short story at a time to the same editor. Do not make a multiple submission unless requested.

Narration. The account of events in a story's plot as related by the speaker or the voice of the author.

Narrator. The person who tells the story, either someone involved in the action or the voice of the writer.

New Age. A term including categories such as astrology, psychic phenomena, spiritual healing, UFOs, mysticism and other aspects of the occult.

Nom de plume. French for "pen name"; a pseudonym.

Novella (also novelette). A short novel or long story, approximately 7,000-15,000 words.

#10 envelope. 4×9½ envelope, used for queries and other business letters.

Novels of the West. Novels that have elements of the western but contain more complex characters and subjects such as fur trading, cattle raising and coal mining.

Offprint. Copy of a story taken from a magazine before it is bound.

One-time rights. Permission to publish a story in periodical or book form one time only.

Outline. A summary of a book's contents, often in the form of chapter headings with a few sentences outlining the action of the story under each one; sometimes part of a book proposal.

Over the transom. Slang for the path of an unsolicited manuscript into the slush pile.

Page rate. A fixed rate paid to an author per published page of fiction.

Payment on acceptance. Payment from the magazine or publishing house as soon as the decision to print a manuscript is made.

Payment on publication. Payment from the publisher after a manuscript is printed.

Pen name. A pseudonym used to conceal a writer's real name.

Periodical. A magazine or journal published at regular intervals.

Plot. The carefully devised series of events through which the characters progress in a work of fiction.

Proofreading. Close reading and correction of a manuscript's typographical errors.

Proofs. A typeset version of a manuscript used for correcting errors and making changes, often a photocopy of the galleys.

Proposal. An offer to write a specific work, usually consisting of an outline of the work and one or two completed chapters.

Prose poem. Short piece of prose with the language and expression of poetry.

Protagonist. The principal or leading character in a literary work.

Public domain. Material that either was never copyrighted or whose copyright term has expired.

Pulp magazine. A periodical printed on inexpensive paper, usually containing lurid, sensational stories or articles.

Purple prose. Ornate writing using exaggerated and excessive literary devices.

Query. A letter written to an editor to elicit interest in a story the writer wants to submit.

Reader. A person hired by a publisher to read unsolicited manuscripts.

Reading fee. An arbitrary amount of money charged by some agents and publishers to read a submitted manuscript.

Regency romance. A genre romance, usually set in England between 1811-1820.

Remainders. Leftover copies of an out-of-print book, sold by the publisher at a reduced price.

Reporting time. The number of weeks or months it takes an editor to report back on an author's query or manuscript.

Reprint rights. Permission to print an already published work whose rights have been sold to another magazine or book publisher.

Roman à clef. French "novel with a key." A novel that represents actual living or historical characters and events in fictionalized form.

Romance. The genre relating accounts of passionate love and fictional heroic achievements.

Royalties. A percentage of the retail price paid to an author for each copy of the book that is sold.

SAE. Self-addressed envelope.

SASE. Self-addressed stamped envelope.

Science fiction. Genre in which scientific facts and hypotheses form the basis of actions and events.

Second serial (reprint) rights. Permission for the reprinting of a work in another periodical after its first publication in book or magazine form.

Self-publishing. In this arrangement, the author keeps all income derived from the book, but he pays for its manufacturing, production and marketing.

Sequel. A literary work that continues the narrative of a previous, related story or novel.

Serial rights. The rights given by an author to a publisher to print a piece in one or more periodicals.

Serialized novel. A book-length work of fiction published in sequential issues of a periodical.

Setting. The environment and time period during which the action of a story takes place.

Short short story. A condensed piece of fiction, usually under 700 words.

Simultaneous submission. The practice of sending copies of the same manuscript to several editors or publishers at the same time. Some people refuse to consider such submissions.

Slant. A story's particular approach or style, designed to appeal to the readers of a specific magazine.

Slice of life. A presentation of characters in a seemingly mundane situation which offers the reader a flash of illumination about the characters or their situation.

Slush pile. A stack of unsolicited manuscripts in the editorial offices of a publisher.

Speculation (or Spec). An editor's agreement to look at an author's manuscript with no promise to purchase.

Splatterpunk. Type of horror fiction known for its very violent and graphic content.

Subsidiary. An incorporated branch of a company or conglomerate (e.g. Alfred Knopf, Inc., a subsidiary of Random House, Inc.).

Subsidiary rights. All rights other than book publishing rights included in a book contract, such as paperback, book-club and movie rights.

Subsidy publisher. A book publisher who charges the author for the cost of typesetting, printing and promoting a book. Also Vanity publisher.

Subterficial fiction. Innovative, challenging, nonconventional fiction in which what seems to be happening is the result of things not so easily perceived.

Suspense. A genre of fiction where the plot's primary function is to build a feeling of anticipation and fear in the reader over its possible outcome.

Synopsis. A brief summary of a story, novel or play. As part of a book proposal, it is a comprehensive summary condensed in a page or page and a half.

Tabloid. Publication printed on paper about half the size of a regular newspaper page (e.g. *The National Enquirer*).

Tearsheet. Page from a magazine containing a published story.

Theme. The dominant or central idea in a literary work; its message, moral or main thread.

Trade paperback. A softbound volume, usually around 5×8, published and designed for the general public, available mainly in bookstores.

Unsolicited manuscript. A story or novel manuscript that an editor did not specifically ask to see.

Vanity publisher. See Subsidy publisher.

Viewpoint. The position or attitude of the first- or third-person narrator or multiple narrators, which determines how a story's action is seen and evaluated.

Western. Genre with a setting in the West, usually between 1860-1890, with a formula plot about cowboys or other aspects of frontier life.

Whodunit. Genre dealing with murder, suspense and the detection of criminals.

Work-for-hire. Work that another party commissions you to do, generally for a flat fee. The creator does not own the copyright and therefore can not sell any rights.

Young adult. The general classification of books written for readers 12-18.

Category Index

The Category Index is a good place to begin searching for a market for your fiction. Below is an alphabetical list of subjects of particular interest to editors listed in *Novel & Short Story Writer's Market*. The index is divided into four sections: Literary and Small Circulation Magazines; Commercial Periodicals; Small Press and Commercial Book Publishers. Some of the markets listed in the book do not appear in the Category Index, because they have not indicated specific subject preferences. Most of these said they accept "all categories." Listings that were very specific also do not appear here. An example of this might be a magazine accepting "fiction about fly fishing only." If you'd like to market your hardboiled mystery novel to a major publishing house, for example, check the Commercial Book Publishers subhead under Mystery. There you will find a list of those publishers interested in the subject along with the page numbers on which their listings appear. Then read the listings *carefully* to find the mystery publishers best suited to your work.

Literary and Small Circulation Magazines

Adventure. A.R.T. 74; Abyss Magazine 75; Aguilar Expression, The 80; Allegheny Review 81; Amateur Writers Journal 82; Amelia 82; Amherst Review, The 83; Anterior Fiction Quarterly 84; Arnazella 86; artisan 87; Ascending Shadows 88; Asian Pacific Journal 88; Belletrist Review, The 91; Big Sky Stories 92; Black Jack 95; Blackwater Review 96; Blue Mesa Review 97; Blue Water Review, The 98; Blueline 98; Bohemian Chronicle 99; BookLovers 99; Boy's Quest 101; Brownstone Review, The 103; Capers Aweigh Magazine 106; Christian Courier 110; Chrysalis Reader 110; Climbing Art, The 112; Cochran's Corner 112; Compenions 114; Dagger of the Mind 119; Dan River Anthology 121; DJINNI 126; Dogwood Tales Magazine 126; Downstate Story 126; Dream International/Quarterly 127; Drinkin' Buddy Magazine, The 128; Earthsongs 128; Echoes 129; 8, Dancing with Mr. D 129; Elf: Eclectic Literary Forum 130; Eureka Literary Magazine 132; Every So Often . . . 133; Expressions 134; Extreme, The 134; FiberOptic Etchings 137; Frayed 141; Fugue 142; Gotta Write Network Litmag 145; Grasslands Review 147; Green Mountains Review 148; Green's Magazine 148; Hawaii Pacific Review 151; Heroic Times 155; Home Girl Press 156; i.e. Magazine 159; Iconoclast, The 159; It's Your Choice Magazine 163; Jeopardy 165; Just Write 166; Lactuca 169; Lacunae 170; Lighthouse 174; Lines In The Sand 174; Liquid Ohio 175; Longneck, The 176; Loop, The 177; Lowell Pearl, The 178; Lynx Eye 179; MacGuffin, The 179; Many Leaves One Tree 182; Medicinal Purposes 184; Mediphors 184; Merlyn's Pen 185; Monolith Magazine 190; Monthly Independent Tribune Times Journal Post Gazette News Chronicle Bulletin, The 190; More Dead Trees 191; Musing Place, The 192; Musk Gland Sally 192; Mysterious Wysteria 192; Mystic Fiction 193; Naked Kiss 193; nerve 194; New Frontiers of New Mexico 196; New Methods 197; New Voices in Poetry and Prose 200; Nimrod 202; Nite-Writer's Literary Arts Journal 202; Northwoods Journal 206; Oak, The 207; Olympia Review, The 208; Ouroboros 212; Pagan Review, The 214; Palo Alto Review 215; Pink Chameleon, The 222; PKA's Advocate 223; Place to Enter, A 223; Poor Katy's Almanac 226; Portable Wall, The 226; Post, The 227; Potpourri 228; Prairie Dog 229; Q Magazine 234; Queen's Quarterly 235; Raconteur 235; Rag Mag 236; Ralph's Review 237; Re Arts & Letters [REAL] 238; Renegade 240; Renovated Lighthouse 240; Robin's Nest 243; Rock Falls Review 243; Rosebud™ 244; S.L.U.G.fest, Ltd. 245; Shift Magazine 250; Short Stuff Magazine for Grown-ups 251; Slate and Style 257; SPSM&H 264; Street Beat Quarterly 267; Surprise Me 269; "Teak" Roundup 272; Texas Young Writers' Newsletter 273; Thema 274; Thresholds Quar-

Magazine 282; Vignette 283; Voices West 284; Vox 284; West Wind Review 286; W!dow of the Orch!d, The 289; Yellow Silk 297; Zero Hour 299

Ethnic/Multicultural. A.R.T. 74; ACM, (Another Chicago Magazine) 76; Acorn Whistle 76; ACTA Victoriana 76; Adrift 77; African American Review 77; Aguilar Expression, The 80; Allegheny Review 81; Amelia 82; Americas Review, The 83; Amherst Review, The 83; Anarchy 83; Antietam Review 84; Arba Sicula 86; Arnazella 86; artisan 87; Art:Mag 87; Asian Pacific Journal 88; Atom Mind 89; Aura Literary/Arts Review 89; Azorean Express, The 89; Bahlasti Papers 90; Bamboo Ridge 90; Beneath The Surface 92; Bilingual Review 93; Black Books Bulletin: WordsWork 93; Black Fire 94; Black Hammock Review, The 94; Black Jack 95; Black Lace 95; Blue Mesa Review 97; Blue Water Review, The 98; Bohemian Chronicle 99; BookLovers 99; Boy's Quest 101; Briar Cliff Review, The 101; Bridge, The 102; Brownbag Press 102; Brownstone Review, The 103; Brújula/Compass 103; Cafe Magazine 104; Callaloo 105; Capers Aweigh Magazine 106; Chaminade Literary Review 107; Chiricú 109; Cimmerian-Journal, The 111; Climbing Art, The 112; Collages and Bricolages 113; Compenions 114; Concho River Review 115; Confluence 115; Crazyquilt 118; Cream City Review, The 118; Crucible 119; Dan River Anthology 121; Daughters of Nyx 122; DJINNI 126; Downstate Story 126; Dream International/Quarterly 127; Drinkin' Buddy Magazine, The 128; Earthsongs 128; Echoes 129; Elephant-Ear, The 130; Elf: Eclectic Literary Forum 130; Epoch Magazine 131; Eureka Literary Magazine 132; Every So Often . . . 133; Excursus 133; Expressions 134; Fault Lines 136; Feminist Studies 137; FiberOptic Etchings 137; Filling Station 138; Fish Drum Magazine 139; Fish Stories 139; Flying Island, The 140; Footwork 140; Four Directions, The 140; Fuel Magazine 142; Fugue 142; Gathering of the Tribes, A 143; Grasslands Review 147; Green Hills Literary Lantern, The 147; Gulf Coast 149; Happy 150; Hawaii Pacific Review 151; Hawaii Review 151; Hayden's Ferry Review 153; Heartlands Today, The 153; Hecate's Loom 154; Heroic Times 155; Hill and Holler 155; hip MAMA 156; Home Girl Press 156; Home Planet News 157; Iconoclast, The 159; Illinois Review, The 159; International Quarterly 161; Intuitive Explorations 162; Iowa Review, The 162; Italian Americana 163; It's Your Choice Magazine 163; Jacaranda 163; Jambalaya Magazine 164; Japanophile 164; Jeopardy 165; Jewish Currents Magazine 165; Just Write 166; Kennesaw Review 168; Kenyon Review, The 168; Kerem 168; Kestrel 168; Left Bank 172; Left Curve 172; Liquid Ohio 175; Longneck, The 176; Lowell Pearl, The 178; Lynx Eye 179; MacGuffin, The 179; Mangrove 181; manna 181; Many Leaves One Tree 182; Many Mountains Moving 182; Mark 183; Maryland Review, The 183; Matriarch's Way 183; Medicinal Purposes 184; Men As We Are 185; Midland Review 187; Minority Literary Expo 189; Mobius 189; Moccasin Telegraph 190; Monolith Magazine 190; More Dead Trees 191; Musing Place, The 192; Mystic Fiction 193; nerve 194; New Frontiers of New Mexico 196; New Letters Magazine 197; Nimrod 202; North Dakota Quarterly 204; Northeast Arts Magazine 204; Obsidian II: Black Literature in Review 207; Olympia Review, The 208; One Hundred Suns 210; Onionhead 210; Oracle Story 210; Orange Coast Review 210; Otisian Directory 212; Owen Wister Review 212; Oxford Magazine 213; Oxygen 213; Pacific Coast Journal 214; Pagan Review, The 214; Painted Bride Quarterly 215; Palo Alto Review 215; Paradoxist Literary Movement, The 216; Pequod 219; Phoebe (NY) 221; Pikeville Review 222; Pink Chameleon, The 222; PKA's Advocate 223; Place to Enter, A 223; Plowman, The 224; Poetry Forum Short Stories 225; Pointed Circle, The 225; Portable Wall, The 226; Poskisnolt Press 227; Possibilitiis Literary Arts Magazine 227; Potomac Review 228; Potpourri 228; Prairie Dog 229; Psychotrain 232; Puck 233; Puerto Del Sol 233; Rafale 236; Rag Mag 236; Raven Chronicles, The 238; Response 240; River Styx 242; RiverSedge 242; Riverwind 242; Robin's Nest 243; Rock Falls Review 243; Rockford Review, The 244; Rosebud™ 244; S.L.U.G.fest, Ltd. 245; Salt Lick Press 245; Sanskrit 246; Seattle Review, The 247; Semiotext(e) 247; Sequoia 248; Shattered Wig Review 250; Shift Magazine 250; Side Show 251; Silence, The 253; Sing Heavenly Muse! 256; Skipping Stones 256; Skylark 257; Slate, The 257; Slightly West 258; Slipstream 258; Snake Nation Review 259; So To Speak 259; South Carolina Review 260; South Dakota Review 261; Southern California Anthology 261; Southern Exposure 261; Spindrift 263; Spirit Magazine 263; Spout 264; SPSM&H 264; Street Beat Quarterly 267; Struggle 267; Suffusion Magazine 268; Sulphur River Literary Review 268; Surprise Me 269; Tamaqua 271; Tampa Review 271; "Teak" Roundup 272; Texas Young Writers' Newsletter 273; Textshop 273; This Magazine 274; Timber Creek Review 275; Troika Magazine 279; Tucumcari Literary Review 279; Unforgettable Fire, The 280; Uno Mas Magazine 280; Urbanus/Raizirr 281; Valley Grapevine 281; Venus Magazine 282; Vignette 283; Vincent Brothers Review, The 283; Virginia Quarterly Review 284; Voices West 284; Vox 284; Welter

285; West Coast Line 286; West Wind Review 286; Western Pocket, The 287; Westview 287; Wordplay 293; Words of Wisdom 293; Writers' Forum 294; Writes of Passage 295; Writing for Our Lives 295; Xavier Review 296; Xib 296; Yarns and Such 297; Yellow Silk 297; Zephyr 299; Zero Hour 299; Zuzu's Petals Annual 299

Experimental. A.R.T. 74; ACM, (Another Chicago Magazine) 76; ACTA Victoriana 76; Adrift 77; African American Review 77; Aguilar Expression, The 80; Al Aaraaf 80; Alabama Literary Review 80; Alaska Quarterly Review 81; Allegheny Review 81; Alpha Beat Press 82; Amelia 82; Amherst Review, The 83; Anarchy 83; Antietam Review 84; Antioch Review 85; Aphrodite Gone Berserk 85; Arnazella 86; Artful Dodge 87; artisan 87; Art:Mag 87; Ascending Shadows 88; Asian Pacific Journal 88; Atom Mind 89; Azorean Express, The 89; Baby Sue 90; Bahlasti Papers 90; Beneath The Surface 92; Bizára 93; Black Hammock Review, The 94; Black River Review 95; Blackwater Review 96; Blink 97; Blood & Aphorisms 97; Blue Penny Quarterly, The 98; Blue Water Review, The 98; Bogg 99; Bohemian Chronicle 99; Boston Literary Review (BLuR) 99; Boulevard 100; Brownbag Press 102; Brownstone Review, The 103; Brutarian 103; Burning Light 103; Cafe Magazine 104; Calliope 105; Cat's Ear 107; Cayo 107; Century 107; Chaminade Literary Review 107; Changing Men 108; Chicago Review 109; Chiron Review 110; Chrysalis Reader 110; Climbing Art, The 112; Clockwatch Review 112; Collages and Bricolages 113; Compenions 114; Conduit 115; Context South 116; Corona 116; Cream City Review, The 118; Crucible 119; Dagger of the Mind 119; Dan River Anthology 121; Deathrealm 123; Denver Quarterly 124; Disturbed Guillotine 125; DJINNI 126; Dodobobo 126; Downstate Story 126; Dream International/Quarterly 127; Dreams & Nightmares 127; Dreams & Visions 128; Earthsongs 128; Echoes 129; 8, Dancing with Mr. D 129; 1812 130; Elephant-Ear, The 130; Entelechy 131; Eureka Literary Magazine 132; Every So Often . . . 133; Excursus 133; Explorations '96 133; Expressions 134; Extreme, The 134; Eyes 134; Fat Tuesday 135; Fault Lines 136; FiberOptic Etchings 137; Fiction 137; Filling Station 138; Fish Drum Magazine 139; Fish Stories 139; Flipside 139; Florida Review, The 139; Flying Island, The 140; Frayed 141; Free Focus/Ostentatious Mind 141; Fuel Magazine 142; Fugue 142; G.W. Review, The 143; Gathering of the Tribes, A 143; Georgia Review, The 144; Gettysburg Review, The 144; Graffiti Off the Asylum Walls 146; Grain 146; Grand Street 146; Grasslands Review 147; Green Hills Literary Lantern, The 147; Green Mountains Review 148; Greensboro Review 148; Gulf Coast 149; Habersham Review 150; Happy 150; Hawaii Pacific Review 151; Hawaii Review 151; Hayden's Ferry Review 153; Heaven Bone 153; Heroic Times 155; hip MAMA 156; Home Planet News 157; Hopewell Review, The 157; Housewife-Writer's Forum 158; Hunted News, The 158; i.e. Magazine 159; Illinois Review, The 159; International Quarterly 161; Iris 162; It's Your Choice Magazine 163; Jacaranda 163; Jack Mackerel Magazine 163; Jeopardy 165; Just Write 166; Kennesaw Review 168; Kenyon Review, The 168; Kestrel 168; Kinesis 169; Left Curve 172; Liberty 173; Lines In The Sand 174; Liquid Ohio 175; Lite 175; Literal Latté 175; Longneck, The 176; Loop, The 177; Lost and Found Times 177; Lost Worlds 177; Louisville Review, The 178; Lowell Pearl, The 178; Lynx Eye 179; MacGuffin, The 179; Magic Realism 180; Many Leaves One Tree 182; Many Mountains Moving 182; Matriarch's Way 183; Maverick Press, The 184; Medicinal Purposes 184; Mediphors 184; Mid-American Review 186; Midland Review 187; Mind in Motion 187; Minnesota Review, The 188; Mississippi Review 189; Mobius 189; Monolith Magazine 190; Monthly Independent Tribune Times Journal Post Gazette News Chronicle Bulletin, The 190; More Dead Trees 191; Musing Place, The 192; Mysterious Wysteria 192; Mystic Fiction 193; nerve 194; New Delta Review 195; New Frontiers of New Mexico 196; New Letters Magazine 197; New Methods 197; New Press Literary Quarterly, The 197; new renaissance, the 199; Next Phase 200; Nexus 201; Nimrod 202; Nocturnal Lyric, The 203; North Dakota Quarterly 204; Northwest Review 205; Northwoods Journal 206; Oak, The 207; Office Number One 207; Ogalala Review, The 208; Ohio Review, The 208; Old Crow Review 208; Olympia Review, The 208; One Hundred Suns 210; Onionhead 210; Orange Coast Review 210; Other Voices 211; Otisian Directory 212; Ouroboros 212; Owen Wister Review 212; Oxford Magazine 213; Oxygen 213; Pacific Coast Journal 214; Painted Bride Quarterly 215; Palo Alto Review 215; Pangolin Papers 215; Paradox Magazine 216; Paradoxist Literary Movement, The 216; Partisan Review 217; PBW 218; Perception Writings 220; Phoebe (NY) 221; Pica 221; Pikeville Review 222; Pink Chameleon, The 222; PKA's Advocate 223; Poetry Forum Short Stories 225; Portable Wall, The 226; Porter International, Bern 226; Portland Review 226; Poskisnolt Press 227; Potomac Review 228; Potpourri 228; Prairie Dog 229; Prairie Fire 229; Psychotrain 232; Puck 233; Puckerbrush Review 233; Puerto Del Sol 233; Quarry 234; Quarterly West

235; Queen's Quarterly 235; RACS/Rent-A-Chicken Speaks 236; Rag Mag 236; Rambunctious Review 237; Rant 237; Raw Fiction 238; Re Arts & Letters [REAL] 238; Renegade 240; Renovated Lighthouse 240; Report to Hell 240; Response 240; River Styx 242; RiverSedge 242; Robin's Nest 243; Rocket Press 243; Rockford Review, The 244; Rosebud™ 244; Round Table, The 244; Ruby's Pearls 245; S.L.U.G.fest, Ltd. 245; Salt Lick Press 245; Samsara 245; Sanskrit 246; Scorpio Moon 246; Screaming Toad Press 246; Seattle Review, The 247; Semiotext(e) 247; Sequoia 248; Shadowdance 250; Shattered Wig Review 250; Shift Magazine 250; Sidewalks 252; Sierra Nevada College Review 252; Sign of the Times 252; Silence, The 253; Silver Web, The 253; sixpack: poems & stories 256; Skylark 257; Slate, The 257; Slightly West 258; Slipstream 258; Snake Nation Review 259; So To Speak 259; South Dakota Review 261; Southern California Anthology 261; Spectrum (MA) 263; Spindrift 263; Spirit Magazine 263; Spitting Image, The 264; Spout 264; SPSM&H 264; Story 266; Street Beat Quarterly 267; Struggle 267; Sub-Terrain 268; Suffusion Magazine 268; Sulphur River Literary Review 268; Supernatural Magazine on Audiobook, The 269; Sycamore Review 270; Tamaqua 271; Tampa Review 271; Textshop 273; Texture 273; Thema 274; This Magazine 274; Trekker News & Views, The 278; Tribute To Officer Dallies 278; Troika Magazine 279; 2 AM Magazine 279; Uno Mas Magazine 280; Urbanite, The 280; Urbanus/Raizirr 281; Venus Magazine 282; Verve 282; Videomania 282; Vignette 283; Vincent Brothers Review, The 283; Voices West 284; Vox 284; Welter 285; West Coast Line 286; West Wind Review 286; Western Humanities Review 286; Western Pocket, The 287; Westview 287; Whetstone 287; Widener Review 289; W!dow of the Orch!d, The 289; Wisconsin Academy Review 291; Wisconsin Review 291; Writes of Passage 295; Writing for Our Lives 295; Xavier Review 296; Xib 296; Yellow Silk 297; Zero Hour 299; Zyzzyva 300

Fantasy. A.R.T. 74; Abyss Magazine 75; Allegheny Review 81; Amateur Writers Journal 82; Amelia 82; Arnazella 86; artisan 87; SPSM&H 264; Art:Mag 87; Ascending Shadows 88; Bahlasti Papers 90; Bardic Runes 91; Beneath The Surface 92; Bizára 93; Black Hammock Review, The 94; BookLovers 99; Bradley's Fantasy Magazine, Marion Zimmer 101; Brutarian 103; Burning Light 103; Capers Aweigh Magazine 106; Century 107; Cimmerian-Journal, The 111; Climbing Art, The 112; Companion in Zeor, A 114; Compenions 114; Corona 116; Cosmic Unicorn, The 117; Crazyquilt 118; Dagger of the Mind 119; Dan River Anthology 121; Dark Kiss 122; Dark Regions 122; Daughters of Nyx 122; Dead of Night™ Magazine 123; Deathrealm 123; DJINNI 126; Dream Forge 127; Dream International/Quarterly 127; Dreams & Nightmares 127; Dreams & Visions 128; Drinkin' Buddy Magazine, The 128; Echoes 129; 8, Dancing with Mr. D 129; Elf: Eclectic Literary Forum 130; Eureka Literary Magazine 132; Every So Often . . . 133; Expressions 134; FiberOptic Etchings 137; Fish Drum Magazine 139; Flummery Press, The 140; Flying Island, The 140; Frayed 141; Fugue 142; Full-Time Dads 143; Galaxy Magazine 143; Gotta Write Network Litmag 145; Grasslands Review 147; Green Egg/How About Magic? 147; Green's Magazine 148; Happy 150; Haunts 151; Hawaii Pacific Review 151; Hayden's Ferry Review 153; Heaven Bone 153; Hecate's Loom 154; Heroic Times 155; Hobson's Choice 156; Home Girl Press 156; i.e. Magazine 159; It's Your Choice Magazine 163; Just Write 166; Lacunae 170; Lamp-Post, The 171; Liberty 173; Lines In The Sand 174; Liquid Ohio 175; Lite 175; Literal Latté 175; Longneck, The 176; Loop, The 177; Lost Worlds 177; Lynx Eye 179; MacGuffin, The 179; Magic Changes 180; Magic Realism 180; Many Leaves One Tree 182; Matriarch's Way 183; Medicinal Purposes 184; Merlyn's Pen 185; Minas Tirith Evening-Star 187; Mind in Motion 187; Mississippi Review 189; Mobius 189; Monolith Magazine 190; More Dead Trees 191; Musing Place, The 192; Mysterious Wysteria 192; Mystic Fiction 193; Mythic Circle, The 193; Nassau Review 194; New Laurel Review 196; New Voices in Poetry and Prose 200; Next Phase 200; Nocturnal Lyric, The 203; Non-Stop Magazine 204; Northwoods Journal 206; Northwords 206; Office Number One 207; On Spec 209; Once Upon a World 209; Otisian Directory 212; Ouroboros 212; Pablo Lennis 214; Pagan Review, The 214; Palo Alto Review 215; Phantasm II 221; Pink Chameleon, The 222; Pirate Writings 223; PKA's Advocate 223; Pléiades Magazine/Philae 224; Poetry Forum Short Stories 225; Poet's Fantasy 225; Poskisnolt Press 227; Potpourri 228; Prairie Dog 229; Primavera 230; Processed World 232; Puck 233; Pulphouse 233; Quanta 234; Quarry 234; Queen's Quarterly 235; Raconteur 235; Rag Mag 236; Ralph's Review 237; Rant 237; Renegade 240; Renovated Lighthouse 240; Riverside Quarterly 242; Robin's Nest 243; Rock Falls Review 243; Rockford Review, The 244; Samsara 245; Scorpio Moon 246; Seattle Review, The 247; Semiotext(e) 247; Sensations Magazine 248; Shadow Sword 249; Shadow Sword Presents: Laughter, The Best Magic of All 249; Shadow Sword Presents: The Heroines of Fantasy 249; Shadowdance 250; Sidetrekked 252; Sidetrekked 252; Skylark

257; Slate and Style 257; Snake Nation Review 259; Southern Humanities Review 261; Spirit Magazine 263; SPSM&H 264; Square One 265; Starblade 265; Street Beat Quarterly 267; Supernatural Magazine on Audiobook, The 269; Surprise Me 269; Tales from the Vortex 270; Tampa Review 271; Texas Young Writers' Newsletter 273; This Magazine 274; Thresholds Quarterly 275; Tickled By Thunder 275; Time Pilot 276; Tomorrow 276; Trekker News & Views, The 278; Twisted 279; 2 AM Magazine 279; Urbanite, The 280; Verve 282; Videomania 282; Vintage Northwest 283; Weirdbook 285; West Wind Review 286; Whisper 288; Whispering Pines Quarterly 288; W!dow of the Orch!d, The 289; Worlds of Fantasy & Horror 293; Writers' International Forum 294; Writes of Passage 295; Xib 296; Yellow Silk 297

Feminist. A.R.T. 74; ACM, (Another Chicago Magazine) 76; Acorn Whistle 76; Adrift 77; African American Review 77; Allegheny Review 81; Amelia 82; Americas Review, The 83; Amherst Review, The 83; Anarchy 83; Antietam Review 84; Aphrodite Gone Berserk 85; Arnazella 86; artisan 87; SPSM&H 264; Art:Mag 87; Asian Pacific Journal 88; Aura Literary/Arts Review 89; Bahlasti Papers 90; Beneath The Surface 92; Black Books Bulletin: WordsWork 93; Blackwater Review 96; Blue Mesa Review 97; Blue Penny Quarterly, The 98; Briar Cliff Review, The 101; Brownbag Press 102; Brownstone Review, The 103; Brújula/Compass 103; Brutarian 103; Callaloo 105; Calyx 105; Capers Aweigh Magazine 106; Century 107; Changing Men 108; Collages and Bricolages 113; Communities: Journal of Cooperation 114; Compenions 114; Confluence 115; Context South 116; Corona 116; Crucible 119; Daughters of Nyx 122; Disturbed Guillotine 125; DJINNI 126; Dodobobo 126; Drinkin' Buddy Magazine, The 128; Earthsongs 128; Echoes 129; Elephant-Ear, The 130; Elf: Eclectic Literary Forum 130; Emrys Journal 131; Entelechy 131; Eureka Literary Magazine 132; Event 132; Every So Often . . . 133; Excursus 133; Expressions 134; Farmer's Market, The 135; Feminist Studies 137; FiberOptic Etchings 137; Filling Station 138; Fish Stories 139; Flying Island, The 140; Free Focus/Ostentatious Mind 141; Fuel Magazine 142; Gathering of the Tribes, A 143; Graffiti Off the Asylum Walls 146; Green Hills Literary Lantern, The 147; Happy 150; Hayden's Ferry Review 153; Hecate's Loom 154; hip MAMA 156; Home Planet News 157; Hurricane Alice 159; Illinois Review, The 159; Iowa Woman 162; Iris 162; It's Your Choice Magazine 163; Jambalaya Magazine 164; Jeopardy 165; Just Write 166; Kennesaw Review 168; Kenyon Review, The 168; Kerem 168; Kestrel 168; Left Bank 172; Liberty 173; Lime Green Bulldozers 174; Longneck, The 176; Lowell Pearl, The 178; Lynx Eye 179; manna 181; Many Leaves One Tree 182; Many Mountains Moving 182; Matriarch's Way 183; Medicinal Purposes 184; Midland Review 187; Minnesota Review, The 188; Mobius 189; Mostly Maine 191; Musing Place, The 192; Musk Gland Sally 192; Mystic Fiction 193; nerve 194; New Frontiers of New Mexico 196; North Dakota Quarterly 204; Northwest Review 205; Obsidian II: Black Literature in Review 207; Olympia Review, The 208; One Hundred Suns 210; Onionhead 210; Orange Coast Review 210; Otisian Directory 212; Oxford Magazine 213; Oxygen 213; Pacific Coast Journal 214; Pagan Review, The 214; Painted Bride Quarterly 215; Palo Alto Review 215; Phoebe (NY) 221; Pica 221; Pikeville Review 222; PKA's Advocate 223; Poetry Forum Short Stories 225; Portable Wall, The 226; Poskisnolt Press 227; Potato Eyes 227; Potomac Review 228; Primavera 230; Psychotrain 232; Puck 233; Rag Mag 236; Rambunctious Review 237; Rant 237; Re Arts & Letters [REAL] 238; Renegade 240; Response 240; River Styx 242; RiverSedge 242; Riverwind 242; Salt Lick Press 245; Sanskrit 246; Seattle Review, The 247; Semiotext(e) 247; Shattered Wig Review 250; Shift Magazine 250; Side Show 251; Silence, The 253; Sing Heavenly Muse! 256; Sinister Wisdom 256; Skipping Stones 256; Skylark 257; Slate, The 257; Slightly West 258; Snake Nation Review 259; So To Speak 259; Southern California Anthology 261; Southern Exposure 261; Southern Humanities Review 261; Spirit Magazine 263; Spout 264; SPSM&H 264; Street Beat Quarterly 267; Struggle 267; Suffusion Magazine 268; Sulphur River Literary Review 268; Tamaqua 271; Texture 273; This Magazine 274; Timber Creek Review 275; Troika Magazine 279; Unforgettable Fire, The 280; Uno Mas Magazine 280; Urbanus/Raizirr 281; Venus Magazine 282; Videomania 282; Vignette 283; Vincent Brothers Review, The 283; Virginia Quarterly Review 284; Vox 284; Welter 285; West Coast Line 286; West Wind Review 286; Women's Work 292; Wordplay 293; Words of Wisdom 293; Writes of Passage 295; Writing for Our Lives 295; Xib 296; Yellow Silk 297; Zephyr 299; Zero Hour 299; Zuzu's Petals Annual 299

Gay. A.R.T. 74; ACM, (Another Chicago Magazine) 76; Adrift 77; African American Review 77; Allegheny Review 81; Amelia 82; Amherst Review, The 83; Anarchy 83; Aphrodite Gone Berserk 85; Arnazella 86; artisan 87; SPSM&H 264; Art:Mag 87; Asian Pacific Journal 88;

Backspace 90; Bahlasti Papers 90; Beneath The Surface 92; Black Fire 94; Blackstone Circular, The 96; Blue Mesa Review 97; Blue Penny Quarterly, The 98; Bohemian Chronicle 99; Brave New Tick, (the) 101; Brownbag Press 102; Brownstone Review, The 103; Brújula/Compass 103; Brutarian 103; Changing Men 108; Crazyquilt 118; Crucible 119; Disturbed Guillotine 125; DJINNI 126; Dodobobo 126; Drinkin' Buddy Magazine, The 128; Earthsongs 128; Echoes 129; Entelechy 131; Evergreen Chronicles, The 132; Every So Often . . . 133; Expressions 134; Extreme, The 134; Feminist Studies 137; Filling Station 138; Fish Drum Magazine 139; Fish Stories 139; Flying Island, The 140; Frayed 141; Gathering of the Tribes, A 143; Gay Chicago Magazine 144; Glass Cherry, The 145; Hayden's Ferry Review 153; Hecate's Loom 154; Home Planet News 157; Illinois Review, The 159; It's Your Choice Magazine 163; Jacaranda 163; Jeopardy 165; Kennesaw Review 168; Kenyon Review, The 168; Left Bank 172; Liberty 173; Libido 173; Lime Green Bulldozers 174; Longneck, The 176; Lowell Pearl, The 178; Lynx Eye 179; Many Leaves One Tree 182; Many Mountains Moving 182; Matriarch's Way 183; Medicinal Purposes 184; Minnesota Review, The 188; Mobius 189; Mostly Maine 191; Musing Place, The 192; nerve 194; 96 Inc. 202; Northeast Arts Magazine 204; Onionhead 210; Orange Coast Review 210; Otisian Directory 212; Oxford Magazine 213; Pagan Review, The 214; Painted Bride Quarterly 215; PBW 218; Perceptions 220; Phoebe (NY) 221; Pica 221; Poskisnolt Press 227; Primavera 230; Psychotrain 232; Puck 233; Puckerbrush Review 233; RFD 241; River Styx 242; Salt Lick Press 245; Sanskrit 246; Seattle Review, The 247; Semiotext(e) 247; Sensations Magazine 248; Shadowdance 250; Shattered Wig Review 250; Shift Magazine 250; Side Show 251; Sign of the Times 252; Slightly West 258; Snake Nation Review 259; Southern Exposure 261; Spout 264; SPSM&H 264; Tamaqua 271; This Magazine 274; Troika Magazine 279; Unforgettable Fire, The 280; Uno Mas Magazine 280; Urbanus/Raizirr 281; Venus Magazine 282; Vignette 283; Vox 284; Welter 285; West Coast Line 286; West Wind Review 286; White Review, The James 289; Wilde Oaks 290; Writes of Passage 295; Xib 296; Yellow Silk 297; Zephyr 299; Zero Hour 299; Zuzu's Petals Annual 299

Historical. A.R.T. 74; Acorn Whistle 76; Allegheny Review 81; Amelia 82; Amherst Review, The 83; Anterior Fiction Quarterly 84; Appalachian Heritage 85; Ararat Quarterly 85; Arnazella 86; Art:Mag 87; Asian Pacific Journal 88; Atom Mind 89; Beneath The Surface 92; Big Sky Stories 92; Black Books Bulletin: WordsWork 93; Blackwater Review 96; Blue Mesa Review 97; BookLovers 99; Boy's Quest 101; Briar Cliff Review, The 101; Brownstone Review, The 103; Callaloo 105; Capers Aweigh Magazine 106; Century 107; Christian Courier 110; Chrysalis Reader 110; Climbing Art, The 112; Cochran's Corner 112; Compenions 114; Concho River Review 115; Crazyquilt 118; Dan River Anthology 121; DJINNI 126; Dodobobo 126; Downstate Story 126; Dream International/Quarterly 127; Drinkin' Buddy Magazine, The 128; Earthsongs 128; Echoes 129; Elf: Eclectic Literary Forum 130; Eureka Literary Magazine 132; Every So Often . . . 133; Expressions 134; FiberOptic Etchings 137; Fugue 142; Gathering of the Tribes, A 143; Gettysburg Review, The 144; Glass Cherry, The 145; Gotta Write Network Litmag 145; Hayden's Ferry Review 153; Hecate's Loom 154; Home Planet News 157; Housewife-Writer's Forum 158; i.e. Magazine 159; Iowa Woman 162; It's Your Choice Magazine 163; Jeopardy 165; Just Write 166; Kenyon Review, The 168; Lamplight, The 170; Left Curve 172; Lighthouse 174; Lime Green Bulldozers 174; Lite 175; Longneck, The 176; Loop, The 177; Lowell Pearl, The 178; Lynx Eye 179; MacGuffin, The 179; Mail Call 180; Many Mountains Moving 182; Medicinal Purposes 184; Mediphors 184; Merlyn's Pen 185; Midland Review 187; Mind Matters Review 187; Minnesota Review, The 188; Mobius 189; Mostly Maine 191; Musing Place, The 192; Mystic Fiction 193; Nassau Review 194; nerve 194; New Frontiers of New Mexico 196; New Methods 197; New Voices in Poetry and Prose 200; 96 Inc. 202; Nite-Writer's Literary Arts Journal 202; North Dakota Quarterly 204; Northeast Arts Magazine 204; Olympia Review, The 208; Oracle Story 210; Otisian Directory 212; Ouroboros 212; Pacific Coast Journal 214; Pagan Review, The 214; Palo Alto Review 215; Pink Chameleon, The 222; Pipe Smoker's Ephemeris, The 223; PKA's Advocate 223; Poetry Forum Short Stories 225; Portable Wall, The 226; Potpourri 228; Prairie Dog 229; Puck 233; Q Magazine 234; Queen's Quarterly 235; Raconteur 235; Rant 237; Re Arts & Letters [REAL] 238; Renegade 240; Renovated Lighthouse 240; Response 240; RiverSedge 242; Riverwind 242; Robin's Nest 243; Rock Falls Review 243; Rosebud™ 244; S.L.U.G.fest, Ltd. 245; Seattle Review, The 247; Sensations Magazine 248; Shift Magazine 250; Short Stuff Magazine for Grown-ups 251; Slate, The 257; Slightly West 258; Southern California Anthology 261; Spectrum (MA) 263; Spindrift 263; SPSM&H 264; Street Beat Quarterly 267; Struggle 267; Tampa Review 271; "Teak" Roundup 272; Texas Young

142; Full-Time Dads 143; G.W. Review, The 143; Gathering of the Tribes, A 143; Gettysburg Review, The 144; Gotta Write Network Litmag 145; Graffiti Off the Asylum Walls 146; Grasslands Review 147; Green Hills Literary Lantern, The 147; Green Mountains Review 148; Green's Magazine 148; Greg's Good Gazette 149; Happy 150; Hawaii Pacific Review 151; Hawaii Review 151; Hayden's Ferry Review 153; Heartlands Today, The 153; Hecate's Loom 154; High Plains Literary Review 155; Hill and Holler 155; hip MAMA 156; Home Girl Press 156; Hopewell Review, The 157; Housewife-Writer's Forum 158; i.e. Magazine 159; Iconoclast 159; International Quarterly 161; It's Your Choice Magazine 163; Jacaranda 163; Jambalaya Magazine 164; Jeopardy 165; Journal of Polymorphous Perversity 166; Just Write 166; Kennesaw Review 168; Kenyon Review, The 168; Kerem 168; Kinesis 169; Lamplight, The 170; Laughing Times 171; Left Bank 172; Legal Fiction 172; Liberty 173; Light Quarterly 173; Lighthouse 174; Lime Green Bulldozers 174; Lines In The Sand 174; Liquid Ohio 175; Lite 175; Literal Latté 175; Longneck, The 176; Loop, The 177; Lowell Pearl, The 178; Lynx Eye 179; MacGuffin, The 179; Many Leaves One Tree 182; Many Mountains Moving 182; Mark 183; Maryland Review, The 183; Matriarch's Way 183; Medicinal Purposes 184; Mediphors 184; Merlyn's Pen 185; Meshuggah 186; Mind in Motion 187; Mississippi Review 189; Mobius 189; Monolith Magazine 190; Monthly Independent Tribune Times Journal Post Gazette News Chronicle Bulletin, The 190; More Dead Trees 191; Mostly Maine 191; Mountain Luminary 191; Musing Place, The 192; Musk Gland Sally 192; Mystic Fiction 193; Nebraska Review, The 194; nerve 194; New Delta Review 195; New Frontiers of New Mexico 196; New Letters Magazine 197; New Press Literary Quarterly, The 197; new renaissance, the 199; New Voices in Poetry and Prose 200; 96 Inc. 202; Nocturnal Lyric, The 203; Nonsense 203; North Dakota Quarterly 204; Nuthouse 206; Oak, The 207; Office Number One 207; Olympia Review, The 208; Onionhead 210; Oracle Story 210; Orange Coast Review 210; Oregon East 211; Other Voices 211; Otisian Directory 212; Ouroboros 212; Owen Wister Review 212; Oxford Magazine 213; Pacific Coast Journal 214; Pagan Review, The 214; Palo Alto Review 215; Pangolin Papers 215; Paradox Magazine 216; Pearl 218; Pegasus Review, The 219; Perceptions 220; Phoebe (NY) 221; Pica 221; Pikeville Review 222; Pink Chameleon, The 222; Pipe Smoker's Ephemeris, The 223; PKA's Advocate 223; Place to Enter, A 223; Poor Katy's Almanac 226; Portable Wall, The 226; Portland Review 226; Poskisnolt Press 227; Possibilitiis Literary Arts Magazine 227; Potato Eyes 227; Potpourri 228; Prairie Dog 229; Primavera 230; Processed World 232; Psychotrain 232; Puck 233; Queen's Quarterly 235; Raconteur 235; RACS/Rent-A-Chicken Speaks 236; Ralph's Review 237; Rambunctious Review 237; Rant 237; Renegade 240; Report to Hell 240; Response 240; River Styx 242; Riverwind 242; Robin's Nest 243; Rock Falls Review 243; Rocket Press 243; Rockford Review, The 244; Rosebud™ 244; Ruby's Pearls 245; S.L.U.G.fest, Ltd. 245; Sanskrit 246; Seattle Review, The 247; Secret Alameda, The 247; Sensations Magazine 248; Shattered Wig Review 250; Shift Magazine 250; Short Stuff Magazine for Grown-ups 251; Side Show 251; Sidewalks 252; Skylark 257; Slate and Style 257; Slate, The 257; Slightly West 258; Slipstream 258; Snake Nation Review 259; South Carolina Review 260; Southern California Anthology 261; Southern Exposure 261; Southern Humanities Review 261; Spout 264; SPSM&H 264; Story 266; Street Beat Quarterly 267; Struggle 267; Sub-Terrain 268; Suffusion Magazine 268; Sulphur River Literary Review 268; Supernatural Magazine on Audiobook, The 269; Sycamore Review 270; Tamaqua 271; Tampa Review 271; "Teak" Roundup 272; Texas Young Writers' Newsletter 273; Thalia: Studies in Literary Humor 274; Thema 274; Thresholds Quarterly 275; Tickled By Thunder 275; Timber Creek Review 275; Time Pilot 276; Touchstone Literary Journal 276; Troika Magazine 279; Tucumcari Literary Review 279; 2 AM Magazine 279; Unforgettable Fire, The 280; Uno Mas Magazine 280; Urbanite, The 280; Urbanus/Raizirr 281; Venus Magazine 282; Verve 282; Videomania 282; Vignette 283; Villager, The 283; Vincent Brothers Review, The 283; Vintage Northwest 283; Virginia Quarterly Review 284; Voices West 284; Vox 284; Wascana Review of Contemporary Poetry and Short Fiction 284; Welter 285; West Wind Review 286; Western Pocket, The 287; Westview 287; Whisper 288; William and Mary Review, The 290; Wisconsin Academy Review 291; Women's Harpoon 292; Words of Wisdom 293; Writers' International Forum 294; Writes of Passage 295; Writing for Our Lives 295; Xib 296; Xtreme 296; Yarns and Such 297; Yellow Silk 297; Zero Hour 299; Zuzu's Petals Annual 299

Lesbian. A.R.T. 74; ACM, (Another Chicago Magazine) 76; Adrift 77; African American Review 77; Allegheny Review 81; Amelia 82; Amherst Review, The 83; Anarchy 83; Aphrodite Gone Berserk 85; Arnazella 86; artisan 87; SPSM&H 264; Art:Mag 87; Asian Pacific Journal 88; Backspace 90; Bahlasti Papers 90; Beneath The Surface 92; Black Lace 95; Blackstone

139; Flipside 139; Florida Review, The 139; Flying Island, The 140; Folio: A Literary Journal 140; Frayed 141; Free Focus/Ostentatious Mind 141; Fuel Magazine 142; Fugue 142; Full-Time Dads 143; G.W. Review, The 143; Gathering of the Tribes, A 143; Georgetown Review 144; Georgia Review, The 144; Gettysburg Review, The 144; Glass Cherry, The 145; Glimmer Train Stories 145; Gotta Write Network Litmag 145; Grain 146; Grand Street 146; Grasslands Review 147; Green Hills Literary Lantern, The 147; Green Mountains Review 148; Green's Magazine 148; Greensboro Review 148; Gulf Coast 149; Gulf Stream Magazine 149; Habersham Review 150; Happy 150; Hawaii Pacific Review 151; Hawaii Review 151; Hayden's Ferry Review 153; Heartlands Today, The 153; Heaven Bone 153; Hecate's Loom 154; High Plains Literary Review 155; Hill and Holler 155; hip MAMA 156; Home Girl Press 156; Home Planet News 157; Hopewell Review, The 157; Housewife-Writer's Forum 158; Hunted News, The 158; i.e. Magazine 159; Iconoclast, The 159; Illinois Review, The 159; Indiana Review 160; International Quarterly 161; Iowa Review, The 162; Iowa Woman 162; Iris 162; Italian Americana 163; Jacaranda 163; Jack Mackerel Magazine 163; Jambalaya Magazine 164; Janus, A Journal of Literature 164; Jeopardy 165; Just Write 166; Kaleidoscope 166; Kalliope 167; Karma Lapel 167; Kelsey Review 167; Kennesaw Review 168; Kenyon Review, The 168; Kerem 168; Kestrel 168; Kinesis 169; Kiosk 169; Lactuca 169; Lacunae 170; Lamplight, The 170; Lamp-Post, The 171; Laurel Review, The 171; Ledge Poetry and Fiction Magazine, The 171; Left Bank 172; Left Curve 172; Legal Fiction 172; Liberty 173; Light Quarterly 173; Lime Green Bulldozers 174; Limestone: A Literary Journal 174; Lines In The Sand 174; Liquid Ohio 175; Lite 175; Literal Latté 175; Literary Review, The 176; Longneck, The 176; Loonfeather 177; Lost and Found Times 177; Louisiana Literature 178; Louisville Review, The 178; Lowell Pearl, The 178; Lynx Eye 179; MacGuffin, The 179; Magic Changes 180; Magic Realism 180; Mangrove 181; Manoa 182; Many Leaves One Tree 182; Many Mountains Moving 182; Mark 183; Maryland Review, The 183; Matriarch's Way 183; Maverick Press, The 184; Medicinal Purposes 184; Mediphors 184; Men As We Are 185; Merlyn's Pen 185; Michigan Quarterly Review 186; Mid-American Review 186; Midland Review 187; Mind in Motion 187; Mind Matters Review 187; Mink Hills Journal 188; Minnesota Review, The 188; Minority Literary Expo 189; Mississippi Review 189; Missouri Review, The 189; Mobius 189; Mostly Maine 191; Musing Place, The 192; Musk Gland Sally 192; Mystic Fiction 193; Nassau Review 194; Nebo 194; Nebraska Review, The 194; nerve 194; New Delta Review 195; New England Review 195; New Frontiers of New Mexico 196; New Laurel Review 196; New Letters Magazine 197; New Orleans Review 197; New Quarterly, The 197; new renaissance, the 199; New Voices in Poetry and Prose 200; Nexus 201; 96 Inc. 202; Nite-Writer's Literary Arts Journal 202; North American Review, The 204; North Dakota Quarterly 204; Northeast Arts Magazine 204; Northeast Corridor 205; Northern Contours 205; Northwest Review 205; Northwoods Journal 206; Oasis 207; Office Number One 207; Ogalala Review, The 208; Ohio Review, The 208; Old Crow Review 208; Old Red Kimono, The 208; Olympia Review, The 208; One Hundred Suns 210; Onionhead 210; Oracle Story 210; Orange Coast Review 210; Oregon East 211; Other Voices 211; Otisian Directory 212; Ouroboros 212; Outerbridge 212; Owen Wister Review 212; Oxford Magazine 213; Oxygen 213; Pacific Coast Journal 214; Pagan Review, The 214; Painted Bride Quarterly 215; Palo Alto Review 215; Pangolin Papers 215; Paradox Magazine 216; Paris Review, The 217; Parting Gifts 217; Partisan Review 217; PBW 218; Pearl 218; Pegasus Review, The 219; Pennsylvania English 219; Pequod 219; Perception Writings 220; Phoebe (NY) 221; Pica 221; Pig Iron 222; Pikeville Review 222; Pink Chameleon, The 222; Pipe Smoker's Ephemeris, The 223; PKA's Advocate 223; Place to Enter, A 223; Pléiades Magazine/Philae 224; Ploughshares 224; Poetry Forum Short Stories 225; Poetry WLU 225; Pointed Circle, The 225; Poor Katy's Almanac 226; Portable Wall, The 226; Porter International, Bern 226; Portland Review 226; Poskisnolt Press 227; Possibilitiis Literary Arts Magazine 227; Potato Eyes 227; Potomac Review 228; Potpourri 228; Prairie Dog 229; Prairie Fire 229; Prairie Journal of Canadian Literature, The 230; Primavera 230; Prism International 231; Processed World 232; Psychotrain 232; Puck 233; Puckerbrush Review 233; Puerto Del Sol 233; Quarry 234; Quarterly, The 235; Quarterly West 235; Queen's Quarterly 235; Raconteur 235; RACS/Rent-A-Chicken Speaks 236; Rag Mag 236; Ralph's Review 237; Rambunctious Review 237; Raven Chronicles, The 238; Raw Fiction 238; Red Cedar Review 239; Renegade 240; Renovated Lighthouse 240; Report to Hell 240; Response 240; Review: Latin American Literature and Arts 241; River Styx 242; RiverSedge 242; Riverwind 242; Robin's Nest 243; Rocket Press 243; Rockford Review, The 244; Rosebud™ 244; S.L.U.G.fest, Ltd. 245; Salt Lick Press 245; Samsara 245; Sanskrit 246; Santa Barbara Review 246; Scorpio Moon 246; Screaming

Mainstream. A.R.T. 74; ACM, (Another Chicago Magazine) 76; Acorn Whistle 76; ACTA Victoriana 76; Adrift 77; African American Review 77; Aguilar Expression, The 80; Alabama Literary Review 80; Alaska Quarterly Review 81; Allegheny Review 81; Amateur Writers Journal 82; Amelia 82; American Literary Review 82; Americas Review, The 83; Amherst Review, The 83; Anterior Fiction Quarterly 84; Antietam Review 84; Antigonish Review, The 84; Antioch Review 85; Ararat Quarterly 85; Arnazella 86; artisan 87; SPSM&H 264; Art:Mag 87; Ascending Shadows 88; Asian Pacific Journal 88; Atom Mind 89; Aura Literary/Arts Review 89; Azorean Express, The 89; Belletrist Review, The 91; Bellowing Ark 91; Beloit Fiction Journal 92; Black Hammock Review, The 94; Black Jack 95; Black River Review 95; Black Warrior Review 96; Blue Mesa Review 97; Blue Penny Quarterly, The 98; Blue Water Review, The 98; Blueline 98; BookLovers 99; Boston Literary Review (BLuR) 99; Boulevard 100; Briar Cliff Review, The 101; Bridge, The 102; Brownstone Review, The 103; Brújula/Compass 103; Brutarian 103; Cafe Magazine 104; Callaloo 105; Calliope 105; Capers Aweigh Magazine 106; Carousel Literary Arts Magazine 106; Cat's Ear 107; Century 107; Changing Men 108; Chariton Review, The 108; Chattahoochee Review, The 108; Chicago Review 109; Chiron Review 110; Chrysalis Reader 110; Cimarron Review 111; Cimmerian-Journal, The 111; Climbing Art, The 112; Clockwatch Review 112; Collages and Bricolages 113; Compenions 114; Concho River Review 115; Confluence 115; Confrontation 116; Corona 116; Crazyquilt 118; Crucible 119; Dan River Anthology 121; Daughters of Nyx 122; Descant (Ontario) 124; Descant (Texas) 124; DJINNI 126; Dogwood Tales Magazine 126; Downstate Story 126; Dream Forge 127; Dream International/Quarterly 127; Dreams & Visions 128; Drinkin' Buddy Magazine, The 128; Eagle's Flight 128; Earthsongs 128; Echoes 129; 1812 130; Elephant-Ear, The 130; Elf: Eclectic Literary Forum 130; Emrys Journal 131; Epoch Magazine 131; Eureka Literary Magazine 132; Event 132; Every So Often . . . 133; Excursus 133; Explorer Magazine 134; Expressions 134; Eyes 134; Farmer's Market, The 135; Feminist Studies 137; FiberOptic Etchings 137; Fiction 137; Filling Station 138; Fish Drum Magazine 139; Flipside 139; Florida Review, The 139; Flying Island, The 140; Folio: A Literary Journal 140; Free Focus/Ostentatious Mind 141; Fugue 142; Full-Time Dads 143; G.W. Review, The 143; Gathering of the Tribes, A 143; Gettysburg Review, The 144; Glass Cherry, The 145; Gotta Write Network Litmag 145; Grain 146; Grasslands Review 147; Green Hills Literary Lantern, The 147; Green Mountains Review 148; Green's Magazine 148; Greensboro Review 148; Gulf Stream Magazine 149; Habersham Review 150; Hawaii Pacific Review 151; Hawaii Review 151; Hayden's Ferry Review 153; Heartlands Today, The 153; Hecate's Loom

154; High Plains Literary Review 155; Hill and Holler 155; hip MAMA 156; Home Girl Press 156; Home Planet News 157; Hopewell Review, The 157; Housewife-Writer's Forum 158; Hunted News, The 158; i.e. Magazine 159; Iconoclast, The 159; Illinois Review, The 159; International Quarterly 161; Iris 162; Jacaranda 163; Jambalaya Magazine 164; Janus, A Journal of Literature 164; Jeopardy 165; Journal, The 165; Just Write 166; Kennesaw Review 168; Kenyon Review, The 168; Kestrel 168; Kinesis 169; Lactuca 169; Lacunae 170; Laurel Review, The 171; Left Bank 172; Left Curve 172; Legal Fiction 172; Liberty 173; Lighthouse 174; Lime Green Bulldozers 174; Limestone: A Literary Journal 174; Lines In The Sand 174; Longneck, The 176; Loop, The 177; Lost and Found Times 177; Louisiana Literature 178; Louisville Review, The 178; Lowell Pearl, The 178; Lynx Eye 179; MacGuffin, The 179; Mangrove 181; Manoa 182; Many Leaves One Tree 182; Many Mountains Moving 182; Mark 183; Maryland Review, The 183; Maverick Press, The 184; Medicinal Purposes 184; Mediphors 184; Men As We Are 185; Merlyn's Pen 185; Mississippi Review 189; Missouri Review, The 189; Mobius 189; More Dead Trees 191; Mostly Maine 191; Musing Place, The 192; Mystic Fiction 193; Nassau Review 194; Nebo 194; Nebraska Review, The 194; nerve 194; New Delta Review 195; New Frontiers of New Mexico 196; New Laurel Review 196; New Letters Magazine 197; New Methods 197; New Orleans Review 197; New Press Literary Quarterly, The 197; New Voices in Poetry and Prose 200; Nexus 201; Nite-Writer's Literary Arts Journal 202; North Atlantic Review 204; North Dakota Quarterly 204; Northern Contours 205; Northwest Review 205; Northwoods Journal 206; Oak, The 207; Ogalala Review, The 208; Ohio Review, The 208; Old Crow Review 208; Olympia Review, The 208; Onionhead 210; Oracle Story 210; Orange Coast Review 210; Other Voices 211; Ouroboros 212; Oxygen 213; Pagan Review, The 214; Painted Bride Quarterly 215; Palo Alto Review 215; Partisan Review 217; Pearl 218; Pennsylvania English 219; Pequod 219; Phantasm Ca 220; Phantasm II 221; Pikeville Review 222; Pink Chameleon, The 222; PKA's Advocate 223; Place to Enter, A 223; Poetry Forum Short Stories 225; Pointed Circle, The 225; Portable Wall, The 226; Portland Review 226; Poskisnolt Press 227; Possibilitiis Literary Arts Magazine 227; Potato Eyes 227; Potomac Review 228; Potpourri 228; Prairie Dog 229; Prairie Fire 229; Prairie Journal of Canadian Literature, The 230; Primavera 230; Prism International 231; Processed World 232; Puerto Del Sol 233; Pulphouse 233; Quarterly West 235; Queen's Quarterly 235; Raconteur 235; Rag Mag 236; Rambunctious Review 237; Raw Fiction 238; Re Arts & Letters [REAL] 238; Redneck Review of Literature, The 239; Renegade 240; Renovated Lighthouse 240; Response 240; River Styx 242; RiverSedge 242; Riverwind 242; Robin's Nest 243; Rock Falls Review 243; Rosebud™ 244; Round Table, The 244; Ruby's Pearls 245; S.L.U.G-.fest, Ltd. 245; Salt Lick Press 245; Samsara 245; Sanskrit 246; Scorpio Moon 246; Screaming Toad 246; Seattle Review, The 247; Sewanee Review, The 248; Shattered Wig Review 250; Shift Magazine 250; Short Stories Bimonthly 251; Short Stuff Magazine for Grown-ups 251; Side Show 251; Sidewalks 252; Sierra Nevada College Review 252; Silence, The 253; Siren, The 256; Skylark 257; Slate and Style 257; Slate, The 257; Slightly West 258; Slipstream 258; Snake Nation Review 259; So To Speak 259; Soft Door, The 260; Soundings East 260; South Carolina Review 260; South Dakota Review 261; Southern California Anthology 261; Southern Exposure 261; Southern Review, The 262; Spectrum (MA) 263; Spindrift 263; SPSM&H 264; Square 265; Square One 265; Story 266; Street Beat Quarterly 267; Stroker Magazine 267; Struggle 267; Suffusion Magazine 268; Sulphur River Literary Review 268; Supernatural Magazine on Audiobook, The 269; Sycamore Review 270; Tamaqua 271; Tampa Review 271; "Teak" Roundup 272; Texas Review, The 273; Texas Young Writers' Newsletter 273; Thema 274; This Magazine 274; Tickled By Thunder 275; Timber Creek Review 275; Touchstone Literary Journal 276; Trekker News & Views, The 278; Triquarterly 278; Troika Magazine 279; Tucumcari Literary Review 279; Unmuzzled Ox 280; Uno Mas Magazine 280; Urbanus/Raizirr 281; Valley Grapevine 281; Venus Magazine 282; Verve 282; Videomania 282; Vignette 283; Vincent Brothers Review, The 283; Virginia Quarterly Review 284; Voices West 284; West Branch 286; West Wind Review 286; Westview 287; Whetstone 287; Whisper 288; Whispering Pines Quarterly 288; Widener Review 289; William and Mary Review, The 290; Wind Magazine 291; Wisconsin Academy Review 291; Wordplay 293; Words of Wisdom 293; Writers' Forum 294; Writers' International Forum 294; Writes of Passage 295; Writing on the Wall, The 296; Xavier Review 296; Xtreme 296; Zyzzyva 300

Mystery/Suspense. A.R.T. 74; Aguilar Expression, The 80; Allegheny Review 81; Amateur Writers Journal 82; Amelia 82; Amherst Review, The 83; Anterior Fiction Quarterly 84; Arnazella 86; artisan 87; SPSM&H 264; Art:Mag 87; Ascending Shadows 88; Belletrist Review, The 91;

From the publishers of <u>Writer's</u> <u>Digest</u> and
Novel *and* *Short* *Story* *Writer's* *Market*

Go One-On-One
With a Published Author

Are you serious about learning to write better? Getting published? Getting paid for what you write? If you're dedicated to your writing, **Writer's Digest School** can put you on the fast track to writing success.

You'll Study With A Professional

Writer's Digest School offers you more than textbooks and assignments. As a student you'll correspond <u>directly with a professional writer</u> who is currently writing **and selling** the kind of material you want to write. You'll learn from a pro who knows from personal experience what it takes to get a manuscript written and published. A writer who can guide you as you work to achieve the same thing. A true mentor.

Work On Your Novel, Short Story, Nonfiction Book, Or Article

Writer's Digest School offers five courses: The Novel Writing Workshop, the Nonfiction Book Workshop, Writing & Selling Short Stories, Writing & Selling Nonfiction Articles and The Secrets of Selling Your Manuscripts. Or, you can put a polish on an existing manuscript with a professional critique from the Writer's Digest Criticism Service. Each course is described on the reverse side.

If you're serious about your writing, you owe it to yourself to check out **Writer's Digest School**. Mail the coupon below today for FREE information! Or call **1-800-759-0963**. (Outside the U.S., call (513) 531-2690.) Writer's Digest School, 1507 Dana Avenue, Cincinnati, Ohio 45207-1005.

Reg. #73-0409H

There are five **Writer's Digest School** courses to help you write better and sell more:

Novel Writing Workshop. A professional novelist helps you iron out your plot, develop your main characters, write the background for your novel, and complete the opening scene and a summary of your novel's complete story. You'll even identify potential publishers and write a query letter.

Nonfiction Book Workshop. You'll work with your mentor to create a book proposal that you can send directly to a publisher. You'll develop and refine your book idea, write a chapter-by-chapter outline of your subject, line up your sources of information, write sample chapters, and complete your query letter.

Writing & Selling Short Stories. Learn the basics of writing/selling short stories: plotting, characterization, dialogue, theme, conflict, and other elements of a marketable short story. Course includes writing assignments and one complete short story.

Writing & Selling Nonfiction Articles. Master the fundamentals of writing/selling nonfiction articles: finding article ideas, conducting interviews, writing effective query letters and attention-getting leads, targeting your articles to the right publication. Course includes writing assignments and one complete article manuscript (and its revision).

Secrets of Selling Your Manuscripts. Discover all the best-kept secrets for mailing out strategic, targeted manuscript submissions. Learn how to "slant" your writing so you can publish the same material over and over, which publishing houses are your best bet, and much more.

Writer's Digest Criticism Service. Give your manuscript the extra edge it needs in today's competitive publishing marketplace. A published writer will offer constructive criticism, advice and tips on articles, stories, books, poetry, novelettes, screenplays, query letters.

Mail this card today for **FREE** information!

NO POSTAGE
NECESSARY
IF MAILED
IN THE
UNITED STATES

BUSINESS REPLY MAIL
FIRST CLASS MAIL   PERMIT NO. 17   CINCINNATI, OHIO
POSTAGE WILL BE PAID BY ADDRESSEE

Writer's Digest School
1507 DANA AVENUE
CINCINNATI OH 45207-9965

Beneath The Surface 92; Blue Water Review, The 98; Bohemian Chronicle 99; BookLovers 99; Brownstone Review, The 103; Brutarian 103; Capers Aweigh Magazine 106; Chrysalis Reader 110; Climbing Art, The 112; Cochran's Corner 112; Compenions 114; Confluence 115; Crazyquilt 118; Dagger of the Mind 119; Dan River Anthology 121; Dead of Night™ Magazine 123; DJINNI 126; Dodobobo 126; Dogwood Tales Magazine 126; Downstate Story 126; Dream International/ Quarterly 127; Drinkin' Buddy Magazine, The 128; Eagle's Flight 128; Echoes 129; 8, Dancing with Mr. D 129; Elf: Eclectic Literary Forum 130; Eureka Literary Magazine 132; Every So Often . . . 133; Excursus 133; Expressions 134; Extreme, The 134; FiberOptic Etchings 137; Flying Island, The 140; Free Focus/Ostentatious Mind 141; Fugue 142; Full Clip: A Magazine of Mystery & Suspense 142; Grasslands Review 147; Green's Magazine 148; Hardboiled 150; Heroic Times 155; Housewife-Writer's Forum 158; i.e. Magazine 159; It's Your Choice Magazine 163; Jacaranda 163; Just Write 166; Lacunae 170; Lamplight, The 170; Liberty 173; Lighthouse 174; Lime Green Bulldozers 174; Lines In The Sand 174; Liquid Ohio 175; Lite 175; Longneck, The 176; Loop, The 177; Lynx Eye 179; Medicinal Purposes 184; Merlyn's Pen 185; Monolith Magazine 190; Monthly Independent Tribune Times Journal Post Gazette News Chronicle Bulletin, The 190; Musing Place, The 192; Mystery Time 192; Mystic Fiction 193; Naked Kiss 193; New Press Literary Quarterly, The 197; New Voices in Poetry and Prose 200; Northeast Arts Magazine 204; Northwoods Journal 206; Oak, The 207; Oracle Story 210; Ouroboros 212; Pagan Review, The 214; Palo Alto Review 215; Pink Chameleon, The 222; Pirate Writings 223; PKA's Advocate 223; Place to Enter, A 223; Pléiades Magazine/Philae 224; Poetry Forum Short Stories 225; Poor Katy's Almanac 226; Possibilitiis Literary Arts Magazine 227; Post, The 227; Potpourri 228; PSI 232; Pulphouse 233; Raconteur 235; Red Herring Mystery Magazine 239; Renegade 240; Robin's Nest 243; Rock Falls Review 243; Ruby's Pearls 245; Seattle Review, The 247; Sensations Magazine 248; Short Stuff Magazine for Grown-ups 251; Skylark 257; Snake Nation Review 259; SPSM&H 264; Square One 265; Street Beat Quarterly 267; Struggle 267; Suffusion Magazine 268; Supernatural Magazine on Audiobook, The 269; "Teak" Roundup 272; Texas Young Writers' Newsletter 273; Thema 274; Tickled By Thunder 275; Timber Creek Review 275; Tribute To Officer Dallies 278; Troika Magazine 279; Tucumcari Literary Review 279; 2 AM Magazine 279; Venus Magazine 282; Villager, The 283; Vincent Brothers Review, The 283; Vintage Northwest 283; West Wind Review 286; Whisper 288; Whispering Pines Quarterly 288; Wordplay 293; Words of Wisdom 293; Writers' International Forum 294; Writes of Passage 295; Yarns and Such 297

New Age/Mystic/Spiritual. Chrysalis Reader 110; Merlana's Magickal Messages 185; New Frontier 196; Renovated Lighthouse 240; Skylark 257

Psychic/Supernatural/Occult. A.R.T. 74; Abyss Magazine 75; Allegheny Review 81; Amherst Review, The 83; Anterior Fiction Quarterly 84; artisan 87; SPSM&H 264; Art:Mag 87; Ascending Shadows 88; Bahlasti Papers 90; Beneath The Surface 92; Black Hammock Review, The 94; Bohemian Chronicle 99; Brownbag Press 102; Brutarian 103; Capers Aweigh Magazine 106; Cat's Ear 107; Century 107; Cimmerian-Journal, The 111; Compenions 114; Crossroads 118; Dan River Anthology 121; Dark Kiss 122; Daughters of Nyx 122; Dead of Night™ Magazine 123; Deathrealm 123; DJINNI 126; Dodobobo 126; Downstate Story 126; Dream International/ Quarterly 127; Drinkin' Buddy Magazine, The 128; Earthsongs 128; 8, Dancing with Mr. D 129; Eldritch Tales 130; Eureka Literary Magazine 132; Every So Often . . . 133; Expressions 134; Fat Tuesday 135; FiberOptic Etchings 137; Flying Island, The 140; Frayed 141; Free Focus/ Ostentatious Mind 141; Galaxy Magazine 143; Green Egg/How About Magic? 147; Grue Magazine 149; Happy 150; Haunts 151; Hayden's Ferry Review 153; Heaven Bone 153; Hecate's Loom 154; Intuitive Explorations 162; It's Your Choice Magazine 163; Lacunae 170; Lime Green Bulldozers 174; Lite 175; Longneck, The 176; Lost Worlds 177; MacGuffin, The 179; Matriarch's Way 183; Medicinal Purposes 184; Monolith Magazine 190; Monthly Independent Tribune Times Journal Post Gazette News Chronicle Bulletin, The 190; More Dead Trees 191; Mysterious Wysteria 192; Mystic Fiction 193; New Voices in Poetry and Prose 200; Night Shadows 201; Nightmares 201; Nocturnal Lyric, The 203; Northwoods Journal 206; Northwords 206; Office Number One 207; Old Crow Review 208; Otisian Directory 212; Ouroboros 212; Pagan Review, The 214; Paradox Magazine 216; Perceptions 220; Poskisnolt Press 227; Psychotrain 232; Puck 233; Quanta 234; Raconteur 235; Ralph's Review 237; Rant 237; Renegade 240; Report to Hell 240; Robin's Nest 243; Rosebud™ 244; S.L.U.G.fest, Ltd. 245; Scorpio Moon 246; Screaming Toad Press 246; Seattle Review, The 247; Semiotext(e) 247; Shadowdance 250; Shattered Wig

Review 250; Snake Nation Review 259; Spout 264; Supernatural Magazine on Audiobook, The 269; Surprise Me 269; Terminal Fright 272; Thema 274; Thresholds Quarterly 275; Tickled By Thunder 275; Trekker News & Views, The 278; Troika Magazine 279; Twisted 279; 2 AM Magazine 279; Urbanite, The 280; Venus Magazine 282; Vignette 283; Vox 284; Weirdbook 285; West Wind Review 286; Wicked Mystic 289; W!dow of the Orch!d, The 289; Worlds of Fantasy & Horror 293; Writers' International Forum 294; Writes of Passage 295; Xib 296; Zero Hour 299

Regional. A.R.T. 74; Above the Bridge 75; Acorn Whistle 76; Allegheny Review 81; Amelia 82; Amherst Review, The 83; Anterior Fiction Quarterly 84; Appalachian Heritage 85; Arnazella 86; Artemis 86; Art:Mag 87; Asian Pacific Journal 88; Aura Literary/Arts Review 89; Azorean Express, The 89; Bamboo Ridge 90; Belletrist Review, The 91; Black Hammock Review, The 94; Blackwater Review 96; Blue Mesa Review 97; Blue Penny Quarterly, The 98; Blue Water Review, The 98; Blueline 98; BookLovers 99; Briar Cliff Review, The 101; Bridge, The 102; Brownstone Review, The 103; Burning Light 103; Callaloo 105; Canadian Author 106; Capers Aweigh Magazine 106; Cayo 107; Chaminade Literary Review 107; Climbing Art, The 112; Clockwatch Review 112; Compenions 114; Concho River Review 115; Confluence 115; Confrontation 116; Corona 116; Cream City Review, The 118; Crucible 119; Dan River Anthology 121; Descant (Texas) 124; DJINNI 126; Dodobobo 126; Downstate Story 126; Drinkin' Buddy Magazine, The 128; Earthsongs 128; Echoes 129; Elephant-Ear, The 130; Elf: Eclectic Literary Forum 130; Emrys Journal 131; Entelechy 131; Eureka Literary Magazine 132; Event 132; Every So Often . . . 133; Excursus 133; Expressions 134; Farmer's Market, The 135; FiberOptic Etchings 137; Filling Station 138; Fish Drum Magazine 139; Fish Stories 139; Fugue 142; Gettysburg Review, The 144; Grasslands Review 147; Green Hills Literary Lantern, The 147; Gulf Coast 149; Habersham Review 150; Hawaii Pacific Review 151; Hawaii Review 151; Hayden's Ferry Review 153; Heartlands Today, The 153; Heaven Bone 153; High Plains Literary Review 155; Hill and Holler 155; Home Girl Press 156; Hopewell Review, The 157; International Quarterly 161; Iowa Woman 162; It's Your Choice Magazine 163; Jambalaya Magazine 164; Japanophile 164; Jeopardy 165; Kennesaw Review 168; Kestrel 168; Kinesis 169; Lactuca 169; Left Bank 172; Left Curve 172; Lighthouse 174; Liquid Ohio 175; Longneck, The 176; Loonfeather 177; Loop, The 177; Louisiana Literature 178; Lowell Pearl, The 178; Mangrove 181; Manoa 182; Mark 183; Matriarch's Way 183; Medicinal Purposes 184; Men As We Are 185; Midland Review 187; Mink Hills Journal 188; Mostly Maine 191; Musing Place, The 192; nerve 194; New Frontiers of New Mexico 196; New Methods 197; New Voices in Poetry and Prose 200; NeWest Review 200; Nexus 201; Northern Contours 205; Northwoods Journal 206; Old Crow Review 208; Olympia Review, The 208; Onionhead 210; Oregon East 211; Otisian Directory 212; Oxford American, The 213; Palo Alto Review 215; Partisan Review 217; Pikeville Review 222; PKA's Advocate 223; Place to Enter, A 223; Pointed Circle, The 225; Portable Wall, The 226; Portland Review 226; Potato Eyes 227; Prairie Dog 229; Prairie Journal of Canadian Literature, The 230; Puck 233; Rag Mag 236; Raven Chronicles, The 238; Re Arts & Letters [REAL] 238; Response 240; RiverSedge 242; Riverwind 242; Robin's Nest 243; Rock Falls Review 243; Rockford Review, The 244; Rosebud™ 244; S.L.U.G.fest, Ltd. 245; Sanskrit 246; Seattle Review, The 247; Shattered Wig Review 250; Shift Magazine 250; Short Stuff Magazine for Grown-ups 251; Sidewalks 252; Sierra Nevada College Review 252; Siren, The 256; Skylark 257; Slate, The 257; Slightly West 258; Snake Nation Review 259; So To Speak 259; South Dakota Review 261; Southern California Anthology 261; Southern Exposure 261; Southern Humanities Review 261; Spindrift 263; Spirit Magazine 263; Spout 264; SPSM&H 264; Struggle 267; Suffusion Magazine 268; Sycamore Review 270; Tamaqua 271; "Teak" Roundup 272; Thema 274; This Magazine 274; Timber Creek Review 275; Troika Magazine 279; Tucumcari Literary Review 279; Valley Grapevine 281; Venus Magazine 282; Vignette 283; Vincent Brothers Review, The 283; Voices West 284; West Wind Review 286; Western Pocket, The 287; Widener Review 289; Wisconsin Academy Review 291; Words of Wisdom 293; Writers' Forum 294; Writers' International Forum 294; Writes of Passage 295; Xavier Review 296; Xib 296; Yarns and Such 297; Zuzu's Petals Annual 299; Zyzzyva 300

Religious/Inspirational. A.R.T. 74; Allegheny Review 81; Amateur Writers Journal 82; Ararat Quarterly 85; Beloit Fiction Journal 92; Chaminade Literary Review 107; Christian Courier 110; Cochran's Corner 112; Dreams & Visions 128; Echoes 129; Every So Often . . . 133; Explorer Magazine 134; Expressions 134; Full-Time Dads 143; Heaven Bone 153; Hecate's

Loom 154; Intuitive Explorations 162; Kerem 168; Liquid Ohio 175; Loop, The 177; manna 181; Many Leaves One Tree 182; Ministry Today 188; Miraculous Medal, The 189; New Voices in Poetry and Prose 200; Nite-Writer's Literary Arts Journal 202; Otisian Directory 212; Oxygen 213; Pagan Review, The 214; Paradox Magazine 216; Pegasus Review, The 219; Pink Chameleon, The 222; Poetry Forum Short Stories 225; Puck 233; Queen of All Hearts 235; Renegade 240; Response 240; Riverwind 242; Robin's Nest 243; Rock Falls Review 243; S.L.U.G.fest, Ltd. 245; Skipping Stones 256; Skylark 257; Spirit Magazine 263; Surprise Me 269; "Teak" Roundup 272; Thresholds Quarterly 275; Tickled By Thunder 275; Troika Magazine 279; West Wind Review 286; Writes of Passage 295; Xavier Review 296; Young Judaean 297

Romance. A.R.T. 74; Aguilar Expression, The 80; Amateur Writers Journal 82; Amherst Review, The 83; Anterior Fiction Quarterly 84; Ascending Shadows 88; Aura Literary/Arts Review 89; Bohemian Chronicle 99; BookLovers 99; Cochran's Corner 112; Compenions 114; Dan River Anthology 121; Dogwood Tales Magazine 126; Downstate Story 126; Dream International/Quarterly 127; Drinkin' Buddy Magazine, The 128; Eagle's Flight 128; Echoes 129; Eureka Literary Magazine 132; Every So Often . . . 133; Explorer Magazine 134; Expressions 134; Eyes 134; FiberOptic Etchings 137; Frayed 141; Fugue 142; Gathering of the Tribes, A 143; Gay Chicago Magazine 144; Gotta Write Network Litmag 145; Hayden's Ferry Review 153; Hecate's Loom 154; Home Girl Press 156; Housewife-Writer's Forum 158; i.e. Magazine 159; Jeopardy 165; Lamplight, The 170; Lighthouse 174; Loop, The 177; Lynx Eye 179; Many Leaves One Tree 182; Matriarch's Way 183; Medicinal Purposes 184; Merlyn's Pen 185; Musing Place, The 192; Mysterious Wysteria 192; New Voices in Poetry and Prose 200; Nite-Writer's Literary Arts Journal 202; Northwoods Journal 206; Otisian Directory 212; Palo Alto Review 215; Peoplenet 219; Pink Chameleon, The 222; PKA's Advocate 223; Place to Enter, A 223; Poetry Forum Short Stories 225; Poskisnolt Press 227; Possibilitiis Literary Arts Magazine 227; Post, The 227; Potpourri 228; PSI 232; Pulphouse 233; Raconteur 235; Ralph's Review 237; Renegade 240; Robin's Nest 243; Rock Falls Review 243; Rosebud™ 244; Scorpio Moon 246; Short Stuff Magazine for Grown-ups 251; Skylark 257; SPSM&H 264; Supernatural Magazine on Audiobook, The 269; Surprise Me 269; "Teak" Roundup 272; Texas Young Writers' Newsletter 273; Trekker News & Views, The 278; Troika Magazine 279; 2 AM Magazine 279; Villager, The 283; Virginia Quarterly Review 284; West Wind Review 286; Writers' International Forum 294; Writes of Passage 295

Science Fiction. A.R.T. 74; Abrupt Edge 75; Absolute Magnitude 75; Abyss Magazine 75; Alabama Literary Review 80; Allegheny Review 81; Amateur Writers Journal 82; Amelia 82; Anarchy 83; artisan 87; SPSM&H 264; Art:Mag 87; Ascending Shadows 88; Aura Literary/Arts Review 89; Bahlasti Papers 90; Beneath The Surface 92; Blackwater Review 96; Blue Water Review, The 98; Bohemian Chronicle 99; Brownstone Review, The 103; Burning Light 103; Callaloo 105; Capers Aweigh Magazine 106; Cat's Ear 107; Century 107; Chrysalis Reader 110; Cimmerian-Journal, The 111; Climbing Art, The 112; Cochran's Corner 112; Communities: Journal of Cooperation 114; Companion in Zeor, A 114; Compenions 114; Confluence 115; Cosmic Landscapes 117; Cosmic Unicorn, The 117; Crazyquilt 118; Dagger of the Mind 119; Dan River Anthology 121; Dark Kiss 122; Dark Regions 122; Daughters of Nyx 122; Dead of Night™ Magazine 123; Deathrealm 123; DJINNI 126; Dodobobo 126; Downstate Story 126; Dream International/Quarterly 127; Dreams & Nightmares 127; Dreams & Visions 128; Drinkin' Buddy Magazine, The 128; Echoes 129; Elf: Eclectic Literary Forum 130; Eureka Literary Magazine 132; Every So Often . . . 133; Explorer Magazine 134; Expressions 134; Extreme, The 134; Federation Standard 136; FiberOptic Etchings 137; Fish Drum Magazine 139; Flummery Press, The 140; Flying Island, The 140; Frayed 141; Fugue 142; Galaxy Magazine 143; Gathering of the Tribes, A 143; Glass Cherry, The 145; Gotta Write Network Litmag 145; Grasslands Review 147; Green's Magazine 148; Happy 150; Hawaii Pacific Review 151; Hayden's Ferry Review 153; Hecate's Loom 154; Heroic Times 155; Hobson's Choice 156; Home Girl Press 156; Home Planet News 157; i.e. Magazine 159; Iconoclast, The 159; It's Your Choice Magazine 163; Jacaranda 163; Jeopardy 165; Lacunae 170; Lamp-Post, The 171; Left Curve 172; Liberty 173; Lines In The Sand 174; Liquid Ohio 175; Lite 175; Literal Latté 175; Loop, The 177; Lost Worlds 177; Lowell Pearl, The 178; Lynx Eye 179; MacGuffin, The 179; Magic Changes 180; Many Leaves One Tree 182; Mark 183; Matriarch's Way 183; Medicinal Purposes 184; Mediphors 184; Merlyn's Pen 185; Mind in Motion 187; Mindsparks 188; Mobius 189; Monolith Magazine 190; More Dead Trees 191; Musing Place, The 192; Mystic Fiction 193; NeuroNet

195; New Voices in Poetry and Prose 200; Nimrod 202; Nocturnal Lyric, The 203; Non-Stop Magazine 204; Northwoods Journal 206; Northwords 206; Olympia Review, The 208; On Spec 209; Once Upon a World 209; One Hundred Suns 210; Other Worlds 211; Otisian Directory 212; Ouroboros 212; Pablo Lennis 214; Pacific Coast Journal 214; Pagan Review, The 214; Palo Alto Review 215; Paradox Magazine 216; Phantasm Ca 220; Pink Chameleon, The 222; Pirate Writings 223; PKA's Advocate 223; Poetry Forum Short Stories 225; Poor Katy's Almanac 226; Portable Wall, The 226; Possibilitiis Literary Arts Magazine 227; Potpourri 228; Prairie Dog 229; Primavera 230; Processed World 232; Puck 233; Pulphouse 233; Quanta 234; Queen's Quarterly 235; Raconteur 235; Ralph's Review 237; Re Arts & Letters [REAL] 238; Renegade 240; Renovated Lighthouse 240; Riverside Quarterly 242; Robin's Nest 243; Rock Falls Review 243; Rockford Review, The 244; Rosebud™ 244; Samsara 245; Scorpio Moon 246; Seattle Review, The 247; Semiotext(e) 247; Sensations Magazine 248; Sidetrekked 252; Silver Web, The 253; Skylark 257; Snake Nation Review 259; Spindrift 263; Spout 264; SPSM&H 264; Square One 265; Starblade 265; Struggle 267; Suffusion Magazine 268; Supernatural Magazine on Audiobook, The 269; Surprise Me 269; Texas Young Writers' Newsletter 273; Thema 274; Thresholds Quarterly 275; Tickled By Thunder 275; Time Pilot 276; Tomorrow 276; Trekker News & Views, The 278; Troika Magazine 279; 2 AM Magazine 279; Urbanite, The 280; Urbanus/Raizirr 281; Videomania 282; Vincent Brothers Review, The 283; West Wind Review 286; Whisper 288; Whispering Pines Quarterly 288; Writers' International Forum 294; Writes of Passage 295; Xib 296; Yellow Silk 297

Senior Citizen/Retirement. A.R.T. 74; Amelia 82; Brownstone Review, The 103; Christian Courier 110; Dan River Anthology 121; Drinkin' Buddy Magazine, The 128; Echoes 129; Expressions 134; Gathering of the Tribes, A 143; Hayden's Ferry Review 153; Lighthouse 174; Lines In The Sand 174; Lowell Pearl, The 178; manna 181; Medicinal Purposes 184; Nite-Writer's Literary Arts Journal 202; Pink Chameleon, The 222; PKA's Advocate 223; Pléiades Magazine/Philae 224; Poetry Forum Short Stories 225; Portable Wall, The 226; Poskisnolt Press 227; Robin's Nest 243; Rock Falls Review 243; Snake Nation Review 259; SPSM&H 264; Struggle 267; Surprise Me 269; Tucumcari Literary Review 279; Vincent Brothers Review, The 283; Vintage Northwest 283; West Wind Review 286; Writers' International Forum 294; Xib 296

Serialized/Excerpted Novel. A.R.T. 74; Agni 77; Al Aaraaf 80; Alabama Literary Review 80; Art:Mag 87; Asian Pacific Journal 88; Atom Mind 89; Bahlasti Papers 90; Bellowing Ark 91; Black Jack 95; Bohemian Chronicle 99; BookLovers 99; Burning Light 103; Callaloo 105; Chaminade Literary Review 107; Cimmerian-Journal, The 111; Crazyquilt 118; Dodobobo 126; Drinkin' Buddy Magazine, The 128; Echoes 129; Entelechy 131; Farmer's Market, The 135; Fat Tuesday 135; Gettysburg Review, The 144; Glass Cherry, The 145; Green Mountains Review 148; Gulf Coast 149; Hunted News, The 158; Lime Green Bulldozers 174; Liquid Ohio 175; Loop, The 177; Lost Worlds 177; Lynx Eye 179; Magic Realism 180; Many Leaves One Tree 182; Matriarch's Way 183; Mid-American Review 186; Musing Place, The 192; Musk Gland Sally 192; Nassau Review 194; Oracle Story 210; Orange Coast Review 210; Other Voices 211; Otisian Directory 212; Paradox Magazine 216; Pléiades Magazine/Philae 224; Prairie Journal of Canadian Literature, The 230; Puerto Del Sol 233; Quarry 234; River City 241; River Styx 242; Rosebud™ 244; Seattle Review, The 247; Shift Magazine 250; Skylark 257; South Dakota Review 261; Southern California Anthology 261; Spindrift 263; Supernatural Magazine on Audiobook, The 269; Surprise Me 269; Trafika 277; Vincent Brothers Review, The 283; Virginia Quarterly Review 284; Vox 284; Widener Review 289; Willow Springs 290; Writing on the Wall, The 296; Xavier Review 296; Zephyr 299

Short Story Collections. Ararat Quarterly 85; Aura Literary/Arts Review 89; Painted Bride Quarterly 215

Sports. A.R.T. 74; Aethlon 77; Amelia 82; Anterior Fiction Quarterly 84; artisan 87; SPSM&H 264; Beloit Fiction Journal 92; Blue Water Review, The 98; BookLovers 99; Boy's Quest 101; Brownstone Review, The 103; Changing Men 108; Christian Courier 110; Chrysalis Reader 110; Climbing Art, The 112; Drinkin' Buddy Magazine, The 128; Echoes 129; Elf: Eclectic Literary Forum 130; Expressions 134; FiberOptic Etchings 137; Fugue 142; Iconoclast, The 159; Lighthouse 174; Lowell Pearl, The 178; Magic Changes 180; Medicinal Purposes 184; nerve 194; Nite-Writer's Literary Arts Journal 202; Northwoods Journal 206; Pink Chameleon, The 222; PKA's Advocate 223; Portable Wall, The 226; Riverwind 242; Rock Falls Review 243; Skylark

257; Spitball 263; "Teak" Roundup 272; Thema 274; West Wind Review 286; Whispering Pines Quarterly 288; Writers' International Forum 294; Writes of Passage 295

Translations. A.R.T. 74; ACM, (Another Chicago Magazine) 76; Adrift 77; Agni 77; Al Aaraaf 80; Alabama Literary Review 80; Alaska Quarterly Review 81; Amelia 82; Amherst Review, The 83; Antigonish Review, The 84; Antioch Review 85; Aphrodite Gone Berserk 85; Ararat Quarterly 85; Arnazella 86; Artful Dodge 87; Art:Mag 87; Asian Pacific Journal 88; Atom Mind 89; Beneath The Surface 92; Blue Penny Quarterly, The 98; Boston Literary Review (BLuR) 99; Brownbag Press 102; Brújula/Compass 103; Cafe Magazine 104; Callaloo 105; Chaminade Literary Review 107; Chariton Review, The 108; Chelsea 108; Christian Courier 110; Cimmerian-Journal, The 111; Columbia: A Magazine of Poetry & Prose 113; Compenions 114; Conduit 115; Confluence 115; Confrontation 116; Cream City Review, The 118; Descant (Ontario) 124; Disturbed Guillotine 125; DJINNI 126; Dream International/Quarterly 127; Drinkin' Buddy Magazine, The 128; 1812 130; Entelechy 131; Eureka Literary Magazine 132; Fault Lines 136; Fiction 137; Filling Station 138; Folio: A Literary Journal 140; G.W. Review, The 143; Galaxy Magazine 143; Gathering of the Tribes, A 143; Glass Cherry, The 145; Grand Street 146; Green Mountains Review 148; Hawaii Pacific Review 151; Hawaii Review 151; Hopewell Review, The 157; Hunted News, The 158; i.e. Magazine 159; International Quarterly 161; Jacaranda 163; Jack Mackerel Magazine 163; Jeopardy 165; Jewish Currents Magazine 165; Karma Lapel 167; Kenyon Review, The 168; Kestrel 168; Left Curve 172; Loop, The 177; Lowell Pearl, The 178; Lynx Eye 179; MacGuffin, The 179; Magic Realism 180; Mangrove 181; Manoa 182; Many Leaves One Tree 182; Many Mountains Moving 182; Men As We Are 185; Mid-American Review 186; Midland Review 187; Mississippi Review 189; New Delta Review 195; New Frontiers of New Mexico 196; New Laurel Review 196; New Letters Magazine 197; New Orleans Review 197; new renaissance, the 199; Nexus 201; Nimrod 202; 96 Inc. 202; Non-Stop Magazine 204; Northwest Review 205; Old Crow Review 208; Olympia Review, The 208; Orange Coast Review 210; Oregon East 211; Otisian Directory 212; Owen Wister Review 212; Oxford Magazine 213; Oxygen 213; Painted Bride Quarterly 215; Palo Alto Review 215; Pangolin Papers 215; Partisan Review 217; Pequod 219; Phoebe (NY) 221; Pikeville Review 222; Portable Wall, The 226; Porter International, Bern 226; Possibilitiis Literary Arts Magazine 227; Potomac Review 228; Prairie Dog 229; Prism International 231; Psychotrain 232; Puck 233; Puerto Del Sol 233; Quarry 234; Quarterly West 235; Renegade 240; Response 240; River Styx 242; RiverSedge 242; Riverwind 242; Rosebud™ 244; Sanskrit 246; Seattle Review, The 247; Semiotext(e) 247; Shift Magazine 250; Silence, The 253; Silverfish Review 253; Siren, The 256; sixpack: poems & stories 256; Slate, The 257; Slightly West 258; So To Speak 259; Spindrift 263; Spitting Image, The 264; Spout 264; SPSM&H 264; Story 266; Struggle 267; Sulphur River Literary Review 268; Sycamore Review 270; Tampa Review 271; Touchstone Literary Journal 276; Trafika 277; Triquarterly 278; Unmuzzled Ox 280; Vincent Brothers Review, The 283; Virginia Quarterly Review 284; Vox 284; Webster Review 285; West Branch 286; West Wind Review 286; Willow Springs 290; Wind Magazine 291; Worlds of Fantasy & Horror 293; Writing for Our Lives 295; Xavier Review 296; Xib 296; Yellow Silk 297; Zephyr 299; Zero Hour 299

Western. A.R.T. 74; Allegheny Review 81; Amelia 82; Amherst Review, The 83; artisan 87; SPSM&H 264; Azorean Express, The 89; Big Sky Stories 92; Black Jack 95; Blue Mesa Review 97; Brownstone Review, The 103; Compenions 114; Concho River Review 115; Dan River Anthology 121; Downstate Story 126; Drinkin' Buddy Magazine, The 128; Echoes 129; Elf: Eclectic Literary Forum 130; Eureka Literary Magazine 132; Expressions 134; FiberOptic Etchings 137; Free Focus/Ostentatious Mind 141; Fugue 142; Grasslands Review 147; i.e. Magazine 159; Lighthouse 174; Lines In The Sand 174; Loop, The 177; Lynx Eye 179; Medicinal Purposes 184; Merlyn's Pen 185; Mystic Fiction 193; New Frontiers of New Mexico 196; Northwoods Journal 206; Palo Alto Review 215; Pink Chameleon, The 222; PKA's Advocate 223; Pléiades Magazine/Philae 224; Poor Katy's Almanac 226; Poskisnolt Press 227; Post, The 227; Potpourri 228; PSI 232; Pulphouse 233; Raconteur 235; Renegade 240; Riverwind 242; Rock Falls Review 243; Seattle Review, The 247; Sensations Magazine 248; Short Stuff Magazine for Grown-ups 251; Skylark 257; Spitting Image, The 264; SPSM&H 264; Supernatural Magazine on Audiobook, The 269; "Teak" Roundup 272; Thema 274; Tickled By Thunder 275; Timber Creek Review 275; Tucumcari Literary Review 279; Valley Grapevine 281; Vincent Brothers Review, The 283; Vintage Northwest 283; West Wind Review 286; Western Pocket, The 287; Western

Tales Magazine 287; Words of Wisdom 293; Writers' International Forum 294; Writes of Passage 295

Young Adult/Teen. Amateur Writers Journal 82; BookLovers 99; Brilliant Star 102; Children's Journal, The 109; Claremont Review, The 111; Cochran's Corner 112; Cosmic Unicorn, The 117; Dream International/Quarterly 127; Drinkin' Buddy Magazine, The 128; Echoes 129; Every So Often . . . 133; FiberOptic Etchings 137; Free Focus/Ostentatious Mind 141; Fudge Cake, The 141; Full-Time Dads 143; Galaxy Magazine 143; India Papers, The 160; It's Your Choice Magazine 163; Lamp-Post, The 171; Lighthouse 174; Lines In The Sand 174; Liquid Ohio 175; Loop, The 177; Majestic Books 181; Medicinal Purposes 184; Merlyn's Pen 185; Mindsparks 188; Mysterious Wysteria 192; Nite-Writer's Literary Arts Journal 202; Oracle Story 210; Pink Chameleon, The 222; PKA's Advocate 223; Poetry Forum Short Stories 225; Poskisnolt Press 227; Raconteur 235; Ralph's Review 237; Shadow 248; Shattered Wig Review 250; Skipping Stones 256; Struggle 267; Supernatural Magazine on Audiobook, The 269; Surprise Me 269; "Teak" Roundup 272; Texas Young Writers' Newsletter 273; Trekker News & Views, The 278; West Wind Review 286; Writers' International Forum 294; Writes of Passage 295

Commercial Periodicals

Adventure. Art Times 315; Bowhunter Magazine 319; Boys' Life 319; Buffalo Spree Magazine 320; Bugle 320; Career Focus; College Preview; Direct Aim; Journey; Visions 321; Companion Magazine 325; Cosmopolitan Magazine 326; Easyriders Magazine 328; Florida Wildlife 330; Gallery Magazine 331; Gold and Treasure Hunter 332; Nu*Real 347; Pockets 349; Power and Light 350; Ranger Rick Magazine 352; Upstate New Yorker Magazine 361; Weekly Synthesis, The 361; Writer's World 363

Children's/Juvenile. American Girl 314; Associate Reformed Presbyterian, The 316; Bear Essential, The 317; Bugle 320; Chickadee 322; Child Life 322; Children's Digest 323; Children's Playmate 323; Cricket Magazine 327; Crusader Magazine 327; Friend Magazine, The 330; Guide Magazine 333; Guideposts for Kids 333; Highlights for Children 334; Humpty Dumpty's Magazine 336; Indian Life Magazine 337; Jack and Jill 338; Junior Trails 339; Ladybug 339; My Friend 345; Odyssey 347; On the Line 348; Pockets 349; Power and Light 350; R-A-D-A-R 351; Ranger Rick Magazine 352; Shofar 354; Story Friends 357; Touch 360; Turtle Magazine for Preschool Kids 360; Venture 361; Wonder Time 362; Writer's World 363

Condensed Novel. Arizona Coast 315; Campus Life Magazine 321; Career Focus; College Preview; Direct Aim; Journey; Visions 321; Upstate New Yorker Magazine 361; Weekly Synthesis, The 361; Writer's World 363

Erotica. Contact Advertising 326; First Hand 330; Gallery Magazine 331; Gent 331; Guys 333; Hustler 336; Hustler Busty Beauties 336; Manscape 343; Nugget 347; Options 348; Swank Magazine 358; Texas Connection Magazine 360; Weekly Synthesis, The 361

Ethnic/Multicultural. African Voices 313; American Citizen Italian Press, The 314; Art Times 315; Boston Review 319; Buffalo Spree Magazine 320; Career Focus; College Preview; Direct Aim; Journey; Visions 321; Emerge Magazine 328; Hadassah Magazine 334; India Currents 337; Indian Life Magazine 337; Inside 337; Interrace Magazine 337; Jive, Black Confessions, Black Romance, Bronze Thrills, Black Secrets 338; Lilith Magazine 342; Live 342; Midstream 345; Pockets 349; Reform Judaism 353; Sassy Magazine 353; Shofar 354; Spirit Talk 355; Upstate New Yorker Magazine 361; Weekly Synthesis, The 361; Writer's World 363

Experimental. Bomb Magazine 318; Boston Review 319; Career Focus; College Preview; Direct Aim; Journey; Visions 321; Gold and Treasure Hunter 332; Sassy Magazine 353; Weekly Synthesis, The 361

Fantasy. Art Times 315; Asimov's Science Fiction 316; Contact Advertising 326; Dragon® Magazine 327; Emerge Magazine 328; Nu*Real 347; Omni 347; Playboy Magazine 349; Power and Light 350; Ranger Rick Magazine 352; Weekly Synthesis, The 361; Art Times 315; Buffalo Spree Magazine 320; Christian Century, The 323; Contact Advertising 326; Lilith Magazine 342; Radiance 351; Sassy Magazine 353; Sojourner 355

Gay. Art Times 315; Contact Advertising 326; Drummer 328; First Hand 330; Guys 333; Hot

Shots 336; In Touch for Men 336; Manscape 343; Options 348; Powerplay Magazine 350; Sassy Magazine 353

Historical. American Citizen Italian Press, The 314; Arizona Coast 315; Art Times 315; Bear Essential, The 317; Beckett Baseball Card Monthly 318; Bugle 320; Career Focus; College Preview; Direct Aim; Journey; Visions 321; Gold and Treasure Hunter 332; Indian Life Magazine 337; Juggler's World 339; Lady's Circle 341; Montana Senior Citizens News 345; Pockets 349; Portland Magazine 349; Upstate New Yorker Magazine 361; Weekly Synthesis, The 361; Writer's World 363

Horror. Bear Essential, The 317; New Mystery 346; Nu*Real 347; Omni 347; Playboy Magazine 349; Upstate New Yorker Magazine 361; Weekly Synthesis, The 361

Humor/Satire. Art Times 315; Baby Connection News Journal, The 317; Balloon Life 317; Bear Essential, The 317; Beckett Baseball Card Monthly 318; Boys' Life 319; Buffalo Spree Magazine 320; Campus Life Magazine 321; Career Focus; College Preview; Direct Aim; Journey; Visions 321; Companion Magazine 325; Emerge Magazine 328; Gallery Magazine 331; Gold and Treasure Hunter 332; Harper's Magazine 334; Inside 337; Juggler's World 339; Lady's Circle 341; Looking Ahead—Napa 342; Mature Living 344; Metro Singles Lifestyles 344; Playboy Magazine 349; Ranger Rick Magazine 352; Reform Judaism 353; St. Joseph's Messenger and Advocate of the Blind 353; Sassy Magazine 353; Upstate New Yorker Magazine 361; Weekly Synthesis, The 361; Writer's World 363; Zelos 364

Lesbian. Art Times 315; Contact Advertising 326; Options 348

Literary. Art Times 315; Atlantic Monthly, The 316; Bear Essential, The 317; Boston Review 319; Buffalo Spree Magazine 320; Buzz 320; Emerge Magazine 328; Esquire 329; Gallery Magazine 331; Inside 337; Metro Singles Lifestyles 344; New Yorker, The 346; Portland Magazine 349; Sassy Magazine 353; Seventeen 354; Upstate New Yorker Magazine 361; Weekly Synthesis, The 361; Writer's World 363

Mainstream/Contemporary. American Citizen Italian Press, The 314; Art Times 315; Associate Reformed Presbyterian, The 316; Atlantic Monthly, The 316; Baby Connection News Journal, The 317; Boston Review 319; Buffalo Spree Magazine 320; Buzz 320; Career Focus; College Preview; Direct Aim; Journey; Visions 321; Christian Century, The 323; Companion Magazine 325; Cosmopolitan Magazine 326; Esquire 329; Gallery Magazine 331; Good Housekeeping 332; Harper's Magazine 334; Inside 337; Ladies' Home Journal 339; Lady's Circle 341; Looking Ahead—Napa 342; New Yorker, The 346; Northeast 346; Pockets 349; Portland Magazine 349; Redbook 352; St. Anthony Messenger 353; St. Joseph's Messenger and Advocate of the Blind 353; Sassy Magazine 353; Upstate New Yorker Magazine 361; Weekly Synthesis, The 361; Writer's World 363

Mystery/Suspense. bePuzzled 318; Boys' Life 319; Buffalo Spree Magazine 320; Career Focus; College Preview; Direct Aim; Journey; Visions 321; Cosmopolitan Magazine 326; Gallery Magazine 331; Gold and Treasure Hunter 332; Hitchcock Mystery Magazine, Alfred 335; New Mystery 346; Nu*Real 347; Pockets 349; Queen's Mystery Magazine, Ellery 351; Ranger Rick Magazine 352; Upstate New Yorker Magazine 361; Weekly Synthesis, The 361; Woman's World Magazine 362; Writer's World 363

Psychic/Supernatural/Occult. Nu*Real 347; Weekly Synthesis, The 361

Regional. Aloha 314; Boston Review 319; Buzz 320; Lady's Circle 341; Northeast 346; Upstate New Yorker Magazine 361; Wy'East Historical Journal 363

Religious/Inspirational. Annals of St. Anne De Beaupré, The 315; Associate Reformed Presbyterian, The 316; Campus Life Magazine 321; Christian Century, The 323; Christian Single 323; Companion Magazine 325; Cornerstone Magazine 326; Crusader Magazine 327; Emphasis on Faith and Living 329; Evangel 329; Family, The 330; Friend Magazine, The 330; Gem, The 331; Guide Magazine 333; Guideposts for Kids 333; High Adventure 334; Home Life 335; Home Times 335; Indian Life Magazine 337; Inside 337; Junior Trails 339; Lady's Circle 341; Liguorian 341; Live 342; Lookout, The 343; Lutheran Journal, The 343; Mature Living 344; Mature Years 344; Messenger of the Sacred Heart 344; Metro Singles Lifestyles 344; My Friend 345; New

Era Magazine 346; On the Line 348; Parabola 349; Pockets 349; Power and Light 350; Purpose 350; R-A-D-A-R 351; Reform Judaism 353; St. Anthony Messenger 353; St. Joseph's Messenger and Advocate of the Blind 353; Seek 354; Shofar 354; Standard 355; Story Friends 357; Straight 357; Student Leadership Journal 358; Teen Life 359; Teen Power 359; Touch 360; Upstate New Yorker Magazine 361; Venture 361; Vista 361; With 362; Wonder Time 362; Writer's World 363; Young Salvationist 364; Zelos 364

Romance. Baby Connection News Journal, The 317; Career Focus; College Preview; Direct Aim; Journey; Visions 321; Cosmopolitan Magazine 326; Good Housekeeping 332; Jive, Black Confessions, Black Romance, Bronze Thrills, Black Secrets 338; Metro Singles Lifestyles 344; Nu*Real 347; St. Anthony Messenger 353; St. Joseph's Messenger and Advocate of the Blind 353; Upstate New Yorker Magazine 361; Weekly Synthesis, The 361; Woman's World Magazine 362; Writer's World 363

Science Fiction. Aboriginal Science Fiction 312; Analog Science Fiction & Fact 315; Art Times 315; Asimov's Science Fiction 316; Bear Essential, The 317; Boys' Life 319; Career Focus; College Preview; Direct Aim; Journey; Visions 321; Expanse® Magazine 329; Juggler's World 339; Nu*Real 347; Omni 347; Playboy Magazine 349; Ranger Rick Magazine 352; Upstate New Yorker Magazine 361; Weekly Synthesis, The 361

Senior Citizen/Retirement. Arizona Coast 315; Gold and Treasure Hunter 332; Grand Times 332; Lady's Circle 341; Looking Ahead—Napa 342; Mature Living 344; Mature Years 344; Montana Senior Citizens News 345; St. Anthony Messenger 353; St. Joseph's Messenger and Advocate of the Blind 353; Writer's World 363

Serialized/Excerpted Novel. Analog Science Fiction & Fact 315; Arizona Coast 315; Bomb Magazine 318; Campus Life Magazine 321; Capper's 321

Sports. Adventure Cyclist 313; American Citizen Italian Press, The 314; Balloon Life 317; Beckett Baseball Card Monthly 318; Black Belt 318; Bowhunter Magazine 319; Boys' Life 319; Career Focus; College Preview; Direct Aim; Journey; Visions 321; Florida Wildlife 330; Junior Trails 339; Playboy Magazine 349; Prime Time Sports and Fitness 350; Ranger Rick Magazine 352; Surfing Magazine 358; Upstate New Yorker Magazine 361; Weekly Synthesis, The 361

Translations. American Citizen Italian Press, The 314; Boston Review 319; India Currents 337; Inside 337; Parabola 349

Western. Arizona Coast 315; Boys' Life 319; Bugle 320; L'Amour Western Magazine, Louis 341; Montana Senior Citizens News 345; Playboy Magazine 349; Weekly Synthesis, The 361; Writer's World 363

Young Adult/Teen. American Newspaper Carrier, The 314; Associate Reformed Presbyterian, The 316; Beckett Baseball Card Monthly 318; Boys' Life 319; Campus Life Magazine 321; Career Focus; College Preview; Direct Aim; Journey; Visions 321; Guide Magazine 333; High Adventure 334; Indian Life Magazine 337; New Era Magazine 346; On the Line 348; Sassy Magazine 353; Seventeen 354; Straight 357; Teen Life 359; 'Teen Magazine 359; Teen Power 359; Weekly Synthesis, The 361; With 362; Writer's World 363; Young Salvationist 364; Zelos 364

Small Press

Adventure. Aegina Press, Inc. 371; Ariadne Press 373; Arjuna Library Press 374; Black Heron Press 378; Brownell & Carroll, Inc. 379; Burning Gate Press 380; Cave Books 381; Crowbar Press 385; Dan River Press 385; EE.M. Press Inc. 387; Earth-Love Publishing Ltd. 387; Ecopress 388; Gryphon Publications 393; Jesperson Press Ltd. 396; Laredo Publishing Co. 397; Mey-House Books 401; Our Child Press 406; Pieper Publishing 408; Read 'n Run Books 412; Reader's Break 413; Rio Grande Press 413; Rose Creek Publishing 414; Shields Publishing 417; Soho Press 418; Story Line Press 421; University Editions 424; Vandamere Press 425; Vista Publications 426; Write Way Publishing 428

Children's/Juvenile. Advocacy Press 371; Annick Press Ltd. 373; Arjuna Library Press 374;

Bagman Press 375; Borealis Press 379; Carolina Wren Press 381; Cool Hand Communications, Inc. 383; Creative with Words Publications 384; Cross-Cultural Communications 384; Distinctive Publishing Corp. 387; E.M. Press Inc. 387; Feminist Press at the City University of New York, The 389; Huntington House Publishers 395; Jesperson Press Ltd. 396; Jones University Press, Bob 396; Kar-Ben Copies Inc. 396; Laredo Publishing Co. 397; Lee & Low Books 397; Lester Publishing Limited 397; Lollipop Power Books 398; Long Publishing Co., Hendrick 399; Mayhaven Publishing 401; Milkweed Editions 401; Orca Book Publishers Ltd. 406; Our Child Press 406; Overlook Press, The 407; Peachtree Publishers, Ltd. 407; Pemmican Publications 408; Pieper Publishing 408; Pippin Press 409; Prairie Publishing Company, The 410; Prep Publishing 410; Quarry Press 412; Read 'n Run Books 412; Shields Publishing 417; Third World Press 422; University Editions 424; Willowisp Press 427; Women's Press 427

Comic/Graphic Novels. Hollow Earth Publishing 395

Erotica. Arjuna Library Press 374; Center Press 381; Circlet Press 382; Creative Arts Book Co. 383; Ekstasis Editions 388; Permeable Press 408; Pieper Publishing 408; Press Gang Publishers 410; Second Chance Press and the Permanent Press 416; Sterling House Publisher 420; Vandamere Press 425

Ethnic/Multicultural. Alaska Native Language Center 372; Arsenal Pulp Press 374; Arte Publico Press 374; Bamboo Ridge Press 375; Bilingual Press/Editorial Bilingüe 378; Brownell & Carroll, Inc. 379; Carolina Wren Press 381; China Books 382; Coffee House Press 382; Cross-Cultural Communications 384; Crowbar Press 385; Feminist Press at the City University of New York, The 389; Griffon House Publications 392; Guernica Editions 393; Heritage Press 393; Kar-Ben Copies Inc. 396; Lincoln Springs Press 398; Loonfeather Press 399; Mage Publishers 400; Mey-House Books 401; Path Press, Inc. 407; Pemmican Publications 408; Pieper Publishing 408; Pocahontas Press, Inc. 409; Press Gang Publishers 410; Read 'n Run Books 412; Rio Grande Press 413; Sand River Press 415; Sandpiper Press 415; Seal Press 416; Second Chance Press and the Permanent Press 416; Seven Buffaloes Press 417; Shields Publishing 417; Soho Press 418; Southern Methodist University Press 418; Stone Bridge Press 420; Story Line Press 421; Third World Press 422; Three Continents Press 422; Tudor Publishers, Inc. 423; University Editions 424; Vista Publications 426; White Pine Press 426; Woman in the Moon Publications 427; Women's Press 427; Zephyr Press 428

Experimental. Aegina Press, Inc. 372; Ageless Press 372; Anvil Press 373; Arjuna Library Press 374; Black Heron Press 378; Burning Gate Press 380; Carolina Wren Press 381; Coffee House Press 382; Cross-Cultural Communications 384; Dan River Press 385; Depth Charge 386; Ekstasis Editions 388; Griffon House Publications 392; Gryphon Publications 393; Heaven Bone Press 393; Lincoln Springs Press 398; New Rivers Press 404; Permeable Press 408; Puckerbrush Press 411; Pyx Press 411; QED Press 411; Quarry Press 412; Read 'n Run Books 412; Red Deer College Press 413; Ronsdale Press/Cacanadadada 414; Shields Publishing 417; Thistledown Press 422; Turnstone Press 423; Ultramarine Publishing Co., Inc. 424; University Editions 424

Family Saga. E.M. Press Inc. 387; Huntington House Publishers 395; Pieper Publishing 408; Rio Grande Press 413; Second Chance Press and the Permanent Press 416; Shields Publishing 417; Write Way Publishing 428

Fantasy. Aegina Press, Inc. 372; Ageless Press 372; Arjuna Library Press 374; Brownell & Carroll, Inc. 379; Circlet Press 382; Dan River Press 385; E.M. Press Inc. 387; Fasa Corporation 388; Hollow Earth Publishing 395; Jesperson Press Ltd. 396; Obelesk Books 406; Our Child Press 406; Overlook Press, The 407; Pieper Publishing 408; Pyx Press 411; Read 'n Run Books 412; Reader's Break 413; Rio Grande Press 413; Rose Creek Publishing 414; Savant Garde Workshop, The 415; Shields Publishing 417; Ultramarine Publishing Co., Inc. 424; University Editions 424; Virtual Press, The 426; W.W. Publications 426; Woman in the Moon Publications 427; Write Way Publishing 428

Feminist. Ariadne Press 373; Arsenal Pulp Press 374; Bagman Press 375; Brownell & Carroll, Inc. 379; Calyx Books 380; Carolina Wren Press 381; Creative Arts Book Co. 383; Eighth Mt. Press, The 388; FC2/Black Ice Books 389; Feminist Press at the City University of New York, The 389; Firebrand Books 389; Hollow Earth Publishing 395; Lincoln Springs Press 398; New Victoria Publishers 405; Nightshade Press 405; Outrider Press 406; Papier-Mache Press 407;

Permeable Press 408; Pieper Publishing 408; Post-Apollo Press, The 409; Press Gang Publishers 410; Quarry Press 412; Ragweed Press Inc./gynergy books 412; Read 'n Run Books 412; Seal Press 416; Shields Publishing 417; Spectrum Press 418; Spinsters Ink 419; Third Side Press, Inc. 421; Tide Book Publishing Company 423; University Editions 424; Véhicule Press 425; Women's Press 427; Zephyr Press 428; Zoland Books, Inc. 428

Gay. Alyson Publications, Inc. 372; Arsenal Pulp Press 374; Bagman Press 375; Brownell & Carroll, Inc. 379; Carolina Wren Press 381; FC2/Black Ice Books 389; Feminist Press at the City University of New York, The 389; Gay Sunshine Press and Leyland Publications 392; Hollow Earth Publishing 395; Outrider Press 406; Permeable Press 408; Shields Publishing 417; Spectrum Press 418; STARbooks Press 419; Woman in the Moon Publications 427

Glitz. Brownell & Carroll, Inc. 379; Write Way Publishing 428

Historical. Aegina Press, Inc. 372; Ariadne Press 373; Bagman Press 375; Brownell & Carroll, Inc. 379; Center Press 381; Creative Arts Book Co. 383; Crowbar Press 385; Dan River Press 385; Goose Lane Editions 392; Huntington House Publishers 395; Lester Publishing Limited 397; Lincoln Springs Press 398; Long Publishing Co., Hendrick 399; Mayhaven Publishing 401; Path Press, Inc. 407; Pieper Publishing 408; Pocahontas Press, Inc. 409; Quarry Press 412; Read 'n Run Books 412; Shields Publishing 417; Soho Press 418; Third World Press 422; Tide Book Publishing Company 423; University Editions 424; Vista Publications 426; Write Way Publishing 428; Zephyr Press 428

Horror. Aegina Press, Inc. 372; Arjuna Library Press 374; Brownell & Carroll, Inc. 379; Burning Gate Press 380; Dan River Press 385; Distinctive Publishing Corp. 387; Gryphon Publications 393; Obelesk Books 406; Pieper Publishing 408; Read 'n Run Books 412; Rose Creek Publishing 414; Shields Publishing 417; University Editions 424; Virtual Press, The 426; Write Way Publishing 428

Humor/Satire. Acme Press 371; Ageless Press 372; Ariadne Press 373; Baskerville Publishers, Inc. 375; Beil, Publisher, Inc., Frederic C. 375; Black Heron Press 378; Black Moss Press 378; Brownell & Carroll, Inc. 379; Catbird Press 381; Center Press 381; Coffee House Press 382; Creative with Words Publications 384; Cross-Cultural Communications 384; Crowbar Press 385; Dan River Press 385; E.M. Press Inc. 387; Jesperson Press Ltd. 396; Lester Publishing Limited 397; Longstreet Press 399; Nightshade Press 405; Pieper Publishing 408; Press Gang Publishers 410; Read 'n Run Books 412; Rio Grande Press 413; Shields Publishing 417; Tide Book Publishing Company 423; University Editions 424; Vandamere Press 425; Write Way Publishing 428

Lesbian. Alyson Publications, Inc. 372; Arjuna Library Press 374; Arsenal Pulp Press 374; Bagman Press 375; Brownell & Carroll, Inc. 379; Calyx Books 380; Carolina Wren Press 381; Eighth Mt. Press, The 388; Feminist Press at the City University of New York, The 389; Firebrand Books 389; Hollow Earth Publishing 395; Madwoman Press 400; Naiad Press, Inc., The 404; New Victoria Publishers 405; Outrider Press 406; Permeable Press 408; Pieper Publishing 408; Post-Apollo Press, The 409; Press Gang Publishers 410; Ragweed Press Inc./gynergy books 412; Rising Tide Press 414; Sand River Press 415; Seal Press 416; Shields Publishing 417; Spectrum Press 418; Spinsters Ink 419; Third Side Press, Inc. 421; Woman in the Moon Publications 427; Women's Press 427

Literary. Aegina Press, Inc. 372; Ageless Press 372; Another Chicago Press 373; Anvil Press 373; Ariadne Press 373; Arsenal Pulp Press 374; Bagman Press 375; Bamboo Ridge Press 375; Baskerville Publishers, Inc. 375; Beil, Publisher, Inc., Frederic C. 375; Bilingual Press/Editorial Bilingüe 378; Black Heron Press 378; Black Moss Press 378; Books for All Times, Inc. 379; Borealis Press 379; Brownell & Carroll, Inc. 379; Burning Gate Press 380; Cadmus Editions 380; Carolina Wren Press 381; Catbird Press 381; Center Press 381; Coffee House Press 382; Confluence Press Inc. 382; Creative Arts Book Co. 383; Cross-Cultural Communications 384; Crowbar Press 385; Dan River Press 385; Daniel and Company, Publishers, John 385; Delphinium Books 386; E.M. Press Inc. 387; Ecco Press, The 387; Ecopress 388; Ekstasis Editions 388; Faber and Faber, Inc. 388; FC2/Black Ice Books 389; Feminist Press at the City University of New York, The 389; Florida Literary Foundation Press 389; Four Walls Eight Windows 391; Goose Lane Editions 392; Graywolf Press 392; Griffon House Publications 392; Guernica Editions 393; Heaven Bone Press 393; Hollow Earth Publishing 395; Homestead Publishing 395;

Huntington House Publishers 395; Lemeac Editeur Inc. 397; Lester Publishing Limited 397; Lincoln Springs Press 398; Livingston Press 398; Longstreet Press 399; MacMurray & Beck, Inc. 400; Milkweed Editions 401; Moyer Bell Limited 404; New Rivers Press 404; NeWest Publishers Ltd. 405; Nightshade Press 405; Orca Book Publishers Ltd. 406; Outrider Press 406; Overlook Press, The 407; Peachtree Publishers, Ltd. 407; Permeable Press 408; Pieper Publishing 408; Post-Apollo Press, The 409; Prairie Journal Press 410; Press Gang Publishers 410; Pucker-brush Press 411; Pyx Press 411; QED Press 411; Quarry Press 412; Read 'n Run Books 412; Reader's Break 413; Red Deer College Press 413; Rio Grande Press 413; Ronsdale Press/Cacana-dadada 414; Rose Creek Publishing 414; Sand River Press 415; Savant Garde Workshop, The 415; Seal Press 416; Second Chance Press and the Permanent Press 416; Shields Publishing 417; Silver Mountain Press 417; Simon & Pierre Publishing Co. Ltd. 417; Soho Press 418; Southern Methodist University Press 418; Spectrum Press 418; Stormline Press 421; Story Line Press 421; Thistledown Press 422; Tide Book Publishing Company 423; Tudor Publishers, Inc. 423; Turnstone Press 423; Turtle Point Press 424; University of Arkansas Press, The 425; Véhicule Press 425; White Pine Press 426; Zephyr Press 428; Zoland Books, Inc. 428

Mainstream/Contemporary. Aegina Press, Inc. 372; Ageless Press 372; Ariadne Press 373; Bagman Press 375; Black Heron Press 378; Books for All Times, Inc. 379; Borealis Press 379; Brownell & Carroll, Inc. 379; Burning Gate Press 380; Carolina Wren Press 381; Catbird Press 381; Coffee House Press 382; Confluence Press Inc. 382; Cool Hand Communications, Inc. 383; Creative Arts Book Co. 383; Cross-Cultural Communications 384; Crowbar Press 385; Dan River Press 385; Daniel and Company, Publishers, John 385; Distinctive Publishing Corp. 387; Dundurn Press 387; E.M. Press Inc. 387; Ecopress 388; Ekstasis Editions 388; Feminist Press at the City University of New York, The 389; Goose Lane Editions 392; Griffon House Publications 392; Guernica Editions 393; Huntington House Publishers 395; Lester Publishing Limited 397; Lincoln Springs Press 398; Longstreet Press 399; MacMurray & Beck, Inc. 400; Mey-House Books 401; New Rivers Press 404; Nightshade Press 405; Orca Book Publishers Ltd. 406; Our Child Press 406; Papier-Mache Press 407; Peachtree Publishers, Ltd. 407; Pieper Publishing 408; Pocahontas Press, Inc. 409; Press Gang Publishers 410; Puckerbrush Press 411; Read 'n Run Books 412; Reader's Break 413; Red Deer College Press 413; Rio Grande Press 413; Rose Creek Publishing 414; Savant Garde Workshop, The 415; Seal Press 416; Second Chance Press and the Permanent Press 416; Seven Buffaloes Press 417; Shields Publishing 417; Silver Mountain Press 417; Simon & Pierre Publishing Co. Ltd. 417; Soho Press 418; Southern Methodist University Press 418; Spectrum Press 418; Sterling House Publisher 420; Tide Book Publishing Company 423; Ultramarine Publishing Co., Inc. 424; University Editions 424; University of Arkansas Press, The 425; Woman in the Moon Publications 427; Women's Press 427; Zephyr Press 428

Military/War. Brownell & Carroll, Inc. 379; Burning Gate Press 380; Crowbar Press 385; Dan River Press 385; E.M. Press Inc. 387; Gryphon Publications 393; Nautical & Aviation Publishing Co. of America Inc., The 404; Pieper Publishing 408; Read 'n Run Books 412; Shields Publishing 417; University Editions 424; Vandamere Press 425; Write Way Publishing 428

Mystery/Suspense. Aegina Press, Inc. 372; Ageless Press 372; Brownell & Carroll, Inc. 379; Burning Gate Press 380; Creative Arts Book Co. 383; E.M. Press Inc. 387; Earth-Love Publishing Ltd. 387; Ecopress 388; Gryphon Publications 393; Homestead Publishing 395; May-haven Publishing 401; Papyrus Publishers & Letterbox Literary Service 407; Pieper Publishing 408; QED Press 411; Read 'n Run Books 412; Reader's Break 413; Rio Grande Press 413; Rose Creek Publishing 414; Second Chance Press and the Permanent Press 416; Shields Publishing 417; Simon & Pierre Publishing Co. Ltd. 417; Soho Press 418; Story Line Press 421; University Editions 424; Virtual Press, The 426; Vista Publications 426; Write Way Publishing 428

New Age/Mystic/Spiritual. Ageless Press 372; Distinctive Publishing Corp. 387; Earth-Love Publishing Ltd. 387; Ekstasis Editions 388; Heaven Bone Press 393; Hollow Earth Publishing 395; Outrider Press 406; Shields Publishing 417

Psychic/Supernatural/Occult. Brownell & Carroll, Inc. 379; Carolina Wren Press 381; Dan River Press 385; Heaven Bone Press 393; Overlook Press, The 407; Permeable Press 408; Pieper Publishing 408; Read 'n Run Books 412; Shields Publishing 417; Woman in the Moon Publications 427; Write Way Publishing 428

Regional. Acadia Press 371; Aegina Press, Inc. 372; Beil, Publisher, Inc., Frederic C. 375; Brownell & Carroll, Inc. 379; Butternut Publications 380; Carolina Wren Press 381; Creative Arts Book Co. 383; Crowbar Press 385; Dan River Press 385; Feminist Press at the City University of New York, The 389; Long Publishing Co., Hendrick 399; Loonfeather Press 399; Mercury Press, The 401; NeWest Publishers Ltd. 405; Nightshade Press 405; Orca Book Publishers Ltd. 406; Overlook Press, The 407; Peachtree Publishers, Ltd. 407; Pieper Publishing 408; Pineapple Press 409; Pocahontas Press, Inc. 409; Read 'n Run Books 412; Rio Grande Press 413; Sand River Press 415; Seven Buffaloes Press 417; Shields Publishing 417; Southern Methodist University Press 418; Story Line Press 421; Three Continents Press 422; Tide Book Publishing Company 423; Times Eagle Books 423; Tudor Publishers, Inc. 423; University Editions 424; Véhicule Press 425; Vista Publications 426; Woodley Memorial Press 428; Zephyr Press 428

Religious/Inspirational. Bethel Publishing 375; Brownell & Carroll, Inc. 379; Distinctive Publishing Corp. 387; Huntington House Publishers 395; Post-Apollo Press, The 409; Prep Publishing 410; Read 'n Run Books 412; Rose Creek Publishing 414; Shaw Publishers, Harold 417; Shields Publishing 417; Starburst Publishers 420; Threshold Books 423; Vine Books Imprint 425

Romance. Aegina Press, Inc. 372; Arjuna Library Press 374; Brownell & Carroll, Inc. 379; Lemeac Editeur Inc. 397; Pieper Publishing 408; Prep Publishing 410; Read 'n Run Books 412; Reader's Break 413; Rose Creek Publishing 414; Shields Publishing 417; University Editions 424; Vine Books Imprint 425; Vista Publications 426

Science Fiction. Aegina Press, Inc. 372; Aegina Press, Inc. 371; Ageless Press 372; Arjuna Library Press 374; Bagman Press 375; Black Heron Press 378; Brownell & Carroll, Inc. 379; Circlet Press 382; Dan River Press 385; Ecopress 388; Fasa Corporation 388; FC2/Black Ice Books 389; Feminist Press at the City University of New York, The 389; Gryphon Publications 393; Heaven Bone Press 393; Mey-House Books 401; Obelesk Books 406; Overlook Press, The 407; Permeable Press 408; Pieper Publishing 408; Pyx Press 411; Read 'n Run Books 412; Reader's Break 413; Rose Creek Publishing 414; Savant Garde Workshop, The 415; Shields Publishing 417; Ultramarine Publishing Co., Inc. 424; University Editions 424; Virtual Press, The 426; W.W. Publications 426; Write Way Publishing 428

Short Story Collections. Aegina Press, Inc. 372; Ageless Press 372; Anvil Press 373; Arsenal Pulp Press 374; Bagman Press 375; Bamboo Ridge Press 375; Beil, Publisher, Inc., Frederic C. 375; Bilingual Press/Editorial Bilingüe 378; Black Moss Press 378; Books for All Times, Inc. 379; Calyx Books 380; Carolina Wren Press 381; Center Press 381; Coffee House Press 382; Confluence Press Inc. 382; Crowbar Press 385; Dan River Press 385; Daniel and Company, Publishers, John 385; Delphinium Books 386; Ecco Press, The 387; Ecopress 388; Eighth Mt. Press, The 388; Ekstasis Editions 388; FC2/Black Ice Books 389; Goose Lane Editions 392; Graywolf Press 392; Gryphon Publications 393; Homestead Publishing 395; Lemeac Editeur Inc. 397; Lester Publishing Limited 397; Lincoln Springs Press 398; Livingston Press 398; Loonfeather Press 399; New Rivers Press 404; Outrider Press 406; Papier-Mache Press 407; Path Press, Inc. 407; Peachtree Publishers, Ltd. 407; Permeable Press 408; Pieper Publishing 408; Prairie Journal Press 410; Press Gang Publishers 410; Quarry Press 412; Read 'n Run Books 412; Red Deer College Press 413; Rio Grande Press 413; Rose Creek Publishing 414; Sarabande Books, Inc. 415; Seal Press 416; Seven Buffaloes Press 417; Shields Publishing 417; Southern Methodist University Press 418; Spectrum Press 418; Sterling House Publisher 420; Story Line Press 421; Third World Press 422; Thistledown Press 422; Ultramarine Publishing Co., Inc. 424; University Editions 424; University of Missouri Press 425; University of Arkansas Press, The 425; Véhicule Press 425; Vista Publications 426; White Pine Press 426; Woman in the Moon Publications 427; Women's Press 427; Zephyr Press 428; Zoland Books, Inc. 428

Sports. Brownell & Carroll, Inc. 379; Path Press, Inc. 407; Pocahontas Press, Inc. 409

Thriller/Espionage. Aegina Press, Inc. 372; Ageless Press 372; Brownell & Carroll, Inc. 379; Burning Gate Press 380; Distinctive Publishing Corp. 387; E.M. Press Inc. 387; Ecopress 388; Gryphon Publications 393; Pieper Publishing 408; Prep Publishing 410; Rose Creek Publishing 414; Shields Publishing 417; Tudor Publishers, Inc. 423; Virtual Press, The 426; Write Way Publishing 428

Translations. Bagman Press 374; Beil, Publisher, Inc., Frederic C. 375; Bilingual Press/Edito-

Commercial Book Publishers

Fantasy. Aspect 435; Avon Books 436; Baen Books 436; Bantam Spectra Books 437; Berkley Publishing Group, The 438; Berkley/Ace Science Fiction 438; Carroll & Graf Publishers, Inc. 442; Daw Books, Inc. 443; Del Rey Books 444; Delacorte/Dell Books for Young Readers 444; Dutton Signet 445; HarperPaperbacks 450; Philomel Books 458; Pocket Books 458; ROC 459; St. Martin's Press 459; Tor Books 462; Vesta Publications, Ltd 463

Feminist. Academy Chicago Publishers 435; Braziller, Inc., George 439; Holt & Company, Henry 452; Morrow And Company, Inc., William 456; Pocket Books 458; St. Martin's Press 459; Vesta Publications, Ltd 463

Gay. Dutton Signet 445; Hyperion 452; Morrow And Company, Inc., William 456; St. Martin's Press 459

Glitz. Harlequin Enterprises, Ltd. 448

Historical. Academy Chicago Publishers 435; Avon Books 436; Ballantine Books 437; Branden Publishing Co. 439; Crossway Books 443; Dell Publishing 444; Dutton Signet 445; Fawcett 446; Fine, Inc., Donald I. 446; Godine, Publisher, Inc., David R. 447; Harcourt Brace & Co. 449; HarperPaperbacks 450; Herald Press 451; Holt & Company, Henry 452; Kensington Publishing Corp. 453; Morrow And Company, Inc., William 456; Philomel Books 458; Pocket Books 458; Presidio Press 458; Random House, Inc. 458; St. Martin's Press 459; Vesta Publications, Ltd 463; Winston-Derek Publishers 464

Horror. Avon Books 436; Dell Publishing 444; Fine, Inc., Donald I. 446; HarperPaperbacks 450; Kensington Publishing Corp. 453; Leisure Books 453; Morrow And Company, Inc., William 456; Pocket Books 458; ROC 459; St. Martin's Press 459

Humor/Satire. Books In Motion 438; Broadman & Holman Publishers 442; Harvest House Publishers 451; Holt & Company, Henry 452; Morrow And Company, Inc., William 456; Pocket Books 458; St. Martin's Press 459; Signal Hill Publications 460

Lesbian. Morrow And Company, Inc., William 456; St. Martin's Press 460

Literary. Bantam Spectra Books 437; Branden Publishing Co. 439; Braziller, Inc., George 439; Carroll & Graf Publishers, Inc. 442; Fine, Inc., Donald I. 446; Godine, Publisher, Inc., David R. 447; Harmony Books 450; Herald Press 451; Holt & Company, Henry 452; Hyperion 452; Knopf, Alfred A. 453; Morrow And Company, Inc., William 456; Multnomah Books 456; Norton & Company, Inc., W.W. 457; Philomel Books 458; Pocket Books 458; Random House, Inc. 458; St. Martin's Press 459; Vesta Publications, Ltd 463; Washington Square Press 463

Mainstream/Contemporary. Avon Books 436; Ballantine Books 437; Berkley Publishing Group, The 438; Branden Publishing Co. 439; Carroll & Graf Publishers, Inc. 442; Crossway Books 443; Dell Publishing 444; Dutton Signet 445; Eriksson, Publisher, Paul S. 445; HarperPaperbacks 450; Harvest House Publishers 451; Holt & Company, Henry 452; Hyperion 452; Kensington Publishing Corp. 453; Knopf, Alfred A. 453; Morrow And Company, Inc., William 456; Pocket Books 458; Random House, Inc. 458; St. Martin's Press 459; Tor Books 462; Vesta Publications, Ltd 463; Weiss Associates, Inc., Daniel 463

Military/War. Avon Books 436; Branden Publishing Co. 439; Dell Publishing 444; Fine, Inc., Donald I. 446; Kensington Publishing Corp. 453; Morrow And Company, Inc., William 456; Pocket Books 458; Presidio Press 458; St. Martin's Press 459

Mystery/Suspense. Avalon Books 436; Berkley Publishing Group, The 438; Books In Motion 438; Carroll & Graf Publishers, Inc. 442; Dell Publishing 444; Doubleday 445; Fawcett 446; Fine, Inc., Donald I. 446; Godine, Publisher, Inc., David R. 447; Harcourt Brace & Co. 449; Harlequin Enterprises, Ltd. 450; HarperPaperbacks 450; Harvest House Publishers 451; Holt & Company, Henry 452; Hyperion 452; Kensington Publishing Corp. 453; Knopf, Alfred A. 453; Morrow And Company, Inc., William 456; Mysterious Press, The 457; Philomel Books 458; Pocket Books 458; Presidio Press 458; Random House, Inc. 458; St. Martin's Press 459; Signal Hill Publications 460; Tor Books 462; Vesta Publications, Ltd 463; Walker and Company 463

New Age/Mystic/Spiritual. Dutton Signet 445

Psychic/Supernatural/Occult. Avon Books 436; Dell Publishing 444; Pocket Books 458; St. Martin's Press 459; Vesta Publications, Ltd 463

Regional. Blair, Publisher, John F. 438; Philomel Books 458; Vesta Publications, Ltd 463

Religious/Inspirational. Baker Book House 437; Bridge Publishing, Inc. 439; Broadman & Holman Publishers 442; Cook Communications Ministry 442; Crossway Books 443; Harvest House Publishers 451; Herald Press 451; Hyperion 452; Lion Publishing 454; Multnomah Books 456; Resource Publications, Inc. 459; Revell Publishing 459; St. Martin's Press 459; St. Paul Books and Media 460; Standard Publishing 462; Tyndale House Publishers 462; Vesta Publications, Ltd 463; Winston-Derek Publishers 464; Zondervan 465

Romance. Avalon Books 436; Berkley Publishing Group, The 438; Bouregy & Company, Inc., Thomas 439; Dell Publishing 444; Doubleday 445; Dutton Signet 445; Harlequin Enterprises, Ltd. 450; HarperPaperbacks 450; Harvest House Publishers 451; Kensington Publishing Corp. 453; Leisure Books 453; Love Spell 455; Loveswept 455; Pocket Books 458; St. Martin's Press 459; Signal Hill Publications 460; Silhouette Books 460; Vesta Publications, Ltd 463

Science Fiction. Aspect 435; Avon Books 436; Baen Books 436; Bantam Spectra Books 437; Berkley Publishing Group, The 438; Berkley/Ace Science Fiction 438; Carroll & Graf Publishers, Inc. 442; Daw Books, Inc. 443; Del Rey Books 444; Dutton Signet 445; HarperPaperbacks 450; Morrow And Company, Inc., William 456; ROC 459; St. Martin's Press 459; Signal Hill Publications 460; Tor Books 462; Vesta Publications, Ltd 463

Short Story Collections. Branden Publishing Co. 439; Braziller, Inc., George 439; Philomel Books 458; Random House, Inc. 458; Resource Publications, Inc. 459; Vesta Publications, Ltd 463

Sports. Signal Hill Publications 460

Thriller/Espionage. Dutton Signet 445; Fine, Inc., Donald I. 446; HarperPaperbacks 450; Hyperion 452; Kensington Publishing Corp. 453; Morrow And Company, Inc., William 456; Presidio Press 458; St. Martin's Press 459

Translations. Branden Publishing Co. 439; Braziller, Inc., George 439; Holt & Company, Henry 452; Interlink Publishing Group, Inc. 452; Morrow And Company, Inc., William 456; Philomel Books 458; Vesta Publications, Ltd 463

Western. Avalon Books 436; Avon Books 436; Bouregy & Company, Inc., Thomas 439; Doubleday 445; Dutton Signet 445; Evans & Co., Inc., M. 445; Fine, Inc., Donald I. 446; Harper-Paperbacks 450; Jameson Books 452; Philomel Books 458; Pocket Books 458; Tor Books 462; Walker and Company 463

Young Adult/Teen. Archway Paperbacks/Minstrel Books 435; Atheneum Books for Young Readers 435; Avon Books 436; Bantam/Doubleday/Dell Books for Young Readers Division 437; Boyds Mills Press 439; Broadman & Holman Publishers 442; Crossway Books 443; Delacorte/Dell Books for Young Readers 444; Flare Books 447; Godine, Publisher, Inc., David R. 447; HarperCollins Children's Books 450; HarperPaperbacks 450; Herald Press 451; Holt & Company, Henry 452; Lerner Publications Company 453; Little, Brown and Company Children's Books 454; Lodestar Books 455; Macmillan Books for Young Readers 456; Morrow Junior Books 456; Philomel Books 458; Scribner's, Books for Young Readers 460; Troll Associates 462; Vesta Publications, Ltd 463; Walker and Company 463; Weiss Associates, Inc., Daniel 463; Winston-Derek Publishers 464

Markets Index

More Great Books For Writers!

1996 Writer's Market—Celebrating 75 years of helping writers realize their dreams, this newest edition contains information on 4,000 writing opportunities. You'll find all the facts vital to the success of your writing career, including an up-to-date listing of buyers of books, articles and stories, plus articles and interviews with top professionals. *#10432/$27.99/1008 pages*

The Writer's Ultimate Research Guide—Save research time and frustration with the help of this guide. Three hundred fifty-two information-packed pages will point you straight to the information you need to create better, more accurate fiction and nonfiction. Hundreds of listings of books and databases reveal how current the information is, the content and organization and much more! *#10447/$19.99/352 pages*

Mystery Writer's Sourcebook: Where to Sell Your Manuscripts—Part market guide, part writing guide, this is an invaluable companion for all mystery, suspense and crime writers. You'll discover in-depth market reports on 120 mystery book and magazine publishers, techniques from top writers and editors and 125 agents who represent mystery writers. *#10455/$19.99/475 pages*

1996 Guide to Literary Agents—Find everything you need to know about choosing an agent! More than 450 listings of agents for literature, television and motion pictures are included in this new edition. Plus you'll find valuable information on the agent-author relationship and answers to the most often asked questions. *#10443/$21.99/236 pages*

How to Write Like an Expert About Anything—Find out how to use new technology and traditional research methods to get the information you need, envision new markets and write proposals that sell, find and interview experts on any topic and much more. *#10449/$17.99/224 pages*

Romance Writer's Sourcebook: Where to Sell Your Manuscripts—Get your romance manuscripts published with this new resource guide that combines how-to-write instruction with where-to-sell-direction. You'll uncover advice from established authors, as well as detailed listings of publishing houses, agents, organizations, contests and more! *#10456/$19.99/475 pages*

Handbook of Short Story Writing, Volume II—Orson Scott Card, Dwight V. Swain, Kit Reed and other noted authors bring you sound advice and timeless techniques for every aspect of the writing process. *#10239/$12.99/252 pages/paperback*

Science Fiction Writer's Marketplace and Sourcebook—Discover how to write and sell your science fiction and fantasy! Novel excerpts, short stories and advice from pros show you how to write a winner! Then over 100 market listings bring you publishers hungry for your work! Plus, you'll get details on SF conventions, on-line services, organizations and workshops. *#10420/$19.99/464 pages*

Description—Discover how to use detailed description to awaken the reader's senses; advance the story using only relevant description; create original word depictions of people, animals, places, weather and much more! *#10451/$15.99/176 pages*

Writing the Blockbuster Novel—Let a top-flight agent show you how to weave the essential elements of a blockbuster into your own novels with memorable characters, exotic settings, clashing conflicts and many other elements. *#10393/$18.99/224 pages*

How to Write Fast (While Writing Well)—Discover what makes a story and what it takes to research and write one. Then, learn step-by-step how to cut wasted time and effort by planning interviews for maximum results, beating writer's block with effective plotting and getting the most information from traditional library research and on-line computer databases. *#10473/$15.99/208 pages/paperback*

20 Master Plots (And How to Build Them)—Write great contemporary fiction from timeless plots. This guide outlines 20 plots from various genres and illustrates how to adapt them into your own fiction. *#10366/$17.99/240 pages*

More Editors Share Their Views —

Here are more useful "inside" views from editors about the book publishing industry and tips about what they want to see from fiction writers.

"I don't care where a particular relationship in a story goes, as long as it's authentic, as long as I get the feeling that the author is hanging out there with me, discovering things, exploring, and is just as surprised as I in the direction the story takes. The closer we as readers can get to the creative process, the more we are rewarded. That's the ideal I'm looking for."
—Jeff Putnam, Baskerville Publishers

"Every editor dreams of discovering a new voice. Nothing excites an editor more than to be the first to publish a writer, to develop that writer and establish a relationship that will last for years. It's not a negative if you haven't been published before. It's a positive in our eyes."
—Jay Schaefer, Chronicle Books

"Because the big houses are searching for instant bestsellers, we're taking on more and more books that were submitted to, and rejected by, major publishers. That's what we're here for, to try and catch these books that otherwise would be neglected and bring them into print."
—Fiona McCrae, Graywolf Press